GROLIER
ENCYCLOPEDIA
OF KNOWLEDGE

Grolier Incorporated
Danbury, Connecticut

1993 Printing

ISBN 0-7172-5300-7 (complete set)
ISBN 0-7172-5313-9 (volume 13)

Printed and manufactured in the United States of America.

This publication is an abridged version of the *Academic American Encyclopedia.*

3 4 5 6 7 8 9 10

mode (mathematics)   see AVERAGE

---

mode (music)   Modes in music refer primarily to melodic scales (see SCALE, music) and in a narrower sense to certain rhythmic patterns in 13th-century music. Ancient Greek music was based on melodic modes, but their precise manner of use is unclear. Medieval and Renaissance music was based on church modes identified by number and by Greek terms, although the church modes are unrelated to those used by the Greeks. Church modes are easily illustrated using the white notes of the piano keyboard. The First Mode, or Dorian, for example, embraces all the white notes from D to the next D an octave higher. Its companion mode, the Second Mode (Hypodorian), begins a fourth lower on A. The three other mode pairs, and their initial notes on the piano, are the Phrygian (E), Lydian (F), and Mixolydian (G). Aeolian (A) and Ionian (C), added in the mid-16th century, correspond to the minor and major modes, which have prevailed in Western music since the mid-17th century.

The concept of mode is important in the music of Eastern cultures, particularly India (see INDIAN MUSIC).

Model T   The Model T Ford, also called the "Tin Lizzie" or the "Flivver," was introduced in 1908. It was Henry Ford's "car for the great multitude" and was an immediate success (see FORD family). Designed for durability and economy of operation, it had a four-cylinder, 20-horsepower engine and a simple planetary transmission operated by foot pedals on the floor. To meet the demand for the car, the Ford Motor Company introduced the moving ASSEMBLY LINE for mass production, completed in 1914. This system not only increased the rate of production but

Henry Ford's Model T revolutionized the consumer-product industries by proving the economic advantages of assembly-line construction. Through mass production, Ford was able to make the Model T available at an affordable price for the average American.

also substantially reduced the price. In 1908 a Model T cost about $850; by 1925 the cheapest model, the coupe, sold for $290. By 1919 three-fifths of all U.S. motor vehicles and one-half of those in the entire world were Model T Fords. The car finally succumbed to a shift in public taste. Production ceased on May 31, 1927, when no. 15,007,003 rolled off the assembly line.

---

modem   A modem is a device that converts digital data into analog signals for transmission over telephone lines and that converts the received analog signals back into digital data. Its name is derived from these two functions of *mo*dulation and *dem*odulation. Modems are used to connect COMPUTERS and COMPUTER TERMINALS to telephone lines, which cannot carry digital signals, so that they can transmit data to one another at a distance. Modems are also able to carry out a number of control functions for coordinating the transmitted data.

If the terminal and the computer can send data to one another, the modems are operating in what is referred to as full duplex mode. If only one of them can send data at any given time, the mode is then called half-duplex.

Modena [moh-day'-nah]   Modena is a city in northern Italy, located in the Emilia-Romagna region on the Panaro River about 40 km (25 mi) northwest of Bologna. It has a population of 176,556 (1988 est.).

Located in one of Italy's great agricultural districts, Modena is a center for the marketing and processing of foodstuffs. Manufactures include automobiles, machine tools, clothing, and leather goods. The University of Modena (1175) is located there. Important buildings include the cathedral (begun 1099) and the ducal palace of the Este family (begun 1634).

An Etruscan settlement until 183 BC when it was conquered by Rome, Modena became a flourishing city on the Aemilian Way, one of the Roman roads. It became a free commune, or republic, in the 12th century but came under the rule of the ESTE family of Ferrara in 1288. The duchy of Modena was created in 1452. Except for a period of French control (1796–1814), Modena was ruled by the Estes until 1859, after which it became part of the kingdom of Italy.

---

modern architecture   Modern architecture is generally agreed to be an identifiable form of building design characterized by the use of unornamented industrial materials—principally steel, glass, and concrete—to form simple, geometric forms standing free in space. Such buildings, which began to appear around 1922 in Germany, the Netherlands, the USSR, and France, were first grouped together under a single stylistic heading in a 1932 exhibition titled "Modern Architecture" held at the Museum of Modern Art in New York City. The exhibition's organizers, the critic Henry-Russell Hitchcock and the architect C. Philip JOHNSON, detected in a variety of post–World War I buildings from several countries a shared

The Pilgrimage Church of Notre Dame du Haut (1950–55), at Ronchamp, France, is one of Le Corbusier's later buildings in poured concrete; it is considered the most revolutionary ecclesiastical structure by a 20th-century architect.

emphasis on volume over form, asymmetrical composition, and avoidance of ornamentation. These elements, Hitchcock and Johnson proclaimed, constituted an INTERNATIONAL STYLE—the result of a century-long search for a style suited to modern materials and engineering techniques, freed from borrowed forms.

Some of the architects cited by Hitchcock and Johnson as exponents of the International Style resisted this narrow, formal definition. The dissenters asserted that their work was only the direct, logical manifestation of contemporary science and society, that it would change as its preconditions changed, and that architecture had in fact finally escaped the limitations of stylistic fashions. The course of architecture since 1932 has proved both camps correct: if the form-system known as the International Style has been universally accepted as the symbolic expression of modernity in building, it has also been shown to be essentially an artificial construct that is neither the inevitable nor necessarily the most logical reflection of 20th-century conditions.

Founders of Modern Architecture

The Bauhaus. Among the architects who developed the International Style, the Germans formed the largest and initially the most important group. By 1918 a group of radical designers, centered in Berlin, had emerged as the champions of an architecture featuring astylistic shapes in steel and glass and based on an industrial and socialist ethic that had as its primary goal the overthrow of 19th-century ECLECTICISM. The strong intuitive flavor of this so-called expressionism in turn triggered a reaction led by Walter GROPIUS and Ludwig MIES VAN DER ROHE, who accepted steel-and-glass construction and pure geometric forms as ideals but sought to use these elements with scientific logic and precision.

The chief theorist of what its adherents called the *Neue Sachlichkeit,* or the new factualism, was Gropius, from 1919 the director of what had formerly been the Weimar Art School, and was now known as the BAUHAUS. When the Bauhaus moved (1925) to Dessau, Gropius implemented his theories in the buildings he designed for the new site. Mies van der Rohe had demonstrated both the practicality and the formal unity of the new architecture in supervising the design of the Weissenhof Siedlung housing project (1925–27) in Stuttgart. Then, in his German Pavilion at the Barcelona Trade Fair of 1929, Mies carried the features of the International Style to their furthest limit of abstraction.

Neoplasticism and Constructivism. The Bauhaus architects' final step from expressionism to the *Neue Sachlichkeit* is widely credited to the influence of two contemporary art movements: Dutch neoplasticism, usually called DE STIJL, and Soviet CONSTRUCTIVISM. The neoplasticist group was assembled (1917) by the poet-painter Theo van DOESBURG, who also founded the group's magazine, *De Stijl* (1917–31). Van Doesburg and Cornelius van Eesteren outlined the neoplasticist ideal in a 1922 Paris exhibition of a series of house projects whose asymmetrical arrangements of colored planes resembled the paintings of abstract artist Piet Mondrian made three-dimensional. This rigorously abstract conception was realized most fully in Gerrit Rietveld's Schröder House (1925) in Utrecht.

Constructivism was initiated in the Soviet Union with the nonobjective sculpture of Vladimir TATLIN. Once brought (1922) to Germany by émigrés such as László MOHOLY-NAGY, the constructivist concept of a building as a technical mechanism in motion soon assumed a key role in European architectural theory.

Le Corbusier. The contemporaneous work of the Swiss architect Charles Édouard Jeanneret, better known as LE CORBUSIER, differed in its premises, if not in its outward appearance, from that of the Germans. His early buildings—the Ozenfant House (1923) in Paris, the Villa Stein (1927–28) in Garches, the Villa Savoye (1929–30) in Poissy—resemble those of Gropius and Mies in their asymmetrical and flowing spatial arrangements, as well as in their unornamented glass and stucco planes.

Le Corbusier's explanation of his art in his immensely influential *Vers une Architecture* (1923; trans. as *Towards a New Architecture,* 1927) emphasized that a new and purer classical architecture of forms could be created by following the logical conceptual processes of the engineer. This organic and somewhat grandiose conception of the new architecture sets Le Corbusier apart from the austere geometricism of the Bauhaus school.

Le Corbusier insisted that the reorganization of the city was the first task of modern architecture. His 1922 exhibition entitled "*Modern City for Three Million Inhabitants*" led eventually to a model apartment tower that he called a Unité d'Habitation, the first of which was erected in Marseille in 1946–52. An overriding concern for URBAN PLANNING made him one of the key figures in the formation (1928) of the Congrès International de l'Architecture Moderne (CIAM). Greatly influenced by Le Corbusier, the CIAM architects overruled the aesthetic goals of the expressionists by setting urbanism, rather than design, as the organization's chief concern.

Frank Lloyd Wright. Also active at the time of the epochal "Modern Architecture" exhibition was another leading exponent of modern architecture, the American Frank Lloyd WRIGHT. Although his work was recognized in the 1932 exhibition, Wright was set apart from the practitioners of the International Style because of his "individualism" and "romantic" attachment to nature. He was also a generation older than his European counterparts and had actually influenced some of their work through the publication (1910) in Berlin of the *Wasmuth Portfolio* of his work. Wright accepted the machine as an aid to architecture and made early use of such modern materials as reinforced concrete in his compositions of cantilevered roof planes, unornamented surfaces, and flowing spaces. On the other hand, he believed in what he termed the "organic" use of building materials and in the close relationship of a building to its site—19th-century ideas rejected by his European contemporaries. His idea of modern organicism is expressed in such works as the Johnson's Wax Company Headquarters (1937–39) in Racine, Wis., a great space wrapped with brick and fiberglass tubing whose roof is supported by slender, mushroom-shaped columns; and in the dramatically cantilevered concrete-and-glass Kaufmann House, "Fallingwater" (1936–37), at Bear Run, Pa.

Triumph of the International Style

In 1932 the International Style embraced only a small proportion of recent architecture; outside of private houses its influence was limited to certain housing projects in Germany, Austria, and the Netherlands. The pre–World War I academic-eclectic tradition had also dominated most postwar building of the 1920s and had produced a "modern architecture" of its own in the simplified historicism of Ragnar Östberg's Stockholm City Hall (1909–23), Bertram Goodhue's Nebraska State Capitol (1919–28), and the skyscrapers of New York City. During the Great Depression of the 1930s, however, the simplicity and economy of the International Style posed a desirable alternative to the extraneous ornamentation and lavish use of space inherent in eclectic architecture, and only CIAM seemed to have any clear solutions to the pressing problem of social housing. This new socioeconomic environment, as much as the aesthetics of modern architecture, paved the way for the triumph of the International Style in France, Great Britain, and the United States.

After World War II the International Style provided the basis for the rebuilding of European cities. In the United States the architects of the building boom of the 1950s and 1960s turned to the International Style in designing technocratic office buildings such as New York City's Lever House (1950–52), by Gordon BUNSHAFT of the firm of Skidmore, Owings, and Merrill (SOM).

Equally attracted to the philosophy and the aesthetics of the new architecture were institutions that sought to project a modern image, such as the Air Force Academy, whose Colorado Springs, Colo., campus was designed (1954–57) and built (1956–62) by SOM. Even the New York City headquarters of the United Nations (1947–50) was rendered in the International Style by a team of architects that included Le Corbusier, who had been passed over (1927) for the design of the League of Nations building.

Limits of the International Style

If the term *modern architecture* is understood to consist of a particular form-vocabulary (the International Style) embodying a certain philosophy (functionalism), then the term cannot be used to signify all the architecture produced in the modern epoch, but only one architectural tradition extending backward and forward from an accepted year of conception (1922). Frank Lloyd Wright's so-called Prairie style (from *c.*1900; see PRAIRIE SCHOOL) clearly prefigures the International Style. In another vein the ART NOUVEAU movement of the 1890s also sought to produce an innovative modern style using the industrial materials of metal, glass, and concrete. As with most other artistic traditions, the aesthetic and philosophical roots of modern architecture can be traced back through a long line of artists and theorists.

The United Nations Headquarters complex (1952), in New York City, was initially conceived by Le Corbusier; his plans were reworked by an international architectural group under Wallace K. Harrison. The glass-walled Secretariat tower dominates the domed General Assembly Building.

Modern architecture claimed to be based on a logical expression of the spatial and structural facts of building, yet its practitioners have rarely approached the structural ingenuity of conceptual technicians such as R. Buckminster FULLER. Similarly, although its apologists claimed that modern architecture represented a democratic style expressing the taste of the general public, its works often have been seen as aloof and oversophisticated by their residents. Finally, modern architecture's efficacy in solving the problems of redesigning cities into finely tuned social organisms has been questioned by those who see it as the destroyer of cohesive neighborhoods through wholesale urban renewal.

Recent Trends

As these contradictions in modern architecture began to emerge clearly in the 1950s, many architects sought to modify the codes of the International Style so as to create buildings at once modern and monumental, as well as functional and responsive to the needs and expectations of a wide audience. An international group of architects formed (1953) under the name Team X succeeded in 1959 in dissolving CIAM and setting its own goals for a new, more humane system of public housing. Team X members such as Alison and Peter Smithson and Aldo van Eyck, working from the aesthetic basis of the International Style, evolved from it more visually complex, texturally rich, and physically substantial buildings. Late in his career Le Corbusier himself became a major figure in this development, particularly with his sculptural concrete chapel (1951–55) at Ronchamp, France. Another convert was Philip Johnson, the theorist of the International Style, who executed a number of monumental public buildings in rich materials.

If Eero SAARINEN turned the International Style to expressionistic ends in works such as his TWA Terminal

The central court of New York City's Guggenheim Museum, flooded with light from its dome, expresses Frank Lloyd Wright's belief that architecture should be derived from natural, organic forms, such as the shell form in the spiraling gallery ramp.

(1956–62) at J. F. Kennedy Airport in New York City, his buildings are scarcely more extraordinary than the later works of Frank Lloyd Wright, whose spiraling, concrete GUGGENHEIM MUSEUM was conceived in 1942 and completed in 1959. Finally, Louis I. KAHN developed a new monumentality that was first expressed in his Yale University Art Gallery (1951–53) and culminated in such buildings as the Exeter Library (1967–72), a symmetrical, almost classical composition of brick, wood, concrete, and glass. Kahn was perhaps the last of the great modern architects. The full emergence of POSTMODERN ARCHITECTURE took place shortly after Kahn's death (1974), and many prominent architects are now pursuing a variety of formal images beyond the doctrinal limitations of the International Style.

---

modern art   The term *modern art* has been used in the past to describe all art produced after the emergence of CUBISM in 1908 and of ABSTRACT ART—in its 20th-century manifestation—in 1910. The avant-garde movements of the subsequent decades—CONSTRUCTIVISM, DADA, DE STIJL, EXPRESSIONISM, FUTURISM, SUPREMATISM, SURREALISM, VORTICISM—were also considered modern art. Paris was the center of the art world, and hence the center of modern art, until the outbreak of World War II. Meanwhile, many of the foremost Austrian, German, and Italian artists fled to the United States to escape the Nazi and Fascist regimes. Mingling with American artists, they created an artistic ferment that made New York City the art capital of the world after 1946. In this article, modern art is taken to mean recent and contemporary art, or art produced since 1946.

Origins of Contemporary Art.   The most pertinent starting point for a discussion of the complex and diverse characteristics of recent art is the period of the 1940s in New York City, where a small number of avant-garde artists, whose styles were later labeled ABSTRACT EXPRESSIONISM, were evolving a way of painting that has profoundly affected many subsequent developments. During the late 1930s some of these artists had worked on the federal art project of the Works Progress Administration. Many were in close contact with members of the American Abstract Artists, advocates of geometric cubist abstraction, organized in 1936. Others were in contact with Hans HOFMANN, who arrived in New York City from Munich in the early 1930s and became an influential exponent of modernist theory during the late 1930s and 1940s. These artists were coming to terms with the work of the recent past, especially the revolutionary work of Pablo PICASSO, and were exposed to European art through a number of exhibitions.

In 1936, Arshile GORKY began his shift from geometric cubism toward biomorphic abstraction, which reached maturity by 1940–1941. From 1939 to 1941 a number of well-known European artists, including André BRETON, Marc CHAGALL, Max ERNST, Fernand LÉGER, André MASSON, and Piet MONDRIAN, emigrated to escape the war in Europe. Their arrival served to reinforce the American artists, who were aware of European modernist art theory,

First Abstract Watercolor *(1910), by Wassily Kandinsky is considered the first entirely abstract or nonrepresentational painting ever produced. (Collection of Mme. Nina Kandinsky, France.)*

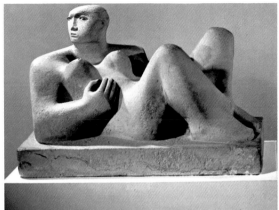

Reclining Woman *(c.1929), by the English sculptor Henry Moore, was carved early in his career, when he was influenced by pre-Columbian sculpture. (National Gallery of Canada, Ottawa.)*

psychology, and philosophy, and were assimilating a complex set of influences including those of cubism, surrealism, Mexican mural painting, Oriental art and ideas, and the American tradition of landscape painting.

Emergence of Abstract Expressionism. During the early 1940s two enclaves were formed, each offering an alternative to prevalent social realism and geometric abstraction.

The first group, termed the *gestural wing*, consisted of Americans Robert MOTHERWELL and William Baziotes and the Chilean surrealist Roberto Sebastián MATTA ECHAURREN and soon included Lee KRASNER and Jackson POLLOCK. They met during 1941–42 and evolved an approach

Three Musicians *(1921), one of Pablo Picasso's most impressive cubist paintings, may be seen as abstractions of commedia dell'arte musicians or as ominous figures disguised as musicians. (Museum of Modern Art, New York City.)*

to art that combined attention to painterly values and psychological content, extending the techniques of surrealism. The second group, termed the *color-field wing* (see COLOR-FIELD PAINTING), consisted of Americans Adolph GOTTLIEB, Barnett NEWMAN, an important theoretician, Mark ROTHKO, and Theodoros Stamos. They advocated the use of myth and primitive styles. During the next few years the second group of artists, along with a few others such as Ad REINHARDT, Clyfford STILL, and Richard Pousette-Dart, continued to condense and intensify their structural forms and images. During the years from 1947 to 1950 abstract expressionism came to full maturity and by the late 1950s dominated the New York City art scene.

Extending the techniques developed by Jackson Pollock from about 1947 to 1951, painters Helen FRANKENTHALER (in 1952) and Morris LOUIS (in 1954) began to use staining technique to develop personal variants of gestural painting. A coloristic, geometric style termed hard-edge painting, typified by neat surfaces, economy of form, and fullness of color, had developed by the late 1950s, notably in the work of Ellsworth KELLY, Alexander Liberman, and Agnes Bernice Martin. In the late 1950s and into the '60s a number of painters such as Kenneth NOLAND, and Frank STELLA developed other kinds of abstraction that were related to the critic Clement GREENBERG'S emphasis on formalist aesthetics.

Pop Art and Happenings. Even as these and other abstractionists were putting metallic and acrylic pigments and new materials such as plastic to use in their canvases, other artists were working in the areas of collage and assemblage, manipulating and combining real objects with paint. Marcel DUCHAMP was an important inspiration for Jasper JOHNS and Robert RAUSCHENBERG who, from the mid-1950s, used common, concrete objects and images to explore the ambiguous relation between art and contemporary life. Allan KAPROW worked his way from assemblage to ENVIRONMENTAL ART to HAPPENINGS. In 1959, in New York City, Kaprow coordinated the first happening

(Right) Blue, Orange, Red *is by Mark Rothko, a prime exponent of the color-field branch of abstract expressionism in which areas of pure color are juxtaposed to achieve complete abstraction. (Private collection.)*

(Below) Three Flags *(1958), a three-dimensional painted sculpture by Jasper Johns, is an early example of American pop art. The startling effects of pop art stem from its transformations of common objects and images. (Whitney Museum, New York City.)*

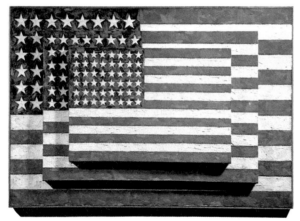

with a number of other artists interested in extending art into the environment: Red GROOMS, Jim DINE, Claes OLDENBURG, George Brecht, and Robert Whitman.

Kaprow's development emphazes art as a transient experience rather than an enduring object, a philosophical search rather than an aesthetic activity. POP ART, as practiced by artists such as Robert INDIANA, Roy LICHTENSTEIN, and James ROSENQUIST, incorporates subject matter from the mass media and objects from our "throwaway" culture, but it also retains the formal values that were inherent in the abstract painting of the time. Pop art had first appeared in London in the collages of Richard Hamilton. The most influential pop art is still that of Andy WARHOL.

Resurgence of Realism. A resurgence of representa-

tional painting during the early 1960s took two forms, the earliest of which, PHOTOREALISM, emerged in 1963–65. Photorealism combined a photographic fidelity to appearances with reference to commonplace objects. The second form is a more painterly realism, closely involved with illusions and sensations received directly from nature. Among its major exponents are the sculptor George SEGAL and the painter Wayne THIEBAUD.

Minimal Art. A number of artists working in New York City during the mid- and late 1960s adopted three-dimensional forms that owed much to the influence of recent geometric abstract painting. This MINIMAL ART, whose principal initiators were Donald JUDD, Robert MORRIS, Sol LeWitt, and Carl Andre, was characterized by monolithic or modular shapes, such as cubes, boxes, or beams made of industrial materials. The aim of these so-called primary structures is to emphasize the concrete visual quality of a simple form and to stress its interaction with the space surrounding it.

Works by Louise BOURGEOIS, Bruce Nauman, and Eva Hesse exemplify a trend in sculpture of the late 1960s away from minimal art's methodical, preconceived systems of geometric shapes. This antiformal or postminimal style is characterized by arbitrary arrangements of standing, leaning and wall-mounted forms.

Earthworks and Conceptual Art. The architectural and enviromental aspects of minimal art were extended by an innovation that took art out of galleries and installed it in the world at large. EARTHWORKS, large, outdoor sculptures intimately connected with the specific sites for which they are made, were conceived by Robert SMITHSON.

Conceptual art places prime importance on the artist's concept rather than the production of a unique, permanent, tangible art object. Conceptual art relates to minimal art, earthworks, and happenings, all of which had shown a concern for the nonvisual, nonpermanent, and experiential aspects of art. In its inclusion of written and photographic material conceptual art is in part a response to the proliferation of art criticism. It is an antipurist form that uses visual and verbal materials to communicate on a sociopolitical level.

Art Since the 1970s. Abstraction, representational painting and sculpture, a variety of conceptual modes, PERFORMANCE ART, and VIDEO ART coexist in this so-called pluralistic period. The newest major trends have been essentially conservative, with painting in the forefront. Most prominent is international neoexpressionism—gestural, emotive painting that uses complex surfaces and large scale in eclectic historical mixes to stress the psychological dilemma for the artist in what has been called the "postmodern" period. Increased commerce has brought rapid recognition to many young artists, a number coming out of New York's East Village galleries, where varied "stylish" modes are seen both in galleries and in nightclubs, creating "art stars" who compete with mass media stars. Graffiti have been co-opted by the art world, its exponents ranging from naive street artists to the formally trained, such as Keith Haring. Warhol's influence continues strong, most evident in photography like that of Cindy Sherman.

modern dance   Modern dance cannot be described as a particular style of dance or a single technical method of movement; it is rather a point of view: DANCE as art. Neither BALLET nor popular show dancing, modern dance is theatrical dancing for a serious artistic purpose that developed largely independently of, and in opposition to, those forms. It stresses individuality of expression over uniformity of method. The artistic movement that came to be recognized as modern dance was led by a small group of dancers in the United States in the 1920s and '30s.

Beginning around 1900, a number of dancers grew dissatisfied with the mechanical sterility of a ballet aesthetic then in decline and with the decorative triviality of conventional theater dance. Loie FULLER discovered illusionistic effects that could be created by colored light and swirling draperies, illustrating the vivid theatrical impact that movement can have. Isadora DUNCAN devised a free style of dance that conveyed great intensity of feeling. Ruth ST. DENIS impersonated Oriental goddesses with an air of spirituality and mysticism that audiences found uplifting. When St. Denis and her husband, Ted SHAWN, founded the DENISHAWN school and company in 1915 in Los Angeles, they laid the basis from which the founders of modern dance emerged.

Three members of Denishawn, finding its pseudoexoticism inappropriate to a post–World War I society, left the company in the 1920s to invent a dance suited to the times. The three—Martha GRAHAM, Doris HUMPHREY, and Charles WEIDMAN—became the founders of modern dance, although others also influenced succeeding generations of dancers.

The creative surge was not strictly an American event. In central Europe a parallel trend was taking place, influenced by the scientific studies of movement conducted by Rudolf von LABAN and his mentor François Delsarte and by the Dalcroze system of rhythmic movement (see Émile

Martha Graham and her company are seen in a performance of Primitive Mysteries *(1931), one of her most important early works. Graham developed a powerful, expressive style integral to the foundations of modern dance.*

Jaques DALCROZE). The German dancers Mary WIGMAN and Harald Kreutzberg (1902–68) toured the United States and Hanya HOLM established a Wigman school in New York City in 1931. Modern-dance activity in Europe ended with World War II, and it was not until American choreographers began working overseas in the 1960s that modern dance again became an international phenomenon.

The early moderns were fiercely independent, even rivals, but they saw themselves as a movement in rebellion against conventional forms of dance. They believed that dance had to express a contemporary spirit and could not be authentic if cast in a borrowed style. Dance had to embody the sense of a machine age, the personality of the particular artist, and the moral concerns of the time. They danced in bare feet, stayed close to the ground, emphasized body weight, eschewed elaborate costumes and sets, worked with simple musical arrangements, and moved with deliberate force, angularity, asymmetry, and distortion. Each dancer had to develop a technique of movement suited to the dancer's own body and to the subject to be expressed.

It was not through the efforts of the pioneering dancers alone that modern dance, after more than 20 years, won its battle for respectability in the United States. The musician Louis Horst (1884–1964), a great supporter of modern dance in its formative period, acted as advisor, composer, and accompanist to many choreographers, particularly to Martha Graham. In 1927 newspapers regularly began assigning dance critics, among them John Martin (1893–1985), Margaret Lloyd (1887–1960), Walter Terry (1913–82), and Edwin Denby (1903–83), who approached performances from the point of view of a movement specialist rather than as a reviewer of music or drama. Educators accepted modern dance into college and university curricula, first as part of physical education and later as a performing art. Many college teachers were trained at the Bennington Summer School of the Dance, which was established at Bennington College in 1934 and continued by Connecticut College in 1948.

With the struggle to establish modern dance largely won, the hostility among different technical schools and between modern dance and ballet lessened, and modern dance styles began to blend, soften, and lighten. José LIMÓN made dances about larger-than-life heroes and grand social schemes. Anna SOKOLOW concentrated on mood rather than plot in dances reflecting the tension and alienation of the 1950s. Alvin AILEY combined ballet and modern dance and concentrated on black themes; other black choreographers adopted a bouncier, looser jazz style influenced by the African and Caribbean native dances presented by Katherine DUNHAM. In the hands of Jack Cole (1913–1974) and other choreographers, the modern-dance impetus reached Broadway musicals and Hollywood films.

Some dancers of the second generation, however, continued in the rebellious spirit of their predecessors. Paul TAYLOR and Erick Hawkins made innovations in the technique and substance of their dances. Alwin NIKOLAIS evolved a multimedia spectacle of sound, shape, move-

Revelations *(1960), performed by the Alvin Ailey American Dance Theater, draws on blues, gospel, and jazz traditions to create a moving expression of African-American experience.*

ment, and light. Merce CUNNINGHAM abandoned plot, characterization, logical sequence, and preconceived emotional coloration, letting his dance movement speak for itself simply as movement occupying time and space.

Cunningham greatly influenced the dancers of the 1960s, many of whom followed his exploration of movement-as-movement and questioned even further what qualified as dance movement. Choreographers working with the Judson Dance Theater used everyday, unemotional movement that could be performed with minimal training. Choreographic minimalists like Rudy Perez experimented with how little could be done. Many choreographers set their dances to be performed in streets, museums, and other nontheatrical spaces.

The generation of dancers that appeared after the

Merce Cunningham appears with Carolyn Brown in his production of RainForest *(1968), for which Andy Warhol designed the set. Cunningham, a major figure of the modern-dance avant-garde, focuses on pure, sometimes random, movement.*

1960s has shown a strong interest in training, technique, and theatricality. Meredith Monk has created an imaginative theater form using poetic combinations of dance images, props, and music. Twyla THARP has developed a casual-looking but rigorous and intricate technique that serves, often, as a commentary on social issues and on other dance styles. The German dancer Pina Bausch, with her Wuppertal Dance Theater, choreographs strongly narrative dances that combine movement with words, song, chant, and mime. Her work has been labeled expressionist and has been influenced by her teacher, the early dance modernist Kurt JOOSS. Avant-garde choreographer Trisha Brown designs dances where multimedia effects create a kind of performance art.

Modern Jazz Quartet The Modern Jazz Quartet (MJQ) was formed in 1952 by the pianist and composer John Lewis, b. La Grange, Ill., May 3, 1920. Lewis, who had been an accompanist and arranger for Dizzy Gillespie and other jazz bandleaders, had also studied and taught classical music. The two musical modes merged in his work with the MJQ, whose other members were closer to the jazz tradition: vibraphonist Milt Jackson, bassist Percy Heath, and, as drummers, first Kenny Clarke, then—after 1954—Connie Kay. The group disbanded in 1974 after 22 years together. During that time they had played as often in concert halls as in nightclubs and had won the Downbeat Critics Poll for five consecutive years (1954–59). Re-formed in 1981, MJQ continues to tour extensively and to record.

modernism Modernism was a loosely defined movement within the Roman Catholic church aimed at adapting Catholic belief to the intellectual, moral, and social needs of modern times. It developed spontaneously toward the end of the 19th century principally in Italy, France, Germany, Spain, Great Britain, and the United States.

Proponents of the movement accepted the findings of modern science and supported the critical view of the Bible, thereby establishing a link with liberal Protestantism and incurring the wrath of traditionalists. In his encyclical *Pascendi dominici gregis* (1907), PIUS X condemned the movement and attempted to carry out the principle established by Pope LEO XIII that made the philosophy and theology of Saint Thomas AQUINAS the norm for the church's teaching. Two leaders of the movement, Father Alfred LOISY of France and Father George Tyrrell of England, were condemned by the church for refusing to accept the papal position.

Modernism, as defined in *Pascendi*, ended when Pope PIUS XII opened the way for the use of biblical criticism in Catholicism by his encyclical *Divino afflante spiritu* (1943). This encyclical was followed by a widespread interest in history and such adventuresome theologies as the evolutionary teachings of Father Pierre TEILHARD DE CHARDIN.

Modersohn-Becker, Paula [moh'-dur-zohn-bek'-ur]   The painter Paula Modersohn-Becker, b. Feb. 8, 1876, d. Nov. 20, 1907, developed an antiromantic, consciously primitive style that anticipated 20th-century German expressionism. While her friends painted vast landscapes at the artists' colony of Worpswede, outside Bremen, Modersohn-Becker singled out individual forms, such as a burly peasant or a massive barn. These compositions—inspired by the works of Paul Cézanne, Vincent van Gogh, and Paul Gauguin—were not well received during the artist's short life. Many of her paintings are preserved in the Paula Modersohn-Becker Museum in Bremen.

Modest Proposal, A   see SWIFT, JONATHAN

Modigliani, Amedeo [moh-dee-lee-ah'-nee, ah-may-day'-oh]   During the early 1900s in Paris, the Italian painter and sculptor Amedeo Modigliani, b. July 12, 1884, d. Jan. 24, 1920, developed a unique style. Today his graceful portraits and lush nudes at once evoke his name, but during his brief career few apart from his fellow artists were aware of his gifts. Modigliani had to struggle against poverty and chronic ill health, dying of tuberculosis and excesses of drink and drugs at the age of 35.

In 1906, Modigliani settled in Paris, where he encountered the works of Henri de Toulouse-Lautrec, Georges Rouault, and Pablo Picasso (in his "blue period") and assimilated their influence, as in *The Jewess* (1908; private collection, Paris). The strong influence of Paul Cézanne's paintings is clearly evident, both in Modigliani's deliberate distortion of the figure and the free use of large, flat areas of color.

His friendship with Constantin Brancusi kindled Modigliani's interest in sculpture, in which he would con-

After settling in Paris in 1906, the Italian artist Amedeo Modigliani devoted himself to portraying the human form, as in this graceful female nude. His portraits are instantly recognizable by their elongated proportions and mood of poetic reverie.

tinue his very personal idiom, distinguished by strong linear rhythms, simple elongated forms, and verticality. *Head* (1912; Guggenheim Museum, New York City) and *Caryatid* (1914; Museum of Modern Art, New York City) exemplify his sculptural work, which consists mainly of heads and, less often, of full figures.

After 1915, Modigliani devoted himself entirely to painting, producing some of his best work. His interest in African masks and sculpture remains evident, especially in the treatment of the sitters' faces: flat and masklike, with almond eyes, twisted noses, pursed mouths, and elongated necks. Despite their extreme economy of composition and neutral backgrounds, the portraits convey a sharp sense of the sitter's personality, as in *Moïse Kisling* (1915; private collection, Milan).

Modoc [moh'-dahk]   The Modoc tribe of North American Indians, closely related linguistically and culturally to the KLAMATH, traditionally occupied a region of lakes and the Lost River Valley in northeastern California and a small adjacent area of Oregon. Both they and the Klamath spoke a Sahaptin-Chinook language of the Penutian stock. Klamath and Modoc lifeways were both adapted to the lake-and-marsh environment; their houses, dugout canoes, and use of rushes for mats and baskets were essentially the same. Both tribes occasionally raided California Indian groups to take captives whom they sold as slaves.

When intensive contacts with white settlers began in the mid-1860s, the Modoc were involved in a series of violent incidents. In 1864 the Modoc and Klamath were forced to cede their lands and were confined together on a reservation in Oregon. Despite their similarities, hostility had long existed between the two tribes. An attempt by a group of dissatisfied Modoc to break away from the reservation was put down in the Modoc Wars of 1872–73, in which federal troops suffered heavy casualties. The rebellious Modocs were subsequently imprisoned in Oklahoma. They formed a tribe there, which numbered 102 in 1989. The Modoc and Klamath of the Northwest lost federal tribal recognition in the 1950s.

modulation [mah-due-lay'-shuhn]   Modulation is the periodic variation of one or more properties of a signal or wave (see WAVES AND WAVE MOTION). A principal application of modulation is communications—the transmission of information. In the case of the TELEPHONE, for example, waves of air that have been modulated in intensity and frequency by the speaker are picked up by a MICROPHONE. The microphone converts the waves into an electrical signal the intensity and frequency of which follow that of the audible signal. This modulated electrical signal is then transmitted through a conducting wire to a receiver, in which the modulated electrical signal is demodulated— that is, converted back into the audible signal.

Information may be conveniently transmitted by means of ELECTROMAGNETIC RADIATION. The wave has several properties that may be altered, or modulated, the most

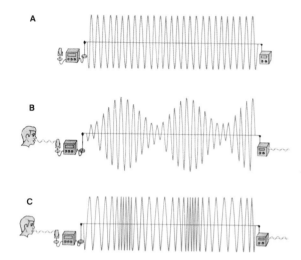

Modulation is a technique for combining a sound signal with a carrier wave (A), which is a specific transmission frequency allotted to a radio station by the government. In AM, or amplitude modulation (B), frequency of the modulated wave is constant, and amplitude is varied in proportion to the sound signal. In FM, or frequency modulation (C), amplitude remains constant, and frequency is changed.

important of which are its amplitude and frequency. The unit for measuring the frequency of a wave, formerly called a cycle per second, is now called a hertz (Hz).

In the field of communications, when the goal is the transmission of information, modulation may be more precisely defined as the process of superimposing the amplitude or frequency of an incoming wave (the signal) upon a transmitted wave (the carrier). Several forms of modulation are in common use.

The transmission of information by varying the amplitude of a fixed-frequency carrier wave in proportion to the amplitude of the signal is called AMPLITUDE MODULATION (AM). This method is employed by commercial radio broadcast stations that transmit worldwide over the frequency band between 540,000 and 1,600,000 Hz (540–1,600 kHz). Amplitude modulation is simple to implement but is susceptible to various types of electromagnetic NOISE.

The transmission of information by varying the frequency of a carrier wave in proportion to the amplitude of the signal is called FREQUENCY MODULATION (FM). Frequency-modulated electromagnetic waves are less susceptible to noise.

The advent of digital electronics has led to a variety of pulse modulation methods. These modulation methods are used to transmit information by means of brief pulses (see PULSE, electronics) of electromagnetic energy rather than continuous waves. In a method called pulse frequency modulation, the frequency of a train of pulses is varied in response to an incoming signal much as in frequency modulation. Other pulse modulation methods are also in use.

Mofolo, Thomas [moh-foh'-loh]   The South African writer Thomas Mokopu Mofolo, b. Aug. 2, 1877, d. Sept. 8, 1948, wrote the first novel in an African vernacular language. *Moeti oa bochabela* (The Traveler to the East, 1907), written in Sesotho, was followed by an autobiographical novel, *Pitseng* (In the Pot, 1910). His masterpiece, *Chaka* (1925; trans. in 1931 as *Chaka, A Historical Romance*), was based on the life of the Zulu chief Shaka. Despite the Christian tone of the work, it was repressed by Mofolo's publishers for more than 13 years but has since been translated into several European and African languages.

Mogadishu [mahg-uh-dish'-oo]   Mogadishu (Somali: Muqdisho) is the capital and chief port of Somalia, situated on the Indian Ocean coast near the equator. The population of 400,000 (1981 est.) is often swelled temporarily by nomads. Food processing, sugar refining, leather tanning, and shoemaking are important. The National University of Somalia (1954) is there. Settled in the 10th century, Mogadishu was one of the earliest Arab trading centers in East Africa. The port was sold to Italy in 1905 and became the capital of Italian Somaliland.

Mogollon culture   see ANASAZI

Mogul art and architecture [moh'-gul]   India produced a unique style of art and architecture under the patronage of its Mogul emperors (r. 1526–1707), in which indigenous traditions of INDIAN ART AND ARCHITECTURE were brilliantly transformed by influences derived from imperial Safavid Persia.

Architecture. The Mogul style of architecture is characterized by such Persian-inspired elements as arched entryways and bulbous domes, as seen in the splendid Delhi tomb (begun 1561) of Humayun (r. 1530–56), the son and successor of the first Mogul emperor Babur (r. 1526–30). Generally considered the first great monument of Mogul architecture, the tomb is composed of red sandstone, the principal Mogul building material in the 16th century, and embellished with marble inlay. Under Humayun's son Akbar the Great (r. 1556–1605) many massive forts were erected, of which those at Agra, Allahabad, and Lahore are the finest. The new capital city Akbar established (1569) at Fatehpur Sikri was a remarkable achievement in both planning and execution. In general, the Hindu elements dominate the structural forms as well as the decoration of Akbar's monuments.

Akbar's own tomb (completed *c.*1614) at Sikandra near Agra consists of four lower stories of red sandstone dressed with marble inlay, with the uppermost section of marble openwork. This monument provided the structural prototype for the Shadera tomb (*c.*1625) of Akbar's son Jahangir (r. 1605–28) and for the even grander Agra tomb (1626) of I'timad ud-Daula, the father of Jahangir's wife Nur Jahan—the first Mogul tombs to be faced en-

(Below) *The Buland Darwaza (c.1575) is the southern gateway of the Great Mosque at Fatehpur Sikri, the capital Akbar founded in 1569. Fatehpur Sikri was abandoned in 1585 because of an inadequate water supply.*

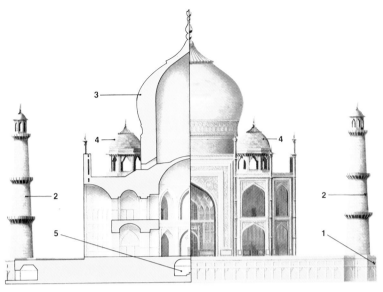

(Above) *The Taj Mahal, Agra, erected (1631–48) by Shah Jahan as a tomb for his wife, Mumtaz Mahal, marks the culmination of Indo-Islamic style. Standing on a raised platform (1), the Taj Mahal features four corner minarets (2). A central dome (3), reflecting Safavid influence, contains an inner dome and is flanked by smaller domes (4). The crypt (5) is underground.*

tirely in white marble. The inlay of semiprecious stones, depicting trees, flowers, and scent-bottles, dominates the walls of I'timad ud-Daula's tomb, and the intricate marble latticework admitting light into the interior of the tomb creates additional highlights.

Jahangir's son Shah Jahan (r. 1628–58) is considered the greatest patron of Mogul architecture. He built (1638–48) a new capital city at Delhi with a vast array of marble palaces within its Red Fort. At Agra, Shah Jahan replaced a large number of red-sandstone buildings erected by his grandfather with marble ones; the new structures were often connected by colonnaded porches and surrounded by geometrically laid out gardens and water fountains. The culmination of Mogul tomb architecture is the TAJ MAHAL, a mausoleum that Shah Jahan commissioned (1631–48) for his favorite wife.

Painting. The art of Mogul miniature painting evolved mainly out of the indigenous Indian fresco tradition associated with AJANTA and out of the imported Persian miniaturist art of Kamal al-Din BIHZAD. In Akbar's reign Persian painters trained about a hundred Hindu painters. In 1585, Akbar's studio was further strengthened by the immigration of an accomplished Central Asian painter, Farrukh Beg Qalmaq.

Early Mogul miniature painting consists largely of illustrations for the many historical manuscripts commissioned by the emperor. The enormous *Hamza-nama*, begun (1567) under the supervision of Sayyid 'Ali and 'Abdu's Samad, contained over a thousand painted illustrations on cotton cloth of the life and legendary exploits of the Islamic hero Hamza. The work, which took 15 years to complete, displays markedly Persian stylistic elements. By the end of the 16th century, however, a distinctly Mogul miniaturist style had emerged, in which the plasticity associated with the Ajanta style is harmoniously fused with the symmetry, proportion, and subtle coloring of the school of Bihzad.

Beginning in the 16th century a number of European prints, portraits, and other paintings were brought to the Mogul court, and late in his reign Akbar often commissioned portraits of himself and his nobles. European influence included the use of shading and *chiaroscuro* and the introduction of distant views of cities forming the background in some Mogul scenes. A clear sense of realism came to dominate late-16th- and early-17th-century Mogul painting, with the gradual abandonment of the flat, highly conventional Persian figure style. The Indian sculptural heritage also seems to have promoted the Mogul artists' apparent desire to express depth and volume in painting.

Mogul painting reached its greatest refinement under the patronage of Jahangir. His imperial studio produced the first full-length portraits, in profile or three-quarter view. He commissioned numerous scientific studies of birds and animals, notable for their lively naturalism, and frequently had artists accompany him on his tours in order to make paintings of special events or hunting scenes. The trend continued in Shah Jahan's reign; his court scenes are grand and the portraits impressive, though lacking in the spontaneous quality that characterized much of the work of the Jahangir period. Mogul traditions in both art and architecture gradually declined during the reign of Aurangzeb (1658–1707), an orthodox Muslim who discouraged the practice of the arts at his court.

Moguls (dynasty) [moh'-gulz]   The Moguls (or Mughals) were a Muslim dynasty of India founded in 1526 by BABUR, a descendant of both GENGHIS KHAN and TIMUR. The dynasty ruled much of the Indian subcontinent until the mid-18th century. The word *Mogul* is the Arabic and Persian version of Mongol.

Babur, who reigned until 1530, was a man of culture as well as a military genius. After defeating the last Lodi king of the DELHI SULTANATE, Babur established a policy of tolerance toward his Hindu subjects. His son, HUMAYUN, spent most of his reign (1530–40, 1555–56) attempting to consolidate Mogul rule over Babur's conquests. Humayun's son AKBAR (r. 1556–1605) laid a firm basis for the administration of the vast Mogul domain. Akbar and his successors, JAHANGIR (r. 1605–27), SHAH JAHAN (r. 1627–58), and AURANGZEB (r. 1658–1707), are generally considered among the finest groups of kings to rule in succession over such a long period.

Although the Moguls remained on the throne until 1858, their territory began to contract after 1707, and they eventually became mere puppets of the British. Following the INDIAN MUTINY of 1857, the British exiled the last Mogul emperor, Bahadur Shah II (1775–1862; r. 1837–58). The Moguls' main legacy to India consisted of an administrative machine, land-tenure patterns, and a system of revenue collection, all of which have proved remarkably durable, plus the magnificent Mogul art and architecture.

mohair   see ANGORA

Mohammed   see MUHAMMAD

Mohammedanism   see ISLAM

Mohave   see MOJAVE

Mohawk   The Mohawk Indians are a tribe of Iroquoian-speaking people who aboriginally inhabited the eastern part of what is now New York State. The name *Mohawk*, meaning "man eater," was given to the tribe by its Algonquian-speaking neighbors. The Mohawks called themselves *Ganiengehaga*, meaning "people of the flint." Members of the Five (later Six) Nations IROQUOIS LEAGUE, they were represented on its Grand Council by nine sachems (chiefs) and were considered "keepers of the eastern door" of the longhouse symbolizing the league. Deganawidah and HIAWATHA, the traditional founders of the Iroquois League, were adopted Mohawks.

As did their neighbors the Seneca, Cayuga, Onondaga, and Oneida, the Mohawks traced kinship through the fe-

male line. Warfare and a concomitant gaining of prestige and honor by males were traditionally of great importance. A calendric cycle of religious ceremonies centered on these activities.

Under the leadership of Joseph BRANT, the Mohawk nation supported the British during the American Revolution. Their descendants live on a number of Indian reserves in Canada, and on the Saint Regis Reserve and in the cities of Brooklyn, Buffalo, and Detroit in the United States.

Mohawk River   The Mohawk River, the largest tributary of the HUDSON RIVER, flows for 238 km (148 mi) in northern New York State. The industrial cities of Rome, Schenectady, and Utica are located along its picturesque banks. The NEW YORK STATE BARGE CANAL, connecting the Hudson and the Great Lakes, parallels the river.

Mohegan   [moh-hee'-guhn]   Much celebrated in the novels of James Fenimore COOPER, the Mohegan are an Algonquian-speaking Indian people who traditionally lived as maize cultivators along the Thames River of Connecticut. They were one of the few tribes to develop successful alliances with the new English colonies in their territory. At the time the English first arrived the Mohegan and the PEQUOT formed a single society under the paramount chief, Sassacus. A subchief however—the famed UNCAS—rebelled and assumed the leadership of one faction. After Sassacus was defeated (1637) in the Pequot War against the English, Uncas assumed control of the reunited Mohegan, who then numbered about 2,300. With the backing of the English, they embarked on a campaign of conquest. By 1673 the Mohegan were the major tribe in New England south of the ABNAKI, but they were soon overwhelmed by expanding white settlement in their area. After selling their lands and settling on reservations, the Mohegan suffered a rapid decline. In 1788 most of the remaining Mohegans joined the Brotherton community of Christianized Indians in New York. Their descendants, of mixed ancestry, are now located in Wisconsin and several other states.

Mohican   see MAHICAN

Moholy-Nagy, László   [moh'-hoh-lee-nahd'-yuh, lahs'-loh]   The Hungarian-born artist László Moholy-Nagy, b. July 20, 1895, d. Nov. 24, 1946, a leading exponent of CONSTRUCTIVISM, was a painter, sculptor, stage designer, photographer, and filmmaker. The immense influence of his art is partly due to his success as a teacher, both at the German BAUHAUS (1923–28) and at his own Chicago Institute of Design (1938–46). He also wrote several important pedagogical works, among them *Painting Photography Film* (1925; Eng. trans., 1969), *The New Vision* (1929; Eng. trans., 1932; rev. ed 1964), and *Vision in Motion* (1947). His first mature paintings, whose hard-edged forms are based on the work of the Russians Ka-

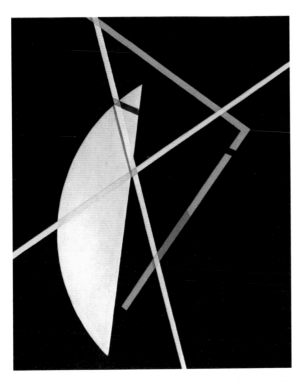

The Hungarian-born artist and theorist Lázló Moholy-Nagy reveals strong affinities with the Russian Suprematists and the Dutch artists of De Stijl in his bold geometric abstraction Construction VII *(1922).*

simir Malevich and El Lissitzky, were made around 1920. At the same time he began to experiment with new plastics and metals in his sculpture and to make some of the first photograms.

Mohorovičić discontinuity [moh-hohr-oh'-vuh-chich] The Mohorovičić discontinuity, or Moho, is the boundary layer or abrupt seismic-velocity discontinuity that separates the Earth's crust from the mantle (see EARTH, STRUCTURE AND COMPOSITION OF). Seismic pressure-wave velocities jump across this boundary from about 7.0 km/sec (4.2 mi/sec) to about 8.1 km/sec (4.9 mi/sec). This discontinuity—the most marked on the Earth except for the mantle-core boundary—was first observed (1909) on seismograms of a Yugoslavian earthquake by the Croatian seismologist Andrija Mohorovičić (1857–1936).

Beneath continents the Moho marks the transition between continental granitic rocks, or sial, and the ultrabasic peridotite rock, or sima, of the Earth's mantle. The Moho is here found typically at a depth of about 35 km (21 mi), but it may be much deeper under the thickened roots of mountains. Beneath ocean basins the Moho is usually only about 6 km (3.6 mi) deep, and it marks the transition between the basic oceanic basalt of the crust and the peridotite of the mantle.

Moi, Daniel arap [may]   The Kenyan political leader Daniel arap Moi, b. 1924, became president of Kenya in 1978. After working (1945–57) as a teacher, he served in a number of government positions before becoming vice-president of Kenya in 1967. He became acting president of Kenya in August 1978, upon the death of Jomo Kenyatta; he was subsequently nominated for the presidency by Kenya's sole political party, the Kenya African National Union, and was elected (1978) with no opposition. Reelected in 1979 and 1983, Moi's policies became increasingly repressive.

Moiseyev, Igor Aleksandrovich [moy-say'-ev, ee'-gohr uhl-yik-sahn'-druh-vich]   The Soviet choreographer, dancer, and company director Igor Aleksandrovich Moiseyev, b. Jan. 21 (N.S.), 1906, helped to renew worldwide interest in folk-dance forms through the performances of his troupe, the State Folk Dance Ensemble (SFDE) of the USSR. He graduated from the Bolshoi Ballet school into the Bolshoi Ballet in 1924 and was a leading character soloist and choreographer with the company until 1939.

Founded in 1937, the SFDE has not endeavored to show the dances in their native form, but rather to present a polished stage version by professional dancers. Many of their dances have been choreographed either to simulate a folk dance, as in *Bulba (Potato),* or to show a vignette, as in *May 1st.* Moiseyev is a Hero of Socialist Labor (1976) and a People's Artist, USSR (1953).

Mojave [moh-hah'-vee]   The Mojave, a North American Indian tribe, lived along the lower Colorado River in present-day Arizona, California, and Nevada. Speakers of a Yuman dialect affiliated with the Hokan stock, they borrowed cultural traits from various California and western Pueblo Indian groups. Living in dispersed hamlets of a few houses, the Mojave had little formal government. Chronic warfare did, however, stimulate a tribal identification expressed in a hereditary chieftaincy and tribal war chief. A clan system traced through the male line regulated marriage but played no part in the political or ceremonial life. Dreams were believed to exert mystical powers over daily life, regulating success, especially in war. Death rites, in which the body was cremated and the dwelling, granary, crops, and personal property of the deceased set afire, formed the most important public ceremonial.

Spanish contact in the 1700s introduced wheat and other food crops, but vital changes in Mojave culture did not begin until 1860. The Colorado River Reservation (106,874 ha/264,092 acres), shared with the Chemehuevi and Kamia, was established in 1865. The reservation's population was about 2,459 in 1989.

Mojave Desert   The Mojave Desert (also spelled Mohave) of southeastern California is situated east of Los

Angeles, south of Death Valley, and west of the Colorado River. It covers 64,750 km² (25,000 mi²), and elevations vary from 600 to 1,500 m (2,000 to 5,000 ft). A part of the GREAT BASIN, the Mojave is a region of salt flats, sand plains, and bare, rocky mountains that was part of the Pacific Ocean until volcanic action cut it off from the sea. The one major river, the Mojave, flows underground for part of its course. The average July temperature is 24° C (75° F), but winter temperatures often drop below freezing. Gale-force winds regularly sweep the desert floor. Borax, potash, salt, silver, and tungsten are mined in the Mojave. Military bases are located there, and suburbs of Los Angeles are rapidly spreading into the desert.

molality   see CONCENTRATION

molar   see TEETH

molarity   see CONCENTRATION

molasses [muh-las'-iz]   Molasses is a thick syrup obtained from the boiling of sugar-cane or sugar beet juice during SUGAR PRODUCTION. It may also be made from processing citrus fruit wastes.

The syrup is produced in different grades. The highest grades are the edible molasses, which are light in color and contain about 90% total sugars, dry weight. Industrial, or blackstrap, molasses is the lowest grade and is the product of the reprocessing of light molasses in order to extract more of its sugar. Blackstrap, which is thicker, darker, and more strongly flavored than edible molasses, contains about 50% total sugars, dry weight.

Edible molasses is used in table syrup blends, as a sweetener and flavoring in cooked and baked foods, and for the manufacture of RUM. Blackstrap molasses is an important constituent of animal feeds. It also serves as a nutrient substrate in YEAST cultivation and is fermented to produce alcohol.

Molasses Act   The Molasses Act, passed by the British Parliament in May 1733, imposed taxes on molasses, rum, and sugar imported into British North America from foreign sources. It was designed to encourage Britain's North American colonists to use sugar products from the British Caribbean islands. North Americans, who profited from a lucrative trade with the French West Indies, resorted to smuggling to avoid compliance with the act. It thus contributed to the disputes that eventually led to the American Revolution.

Moldavia [mohl-day'-vee-uh]   Moldavia is a former principality located in the BALKANS along the lower Danube River. The region is now divided between Romania and Moldova, and the principal cities are Galaţi, Iaşi, and Suceava (all in Romania). In addition to the DANUBE, the region is drained by the DNESTR and Prut rivers. Molda-

via's fertile soils produce vines and other fruits, wheat, and tobacco, and it is an important industrial area.

The region was part of the Roman province of Dacia. Early in the 13th century the Slavic Vlachs migrated into the area, achieved independence from Hungary, which had controlled the region, and established their own principality. By the mid-16th century, however, Moldavia had become a subject state of the Ottoman Empire. Turkish control continued, except for brief interruptions, until 1791 when part of the area passed to Russia.

In 1812, Russia secured all of eastern Moldavia, the section called BESSARABIA. The rest of Moldavia remained under Turkish control, but in 1822, after a Greek insurrection, the Turks replaced the Greek Phanariot governors of the region with local appointees. During the Crimean War (1854–56), Russia occupied Moldavia. In 1856, however, both Moldavia and the neighboring WALACHIA were established as principalities under Turkish suzerainty. They were formally united as Romania in 1861–62 and granted independence from Turkey in 1878.

In 1918, Romania seized Bessarabia. It was forced to return it in 1940, when the boundary between Romania and the USSR was drawn. At the same time, Bessarabia was included in the Soviet republic of Moldavia.

Moldova [mohl-doh'-vuh]   Moldova, formerly the Soviet republic of Moldavia, became independent in 1991. A small land-locked country northwest of the Black Sea, it is bordered by Ukraine on the north, east, and south, and by Romania on the west. The area is 33,700 km² (13,010 mi²), and the population is 4,366,100 (1991 est.). The capital is KISHINEV, with a population of 665,000 (1989). Known historically as BESSARABIA, Moldova forms the eastern half of the historic region of Moldavia.

The republic's topography is a gently rolling plain between the DNESTR RIVER, which lies on the border with Ukraine on the east, and the Prut River, which forms the frontier with Romania.

Moldavians, who represent 64% of the republic's population, speak Romanian. The principal minorities in the republic are Ukrainians (14%), Russians (13%), Jews (2.5%), and the Gagauz people (3.5%), a Turkish-speaking group. In addition to Kishinev, the capital, the largest cities are Tiraspol (182,000), Beltsy (159,000), and Bendery (130,000; all 1989).

Moldova is an important agricultural region, with large wine and tobacco industries. It is also a major producer of canned fruit and vegetables, essential oils, and sugar. Industry in the cities focuses on light manufacturing and the processing of farm products.

Russia incorporated Bessarabia, the eastern part of historical Moldavia, in 1812 but lost it to Romania in 1918. To affirm its claim to the area, in 1924 the USSR established a small token Moldavian Autonomous SSR within the Ukrainian SSR, on the east bank of the Dnestr River. In 1940 the USSR recovered Bessarabia and transformed it into a Soviet republic.

Following the declaration of independence in 1991, an armed conflict erupted between the Russian-Ukrainian separatists in the Trans-Dnestr region and the Moldovan government. Boris Yeltsin, Leonid Kravchuk, and Mircea Snegur, the presidents of Russia, Ukraine, and Moldova, tried to resolve the conflict in the summer of 1992.

molds   Mold is the common name for a group of fungi often characterized by the presence of threadlike filaments, called hyphae, that mass together to form mycelia, vegetative bodies that resemble cotton. Some molds, however, such as the SLIME MOLDS, are more amoebalike and form multinucleate masses of protoplasm called plasmodia. Molds grow over many surfaces, such as wood and food, and thrive best in warm and moist conditions. Many, however, do well at freezing temperatures, presenting problems for refrigerated foods.

Perhaps the most widely studied mold is the familiar bread mold, *Rhizopus nigricans*, which appears on bread that has been moistened, exposed to air, and placed in a warm, dark place. Bread molds have different types of hyphae. Those which spread along the surface are called stolons. At intervals along the stolons, clusters of shorter hyphae, called rhizoids, extend down into the food supply and secrete enzymes that break down sugar and starch into digestible food. The rhizoids absorb the food, and water as well.

Molds can reproduce both asexually and sexually. To produce asexually, some molds develop special reproductive hyphae (sporangiophores), which extend into the air. Black knobs, or spore cases (sporangia), appear at the ends of these hyphae after a few days. When mature, the sporangia break open and release their spores, which will germinate if they reach a suitable environment. Sexual reproduction is accomplished through a form of conjugation. Two different mating types of hyphae, termed *plus* and *minus*, form short, specialized side branches. If the tip of a plus branch meets the tip of a minus branch, conjugation occurs. Each tip becomes a gamete cell, with two fusing to form a zygote. The zygote matures into a zygospore, which may germinate after one to several months if conditions are favorable.

Green mold is an important source of the antibiotic drug penicillin, a substance that destroys many species of infectious bacteria.

mole (animal)   Moles are small burrowing mammals; they include true moles, golden moles, and marsupial moles. The true moles constitute the family Talpidae in the order Insectivora. DESMANS and shrew moles are also members of this family.

True moles comprise 12 genera and 22 species found in North America, Europe, and Asia, primarily in the temperate regions. They feed largely on insects, worms, and other small animals. True moles have cylindrical, stocky bodies; a long, tubular, hairless snout; tiny eyes that are either hidden in the fur or, in some species, actually covered with skin; small ears or, more commonly, no external ears at all; and broad, five-fingered front feet, which are as wide as or wider than they are long and are permanently turned to the side with the thumb down. The front feet are used in digging and possess large, strong claws. In the shrew moles the front feet are longer than they are wide and can be turned palm down. The mole's fur ranges from gray to brown to black, is thick and velvety, and can lie flat in any direction, enabling the mole to move easily either forward or backward in close-fitting tunnels. Moles range in length from 63 to 215 mm (2.5 to 8.5 in) long, plus a tail of 15 to 215 mm (0.6 to 8.5 in), and weigh from 9 to 170 g (0.3 to 6 oz).

Moles dig shallow tunnels, sometimes raising the soil to form extended ridges of broken earth. They also dig deeper tunnels as living quarters and as nurseries. There is an average of two to five young in a litter.

The golden moles, family Chrysochloridae in the order Insectivora, are an African group of 15 to 20 species resembling the true moles in size, form, and habits. They differ in having four fingers on each front foot and in having a broad, horny pad at the end of a relatively short

The common European mole uses its large claws to tunnel up to 18 m (20 yd) daily in search of insects. Its highly sensitive snout compensates for its poor eyesight, enabling the mole to find and consume its weight in food each day. The star-nosed mole (inset) develops fleshy tentacles on its snout, which are thought to aid in sound perception.

nose. The vestigial eyes are covered with skin. The fur is brightly colored, with a metallic sheen, and may be yellow, bronze, red, green, or violet. Golden moles feed largely on insects and lizards.

The MARSUPIAL moles, family Notoryctidae in the order Marsupialia, comprise one or possibly two species found in dry areas in northwestern and south central Australia. Although molelike in appearance, they are true marsupials, the female having a pouch for carrying her young. They have a horny pad on the front of the head, vestigial eyes covered with skin, and no external ears. The silky, iridescent coat varies from white to golden red. Marsupial moles are not as subterranean as are true moles. They are believed to eat insects and worms.

mole (dermatology) Moles are pigmented nodules found on the SKIN of almost all humans. Made up of groups of melanocytes (epidermal cells), or nevus cells, they vary greatly in size and shape and range from flat to raised and smooth to hairy. Moles are flesh colored, brownish yellow, or black. They appear in childhood, and at adolescence or during pregnancy they may enlarge and darken. They often disappear with age.

Moles are generally benign. Rarely, they become involved with the skin CANCERS called malignant melanomas. Only 20 to 30 percent of all such tumors result from melanocytes in moles, so mole removal purely for preventive reasons is not recommended. Moles that enlarge suddenly, change color, bleed, become painful, or are subject to infection and irritation, however, may safely be removed. They should then be analyzed in a laboratory to determine if they are cancerous.

mole (unit of substance) A mole, in chemistry, is a quantity of substance and one of the base units of the SI system, or International System of Units, a modernized version of the METRIC SYSTEM. A mole is the amount of a substance for which the weight in grams has the same numerical value as the substance's molecular weight. A mole of any chemical species (atom, molecule, ion) always contains 6.02×10^{23} particles (AVOGADRO NUMBER). In addition, a mole of any gas occupies a volume of 22.4 liters when maintained at $0°$ C and 1 atmosphere pressure.

molecular biology   see BIOCHEMISTRY; BIOLOGY

molecular weight [muh-lek'-yuh-lur] The molecular weight of a substance is the weight of one molecule of the substance relative to the weight of an atom of the most abundant isotope of carbon, which is taken as exactly 12. Thus, a substance whose molecular weight is 144 has molecules exactly 12 times heavier than a ^{12}C atom. In practice, the molecular weight is found by taking the sum of the ATOMIC WEIGHTS of all the atoms represented, or shown, in the chemical formula.

molecule [mahl'-uh-kuel] A molecule is the smallest particle of a substance that exhibits the chemical properties of that substance. Molecules are groups of ATOMS held together by relatively strong forces called CHEMICAL BONDS. Each molecule of a given substance always contains the same number and kinds of atoms, and the number may range from one (Ne, for example) to many thousands (PROTEINS, for example). In a chemical reaction the chemical bonds are broken, and rearrangement of atoms takes place to form molecules of new compounds (see REACTION, CHEMICAL).

The concept of the molecule dates back to approximately 1800, when a great deal of effort was being directed toward the study of gases and reactions of gases. The results of the experiments led Amadeo Avogadro (see AVOGADRO'S LAW) to suggest that some gases consisted of groups of atoms, or molecules.

dimethyl ether   ethyl alcohol

Molecules with the same number and kinds of atoms but different properties are called ISOMERS. There are two general kinds: structural isomers and stereoisomers (see STEREOCHEMISTRY). Structural isomers are molecules that differ in the order in which the atoms in the molecule are bonded to each other. Stereoisomers are molecules that differ only in the arrangement of their atoms in space.

cis-isomer   trans-isomer

The attractive forces between molecules (see INTERMOLECULAR FORCES) are responsible for whether a substance is a solid, liquid, or gas. Gases have weak attractive forces between molecules, whereas liquids and solids have stronger forces. All intermolecular forces are weak compared to CHEMICAL BONDS, which in a molecule are covalent. Covalent chemical bonds arise because of the attractive forces between the positive nuclei and the negative ELECTRONS of the bonded atoms.

Molière [mohl-yair'] Molière, b. Jean Baptiste Poquelin, Jan. 15, 1622, d. Feb. 17, 1673, composed 12 of the most durable and penetratingly satirical full-length comedies of all time, as well as six shorter farces and comedies.

He was also the leading French comic actor, stage director, and dramatic theoretician of the 17th century. In a theatrical period, the early baroque, dominated by formal neoclassical tragedies, Molière affirmed the potency of COMEDY. He also wrote pastorals and other divertissements, such as his popular comedy-ballets, that depended on a formidable array of stage machinery capable of providing swift and startling changes of sumptuous scenic effects.

Jean Baptiste was the son of Marie and Jean Poquelin, who was a Parisian furniture merchant and upholsterer to the king. He received his early education at the Collège de Clermont, a Jesuit school, becoming a promising scholar of Latin and Greek. Although he proceeded to study law and was awarded his law degree in 1642, he turned away from both the legal profession and his father's business. Instead, he incorporated (1643) an acting troupe, the Illustre Théâtre, in collaboration with the Béjart family, probably because he had fallen in love with their oldest daughter, Madeleine, who became his mistress. At roughly the same time he also acquired the pseudonym Molière. With this company Molière played an unsuccessful season in Paris and went bankrupt, then left to tour the provinces. In 1658 the troupe returned to Paris and played before Louis XIV. The king's brother became Molière's patron; later Molière and his colleagues were appointed official providers of entertainment to the Sun King himself.

In the following 24 years, starting with *The Precious Maidens Ridiculed* (1659) and ending with *The Imaginary Invalid* (1673), Molière advanced from being a gifted adapter of Italian-derived sketches and an entertainer who put on extravaganzas to a writer whose best plays had the lasting impact of tragedies. The clergy mistakenly believed, however, that certain of his plays were attacks on the church. Other playwrights resented his continual experiments with comic forms (as in *The School for Wives*) and with verse (as in *Amphitryon*). Tragedians such as Montfleury and Hauteroche envied his success with the public and the royal protection he enjoyed. Molière responded by incorporating some of his detractors into his comedies as buffoons.

In 1662 he married Armande Béjart, a 19-year-old actress who was either Madeleine's sister or (as rivals claimed) her daughter by Molière. They had one child, Esprit-Madeleine, born in 1665.

In the late 1660s, Molière developed a lung ailment from which he never recovered, although he continued to write, act, direct, and manage his troupe. He finally collapsed and died after the fourth performance of *The Imaginary Invalid*. Church leaders refused to grant his body a formal burial. Seven years later the king united Molière's company with one of its competitors; since that time the French national theater, the COMÉDIE FRANÇAISE, has been known as the House of Molière.

The strongest influence on Molière came from the Italian COMMEDIA DELL'ARTE troupes—with their stock characters and situations—that he encountered during his travels. This was enhanced by Molière's sharing of the Théâtre du Petit-Bourbon in Paris with the Italian Players,

The 17th-century French playwright Molière was a master of sophisticated comedy that satirized the social mores of his time. Also an actor and theater manager, he was an innovator of the French stage during the classical period. His use of type caricature is exemplified in one of his most popular plays, Le Bourgeois Gentilhomme (1670).

led by the celebrated Scaramouche. In his longer comedies Molière immensely refined the commedia themes and techniques, raising neoclassical French comedy to a plane of artistry and inventiveness never attained before or since. He applied the alexandrine, or rhymed hexameter line, to a relaxed dialogue that imitated conversational speech. He also created a gallery of incisive portraits: Tartuffe the religious hypocrite, Jourdain the social climber, Alceste the stony idealist, Harpagon the miser, Argan the hypochondriac, Philaminte the pretentiously cultured lady, and many more.

Molière's principal short plays are *The Jealous Husband* (1645?), *The Flying Doctor* (1648?), *Sganarelle* (1660), *The Rehearsal at Versailles* (1663), and *The Forced Marriage* (1664); the longer plays include *The School for Husbands* (1661), *The School for Wives* (1662), *Tartuffe* (1664), *Don Juan* (1665), The *Misanthrope* (1666), *The Doctor in Spite of Himself* (1666), *Amphitryon* (1668), *The Miser* (1668), *George Dandin* (1668), The *Bourgeois Gentleman* (1670), *Scapin* (1671), *The Learned Ladies* (1672), and *The Imaginary Invalid* (1673).

Molina, Luis de [moh-lee'-nuh, loo-ees' day]   Luis de Molina, b. September 1535, d. Madrid, Oct. 12, 1600, a Spanish Jesuit theologian, is known for his teachings on divine GRACE. His theory, known as Molinism, was that God has foreknowledge that those to whom he gives grace will freely consent to it. Thus, he believed, the effectiveness of grace remains certain, but human freedom is preserved. This concept was widely accepted by the Jesuits but attacked by the Dominicans, who objected to its Pelagian (see PELAGIANISM) emphasis on human freedom and its particular theory of divine foreknowledge.

Molinos, Miguel de [moh-lee'-nohs]   Miguel de Molinos, b. June 29, 1628, d. Dec. 28, 1696, was a Spanish priest and a proponent of QUIETISM who went to Rome and acquired a following there. Influenced by Neoplatonism and medieval mysticism, he emphasized annihilation of the will, oneness with God, and elimination of external religious practices in his *Spiritual Guide* (1675). Molinos's position was attacked vigorously by Jesuits and Dominicans as being in theological error and leading to spiritual laxity. Accused of personal immorality, he was arrested in 1685, tried, condemned, and incarcerated for life.

mollusk   Mollusks are invertebrate animals comprising the phylum Mollusca, which is the second-largest phylum in the animal kingdom with more than 65,000 living species described, and which includes CLAMS, OCTOPUSES, SLUGS, SNAILS, and SQUID. The phylum name derives from the Latin term *mollis*, meaning "soft," to indicate the soft body that is often, but not always, enclosed in a calcareous shell.

General Anatomy

In spite of great anatomical diversity between members of the molluscan phylum, most have a similar body plan. The muscular head-foot region varies in degree of specialization among the classes; it contains sensory and motor apparatuses and often the major portion of the central nervous system. The visceral mass consists of the digestive, excretory, circulatory, and other internal organ systems. A fold of tissue called the mantle covers the visceral mass and secretes the shell in those species in which a shell is present.

Mollusks breathe by way of gills, except in the case of land snails and slugs and some aquatic snails, where a cavity associated with the mantle serves as a modified lung. Most mollusks have open circulatory systems, with three-chambered hearts. Blood circulates from the gills or modified lungs, where it is oxygenated, to the heart, which pumps the blood into sinuses, where it bathes body tissues directly before proceeding to the gills again. Exceptions include cephalopods (squid and octopuses), which have closed circulatory systems.

The digestive system of mollusks is convoluted and ciliated and contains several subdivisions for specialized digestive functions. The most anterior section consists of the mouth and esophagus. A specialized, rasping, filelike radula in the mouth is used for feeding in the majority of mollusks and is found only in the molluscan phylum. Bivalve mollusks such as clams, oysters, and mussels are filter feeders and do not have a radula. The midsection of the digestive tract consists of the stomach and liver. In many mollusks a crystalline style found in the midgut secretes digestive enzymes and rotates, stirring stomach contents. The last section of the digestive tract comprises the intestine and anus.

The nervous system of mollusks consists of ganglionic centers (small integrating "brains"), connecting nerve cords, sensory organs, and motor organs. In lower mol-

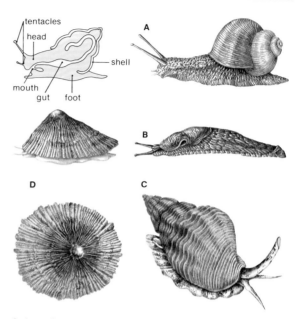

A class of mollusks known as gastropods includes the land snail (A) and slug (B), which are terrestrial, and whelk (C) and limpet (D), which live in oceans. All have similar internal anatomy.

lusks, such as chitons, the nervous system is ladderlike, with ganglia distributed in bilateral pairs running anterior to posterior in the body and connected by long, longitudinal nerve cords and shorter, laterally running connectives. In higher forms (snails, octopuses, and squid) there is a tendency to concentrate ganglia in the head region (cephalization).

Sexes within the mollusks are generally separated, but some cases of hermaphroditism have been found in the gastropods (snails and slugs). Courtship is either nonexistent, as in more primitive forms, or highly complex, as in the gastropods and cephalopods. Fertilization can be external or internal, and eggs are laid singly or in masses.

OYSTERS and clams, both BIVALVE mollusks, are commercially important, and oyster breeding in particular constitutes a major industry in the United States, Europe, and Asia. On the other hand, gastropod mollusks (snails and slugs) are crop pests and cause significant damage.

Molluscan Classes

Monoplacophora. The class Monoplacophora was once known only in fossil form and was thought to be extinct for some 350 million years. In 1952 several living specimens of the genus *Neopilina* were discovered in deep water off the Pacific coast of Costa Rica and were assigned to the monoplacophorans. Like its fossil ancestors, *Neopilina* is unique among the mollusks in showing internal segmentation: it is bilaterally symmetrical with eight pairs of foot-retractor muscles, five or six pairs of gills, six pairs of nephridia (kidneylike structures used in excretion), and other elements indicating a segmented body

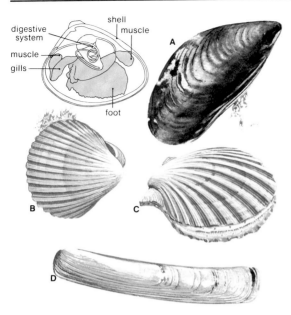

Bivalve mollusks, or pelecypods, include the mussel (A), cockle (B), scallop (C), and razor shell (D). All bivalves have two shells hinged by powerful adductor muscles, a digestive system, gills, and a foot.

plan. The ladderlike nervous system is similar to that of the more advanced chitons but with little ganglionation.

Scaphopoda. Scaphopods, also called tusk shells, are a small group of marine mollusks with long, tubular shells. The head and foot extend into mud or sand, through an opening in one end of the shell. At the opposite end, a smaller opening is exposed above the substrate to provide a pathway for both inhalant and exhalant water currents. Tentacles, coupled with a strong rasping radula, aid in ingestion of food.

Amphineura. Amphineura comprise two subclasses. Aplacophora are small, wormlike animals without a shell that live in moderately deep ocean water. Polyplacophora are the more familiar CHITONS, with eight serially arranged dorsal plates, bilateral symmetry, and a strong muscular foot that clamps the animals onto rocks in shallow water.

Pelecypoda. The class Pelecypoda is also known as Bivalvia. Bivalvia consist of some 30,000 species and include such members as MUSSELS, clams, oysters, and SCALLOPS. The flattened body of the bivalve is enclosed in two shells (called valves) hinged at the dorsum by a strong ligament. These animals are further characterized by a great reduction in the head and by a strong muscular foot (*pelecypoda* means "hatchet foot"), which is often used for rapid digging into sand or mud. Most bivalves are sedentary as adults, although some, such as scallops, can swim by rapidly opening and closing the valves. Bivalves are filter feeders and thus lack a rasping radula to obtain food. The nervous system is composed of three pairs of ganglia connected by two pairs of long nerve cords. Sensory cells discriminate touch, light, and chemical stimuli. A statocyst is used for balance control.

Gastropoda. Gastropods are the largest and most diverse of the molluscan classes and include ABALONES, WHELKS, periwinkles, slugs, and snails. The majority are marine, but there are many terrestrial and freshwater forms. Many gastropods have single coiled external shells. In some the shell has been greatly reduced, internalized, or, in a few cases, lost completely. Gastropods have a well-developed head, in which the central nervous system is concentrated in many species.

Whereas early embryonic development is bilateral in gastropods, they undergo a 180° torsion of the internal organs, shell, and mantle, such that the posterior anus is brought anteriorly toward the mouth. In many, the organs of one side atrophy and development proceeds asymmetrically.

Most aquatic and marine gastropods have gills used for respiration. In land dwellers the gills are replaced with a highly vascularized area in the mantle cavity that serves as a lung.

Cephalopoda. A well-developed head (*cephalopoda* means "head-foot") and a muscular foot modified into arms or tentacles characterize the class Cephalopoda, which contains approximately 650 species of marine mollusks. These include cuttlefish, chambered nautiluses, octopuses, and squid. Among the cephalopods only the chambered nautilus has an external shell. Cephalopods have well-developed nervous systems and are capable of a wide range of complex behaviors, including simple learned behaviors. A funnel, or siphon jet, in the head

Cephalopod mollusks, including the squid (A), cuttlefish (B), and octopus (C), swim through the ocean by sucking water into the body and shooting jets of water out of a siphon. Most cephalopods possess ink sacs containing dark fluid, which they squirt when attacked. Cuttlefish and squid have an internal shell; the nautilus has an external shell, and the octopus has none at all.

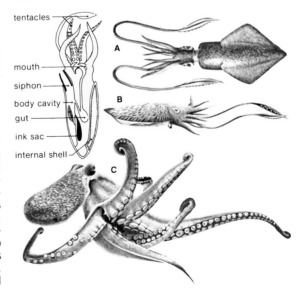

can squirt water in rapid escape from predators, and "ink" sacs can release a cloud of dark fluid to confuse enemies and to cover the animal's retreat.

molly Mollies are a genus, *Poecilia*, of live-bearing killifishes in the family Poeciliidae found from northern South America into southern North America. They range in size from 5 to 13 cm (2 to 5 in). Males have the anal fin developed into a gonopodium for depositing sperm within the female; females can retain the sperm over a period of time to fertilize several successive batches of eggs. One species, *P. reticulata*, is the well-known GUPPY (formerly *Lebistes reticulatus*). The sailfin molly, *P. latipinna*, ranges from Mexico into North Carolina and lives in both fresh and brackish waters. The Amazon molly, *P. formosa*, found from northeastern Mexico into southern Texas, is virtually an all-female species. Female Amazon mollies must mate, usually with males of *P. latipinna* or *P. sphenops*, to produce offspring, but the sperm only stimulates egg development and does not contribute to the young. Rarely—about one in 10,000—a male Amazon molly will be born, but nothing is known about contribution to the species.

Molly Maguires The Molly Maguires, a secret terrorist society, operated in the anthracite coal region of eastern Pennsylvania from the mid-1860s to the late 1870s. Named after a secret antilandlord group in Ireland, the largely Irish-American organization attempted to improve living and working conditions in the mining industry. To achieve this the "Mollies" intimidated and murdered mineowners and superintendents, police officers, and judges, initiated several coal strikes, and formed a union. In 1874, Pinkerton detectives were hired to infiltrate the group, which was crushed by a series of murder convictions between 1875 and 1878.

Molly Pitcher Molly Pitcher was the name given to Mary Ludwig Hays (later McCauley), b. near Trenton, N.J., Oct. 13, 1754, d. Jan. 22, 1832, who carried pitchers of water to the American soldiers at the Battle of MONMOUTH (June 28, 1778) during the American Revolution. Like numerous other women in that war, she accompanied her husband as a camp follower. According to some accounts, she fought in his place when he was overcome by heat or wounded. Her heroism made her a legendary figure.

Molnár, Ferenc [mohl'-nahr, fair'-ents] Ferenc Molnár, b. Jan. 12, 1878, d. Apr. 2, 1952, is perhaps the best-known Hungarian author. His plays have been translated into more than 25 languages, and several have been adapted for the screen. *Liliom* (1909; Eng. trans., 1921) and *The Swan* (1920; Eng. trans., 1922) are frequently staged in the West. A keen observer, he was especially adept at depicting middle- and upper-class urban life.

His plays display a mastery of stagecraft, witty dialogue, and a polished style. Some of his best short stories are collected in *Muzsika* (Music, 1908). Molnár was also the author of several novels, the most successful being *The Paul Street Boys* (1907; Eng. trans., 1927), written for young people. He left Hungary in the 1930s to settle in New York.

Molniya [mohl'-nee-ah] Molniya is a Soviet COMMUNICATIONS SATELLITE program using a distinctive high-inclination 12-hour orbit. First launched on Apr. 23, 1965, the Molniya series consists of three variants, each of which now forms an operational communications-satellite network in connection with ground stations in the "Orbita" program. The inclination of 65° allows the satellites to remain, for long periods, high (39,200-km/24,500-mi apogee) over northern regions of the USSR, whereas satellites in the more common 24-hour geosynchronous equatorial orbits would be very near the horizon. Because the orbits of the Molniyas are not geosynchronous, a pattern of at least three satellites is needed to provide full 24-hour coverage.

Molniya 1 satellites, each weighing about 1,000 kg (2,200 lb), were first launched in 1965; the second-generation *Molniya 2* satellites, each weighing 1,250 kg (2,750 lb), were introduced in 1971; and the third-generation *Molniya 3* satellites appeared in 1974.

Molotov, Vyacheslav Mikhailovich [maw'-luh-tuhf, vyeh-chis-lahf' mee-ky'-luh-vich] Vyacheslav Mikhailovich Molotov (originally Vyacheslav Skriabin), b. Mar. 9 (N.S.), 1890, d. Nov. 8, 1986, was for many years a leading official of the USSR. He joined the Bolsheviks in 1906, helped found the party newspaper *Pravda*, and during the Russian Revolutions of 1917 helped plan the Bolshevik seizure of power. In 1930–41 he was chairman of the Council of People's Commissars, a post equivalent to prime minister, and in 1939–49 and 1953–56 he served as foreign minister. He negotiated the NAZI-SOVIET PACT of August 1939 and played a key role in Soviet wartime and postwar relations with the Western powers. A faithful lieutenant of Joseph Stalin, he broke with Stalin's successor Nikita Khrushchev in 1957. Molotov was dismissed from his government posts and from the party's leading bodies and named ambassador to Mongolia (1957–60) and representative to the International Atomic Energy Agency in Vienna (1960–61). He was expelled from the Communist party in 1962, but was later reinstated.

molting Molting, also called ecdysis or shedding, is the periodic loss and replacement of the cuticle (protective outer covering), skin, feathers, or hair. It occurs in a wide variety of animals.

Nematode worms undergo four molts between hatching and maturity, each time shedding the entire thick cu-

Lizards, such as this gecko, as well as snakes and amphibians, periodically shed their outer layer of skin. This is replaced by an underlying epidermal layer.

ticle along with the attached linings of the body openings. These molts often begin or end distinctive phases in the life cycle.

In the arthropods the cuticle is the rigid supporting frame of the body—an external skeleton. Because this exoskeleton does not grow after it is formed, it must be shed to permit body growth. Molting involves the secretion of enzymes by the epidermis and the loosening and partial dissolving of the old cuticle, which then splits, allowing the arthropod to emerge. Molting is under hormonal control and, in insects, may be begun by the pressure of growth in the abdomen.

A cuticle is definitely present on the skin of some fishes, and it probably occurs on the skin of many others as well. This cuticle is regularly shed in some species, but almost nothing is known about either the structure and composition of the cuticle or its shedding mechanism.

Amphibian molting may occur from every few days to every few weeks except in very cold weather, when it ceases completely. Two molt-control mechanisms are involved, one for the salamanders and another for the frogs and toads. Both mechanisms have a natural internal rhythm of occurrence, and both are influenced by light and temperature. In the salamanders the anterior lobe of the pituitary gland secretes a thyrotropic hormone, which stimulates the thyroid gland to release its hormone or hormones, triggering molting. In frogs and toads the anterior lobe of the pituitary secretes a hormone that stimulates the outer layer, or cortex, of the adrenal glands, which release compounds to begin the molt.

The reptilian epidermis consists of at least six layers, the lowest being the cell-producing stratum germinativum. Above the stratum germinativum the epidermis is typically divided into two distinct tissues. In molting, the two tissue layers separate, and the outer tissue is shed. After about a week the stratum germinativum produces a new inner tissue layer.

Birds undergo both developmental and cyclic molts. The molting process is mechanically simple: the new feathers arise in the same follicles as the old and push them out. The process is thought to be generally controlled by an internal rhythmic cycle and by the changing amounts of seasonal daylight, which effect the release of hormones.

Many mammals undergo at least two developmental molts, the first when they change from their baby, or juvenile, coat to that of the subadult, and the second when they change from the subadult to the adult coat pattern. In temperate regions many mammals undergo two annual molts, one in the spring to produce the summer coat, the other in the fall to produce the winter coat. The new hairs grow alongside the old ones, and both may be present for varying lengths of time. Factors that regulate the process include a natural rhythm, seasonal changes in light duration, and hormones.

Moltke, Helmuth Johannes Ludwig, Graf von

[mohlt'-ke, hel'-moot yoh-hah'-nes lood'-vik, grahf fuhn] Helmuth Johannes Ludwig, Graf von Moltke, b. May 25, 1848, d. June 18, 1916 (a nephew of Helmut Karl Bernhard von Moltke), chief of the German General Staff (1906–14), failed in his bid for a quick victory in World War I. Employing the plan devised by his predecessor, Alfred von SCHLIEFFEN, Moltke concentrated his troops on the Belgian and French frontiers while making minimal efforts on the Russian front. Moltke modified Schlieffen's plan, however; his coordination of the western forces was poor, and in the middle of his offensive he diverted some troops to the east. The German attack on France was stopped at the Marne in early September 1914, and Emperor William II relieved Moltke of his command on September 14.

Moltke, Helmuth Karl Bernhard, Graf von

[mohlt'-ke, hel'-moot kahrl bairn'-hahrt, grahf fuhn] The Prussian general Helmuth Karl Bernhard, Graf von Moltke, b. Oct. 26, 1800, d. Apr. 24, 1891, was the strategist who designed the military victories leading to German unification under Otto von BISMARCK. Moltke entered the Prussian army in 1822 and the General Staff in 1832. Appointed chief of the Prussian General Staff by WILLIAM I in 1857, he held the post until 1888. Greatly influenced by Napoleon I's campaigns and Carl von CLAUSEWITZ's writings, Moltke developed a strategy aimed at annihilating enemy forces by offensive action and decisive battles. His planning led to Prussian victories in the war with Denmark (1864), the SEVEN WEEKS' WAR (1866), and the FRANCO-PRUSSIAN WAR (1870–71). Moltke's battle plans were distinguished by his use of technological innovations—notably railroads—and the skillful training of his officers, who were imbued with his ideas but were nevertheless left free to exercise great latitude on the battlefield.

Moluccas

Moluccas [muh-luk'-uhz] The Moluccas (formerly the Spice Islands and now called Maluku) form a province in eastern Indonesia. They comprise many islands (including Ambon, Buru, and Ceram) and island groups, totaling about 74,500 km^2 (28,800 mi^2). The population is 1,786,200 (1989 est.).

Most of the islands are heavily forested and mountainous, reaching 3,055 m (10,023 ft) on Ceram Island, and several active volcanoes are found there. The islands have long been famous for cloves, mace, and nutmeg; today forest products and copra are the leading exports. In 1511, Ferdinand Magellan was the first European to explore the islands, and in 1512, Portuguese settlers arrived. In the early 17th century the Dutch seized the islands and secured a monopoly of the SPICE TRADE. During World War II the Japanese occupied the islands. Soon after Indonesian independence, a separate, short-lived South Moluccan Republic was proclaimed in 1950. The insurgency, led by the AMBONESE, was crushed by 1956. Promised Dutch support for the campaign to gain independence for the Moluccas failed to materialize, and during the 1970s some South Moluccans living in the Netherlands engaged in terrorist activities to draw attention to their cause.

molybdenum [muh-lib'-duh-nuhm]

Molybdenum is a silver white metallic chemical element of Group VIB in the periodic table, in the second transition series (see TRANSITION ELEMENTS). Its symbol is Mo, its atomic number is 42, and its atomic weight is 95.94. The name is derived from the Greek *molybdos*, meaning "lead." In 1778, Carl Scheele of Sweden recognized molybdenite as a distinct ore of a new element; the ore had previously been confused with graphite and lead ore. The metal was first prepared (in an impure form) in 1782. The free element does not occur in nature, but it is extracted from molybdenite (MoS_2), wulfenite ($PbMoO_4$), and powellite ($Ca[MoW]O_4$) and is recovered as a by-product of copper and tungsten mining. The pure metal is prepared by the reduction of purified molybdic trioxide (MoO_3) or ammonium molybdate ($[NH_4]_2MoO_4$) with hydrogen.

Properties. Molybdenum has a melting point of 2,617° C, a boiling point of 4,612° C, and a density of 10.22 g/cm^3. It exhibits oxidation states of 0, +1, +2, +3, +4, +5, and +6. The metal is very hard but more ductile than the chemically similar tungsten. Of the more readily available metals only tungsten and tantalum have higher melting points.

Uses. Molybdenum is a valuable alloying agent. Almost all high-strength steels contain the metal in amounts ranging from 0.25% to 8% by weight. It is also used in the Hastelloys, which are heat- and corrosion-resistant, nickel-based alloys. Molybdenum wire is used as a filament, grid, and screen material in electron tubes. The metal is also employed as an electrode material for electrically heated glass furnaces, and the sulfide is widely used as a high-temperature lubricant.

Biological Functions. In human metabolism, molybdenum is a trace element that is involved in protein synthesis and oxidation reactions. It is also an essential trace element for plants and is important for soil fertility.

Momaday, N. Scott [mahm'-uh-day]

The writer Navarre Scott Momaday, b. Lawton, Okla., Feb. 27, 1934, is known for his powerful portrayal of the American Indian experience. His Pulitzer Prize–winning novel, *The House Made of Dawn* (1968), is about the dilemma of the modern Indian who can neither totally assimilate into white society nor return to the tribal community. *The Way to Rainy Mountain* (1969) tells in the contrapuntal voices of myth and history the story of Momaday's tribe, the Kiowa. *The Ancient Child*, a novel, and *Ancestral Voices: Conversations with N. Scott Momaday* both appeared in 1989.

Mombasa [mahm-bas'-uh]

Mombasa, a city in southern Kenya situated on the Indian Ocean, is the nation's main port. It has a population of 425,600 (1984 est.). Most of the city is located on Mombasa Island, which is connected to the mainland by causeways and bridges. Mombasa's modern, deepwater harbor is the only port for both Kenya and landlocked Uganda. Mombasa's industries include petroleum refining and cement, automobile production, and food processing.

By the 8th century, Arab traders had settled there. Mombasa was visited by Vasco da Gama in 1498, and the city was essentially controlled by the Portuguese in the 16th and 17th centuries. The sultan of Zanzibar controlled the port from 1840 to 1895, when the British took over and made Mombasa the capital (until 1907) of their East Africa Protectorate.

moment of inertia

A rotating body has the same tendency to maintain its state of rotational motion that a body moving in a straight line has to maintain its linear motion. The moment of inertia is a measure of a body's resistance to changes in rotation rate, analogous to mass as the measure of resistance to changes in translational motion. Specifically, torque T and angular acceleration α are related through the moment of inertia I by the equation $T=I\alpha$, just as force f and acceleration a are related through the mass m by the equation $f=ma$.

The moment of inertia depends not only on the mass of the body but also on the distribution of mass relative to the axis. This distribution accounts for the fact that objects of various shapes with the same masses and diameters (such as sphere, solid cylinder, hollow cylinder, or wheel and axle) will not take the same time to roll down an inclined plane. Objects whose mass is concentrated near the axis have the smallest moment of inertia and thus reach the bottom of the plane sooner than the others.

See also: ANGULAR MOMENTUM; INERTIA.

momentum

Momentum is a property possessed by an object by virtue of its motion. The linear momentum of an object is equal to its mass times its velocity. The momentum of a group of particles is the vector sum of the individual momenta of the particles within the group.

Newton's second law of motion, in its original form, states that the sum of the external forces acting on an object or a system of particles is equal to the time rate of change of momentum of the system.

See also: ANGULAR MOMENTUM; CONSERVATION, LAWS OF.

Mommsen, Theodor [mawm'-sen] Theodor Mommsen, b. Nov. 30, 1817, d. Nov. 1, 1903, was a German historian noted for his studies of ancient Rome. His famous *History of Rome* (1854–85; Eng. trans., 1862–86) combines a focus on the political history of the Roman republic with broad concern for aspects of social and cultural life. He stressed the critical examination of texts, artifacts, and monuments.

Mommsen was also involved in German politics, serving in the Reichstag from 1881 to 1884. In 1902, Mommsen was awarded the Nobel Prize for literature.

Mon The Mon (also sometimes called Talaing) people have for centuries lived in the area of present-day Thailand and Burma. They speak the Mon language, part of the widely distributed Mon-Khmer language group (see SOUTHEAST ASIAN LANGUAGES). Although no reliable population figures exist, Mon speakers are estimated to number about 400,000 in Burma and fewer than 100,000 in Thailand.

Mon kingdoms in Thailand disappeared as Thai influence expanded in the 13th century. Those in Lower Burma frequently were at war with Burmese states that were located further north. Even after the last important Mon kingdom fell in the 16th century, Mon resistance continued; many refugees fled to Thailand, their descendants comprising the present Mon population there. The Burmese adopted much from Mon culture, including their writing system. Inscriptions in the Mon language have been found dating from as early as the 6th century. The Mon are said to have been the first Theravada Buddhists in Southeast Asia; their monastic discipline and ritual are highly respected even today. A political movement actively seeking the formation of a new Mon state has developed within the Burmese nation but has as yet been unsuccessful.

Mon-Khmer languages see SOUTHEAST ASIAN LANGUAGES

Mona Lisa The Mona Lisa (Louvre, Paris), also known as *La Gioconda*, is a portrait of the wife of Francesco del Giocondo, painted by LEONARDO DA VINCI between 1503 and 1505. This figure of a woman, dressed in the Florentine fashion of her day and seated in a visionary, mountainous landscape, is a remarkable instance of Leonardo's sfumato technique of soft, heavily shaded modeling. The Mona Lisa's enigmatic expression, which seems both alluring and aloof, has given the portrait universal fame.

Monaco [mahn'-uh-koh] The Principality of Monaco is located along the Mediterranean Sea on the CÔTE D'AZUR. Only 14 km (9 mi) west of the French city of Nice and 8 km (5 mi) east of the Italian border, Monaco is surrounded by France on three sides. With an area of 1.8 km² (0.7

AT A GLANCE

PRINCIPALITY OF MONACO

Land: Area: 1.90 km² (0.734 mi²). Capital: Monaco-Ville. Largest community: Monte Carlo.

People: Population (1990 est.): 29,453. Density: 15,502 persons per km² (40,127 per mi²). Distribution (1990): 100% urban, 0% rural. Official language: French. Major religion: Roman Catholicism.

Government: Type: constitutional monarchy. Legislature: National Council. Political subdivisions: 4 districts.

Economy: Labor distribution (1985): agriculture, manufacturing, and construction—33%; trade, utilities, and services—47.6%; public administration and others—19.4%. Currency: 1 French franc = 100 centimes.

Education and Health: Literacy (1990): 99% of adult population. Universities (1986): none. Hospital beds (1990): 537. Physicians (1990): 90. Life expectancy (1990): women—80; men—72. Infant mortality (1990): 9 per 1,000 live births.

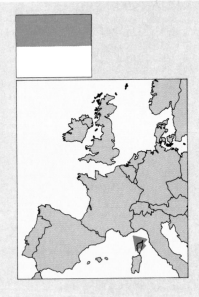

mi²) it is the smallest state in Europe after Vatican City. Thanks to its beaches, well-known gambling casino, and luxurious hotels, it has long been a famous resort.

Land and People

Monaco is divided into four distinct areas. Monaco-Ville, the official capital, is located about 60 m (200 ft) above sea level on the flat top of a rocky promontory extending into the Mediterranean. The 16th-century prince's palace, government buildings, and the cathedral (built 1876–90) are there. The Museum of Oceanography, headed by Jacques COUSTEAU, and several other museums are also in Monaco-Ville. La Condamine is the commercial port area. Monaco's light manufacturing industries are concentrated in Fontvieille. MONTE CARLO is the tourist center, with beaches, hotels, and the gambling casino.

Natives of Monaco, called Monégasques, constitute only about 16% of the population. French citizens, who make up 47% of the population, are the largest group living in Monaco. Italians account for 16% of the population. French is the official language, but English, Italian, and Monégasque, a language with French and Italian roots, are widely spoken. Roman Catholicism, the state religion, is adhered to by 95% of the population. Monaco's population density is the highest of any nation in the world.

Economic Activity

More than half of Monaco's national income is derived from tourism. In 1967 the government bought the casino and main hotels and has expanded the tourist facilities since then. The casino is only for tourists; citizens of

Monaco, an independent principality that forms an enclave on the Mediterranean coast of France, derives much of its revenue from tourism. It is most famous for its resorts and casino.

Monaco are not permitted access. Monaco has encouraged an influx of private and corporate capital by providing a favorable tax structure that does not tax corporate or personal income. Instead, various indirect taxes, including excise, stamp, estate, and export taxes, are levied. Many foreign corporations, particularly French and American, have established headquarters in Monaco. Considerable revenue is derived from the sale of postage stamps to collectors. The French franc is the legal currency of Monaco. An economic union originally established in 1865 regulates economic affairs between Monaco and France.

History and Government

The Phoenicians are thought to have established a settlement in Monaco, attracted by the natural harbor. Subsequently it was held by Greeks, Carthaginians, and Romans. Acquired by the Genoese in 1162, it became the property of the Grimaldi family of Genoa in 1297. In 1304 the first Grimaldi prince ascended to the throne of Monaco. In 1861, Monte Carlo's famous casino was built, and Monaco subsequently became a resort for the wealthy of Europe. In 1949, RAINIER III, the present prince, became the ruler.

The government is a constitutional monarchy in which the prince retains limited powers. As chief of state he may initiate legislation and dissolve the unicameral national council, consisting of 18 members elected to 5-year terms by universal adult suffrage. The prince cannot, however, alter or suspend the constitution. The minister of state, who heads the cabinet, must always be French. In return, France provides Monaco with military protection. According to a treaty of 1919, if the prince dies without a male heir, Monaco will become incorporated as an autonomous state under French protection.

monadnock [muh-nad'-nahk] A monadnock, a hill rising conspicuously above a peneplain (see LANDFORM EVOLUTION), is a partially eroded remnant left behind in the general leveling of an area. Rocks particularly resistant to weathering and erosion usually lie underneath a monadnock. The type example, Mount Monadnock (950 m/ 3,165 ft) in southwest New Hampshire, rises more than 300 m (1,000 ft) above the low hills that surround it.

Monaghan [mahn'-uh-guhn] Monaghan is a county in the traditional province of Ulster in northeastern Ireland just south of the border with Northern Ireland. The county covers 1,290 km² (498 mi²) and has a population of 52,379 (1986). The town of Monaghan is the county seat. Monaghan is a region of low, undulating hills, and agriculture is the principal economic activity, with oats, hay, potatoes, flax, and livestock the major products. Light industry takes place in the urban centers.

In AD 330, Monaghan became part of the kingdom of Oriel. From the 13th to the 16th century the powerful MacMahon family controlled Monaghan, but in 1589 control passed to the British crown.

monarchy Monarchy is a political system in which one individual is sovereign, usually for life. An absolute monarch (see DESPOTISM) is above the law; a constitutional monarch is subject to the provisions of a constitution and the acts of a legislature.

Monarchy is probably the oldest form of government; most early peoples knew no other system. Absolute monarchs assumed a new importance in Europe during the 16th and 17th centuries, when the nation-states were formed. Monarchs such as Louis XIV defended their right to rule with the doctrine of DIVINE RIGHT. But monarchy as a system of government was already beginning to decline. The English in the GLORIOUS REVOLUTION (1688) established the supremacy of Parliament. The American (1776) and French (1789) revolutions set up republics in the place of kings. By the mid-20th century monarchies were to a large degree eliminated as a common form of government. In the constitutional monarchies that survive today the role of the monarch is chiefly ceremonial.

monastic art and architecture A monastery is the place of prayer, worship, and residence of a religious community whose members are bound by religious vows that cut them off from the world and its distractions and make them economically self-sufficient. In the West, monasticism, or monachism, was a strong force in the shaping of political, social, and artistic events for about 1,200 years, from the 6th through the 18th centuries. Western monasticism is closely associated with Saint Benedict of Nursia (c.480–c.550), who founded the Benedictine order and the Abbey of MONTE CASSINO in southern Italy about 529. The architectural implications of the Rule of Saint Benedict are perhaps most fully spelled out in the ideal plan of Saint Gall (c.820), Switzerland.

Central to the monastery plan, as it had evolved by the 9th century, was the CLOISTER, from the Latin word *claustrum*, "a shut-in place." All the buildings normally used by the inhabitants opened off the cloister—in particular the church (see CATHEDRALS AND CHURCHES), the chapter house for meetings of the community, the dormitory, the refectory, and storage facilities. Usually at a slight distance was the infirmary and the quarters of the community's leader, the abbot or prior. Usually sited near a stream, the entire complex was oriented so that water could be diverted to the drinking fountains and kitchen before reaching the wash houses and latrines. The domi-

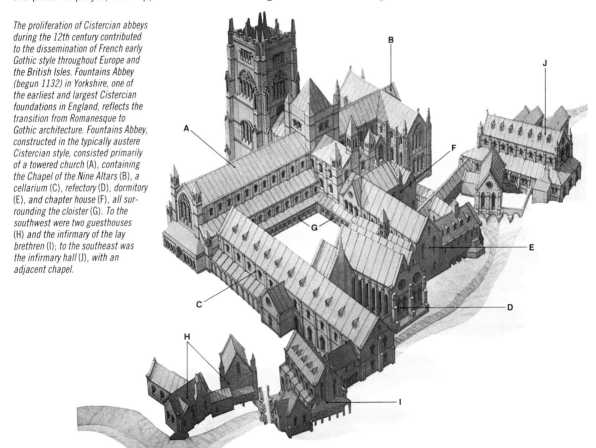

The proliferation of Cistercian abbeys during the 12th century contributed to the dissemination of French early Gothic style throughout Europe and the British Isles. Fountains Abbey (begun 1132) in Yorkshire, one of the earliest and largest Cistercian foundations in England, reflects the transition from Romanesque to Gothic architecture. Fountains Abbey, constructed in the typically austere Cistercian style, consisted primarily of a towered church (A), containing the Chapel of the Nine Altars (B), a cellarium (C), refectory (D), dormitory (E), and chapter house (F), all surrounding the cloister (G). To the southwest were two guesthouses (H) and the infirmary of the lay brethren (I); to the southeast was the infirmary hall (J), with an adjacent chapel.

Fra Angelico's The Stoning of Saint Stephen *is considered one of the highest achievements of iconographic art. Angelico was a Dominican monk and a major figure of the Italian Renaissance. (Chapel of Nicholas V, Vatican City.)*

nant feature of monasticism was its communal character. The size of individual communities varied enormously according to their financial endowments and prestige: an average number of members for a foundation based on the Rule of Saint Benedict was probably from 10 to 50. Central to all monastic life were the devotions in the church and the liturgical requirements of the Hours and the Mass.

Numerous reforms initiated in the late 11th century led to the establishment of new orders that encouraged missionary and parochial work beyond the cloister. Among the preaching orders of friars were the Franciscans, or Grey Friars (founded 1210), the Dominicans, or Black Friars (founded *c.*1210), and the Carmelites, or White Friars (reorganized *c.*1250).

Institutionally, monasticism was the setting for much of the surviving creative artistic activity of the Middle Ages. SAINT BERNARD in his *Apologia* (1127) warned against artistic adornment, principally that of architecture, but Abbot SUGER of Saint-Denis, Paris, one of the most important statesmen of his age (d. 1151), demurred. Suger wrote a treatise—*Libellus de consecratione ecclesiae sancti Dionysii* (1154; A Little Book on the Consecration of the Church of Saint Denis)—concerning the rebuilding and decorating in the new Gothic style of a large part of the abbey church of Saint-Denis under his leadership. It justified the use of fine and rich art as a fitting tribute to the living presence of Christ in the mass. Suger went on to describe the ideal church, which glowed

with color and splendor from paintings, precious stones and metals, and stained-glass windows.

Monastic Church Architecture and Embellishment. The church was always the most imposing feature of a monastic complex. By its size and hierarchical elaboration, it expressed many of the aspirations of the community to which it belonged. It also gave some indication of the wealth and prosperity of the monastery and, inside, would probably commemorate patrons who provided sustained support to the community; many lay patrons were buried inside monastic churches. The most precious human remains in a monastic church were the relics of saints preserved in shrines behind the high altar.

Most churches belonging to the preaching orders have large naves as in the Dominican Church of Santi Giovanni e Paolo (Saints John and Paul; 1234–1430) in Venice, because public preaching and teaching were important. The early austere ideals of Cistercianism can be seen in the architecture of their surviving 12th-century churches, as at Fontenay (*c.*1140) in France. The declining simplicity of a once reformed and austere order can be traced at the Cistercian abbey church of Pontigny; it was rebuilt in 1186 with an elaborate Gothic east end, or chevet, with radiating chapels, an architectural magnificence that would have scandalized Saint Bernard.

The patronage of a monastic house waxed and waned with the popularity of the order itself. The great period of Benedictine patronage ended in the 13th century; the greatest period of popularity for the preaching orders was the 13th and 14th centuries. The Carthusians remained universally respected for their high ideals throughout the Middle Ages.

Despite the chronologically haphazard nature of this process of patronage, extremely fine collections of objects amassed by the wealthier houses have survived. An early treasury (mainly 9th–12th centuries) remains, for example, at the Benedictine house of Sainte-Foy, Conques, France. A splendid group of 11th- and 12th-century manuscripts from the Benedictine Abbey of Saint-Martial, Limoges, survives in the Bibliothèque Nationale, Paris, and a large portion of the 11th- and 12th-century library survives at its original location in the Benedictine priory of Durham Cathedral in England.

Monastic Artists. The monastic orders were much concerned with preservation of texts and of objects. Although the English painter John Siferwas (*c.*1400) and the Italian artist Fra ANGELICO were both Dominican friars, it is less clear how deeply members of religious orders were involved in artistic creation. It is possible to produce a scattering of names of Benedictine monks who were also painters and illuminators, including Eadwine (*c.*1149), creator of the Eadwine Psalter (Trinity College, Cambridge, England) at Canterbury and Matthew Paris (d. 1259) at Saint Albans. The writing of Theophilus clearly indicates that in certain circumstances metalwork and stained glass might have been made in monasteries by monastic craftsmen, but if they did exist, schools of monastic art flourished only spasmodically and infrequently, and from the 11th century onward a growing body of evidence points to the use of outside lay professionals for the creation of art in monastic houses. Spectacular examples of this process are apparent in the great mendicant churches of Florence, decorated in the 14th century by GIOTTO DI BONDONE and his followers. The members of an order who were practicing artists can often be shown to have been fully trained professionals prior to joining the order; indeed, both the development of style and of technical expertise—particularly in architecture—would demand experience based on a mobility that was impossible for most professed monks.

Final Developments. In some areas of Europe, notably in Spain, France, South Germany, and Italy, the great medieval monastic institutions survived until the widespread social changes inspired by the French Revolution in 1789. In an even smaller area, especially in Spain, South Germany, and Austria, they have had a continuous history to the present. During the 17th and 18th centuries a considerable amount of genuine modernization was effected to bring conventual buildings into line with revised conceptions of physical comfort and privacy. Rebuilding often included the church and was carried out on a palatial scale. Thus the great Carolingian foundations of Saint Gall, Switzerland, of Ottobeuren, and of Saint Emmeram, Regensberg, both in Germany, were all substantially and magnificently altered in the 18th century to become outstanding baroque and rococo monuments. At other monasteries such as Bec-Héllouin or Saint-Etienne, Caen, France, the medieval churches were left as they were, but the conventual buildings were dramatically transformed, mostly during the first half of the 18th century. The only monastic art and architecture of note in the 20th century were produced by the Swiss-French architect LE CORBUSIER. They are the startling free-form Pilgrim Church of Nôtre Dame du Haut (1950–55) at Ronchamp and the austere cast-concrete Dominican Monastery of La Tourette (1954–59) at Évreux-sur-l'Arbesle, both in France. The history of significant monastic patronage of art and architecture, however, ends in effect with the political and social changes initiated by the French Revolution.

See also: BAROQUE ART AND ARCHITECTURE; GOTHIC ART AND ARCHITECTURE; ILLUMINATED MANUSCRIPTS; ROMANESQUE ART AND ARCHITECTURE.

monasticism Monasticism (from the Greek *monos,* meaning "single" or "alone") usually refers to the way of life—communitarian or solitary—adopted by those individuals, male or female, who have elected to pursue an ideal of perfection or a higher level of religious experience through leaving the world. Monastic orders historically have been organized around a rule or a teacher, the activities of the members being closely regulated in accordance with the rule adopted. The practice is ancient, having existed in India almost ten centuries before Christ. It can be found in some form among most developed religions: Hinduism, Buddhism, Jainism, Daoism, the Sufi branch of Islam, and Christianity. In the time of Christ, the ESSENES at Qumran were Jewish monks.

Technically, monasticism embraces both the life of the hermit, characterized by varying degrees of extreme solitude, and the life of the cenobite, that is, the monk living in a community offering a limited amount of solitude. Monasticism always entails ASCETICISM, or the practice of disciplined self-denial. This asceticism may include fasting, silence, a prohibition against personal ownership, and an acceptance of bodily discomfort. Almost always it includes poverty, celibacy, and obedience to a spiritual leader.

Christian monasticism began in the deserts of Egypt and Syria in the 4th century AD. Saint ANTHONY the Great was connected with the first Egyptian hermits; Saint Pachomius (d. 346), with the first communities of cenobites in Egypt. Saint BASIL THE GREAT (fl. 379), bishop of Caesarea, placed monasticism in an urban context by introducing charitable service as a work discipline.

The organization of Western monasticism is due primarily to Saint BENEDICT of Nursia (6th century), whose Benedictine rule formed the basis of life in most monastic communities until the 12th century (see BENEDICTINES). Among the principal monastic orders that evolved in the Middle Ages were the CARTHUSIANS in the 11th century and the CISTERCIANS in the 12th; the mendicant orders, or friars—DOMINICANS, FRANCISCANS, and CARMELITES—arose in the 13th century.

Although Protestantism rejected monasticism in the 16th century, the Anglican church since the 19th century has sponsored a number of monastic orders. Buddhist monks, for their part, continue to play an important social as well as religious role in contemporary Southeast Asia and Japan.

monazite [mahn'-uh-zyt] The chief ore of thorium and the rare earths is the PHOSPHATE MINERAL monazite [(Ce, La, Y, Th) PO_4]. It commonly forms small flattened or elongated crystals (monoclinic system) that are a resinous, reddish to yellowish brown. Hardness is $5–5\frac{1}{2}$, streak is white, and specific gravity is 4.6–5.4. Monazite occurs as an accessory mineral in granites, gneisses, and pegmatites and as rounded grains in the sands formed from their weathering. The thorium-rich varieties are radioactive and have been used in RADIOMETRIC AGE-DATING.

Monck, Charles Stanley Monck, 4th Viscount [muhnk] Charles Stanley Monck, b. Ireland, Oct. 10, 1819, d. Nov. 29, 1894, was the first governor-general of the Dominion of Canada. A Liberal, he served (1855–58) as a treasury lord in the British government before being named governor-general of British North America in 1861. He worked both to avoid a breach with the United States during the U.S. Civil War and to promote Canadian Confederation. After Confederation was achieved (1867) he remained in Canada for one year as governor-general of the new dominion.

Monck, George, 1st Duke of Albemarle The English general George Monck, b. Dec. 6, 1608, d. Jan. 3, 1670, fought for the parliamentarians during the English Civil War but helped bring republican government to an end in 1660 by securing the peaceful restoration of the Stuart monarchy. After 1646 he served the Commonwealth and the Protectorate by subduing Scotland and fighting at sea against the Dutch. Following Oliver CROMWELL's death (1658) and the fall of his son Richard Cromwell, Monck broke with the new military government established in 1659. He led his troops south from the Scottish border early in 1660 to restore a free Parliament and to negotiate the return of CHARLES II from France. In gratitude Charles made Monck duke of Albemarle in 1660.

Moncton [muhnk'-tuhn] Moncton (1986 pop., 55,468) is a port and the second largest city in New Brunswick, Canada, located in the southeastern part of the province. It is situated along the Petitcodiac River, about 40 km (25 mi) from its mouth at the Bay of Fundy. The city is an important transportation center, and its manufactures include textiles, paper, and processed foods. The University of Moncton (1864) is a center for the study of French-Acadian culture. The tidal bore, a 1-to-2-m (3-to-6-ft) wave that rushes up the river from the bay twice daily, is a well-known tourist attraction. Moncton was settled in 1763 by German immigrants from Pennsylvania, urged by British colonial authorities.

Mondale, Walter F. [mahn'-dayl] Walter Frederick "Fritz" Mondale, b. Ceylon, Minn., Jan. 5, 1928, served as vice-president of the United States from 1977 to 1981 under President Jimmy Carter. Mondale was also the Democratic party's presidential candidate in 1984.

Trained in law at the University of Minnesota, Mondale served (1960–64) as state attorney general and was chosen to fill out the Senate term of Hubert Humphrey, who was elected vice-president in 1964. Mondale was elected to the Senate in his own right in 1966 and 1972. He pressed for open-housing legislation and federal urban aid. His initial support of the Vietnam War changed to opposition.

As vice-president, Mondale was a key advisor to President Carter. Mondale campaigned vigorously as Carter's running mate in 1980, but Carter and Mondale were defeated for reelection by the Republican ticket of Ronald Reagan and George Bush.

After difficult primary-election battles, Mondale won the Democratic nomination in July 1984. Campaigning with his running mate, Geraldine FERRARO, he attacked the Reagan record on such issues as the large budget deficit and the need for arms control. In the election Mondale won only 13 electoral votes to Reagan's overwhelming 525. Mondale then returned to the private practice of law in Washington.

Monday see CALENDAR

Mondrian, Piet [mohn'-dree-ahn, peet] Piet Mondrian, b. Mar. 7, 1872, d. Feb. 1, 1944, among the most

prominent of the 20th century's geometric painters, evolved an austere art of black lines and colored rectangles placed against white backgrounds. His early paintings are fairly conventional Dutch landscapes, but after 1908—when he became aware of recent and avant-garde art movements of that time (symbolism and Fauvism)—he began to withdraw from imitation of nature.

In 1911, Mondrian discovered the cubist works of Pablo Picasso and Georges Braque. Thereafter, in Paris (1912–14), he produced his own version of CUBISM. It was to be a very short step from his cubist trees and still lifes to the pure abstractions that he produced from 1916 onward.

Throughout World War I, Mondrian remained in Holland, which was a neutral nation. Isolation from Paris at this time fostered an independent modern movement in Holland, leading Mondrian and several other Dutch artists to form the DE STIJL group (1916), which published its own periodical (*De Stijl*, 1917–32). There, Mondrian explained his ideas, which were later codified in the pamphlet *Neoplasticism* (1920). He used straight lines joined at right angles because he believed this to be the angle of perfect equilibrium. He used red, yellow, blue, black, white, and gray because they are not found in their purest form in nature and are therefore the most abstract colors. Mondrian wanted his art to express a universal, spiritual, and harmonious conception of the universe and of humanity's place within it.

Mondrian emigrated to the United States in 1940 and died in New York City four years later. He influenced not only artists slightly younger than himself, such as Ben Nicholson and Max Bill, but also, in the 1950s and '60s, some of the American hard-edge abstractionists. An extensive collection of Mondrian's work is preserved in the Gemeente Museum, The Hague.

Piet Mondrian's Composition with Red, Yellow and Blue *(1920), shows his characteristic use of straight lines, right angles, and primary colors. (Private collection, Amsterdam.)*

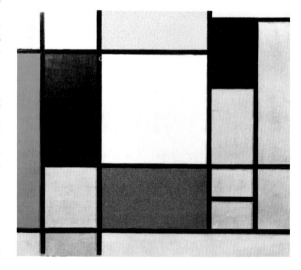

Monera [muh-nair'-uh]   In the classification of living organisms, the group known as Monera contains the smallest and most abundant organisms on Earth, the microbes. Originally a term proposed by Ernst H. Haeckel in 1866, it now includes bacteria, blue-green algae, and spirochetes. In some classification systems Monera is a kingdom; others assign bacteria and blue-green algae to the kingdom Protista or to the plant division Schizophyta.

Most members are characterized by a nucleus that is not distinctly separated from cytoplasm by a membrane. The nucleus contains a single chromosome composed of deoxyribonucleic acid (DNA) and polyamines. Bacteria often have flagella by which to move. Most forms within this group reproduce asexually by means of binary fission of the cells.

Monet, Claude [moh-nay', klohd]   The most lyrical of the impressionist painters, Claude Oscar Monet, b. Nov. 14, 1840, d. Dec. 5, 1926, was also the most committed to recording transient effects of light and atmosphere. This aim led Monet and his colleagues to develop the techniques of IMPRESSIONISM. Monet advised his fellow painters to concentrate on the play of light and color of the objects that they had before them. The goal was to capture temporary phenomena, and this was pursued in a systematic manner, according to the laws of optics and complementary color relationships; yet the result was often a sheer celebration of painting itself, an expression of Monet's delight in the colors, textures, and shapes of the landscape.

At the studio of Charles Gleyre he met Pierre Auguste Renoir, Frédéric Bazille, and Alfred Sisley. By 1865 he had embarked on a program of outdoor painting of marine and forest subjects, townscapes, and figures in landscape settings. In the summer of 1869, Monet worked alongside Renoir and began to emerge as the leading figure in the creation of the techniques of outdoor impressionism. He consolidated this role in 1872–75, especially favoring river subjects with light-dappled water, and garden scenes in which vigorous brushstrokes and patches of bright color break into the contours of objects, dissolving their forms in the play of light. In 1876–77 he embarked on the plan of painting a single subject from various viewpoints, choosing for this purpose the Gare Saint-Lazare, a Parisian railway station (one of these canvases is in the Fogg Art Museum, Cambridge, Mass.).

The Houses of Parliament (1903) is one of several views of the site painted by the French impressionist Claude Monet from across the River Thames. Monet was attracted to London's enveloping fog, which gave architecture, water, and air a mysterious weightlessness in the diffused light of the veiled sun. (Chester Dale Collection, New York City.)

Until the 1880s, Monet endured extreme poverty. During this decade, however, his works began to sell at higher prices, allowing him to live and paint as he wished. In the early 1890s he again took up the idea of producing a series of views of the same subject which he intended to be shown as a group. His subjects included haystacks, poplars, the facade of Rouen Cathedral as it altered from dawn to dusk, the Seine at Giverny, and views of the Thames and the Houses of Parliament. But Monet's key subject after 1890 was the lily pond he had built at his home in Giverny. His various versions of it culminated in several groups of large, decorative paintings of water lilies, called *Nymphéas*. These now hang in the Museum of Modern Art, New York City, and in the Musée de l'Orangerie, Paris. These paintings show the vitality and complexity of Monet's brushwork at its height. Sky, water, and vegetation are transformed into swirling, vibrant masses of color.

monetary policy Monetary policy is action by monetary authorities (in the United States, the Board of Governors of the FEDERAL RESERVE SYSTEM) to induce changes in the money supply and interest rates for the purpose of stimulating or restraining economic activity. Monetary policy is often contrasted to FISCAL POLICY, which affects the economy through taxation and government expenditures, and to INCOMES POLICY, which attempts to influence the economy through wage and price guidelines.

The primary impact of monetary policy is on the availability and cost of loanable funds to businesses. Through a "tight" money policy, the supply of money is restricted, the cost of loanable funds (the interest rate) rises, and business investment spending is thereby discouraged. An "easy" money policy tends to promote the expansion of the money supply, lowers the interest rate, and thereby encourages business to invest in capital facilities. A tight money policy is theoretically appropriate in containing INFLATION; easy money is appropriate in ameliorating a recession.

Monetary policy is effected through certain control mechanisms that the monetary authorities use to alter the excess reserves of commercial banks. The most important and most frequently used technique for changing bank reserves is through open-market operations—the purchase and sale of government securities by the monetary authorities. In the simplest case the monetary authorities order the Federal Reserve banks to purchase government securities from the commercial banks, thus increasing the commercial banks' reserves and their ability to lend. Conversely, when the Federal Reserve banks sell securities to commercial banks, the commercial banks' excess reserves are reduced.

monetary theory Monetary theory attempts to explain the level of total nominal income (income in current dollars), as well as the price level, and hence the value of money within a national economy (see ECONOMY, NATIONAL). Like macroeconomics, with which it overlaps, monetary theory deals with aggregate (total) demand but focuses more on the supply and demand for money. Money is important for aggregate demand because if people want to hold more money they divert expenditures away from items produced by labor and capital, so that employment and the inflation rate decline.

Quantity Theory. The basic insight of the quantity theory of money is that people want to hold a certain *real* (inflation-adjusted) quantity of money. If the nominal quantity of money increases, they find that they are holding more money than they feel is appropriate, and therefore spend this extra money. When a dollar is spent, some of it becomes income to the current recipient, and the remainder becomes income to others as the current recipient and subsequent recipients spend it, increasing the velocity effect of the increase in the money supply. This raises prices, thereby reducing the quantity of money in circulation, a process that continues until the real quantity of money has returned to its old desired level.

Keynesian Model. John Maynard KEYNES, in his 1936 criticism of the quantity theory, focused on the role of interest rates, which quantity theorists had usually ignored. He believed that the demand for money is highly unstable and that there is a speculative demand for money—that is, people do not necessarily spend their extra money; they may hold on to it in the expectation of higher interest rates.

Modern Quantity Theory. Milton FRIEDMAN has combined aspects of Keynesian theory with aspects of traditional quantity theory in his modern quantity theory. He concedes that the demand for money is not constant but argues that it is a stable function of other variables, namely, income and the cost of holding money, which is the interest rate and the loss of purchasing power through inflation. Because, in his view, inflation is a function of the amount of money in circulation, the nominal income is therefore dependent on the current and previous growth rates in the supply of money, a refined version of the traditional quantity-theory conclusion.

money Money is one of the most important inventions of humankind. Without it a complex, modern economy based on the division of labor, and the consequent widespread exchange of goods and services, would be impossible.

Functions of Money. Because many things, ranging from gold to dead rats to entries on computer tape, have been used as money, it cannot be defined as some particular object but must instead be defined by the functions it serves—to act as a medium of exchange and as a standard of value. A third function of money—as a store of wealth—is something money shares with many other types of objects.

A medium of exchange is simply an item used to make it easy to exchange things. In a very primitive economy, and in a few isolated cases in a complex economy, people directly barter goods and services. Direct barter is extremely inefficient, however, because it requires that one locate someone who wants the particular good one provides, and just by coincidence happens to have available for exchange a particular good one wants. In a modern economy with millions of products it would require an extensive search to locate such a person, but the use of money as a medium of exchange allows one to split this barter process into two parts. All one has to do is locate a person who wants one's particular good, receive money in exchange for it, and then locate another person who has available the good one wants and who is sure to take money in payment for it.

Another function of money is to serve as a standard of value or unit of account—so that economic values in terms of money can be measured; in this respect, money serves as an abstract unit. This standard-of-value function is overwhelmingly important because a modern economy requires numerous comparisons of values.

In principle, this standard of value need not be the same as the medium of exchange. In colonial America, for example, merchants kept their financial records in British pounds, but most of the medium of exchange they received consisted of Spanish coins. Obviously, however, it is convenient to use the same item both as a medium of exchange and as a standard of value, and modern money normally fulfills both roles.

The third function of money is to serve as a store of wealth. This is not a distinctive function of money, but money has certain peculiarities as a store of wealth. Unlike other forms of wealth, it has no transactions costs. Someone who decides to hold wealth in, for example, corporate stock has to undergo a certain amount of trouble and cost—first to buy stock and then to sell it again in order to buy another item. All of these costs and inconveniences can be avoided by holding one's wealth in the form of money. Economists term this ease of using money, as opposed to other forms of wealth, as a medium-of-exchange *liquidity*.

It is convenient to classify the numerous moneys that exist into three types. One is full-bodied commodity money—money that has a value as a commodity (gold or silver, for instance) fully equal to its value as money. Because coins can be awkward to carry, representative full-bodied money was developed, which consists of paper money that is freely convertible into full-bodied money. (In the late 19th and early 20th centuries most Western countries based their currencies on gold; see GOLD STANDARD.) Neither of these types of money, however, now exists in the United States or in most other countries. All U.S. money is credit money, or fiat money—money that does not have a value as a commodity equal to its face value and that cannot be exchanged for full-bodied commodity money.

One might well ask why people are willing to exchange valuable goods and services for pieces of paper called $10 bills. The answer is that these pieces of paper are valuable because people know that other people are willing to take them in exchange for their goods. The same is ultimately true of gold—it is considered valuable because people know that other people treat it as valuable. Hence, many of those who advocate a return to the gold standard do so primarily because this would limit the government's ability to create money, rather than because of any inherent value attached to gold.

Definitions of Money. What items should be counted as money in the modern U.S. economy? It is clear that one component of money is currency. The definition of money must include, however, more than just currency because the great bulk of the dollar value of payments is made by transferring bank deposits and not by currency. Currency is merely the small change of the U.S. system. Obviously, checking accounts must be included in the definition of money.

Beyond this basic definition, though, there is disagreement. Some economists prefer to define money by its essence—the fact that it is a medium of exchange and is liquid. According to this criterion, money is narrowly

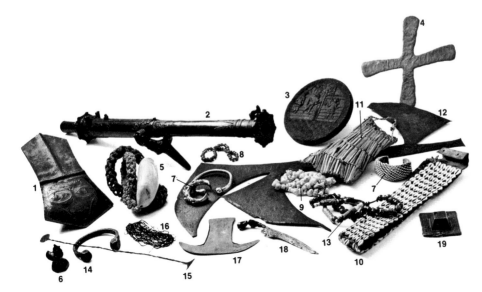

Forms of money include: copper plate (1) *used by the Haida Indians, North America; model of a cannon* (2), *Borneo; brick of pressed tea* (3), *China; copper ingot* (4), *Zaire; tooth of a sperm whale* (5), *Fiji Islands; opium weights* (6) *and bracelets* (7), *Thailand; beads* (8), *Alaska; cowrie-shell necklace* (9) *and belt* (10), *Solomon Islands; tobacco pouch* (11), *knife* (12), *"aggry" beads* (13), *manilla* (14), *and Kissi money* (15), *Africa; beetles' legs* (16), *Mussau Islands; ax head* (17), *Mexico; knife, or* kris (18), *Java; and "tin hat" money* (19), *Melanesia.*

defined as currency plus checkable deposits.

Other economists, however, notably Milton FRIEDMAN and Anna Schwartz, prefer a broader approach. Economists and policy makers are primarily interested in the supply of money because changes in the supply of money bring about changes in prices and output, and hence in income (see MONETARY POLICY; MONETARY THEORY). They therefore define money as that total which gives the best explanation and prediction of changes in income, rather than by money's inherent characteristics. In addition, they believe that the total should be subject to control because policy makers want not only to predict income but to change it if necessary. This approach to the definition of money and the previously discussed approach are not in fundamental conflict; essentially, it is a disagreement about whether to use the word *money* for one thing or the other.

On a more practical level, what specific items should be included in money? Until recently, the FEDERAL RESERVE SYSTEM used the following rule. So-called narrow money, or M_1, was defined to include currency and checking deposits, and broad money, M_2, was defined as M_1 plus time and savings deposits in banks. M_3 included, in addition, deposits held in savings and loan associations and savings banks.

This set of definitions had to be changed in 1980, when all savings and loan associations and mutual savings banks were allowed to offer checkable deposits to their customers in the form of NOW (Negotiable Order of Withdrawal) accounts, which are interest-bearing demand deposits. (Commercial banks may also offer NOW accounts.) First, there is M-1A, which is essentially the old M_1. (Federal government deposits are excluded from both the old and the new measures.) This measure of money will probably be phased out. A more important one is M-1B, which adds in checkable deposits in savings and loan associations, savings banks, and credit unions. Then there is M-2, which adds to M-1B savings and time deposits below $100,000, shares in money-market mutual funds, and some other very liquid items. M-3 then adds to M-2 all savings and time deposits of more than $100,000 plus a few minor items.

The Supply of Money. U.S. currency is issued by the Federal Reserve (paper money) and by the U.S. Treasury (coins), but they do this in a passive way; they provide banks with as much currency as banks want, debiting the banks' account with the Federal Reserve in exchange. A restrictive monetary policy is never carried out by restricting the quantity of currency because banks must always be provided with enough currency. Instead, the Federal Reserve controls the volume of bank deposits in the BANKING SYSTEM. This is done by Federal Reserve purchases and sales of securities, which alter bank reserves. Because banks keep reserves against their deposits, increases in reserves allow banks to increase loans, causing the money supply to increase.

moneywort   Moneywort, *Lysimachia nummularia*, is a creeping perennial plant of the primrose family, Primu-laceae; it is a species of loosestrife. Its name is derived from its rounded, coinlike leaves, which are borne in pairs along the stem. It produces solitary, yellow flowers on slender stalks from June through August. Also called creeping Jennie or creeping Charlie, moneywort is native to Europe but now grows wild in many parts of eastern North America, commonly in damp places.

Monge, Gaspard [mohnzh, gahs-pahr']   Gaspard Monge, b. May 9, 1746, d. July 28, 1818, was a French mathematician who founded descriptive geometry (see PROJECTIVE GEOMETRY)—a method for representing three-dimensional solids in a two-dimensional plane, such as a sheet of paper. Monge taught at the prestigious École Royale de Genie at Mezieres and later became director of the École Polytechnique. He was politically active and accompanied Napoléon in his invasion of Egypt to set up educational facilities there. Instrumental in reviving the study of geometry at the École Polytechnique, Monge also initiated the development of descriptive geometry, the foundation for MECHANICAL DRAWING. Monge's *Géométrie descriptive* (1799) was based on his lectures in this area.

Mongkut, King of Siam [mawng'-koot]   Mongkut, b. Oct. 18, 1804, d. Oct. 1, 1868, king of Siam (now Thailand) from 1851 to 1868, was the first of two successive outstanding rulers whose willingness to modernize and to establish friendly relations with the Western powers enabled their country to escape colonial conquest. Before succeeding his brother on the throne, Mongkut served 27 years as a Buddhist monk and studied Western history and science. As king, Mongkut, also known posthumously as Rama IV, introduced European-style education and hired foreign experts to modernize Siam's government and economy. He was succeeded by his son, CHULALONGKORN. Mongkut was a model for the king in Margaret Landon's book *Anna and the King of Siam* (1944), from which the musical comedy *The King and I* was adapted.

Mongolia [mahn-goh'-lee-uh]   Mongolia (sometimes called Outer Mongolia), a nation in eastern Central Asia, is bordered by the USSR to the north and China to the south. Mongolia has one of the lowest population densities in the world. From the 13th century onward the Mongols ruled a huge empire, but following its disintegration in the 17th century Mongolia was ruled by China until 1921, when it became independent. It became the world's second Communist nation (after the USSR) in 1924.

Land and Resources

The ALTAI MOUNTAINS of Central Asia extend into western Mongolia. Their permanently snow-covered peaks include Mount Monch Chajrchan (4,362 m/14,311 ft), the highest point in the country. East of the Altai Mountains is a depression with more than 300 lakes known as the Great Lakes Region. This is bounded in the east by the

AT A GLANCE

MONGOLIAN PEOPLE'S REPUBLIC

Land: Area: 1,564,619 km^2 (604,103 mi^2). Capital and largest city: Ulan Bator (1988 est. pop., 528,400).

People: Population (1990 est.): 2,187,275. Density: 1.4 persons per km^2 (3.6 per mi^2). Distribution (1988): 52% urban, 48% rural. Official language: Mongol. Major religion: Tibetan Buddhism.

Government: Type: republic. Legislature: bicameral; People's Great Hural, People's Small Hural. Political subdivisions: 18 provinces, 3 municipalities.

Economy: GDP (1985 est.): $1.7 billion; $880 per capita. Labor distribution (1987): agriculture—59%; mining and manufacturing—11%; trade and services—24%; construction—3%. Foreign trade (1988): imports—$1.15 billion; exports—$792 million. Currency: 1 tughrik = 100 mongo.

Education and Health: Literacy (1985 est.): 80% of adult population. Universities (1988): 1. Hospital beds (1987): 22,600. Physicians (1987): 5,200. Life expectancy (1989): women—67; men—63. Infant mortality (1989): 65–75 per 1,000 live births.

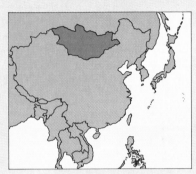

Hangayn-Hentiyn mountain complex. These mountains encircle a fertile basin, drained by the Selenge and Tuul rivers, which is the traditional focus of Mongolian culture. ULAN BATOR, Mongolia's capital and commercial center, is located in the southeastern corner of the basin. The Plateau of Mongolia is further to the east. The northern edge of the GOBI Desert covers southeastern and southern Mongolia. Mongolia's mountains form part of the great divide of Central Asia, which separates waters flowing to the Arctic and Pacific oceans.

Mongolia has a continental climate with long, cold winters (October to April) and short, humid summers. Temperatures average –26° C (-15° F) in January, the coldest month, and 16° C (61° F) in July, the warmest, at Ulan Bator. Rainfall varies from about 460 mm (18 in) in the mountains to about 100 mm (4 in) in the Gobi.

The country's steppe vegetation supports an estimated 24.5 million (1989) horses, cattle, sheep, goats, and camels. Coal, copper, fluorspar, gold, and silver are found there.

People

The population of Mongolia is highly homogeneous. About 90% of the population are MONGOLS. The KHALKHA (about 75% of the total population), Buryat, Dariganga, and Darbet Mongol tribes are important. The largest minority group is the Kazakh, a Turkic people who live primarily in the west. The Mongolian language has been written in the CYRILLIC ALPHABET since the 1940s. The traditional Mongolian script, which resembles Arabic but is written vertically, has been regaining popularity and is

taught, along with English, in the schools. The majority of the population practiced TIBETAN BUDDHISM until the Communist government instituted an antireligious movement in 1937–39.

Population growth has been rapid since 1963, and more than half of all Mongolians are less than 15 years old. Medical treatment is free, and primary education is free and compulsory. Eleven years of schooling are required. The Mongolian State University in Ulan Bator was founded in 1942.

Economic Activity

Mongolia's traditional economy was nomadic and pastoral, with the people traveling with their herds. Absentee owners held the land and exacted taxes in exchange for use of pastureland. Pastoral activities still dominate the economic structure, but control of the economy has been shifted to the government, whose official policy has encouraged sedentarism. Most agricultural activities, including the growing of food and fodder crops, were collectivized by 1959. Of the total land area, about 85% is in pasturage. Until recently, almost all livestock was owned by the government.

Since 1948, the government has tried to diversify the economy by developing industry and increasing the production of food crops. The principal manufactured products are building materials and light consumer goods. Ulan Bator is the largest manufacturing center, followed by Darhan. Both cities are located near coal mines and along road and rail routes to the USSR, which receives 80% of Mongolia's exports. A large copper and molybde-

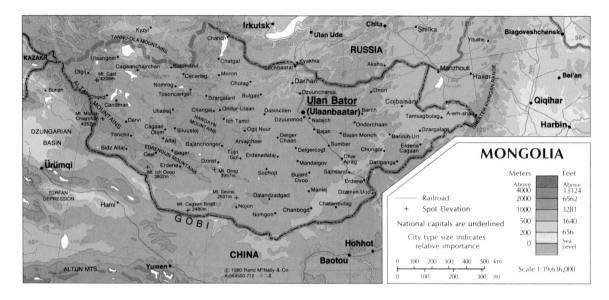

num mining complex built with Soviet aid at Erdenet, east of Darhan, provides 40% of exports. A December 1991 cutoff of Russian oil shipments, the end of Soviet subsidies, and Russia's insistence that Mongolia owes a huge accumulated debt have combined with near chaos in the domestic economy to make Mongolia's economic reforms very painful. Nevertheless, the country is moving rapidly in the direction of privatization and a market economy and is trying to find new trade partners to replace the former USSR and Eastern Europe.

Government

Mongolia is a republic, with a nascent multiparty system. The dominant Mongolian People's Revolutionary party (MPRP), formerly a typical Communist party, has renounced Communism and no longer holds a monopoly on political power. Under a new constitution effective in 1992 the name of the country was changed from People's Republic of Mongolia to Republic of Mongolia and socialism was renounced. The president and members of the unicameral legislature, the People's Great Hural, are directly elected to 4-year terms. A prime minister serves as head of government.

History

The first tribal peoples known to have inhabited Mongolia were the Xiongnu (Huns) during the 4th century. They created a great tribal empire, engaging in warfare with their neighbors the Chinese until the Xiongnu empire was broken up several centuries later. In AD 744 the UIGHUR seized Mongolia and held it until 840, when the Kirghiz took control.

The Mongol tribes were unified and reached the height of their power during the 13th century under GENGHIS KHAN, who established his capital at Karakoram. He and his heirs conquered China and extended their empire to eastern Europe. The Mongol empire gradually declined in

power, and in 1691 it came under the control of the QING dynasty of China. Under the Qing, present-day Mongolia was administered as the province of Outer Mongolia while the adjacent area to the southeast was the province of INNER MONGOLIA. Outer Mongolia remained a province until 1911, when it claimed its independence. The Chinese reoccupied Outer Mongolia in 1919 but were driven out in 1921 by Russian Baron von Ungern-Sternberg, who also massacred thousands of Mongolians. Later that year, Mongolian revolutionaries Sukhe Bator and Khorloin Choybalsan ousted Ungern-Sternberg with Soviet help, and independence was finally won. The Mongolian People's Republic was declared in 1924. It served as a buffer between the USSR and China, which did not recognize it until 1946. Yumjaagiyn Tsedenbal, who headed the MPRP from 1940 to 1954 and again from 1958 and served as president from 1974, resigned in 1984.

The withdrawal of Soviet military forces and the revolutionary changes occurring in Eastern Europe in the fall of 1989 encouraged calls for political and economic change. Swelling public protests in Ulan Bator forced Tsedenbal's successor, Dzhambiyn Batmunkh, to resign in March 1990. A new and substantially more democratic regime followed. Reform-minded Communists retained a legislative majority in multiparty elections held later that year, but the regime and system that essentially ruled the country from 1921 to 1990 was dead. Elections under a new constitution, held in June 1992, were also won by the MPRP.

Mongolian   see RACE

Mongolian language   see URAL-ALTAIC LANGUAGES

mongolism   see DOWN'S SYNDROME

Mongoloid   see RACE

Mongols [mahng'-gulz] The Mongols, whose homeland is the elevated plateau land of east central Asia, emerged as a major force in history early in the 13th century. For nearly two centuries they raided, invaded, conquered, and destroyed many more highly developed countries and peoples, but their impact on the outside world was as brief as it was bloody. Independent since the overthrow of the Manchu (Qing) dynasty in China in 1911–12, the northernmost Mongols today constitute the independent nation of MONGOLIA, with a population of 2,200,000 (1990 est.). An estimated 3.5 million Mongols to the south remain under Chinese rule (particularly in INNER MONGOLIA), and another 500,000 live in the USSR.

Mongolia was inhabited by a variety of nomadic peoples in ancient and medieval times, notably the Xiongnu (HUNS), Orkhon Turks, and UIGHURS. Early in the 13th century, GENGHIS KHAN united the tribes of the area. From his capital of Karakorum, he ruthlessly expanded his empire until, by the time of his death in 1227, it extended from the Pacific Ocean to the Black Sea and from Siberia to Tibet. After Genghis's death the empire was divided among his sons, and by the late 13th century four khanates existed: the empire of KUBLAI KHAN (the Great Khan), who founded the short-lived YUAN dynasty (1279–1368) of China; the Hülagu Khanate in Persia; the Jagatai Khanate in Turkistan; and the Khanate of the GOLDEN HORDE, established by Batu Khan in southern Russia. In the 14th century the Persian and Turkistan khanates were largely conquered by TIMUR, who claimed descent from Genghis Khan. He was, in fact, a Turk, but by this time the Mongols had mixed substantially with Turkic peoples, the TATARS among them. Another conqueror who claimed descent from Genghis Khan was BABUR, founder of the MOGUL Empire in India. The true Mongol states had largely disappeared by the end of the 14th century, and the Mongols returned to their steppe homeland.

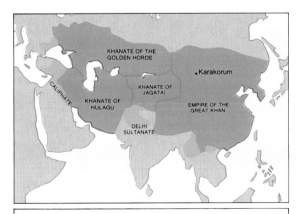

MONGOL RULE AT GREATEST EXTENT

■ Mongol expansion, 1206-79   ■ Intermittent rule

The banded mongoose, a small mammal of Africa, is an aggressive hunter that preys on birds, reptiles, and the eggs of both. It is related to the Indian mongoose, made famous through Rudyard Kipling's character, Rikki-tikki-tavi, in The Jungle Book.

mongoose Mongooses are small carnivores of the family Viverridae. The true mongooses make up the subfamily Herpestinae and include 13 genera and about 30 species, almost all native to Africa. The Madagascan mongooses, a second group, constitute the subfamily Galidiinae and consist of four genera and seven species. In addition, some of the banded palm civets, subfamily Hemigalinae, are also known as mongooses. Conversely, certain mongooses are popularly called suricates, meerkats, cusimanses, or ichneumons.

Mongooses typically have a pointed head, a long tail, and thick hair except on the lower legs. They are commonly terrestrial, diurnal, and solitary. The suricate, *Suricata suricatta*, of southern Africa, however, lives in colonies; the African marsh mongoose, *Atilax paludinosus*, is semiaquatic; and the little-known Madagascan mongoose, *Galidia*, can be found in trees. Mongooses feed on a wide variety of foods, including small mammals, reptiles, birds' eggs, and insects.

Among the better-known mongooses are those of the genus *Herpestes*, which range from southern Europe into Africa and southern Asia. The gold-spotted mongoose, *H. javanicus* or *H. auropunctatus*, was introduced into the Hawaiian and Caribbean islands to control rats and snakes; although it did feed on rats and snakes, it concentrated on and seriously depleted populations of native birds and mammals. Mongooses of this genus are often portrayed fighting a cobra. Research has shown that although the mongoose is tolerant of small dosages of cobra venom, it is not immune to it. Mongooses are almost always victorious because of their speed, agility, and timing and also because of their thick coat.

moniliasis see CANDIDIASIS

monism [moh'-nizm] Monism is any doctrine based on the assumption of a single underlying principle. Metaphysical monism allows that only one being or type of being exists. A substantial metaphysical monism asserts that the variety in our phenomenal experience is due to the different states of a single all-encompassing substance, for example, PARMENIDES' Plenum or Baruch SPI-NOZA's God or Nature. An attributive monism admits many substances but asserts that they are all of the same kind, for example, atoms or G. W. von LEIBNIZ's monads.

Epistemological monism identifies that which is immediately present to the knowing mind with the real object known. Either the content of the mind is equated with the object known (epistemological realism), or the object known is equated with the knowing mind (epistemological idealism). Monism as a philosophical term was first used by Christian WOLFF to designate philosophies that attempted to eliminate the mind-body dichotomy.

monitor   Monitors are about 30 species of lizards constituting the genus *Varanus* in the family Varanidae. They are found in Africa, Asia, Indonesia, New Guinea, and Australia. One species, the Pacific, or Indian, monitor, *V. indicus*, is believed to have been brought by natives to the Polynesian Islands as a source of food. Monitors range in size from the short-tailed monitor, *V. brevicauda*, which may be 20 cm (8 in) long and 20 g (0.75 oz) in weight, to the KOMODO DRAGON, *V. komodoensis*, which grows to 3 m (10 ft) long and 135 kg (300 lb) in weight. Monitors are characterized by small, non-overlapping, beadlike scales; a tapered head; a slender neck; a tail twice as long as the body (except in the short-tailed monitor); four well-developed legs, each with five sharp-clawed toes; and—unique among the lizards—the ability to greatly increase the size of the mouth cavity by spreading the hyoid apparatus (the structure involved in tongue support and movement) and dropping the lower jaw. Monitors are daytime predators, feeding on almost any animal of suitable size. All monitors are egg-layers. The earless monitor, *Lanthanotus borneensis*, the only known member of the family Lanthanotidae, is a large-scaled, semiaquatic lizard native to Borneo.

Monitor and Merrimack   The U.S. Civil War battle between two ironclad warships, the U.S.S. *Monitor* and the converted steam frigate *Merrimack*, fought at Hampton Roads, Va., on Mar. 9, 1862, marked the end of the age of sail-driven, wooden-hulled warships. In 1861, as they withdrew from Norfolk at the beginning of the war, the Union forces had scuttled the U.S.S. *Merrimack*. The Confederates raised the abandoned ship, added a ram to its bow, stripped the superstructure of sail and rigging, and placed a protective, sloped iron casemate over the hull and deck. With this ironclad, renamed the C.S.S. *Virginia*, the South intended to break the Union's strangling blockade of the Southern coast by wooden warships. To meet the threat, John ERICSSON designed and built the *Monitor*, an all-iron steam-driven vessel with a single turret housing two guns.

Neither ship proved able to destroy the other, but the tactical stalemate was a strategic victory for the North. By its presence, the *Monitor* prevented the *Virginia* from dispersing the Union blockaders. (Unable to retreat up the James River from Norfolk, the *Virginia* was destroyed by the Confederates on May 10, 1862.) The Union built

The Union Navy's ironclad Monitor *and the Confederate* Virginia *(previously named* Merrimack) *fought a duel in Hampton Roads, Va., that ended in stalemate on Mar. 9, 1862. This was the first confrontation between ironclad men-of-war.*

many *Monitor*-type vessels, but the Confederacy lacked the industrial capacity necessary for large-scale construction of blockade-breaking ironclads. On Dec. 31, 1862, the unseaworthy *Monitor* foundered off Cape Hatteras, N.C. It was located by underwater archaeologists in 1973, and its anchor was recovered in 1983.

Monk, Thelonious [thel-oh'-nee-uhs]   Pianist and composer Thelonious Sphere Monk, b. Rocky Mount, N.C., Oct. 10, 1918, d. Feb. 17, 1982, was one of the founders of the jazz style that became known as BEBOP. Although he played in bands with Dizzy Gillespie, another bebop originator, and with Coleman Hawkins, most of Monk's work was as a soloist or as the leader of small groups. As a composer he contributed numerous pieces that are still standards in the jazz repertoire. Among them are "Round Midnight" and "Straight No Chaser." Because of his harmonic manipulations, which stretched the boundaries of tonality, he is considered one of the principal influences on avant-garde jazz.

monkey   The term *monkey* is commonly applied to a large number of primates, excluding only the tree shrews, the lemurlike forms, the apes, and humans, and therefore embraces an enormous evolutionary and adaptive array of animals. This array, however, can be divided into two main groups—the New World monkeys and the Old World monkeys—which represent quite separate evolutionary histories. These two major divisions—technically called the Platyrrhini (New World monkeys) and the Catarrhini (Old World monkeys, but also including apes and humans)—were established in 1812 by the French zoologist Étienne Geoffroy de Saint-Hilaire. The terms chosen by Geoffroy refer to the external structure of the nose (*-rhini* is from the Greek word for "nose"): the Old World monkeys, or catarrhines, are characterized by nostrils that are close together and tend to open downward, whereas the New World monkeys, or platyrrhines, have nostrils that are wide apart and open toward the sides. (Not all monkeys clearly exhibit these differences.) The two groups also show differences in the bony parts of the ear and in

Abyssinian guereza

De Brazza's monkey

squirrel monkey

Hanuman langur

black howling monkey

mandrill

proboscis monkey

the teeth. In the New World monkeys the eardrum (tympanum) is encased in a bony ring (tympanic ring), and both the eardrum and the bony ring are at the surface of the skull. In the Old World monkeys the eardrum is situated within the skull, and the bony ring is formed into a tube (the external auditory meatus) that leads to the outside. New World monkeys have three premolar teeth on each side of the upper and lower jaws, whereas Old World monkeys have only two premolar teeth in each of these quadrants.

The most important distinction between the two groups, however, is their separate evolutionary development. It is thought that both arose from the same primitive lemurlike primates inhabiting the formerly connected landmasses of North America and Europe, but that the two groups probably diverged from this common ancestral stock at least 55 million years ago, at about the end of the Paleocene Epoch, with the ancestors of the New World forms moving toward Central and South America and those of the Old World monkeys toward Africa.

Old World Monkeys

Despite their wide geographic distribution, the Old World monkeys are a relatively similar group and are classified as the superfamily Cercopithecoidea, whose members are referred to as cercopithecoids. This superfamily contains a single living family, the Cercopithecidae, which is divided into two subfamilies, the Cercopithecinae and the Colobinae. The cercopithecoids are the only primates, apart from humans, with representatives outside the tropics and subtropics. The Japanese macaque, *Macaca fuscata*, the stump-tailed macaque, *M. arctoides*, and the langur, *Presbytis entellus*, have all been observed living successfully in snow-covered habitats. The subfamily Colobinae, which contains the colobus monkeys, langurs, and related forms, is primarily Asiatic, with only one genus, *Colobus* of Africa, found elsewhere. In contrast, the subfamily Cercopithecinae, containing the baboons, macaques, guenons, and others, is largely African, with two genera, *Papio* and *Macaca*, also occurring in Asia.

All Old World monkeys possess special pads on their buttocks, which aid in sitting for long periods of time, as in nighttime sleeping. These pads, called ischial callosities, are thick, horny calluses that cover swellings of the ischial bone at the bottom rear of the pelvis, or hipbone. In virtually all species the forelimbs and hind limbs are of almost equal length, which generally indicates a quadrupedal, or four-legged, locomotion; however, all species climb well. Some cercopithecoids, especially the macaques, show a reduction in the length of the tail. All species except the colobus monkeys have hands and feet of moderate length and with opposable first digits (thumbs and big toes); in the colobus monkeys the thumb is reduced to a small nub or may be totally lacking. Opposability means that the thumb or big toe is set apart from the other digits and can be moved so as to bring its fleshy lower portion into contact with the fleshy lower portions of one or more of the other digits. Opposability is an adaptation for grasping and for the finer manipulation of objects; it also permits eating with one hand, in con-

trast to the manner of rodents or other animals that must hold food with two hands. Each molar tooth has four projections, or cusps, and is bilophodont, that is, each pair of cusps, front and rear, are joined together by a cross ridge, or "loph." Many species, particularly those in the subfamily Cercopithecinae, show a pronounced sexual dimorphism, the males being considerably larger than the females. The size range among the Old World monkeys is also substantial; fully grown talapoins, *Cercopithecus talapoin*, may weigh only about 2.25 kg (5 lb), whereas large male mandrills, *Mandrillus sphinx*, or baboons, *Papio ursinus*, may tip the scales at 45 kg (100 lb).

One of the chief characteristics of the subfamily Cercopithecinae is the cheek pouches, which are lacking in the members of the subfamily Colobinae. Cheek pouches are muscular cavities in the cheeks that extend below the jaws and are used for the temporary storage of food. The most striking specialization of the subfamily Colobinae is the complex stomach, which is divided into pockets, or chambers (sacculations), and banded by two longitudinal muscular strips. The sacculated stomach is involved in the processing of the cellulose contained in leaves eaten by these monkeys.

Longevity in the wild is difficult to estimate, but members of both subfamilies have lived from 20 to 30 years in zoos. Usually only single infants are born; twin births do occur but are relatively rare in all species. Old World monkeys share the primate tendency toward lengthening the time an infant is dependent on its mother and the duration of the maturation process; most female cercopithecoids reach sexual maturity only at about 3 ½ years of age, and males up to a year or more later. Gestation periods vary; an average for both subfamilies would be about 6 months (170 to 190 days). Females show a regular menstrual cycle of about 30 days; estrus, the period within which ovulation occurs and when the female is fertile, lasts from 5 to 9 days and may or may not be accompanied by external signs such as the swelling and color changes of skin in the genital region. Sexual skin swelling is pronounced in the baboons.

New World Monkeys

The New World monkeys also constitute a single superfamily, the Ceboidea, but because they are more diverse than the Old World monkeys, their superfamily comprises three families: the Callitrichidae (or Callithricidae), containing the marmosets and tamarins; the Cebidae, containing the capuchins, squirrel monkeys, and others; and the Callimiconidae, containing only Goeldi's monkey, which possesses characteristics of the other two families and has often been classified in one or the other.

New World monkeys are all arboreal; there are no ground-dwelling species as occur in the Old World. They inhabit forests from sea level to altitudes of about 1,500 m (5,000 ft). New World monkeys are usually slender-bodied animals with slender limbs and long tails. Unlike that of the Old World monkeys, the tail may be prehensile and used as a "fifth hand." New World monkeys lack the buttock pads (ischial callosities) of the Old World species and frequently sleep in a horizontal position. Females also lack the sexual skin around the genitals that enlarges and changes color when the female is in a sexually receptive state, but many females have external genitals which themselves may be enlarged and swollen in appearance. The opposability of the thumb in New World monkeys is more limited and has been termed pseudo-opposability because although there is no rotation at the wrist-thumb joint as in true opposability, a downward movement of the thumb and the bending of the hand result in the meeting of the thumb and one or more fingers for a functionally opposable grip. Marmosets have short thumbs and do not possess even pseudo-opposability, but their hands are long enough to be folded upon themselves to permit grasping and one-handed feeding. Thumb opposability is also lacking in the spider monkeys, *Ateles*, which have vestigial thumbs or are thumbless, and in the woolly spider monkey, *Brachyteles*, in which the thumb is also reduced or missing. The big toe of New World monkeys, however, is opposable in the same manner as that of the Old World species. New World monkeys range in size from the pygmy marmoset, *Cebuella pygmaea*, which may weigh as little as 70 g (2.5 oz), to the hefty howler monkey, *Alouatta*, which reaches 9 kg (20 lb).

The marmosets and tamarins, family Callitrichidae, are small, most of them weighing about 500 g (1 lb), and are strikingly distinguished by possessing clawlike nails on all digits except the first toe and by the presence of only two molar teeth instead of the more typical three on each side of the upper and lower jaws. As in most quadrupeds, the forelimbs are only slightly shorter than the hind limbs. The marmosets are found in both moist and dry forests in the Amazon River basin and differ from the tamarins in being somewhat smaller and in having elongated incisor teeth. They appear to be monogamous, staying with a single mate; females often bear twins, and the male may assist in the birth and carry the young about. Primarily arboreal and diurnal, marmosets supplement their vegetarian diet with insects. Tamarins are found primarily in the rain forests of Central and South America and appear to resemble the marmosets in their diet and activity pattern, although they may form larger social groups. The Goeldi's monkey, *Callimico goeldii*, the only member of the family Callimiconidae, is generally similar to the marmosets but possesses three molar teeth. Little is known of its behavior in the wild.

The members of the family Cebidae—all distinguished by the possession of three molar teeth on each side of the upper and lower jaws and by digits carrying flat nails—cover a great diversity of types; consequently, usually five and recently seven subfamilies have been recognized.

The subfamily Aotinae contains the douroucouli and usually the titis, but the latter are now considered by some authorities to constitute a separate subfamily, the Callicebinae. The douroucouli, or owl monkey, *Aotus trivirgatus*, is the only nocturnal monkey in the world.

The squirrel monkeys, *Saimiri*, usually classified in the subfamily Cebinae, are now also considered by some authorities to form a separate subfamily, the Saimiriinae. There are two species, both feeding primarily on fruit and insects.

The uakaris, *Cacajao*, and the sakis, *Pithecia* and *Chiropotes*, are representatives of the subfamily Pitheciinae. They are found from the Guianas down to the Amazon basin. The uakaris, which are the only short-tailed New World monkeys, are almost hairless on the face and top of the head and appear bald. In contrast, the sakis have thick hair on the head, forming a hood or a crest with a coiffured look.

The capuchins, *Cebus*, in the subfamily Cebinae, are famous for their impressive performances in laboratory tests of intelligence. They are found throughout Central America and forested South America, where they live usually in small multimate groups. They apparently have quite complex patterns of social relationships.

The howler monkeys, *Alouatta*, in the subfamily Alouattinae, are one of the best-known New World monkeys. Their name is derived from their formidable roaring displays used in defending their territories. These remarkable vocalizations are produced with the aid of highly specialized structures. The hyoid, a supportive bone at the base of the tongue, is enlarged and formed into an egg-shaped hollow box, which acts as a resonating chamber. The thyroid cartilage of the larynx (voice box) and the lower jaw are also enlarged.

The subfamily Atelinae contains the spider monkeys, *Ateles*, the woolly monkeys, *Lagothrix*, and the woolly spider monkey, *Brachyteles*, which are the most specialized in their locomotor apparatus of all the New World monkeys. Like the howlers they possess a fully prehensile tail with a sensitive tactile surface at its tip, but they are much more active and acrobatic. Unlike the quadrupedal howlers, the atelines have rather elongated forelimbs and regularly use their long tail as a "fifth limb" in locomotion; they frequently suspend or propel themselves by their arms or even hang by the tail alone. The spider monkeys and the woolly spider monkey lack thumbs, the hand being essentially modified into a long hook, but the woolly monkeys do possess them.

As one might expect, the reproductive biology of the New World monkeys is much more variable than that of the Old World monkeys, although it is generally poorly known. Twin births are the rule among the marmosets and tamarins; single offspring are normal for members of the family Cebidae. Gestation periods range from about 140 days in the marmosets to 225 days in the woolly monkeys. Sexual maturity is reached in 3 to 4 years among the large forms and in a little over a year in some of the smaller ones. Longevities in the wild are unknown but probably range from about 10 years to upwards of 20.

monkey puzzle tree The monkey puzzle tree, or Chilean pine, *Araucaria araucana*, is an evergreen coniferous tree of the Araucariaceae family native to the Andes Mountains of Chile. It grows to more than 30 m (100 ft) high, with tiers of usually five, mostly horizontal branches spaced along its trunk. The leaves are small, stiff, and pointed and overlap the branches completely, possibly puzzling and deterring a would-be climber, such as a monkey. Male plants bear catkinlike cones up to 13 cm (5 in) long; female trees, rounded cones up to 18 cm (7 in) long and 13 cm (5 in) or more in diameter, containing up to 180 seeds.

---

monkshood   Monkshood is a common name for about 100 species of perennial herbaceous plants in the genus *Aconitum* in the buttercup family, Ranunculaceae. These showy herbs, also called aconite or wolfsbane, are native to the temperate regions of the Northern Hemisphere. The leaves and roots of many species are poisonous; some are a source of drugs. Often planted in gardens, *Aconitum* has spikelike clusters of hood-shaped flowers that are usually blue or purple.

Monmouth, Battle of [mahn'-muhth]   The Battle of Monmouth was an indecisive engagement in the AMERICAN REVOLUTION fought on June 28, 1778, near Monmouth Courthouse (now Freehold), N.J. The British, under Sir Henry CLINTON, evacuated Philadelphia on June 18 and marched across New Jersey toward Sandy Hook, where they were to embark for New York City. At Monmouth, Gen. George WASHINGTON decided to deliver a strong blow and ordered Maj. Gen. Charles LEE to attack the British rear. After some fighting, Lee led a disorderly retreat until halted by Washington, who engaged the heavily reinforced British in fierce but deadlocked combat until dark. During the night Clinton was able to withdraw and complete his march to the sea. Lee was court-martialed for disobeying orders. During the battle, the heroism of the wife of one of the American soldiers who assisted the American forces gave rise to the legend of MOLLY PITCHER.

Monmouth, James Scott, Duke of   James Scott, duke of Monmouth and Buccleuch, b. Apr. 9, 1649, d. July 15, 1685, an illegitimate son of CHARLES II of England, led a rebellion against Charles's successor, JAMES II, in 1685. He married Anne Scott, countess of Buccleuch, whose name he adopted, and was created a duke in 1663. When the 1st earl of SHAFTESBURY started his efforts to exclude the Roman Catholic James from the succession, he put forward the Protestant Monmouth as a possible heir. It was claimed that King Charles had married Monmouth's mother, Lucy Walter, and that Monmouth was therefore legitimate. In 1684, Monmouth had to flee to Europe after exposure of a plot to murder both Charles and James.

On June 11, 1685, four months after Charles's death, Monmouth landed at Lyme Regis, Dorset. On July 6, however, his rebel force was smashed at Sedgemoor, Somerset, by troops led by John Churchill (later duke of MARLBOROUGH). Monmouth was executed, and his supporters were rounded up.

Monmouthshire   see GWENT

Monnet, Jean [maw-nay']   Jean Monnet, b. Nov. 9, 1888, d. Mar. 16, 1979, a French businessman and diplomat, was a leader of the movement for European unity after World War II. Monnet served as deputy secretary general of the League of Nations (1919–23) and worked as an investment banker. During World War II he was part of the French Committee of National Liberation. After the war he became head of the National Planning Board (1947) and was responsible for the nationalization of France's mines, railroads, and electric utilities. He is credited with originating the proposal presented by French foreign minister Robert SCHUMAN that culminated in the European Coal and Steel Community (ECSC); Monnet headed the ECSC in 1953–55.

---

monoclinic system   CRYSTALS belong to the monoclinic system if they have three crystallographic axes of unequal length, two of which are not perpendicular. These possess either a single twofold axis, a symmetry plane, or a combination of both. Monoclinic crystals are usually easily identified by recognition of a single twofold element. The departure from 90° between the *a* and *c* axes is generally marked enough to be easily distinguishable. Crystallographic convention has led to two alternative methods of choosing the crystal axes in the monoclinic case. Because a single twofold axis must be present, this axis is referred to as the unique axis. Should this axis be chosen as the *c* axis, the crystal is said to be oriented in the first setting. If the *b* axis is taken as unique, the crystal is said to be oriented in the second setting; the latter is more widely used at the present time. Crystals belonging to the monoclinic system are optically biaxial. One of the three major optical directions is always chosen to coincide with the unique crystallographic direction. Optical extinction in this class is usually inclined to the crystallographic axis. Minerals that crystallize in the monoclinic system include the AMPHIBOLES, CHLORITE MINERALS, epidote, GYPSUM, orthoclase (see FELDSPAR), the PYROXENES, and TALC.

---

monocot   see ANGIOSPERM; COTYLEDON

---

monogamy   Monogamy is the form of MARRIAGE of one man and one woman at a time. At its extreme, it takes the form of a lifelong commitment to one spouse, even precluding remarriage when the spouse dies. More commonly, monogamy involves the possibility of changing spouses several times, but having only one at a time.

In most of the world's societies the preferred and ideal form of marriage is POLYGAMY, or plural marriage, particularly polygyny, or marriage of a man to more than one woman at a time. Even in societies where polygyny is preferred, however, most marriages are monogamous because of the relatively even ratio of the sexes in all human populations. Those men who marry plurally normally must wait for several years before they take an additional wife or wives.

Anthropologists observe that monogamy is most likely to be found in societies in which the overall economic contribution of the sexes is relatively equal and a small family unit is as efficient as a larger one. Like the nuclear family, monogamy is particularly characteristic of hunting-and-gathering societies and also of industrialized societies. However, monogamous marriage can be found in conjunction with other forms of the family besides the nuclear family—for example, in the patrilineal joint or extended family, such as that of India.

monomer [mahn'-uh-mur]   In chemistry, a monomer is any molecule capable of bonding to others of its species at two sites to form a long chain. Thus, a monomer, which means "single member," is the single repeating unit of any polymer (see POLYMERIZATION). Ethylene oxide, for example, is the monomer of polyoxyethylene.

Monongahela River [muh-nahn'-guh-hee'-luh]   The Monongahela River is formed by the junction of the Tygart and West Fork rivers near Fairmont, in northern West Virginia. It flows northward 206 km (128 mi) past Morgantown, W.Va., to Pittsburgh, Pa., where it joins the Allegheny River to form the Ohio River. The Monongahela was the first river in the United States to be improved for navigation, and today a series of locks and dams, extending 171 km (106 mi), supply hydroelectric power and permit barges carrying iron, steel, coke, and coal to travel its course.

mononucleosis [mahn'-oh-noo-klee-oh'-sis]   Mononucleosis is an acute infectious disease of humans in which the blood and tissues contain increased numbers of mononuclear leukocytes (white blood cells with only one nucleus), either monocytes or lymphocytes. It is sometimes called glandular fever because it produces fever and swelling of the lymph glands, or nodes, throughout the body. The causative agent is Epstein-Barr virus (EBV), a herpesvirus (see HERPES), and the incubation period is 30 to 50 days. The disease occurs most commonly in adults 15 to 30 years old. It is characterized by fever, malaise, sore throat, swelling of the lymph nodes (particularly noticeable in the neck), and skin rashes. Mild jaundice from liver inflammation may occur. Other symptoms include headache and other neurological manifestations reflecting infection of the central and peripheral nervous systems. During the illness antibodies develop; these are detected in the Paul-Bunnell test, one means of diagnosis. The disease is not highly contagious. EBV is present in the saliva of patients, and infection spreads by oral contact—as in kissing or sharing a cup. The illness is generally mild to moderate in severity; death is extremely rare. There is no specific treatment, but bed rest is indicated if jaundice develops. Complete recovery may take several months.

The disease known as CHRONIC FATIGUE SYNDROME, or "yuppie disease," resembles infectious mononucleosis. For a while it was suspected of also being caused by EBV, but this theory has been discounted.

Monophysitism [muh-nahf'-uh-sit-izm]   Monophysitism is the doctrine that JESUS CHRIST had only one nature,

rather than two—divine and human. This belief is sometimes known as Eutychianism, for EUTYCHES, a mid-5th-century archimandrite of a Constantinople monastery. Eutyches taught that in Jesus Christ the humanity was absorbed by the divinity, "dissolved like a drop of honey in the sea." Eutyches fought against the Nestorian doctrine (see NESTORIANISM) that the two natures of Christ represented two distinct persons. His doctrine was condemned as heretical, however, at the Council of CHALCEDON in 451. Nonetheless, by the 6th century Monophysitism had a strong institutional basis in three churches: the ARMENIAN CHURCH, the COPTIC CHURCH, and the JACOBITE CHURCH, all of which remain nominally Monophysite today.

monopole, magnetic   Magnetic monopoles are hypothetical particles that would contain only a "north" or a "south" magnetic pole. They would form the magnetic equivalent of particles with a single electric charge, such as the electron or positron. Thus the existence of magnetic monopoles, predicted by a theory developed by physicist Paul DIRAC in the 1930s, would complete the symmetry between the phenomena of electricity and MAGNETISM. This in turn would satisfy the GRAND UNIFICATION THEORIES being developed by physicists in an attempt to unify all of physics within one comprehensive framework.

No magnetic monopoles have yet been isolated; any known magnetic particle, however small, consists of a magnetic dipole (both a "north" and "south" pole). If a magnetic monopole did exist, however, its movement would induce an electric field, and if it were to pass through a loop of electrically conducting material, a sudden rise in voltage would be observed across the loop. Experiments of this nature are being conducted, using niobium loops connected to a superconducting quantum interference device (SQUID). The most promising possible monopole detection thus far occurred at Imperial College, London, in 1986.

Monopoly   Monopoly is a board game for 2 to 8 players. The object of the game is for one player to bankrupt the other players by buying, selling, and trading properties and by charging rent for buildings on them. The buildings are on streets named for those in the resort town of Atlantic City, N.J. Monopoly was invented in 1933 by Charles Darrow; since 1935 it has been distributed by Parker Brothers.

monopoly and competition   A holder of a monopoly (Latin, *monopolium*, the exclusive seller of something) is a single seller who has exclusive control of the supply and marketing of some product or service. This exclusivity frequently enables the monopolist to set a selling price that is likely to be higher than it would be if competition with other sellers of the same product existed. A telephone company serving a community is an example of a monopolist. In the United States, however, because every telephone company is treated as a PUBLIC UTILITY, the prices it charges are subject to approval by state and federal regulatory agencies (see GOVERNMENT REGULATION). COPYRIGHTS and PATENTS are forms of monopolies granted by the government.

Competition and Market Power

Economists have coined the term *perfect competition* to describe the situation in which so many sellers compete that no one of them can influence the selling price. Few examples exist of perfect competition as defined by economists. Wheat farmers perhaps come closest to it. Such sellers are sometimes referred to as "price takers" rather than "price makers," and they theoretically have free entry and exit from markets, are independent, and have a homogeneous product to sell.

Market power is the term economists use to describe the ability to hold control over prices and profits. A monopoly has the greatest market power, and the seller under perfect competition has no market power at all. In the United States most businesses operate in industries falling between the polar extremes of monopoly and perfect competition. To explain the behavior of firms in the broad spectrum of markets between these extremes, economists have developed theories about the differences in market power in various industries. The most widely held theory assumes that the extent of a firm's market power depends on certain characteristics existing in the market where it operates. Three characteristics are believed to be especially important: (1) the share of an industry's sales held by its leading firms; (2) the ease with which new firms can enter an industry; and (3) the extent to which the products of a seller are differentiated from those of other sellers of similar products. According to this theory, originating in the works of the American economists Edward H. Chamberlin and Joe S. Bain, a firm's power will be greatest if it shares an industry with few competitors, if it is shielded almost completely from the threat of entry by new competitors, and if it sells a highly differentiated product that is distinct from all similar products. When a "big three" or "big four" dominates an industry, that situation is called a shared monopoly, because such firms are believed to behave almost like a single-firm monopoly. If these firms act together to control the supply and marketing of goods, they are known as an oligopoly or CARTEL.

Industrial Concentration

Much of the present competitive structure of U.S. industry evolved from events beginning in the last decades of the 19th century. Until then, nearly all businesses were small proprietorships or partnerships—therefore the control of industry was dispersed among many hands. With the relaxation of state incorporation laws, the industrial CORPORATION burst on the scene.

An enormous MERGER and consolidation movement began about 1900. In the two decades from 1890 to 1910, swift and irreversible changes occurred in many leading industries. The most familiar consolidations involved tobacco (American Tobacco), petroleum (Standard Oil), explosives and chemicals (Du Pont), and tin cans (American

Can). Although some of the great trusts of that day were later partially broken up, the pattern had been set.

A variety of complex, interacting forces determine the level of concentration in industry. On the one hand, the growth of the economy creates opportunities for more firms to enter an industry and to grow to efficient size. On the other hand, the number of firms can be limited by the requirements of large-scale production, the necessity to be large enough to support research laboratories and to finance new products and new methods of production, and the advantages enjoyed by large firms in distribution and advertising. Market concentration is also influenced by various business practices and the general institutional environment in which businesses operate. These include such factors as federal antitrust laws and the way these laws are enforced.

The most important single force promoting concentration in many industries is advertising, which plays an important role in the marketing process. The advent of television as a preferred medium of advertising for many products has been a major factor in promoting concentration. For various reasons, television advertising has favored large companies in many consumer-product industries; the result is a persistent trend toward increased centralization of business among a few corporations.

Another factor promoting concentration is mergers among business firms. Extensive merger activity occurred in the 1960s—when about one-tenth of the manufacturing companies with assets over $10 million were acquired by other firms—and again beginning about 1980. During the course of the 1980s, merger activity accelerated; as it reached new heights, commentators dubbed the phenomenon "merger mania." The merger movement created enormous CONGLOMERATE enterprises that have subsidiaries in many industries. Economists do not agree about the effect of industrial conglomeration on the competitive process. Especially when small companies are involved, mergers may increase efficiency and heighten competition. Mergers among large firms, however, clearly work to centralize control over the economy in ever fewer hands. Huge enterprises, straddling many industries and nations, possess a great deal of potential power over smaller firms and lead to further industrial concentration.

Estimates of the total costs of this concentration of market power in the U.S. economy are hazardous at best. The best evidence suggests that costs are substantial. One authority on the subject, F. M. Scherer, estimates the wastes and inefficiencies resulting from monopoly power at 6.2% of gross national product. Other effects exist as well.

Market power also redistributes income from consumers to the owners of the firms with power. The amount of this redistribution has been estimated at 3% of the gross national product.

These are only the most obvious costs of excessive market power. Some observers claim that market power prevents the economy from achieving full employment with stable prices. In economic theory, perfect competition leads to full employment of people and resources without inflation. Limitations on competition lead to less employment and higher prices. Each 1% rise in the unemployment rate reduces the gross national product by about $100 billion. To the extent that market power forces the country to accept higher unemployment in an effort to keep down inflation, it causes an enormous loss in national income.

Critics of industrial concentration charge that it also leads to the corruption and misuse of political institutions. They point to the tremendous political pressures brought to bear on legislators in Washington and the state capitals by LOBBYISTS and SPECIAL-INTEREST GROUPS, many of them financed by industrialists. Indeed, many monopolies could not exist if they did not have the backing and protection of the government.

Efforts to Combat Monopoly

A great debate over the monopoly question began around the turn of the 20th century; the debate has waxed and waned ever since. Three alternative approaches have been tried to limit monopolies: (1) antitrust legislation designed to prevent monopoly or to foster competition; (2) the regulation of holders of market power through state and federal public-utility laws; and (3) the public ownership of large enterprises (advocated by SOCIALISM).

In the United States the least-used approach has been that of publicly owned enterprise. In Europe and in developing countries, this approach has been a much more common device. Americans have relied mainly on public-utility regulation and the antitrust laws to police business behavior. The first federal legislation to deal with the monopoly problem created the INTERSTATE COMMERCE COMMISSION in 1887 to regulate the railroads.

The SHERMAN ANTI-TRUST ACT of 1890 was intended to prevent monopoly from developing and to strengthen competition. Under the Sherman Act the federal government brought a number of legal actions in the early 1900s that resulted in the breaking up of several large corporations, or trusts as they were then called, including Standard Oil of New Jersey, American Tobacco, and Du Pont. The most far-reaching antitrust settlement in recent years was the 1982 decision that divested the American Telephone and Telegraph Corporation (AT&T) of its 22 local operating companies. Although the Sherman Anti-Trust Act and subsequent antitrust laws such as the ROBINSON-PATMAN ACT of 1936 have attempted to strengthen competition, many industries remain highly concentrated, a trend that is likely to continue.

Other countries have also adopted forms of antitrust legislation, although none are as extensive as the U.S. laws. After World War II the Japanese proceeded to break up some of their large family-owned combines, the Zaibatsu. Japan also established a Fair Trade Commission, but it has been much less active than its U.S. counterparts, the FEDERAL TRADE COMMISSION and the Antitrust Division of the Department of Justice.

When Western European nations formed the EUROPEAN COMMUNITY in 1958, they also adopted a common antitrust law. The law has been generally effective in preventing the reemergence of cartels, or formal agreements to limit competition, that were common in Europe before World War II. It does little, however, to prevent mergers,

which have been widespread among European companies in recent years.

Some less developed nations, including South Korea and Pakistan, also have antitrust laws. These laws are usually aimed particularly at price-fixing cartels. In recent years state-controlled cartels have reappeared on the international scene, most notably the ORGANIZATION OF PETROLEUM EXPORTING COUNTRIES (OPEC).

monorail   see ELEVATED RAILROAD

monosaccharide [mahn'-oh-sak'-uh-ryd]   Monosaccharides are simple SUGARS and are the simplest members of the major class of biomolecules known as CARBOHYDRATES. They can combine to form more complex sugars, or carbohydrates. Monosaccharides have the general carbohydrate formula $C_n(H_2O)_n$. The variable n ranges from 3 to 7 and includes all the important simple sugars, which are classified according to this number as trioses, tetroses, pentoses, hexoses, or heptoses. The sugars are also classified as aldehyde sugars, or aldoses, and ketone sugars, or ketoses, according to whether the molecules of the sugar contain an aldehyde group (–C–CHO) or a ketone group (–C–CO–C–).

Several simple sugars are ISOMERS of each other—for example, galactose and glucose. They have structural formulas that differ only in the spatial arrangement of the hydroxyl (–OH) groups along the chain of carbon atoms. Monosaccharides also exhibit optical activity according to this arrangement, rotating polarized light to either the left or the right. Today the terms *levo,* or *L-,* sugar and *dextro,* or *D-,* sugar refer simply to the placement of the OH group next to the end of the carbon chain, not to the direction of rotation.

See also: POLYSACCHARIDE.

monosodium glutamate [mahn'-oh-soh'-deeuhm gloot'-uh-mayt] Monosodium glutamate, commonly known as MSG, is a flavor enhancer that is widely used in foods. A white, crystalline powder, it is the sodium salt of glutamic acid and occurs naturally in sugar beets, soybeans, and seaweed. It can also be synthetically produced. MSG intensifies and enhances the flavor of foods but has no flavor of its own. The substance is widely used in commercially prepared foods containing meat and fish and in home kitchens under a variety of trade names.

Although MSG is on the Food and Drug Administration's Generally Recognized as Safe (GRAS) list, controversy regarding its safety has arisen in recent years. Some individuals appear to be sensitive to MSG, and the substance is believed to produce the complex of symptoms (chest pain, facial pressure, burning sensations) known as Chinese Restaurant Syndrome. In addition, recent studies have found signs of brain damage in mice that have been injected with or fed diets containing high levels of MSG. As a result, the food industry has voluntarily removed MSG from baby foods until the results of further research become available.

monotheism [mahn'-uh-thee-izm] Monotheism is the religious conception of a single and transcendent God. It contrasts particularly with POLYTHEISM, belief in many gods, and PANTHEISM, belief in God as synonymous with the universe. Judaism, Christianity, and Islam are the principal monotheistic religions. Zoroastrianism was monotheistic in its beginnings, and Greek religion became monotheistic in its late phase.

Monothelitism [muh-nahth'-uh-lit-izm] Monothelitism was a 7th-century Byzantine doctrine that accepted the teaching of two natures in JESUS CHRIST, as defined (451) at the Council of CHALCEDON, but declared that he had only one will or mode of activity (*energeia*). The Monothelitic formula was adopted (624) by Byzantine Emperor HERACLIUS as a compromise that might be acceptable to the Monophysites (see MONOPHYSITISM) of Egypt and Syria. Sergius, patriarch of Constantinople, championed the doctrine and won the support of the Egyptian and Armenian Monophysites. The Christological controversies of an earlier age soon reappeared, however. Sergius sought the support of Pope HONORIUS I, who approved the Monothelitic formula, specifically rejecting the Chalcedonian teaching of "two wills." Monothelitism was condemned by Honorius's successors and by the Third Council of Constantinople (680; see CONSTANTINOPLE, COUNCILS OF). Because the writings of Honorius had contributed to the spread of this teaching, he also was condemned, although he was not accused of the formal teaching of heresy.

monotreme [mahn'-uh-treem] Monotremes are mammals of the order Monotremata and include the DUCK-BILLED PLATYPUS and the echidnas, or SPINY ANTEATERS. The name of the order means "single opening" and refers to the fact that in these mammals, as in birds and reptiles, the intestinal tract, the urinary ducts, and the genital ducts all open into one chamber, the cloaca, which has a single opening to the outside.

Monotremes are classified as mammals because they possess certain strictly mammalian characteristics, including milk glands (but not teats or nipples) to nourish their young, warm-bloodedness, a muscular diaphragm separating the lungs from the abdominal cavity, a single

The duck-billed platypus is a monotreme, a mammal that lays eggs and possesses other reptilian characteristics.

bone making up each side of the lower jaw, three middle ear bones, and hair. They are unique among mammals, however, because they possess many reptilian characteristics, perhaps the most notable being that they lay eggs rather than bear the young alive. Other reptilian features include the presence in the shoulder girdle (front-limb support) of well-developed coracoid bones and an interclavicle bone. In other mammals the coracoids are reduced and fused to the shoulder blades, and the interclavicle occurs at most as a tiny vestige.

The order Monotremata is classified in the mammalian subclass Prototheria and contains two families, the Ornithorhynchidae (duck-billed platypuses, found in Australia) and the Tachyglossidae (echidnas, found in Australia and New Guinea). The earliest known fossils of this group are from the Australian Pleistocene, about 2 million years ago; little is known about the origins or evolution of this group.

Monotype The Monotype is a machine used for mechanical typesetting (see TYPE AND TYPESETTING). It consists of two separate mechanisms (a keyboard and a typecaster), casts type consisting of individual characters, and sets justified lines (lines that are spaced out to uniform length). It was invented and patented in 1887 by Tolbert Lanston (1844–1913). The versatility of the composition of individual characters and the ability to cast new type caused the Monotype system to be widely used throughout the world, particularly for book work and the setting of tabular material, although it has now been largely superseded by phototypesetting techniques.

Monroe Monroe, a city on the Ouachita River in northeastern Louisiana, is the seat of Ouachita Parish. It has a population of 54,909 (1990). Situated on one of the largest natural gas fields in the United States (discovered 1916), Monroe has plants that produce carbon black, chemicals, pulp, paper, and furniture. Northeast Louisiana University is located there. The city, first called Fort Miro (1785), was renamed (1819) in honor of the *James Monroe,* the first steamship to navigate the river.

Monroe, Harriet The American poet Harriet Monroe, b. Chicago, Dec. 23, 1860, d. Sept. 26, 1936, is remembered not for her own work but for her efforts on behalf of such major modern poets as T. S. Eliot, Ezra Pound, Wallace Stevens, and William Carlos Williams. As the founder and editor (1912–36) of *Poetry,* a journal published in Chicago, Monroe became a crucial figure in the development of modern verse. Ezra Pound, who corresponded with her from Europe, did much to direct the policy of the journal and expounded the doctrine of imagism in its pages. T. S. Eliot's "The Love Song of J. Alfred Prufrock" first appeared there in 1915, and *Poetry* also published the work of American poets such as Vachel Lindsay and Carl Sandburg. Monroe's own verse includes the patriotic "Columbian Ode," which she recited (1892) at the opening of the World's Columbian Exposition in Chicago.

AT A GLANCE

JAMES MONROE
5th President of the United States (1817–25)

Nicknames: "The Last Cocked Hat"; "Era-of-Good-Feeling President"

Born: Apr. 28, 1758, Westmoreland County, Va.

Education: College of William and Mary (2 years; left in 1776)

Profession: Lawyer

Religious Affiliation: Episcopalian

Marriage: Feb. 16,1786, to Elizabeth Kortright (1768–1830)

Children: Eliza Kortright Monroe (1786–1835); James Spence Monroe (1799–1800); Maria Hester Monroe (1803–50)

Political Affiliation: Democratic-Republican

Writings: *Writings of James Monroe* (7 vols., 1898–1903), ed. by S. M. Hamilton; *Autobiography* (1959), ed. by Stuart G. Brown and Donald G. Baker

Died: July 4, 1831, New York City

Buried: Hollywood Cemetery, Richmond, Va.

Vice-President: Daniel D. Tompkins

James Monroe

Monroe, James   James Monroe, fifth president of the United States (1817–25), presided over an era sometimes called one of Good Feelings but actually filled with intense factional strife. The MONROE DOCTRINE climaxed a series of brilliant foreign-policy successes during his administrations.

Early Life. Monroe was born Apr. 28, 1758, on his parents' small plantation in Westmoreland County, Va. After spending two years at the College of William and Mary, Monroe left in March 1776 to fight in the American Revolution. He was commissioned lieutenant in a Virginia regiment and marched to join George Washington's army. He fought in the battles around New York that summer and was one of the conspicuous heroes of the Battle of Trenton in December 1776.

In 1779, Monroe formed the most important association of his life when he began the study of law under Thomas Jefferson, who was then governor of Virginia. Jefferson came to value Monroe for his persistence, patriotism, and devotion to republican principles. The two men, together with James Madison, formed political and personal bonds that lasted for half a century. Monroe soon began a steady accumulation of offices: member of the Virginia legislature (1782); delegate to the Continental Congress (1783–86); member of the Virginia ratifying convention (1788), where he opposed adoption of the new federal Constitution; U.S.

senator from Virginia (1790–94); minister to France (1794–96); and governor of Virginia (1799–1802). By 1800 he was among the national leaders of the Jeffersonian, or Democratic-Republican, party.

President Jefferson sent him on a second diplomatic mission in 1803 to help Robert R. Livingston (see LIVINGSTON family) negotiate the purchase of New Orleans from the French. The two Americans were astonished when Napoleon I offered to sell the entire Louisiana Territory, which they quickly and adroitly negotiated to purchase for the United States (see LOUISIANA PURCHASE). The rest of Monroe's mission in Europe was less successful. He spent 18 months in Madrid negotiating inconclusively for the purchase of Florida from Spain. After a further 18 months of negotiation he and William Pinkney obtained a commercial treaty with the British. It did not, however, prohibit impressment—the chief American grievance against Britain. Therefore Jefferson refused to submit the treaty to the Senate for ratification. Monroe felt betrayed and unappreciated and was enough estranged from his colleagues to challenge Madison for the presidency in 1808. When Madison won, the unhappy Monroe kept his distance from the new administration for two years but was elected governor of Virginia again in 1811.

In 1811, Madison, who had always regretted the break with his old friend, invited Monroe to become his secretary of state. Monroe accepted and was thus Madison's chief counselor as the WAR OF 1812 began. After the British capture of Washington in August 1814 he also became secretary of war.

Presidency. As Madison's heir apparent, and with the Federalists in disgrace for having opposed and even hindered the war, Monroe was elected president by an overwhelming majority in 1816. His unopposed reelection in 1820 ranks him with Washington as the least partisan of American presidents. This apparent political harmony gives some justification to the label Era of Good Feelings, an expression coined by a Federalist newspaper.

Monroe hoped that the period of factionalism, and even of political parties, had indeed ended. The tensions and disputes inherent in a free political system, however, left him entangled in sectional differences and beset by personal rivalries—especially among John Quincy ADAMS, John C. CALHOUN, and William H. CRAWFORD (all members of his cabinet) for succession to the presidency. Monroe gave some direction to domestic events—by supporting increases in the tariff, opposing restrictions on slavery in Missouri as a prerequisite to statehood (see MISSOURI COMPROMISE), and rejecting federal subsidy of internal improvements except by constitutional amendment—but, in general, partisan and sectional jealousies overwhelmed his good intentions.

In foreign affairs, however, Monroe's presidency was triumphant, thanks largely to the efforts of the brilliant secretary of state, John Quincy Adams. Monroe approved the Rush-Bagot Agreement (1817), demilitarizing the long boundary with Canada; a treaty (1818) that provided for joint Anglo-American occupation of the Oregon Territory; the Adams-Onís Treaty (1819), which purchased Florida from Spain and demarked the U.S. boundary with Spanish territory across the Rocky Mountains all the way to the Pacific Ocean; and a Russo-American treaty (1824) limiting Russian expansion down the Pacific coast. These treaties, establishing the United States for the first time as a transcontinental power, together with the declaration of the Monroe Doctrine (1823), which validated Anglo-American cooperation in supporting the newly won independence of Spain's Latin American colonies, set the outlines of both U.S. westward expansion and relations with the rest of the world for nearly a century. Monroe left the presidency in 1825 and retired to his Virginia estate. He died July 4, 1831.

Monroe, Marilyn   Marilyn Monroe, b. Norma Jean Baker, Los Angeles, June 1, 1926, d. Aug. 5, 1962, after rising from bit parts, became one of the most celebrated film personalities of her time. Hers was the classic showbusiness tragedy. Stardom seemed a burden; being an international sex goddess, even more so. Her second husband was baseball star Joe DiMaggio. Following her third marriage, to playwright Arthur Miller, she struggled to understand theories of acting and wanted to star in the classics. When this effort proved fruitless, she became so difficult to work with that she was virtually unemployable. Yet in the handful of comedies in which she starred her personal ebullience and freshness transcend her limita-

The American actress Marilyn Monroe was originally publicized as a Hollywood sex symbol but was later recognized as a sensitive and talented performer. Monroe's comedic skill and vulnerable charm were best seen in such films as The Seven Year Itch *(1955) and* Some Like It Hot *(1959).*

tions: *Gentlemen Prefer Blondes* (1953), *How to Marry a Millionaire* (1953), *The Seven Year Itch* (1955), *The Prince and the Showgirl* (1957), and *Some Like It Hot* (1959). She also performed competently in two dramatic roles, *Bus Stop* (1956) and *The Misfits* (1961). Among the many books written about her, Norman Mailer's biography, *Marilyn* (1973), made headlines in its own right. Miller's play *After the Fall* (1964) is the playwright's thinly disguised interpretation of their tense, unhappy marriage; Paddy Chayevsky's screenplay *The Goddess* (1958) is a fictional account of her checkered professional career. She died from an overdose of sleeping pills, possibly a suicide, at age 36.

Monroe Doctrine   President James MONROE's annual message to the U.S. Congress of Dec. 2, 1823, outlined three essential points: (1) "the American continents, by the free and independent condition which they have assumed and maintain, are henceforth not to be considered as subjects for future colonization by any European powers"; (2) "we should consider any attempt [by the nations of Europe] to extend their system to any portion of this hemisphere as dangerous to our peace and safety"; and (3) "in the wars of the European powers in matters relating to themselves we have never taken part, nor does it comport with our policy so to do."

Monroe feared that France, prompted by the Holy Alliance, would dispatch troops to the New World to put down the revolts in the Spanish colonies. The British foreign secretary George CANNING had proposed a joint Anglo-American protest against European intervention in the New World, but on the advice of his secretary of state, John Quincy Adams, Monroe opted for a unilateral U.S. statement. By the time Monroe sent his message to Congress, however, Canning had persuaded the French government to renounce any intention of conquest or annexation in the New World. Monroe considered the warning to Europe a prudent diplomatic move, and he knew that the British government would take care of its enforcement. The principles he enunciated did not receive the name *Monroe Doctrine* until 1853, were not invoked until 1895 (see VENEZUELA BOUNDARY DISPUTE), and obtained international recognition only in the 20th century.

Monrovia [muhn-roh'-vee-uh]   Monrovia is the capital, largest city, and chief port of Liberia, situated on Cape Montserrado on the coast of West Africa. Its population is 421,058 (1984 est.). Industries include oil refining, food processing, and the manufacturing of cement, pharmaceuticals, and paints. Rubber, iron ore, and palm kernels and fiber are exported. A modern deepwater harbor on Bushrod Island, developed after World War II with U.S. aid, is connected with the city by a bridge. The city was founded in 1821, when the American Colonization Society settled freed U.S. slaves on the site, and it was named for U.S. president James Monroe. The University of Liberia was established there in 1822. The city was badly damaged during a civil war in 1989–90.

Mons [mohns]   Mons (Flemish: Bergen) is the capital of Hainaut province in southwestern Belgium, located about 50 km (30 mi) southwest of Brussels, at the junction of the Conde-Mons Canal and the Canal du Centre. It has a population of 89,515 (1988 est.). Mons is primarily a coal-mining center and has a mining college, established in 1837. Other manufactures include cloth, lace, and pottery. Historic buildings include a 12th-century castle chapel and the 15th-century town hall.

First settled as a Roman camp in the 3d century, the town grew up around an abbey built there about 650. During the Middle Ages, Mons was a prosperous cloth-weaving center. It was later repeatedly attacked and occupied by the French, Spanish, Dutch, English, and Austrians. In August 1914 it was the scene of the first battle of World War I between the British and the Germans.

monsoon [mahn-soon']   The term *monsoon,* from the Arabic *mausim,* "season," originally referred to the WIND condition in the Arabian Sea: the wind blows from the southwest during half of the year and from the reverse direction during the other half. The monsoon formed the basis for Arabian trade; merchants moved southward along the African coast during winter and returned with the wind in summer. The term now refers to any wind system characterized by seasonal reversibility. Monsoons occur in Chile and parts of North America, but the largest and most vigorous—the Asian-Australian and African systems—occur in the Eastern Hemisphere.

An important aspect of monsoon systems is the existence of subseasonal, or short-term, weather variations. In monsoon regions rainfall does not occur continuously through the summer; rather, most rainfall is tied to the occurrence of monsoon disturbances and depressions. Occasionally, prolonged periods—monsoon breaks that may last 2 weeks or longer—occur in which no disturbance develops. Such periods are the cause of DROUGHT

and significant hardship to farmers. Even in the winter monsoon cold surges of air spread from cold central Asia and may affect weather as far south as the equator.

The monsoon patterns are rendered even more complicated by the effects of large mountain chains such as the Himalayas, the irregularity of continental shape, and the presence of oceans to the east and west of the continents. Monsoon circulations thus possess considerable local character.

The social and economic implications of monsoon meteorology are great. A late monsoon onset or a prolonged monsoon break may signify drought, and a few more monsoon disturbances than normal may produce flood. Because the majority of nations in the monsoon regions are agrarian societies, forecasting the seasonal vagaries of the monsoon circulation is critically important. One of the most important problems in meteorology is to learn how to forecast monsoon events with sufficient lead time to be of use.

monstera   The genus *Monstera* of the arum family, Araceae, contains 25 to possibly 50 species of tropical American plants that are typically woody vines (lianas). Young plants are usually climbers with small, solid leaves that cling closely, like shingles, to trees; and certain species, such as *M. acuminata,* are called shingle plants. Later the plants tend to become epiphytes, independent of the soil. Areas of leaf tissue between the veins may cease their growth, become dry, and break away, forming holes in the leaves; parts of the leaf margins may similarly fall away to produce deep notches. Monsteras are well-known foliage houseplants. The most popular is the split-leaf philodendron, *M. delicosa,* which has large, leathery, perforated leaves and long, cordlike aerial roots and may grow to 9 m (30 ft) or more in height. It has tiny flowers that are densely clustered on a thick spike, called a spadix, which is surrounded by a creamy white, leaflike bract (spathe).

Mont-Saint-Michel   [mohn-san-mee-shel']   Mont-Saint-Michel is a 1-ha (3-acre) rocky islet topped by a famous Gothic abbey, 1.6 km (1 mi) off the northwest coast of France in the Bay of Mont-Saint-Michel in the English Channel. The island, located 5 km (3 mi) from the shore during the Middle Ages, is now surrounded by water only two times a month. Its one cobblestone street climbs in three layers from a great granite base to the towering Benedictine abbey of Mont-Saint-Michel, an architectural masterpiece built in the 13th century, replacing the original abbey, which was founded in 708 by St. Aubert, bishop of Avranches, but destroyed by King Philip II of France in 1203. Its fortifications enabled the islet to withstand repeated English assaults during the Hundred Years' War. The abbey served as a prison during Napoleon's reign. Restored after 1863, and connected to the mainland by a causeway (completed 1875), the abbey is preserved as a national historical monument and is one of France's great tourist attractions.

Montagnards [mohn-tahn-yahr'] Montagnards (French for "mountain people") are the members of more than 30 primitive societies located mainly in the mountainous, forested spine separating Vietnam and Laos. Among the largest groups are the Jarai, Rhadé, and Sedang. The Vietnamese often refer to these groups as *Moi,* a derogatory name meaning "savage"; the official government name for them is *Nguoi Thuong* ("upland people"). Their population is estimated at 700,000; they speak languages related to both the Malayo-Polynesian and the Mon-Khmer linguistic families (see SOUTHEAST ASIAN LANGUAGES).

The village is traditionally the most important political and economic unit in Montagnard society. The economy is based on rice growing, gathering of forest products (lacquer, resins, and rattan), and hunting of game with the crossbow. Some villages have longhouses occupied by a number of related families; in other communities young men live in bachelor houses until they are married. Traditionally animists, the Montagnards believe in numerous spirits and ghosts of the dead who are thought to bring either success or misfortune. During and since the Vietnam War efforts have been made to integrate the isolated and often exploited Montagnard groups into Vietnamese society.

Montaigne, Michel de [mohn-tayn', mee-shel' duh] Michel Eyquem de Montaigne, b. Feb. 28, 1533, d. Sept. 13, 1592, is the most widely read writer of the French Renaissance. His *Essays* is one of the great works of European literature, and he is generally accounted the inventor of the personal, or familiar, ESSAY as a modern genre. Although in his work Montaigne describes himself as an unimportant person, that description is misleading. He succeeded (1557–70) his father as counselor of the

The 16th-century French author Michel de Montaigne developed the literary genre of the personal essay, establishing its importance in Western literature. His Essays, *which record his observations on such diverse subjects as friendship, education, and government, are valuable historical records of an individual's reaction to the immediate environment. (Musée Condé, Chantilly.)*

parlement of Bordeaux, was twice elected (1581 and 1583) mayor of Bordeaux, and participated in high-level diplomatic negotiations during the turbulent years of the French Wars of Religion.

Montaigne's personal life was lonely and not especially happy. His one close friend, Étienne de La Boétie, in whose memory he wrote the essay "On Friendship," died young in 1563. His relationship with his wife was not close, and all his children except one daughter, for whom he did not greatly care, died in infancy. His last years were cheered by his friendship with Marie de Gournay, whom he called his adopted daughter and who supervised the posthumous edition of his *Essays* in 1595.

Montaigne's first published work (1568–69) was a translation of the *Natural Theology* of Raymond Sebond, a 15th-century Catalan theologian. Montaigne was fond of traveling, and on a trip to Switzerland, Germany, and Italy in 1580–81 he half wrote, half dictated a travel journal published posthumously in 1774. His masterpiece, however, remains the *Essays,* published in three volumes in 1580 and 1588 and first translated into English in 1603.

Montaigne deals perceptively and sensitively with many universal problems: death and how to prepare for it, the pain of illness and the disillusionment of old age, friendship, and true and false repentance. Many, however, find the greatest charm of the *Essays* in the author's self-portrait. Montaigne presents himself as endearingly ordinary, with a poor memory and slow intelligence, full of paradox and contradiction, but always interesting because he is the only thing he can fully know in a world of change and uncertainty. Montaigne's essays constitute the earliest such detailed self-portrait in European literature and have had a decisive influence on writers as different as Pascal, Rousseau, and Proust. His style and approach have had an equal influence on the development of the essay form in English-speaking countries.

Montale, Eugenio [mohn-tah'-lay, ay-oo-jen'-yoh] The Italian poet and essayist and winner of the Nobel Prize for literature in 1975, Eugenio Montale, b. Oct. 12, 1896, d. Sept. 12, 1981, contributed a genuinely new voice to Italian poetry with his first volume of verse, *Ossi di seppia* (Cuttlefish Bones, 1925), depicting a barren world emblematic of human suffering and fate. From the outset Montale's poetry was associated with hermeticism, a school of poetry that rejected flamboyant rhetoric and traditional forms, and was compared with the work of T. S. Eliot, notably *The Waste Land,* which he translated along with the works of Shakespeare, Herman Melville, Emily Dickinson, and Gerard Manley Hopkins. Later collections, many of which have been translated in whole or in part, include *Le occasioni* (The Occasions, 1939); *La bufera e altro* (The Storm and Other Poems, 1956); a collection of short stories and prose poems, *The Butterfly of Dinard* (1956; expanded 1960; Eng. trans., 1970); and *Satura, 1962–1970,* noted for its "Xenia" poems, written in memory of his wife and translated into English as *Xenia Poems* (1970).

MONTANA

Land: Area: 380,847 km² (147,046 mi²); rank: 4th. Capital: Helena (1990 pop., 24,569). Largest city: Billings (1990 pop., 81,151). Counties: 56. Elevations: highest—3,901 m (12,799 ft), at Granite Peak; lowest—549 m (1,800 ft), at the Kootenai River.

People: Population (1990): 803,655; rank: 44th; density: 2.1 persons per km² (5.5 per mi²). Distribution (1990): 52.5% urban, 47.5% rural. Average annual change (1980–90): +0.22%.

Government (1993): Governor: Marc Racicot, Republican. U.S. Congress: Senate—1 Democrat, 1 Republican; House—1 Democrat. Electoral college votes: 3. State legislature: 50 senators, 100 representatives.

Economy: State personal income (1989): $11.3 billion; rank: 46th. Median family income (1989): $28,044; rank: 43d. Agriculture: income (1989)—$1.6 billion. Lumber production (1991): 1.4 billion board feet. Mining (nonfuel): value (1988)—$458 million. Manufacturing: value added (1987)—$1.1 billion. Services: value (1987)—$2.46 billion.

Miscellany: Statehood: Nov. 8, 1889; the 41st state. Nicknames: Treasure State and Big Sky Country; tree: ponderosa pine; motto: *Oro y Plata* ("Gold and Silver"); song: "Montana."

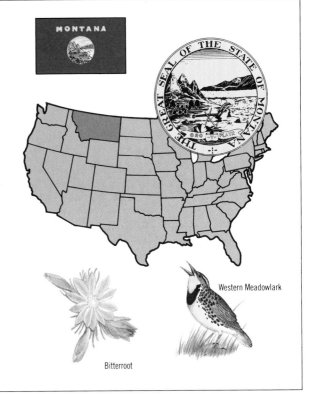

Western Meadowlark

Bitterroot

Montana   Montana, one of the Mountain states, ranks fourth in size but is among the ten least populous of all the U.S. states. Bordering it are the Canadian provinces of British Columbia, Alberta, and Saskatchewan on the north; North Dakota and South Dakota on the east; Wyoming on the south; and Idaho on the west and southwest. Montana stretches for about 885 km (550 mi) from the ROCKY MOUNTAINS and Continental Divide in the west to the rolling plains in the east. The name Montana comes from the Spanish word *montaña,* meaning "mountainous region." Among the state's nicknames are "Treasure State," "Big Sky Country," and the Indian designation, "Land of the Shining Mountains."

Land and Resources

The western third of Montana is rugged and mountainous, and the remaining eastern portion consists of rolling plains. Granite Peak, Montana's highest point, rises to 3,901 m (12,799 ft) in the Beartooth Range near Yellowstone National Park; the lowest elevation, 549 m (1,800 ft), occurs in the northwest, where the Kootenai River crosses into Idaho.

Physiographic Regions. Montana contains parts of three major physiographic regions—the Great Plains, a small section of the Middle Rocky Mountains, and a large section of the Northern Rocky Mountains. The GREAT PLAINS in eastern Montana have a general elevation range of 600 to 1,000 m (2,000 to 3,300 ft) and a deceptively flat-to-rolling overall appearance. On closer inspection, however, it is apparent that they are broken by small mountain masses near the eastern edge of the Rockies and by the angular outlines of mesas, buttes, gullies, canyons, badlands, and naturally sculptured rock outcrops. The Middle Rocky Mountains rise west of the plains and include a small section of the Yellowstone Plateau, along with the rugged Absaroka and Beartooth ranges. The parallel ranges of the Northern Rockies form a 322-km-wide (200-mi) belt of rugged mountains in western Montana.

Rivers and Lakes. Montana rivers drain toward the north, east, and west. A small area in the north central part of the state drains to the north by way of the Saint Mary and Belly rivers. Lands east of the Continental Divide drain into the Gulf of Mexico and Atlantic Ocean through the Missouri-Mississippi river system, and lands west of the divide drain into the Pacific Ocean by the Clark Fork and Kootenai rivers. Montana's principal river

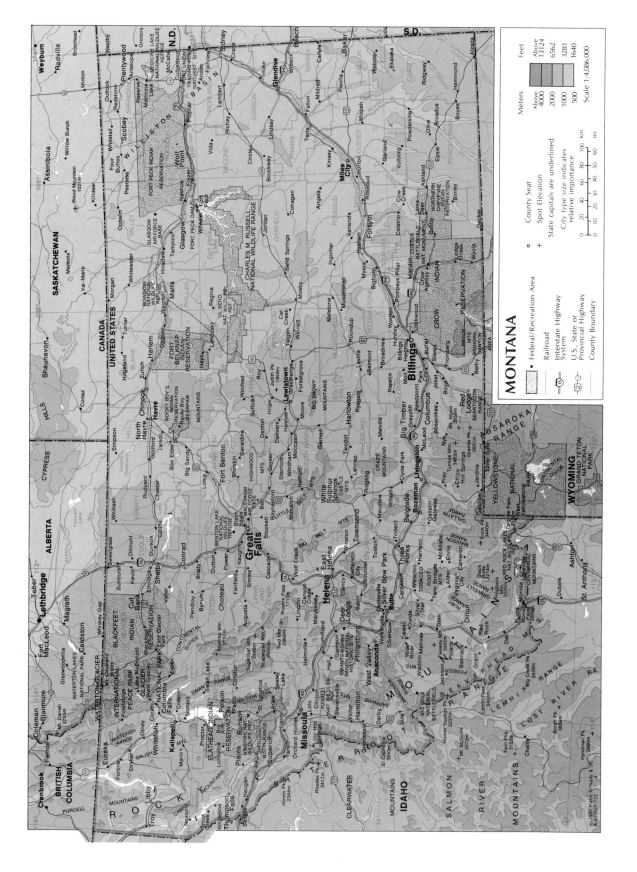

is the MISSOURI. Its source is at Three Forks, where the Jefferson, Gallatin, and Madison rivers unite. It flows eastward, where it receives its major tributaries—the Milk, the Musselshell, and, east of the state border, the YELLOWSTONE. Flathead Lake is the largest natural lake, and Fort Peck Lake on the Missouri River is the largest of many artificial water bodies created for irrigation and production of hydroelectricity.

Climate. January temperatures range from −12° C (11° F) in the northeast to −6° C (22° F) in the southwest, but in unusually cold years the average may be −18° C (0° F). Winters usually bring short-lived cold spells of high winds, blowing snow, and colder temperatures, interspersed with mild periods of chinook weather—warm, dry winds that evaporate the snow cover to the east of the Continental Divide. In 1954, Montana experienced the coldest temperature of any state in the conterminous United States when a low of −57° C (−70° F) occurred at Rogers Pass, northwest of Helena. July temperatures average between 23° C (73° F) in the southeast and 18° C (64° F) in the southwest. Precipitation, concentrated in late spring, is sparse, averaging 380 mm (15 in) over most of the state, with extremes of more than 2,540 mm (100 in) in exposed mountain areas and less than 178 mm (7 in) in the south central areas. Severe hailstorms occasionally strike in summer. Droughts, blizzards, and unexpectedly early or late snows are other climatic hazards.

Vegetation and Animal Life. Most of the plains are treeless and where not farmed are covered with a natural vegetation of buffalo and blue grama grasses, giving way to sagebrush and bunch grass in drier areas. Aspen and cottonwood trees grow along the river valleys, and stands of ponderosa pines top some of the upland areas. In the Rockies, conifers extend up to the tree line. Spruce, Douglas fir, and tamarack are common in wetter areas and lodgepole pine in drier locations. Higher elevations support a low-growing alpine vegetation, with a profusion of wildflower blooms in early summer. Montana's most distinctive animal, the buffalo, was wantonly slaughtered before 1894 and is now found only in the National Bison Range in the Flathead Valley and other protected areas. Other animals found in the mountains are bobcats, coyotes, lynx, mink, puma, and such larger game animals as elk, deer, bighorn sheep, moose, and grizzly and black bears. Numerous national forests and federal and state wildlife refuges protect the state's natural resources.

Mineral Resources. Montana has rich deposits of gold, copper, lead, silver, zinc, manganese, and other metals in the Rocky Mountains. Vast deposits of coal, petroleum, natural gas, and bentonite underlie much of the Great Plains. Especially valuable are the coal deposits found under the entire eastern fourth of the state. Abundant runoff and snowmelt from the mountains provide sufficient surface water for irrigation and hydroelectricity; additional water resources are available from aquifers.

People

One of the least populated of all the states, Montana has a population density that is less than one-tenth the national average. From 1970 to 1980, Montana experienced a growth rate of about 1.3% annually, higher than the national rate, and a net in-migration of 16,000. Growth during 1980–90 slowed, however; the state grew by 2.2%, compared with a national rate of 10.2%. White ethnic groups account for about 95% of the population, with Norwegian, German, and Canadian ancestries predominating. Most Montanans are Protestants, but the largest single religious group is the Roman Catholic. The HUTTERIAN BRETHREN live in a number of colonies in the state.

The Indian population in 1990 numbered 47,679, most of whom lived on reservations. The black population is one of the smallest in any state. Only about half the population are urban. The largest cities are BILLINGS and GREAT FALLS, each with a population of more than 55,000, and MISSOULA, BUTTE, HELENA, and Bozeman, each with more than 20,000 residents.

Educational and Cultural Institutions. In 1893 the legislature established free public schools and in 1897 county high schools. The Montana University System, including the University of Montana (1893) at Missoula and Montana State University (1893) at Bozeman, and a number of private institutions provide higher education. The state's major museums are the Montana Historical Society Museum in Helena, the Charles M. RUSSELL Museum and Original Studio in Great Falls, the Museum of the Plains Indian and Crafts Center at Browning, the Museum of the Rockies in Bozeman, the World Mining Museum in Butte, and the Western Heritage Center in Billings.

Historic Sites. Historical markers identify the 3,122-km-long (1,940-mi) Lewis and Clark Trail of the early explorers. The Custer Battlefield National Monument commemorates Custer's Last Stand against the SIOUX and CHEYENNE in the 1876 Battle of the LITTLE BIGHORN. Big Hole National Battlefield marks the 1877 victory of the NEZ PERCÉ Indians under Chief JOSEPH, and Chief Joseph Battleground State Monument commemorates the chief's surrender. Chief Plenty Coups State Monument preserves the home of this famous CROW leader. Saint Mary's Mission log church and pharmacy are remains of Montana's first permanent settlement. Ghost towns at Bannack, Elkhorn, Virginia City, and Pony recall gold-rush days.

Communications. Montana is well supplied with commercial radio and television stations. The most influential of the state's daily newspapers are the *Montana Standard* of Butte, the *Billings Gazette,* the *Great Falls Tribune,* and the *Missoula Missoulian.*

Economic Activities

Agriculture, mining, and lumbering are the most important elements of Montana's economy. In the 1950s eastern Montana's petroleum and natural-gas industries grew rapidly, and the 1960s, '70s, and '80s brought new wealth from tourism and strip-mining of coal on the Great Plains.

Agriculture. Large-scale farming and ranching predominate in Montana. Beef cattle, sheep, and lambs are raised in large numbers; Montana also produces substan-

The sharp majesty of Glacier National Park in northwestern Montana attracts thousands of visitors each year. The park, stretching across the Continental Divide, is part of the Rockies.

tial numbers of pigs. Wheat is the chief crop. Other crops are hay, sweet cherries, barley, oats, sugar beets, and alfalfa.

Forestry. Approximately one-fourth of Montana's area is covered with forest, much of it in national parks or other reserves. The principal woods cut are ponderosa pine, larch, and Douglas fir; lumber, plywood, pulp, and paper are leading wood products.

Mining. Traditionally a mining state, Montana fluctuates in its metals—gold, silver, and copper—output, depending on prices and labor conditions. Copper was long mined at Butte and was for many years the principal state export, but many of the copper mines were shut down in the early 1980s. Petroleum and coal are the leading minerals today. Most coal is extracted from strip mines in the eastern coalfields. Vermiculite, talc, tungsten, and phosphate rock are also mined.

Manufacturing. Montana's sparse population, small labor supply, and high transportation costs to other parts of the nation restrict industrial development to the processing of raw materials and agricultural commodities. The processing of lumber and wood products, including paper, is Montana's most important manufacturing activity. The growing of Christmas trees is significant economically. The second most important industrial activity in the state is food processing—particularly sugar refining and flour milling.

Other industry involves the processing of mineral products; East Helena is a center for mineral processing. There are petroleum refineries at Great Falls, Billings, Laurel, and Cut Bank. Other manufactures include bricks and cement.

Transportation. Major transportation routes follow—as in the past—the Missouri, Yellowstone, and Clark Fork river valleys. The major highway routes are interstate highways 15, 90, and 94, and major rail lines provide passenger as well as freight service. Historically, the railroad was important in the development of Montana; the first railroad to enter the territory of Montana was the Utah & Northern, in 1880. Major airports are at Billings and Great Falls.

Tourism. Montana's tourist attractions include Glacier National Park and Yellowstone National Park; Bighorn Canyon National Recreation Area; vast mountain and wilderness areas; excellent hunting, fishing, and camping; and dude ranches, ski resorts, and annual rodeo events. Bozeman, Missoula, Whitefish, and Red Lodge are tourist centers.

Energy. Most power in Montana is hydroelectric, with major sites at Great Falls, Columbia Falls, and Fort Peck, and the Hungry Horse, Canyon Ferry, and Libby dams. Montana is one of the leading states in the production of hydroelectricity. Steam generating plants using coal are also important; there are also oil-fired and gas-fired generating plants in the state.

Government

In 1972, Montanans approved a new constitution, effective as of July 1, 1973. It replaced the outdated and overly amended constitution adopted in 1889. Executive power rests with the governor, assisted by a lieutenant governor, both of whom are elected to 4-year terms. The bicameral legislature is composed of 50 senators (elected for 4-year terms) and 100 representatives (elected for 2-year terms).

The Cathedral of Saint Helena (foreground), *in Helena, the capital of Montana, is based on the Cologne Cathedral in West Germany. Helena is a commercial and shipping center.*

Montana's political outlook is evenly balanced between conservative and liberal factions. Although considered a liberal state nationally, Montana has historically been dominated by conservative industrialists on state and local levels. Growing urbanization has brought increased local liberalism.

History

In the early 1700s, Indian tribes, including the BLACKFOOT, Sioux, Crow, and Cheyenne who had been displaced from lands farther east, began moving into Montana, pushing local tribes—including the FLATHEADS, Shoshoni, and Kutenai—westward toward the mountains. The first recorded visit by Europeans occurred in 1805, when the explorers Meriwether LEWIS and William CLARK, accompanied by their Shoshoni Indian guide SACAGAWEA, ascended the Missouri and Jefferson rivers to cross the Rocky Mountains (see LEWIS AND CLARK EXPEDITION). In 1807, Manuel Lisa established the first fur-trading post on the Big Horn River. Many trappers and traders, the so-called MOUNTAIN MEN, soon followed. Montana's first permanent white settlement did not appear until Father Pierre Jean DE SMET founded Saint Mary's Mission in 1841.

The discovery of gold brought a large influx of white settlers in the early 1860s. In 1863 western Montana, which had been successively part of Oregon and Washington territories, was united with eastern Montana, previously part of the territories of Louisiana (1805), Missouri (1812), Nebraska (1854), and Dakota (1861), in the Idaho territory. In 1864 separate territorial status was achieved, with the capital first at Bannack, then Virginia City, and, after 1875, at Helena.

In the 1860s stockmen began trailing cattle northward from Texas, copper mining began, and conflict with the Indians intensified. In the Sioux War of 1875–76, the forces of Lt. Col. George Armstrong CUSTER were annihilated at Little Bighorn, but government troops subsequently subdued and removed the hostile Indians to reservations. Railroads crossed the region in the 1880s, further stimulating cattle and sheep ranching and indirectly setting off a fierce struggle between cattle- and sheepherders for priority grazing rights. In the mountains copper king Marcus DALY developed Butte Hill from a rough silver camp to a vast industrial complex of copper mines, mills, and smelters. Political life came increasingly to revolve around copper and Daly's bitter rivalry with two other copper kings, William Andrews CLARK and F. ("Fritz") Augustus Heinze. On Nov. 8, 1889, Montana became the 41st state.

From 1909 to 1918 homesteaders arrived by the thousands to fence and plant the range with grain crops. Their farms flourished until a series of dry years beginning in 1917 forced abandonment of many homesteads. In the DEPRESSION OF THE 1930s, many mines closed. Since then greater diversity and stability have been introduced in the state by the development of irrigation facilities, tourism, and petroleum and coal resources. Copper's dominance has been broken, and coal mining holds great promise for future economic growth. Strip-mining of coal began in the 1960s, but that is strongly opposed by Indi-

ans on whose reservations much of the coal is located. Environmentalists are seeking to preserve and conserve water quantity and quality, reclaim mined-over land, prevent air pollution from mining operations and other emissions, and protect scenic amenities.

Montana, Joe Joseph Clifford Montana, b. New Eagle, Pa., June 11, 1956, was the National Football League's premier quarterback during the 1980s, and at the start of the next decade he was considered by experts as one of the best ever at his position. After graduating from Notre Dame in 1978, Montana began playing for the San Francisco 49ers, who under his direction won 4 Super Bowls (for the 1981, 1984, 1988, and 1989 seasons). He was the NFL's Most Valuable Player in 1989, as well as the Super Bowl MVP 3 times. Under the NFL's complex rating system for quarterbacks, Montana's career rating is the highest in NFL history, as is his percentage of passes completed—about 64%. He holds many regular-season and Super Bowl records.

Montanism Montanism was a Christian apocalyptic movement that arose in the 2d century. It took its name from Montanus, a Phrygian, who, shortly after his baptism as a Christian (AD 156 or 172), claimed to have received a revelation from the Holy Spirit to the effect that he, as representative prophet of the Spirit, would lead the Christian church into its final stage.

Aided by two women, Maximilla and Priscilla (or Prisca), Montanus founded a sect of enthusiasts who preached the imminent end of the world, austere morality, and severe penitential discipline. They forbade second marriages, denied the divine nature of the church, and refused forgiveness for sins that persons committed after baptism. Montanus called for less church hierarchy and more charismatic prophecy. He regarded a life of seclusion and contempt of the world as the only true Christian ideal.

The Montanists seem to have sought renewal of the church from within through a rebirth of the religious enthusiasm that had marked Christian beginnings. By the 3d century, however, they had established separate communities in which women and men were admitted to presbyterate and episcopacy. Montanism did not disappear until about the 6th century.

Montauk Montauk was the name given by English colonists to the Algonquian-speaking tribe that lived in present-day Suffolk County, Long Island, N.Y., as well as to most other tribes on the island. These peoples, collectively called the Metoac, were most closely related to the tribal groups of Massachusetts and Connecticut. They were a village-dwelling, horticultural people, significantly engaged in fishing, hunting, and trade. Their land was the center for the manufacture of the best WAMPUM in northeastern North America.

Early in the 17th century the Montauk were violently

attacked by the PEQUOT of Connecticut, who sought control of wampum production. The Montauk paid tribute to the Pequot until that confederacy's destruction (1637), after which the NARRAGANSETT invaded Montauk territory. By 1659 the Montauk had lost most of their population through war and disease, and that year they retreated to Easthampton, where they sought the protection of the English colonists. Few Metoac groups survived into modern times as identifiable populations.

Montauk Point

Montauk Point, a promontory at the tip of Long Island, is the easternmost point in New York State, about 185 km (115 mi) east of Manhattan. It is the site of a lighthouse (built 1796), a state park, and a military reservation, Camp Hero.

Montcalm, Louis Joseph, Marquis de

[mohn-kahlm', loo-ee' zhoh-zef', mar-kee' duh] Louis Joseph, marquis de Montcalm, b. Feb. 28, 1712, was the victorious French army commander in the FRENCH AND INDIAN WAR battles of Oswego (1756), Fort William Henry (1757), and Carillon (or Ticonderoga, 1758). He was finally defeated by James WOLFE on the Plains of Abraham, outside Quebec, a battle in which both generals were killed.

Born at the Château de Candiac, near Nîmes, France, of an old noble family, Montcalm entered the French army in 1724 and was a seasoned veteran of military service in Europe when he was named (1756) general officer in command of the French regular army contingent in North America. Montcalm was convinced that France was militarily unable to hold Canada against the numerically superior British forces. He therefore advocated delaying tactics, withdrawal to defend the Montreal-Quebec axis and the honor of his army, and then capitulation on the best possible terms. By 1758, when Montcalm was promoted to lieutenant general and commander of all military forces in Canada, the French government had adopted his strategy.

In 1759, Montcalm held Quebec against British siege

The marquis de Montcalm, French military commander in Canada during the French and Indian War, led successful efforts to regain control of Lake Ontario and to repulse British attacks during the early years of the conflict. His defeat, outside Quebec in 1759, marked the end of French efforts to hold Canadian territory against British forces.

from the end of May until early September 13, when the British scaled the cliffs rising from the St. Lawrence River to take up position west of Quebec on the Plains of Abraham. The surprised Montcalm prematurely and perhaps even unnecessarily attacked the British lines, suffering defeat in what might otherwise have been a stalemate. Fatally wounded, he died on Sept. 14, 1759. Four days later Quebec surrendered.

Monte Albán

[mohn'-tay ahl-bahn'] Monte Albán, atop a ridge on the outskirts of present-day Oaxaca city in Mexico, was the center of ZAPOTEC civilization. By 400 BC a modest civic-ceremonial center with stone temple platforms and a small resident population existed at the site. Early Monte Albán art, especially the distinctive *danzante* carvings depicting slain enemies, shows OLMEC influence. Early Monte Albán glyphs contain the oldest evidence of the development of the Mesoamerican calendar yet discovered.

By 200 BC, Monte Albán had become the most prominent center in Zapotec territory, and by AD 200 it dominated the area surrounding the central valley of Oaxaca. The civic center atop the ridge included temple-pyramids, palaces, richly furnished tombs, and an astronomical observatory. The lower slopes were terraced for dwellings, which housed a population of 30,000 or more. Although there are indications of ties with TEOTIHUACÁN in the period AD 200–600, Monte Albán maintained its independence. About AD 700, Monte Albán was abandoned but MIXTEC and Zapotec nobles were buried there during the following centuries.

Monte Carlo

[mahn'-tee kahr'-loh] Monte Carlo (1982 pop., 13,154), a resort town in the principality of Monaco, lies on an escarpment overlooking the French Riviera and the Mediterranean Sea. The town grew up around the world-famous gambling casino (built 1858) and has luxury hotels, fine villas, and beautiful gardens.

Monte Cassino

[mohn'-tay kahs-see'-noh] Monte Cassino is a 519-m-high (1,703-ft) hill to the west of the town of CASSINO, Frosinone province, central Italy. It is topped by the Benedictine abbey of Monte Cassino. Founded by Saint BENEDICT of Nursia in AD 529, the abbey is considered the cradle of the Roman Catholic order of BENEDICTINES and of Western monasticism. It was destroyed by an earthquake in 1349 and was largely rebuilt between the 16th and 18th centuries.

In World War II, Monte Cassino was the scene of heavy fighting in 1944, when Allied bombers demolished the abbey. Most of the art collection was destroyed, but many manuscripts were saved. Reconstruction was completed in 1964.

Montefiore, Sir Moses

[mahn-ti-fee-ohr'-ee] Moses Haim Montefiore, b. Oct. 24, 1784, d. July 28, 1885, was an outstanding British-Jewish philanthropist. He married into the Rothschild family, made a fortune on the London stock exchange, and retired (1824) to devote his resources to public and private charities, building schools and hospitals, and founding agricultural settlements in Palestine. He was knighted in 1837 and served as sheriff of London the same year. New York's Montefiore Hospital is named for him.

Montenegro [mahn-tay-nay'-groh]   Montenegro (Serbo-Croatian: Crna Gora) joined Serbia in forming a new, smaller YUGOSLAVIA in 1992, after the secession of the other four republics. Located in the Dinaric Alps, Montenegro has an area of 13,812 km² (5,333 mi²) and a population of 639,000 (1989 est.), most of whom are Serbs. Podgorica, formerly TITOGRAD, is the capital.

Montenegro is bounded by Albania on the southeast, by the Adriatic Sea on the southwest, by Serbia on the northeast, and by Bosnia and Hercegovina on the northwest. The topography is primarily mountainous. Livestock raising is the dominant economic activity, with some farming. Forestry and mineral products are also important.

Part of the Roman province of Illyria in ancient times, Montenegro was settled by Slavs in the 7th century AD. It became part of Serbia in the 12th century and achieved independence after the conquest of Serbia by the Ottoman Turks in 1389. From the 16th to the 19th century it was ruled by a series of popularly elected Orthodox bishops (*vladike*) who kept it free of Turkish rule. Montenegro was made a secular principality in 1851 and a kingdom in 1910. In 1918 it was reunited with Serbia in the Yugoslav state, and after World War II it became a republic of Yugoslavia.

Monterey [mahn-tuh-ray']   Monterey is a city in Monterey County, Calif., located on Monterey Bay about 200 km (125 mi) south of San Francisco. Its population is 31,954 (1990). Once a fishing port, it is now a tourist resort. Settled in 1770, it became the capital of Alta California (1774) under both Spanish and Mexican rule. Many buildings from this era have been preserved or restored.

Monterrey [mohn-ter-ray']   Monterrey, the capital of Nuevo León state and Mexico's third largest city, is an industrial center in the northern part of the country on the floodplain of the Río Santa Catarina. Its population is 1,064,197 (1990).

Monterrey leads the nation in steel production; cotton textiles and ore processing are also important. Its Carta Blanca brewery is one of the world's largest. Many factors contribute to Monterrey's industrial concentration: its strategic location, its good transportation connections, its access to raw materials nearby, and its skilled work force. The city's proximity to Texas makes it a popular destination for short-term tourists, and it also serves as a market and service center for nearby agricultural districts. The

Monterrey Institute of Technology and Higher Education (1943) and a large army base are located there.

Founded in 1579, the city began its major growth in the 19th century when it was linked by rail to major cities. Monterrey was captured during the MEXICAN WAR by U.S. forces under Zachary Taylor.

Montespan, Françoise Athénaïs de Rochechouart, Marquise de [mohn-tes-pahn', frahn-swahz' ah-tayn-ah-ees' duh rohsh-oo-ahr', mahr-keez' duh]   Françoise Athénaïs de Rochechouart, marquise de Montespan, b. Oct. 5, 1641, d. May 27, 1707, was the mistress of King LOUIS XIV of France. Married (1663) to Louis, marquis de Montespan, she became maid of honor to Queen Marie Thérèse in 1664 and the king's mistress in 1667. She bore King Louis seven children. During the Affair of the Poisons (1679), Montespan was accused of participating in black masses and buying potions from the poisoner La Voisin. Although she remained at court, she was supplanted by Madame de MAINTENON. In 1691, Montespan retired to a convent.

Montesquieu, Charles Louis de Secondat, Baron de la Brède et de [mohn-tes-kee-u', shahrl looee' duh suh-kohn-dah', bah-rohn' duh lah bred]   Charles Louis de Secondat, baron de la Brède et de Montesquieu, b. Jan 18, 1689, d. Feb. 10, 1755, was a French political philosopher, historian, and jurist who is best known today for *The Spirit of the Laws* (1748) and for his influence on liberalism. A member of a wealthy family, Montesquieu carried on the family tradition of studying law; in 1716 he inherited a fortune, a title, and an important judicial office in Bordeaux. He held this office for 10 years, using the time also to develop his interests in philosophy, natural science, and other fields. In 1721 he published *Persian Letters,* a satire on French institutions, and quickly became a leading literary figure in Paris. In 1728 he was made a member of the French Academy. In 1734,

Baron de Montesquieu exerted considerable influence on the U.S. Constitution through his analysis of human behavior and institutions, The Spirit of the Laws *(1748).*

Montesquieu published *Considerations on the Causes of the Greatness of the Romans and their Decline,* emphasizing the strength of republican civic virtue as opposed to the inevitable weakness of tyranny and conquest. This work is considered to be one of the first important works dealing with the philosophy of history.

The Spirit of the Laws is a comparative study of three types of government—republic, monarchy, and despotism. Abandoning any absolute statement of human nature, it asserts instead that multiple solutions exist to the problems of government and freedom, and that these solutions depend on the differing guiding principles of societies. Its thesis that the powers of government ought to be separated in order to ensure individual freedom had a strong influence on the writers of the U.S. Constitution.

Montessori, Maria [mohn-tes-soh'-ree]   Maria Montessori, an Italian physician-educator, b. Aug. 31, 1870, d. May 6, 1952, devised the educational method that bears her name. She was the first woman in Italy to receive a medical degree and began her career working at the University of Rome's psychiatric clinic. Her experience there with retarded children led her to found the State Orthophrenic School of Rome. She extended her methods to normal children in 1907 by opening her first Casa dei Bambini (Children's House) in a Rome slum. This house also proved successful, and many other Montessori schools were established. After she fled the Italian Fascist government in 1934, she worked in Spain and South Asia before settling in the Netherlands.

Montessori method   In reaction to systems of teaching that require physical compulsion to gain a child's attention, Maria Montessori established an educational system that uses a set of didactic materials that arouse the child's spontaneous interest. This arousal of interest produces a natural concentration on Montessori tasks that does not tire or annoy the child. Children are free to move from one set of materials to another as they wish.

Montessori education emphasizes sensory training, muscular education, and the early learning of reading and writing. Children in Montessori schools often learn to read and write before the age of five. Pupils learn, for example, by manipulating objects, such as vertical, horizontal, and oblique lines made of textured materials, and by fitting cylinders of various thicknesses into the several holes in a block. Self-motivated learning is the core of the Montessori method, which strives to develop self-discipline and self-confidence.

Monteux, Pierre [mohn-tu', pee-air']   Pierre Monteux, b. Paris, Apr. 4, 1875, d. July 1, 1964, was one of the most versatile conductors of the 20th century. He gained early conducting experience at the Concerts Colonne and the Concerts Berlioz. As conductor of Diaghilev's Ballets Russes (1911–14 and 1917) he gave premiere performances of masterpieces by Stravinsky, Debussy, and Ravel. From 1917 to 1919 he conducted at the Metropolitan Opera, and from 1919 to 1924 he led the Boston Symphony. He was associate conductor of the Amsterdam Concertgebouw from 1924 to 1934. In 1929 he founded and conducted (until 1938) the Orchestre Symphonique de Paris, and he directed the San Francisco Symphony from 1936 to 1952. From 1961 until his death he was principal conductor of the London Symphony.

Monteverdi, Claudio [mohn-tay-vair'-dee, klowd'-ee-oh]   The great Italian composer Claudio Monteverdi, b. Cremona, May 1567, d. Venice, Nov. 29, 1643, was an outstanding figure in the development and perfection of early baroque music.

In his early twenties he moved to Mantua and in 1601 was appointed director of music to Duke Vincenzo Gonzaga. He built a brilliant reputation in every type of music—dramatic madrigals, lavishly orchestrated operas, ballet music, dialogues, songs and *scherzi musicali, intermezzi* for plays, outdoor music for tournaments, besides a wealth of church compositions including masses and vespers.

When Monteverdi became music director at St. Mark's, Venice, in 1613, his name and publications were already famous throughout Europe. Musicians came from England, Germany, and Scandinavia to study with him; publishers in northern cities vied with the Venetians to bring out the newest edition of his works. He shouldered the many responsibilities at St. Mark's for 30 years, and in addition to building its choral repertoire and fulfilling his duties with regard to special music required for state occasions, he also managed to keep alive his interest in secular and dramatic music.

In Monteverdi's last years in Venice he achieved further successes in the field of opera, now transformed from the opulence of private patronage to the musically simpler needs of public entertainment. Whereas the elaborate and fantastic features of scenic effects grew in complexity, the operatic orchestra underwent a reduction in numbers and in instrumental color. These changes presented the composer with few real problems, for the strength of his music was inherent in the notes rather than in external appurtenances.

A brief list of Monteverdi's masterpieces would include works that have already won a place in the international repertoire of early music. The setting of a lengthy passage (Ch'io t'ami) from act 3 of Guarini's *Il Pastor fido* (1605) displays his mastery of the classic five-part unaccompanied vocal texture, which may be contrasted with the vocal and instrumental richness of "Hor che 'l ciel" (1638), based on a Petrarch sonnet. From Tasso's *Jerusalem Delivered* he set passages in radically different ways: in the early sequence of madrigals *Vattene pur crudel* (1592) and the later secular oratorio *Il Combattimento di Tancredi e Clorinda* (1624). In church music, the popular *Vespers of 1610* represents only the tip of the iceberg: other vesper services are included among the psalms and hymns of the *Selva morale e spirituale* (1640). Regrettably, almost all of Monteverdi's stage music between *L'Orfeo* (1607) and *Il Ritorno d'Ulisse in pa-tria* (1640) has been lost, as a result of the ravages of time, fire, or negligence.

Montevideo [mohn-tay-vee-day'-oh]   Montevideo is the capital of Uruguay and its commercial, financial, industrial, and cultural center. The city is located in southern Uruguay on the north shore of the Río de la Plata estuary and is one of South America's leading ports. It has a population of 1,246,500 (1985).

Montevideo contains the slaughterhouses, packing plants, freezing facilities, and wool- and leather-processing plants that support Uruguay's livestock industry. The city is also the home port of a large commercial South Atlantic fishing fleet. Textiles and other consumer goods are manufactured, as are building materials. Tourism is also important.

The national university (founded 1849) is located in Montevideo. The city has numerous impressive public buildings, fine beaches, public parks, and promenades.

Montevideo was founded in 1726 as a Spanish outpost against the encroachment of the Portuguese in Brazil to the north. The area of present-day Uruguay was the scene of constant fighting between Spain and Portugal and between Argentina and Brazil after their independence. In 1828, the buffer state of Uruguay was established between the two rivals, and Montevideo became its capital. During the period of civil war, the city was under siege for eight years (1843–51). It has been the major Uruguayan city ever since. Over the decades, the city has received hundreds of thousands of European immigrants, especially settlers from Spain and Italy.

Montez, Lola [mahn-tez']   Lola Montez, b. 1818, d. Jan. 17, 1861, an Irish-born dancer, originally named Marie Dolores Eliza Rosanna Gilbert, is famous for her affairs with such notables as Franz Liszt, Alexandre Dumas *père*, and King Louis I of Bavaria. Her interference in Bavarian affairs helped provoke a revolution (1848) in which her royal lover was deposed.

Montezuma II [mahn-tuh-zoo'-muh]   The AZTEC emperor Montezuma (r. 1502-20) occupied the throne when the Spaniards under Hernán CORTÉS landed (1519) in Mexico. He is also known as Montezuma II, to avoid confusion with Montezuma I (r. 1440–69). Unlike previous Aztec rulers, who were great warriors, Montezuma II was more interested in sorcery and philosophy than in war. When a study of omens and prophecies convinced him that the Spaniards were gods, he concluded that he was doomed. Instead of fighting the Europeans he tried to deter them by trickery, magic, and offering gifts; when that failed, Montezuma allowed Cortés to enter (1519) the island capital of TENOCHTITLÁN without a battle and received him in his court. Montezuma was taken prisoner without resistance, but the brutal conduct of the invaders aroused the anger of the Aztec city's inhabitants. The Az-

This manuscript illustration portrays the Aztec emperor Montezuma II receiving a ceremonial headdress. A weak ruler, Montezuma governed an extensive realm that was constantly disrupted by internal unrest and succumbed to Spanish conquest. (Biblioteca Nacional, Madrid.)

tecs managed to drive the foreigners out for a short while, but during the ensuing battle Montezuma died under mysterious circumstances; he was killed either by the Spaniards or by his own people.

Montezuma Castle National Monument   Montezuma Castle National Monument, one of the Southwest's best-preserved cliff dwellings (see CLIFF DWELLERS), is located in central Arizona about 130 km (80 mi) north of Phoenix. It is called a castle because it is a structure of 5 stories and 20 rooms, built in a cliff cave about 35 m (120 ft) above the valley floor. Constructed by Indians about AD 1100, it remains almost completely intact. The national monument, which covers about 3.5 km^2 (1.4 mi^2), was established in 1906.

Montfort, Simon de, Earl of Leicester [mahnt'-furt, les'-tur]   Simon de Montfort, b. *c.*1208, d. Aug. 4, 1265, led the baronial revolt against England's King HENRY III. French by birth, he joined Henry's court and in 1238 married the king's sister, Eleanor. Simon took part in Henry's invasion of France (1242), and later he returned (1248) to southwestern France to restore order in English-ruled Gascony. The local nobles rebelled (1250) against his oppressive administration, however, forcing a royal inquiry.

Simon was introduced to idealistic views of politics through his association with Oxford philosophers, notably Robert GROSSETESTE. In 1258, Simon was among the supporters of the Provisions of Oxford, which created a formal council of baronial advisors to the king. Simon also supported the Provisions of Westminster (1259), which further strengthened the baronial position.

The hostility of the king and his court forced Simon to flee (1261), but he returned to England in 1263 to lead the Barons' War in support of the provisions. With a coalition of barons and representatives of the towns, Simon won a crushing victory at Lewes in 1264 that made him in effect the ruler of the country. In order to enlarge his support, he summoned representatives of the shires and boroughs to Parliament for the first time in 1265. Nonetheless, he was defeated and killed by the king's son (later EDWARD I) at Evesham.

Montgolfier brothers [mohn-gohl-fee-ay'] The Montgolfier brothers, Joseph Michel, b. Aug. 26, 1740, d. June 26, 1810, and Jacques Étienne, b. Jan. 6, 1745, d. Aug. 2, 1799, were inventors of the first practical BALLOON. The two Frenchmen were papermakers by trade and discovered in 1782 that smoke from a fire directed into a silk bag made the bag buoyant. On June 5, 1783, in the town of Annonay, they gave a public exhibition of their discovery with a balloon made of silk and lined with paper to trap the gas. It rose to an altitude of about 1,830 m (6,000 ft), traveled more than 1.6 km (1 mi) from its takeoff point, and stayed aloft for 10 minutes. At the time, the Montgolfiers were believed to have discovered a new gas; in 1785 the buoyancy was shown to be caused by heated air, which is less dense than the surrounding atmosphere. Almost simultaneously in 1783, Jacques CHARLES developed and demonstrated a hydrogen-inflated balloon; hydrogen soon replaced hot air as the buoyant gas for balloons.

Montgomery Situated on the Alabama River in the south central part of the state, Montgomery is the capital of Alabama. It is also the seat of Montgomery County. It has a population of 187,106 (1990) within the city and 292,517 in the metropolitan area. Although the city is still an economic focal point for cotton, livestock and dairying interests are now predominant, and industry, including the manufacture of machinery and wood products as well as food processing, is important. The city is known for its many fine antebellum houses and buildings, including the capitol with its stately white columns. Montgomery is the seat of Alabama State University (1874) and Auburn University at Montgomery (1963).

Often called the Cradle of the Confederacy, Montgomery holds a special place in the history of the South. The city was first settled in 1817, and after the state capital was moved there from Tuscaloosa in 1847, Montgomery thrived as a great cotton market and river port. In February 1861 the government of the Confederate States of America was formed in Montgomery by the seven seceding states, and Jefferson Davis was inaugurated as its president on the capitol steps. The city served as the capital of the Confederacy until it was replaced by Richmond, Va., in July 1861. Federal troops occupied the city

in April 1865, and recovery was slow and painful. In 1955–56 the black population, led by the Rev. Martin Luther King, Jr., boycotted the city buses in a successful protest against the segregation of public transportation.

Montgomery, Richard Richard Montgomery, b. Dec. 2, 1738, d. Dec. 31, 1775, was a general in the Continental Army during the American Revolution. Born in Ireland, he served (1756–72) in the British army in Canada but left to move to New York, where he married into the prominent Livingston family. In 1775 he was elected to the New York Provincial Congress, and he became a brigadier general in the Continental Army the same year. After Gen. Philip J. Schuyler became ill, Montgomery took over command of the expedition invading Canada. He captured Fort Chambly, Fort Saint John, and Montreal, but he was killed during the unsuccessful attack on Quebec.

Montgomery of Alamein, Bernard Law Montgomery, 1st Viscount [al-uh-mayn'] Bernard Law Montgomery, b. Nov. 17, 1887, d. Mar. 24, 1976, has been described as the finest British field commander since the duke of WELLINGTON. He entered the army in 1908 and distinguished himself during World War I. In World War II he led (1939–40) a division in France, was involved in the Dunkirk (Dunkerque) evacuation, and took charge of the controversial Dieppe commando raid of 1942 before being sent to North Africa as Eighth Army commander. There his decisive victory over the Afrika Korps at El Alamein (1942) and his pursuit of the Germans across Libya and Tunisia captured the imagination of the British public, and he became a national hero, popularly known as "Monty."

He subsequently commanded the Eighth Army in the Sicilian and Italian campaigns, the 21st Army Group in the Normandy Invasion, and the sweep through France and western Germany (1944–45). Montgomery's performance in 1943 and 1944 was controversial. His strategy

British field marshal Bernard Law Montgomery played a major role in the defeat of Germany during World War II. As commander of the British Eighth Army, he forced German forces out of Africa in 1942–43. He was largely responsible for the successful Allied invasion of Sicily in May 1943, and in June 1944 he commanded Allied ground forces in the invasion of Normandy.

disputes with the Allied supreme commander Dwight D. EISENHOWER were aired openly in the newspapers during the war and later in their memoirs. After the war, Montgomery, created viscount in 1946, was commander of British occupation forces in Germany (1945–46), chief of the British general staff (1946–48), and deputy supreme commander of NATO (1951–58).

Montgomeryshire   see POWYS

month   see CALENDAR

Monticello [mahn-ti-sel'-oh]   Monticello ("little mountain"), in Albemarle County, Va., near Charlottesville, designed by Thomas Jefferson as his own home, was erected in two building campaigns, in 1770–82 and 1793–1809, from timber and brick produced on Jefferson's own lands. The earlier house, essentially a block elaborated with bays and a two-story portico, was modeled on works in Robert Morris's *Select Architecture* (1775) and in elevation on designs by Andrea Palladio. It was probably unfinished when Jefferson became minister to France in 1784. He returned to Monticello deeply impressed by recent French architecture and determined to achieve something of its neoclassical aesthetic and standards of comfort in his own house. He detailed its interiors according to classical models and filled the house with labor-saving devices of his own invention. Set in a U-shaped complex of subsidiary structures, with landscaping also designed by Jefferson, Monticello is one of the great American houses: imaginative and harmonious in form, gracious and intensely personal in character.

   See also: AMERICAN ART AND ARCHITECTURE; COLONIAL STYLES IN NORTH AMERICA.

Monticello, designed by Thomas Jefferson for his own use, is a graceful and elegant synthesis of colonial and classic revivalist styles. Located in Albemarle County, Va., Monticello was constructed in two stages, in 1770–82 and 1793–1809. Its interior of 35 rooms features irregular shapes and a number of design innovations.

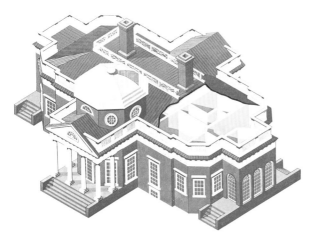

Montmorency, Anne, Duc de [mohn-mohr-ahn-see']   Anne, duc de Montmorency, b. Mar. 15, 1493, d. Nov. 12, 1567, was a French political and military leader. Born into one of the most illustrious families in France, Montmorency was the boyhood companion of FRANCIS I, who in 1538 appointed him constable of France and accepted his policy of alliance with Holy Roman Emperor CHARLES V. Montmorency fell from royal favor in 1541 as new hostilities arose between France and the emperor. When HENRY II became king in 1547, however, he restored Montmorency to authority. The duke was captured by the Spanish at Saint-Quentin in 1557 and held prisoner until the Treaty of Cateau-Cambrésis in 1559. At the onset of the Wars of Religion (1562–98; see RELIGION, WARS OF) he held the balance between the GUISE and BOURBON factions before declaring for the Catholic cause.

Montpelier [mahnt-peel'-ee-ur]   Montpelier, a city in central Vermont, is located in the Green Mountains on the upper Winooski River. It is the seat of Washington County and has been the state capital since 1805. Its population is 8,247 (1990). Settled in 1787, it was named for Montpellier, France. The granite industry in the area contributed to the city's growth; the granite State House was built in 1859. The city's economy centers on insurance companies, state government, and light manufacturing, as well as tourism from nearby ski resorts.

Montpellier [mohn-pel-ee-ay']   Montpellier is the capital city of Hérault department in the Languedoc region of southern France, about 125 km (75 mi) northwest of Marseille and 12 km (7 mi) north of the Mediterranean coast. The population is 197,231 (1982). A manufacturing and trade center, the city has textile, food processing, and metallurgy industries. It is also a health resort.

   Founded in the 8th century on the site of a Benedictine abbey, the city is formed around a central hub with radiating streets and is surrounded by a belt of modern apartment buildings and factories. Long a center of intellectual life, it is the home of the University of Montpellier (founded 1289), with its famous medical faculty.

Montpensier, Anne Marie Louise d'Orléans, Duchesse de [mawn-pen-see-ay', dohr-lay-ahn', doo-shes' duh]   Anne Marie Louise d'Orléans, duchesse de Montpensier, b. May 29, 1627, d. Apr. 5, 1693, was a French princess known as Mademoiselle at the court of LOUIS XIV. The daughter of Gaston, duc d'Orléans (see ORLÉANS family), younger brother of Louis XIII, she took part in the revolt known as the princely FRONDE, leading troops to relieve the city of Orléans and opening the gates of Paris to Louis II, prince de Condé (see CONDÉ family), in 1652. She was exiled for this action until 1657 and again (1662–64) for refusing to marry King Alfonso VI of Portugal.

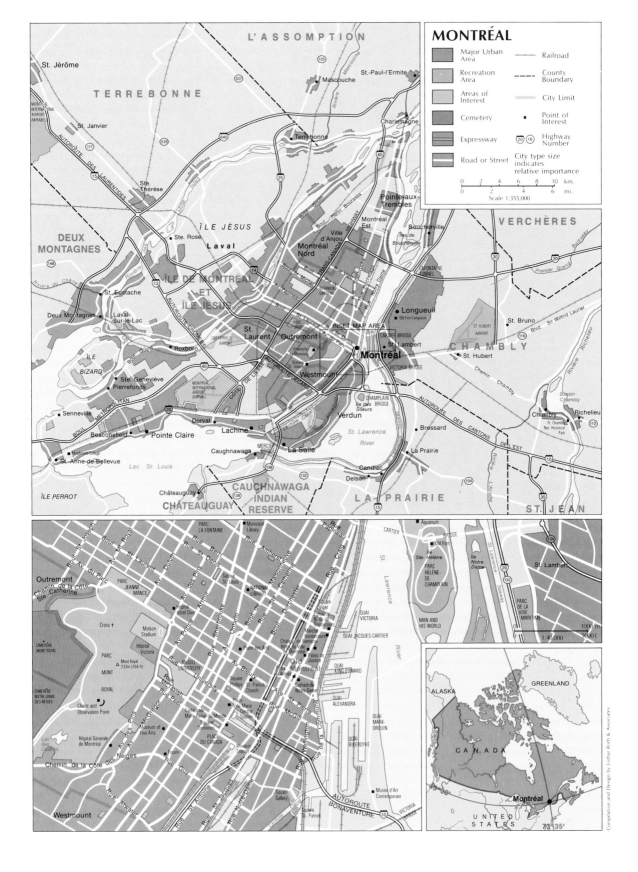

Montreal [mahn-tree-awl' or mawn-ray-ahl']   Montreal (French: Montréal), located in eastern Canada in Quebec province, is Canada's largest city and leading port. The population of the city proper is 1,015,420 (1986); that of the metropolitan area, 2,921,357. The city spreads over most of Montreal Island, in the St. Lawrence River near its confluence with the Ottawa River. The urbanized area also overflows onto several other nearby islands (notably Île Jésus) and eastward across the St. Lawrence onto the mainland. Its site is dominated by the volcanic hill of Mount Royal, which rises to 233 m (764 ft) directly behind the central business district, and for which the city was named.

Contemporary City. Montreal is about two-thirds Francophone (French-speaking) and is the second largest French-language city in the world (after Paris). The remaining third of the populace is almost evenly divided between people of British ancestry and those of neither British nor French descent. The latter include large communities of Germans, Italians, Jews, and Central and Eastern Europeans. Roman Catholicism is the predominant religion.

Montreal and Toronto are virtually equal in most measures of economic activity. Montreal is, however, unrivaled as the nation's leading port. Many of Canada's banks and insurance and railroad companies have their headquarters in Montreal. Trade, industry, and services are the main areas of economic activity. The city's major industries are metal products, chemical products, transportation equipment, textiles, and food processing.

During the 1960s and '70s the center of Montreal was greatly transformed. Many large buildings were constructed, but the most striking development was the integration of skyscrapers with underground shopping complexes to provide largely self-contained indoor environments for winter living. This climate-controlled area exists beneath the streets and buildings of Montreal. Also recently constructed is the excellent subway system, the Metro, which connects with the underground city. All of the past has not been uprooted, however. A strong Old World flavor is maintained in the preserved historic section of the city along the river called Old Montreal. It is the site of McGill University (1821) and the Université de Montréal (1878). Among Montreal's many museums is the Museum of Fine Arts. The Place des Arts is a complex of concert and theater halls. Montreal has many buildings of historical significance, of which the most notable are the cathedral Church of Notre Dame (completed 1829), St. Sulpice Seminary (c.1685), and the Château de Ramezay (1705), the former residence of French and British governors.

In recent decades Montreal has hosted two world events. A world's fair, called Expo '67, was held in 1967 as a centenary celebration of Canada's independence, and a very popular permanent exhibition, Man and His World, continues to occupy the fairgrounds on islands in the river. In 1976, Montreal was the site of the Summer Olympic Games.

History. Jacques Cartier discovered a Huron Indian village (Hochelaga) at the base of Mount Royal when he visited the site in 1535. More than a century passed, however, before the first European settlement, a fortified mission station called Ville-Marie de Montreal, was established (1642) on the site by the sieur de MAISONNEUVE. The settlement's first real development came in the early 1700s, when Montreal became an important base for westward explorers and fur traders. The British captured the city from the French in 1760. It served as Canada's capital from 1844 to 1849. At the time of confederation in 1867, Montreal had become the dominant city of Canada, with a population of about 100,000.

Montrose, James Graham, 1st Marquess of [mahn'-trohz, mar'-kwes]   James Graham, marquess of Montrose, b. 1612, d. May 21, 1650, was the leading royalist commander in Scotland during the ENGLISH CIVIL WAR. He became a COVENANTER in 1637 and served in the Scottish army that invaded England (1640) in the Bishops' Wars. Later, however, Montrose came into conflict with the Covenanters; he adhered to CHARLES I's cause after the Covenanters allied (1643) with the parliamentarians in the English Civil War. Organizing a force of Highlanders, he won a series of brilliant victories over Covenanter forces in 1644–45, but defeat at Philiphaugh (1645) forced him to retire abroad. Montrose returned to Scotland in March 1650 on behalf of the exiled CHARLES II. He was abandoned by Charles, however, and was captured and hanged.

Monts, Pierre du Gua, Sieur de [mohn, peeair' due gwah, sur duh]   Pierre de Gua (or Guast), sieur de Monts, c.1558–1628, was a French explorer and trader in Canada whose organizational ability sustained the infant colony of New France during the first 20 years of the 17th century. He was born in the French province of Saintonge, probably at Le Gua. From 1603 to 1617, Monts directed a succession of fur-trading companies that promoted emigration to North America. With Samuel de CHAMPLAIN as his cartographer, he founded Port Royal (now Annapolis Royal) in ACADIA in 1605. Monts organized the financing of Champlain's later explorations and the post he founded at Quebec.

Montserrat (island) [mahnt-suh-rat']   The Caribbean island of Montserrat is a British crown colony. One of the LEEWARD ISLANDS in the Lesser Antilles of the West Indies, it has an area of 106 km^2 (40 mi^2) and a population of 11,900 (1986 est.). Plymouth is the capital and only port. The island is rugged and lush, with steep, thickly forested mountains, many of them active sulfurous volcanoes; deep valleys; and beaches of dark volcanic sands. Sea-island cotton, limes, and tomatoes and other vegetables are grown. Tourism and light industry are also important.

The island was discovered by Christopher Columbus in 1493, and it was named Montserrat for the mountain monastery in Spain. The island was colonized by Irish settlers in 1632, but the French took possession of it in 1664–68 and in 1782–84. It has been a British crown colony since 1871.

Montserrat (mountain) Montserrat is a 1,236-m-high (4,054-ft) jagged mountain ridge about 48 km (30 mi) northwest of Barcelona in Barcelona province, Spain. It is best known as the site of the Benedictine monastery of Santa María de Montserrat and its many hermitages. A site of religious pilgrimage for centuries, the monastery contains the Shrine of Our Lady of Montserrat (La Moreneta), a wooden statue said to have been carved by Saint Luke. During the Middle Ages, the monastery was the legendary home of the Holy Grail. It is the place where Saint Ignatius of Loyola, founder of the Jesuit order, began his religious devotions.

The hermitages of Montserrat were founded about 880. The first monastery was built during the 11th century. The basilica of the shrine (16th century) and the present structure of the monastery (18th century) are on the east side of the mountain. The San Gerónimo Hermitage is at the summit.

Monument Valley Monument Valley is a scenic region encompassing approximately 5,180 km^2 (2,000 mi^2) in northeastern Arizona and southeastern Utah. The landscape is characterized by tall, red sandstone buttes, mesas, and arches created by erosion, rising up to 300 m (1,000 ft) from a sandy plain. Monument Valley is part of the Navajo Indian Reservation; the Navajo have occupied the valley since the 1860s. Rainbow Bridge and Natural Bridges national monuments are nearby.

Monza [mohnt'-sah] Monza (1988 est. pop., 122,726) is an industrial city in the Lombardy region of northern Italy, 16 km (10 mi) northeast of Milan. The city's numerous manufactures include furniture, machinery, textiles, glass, and plastic. The Cathedral of Saint John the Baptist, built on the site of a church founded (895) by the Lombard queen Theodolinda, houses the iron crown of Lombardy, which is said to contain a nail from the cross of Christ; the crown was used at the coronations of both Charlemagne and Napoleon I, among other notable rulers. Monza is now famous for its auto racing.

Called Modicia by the Romans, Monza was a key city of the Lombard kingdom (568–774). In 1900, King Humbert I of Italy was assassinated there.

Moody, Deborah A pioneer of religious liberty, Deborah Dunch Moody, c.1600–1659, migrated to Massachusetts about 1640 to secure the freedom she despaired of gaining in England. She was the widow of Sir Henry Moody (and thus properly called Lady Moody). At Salem she was brought before the court for denying that infant baptism was an ordinance of God, but she refused to change her views. Subsequently, she and a number of her followers moved to the Dutch province of New Netherland and settled in Gravesend on Long Island, the first English settlement in what is now Kings County and the first colonial enterprise to be headed by a woman. Moody welcomed the Quakers who arrived in 1657, and the settlement soon became a center of the Society of Friends.

Moody, Dwight L. Dwight Lyman Moody, b. Northfield, Mass., Feb. 5, 1837, d. Dec. 22, 1899, was a lay evangelist who took his revival campaigns to major American and British cities with phenomenal success. After YMCA service during the Civil War, Moody began preaching and doing revival work. He invited Ira D. Sankey to join him as a chorister. In 1873, Moody and Sankey went to Britain on an extended revival tour. They achieved remarkable success there and were equally successful after returning (1875) to the United States. For almost 20 years the team of Moody and Sankey moved their revivals from one major urban center to the next, preaching to millions and converting thousands. They avoided theological and denominational labels and encouraged those who made a commitment to Christ to join the church of their choice. When Moody retired in 1892, he turned his attention to his schools, which included the Moody Bible Institute in Chicago.

Moody, Helen Wills see WILLS, HELEN NEWINGTON

Moon The Moon is the only natural satellite of the Earth and a unique member of the solar system in several respects. With a radius of 1,738 km (1,080 mi), it is approximately one-quarter of the size of the Earth and 81.3 times less massive. Although the solar system contains both larger and more massive satellites than the Moon, none except Pluto's newly discovered moon differs so little from its planet in mass or size. Indeed, the Earth-Moon system constitutes a veritable double planet.

Astronomical Data. The Moon moves around the Earth in an elliptical orbit of small eccentricity, inclined by 5° 8' 43.4" to the plane in which the Earth revolves around the Sun. Its distance from the Earth varies between 356,000 and 407,000 km (221,000 and 253,000 mi) in the course of each month; the average distance is 384,400 km (238,900 mi), less than 1% of the distance to Venus and Mars, even at the time of their closest approach. The lunar globe appears in the sky as a disc of a little over half a degree (31' 5.2") in apparent diameter.

The period in which the Moon completes an orbit around the Earth and returns to the same position in the sky—the sidereal month—is 27 days, 7 hr, 43 min, and 11.6 sec. Because the Earth is moving in its orbit around the Sun in the same direction as the Moon, the time needed to return to the same phase—the synodic month—is longer: 29 days, 12 hr, 44 min, and 2.8 sec. This period is the time interval that, for example, elapses between two successive full moons, a period that was known within a second even in ancient times. The Moon's average velocity is 1.023 km/sec (0.635 mi/sec), corresponding to a mean angular velocity in the sky of about 33 minutes of arc per hour, a little greater than the apparent diameter of the Moon.

In addition to its motion through space, the Moon also

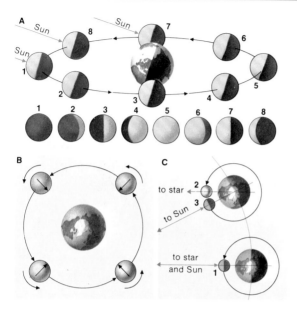

The Moon's phases (A) *depend on what fraction of its sunlit hemisphere can be seen from Earth. As the Moon orbits Earth, it grows in size from new moon* (1) *to crescent* (2), *first quarter* (3), *gibbous* (4), *and full moon* (5). *It then decreases in reverse order to gibbous* (6), *third quarter* (7), *crescent* (8), *and back to new moon. The same side of the Moon always faces the Earth* (B) *because the Moon rotates on its axis in the same period that it revolves around the Earth. The Moon* (C) *takes 27.3 days to complete one revolution around the Earth with respect to the stars* (1 to 2), *but 29.5 days with respect to the Sun* (1 to 3) *because of the Earth's simultaneous motion around the Sun.*

rotates about its axis in a period of one sidereal month, so that it keeps approximately the same side toward the Earth at all times. Nonuniformities in its orbital motion, however, together with the inclination of the orbit to the ecliptic, cause "optical librations" that allow 59% of the entire lunar surface to be seen from the Earth at one time or another. The remaining 41% was hidden until the Russian LUNA *3* spacecraft photographed the far side in October 1959. It has since been thoroughly mapped.

Internal Structure. The essential clues to the internal structure of the Moon are provided by its mass and size, which give a mean density of 3.34 g/cm^3 (208.51 lb/ft^3). Because the average density of lunar rocks brought back during the APOLLO PROGRAM ranges between 3.1 and 3.5 g/cm^3, this finding precludes any large differentiation of lunar material in the interior, which would be accompanied by density changes.

The lithostatic pressure inside a globe of lunar size and mass should accordingly vary from zero on the surface to 47.1 kilobars at the center, and average 10 kb throughout most of its mass. This value is well in excess of the crushing strength of typical lunar rocks, and the prevalent pressure will therefore force the lunar globe to assume the spherical form even though its material remains solid throughout most of its mass. Its rigidity has been confirmed independently by the "seismic signa-

tures" of moonquakes as registered by seismometers installed on the Moon during several Apollo missions. In light of their combined evidence, the Moon proved to be seismically much quieter than the Earth.

The centers of the moonquakes that registered were found to be located 600 to 900 km (375 to 560 mi) below the Moon's crust. Seismic records of such disturbances, however, contain evidence of both pressure and shear elastic waves, which could not be true if the layers through which these waves propagate were fluid or even plastic. The very long decay times of such disturbances imply that the lunar surface layers must be highly fractured to scatter seismic waves to the observed extent.

Consistent with degree of rigidity evidenced by seismic records, the interaction of the lunar globe, on its journey through space, with the solar wind, registered by spacecraft, indicates that the lunar globe behaves as an insulator exhibiting an electrical conductivity consistent with that of silicate rocks at a temperature less than 1,500° C, where such rocks can still behave as solid. The virtual absence of any dipole magnetic field of the lunar globe, attested to by many spacecraft, discloses that the Moon does not have a metallic core.

Chemical Composition. Direct information on the chemical composition of the Moon became available in 1969 with the return of the first Apollo mission. Although the data refer only to the rocks collected on the surface, there is no reason to believe that the composition of the interior of the Moon would be essentially different. By atomic composition, the most abundant element found on the Moon is oxygen. It composes 60% of the Moon's crust by weight, followed by 16–17% silicon, 6–10% aluminum, 4–6% calcium, 3–6% magnesium, 2–5% iron, and 1–2% titanium. All other elements are present in amounts very much smaller than 1% by weight. The elements oxygen, silicon, and aluminum are present on the Moon in amounts comparable to their existence in the crust of the Earth. Iron and titanium contents are distinctly enhanced on the Moon, by comparison to Earth, while the alkali metals are less abundant, as are carbon and nitrogen.

Of the compounds formed by these elements, silica (SiO_2) constitutes between 40% and 50% of the Moon's crust by weight, compared to 48.5% in the crust of the Earth, while ferrous oxide (FeO) or calcium oxide (CaO) constitute 10% to 20% of each. All oxidized compounds appear to be present on the Moon only in their lowest states of oxidation, because they solidified at temperatures between 1,100° and 1,200° C (2,000° and 2,200° F). The oxide of hydrogen in the form of H_2O is totally absent on the Moon; no trace of water in any form has been found. The only form of hydrogen present on the Moon is that imported by the solar wind, and any water produced by its oxidation would be quickly dissociated by sunlight.

Surface Features. Naked-eye as well as more detailed telescopic and satellite observations disclose that the lunar surface consists mainly of two different types of terrain: the first is rough, relatively bright, and replete with mountains and occupies more than two-thirds of the visi-

THE MOON

NORTH POLE

60°N · 60°N

30°N · 30°N

0° · 0°

30°S · 30°S

60°S · 60°S

SOUTH POLE

NEAR SIDE

Legend of major lunar features

Palus Putredinis

Marsh

MARE TRANQUILITATIS

(SEA OF TRANQUILLITY)

Ocean or sea

Lacus Somniorum

(Lake of Dreams)

Lake

Sinus Iridum

Bay

+ Manned landing sites

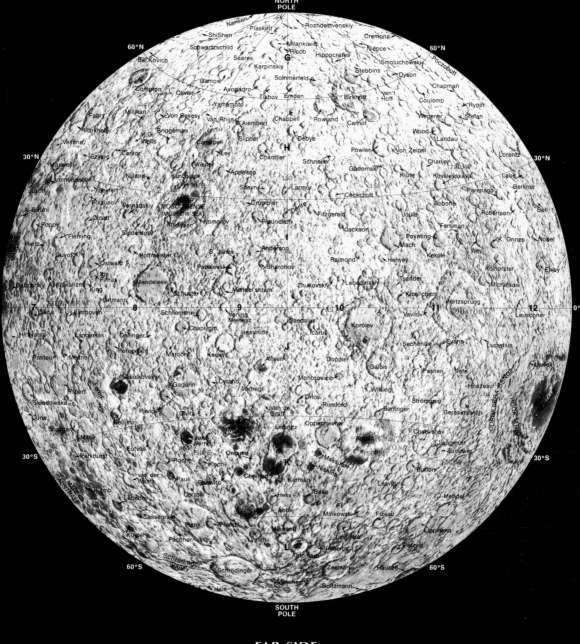

NORTH POLE

Nansen · Plaskett · Rozhdestvenskiy · Cremona
ShiShen · Milankovic · Niépce
60°N · Schwarzschild · Ricco · Hippocrates · Smoluchowskiy · Poczobutt · 60°N
Bel'kovich · Séares · G · Stebbins · Dyson
Compton · Karpinskiy · Sommerfeld · Birkhoff · Chapman
Olivier · Gamow · Avogadro · Emden · van't Hoff · Coulomb · Rynin
Fabry · Millikan · Yamamoto · Tikhov · Wegener · Stefan
Von Bekesy · Van Rhijn · D'Alembert · Chappell · Rowland · Carnot · Wood · Landau
Harkheby · Briggeman · Campbell · Slipher · Debye · Fowler · Von Zeipel · Lorentz
30°N · Vestine · Szilard · H.G. Wells · Ley · Chandler · Schneller · Gadomski · Charlier · Laue · 30°N
Maxwell · Cantor · Wiener · Appleton · Larmor · Henyey · Klute · Kovalevskaya · Berkner
Lomonosov · Niland · Kurchatov · Shayn · Trumpler · Cockcroft · Bobone · Bell
Seyfert · Dante · Fitzgerald · Joule · Fersman · Robertson
Al-Biruni · Polzunov · Vernadskiy · Komarov · Freundlich · Jackson · Poynting · K. Onnes · Nobel
Popov · Olcott · Sliedentop · Anderson · Mach · Kekulé · Wey
Fleming · Hoffmeister · S. Janes · Sharonov · Raimond · Lebedinskiy · Kibal'chich · Kohlhörster · Elvey
Guyot · Ostwald · Papaleksi · Zhukovskiy · Tsander · Michelson
Babcock · Ibn Firnas · Mendeleev · Schuster · Mandel'shtam · Vavilov · Hertzsprung
Al-Kwarizmi · King · Schliemann · Vening · Daedalus · Korolev · Leuschner
0° · 7 · Saha · Hartmann · 8 · Meinesz · 9 · Icarus · 10 · 11 · 12 · 0°
Einthoven · Chaplygin · Heaviside · Sechenov · Evans · Lucretius
Hirayama · Dellinger · Keeler · Aitken · Doppler · Galois · Paschen · Mofe
Langemak · Perepelkin · Marconi · Mohorovicic · Wilsing · Houzeau
Pasteur · Meitner · Tsiolkovskiy · Cyrano · Orlov · Stromgren · Upwell
Hilbert · Gagarin · Levi · Vertregt · Rumford · Barringer
Sklodowska · Pavlov · Civita · Van de Graff · Oppenheimer · Gerasimovich
Curie · Neujmin · Leibnitz · Chebyshev · Langmuir
Scaliger · Jules · Apollo · Brouwer
30°S · Milne · Verne · Orenme · Makarov · Button · 30°S
Parkhurst · Eotvos · Roche · Koch · Nishina · Leavitt
van der · Chretien · Bose · Mendel
Lamb · Waals · Pauli · Galvito · Von Karman
Lebedev · Geraski · Hess · Minkowski · Fizeau
Cassegrain · Poincare · Abbe · Lippmann
Kugler · Plank · Prandtl · Antoniadi · Minnaert · Lebiga · Petzval
Pechner · Lyman · Namerby
60°S · Schroedinger · Schrödinger · Antoniadi · Zeeman · Hausen · 60°S
Valley · Hale · Avecher · Boltzmann

SOUTH POLE

FAR SIDE

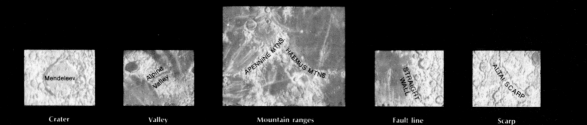

Mendeleev

Alpine Valley

APENNINE MTNS · HAEMUS MTNS

STRAIGHT WALL

ALTAI SCARP

Crater · **Valley** · **Mountain ranges** · **Fault line** · **Scarp**

(Right) *This panorama of the Taurus-Littrow Valley on the Moon was photographed during the last excursion by Apollo 17 astronauts.*

(Below) *Every detail of the bootprint of Apollo 11 astronaut Neil Armstrong is clearly defined in this photograph taken in Mare Tranquillitatis on the Moon's surface.*

ble hemisphere of the Moon and nine-tenths of its far side; the other type is much darker as well as smoother. The first type of terrain is usually referred to as "continents" and the second type is called *maria*, Latin for "seas." The term *highlands*, sometimes used for continents, is a misnomer in the literal sense, for not all continental ground is elevated; *maria* is an even worse misnomer, because water never wetted their surfaces.

A telescopic inspection of the Moon reveals that both types of ground are replete with formations commonly called craters. Their number is immense, and they range in size from formations such as Mare Imbrium (Sea of Rains) or Mare Orientale (Eastern Sea), which are more than 1,000 km (620 mi) across, down to 10–20 micron pits etched on crystalline rocks brought to the Earth by the Apollo missions. The origin of all such formations is no longer in doubt: they arise directly or indirectly from impacts of celestial bodies ranging from ASTEROIDS and COMETS to interplanetary dust. In the case of circular maria, the largest impact formations encountered on the Moon, the excavation of the initial basin appears to have been followed by its lava flooding only after a few hundred million years (see METEORITE CRATERS).

From the mineralogical point of view, the backbone of the dark crystalline material that fills the basins of lunar maria can be described as gabbroid basalts—material akin to lavas known on the Earth but enriched with iron and titanium. In contrast, the continental areas of high reflectivity appear to consist of feldspathic rocks similar to terrestrial granites, including a nearly pure feldspar called anorthosite.

Lunar-orbiting spacecraft have revealed regions of unusually high gravitational attraction. These regions, called mascons (for mass concentration), are primarily found beneath most of the maria. They are believed to be local concentrations of deeply buried fragments of dense material either from the impacting bodies that initially created the maria or from igneous (volcanic) rocks brought from the molten interior during the lava flooding of the maria.

Temperature. Because the sole source of the Moon's heat is derived from its illumination by the Sun, its mean temperature would be essentially equal to that of the Earth were it not for the lack of atmosphere. Its extremes are very different. At the point in the lunar tropics directly below the Sun the surface temperature has been measured at 130° C (266° F), although the surface cools off rapidly toward the sunset and between midnight and dawn descends to −173° C (−280° F). Therefore, the daily variation of temperature over the exposed surface in the lunar tropics can exceed 300 Celsius degrees (575 Fahrenheit degrees), ranging from a temperature above that of boiling water to that of liquid air. These extremes are, however, attained only in the tropics and only on the surface exposed to outer space.

Formation and Evolution. Radiometric age-dating of rocks brought back by the 1969–72 Apollo missions from different parts of the Moon disclosed evidence of its geologic history. The oldest particles of lunar material found in every locality are 4.5–4.6 billion years old. Because this age coincides approximately with the radiometric ages of the oldest known chondritic meteorites, the age of the entire solar system with all its constituents may well be 4.6 billion years. Because no material that old survives in larger pieces, these must have been shattered and transported all over the Moon in the course of an initial heavy bombardment of the lunar surface during the first 200 or 300 million years of its existence, before the supply of interplanetary material available for bombardment became largely exhausted.

The dating results also indicated that a large part of the crater-forming impacts that disfigured the mountainous parts of the Moon occurred in the first half-billion years of lunar existence. The largest of them, which gave rise to scars known to us as circular maria, occurred 400–800 million years after the Moon was formed. The flooding of the basins excavated by these impacts with basaltic magmas occurred some 400–700 million years later, or 3.3–3.8 billion years before the present time. No more basalts appeared on the lunar surface in the first 800 million years of its existence, nor were any added more than 600 million years later. In the past 3 billion years, more than two-thirds of the age of the satellite, nothing much has happened on the Moon.

Moon, Sun Myung [myuhng] The Reverend Sun Myung Moon, b. Jan. 6, 1920, is a Korean religious leader who in 1954 founded the Unification Church. A Presbyterian minister, Moon in 1946 began to proclaim his own version of Christianity, the doctrines of which he explained in *The Divine Principle* (1952). The Holy Spirit Association for the Unification of World Christianity, established two years later, rapidly won converts in Korea, Japan, and, in the 1960s, the United States. In 1973, Moon moved the church's headquarters to Tarrytown, N.Y., and has since lived mostly in the United States. Many of his followers, popularly called "Moonies," regard their leader as a new messiah; the most devoted practice a rigorous discipline and communal living. Moon's critics have accused the organization of brainwashing recruits and of devoting more time to anti-Communist propaganda than to religious ideals. Moon himself has been charged with financial irregularities and illegal political activities on behalf of the South Korean government. The church has been involved in frequent lawsuits, and in 1982, Moon, convicted of tax evasion by a U.S. court, was sentenced to an 18-month prison term.

moonfish Several species of fishes characterized by a thin, rounded, moonlike body are called moonfishes. They include the opah, *Lampris guttatus*; the fingerfish, *Monodactylus argenteus*; *Mene maculata*; and *Vomer setapinnis* and *V. declivifrons*. In addition, the platy, *Xiphophorus maculatus*, a popular aquarium fish, is sometimes called the moon or moonfish.

Monodactylus argenteus, of the family Monodactylidae, is found in both fresh and marine waters of the Indo-Pacific region and grows to 20 cm (8 in) long. It has a silvery body, with yellowish fins that are bordered with black in the front, and two black vertical stripes crossing the front of its body.

Mene maculata, the only member of the family Menidae, is found from the eastern coast of Africa to Hawaii in shallow, tropical marine waters. It grows to 20 cm (8 in) long and is silvery, with a very thin, disk-shaped body, large eyes, and a small, steeply upturned mouth.

Vomer setapinnis is found on both sides of the Atlantic Ocean; on the coasts of the Americas it ranges from Nova Scotia to Uruguay. *V. declivifrons* is found in the Pacific Ocean from southern California to Peru. Both species, members of the jack family, Carangidae, are similar in appearance. They are blue green above, with silvery lower sides, and reach about 30 cm (1 ft) long. Their heads are deeper than long, giving them a steep forward profile.

moonstone Moonstone—one of the birthstones for June—is a semiprecious FELDSPAR that exhibits a bluish, silvery, or pearly light. The term *moonstone* is correctly applied to the alkali orthoclase feldspar adularia, which consists of submicroscopic intergrowths of albite ($NaAlSi_3O_8$) and orthoclase ($KAlSi_3O_8$). The chief commercial source is Sri Lanka, where moonstones occur in the Dumbara district gem gravels and pegmatites. Sacred in India, moonstone is believed to bring good fortune and to arouse the passions of lovers.

Moonstone is a transparent to translucent semiprecious feldspar with a bluish, silvery, or pearly opalescence. It is generally milky white to colorless but may be found in other colors.

Moor Moor (from Latin, *Maurus*) is sometimes used to denote a member of the Muslim populations of North Africa and, by extension, the Arab and Arabicized Berber conquerors of Spain, who established Muslim rule in the Iberian peninsula from the 8th to the 17th century. The term has also been applied specifically to the populations of Morocco and Mauritania; it occasionally has been used to refer to Muslims in general, as in the Moors of the Philippines and Sri Lanka (Ceylon). Today the term is rarely used except in reference to the style of art and architecture that arose during the early medieval florescence of Muslim power in North Africa and Spain.

Moore, Brian A Northern Irish writer with a superior gift for characterization, Brian Moore, b. Belfast, Aug. 25, 1921, established his reputation with his first novel, *The Lonely Passion of Judith Hearne* (1956), a powerful story of a Belfast spinster. The religious, social, and personal bonds of Irishness were further scrutinized in *The Feast of Lupercal* (1957), *The Luck of Ginger Coffey* (1960), *The Emperor of Ice-Cream* (1965), and *Catholics* (1972).

I Am Mary Dunne (1968) and *The Great Victorian Collection* (1975) best illustrate his compassion and humor.

Moore, Charles Willard   The architect, teacher, and author Charles Willard Moore, b. Benton Harbor, Mich., Oct. 31, 1925, is the wittiest and most accessible figure of the 1960s reaction against the International Style. His joyful, colorful works appeal to both professionals and the public, attesting to the strength of POST-MODERN ARCHITECTURE.

In small private homes, multimillion-dollar housing commissions (The Sea Ranch, Glendale, Calif., 1965; Huntington Plaza, Long Island, N.Y., 1974), commercial projects, and public works projects (sewage treatment plant, Cold Spring Harbor, N.Y., 1974), Moore has pioneered the revival of traditional styles and the use of color and decoration in architecture, and has devised novel approaches to lighting.

Moore, Clement Clarke   A biblical and Hebrew scholar at General Theological Seminary in New York City, Clement Clarke Moore, b. New York City, July 15, 1779, d. July 10, 1863, is popularly known for his amusing poem "A Visit from St. Nicholas," which begins "Twas the night before Christmas...."

Moore, Douglas Stuart   The American composer Douglas Stuart Moore, b. Cutchogue, N.Y., Aug. 10, 1893, d. July 25, 1969, is best known for his operas written in a simple, melodious, folklike idiom, particularly those dealing with American subject matter. His operas include *Giants in the Earth*, which won the 1951 Pulitzer Prize for music, *The Devil and Daniel Webster* (1938), *The Ballad of Baby Doe* (1956), *The Wings of the Dove* (1961), and *Carry Nation* (1966). His other works include orchestral pieces, such as the symphonic poem *Moby Dick* (1928), and chamber music.

Moore taught (1926–62) at Columbia University and was chairman of the music department there from 1940 to 1962.

Moore, G. E.   Highly influential in contemporary Anglo-American philosophy, George Edward Moore, b. Nov. 4, 1873, d. Oct. 24, 1958, was a British philosopher whose methods helped form the basis of ANALYTIC AND LINGUISTIC PHILOSOPHY.

Moore took the lead in rebelling against absolute IDEALISM, the prevailing philosophical movement at the turn of the century. He tried to show that every argument on behalf of idealism contained a crucial premise that, under all interpretations, was either false or self-contradictory.

The philosophical position that Moore defended was REALISM, and he was a realist in almost all senses of the term. He also, in various works, placed an emphasis on common sense. Using this approach, along with a meticulous analysis of concepts, he claimed to prove, or at least know, with certainty, many things that some philosophers had held to be unknown, or doubtful, or at best probable—for example, the existence of an external world of material objects.

Moore also wrote two books (and many articles) on ethics. The first, *Principia Ethica* (1903), was very influential among nonphilosophers as well as philosophers. The second, shorter book, *Ethics* (1912), has often been used as a text. One of Moore's chief claims in this area is that the notion of good is indefinable. With Bertrand Russell and Ludwig Wittgenstein, Moore exerted a seminal influence on 20th-century British and American philosophy.

Moore, George   The Irish writer George Moore, b. County Mayo, Feb. 24, 1852, d. Jan. 21, 1933, introduced NATURALISM into English literature. His best-known novel, *Esther Waters* (1894), relates the story of a religious young woman with an illegitimate son and her struggles against hardship and poverty. Greatly influenced by Balzac, Flaubert, and Zola, Moore contributed important works to the IRISH LITERARY RENAISSANCE, among them *The Untilled Field* (1903), a collection of short stories; a psychological novel, *The Lake* (1905); and the trilogy *Hail and Farewell* (1911–14), an autobiographical account of his ten years in Dublin. Moore also published the verse volumes *Flowers of Passion* (1878) and *Pagan Poems* (1881).

Moore, Henry   The British abstract sculptor Henry Spencer Moore, b. July 30, 1898, d. Aug. 31, 1986, was acclaimed as one of the great sculptors of the 20th century. From the beginning of his artistic career Moore displayed a predilection for the sculpture of primitive and

During his later career British sculptor Henry Moore experimented with cast-metal forms, such as his bronze Locking Piece *(1962).*

ancient peoples. His early works reflect his rejection of the mainstream traditions of Western art. Simplicity, monumentality, and an underlying sense of deep humanity mark such early works as his *Reclining Figure* (1929; Leeds Art Gallery).

Nearly all of Moore's work before the mid-1940s was carved directly in wood or stone. For his first major commission—the large relief *North Wind*, executed (1928–29) in Portland stone for the headquarters of the London underground railway—Moore carved a simple, massive figure that is characteristic of much of his work.

During World War II, Moore executed many drawings, most notably a series depicting air-raid shelters (1940–41; British Museum, London), that reflected his deep-seated concern with the human situation. Most of his postwar sculpture, both large- and small-scale, was modeled in clay and cast in metal. The bronze *Family Group* (1948–49; Museum of Modern Art, New York City) and the lead and bronze series *Helmet Heads* (1950; numerous collections) are representative of his later cast pieces.

Moore continued to be creatively active into his eighties, producing graphics as well as sculpture. In 1983 the Metropolitan Museum in New York City mounted the first American retrospective exhibition of his work.

Moore was perhaps the preeminent 20th-century master of monumental sculpture. His large sculptures often take on the appearance of primeval humans or giants that symbolize the invincibility of humanity in a complex environment continually in flux.

The Hall of Justice is located at the east end of the 14th-century Alhambra, the castle-palace of the Nasrid dynasty in Granada.

Moore, Marianne   Marianne Moore, b. St. Louis, Mo., Nov. 15, 1887, d. Feb. 5, 1972, was a major American poet who is best known for her meticulously written, witty, ironic verse. She wrote many poems about animals, celebrating them as ironic counterparts of people. Her famous definition of poetry as containing "for inspection, `imaginary gardens with real toads in them'" has been widely quoted.

After graduating from Bryn Mawr College in 1909, Moore taught stenography, worked as a librarian, and from 1926 to 1929 edited the literary magazine *The Dial*. In 1921 her first book, *Poems*, was published. Her other volumes include *Marriage* (1923), *The Pangolin and Other Verse* (1936), *Nevertheless* (1944), *Like a Bulwark* (1956), *O To Be a Dragon* (1959), and *Tell Me, Tell Me* (1966). She translated (1954) the *Fables* of La Fontaine and wrote the essays and reviews later collected in *Predilections* (1955) and *Poetry and Criticism* (1965). Her *Collected Poems* (1951) was awarded the Pulitzer Prize, the National Book Award, and the Bollingen Award.

Moorish art and architecture   The term *Moor* (Spanish: *Moro*) is derived from *Mauretania,* the Roman name for the part of northwest Africa that includes present-day Morocco and Algeria. As the tide of Islam swept across Africa, it was joined by the Berbers of this region, and thus it was a predominantly "Moorish" army that invaded Spain in 711, pushing the Visigoths north-

ward across the peninsula. The Christian reconquest of the area did not occur for nearly eight centuries, during which the Moors remained a political and military force, establishing brilliant courts and erecting outstanding architectural monuments. The center of Moorish civilization was in southern Spain, and it was there that the Moorish style developed, spreading northward and also back to Africa. It penetrated Christian territories first through the agency of Christians working under Moorish influence, called Mozarabs, and, later, through Moorish artisans in Christian employ, working in the so-called Mudejar style.

The formative influences of the Moorish style came not from the Berber invaders but from Syrian Arabs, founders of the Umayyad caliphate (661) in Damascus and later of a Cordovan emirate (756), and from the Romano-Visigothic tradition of the Christians, who at first lived peacefully under the Islamic rulers. Both eastern and Visigothic elements appear in the first and most influential of Umayyad monuments, the oldest section of the Great Mosque of Córdoba (begun 785).

As Córdoba grew, so did the mosque. By the 10th century the city was the seat of a caliph and was known as the most brilliant caliphate of Europe. Dating from this period is the third section of the mosque, with such extraordinary features as interlacing polylobed arches, a ribbed dome, and a mihrab (niche in the wall facing Mecca) decorated with exquisite carving and Byzantine mosaics. By the mid-11th century the Cordovan caliphate had broken up into petty warring factions, but this very decentralization led to the further spreading out of skilled Moorish artisans.

During the late 11th and early 12th century, two warlike, fanatically religious Berber dynasties held power, successively, in North Africa and Spain, bringing significant changes to Moorish art. The ALMORAVIDS crossed to Spain in 1086, restoring a centralized Moorish power. Their architecture survives only in North Africa, notably in the mosques of Algiers (late 11th century) and Tlemcen (mihrab dated 1136). Features important for the future of Moorish art appear at Tlemcen: stalactite vaulting (an eastern import) and increasing use of carved plaster.

In the 12th century the Almohads, even more warlike and religiously fanatical, established themselves across North Africa and deep into Spain. They were builders with a sense of scale, strength, and restrained decoration unusual in the Moorish tradition. Their mosques in Tinmal and Marrakesh, both built in the early 1150s, still exist. The mosque in Seville (built 1172–76) provided the site for the enormous Seville cathedral, begun in the 15th century. The cathedral's bell tower, the Giralda, preserves the minaret, the greatest surviving Almohad monument in Spain.

The Almohad empire split apart in the 13th century. In Spain the Moorish dominion gradually shrank to the Nasrid kingdom (founded 1238) of Granada, which persisted until the final defeat of the Moors in 1492. The castle-palace of the Nasrids, the Alhambra, dating from the 14th century, is considered the most spectacular of Moorish monuments, with magnificent gardens, richly colonnaded courts, and fantastically vaulted halls.

Handsome structures of the same period also exist in Africa, particularly in Fez, but it was in Spain after the reconquest that the late Moorish style, grafted onto Christian buildings, found a final hybrid flowering. From the 13th through the 15th century, city gates, synagogues, churches, palaces, and castles were given Mudejar decoration in regions as far apart as Andalusia, Castile, and Aragon. Outstanding examples are the Alcázar of Seville (14th century), the fantastic castle of Coca (15th century), the former synagogue of Santa Maria la Blanca (13th century) in Toledo, and the old cathedral of La Seo in Saragossa (14th century). Typical of the style are exteriors of patterned brickwork, horseshoe arches, carved wood ceiling panels (*artesonado*), and interior walls covered with carved plaster and glazed tiles. The Moorish heritage in the decorative arts is found in Spain to this day in the patterns employed in wood paneling, metalwork, and ceramics.

moose   The moose, *Alces alces,* is the largest member of the deer family, Cervidae. It is found in North America from Alaska to eastern Canada, south into the northwestern United States, and in Europe and Asia from Norway to Mongolia. The name *moose* is an American Indian word, and in Europe the moose is known by the old Germanic name *elk.* An elk in North America, however, is an entirely different deer, *Cervus canadensis.* The moose is a massive animal with long legs, a large head, and an elon-

The moose is the largest member of the deer family, standing 2.3 m (7.5 ft) at the shoulders and weighing up to 825 kg (1,800 lb). Inhabiting forests of North America and Eurasia, the moose feeds largely on leaves and twigs.

gated, overhanging muzzle. A long flap of skin, called the bell, hangs beneath its throat. Large bulls may be 3.1 m (10 ft) in length, plus a short tail, more than 2.3 m (7.5 ft) high at the shoulder, and up to 825 kg (1,800 lb) in weight. Bulls typically also have large, broad, spoon-shaped spiked antlers, which may be 1.8 m (6 ft) across. Moose are found principally in moist woods of willows, poplars, and birch, on which they browse. They also wade into lakes to feed on such aquatic plants as water lilies. Mating occurs in early fall, and gestation lasts 8 months, with one, often two, and occasionally three young being born in late spring.

Moose Jaw   Moose Jaw, a Canadian city with a population of 35,073 (1986), is located in south central Saskatchewan, on Moose Jaw River at its confluence with Thunder Creek. Founded in 1882 with the arrival of the Canadian Pacific Railway, Moose Jaw grew as a rail terminus and distribution center for the large surrounding wheat-growing area. The city has stockyards, slaughterhouses, flour-mills, and grain elevators, but the biggest employer is its Canadian military jet-training base.

moped   A motorized bicycle, or moped, is a bicycle with a small gasoline engine, as well as pedals, for propulsion. The pedals are used for starting and assisting the engine. A moped (the term was coined from *mo*tor plus *ped*al) shares some features with the bicycle, motorcycle, motor scooter, and minibike but is a unique vehicle. The distinguishing feature is its single-cylinder engine whose size (displacement of cylinder) is no greater than 50 cubic centimeters (cc; 50 cm^3/3 in^3), producing no more than 1–2 horsepower and enabling a top speed of 48 km/h (30 mph) to be attained on level ground. For information on the distinctions among various two-wheeled motorized vehicles, see MOTORCYCLE.

Mopeds have been popular in Europe and Asia for about 40 years, and millions of mopeds are in use worldwide. They did not become popular in the United States, however, until the 1970s. Advantages include low price, energy efficiency, simplicity of design and construction, and ease of operation. For example, some mopeds get more than 63 km/l (150 mi/gal) of gasoline. Sales of mopeds in the United States increased extraordinarily in the mid-1970s.

moraine [muh-rayn'] A moraine is a deposit of till (see TILL AND TILLITE), rock debris picked up and transported by the moving ice of mountain glaciers and continental ice sheets and laid down during both the advance and the retreat of the ice. This unstratified rock debris may range in size from clay and sand to large boulders; it originates from many locations along the glacial advance. Several kinds of moraines are recognized. Terminal, lateral, and median moraines are classified according to their position relative to a glacier or ice sheet (see GLACIER AND GLACIATION). The ridgelike terminal, or end, moraines, which form at the front of a glacier or ice sheet, indicate either a temporary halt in the ice advance or the furthermost advance of the ice. Ground and ablation moraines form blankets of till that may be up to 20 m (70 ft) thick (and still thicker when deposition occurs in valleys); they are made up of debris carried on, or incorporated into, the ice and laid down when the ice melted away. A recessional moraine occurs when a glacier halts in its retreat.

Moral Majority Founded by the Rev. Jerry FALWELL of Lynchburg, Va., Moral Majority was established in 1979 to mold conservative Christians into a potent voting bloc and to press for the enactment of laws reflecting conservative values. The 4-million-member organization appealed mainly to Protestant fundamentalists. Its positions have included opposition to abortion, homosexuality, pornography, and the EQUAL RIGHTS AMENDMENT. It has advocated increased U.S. military spending, prayer in the public schools, and the teaching of biblical CREATIONISM.

In 1986, Moral Majority Foundation Incorporated, the tax-deductible arm of the organization, became Liberty Federation; it has concentrated mainly on moral issues. Moral Majority Incorporated, which was dissolved in 1989, had concerned itself more with political matters. Falwell stepped down as president in 1987.

Moral Re-Armament Moral Re-Armament, also known as MRA, the Oxford Group, or Buchmanism for its American founder, Frank Buchman, is an international, nondenominational, evangelistic movement devoted to the moral regeneration of the world through the spiritual reconstruction of individual lives. Buchman first organized a group at the University of Oxford, England, in 1921. Through vigorous proselytization the movement spread to many countries, assuming the name Moral Re-Armament in 1938. MRA stresses conversion through personal confession and the development of altruistic values among members. Politically, it is vehemently anti-Communist.

Morales, Luís de [moh-rah'-lays] The Spanish painter Luís de Morales, c.1510–1586, is considered, after El Greco, Spain's greatest Mannerist painter. Among his early works are five panels in the Badajoz Cathedral. Nicknamed El Divino for the intense spirituality of his work, Morales chose as his favorite themes the Virgin and Child and the Pietà (the dead Christ being mourned by the Virgin). In two versions of the first subject (both undated; National Gallery, London, and Hispanic Society, New York City) the influence of Leonardo da Vinci is evident in Morales's use of sfumato, or imperceptible gradations of light and dark. This technique is also apparent in another undated work, the *Pietà*, at the Academia de San Fernando, Madrid. The inspiration of the German painters Martin Schongauer and Albrecht Dürer can be detected in Morales's many versions of the *Ecce Homo* (such as the undated canvas in London's National Gallery), especially in the exaggerated ugliness of Christ's tormentors.

morality play SEE MEDIEVAL DRAMA

Moran, Thomas [moh-ran'] An American painter of western mountain ranges, Thomas Moran, b. Bolton, Lancashire, England, Jan. 12, 1837, d. Aug. 26, 1926, traveled (1860) to the Lake Superior region and went farther west with surveying parties in 1871 and 1873, painting the Grand Canyon, the Teton Range, and the Sierra Nevada. Moran endowed his mountainscapes with great depth and panoramic sweep and took artistic license to dramatize these vistas. His *Grand Canyon of the Yellowstone* (1872; National Collection of Fine Arts, Washington, D.C.) was bought by Congress for $5,000; this work much impressed the nation's legislators and helped establish the U.S. system of national parks. Officials also named a peak in the Tetons for the artist. *The Teton Range* (1897; Metropolitan Museum of Art, New York City) is another of Moran's well-known works.

Morante, Elsa [moh-rahn'-tay] The Italian writer Elsa Morante, b. Aug. 18, 1918, d. Nov. 25, 1985, won recognition as the author of several short, beautifully composed novels, among them *House of Liars* (1948; Eng. trans., 1951) and *Arturo's Island* (1957; Eng. trans., 1959). *History* (1974; Eng. trans., 1977) explores the war-devastated lives of several ordinary Italians; *Aracoeli* (1982; Eng. trans., 1985) is a Freudian-influenced narrative.

moratorium A moratorium is a government declaration permitting debtors to postpone payment of their obligations for a certain time. Moratoria have been declared many times throughout history for conscripted soldiers.

During the financial panic of 1933 in the United States, numerous moratoria, or bank holidays, were declared by state governments, allowing banks to suspend their operations and thus avoid massive withdrawals by depositors. On Mar. 6, 1933, the new administration of Franklin D. Roosevelt declared a national bank holiday to give banks a chance to organize their accounts. Some banks remained closed for weeks, and many never reopened. The widespread losses suffered by depositors led to the establishment of the FEDERAL DEPOSIT INSURANCE CORPORATION, which insures the deposits of most U.S. banks.

The Italian author Alberto Moravia focused on the themes of alienation and dehumanization throughout his writings. His first novel, Gli Indifferenti *(1929;* The Time of Indifference, *1953) was a forerunner of the European existential novel.*

Photo Jill Krementz © 1974

Moravia [muh-ray'-vee-uh]   Moravia is a historic region in the eastern part of the Czech Republic. It is now divided into two administrative districts: South Moravia, where BRNO is the principal city, and North Moravia, with OSTRAVA as the main city. Moravia is bordered by the Carpathian Mountains in the east and the Sudeten Mountains in the north. It is a rich agricultural and horse-breeding area. Coal is mined, and both Ostrava and Brno are large industrial centers.

Moravia was first peopled by Celts, then by Germanic tribes, and finally by Slavs by the 6th century. It was Christianized by the 9th-century missionaries Cyril and Methodius. In the 10th century the Magyars overran the area, but they were forced back by the German king OTTO I, and Moravia became a march (frontier area) of the Holy Roman Empire. In the 11th century it became attached to BOHEMIA. Although it largely shared Bohemia's history thereafter, Moravia was quieter under Austrian Habsburg rule (from 1526) than Bohemia and was more heavily Germanized. After World War I, Moravia became part of Czechoslovakia. In 1939, Germany, which had already annexed the SUDETENLAND, established a protectorate over Bohemia and Moravia. With the reconstitution of Czechoslovakia after World War II, most of Moravia's German-speaking population was expelled.

The region of Moravia, located in the eastern portion of the Czech Republic, was once an independent kingdom that expanded during the 9th century to include Bohemia and parts of Poland and Hungary.

Moravia, Alberto [moh-rah'-vee-ah, ahl-bair'-toh]   Alberto Moravia is the pen name of Alberto Pincherle, b. Rome, Nov. 28, 1907, d. Sept. 26, 1990, Italy's most famous contemporary novelist. Even his first novel, *The Time of Indifference* (1929; Eng. trans., 1953), was significant; its harsh realism broke with Italian literary tradition, foreshadowed the European existentialist novel, and introduced the major themes of Moravia's subsequent work: the superficiality of the bourgeoisie, the importance of sex and money in human affairs, and the alienation of modern people. Such works as *The Wheel of Fortune* (1935; Eng. trans., 1937) and *Agostino* (1944; Eng. trans., 1947) dealt, respectively, with middle-class values and an adolescent's painful initiation into sex.

After World War II, Moravia wrote neorealistic fiction about the lives of working-class Romans. *The Woman of Rome* (1947; Eng. trans., 1949), *Two Women* (1957; Eng. trans., 1958; film, 1961), and several volumes of short stories—especially *Roman Tales* (1954; Eng. trans., 1957) and *More Roman Tales* (1959; Eng. trans., 1964)—were popular as well as critical successes. Moravia's later works repeated earlier themes: *Time of Desecration* (1979; Eng. trans., 1980) is a sexual morality tale, *1934* (1982; Eng. trans., 1983) examines the intellectual corruption created by fascism, and the stories in *Erotic Tales* (Eng. trans., 1986) concern the sexual obsessions that Moravia interpreted as symptoms of alienation.

Moravian Church [muh-ray'-vee-uhn]   The Moravian Church is a Protestant communion closely linked to LUTHERANISM. It has its roots in the Czech REFORMATION and is a direct continuation of the Bohemian Brethren.

Influenced by the spiritual heritage of John HUSS, Brother Gregory founded the Bohemian Unity of Brethren, which, having functioned within the Utraquist group of HUSSITES for a decade, separated in 1467 and established an independent ministry. The reform movement based itself solely on the Bible, and its leaders were able to procure non-Roman ordination from a bishop of the WALDENSES. Occasional persecution of the Unity became systematic in the 16th century, a period marked by the theological creativity of Lukas of Prague (c.1460–1528) and Jan Augusta (1500–72) and by contact with other Protestant reformers. Toleration obtained in 1609 was short-lived as the Czech Protestants were expelled by Catholic advances in the THIRTY YEARS' WAR (1627). Educator John Amos COMENIUS, the Unity's last bishop, led the group into exile. A century later, representatives of German PIETISM encouraged survivors of the Unity to migrate from Moravia to Saxony, where in 1722 the community of Herrnhut was founded. Graf von ZINZENDORF assumed leadership, and a spiritual awakening swept the congregation in 1727, which is often taken as the founding date of the Moravian Church.

The Moravians were pioneers in Protestant home and foreign missions, seeking renewal of European Christianity and the evangelization of the non-Christian world. Augustus Gottlieb SPANGENBURG, sent to America in 1735, founded churches in Georgia, Pennsylvania, and North Carolina. Zinzendorf stimulated the church by his missionary leadership and religious genius, especially in community formation and cultic celebration. He also troubled the church with financial instability and devotional excesses that nearly wrecked it in the 1740s. After his death more moderate leadership was introduced by Spangenberg.

Moravianism is basically presbyterian in structure, and its bishops are chosen on spiritual merit to serve in pastoral and cultic roles rather than in administrative ones.

Moray [mur'-ee]   Moray (also Elginshire) is a former county in northeastern Scotland, located along the coast of Moray Firth. Farming takes place in the coastal lowlands, and farther inland hills reaching 710 m (2,329 ft) are used for sheep grazing. Fishing is also a major economic activity, and textiles, whiskey, and processed foods are produced in the towns. Moray was settled by Picts and invaded by Norsemen. In 1050, MACBETH, the lord of Moray immortalized by William Shakespeare, killed King Duncan and seized the Scottish throne. In 1975, during the reorganization of local government in Scotland, Moray was integrated into the GRAMPIAN region.

moray eel [mohr'-ay]   Moray eels, family Muraenidae, comprise 100 species of snakelike fishes typically found in reefs or rocky areas in warm or tropical seas. They lack paired fins (pectorals and pelvics) and have a thick, scaleless skin, a small, round gill opening on each side, a bulky head region, and a large mouth, usually with long, slender, depressible teeth. Either or both pairs of nostrils may be projected into tubes. Morays range in size from 15 cm (6 in) to 3 m (10 ft). Some are strikingly marked, others are uniformly colored; the green moray, *Gymnothorax funebris*, actually has a blue-gray skin that is usually covered with yellowish algae, giving it its greenish hue. Morays are generally nocturnal feeders and commonly eat fish and also mollusks; morays of the genus *Echidna* have flattened teeth for crushing sea urchins and

Moray eels, Gymnothorax undulatis *(left)* and *G.* favagineus *(right), are plentiful in rock outcrops and coral reefs of the Indo-Pacific.*

other echinoderms. Although morays can inflict serious bites, they have an unearned reputation for consistent aggressiveness.

Morazán, Francisco [mohr-ah-sahn', frahn-sees'-koh]   The guiding force behind the CENTRAL AMERICAN FEDERATION (1823–39)—the union of Costa Rica, El Salvador, Guatemala, Honduras, and Nicaragua—was the Honduran soldier and statesman Francisco Morazán, b. Oct. 3, 1792, d. Sept. 15, 1842. When the Mexican empire of Agustín de ITURBIDE broke up, Morazán forged the five Central American republics into a loose federation and became its president.

Although Morazán accomplished notable reforms, internal disputes between liberals and conservatives and among the five national groups finally broke up the federation in 1839. Morazán went into exile in 1840. In 1842 he was recalled to Costa Rica and became its president, but after a few months civil war broke out; Morazán was captured and executed by the opposing faction.

Mordecai   see ESTHER, BOOK OF

More, Henry   The English philosopher and poet Henry More, b. Oct. 12, 1614, d. Sept. 1, 1687, spent most of his life as a Cambridge fellow. He was perhaps the best known of the Cambridge Platonists, a group of philosophers who, drawing inspiration from the tradition of Platonic philosophy, defended Christianity against the materialism represented by Thomas HOBBES. In the scholastic tradition, More perceived all nature as permeated by spirit, an essence constantly reflecting the universal reason, God's mind. More influenced the scientist Sir Isaac Newton.

More, Saint Thomas   Sir Thomas More, b. Feb. 6, 1478, d. July 6, 1535, a leading English intellectual and statesman, was executed for his adherence to the Roman Catholic faith. The son of John More, a prominent jurist, Thomas was educated at Oxford and at Lincoln's Inn, where he studied law. His humanist philosophy was shaped by the "new learning" of the Renaissance and by

Sir Thomas More, English scholar and statesman, was executed under Henry VIII for his refusal to deny papal supremacy and acknowledge the king as head of the English church. (Hans Holbein, 1527; Frick Collection, New York City.)

his friendship with the scholar Desiderius Erasmus. As speaker of the House of Commons in 1523, More helped establish the parliamentary privilege of free speech. He refused (1527) to endorse King HENRY VIII's plan to divorce CATHERINE OF ARAGON. Nevertheless, after the fall (1529) of Thomas WOLSEY, More became lord chancellor. His work in the law courts was exemplary, but he resigned in 1532, citing ill health and probably feeling that he could not in conscience serve a government that was interfering with the church. Two years later he was imprisoned in the Tower of London for refusing to acknowledge Henry as supreme head of the Church of England. He was found guilty of treason, on evidence that was probably perjured, and was beheaded. More was canonized in 1935.

Utopia (written in Latin, 1516; Eng. trans., 1551), More's most noted book, assails the inequitable social and economic conditions in Europe and describes an ideal state based on reason. His other writings include a history of the reign of Richard III and a number of religious treatises intended to refute the views of Martin Luther and other Protestant theologians. A complete edition of his works (1963–) has been undertaken under the auspices of Yale University. Feast day: June 22 (with Saint John Fisher; formerly July 9).

Moreau (family) [moh-roh'] The painters Jean Michel Moreau, b. Mar. 26, 1741, d. Nov. 30, 1814, known as Moreau le Jeune, and his brother, Louis Gabriel Moreau, b. Apr. 24, 1739, d. Oct. 12, 1805, were among the keenest observers of French rococo society during the last quarter of the 18th century. **Louis Gabriel** is known primarily for his calm landscapes depicting the vicinity of Paris, sensitively worked in watercolor, gouache, etching, and occasionally oil.

Figures were sometimes drawn in by Louis Gabriel's more talented younger brother **Jean Michel**, who in more than 2,000 prints and drawings left a minutely detailed chronicle of the capricious atmosphere of the royal court prior to the French Revolution. Most of Moreau le Jeune's

works are delicate, small-scale drawings intended for book illustrations, only a few of which he engraved himself. A large-format series of etchings, representative of his finest work, appeared in Paris in 1776 as *Le Monument du Costume*.

Moreau, Gustave The French painter Gustave Moreau, b. Apr. 6, 1826, d. Apr. 18, 1898, was a major figure among those painters and writers of the late 19th century who turned away from realistic depiction of the material world to cultivate a visionary and symbolic art.

He found his first success at the Paris Salons of 1864–66 but withdrew from 1869 to 1876 in response to hostile criticism. After 1880 he stopped exhibiting and became a recluse until, in 1888, he began teaching at the École des Beaux-Arts, where his pupils included Georges Roualt and Henri Matisse. Moreau's disquietingly perverse treatments of mythological and biblical subjects were greatly admired by many avant-garde literary figures of his time. The novelist J. K. Huysmans praised his glowing watercolors in *À Rebours* (1884) and described his art as the epitome of morbid and decadent perception. His *Oedipus and the Sphinx* (1864; Metropolitan Museum of Art, New York City) inspired Odilon Redon to paint, and Moreau was much admired by the surrealists.

Moreau, Jean Victor Marie Gen. Jean Victor Moreau, b. Feb. 14, 1763, d. Sept. 2, 1813, commanded French forces in the FRENCH REVOLUTIONARY WARS and NAPOLEONIC WARS but later opposed Napoleon's regime and assisted the troops of the powers allied against France. At the outbreak of the French Revolution (1789), he formed a national guard unit at Rennes. He was promoted to general of a division in 1794, and in 1796 he executed a brilliant retreat from Germany. The government recalled Moreau in 1797 for suspected dealings with Gen. Jean Charles PICHEGRU, who was in contact with royalist exiles, but reinstated him two years later. Under Napoleon (see NAPOLEON I), Moreau was victorious at Hohenlinden against the Austrians in December 1800. Not involved in royalist intrigues but refusing to reveal them, Moreau was banished in 1804. He went to the United States but returned to join the forces allied against France in 1813; he was fatally wounded at Dresden.

Moreau, Jeanne Jeanne Moreau, b. Paris, Jan. 23, 1928, is a French actress whose popularity stems from her work with such New Wave film directors as Louis Malle and François Truffaut. After training at the Comédie Française, she acted in several undistinguished films before Malle's *The Lovers* (1959) brought her stardom. It was followed by roles in Roger Vadim's *Liaisons Dangereuses* (1959), Michelangelo Antonioni's *La Notte* (1961), Truffaut's *Jules et Jim* (1961), and Luis Buñuel's *Diary of a Chambermaid* (1964). Since the early 1960s she has appeared frequently in English-language films, including *Viva Maria!* (1965), *Chimes at Midnight*

(1966), and *Monte Walsh* (1971). She made her own directorial debut with *Lumière* (1976), followed by *L'Adolescente* (1979).

Morehouse College   Established in 1867 and associated with the Baptist church, Morehouse College is a private liberal-arts school for men in Atlanta, Ga. The college, established for the higher education of blacks, is part of the Atlanta University Center, a consortium of seven schools that shares various programs and facilities, including a library.

Morelia [moh-rayl'-ee-ah]   Morelia is the capital city of MICHOACÁN state in west central Mexico. Its population is 353,055 (1983 est.). Located in the central plateau, Morelia is the trade and manufacturing center for an irrigated agriculture and cattle-raising region and is known for local crafts. The city's colonial buildings include the Renaissance-style cathedral (1640–1744) and many other churches. The city's universities include one of the oldest in Latin America, Colegio San Nicolás (founded 1540), also known as Michoacana University of San Nicolás of Hidalgo, and the Autonomous University of Morelos (1939).

Originally the site of the capital of the Tarascan Indian kingdom, the city was founded in 1541 as Valladolid and renamed (1828) in honor of José María Morelos y Pavón, philosopher of the Mexican independence movement, who studied there.

Morelos [moh-ray'-lohs]   Morelos is the second smallest state in Mexico, covering only 4,950 km^2 (1,911 mi^2). It has a population of 1,195,381 (1990). Morelos lies south of Mexico City and is extremely mountainous. Its capital is CUERNAVACA. The main crops of this important agricultural region are sugarcane, wheat, rice, corn, coffee, fruits, and vegetables. Tourism is also important. Morelos became a state in 1869 and was named for the country's national hero, José María Morelos y Pavón. In 1910–17, Morelos was a stronghold of Emiliano Zapata, one of the leaders of the Mexican revolution.

Morelos y Pavón, José María [moh-ray'-lohs ee pah-vohn']   A poor parish priest, José María Morelos y Pavón, b. Sept. 30, 1765, d. Dec. 22, 1815, became a leader of the movement to achieve Mexico's independence from Spain. He served as a parish priest until 1810, and the following year he joined the independence movement. After the execution (1811) of Miguel HIDALGO Y COSTILLA, Morelos assumed leadership and led his troops to significant victories at Oaxaca (1812) and Acapulco (1813). He called the Congress of Chilpancingo, which issued a formal declaration of independence on Nov. 6, 1813, and declared him the supreme executive. Morelos was captured by royalist forces, however, and defrocked; he was then shot as a traitor by the Spaniards.

J. P. Morgan (1837–1913), son of a London-based American banker, headed a financial empire that profoundly influenced the American economy of the late 19th and early 20th centuries. Morgan specialized in the creation of enormous business consolidations, the most famous of which was the U.S. Steel Corp. (1901).

Morgan (family)   The Morgan family was active in U.S. finance and banking for three generations. **Junius Spencer Morgan**, b. West Springfield, Mass., Apr. 14, 1813, d. Apr. 8, 1890, was an important financial link between the United States and Britain during the middle of the 19th century. After some experience in American mercantile firms, he joined the London-based international banking house of George Peabody & Co., becoming a partner in 1854. When Peabody retired, Morgan took over, changing the firm's name to J. S. Morgan & Co. He directed this company until his death. **John Pierpont Morgan**, known as J. P. Morgan, b. Hartford, Conn., Apr. 17, 1837, d. Mar. 31, 1913, the son of Junius, was a major figure in international finance before World War I. An agent for his father in New York, he formed (1871) the banking house of Drexel, Morgan, & Co., which 24 years later was renamed J. P. Morgan & Co. After the crash of 1893, Morgan was active in railroads, reorganizing several lines in the eastern United States. In 1898 he entered the field of industrial consolidation, forming the Federal Steel Company and (1901) the United States Steel Corp. The latter firm included the Carnegie steel interests, which were purchased for $400 million. Morgan had wide-ranging influence over many of the companies that he financed, an influence that was, however, probably exaggerated in public opinion. A great art collector, he gave many works to the Metropolitan Museum of Art in New York City.

His son **John Pierpont Morgan, Jr.**, b. Irvington, N.Y., Sept. 7, 1867, d. Mar. 13, 1943, inherited the family's banking house. He was instrumental in financing $1.5 billion in Allied military purchases during World War I and in arranging $1.7 billion in reconstruction loans after the war.

Morgan (horse)   The Morgan is a compact, muscular horse standing 14–15 hands high (1.42–1.52 m/56–60

The Morgan, a light horse first bred in the United States, is a popular utility breed. The breed is noted for its handsomeness, temperament, and endurance.

in) at the withers and weighing 360–500 kg (800–1,100 lb). Morgans are usually bay or dark chestnut but may also be black or brown. Developed in the United States, the Morgan is used for general riding, steeplechasing, and light draft work. Its origins can be traced to one Justin Morgan (1748–98) of Randolph, Vt., who acquired (1790) the colt named for him. The horse lived until 1821. Its parentage is uncertain. The Morgan has contributed to several other American breeds.

Morgan, Daniel   Daniel Morgan, b. Hunterdon County, N.J., 1736, d. July 6, 1802, was the commander of a band of Virginia sharpshooters in the American Revolution. In 1775, Morgan took part in Benedict Arnold's expedition against Canada; taken prisoner, he was later released. During the Battles of Saratoga (1777) he and his frontier riflemen played a major part in defeating the British at Freeman's Farm and Bemis Heights. Promoted to brigadier general, Morgan won (1781) a notable victory over Col. Banastre Tarleton in the Battle of COWPENS. As commander of the Virginia militia, he helped suppress (1794) the WHISKEY REBELLION. Morgan also served a term (1797–99) in the U.S. House of Representatives.

Morgan, Sir Henry   A Welsh adventurer, Sir Henry Morgan, b. 1635, d. Aug. 25, 1688, was one of the buccaneers who, with the unofficial support of the English government, preyed on Spanish shipping and colonies in the Caribbean. In 1668 he captured Puerto Príncipe (now Camagüey, Cuba) and sacked Portobelo (now in Panama). He raided Maracaibo (now in Venezuela) in 1669. His spectacular capture (1671) of the city of

Panama was marked by great brutality and debauchery. Afterward much of the booty was lost, and Morgan's crew claimed that he had cheated them. Captured and sent back (1672) to England to answer piracy charges, Morgan was treated like a hero, knighted, and appointed lieutenant governor of Jamaica, where he lived quietly thereafter.

Morgan, Joe   Joseph Leonard Morgan, b. Bonham, Tex., Sept. 19, 1943, was one of professional baseball's greatest 2d basemen. In a long career (1963–84), Morgan was most famous for his period (1972–79) with the Cincinnati Reds. He was the team leader of the so-called Big Red Machine that won the World Series in 1975 and 1976; in both years he was the National League's Most Valuable Player. Morgan accumulated 1,865 walks (3d all time), 689 stolen bases, 2,518 hits, and 5 Gold Gloves as the NL's top defensive 2d baseman. He was elected to the Hall of Fame in his first year of eligibility (1990).

Morgan, John Hunt   John Hunt Morgan, b. Huntsville, Ala., June 1, 1825, d. Sept. 4, 1864, a Confederate scout in the U.S. Civil War, was made a brigadier general for capturing a garrison of Union troops in Tennessee (December 1862). He led many successful raids behind Union lines; the most famous was through Kentucky, Indiana, and Ohio during the summer of 1863. It led to his capture, however, and the virtual destruction of his division. Morgan escaped, and in April 1864 he became a commander in Virginia. He was killed in Tennessee by Union forces.

Morgan, Julia   The American architect and engineer Julia Morgan, b. San Francisco, 1872, d. Feb. 2, 1957, was the first woman to be licensed to practice architecture in California. A student of Bernard Maybeck, she was the first woman ever admitted to architectural studies at the École des Beaux-Arts in Paris. When Morgan set up her practice in 1904 she created a sensation in a profession historically dominated by men. However, when her reinforced-concrete Mills College Campanile (1904) withstood the 1906 San Francisco earthquake, her reputation was made. Morgan's most famous work—also of reinforced concrete—is La Cuesta Encantada (The Enchanted Hill, begun 1919), William Randolph Hearst's mountaintop palace at San Simeon.

Morgan, Lewis Henry   The American anthropologist Lewis Henry Morgan, b. Aurora, N.Y., Nov. 21, 1818, d. Dec. 17, 1881, developed comprehensive early theories of kinship systems and of cultural evolution based on his extensive studies of the Indians of upstate New York, upper Michigan, and the Hudson Bay area of Canada. He practiced law in Rochester, N.Y., from 1844 and served in the state assembly (1861–68) and senate (1868–69). For his labors in defending land claims for the SENECA

Indians, he was made (1847) an honorary tribesman. Morgan's anthropological work focused on the origins, migrations, and present-day survival of Indian cultures. His writings, because of their theme of cultural evolution, attracted the attention of Marxists outside the United States.

Morgan, Thomas Hunt   The American zoologist Thomas Hunt Morgan, b. Lexington, Ky., Sept. 25, 1866, d. Dec. 4, 1945, was awarded the 1933 Nobel Prize for physiology or medicine for his work in the field of genetics. He was a professor of experimental zoology at Columbia University (1904–28), where he conducted extensive breeding experiments with the fruit fly *Drosophila melanogaster*. From this research he concluded that the units of heredity, genes, are arranged in a line on the chromosomes—a theory known as the chromosome theory of heredity.

In 1926, Morgan wrote *The Theory of the Gene,* in which he stated that genes are held together in linkage groups and that there is an interchange of alleles, genes affecting the same trait. This interchange, known as crossing-over, allowed Morgan to construct chromosome maps showing the relative locations of many genes.

Morgantown   A north central West Virginia port city located 90 km (55 mi) south of Pittsburgh on the Monongahela River, Morgantown is the seat of Monongalia County. It has a population of 25,879 (1990). The city, founded in 1767, is known for its glass industry. It is the site of West Virginia University (1867).

Morgenthau (family) [mohr'-guhn-thaw]   The Morgenthau family has been prominent in U.S. business, law, and public service for more than a century. **Henry Morgenthau**, b. Apr. 26, 1856, d. Nov. 25, 1946, emigrated (1865) from Germany to New York City, where he practiced real-estate law and made highly profitable land transactions. Morgenthau was finance chairman of the Democratic National Committee during Woodrow Wilson's presidential campaigns (1912, 1916) and was U.S. ambassador to Turkey (1913–16). His son, **Henry Morgenthau, Jr.**, b. New York City, May 11, 1891, d. Feb. 6, 1967, a longtime friend of Franklin D. Roosevelt's, chaired the Federal Farm Board (1933) and was secretary of the treasury (1934–45) during Roosevelt's presidency. An early advocate of resistance to Adolf Hitler, he coordinated aid to the Allies from 1938 to 1941. He resigned from the cabinet in 1945 because of President Harry Truman's opposition to the so-called Morgenthau Plan for the permanent partition of Germany and the dismantling of its industries.

Mörike, Eduard [mur'-ik-e, ay'-dwahrt]   Eduard Friedrich Mörike, b. Sept. 8, 1804, d. June 4, 1875, was the greatest German poet between Goethe and Rilke. He lived an outwardly idyllic life but was inwardly aware of death, conflicts of conscience (he resigned from the Lutheran ministry in 1843), and unhappy love. Mörike's poems range from classical hexameters to folk song and from tragedy to broad humor. Some anticipate Rilke's *Ding-Gedicht,* or "object poem," and many were set to music by Hugo Wolf. In prose Mörike is noted for his romantic novel *Maler Nolten* (Painter Nolten, 1832) and for short stories. His novella *Mozart on the Way to Prague* (1854; Eng. trans., 1913–15) probes the mystery of artistic creation.

Moriscos [mohr-is'-kohz]   Spanish Muslims who converted to Christianity during and after the expulsion of the Moors from Spain were known as Moriscos; although baptized, they continued to maintain their Islamic customs. After King FERDINAND II and Queen ISABELLA I completed the Christian reconquest in 1492, they guaranteed the vanquished Muslims freedom of religion. Soon, however, forcible conversions were carried out, and a royal edict of 1502 required all Muslims to accept baptism or go into exile. Most Muslims chose to convert rather than abandon their ancestral homes, but their loyalty to the Spanish crown remained suspect. After King PHILIP II forbade the Granada Moriscos to use Arabic, wear their traditional dress, and continue other customs, a widespread but unsuccessful revolt occurred (1569–71). In 1609 the difficulty of assimilating the Moriscos prompted King PHILIP III to order their deportation. Over the next several years an estimated 300,000 Moriscos were expelled from Spain.

Morison, Samuel Eliot [mohr'-i-suhn]   Samuel Eliot Morison, b. Boston, July 9, 1887, d. May 15, 1976, an American historian, was a professor at Harvard (1925–55). He retraced Columbus's voyages before writing his biography, *Admiral of the Ocean Sea* (2 vols., 1942), a Pulitzer Prize winner. Morison wrote the acclaimed *History of U.S. Naval Operations in World War II* (15 vols., 1947–1962) and won a second Pulitzer Prize for *John Paul Jones* (1959). His many other works include *The Growth of the American Republic* (1930), a textbook written with Henry Steele Commager, and *The European Discovery of America,* 2 vols. (1971–74).

Morisot, Berthe [mohr-ee-zoh', bairt]   The first woman to join the circle of the French impressionist painters, Berthe Morisot, b. Jan. 14, 1841, d. Mar. 2, 1895, exhibited in all but one of their shows. Unlike most of the other impressionists, who were then intensely engaged in optical experiments with color, Morisot and Édouard Manet, her brother-in-law, agreed on a more conservative approach, confining their use of color to a naturalistic framework. Morisot, however, did encourage Manet to adopt the impressionists' high-keyed palette and to abandon the use of black. Her own carefully composed, brightly hued canvases are often studies of wom-

The Cradle *was painted by the French impression-ist Berthe Morisot in 1872. The figures are depicted natu-ralistically, showing Morisot's extraordi-nary ability to cap-ture a tender, fleet-ing moment through direct observation of an everyday event. (Musée d'Orsay, Paris.)*

en, either out-of-doors or in domestic settings. Morisot and American artist Mary Cassatt are generally considered the most important women painters of the later 19th century.

Mormonism Mormonism is a way of life practiced by members of the Church of Jesus Christ of Latter-day Saints, often called Mormons or Latter-day Saints.

History. Joseph Smith organized the church in Fayette, N.Y., in 1830. Earlier he reported having visions of God, Jesus Christ, and other heavenly beings in which he was told that he would be the instrument to establish the re-stored Christian church. According to Smith, one of the heavenly messengers directed him to some thin metal plates, gold in appearance and inscribed in a hieroglyph-ic language. Smith's translation of the plates, the Book of Mormon, describes the history, wars, and religious beliefs of a group of people (*c.*600 BC–AD 421) who migrated from Jerusalem to America, and focuses on the appear-ance of the resurrected Christ in the Western Hemi-sphere. Smith attracted a small group of followers who settled in Kirtland, Ohio, and Jackson County, Mo. Be-cause of persecution the church moved to northern Mis-souri and then to Nauvoo, Ill. In 1837 missionaries were sent to England and later to Scandinavia; most of their converts eventually immigrated to the United States.

Although the church prospered in Nauvoo, it faced difficult times. Neighbors resented Mormons' voting as a bloc and became irate when rumors spread that Smith had introduced polygamy into Mormonism. Feelings peaked on June 27, 1844, when an armed mob assassi-nated Smith in Carthage, Ill. Brigham Young, the head of the church's Council of the Twelve Apostles, was named as new leader of the church. In 1846 he organized and directed the epic march from Nauvoo across the plains and mountains to the Great Salt Basin.

In Utah the church continued to grow but was chal-lenged by the U.S. government because of the acknowl-edgment of polygamy as a Mormon tenet. A war almost

developed, but Mormon leaders decided to compromise after only sporadic fighting. In 1862 and 1882, Congress passed antibigamy laws, and in 1870 the Supreme Court ruled that religious freedom could not be claimed as grounds for the practice of polygamy. In 1890 the Mor-mons officially ended the practice of plural marriage.

Not everyone supported Young as church leader. The opposition eventually withdrew to form other churches, the largest of which is the Reorganized Church of Jesus Christ of the Latter-day Saints, headquartered at Inde-pendence, Mo. The Reorganized Church holds that lead-ership rightfully belongs to the direct descendants of Joseph Smith.

Organization and Beliefs. A 3-member First Presidency and a 12-man Council of Apostles constitute the major policy-making body of the Utah-based church. Two Quo-rums of Seventy and a Presiding Bishopric are the other general authorities who provide guidelines to local units. General conferences are held semiannually in Salt Lake City, and regional conferences periodically in other areas. Local and regional leadership is provided by unpaid lay clergy.

Mormons use the Bible, the *Book of Mormon*, and two other books of revelations to Joseph Smith—*Doctrine and Covenants* and the *Pearl of Great Price*—as their stan-dard scriptures. Thus they share most of the beliefs of traditional Christianity but with some modification. Mor-mons believe that God continues to reveal his word to in-dividuals who seek it for their own benefit, to leaders of local units for their own jurisdiction, and to the President-Prophet for the church as a whole. In 1978, for example,

The Mormon Temple in Salt Lake City, Utah, a majestic structure that dominates the city, is one of 43 temples located throughout the world.

Mormon church authorities announced that they had been instructed by revelation to strike down the church's former policy of excluding black men from the priesthood.

The church baptizes by immersion at age 8 or older. Vicarious baptism for those who have died and marriage for eternity are two distinctive Mormon practices. Latter-day Saints believe in the eternal progress of humans from a spiritual state to mortality and then to an afterlife where resurrected individuals will receive their reward. The church lays great emphasis on genealogical research in order that members may undergo vicarious baptismal rites on behalf of their ancestors.

Church members pay a tithe to support numerous church activities and building construction and work on welfare farms or other projects to produce items for the poor. Local members operate the full program in each congregation, including individual weekly meetings for men, women, children, and young people, and two meetings—Sunday School and Sacrament—for the entire church body. Many young men and women devote two years of their lives as missionaries.

Mornay, Philippe de [mohr-nay', fee-leep' duh]

Philippe de Mornay, also known as Philippe Duplessis-Mornay, b. Nov. 5, 1549, d. Nov. 11, 1623, was a French Protestant writer and statesman during the Wars of Religion (1562–98; see RELIGION, WARS OF). He became (1576) counselor to Henry of Navarre, for whom he negotiated (1589) a reconciliation with HENRY III of France. In recognition of his services, Navarre appointed Mornay governor of Saumur. After Navarre became king (1589) as HENRY IV and then converted (1593) to Catholicism, Mornay—who had advocated an alliance of France and the Protestant powers against Catholic Spain—continued to work for toleration of the French Protestants, known as HUGUENOTS.

Mornay later acted (1611) as moderator of the Huguenot assembly at Saumur, which had become a center of the Protestant movement, and opposed the renewal of armed resistance to the crown. His opposition to the policies of Louis XIII brought about his removal from the governorship in 1621.

morning glory

Morning glory is a common name for various herbaceous plants of the morning-glory family, Convolvulaceae, but refers particularly to certain plants of the genus *Ipomoea*, which are annual or perennial vines of warm and tropic regions. Some species of *Ipomoea*, have seeds containing narcotic alkaloids similar to LSD. The common morning glory, *I. purpurea*, native to tropical America, is an annual vine with hairy stems, broad, heart-shaped leaves, and showy, funnel-shaped flowers of blue, purple, pink, or white.

Moro, Aldo [moh'-roh, ahl'-doh]

Aldo Moro, b. Sept. 23, 1916, d. May 9, 1978, was an Italian political leader who headed five governments in the 1960s and '70s.

Moro was first elected to the Chamber of Deputies as a Christian Democrat in 1948 and served (1955–57) as minister of justice. Between 1963 and 1968 he was prime minister in three coalition governments with the Socialists, and in 1974 he became head of a minority government of Christian Democrats and Republicans.

As president of the Christian Democratic party from 1976, Moro helped arrange the inclusion of the Communist party in the Christian Democratic government's official parliamentary majority. Expected to be elected president of Italy in 1978, he was abducted by the terrorist organization the Red Brigades and later killed.

Morocco [muh-rah'-koh]

The Kingdom of Morocco (Arabic: Al Maghrib) is located in northwestern Africa. Bounded by the Atlantic Ocean on the west and the Mediterranean Sea on the north, Morocco is separated from Europe to the north by the Strait of Gibraltar. Morocco's eastern and southern neighbor is Algeria. In the far southwest, Morocco adjoins the disputed territory of WESTERN SAHARA, a former Spanish possession claimed by Morocco.

Morocco became a Muslim country with the Arab conquest in the 7th century. Maintaining independence longer than any of its neighbors, Morocco never came under the control of the Ottoman Empire and was a French, and then a Spanish, protectorate for only 44 years (1912–56). The country regained independence on Mar. 2, 1956.

Land and Resources

In the west a narrow plain stretches along the Atlantic coast. The Mediterranean coast in the north is rimmed by the RIF mountains. Most of Morocco's interior is composed of mountains and plateaus. The major mountain system, the ATLAS MOUNTAINS, consists of three parallel ranges situated in the center of the country and extending for about 2,400 km (1,500 mi). Jebel Toubkal, the nation's highest peak, rises to 4,165 m (13,665 ft) in the southwest. Rolling plateaus east of the mountains gradually lead into the SAHARA.

Alluvial soils predominate along the Atlantic coast, the Rharb Plain in the southwest, and the Moulouya River valley at the Mediterranean coast. Good soils are also found at the oases located in the foothills of the Atlas. Much of the Sahara in Morocco is composed of bare rock outcroppings.

Climate. A Mediterranean climate with warm summers and mild winters prevails in most of the northern lowlands of Morocco. Average temperatures in Rabat are 23° C (74° F) in August and 12° C (54° F) in January. By comparison, temperatures in the region between the coastal strip and the mountains have a greater range and are higher in summer and lower in winter. The Atlas ranges have cool summers and cold winters.

Rainfall is most plentiful in the north and decreases southward. Tangier, located near the Strait of Gibraltar, receives 890 mm (35 in) annually, whereas Agadir, located along the southern Atlantic coast, receives only 230 mm (9 in). Precipitation in the Atlas Mountains av-

KINGDOM OF MOROCCO

Land: Area: 446,550 km² (172,414 mi²). Capital: Rabat (1987 est. pop., 610,00). Largest city: Casablanca (1987 est. pop., 2,904,000).

People: Population (1990 est.): 25,648,241. Density: 57.4 persons per km² (148.8 per mi²). Distribution (1989): 45% urban, 55% rural. Official language: Arabic. Major religion: Islam.

Government: Type: constitutional monarchy. Legislature: Majlis al-Nuwab. Political subdivisions: 35 provinces, 2 prefectures.

Economy: GNP (1989 est.): $21.9 billion; $880 per capita. Labor distribution (1985): agriculture—50%; manufacturing—15%; services—26%. Foreign trade (1989): imports—$5.1 billion; exports—$3.1 billion. Currency: 1 dirham = 100 cents.

Education and Health: Literacy (1985): 33% of adult population. Universities (1987): 6. Hospital beds (1988): 26,066. Physicians (1988): 4,946. Life expectancy (1990): women—66; men—63. Infant mortality (1990): 78 per 1,000 live births.

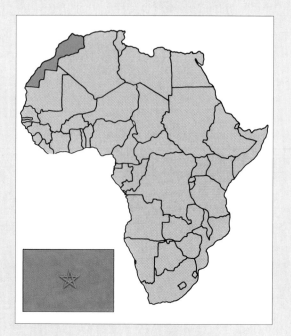

erages more than 1,000 mm (40 in) annually, some of it in the form of snow. In the Sahara, rainfall is unpredictable and amounts to an annual average of 100 mm (4 in).

Drainage. All the rivers of Morocco rise in the Atlas Mountains. The Moulouya flows north, and the Sebou, Oum er Rbia, Sous, and Tensift rivers drain westward to the Atlantic. Rivers flowing southward are seasonal. In summer many of the country's lakes evaporate, and the exposed lake beds are used for agricultural purposes.

Vegetation and Animal Life. Forests of Mediterranean evergreen, cedar, and eucalyptus remain on the mountains at high altitudes. Some of the lower slopes and inland areas have been cleared of trees or are covered with scrub forests. Esparto grass grows over much of eastern Morocco. Animals include camels, mouflons, gazelles, and macaco monkeys.

Resources. Morocco controls 75% of the world's known phosphate reserves (including those in Western Sahara) and has deposits of copper, rock salt, petroleum, iron ore, coal, lead, manganese, and zinc. About 12% of the total land area is forested. Offshore waters contain abundant fish.

People

ARABS constitute the majority of the population, although BERBERS, the original inhabitants, form a larger minority in Morocco than in any other North African country. Most foreign residents are French and Spanish.

Arabic is the official language, but the three Berber dialects remain in use, particularly in mountain areas, and French is still spoken, especially in government and business. Almost all Moroccans adhere to Islam, the official religion.

Demography. Morocco's population has increased steadily, and more than 40% of the total population are under 15 years of age. Migration from rural to urban areas has increased the percentage of urban inhabitants. The historic cities, such as the former capitals FEZ, MARRAKECH, and MEKNES, and the present capital, RABAT, were established during the 10th and 12th centuries. CASABLANCA is the country's largest city and leading port. TANGIER, an international port from 1925 to 1956, became part of Morocco again after independence.

Education and Health. Primary education is free and compulsory for all children between the ages of 7 and 13, and about 75% of them attend school. The Islamic University of Karouine (859) and the secular Muhammad V University (1957) are the country's major institutions of higher education.

Health-care facilities are being expanded, but diseases such as malaria, typhoid, trachoma, tuberculosis, and gastrointestinal infections remain widespread.

Economic Activity

Agriculture contributes about 11% of the gross national product. Commercial agriculture, including cash crops grown for export, is concentrated on the Atlantic coastal plain and in the Rharb basin. Wheat and barley, sugar beets, rice, and cotton constitute the chief crops for domestic consumption, and citrus fruits, winter vegetables, and grapes for wine are the principal export crops. Large, mechanized farms cover about one-third of the land presently available for cultivation and account for 85% of the total agricultural output. There are irrigation projects along most major rivers.

Morocco leads the world in the production and export of phosphates. Manufacturing is concentrated around Casablanca and Rabat. Industries in addition to the processing of phosphates include food processing and the manufacture of textiles, plastics, leather goods, glassware, furniture, machine tools, and electrical equipment. Manufactured goods rose from only 5% of exports in 1970 to 35% in 1986. The fishing industry has also increased in importance. Tourism and salaries earned by Moroccan workers in Western European countries, princi-

pally in France, are significant sources of foreign exchange. In the 1980s and early 1990s the economy was adversely affected by drought, a depressed world market for phosphates, and the continuing costs of the war in Western Sahara.

Government

According to the Constitution of 1972, Morocco is a constitutional monarchy. The king holds executive power; he appoints the prime minister and cabinet and can dismiss cabinet members and disband the legislature. The reigning monarch, HASSAN II, succeeded to the throne in 1961. Members of the unicameral legislature serve six-year terms; two-thirds of them are directly elected. Morocco proper is divided into 35 provinces, each headed by a governor appointed by the king, and two prefectures. There are four additional provinces in disputed Western Sahara.

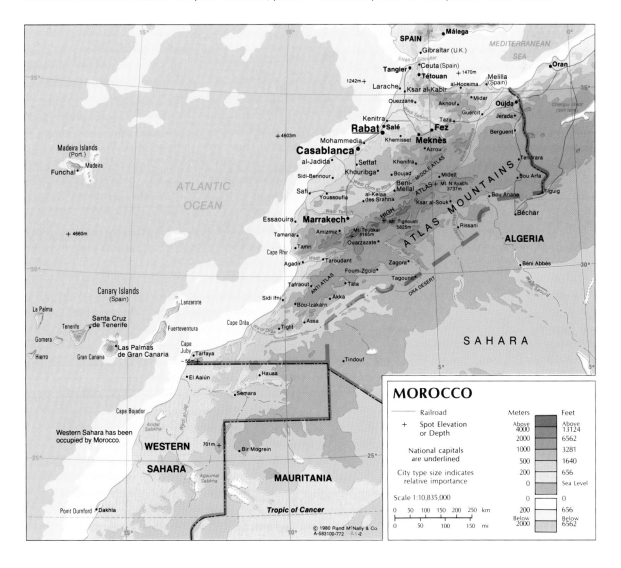

Casablanca, the largest city and principal commercial center of Morocco, is located on the Atlantic Ocean in western Morocco. The city was important during World War II as the site of an Allied landing (1942) and the Casablanca Conference (November 1943).

History

Between 475 and 450 BC, Morocco was colonized by the Carthaginians, who named it Barbary because of the Berber inhabitants. The Romans established a province, Mauretania Tingitana, during the 1st century AD in the area between Tangier and Rabat; however, Berbers remained in possession of the land in the mountains and south of Rabat. Arab proselytizers for Islam arrived in 683. The indigenous Berber people accepted the new religion, and Arab culture and language gradually diffused throughout the land.

The first dynasty to unify all of Morocco under a single government was that of the Berber Almoravids during the 11th century. They subsequently conquered Spain, but in 1174 they were conquered by another Berber dynasty, the Almohads. The Almohads were expelled from Spain in 1212, but they continued to rule in Morocco until the end of the 15th century.

By the 15th century both the Spanish and Portuguese had begun to encroach on Moroccan territory, and the Portuguese had taken the coastal cities of Agadir, Ceuta, and Tangier. *Jihad* (holy Islamic war) was declared against the invaders, culminating in the Battle of Alcazarquivir (1578), in which the Portuguese king SEBASTIAN was killed. Pirates from Morocco and the other BARBARY STATES along the Mediterranean coast of North Africa continued to antagonize the European nations by raiding their ships. The present Alawite dynasty first came to power in 1666, but these sultans controlled very little of their country outside the capital city.

During the 19th century European involvement in Morocco continued. After conquering Algiers in 1830 the French turned their attention westward. In 1884, Spain claimed a protectorate along Morocco's southern coastal zone. Heightened competition among the European powers for control of North Africa culminated in the Moroccan crises of 1905 and 1911–12, in which Germany sought to isolate France diplomatically by impeding its designs in Morocco. In 1911, however, Germany recognized French rights in Morocco, and in 1912 most of the area became a French protectorate.

The first French resident-general, Louis LYAUTEY, was able to extend French control across the mountains, and in 1926, French troops finally subdued the tribal rebellion led by Abd el-Krim. With the invasion of France by Germany in 1940, Morocco remained loyal to the VICHY GOVERNMENT until Allied forces landed in Morocco in November 1942. After World War II, Sultan Muhammad V became the symbol of the growing nationalist movement when the French exiled him. He was reinstated as king after independence in 1956.

In 1976, Spain ceded the northern two-thirds of Spanish Sahara (now Western Sahara) to Morocco and the remainder to Mauritania. Algeria, and later Libya, supported the Polisario Front, a group fighting for Saharan independence. When Mauritania renounced its claim to Western Sahara in 1979, Morocco annexed the entire area, building a fortified wall around most of it and encouraging Moroccan settlement there. A prolonged drought and the costly desert war, which had broad popular support, damaged the Moroccan economy and led to opposition gains in the 1984 parliamentary elections. In 1988, two years after withdrawing from a 1984 treaty of union with Libya, Morocco restored diplomatic relations with Algeria and agreed to direct talks with the Polisario Front. In 1989 voters agreed to postpone elections until 1992 so that a referendum on self-determination could be held in Western Sahara. That same year, Hassan celebrated his 60th birthday with the opening of the world's largest mosque, in Casablanca. Morocco joined the anti-Iraq coalition in the 1991 GULF WAR.

Moroni [moh-roh'-nee] Moroni (1988 est. pop., 22,000), on the island of Grande Comore, is the capital of the Republic of the Comoros. Located at the northern entrance of the Mozambique Channel, the city is a port, trading in vanilla, cacao, and coffee.

Moronobu [moh-roh-noh'-boo] Moronobu, c.1618–1694, was a Japanese print artist, illustrator, and painter who is regarded as one of the major founders of the UKIYO-E genre of decorative prints. He rose to prominence as a book illustrator in Edo (modern Tokyo), where he produced (from 1658) more than 130 black-and-white illustrations; a typical example is the print *Street Scene in the Yoshiwara* (c.1680; Metropolitan Museum of Art,

New York City). Perhaps his finest works are the erotic album designs he executed (1680s) in a graceful linear style. Moronobu is often hailed as the first Ukiyo-e artist to sign his work.

—

Morpheus [mohr'-fee-uhs]   The god of dreams in Greek and Roman mythology, Morpheus was the son of Hypnos (or Somnus), god of sleep. He appeared in dreams in human form and was able to assume the form of any person. Generally portrayed as winged and carrying clusters of poppies, whose seeds he scattered to induce sleep, Morpheus was sometimes represented as a slumbering child.

—

morphine [mohr'-feen]   One of the principal alkaloids of OPIUM, morphine is a narcotic drug used in medicine for its ANALGESIC effects. Morphine is extracted from the dried milky juice of the unripe seed capsule of the opium poppy. It was first isolated by the German chemist F. W. A. Serturner in the early 1800s. Morphine is extremely effective in relieving severe pain, such as that encountered in connection with gallstones and terminal cancer and in cases where other analgesics fail. It is also used for its calming or sedating effects. Morphine has a euphoric effect on patients, as well as side effects that may be manifested in either the respiratory, circulatory, or gastrointestinal system. In addition, morphine has an emetic effect (induces vomiting) and is a general depressant. The most serious consequence of morphine use is addiction. Morphine can be converted into HEROIN, which can be even more addicting than morphine. Synthetic compounds, such as meperidine and METHADONE, have largely replaced morphine in medical use.

See also: DRUG ABUSE; PSYCHOPHARMACOLOGY.

morphology   see PHONOLOGY AND MORPHOLOGY

—

Morrill, Justin S. [mohr'-ul]   The American politician Justin Smith Morrill, b. Strafford, Vt., Apr. 14, 1810, d. Dec. 28, 1898, was often called the father of the Senate for his long service there. Morrill was elected to the U.S. House of Representatives as a Whig from Vermont in 1854, helped organize (1855) the Republican party in Vermont, and served in the U.S. Senate from 1867 until his death. He introduced (1857) the Morrill Act, passed in 1862, which provided for grants of public lands for educational facilities, later called LAND-GRANT COLLEGES. He was responsible for a measure (1890) that supplemented the original grants with monetary aid. Morrill also sponsored the TARIFF ACT of 1861, which inaugurated a period of increasing protectionism.

Morrill Acts   see LAND-GRANT COLLEGES

—

Morris (family)   The Morris family of New York produced three generations of distinguished judges and statesmen. The American line began with **Richard Morris**, d. 1672,

Cromwellian soldier and Barbados merchant, who bought land north of the Harlem River. His son **Lewis Morris**, b. Oct. 15, 1671, d. May 21, 1746, acquired the 2,000-acre (809-ha) manor "Morrisania," plus 3,500 acres (1,416 ha) in New Jersey; he was chief justice of New York (1715–33) and governor of New Jersey (1738–46).

Lewis's son **Robert Hunter Morris**, b. c.1700, d. Jan. 27, 1764, inherited the Jersey estate and served as chief justice of New Jersey (1738–64) and governor of Pennsylvania (1754–56). Robert's son, **Robert Morris**, b. c.1745, d. June 2, 1815, was also chief justice of New Jersey and a federal district court judge (1789–1815). Lewis's son **Lewis Morris II**, 1698–1762, tended to the manor, but his sons continued the tradition of government service. His marriage to Tryntje Staats produced **Lewis Morris, Jr.**, b. Apr. 8, 1726, d. Jan. 22, 1798, third lord of the manor, lawyer, judge, militia general, state senator, and signer of the Declaration of Independence; **Staats Long Morris**, 1728–1800, a British army officer who served in India; and **Richard Morris**, 1730–1810, chief justice of New York. Another son, **Gouverneur Morris**, b. Jan. 31, 1752, d. Nov. 6, 1816, was born to Lewis II and Sarah Gouverneur Morris. He sat in the Provincial and Continental Congresses and coauthored the New York State Constitution; on moving to Philadelphia in 1780, he represented Pennsylvania in the Federal Convention of 1787. He served briefly as minister to England and France in the 1790s and as U.S. senator from New York (1800–03).

—

Morris, Esther   Esther Morris, b. Tioga County, N.Y., Aug. 8, 1814, d. Apr. 2, 1902, was called the mother of woman suffrage in Wyoming. Settling in Wyoming Territory in 1869, she was reportedly instrumental in securing passage (1869) in the territorial legislature of the bill, the first in the nation, granting women the vote. Morris was also the first woman justice of the peace (1870) in the United States.

—

Morris, Robert (artist)   The American artist Robert Morris, b. Kansas City, Mo., Feb. 9, 1931, has been associated with a variety of sculptural, environmental, and conceptual art movements. Influenced by Jackson Pollock in the 1950s, by the early 1960s he had begun to work in severe, impersonal geometric forms, such as the nine steel units of *Untitled* (1967; Guggenheim Museum, New York City). Morris's cubes, L shapes, and rectangles became central to the development of the minimalist movement (see MINIMAL ART). Subsequently he abandoned clarity of form in favor of EARTHWORKS. During the 1980s, Morris exhibited large works combining painting, sculpture, and architecture. Many of these ambitiously conceived pieces are based on images from concentration camps.

—

Morris, Robert (merchant)   Robert Morris, b. Jan. 31, 1734, d. May 8, 1806, was an American merchant and revolutionary leader who came to be known as the financier of the American Revolution. After emigrating from England in 1747, he settled in Philadelphia, where he became a partner in Willing, Morris and Co., one of the largest mercantile firms in the British North American colonies. In 1775 he was made a member of the Pennsylvania Council of Safety. A member of the Continental Congress from 1775 until 1778, he was a signer of the Declaration of Independence. He rendered invaluable service on purchasing committees.

In 1781, Congress, in an attempt to bring order to the financial chaos of the new nation, made Morris superintendent of finances. During his tenure (1781–84), Morris brought greater efficiency into accounting and military purchasing, worked toward the establishment of a national mint, and organized the Bank of North America, the nation's first bank.

An advocate of strong government, he was a member of the Constitutional Convention of 1787. As U.S. senator from Pennsylvania (1789–95) he supported the programs of the Federalist party. Because of overinvestment in western lands, Morris was arrested for debt in 1798 and forced into bankruptcy; after his release (1801) from debtor's prison he lived on his wife's annuity.

Morris, William   The English poet and socialist William Morris, b. Mar. 24, 1834, d. Oct. 3, 1896, was also the most important designer-artisan of the late Victorian era. Leader of the ARTS AND CRAFTS MOVEMENT, Morris valued artisanship over mechanical production. He designed and manufactured objects in a Gothic style using manual skills and simple machinery, believing that the beauty of handmade objects was an expression of the artisan's joy in everyday work.

In 1856, after meeting Dante Gabriel Rossetti, the leader of the PRE-RAPHAELITES, Morris abandoned architecture for painting. Between 1857 and 1859, Morris lived with the painter Edward Burne-Jones in London, where they designed and decorated furniture. At the same time, under the guidance of Rossetti, they were involved in decorating the Oxford Union Debating Hall with frescoed scenes from Lord Tennyson's medieval romance "Mort d'Arthur" (1842). At Oxford Morris met Jane Burden, whom he married in 1859 and for whom he commissioned Philip Webb to build the Red House at Upton in Kent. This led to the foundation (1861) of the decorating firm Morris, Marshall, Faulkner, and Company.

The firm produced stained glass, metalwork, jewelry, sculpture, embroidery, and furniture that were first publicly shown at the London International Exhibition of 1862. At this time Morris also attempted to print wallpapers himself, but since 1864 all of the firm's wallpapers have been printed by Jeffrey & Co. (until 1930) and Sanderson and Son, Ltd. In 1865 the firm moved to larger premises, and George Warrington Taylor was appointed business manager; Taylor encouraged the development of such inexpensive, functional furniture as the rush-seated

Sussex chair (1864) and the Morris chair with adjustable back (1866). During the 1870s and early 1880s, Morris designed patterns for machine-made carpets, wallpapers, and printed and woven textiles. Morris's interest in weaving, dyeing, and cotton printing led him to look for additional factory premises. In 1880 he established at Hammersmith, London, a workshop for the production of hand-knotted carpets; in 1881 he discovered an old silk-weaving factory at Merton Abbey, Surrey, where he produced tapestries, woven fabric, and printed chintzes. At the end of 1889, Morris decided to set up his own printing press; the Kelmscott Press, which produced beautifully printed books from 1891, occupied him until his death. During the last three decades of his life, Morris also wrote poetry and prose romances and from 1883 was engaged as a socialist in writing and public speaking.

Today Morris's poems, although a valuable record of his enthusiasm for medieval culture and Norse mythology, command less interest than his wallpaper designs and socialist theories. His contribution to the theory and practice of INDUSTRIAL DESIGN continues to exert a profound influence on modern thought.

William Morris's triumph as a book printer was the Kelmscott Chaucer (1896), illustrated by his partner, Edward Burne-Jones. Seen here is the richly ornate colophon page, containing the conclusion of the text and an emblematic drawing from Chaucer's Troilus and Criseyde.

Morris, Wright   Wright Morris, b. Central City, Nebr., Jan. 6, 1910, is an American novelist whose work, which frequently explores relations between the folklore of the American past and contemporary society, bears some affinities to the tales of Mark Twain. His first novel, *My Uncle Dudley* (1942), set in the 1920s, is the rambling narrative of a small boy who travels across the United States in an old car in company with an aging vagabond. Wright's later work includes *The Home Place* (1948), illustrated with his own photographs; *The World in the Attic* (1949); and *Field of Vision* (1956), for which he won a National Book Award.

morris dance The morris dance is the English version of a FOLK DANCE that probably originated in 15th-century Spain (where it was called the *Moresca* or *Morisco*, both meaning "Moorish"), as a Moorish dance, or in imitation of one. In rural England, the dance was a feature of May Day celebrations and was performed by six dancers in bizarre costumes, with bells tied around their ankles and occasionally with blackened faces. The dance is part pantomime, using such stock characters as a Fool, Maid Marian, the Queen of the May, and a hobbyhorse to mime traditional stories.

Morrison, Robert Robert Morrison, b. England, Jan. 5, 1782, d. Aug. 1, 1834, was the first Protestant missionary to China. In 1807 he was sent to Guangzhou (Canton); he traveled via the United States because the British East India Company would not transport missionaries.

The imperial edicts against foreigners and their religions made his first years in China difficult. Seven years were required for him to make his first convert. Meanwhile he learned Chinese and translated the Bible—the New Testament in 1814 and the Old Testament four years later. His greatest work was a 6-volume Chinese dictionary (1815–25). Morrison also sought to spread appreciation of Chinese culture and civilization in the West.

Morrison, Toni The novelist Toni Morrison, b. Chloe Anthony Wofford in Lorain, Ohio, Feb. 18, 1931, has shown an extraordinary insight into the maturation of her African-American characters. *The Bluest Eye* (1970) traces a black child's descent into madness, and *Sula* (1973) traces the estrangement of childhood friends through their different definitions of adulthood. *Song of Solomon* (1977) tells of a black man's discovery of his identity in the achievements of previous generations. *Tar Baby* (1981) is a fable of race and eroticism. Morrison's novel *Beloved* (1987; Pulitzer Prize) knits together her previous themes and adds the supernatural in a story about slavery.

Morristown A town in northern New Jersey along both banks of the narrow Whippany River, Morristown is the seat of Morris County and has a population of 16,189 (1990). It is primarily a residential city. The area was settled about 1710. Morristown was a key point in the American Revolution, and Washington and his army were quartered there in the winters of 1776–77 and 1779–80. Samuel F. B. Morse and Alfred Vail perfected the magnetic telegraph there. Morristown National Historic Park includes Revolutionary War objects.

Morrow, Dwight Dwight Whitney Morrow, b. Huntington, W.Va., Jan. 11, 1873, d. Oct. 5, 1931, an American lawyer, banker, reformer, and diplomat, helped to improve U.S.-Mexican relations. Morrow served on various New Jersey state commissions, helping to write a workmen's compensation law, to improve the prisons, and to reform state agencies. As U.S. ambassador to Mexico (1927–30), he helped to resolve a disagreement over oil rights, to improve relations between the Mexican government and the Roman Catholic church, and to set into motion a policy of Mexican-U.S. cooperation. A Republican, Morrow was elected U.S. senator from New Jersey in 1930. He was the father of Anne Morrow Lindbergh.

Morse, Jedidiah [jed-uh-dy'-uh] Jedidiah Morse, b. Woodstock, Conn., Aug. 23, 1761, d. June 9, 1826, often called the father of American geography, was also a prominent Congregational minister. Morse wrote *Geography Made Easy* (1784), the first book published in the United States on American geography.

Morse, Samuel F. B. Samuel Finley Breese Morse, b. Charleston, Mass., Apr. 27, 1791, d. Apr. 2, 1872, achieved distinction both as an artist, particularly as a painter of miniatures, and as an inventor. Morse was the son of Jedidiah Morse. He was educated at Yale College but also went to Europe for art training. It was during the return voyage from one such trip (1832) that he conceived of an electromagnetic signaling system.

Although Morse continued with his artistic activities in New York and became first president of the National Academy of Design, serving from 1826 to 1845, his main activity after 1837 was the development of an electric TELEGRAPH. Systems making use of a deflecting magnetic needle had already been developed by a number of workers, particularly Sir William Cooke and Sir Charles Wheatstone, who installed the first railway telegraph system in

The American inventor and artist Samuel F. B. Morse developed the electric telegraph and the signaling code used with it. On May 24, 1844, Morse wired Congress the message "What hath God wrought!" and inaugurated instantaneous long-distance communication.

England in 1837. Morse's important contribution was that he based his receiver on the ELECTROMAGNET. This feature ultimately ensured the universal adoption of his system. When the electromagnet was energized by a pulse of current from the sender, a soft iron armature with a pen or pencil attached to it was attracted to the magnet, producing a V-shaped deflection in the straight line being recorded on a moving strip of paper. The grouping of a succession of such marks symbolized the words of a message.

Morse soon devised a code whereby letters and numbers were represented by combinations of dot-and-dash symbols, which corresponded to signals of short and long duration (see MORSE CODE). With the aid of Alfred Vail, the original receiver was greatly improved and adapted to print the dot-and-dash symbols. Such a system was used in the first U.S. telegraph link that Morse set up in 1844 between Baltimore, Md., and Washington, D.C. Morse defended his patent vigorously and secured recognition by the Supreme Court in 1854. He also held a chair in natural science at Yale.

___

Morse, Wayne Lyman   Wayne Lyman Morse, b. Madison, Wis., Oct. 20, 1900, d. July 22, 1974, was an American legal scholar whose career in the U.S. Senate (1945–69) was notable for his liberal positions on social issues and for his opposition to the Vietnam War. Morse served (1931–44) as dean of the University of Oregon Law School and was a nationally known labor mediator when he entered the Senate as a liberal Republican in 1945. He left the Republican party and became an independent in 1953 but joined the Democrats in 1956. His opposition to the Vietnam War led to his defeat in 1968. Morse won the 1974 Democratic nomination for the Senate but died before the election.

___

Morse code   Morse code is a SIGNALING code first devised by Samuel F. B. MORSE in 1838 for use with his electromagnetic TELEGRAPH. The code used two basic symbols or signaling elements: the "dot," a short-duration electric current, which gave a quick deflection of the armature of Morse's receiver and so caused a dot to be printed on the strip of paper moving beneath the ink pen carried by the armature; and the "dash," a longer-duration signal that caused a dash to be printed. Using this code, the various alphanumeric characters (letters and numerals) that compose a message could be represented by groups of these two signal elements. In the International Morse code, for example, one dot followed by one dash (• -) symbolizes the letter A; the number *seven* appears as "dash dash dot dot dot" (-- •••). The dot-and-dash elements are separated by an interval that has the duration of one dot; the dash has a duration equal to three dots. The space between characters, whether letters or numbers, is equal to three dot units; the separation between words is six units. Morse's code rapidly gained acceptance and evolved into several forms—Early Morse, American Morse, and International Morse. In its international form it is still in use.

Although Morse devised his code for use with a printing telegraph, he and his colleague Alfred Vail soon realized that messages could easily be read from the sound of the clicking armature. When the printer was replaced by a simple buzzer, the operator could read the message from the sequence of dots and dashes. Radio telegraphy was introduced in 1897, and Morse code was again employed. In early use the radio signal would cause a sensitive relay to operate the local printer or buzzer circuit. Similarly, Morse code was applied to the left and right beats of the needle of the submarine telegraph and the light flashes produced by a signaling lamp used on ships at sea. Morse's work dominated signal coding until well into the 20th century.

mortality   see DEMOGRAPHY; LIFE SPAN; POPULATION

___

mortar   A mortar is a short-barreled weapon used to fire relatively slow-moving projectiles in high-angle trajectories. Originally a stubby, wide-bored barrel (early mortars had barrel lengths only 1½ to 2 times the bore diameter) used as an artillery weapon, by World War I the mortar had become an important infantry weapon, highly effective in trench warfare. The 1915 Stokes mortar was a lightweight tube; the shell was dropped into the tube's muzzle, and a firing pin mounted in the tube's base ignited the shell's propellant. Contemporary mortars are usually variations of the Stokes and use solid-rocket or explosive propellants. Lightweight and simple to operate, their portability and low cost have made them a favored weapon in guerrilla warfare.

Morte Darthur   see ARTHUR AND ARTHURIAN LEGEND

mortgage A mortgage is the pledging of property by a borrower to a lender as security for the payment of a debt. A familiar example is the home mortgage: the mortgagor (buyer) gives a mortgage on the house being bought to the mortgagee (a bank, savings and loan association, or other institution that deals in mortgage loans), which provides money for the transaction. The buyer agrees to repay the principal amount of the loan and interest in a specified period of time, usually 20 to 30 years. In most states a mortgage gives the mortgagee a LIEN—as opposed to the common-law practice of granting condition title—on the house or property as security for the loan. If the borrower fails to make payments on the loan and interest due, the lender may begin foreclosure proceedings, through which the property is sold in order to satisfy the claim of the lender. A person with no real estate may borrow by giving a bank or loan company a chattel mortgage on personal property, such as a car, as security for a loan. Corporations often borrow by issuing mortgage bonds, which are secured by mortgages on their business property. In the United States, interest-rate ceilings for mortgages, as for other forms of credit, vary from state to state.

The owner of a mortgaged house who wants to obtain another loan sometimes applies for another mortgage, which is called a second mortgage because it is second in priority to the first mortgage. The interest charged on a second mortgage is higher than that on a first mortgage. In case of foreclosure, the holder of the second mortgage can recover only after the first mortgage holder has been paid.

The U.S. government has entered the mortgage market to make it easier for home buyers to obtain mortgages. The Federal Housing Administration (FHA) insures mortgages by private lenders, and the Department of Veterans Affairs guarantees part of the principal on loans made to veterans. The FEDERAL NATIONAL MORTGAGE ASSOCIATION is a privately owned corporation established to buy and sell government-backed mortgages.

Mortimer (family) The Mortimers were an Anglo-Norman family that settled on the Welsh marches (the frontier area along the English border) in the 11th century and later became one of the richest and most powerful families in the kingdom of England.

Ralph de Mortimer, d. *c.*1104, settled in the marches and acquired holdings, chiefly in Herefordshire and Shropshire, that included Wigmore. A descendant, **Roger de Mortimer**, d. 1282, increased the family's wealth and power through an advantageous marriage. Often at war with the Welsh prince Llewelyn Gruffyd, Roger supported King EDWARD I of England against Llewelyn in 1277. Roger's grandson, **Roger de Mortimer, 1st earl of March**, b. *c.*1287, d. Nov. 29, 1330, became the lover of Isabella of France, queen of EDWARD II.

The Mortimers established a claim to the English throne through the marriage of **Edmund de Mortimer, 3d earl of March and 1st earl of Ulster**, 1351–81, to Philippa, a granddaughter of Edward III. Their grandson, **Edmund de Mortimer, 5th earl of March and 3d earl of Ul-**ster, 1391–1425, was imprisoned after the Lancastrian HENRY IV usurped the throne in 1399. His uncle **Sir Edmund Mortimer**, 1376–1409, joined with Owen GLENDOWER and the PERCY family in an unsuccessful rebellion against Henry. The 5th earl was released from prison in 1413, served Henry V, and became (1422) a member of the regency council of Henry VI. On his death the family estates passed to his sister Anne, who had married Richard, earl of Cambridge, also descended from Edward III. Their son was Richard, duke of York (see YORK dynasty).

Morton, Jelly Roll The jazz pianist and composer Ferdinand Joseph La Menthe "Jelly Roll" Morton, b. Gulfport, La., Sept. 20, 1885, d. July 10, 1941, was one of the first great New Orleans jazz artists and orchestrators and perhaps the first jazz theorist. Morton learned his art as a RAGTIME pianist in New Orleans bordellos and then played in other cities as a part-time musician; he was also a pool shark, vaudeville comic, and nightclub owner. His most memorable recordings were made in the 1920s: a number of piano pieces recorded in 1923–24, and a series of instrumentals (1926–30) made with his group, The Red Hot Peppers.

Morton was proud to the point of arrogance both of his talents and of his Creole heritage, which separated him, he felt, from his black jazz colleagues. His claim to have invented JAZZ is treated seriously by many musicologists. The recordings Morton made (1938) for the Library of Congress are an invaluable contribution to the history of jazz.

Morton, Levi P. Levi Parsons Morton, b. Shoreham, Vt., May 16, 1824, d. May 16, 1920, was an American banker and vice-president of the United States (1889–93) under Benjamin Harrison. He founded (1863) Levi P. Morton and Company, a banking firm that helped float the government's Civil War loans. In 1869 the firm became Morton, Bliss and Company and embarked on broad international operations as a leading business agent for the U.S. government. Morton served as a U.S. representative (1879–81), as minister to France (1881–85), and as governor of New York (1895–97).

Morton, Oliver Oliver Perry Morton, b. Salisbury, Ind., Aug. 4, 1823, d. Nov. 1, 1877, an American political leader, served (1861–67) as governor of Indiana during the U.S. Civil War. He helped organize the Republican party in Indiana, firmly backed Abraham Lincoln, and helped finance the state's war effort through private contributions and federal loans. As a U.S. senator (1867–77), Morton was a radical Republican, supporting thorough RECONSTRUCTION in the South.

Morton, Thomas Thomas Morton, d. *c.*1647, an English fur trader and adventurer, settled *c.*1624 at Merry Mount (now Quincy), Mass., and came into frequent conflict with his Pilgrim and Puritan neighbors. He was arrested three times on such charges as licentiousness and selling firearms to the Indians and was deported twice to England.

▬

Mosaddeq, Muhammad   The militant Iranian prime minister Muhammad Mosaddeq, b. 1880, d. Mar. 5, 1967, nationalized the country's oil resources in 1951. Mosaddeq (whose name also appears as Mossadegh or Mussadegh) was educated in Europe and well connected. He held major ministerial portfolios and was elected (1923) to the Iranian parliament, but he earned the enmity of REZA SHAH PAHLAVI, who became shah in 1925 and caused Mosaddeq's retirement from parliament that year.

Following Reza Shah's abdication (1941), Mosaddeq gained a reputation as an honest, uncompromising nationalist equally opposed to Russian and British interference in Iranian affairs. In 1951 he became prime minister. When he attempted to dethrone Reza Shah's son and successor, MUHAMMAD REZA SHAH PAHLAVI, in 1953, however, Iran's army—backed by U.S. aid—toppled Mosaddeq. He was imprisoned for three years and spent his last years under house arrest.

▬

mosaic   Mosaic is the art of embedding small pieces of cut stone or pigmented glass in a plaster bed to serve as floor or wall decoration. Developed principally in ancient Greece, mosaic was a leading artistic medium in the Greco-Roman world and reached its greatest heights in Early Christian art and architecture and Byzantine art and architecture.

Solidity, resistance to moisture, durability, and colorfastness made mosaic a practical form of architectural decoration in the warm and humid areas of the Mediterranean basin. The process of constructing a mosaic begins with cubes of cut stone, pigmented glass, or gold or silver leaf sandwiched by glass. These cubes, known as tesserae (singular: tessera), average 1 to 2 cm^2 (0.155 to 0.310 in^2) in size; highly detailed and refined work can demand tesserae one-tenth as large.

Classical and Hellenistic Mosiacs.   The sophisticated mosaics of the classical and medieval worlds evolved from the practice, widespread in ancient Crete and Anatolia, of gathering pebbles from the beach and setting them in a cement bed to provide durable flooring in homes and temples. About 400 BC, pebble mosaics began to take pictorial form. In these early efforts, such as the Bellerophon mosaic (before 348 BC; Olynthos, Greece), white pebbles were set in a black-pebble background in order to depict mythological figures and scenes. In the 3d century BC, cut stones were combined with pebbles for more detailed renderings and to widen the range of colors.

Pebble mosaics were largely displaced in the Hellenistic era (323–31 BC) by tessellated mosaics of cut stone, colored glass paste, and occasionally of mother-of-pearl, shells, and terra-cotta. Important Hellenistic schools of mosaicists were located at Alexandria in Egypt and Pergamum in Anatolia. Prefabricated mosaic panels, called emblemata, were exported from these cities and were used as the centerpieces for mosaic pavements that became (3d century BC) the fashion in the homes and villas of the wealthy throughout the Mediterranean area and the Near East.

Roman Mosaics.   Hellenistic examples served as models for Roman mosaics until the 1st century AD, when polychrome pictorial mosaics were displaced by a black-and-white mosaic style (see ROMAN ART AND ARCHITECTURE). Roman settlers conveyed mosaic art to the farthest reaches of the Empire. Some of the finest Roman mosaics outside Italy have been found in North Africa and Syria. Athletic contests, the circus, seascapes, and scenes from mythology were popular subjects in Late Roman floor mosaics. Geometric pavements carpeted innumerable secular and religious buildings in the 4th and 5th centuries with colorful and intricate patterns, including the cosmographical and topographical designs favored in Greek and Near Eastern churches. A last, nostalgia-laden effort at emulating classical mosaics appears in the beautiful hunting vignettes bordered by a lush vine scroll that paved the huge court of the imperial palace in Constantinople (now Istanbul), a late-6th-century testimonial to the survival in Byzantine art of classical motifs and styles.

Early Christian and Byzantine Mosaics.   Mosaic as a form of wall decoration achieved its greatest expression in EARLY CHRISTIAN ART AND ARCHITECTURE and BYZANTINE ART AND ARCHITECTURE. The earliest example of the extensive use of mosaic as wall covering is preserved in Rome's Santa Costanza (c.350), the mausoleum of one of the daughters of Emperor Constantine I. Floor mosaics include a splendid version of the popular Hellenistic motif called the "unswept floor"—a scattering of branches, shells, pitchers, bowls, and birds that might have littered a floor after a banquet. Perhaps the richest Early Christian mosaics are those executed for the churches, baptisteries, and mausoleums of RAVENNA in the 5th and 6th centuries. In the Mausoleum of Galla Placidia (c.430), patterns of rosettes, meanders, ribbons, and vine scrolls set against a brilliant blue ground cover the vaults, while figurative scenes fill flat areas of wall and a vision of the cross crowns the swirling, star-studded heaven of the dome. The play of light on the polished, tessellated, curving surfaces of the vaults in this and other buildings produces effects unmatched in MURAL PAINTING. The shimmering surface and the impression of flickering images and of movement render mosaic a lively and luxurious form of decoration.

In the octagonal Church of SAN VITALE (526–47), Ravenna, the sanctuary is decorated with an elaborate mosaic program. Figures appear to be weightless and without volume, overlapping and impinging on one another like cutouts. This dematerialization of physical form, basic to Byzantine art, was used to great effect in mosaics, where beautifully costumed figures seem to hover weightlessly before a golden surface.

In Constantinople, the center of Byzantine civilization, relatively few schemes of mosaic decoration are preserved

The Empress Theodora and Her Retinue (left), *a 6th-century companion piece to the mosaic of the emperor Justinian in the Church of San Vitale, Ravenna, Italy, exemplifies the static figural representation and the brilliant use of color characteristic of Byzantine art. The mosaics of San Vitale are notable for the regularity of size and shape of the tesserae, as seen in the detail* (below) *of Theodora's head.*

because of natural loss and the destruction wrought by iconoclasts, the Crusaders, and the Ottoman Turks. HAGIA SOPHIA, the focus of Byzantine spiritual life, retains little of its original mosaic decoration, but what remains testifies to the unparalleled achievements of Byzantine mosaicists. Larger-than-life figures of the Virgin and Saint John flank the central figure of Christ in the *Deësis*, a mosaic probably executed in the 13th century. Small, finely graded tesserae are closely set in patterns and lines that suggest the sculptured planes of the faces and depict in detail the Virgin's locks of hair and the saint's beard. The mosaicists' precise placement of the tesserae adds to the quality and power of the design; by varying the cubes' angles of insertion into the plaster bed, the artists were able to differentiate, for example, between the golden halos and the golden ground.

In the 11th century, Byzantine artists perfected a decorative scheme in which the symbolic associations of different parts of a church are enhanced by the selection and hierarchy of figures and scenes. Epitomizing this canon of mosaic decoration is the interior of the small 11th-century monastery church at Daphni, near Athens. In the church's dome, the symbol of heaven, is a huge image of Christ Pantocrator, Lord of the Universe; circling the drum are 16 Old Testament prophets. The apse, the next-highest surface, holds an image of the Virgin. Prophets are situated in the drum of the dome. On the wall areas in and around the nave are scenes from Christ's earthly life, including, in the squinches beneath the dome, the Annunciation, the Nativity, the Baptism, and the Transfiguration. Lowest in the hierarchy and placed closest to the faithful are images of saints and martyrs. In addition to symbolizing the microcosm, this decorative scheme evokes the church calendar and local cults, for

the scenes illustrating Christ's life parallel the major festivals of the Christian year, and the saints and martyrs represented include those both universally and locally revered.

The refinement of mosaic is evident in the small icons of miniature mosaic intended for private devotion. The tesserae, never larger than 1 mm (.039 in), are set in wax on a wooden plaque. The icons range in size from 5×10 cm (2×4 in) to 20×25 cm (8×10 in). One of the most exquisite examples is *Saint John Chrysostom* (12.7×17.8 cm/5×7 in; Dumbarton Oaks Collections, Washington, D.C.), executed in Constantinople in the first half of the 14th century.

Economic factors and a change in aesthetic standards contributed to the decline of mosaic after the 14th century. Because it emphasizes the surface it covers, mosaic and the new aesthetic stressing figural volume and spatial depth came into conflict. Fresco, more suited to this aesthetic and far less expensive, then became the leading form of mural decoration in Europe.

Other Medieval Mosaics. The nature of its materials and production made mosaic a luxury art prized by Western emperors, princes of the church and state, and wealthy individuals. In medieval Rome the popes kept the art of mosaic alive by sponsoring mosaics in new churches and by restoring works in older churches. The attempt to revive the spirit of Early Christianity during the Carolingian period (see CAROLINGIAN ART AND ARCHITECTURE) resulted in the building and decoration of a number of churches following traditional architectural types and decorative schemes, as at Santa Maria in Dominica (early 9th century) in Rome. Charlemagne, who was crowned emperor in Rome, was so impressed by its art that he ordered mosaics installed in his octagonal palace chapel (792–805) at Aix-la-Chapelle (now Aachen) and elsewhere.

Byzantine mosaicists were called to other cultures to beautify secular and religious monuments. Islamic caliphs, for example, employed Byzantine mosaicists in the 7th and 8th centuries to decorate the Dome of the Rock (c.700) in Jerusalem and the Great Mosque (c.715) in Damascus. During the 11th century, Constantinopolitan artists worked in new churches in Kiev, where, by adapting standardized decorative schemes and training local assistants, they helped implant Byzantine culture in Russia. The Norman rulers of Sicily also employed teams of Byzantine mosaicists to decorate their churches and chapels, as in Monreale Cathedral (c.1180–90).

In northern Italy, Byzantine-inspired mosaics fill the churches of Venice and of the neighboring island of Torcello. The decorative program in Saint Mark's Church (see SAINT MARK'S BASILICA), executed in the 12th and 13th centuries by successive generations of local artists, has Byzantine antecedents, but it is largely a Venetian creation.

The Modern Era. After the 14th century the art of mosaic was all but abandoned. Only with the GOTHIC REVIVAL, beginning in the 18th century, were mosaics used once again for architectural decoration, as in the Houses of Parliament (1840–65; see WESTMINSTER PALACE) in London and in the basilica of Sacré-Coeur (1875–1914) in Paris. In the 20th century, mosaics have been revived as appropriate decorations for harsh urban environments that demand durable surface adornment, such as the Mexico City subway system (opened 1968).

mosaic disease   see DISEASES, PLANT

mosasaur [moh'-zuh-sohr]   Mosasaurs were large (up to 12.2 m/40 ft long) marine lizards of Late Cretaceous age (100 to 65 million years ago). Distant relatives of the existing monitor lizards, mosasaurs evolved exceptional adaptations for swimming, including paddlelike limbs and a broad, rudderlike tail. They probably fed mostly on fish; one species had bulbous teeth, suggesting that it fed mostly on mollusks. Their remains, distributed worldwide, are common in the chalk deposits of western Kansas. The first specimen, found in 1780 in a mine at Maastricht, Holland, later became a celebrated prize of war when that city fell to Napoleon in 1795. The name alludes to the Meuse River, near Maastricht.

Mosby, John Singleton [mawz'-bee]   John Singleton Mosby, b. Edgemont, Va., Dec. 6, 1833, d. May 30, 1916, won fame as a Confederate scout and guerrilla leader during the U.S. Civil War. In December 1862, Mosby was authorized to create an independent cavalry battalion that came to be called the Partisan Rangers. The rangers operated mainly in northern Virginia and Maryland, an area dubbed "Mosby's Confederacy." The guerrilla operations that Mosby led behind enemy lines may have delayed the war's end for several months. Entering politics as a Republican after the war, Mosby held various minor government positions.

Mosconi, Willie [mohs-koh'-nee]   William Joseph Mosconi, b. Philadelphia, June 21, 1913, is generally considered the greatest pocket billiards player of all time. His father, a billiard parlor proprietor, forbade his learning the game, but he practiced in secret. A scarcity of jobs during the 1930s led Mosconi, at the age of 19, to join the staff of a billiard equipment manufacturer. He went on to win the world pocket billiards championship 14 times during the period 1941–57.

During Mosconi's career few challengers won a single game from him, and he set a record (now surpassed) by pocketing consecutively 526 balls without a miss. After retiring from competition, Mosconi devoted his time to promoting the sport through exhibition play and publicity.

Moscow   Moscow (Russian: Moskva) is the capital and largest city of the Russian Federation and the former headquarters of the world Communist movement. With the collapse of the USSR in 1991, Moscow lost its position as capital of an empire, but it remains the seat of the Russian government and one of the world's major cities. It is located in the center of the Russian Plain on the Moscow River, a tributary of the Oka, which in turn flows to the Volga River. It has long, cold winters, and hot, humid summers. The population is 8,801,500 (1991 est.), and the city's area is 879 km^2 (339mi^2). The city limits were expanded in 1960 as far as a newly built multilane ring highway. Nearly half the city area comprises forests, parks, and other greenery.

Moscow's main thoroughfares radiate outward from the Kremlin at the city center, connected by a succession of broad, circular streets. The historical heart of Moscow, within the Sadovaya Ring, has remained largely unreconstructed. New residential areas and other new construction projects are located mainly on the outer fringes of the city. The population is overwhelmingly ethnic Russian.

Economy. Moscow is Russia's leading manufacturing center, producing a wide range of machinery and

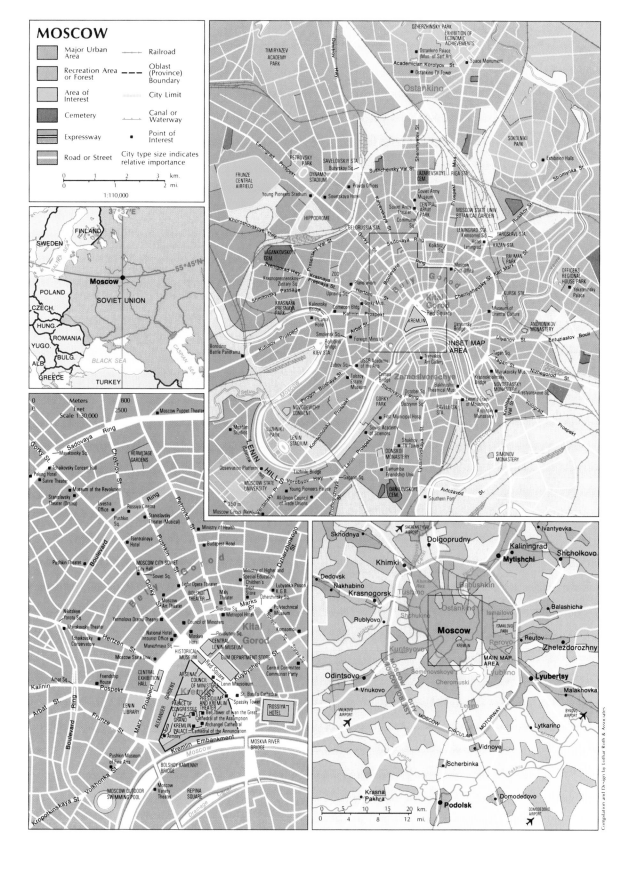

MOSCOW

Legend

- Major Urban Area
- Recreation Area or Forest
- Area of Interest
- Cemetery
- Expressway
- Road or Street

- Railroad
- Oblast (Province) Boundary
- City Limit
- Canal or Waterway
- Point of Interest

City type size indicates relative importance

0   1   2   3 km.
0   1   2 mi.

1:110,000

Locator map

37°37'E
55°45'N

SWEDEN
FINLAND
POLAND
CZECH.
HUNG.
YUGO.
ALB.
ROMANIA
BULG.
GREECE
TURKEY

Moscow

SOVIET UNION

BALTIC SEA
BLACK SEA
CASPIAN SEA

Central inset map

Meters 800
Feet 2500
Scale 1:30,000

Gorky St.
Sadovaya Ring
Mayakovsky Sq.
HERMITAGE GARDENS
Tchaikovsky Concert Hall
Peking Hotel
Satire Theater
Stanislavsky Theater (Drama)
Izvestia Office
Pushkin Sq.
Museum of the Revolution
Rossiya Cinema
Stanislavsky Theater (Musical)
Pushkin Theater
Moscow Puppet Theater
Tsentralnaya Hotel
Budapest Hotel
MOSCOW CITY SOVIET (City Hall)
Soviet Sq.
Light Opera Theater
BOLSHOI THEATER
Maly Theater
Ministry of Higher and Special Education
Children's Dept. Store
Lubyanka Prison K.G.B.
Dzerzhinsky Sq.
Polytechnical Museum
Moscow Art Theater
Sverdlov Sq.
Metropol Hotel
Niikitskye Vorota Sq.
Mayakovsky Theater
Yermolova Drama Theater
Council of Ministers
Komsomol
Tchaikovsky Conservatory
National Hotel Intourist Office
Manezhnaya Sq.
Revolution Sq.
Moskvy Hotel
CENTRAL LENIN MUSEUM
Moscow State Univ.
HISTORICAL MUSEUM
GUM DEPARTMENT STORE
Central Committee Communist Party
ARSENAL
COUNCIL OF MINISTERS
Friendship House
CENTRAL EXHIBITION HALL
Arbat Sq.
Kalinin
Arbat St.
Frunze St.
LENIN LIBRARY
PALACE OF CONGRESSES
GRAND KREMLIN PALACE
PRESIDIUM AND KREMLIN THEATER
Spassky Tower
St. Basil's Cathedral
Bell Tower of Ivan the Great
Archangel Cathedral
Cathedral of the Assumption
Cathedral of the Annunciation
Armory
Lenin Mausoleum
ROSSIYA HOTEL
Red Square
Kremlin
Kitai Gorod
Bely Gorod
Pushkin Museum of Fine Arts
MOSKVA RIVER BRIDGE
BOLSHOY KAMENNY BRIDGE
Moscow Variety Theater
REPINA SQUARE
Kremlin Embankment
Kropotkinskaya St.
Volkhonka St.
MOSCOW OUTDOOR SWIMMING POOL
Boulevard Ring
Marx Prospect
Hertzen St.

250 m

Main map

DZERZHINSKY PARK
EXHIBITION OF ECONOMIC ACHIEVEMENTS
TIMIRYAZEV ACADEMY PARK
Ostankino Palace (Mus. of Serf Art)
Academician Korolyov St.
Space Monument
Ostankino TV Tower
Ostankino
SOKOLNIKI PARK
Exhibition Halls
Stromynka St.
FRUNZE CENTRAL AIRFIELD
PETROVSKY PARK
SAVELOVSKIY STA.
Butyrsky Sq.
Pravda Offices
Sushchevsky Val St.
AZAREVSKOYE CEM.
RIGA STA.
Mira
Young Pioneers Stadium
DYNAMO STADIUM
Sovetskaya Hotel
Soviet Army Museum
CENTRAL ARMY PARK
MOSCOW STATE UNIV. BOTANICAL GARDEN
HIPPODROME
BELORUSSIA STA.
Soviet Army Theater
Communist Sq.
LENINGRAD STA.
Komsomol Sq.
YAROSLAVL STA.
Hotel Leningrad
KAZAN STA.
VAGANKOVSKOYE CEM.
Zvenigorod St.
Krasnaya Presnya St.
Krasnopresnensky Zastavy Sq.
Shmitovsky passage
KRASNAYA PRESNYA PARK
ZOO
Planetarium
Uprising Sq.
Hertzen St.
Gorky Mus.
Comecon Bldg.
Ukraina Hotel
Kalinnsky Bridge
Kalinin Prospekt
Smolensk Sq.
Arbat St.
Foreign Ministry
Borodino Bridge
KIEV STA.
Borodino Battle Panorama
Kutuzov Prospect
USSR Academy of the Arts
Zubov Sq.
Tolstoy Estate Museum
Pirogov St.
Bolshaya St.
Crimea Bridge
October Sq.
Bakhrushin Theatrical Mus.
GORKY PARK
Dobrynin St.
Lenin Prospekt
PAVELETSK STA.
First Municipal Hosp.
Soviet Academy of Sciences
Shukhov TV Tower
DONSKOI MONASTERY
SIMONOV MONASTERY
Mosfilm Studios
LUZHNIKI PARK
LENIN PARK
LENIN STADIUM
Komsomolsky Prospekt
Observation Platform
LENIN HILLS
Luzhniki Bridge
Vorobyov Hwy.
MOSCOW STATE UNIVERSITY
Young Pioneers Palace
Gagarin Sq.
All-Union Council of Trade Unions
Moscow Circus (New)
Vernadsky Prospekt
Profsoyuznaya St.
DANILOVSKOYE CEM.
Southern Port
Avtozavod St.
Simonovsky Val St.
Kuibyshev St.
KRUTITSK MONASTERY
NOVOSPASSKY MONASTERY
Krestyanskoye Sq.
Krasnokholmsky Bridge
Mayakovsky Mus.
Taganskaya Sq.
Tagan Sq.
ANDRONIKOV MONASTERY
Ulyanov St.
Entuziastov Boull.
Nizhegorod St.
Vologad St.
OFFICERS' REGIONAL HOUSE PARK
Yekaterinsky Palace
KURSK STA.
Museum of Oriental Culture
ANDRONIKOV MONASTERY
Museum of Oriental Culture
BAUMAN PARK
MOSCOW POST OFFICE
Chernyshevsky St.
Karl Marx St.
Red Square
KREMLIN
KITAI GOROD
Bely Gorod
Ustynsky Bridge
Tretyakov Art Gallery
Setun
Moskva
Zamoskvorechye
NOVODEVICHY CONVENT

INSET MAP AREA

Regional map

Skhodnya
SHEREMETYEVO AIRPORT
Ivantyevka
Dolgoprudny
Kaliningrad
Khimki
Shcholkovo
Mytishchi
Dedovsk
Nakhabino
Babushkin
Tushino
Krasnogorsk
Ostankino
Ismailovo
Balashicha
Shchukino
ISMAILOVO PARK
Rublyovo
Moscow
Perovo
KREMLIN
Reutov
Kuntsyovo
MAIN MAP AREA
Zhelezdorozhny
Odintsovo
Semenovskoye
Cheromuski
Lyublino
Lyubertsy
Vnukovo
Lenino
Malakhovka
VNUKOVO AIRPORT
BYKOVO AIRPORT
Lytkarino
Vidnoye
Desna
Pakhra
Scherbinka
Krasna Pakhra
Podolsk
Domodedovo
DOMODEDOVO AIRPORT
MOSCOW CIRCULAR MOTORWAY
MOSCOW OBLAST

0 5 10 15 20 km.
0 4 8 12 mi.

Compilation and Design by Lothar Roth & Associates

equipment, chemicals, consumer durables, apparel, leather ware, and food products. The city is served by airports, major rail lines, and highways. Its inland ports connect with the rest of the country via the Moscow River and the Moscow-Volga Canal. Mass transit in Moscow is served by a subway system (begun 1935), trolley buses, motor buses, and streetcars.

Moscow is Russia's leading educational and scientific research center. The chief institution of higher learning is Moscow University. As the home of the Russian Academy of Sciences and the nation's industrial ministries, Moscow has a large number of scientific institutes.

Cultural Life. Moscow has more than 4,000 libraries, 100 museums, and 60 theaters. The Russian State Library (formerly the Lenin Library) is the nation's main book repository. The principal museums are the Armory and Diamond Fund in the KREMLIN, with a collection of tsarist treasures, and the State History Museum on Red Square. Best known for art collections are the Tretyakov Gallery, with old Russian art, and the Pushkin Museum, with more recent Russian and Western works. Moscow contains some of the world's most famous theaters, including the Bolshoi Theater of Opera and Ballet (see BOLSHOI BALLET) and the Moscow Art Theater. The modernistic Palace of Congress in the Kremlin is used for both spectacles and official gatherings.

The Luzhniki sports complex includes a stadium and an indoor sports palace. Large parks, including Gorky Park, Sokolniki Park, and Izmailovo Park, are important centers of recreation.

Moscow's city government, headed by an executive committee and its chairman or mayor, is equivalent to that of an oblast and comes directly under the government of Russia. The city is divided into 10 administrative regions (okrugs).

History. First mentioned in old Russian chronicles dated 1147, Moscow was an early trading settlement. In the 14th century it assumed the leadership in Russian resistance against the Tatar-Mongol forces and became the capital of a unified Russian state in the 15th century. Under Ivan III (r. 1462–1505) and Ivan IV (r. 1533–84) this Muscovite state extended its control west toward the Baltic Sea and east into Siberia, laying the groundwork for the later Russian empire. The city of Moscow itself gradually expanded around its inner fortress, the Kremlin, and became Russia's leading economic center. Emperor Peter I (the Great), however, in an effort to orient Russia toward the West, moved his capital in 1712–13 from Moscow to the new city of Saint Petersburg (later Leningrad), on the Baltic Sea.

In 1812, Moscow was damaged by fire when it was briefly occupied by Napoleon. After the Bolshevik Revolution of 1917, Russia resumed its isolationist stance. Lenin reestablished the national capital in Moscow in 1918, and the city's growth accelerated. Its population more than doubled from 1.8 million in 1918 to more than 4 million in 1939. During World War II, German forces approached within 16 km (10 mi) of its northwest limits but were repulsed in the decisive Battle of Moscow (October 1941–April 1942). Moscow was the site of the 1980 Summer Olympics, boycotted by the United States and many other countries to protest the 1979 Soviet invasion of Afghanistan.

In August 1991 the Russian president Boris Yeltsin and his supporters organized the successful resistance against the putsch by Soviet hard-liners from the Moscow seat of the Russian government. That building was dubbed the "White House."

Moscow Art Theater The Moscow Art Theater, known officially as the Maksim Gorky Moscow Art Academic Theater, was founded in 1898 by Konstantin STANISLAVSKY and Vladimir Ivanovich NEMIROVICH-DANCHENKO as a public theater that would present the meaning of contemporary drama by using new, naturalistic methods of staging. Its opening production was a historically authentic adaptation of Aleksei Konstantinovich Tolstoy's Tsar Fyodor Ivanovich (1898). The theater then reflected contemporary life in a production of Anton CHEKHOV's The Seagull (1898), with its lengthy pauses, apparently aimless dialogue, and lack of a conventional plot. The seagull emblem of the Moscow Art Theater commemorates this early success and Chekhov's association with the theater, which continued to reflect literary innovations of the times.

Moselle River [moh-zel'] The Moselle (German: Mosel) is a 515-km-long (320-mi) tributary of the Rhine River. From its source near Remiremont in Vosges department of northeastern France, it flows north past Nancy and Metz, follows the Luxembourg-Germany border for 40 km (25 mi), and continues northeast past Trier, Germany, to join the Rhine at Koblenz. The Moselle drains an area of about 28,000 km^2 (11,000 mi^2). Its main tributaries are the Orne, Sauer, Saar, and Meurthe rivers.

Completely navigable since the completion of the Moselle Canal in 1964, the Moselle is one of the main water routes from Lorraine to the Ruhr. The river flows through steel-producing regions, and the famous German Mosel wine grapes are grown along the river below Koblenz.

Moses Moses was a leader of the ancient Hebrews who brought them out of Egypt in the so-called Exodus (c.1250 BC), mediated the covenant between them and Yahweh at Sinai, and guided them through the desert to the borders of Canaan. The biblical tradition assigns him a life span of 120 years, but the reliability of this figure is questioned.

The books of Exodus through Deuteronomy in the Bible are the only available sources for details about Moses' life. No contemporary Egyptian documents yet found mention him, and the later traditions about him recorded in the work of Philo of Alexandria and in Josephus and rabbinic sources appear to be mere elaborations of the biblical story. Moreover, the biblical story is a composite of sources, the earliest of which postdates Moses by more

Moses receives the Ten Commandments and presents them to the Israelites in this miniature from the Regensburg Pentateuch (c.1300). According to the Book of Exodus, Moses smashed the first set of tablets, after he returned from Mount Sinai and found the Israelites worshiping the Golden Calf.

than 200 years and allows ample time for legendary accretions. The story of the baby Moses in the reed basket on the Nile, for example, is a typical legend about a famous man's childhood. The same basic story is also told about Sargon, king of Akkad (c.2350 BC).

According to the biblical account, Moses grew up at the pharaoh's court but was forced to flee to Midian after killing an Egyptian whom he had seen strike an Israelite. Moses' presence at the pharaoh's court may be explained by the Egyptian practice of taking hostages from their Semitic vassals, giving them Egyptian training, and sending them back to lead their people with an ingrained Egyptian point of view. Such a background might also explain the story of Moses' adoption by the pharaoh's daughter.

In exile Moses married the daughter of the high priest of Midian. While he was keeping his father-in-law's flock, God spoke to him at a burning bush and commissioned him to lead Israel out of Egypt. After the Exodus, Moses met again with his father-in-law, who performed sacrifices and advised him regarding an improved judicial system. These traditions suggest that certain aspects of Moses' religious and legislative reforms, perhaps even God's new name, *Yahweh*, were derived from beliefs of the MIDIANITES.

Moses returned to Egypt to confront the pharaoh with Yahweh's demand. After a long struggle involving ten plagues and culminating in the slaying of the first-born of the Egyptians, the pharaoh permitted Israel to leave. He then changed his mind, but God drowned the pursuing Egyptians in the Reed (traditionally, Red) Sea. The ancient poem in Exodus 15 celebrates this victory, but the actual event cannot be reconstructed from this poetic account.

After the Israelites experienced Yahweh's deliverance in the Exodus, Moses led them to the sacred mountain—named Sinai in one source, Horeb in another. There God appeared to them in a frightening display of thunder and lightning. Moses went up onto the mountain and returned with God's instructions, including the TEN COMMANDMENTS.

Thus Moses mediated the COVENANT God made with the people of Israel. As covenant mediator Moses was a law-giver, and his status became such that all of Israel's laws were attributed to him, even much later ones (see TORAH).

Israel remained in the desert under Moses' leadership for a number of years, camping at Qadesh and other oases. The Old Testament tells of many conflicts between Moses and the people during this time. The most dramatic one concerned the GOLDEN CALF set up by Moses' brother AARON while Moses was on Mount Sinai (or Horeb).

See also: DEUTERONOMY, BOOK OF; EXODUS, BOOK OF; NUMBERS, BOOK OF.

Moses, Edwin   The 1983 Sullivan Award winner as America's finest amateur athlete, Edwin Corley Moses, b. Dayton, Ohio, Aug. 31, 1955, is the best 400-m hurdler in track history. Moses won the gold medal in that event at the 1976 Olympics in Montreal with a time of 47.64 sec, breaking John Akii-Bua's 4-year-old world record. He lowered the record 3 more times—to 47.45 (1977), 47.13 (1980), and 47.02 (1983)—before winning another gold medal at the 1984 Games in Los Angeles. Moses earned only a bronze at the 1988 Games in Seoul, but his domination of a single event remains unchallenged in track history—from 1977 to 1987 he was undefeated in 107 consecutive meets.

Moses, Grandma   America's most renowned primitive painter, Grandma Moses, or Anna Mary Robertson Moses, b. Greenwich, N.Y., Sept. 7, 1860, d. Dec. 13, 1961, was in her seventies when she began to paint seriously and had won universal acclaim by the time of her death. Her paintings were discovered about 1939 by the

The paintings of Grandma Moses belong to the American primitive school of the 1940s. Look, It's a New Little Colt (1945) is typical of her folk-art style. (Clemens-Sels Museum, Neuss, Germany.)

art dealer Otto Kallir, who first exhibited her work in 1940 at his Gallerie Saint Etienne in New York City. The basic theme of her painting is American rural life. Self-taught, she said that she liked bright colors and preferred to work from memory. She wrote *My Life's History* (1952).

Moses, Robert Robert Moses, b. New Haven, Conn., Dec. 18, 1888, d. July 29, 1981, was for 40 years an important figure in New York politics—particularly in the area of public works. As chairman of New York's state park commission (1924–63), head of the Triborough Bridge and Tunnel Authority (1946–68), and New York City park commissioner (1934–60), Moses undertook vast and often controversial programs of park and beach-front development, highway construction, and bridge building. He was responsible for creating Jones Beach and Robert Moses state parks and for building the Triborough and Verrazano-Narrows bridges.

Mosheshwe, King of the Sotho [moh-shesh'-way] Mosheshwe, b. *c.*1790, d. Mar. 11, 1870, was the founder of the SOTHO (Basuto) nation and first paramount chief of Basutoland (now LESOTHO) in southern Africa. By superior military and political skill he united a variety of small African groups into one people known as the Sotho in the early years of the 19th century. Mosheshwe defended his nation against a multitude of enemies, both black (primarily the ZULUS) and white, and encouraged Christian missionaries to come to his country. In 1868 he accepted British protection to safeguard his country against the Boers, and although his kingdom sustained heavy territorial losses, he managed to preserve its existence. His name appears in several other forms, including Msheshwe and Moshoeshoe.

Mosley, Sir Oswald [mohz'-lee] Sir Oswald Ernald Mosley, b. Nov. 16, 1896, d. Dec. 2, 1980, was for many years the leader of British fascism. First elected to Parliament in 1918 as a Conservative, he later joined (1924) the Labour party and was a junior cabinet minister in 1929–30. In 1931 he founded the left-wing New party, but the following year, having moved dramatically to the Right, he established the British Union of Fascists. After his first wife, the daughter of Lord Curzon, died, he married (1936) Diana Guinness, a member of the MITFORD family. His and his wife's open support of Hitler and Nazi Germany led to his imprisonment during World War II.

---

mosque [mahsk] A mosque (from the Arabic *masjid*, "a place to prostrate one's self [in front of God]") is a place of public worship in the Muslim religion. It must be oriented toward Mecca, have a place for ritual ablutions, and a place from which a preacher (*khatib*) can speak and a leader (*imam*) can start the action of prayer. The preacher speaks from a *minbar*, a high pulpit originally used by judges administering the law. The *imam* stands in or before the *mihrab*, a niche inserted in the *qiblah* wall, which indicates the direction of Mecca. Early in Islam the *mihrab* became the focal center of the mosque and together with the wall around it often acquired a wealth of abstract decoration. An additional liturgical requirement is the MINARET, a high, generally pointed tower from which Muslims are called to prayer.

In the Koran, the term *masjid* refers either specifically to the Holy Sanctuary (the Kaaba Mosque) in Mecca or to religious buildings in general. Early Islam did not require a specially built space for the performance of the principal liturgical obligation of common prayer. The obligation could be met anywhere, provided the direction in which worshippers must face during prayer (the *qiblah*) was properly determined. Soon after the Prophet Muhammad's death (632), his house in Medina, which had often been used for gatherings of the faithful, became a model of the proper kind of meeting place in which to pray at formally appointed times as well as to perform a variety of social, political, and administrative functions related to the Muslim faith.

The Masjid-i-Jami is the congregational mosque used for Friday (Sabbath) services in Isfahan, Iran. The mosque's interior, based on the architectural design of the traditional Iranian mosque, consists of four vaulted halls (eyvans) surrounding a central court where the prayer room is located.

Generally, but with notable exceptions, mosques have assumed the form of large enclosed spaces serving the collective needs of the Muslim community and decorated with quotations from the Koran and with ornaments intended to heighten the unique quality of the monument. Statuary or other images of living beings are uniformly absent from the mosque; geometric or floral motifs predominate in its carved-wood, plaster, tile, or mosaic decoration. The floors of mosques are generally covered with rugs; hanging lamps, candlesticks, stands for holy books, and platforms for readers are often placed within the interior. Other features may include a screened area reserved for princes (*maqsurah*), elaborate entrances, and stores for community treasures.

Stylistically, mosques can be divided into three major types. The first is often called the Arab type, because it first appeared in the earliest conquered lands of the Fertile Crescent area and Egypt. Also called the hypostyle type, this widely occurring style of mosque is characterized by a large space, often composed of many parallel galleries, organized through naves or bays supported on a mass of piers or columns around an open courtyard. Notable examples include the mosque of Damascus (8th century); the great Cairene mosques of Ibn-Tulun (8th century) and of al-Azhar and Hakim (both 9th century); the mosques of Kairouan, Tunisia (9th century), and of Córdoba, Spain (8th–10th century); and the 12th-century Delhi mosque in India.

The second basic mosque type is the Iranian mosque. Of uncertain origin, this type is first clearly evident in Western Iranian mosques of the late-11th through the 12th century, such as at Isfahan, Zavareh, and Ardistan. The Iranian mosque, which drew on pre-Islamic Iranian architectural features, is based on four *eyvans* (vaulted halls opening on an open space) around a central court. In addition to the early examples in Western Iran, the major masterpieces of the Iranian type are the 15th-century mosques of Samarkand in Soviet Central Asia and the 17th-century Masjid-i shah in Isfahan. In addition to the striking effect of its monumental synthesis of diverse architectural forms—*eyvans*, domes, and minarets—the Iranian-type mosque is characteristically emblazoned with spectacular decorative patterns both inside the building and on its facades.

The third mosque type, called Turkish or Ottoman, was created under the influence of the local Anatolian architecture of the 13th and 14th centuries. It is characterized by the domination of a single dome covering the main prayer hall. Inside, brilliantly patterned supports extend gracefully from the top of the cupola, and in the exterior courtyard tall minarets frame the soaring dome. The Ottoman-type mosque appeared in all the lands that came under Ottoman rule, but its masterpieces are the 16th-century Selimiye mosque in Edirne and the Suleimaniye mosque in Istanbul.

See also: ISLAMIC ART AND ARCHITECTURE.

Mosquito [muh-skee'-toh]   One of the most versatile and successful of all combat aircraft, the two-seat Mos-

quito originated in October 1938 as a project for a British private-venture, high-speed, light bomber. Perhaps its most distinctive feature was its all-wood construction, designed to conserve strategic materials. The Mosquito (full name de Havilland D.H. 98 Mosquito) had a 16.5-m (54-ft 2-in) wing span; twin 1,710-horsepower Rolls-Royce Merlin engines cooled through leading-edge radiators; and fully retractable landing gear. It was able to operate without defensive armament because it was faster than the fighter aircraft of the enemy, its top speed being 655 km/h (407 mph) at an altitude of 8,500 m (28,000 ft). The first prototype was a bomber; then came a fighter variant, and the third was designed for photo-reconnaissance.

---

mosquito   Mosquitoes are small, delicate, two-winged flies, the adult females of which are pests to humans and many other animals because they feed on blood. Because of this habit several species serve as carriers of diseases such as malaria, filariasis, dog heartworm, arboviral encephalitis, and yellow fever.

Mosquitoes can be distinguished from other true flies by an elongated sucking proboscis and scales along the wing veins and on the body. The scales vary in color and arrangement, giving each species a characteristic appearance. The species belong to the insect order Diptera, family Culicidae. The more than 2,600 species are divided into 31 or more genera, 12 of which are found in the

The female Anopheles *mosquito carries the malaria parasite, which is dangerous to humans. The insect's population can be suppressed by methods appropriate to stages of its life cycle (outer band). Eggs (1) are laid in still water, where they become larvae (2) and then pupae (3). The introduction of such fish as the guppy can effectively inhibit the population during the aquatic stage (blue). Spraying oil on water kills larvae and pupae by preventing them from breathing (green). In the adult stage (4) mosquitoes are curbed by insecticide (red).*

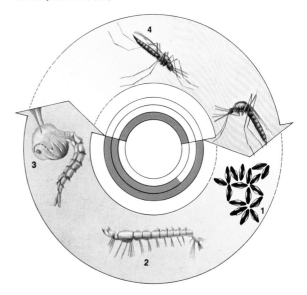

United States. Mosquitoes are distributed worldwide in all but the most extreme habitats.

Mosquitoes pass through four stages: egg, larva, pupa, and adult. Mosquito larvae can live only in water, and they usually feed on microplankton. They move by wiggling their bodies—hence the common name "wiggler"—and by the waving motion of their mouth brushes. Larvae are transformed into adults during the comparatively brief, nonfeeding pupal stage. Unlike most other insects, mosquito pupae are active, diving in response to potentially threatening stimuli. Most breathe at the water's surface by means of respiratory tubes, or "trumpets." Adults emerge at the water's surface.

Only females are blood-feeders, although both males and females feed on flower nectar. Most females require a blood meal to produce a batch of eggs. A mosquito may be attracted to its victim by warmth, odor, moisture, and even carbon dioxide. Using carbon dioxide gradients, the mosquito may be able to follow a sleeping person's breath to its source.

The mosquito's mouthparts consist of two pairs of needlelike maxillae and mandibles; a food channel, which sucks up the blood or nectar; a saliva channel; and a sheath. When a mosquito bites, it first inserts the pointed, barbed pair of maxillae, which anchor the mouthparts in the skin and provide leverage for the insertion of the remaining four parts. The sheath slides back as the other mouthparts pass through its tip. The mosquito's saliva—which contains anticoagulants to stop the blood from clotting—is injected into the skin, causing the area around the bite to swell and itch.

Mosquito control is effected in several ways, including draining breeding areas, applying thin oil to water to kill the larvae, spraying with insecticides, and employing biological agents, such as small fishes that eat mosquito larvae. The incidence of mosquito-borne disease, however, is increasing rapidly. The tiger mosquito, *Aedes albopictus*, unlike other mosquitoes, is able to carry many disease-causing viruses. Native to Asia, it is now also found in the United States.

Mosquito Coast   The Mosquito Coast is a 65-km-wide (40-mi) littoral bordering the Caribbean Sea for about 360 km (225 mi) in eastern Nicaragua and Honduras. The term is a corruption of Miskito Coast, named for the MISKITO Indians. It is a lowland region of tropical forests, with many swamps and lagoons along the coast and banana plantations inland. The area is sparsely populated. Bluefields, Nicaragua, is the principal town. The region was a British protectorate from 1740 to 1860, when it was returned to the Miskito. Their territory was incorporated into the Nicaraguan Republic in 1894. In 1960 the northern portion of the Mosquito Coast was awarded to Honduras.

mosquito fish   The term *mosquito fish* may refer to any small species of fish used in mosquito control or to certain members of the live-bearing topminnow family,

Poeciliidae, such as the dwarf mosquito fish, *Heterandria formosa,* but more specifically it refers to the topminnow *Gambusia affinis,* native to the eastern United States. This fish is usually brownish to silvery in color, but some individuals may be irregularly blotched with black. Females reach 6 cm (2.5 in) in length; males, 4 cm (1.5 in). The anal fin of the male is modified into an organ, the gonopodium, for transferring sperm to the female. *G. affinis* often feeds extensively on mosquito larvae and for this reason has been widely introduced around the world.

moss   Mosses comprise about 23,000 species of small, delicate green plants in the class Musci. With hepatics, or liverworts (class Hepaticae), and hornworts (class Antherocerotae), they comprise the division Bryophyta of the plant kingdom. Most mosses grow in moist and shaded woods and forests, rarely in open places, although a relatively few kinds are adapted to an aquatic habitat in standing or running water, and some even live in the desert. All, however, require fresh water in some greater or lesser quantity. They are widely distributed around the world. In the tropics they are most luxuriant in mountain rain forests.

A number of plants commonly referred to as mosses are actually different plants, such as Spanish moss (an epiphyte), Irish moss (an alga), club moss (a primitive vascular plant), and reindeer moss (a lichen).

Classification. Mosses are rather primitive plants. Biochemical evidence indicates that they are an evolutionary offshoot from simple higher plants, from which they separated at some time before the Devonian geological period.

By far the largest group of Bryophyta, mosses consist of three major subgroups: the so-called true mosses (Bryales), the PEAT MOSSES (Sphagnales), and the granite mosses (Andreaeales). True mosses are by far the most common and familiar. Peat mosses comprise one genus, *Sphagnum*, and widely occur in wet habitats. In cool or cold temperate climates, as in the northernmost United States and in much of Canada, *Sphagnum* may produce vast peat bogs. The carbohydrate materials accumulated by the continuing growth of peat mosses over long periods of time are a source of fuel (see PEAT). Granite mosses consist of fewer than a hundred species, almost all of them in the genus *Andreaea*, that grow directly on acidic rock in the mountains.

Structure. All mosses and most liverworts have a leafy stem that may be so short as to be imperceptible or, rarely, may extend to as much as a meter or more in length. Normally the stem rises above the ground from 2.5 to 15 cm (1 to 6 in) in height. The stem is not woody, although it does contain groups of cells that strongly resemble primitive conductive strands. The stem is not, however, vascular. Most of the water used by the plant is probably conducted upward to the leaves on the outside of the stem by means of capillarity. The leaves of all but a very few species are only a single layer of cells thick, giving them a very delicate appearance and consistency, even though the walls may be surprisingly thick and strong. A leaf consists mainly of the green photosynthetic tissue of

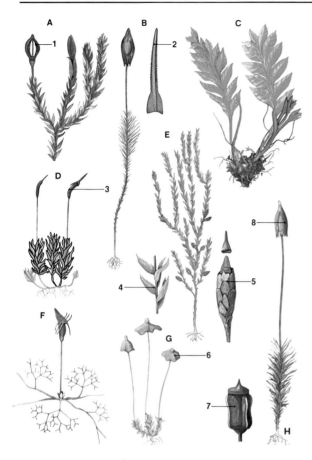

Andreaea rupestris (A) *is a reddish brown moss that sheds spores through four slitlike valves in the capsule* (1). *The Australian species* Dawsonia polytrichoides (B) *has thin, pointed leaves* (2). Schistostega pennata (C) *is a luminous European moss.* Atrichum undulatum (D) *has a long, pointed cap* (3) *on the capsule.* Fontinalis antipyretica (E), *an aquatic moss with boat-shaped leaves* (4) *and elongated capsules* (5), *is among the largest species;* Ephemeropsis tjibodensis (F) *is among the smallest.* Splacnum luteum (G) *has a yellow umbrella-shaped apophysis* (6). *The four-sided capsule* (7) *of* Polytrichum commune (H) *is protected by a long brown cap* (8).

which produces thousands of microscopic, motile sperm cells, or spermatozoids. During a light rain or heavy dew, the ripe antheridium breaks open by the swelling and bursting of its apical cells, and the numerous sperm escape into the surrounding film of water. At the same time, the contents of the neck canal of the archegonium are expelled by swelling. These contents contain a potent chemical attractant for spermatozoids, which swim through the water to the archegonium and down the neck canal until finally one of them reaches the egg and unites with it.

Mosses and liverworts, as well as the archegonia and antheridia they produce, all belong to the sexual, or gametophyte, generation, which is characterized by having a single set of chromosomes (haploid) in each cell. The fertilized egg, or zygote, however, begins a new generation or phase in the life history, because it now has two sets of gamete chromosomes (diploid), one from the egg and another from the sperm. The diploid zygote then begins to divide within the archegonium, producing a sporophyte, or spore-producing plant, representing the nonsexual phase of mosses. When mature, the sporophyte consists of a basal foot that remains embedded in the tissue of the gametophyte plant and that serves to absorb water and some nutrients from that tissue. Above the foot is the stalk, or seta, which bears a capsule in which spores are produced. The spores are haploid cells produced from a single diploid cell, the spore mother-cell.

The capsule usually has a specialized cap, plus a fringe of teeth around the mouth of the cap, which governs the shedding of spores by restricting them in wet weather and pushing them out in dry weather. The spores germinate under conditions of abundant moisture and produce a web or a thallose plate of cells. Eventually these cells grow into new leafy plants and complete the life cycle.

Importance. Individual moss plants have very little economic importance, but through their aggregations into enormous mats and their frequent dominance in cool, wet habitats they have very real significance in their ability to absorb and hold water. The reputation of forests for holding water, both as a water supply in times of drought and as a retention system in times of flood, depends largely on the mosses they shelter.

the thin blade. Mosses and liverworts lack true roots and so must depend on small, threadlike, delicate cells called rhizoids for the absorption of water and nutrients, as well as for a limited amount of anchorage. Thus, the nutrition of mosses and liverworts is relatively simple. Photosynthesis produces energy-containing carbohydrates; biochemical synthesis then transforms the carbohydrates into the other materials needed for nutrition.

Life Cycle. In the reproductive life cycle of mosses and liverworts the male and female sex organs are produced on one or on separate gametophyte plants (see below). The female sex organ is a small, flask-shaped structure called the archegonium. The swollen base of the flask contains one relatively large egg; the long, narrow neck contains the neck canal. The male sex organ is an elongated, often cigar-shaped structure, the antheridium,

Moss, Stirling Stirling Moss, b. Sept. 17, 1929, was one of the central figures in the post–World War II automobile-racing boom. Moss, an Englishman, was the son of a former Indianapolis 500 driver and by age 14 was a skilled racing-car driver himself. In 1954 he joined the Mercedes-Benz racing team as the number 2 driver, behind Juan Fangio. Moss won 16 Formula 1 races in his 16-year career, but he never won the World Driving Championship; his forte was endurance and sports-car racing. Moss retired from racing in 1961, after he recovered from a crash.

most-favored-nation status Most-favored-nation status is a provision in a commercial treaty that grants each signatory the automatic right to any tariff reduction that may be negotiated by one of them with a third country. For example, if the United States were to negotiate a tariff reduction on automobiles with Japan, it would also be committed to such reductions with all its other trading partners to whom it has granted most-favored-nation status. All nations belonging to GENERAL AGREEMENT ON TARIFFS AND TRADE (GATT) have agreed to the most-favored-nation principle as a condition of membership.

Mostel, Zero [mahs-tel', zeer'-oh] One of the most versatile modern comic actors, Zero Mostel, stage name of Samuel Joel Mostel, b. Brooklyn, N.Y., Feb. 28, 1915, d. Sept. 8, 1977, began his career in the 1940s as a stand-up comic in Greenwich Village clubs to support himself as a painter. Mostel appeared in stage, screen, and television roles until the mid-1950s, when he was blacklisted for his liberal political views. In 1958 he returned to acting in the choice part of Leopold Bloom in *Ulysses in Nighttown*, which brought him an Obie Award. His Broadway roles in Ionesco's *Rhinoceros* (1961; film 1974), *A Funny Thing Happened on the Way to the Forum* (1962; film 1966), and *Fiddler on the Roof* (1964) all earned him Tony Awards. Mostel was also memorable in two later films, *The Producers* (1968) and *The Front* (1976), a serious commentary on the 1950s blacklistings instigated by Sen. Joseph R. McCarthy.

Mosul [moh'-suhl] Mosul (Arabic: Al-Mawsil), the capital of Nineveh province, Iraq, is situated on the west bank of the Tigris River, about 354 km (220 mi) upstream from Baghdad. It is Iraq's third largest city and has a population of 570,926 (1985 est.). The city lies across the river from the ancient Assyrian capital, NINEVEH. Mosul itself contains many historic buildings, including the Red Mosque. Mosul University was founded in 1967.

Mosul's population is primarily Arab, but the surrounding area is predominantly Kurdish. The economy in earlier times was based on fine cotton goods (muslin). Today it is centered on varied manufacturing industries and on the marketing of agricultural commodities. Petroleum fields are nearby.

Mosul has been the chief city of northern Mesopotamia since the 8th century AD. Subject to various rulers, including Mongols, Persians, and Turks, it was part of the Ottoman Empire from 1534 to 1918 and was then held by the British until 1920. There was fighting in the city during the unsuccessful Kurdish revolt after Iraq's defeat in the 1991 Gulf war.

motel see HOTEL

motet [moh-tet'] In current musical usage *motet* refers to an unaccompanied, sacred choral piece, often with a Latin text, and often composed in a deliberately archaic style that looks back to the polyphonic composers of the Renaissance. But the term—derived from the French *mot*, or "word"—has been in use since about 1250 and has undergone many changes of meaning.

An outgrowth of the 12th-century clausula, the motet combined, in different vocal parts, a few words of liturgical Latin with a poetic, comic, or even bawdy text in French. The motet was as much a secular entertainment as a church piece. By the 14th century the isorhythmic motet, in which rhythmic patterns were repeated in some or all of the voices, was a fixture of court and church music in France, Germany, and England.

At the beginning of the 15th century a new kind of motet appeared. Guillaume Dufay and John Dunstable, two composers who had lived in Italy, composed not only isorhythmic works, but also motets that resembled madrigals in their rhythmic freedom and single text. In the "Flemish school" of Jean d'Ockeghem, Jacob Obrecht, and Josquin des Prez, this type of motet became a complex composition in several sections, using three to six voices.

A continent-wide flowering of the motet took place in the last half of the 16th century. The complex choral works of the Gabrielis, Giovanni Palestrina, Thomas Tallis, and William Byrd fixed the definition of *motet* for the 19th and 20th centuries.

During the baroque and classical eras, however, usage of the term loosened to the point where almost any vocal piece for church use could be called a motet. Some motets were unaccompanied contrapuntal choral pieces. Others used orchestra and soloists in the most up-to-date operatic style, which was all but indistinguishable from the cantata.

moth see BUTTERFLIES AND MOTHS

mother goddess The symbol and mythology of the mother goddess is found in many diverse cultures of the ancient world. She represents the creative power of all nature and the processes of fecundity, along with the periodic renewal of life. As a mythological and cult figure the mother goddess has appeared in many localized forms, such as ISIS, the "goddess of many names," and the Phrygian Magna Mater. She represents different aspects of the feminine archetype as typified in KALI, LAKSHMI, and the other goddesses of Hindu mythology (see SHAKTI), or in Coatlicue in the Aztec world.

The Neolithic settlement of Çatal Hüyük (c.7000 BC) in Anatolia provides archaeological evidence that the cult of the mother goddess experienced a long continuity. The chief deity was a goddess who simultaneously incorporated the roles of young woman, mother in childbirth, and old woman. Between the 5th and 3d millennia BC the cult became established in the Fertile Crescent, in the Indus Valley, and around the Aegean Sea.

The worship of a great goddess was particularly dominant in Middle Eastern religions, especially in the cults of CYBELE and ISHTAR. Both were fertility goddesses involved with a young male consort who died and was continually reborn. This element of the dying male deity, representing vegetation, is a later development in the cult of the mother goddess and is regarded as a transition from her primal state of being an unmarried mother to having a son, a lover, or both. The Egyptian cult of Isis is concerned with a variant of this relationship, focusing on the death and resurrection of her brother-husband, OSIRIS. The most important cult activity in Greco-Roman culture—the initiation rites of the ELEUSINIAN MYSTERIES—was based on the power of DEMETER and her daughter PERSEPHONE to ensure the yearly renewal of all life-forms.

The Greco-Roman world adopted the Egyptian Isis cult, incorporating local forms of Greek and Roman goddesses and identifying Isis with a fertility mystery cult. The cult of Isis persisted during the first four centuries AD, until persecution finally halted cult activities.

In Christianity the figure of the Virgin Mary as *theotokos*, or the "Mother of God," has clear affinities with that of the ancient mother goddess. Her role, however, is diminished, and that of the divine child—the dying and resurrected male god—is central.

Mother Goose   see PERRAULT, CHARLES

mother-of-pearl   Mother-of-pearl, or nacre, is an iridescent substance that lines the shells of some mollusks. Like the pearl (see PEARLS AND PEARLING), it is made up of layers of calcium carbonate and conchiolin that are secreted by the mantle, or sheath of skin that envelops the body of the mollusk. Mother-of-pearl is used for buttons, for delicate inlay work, and for many other decorative purposes. Its chief sources are the pearl oyster, found in the tropical seas of the Far East; the freshwater pearl mussel, from American and European rivers; and the abalone, taken from the Pacific Ocean off Japan and California.

Motherwell, Robert   The American painter Robert Motherwell, b. Aberdeen, Wash., Jan. 24, 1915, d. July 16, 1991, was one of the originators of ABSTRACT EXPRESSIONISM as well as a printmaker, teacher, lecturer, and writer. An initial interest in psychoanalysis led Motherwell to explore surrealism, but in 1941 he chose to devote himself to painting. One of his earliest works, *The Little Spanish Prison* (1941; collection of the artist), introduced the striped format that was to dominate much of his later work. *Pancho Villa Dead and Alive* (1943; Museum of Modern Art, New York City) is representative of Motherwell's collages, a medium in which he continued to work. *Elegy to the Spanish Republic* (1949–76) is a series of more than 100 paintings in reaction to the Spanish Revolution, each composed of vertical black planes and suspended ovoids on a white ground. Motherwell's expressionist style underwent further development in the late 1960s when he began a second series—the so-called "open" or "window-and-wall" canvases that often display a rectangle on a field of solid color. In 1944 he became editor of *Documents of Modern Art*, a series of anthologies to which he contributed several introductions.

motion, circular   Circular motion is one of the most widespread forms of motion, both in nature and in artifi-

cial devices; the planets go around the Sun in orbits that are almost circular; the daily rotation of the Earth makes the stars appear to travel in circular paths through the sky; and the machinery of modern industrial civilization depends on rotating wheels. The Greek philosophers and their scholastic successors in the Middle Ages thought that circular motion was the most perfect kind of motion. Necessarily, they argued, the motions of the heavenly bodies must be circular.

If a moving object is free of external influence, it will continue moving with constant velocity in a straight line. If the object is subjected to a force that continually changes direction so that it is always perpendicular to the velocity, the object will travel in a circle. This constant perpendicular force is called centripetal force (see CENTRIFUGAL AND CENTRIPETAL FORCES). Because the velocity of the revolving object is always tangential, the centripetal force is necessarily radial. For an object of mass m to travel in a circular path of radius r with constant speed v, the centripetal force must be equal to mv^2/r. Gravitation supplies the centripetal force for the planets.

The time taken for one complete revolution is called the period T. The number of revolutions per unit time is the frequency f, and $T = 1/f$. The angular speed ω in radians/sec is equal to $2\pi f$, where f is given in revolutions/sec. The tangential speed v is equal to ωr.

The measures of linear motion have their counterparts in circular motion. Linear displacement, x, corresponds to angular displacement, θ, and linear speed, v, corresponds to angular speed, ω. The inertia of the revolving object is called the MOMENT OF INERTIA, I. Linear momentum, mv, corresponds to ANGULAR MOMENTUM, $I\omega$.

The projection on an axis (in some cases, the shadow) of an object in circular motion with constant speed executes the special type of oscillation known as simple harmonic. In nature this effect is responsible for the sinusoidal pattern of lengthening and shortening of daylight throughout the year.

motion, harmonic   Motion that exactly repeats itself in regular time intervals is called periodic motion; the simplest type of periodic motion is harmonic, or sinusoidal, motion. Harmonic motion is important not only because it is commonly observed and is simple to describe and analyze but also because any periodic motion, no matter how complicated, can be expressed as a sum of harmonic motions.

The two general physical quantities that must be present for harmonic motion to occur are inertia, which is the tendency of a system to continue doing what it is currently doing, and a restoring force that tries to return the system to its equilibrium or natural rest position. The strength of the restoring force is directly proportional to the displacement from equilibrium; that is, the greater the displacement, the greater the restoring force. This type of restoring force, called an elastic force, was first described by Robert Hooke in the 17th century. The proportionality of the elastic restoring force to the displacement is called Hooke's law.

A simple example of harmonic motion is that of a body attached to a spring. When the spring is stretched or compressed by the motion of the body, it exerts an elastic restoring force that causes the body to oscillate. The body itself exhibits the property of inertia; it would remain in uniform motion in the absence of forces. The resultant motion of the body, therefore, is simple harmonic.

In an electrical CIRCUIT, the combination of an inductor and a capacitor provides the ingredients for harmonic oscillation of the current and the voltage. The inductor provides inertia by resisting changes in the current; the capacitor provides restoring force by becoming more difficult to charge in direct proportion to the amount to which it has already been charged. Electrical oscillations based on this idea have been developed to a high degree of sophistication in modern electrical and electronic equipment.

Another example of periodic motion is that of a simple PENDULUM—a weight swinging on the end of an inextensible, massless string. Gravity provides the restoring force, but because the path of the weight is an arc, the force is not directly proportional to the displacement, and therefore the motion is not exactly harmonic. For small displacements, up to an angle of approximately 10°, the motion may be treated as harmonic because its departure from ideality is less than 1%.

Harmonic motion is called sinusoidal motion because the mathematical relation between the displacement x of the oscillating object and time t is a SINE (or cosine) function.

A close relationship exists between simple harmonic motion and circular motion. If an object moving at constant speed in a circular path were viewed from within the plane of its motion (so that the circle is seen on edge), the object would appear to move back and forth in a straight line, obeying the rules of simple harmonic motion. A circular path may therefore be considered the path of an object subjected to two restoring forces acting at right angles to each other. Each would have the same frequency and produce the same maximum displacement, but they would be 180° out of phase with each other (one reaches a minimum when the other is at a maximum).

Elliptical motion may also be considered as the result of two separate perpendicular harmonic motions. As in circular motion, the frequencies of the two forces are the same but either the maximum displacements are different or the phase difference is a value other than 180° (or 0°, in which case the resulting path is a straight line).

Harmonic motion is characterized by symmetric movement about the equilibrium position. If each maximum displacement is instead slightly less than the previous one, the motion is said to be damped. Damping is the dissipation of the kinetic energy of the oscillator and causes vibrations to die out. Energy-absorbing devices, which may be something as simple as rubber cushions, are useful wherever vibrations are undesirable.

See also: WAVES AND WAVE MOTION.

motion, laws of　see LAWS OF MOTION

motion, planar　An intuitive definition of motion is "a continuous change in time." Such a description was used by the ancient Greek philosophers, for whom the interpretation of the concept of change in general constituted a great problem. The description of motion in classical mechanics requires the use of mathematics. In order to be able to analyze motion systematically, precise definitions for the concepts of velocity and acceleration must be formulated, and if the values for these quantities are known for an object at every moment, its complete trajectory can be determined. In this way it is possible to solve most problems of motion, from the motion of atoms to that of planets.

Velocity. The velocity of an object can be calculated from the distance it travels within a certain time. Distance divided by elapsed time is then called the average velocity, given in units such as meters per second (m/sec) or miles per hour (mph). The average velocity of an object during a particular period of time conveys only a rough impression of the way the object actually moved during that period. To obtain the velocity v for a particular moment in time (instantaneous velocity), one must know the infinitesimal change in position, dr, that occurs in an infinitesimally short moment dt; then, $v = dr/dt$.

Velocity is a vector quantity; it has not only magnitude but also direction. When the velocity of an object remains in the same direction and has constant magnitude, that object is moving with uniform motion. Such motion is quite common; once airplanes, trains, and ships have come up to speed, they endeavor to continue their journey at constant speed and—if the route permits—in a constant direction. Uniform motion is special because it is the only motion in nature that can be achieved without a net force of any kind. A passenger in a vehicle undergoing uniform motion will neither be pressed into his or her chair nor pulled to one side.

Acceleration. As soon as forces that do not cancel each other out act on an object, uniform motion no longer takes place. A simple idea of the concept of acceleration can be obtained when the change in velocity occurs only in the direction of the velocity itself. The acceleration is usually expressed as the change in speed, say, in m/sec, that takes place in one second; in this case, in meters per second per second (m/sec^2). An automobile that accelerates from rest up to 72 km/hr (20 m/sec) in 10 seconds has undergone an acceleration of 2 m/sec^2. The force responsible for the acceleration is provided by the motor, and the occupant undergoes the same accelerating force by being pressed into the seat. A deceleration (negative acceleration) slows the car. Unless an occupant is secured by a seat belt, there is no decelerating force on him or her, and he or she persists in the forward motion.

Acceleration is also a vector. If the force causing the acceleration does not act in the same line as the velocity, the acceleration may be divided into two perpendicular components, the tangential acceleration and the radial acceleration. Even if an object is undergoing uniform motion, its path will become curved under the influence of radial acceleration.

Calculating Position. The exact location of an object moving uniformly along a straight line can easily be calculated from $x = vt$, where x is the distance covered. The velocity of an object that was initially at rest and subsequently exposed to a uniform acceleration can also be calculated from $v = at$. In both cases calculations must be made consistently with meters and seconds or, alternatively, with kilometers and hours, or whatever units of measure are being used.

A uniformly accelerated motion is the motion caused when an object is constantly accelerated at the same rate, such as by gravity. Such an object's motion is determined by $x = \frac{1}{2} at^2$. The distance covered thus increases with the square of the time. If the object in question was already in motion at the time that acceleration began, then the distance covered prior to that time, $v_o t$, has to be included and $x = v_o t + at^2$. The initial velocity need not be in the same direction as the acceleration. In such a case a distance equal to $v_o t$ is covered in one direction and at the same time a distance equal to $\frac{1}{2} at^2$ is covered in another direction.

Falling Motion. A well-known case of objects being subjected to a uniform acceleration is when they are released (dropped) in the gravitational field of the Earth (see FREE FALL). The velocity of such an object increases every second by an amount of 9.8 m/sec (32.2 ft/sec). The acceleration of gravitational force is in fact not a constant, but up to an altitude of 30 km (19 mi) the deviations of this value are less than 1%. An object that is thrown horizontally will move uniformly in a straight line across the Earth's surface and at the same time will undergo the accelerating falling motion caused by gravity. The actual motion resulting from these two motions is then no longer a straight line, and the object will traverse increasingly greater distances downward in proportion to forward; a parabolic trajectory is thus formed.

The height h in meters at which an arbitrarily thrown object is located after a particular time t may be calculated from the previous formula for distance by adding its starting height to h: $h = v_o t - \frac{1}{2}(9.8)t^2$. If distance is measured in feet, 32.2 is substituted for 9.8. Because the last factor in this formula will ultimately always gain the upper hand, the height will eventually decrease in the end and the object will ultimately land on the Earth. The horizontal distance it will have traveled in that time is $v_o t$. The initial horizontal velocity v_o is different from the initial vertical velocity v_o. Air resistances and other forces are not included in this calculation.

Motion Picture Arts and Sciences, Academy of   see ACADEMY AWARDS

motion picture technology   see CINEMATOGRAPHY

motion pictures   see ANIMATION; CINEMATOGRAPHY; DOCUMENTARY; FILM, HISTORY OF; FILM PRODUCTION

motion sickness   Motion sickness is a syndrome that occurs in some people when they travel in a convey-

ance such as an automobile, airplane, or ship. Its symptoms include dizziness, nausea, vomiting, drowsiness, pallor, and sweating. Why some people experience motion sickness and others do not is uncertain. The syndrome appears to arise from a disturbance in the organs of balance found in the inner EAR. Psychological factors may also be involved. In the course of a long journey, the syndrome may disappear on its own, and in general such symptoms quickly cease once travel is ended. Certain steps may also be taken to reduce nausea, such as minimizing head motions or adopting a prone position. Medications such as the antihistamine dimenhydrinate (Dramamine) are effective against motion sickness. Tranquilizers are also used.

motivation   Motivation is the hypothesized cause of behavior: the determinant of behavior's arousal, vigor, direction, and persistence. Motivation is often considered an answer to the question *why* an action is performed.

Common sense provides a rich vocabulary of motivational terms. Needs, drives, motives, and desires are typically cited as internal states that explain actions. Motives and emotions are thought to provide the push, and incentives the pull, in commonsense accounts. Much of "common sense" is based on the legacy of Western philosophy. Early philosophers sharply distinguished between lower animals, guided by blind instinct, and humans, operating more rationally. Darwin's theory of evolution made this distinction untenable.

Formal approaches distinguish sources of motivation variously labeled primary, survival, or viscerogenic, from those termed secondary, social, or psychogenic. Primary motivations, such as hunger, thirst, and the avoidance of bodily injury, must be satisfied for the organism to survive. Secondary motivations, such as affiliation, sex, aggression, and achievement, are important but need not be satisfied for survival. Abraham MASLOW proposed five need categories: physiological; safety; love or belongingness; esteem or status; and self-actualization.

The primary dynamic principle in motivational theories is HOMEOSTASIS. As in cybernetics, deviation from a desired state leads to corrective measures—in this case behavior—to regain the state. There can be little doubt that many physiological systems operate in this manner.

The most ubiquitous assumption in psychological theories has been an optimal state of no stimulation. Because needs or drives are sources of stimulation, the desired state becomes their absence. Sigmund FREUD believed the goal of the psychic apparatus to be the reduction of stimulation to its lowest possible level. The presence of tension, for Kurt LEWIN, and the presence of drive, for Clark HULL, were states the organism acted to eliminate. Homeostasis has also been applied to cognition: Leon Festinger proposes that inconsistencies between two cognitions, or between cognitions and behavior, produce a state of dissonance that is reduced by bringing about consistency. Fritz Heider and Theodore Newcomb suggest that individuals attempt to achieve states of balance between their own attitudes and those of other persons with regard to common issues.

Homeostasis, with its optimal state of zero, has difficulty explaining behavior such as curiosity, exploration, and sensation seeking, which ostensibly seek to increase rather than decrease stimulation. A solution proposed by Daniel Berlyne would set the optimal level of stimulation at some point above zero. Deviations in the level of stimulation either above or below that point would lead to arousal and behavior directed toward restoring optimality. Another solution is to assume additional motives or drives, such as a curiosity, exploratory, or manipulation drive.

At present there is no accepted scientific theory of motivation. Instead, several behavior theories exist that can be described as motivational. Association or reinforcement theories are completely mechanistic, accounting for behavior in terms of learned stimulus-response connections without postulating any separate motivational construct. Several formulations are modeled on the human being as a rational decision maker. Although slightly different terms are used, each assumes behavior to depend on that course of action for which the subjective expected utility (SEU) is highest. The theories are cognitive because they involve expectancy as a construct along with the assumption that alternatives and their consequences are considered.

Moton, Robert Russa [moh'-tuhn, ruhs'-uh]   Robert Russa Moton, b. Amelia County, Va., Aug. 26, 1867, d. May 31, 1940, was a black American educator. From 1891 to 1915 he served as commandant of cadets at Hampton Institute in Virginia, from which he had graduated in 1890. In 1915, Moton succeeded Booker T. WASHINGTON as principal of Tuskegee Institute in Alabama, a vocational school for blacks, where he raised the curriculum to college level. In 1930 he was named chairman of the U.S. Commission on Education in Haiti and became a member of the National Advisory Commission on Education and the Commission to Study Education in Liberia.

Motonobu [moh-toh'-noh-boo]   Motonobu, or Kano Motonobu, 1476–1559, was a Japanese painter of the Kano school. He was the son of the painter Masanobu (1453–1540), the official founder of the Kano school, but only in Motonobu's works did the decorative style of the Kano burst into full flower.

Motonobu's paintings in ink and soft color, such as *Stork on a Branch* (c.1545; Reiun-in, Kyoto), exhibit a brilliant synthesis of bold Chinese-style brushwork and the decorative color and lyric mood of traditional Japanese painting.

---

motor   A motor is a machine that converts electrical energy into mechanical energy. It is an extremely efficient energy-conversion device; more than 90 percent of the energy fed into a motor can be converted into work. Motors are built in a great variety of sizes, from small fractional-horsepower motors used in instruments to new designs approaching 100,000 horsepower in size. Motors are rated according to the horsepower they can deliver without overheating. (See also ENGINE.)

The principle utilized in motors dates back to 1819, when the Danish physicist Hans Christian Oersted showed that electricity and magnetism were related. By 1821 the English scientist Michael FARADAY had built a simple electric motor, laying the foundation for the development of practical electric motors and GENERATORS.

Electric motors are classified as direct-current motors and alternating-current motors, depending on the type of electric power required. Direct-current (DC) electric motors were used in industry by the late 1800s. In 1888, Nikola TESLA patented the alternating-current (AC) motor.

DC Motor. A DC motor consists of two basic parts: a field-frame assembly and an armature assembly. The armature rotates in a magnetic field that acts upon the current-carrying wires. The motor operates because a coil of wire that current is flowing through will rotate when placed in a magnetic field, until the coil aligns itself with the magnetic field. At the point just before the rotation would stop, brushes and a commutator are used to reverse the current in the coil. This commutator action causes the coil to continue rotating. The amount of torque developed in the coil depends on the strength of the magnetic field, the number of turns of wire in the coil,

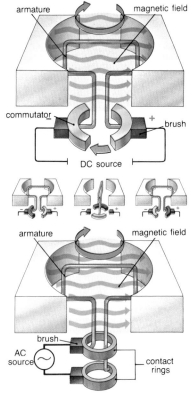

In a direct-current (DC) motor, current flows from a DC source to half-rings of copper—known as a commutator—and into a wire coil—the armature. Situated within a magnetic field, the wire, when electromagnetized by the current, rotates until the half-rings break contact with the brushes. Momentum keeps the coil moving until the half-rings are again in contact with the brushes, and an electromagnetic field opposite to the previous field is created, which keeps the coil turning in one direction. In an alternating-current (AC) motor, the current from the AC source alternates charge as the coil aligns itself at a certain point within the field, thus continuing the momentum of rotation.

and the position of the coil in the magnetic field. Since there is a torque acting on each turn in the coil, the greater the number of turns, the greater the torque.

In most motors the magnetic field is furnished by an ELECTROMAGNET, which can be made much stronger than a permanent MAGNET. The current to energize the electromagnet comes from the same source that supplies current to the armature.

AC Motor. Alternating-current motors are used more widely than direct-current motors, because most utility companies distribute only AC electric power. Also, DC motors have commutators and brushes that arc while the motor is operating and require periodic service. In addition, under certain conditions the arcing may present a serious fire and explosion hazard.

The AC motor is used today in clocks, clothes dryers, fans, vacuum cleaners, washers, and other home appliances. Almost all motors used on cars and trucks, however, are DC motors, because automotive batteries supply direct current. The starting motor, windshield-wiper motor, and windshield-washer motor are all DC motors.

motorboat   see BOAT AND BOATING

motorcycle   The term *motorcycle* usually refers to a self-propelled two-wheeled vehicle, most commonly powered by a gasoline-fueled internal-combustion engine. There are exceptions, such as the occasional electrically powered bike and certain open three-wheeled vehicles that fall into the same category. The broad term also includes MOPEDS, motorized bicycles that are fitted with pedals and have engines no greater than 50 cubic centimeters (cc) displacement. Included as well are motor scooters, characterized by medium-sized engines (averaging about 200 cc) and fitted with relatively wide, small-diameter wheels. The term also includes minicycles, or "minibikes," which have rather small frames and small wheels, have engines under 85 cc, and are usually ridden by young people.

History. Some of the earliest motorcycle experiments involved fitting steam engines to modified bicycles. Not until the advent of the gasoline engine, however, did motorcycle designs assume serious and practical forms. The men most often credited with laying the groundwork for modern motorcycles are Nikolaus A. OTTO, who developed the concept of a four-stroke engine, and Gottlieb DAIMLER,

Motorcycles became practical vehicles with the development of the internal combustion engine during the late 19th century. Contemporary motorcycles include many basic engineering features developed before World War I. Over the years, however, motorcycles gradually have been refined through manufacturing methods and materials technology so that modern cycles are both lighter and swifter than their predecessors. (See also next page.)

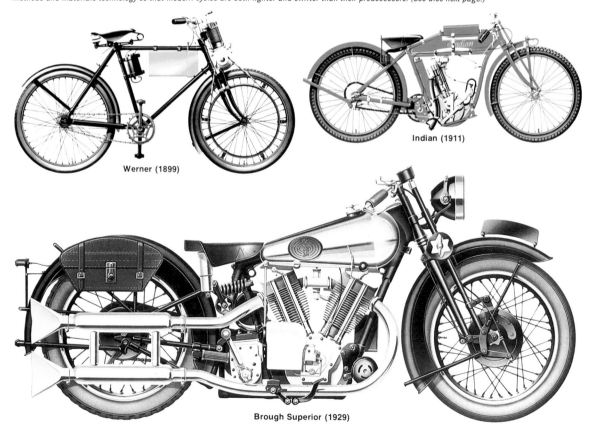

Werner (1899)

Indian (1911)

Brough Superior (1929)

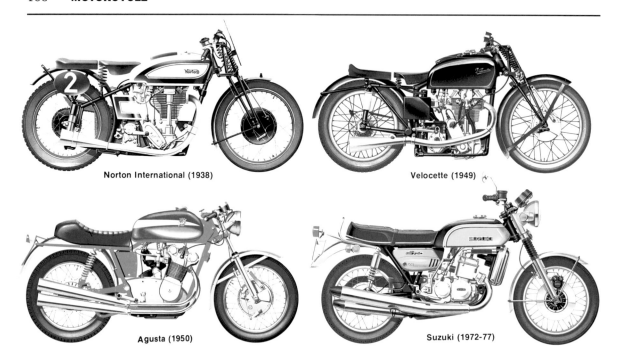

Norton International (1938)

Velocette (1949)

Agusta (1950)

Suzuki (1972-77)

who used Otto's idea and in 1885 built a motorcycle powered by a single-cylinder air-cooled engine, which developed one-half horsepower. The Hildebrand brothers of Munich called their design a *Motorad*. With their assistant, Alois Wolfmüller, they produced the Hildebrand-Wolfmüller, the first commercially practical motorcycle. With a water-cooled, 1,488-cc, four-stroke, two-cylinder engine, it was capable of approximately 40 km/h (25 mph).

Several technical problems remained, including the lack of an effective means of transmitting power to the driving wheel. Customarily, a leather belt was employed, but this tended to slip when wet, and it frequently broke because of the jerky power impulses of early engines.

About 1900, steel chain was first used to replace leather belts for power transmission. Roc, a British company, introduced a friction clutch and four-speed transmission in 1904.

Disc brakes were employed on the motorcycles built by the Imperial Company of Great Britain as early as 1901. Overhead cams and valves, fuel injection, multigear transmissions, shaft drive, and telescopic suspension all appeared prior to 1918.

The Present. Modern motorcycles have become lighter, faster, and very specialized. Today a typical street bike has four cylinders with four carburetors, cast-aluminum wheels, at least one disc brake, a 5- or 6-speed transmission, and a sophisticated electronic ignition system. Most larger street bikes are powered by four-stroke engines. Dirt, or off-road, bikes, on the other hand, typically have two-stroke, single-cylinder engines, although four-stroke singles are regaining popularity.

National governments generally prescribe certain equipment standards for motorcycles used on the streets.

For example, in the United States electrical switches and lighting equipment, hydraulic hoses and brakes, tires, and many other items must meet strict federal requirements.

Following World War II there were a large number of motorcycle manufacturers, but by the 1970s many had gone out of business. Although Japanese manufacturers (Honda, Kawasaki, Yamaha) continued to dominate the market, by the late 1980s the once-popular U.S. firm of Harley-Davidson was retaking some of its lost market share.

motorcycling Motorcycling is not only a popular form of transportation and recreation; it is also an organized, competitive sport. In the late 1980s more than 4 million motorcycles were registered in the United States. Their uses ranged from traffic control, to special off-road races, to daily commuting. The American Motorcyclist Association (AMA), which had 187,000 members in 1991, is the national governing body that oversees motorcycle racing in the United States. Each year about 3,000–3,500 AMA-approved races are held, of which 80–90 are for professionals and the remainder for amateurs.

International motorcycle racing is regulated by the Fédération Internationale Motocycliste (FIM), which sanctions the Grand Prix series of races.

The two basic types of motorcycle races are road races and motocross races. Others include hill climbs, flat-track racing, sidecar racing, indoor racing, and drag racing.

U.S. road racers compete in several engine-size categories—250 cubic centimeters (cc): Grand Prix; 600 and 750 cc: Supersport; 750 and 1,200 cc: Superbike. The number of cylinders may differ from class to class. Road-racing machines, powered by multicylinder engines, have

Popular forms of competitive motorcycling include road races, speedway races, and motocross. Road races (left) are conducted on paved courses similar to those used in automotive. Cycles used in speedway racing (center) are lightweight and have no brakes. The unpaved course is flat, and cyclists turn by sliding sideways around curves. Motocross (right) racing is conducted over a closed course on natural terrain featuring hills, gullies, and mud holes.

low-slung chassis, short handlebars, and footrests near the rear wheel. The rider sits behind a streamlined windshield in a tight crouch that lowers the center of gravity. Road races are run on oval or irregular tracks with straightaways that may allow speeds of up to 298 km/h (185 mph). The major U.S. road race is the 200-mi (321.8-km) event that is held annually at the Daytona International Speedway in Daytona, Fla.

Motocross races are run over natural-terrain courses chosen for their ruggedness and unevenness. The machines that the racers use are designed to meet strictly enforced regulations and at the same time deliver maximum power and tractability. Motocross machines are also divided into competitive categories according to engine size; 125, 250, and 500 cc are the three groups. These machines, which are powered by single-cylinder engines, have knobby tires for traction, wide-set handlebars for steering leverage, and long-travel suspension that can absorb the bumps and jolts of a motocross course. One of the most important AMA-certified motocross races is the annual 1,000-mi (1,609-km) event held on the Baja California peninsula.

Motown

Motown [moh'-town]   Motown, the most successful black-owned American record company, was founded in 1960 in Detroit by Berry Gordy, Jr. Derived from "Motor Town," the name also denoted the company's musical style, which featured unusual song structures, heavy rhythms, and large orchestras. Live performances by Motown artists required carefully controlled choreography, set routines, and elaborate costumes and grooming, to produce what was in effect a Motown-style package.

The Motown formula created a number of stars during the 1960s, including Stevie WONDER, Marvin Gaye, and Diana ROSS and the Supremes; in the 1970s, The Jackson Five (see JACKSON, MICHAEL); and in the 1980s, Lionel Richie. At the peak of its success, Motown represented the best of mass-produced, black-derived pop music. Al-though its later productions were less inspired and more obviously the products of a musical assembly line, Motown was largely responsible for introducing the sounds of contemporary black music to a large white audience.

See also: ROCK MUSIC.

Mott, Lucretia Coffin

Mott, Lucretia Coffin   Lucretia Coffin Mott, b. Nantucket, Mass., Jan. 3, 1793, d. Nov. 11, 1880, was an American Quaker preacher, abolitionist, and leading women's-rights advocate. She began preaching in 1818 and was soon an acknowledged minister. When the Society of Friends split in 1827, she affiliated with the liberal faction led by Elias HICKS. Influenced by Hicks and other abolitionists, she attended the founding convention of the American Anti-Slavery Society in 1833 and four years later helped establish the Anti-Slavery Convention of American Women. After 1840, when an international antislavery conference in London rejected her credentials and those of other American women delegates because of their sex, Mott gave greater attention to women's-rights issues. In 1848 she and Elizabeth Cady STANTON organized the SENECA FALLS CONVENTION; she also participated in the founding of the American Equal Rights Association in 1866.

Mound Builders

Mound Builders   *Mound Builders*, in archaeology, is a general term used to refer to the peoples who constructed earthen mounds and other earthworks in eastern and central North America during prehistoric times. Far from being the product of a single, uniform culture, the mounds and earthworks were built at various times from about 1000 BC to after AD 1500 by many different Indian societies in a large area extending from the Appalachian Mountains west to the eastern edge of the prairies and from the Great Lakes area to the Gulf of Mexico.

Archaeological work has documented prehistoric mounds and earthworks numbering in the tens of thou-

The sinuous earthwork known as the Great Serpent Mound, located near Hillsboro, Ohio, is an effigy mound constructed about 2,000 years ago by the Adena culture of the Woodland tradition.

sands. The total number constructed will never be known, however, because a great many have been destroyed by natural forces such as floods, by farming, and by other human activities.

The earthen constructions have been classified into three principal categories: burial mounds; platform or temple mounds, on which important buildings were placed; and circular and geometric ceremonial earthworks. Archaeologists recognize two major traditions of the mound-building cultures—the Woodland and the Mississippian.

Woodland Tradition. Woodland cultural complexes are known to have developed in eastern North America from about 1000 BC to the early historic period (AD c.1700). The mounds associated with the Woodland tradition are primarily burial mounds, although circular and geometric earthworks also appeared in some areas.

One of the best-known Early Woodland complexes is referred to as the Adena culture. This mound-building cultural complex was located in the central Ohio Valley and in the lower Kanawha Valley of West Virginia. The Adena mounds were constructed from the first half of the 1st millennium BC to early in the 1st century AD. Many of the late Adena mounds were large (from 6 to 24 m/20 to 80 ft high), were apparently constructed over many years, and contained numerous burials, some of them in log tombs. The Adena people also constructed earthen circles enclosing an interior ditch with an entryway. Some of the larger examples, such as Braddock Mound, near Fredericktown, Ohio, had a burial mound in the center of the circle.

The late 1st century BC to about AD 400 marks the major period of burial-mound construction from southern Florida to northeast Texas and from New York to Minnesota. Most of the Middle Woodland societies were connected through trade, exchange, and common cultural patterns with the Hopewellian societies, which represent the most highly developed culture of the period, centered in south-

ern Ohio and the Illinois Valley. The largest and most elaborate mounds, built in southern Ohio, were often associated with complex geometric earthworks in the form of circles, rectangles, octagons, parallel walls, hilltop fortlike constructions, and other forms. The precise function of these earthworks is unknown. The largest and best preserved, at Newark, Ohio, covered about 5 km^2 (2 mi^2).

Late Woodland societies in the upper Mississippi valley of Illinois, Iowa, Wisconsin, and Minnesota erected effigy mounds in the period from about 400 to 1100. These burial mounds were sculpted in dome-shaped, curvilinear patterns or in the form of bird, animal, and human representations, such as the Marching Bears Mound in Wisconsin. The burials were apparently placed in the area corresponding to the heart of the effigy figures, which were often more than 100 m (325 ft) long but generally only about 1 to 2 m (3 to 6 ft) high.

Elsewhere during the Late Woodland period (400–700) conical mounds of simple construction continued to be erected. New burial techniques at mound sites in the Ohio, Indiana, Kentucky, Illinois, and Missouri areas included the use of stone vaults and cists to enclose human remains.

Mississippian Tradition. The large-scale farming of maize and beans was a major factor in the development of a new cultural tradition—the Mississippian—and the increased size of Mississippian settlement populations. Beginning about 700 in the flood plains of the central and lower Mississippi and its tributaries, many towns and villages developed, characterized by the erection of palisades and flat-topped, rectangular mounds that served as bases for temples and other important structures. Large political and religious centers, such as the CAHOKIA MOUNDS, across the Mississippi from present-day St. Louis, Mo., contained 10 to 50 or more platform mounds and accommodated populations of 500 to perhaps 10,000 people.

Although most Mississippian groups buried their dead in cemeteries, the construction of the Woodland-type burial mounds did not disappear entirely. At the larger centers the elite families were sometimes placed in special burial mounds with elaborate grave goods representing their status in the society. These burials took place from about 1000 to 1500, when Mississippian culture was at its peak; the imposing monuments and associated artifacts—including outstanding pottery, weavings, and stone carvings—are a reflection of the most advanced prehistoric Indian groups in eastern North America.

The powerful chiefdoms of the Mississippian tradition were still flourishing when early European explorers such as Hernando de Soto visited southeastern North America in the 16th century. By the mid-17th century, however, mound building had ceased, and the populations of these groups had vastly declined, in part the result of internal warfare and epidemic diseases of European origin.

Mount, William Sidney   William Sidney Mount, b. Setauket, N.Y., Nov. 26, 1807, d. Nov. 19, 1868, was one of the first American genre painters; his scenes of dancers, musicians, and other rural activities were set in his native Long Island. Although he began his career as a religious and portrait painter, Mount soon turned (c.1830) to genre subjects. He was one of the first American artists to depict black people, in scenes or in individual portraits. His realistic and detailed paintings captured the warmth and humor of rural American life.

Mount Holyoke College   Established in 1837, Mount Holyoke College is a private 4-year liberal arts school for women in South Hadley, Mass. It is one of the SEVEN SISTERS COLLEGES, sharing with another of them, Smith, cooperative study programs at Amherst and Hampshire colleges and the University of Massachusetts.

Mount of Olives   The Mount of Olives is a ridge or mountain located east of JERUSALEM across the Valley of Kidron and known as the site of various New Testament activities of Jesus. The Garden of Gethsemane is at its foot. Jesus' entrance into Jerusalem (Luke 19:37) was over this route, and the Ascension is traditionally located there (Acts 1:12). It is the site of many Christian shrines.

Mount Rushmore   see RUSHMORE, MOUNT

Mount Vernon (city in New York)   Mount Vernon is a city in New York on the Bronx and Hutchinson rivers and adjacent to New York City. It has a population of 67,153 (1990) and is regarded primarily as a residential suburb. There is some industry in the city, including food processing and the manufacture of electrical products and pharmaceuticals. Saint Paul's Church (1761) was designated a national historic site in 1943 because of its connection with John Peter ZENGER.

Mount Vernon was first settled in 1664. In 1852 it was laid out as a planned community by a group of workmen seeking moderately priced homesites for their families; it was named for George Washington's Virginia home.

Mount Vernon (Washington's home)   Mount Vernon, near Alexandria, Va., the home of George WASHINGTON, was a small house, probably built before 1700, that Washington enlarged in stages. The exterior walls were finished in wood that was painted and sanded to resemble rusticated stone, probably inspired by illustrations in William Adam's *Vitruvius Scotticus* (c.1780), a neoclassical architectural pattern-book. The interiors were remodeled using decorative details culled from English publications of the contemporary classicizing style of Robert Adam. The familiar portico, with eight slender piers, was added to the Georgian structure in 1784, and the cupola over the center of the house was completed in 1787. The effect of the whole is that of a composition of borrowed English motifs rendered with a distinctively graceful naiveté that gives American colonial architecture its special character.

Mount Wilson Observatory   Mount Wilson Observatory, located northwest of Los Angeles, was established in 1904. It was operated by the Carnegie Institute, Washington, D.C., until 1989, when a new organization, the Mount Wilson Institute of Pasadena, Calif., took over its operation. With PALOMAR OBSERVATORY it constituted (1970–80) the Hale Observatories, named for their founder and Mount Wilson's first director, George Ellery HALE. Mount Wilson's 100-in (254-cm) Hooker reflecting telescope, installed in 1918, was the world's largest until 1948, when the 200-in (508-cm) Hale telescope became operational at Palomar. Other Mount Wilson instruments include a 60-in (152-cm) reflector and two solar telescopes. Observations made and research carried out at Mount Wilson have revealed the structure of galaxies and the enormous size of the observable universe.

mountain   Mountains are landforms with a narrow summit area that rise sharply and prominently above their surroundings. Occurring worldwide, mountain ranges are often a major factor affecting regional weather patterns. In many places they have been a hindrance to travel and communication. Mountains are important economically for their metallic mineral deposits.

Classification

Isolated mountains are those not associated with others in age, origin, or geographic distribution. Single mountain peaks are most commonly the result of volcanic activity.

A mountain range is a long, narrow belt of mountains of similar age and origin. The Sangre de Cristo Range in Colorado and New Mexico, for example, is more than 400 km (250 mi) long and less than 24 km (15 mi) wide. When geographically associated mountains of similar age

Mount McKinley, in central Alaska, is the highest mountain in North America. Numerous glaciers cover its summit and flow down the southern and eastern sides.

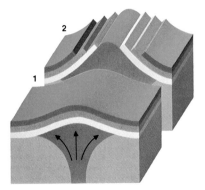

(Left) *Dome mountains are formed when molten magma (1) from the Earth's interior rises and spreads between layers of sedimentary rock near the surface, causing them to arch upward. Erosion (2) eventually exposes the various overlying rock strata and the underlying igneous rock.*

(Right) *Folded mountains result when horizontal compressive forces bend, or fold (3), the rock strata into regular upfolds, or anticlines, and downfolds, or synclines. Erosion (4) along the fold crests subsequently leads to the formation of a series of parallel ridges and valleys.*

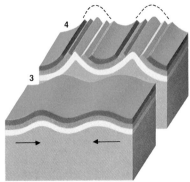

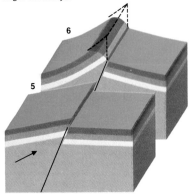

(Left) *Block mountains are created when movements (5) along faults, or cracks, in the Earth's solid rock crust raise large masses, or blocks, of the crust above the surrounding area. Erosion (6) gradually rounds off the upthrust overhang and exposes the different strata.*

(Right) *A volcano erupts (7) when hot liquid magma and dissolved gases from deep within the Earth's crust are expelled through cracks at the surface. Various types of peak (8) may be built up around a volcano's opening by gradual accumulation of lava, ash, and solid fragments ejected in successive eruptions.*

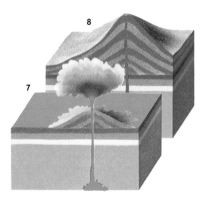

and origin are not arranged along a narrow belt—the BLACK HILLS in South Dakota are an example—they form a mountain group.

A mountain system is composed of ranges and groups of similar age and origin. The ROCKY MOUNTAINS comprise a mountain system that includes the BROOKS, TETON, WASATCH, and many other ranges. A mountain cordillera may include ranges, groups, and systems of differing origins and ages. The North American cordillera, for example, includes the COAST RANGES, the CASCADE RANGE, the SIERRA NEVADA, the ALEUTIAN ISLANDS chain, and the Rocky Mountains.

Geology

Mountains are generally placed in four categories on the basis of geology: folded, volcanic, erosional, and fault-block.

Folded Mountains. Mountains of the folded type have been formed by the interactions of the borders of moving crustal plates (see PLATE TECTONICS). This type of mountain-building, called orogeny or orogenesis, is preceded by a long buildup of erosional deposition along a continent's edge. When the crustal plate the continent rests upon collides with another crustal plate, the sediments deposited along the edge of the continent are crumpled. Sedimentary rocks in crustal areas squeezed between converging crustal plates are subject to intense pressure and eventual uplift as the crustal blocks buckle.

The multiple collisions of the North American and Eurasian plates, from late Precambrian time (prior to 570 million years ago) through the Appalachian orogeny (250 million years ago), are thought to have created the APPALACHIAN MOUNTAINS. The complex interactions of the North American and Pacific plates, extending from the Nevadan (160 to 104 million years ago) through the Laramide orogeny (65 to 35 million years ago) to the present, formed the ranges in the North American cordillera. The convergence of the African and Eurasian crustal plates resulted in the formation of the PYRENEES and the ALPS (225 to 200 million and 65 to 2 million years ago, respectively). The convergence of the South American and Pacific plates (begun 70 million years ago) has formed the ANDES, flanking the western coast of South America. The ongoing convergence of the Eurasian and Indian crustal plates (begun less than 65 million years ago) has produced the HIMALAYAS in the Asian cordillera. The Himalayas continue to rise at a rate of about 5 cm (2 in) per year.

Volcanic, Erosional, and Fault-Block Mountains. Volcanic mountains may be isolated, as is Mount Rainier, or in long chains, exemplified by the Hawaiian Islands (see HAWAII, state). MAUNA KEA and MAUNA LOA, both over 4,000 m (over 13,000 ft) are two of the Hawaiian chain of volcanic mountains (not all exposed above water) stretching 2,400 km (1,500 mi) across the Pacific Ocean. Volcanic mountains are of two basic types: cinder cones, such as VESUVIUS (1,277 m/4,190 ft), characterized by a rhyolitic lava and explosive eruptions; and shield VOLCANOES, such as Mauna Loa, characterized by a flattened dome originating from flows of fluid, basaltic lava.

The processes of erosion that wear down the land act to carve out and carry away those rocks that are less re-

HIGHEST MOUNTAINS IN VARIOUS REGIONS

Name	Feet	Meters	Location
Africa			
Kilimanjaro	19,340	5,895	Tanzania
Kenya	17,058	5,200	Kenya
Margherita	16,765	5,110	Uganda-Zaire
Antarctica			
Vinson	16,864	5,140	
Tyree	16,289	4,970	
Asia*			
Everest	29,028	8,848	Nepal-Tibet
K-2	28,250	8,611	Kashmir
Kanchenjunga	28,168	8,586	Nepal-Sikkim
Lhotse I	27,923	8,511	Nepal-Tibet
Makalu	27,790	8,470	Nepal-Tibet
Lhotse II	27,560	8,400	Nepal-Tibet
Dhaulagiri	26,810	8,172	Nepal
Australia and New Zealand			
Cook	12,349	3,764	New Zealand
Kosciusko	7,314	2,229	Australia
Europe*†			
Blanc	15,771	4,807	France-Italy
Rosa	15,203	4,634	Switzerland
Dom	14,911	4,545	Switzerland
North America			
McKinley	20,320	6,194	U.S. (Alaska)
Logan	19,520	5,950	Canada
Citlaltepetl	18,700	5,699	Mexico
St. Elias	18,008	5,489	U.S.-Canada
Popocatépetl	17,889	5,453	Mexico
Oceania			
Wilhelm	14,793	4,509	Papua New Guinea
Giluwe	14,331	4,368	Papua New Guinea
Mauna Kea	13,796	4,205	U.S. (Hawaii)
South America			
Aconcagua	22,831	6,959	Argentina
Ojos del Salado	22,574	6,881	Argentina
Bonete	22,546	6,872	Argentina-Chile
Tupungato	22,310	6,800	Argentina-Chile
USSR†			
Communism	24,590	7,495	
Pobedy	24,406	7,439	USSR-China
Lenin	23,405	7,134	
Korzhenevski	23,310	7,105	
Revolution	22,880	6,974	

*Excluding USSR.
†The two peaks of Elbrus (5,642 m/18,510 ft and 5,633 m/18,481 ft), followed by several other peaks in the Caucasus of the European USSR, are the highest mountains in Europe. Within the USSR, however, they are dwarfed by many peaks in Central Asia.

sistant. Erosional mountains, typified by the CATSKILL MOUNTAINS of New York, are those formed by the residual relief of resistant strata.

The vertical movement, by faulting, of large blocks of crustal material results in the formation of fault-block mountains and fault-block valleys. Mountains and valleys such as these, called HORSTS AND GRABENS, characterize the landscape of the BASIN AND RANGE PROVINCE in Nevada and Utah.

—

mountain climbing Mountain climbing, or mountaineering, is an amateur pursuit that is internationally popular. Since the 1960s the popularity of mountain climbing has grown enormously. In an average year about half a million people climb mountains.

Anyone attempting a climb should be aware that the sport is dangerous, especially to those with little experience. The growing number of climbers has led to an increase in accidents and deaths. More than 100 climbers are killed each year in the Alps; in 1988, 24 persons were killed in the United States, and 4 died while climbing in Canada.

History. Prior to the 18th century mountains were believed by most Europeans to be the abode of spirits and therefore best avoided. In 1760 a wealthy Genevan, Horace Benedict de Saussure, began to make ascents in the Swiss Alps. He hoped to become the first to scale Mont Blanc—at 4,807 m (15,771 ft) the highest point in Europe—but two other Swiss, Dr. Michel Paccard and Jacques Balmat, reached the summit first, in 1786. The British soon adopted mountain climbing as a sport, and between 1854 and 1870, Britons scaled every major peak in Europe. In the next 30 years climbers ascended all of the most formidable peaks in North and South America and Africa. They finally turned their attention to the greatest mountain range on Earth, the Himalayas. In 1902 a British team tried to climb K-2 (Mount Godwin Austen); at 8,610.6 m (28,250 ft) it is the second highest mountain in the world. In 1922 and 1924 other British groups made attempts on the world's highest peak, Mount Everest (8,848 m/29,028 ft). It was not until 1950 that a French team scaled Annapurna (8,078 m/ 26,504 ft). Between 1950 and 1964 the world's 14 highest mountains, all in the Himalayas, were climbed. Mount Everest was scaled in 1953 by Sir Edmund HILLARY of New Zealand and Tenzing Norgay, a Sherpa native, and K-2 was conquered in 1954 by an Italian expedition.

Equipment. The equipment used in mountain climbing has evolved with the increased popularity of the sport. In the 19th century climbers wore heavy, protective clothing and boots with iron spikes in the soles. They carried wooden poles called alpenstocks from which the modern ice ax, a more sophisticated tool designed for use on snow and ice, is derived. The crampon—a set of removable steel spikes worn on the boot for climbing on snow and ice—was developed in 1908. Modern rock climbers wear nonrestrictive, lightweight clothing and are aided by nylon rope, pitons (metal spikes with a ring in one end), and carabiners (oblong metal rings with spring-loaded closing gates), which are used to clip the rope to the piton. Many climbers also wear helmets. A prerequisite for any type of climbing is to be physically fit enough to hike over many kilometers of rugged terrain in order to reach the base of a mountain.

Types of Climbing. Today many climbers are proficient in only one particular kind of climbing, such as scaling vertical rock walls or making winter ascents of frozen waterfalls. Rock climbing is further divided into free climbing (in which only hands and feet are used and the rope is merely a safety device) and direct-aid climbing (in which the climber fixes a piton or an aluminum wedge called a chock in the rock and then attaches a stirrup ladder that is used to climb a meter or so at a time in order to emplace the next piton or chock).

Conservation of Mountains. In the United States since 1970, rock climbing has seen important changes in technique and equipment. Before the 1960s most ascents were made using pitons made of hard steel. Mountaineers noticed that constant placement and removal of pitons on popular climbing routes was causing permanent damage to the rocks. The solution was to use aluminum chocks, which, because they are wedged and not hammered and are made of relatively soft material, cause no damage to the rocks. Today nearly all climbers in the United States use these chocks, and this practice is called clean climbing.

Changing Techniques. Recent changes in technique have been introduced by climbers in the Himalayas. Traditional Himalayan expeditions were paramilitary-type operations involving dozens or hundreds of porters. In 1975 two Austrians, Reinhold Messner and Peter Habeler, made the first ascent of the northwest face of Hidden Peak (8,068 m/26,470 ft) in the Karakoram range of the Himalayas. The two made the climb by themselves in three days with only a dozen porters to help carry gear to the mountain base. In 1978, Messner and Habeler again defied orthodox technique when they became the first to reach the summit of Mount Everest without relying on pressurized bottled oxygen. Messner made the first solo climb of Everest in 1980, again without bottled oxygen.

mountain goat The mountain goat, *Oreamnos americanus,* in the family Bovidae, is not a true goat (*Ca-*

The mountain goat is really a small antelope that inhabits the mountains of North America. Mountain goats feed on mosses and other vegetation found above the timberline.

pra) but rather a member of a group (tribe Rupicaprini) known as goat-antelopes. Mountain goats stand about 1 m (39 in) high at the shoulder and weigh up to 140 kg (300 lb). The coat is white, sometimes tinged with yellow, with a thick, woolly underfur. The hair above the shoulders and on the neck is long and stiff. Both sexes have beards and permanent, black, unbranched horns that seldom exceed 23 cm (9 in) long. The hooves are hard and sharp and surround soft pads, enabling the animals to obtain footing on ice and rocks. Mountain goats are found from southwestern Alaska along the Rocky Mountains into the northern United States. Mating occurs in November, and one or two kids are born in the spring.

mountain laurel Mountain laurel, *Kalmia latifolia,* is an evergreen shrub or small tree of the heath family, Ericaceae, found in eastern North America. Mountain laurel grows to 9 m (30 ft) high and is commonly found in hardwood forests, where it may form dense thickets. It bears clusters of white or rose flowers with purplish markings. Its leaves are leathery, dark on the upper surface, lighter beneath, and poisonous to livestock.

mountain life Mountains present a unique and often formidable set of conditions to which life must adapt in order to survive. As the elevation increases the air becomes thinner and temperatures cooler, the growing season is shorter, and soils tend to be thinner and less fertile. Organisms inhabiting mountains have evolved the ability to withstand high winds, widely fluctuating temperatures, floods, drought, rockslides, avalanches, and bursts of solar radiation. Furthermore, conditions can vary among mountains of the same range or among different elevations on the same mountain.

Plant Life. Alpine tundra plants in general are small, often ground-huggers, and either woody or herbaceous but almost always perennial. To survive they must retain as much of the little available heat as is possible. A low, tufted, dense growth habit contributes to heat retention; hairiness is also useful. The leaves of many alpine plants are a deep, dark green: the darker the color, the more heat will be absorbed.

As forests give way to alpine tundra at the timberline, trees become smaller and smaller, until they adopt a unique shape called *krummholz* (German for "crooked wood"). Krummholz plants are woody plants (usually trees) that bend with the force of the prevailing wind. They become stunted, wind-bent, and scraggly and commonly hug the ground.

Many alpine plants can grow (metabolize) and even flower (reproduce) at very low temperatures. Their cells are very small and contain high concentrations of solutes. This protects the cells from freezing by lowering the freezing point of the cell sap—a mechanism similar to that of antifreeze.

Alpine tundra plants can be broadly classified as xerophytes, or plants adapted to dry environments. Although alpine tundra may be snow-covered most of the year, water is usually lacking during the growing season. Many of these plants have deep taproot systems for obtaining water and can thus offset the drying effects of harsh winds.

Animal Life. Because of their limited combination of acceptable living space and water, mountains can support only a relatively few animals. These animals often need to be specially adapted to severe cold conditions, although—unlike plants—they can move to different locations in response to environmental fluctuations. Most mountaintops support all kinds of animals except reptiles and amphibians. The ecological relationships among the resident animals are fairly simple and very fragile compared to animal relationships among the lower mountain zones, because food webs in alpine tundra comprise fewer predators, consumers, and primary producers.

In general, mountain cold is not a limiting factor for the larger animals. Most are well insulated by their fur and fat. Nonetheless, the Rocky Mountain goat is one of the few animals that can withstand even mild winter days exposed above the timberline. Most large mountain animals, such as the bighorn sheep and the elk, migrate downslope in autumn and upslope in spring. The ground squirrel passes through winter by hibernating. The meadow vole actively spends the winter under the insulating cover of snow, where it is able to gather sufficient food and water to survive.

Certain animals can live at extremely high altitudes. The jumping spiders, the highest permanent resident organisms known, have been observed at 6,700 m (22,000 ft) on Mount Everest. They prey on small flies and springtails, which in turn feed on fungi and rotting vegetation.

mountain lion   see PUMA

Mountain Meadows Massacre   Mountain Meadows Massacre is the name given to the slaughter, in September 1857, by a group of Mormons and PAIUTE Indians of about 120 settlers traveling through Utah Territory on their way to California. The attack, apparently led by Mormon elder John Doyle LEE, stemmed from the hostility of some of the settlers toward the Mormons and from Mormon anger over federal troop intervention in the territory.

mountain men   Mountain men roamed the Rocky Mountain region of the United States in search of the valuable furs of animals, especially beaver, during the first half of the 19th century. Although motivated mainly by the desire for personal gain, they established trails and accumulated information that later greatly aided settlement of the far western FRONTIER. The heyday of the mountain men began with William Henry ASHLEY and Andrew Henry's expedition to the upper Missouri River in 1822. During the next 15 years American and some French and Spanish trappers discovered passes through the Rocky Mountains, including the South Pass, explored the Great Basin and far Southwest, and developed several useful routes to California and Oregon. Explorers such as James BRIDGER, Thomas FITZPATRICK, and, preeminently,

Jedediah S. SMITH contributed greatly to the knowledge of the region and solved many geographical mysteries.

During this time perhaps as many as 3,000 mountain men operated in the Far West. Some worked for fur companies; others worked independently and sold their furs to the highest bidder at the summer rendezvous held annually from 1825 to 1840. Mountain men lived in isolation for much of the year, and most learned the techniques and adopted the style of life of the Indians in order to survive the dangers of the wilderness. Some returned to civilization once the FUR TRADE began to decline after about 1840, whereas others such as Bridger, Fitzpatrick, and Kit CARSON stayed in the West and worked as immigrant guides, Indian agents, or government scouts.

mountain sheep   Mountain sheep are members of the genus *Ovis* in the family Bovidae and are characterized by narrow muzzles, pointed ears, and massive curling horns in the older males (rams). Unlike true goats, *Capra*, they lack beards and have dished, or concave, foreheads. The largest of the mountain sheep, the argali, reaches 1.2 m (4 ft) in height at the shoulder and 160 kg (350 lb) in weight. Coat colors range from white to gray or dark brown. The coat is generally short and coarse, with only the mouflon species developing a woolly undercoat in winter. Some forms have a mane of hair down the front of the neck. Mountain sheep generally inhabit dry upland areas, from craggy mountains into semideserts. During the summer months the adult males live in groups apart from the females and their young. In late fall and early winter the males battle for possession of females, which they gather into harems of up to 12 ewes. Gestation lasts 5 to 6 months, and from one to three lambs are born in the spring.

Mountain sheep are usually classified into six species: the bighorn, *O. canadensis*, of the western United States and southwestern Canada; the Dall sheep, *O. dalli*, of Alaska and northwestern Canada; the argali, or Marco Polo sheep, *O. ammon*, of central Asia; the red sheep, *O. orientalis*, of southwestern Asia; the Laristan sheep, *O. laristanica,* of southern Iran; and the mouflon, *O. musimon*, of Sardinia and Corsica.

mountain and valley winds   Mountain and valley WINDS are small-scale breezes that develop locally in response to daily changes in air temperature and pressure. The mountain, or katabatic, wind blows from the upper slopes down into valleys at night. The valley, or anabatic, wind blows from lower elevations upslope in the daytime.

The higher slopes of mountains and plateaus lose heat by radiation more rapidly at night than do valley bottoms. Air lying over the cooler surfaces is cooled, becomes more dense, and flows down the slopes as a mountain wind. The local circulation system thus created between slope and valley is easily disrupted by a large-scale storm. Ordinarily, a mountain wind begins before midnight and continues until after sunrise. The flow of air into partially enclosed valleys can result in cool pools of air and temperature inversions.

Valley winds develop greatest strength where mountain sides face the noon Sun and valleys are deep. Unlike the mountain wind, which is a cooling phenomenon, the valley wind results from heating of slopes. As the overlying air heats, it expands, becomes less dense, and rises. The pressure gradient, which determines the direction of flow, is from the free air over the valley toward the upper slopes. Valley winds usually begin well before noon and continue until sunset.

See also: CHINOOK.

mountaineering   see MOUNTAIN CLIMBING

Mountbatten of Burma, Louis Mountbatten, 1st Earl

[mownt-bat'-uhn]   Louis Francis Albert Victor Nicholas Mountbatten, b. June 25, 1900, d. Aug. 27, 1979, was one of Britain's great war heroes. A great-grandson of Queen Victoria, he entered the Royal Navy in 1913. (At that time his father, Prince Louis of Battenberg, was first sea lord; after the outbreak of World War I, however, he was forced to resign because of his German birth, and he later changed the family name to Mountbatten.) While chief of British combined operations (1942–43) in World War II, Mountbatten directed the invasion of Madagascar and commando raids on Norway and France. As supreme Allied commander for Southeast Asia (1943–46), he was responsible for the recapture of Burma from Japan. The last viceroy of India, he supervised the creation of the states of India and Pakistan in 1947. He was created Lord Mountbatten of Burma that same year. Subsequently, he was first sea lord (1955–59). Mountbatten retired in 1965, although he remained a confidant of Queen Elizabeth II, whose husband, Prince Philip, was his nephew. He died when a bomb, planted by the Irish Republican Army, demolished his fishing boat in waters off the northwest coast of Ireland.

mouse   Mice are small RODENTS. Like all rodents they have gnawing teeth. The word *mouse*, however, has been applied loosely to many rodents simply because of their size and superficial similarities, such as a somewhat pointed snout, a slender and sparsely haired tail, relative-

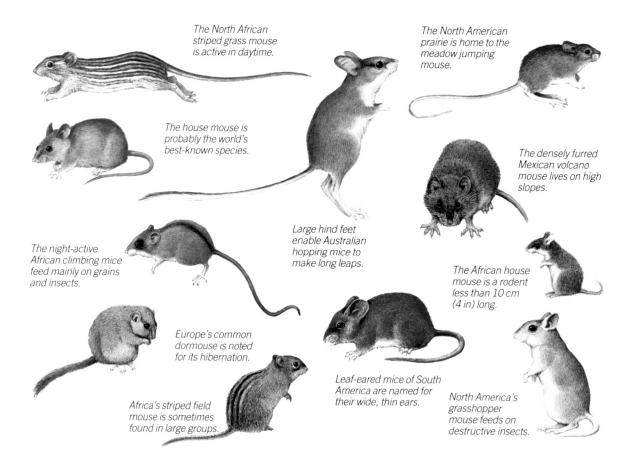

The North African striped grass mouse is active in daytime.

The North American prairie is home to the meadow jumping mouse.

The house mouse is probably the world's best-known species.

The densely furred Mexican volcano mouse lives on high slopes.

The night-active African climbing mice feed mainly on grains and insects.

Large hind feet enable Australian hopping mice to make long leaps.

The African house mouse is a rodent less than 10 cm (4 in) long.

Europe's common dormouse is noted for its hibernation.

Africa's striped field mouse is sometimes found in large groups.

Leaf-eared mice of South America are named for their wide, thin ears.

North America's grasshopper mouse feeds on destructive insects.

ly conspicuous ears, and an elongate body. In terms of these characteristics, mice are grouped below into New World and Old World families, although both contain many species other than those called mice. In addition, many small rodents with distinctly different characteristics are known as mice, including the short-tailed field mice, or field voles, *Microtus*; the pocket mice, family Heteromyidae; the jumping mice, family Zapodidae; and the squirrellike dormice and related forms, families Gliridae, Platacanthomyidae, and Seleviniidae.

Many mice carry viral, bacterial, and parasitic diseases. Mice also have considerable economic impact through crop damage, destruction of trees, and food contamination.

New World Mice. The family Cricetidae, which also contains hamsters, rats, lemmings, voles, and gerbils, comprises about 177 species of mice, grouped into 30 genera. The best-known native North American forms are the white-footed or deer mice, *Peromyscus*, represented by approximately 57 species ranging from northern coniferous forests into tropical habitats in Central America. The most widespread species is the deer mouse, *P. maniculatus*. Other common North American mice are the harvest mice, *Reithrodontomys*, and the grasshopper mice, *Onychomys*. The smallest New World form is the pygmy mouse, *Baiomys*, which may be less than 100 mm (4 in) in length, including the tail.

Old World Mice. The family Muridae, which also contains rats and gerbil mice, comprises about 130 species of mice, grouped into 30 genera, including *Mus*, the house mice, and *Apodemus*, the Old World field mice. These mice are found naturally only in the Eastern Hemisphere. They are common throughout Eurasia and Africa and through Indonesia into Australia, being absent only on Madagascar. Their diet consists mainly of plant materials, but small animals, such as insects, may also be eaten. Forms living in association with humans may eat almost any food. Most species are terrestrial, although some may spend most of their time in trees or shrubs. Some dig burrows or use those of other animals; some occupy abandoned birds' nests; and many use crevices, hollow logs, or other natural features. The most widely distributed mammal other than humans is the house mouse, *Mus musculus*, which has been introduced into almost every place inhabited by humans. Many genetic variations, such as the white (albino) mouse, are bred as laboratory animals or pets.

mousebird   The six species of the genus *Colius* are commonly called mousebirds or colies. Gregarious, mainly fruit-eating, brown or gray birds of African forest edges and brushland, they are called mousebirds possibly from their habit of creeping about trees and brush. Because their relationships to other birds are obscure, mousebirds are placed by themselves in the family Coliidae, in its own order, Coliiformes. Mousebirds range from 29 to 35.5 cm (11 to 14 in) in length, two-thirds of which is the long, stiff, pointed tail. The hind toe can be reversed so that all four toes extend forward. A hibernationlike state of torpidity occurs in the speckled mousebird, *C. striatus*.

Mousterian [moos-teer'-ee-uhn]   The Mousterian, a PALEOLITHIC tool culture, was first identified at Le Moustier, in southwest France, as encompassing tools of the "Cave Bear Age." Mousterian assemblages are best represented in Europe, North Africa, and the Near East, although they have also been recognized in South Africa and in China. The Mousterian tradition is characterized by numerous variations in the frequency of particular tool types, which include scrapers, points, notched and denticulate (toothed) flakes, hand axes, and backed-blade knives. Significant variations also exist in the presence or frequency of the LEVALLOISIAN technique and in the frequency of steeply retouched thick side scrapers. These variations have been variously described as functional differences, as chronological differences, or as the work of different social groups.

Mousterian, or Middle Paleolithic, tools range in date from about 125,000 years ago to 32,000 years ago. They represent the transition from the Lower Paleolithic Acheulean industry to the Upper Paleolithic AURIGNACIAN and Gravettian industries. Most of the hominid remains associated with Mousterian tools have been of NEANDERTHALERS, *Homo sapiens neanderthalensis*, although fully modern *Homo sapiens sapiens* remains have frequently been found in association with late Mousterian tools.

movies   see ANIMATION; CINEMATOGRAPHY; DOCUMENTARY; FILM, HISTORY OF; FILM PRODUCTION

Mowat, Farley [moh'-uht]   Author Farley Mowat, b. Belleville, Ontario, May 12, 1921, is best known for his books about the people and wildlife of northern Canada. His subjects are often personal. *A Whale for the Killing* (1972; film, 1981) chronicles his efforts to save a whale trapped in a tide pool, *Never Cry Wolf* (1963; film, 1983) describes his solitary study of Arctic wolves, and *The Dog Who Wouldn't Be* (1957) and *Owls in the Family* (1962) recall his childhood pets. His *Sea of Slaughter* (1985) is a history of the destruction of North American wildlife.

Mowat, Sir Oliver   Sir Oliver Mowat, b. Kingston, Upper Canada (now Ontario), July 22, 1820, d. Apr. 19, 1903, was premier of Ontario from 1872 until 1896 and a leader in the fight for provincial rights. Mowat was elected to the Legislative Assembly of the Province of Canada in 1857. As a delegate to the Quebec conference in 1864, he helped draft the articles of confederation. After his service as premier he was minister of justice in the cabinet of Sir Wilfrid Laurier (1896) and lieutenant governor of Ontario (1897–1903). He was knighted in 1892.

Moynihan, Daniel Patrick [moy'-nuh-han]

The American sociologist and political figure Daniel Patrick Moynihan, b. Tulsa, Okla., Mar. 16, 1927, has served as Democratic senator from New York since January 1977. Earlier, Moynihan had been a professor of government at Harvard University and had served as a labor advisor (1961–66) under Presidents Kennedy and Johnson and as ambassador to India (1973–75) and ambassador to the United Nations (1975–76) under Presidents Nixon and Ford. His writings include *Beyond the Melting Pot* (with Nathan Glazer, 1963), *Maximum Feasible Misunderstanding* (1969), *Counting Our Blessings* (1980), *Loyalties* (1984), and *Family and Nation* (1986).

Mozambique [moh-zam-beek']

Mozambique emerged from four centuries of Portuguese rule when, after ten years of bush warfare, it won independence on June 25, 1975. Located in southeastern Africa, it is bordered by Tanzania to the north, Malawi and Zambia to the northwest, Zimbabwe to the west, and South Africa and Swaziland to the southwest. The Mozambique Channel separates Mozambique from the island of Madagascar. Famine, drought, and a ruthless guerrilla war have crippled the country in recent years.

Land and Resources

Lowland coastal plains, with altitudes to 180 m (600 ft), account for 44% of Mozambique's area. Plateaus with elevations to 540 m (1,800 ft)—the central uplands—cover 17%, and high plateaus reaching 900 m (3,000 ft) make up 26%. Mountains in the northwest, near Lake NYASA, reach 2,200 m (7,420 ft), and a lower range rises on the border with Tanzania. The highest peak is Monte Binga (2,436 m/7,992 ft), on the border with Zimbabwe. Excellent harbors include those at MAPUTO, Quelimane, BEIRA, and Pemba. Rivers flow eastward to the Indian Ocean. The ZAMBEZI RIVER, Africa's fourth largest, bisects the country. The LIMPOPO RIVER is the major river in the south, and the Rovuma is important in the north.

Most of Mozambique is tropical or subtropical in climate, with temperatures ranging from 18° C (65° F) to 28° C (85° F). Warmer temperatures prevail in the rainy season (October to April), when up to 1,522 mm (60 in) of rain falls in the north, but only 760 mm (30 in) in the south.

Savanna covers about two-thirds of Mozambique, but there are extensive hardwood forests. Significant deposits of diamonds, gold, uranium, tantalite, beryl, iron ore, coal, graphite, titanium, bauxite, copper, and natural gas exist.

People

Mozambique is predominantly rural. About 99% of all

AT A GLANCE

REPUBLIC OF MOZAMBIQUE

Land: Area: 801,590 km² (309,496 mi²). Capital and largest city: Maputo (1989 est. pop., 1,069,727).

People: Population (1990 est.): 14,565,656. Density: 18.2 persons per km² (47.1 per mi²). Distribution (1988): 19% urban, 81% rural. Official language: Portuguese. Major religions: traditional religions, Christianity, Islam.

Government: Type: republic. Legislature: People's Assembly. Political subdivisions: 10 provinces.

Economy: GNP (1988): $1.6 billion; less than $110 per capita. Labor distribution (1990): agriculture—90%. Foreign trade (1988): imports—$764 million; exports—$100 million. Currency: 1 metical = 100 centavos.

Education and Health: Literacy (1985): 17% of adult population. Universities (1988): 1. Hospital beds (1988): 12,129. Physicians (1988): 342. Life expectancy (1990): women—49; men—45. Infant mortality (1990): 138 per 1,000 live births.

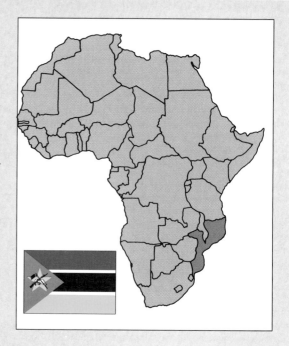

Mozambicans are black Africans belonging to one of ten major ethnic groups. About 60% of the people practice traditional religions, 30% are Christians, and 10% are Muslims. The official language is Portuguese, but many speak indigenous languages. Maputo (the capital) is by far the largest city.

Medical care is poor at best and often nonexistent. The infant mortality rate is one of the world's highest, and life expectancy is one of the shortest. Malnutrition and even starvation are common, and one-third of the population are dependent on international food aid. By 1990 as many as 1 million people had fled Mozambique; another 2 million were internal refugees, swelling the urban population. Illiteracy remains high despite significant postindependence gains.

Economic Activity

Although Mozambique possesses significant mineral resources, agriculture is by far the leading sector of the economy. After independence the government embarked on a poorly conceived effort to reorganize the economy along doctrinaire socialist lines, including the creation of state farms and communal villages. In 1983 it reversed direction and began to revive a free-market system, but civil war hampered efforts to revive the agricultural sector. One of the few bright spots is commercial fishing; shrimp has become the leading export. Mozambique also has yet to recover from the 1975 exodus of 200,000 Portuguese, who made up most of the skilled labor force. Manufacturing is limited to the domestic market. The Cabora Bassa Dam, one of the largest hydroelectirc complexes in Africa, seldom operates to capacity due to sabotage, although South Africa and Portugal have pledged to bring it back into full service.

Roads are often in poor condition and dangerous. The rehabilitation of the railroad, road, and pipeline linking Beira with Harare, Zimbabwe, has attracted international support as a way to reduce the dependence of the southern African states on South Africa and to aid Mozambique.

History and Government

The area was first inhabited by hunter-gatherers. Nearly 2,000 years ago Bantu-speaking people swept into the region and settled there. The Portuguese explorers who reached what is now Mozambique in 1498 were preceded by Arab traders. About 1500, Portugal established coastal forts and conducted a thriving trade in gold, slaves, and ivory. Fixed colonial boundaries were drawn around Mozambique in the late 1800s, but little was done to develop the colony except what was necessary to facilitate exploitation. In fact, Portugal made no pretense of social development. By 1975 only 10% of the population were literate.

In 1962 the Front for the Liberation of Mozambique (FRELIMO) was created, and by 1964 an armed campaign against Portuguese rule was launched. In 1974, after a momentous coup in Lisbon ended half a century of dictatorship there, Portugal agreed to leave Mozambique. After a short period of joint rule, Mozambique became

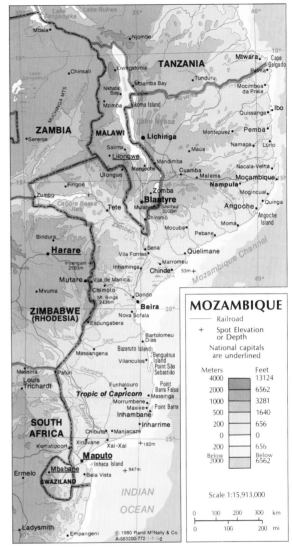

fully independent in 1975. FRELIMO leader Samora Machel became president, with FRELIMO the sole legal party. The constitution established an indirectly elected legislature as the supreme state institution. In reality, most key decisions were made by the political bureau of FRELIMO, and FRELIMO elected the president.

Independence presented the new government with a daunting array of social and economic problems and few institutions equipped to address them. As the government later conceded, it committed some disastrous blunders, especially in economic policy, but it made impressive headway in health care and education. It also provided crucial support to rebel opponents of the white supremist regime in Rhodesia (now Zimbabwe). In response, Rhodesia created the Mozambique National Resistance (RE-NAMO) to attack rebel bases in Mozambique. When Zimbabwe gained black majority rule in 1980, South Africa adopted RENAMO, which embarked on a campaign of violence calculated to destabilize Mozambique and end its support for opponents of South Africa's regime. In 1984, faced with a ruined economy and unable to suppress RE-NAMO, Mozambique signed a nonaggression pact with South Africa. Mozambique kept the agreement, but South Africa continued to aid RENAMO for several more years.

President Machel died in a 1986 plane crash and was replaced without incident by Joaquím A. Chissano. In 1990 the government abandoned Marxism-Leninism and adopted a new constitution providing for a multiparty system of government with a directly elected president and legislature. In 1992, Chissano and RENAMO leader Afonso Dhlakama met face-to-face for the first time and reached tentative agreement on a cease-fire and democratic elections based on proportional representation. The cease-fire became effective in October, but the nation's problems remained formidable.

Mozarabic art   see Spanish art and architecture

Mozarabs [moh-zair'-uhbz]   Mozarabs were Christians living in Moorish Spain. After the Muslim, or Moorish, invasion of Spain in 711 many Christians converted to Islam. Those who remained faithful to Christianity came to be known as Mozarabs; they were strongest in Córdoba, Seville, and, especially, Toledo. Although they were generally tolerated by the Muslims, they suffered some persecution, especially in the 11th century. Most of the Mozarabs were assimilated into Christian Spain as the reconquest advanced in the 12th century; vestiges of their liturgy, the Mozarabic rite, persist.

Mozart, Wolfgang Amadeus [moht'-sahrt, vohlf'-gahng ah-mah-day'-us]   Probably the greatest genius in Western musical history, Wolfgang Amadeus Mozart was born in Salzburg, Austria, Jan. 27, 1756, the son of Leopold Mozart and his wife, Anna Maria Pertl. Leopold was a successful composer and violinist and assistant concertmaster at the Salzburg court, whose archbishop, Sigismund von Schrattenbach, encouraged the activities of Leopold and his remarkable children.

Boyhood

Wolfgang began composing minuets at the age of 5 and symphonies at 9. When he was 6, he and his older sister, Maria Anna (known as Nannerl), embarked on a series of concert tours to Europe's courts and major cities. Both children played the keyboard, but Wolfgang became a violin virtuoso as well. In London, the 8-year-old Wolfgang wrote his first symphonies and was befriended by Johann Christian Bach, whose musical influence on Wolfgang was profound. Between 1769 and 1772, Leopold and Wolfgang undertook three tours through Italy.

In 1772, Archbishop von Schrattenbach died, to be

succeeded by Hieronymus von Colloredo. The latter eventually became irritated by Wolfgang's prolonged absences and stubborn ways. In 1772, von Colloredo retained Wolfgang as concertmaster at a token salary. In this capacity Mozart composed many sacred and secular works. Wishing to secure a better position outside Salzburg, he obtained permission to undertake another journey in 1777. With his mother he traveled to France, where he composed the *Paris* Symphony (1778); he could find no permanent position, however. His mother died in Paris.

Maturity

When he returned to Salzburg, Mozart was given the position of court organist (1779) and produced a splendid series of church works, including the famous "Coronation" Mass. He was commissioned to compose a new opera for Munich, *Idomeneo* (1781), which proved that he was a consummate master of opera seria (see OPERA). He was summoned by von Colloredo to Vienna in 1781 and after a series of violent arguments was dismissed.

Mozart's career in Vienna began promisingly, and he was soon commissioned to write the Singspiel *The Abduction from the Seraglio* (1782). His concerts were a great success, and the emperor, Joseph II, encouraged him, later (1787) engaging him as court composer. In 1782 the now-popular Mozart married Constanze Weber from Germany, much to his father's dismay. The young pair visited Salzburg in 1783; there, the *Kyrie* and *Gloria* of Mozart's great Mass in C Minor, composed in Vienna and never finished, were performed.

Mozart's greatest success was *The Marriage of Figaro* (1786), composed for the Vienna Opera. The great piano concertos and the string quartets dedicated to Josef Haydn were also composed during this period.

Final Years

Mozart's fame began to wane after *Figaro*. The nobility and court grew increasingly nervous about his revolutionary ideas as exemplified in *Figaro*. He sank into debt and was assisted by a brother Freemason, Michael Puchberg (Mozart had joined the Masons in 1784 and remained an ardent member until his death). His greatest operatic success after *Figaro* was DON GIOVANNI (1787), composed for Prague, where Mozart's art was especially appreciated. This was followed in 1790 by *Così fan tutte*, the third and final libretto provided by the Italian poet Lorenzo DA PONTE; and in 1791 by *The Magic Flute*, produced by a suburban theater in Vienna. During this period of financial strain, Mozart composed his last three symphonies (E flat, G minor, and the *Jupiter* in C) in less than seven weeks (summer 1788). These had been preceded by a great series of string quintets, including the two in C and in G minor, 1787.

In 1791, Mozart was commissioned to write a requiem (unfinished). He was then quite ill—he had never known very good health—and imagined that the work was for himself, and so it proved. His death, on Dec. 5, 1791, which gave rise to false rumors of poisoning, is thought to have resulted from kidney failure. After a cheap funeral at Saint Stephen's Cathedral he was

Wolfgang Amadeus Mozart began writing minuets at the age of 5, and, by the time of his death at age 35, he had produced 626 catalogued works. His works include the famous last symphonies and the operas The Marriage of Figaro *(1786),* Don Giovanni *(1787), and* The Magic Flute *(1791).*

buried in an unmarked grave at the cemetery of Saint Marx. At that time such burial was legally required for all Viennese but aristocrats and the nobility.

Mozart excelled in every form in which he composed. His contemporaries found the restless ambivalence and complicated emotional content of his music difficult to understand. Accustomed to the light, superficial style of ROCOCO MUSIC, his aristocratic audiences could not accept the music's complexity and depth. Yet, with Josef Haydn, Mozart perfected the grand forms of symphony, opera, string quartet, and concerto that marked the CLASSICAL PERIOD IN MUSIC. In his operas Mozart's uncanny psychological insight, particularly into his female characters, is unique in musical history. His music informed the work of the later Haydn and of the next generation of composers, most notably Beethoven. The brilliance of his work continued until the end, although darker themes of poignancy and isolation grew more marked in his last years. Couched as they are in a language of shining technical perfection, his compositions continue to exert a particular fascination for musicians and music lovers.

Mrożek, Sławomir [mroh'-zhek, swa-voh'-meer]
Sławomir Mrożek, b. June 26, 1930, is the outstanding Polish dramatist of the postwar period. To show the arbitrariness of politics, Mrożek invents preposterous situations pushed to logical conclusions. His short plays *Out at Sea* (1960; Eng. trans., 1967), *Striptease* (1962; Eng. trans., 1972), and *Charlie* (1962; Eng. trans., 1967) are slapstick parables of power. His best-known work, *Tango* (1964; Eng. trans., 1968), uses the collapse of a farcical family to trace the history of Europe from liberalism to totalitarianism. His two-character play *Emigrés* (1974; Eng. trans., 1976) treats with comic verve the problems of Eastern Europeans seeking freedom in the West.

Muawiyah I, Umayyad Caliph [moo-ah'-wee-ah]
Muawiyah I, b. *c.*602, d. April 680, the 6th caliph, was the founder of the UMAYYAD dynasty. Converted to Islam in 630, he became a secretary to the Prophet Muhammad. After the death of the Prophet, Muawiyah led the Muslim conquest of Syria, which he then governed for 20 years. From that position he challenged the power of ALI, the 4th caliph and the son-in-law of Muhammad. In 661 he usurped the CALIPHATE from Hasan, Ali's son and successor, creating Islam's great schism between the SUNNITES and the SHIITES. Muawiyah transformed the early Muslim patriarchy into an imperial monarchy, pacifying the empire and greatly extending its frontiers.

Mubarak, Muhammad Hosni [moo-bahr'-uhk]
Muhammad Hosni Mubarak, b. May 4, 1928, became president of Egypt in October 1981 after the assassination of Anwar al-SADAT. A former commander of the air force (1972–75) and one of Sadat's closest advisors, Mubarak had been vice-president of Egypt since 1975. As president, he continued Sadat's close ties with the United States and restored Egypt's position as a leader of the moderate Arab world. After Iraq's 1990 invasion of Kuwait, he convened the Arab League summit that approved sanctions against Iraq and sent Egyptian troops as part of a pan-Arab force to defend Saudi Arabia.

Mucha, Alfons [muk'-ah, ahl-fawns']   Alfons-Maria Mucha, b. July 24, 1860, d. July 14, 1939, was a Moravian (Czech) decorative artist closely associated with the foundation and development of ART NOUVEAU. In Paris, he was influenced by Jean Paul Laurens, and in Munich, by Hans Mackart. In 1894 he was discovered by actress Sarah Bernhardt in Paris; his poster of Bernhardt playing the lead in Victorien Sardou's *Théodora* brought Mucha into prominence. His work has an almost bejeweled richness and grace but is unmistakably fin de siècle and highly formalized. His designs are often dominated by richly curvaceous women and by peacock feathers and large flowers, especially lilies, which emphasize the sinuosity of his outlines.

muckrakers [muhk'-rayk-urz]   Those American writers who early in the 20th century exposed both in fiction and in nonfiction corruption in business and politics were called the *muckrakers*, a term first used by President Theodore Roosevelt in 1906. Most of their sensational exposés appeared in popular magazines such as *McClure's* and *Collier's*. Upton SINCLAIR's novel *The Jungle* (1906) about the Chicago meat-packing industry gained instant fame and influenced passage of the Pure Food and Drug Act (1906). The muckrakers' work is described by Lincoln STEFFENS in his autobiography (1931).

Prominent among the muckrakers were Ray Stannard Baker, who focused on racial discrimination in *Following the Color Line* (1908); Edwin MARKHAM, who crusaded against child labor; David Graham Phillips, whose series "The Treason and the Senate" (1906) was influential in the adoption of the 17th Amendment; Ida M. TARBELL, who wrote of corruption in big business; Thomas Lawson, whose *Frenzied Finance* (1905) delved into corporate stock manipulation; and Charles Edward Russell, who dealt with social dislocation. The revelations of the muckrakers gained support for the reforms of the PROGRESSIVE ERA.

---

mud puppy Mud puppies are four to six species of nocturnal, strictly aquatic salamanders making up the genus *Necturus* in the family Proteidae. They are sometimes called water dogs. Both common names refer to the erroneous belief that these salamanders produce barking sounds. Mud puppies are found in permanent ponds, lakes, or streams in the eastern half of the United States and Canada. They retain larval characteristics (neoteny) and reach sexual maturity in the larval form. Adults retain three pairs of gills and two pairs of gill openings. They do develop lungs, but the bright red gills are the principal respiratory organs. Eyelids also fail to develop, but both front and hind legs are present, with four toes on each foot. Mud puppies are usually 20 to 33 cm (8 to 13 in) in length and are gray or brown in color. They eat small aquatic animals.

---

mud turtle The mud turtles comprise about 16 species of small turtles making up the genus *Kinosternon* in the family Kinosternidae. They are found from the middle latitudes of the United States to northern Argentina. Mud turtles are drably colored yellow, olive, brown, or almost black. They are among the smallest of turtles, usually reaching no more than 150 mm (6 in) in shell length. Mud turtles have large heads, strong jaws, and scent glands from which musk can be emitted, producing a foul smell. Males have two patches of horny scales on the inner side of each hind leg and a strongly developed spine at the tip of the tail. Mud turtles resemble snapping turtles, but unlike the snappers they have a large lower shell (plastron) with two hinged ends that allow most species to close their shells tightly. They are omnivorous, eating insects, snails, tadpoles, carrion, and aquatic vegetation.

---

mudflow A mudflow is a sudden and destructive variety of landslide in which predominantly fine-grained earth material, mobilized by saturation of loose materials on steep slopes, flows down a channel or canyon. The term *debris flow* is used if more than half of the solid fraction is larger than sand size. The water content of mudflows may range up to 10 to 60 percent by volume. Their high specific gravity permits transport of huge boulders for great distances down gentle slopes. Mudflows generally move faster than walking speed but slower than running water, often advancing in surges.

Three types of mudflow are recognized. Desert mudflows occur when infrequent thunderstorms saturate surficial materials on sparsely vegetated slopes. The mass mixes as it moves downslope and then flows downcanyon, commonly onto ALLUVIAL FANS. Most desert mudflows are less than 2 m (7 ft) thick, but they have destroyed much life and property in areas such as Los Angeles. Alpine

mudflows, which gain water from thaw or snowmelt, can be enormous, and they have demolished whole villages in the Alps and Himalayas. Volcanic mudflows, or lahars, occur on the flanks of volcanoes during or shortly after explosive eruptions and can be particularly destructive. Mudflows from Mount Vesuvius buried the town of HERCULANEUM in AD 79. The 1985 eruption of Nevado del Ruiz in Colombia triggered a mudflow that took more than 25,000 lives.

See also: LANDSLIDE AND AVALANCHE.

Mugabe, Robert [moo-gah'-bay] Robert Gabriel Mugabe, b. 1924, is executive president of Zimbabwe and president of its ruling party, the Zimbabwe African National Union-Patriotic Front (ZANU-PF). Originally a teacher, Mugabe joined the opposition to Rhodesia's white minority government under Ian SMITH and helped found ZANU in 1963. He was imprisoned in Rhodesia from 1964 to 1974. In 1976 he joined Joshua NKOMO in the Patriotic Front, which began to wage guerrilla warfare against the Smith government, Mugabe's forces operating out of Mozambique. He participated in the 1979 London conference that led to black majority rule and assumed leadership of the new republic of Zimbabwe in April 1980. In 1984, Mugabe was named head of a new ZANU-PF politburo. ZANU-PF won the 1985 elections, and Nkomo's party merged with it in 1988. Mugabe easily won the March 1990 presidential election. In September his party abandoned his controversial plan to make Zimbabwe a one-party state.

Mughal art and architecture see MOGUL ART AND ARCHITECTURE

---

mugwumps In U.S. history, *mugwumps* was a derisive term applied to independent Republicans who opposed their party's national ticket in the 1884 presidential campaign and thus backed Grover Cleveland, the Democratic candidate. Advocates of civil service reform, they distrusted Republican nominee James G. Blaine.

Muhammad [muh-ham'-uhd] The Prophet Muhammad founded the religion of ISLAM. Muslims believe the KORAN to be the words of God revealed to the Prophet.

Muhammad's Life and Work. Muhammad was born about AD 570 in the city of MECCA, an important trading center in western Arabia. He was a member of the Hashim clan of the powerful Quraysh tribe. Because Muhammad's father, Abd Allah, died before he was born and his mother, Amina, when he was 6 years old, he was placed in the care of his grandfather Abd al-Muttalib and, after 578, of his uncle Abu Talib, who succeeded as head of the Hashim clan. At the age of about 25, Muhammad entered the employ of a rich widow, Khadijah, in her commercial enterprise. They were married soon after. Two sons, both of whom died young, and four daughters were born. One of the daughters, FATIMA, acquired special prominence in later Islamic history because of her marriage to Muhammad's cousin ALI.

About 610, Muhammad, while in a cave on Mount Hira outside Mecca, had a vision in which he was called on to preach the message entrusted to him by God. Further revelations came to him intermittently over the remaining years of his life, and these revelations constitute the text of the Koran. The opening verses of chapters 96 and 74 are generally recognized as the oldest of these revelations; Muhammad's vision is mentioned in 53:1–18 and 81:19–25, and the night of the first revelation in 97:1–5 and 44:3. At first in private and then publicly, Muhammad began to proclaim his message: that there is but one God and that Muhammad is his messenger sent to warn people of the Judgment Day and to remind them of God's goodness.

The Meccans responded with hostility to Muhammad's monotheism and iconoclasm. As long as Abu Talib was alive Muhammad was protected by the Hashim, even though that clan was the object of a boycott by other Quraysh after 616. About 619, however, Abu Talib died, and the new clan leader was unwilling to continue the protective arrangement. At about the same time, Muhammad lost another staunch supporter, his wife Khadijah. In the face of persecution and curtailed freedom to preach, Muhammad and approximately 70 followers reached the decision to sever their ties of blood kinship in Mecca and to move to MEDINA, a city about 400 km (250 mi) to the north. This move, called the hegira, or *hijra* (an Arabic word meaning "emigration"), took place in 622, the first year of the Muslim calendar. (Muslim dates are usually followed by AH, "Anno Hegirae," the year of the hegira.)

In Medina an organized Muslim community gradually came into existence under Muhammad's leadership. Attacks on caravans from Mecca led to war with the Meccans. Muhammad's followers obtained (624) victory at Badr but were defeated at Uhud a year later. In 627, however, they successfully defended Medina against a siege by 10,000 Meccans.

Mecca was considered of primary importance to the Muslim community because of the presence there of the KAABA. This sanctuary was then a pagan shrine, but according to the Koran (2:124–29), it had been built by Abraham and his son Ishmael and had therefore to be reintegrated in Muslim society. In January 630, Muhammad and his men marched on Mecca. The Quraysh offer to surrender was accepted with a promise of general amnesty, and hardly any fighting occurred. Muhammad's generosity to a city that had earlier forced him out is often cited as an example of remarkable magnanimity.

In his final years Muhammad continued his political and military involvements, making arrangements with nomadic tribes ready to accept Islam and sending expeditions against hostile groups. A few months after a farewell pilgrimage to Mecca in March 632 he fell ill. Muhammad died on June 8, 632, in the presence of his favorite wife, Aisha, whose father, ABU BAKR, became the first caliph (see CALIPHATE).

God's Messenger. According to Muslim belief, God sent Muhammad as a messenger (*rasul*, or "apostle") from among the Arabs, bringing a revelation in "clear Arabic" (Koran 26:192–95); thus, as other peoples had received their messengers, so the Arabs received theirs. In his sermon during the farewell pilgrimage Muhammad testified that he had fulfilled his mission by leaving behind "God's Book and the *sunna* [custom] of the Prophet." Imitation of the Prophet—following the example of his life in all circumstances—is a prerequisite for every Muslim.

—

Muhammad, Elijah   Elijah Muhammad, b. Sandersville, Ga., Oct. 7, 1897, d. Feb. 25, 1975, served as the "Messenger" of Allah and leader of the Nation of Islam, or BLACK MUSLIMS, from 1934 until his death. Originally named Elijah Poole, the son of a Baptist minister, he left his Georgia home when he was 16 and finally settled in Detroit. In 1930 or 1931 he met W. D. Fard, who called himself Master Farad Muhammad, or The Prophet, and who had founded the Temple of Islam. Elijah became a follower and, when Fard disappeared in 1934, the new leader of the sect. He subsequently moved to Chicago and established Temple No. 2. It became the center of a movement that included schools in many cities, restaurants, a publishing company, stores, and extensive farms. Elijah wrote *Message to the Black Man* (1964). He was succeeded by his son Wallace D. Muhammad as leader of the movement, which the son identified as part of worldwide Islam in 1985.

—

Muhammad Ali Pasha   As ruling pasha of Egypt, Muhammad Ali, b. 1767, d. Aug. 2, 1849, initiated the process that transformed Egypt from a traditional into a modern country and established a dynasty that survived until the mid-20th century.

He rose through the ranks in the Turkish army and assisted in restoring Ottoman rule over Egypt following the invasion by Napoléon Bonaparte (see NAPOLEON I). In 1805 the Ottoman sultan appointed him Egypt's

Muhammad Ali, a Balkan-born officer in the Turkish army, was appointed governor of Egypt in 1805 by the Ottoman sultan as a reward for his military successes. Muhammad Ali built up Egypt's economic and military strength and twice waged successful war against his overlord.

governor, or viceroy, with the rank of pasha. Muhammad Ali overcame the last obstacle to his complete control in 1811, when he massacred members of the powerful MAMELUKE aristocracy. To support his personal political ambitions, he built a powerful Western-style military apparatus between 1815 and 1838. He hired Westerners as advisors, officers, teachers, and managers; sent Egyptians to Europe to learn modern methods; and introduced new cash crops, such as cotton, to pay for his innovations.

By the late 1830s, Muhammad Ali ruled the Middle East's most powerful state. He had helped suppress rebellions against Ottoman rule in Arabia and Crete and had annexed much of the Sudan and Syria, the latter having been wrested from Ottoman sultan MAHMUD II. In 1841 those European powers which wanted the area's political equilibrium preserved forced Muhammad Ali to abandon his conquests and reduce his army in return for Ottoman recognition of his family's hereditary rights to Egypt. His son (or adoptive son) Ibrahim Pasha became governor in 1848.

Muhammad Reza Shah Pahlavi

Muhammad (or Mohammed) Reza Shah Pahlavi, Shahansha (Farsi, "King of Kings") of Iran, b. Oct. 26, 1919, d. July 27, 1980, ruled Iran from 1941 to 1979. He was the son of Reza Khan, who became shah of Iran in 1925 as Reza Shah Pahlavi. Muhammad Reza succeeded his father as shah when the latter was deposed by British and Soviet forces in 1941. In August 1953, Prime Minister Muhammad Mosaddeq deposed the shah. Mosaddeq, however, was quickly ousted by the army with clandestine U.S. help. The shah returned to power and, at the same time, began to cooperate closely with the United States.

In 1963 the shah launched the so-called White Revolution to bring Iran into the modern world. He initiated land reform, emancipated women, and vastly expanded public education. As oil revenues grew, the pace of modernization quickened. With modernization, however, came greater inflation, corruption, and social unrest, which the shah sought to control with the help of his bru-

tal secret police, the SAVAK. In 1978 opposition to the shah crystallized around the exiled religious leader Ayatollah Ruhollah KHOMEINI. In January 1979 the shah went into exile, and Khomeini was swept into power. The shah's admission into the United States for medical treatment in October 1979 triggered an international crisis when Iranian militants took hostages at the U.S. embassy in Tehran. The shah departed for Panama and finally settled in Egypt, where he died.

Muhlenberg

Muhlenberg (family) [mue'-len-bairk]   An American family of German origin, the Muhlenbergs served the Lutheran church and the United States with distinction for several generations. **Henry Melchior Mühlenberg**, b. Germany, Sept. 6, 1711, d. Oct. 7, 1787, began his ministry in Pennsylvania in 1742 and, in 1748, helped found a Lutheran synod in Pennsylvania that became the nucleus of the Lutheran movement in America.

His eldest son, **John Peter Gabriel Muhlenberg**, b. Oct. 1, 1746, d. Oct. 1, 1807, served as pastor of a Lutheran congregation in Virginia and as major general in the Continental Army. He was vice-president of Pennsylvania (1785–88) and a U.S. representative.(1789–91, 1793–95, 1799–1801). His brother **Frederick Augustus Conrad Muhlenberg**, b. Jan. 1, 1750, d. June 4, 1801, was ordained by the Lutheran synod of Pennsylvania in 1770 and was elected to the Continental Congress in 1779. A member of the U.S. House of Representatives (1789–97), he was its first Speaker. Another brother, **Gotthilf Henry Ernest Muhlenberg**, b. Nov. 17, 1753, d. May 23, 1815, was a pastor and a well-known botanist. A son of Gotthilf's, **Henry Augustus Philip Muhlenberg**, b. May 13, 1782, d. Aug. 11, 1844, also a Lutheran pastor, served as a Democratic U.S. representative (1829–38) and as the first U.S. minister to Austria (1838–40).

Muir, Edwin

Muir, Edwin [muer]   The poet, translator, and critic Edwin Muir, b. May 15, 1887, d. Jan. 3, 1959, was one of the most important 20th-century Scottish poets to write in English. The son of an Orkney Islands farmer, Muir received no formal schooling beyond the age of 15. After his marriage (1919) he moved to London, worked as a literary reviewer, and taught (1921–24) English in Austria, Czechoslovakia, and Germany. In the mid-1920s he began to publish poems, and in 1927 his first novel, *The Marionette*, appeared. His many books of criticism, which include *The Structure of the Novel* (1928), are notable for their perceptive appreciation of modern writers. In 1955–56 he was Norton Professor at Harvard University, where he delivered the lectures later published as *The Estate of Poetry* (1962).

Muir, John

Muir, John   John Muir, b. Scotland, Apr. 21, 1838, d. Dec. 24, 1914, is known as an American naturalist who worked toward gaining popular and federal support of forest conservation. He traveled throughout the United States and Alaska; in the latter he discovered what is now

Muhammad Reza Shah Pahlavi, pro-Western ruler of Iran (1941–79), promoted industrial development and modernization during his 38-year ascendancy. Ruling as virtual dictator from 1953, he was deposed (January 1979) by Muslim revolutionaries and fled the country.

known as Muir Glacier. He spent six years in Yosemite Valley studying its forests and glacial rock formations. In 1908, Theodore Roosevelt established the Muir Woods National Monument in Marin County, Calif., in acknowledgment of Muir's achievements.

Mujibur Rahman [moo-jee-boor' rah-mahn'] Mujibur Rahman, b. Mar. 17, 1920, d. Aug. 15, 1975, was prime minister of Bangladesh from 1972 until 1975, when he became president. He was known popularly as Sheikh Mujib. Born in East Bengal, he fought for Bengali rights both during British colonial rule and, after 1947, within the new nation of Pakistan. In 1949 he was the cofounder of the Awami (People's) League, which became Pakistan's first opposition party. In 1955 he was elected to Pakistan's National Assembly. Civil war between the Punjabis of West Pakistan and the Bengalis of East Pakistan erupted in 1971, and India intervened on the side of the Bengalis (see INDIA-PAKISTAN WARS). The rapid Indian victory led to recognition of the independence of East Pakistan as Bangladesh. Mujib was killed in a coup d'etat at Dacca.

Mukden see SHENYANG

Mukden Incident see SINO-JAPANESE WARS

mulatto [moo-laht'-oh] Mulatto, meaning a person of mixed Negro and European parentage, is a term most used in parts of the New World that were formerly colonies of Spain, Portugal, or France. The social implications of the term vary considerably according to the cultural framework in which it is used. In French-speaking Louisiana, mulattoes are regarded legally as blacks. Haitian mulattoes traditionally have constituted a social elite in that country; Brazil's mulattoes also enjoy a respectable social and economic status. In the traditional Peruvian social hierarchy, mulattoes are ranked below cholos (persons of mixed Indian and European ancestry) and above zambos (persons of mixed Negro and Indian ancestry).

mulberry Mulberries are about ten species of long-lived trees or shrubs of the genus *Morus* in the mulberry family, Moraceae; they are native to temperate regions of the Northern Hemisphere. Mulberries have variable leaves, with several shapes occurring on the same tree. They are cultivated for their edible fruits, and their foliage is the preferred food of silkworms. Mulberry trees have scaly bark and shed their leaves in the fall. The flowers are small and are borne in densely packed, small clusters (spikes or catkins). The clusters typically contain either all male or all female flowers. Each mature female flower develops into a nutlet (achene), surrounded by the thick, fleshy calyx (sepals) of the flower. The densely crowded and partially united fruitlets of each female cluster form a single mulberry. The sweet, juicy fruits are often made into jellies and preserves.

Muldoon, Robert David The New Zealand political leader Robert David Muldoon, b. Sept. 21, 1921, d. Aug. 5, 1992, was prime minister of New Zealand from 1975 to 1984. After a career in public accounting, he was elected to Parliament in 1960 as a member of the National party. He was minister of finance (1967–72) and leader of the opposition (1974–75). When the National party returned to power in December 1975, Muldoon became prime minister. Labour leader David LANGE replaced Muldoon after the July 1984 elections.

mule A cross between an ass, or donkey, and a horse is called a mule or a hinny. A mule is the offspring of a male donkey, or jack, and a female horse, or mare. It is much like the horse in size and body shape but has the shorter, thicker head, long ears, and braying voice of the donkey; it also lacks, as does the donkey, the horse's calluses, or "chestnuts," on the hind legs. The reverse cross between a male horse, or stallion, and a female donkey (called a jennet or jenny) is a hinny, sometimes also called a jennet. It is similar to the mule in appearance but is smaller and more horselike, with shorter ears and a longer head; it has the color patterns of the donkey. It is more difficult to produce hinnies than mules. There are no records of fertile male mules or hinnies. Rarely, a female mule or hinny may produce a foal.

An important farm animal, the mule can carry heavy loads over rough, treacherous terrain. It is also adaptable to harsh climatic conditions.

Mülheim an der Ruhr [muel'-hym ahn dair roor] Mülheim an der Ruhr is a city in Germany in the state of North Rhine–Westphalia. Its population is 176,000 (1989 est.). On the Ruhr River just southwest of Essen, the city is an important center for rail, road, and river transportation. Manufactures include iron and steel, electrical machinery, wire, cement, leather, paper, and food products. A coal research center of the Max Planck Institute is located in the city, as is a 13th-century castle. Mülheim existed as early as the 11th century. It became part of Prussia in 1814 and developed in step with the exploitation of its iron and coal.

mullah In Islamic countries a mullah (from the Arabic for "teacher" or "master") is a religious leader or a person who is considered an authority in religious law. Although the title is honorary and may be conferred on the basis of reputation alone, most mullahs have received formal religious training. The title generally refers to a learned teacher of the laws and doctrines of ISLAM.

Mullard Radio Astronomy Observatory [muhl'-urd]   Located 8 km (5 mi) southwest of Cambridge, England, the Mullard Radio Astronomy Observatory (opened in 1957) is one of the foremost British research institutions. Led by 1974 Nobel Prize laureates Antony Hewish and Sir Martin Ryle, scientists at Mullard have constructed large dish antennas and extensive lines and fields of dipoles that are capable of great resolving power, extreme positional accuracy, and high sensitivity for detecting faint sources of radio emission. PULSARS—hot neutron stars that rotate like beacons—were detected at Mullard in 1967 by Jocelyn Bell-Burnell and explained by Hewish. Several catalogs of radio sources in space have become world standards for reference; they use "Cambridge" numbers because Mullard is part of Cambridge University.

mullein [muhl'-uhn]   Mulleins are mostly biennial plants of the genus *Verbascum* in the figwort family, Scrophulariaceae. Native to Europe and Asia, they are now common weeds in North America. Mulleins may grow to 1.8 m (6 ft) high and have woolly or downy foliage and tall spikes of usually yellow flowers.

Müller, Hermann [mue'-lur, hair'-mahn]   Hermann Müller, b. May 18, 1876, d. Mar. 30, 1931, was a German politician who served as chancellor (1920, 1928–30) during the Weimar Republic. A Social Democrat, he was foreign minister in 1919 and signed the Treaty of Versailles. In 1928 he became chancellor under a coalition of Social Democrats, the Center party, and the rightwing German People's party. His government—prewar Germany's last based on a parliamentary majority—fell in 1930, the victim of the worldwide depression, fears of Communism, and the rise of Nazism.

Müller, Johann   see REGIOMONTANUS

mullet   Mullet are about 100 species of small-mouthed, torpedo-shaped, schooling fishes in the family Mugilidae. They inhabit shallow, mostly marine or brackish waters throughout the world. Some species normally inhabit fresh water. The striped mullet, *Mugil cephalus,* is found worldwide in warmer marine waters. It is usually less than 30 cm (1 ft) long but may occasionally reach 90 cm (3 ft) in length and weigh more than 6.5 kg (14 lb). It is blue gray and green above and silvery below, with dark stripes along the length of the body. Mullet feed by grubbing into sandy or muddy bottoms for organic (mostly plant) material, which they strain out by means of their gill rakers. Spawning occurs offshore in late fall and early winter, and the silvery young move inshore when about 25 mm (1 in) long. There is an extensive commercial fishery.

Mulroney, Brian [mul-roon'-ee]   Martin Brian Mulroney, b. Baie Comeau, Quebec, Mar. 20, 1939, became prime minister of Canada in September 1984. He received a B.A. degree from St. Francis Xavier College in Nova Scotia and a law degree from Laval University before being called to the bar of Quebec in 1965. Acquiring a formidable reputation as a businessman, Mulroney became (1977) president of the Iron Ore Company of Canada.

In 1976, Mulroney was candidate for the leadership of the Progressive Conservative party but lost the contest to Joe Clark. When, however, party pressure forced Clark to call another leadership convention, Mulroney triumphed: in June 1983 he was elected leader. Two months later he won a seat in the House of Commons in a by-election in Nova Scotia—his first elective office. Liberal Prime Minister John Turner called an election in 1984, and Mulroney led the Conservatives to a historic victory (211 of 282 House seats) over the Liberals. The bilingual Mulroney, who calls himself a pragmatist and a centrist, became prime minister on Sept. 17, 1984. Subsequently, he took measures to promote federal-provincial harmony, including the Meech Lake agreement of 1987 (amending Canada's CONSTITUTION ACT to make it acceptable to Quebec) that failed in 1990. Mulroney also fostered close relations with the United States. Although differences over acid rain persisted, Mulroney and President Ronald Reagan in 1988 signed a pact to eliminate remaining trade barriers. Facing stiff opposition to this pact, Mulroney called a general election in late 1988, and won it. Since 1989 he has forged strong ties with President George Bush.

In 1984, Brian Mulroney became the 18th prime minister of Canada, having led the Progressive Conservative party in an overwhelming electoral victory. Four years later, after an intense campaign in defense of his free-trade pact with the United States, Mulroney and the conservatives won a second majority.

Multan [mul-tahn']   Multan (1981 pop., 730,000) is a city in the Punjab province of Pakistan, on the east bank of the Chenab River about 320 km (200 mi) southwest of Lahore. A transportation and trade center, the city is also known for its carpet weaving and tile and enamel work. A university (1975) and several 13th-century shrines and tombs are landmarks.

Multan was conquered by Alexander the Great during his invasion of India (326 BC). It was taken by the Arabs about 712, by Mahmud of Ghazni in 1005, and by Timur in 1398. Part of the Mogul Empire from 1526, it fell to the Sikh leader Ranjit Singh in 1818. The British occupied Multan in 1849.

multiple birth Multiple births are rare among human beings and other large mammals. More than 98 percent of all human pregnancies result in single offspring; multiple births, which account for the rest, occur with rapidly decreasing frequency the higher the multiple. An increase in the number of such births has been observed, however, since the introduction of so-called fertility drugs in the 1960s (see FERTILITY, HUMAN). These hormonal drugs tend to cause polyovulation in women—the release of more than one egg at a time for fertilization.

Multiple births may be identical, fraternal, or (in cases other than twins) some combination of these. Identical births are monozygotic; that is, they arise from a single fertilized egg (zygote) that at some stage in its development separates into two or more embryos. (SIAMESE TWINS result from very late or incomplete division.) Such births share the same genetic material and are always of the same sex. Fraternal births are polyzygotic; they arise from two or more fertilized eggs and may be of either sex.

Because identical twins are genetically equivalent and are also relatively common, compared to higher-multiple births, they have been frequent subjects of study in such fields as BEHAVIORAL GENETICS and INTELLIGENCE research. These studies probe the relative importance of cultural and genetic influences in determining the characteristics of individuals.

Multiple Independently Targeted Reentry Vehicle see MIRV MISSILE

multiple myeloma [my-uh-loh'-muh] Multiple myeloma, or myelomatosis, is CANCER of the plasma cells, the main function of which is the synthesis of specific proteins involved in immunity. Diagnosis is mainly based on the presence of increased numbers of plasma cells in the bone marrow and the detection of nonfunctional, abnormal "M type" proteins usually found in the serum or urine. A progressive disease, myelomatosis can exist in a presymptomatic phase for up to 20 years, during which the chief difficulty is high susceptibility to bacterial infections. In addition, anemia and kidney damage may be present. Bone pain, the first prominent symptom, is due to the dissolution of bone in patchy areas throughout the skeleton. Treatment is mainly with chemotherapy and radiation.

multiple personalities see PERSONALITY, MULTIPLE

multiple sclerosis [skluh-roh'-sis] Multiple sclerosis is a chronic disease of the central nervous system characterized by the degeneration and loss of myelin (a white, fatty substance that acts as an electrical insulator for nerve fibers) in the brain and spinal cord. Patients develop weakness or paralysis, incoordination, mental disturbances, impaired sensation, and vision problems. Although multiple sclerosis is not an inherited disease, a predisposition may be inherited. No cause has yet been proved, but some researchers propose that it is an autoimmune disorder; others believe that a viral infection may trigger the disease. It is more common in temperate climates and is relatively rare in Asia and Africa. In the United States it is usually diagnosed between the ages of 20 and 40.

In most cases, multiple sclerosis follows a course of repeated remissions and worsenings over a period of years. About two-thirds of the patients are able to continue working during the first 5 years after onset. This number drops to one-half after 10 years, and about one-third after 20 years. Although some patients die within weeks and others survive more than 50 years, the average life expectancy after onset is about 20 to 30 years. Respiratory infections are a common cause of death. No specific treatment yet exists for multiple sclerosis, although experimental trials of many drugs have been conducted. Radiation treatments have also shown some promise in slowing the progress of the disease.

multiplexer A multiplexer is an apparatus for communicating two or more continuing messages at the same time on the same channel. A simple example is the frequency-division multiplexer, which can send two or more voice-frequency messages over one channel by combining each message with a distinct carrier frequency at the transmitter end (a process known as MODULATION) and separating the voice-frequency messages from the carrier at the receiving end (demodulation).

The channel to be used for multiplexing must have sufficient capacity, or bandwidth, to accommodate all the messages. Modern communication theory has demonstrated that not all of a continuous voice message needs to be sent over the channel; instead, the original can be reconstructed at the receiving end if just a suitable number of regular samples are sent. This discovery led to the modern sampled-data and pulse-code modulation techniques of multiplexing, which employ ANALOG-TO-DIGITAL CONVERTERS and DIGITAL-TO-ANALOG CONVERTERS, together with computers. These converters efficiently pack many messages into a given channel for effective TIME-SHARING. In a CENTRAL PROCESSING UNIT, a multiplexer is a device that transfers data between computer registers and other devices.

multiplication see ARITHMETIC

Mumford, Lewis [muhm'-furd] Lewis Mumford, b. Flushing, N.Y., Oct. 19, 1895, d. Jan. 26, 1990, was a cultural historian, social philosopher, and authority on architecture and urban planning. Early books by Mumford, such as *Sticks and Stones* (1924) and *The Brown Decades* (1931), were studies of American art and architecture. In *The Culture of Cities* (1938) and subsequent books he emerged as a critic of modern technological society who retained belief that humans have the capacity to renew their world. After World War II, Mumford expressed concern over the destructiveness of nuclear warfare in *In the Name of Sanity* (1954). His *The City in History* won a National Book Award in 1962. Later works include the two-volume *Myth of the Machine* (1967–70) and the autobiographical *Sketches from Life* (1982).

mummy A mummy is an embalmed body dating from ancient Egyptian times. The word is derived through Arabic from the Persian *mumiai* ("pitch" or "asphalt"), presumably because Egyptian mummies of the late period were often coated with a layer of black resin resembling pitch. The ancient Egyptians placed great stress on the preservation of the human body after death because they believed that the spirit of the deceased returned to it when visiting the tomb. Animals and birds sacred to various deities were also mummified and buried in special cemeteries, the most famous being the catacombs of the sacred bulls, known as the Serapeum, at SAQQARA.

In the shallow graves of the Predynastic Period, when bodies were simply wrapped in matting, close contact with the warm, dry sand caused dehydration and prevented decay. Deeper and more elaborate tombs, combined with the use of wooden coffins, gave greater protection from disturbance by robbers and wild beasts, but at the

(Right) *This mummy case and portrait of Artemidorus, dating from the 2d century AD, was found in a Roman cemetery in the Faiyum, near Cairo. (British Museum, London.)* (Below) *The sophisticated embalming techniques of the ancient Egyptians, which preserved the human body for centuries, are exemplified by the unwrapped mummy of King Ramses II.*

same time removed the body from the elements that had previously been responsible for its preservation. Early in the Dynastic Period the shrunken body of a deceased person was restored to its former shape by the placing of pads soaked in resin under linen bandages wrapped separately around each physical member. By the 5th dynasty (*c.*2350 BC) the bandaged body was coated with a layer of plaster, colored light green, and the facial features were represented in paint like a mask.

When fully developed, the process of mummification consisted of extracting the brain through the nose; removing the lungs and the abdominal organs (but not the heart) through an incision cut in the left flank; placing the body in natron, a naturally occurring compound of sodium carbonate and sodium bicarbonate; and finally wrapping the body in many layers of bandages with appropriate amulets sandwiched between the layers. As early as the 4th dynasty (*c.*2600 BC) the internal organs were sometimes embalmed separately and put in four vessels known as Canopic jars.

Researchers are now gleaning genetic information about ancient peoples by studying mummies with modern medical techniques.

mumps Mumps, an acute viral infection in humans, characteristically causes swelling of the parotid glands, a pair of salivary glands located in front of the ears; both glands are affected in most cases. Other parts of the body may also be affected. Mumps is communicable and occurs with great frequency in heavily populated areas. Although the disease can occur at any age, children ages 5 to 15 are primarily affected.

Paramyxovirus, the mumps virus, is spread by infected saliva. It probably enters the body through the respiratory tract. After a 16- to 21-day incubation period, onset of mumps occurs with chills, headache, and a fever lasting up to 24 hours before infection of the parotid glands is apparent. In adult males inflammation and swelling may first occur in the testicles. Testicular inflammation, orchitis, occurs in about 20 percent of adult males who have mumps, and it can be extremely painful. An analogous situation involving the ovaries, oophoritis, occurs occasionally in women. Oophoritis causes high fever, chills, and low-back pain. A condition called aseptic MENINGITIS sometimes occurs when the virus enters the central nervous system. Involvement of the pancreas occurs in less than 10 percent of cases. Bed rest and relief of pain are the only available treatments for mumps, but the disease usually runs its course in 2 to 3 weeks. A vaccine is available to prevent the disease. A single attack of mumps usually confers permanent immunity.

Muncey, Bill [muhn'-see] Bill Muncey, b. Ferndale, Mich., Nov. 12, 1928, d. Oct. 18, 1981, was the most successful hydroplane racer ever. Hydroplanes are boats of up to 3,000 horsepower designed to reach speeds of 322 km/h (200 mph). Muncey won 6 President's Cups, 8 American Power Boat Association Gold Cups, 7 national championships, and 4 world titles. He had 62 career victories—more than twice the total of any other racer—before dying in a hydroplane crash.

Munch, Charles [moonsh, shahrl]   Charles Munch (originally Münch), b. Strasbourg, Alsace (now in France), Sept. 26, 1891, d. Nov. 6, 1968, is remembered principally as the conductor of the Boston Symphony Orchestra (1949–62). He began his career as a violinist and then studied conducting with Wilhelm Furtwängler in Leipzig before making his professional debut (1933) as a conductor with the Lamoureux and Strarum orchestras in Paris. He made his U.S. debut with the Boston Symphony in 1946 and two years later was named permanent conductor. He was an exemplary interpreter of French music.

Munch, Edvard [munk, ed'-vahrt]   The Norwegian painter and graphic artist Edvard Munch, b. Dec. 12, 1863, d. Jan. 23, 1944, was one of the great masters of modern European art and a key figure in the development of modern EXPRESSIONISM.

After an early flirtation with impressionism, Munch set out to record the anguished psyche of modern humanity. In several stunning expressionist paintings, such as *The Scream* (1893; National Gallery, Oslo) and *The Red Vine* (1898; Munch Museum, Oslo), he succeeded in creating stark and terrifying images of modern alienation and despair. *The Scream* belonged to an unfinished series of paintings Munch titled the *Frieze of Life*. So fearsome were the images and so threatening the symbolism of this series that when six of the paintings were exhibited at a major Berlin art show in 1892, shocked authorities ordered the show closed. In spite of, or perhaps because of, the Berlin fiasco, Munch's influence on German painting was immense. His works of the 1890s played a large part in the founding of modern German expressionism by the Munich expressionist group *Der Blaue Reiter* (The Blue Rider) and the Dresden expressionist group *Die Brücke* (The Bridge).

Stylistically, Munch's forceful technique and free, intense brushstrokes have antecedents in the postimpressionist paintings of Vincent VAN GOGH and Paul GAUGUIN, but his works reflect an intensity and emotional depth unparalleled in modern art. Munch's facility with diverse pictorial media is demonstrated by his innovative series of woodcuts, including *The Kiss* (1895), and his deserved reputation as one of the finest modern lithographers.

Powerful inner torments and setbacks in his personal life, combined with widespread public distaste for his art, left Munch in an agitated and isolated state that is graphically evoked in his *Self Portrait by the Wine* (1906; Munch Museum). In 1908 he suffered a severe nervous breakdown brought on by depression and heavy drinking, and although he recovered after electroshock treatment, his art underwent a profound change. The obsessional quality of his early work is no longer apparent in later paintings such as *Model beside the Armchair* (1929; Munch Museum). Perhaps the major works of his post-

The Scream *(1893) typifies the emotionally charged work of Edvard Munch, one of Norway's most original artists. (National Gallery, Oslo.)*

breakdown period are the murals that he executed (1909–14) for the University of Oslo, in which he turned from visions of personal anguish to simpler and more universal imagery depicting nature at its most imposing.

Muni, Paul [myoo'-nee]   Paul Muni, b. Muni Weisenfreund in Lemberg, Austria (now Lvov, USSR), Sept. 22, 1895, d. Aug. 25, 1967, was a character actor who became a top Hollywood star in the 1930s. He came to the United States with his family in 1907. As a young man, Muni gained experience touring with the Yiddish Art Theatre company; he first brought his conscientious approach and animated acting style to the screen in 1928. His powerful performances in films include *Scarface* (1932), *I Am a Fugitive from a Chain Gang* (1932), *The Story of Louis Pasteur* (1936; Academy Award), *The Good Earth* (1937), *The Life of Emile Zola* (1937), *Juarez* (1941), and *The Last Angry Man* (1959).

Munich [mue'-nik]   Munich (German: München) is the capital and principal city of the German state of Bavaria and the third largest city in Germany (after Hamburg and Berlin). Munich is situated near the Austrian border on the Isar River about 48 km (30 mi) north of the Alps. The city has a population of 1,211,617 (1989 est.). Its name is derived from *Munichen*, which means "home of the monks." Munich was established in 1157 when HENRY THE LION, duke of Bavaria, granted trade, coinage, and customs privileges to a market center established by monks near their monastery, probably founded in 750.

Contemporary City. Munich is a major transportation, commercial, and industrial center. The city is famous for its beer, but machinery, automobiles, furniture, clothing, optical instruments and electronic equipment are more significant manufactures. Publishing, filmmaking, and tourism are important, and Munich is one of Europe's leading financial and wholesale trade centers.

Munich has numerous cultural, artistic, and educational institutions. The Glyptothek is a world-famous sculpture museum; the Alte Pinakothek contains an excellent collection of German and Flemish paintings; and the Deutsches Museum is the largest technological museum in Europe. The National Theater has an excellent reputation. Summer concerts are held in the impressive NYMPHENBURG PALACE, near the Amalienburg Pavilion. The Ludwig Maximilian University, founded in 1472 and located in Munich since 1826, is among Germany's best. Munich's *Oktoberfest, a* beer festival, is celebrated in October.

The center of the oldest part of the city, dating from the 12th to 14th centuries, is the Marienplatz, near which are the Old Town Hall, a Gothic structure dating from the 1470s, and the Frauenkirche, built between 1468 and 1488 and restored following damage in World War II. The huge palace (Residenz) of the dukes and kings of Bavaria, built from the 15th to the 19th century, is now a museum.

History. The city's rise to prominence began in the 13th century, when the WITTELSBACH family, who ruled Bavaria from 1180 to 1918, made Munich their capital. Following a disastrous fire in 1327, Holy Roman Emperor LOUIS IV oversaw the rebuilding of much of the city. In 1806, Munich became the capital of the Kingdom of Bavaria. Under King LOUIS I, Munich once again experienced much growth. LOUIS II brought Richard Wagner to Munich, which became a musical and artistic center.

Following World War I Munich was the site of severe revolutionary fighting, especially after the assassination of Socialist premier Kurt EISNER, when workers attempted to establish a Communist government in April 1919. The National Socialist (Nazi) party was founded in Munich, and Adolf Hitler attempted to launch a coup there in 1923 (see MUNICH PUTSCH). The Munich Conference took place in the city in 1938. Munich suffered heavy Allied bombing during World War II. The city hosted the 1972 Summer Olympic Games.

Munich Conference   At the Munich Conference (Sept. 29–30, 1938), which was attended by Neville CHAMBERLAIN, Édouard DALADIER, Adolf HITLER, and Benito MUSSOLINI, Britain and France acceded to Hitler's demand for immediate German occupation of the predominantly German-speaking SUDETENLAND in western Czechoslovakia. The conference created an international commission to demarcate the area and provided for plebiscites in some parts of the Sudetenland to give residents a choice of Czech or German nationality. The plebiscites were never held, however. Chamberlain stated that the agreement had secured "peace in our time," but Winston CHURCHILL insisted that the surrender to the Nazi government was a "total and unmitigated defeat." The Munich Conference became the primary symbol of the West's appeasement of Germany in the years before the outbreak of WORLD WAR II.

Munich Putsch   The unsuccessful coup, or putsch, launched by Adolf HITLER in a Munich beer hall on the night of Nov. 8, 1923, was the first effort of the National Socialist (NAZI) party to gain power. Munich, the cradle of the Nazi movement (see NAZISM), was also beset by other right-wing elements that challenged Hitler for leadership. The Munich Putsch (also known as the "beer-hall putsch") was thus aimed at consolidating Hitler's own political position as well as overthrowing the alleged government of Jews and Marxists in Berlin. On November 8, Hitler and Gen. Erich LUDENDORFF announced the "National Revolution," and the next day they led a Nazi march on the Bavarian War Ministry. Tried for high treason, Hitler used his trial to attract nationwide publicity for the Nazi cause. He served less than a year of a 5-year prison sentence, during which he wrote MEIN KAMPF.

municipal government   Municipal government is the political administration of urban, suburban, and rural communities that are not run directly by central, state, or county governments. In a modern CITY, municipal government is concerned with such matters as FIRE PREVENTION AND CONTROL, HOUSING, POLICE, SEWERAGE, TRAFFIC CONTROL, URBAN PLANNING, WASTE DISPOSAL SYSTEMS, ZONING and the paving of streets and sidewalks.

Forms of Municipal Government

In the United States most cities have representative government rather than a direct system. The latter is found in the New England town meeting, but such towns rely on boards of elected representatives to administer affairs in intervals between meetings. The major forms of municipal government are the mayor-council system, the commission system, and the council-manager system.

Mayor-Council Government. The mayor-council system was for many years the predominant form of municipal government in areas outside New England. In structure it resembles state government: an elected mayor is the chief executive of the municipality, and an elected council, whose members represent individual districts (or wards), acts as the legislative and policymaking body. The powers of a MAYOR vary widely. Some cities have what is called a weak-mayor system, in which the mayor has no more power, apart from the prestige of the office, than an individual councilman. In years past, cities with weak mayors were often run by a political boss who, though he held no major office, controlled the workings of the city. Other municipalities adopted a strong-mayor system, in which the mayor has a number of important powers such as the right to appoint city officials, to draft budgets, and to veto acts of the council.

By the late 19th century the growing complexity of life in urban areas had exposed some basic inefficiencies in city government, and these shortcomings, coupled with instances of widespread official corruption, gave rise to reform movements. Two new types of municipal government were developed: the commission type and the council-manager type.

Commission System. The commission system emerged in the wake of a crisis in Galveston, Tex., which in 1901 was virtually destroyed by a hurricane and tidal wave. In 1903, after it had become clear that the existing city government was incapable of coping with the task of rebuilding the city, executive and legislative authority was turned over to an elected 5-member commission. Each commissioner, who was chosen by the voters at large rather than in a given district, functioned as a department head as well as a legislator. Reformers saw in the commission plan an efficient way of mobilizing power. By 1920 it had been adopted by about 500 municipalities. The system has been opposed by some minority groups, who feel that this form of government is not sensitive to their particular needs and interests.

Council-Manager System. The council-manager plan, developed between 1900 and 1920, is based on the model of the private corporation run by a board of directors and an appointed executive. The council, whose members are nonpartisan and usually elected at large rather than from particular districts, appoints a city manager. The city manager runs the municipality on a daily basis, recommends the budget, and advises the council on policy matters. The tenure of the city manager depends on the will of the council. This type of government has become increasingly popular among municipalities of all sizes except the very largest, which continue to adhere to the mayor-council system.

Forms of Municipal Government in Other Countries. Municipal government may vary significantly in form and function. Canada's municipalities, for example, are governed mostly by the mayor-council plan and, to a lesser extent, by the council-manager system. Varieties of cabinet-type municipal government also exist. In Great Britain municipal government is either by the executive and legislative borough council—in which elected councilors pick aldermen and the mayor—or by an urban district council, which selects a chairman. In France the communes—the municipal units into which all of France is partitioned—also have elected councils that select mayors. French communes, however, unlike in the British, Canadian, and U.S. systems, are closely controlled by the central government. The French pattern of city government has been adopted elsewhere in Europe and in many parts of South America and Asia.

Munk, Kaj [munk, ky]   Kaj Harald Leininger Munk, b. Jan. 13, 1898, d. Jan. 4, 1944, was a rural priest, a leading Danish playwright of the 1930s, and a spokesperson for Danish resistance to German aggression during World War II. He suffered martyrdom at the hands of the Nazis. *The Victory* (1936) dealt with Mussolini and Ethiopia, and *He Sits at the Melting-Pot* (1938; Eng. trans., 1953) attacked Hitler's anti-Semitism. Munk's finest dramatic achievement, however, may be *Cant* (1931; Eng. trans., 1953). Written in blank verse, the play is set in the reign of Henry VIII of England and condemns the policy that might makes right.

Muñoz Marín, Luis [moon-yohs' mah-reen', looees']   José Luis Alberto Muñoz Marín, b. San Juan, Feb. 18, 1898, d. Apr. 30, 1980, was the first popularly elected governor of Puerto Rico. In 1926 he became editor of the Puerto Rican daily *La Democracia*. In 1932 he was elected to the Puerto Rican Senate, and in 1938 he founded the Popular Democratic party. Reelected as governor three times, Muñoz Marín served in this post from 1949 to 1965, working to develop industry and improve conditions in transportation, agriculture, health, education, and housing. Originally a supporter of Puerto Rican independence, he subsequently opted for the commonwealth status, regarding it as economically more viable.

Muñoz Rivera, Luis [ree-vay'-rah]   The Puerto Rican statesman, journalist, and publisher Luis Muñoz Rivera, b. July 17, 1859, d. Nov. 15, 1916, led his island's struggle for greater home rule. The founder (1889) of the newspaper *La Democracia*, which advocated autonomy for Puerto Rico, he helped win home-rule powers from Spain in 1897 and was president of the first quasi-independent cabinet. After the United States gained control of Puerto Rico in 1898, Muñoz Rivera resigned and went to Washington, D.C., to lobby for fuller autonomy. Elected Puerto Rico's resident commissioner in the United States in 1910, he worked for passage of the Jones Bill, which offered Puerto Ricans an elected legislature and American citizenship. The bill was passed in 1917. Muñoz Rivera was the father of Luis Muñoz Marín.

Munro, H. H.   see SAKI

Munsey, Frank Andrew   The freewheeling newspaper and magazine magnate Frank Andrew Munsey, b. Mercer, Maine, Aug. 21, 1854, d. Dec. 22, 1925, began his publishing career by founding a juvenile weekly, *The Golden Argosy*, which six years later he renamed *Argosy Magazine* and changed to a monthly for adults. In 1889 he founded the New York weekly *Munsey's*; two years later he bought his first newspaper, the *New York Star*. In 1901 he purchased the *New York Daily News* and changed it from an evening paper with strong Tammany Hall connections to a Republican morning paper.

Münster [muen'-stur]   Münster is a city in Germany in the state of North Rhine–Westphalia, with a population of

267,600 (1987 est.). Situated on the Dortmund-Ems Canal about 52 km (32 mi) north of Dortmund, the city is a trade and shipping center for grain and lumber; manufactures include heavy machinery, hardware, furniture, textiles, flour, and beer. Rebuilt since World War II, Münster has restored such landmarks as the 13th-century cathedral and the 14th-century Rathaus. Westfalische Wilhelms-Universität (1773) is in Münster.

The city was founded by Ludger, a missionary, about 804 and took the name Münster ("mission church") in 1068. Prince-bishops ruled it until 1803, except for a brief period (1534–35) when it was the center of the ANABAPTIST "kingdom." The Peace of Westphalia ending the Thirty Years' War was signed in the Rathaus in 1648. From 1815 until World War II, Münster was the capital of the Prussian state of Westphalia.

Munster [muhn'-stur]   A province in southwestern Ireland that was once an ancient Irish kingdom, Munster includes the counties of CLARE, CORK, KERRY, Limerick, TIPPERARY, and Waterford. Its area is 24,127 km² (9,315 mi²), and the population is 1,020,577 (1986). CORK, LIMERICK, and WATERFORD are the chief cities.

Münter, Gabriele [muen'-tur, gah-bree-el']   Gabriele Münter, b. Feb. 19, 1877, d. 1962, was a member of Der BLAUE REITER, the German expressionist group that she helped organize along with Wassily KANDINSKY and Franz MARC. She and Kandinsky announced (1903) their common-law marriage and lived and worked together in a studio-home in Murnau, where Münter perfected her own style of EXPRESSIONISM, which had a power and lyricism evident in her *Man Seated at a Table, Portrait of Kandinsky* (1911; Städtische Galerie, Munich). After Kandinsky left her (1914), Münter withdrew from public life completely until about 1930, when she was hindered in developing her art further by the repressive Nazi authorities.

muntjac [muhnt'-jak]   Muntjacs are small deer of the genus *Muntiacus* in the deer family, Cervidae. They are found from India to China through southeast Asia into the East Indies. They are also called barking deer because of their short, hard cry, which resembles a dog's bark. Muntjacs are variously classified as one species, *M. muntjak,* to six species, with many subspecies. Muntjacs are chestnut to yellowish brown in color and are about 60 cm (2 ft) high at the shoulder, about 1 m (39 in) in body length, and usually less than 23 kg (50 lb) in weight. Adult males have small antlers, usually unbranched except for a small front tine; each antler is set on top of a permanent bony structure about as long as the antler. Males also have the upper canine teeth developed into small tusks. Muntjacs are typically solitary inhabitants of forests. The gestation period is about 6 months; does usually bear one to two fawns.

Münzer, Thomas [muent'-sur, toh'-mahs]   An Anabaptist and social radical of the early REFORMATION, Thomas Münzer, b. Stolberg, Saxony, c.1490, d. May 27, 1525, was a leader of the PEASANTS' WAR in Thuringia.

Münzer developed religious ideas based upon immediate revelation by the Holy Spirit and claimed insights based upon visions and dreams. He denounced the princes and preached the imminent coming of the Kingdom of God in which all people would be equal and all property held in common. As a leader of the revolting peasants in Thuringia, he made his headquarters at Mühlhausen. On May 15, 1525, Duke George of Saxony and Count Philip of Eisenach attacked the peasant army and demolished them with artillery and cavalry. Münzer was found hiding and, under torture, recanted his radical ideas; he was executed. Münzer's alleged communism was a part of his apocalyptic vision, and the peasants' revolt gave him an opportunity to dramatize his role as a prophet and suffering "servant of God against the godless."

muon [mue'-ahn]   The muon (a contraction of mu meson) is a subatomic FUNDAMENTAL PARTICLE with a mass equal to 207 electron masses (105.6 MeV). The existence of both positive and negative muons (one is the antiparticle of the other) was established by the American physicist Carl Anderson in 1937. Unlike other mesons, the muon is classified as a lepton because it does not display the strong interaction (see FUNDAMENTAL INTERACTIONS). The average life of a muon is 2.2×10^{-6} seconds, after which it decays to an electron and a pair of neutrinos.

Muppets   Created by the puppeteer Jim Henson (1936–90), the Muppets won international recognition on the children's program SESAME STREET, initiated by the Public Broadcasting System in 1969 and featuring such Muppet characters as Big Bird, Bert and Ernie, Cookie Monster, and Oscar the Grouch.

In 1976 the Muppets, expanded to include more characters, made their debut on evening television with a weekly series, "The Muppet Show," which aired until 1981. The award-winning show appealed to both adults and children and was seen by millions of people in more than 100 countries. The Muppets, led by Kermit the Frog, made their way to Hollywood for *The Muppet Movie* (1979). That film and others, including *The Muppets Take Manhattan* (1984), featured live stars in interaction with the Muppets and the invisible puppeteers, notably Henson and his principal associate, Frank Oz, the voice for such diverse characters as Miss Piggy, Animal, and Sam, the self-righteous American eagle.

Muqi (Mu-ch'i) [moo-chee]   The Chinese painter Muqi, fl. c.1260, was a master of the Chan (Zen) school that flourished during the Song dynasty (960–1279). From Sichuan province, Muqi settled eventually in Hangzhou, where he became the abbot of a Chan temple. He executed ink monochrome works in a bold, abbreviated mode that represented the culmination of the vigorous and intuitive style of Chan painting. Rapid and spontaneous brushwork characterizes his extant masterpieces, the painting *Six Persimmons* (Daitoku-ji, Kyoto, Japan) and the triptych *Kuan-yin, Monkeys, and Crane* (Daitoku-ji). Muqi exerted a great influence on Japanese Zen painters.

Murad I, Sultan of the Ottoman Empire

[moo-rahd']   Sultan Murad I, b. *c.*1326, d. June 1389, extended Ottoman rule into Anatolia and the Balkans and introduced the infantry corps known as the JANISSARIES. He became sultan of the OTTOMAN EMPIRE in 1360. After Murad's victories in western Thrace in 1362 and 1363, the Byzantine emperor John V Palaeologus became his vassal. Murad crushed the south Serbian states in 1371 and won additional Balkan victories at Sofia (1385) and Nis (1386). In Anatolia he defeated (1387) a coalition of Turkmen principalities near Konya. Killed at the first Battle of Kosovo (with Serbians), Murad was succeeded by his son BAYEZID I.

Murad II, Sultan of the Ottoman Empire

Sultan Murad II, b. 1404, d. Feb. 5, 1451, completed the restoration of the OTTOMAN EMPIRE's unity after the invasion (1400–02) of TIMUR. Succeeding Mehmed I in 1421, Murad, by 1430, had reestablished Ottoman control of Thessaly and Macedonia, occupied Anatolia's Aegean coast, and won Salonika in a war with Venice. During the next decade he extended his sway to the Adriatic. At home he expanded the elite infantry corps of the JANISSARIES, developing the *devshirme* system of recruiting its members. He tried to leave the throne to his young son, MEHMED II, in 1444 but returned to power in 1446. Murad defeated (1444) a crusade organized by the pope and János HUNYADI of Hungary at Varna. He later defeated (1448) the Hungarians in the second Battle of Kosovo.

mural painting

Mural painting, one of the oldest forms of artistic expression, includes all painting executed for the express purpose of embellishing or decorating a wall. The word *mural* is derived from the Latin *murus* ("wall").

A variety of techniques can be subsumed under the general heading of mural painting. The term *fresco* (see FRESCO PAINTING) sometimes incorrectly used interchangeably with *mural,* refers to only one technique. Others include ENCAUSTIC PAINTING; painting on canvas which is then affixed to a wall; painting in various pigments directly on the surface of the wall; scratching designs into a wall; MOSAIC; STAINED GLASS; baked ENAMEL; and photographic murals.

The earliest evidence (14,000–10,000 BC) of mural art is provided by the cave paintings discovered at ALTAMIRA, Spain (1879), and LASCAUX, France (1940), in which animals are depicted in yellow, red, black, and brown earth-pigments. Another form of prehistoric mural, called rock art, consists of incised designs on exposed rocks or rock shelters.

Beginning in the 3d millennium BC, Egyptian artists decorated the walls of tombs with formal scenes of warfare, hunting, and ceremonies. Fresco was first used (*c.*1700 BC) in the lively work of the Minoan art of Crete, although little remains of these early efforts. Largely vanished also are the epic murals of classical Greece (6th–5th centuries BC). Most direct knowledge of Greek wall

For the convent refectory of Milan's Santa Maria delle Grazie, Leonardo da Vinci created The Last Supper *(1495–98) using a new technique of oil and tempera painted on a mastic-and-pitch base covering the stone wall.*

painting comes from the sophisticated and action-filled mosaics of the Hellenistic Age, of which the Olynthos mosaics (c.400 BC) are the prime example. Roman artists adopted and developed the art of mosaic, and they filled the walls of homes and temples with naturalistic wall paintings such as those preserved at POMPEII and HERCULANEUM. Pompeiian paintings reflect the great range and expertise of classical muralists, who were adept at depicting illusionistic architectural settings and realistic landscape, animals, and portraits.

From approximately the 4th through the 13th centuries mosaics dominated European mural decoration, reaching an unsurpassed peak of richness and color in EARLY CHRISTIAN and, especially, BYZANTINE ART AND ARCHITECTURE. The notable centers of mosaic production were Ravenna, Italy, and Constantinople (now Istanbul), where Byzantine artists perfected a stately, hieratical, and two-dimensional style.

In 14th-century Italy, fresco was reborn in the genius of GIOTTO and Simone MARTINI and broadened by the great fresco painters of the Early RENAISSANCE period (c.1420–1500), the most notable of whom were Fra ANGELICO, MASACCIO, and PIERO DELLA FRANCESCA. The high point of Renaissance fresco—and one of the greatest expressions of mural art—came in a brief span of 20 years (1495–1515), with the unparalleled freedom and beauty of LEONARDO DA VINCI's *Last Supper* (1495–98; Santa Maria delle Grazie, Milan), RAPHAEL's *School of Athens* (1510–11; Stanza della Segnatura, Vatican); and MICHELANGELO's Sistine Chapel ceiling (1508–12). Throughout the remainder of the 16th century, Italian Late Renaissance and Mannerist painters such as Paolo VERONESE and GIULIO ROMANO experimented with illusionistic ceiling and wall frescoes that emphasize technical virtuosity.

During the baroque period (see BAROQUE ART AND ARCHITECTURE) of the 17th century, fresco gave way to panel painting in mural art, and dramatic, exuberant wall decorations such as Peter Paul RUBENS's Marie de Medici cycle (1622–25; Louvre, Paris) filled the palaces and villas of northern Europe. The kinetic drama of baroque wall painting was followed by the bold romanticism of Eugène DELACROIX's murals for Saint Sulpice (1856–61) and the Louvre (1850–51) in Paris.

Mural painting generally declined in importance during the 19th century, although neo-Gothic movements such as the English PRE-RAPHAELITES and the German NAZARENES resurrected some forms of medieval mural art. Modern interest in this ancient art form was rekindled, however, by the murals executed in the 1890s for the 1893 Chicago World's Fair (by Mary CASSATT, Kenyon Cox, and others) and the Boston Public Library (by Pierre PUVIS DE CHAVANNES, John Singer SARGENT, and others). These public works led directly to the three major movements that have dominated 20th-century mural painting: the Mexican muralists of the 1920s and '30s (especially Diego RIVERA, José Clemente OROZCO, and David Alfaro SIQUEIROS), the New Deal muralists of the 1930s and early '40s (the most renowned of whom are Stuart DAVIS, Ben SHAHN, and Thomas Hart BENTON), and the outdoor-urban muralists of the 1960s and '70s.

Murasaki Shikibu [moo-rah-sah'-kee shee-kee-boo'] Murasaki Shikibu, b. c.978, d. c.1026, a Japanese author and lady of the court in the Heian, or Fujiwara, period, wrote the classic *Tale of Genji* (c.1000; Eng. trans., 1925–33), considered by many the world's first novel. It narrates the amorous adventures of a prince and, though lacking a well-developed plot, is far ahead of its time in delineation of character and analysis of subtle feelings. Murasaki also left a diary (1007–10), an invaluable source of information about Japanese court life and the period in general.

Murat, Joachim [mue-rah', zhoh-ah-sham'] A brilliant French cavalry officer, Joachim Murat, b. Mar. 25, 1767, d. Oct. 13, 1815, became marshal of France and king of Naples under Napoléon Bonaparte (see NAPOLEON I). Murat studied theology at Toulouse but joined a cavalry regiment in 1787. He aided Bonaparte on 13 Vendémiaire (Oct. 5, 1795) in defending the National Convention. He served Bonaparte in Italy and Egypt and then helped him seize power on 18 Brumaire (Nov. 9, 1799). The following year he married Bonaparte's sister Caroline.

Murat led the cavalry at Marengo (1800) and was made a marshal in 1804. He took part in the battles of Ulm (1805), Austerlitz (1805), and Jena (1806) and was named (1806) grand duke of Berg and Cleves. After engaging the Russians at Eylau and Friedland (1807), he directed the occupation of Spain (1808).

As king of Naples (1808–15), Murat introduced social and economic reforms. He headed Napoleon's Grand Army during the retreat (1812) from Russia but fled to Naples to protect his throne. Following Napoleon's defeat (1813) at Leipzig, Murat negotiated an armistice with Austria to protect his own Neapolitan throne, but Austria later defeated his army at Tolentino (1815). When he returned from Elba in 1815, Napoleon rejected Murat's services. Murat then attempted to reconquer Naples but was captured, tried, and shot.

See also: NAPOLEONIC WARS.

Murcia (city) [moor'-thee-ah] Murcia is the capital of Murcia province, southeastern Spain, at the junction of the Segura and Guadalentín rivers; it has a population of 305,278 (1987 est.). Silk manufacturing has been important for centuries; other industries include the manufacture of wool and linen, food products, and chemicals. The University of Murcia (1915) is located there.

Although Murcia was settled during Roman times, its recorded history dates to 825, when it came under Moorish rule. It was the capital of the Moorish kingdom of Murcia in the 11th and 12th centuries but was annexed to Castile in 1266. During the Spanish Civil War (1936–39), Murcia was the site of intense fighting.

Murcia (region) Murcia, a historic region in southeastern Spain on the Mediterranean coast, comprises the present-day provinces of Albacete and Murcia. The

Carthaginians established a colony, Carthago Nova (CARTAGENA), in the region about 200 BC. The area was captured by the Moors in the 8th century AD, and after the fall of the Umayyad caliphate of Córdoba, Murcia became (1063) an independent Moorish kingdom. In 1092 the North African Almoravids took possession of the kingdom, but an uprising in 1144 reestablished independence. In 1168, Murcia became a province of the North African Almohad empire. Murcia was taken by the Christians in 1243 and incorporated into the kingdom of Castile.

murder   Murder, in criminal law, is the unlawful killing of another human being (see HOMICIDE) with MALICE aforethought (an intentional or evil criminal intent). In traditional common law, different degrees of murder were not particularized. Most states of the United States, however, have divided murder into two or more degrees by statute. First-degree murder is characterized by premeditation or deliberate design. It usually includes the killing of another while committing a felony. In some states a person convicted of first-degree murder can be sentenced to death (see CAPITAL PUNISHMENT). Second-degree murder is characterized by a lack of premeditation but includes intentional and reckless behavior accompanied by malice, express or implied.

Murdoch, Iris   The English writer Iris Jean Murdoch, b. July 15, 1919, is a prolific and popular novelist. She taught modern philosophy at Oxford University from 1948 to 1963, and her philosophical knowledge is often reflected in her intricate, comic plots. Her first book (1953) was a study of Jean Paul Sartre, but her first novel, *Under the Net* (1954), is sometimes regarded as an implicit rejection of existentialism. She has since published several plays, philosophical essays, and numerous novels. The most acclaimed of the last are *The Bell* (1958) and *A Severed Head* (1961). Other novels include *The Philosopher's Pupil* (1983), *The Good Apprentice* (1985), and *The Book and the Brotherhood* (1988).

Murdoch, Rupert   The Australian-born publisher Keith Rupert Murdoch, b. Mar. 11, 1931, is owner of an international newspaper-publishing-broadcasting empire. He graduated from Oxford in 1953 and shortly afterward returned to Australia to his family-owned *Adelaide News*. From his initial success there he established Australia's first national paper, the *Australian* (1964), and purchased London's *News of the World* and *Sun* in 1969 and, in 1976–77, the *New York Post* (sold in 1988) and New York Magazine Company, comprising *New York* magazine, *New West* (sold in 1980), and the *Village Voice* (sold in 1985). Despite a reputation for sensationalism, he overcame British opposition to his purchase of London's esteemed *Times* and *Sunday Times* in 1981. Four years later Murdoch bought a half interest in 20th Century–Fox Films, and soon thereafter the Fox partners bought seven U.S. television stations from Metromedia,

Inc. (selling one immediately). In 1987, Murdoch's Fox Broadcasting Company began national programming. Recent major acquisitions include Harper and Row in 1987 and Triangle Publications, Inc., publishers of *TV Guide*, in 1988. Murdoch also owns a large interest in a satellite service broadcasting to much of Europe.

Murillo, Bartolomé Esteban   [moo-ree'-oh, bahr-toh-loh-may' es-tay'-bahn]   Bartolomé Esteban Murillo, one of the most prolific and renowned painters of the Spanish baroque era, was born in 1617 in Seville, where he executed most of his works. Paintings from his early period, characterized by dramatic lighting contrasts, are intimate devotional works such as his *Holy Family with a Bird* (c.1646; Prado, Madrid), in which divine figures seem more kindly and accessible than was usually the case in contemporary Spanish art. Murillo also executed more than 30 versions of the Immaculate Conception and the Virgin and Child motifs, in response to the mid-17th-century popularity of the cult of the Virgin.

In 1660, Murillo cofounded the Seville drawing academy and embarked on a series of major works for Seville's monasteries and churches, including his famous series of eight canvases (c.1670–74) depicting works of mercy, executed for the Church of the Hospital of Charity. During the same period, he painted several portraits and under-

The Young Beggar *(1645–55) is one of a group of genre paintings of children by the Spanish baroque painter Bartolomé Esteban Murillo. (Louvre, Paris.)*

took a series of genre subjects whose naturalism and vivacity anticipated the rococo style, inspiring the so-called fancy pictures of Gainsborough. Murillo died Apr. 3, 1682, as the result of a fall from a scaffold while working on the *Mystic Marriage of Saint Catherine* (Museo de Bellas Artes, Cádiz) for the Capuchin church in Cádiz.

Murmansk [mur-mahnsk'] Murmansk is the capital of Murmansk oblast in Russia, a republic of the USSR. The city's population is 412,000 (1984 est.). Murmansk, situated on Kola Gulf (an inlet of the Barents Sea), is a fishing port and fish-processing center. Although situated on the Arctic Ocean, warm water from the North Atlantic Current keeps the harbor ice-free all year. The naval base of Severomorsk, to the north, is the headquarters of the Soviet Navy's Northern Fleet.

Murmansk was founded in 1916 as the terminal of the Murmansk railroad, which extends from the Russian rail network to the Arctic coast. The city resisted attacks by German and Finnish forces during World War II.

Murnau, F. W. [moor'-now] Friedrich Wilhelm Murnau, originally surnamed Plumpe, b. Dec. 28, 1888, d. Mar. 11, 1931, directed films during the German cinema's most experimental period and was perhaps the greatest of all filmmakers of the 1920s. Fewer than half of his 22 films have been preserved, but what remains is proof that he excelled in every genre he tried: the horror film, as in *Nosferatu* (1922); realistic lowlife drama, as in *The Last Laugh* (1924); and classical adaptation, as in *Faust* (1926). His command of lighting and composition, together with his fluent moving-camera style, are also apparent in his Hollywood films—especially his masterpiece, *Sunrise* (1927), which transmutes melodrama into the purest cinematic poetry.

Murphy, Audie [aw'-dee] Audie Murphy, b. near Kingston, Tex., June 20, 1924, d. May 28, 1971, was the most decorated U.S. soldier in World War II. He enlisted in the infantry at age 18. In 1945, Murphy won the Medal of Honor for killing about 50 German soldiers single-handedly. Altogether he won 24 U.S. and 4 foreign citations. Later, Murphy became a movie actor.

Murphy, Frank Frank Murphy, b. Harbor Beach, Mich., Apr. 13, 1890, d. July 19, 1949, served as Associate Justice of the Supreme Court from 1940 to 1949. In 1930, Murphy was elected mayor of Detroit, where he was noticed by President Franklin D. Roosevelt. Roosevelt appointed him governor-general (1933–35) and U.S. high commissioner (1935–36) of the Philippines. In 1936, Murphy returned to Michigan to run for governor. He won that election but failed in his bid for reelection two years later. In 1939 he was appointed U.S. attorney general. Murphy developed a strong reputation as an advocate of civil liberties and minority rights throughout his career.

Murphy, Isaac Isaac Murphy, b. Lafayette County, Ky., 1856, d. Feb. 12, 1896, was a highly successful Thoroughbred racehorse jockey during the 19th century, before racial prejudice prevented blacks from riding in major races. During his career, which lasted from 1873 to 1896, black jockeys won 13 of the first 27 Kentucky Derbies. Murphy was the first to ride 3 Derby winners (1884, 1890, 1891), a record until Eddie Arcaro won his 4th Derby in 1948. His best year was 1879, when he won 35 races on 75 mounts. By the end of Murphy's career he had 628 victories out of 1,412 races. His other major wins included 4 American Derbies (1884–86, 1888).

Murray, James James Murray, b. Scotland, *c.*1721, d. June 18, 1794, was the first British governor (1764–68) of Canada, then known as the Province of Quebec. During the French and Indian War (1754–63) he participated in the British capture of Louisbourg (1758) and Quebec (1759), serving as military governor of Quebec from 1760. After France ceded Canada to Britain in 1763, he became civil governor. Murray was accused of favoring French subjects, however, and he returned to England in 1766 to face charges. He was cleared and retained the office of governor until 1768, but he did not return to Canada.

Murray, Sir James The Scottish lexicographer James Augustus Henry Murray, b. Feb. 7, 1837, d. July 26, 1915, was the first editor and the person most responsible for the compilation of The Oxford English Dictionary (*OED*). Murray was a teacher for 30 years (1855–85), during which time he provided (1878) the article on the English language for the *Encyclopaedia Britannica* and assumed (1879) editorship of the *OED*. In 1885 he moved to Oxford, working tirelessly on the dictionary. Murray completed about half the *OED* (A–D, H–K, O, P, T) before his death. He was knighted in 1908.

Murray, John Founder of the Universalist Church in America, John Murray, b. England, Dec. 10, 1741, d. Sept. 3, 1815, believed that "every individual shall in due time be separated from sin." Of Calvinist background, he was influenced by the Methodism of John Wesley but was converted to Universalism, the doctrine of universal redemption, by the preacher James Relly. An emotional collapse left him a broken man and led to his immigration to America in 1770. After preaching in several states he settled in Gloucester, Mass., and in 1775 was appointed chaplain to the Rhode Island troops by George Washington. Murray organized the first American Universalist Church in 1779 at Gloucester.

Murray, Sir John The Scottish oceanographer and marine geologist John Murray, b. Cobourg, Ontario, Mar.

3, 1841, d. Mar. 16, 1914, edited the *Report on the Scientific Results of the Voyage of H.M.S. Challenger During the Years 1872–1876,* a series of 52 volumes that represented a major step in the organization of OCEANOGRAPHY as a distinct science. Murray spent 3½ years aboard the H.M.S. *Challenger,* naming and mapping the distribution of all of the major oceanic sediment types and thereby contributing toward an understanding of the origin of such sediments. Upon the death of the leader of the Challenger Expedition, Murray assumed responsibility for preparing the report of the findings, a task he completed in 1895. *Deep-Sea Deposits* (1891), a volume in the *Challenger* report that Murray cowrote with Alphonse Renard, was the first treatment of the subject for the entire ocean.

Murray, Pauli A black lawyer, writer, teacher, civil rights activist, and early feminist, Pauli Murray, b. Baltimore, Md., Nov. 20, 1910, d. July 1, 1985, became (1977) one of the first of her sex and race to be ordained an Episcopal minister. While a law student at Howard University in Washington, D.C., in the 1940s she participated in some of the first nonviolent civil rights demonstrations. Later she took an active role in arguing sex-discrimination cases. After serving on President Kennedy's Commission on the Status of Women (1962–63), she helped found (1966) the National Organization for Women. From 1968 to 1973 she taught law and constitutional history at Brandeis University but left academic life to fulfill a long and deep commitment to her religion. Her published works include *Proud Shoes* (1956; repr. 1978), a family memoir, and a volume of poetry, *Dark Testament* (1970).

Murray River The Murray River is the principal river of Australia; it rises near Mount Kosciusko in the Snowy Mountains of eastern Victoria and southeast New South Wales, flows northwest following the border between Victoria and New South Wales, and then south through South Australia to its outlet at Lake Alexandrina and Encounter Bay on the Indian Ocean. The main tributaries of the 2,589-km (1,609-mi) waterway are the Murrumbidgee and the Darling. The Murray is important for irrigation projects, and many hydroelectric plants and reservoirs have been built along its course.

The Murray River was first explored by William H. Hovell and Hamilton H. Hume in 1824; Charles Sturt was the first to navigate the river, which he named for Colonial Secretary Sir George Murray in 1830.

Murrow, Edward R. The broadcaster Edward R. Murrow, b. Egbert Roscoe Murrow, Pole Creek, N.C., Apr. 27, 1908, d. Apr. 23, 1965, almost single-handedly brought integrity to television journalism. In 1932 he became assistant director of the Institute of International Education, and in 1935 he joined CBS as director of talks and education. Murrow was subsequently assigned

Edward R. Murrow's career is often studied as a model for accurate, responsible journalism. As a World War II correspondent, Murrow described the Battle of Britain. Murrow left radio for television to host the "See It Now" series (1948–58), regarded as the first modern news program.

to Europe, where he served as the network's one-man news staff. After 11 years as an outstanding war correspondent, he returned to the United States to become vice-president of CBS news operations. In 1948 his "Hear It Now" radio program was given a new name, "See It Now," and moved to television. Probably the most important show was that of Mar. 9, 1954, which attacked the investigative methods of Senator Joseph R. McCarthy. After leaving CBS, Murrow served as director of the U.S. Information Agency from 1961 until December 1963.

Murrumbidgee River [muh-ruhm'-bi-jee] The Murrumbidgee River of Australia rises in the Great Dividing Range of southeast New South Wales, flows through Canberra, and, after a course of about 1,690 km (1,050 mi), joins the Murray River near the Victoria border. The Murrumbidgee is important for irrigation. Its main tributary is the Lachlan. Charles Sturt explored the river in 1829–30.

Muscat [muhs'-kat] Muscat (1982 est. pop., 85,000), the capital of Oman, is located at the southeastern end of the Arabian Peninsula. A port on the Gulf of Oman, it handles the country's exports of petroleum and its imports (primarily foodstuffs). A sizable minority of Muscat's population is non-Arab. Controlled by the Portuguese from 1502 to 1650, Muscat became Oman's capital in 1741, when the present dynasty came to power.

Muscat and Oman see OMAN

muscle Muscle tissue, which comprises about 40 percent of human body weight, consists of threads, or muscle fibers, supported by connective tissue. All living cells can move to some degree, but this ability is highly developed in muscles, which act by fiber contraction: the fibers can shorten to two-thirds of their resting length. Muscles vary greatly in structure and function in different organs and animals. Based on structure there are two types of muscles: smooth and striated. "Involuntary," or smooth, muscles are found in the walls of all the hollow organs and tubes of the body (for example, blood vessels and intestines). These react slowly to stimuli from the autonomic nervous system. The "voluntary," or striated, muscles of the body attach mostly to the bones to move the skeleton, and under the microscope their fibers have a cross-striped appearance. Striated muscle is capable of fast contractions. The heart wall is made up of special muscle fibers (cardiac muscle), a type of striated muscle. Some invertebrates have only smooth muscles. All arthropods have only striated muscles.

Structure and Function

All muscles have basically the same structure. Each muscle has an attachment at both ends, called the origin and the insertion, and a fleshy contractile part, known as the muscle belly. Origins and insertions are usually noncontractile tendons; however, a great variety of muscle architecture is found that obtains the special mechanical advantages required at specific JOINTS.

Motor Units. The nerve control of the muscle fibers is organized in an economical fashion. Each motor nerve fiber running in a motor nerve to a muscle supplies a group of muscle fibers, which twitch each time an impulse is sent down the nerve fiber from the spinal cord. The frequency of these twitches can be increased and the number of motor units involved can be increased until all units are twitching rapidly. The blending of all the twitches results in a smooth contraction of the entire muscle. If the twitches fail to blend well but instead come in bursts, an obvious tremor results.

Mechanics. A muscle produces movements of a joint and can act only on the joints it crosses; muscles also steady joints, preventing movements in the direction opposite to those intended. For instance, the triceps brachii on the back of the arm not only is a powerful extensor straightener of the elbow joint, it also contracts to prevent the elbow from bending when pushing with the hand. In many muscles of the lower limb it is gravity that must be counteracted; for example, muscles are just as important to keep a person erect as they are in raising the heels off the ground.

In mechanical terms, the skeleton provides leverage, the muscles are the motors that act on the levers, and the joints provide fulcrum. The body employs all the typical leverage forms known to engineers. Most levers in the human body are levers of the first class; these are exemplified by the familiar seesaw and the crowbar. Levers of the third class are also common in the body; the ordinary hinged door is an example, the handle being the point at which the force is applied. In the body, this force is exerted by a tendon attached to a bone.

Actions. The brain needs to be specifically trained in order to contract individual muscles. Animals, including human beings, "will" movements of joints and limbs. Individuals do not consider the amount of contraction necessary in biceps brachii, brachialis, and brachioradialis muscles to develop the force and speed required to move an elbow. Voluntary movement takes learning, perhaps over many months and years, and it becomes automatic

or semiautomatic, reaching its finest expression in the virtuoso performance of a great musician or a champion athlete. All human movements and postures, with the exception of a few primitive, life-sustaining reflexes, are learned and patterned by repetition. Coordination of muscle actions is also learned and depends on the cerebellum and brain stem for a form of subconscious training.

Training not only improves coordination, it also makes muscles stronger. This occurs because individual muscle fibers become thicker and more powerful; they do not, however, increase in number. Each creature is born with its full quota of fibers. Normal growth and the increase in volume that comes from exercise depend on enlarging this set number of fibers. Conversely, a muscle atrophies (shrinks and weakens) when it is not used or has had its nerve supply cut. If the nerve supply remains intact or is restored, exercise will bring the muscle back to its former condition.

Classification

The 700 or more muscles of the HUMAN BODY are grouped in various ways. For example, they can be divided into dynamic (fast) and postural (slow) muscles, depending on how each muscle is most often used. Even the metabolic character of the muscle fibers is different in these muscles, although in humans there are no exclusively fast or slow muscles.

Muscles may also be subdivided regionally into axial muscles (trunk, head, and neck) and limb muscles (upper and lower). The limb muscles may be further divided into flexors (benders) and extensors of the various joints. In some joints movements also occur in a crosswise direction; hence, abductors are muscles that move the bone away from the midline axis of the body; adductors act in the opposite direction.

Most muscles have Latin·names that refer to their primary function, location, shape, or size. Thus, *flexor digitorum profundus* means the "deep bender of the fingers," and the *adductor magnus* of the hip joint is the "big (muscle) that pulls (the thigh) toward (the midline)."

Supplementary Structures

Muscles are surrounded and supported by essential structures. Each muscle is enveloped within a fibrous-tissue sheath; regional groups of muscles are further wrapped in fibrous connective tissue, or deep fascia. Deep fascia often becomes specialized retinacula (singular, retinaculum) that hold down tendons and prevent them from bowstringing.

An antifriction device called the bursa develops in the connective tissues wherever a tendon rubs hard against a bone or a similar hard structure (such as another tendon). The bursa is like a collapsed bag, lubricated inside by synovial fluid, which is also found inside the joints. When the friction is too great or the tendon is injured or inflamed, the bursa becomes inflamed, producing a condition called BURSITIS.

Because many tendons run through retinacula, they experience friction all around them. Tubular synovial sheaths surround and protect these tendons. They are particularly important in the wrist, hand, fingers, and ankles.

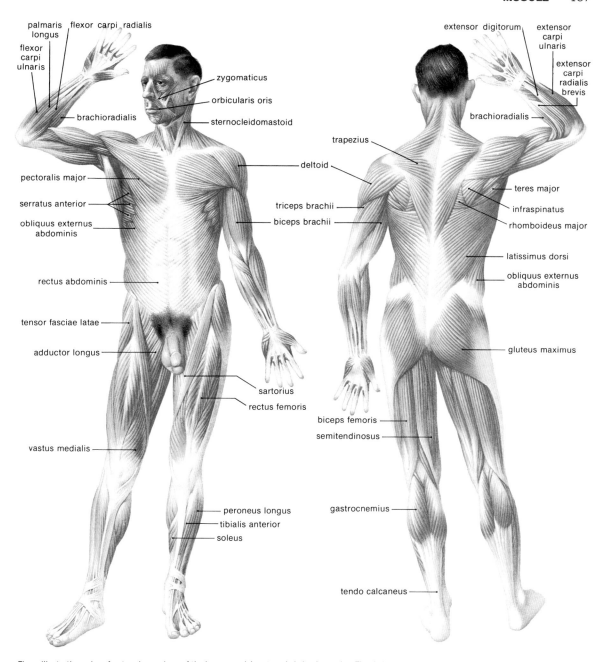

palmaris longus
flexor carpi radialis
flexor carpi ulnaris
brachioradialis
zygomaticus
orbicularis oris
sternocleidomastoid
pectoralis major
serratus anterior
obliquus externus abdominis
rectus abdominis
tensor fasciae latae
adductor longus
sartorius
rectus femoris
vastus medialis
peroneus longus
tibialis anterior
soleus
deltoid
triceps brachii
biceps brachii

extensor digitorum
extensor carpi ulnaris
extensor carpi radialis brevis
brachioradialis
trapezius
teres major
infraspinatus
rhomboideus major
latissimus dorsi
obliquus externus abdominis
gluteus maximus
biceps femoris
semitendinosus
gastrocnemius
tendo calcaneus

These illustrations show front and rear views of the human male's external skeletal muscles. The skeletal, or voluntary, muscular system is responsible for the body's movement and support. The 700 or more muscles pull on bones—as forces act on levers—to produce motion. Limb muscles often work in opposing groups. For example, contraction of the biceps brachii causes flexion of the arm at the elbow joint; contraction of the triceps brachii produces extension of the arm. The cerebral cortex of the brain controls and coordinates voluntary muscular activity.

Major Muscles and Muscle Groups

Facial Muscles. The muscles used in facial expression are unique in that they are attached to various parts of the facial skin. They surround and radiate from the vital orifices of the face: the mouth, nostrils, eyes, and ears. Some muscles open these orifices wide; others narrow or close them.

Muscles of Mastication. Four large muscles on each side move the jaw. The *temporalis* (in the temple) and the masseter (on the side of the jaw) can be felt when a person bites forcibly. The other muscles help provide the motions needed for grinding food between the molars.

Tongue, Swallowing, and Speech Muscles. The tongue is almost all muscle, and it is capable of very precise, complicated, and elaborate movements. In eating, the tongue moves food around; in swallowing, it pushes food into the throat; and in talking, it articulates the sounds coming from the larynx. Once food enters the pharynx (the throat) it is moved down into the esophagus by waves of muscle contraction. Special sets of muscles guard the larynx. Others alter the tension and position of the vocal cords.

Respiratory Muscles. Deep in the neck and between the ribs are muscles that lift and regulate the ribs during inspiration; they relax completely during expiration. Even more important to breathing is a dome-shaped horizontal partition—the diaphragm—below the lungs and above the abdominal cavity. Its contraction greatly enlarges the chest and draws air into the lungs with each inspiration.

Abdominal Wall Muscles. Layers of muscle enclose and can greatly compress the contents of the abdomen. This forceful compression is required to expel urine from the bladder, the contents of the colon and rectum during bowel movements, and the baby from a woman's uterus. In each of these cases, smooth muscles in the walls of the hollow organs also take part in the expulsion of the contents. Further, each of the outlets is guarded by a ring of striated (voluntary) muscle that can be trained to prevent uncontrolled expulsions.

Back Muscles. The vertebral column has a great number of muscle bundles that help to position and move it. When caught off guard, these muscles can be strained, causing spasms and pain.

Shoulder and Hip Muscles. The scapula (shoulder blade) must be kept constantly in a proper position so that the upper limb and hand may be used. Large muscles radiate from it to the chest wall, spinal column, and skull. The shoulder joint is capable of many movements, because it has flexors, extensors, abductors, adductors, and rotators.

The hip bones are much less mobile; the huge muscles at the hip are concerned mostly with moving and stabilizing the hip joint. This joint also requires a complete complement of muscles, the largest of which is the *gluteus maximus* ("biggest in the buttock"), which is important in climbing and running.

Limb Muscles. Emphasis in the arms and legs is on opposing groups of flexor and extensor muscles on the front and back of each limb. Almost all the muscles act on the joints just below them; some go on into the hand or foot to act as flexors and extensors of the digits. In addition, the digits have many small local muscles that produce fine movements.

---

muscle contraction Muscles produce force through the process of contraction. When a MUSCLE contracts it may change its shape, but its volume remains the same; it does not become smaller. During the process of contraction the energy from chemical reactions in the muscle can be converted into useful work. Thus, contraction of muscle enables human beings to move about (locomotion) and perform direct actions on the environment. A great variety of muscles are found in the bodies of different animals, and the structure of each muscle is suited to its particular function. Despite this great diversity among muscles, it appears that the basic mechanism of contraction is the same: the coupling of the splitting of adenosine triphosphate (see ATP) to the interaction of two proteins, myosin and actin.

Filaments

A skeletal muscle consists of a number of cells, called muscle fibers. Muscle fibers contain many of the same chemicals, ions, and organelles as do other cells. The structures that are particularly characteristic of muscle fibers and important for their function are the filaments and the membranes.

The filaments, which are directly involved in the contractile process, are of two sizes: thick filaments, which are about 1.6 μm (1 μm = 0.001 mm) in length, and thin filaments, which are about 2 μm in length. They are arranged parallel to the long axis of the fiber in cylindrical-shaped columns called myofibrils, or fibrils. Along the length of each myofibril, the sets of filaments interdigitate, forming alternate regions. The "unit pattern," or sarcomere, has an A band region that contains both thick filaments and thin filaments overlapping with them, and an I band region that contains only thin filaments. The H zone is the part of the center of the A band that contains only thick filaments. At the edge of a sarcomere, membranes called Z lines connect the thin filaments.

It is the splitting of the ATP molecule along with the interaction of myosin with actin that is the fundamental process of contraction. This process is controlled by the action of troponin, tropomyosin, and calcium ions. Interaction of actin and myosin can occur only when calcium ions are bound to particular sites on troponin; in relaxed muscle, calcium ions are not bound to these sites, and troponin and tropomyosin act together to prevent the interaction of actin and myosin.

Two separate membrane systems in skeletal muscle are involved in controlling contraction. The first consists of the plasma or cell membrane, which surrounds each fiber, and the transverse tubules, which are tube-shaped continuations of cell membrane. The tubules penetrate into the fiber and form rings around the myofibrils.

The second membrane system is the sarcoplasmic reticulum, which is analogous to the endoplasmic reticulum of other cells. It is like a closed bag inside the fiber itself. The calcium ions that act as a trigger for contraction are stored in the sarcoplasmic reticulum when the muscle is resting. At particular locations the walls of the transverse tubules and the sarcoplasmic reticulum lie very close together in a characteristic pattern that is called the triad.

Sequence of Events During Contraction

Signal. The communication between nerve and muscle actually occurs at the neuromuscular junction, a specialized area in which the nerve endings lie close to the end-plate region of the muscle fiber. When an action potential—an electrical signal—reaches the nerve endings, a chemical transmitter, acetylcholine, is released, and it diffuses across the small gap between the nerve and the muscle. If enough acetylcholine reaches the end-plate region of the muscle fiber, an action potential is triggered that spreads over the cell membrane and down into the fiber along the transverse tubules. When the action potential reaches the triads, the signal is communicated to the sarcoplasmic reticulum. Calcium ions are then released from the sarcoplasmic reticulum, and the level of calcium in the region of the filaments increases. Calcium ions combine with the troponin in the thin filaments, and troponin is stopped from inhibiting the myosin-actin interaction. This allows the thick and thin filaments to interact, and contraction takes place. When the "command" for contraction ceases, the release of calcium ions ends and calcium ions are pumped back into the sarcoplasmic reticulum. As this process lowers the level of calcium ions in the sarcoplasm, the calcium ions dissociate from the troponin and the myosin-actin interaction is inhibited. As a result, tension produced by the muscle diminishes, and it relaxes back to the resting state.

Sliding Filament Theory. A major advance in the understanding of muscular contraction was the realization that the thick and thin filaments slide past each other during contraction. Essentially, the "sliding filament" theory holds that the filaments do not change in length during contraction. Instead, a muscle shortens when the thin filaments slide over the thick ones, so that they penetrate farther into the region of the thick filaments (A band). The region containing only thin filaments (I band) becomes smaller.

A part of each myosin molecule in the thick filament is able to bind to actin in the thin filament and to act as an enzyme to catalyze the splitting of ATP. This region of the myosin molecule protrudes from the main backbone of the thick filament and forms what is called a cross-bridge. It appears that during contraction a cross-bridge splits a molecule of ATP and stores the energy from this reaction. The cross-bridge then interacts with actin, forming a physical link between them; this link then changes shape so that the filaments slide past each other to produce shortening and tension. At this step, the energy from ATP splitting appears as mechanical work being done by the muscle. The link between the myosin and actin then breaks. The distance that the filaments move in one such cycle is very small compared to the total shortening that can occur. Thus, each cross-bridge goes through this cycle repeatedly in order to shorten the muscle a large distance.

ATP Splitting and Metabolic Reactions

The splitting of ATP to form adenosine diphosphate (ADP) and inorganic phosphate is the only reaction that can directly supply energy to myosin and actin for normal muscular contraction. Thus, it is essential that the muscle have an adequate supply of ATP to fuel the contractile process. This requirement is met by the actual rebuilding of ATP as it is used rather than by storing a very large amount in the muscle.

During brief contractions, ATP is rebuilt by the transfer of a phosphate group from phosphocreatine to ADP to form ATP and creatine. This reaction is catalyzed by the enzyme creatine phosphokinase. If contractions last more than a few seconds, ATP is supplied by a more complex set of reactions, including the glycolytic and oxidative metabolic pathways. The original starting materials for all metabolic reactions are the food ingested and the oxygen breathed.

muscovite see MICA

---

muscular dystrophy [dis'-truh-fee] *Muscular dystrophy* is a term that encompasses several hereditary diseases characterized by progressive weakness and degeneration of skeletal muscle. The most common form was described by the French neurologist Guillaume B. A. Duchenne in 1868. Duchenne muscular dystrophy is inherited as a recessive disorder. As a result the disease is sex-linked, affecting males (see GENETIC DISEASES). Symptoms of weakness begin in early childhood. The muscles—especially those of the calves—become abnormally enlarged. This is partially caused by infiltration of the muscles with fat. Progressive destruction of muscle leads to a wheelchair existence, usually by age 13. Death usually occurs in the late teens or early twenties. Female carriers can be detected in many instances by a simple blood test that measures an enzyme known as creatine kinase, and in 1985 detection also became possible through tests for genetic markers indicating the presence of the Duchenne gene. The location of the large gene on the X chromosome was determined in 1986. Before the 20th gestational week, pregnancies at risk for the disease can be monitored by analyzing fetal blood.

Other forms of muscular dystrophy follow various patterns of inheritance and may affect children and adults of both sexes. Some are less severe and less progressive than the Duchenne form. No cure exists as yet for any form of the disease. In 1987 researchers identified a protein that the abnormal Duchenne gene produces in abnormal form or not at all and named this protein dystrophin. The protein was later located in the outer membrane of normal muscles. A lack of the protein was shown to lead to Duchenne and other forms of muscular dystrophy. Such knowledge suggests further avenues of approach in the search for a cure. Scientists are also studying the potential value of calcium-blocking drugs in treatment of the disease.

---

muses The muses were the nine Greek goddesses of inspiration in learning and the arts. Since ancient times writers, especially poets, have invoked the appropriate muse for aid: Calliope for epic and heroic poetry, Clio for history, Erato for love poetry, Euterpe for music and lyric poetry, Melpomene for tragedy, Polyhymnia for songs or hymns to the gods, Terpsichore for dance, Thalia for comedy, and Urania for astronomy. The muses were the daughters of ZEUS and MNEMOSYNE, or Memory; their leader was APOLLO. Sometimes called the Pierides, after their early home, Pieria, in Macedonia, they frequented the fountain of Aganippe on Mount Helicon.

Museum of Modern Art, The

The Museum of Modern Art (MOMA), perhaps the world's most comprehensive repository of modern art, was founded (1929) by prominent New York City art collectors for the purpose of acquiring and exhibiting the best modern works of art. In its first few years the museum presented only temporary exhibitions. The nucleus of the permanent collection was provided by the Lillie P. Bliss donation in 1934; the collection now comprises more than 100,000 items. The first director of the museum, Alfred H. BARR, Jr. (retired 1967), seeking to establish MOMA as a multidisciplinary institution, presided over the founding of the departments of architecture and design, photography, and film, as well as the opening (1960) of the print collection. The drawings collection was added in 1971.

In 1945 the museum moved to its present location. The original structure, designed (1939) by the architects Philip Goodwin and Edward Durell Stone, was enlarged by an addition (1962–63) by Philip Johnson. Cesar Pelli designed the extensive addition and renovation completed in 1984, which doubled the museum's space.

The present collection features important works of painting and sculpture representative of all major late-19th-century and 20th-century European and American movements. The sculpture collection is exhibited both in the garden and in the galleries.

In addition to its permanent collection, MOMA carries on a loan and circulating-exhibitions program, as well as educational and film-and-video programs. An extensive library is available to scholars and students.

museums, art

Art museums are institutions or buildings where objects of aesthetic value are preserved and displayed. Functions of the art museum include acquiring, conserving, and exhibiting works of art; providing art education for the general public; and conducting art historical research.

Art museums may be classified into two major categories: public museums, administered directly by the national or local government; and private museums, under the authority of a board of trustees, which is composed of private citizens and a director chosen by the board. In addition, art museums are of two basic types: the general museum, which presents a broad range of works from early times to the present, and the specialized museum or gallery, in which the collection is restricted to the works of a single artist or is concentrated on a particular type of art, historical period, or geographical area. In addition to exhibiting objects in their own collections, many museums develop special temporary or "traveling" exhibitions that are later displayed in other institutions.

Historical Development. The word *museum* is derived from the ancient Greek name for the temple of the Muses, the patron goddesses of the arts. The term was originally used to refer to institutions of advanced learning. It did not assume its present meaning until the Renaissance, when the first great collections of art were formed in Italy, the result of a burgeoning desire for knowledge of the past, especially classical antiquity. The impulse to collect art soon passed to princes, nobles, and clergy (see ART COLLECTORS AND PATRONS).

Art collectors began not only to acquire ancient Greek and Roman art objects and relics of the Middle Ages but also to patronize works by contemporary artists. These collections became, in some cases, the foundations of today's most famous museums. For example, the powerful MEDICI family of Florence amassed a vast collection of ancient and modern works of art that formed the basis of, among other museum collections, the UFFIZI Gallery, one of the richest repositories of art in the world. Hundreds of private collections were formed throughout Europe in the 17th and 18th centuries. However, as in the Renaissance period, almost all collections were private, and public access to them was extremely limited. A notable exception was the collection of Elias Ashmole in England, which became (1683) the Ashmolean Museum, Oxford, the first university museum. Seventy years later, the collection of Sir Hans Sloane was bequeathed to the nation, resulting in the establishment of the first museum organized as a public institution, the BRITISH MUSEUM.

Beginning in the late 18th century, a number of public art museums were founded, formed principally of royal or princely collections. The principle of public control over art and art collections was firmly established in France during the Revolution, when the royal collection was nationalized (1793) and opened to the public as the LOUVRE Museum. Inspired by the creation of the Louvre, King Frederick William III of Prussia declared his collection public in 1797, leading to the establishment of the Kaiser Friedrich Museum, Berlin. In 1809 the Brera Picture Gallery, Milan (originally the collection of the Accademia di Belle Arti), was opened to the public. The National Gallery, London, one of the few major European museums not originating from a royal collection, was founded in 1824. In 1852 the HERMITAGE MUSEUM, Saint Petersburg (now Leningrad), containing the tsar's private art collection, was opened to public view on a regular basis.

In the second half of the 19th century, a number of specialized museums were created in Europe, such as the Bavarian National Museum (1855), Munich, devoted almost exclusively to the fine and applied arts of South Germany, and the Museum of Ornamental Art, London (1852), renamed the Victoria and Albert Museum in 1899, originally established to display and encourage modern handicrafts. The first museums to be established as public institutions in the United States were the Museum of Fine Arts, Boston (1870), and the METROPOLITAN MUSEUM OF ART, New York City (1872), followed (1879) by the Art Institute of Chicago (see CHICAGO, ART INSTITUTE OF), which originated as an art school and museum.

In recent years a number of the world's largest museums have attempted to reduce the size and refine the quality of their collections by selling less important works of art and concentrating available funds on acquiring

The Musée d'Orsay in Paris, created from a former railway station and opened in 1986, holds a major collection of paintings from the impressionist era.

works of greater artistic merit or historical significance. Some have also embarked on vast programs of expansion, such as the NATIONAL GALLERY OF ART, Washington, D.C., which opened (1978) a new wing designed by I. M. Pei. Major museums devoted entirely to modern art include the MUSEUM OF MODERN ART, New York City (1929); the Gallery of the Twentieth Century, Berlin (1949); and the BEAUBOURG, Paris (1977), home to the National Museum of Modern Art. The latest addition to Paris's magnificent museum collection is the Musée d'Orsay, reconstructed in 1986 from the old railroad station, the Gare d'Orsay, and housing thousands of pieces of art and artifacts from the last half of the 19th century.

Since older works of European and American art, as well as Oriental and primitive art, have become scarce and therefore costly, museums are now acquiring relatively less expensive contemporary art. While this recognition of practicing artists is invigorating (in that it alerts the community to potentially stimulating current ideas), it has altered attitudes that have long governed the making and collecting of art. New art, often purchased from the artists' studios and donated to museums by patrons (partially as tax-exempt gifts), receives sanction simply by its association with the institution, and not by any other recognition of its artistic worth. This acceleration of museums' perhaps premature recognition of young artists pushes and is pushed by art-market forces. Public appreciation of art then becomes more an appreciation of art's economic rather than its aesthetic values.

Museum Staff. Museums are staffed by highly trained professionals who are responsible for the preservation of the collection and for implementing its visual accessibility for the public. Fulfilling these sometimes conflicting requirements is the task of the curator, an art historian who is knowledgeable regarding the physical properties of handmade objects. While curators have a general background in the history of art, they usually specialize in a given area. Large museums having diversified collections employ several curators for such departments as Europe-

an, Modern, American, Oriental, Primitive, and Decorative Arts, as well as Photography. Curators oversee existing objects in the collection and assist in obtaining new acquisitions. Works of art are chosen for their aesthetic value (excellence of composition, form, color, and so on) and historical significance (either as a representation of a stylistic movement or as an example of a period within an artist's oeuvre). Curators verify the authenticity of an object by researching its provenance, a compilation of facts relating to the work's previous owners and exhibitors. This documentation is made available to other scholars and the public in catalogs, museum publications, and annotated wall labels.

The installation of the museum's permanent collection is planned and supervised by the curator, who determines the number of objects to be shown and organizes their sequence and arrangement for maximum historical, contextual, and aesthetic coherence.

Most major art museums have their own conservators who evaluate the condition of objects and, using mechanical and chemical procedures, clean and stabilize works to guard against deterioration. Occasionally, conservators restore objects to resemble their original state, but they do so only after recording and photographically documenting the work in its initial disrepair (see ART CONSERVATION AND RESTORATION).

Because works of art are often moved within a museum, or transported to distant exhibitions, it is necessary to maintain files specifying their location. These files are handled by a registrar, who also negotiates for all shipping and insurance.

Educational programming has become important in all museums, and most have departments that organize lectures and symposiums and provide information in the galleries through the use of automated video and slide presentations and audiocassette recordings. Tours of exhibitions are led by staff members and volunteer guides called docents.

A wall of immense paintings by Rubens greets visitors to the Louvre, France's greatest art museum. Mounted in heavy frames and hung on velvet-covered walls, these works seem designed to fit their setting.

This soap-film painting creates a rainbow of colors visible to onlookers when reflected light waves interfere with the wave patterns that form in a vibrating membrane. It is one of the nearly 450 exhibits at the Exploratorium, a science museum in San Francisco that emphasizes the teaching of science.

museums of science and industry

Museums of science and industry can be classified into two general types: historical museums, which preserve and display objects that have been important to the development of science and technology, and centers, which teach the principles related to these fields. The two types are not necessarily mutually exclusive, although most institutions fall into one category or the other.

Origin and Development. Science museums have their origin in the "cabinets of curiosities," or miscellanea, assembled by scientifically minded people. These collections became numerous during the Renaissance, and from them full-scale museums began to emerge in the 17th century. They embodied the basic elements of the modern science museums: a desire to interest visitors in history, to enlighten them about the nature of science, and to entertain.

In 1794 the museum of the Conservatoire National des Arts et Métiers was born in Paris, with the expressed purpose of explaining "the construction and use of tools and machines employed in arts and trades." Similar museums in London and Washington grew out of the public enthusiasm generated by the CRYSTAL PALACE Exhibition in London in 1851 and the 1876 CENTENNIAL EXPOSITION in Philadelphia. The development reached its peak when Oskar von Miller founded the Deutsches Museum in Munich in 1903.

In the late 1920s a new type of museum appeared, exemplified by the Palais de la Découverte (which opened in Paris in 1937), where there were few historical objects, but where the operation of the latest scientific and technical devices was demonstrated.

Since World War II increasing attention has been paid to the aesthetics of museum design in an attempt to appeal to a more general public. Objects are placed in a context that emphasizes the impact that science and technology have had on modern society.

Methods and procedures differ in the two types of mu-

seums. In the historical institutions scholars with historical expertise are responsible for collecting and caring for the objects and arranging the exhibitions. In the science and technology centers the principal staff members are apt to be scientists with an interest in teaching.

Notable Science Museums. Among large historical museums three are preeminent: the Science Museum in London, the Deutsches Museum in Munich, and the science and technology portions of the Smithsonian's National Museum of History and Technology in Washington, D.C. Although the collections of each of these museums tend to have a nationalistic base, all three give broad coverage to the major areas of science and technology. They all place strong emphasis on display technique. There are also a number of specialized museums—notably in the field of transportation—including the Science Museum's Railway Museum in York, England, and the Smithsonian's National Air and Space Museum in Washington.

Some museums that emphasize teaching the principles of science and technology are the Museum of Science in Boston, the Franklin Institute in Philadelphia, and the Museum of Science and Industry in Chicago. The number of science centers in which almost exclusive attention is paid to teaching is rapidly increasing. All of them emphasize participatory exhibits designed to help visitors to become better acquainted with scientific and technological principles.

mushrooms

Mushrooms and toadstools are FUNGI; the term *toadstool* is commonly but not precisely reserved for nonedible, sometimes violently poisonous species of mushroom. More precisely, mushrooms are the fruiting structures, or spore-bearing organs, of higher fungi. They are produced by the fungi's vegetative bodies, the mycelia (singular, mycelium) growing in the soil, on wood, or in or on other substrates. More than 3,000 kinds of mushrooms grow in North America alone. Some are very common, but many are found only rarely in special habitats.

Mushrooms colonize by means of mycelial growth. For example, the fairy ring mushroom, *Marasmius oreades*,

A typical mushroom of the subdivision Basidiomycotina is a small, fruiting body that begins as a "button" mushroom (left). During the mushroom's growth the outer layer, or veil, is torn, exposing the cap, with its gills beneath, and the supporting stalk (center). The remains of the veil may form a ring around the stalk, and the gills eventually mature into spore-bearing basidia cells (right).

Although most mushrooms are edible, several species cause serious poisoning. The fly agaric (left) *contains the poison muscarine, which may cause slowed heart rate, delirium, and convulsions; its red or orange cap bears white scales.* Gyromitra esculenta *(center), distinguished by its convoluted cap, can be deadly if eaten raw but may be edible if cooked or dried. The death cap* (right) *leads to severe abdominal pain, weakness, convulsions, and usually death; symptoms can appear as late as two days after eating this mushroom.*

produces an expanding ring of mushrooms that appears each year. Many species produce rootlike structures, called rhizomorphs, composed of large numbers of mycelial filaments, or hyphae, surrounded by an outer rind. These produce branches and spread out over the surface of logs or roots of plants.

Many mushrooms and puffballs are saprobic, deriving all their nutritional needs from organic material in soil, such as dead plants, or fallen trees. Saprobic fungi serve an important role in degrading dead plant materials and in recycling nutrients and carbon for reuse by plants. Others are parasitic on living trees and cause considerable damage.

A number of mushrooms have a symbiotic relationship, known as mycorrhiza, with higher plants. The fungal hyphae form a thick sheath around the surface and outer cells of the small rootlets of certain trees, such as pine or beech, causing them to branch and suppressing the normal development of root hairs. Other mycorrhizal fungi do not form the sheath and instead penetrate many of the root cells. The fungi obtain organic nutrients from the plant "host" and benefit it by providing certain needed elements, such as phosphate.

Classification. Mushrooms generally are members of the fungi subdivision Basidiomycotina, class Hymenomycetes, although certain fungi commonly called mushrooms—such as the edible morels, *Morchella*—are members of the subdivision Ascomycotina. The typical basidiomycotinan has a stalk (stipe) and cap (pileus). Ascomycotinan fungi are broadly characterized by a fruiting structure, called an ascocarp, usually the shape of an open cup or a nearly closed sphere.

Mushrooms of the class Hymenomycetes are separated into different orders and families on the basis of the arrangement of the hymenia, the spore-bearing layers of the fruit. They are usually classified into two separate orders, the Agaricales, which contains almost entirely the soft-bodied gill fungi, and the Polyporales, which contains hard-bodied fungi whose hymenial layers are not borne on gills. Agaricales include the commercial mushroom, *Agaricus bisporus*; its relative the wild mushroom, *A. capestris*; the oyster mushroom, *Pleurotus ostreatus*; and the fairy ring mushroom. Deadly poisonous species such as *Amanita phalloides* are also agaricales. Among the polyporales are the coral fungi, which produce coral-shaped, branched, or unbranched fruits; and the cantharelloid fungi, which usually have funnel-shaped fruits.

Mating and Growth. Tiny spores produced by the fruits in large numbers are called basidiospores. If they fall in an area that will support growth, they germinate to produce a primary mycelium, which may grow extensively; or, if they meet the filaments of another compatible primary mycelium, they will fuse together to form a secondary mycelium, or dikaryon.

This mycelial stage may grow for years in the same area and produce the fruiting bodies, or mushrooms; the way these mushrooms develop is characteristic of different genera and species. Typical mushrooms, such as the common meadow mushroom, *A. campestris*, form a small embryonic fruit (the "button") just below the soil's surface, made up of specialized hyphal strands. The button expands rapidly in size to produce the mature mushroom. This expansion ruptures the outer layer, or veil, connecting the cap and stalk of the button stage. As the cap expands, the tips of hyphal filaments on the surface of the gills become spore-bearing cells called basidia.

Most basidiomycotinans discharge very large numbers of basidiospores to ensure that at least a few will fall in places where new colonies can grow. A single *A. campestris* mushroom may release 40 million spores an hour for two days. A large specimen of the giant puffball, *Calvatia gigantea*, may produce a total of 7 trillion basidiospores.

Mushrooms as Food. The mushroom *A. bisporus* is grown commercially for food on a large scale in the United States; in Asia, other species, such as the shiitake mushroom, *Cortinellus berkeleyanus*, are cultivated. Wild mushrooms are regularly collected for sale and as a popular pastime in Europe and Asia. Proper care must be taken in mushroom collection because only a relatively small number of mushrooms are considered both edible and desirable. The collector must be able to identify them accurately because, for instance, two mushroom species, one poisonous and one not, may superficially resemble each other. A few mushrooms cause hallucinations when consumed, such as *Amanita muscaria*, which is also poisonous, and *Psilocybe* species, used to induce hallucination during ritual ceremonies by Mexican Indians.

See also: POISONOUS PLANTS AND ANIMALS.

Musial, Stan [myoo'-zee-ul]   Stanley Frank Musial, b. Donora, Pa., Nov. 21, 1920, an American professional baseball player, was one of the game's greatest hitting stars. A member of the St. Louis Cardinals from 1941 to 1963, he was affectionately referred to as "Stan the Man." Musial became a pitcher with the St. Louis organization in 1938 and in the next 3 years compiled a minor league record of 33 wins and 13 losses. His pitching career came to an end when he was playing outfield, between pitching assignments, and injured his throwing arm while attempting a difficult catch. He played for the Cardinals briefly in 1941, then hit over .300 in each of the next 16 full seasons, winning the National League batting championship 7 times. Musial ended his 22-year career with a .331 lifetime batting average, compiling a total of 3,630 hits, until 1981 the most in National League history. A bona fide long-ball threat (he hit 475 home runs during his career), he set a major league record on May 2, 1954, by hitting 5 home runs during a doubleheader. He played in 24 All-Star Games and 4 World Series and was the National League's Most Valuable Player in 1943, 1946, and 1948. In 1969, Musial was elected to the Baseball Hall of Fame.

---

music   Music has been called both the most mathematical and the most abstract of the arts. Unlike words, pictorial images, or bodily movements, however, musical tones in themselves have no concrete associations, and gain meaning only when they are combined into musical patterns.

Philosophers have always been intrigued by the problems inherent in attempts to define music. Three centuries before the birth of Christ the Greek philosopher Aristoxenes distinguished between speculations on the nature of music and attempts to explain actual musical practice. Like most medieval theorists and their Greek predecessors, Boethius (*c.*480–*c.*524) held a very broad view, dividing music into the harmony of the universe, the harmony of soul and body, and the harmony of sounding tones. Many non-Western cultures and some Western writers as well—believing the power of music to be less tied to the material world than are the other arts and sciences—have perceived it as an inherently mystical or occult force, able to unlock elemental truths or principles that cannot be otherwise translated into written or graphic form. "Music is born of emotion," Confucius observed. Whether vocal or instrumental, music has also been viewed both literally and figuratively as a form of language or speech, with less specificity than the spoken word but possessing subtler shades of meaning and more emotive force. It is not a "universal language," however, but rather, like speech, an acquired one for which humans have innate capacity.

Some recent definitions of music include "organized sound," "the motion of tones," "sounding form in motion," and "time given shape by the energy of sound." Of course, no single definition can encompass all the diverse practices of music, or be free of some aesthetic bias. Robert Schumann noted that "perhaps it is precisely the mystery of her origins which accounts for the charm of her beauty."

Archaeologists have discovered musical instruments dating back almost 30,000 years. Ceremonial music predates recorded history and, according to certain theories, may predate human speech. Folk music is also common to all societies. Although folk songs, too, can be associated with certain functions (work songs, spiritual music, and so on), they are often performed solely for the pleasure they bring. More-structured musical traditions evolve from ceremonial, folk, and related types of practice to become, over time, classical (or "art music") traditions. The music is now increasingly performed for its own sake, in its own time and place, and it has its own meaning.

To comprehend and enjoy a musical performance, one must have some familiarity with its choice of sounds, its nuances, and its organizing principles and a grasp of its function—of how the music is intended to be heard. When considering the quality of a sound or of a musical passage, it is often necessary to distinguish among the acoustical properties of the source, the subjective mental perception of what is heard, and the ways in which musical training and experience color a listener's response. These considerations involve such disciplines as acoustics (the science of physical properties of sound) and psychoacoustics (the study of how sounds are interpreted). Music theories are attempts to codify the elements, techniques, and forms of music. Musicology traces the historical development of styles and forms. Aesthetics examines artistic values and judgments. Branches of psychology and sociology consider broader issues in the relation of music to mental processes and social changes.

The remainder of this article surveys important facets of music making and listening. More detailed information on historical periods (for example, BAROQUE MUSIC), composers, musical forms, and national musics (AMERICAN MUSIC, RUSSIAN MUSIC, and so forth) can be found in separate articles.

The Elements of Music

The physical qualities of sound include duration; amplitude (a measure of force or strength) and its temporal en-

Common Musical Notational Signs

a. Treble clef, used to notate pitches in higher registers.

b. Key signature. (Two flats denotes the key of B-flat major.)

c. Time signature. (¾ specifies triple meter — three quarter notes per measure.)

d. Tempo indication. (*Vivace*, Italian for "quick, lively," is denoted precisely in the metronome marking of 50 measures per minute. The dotted half note within the metronome marking is equivalent to three quarter notes.)

e. Dynamic markings. f = *forte*, Italian for "loudly;" *cresc.* = crescendo, "gradually increase volume;" ff = *fortissimo*, "very loudly;" the sign for *decrescendo*, "gradually softer;" p = *piano*, softly; *scherz.* = *scherzando*, "in a lively, joking fashion."

f. Ornaments: tr = trill, a rapid alternation of two adjacent tones. Grace notes (the smaller notes in the fourth and fifth measures) are played rapidly just before the beat.

velope, or evolution (attack, sustaining, and decay characteristics); and frequency (the fundamental rate of vibration, measured in cycles per second, also called hertz). (See SOUND AND ACOUSTICS.)

Audible vibrations occur within a range of roughly 20 to 20,000 hertz (Hz). The lowest and highest tones of the piano vibrate, respectively, at frequencies of 27.5 and 4,186 Hz. The complex vibrating patterns of natural sounds actually contain many frequencies, called partials, of varying strength. In sung tones, and in most tones produced by stringed and wind instruments, most or all of these partials are harmonically related by simple integer ratios (double the fundamental frequency, three times the fundamental, four times, and so on). In percussive, spoken, and noiselike sounds, by contrast, partial frequencies are not harmonically related, and so one does not hear a well-defined fundamental pitch.

A straightforward relationship exists between frequency and PITCH: the higher the fundamental frequency, the higher the perceived pitch. Loudness depends both on amplitude and on the frequency spectrum, since sounds with more high frequency energy are perceived as more intense. Timbre is the characteristic tonal quality of a sound, which enables one to distinguish the voices of two people, or a clarinet from a flute. Several physical factors influence the perception of timbre: the envelope; the frequency spectrum; and the formants, one or more regions in an instrument that resonate and amplify any frequencies that pass through them.

The melodies and harmonies of a culture's music consist of a limited number of pitched tones that reflect a tuning system. This collection of available tones can be arranged in ascending or descending order to form a SCALE. The scales of ancient Greece and the Middle Ages comprised seven tones. Such scales, corresponding to the white keys of the piano, are termed diatonic, and remain the basis for most Western music. Since the 16th century, however, Western music has made increasing use of five additional chromatic tones (the black keys), which lie between the original seven. Non-Western cultures employ different tuning systems, which may consist of as few as two or three tones (in some African tribal music) or of more than twelve (in some Asian music). Scales of five, six, or seven tones are most common.

The characteristic sound of a scale is determined by the intervals (distances) between adjacent tones. The most basic musical interval is the octave, which occurs when the frequency of any tone is doubled or halved. Two tones an octave apart sound "identical," as if a single pitch were duplicated in a higher or lower register. The Greek mathematician Pythagoras discovered similar simple ratios for other important intervals (for example, a 2/3 ratio for the perfect fifth). These acoustically "pure" intervals, however, lead to mistunings and other problems in chromatic music. Various temperaments—tuning systems in which minor adjustments are made in the size of Pythagorean intervals—have been devised to deal with this problem. The system of equal temperament, first proposed in the 1500s, became standardized during the 18th and early 19th centuries. This system divides the octave into 12 equally spaced intervals. The interval between any two adjacent tones (a frequency ratio of 1.05946) is called a half step. An interval equal to two half steps (such as between two white keys separated by a black key) is termed a whole step.

Diatonic scales consist of patterns of five whole steps and two half steps. Several such scales, called MODES, were used in medieval and Renaissance music. Medieval theorists, like their Greek predecessors, attributed particular expressive qualities and suitabilities to each mode.

Scales are usually rooted on a central tone, to which melodies frequently return and on which they end. TONALITY—the relationship of all scale tones to a home tone—is among the few principles common to all musical cultures. The term is also used in a more restricted sense, however, to refer to the harmonic system of major-minor tonality. This system governed virtually all Western art music between the mid-17th and the early 20th century and remains the basis for most popular and much concert music. Tonal music employs only two diatonic modes, major (where the step arrangement on the piano is 1-1-½-1-1-1-½) and minor (1-½-1-1-1-1-½).

The most important elements of music are rhythm, melody, counterpoint, harmony, form, and tone color. Other elements, such as dynamics (variations in loudness), texture, and density, can also be identified, but these are usually employed to underscore formal or expressive patterns.

Rhythm. A rhythmic pulse marks off divisions of time. Pulses may be stressed or unstressed. Many early medieval and some Renaissance works are unstressed, with subtly shifting accents determined by the sung text. Most familiar musical styles, however, feature regular patterned groupings of accented and unstressed pulses, which result in a number of common meters. Duple meters, with alternating stressed and unstressed beats, are characteristic of marches; triple meters (in which every third beat is stressed), of waltzes. Before the early 20th century almost all Western music employed relatively simple metrical patterns of two, three, four, or six beats. Great variety in duration and secondary accents is possible within such simple frameworks, however. Asymmetric meters, typically of five or seven beats, and polyrhythms (different meters played simultaneously) are widespread in non-Western folk music and in 20th-century concert music. (See RHYTHM.)

Melody. A MELODY is a succession of tones in rhythm. Melodies are structured into phrases, each of which ends with a cadence, a relaxation or breathing point. Sometimes a fragmentary but incisive pitch or rhythmic figure of a few notes, called a motive, is repeated several times. Motives, phrases, or entire melodies can also be varied (repeated with alterations) or developed (broken into smaller units that are combined in new ways or transposed to a new pitch level). Melodies are frequently referred to as "lines" because of the audible shapes they trace. In large-scale works the principal melodies are called themes.

"Originality" in melodic construction is highly prized in the West, but in some traditions melodic invention takes the form of variations on well-known melodic formulas, motivic figures, or scalelike models. The raga of Indian music, for example, provides a structural and expressive framework for continuous improvisational variations.

The development of melodic resources in Asian and African cultures has led to many intricate tuning systems. The development of Western music, by contrast, has been characterized largely by the combination of tones and melodies in ever new ways, through POLYPHONY ("many sounds") and COUNTERPOINT ("point against point"). The separate melodies, usually called "voices" even in instrumental works, maintain independent contours and may end at different places, but they are also interrelated to produce a composite formal design.

Harmony. Groups of tones sounded together create HARMONY. Harmonic practice, which evolved out of melodic and polyphonic procedures, is among the most distinctive features of Western music. The basic unit of harmony is the chord, two or more tones that fuse into a single musical sound. The harmonic quality of a chord is determined by the intervals between its tones and by its relation to other chords in a passage. Consonant intervals

A panel from the Ghent altarpiece painted (1432) by Jan van Eyck shows angel musicians playing organ, viol, and harp. The organ is a positive: that is, air is supplied by bellows attached to the back of the instrument and worked by a person other than the player. With the portative, another early organ type, the player operated a pair of bellows with one hand while playing a small keyboard with the other.

(which generally result from simpler frequency ratios) produce a sense of stability or relaxation, whereas dissonant intervals create a feeling of tension and a need for resolution. Intervals and chords that are perceived as dissonant in one era or culture are often treated as consonances elsewhere. Furthermore, an acoustically consonant chord can function as a dissonant harmony in certain contexts, especially if it is unexpected.

The basic chord of tonal music is the triad, consisting of three tones, each two diatonic scale steps apart (for example, tones 1, 3, and 5 of a major or minor scale). Triads, and more complex chords with additional tones, can relate to each other in changing ways, resulting in modulation, a temporary shift into some other key. In later-19th-century music increasing use of chromatic inflections, strings of dissonant or coloristic harmonies, and prolonged passages of restless tonal movement gradually weakened the underlying principles of tonality. Several alternative methods of harmonic organization—some linked to tonal practice, others based on new procedures—have been employed in 20th-century music.

Form. Form is the architectural structure of music—the process through which the tiniest details are linked and related through points of tension, climax, and resolution to create the overall design of a work. Formal principles can be grouped into two broad categories, outlines and procedures. An outline, or scheme, consists of a general sequence of events. The most important arrival points are full cadences—the points of harmonic repose that mark off sectional divisions. Two-part forms present a statement and a response. The second section may begin with contrasting ideas, or with a restatement of the initial material. In either case, it will lead to a strong final closure and a feeling of resolution. Most three-part forms are derived from the related principle of statement, contrast, and return (A-B-A). Individual sections may themselves contain exact or varied repetitions, groups of themes, transitions and developmental passages, and internal two- or three-part patterns. In tonal music, unity, contrast, and overall structure result primarily from harmonic motion between secondary tonal goals and the home, or tonic, chord.

Many common forms, however, are based on particular procedures rather than on a given sequence of events. Imitation, for example, is the primary organizing principle in many polyphonic and contrapuntal works and is the basis for such forms as the FUGUE and CANON. Individual fugues vary widely in the number and placement of thematic statements, modulations, and cadences, but they share a common method of development.

Sometimes confused with forms, musical genres are particular performance mediums, many of which, such as the string quartet or accompanied song, have developed their own distinctive idioms and extensive literatures. For certain periods, some genres are associated with particular forms. Most 18th- and 19th-century string quartets, for example, follow roughly the same formal outline.

The musical language, conventions, and working procedures of a culture, historical period, or individual composer or performer constitute a musical style. In both their conventional and individual aspects, styles reflect the responses of musicians to the values and aspirations of society.

Development of Western Musical Forms

Throughout the long period of MEDIEVAL MUSIC, encompassing roughly a thousand years from the early Christian era to the mid-15th century, the Roman church was the dominant and unifying force in Western music. The most important musical developments were the establishment and codification of the repertory of PLAINSONG chants of

The baroque composer Antonio Vivaldi wrote nearly 450 concertos for the violin and other instruments. (Liceo Musicale, Florence.)

French artist Louis Carmontelle painted this watercolor portrait of Leopold Mozart and his children in 1763. Wolfgang was 7, his sister, Nannerl, 12. In 1763–66, they performed on the continent and in England to the astonishment of audiences.

the Mass and Offices, which would serve as the structural basis for countless secular as well as sacred compositions in ensuing centuries; the rise of polyphonic techniques and forms; and the development of metrical rhythms and principles of rhythmic organization.

Organum, the earliest form of polyphony, featured the addition of one, two, or three melodic lines to a plainsong melody. Later the technique of isorhythm (reiterated rhythmic patterns) was cultivated in the major genre of medieval polyphony, the MOTET. Cantus-firmus techniques, in which the "fixed melody" (usually borrowed, most often from plainsong) is sung or played in the tenor voice against more rapid, freely composed upper voices, remained a common basis for most polyphonic forms until the late 16th century.

During the 12th and 13th centuries an independent tradition of secular songs developed among minstrels at feudal courts (see MINSTRELS, MINNESINGERS, AND TROUBADOURS). The musical structures of the ballade, rondeau, virelai, and other types of SONGS were derived from the French poetic forms of the same names. In Italy the primary 14th-century forms were the ballata, with a refrain structure; the caccia, which involved continuous imitation between the upper two voices against a slower-moving tenor; and the MADRIGAL (not to be confused with a 16th-century form of the same name).

In contrast to such rigid late-Gothic techniques as isorhythm, RENAISSANCE MUSIC (c.1450–1600) is characterized by imitative polyphonic styles of seamless textures, rhythmically flowing lines, equality among voice parts, and a growing emphasis on sonorous harmonies. The two major genres of sacred polyphony, the motet and settings of the ordinary of the mass (see MASS, musical setting), were brought to their highest levels of mastery by Josquin des Prez and Giovanni Palestrina. Following the Reformation, Martin Luther and his followers assembled collections of CHORALES (Protestant hymns), derived mostly from secular songs and Catholic hymns and designed for congregational singing.

The humanistic spirit of the Renaissance is reflected in the rise of distinct secular styles and forms. Polyphonic secular songs, including the French chanson, the Italian frottola, the German polyphonic lied, the Spanish villancico, and the Italian and English madrigal, were lighter in texture (with a solo singer on each part) as well as in spirit.

Instruments were no longer used only to accompany or replace singers. Repertoires of keyboard music (often played on ORGANS, HARPSICHORDS, or CLAVICHORDS) and LUTE music developed in such forms as the fantasia, ricercar, canzona, and sets of VARIATIONS on secular tunes. A similar repertoire was composed for consorts of instruments.

Major developments at the beginning of the period of baroque music (c.1600–1750) were concentrated in vocal music. The simplified vocal style of monody, with a solo vocal line in speechlike rhythms over a sparse harmonic accompaniment, provided the basis for the first OPERAS, notably those of Claudio Monteverdi. Distinct national and regional serious and comic operatic forms arose, comprising ARIAS, RECITATIVES, and choruses, as well as less elaborate types of music drama such as the English MASQUE. The ORATORIO, originally similar in outline to opera (but without stage action), and the CANTATA, a narrative work in several movements for soloists, chorus, and orchestral accompaniment, incorporated operatic forms and conventions. Chorale melodies were incorporated within the church cantata, passion, and other genres of Lutheran music (see CHORAL MUSIC) and functioned in the manner of cantus firmus in many organ works.

Vivid emotional portrayals characterized many vocal

The anonymous caricature "Chromatic Gallop by the Devil of Harmony, April 18, 1843," mocks the 19th-century composer Franz Liszt, who aroused the ire and envy of contemporaries with his innovative compositions and dazzling virtuosity.

works. The fundamental formal principle in most instrumental works, however, was the contrast in patterns between opposing groups, sections, dynamic levels, soprano and bass voices, or other elements of structure. The sonata ("sound-piece"), a term originally used to designate various types of music for instruments, evolved into the most important genre of CHAMBER MUSIC and music for harpsichord, notably in the works of Domenico Scarlatti. Sonatas for violin and continuo (an accompanying instrumental group; see FIGURED BASS), and trio sonatas, typically for two violins and continuo, included three or four contrasting slow and fast movements. The CONCERTO ("contrasting instrumental bodies") evolved in the works of Antonio Vivaldi and his contemporaries into an orchestral form characterized by alternation between a small group of instruments and the larger string ensemble (the concerto grosso), or between a soloist (usually a violinist) and an orchestra.

The keyboard forms of the late 16th century remained popular, but new forms also developed, notably the TOCCATA, a "touch piece" for organ or harpsichord featuring rapid scalelike runs and similar idiomatic figures. The long history of Renaissance and baroque imitative polyphony culminated in the perfection of the fugue by J. S. Bach.

Sonata procedures that were first developed in the CLASSICAL PERIOD IN MUSIC (c.1750–1825) dominated major instrumental genres through the early 20th century and remain vital components of many recent works. The sonatas for piano or for another instrument with piano of Franz Joseph Haydn, Wolfgang Amadeus Mozart, and Ludwig von Beethoven are expansive three- or (in many of Beethoven's works) four-movement cycles featuring clearly articulated tonal schemes and extensive thematic development. These features are most prominent within the first movement of the cycle, where they constitute a structural procedure known as the sonata form. (The principles of "sonata form," through which a single movement is developed, should not be confused with the overall multimovement scheme of the sonata as a whole.)

The formal outline of the sonata, and the procedures of sonata form, were applied in other mediums to produce the SYMPHONY, the classical concerto, and the STRING QUARTET (and such related genres as the piano trio and the string quintet). The overall design of each of these genres consists of a fast movement in sonata form; a slow movement; a third movement (not included in concerti or early sonatas) in MINUET-and-trio or SCHERZO-and-trio form; and a finale, most often in RONDO, sonata-rondo, or theme-and-variation form. Sonata-form procedures were also widely employed in simplified form within single-movement OVERTURES.

Opera remained the primary genre of vocal music, given new life through the reforms first implemented by Christoph Willibald Gluck. The comic opera and Singspiel attained greatest expressive power in the works of Mozart.

Classical forms underwent considerable expansion during the period of ROMANTICISM (c.1830–1910). Such composers as Felix Mendelssohn and Johannes Brahms sought to extend classical practice with a more expansive

Stravinsky (especially *Le Sacre du Printemps*, 1913) unleashed a torrent of asymmetric rhythmic energy, bristling dissonances, and orchestral color within highly sectional structures. Whereas the music of Debussy and early Stravinsky often maintained tonal references, Arnold Schoenberg carried the dense chromaticism of late German romanticism to its final stage, employing all 12 tones equally and consciously avoiding tonal implications (see ATONALITY). Seeking a more systematic method of atonal composition, Schoenberg formulated the principles of serial composition, manipulating an ordered series, or "row," of the 12 tones. Adopted in both rigorous and freer forms by Schoenberg's pupils Anton von Webern and Alban Berg, and by Stravinsky and many later composers, serial principles were later applied to rhythmic procedures and other structural elements (see SERIAL MUSIC).

Composers seeking clarity of design and well-defined frameworks have frequently sought to revive and update historical models. Between 1920 and 1950 this movement was termed *neoclassicism*, although baroque procedures such as the fugue were employed nearly as often as classical forms and genres. Within the past decade, several leading composers of atonal music have added tonal elements to their works.

Tone color has become an increasingly significant element of structure. Seeking "to focus interest on the harmonies of sound quality alone," Edgard Varèse used percussion instruments extensively in the creation of sharply drawn melodic, timbral, and rhythmic textural layers. By means of tape manipulation and other sound-processing procedures, collectively called *musique concrète* ("concrete music"), composers of ELECTRONIC MUSIC have altered, superimposed, and reshaped recorded sounds. COMPUTER MUSIC procedures have enabled musicians to manipulate lifelike synthetic or processed sounds with great precision.

Musical Notation

Aural traditions, in which musical practices are learned by ear through years of imitation and memorization, can be found among highly trained professional musicians as well as in preliterate societies. Many classically trained musicians of India and some of the leading jazz performers of the first half of the 20th century have attained consummate performing skills without learning to read music. Most Western traditions, however, rely heavily on written notation to transmit music.

The Audubon Quartet plays a concert. Chamber music was once the favorite of amateur players. From the 19th century, however, compositions grew increasingly difficult and playable, usually, only by professional musicians.

harmonic palette. Other romantics, including Hector Berlioz, Franz Liszt, and Richard Wagner, however, believed that the enriched, often highly chromatic tonal language of the age and the romantic imperative for intense personal expression required free adaptation or the development of new forms, sometimes based on literary or pictorial themes, as in the SYMPHONIC POEM. Conceiving of opera as a "total art work" (*Gesamtkunstwerk*) seamlessly combining music, drama, and other arts, Wagner replaced conventional set numbers with vocal lines midway between aria and recitative, accompanied by continuous, constantly evolving orchestral colors and textures. Giuseppi Verdi, by contrast, accepted the conventions of Italian serious opera, composing "singers' operas" with rapid stage action and melodramatic plots.

The tendencies toward increased brilliance and breadth, also reflected in the virtuosic piano works of Liszt, were counterbalanced by an opposing desire for intimate expression in simple forms, most notably in the flowering of the romantic lied (German art song). The lieder of Franz Schubert, Robert Schumann, and later composers served as models for lyrical instrumental themes. The character piece, a brief piano work that depicts particular moods or qualities, was pioneered by Frédéric Chopin. Popular genres of this type included "songs without words," impromptus, NOCTURNES, INTERMEZZOS, rhapsodies, and PRELUDES.

During the years immediately before and after World War I, the principles of tonality and the romantic aesthetic were challenged by an array of aesthetic, stylistic, and structural alternatives. The resulting musical pluralism, in which style becomes a matter of choice rather than of accepted conventions, has been the most prominent characteristic of a fertile but unsettled artistic age that continues through the present day.

Claude Debussy sought to create musical forms that evolve organically and continuously out of opening figures or a "precise sound" (*ton juste*). The early ballets of Igor

STANDARD DURATIONAL NOTATION

British		American	corresponding rest signs
semibreve	o	whole note	
minim	♩	half note	
crochet	♩	quarter note	
quaver	♪	eighth note	
semiquaver	♪	sixteenth note	
demi semiquaver	♪	thirty-second note	
hemi demi semiquaver	♪	sixty-fourth note	

Various types of notation have been devised to represent different kinds of performance practices. In improvisatory traditions, shorthand sketches are sometimes sufficient. Tablature systems employ signs that show where to position the fingers on a keyboard or stringed instrument to produce the desired notes. When several performers must realize a composer's detailed intentions, however, means of precise indication of pitch and durations, supplemented by directions for tempo, loudness, character of the music, various types of accents, special effects, and ornamentation, become necessary.

The symbols of modern Western notation were derived from grammatical and phonetic symbols, originally placed above or below the texts of plainsong chants as memory aids to rising and falling melodic inflections. These rudimentary symbols gradually evolved into a system of neumes, signs representing single tones, groups of notes, or melodic formulas. Neumes were positioned at various heights above and below a horizontal line that designated the pitch "F." Additional lines were gradually added to indicate pitch level more precisely, and by the 13th century the familiar five-line staff appeared in notations of polyphonic music. At about the same time, a proportional system of durational values was devised, employing four square-shaped note symbols: the double-long ◗; the long ◖; the breve ■; and the semibreve ♦. Mensural notation (c.1450–1600) enabled composers to indicate either duple or triple division of beats. The present system, dating from the early 17th century, is based on the duple division of each successive note and rest symbol (one whole note = two half notes = four quarter notes, and so on). Meters are indicated by means of time signatures and bar lines, major and minor keys by means of key signatures (sharps and flats). Additional symbols, such as those needed for microtonal tunings or special effects, have been introduced in recent years, and alternative graphical and proportional systems, which sometimes bear little resemblance to common musical notation, are frequently employed by contemporary composers.

(Above) *This 17th-century Indian miniature illustrates a courtly musical entertainment. Indian music is based on a system of modes (ragas) that are used as a framework for improvisation.* (Right) *Musicians are seen practicing Tokiwazu music, used in Kabuki theater, in this 18th-century woodcut. The samisen, a long-necked lute, is used as accompaniment in Tokiwazu music, a type of chanted narrative.*

Non-Western Musical Traditions

The term *non-Western* is most often applied to the music of Asia and Africa, but it denotes all musical practices outside of the European traditions. See such articles as AFRICAN MUSIC; ARABIAN MUSIC; CHINESE MUSIC; INDIAN MUSIC; INDIANS OF NORTH AMERICA, MUSIC OF THE; JAPANESE MUSIC; LATIN AMERICAN MUSIC AND DANCE.

Some of the cultures listed above have very long musical histories. Chinese writings as old as the 6th century BC refer to musical performances. Within the Far Eastern countries distinct traditions of classical practice (concentrated in the courts, temples, and major urban centers) and related but simpler folk musics have coexisted for many centuries.

A few striking parallels among civilizations that until recently had little or no contact can be observed. These include the nearly universal recognition of the intervals of the octave and perfect fifth as having a special structural importance and consonant quality, and the widespread use of pentatonic ("black key") scales in Chinese, Afri-

can, American Indian, and other cultures. Attempts to discover universal or consistent principles beyond certain acoustical fundamentals, however, have proved elusive. Ethnomusicologists are concerned with understanding how and why a music sounds as it does, chiefly through study of the music within its cultural context.

Studies of non-Western music often require different methods from those used in conventional musicology. Some types of African drums, for example, can produce ten or more distinct tones of varying pitch and tone color, depending on where and how the instrument is struck. Such music cannot be transcribed in common Western notation, of course.

Western concepts of abstract music ("music for its own sake") are foreign to many other cultures. In many folk traditions particular types of songs, dances, and instrumental music are performed in connection with particular ceremonies and entertainments associated with hunting, farming, birth, and rites of passage. Within some classical traditions, to an even greater degree, elements

A quartet of musicians from the Central African Republic play on the 10-string arched harp, called ngombi (left and center), and on two membrane-headed drums. The complexity of African music requires a high order of performance.

of structure may be determined by the function of the music. Each of the hundreds of Indian ragas, for example, prescribes not only unique melodic formulas but also an emotional quality, such as happiness or longing, and suitability for performance at a certain time of day. When viewed as the aural embodiment of shared experience or metaphysical harmonies, music is often closely allied with other arts, which reflect this same source in visual form. African music is generally associated with dance, music of the Far East with drama.

Given such musical values, at once mythic and very utilitarian, it is not surprising that musical practice in many parts of the world has remained virtually unchanged for long periods, in marked contrast to the continuous evolution of Western styles. Japanese *gagaku* (orchestral court) music exists today much as it did in the 8th century; *guenzhen*, a 16th-century genre of music drama that dominated Chinese music for almost 400 years, can be heard today in its original form. Clues to the nature and instruments of distant classical practices that were superseded can often be found in contemporary folk music, where these elements sometimes survive for even longer periods.

Within the past hundred years, world musics have increasingly been influenced by Western elements. The spread of technology, particularly of radio and recordings, has accelerated this trend. Some traditions now exist only in hybrid form, and others are passing from use. Fortunately, the same technological tools are now assisting scholars from many areas of the world in recording, studying, and preserving the musical heritage of diverse cultures.

Interactions between Musical Traditions

Most Western music is goal oriented, or narrative in structure, consisting of a series of events that create listener expectations as to "where the music is going." Much non-Western music, by contrast, is characterized by stasis—

the prolongation of one quality or pattern—throughout a performance. The availability of recordings and ease of global travel have enabled Western audiences to gain increased understanding and appreciation of such types of musical expression. Eastern and African influences within recent Western concert music have been extensive, and can be readily discerned in John Cage's attempts to free music of personal elements, often through chance procedures (see ALEATORY MUSIC). Minimalist music by such composers as Steve Reich often features a single, elemental formal process that unfolds continuously throughout a work. Some works also reflect the influence of ROCK MUSIC, which itself incorporates elements of rhythm and blues, gospel, country, and black folk music.

Such interactions between musical cultures and tradi-

(Above) *Master artists from different worlds, violinist Yehudi Menuhin and sitarist Ravi Shankar found a common musical language during the 1960s.* (Below) *George Balanchine and Igor Stravinsky (right) had an enduring collaboration that produced such ballets as* Apollo *(1929) and* Agon *(1957).*

tions have always been an important means of renewal and a catalyst in the rise of new styles and forms. Medieval European music developed from Greek, Jewish, Oriental, and local folk sources. Nationalist composers of many periods have incorporated local folk tunes, rhythms, and harmonies within concert and operatic works, seeking to reflect in their music the character and aspirations of their native peoples. JAZZ, the product of African rhythmic and melodic practices applied to European tuning, harmonic, and metrical frameworks, has evolved rapidly into several distinct idioms, many of which have had a significant impact on contemporary concert music.

See also: separate articles on individual composers mentioned.

music box A music box is a mechanical instrument whose sounds are produced by a metal comb—although metal prongs in other shapes are also used—the teeth of which are tuned to specific pitches. The teeth are plucked by pins protruding from a barrel that is rotated by a wound spring.

This mechanism, used today in children's toys as well as in elaborate ornaments, was invented in 1796 by the Swiss watchmaker Antoine Favre. It was originally placed in snuff boxes, watches, and various ornamental objects. In the 1820s a mass-production industry began as music boxes became popular in homes.

By the mid-19th century further developments had been made: barrels could be replaced for a wider selection of music, and long-playing barrels could provide hours of music and could pluck several combs simultaneously, thereby reproducing—in boxes that were by now massive pieces of furniture—elaborate orchestral works.

In 1885 a box was invented using metal disks instead of cylinders. Costing much less than the earlier box, it sold in vast quantities, but the industry was halted by competition from the newly invented phonograph. By 1914 the manufacture of high-quality music boxes had ended.

music festivals Music festivals, which date as far back as the mid-17th century, have become increasingly popular within the past few decades. Summer festivals now form an important and permanent aspect of musical life, completing what has become a 12-month musical season. A recent count of festivals in the United States alone found some 300.

The earliest festivals were choral events, closely tied to church sponsorship. The Three Choirs Festival in England, for example, begun in 1715, was held in the cathedral cities of Gloucester, Worcester, and Hereford. Westminster Abbey was the site of the colossal Handel Commemoration, first held in 1784, in which more than 500 professional musicians participated. In the United States, festivals like those held in Europe began in the mid-19th century, although the Handel and Haydn Society of Boston has presented concerts in that city since 1815, thus establishing the country's oldest music festi-

val. Later, large open-air centers were built in parks and summer resorts, such as those in Saratoga Springs, N.Y. (summer home of the Philadelphia Orchestra), and Ravinia, Ill. (where the Chicago Symphony plays in summer). The Berkshire Music Festival at Tanglewood (see TANGLEWOOD FESTIVAL), now one of the country's largest, opened in Lenox, Mass., in 1937. Berkshire, along with many other festivals, offers summer courses for music students.

The most prestigious European festivals are the Bayreuth Wagner Festival in Germany; the Glyndebourne Opera Festival in England; the Salzburg Festival in Austria; and the Maggio Musicale in Florence, Italy, a month-long festival in May. Jazz, popular, and folk music are well represented, with festivals in Vienne, France; Montreux, Switzerland; New York City; New Orleans, La.; and Austin, Tex., among many others. Martinique, in the West Indies, presents an annual guitar festival. Festivals are held for many reasons: to celebrate a composer's anniversary; to honor a particular performer; to present music related to a particular theme; or simply to take advantage of a beautiful setting.

music hall, vaudeville, and burlesque Music hall, vaudeville, and burlesque were popular entertainment forms that developed in the 19th century to meet the needs of the masses of working people who lived in the rapidly growing cities of Great Britain and the United States and—to a lesser extent—in many cities on the Continent. Vaudeville in America and music hall in England were variety shows of unconnected musical, dancing, comedy, and specialty acts. Burlesque began as comic parodies of well-known topics or people. The word came from the Italian *burla*, "jest."

Music Halls. Early-19th-century English urban taverns were places where the clientele enjoyed communal singing along with the ale. The Theatre Regulation Act of 1843 banned drinking in legitimate theaters, but allowed it in "music halls," prompting many tavern owners to expand into larger rooms and to arrange their tables in front of a platform, where entertainment was supplied by singers, comics, and actors who recited monologues from famous plays. With the addition of a proscenium arch over the platform, and wings and a backstage, the hall grew into a theater, where audiences now came solely to hear professional entertainers. Between 1850 and 1870, music halls went up all over England, and variety shows became the most popular form of entertainment in the country. Although comedy, dance, magic, and other kinds of acts were all presented, popular songs were still the main attraction.

In France, where the café and, later, the beer hall took the place of England's taverns, the 19th century saw somewhat similar developments. Paris's Moulin Rouge, for example, dispensed beer, wine, and champagne to its customers along with a dance orchestra and a string of singers and entertainers. The French were also the inventors of the CABARET, a type of nightclub featuring satiric entertainment.

(Below) *The Kiddie Kar Girls and the Midnight Frolic Collies unleash their charms in this early Ziegfeld production. Exotic pageantry and beautiful chorus girls made Ziegfeld's revues, staged annually from 1907 through 1931, celebrated Broadway entertainments.*

(Above) *Drane and Alexander was among the many comedy teams that flourished on American vaudeville and British variety circuits of the early 1900s. The fast-paced programs included as many as 15 acts.*

Minstrel Shows. In the United States, variety first took the form of the minstrel show, a blend of popular music, dance, and comedy performed by white men wearing burnt-cork facial makeup and speaking and singing in black dialects. Minstrel shows originated in the 1820s and quickly spread throughout America and to England, where blackface acts became part of the music hall shows. Led by the Christy Minstrels, the shows settled into a three-part format. The first part, with all the performers sitting on stage in a semicircle, featured such popular songs as Stephen Foster's "Camptown Races" and "Old Folks at Home" and snappy comic one-liners, riddles, and puns. The second part, the olio, was a black-face variety show with the performers appearing one at a time to do their specialties. Eventually, as the burnt cork was discarded, this section evolved into vaudeville. The third part of the minstrel show was a skit, combining music and comedy in a farce that often parodied current events or fads. The success of these parodies led to burlesques of popular plays and musicals, which reached their high point in the full-length musical burlesques staged by Joe Weber and Lew Fields at the turn of the 20th century.

Burlesque. Although such parodies continued in show business, the word *burlesque* by the late 19th century was more commonly used to mean "girlie" shows—shows featuring the display of women's bodies. In 1868, Lydia Thompson and her British Blondes brought their burlesques of classical drama to America. To play the male roles, the women wore tights and short tunics, which were considered very revealing in the Victorian age.

In the 1870s these burlesque troupes traded their parodies for material like the "can-can" and added male comics to their casts. Although best known for its dancing girls, burlesque produced many great comedians, including Bert LAHR, Fanny BRICE, and ABBOTT AND COSTELLO. To compete with daring vaudeville stars such as Mae WEST and revues such as The ZIEGFELD FOLLIES, burlesque became increasingly racy after 1900.

Variety shows were considered off-color saloon entertainment suitable for men only until Tony Pastor, the "father of American vaudeville," opened (1865) his first variety theater and presented family entertainment.

Vaudeville. Benjamin Franklin Keith and Edward Franklin Albee adopted Pastor's successful approach and called the shows vaudeville to give them a refined new image. (The word *vaudeville* originated in France, and probably derived from the satiric songs typically sung in the Vau de Vire, the Vire River valley in Normandy.) Keith and Albee staged their first vaudeville show in Boston in 1885. They demanded that every performer eliminate anything that might offend anyone. Families flocked to their shows, which ran continuously from early morning to late at night. In 1894, when Keith and Albee opened their Colonial Theater in Boston, it was rivaled in opulence only by the Imperial and Savoy hotels in New York. Anyone with 25 cents could feel like an honored guest in an ornate mansion that had uniformed attendants who provided refreshments, escorted people to their seats, and assisted women in lavish powder rooms. By the turn of the century vaudeville had replaced the minstrel show as America's most popular form of entertainment.

Similar developments took place in Great Britain, where "palaces of variety," such as the Empire, Palace, and Alhambra, replaced music halls, and the Moss and Stoll circuits blanketed the provinces with variety shows.

There was considerable interchange between American and British variety, especially with singers. Harry Lauder and Beatrice Lillie were two of the many British stars who also starred in America, just as Sophie Tucker, Eddie Cantor, and many other Americans found success in England. In both countries, big-time variety offered the widest possible range of entertainment, everything from opera singers to jugglers, from tragedians to trained seals.

The typical show opened with an action-packed "dumb act," such as acrobats or cyclists, that did not need to be heard while people were coming in. The second spot went to a typical vaudeville act, such as a song-and-dance or comedy team, that performed in front of a curtain while stage hands set up scenery for the production to follow, which might be a musical number or a comedy sketch—something that stressed the show's diversity. The first star came next, and the first half climaxed with an exciting headliner. The second half opened with an act that regained the fun and pace of the show and settled the audience down. Next came a production, often a dramatic scene with a famous actor doing a "bit" of a play. In the eighth spot on the typical nine-act bill came the biggest star of the show, often a comedy act. The program closed as it opened—with a showy act that left the audience with a sense of action and abundance but also kept early leavers from disrupting the show.

Vaudeville differed from every other entertainment form in that each performer—no matter how famous or well paid—appeared only once in each show, and rarely for more than 20 minutes. Vaudeville forced performers to select only excellent material and to perfect their timing and delivery, which made it an almost ideal school for comedians.

Competition from Movies. Forced to face the competition of talkies and the economic despair of the Great Depression of the 1930s at the same time, stage entertainment in general declined sharply in popularity. The exception was burlesque. With striptease dances performed by sophisticated artists like Gypsy Rose Lee, burlesque was far racier than movies, and it flourished despite the depression, but because of excesses that led to public censorship, and because it lost its best performers and best features to other entertainment forms, it quickly faded.

In 1932, New York's Palace Theater, the hub of big-time vaudeville, became a movie theater. Live vaudeville with its high operating costs could not compete with the mass media. The greatest impact of vaudeville on modern audiences came through such television variety shows as the "Ed SULLIVAN Show" and through the prominent roles played by ex-vaudevillians and ex-burlesque performers in other branches of show business.

--

musical comedy   The term *musical comedy* is generally applied to theater works in which the play is interwoven with music, lyrics, and, often, dance sequences. Some critics insist that musical comedy is America's distinctive and major contribution to theater, but the genre is not exclusively a U.S. invention.

Henry Higgins (Rex Harrison) notes the nuances of Eliza Doolittle's (Julie Andrews) cockney speech in Lerner and Loewe's My Fair Lady *(1956). This adaptation of George Bernard Shaw's* Pygmalion *became a highly successful Broadway musical.*

Classification. Creators of works for the musical theater frequently designate a new show as either a musical comedy or a play with music. The term *musical comedy* is ambiguous as a genre label. Some notable works, owing to the serious treatment of their characters and plots, can hardly be called comic. Increasingly, therefore, the more general term *musical* is used. If songs and other music are omitted from a production of the work and the work remains an effective drama, then it can best be described, in its original form, as a play with music. Since the advent of musicals such as *Showboat* (1927) and *Oklahoma!* (1943), authors and composers usually have striven to integrate the book, the music and lyrics, and the dances to tell their story so effectively that none of these elements can be diminished or subtracted without severely damaging the structure of the musical.

The distinctions separating the musical from operetta and opera concern the treatment of subject matter and the treatment of music. Operettas have tended to deal with romance and sentiment, often involving picturesque European locales and aristocratic people, whereas musicals have frequently dealt with ordinary people and situations, and have even exaggerated these for comic effect. Operetta scores also make greater musical demands on performers than do musicals, in which the stars are occasionally noted for their inability to sing. Opera—unless it is comic opera—treats its themes and characters with great seriousness, and it also makes major demands on its performers' musical abilities, much more than it does on their acting talents. Thus, the seriousness with which the tale of Porgy and Bess is told, as well as the remarkable Gershwin score, causes some admiring critics to insist that *Porgy and Bess* (1935) is indeed an opera and not a musical.

History. *The Black Crook* (1866), by Charles M. Barras is often cited as the first musical comedy, but this American stage success did not create a new genre. It was a combination of extravaganza, burlesque, ballet, and melodrama, and its book was strongly influenced by Carl Maria von Weber's opera *Der Freischütz*. As the musical theater developed on 19th-century British and American stages, it accommodated a variety of formats and specialty performers. (See MUSIC HALL, VAUDEVILLE, AND BURLESQUE.) Nate Salsbury's *The Brook* (1879) was the first American show to use the term *musical comedy,* but its loosely constructed story was not integrated with the musical numbers. Similar concoctions of music and comedy were provided by such teams as Harrigan and Hart, Weber and Fields, and the Rogers Brothers.

In London producer George Edwardes launched a special kind of musical featuring the talents and charms of attractive young actresses. *The Nautch Girl* (1891), *The Shop Girl* (1894), and others were constructed following a simple formula. These shows inspired many American imitations.

Much of the musical fare before World War I in both London and New York was devoted to spectacular scenery, lavish costumes, attractive chorus girls, vaudeville acts, and glamorous stars, with only the most tenuous or improbable plots to hold the shows together. *The Ziegfeld Follies, The Passing Show,* and George White's *Scandals* were among the most successful of these revues.

George M. COHAN was one of the first to develop an effective format for making comedy, music, and dance into a unified show. Cohan was author, composer, lyricist, director, and performer. Today, his musicals seem naive, but his energy can still be discovered in *Little Johnny Jones* (1904) or *Hello, Broadway* (1914).

It was in the 1920s that the American musical first made its mark, both in the United States and in Europe. A group of immensely talented composers and lyricists produced a series of musicals that became famous for their songs (plots were still sophomoric, when they existed at all). From his first shows (*Very Good, Eddie,* 1915; *Oh Boy!,* 1917; *Sally,* 1920), Jerome KERN's songs were always catchy, and his great work *Showboat* (1927), with libretto and lyrics by Oscar HAMMERSTEIN II, provided the model for the perfection of the musical form. George and Ira GERSHWIN wrote a number of musicals that seemed to fit the mood of the 1920s: their stories were instantly forgettable, but the songs and lyrics were brilliant. Eubie

Sidney Poitier plays the role of Porgy in the 1959 film of George Gershwin's Porgy and Bess *(1935). Gershwin's last Broadway production,* Porgy and Bess *combines the serious musical and dramatic treatment of opera with the idioms of folk and jazz.*

Riff (Tom Hasson) and Bernardo (George Marcy) begin the powerfully choreographed gang rumble in a 1960 performance of Leonard Bernstein's West Side Story *(1957).*

BLAKE and Noble Sissle's 1921 *Shuffle Along* set a successful precedent for black musicals on Broadway and introduced jazz to the musical stage. Sigmund ROMBERG and Rudolf FRIML brought the European tradition of the romantic musical play to the United States with great success.

The 1930s began with the lighthearted, witty songs of Cole PORTER (*The New Yorkers,* 1930; *Gay Divorce,* 1932; *Anything Goes,* 1934) and ended with *Pal Joey* (1940), the acid portrait of a heel, created by the brilliant team of Richard RODGERS and Lorenz HART, and *Lady in the Dark* (1941), Kurt WEILL's stylish comment on psychoanalysis. The years between saw the beginnings of the musical-with-a-message: the Gershwins' Pulitzer Prize–winning *Of Thee I Sing* (1931), about American politics; Weill's antiwar *Johnny Johnson* (1936); and Marc BLITZSTEIN's *The Cradle Will Rock* (1937), satirizing capitalism.

The 1940s seemed to belong to the innovative duo Richard Rodgers and Oscar Hammerstein. From their first collaboration, *Oklahoma!* (1943), through *South Pacific* (1949) and *The King and I* (1951), the two produced musicals whose plots developed logically and whose songs were a perfect blend of words and music. The composer and conductor Leonard BERNSTEIN—whose 1944 *On the Town* had already proved his adeptness at musical comedy—helped shape the 1950s with the almost operatic *Candide* (1956) and *West Side Story* (1957). Frank Loesser was equally successful with *Guys and Dolls* (1950), among other musicals, and Lerner and Loewe (see LERNER, ALAN JAY, AND LOEWE, FREDERICK) produced their elegant hit *My Fair Lady* (1956).

Other composers of hit musicals include Jule STYNE, with *Gypsy* (1959); Jerry Herman, with *Hello Dolly!* (1964) and *La Cage aux Folles* (1983); Meredith WILLSON, with *The Music Man* (1957); and Stephen SONDHEIM, with such innovative works as *Company* (1970), *Sweeney Todd* (1979), *Sunday in the Park with George* (1984), and the grown-up fairy tale *Into the Woods*

violin

lute

banjo

guitar

zither

harp

cello

(1987). Hit British musicals include Sandy Wilson's *The Boy Friend* (1954), a parody of musical comedies of the 1920s, and Lionel Bart's darker-hued *Oliver* (1960), based on Dickens's *Oliver Twist.* More recently, the highly diverse works of British composer Andrew Lloyd Webber have enlivened the Broadway scene. They include the rock opera *Jesus Christ Superstar* (1971), *Evita* (1979), a musical based on the life of the Argentinian Eva Perón, the feline-populated *Cats* (1982), and *The Phantom of the Opera* (1988).

musical instruments   Although vocal performance is common to practically all musical traditions, instrumental performance has a more varied history. Stringed and wind instruments are mentioned in the Bible, and they fulfilled important functions in the ceremonies and entertainments of the Greek and Roman civilizations. Although central to the religious rituals of many non-Western cultures, instrumental music was considered distracting or inappropriate to worship by the church authorities of medieval Europe, who severely restricted its use. Such instruments as the harp, lyre, psaltery, and various winds and drums—most of which were derived from Oriental models—were, however, employed in small ensembles to accompany songs and to play single-line (monophonic) dance pieces. Because only a few instruments from the Middle Ages still exist, much of the present knowledge comes from pictorial and literary sources and from folk music that preserves these traditions.

During the 16th and early 17th centuries viols, recorders, and other winds and strings were constructed in various sizes to form homogeneous consorts, and a repertoire of polyphonic keyboard, lute, and consort music developed independently of vocal music. Rare in music before the mid-1500s, larger ensembles consisting primarily of strings became common at European courts, leading to the standardization of the basic orchestral instrumentation in the late 1700s. For the past 250 years the profusion of instrumental music, in various solo, chamber, and orchestral or large-ensemble genres, has been among the most prominent characteristics of European music.

The comparatively rapid evolution of Western musical genres and instruments (in marked contrast to the stability of many other musical cultures) was frequently accompanied by a disdain for those of previous generations. Older instruments were often altered, "improved," or simply discarded, sometimes surviving intact only in private collections. Renewed interest in the performance of early music, and the revival of such instruments as the harpsichord since World War II, however, have resulted in a growing appreciation for performances on restored in-

Stringed instruments, or chordophones, produce musical tones by one or more strings under tension, sounded by plucking, striking, or bowing. Two primary divisions of chordophones are zithers, where strings are stretched between two ends of a flat body, and lutes, which have a body and a neck. The plucked lutes include the lute, guitar, and banjo, and the bowed lutes include the violin and cello. The harp is unique in that its plane of strings is perpendicular rather than parallel to the soundboard; pitch is controlled with pedals.

struments or authentic reconstructions of early instruments. Many soloists and ensembles now specialize in early music played on these instruments.

Classification

Musical instruments are popularly divided into the stringed, woodwind, brass, percussion, and keyboard families of the symphony orchestra and concert solo repertoire, but these distinctions are not adequate for serious study. The piano, for example, is at once a string, percussion, and keyboard instrument. Medieval trumpets and other brasslike instruments were made of wood, whereas such "woodwinds" as the modern flute and saxophone are constructed from metal. Those who study the origins, construction, and performance of instruments—including non-Western, folk, popular, and ancient, as well as those of concert and liturgical music—require a more precise and inclusive method of classification.

Most instruments incorporate both a vibrating source of sound (such as a stretched string) and a resonator, a larger solid or hollow object that amplifies, prolongs, and adds distinctive tonal coloration to the sound. The most widely used classification scheme, developed by Curt Sachs and Eric M. von Hornbostel in 1914, divides instruments into four broad categories according to the source of vibration: (1) chordophones, from the Greek words *chordos* ("string") and *phonos* ("sound"), include all stringed instruments; (2) aerophones ("air-sound") are wind instruments; (3) idiophones ("self-sound") are made from resonant wood or metal, as in the xylophone and cymbals, and are usually struck; (4) membranophones include drums and other instruments on which a stretched skin or membrane is played. The latter two percussive classes are particularly important in the study of African, Middle Eastern, Asian, and folk music. Twentieth-century applications of technology to musical performance have led to a fifth category, the electrophones, which include electronic and computer-based instruments and sound-processing devices. For the following overview, however, the familiar orchestral family names will suffice.

Stringed Instruments

The many varieties of stringed instruments are distinguished by the positioning of the strings and resonating box (usually a hollow wooden case), and by the manner of playing. Strings can be bowed; plucked with the fingers; plucked with a plectrum or some other device; or hammered. Whereas bowing produces a sustained tone, plucking or striking produces a short percussive sound.

The largest category of chordophones includes members of the LUTE family and its principal derivatives, the

The aerophones include all wind instruments whose musical tones are produced by vibration of air. Two major divisions of aerophones are illustrated: the lip-vibrated aerophones, which include the trumpet, French horn, trombone, and tuba; and the reed pipes, which include the oboe, clarinet, bassoon, and saxophone. The lip-vibrated aerophones are commonly identified as horns, or brass instruments, and have cup-shaped mouthpieces. The reed pipes, or woodwinds, are played with a single or a double reed.

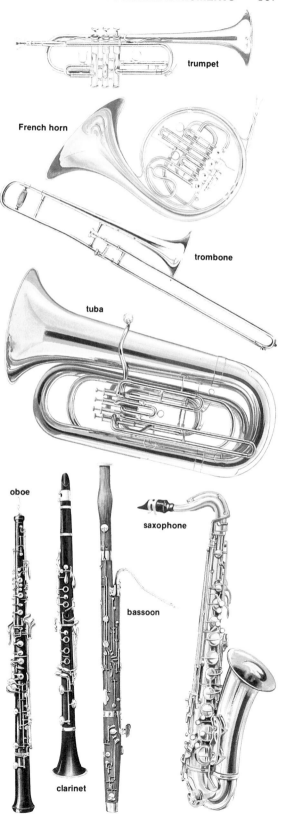

trumpet

French horn

trombone

tuba

oboe

saxophone

bassoon

clarinet

timpani

bass drum

snare drum

triangle

bongo drums

cymbals

xylophone

tambourine

chimes

orchestral gong

violin family. The sound box is attached to one end of a narrow neck against which the strings can be pressed (stopped) to vary the vibrating length and thus the pitch. Lutes (pear-shaped, plucked instruments most popular in the Renaissance but dating back at least 2,000 years), GUITARS, BANJOS, and many similar types of folk instruments usually include frets of wood, metal, or catgut attached to the fingerboard to indicate the position of scale tones. The Indian SITAR is a long-necked lute with three to seven melody strings with movable frets and an additional dozen or so resonating, or drone, strings. Common in folk instruments, drone strings may be plucked or (as in the sitar) simply allowed to vibrate sympathetically with other strings.

Fiddles have been the most important Western stringed instruments since the Middle Ages. The violin family (VIOLIN, VIOLA, and CELLO) evolved during the 17th century out of the Renaissance viols, softer instruments that were held vertically, often with six fretted strings. With its more curved shape, the DOUBLE BASS (or bass viol) is a more direct descendant of the larger viols. The bows with which orchestral strings are played, made of horsehair stretched over a slightly curved stick, developed over the centuries from simple archery-type bows, reaching their present forms in the late 18th century.

HARPS form a second major category of chordophones. The strings are stretched perpendicularly or obliquely to the sound box, which is usually the bottom arm of a triangular frame. Because the strings are not stopped, a separate string is required for each tone. Among the oldest musical instruments, antecedents of the modern harps can be traced back to about 3000 BC in the Mesopotamian region, and a thousand years earlier in Africa.

With the ZITHER and similar instruments (for example, the PSALTERY), the strings are supported by a flat sound box. The most common type of zither incorporates four or five fretted melodic strings, played with a plectrum on the right-hand thumb, and many drone strings, plucked by the right-hand fingers. DULCIMERS are hammered zithers, a category that includes the piano.

Wind Instruments

The sound of wind instruments results from the vibration of air inside a length of tubing or other enclosed cavity. This vibration can be initiated in several ways: when the player blows through a narrow hole in the instrument, as in the flutes; through the movement of reeds, as in the other orchestral woodwinds and the pipe organ; by the buzzing movement of a player's lips, as in the brass instruments; or, less frequently, through direct stimulus from the surrounding air (the so-called "free-aerophones," mostly ancient and folk instruments).

Percussion instruments are divided into idiophones, instruments consisting of metal or wood that is struck to produce sounds, and membranophones, for which a stretched skin is the sound-producing agent, as in drums. Percussion instruments of definite pitch are represented by the timpani, chimes (tubular bells), and xylophone. The bass drum, snare drum, triangle, bongo drums, cymbals, tambourine, and orchestral gong (tam-tam) are percussion instruments of indefinite pitch used for special orchestral effects.

The familiar transverse FLUTE is actually a member of a fairly large class of mouth-blown, hand-held pipe instruments generically called "flutes." Tone holes spaced at intervals along the pipe are covered by the fingers to vary the length of the vibrating air column. On the orchestral flute a key-and-pad mechanism is used to cover the holes, vent the instrument, and extend its pitch compass.

The other orchestral woodwinds have similar keying systems but are examples of reed pipes. The CLARINET and SAXOPHONE incorporate a single flat cane reed that vibrates against a mouthpiece, whereas the OBOE and BASSOON employ a pair of curved reeds. The BAGPIPES and the medieval and Renaissance SHAWMS and KRUMMHORNS exemplify the characteristic nasal tone quality of most double-reed instruments.

The earliest precursors of brass instruments were animal horns and shells (see SHOFAR). The lips of a brass player function like double reeds, but by varying the tension of the lip muscles the player can produce various harmonically related pitches that will resonate within the tubing. Additional tones have been available on the TROMBONE since the 15th century by means of a slide mechanism to vary the length of the tubing, but the TRUMPET, horn, and TUBA and their antecedents were capable of only a limited number of tones, mostly at the upper end of their compass, until the introduction of valves in the early 19th century.

The external shape and composition of the resonator are generally less important to the tonal quality of wind instruments than are the source of vibration and the internal shape (bore) of the air cavity. Cylindrical bore instruments include the clarinet, trumpet, and trombone. Conical bores, which are wider at one end than the other, are found in the oboe, saxophone, horn, and tuba.

Percussion Instruments

Percussion instruments, usually played by striking or shaking, form the oldest and most universal of instrumental groups. Drums and other membranophones were introduced to ancient Greece and medieval Europe from the Orient but were generally limited to ceremonial and military functions and song accompaniment. The KETTLE-DRUMS (timpani), which originated in the Middle East, were introduced into Europe before 1400 and first used orchestrally during the 17th century. During the next two centuries such idiophones as the CYMBAL and TRIANGLE were increasingly used in orchestral works. Only within the present century, however, during which sharply drawn rhythms and tonal colors have been widely explored, have percussion instruments achieved an importance in Western music comparable to the status they have long enjoyed in other cultures.

The keyboard instruments are represented by (top to bottom) the grand piano, the clavichord, the harpsichord, and the organ (harmonium). Keyboard instruments, having a wide range of pitch and expression, are suitable for performing a great variety of compositions. The piano, clavichord, and harpsichord share a common technical feature in their use of strings, which are either plucked or struck when the keys are depressed. The first stringed keyboard instruments appeared during the 14th century.

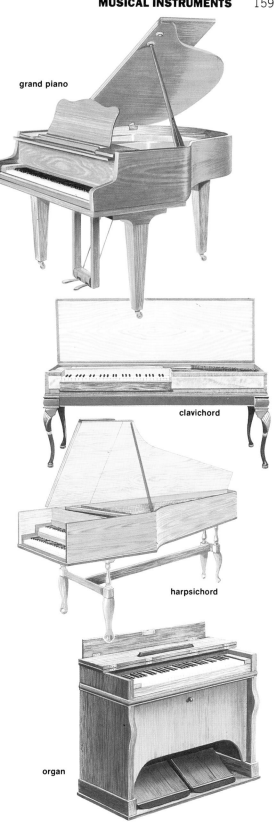

grand piano

clavichord

harpsichord

organ

Percussion instruments are often divided into groups of definite pitch (such as the XYLOPHONE) and indefinite pitch (such as the SNARE DRUM). In fact, the division is not always clear-cut. Such indefinite-pitched instruments as the triangle and temple blocks (carved wood ovals that produce a hollow wooden sound when struck) often produce well-defined tones, but these will vary from instrument to instrument and are not standardized. Among the membranophones, timpani and roto toms (small, tunable drums) are capable of melodic passages, whereas most other drums vibrate in a more complex, less tonal manner. Definite-pitched wooden instruments include those with tuned bars (MARIMBA, xylophone). Wooden idiophones without strong pitch definition include the CASTA-NETS and such Latin American instruments as the claves (pairs of wooden sticks) and maracas (rattles made from bean-filled gourds). Tuned bronze or metallic gongs form the core of many gamelan and other Eastern ensembles. Western examples of tuned metallophones are the VIBRA-PHONE, GLOCKENSPIEL, tubular chimes, CELESTA, hand bells, and steel drums. Cymbals, triangles, sleigh bells, cow bells, and some tam tams (Chinese gongs) are among the many untuned metallic instruments.

Keyboard Instruments

Strictly speaking, keyboard instruments do not constitute a separate category, since the keyboard itself produces no vibration but, rather, is linked to some external sound source. Keyboard mechanisms have been devised for strings (the PIANO and HARPSICHORD), winds (the pipe OR-GAN), idiophone percussion (the celesta), and electro-phones (the synthesizer and electronic organ). Despite their differences in action (linkage to the sound source) and resulting differences in playing techniques, these instruments share many common features, so that it is often useful to consider them together. The familiar pattern of seven white and five raised black keys to the octave results from Western scale patterns and tone intervals. Keyboard mechanisms, in fact, are unique to European musical traditions. By enabling players to control many notes simultaneously with relatively small finger movements, keyboards facilitate the performance of polyphonic lines and chordal textures, distinguishing features of Western music and the keyboard repertoire in particular.

The history of keyboards begins with the organ, specifically with the Greek hydraulos (c.250 BC), which was described in considerable detail by writers shortly before the time of Christ. Early European organs had only a few large keys. This number increased steadily after the 12th century to the present complement of 61 keys on each of two or more manuals (keyboards), each of which controls several complete sets of pipes, and an additional pedal (foot) manual.

Between the 16th and 18th centuries the harpsichord, a plucked string instrument, and its smaller, softer cousin, the CLAVICHORD, with hammered strings like the piano, became the most important European solo instruments for dance and other secular music. Keyboard works of the period are often labeled simply "for clavier" (keyboard), without specifying a particular instrument. The

piano, invented about 1709, is more responsive to variations in touch and has a larger, more continuous range than its predecessors. For these reasons it was originally called *gravicembalo col piano e forte* ("harpsichord with soft and loud").

Electronic and Computer-Based Instruments

The vibrating source of an electronic instrument is a loudspeaker, driven by an alternating current that is proportional in shape and amplitude to the resulting sound wave. The sound source may be purely electronic, as in the synthesizer and electronic organ, or it may be a live or recorded acoustical sound, as in the electric guitar and various types of sampling devices. Electronic instruments can be designed to mimic orchestral and other acoustic sounds, or to achieve tone colors and performing techniques not possible by traditional means. In the 1970s and '80s digital synthesizers and sound-modification processors achieved rapid acceptance as instruments for live performance (see ELECTRONIC MUSIC and COMPUTER MUSIC).

Musil, Robert [moo'-zil, roh'-bairt] The Austrian writer Robert Musil, b. Nov. 6, 1880, d. Apr. 15, 1942, is best known for his long, unfinished novel, *The Man without Qualities* (1930–43; Eng. trans., 1953–60). He also wrote a successful short novel, *Young Törless* (1906; Eng. trans., 1955), as well as a series of short stories (1911–24) translated as *Five Women* (1966). *Young Törless* is a powerfully realistic account of the psychological and sexual problems of a group of adolescent boys at a military academy. His much more ambitious work, *The Man without Qualities*, diagnoses the ills of modern society on the brink of collapse before World War I. Because of the dizzying range of possibilities offered by modern life, the protagonist, Ulrich, is virtually identityless.

musk Musk, a scent and fixative used in PERFUMES, is obtained from the sex glands of the male musk deer, a small, tusked, antlerless deer (*Moschus moschiferus*), native to mountainous regions from Siberia to the Himalayas. The odor of musk, penetrating and persistent, is believed to act as an aphrodisiac. In animals, musk serves the functions of defining territory, providing recognition, and attracting mates.

The pods from which musk is obtained are lodged in a pouch near the deer's sex organs and contain a substance whose essential ingredient is the organic compound muscone. Dried, the substance yields a grainy powder that is prepared for perfume by making a tincture with alcohol. Musk is exported from India, Nepal, and the USSR.

musk deer The musk deer, *Moschus moschiferus*, in the family Cervidae, is a small, usually solitary deer commonly found in forests at high altitudes in central and northeastern Asia. It stands about 60 cm (24 in) tall at the shoulder and weighs up to 11 kg (24 lb). Its hind legs are longer than the front legs, raising the rump about 50 mm (2 in) higher than the shoulders. Its coarse coat is typically a mottled dark brown color. Its head is small, with large, rounded ears but no antlers. The upper canine teeth of males are developed into tusks up to 75 mm (3 in) long. Adult males also possess a musk gland, in the skin of the abdomen, that secretes a waxlike, musky substance during the rutting season. This musk is used in perfume.

musk-ox The musk-ox, *Ovibos moschatus*, in the family Bovidae, lives on open tundra to well-vegetated terrain in northern Canada and Greenland and has been introduced into Alaska. It is short-legged but massively built, reaching 1.5 m (5 ft) high at the shoulder and more than 400 kg (900 lb) in weight. The large head bears broad, down-curving horns. Musk-oxen are protected from the cold by an ankle-length dark brown outer coat covering a light brown, soft, dense undercoat. The coat's musky odor gives the musk-ox its name. Musk-oxen live in herds of 20 to 100. When under attack they form a circle, horns outward, with the young on the inside.

The male musk-ox weighs more than the female and has longer horns. The extremely long outer coat and short, dense inner coat provide the musk-ox with excellent insulation against the cold temperatures of the far north.

musk turtle The three to four species of musk turtles making up the genus *Sternotherus* in the family Kinosternidae are found from southern Ontario, Canada, to the U.S. Gulf Coast. Characterized by glands on the underside of the body that emit a musky secretion, musk turtles are usually less than 120 mm (4.7 in) in shell length. They seldom leave the water and typically can be seen creeping along the bottom of a pond or slow-moving stream. They can be distinguished from their close relatives, the mud turtles, by the comparatively smaller lower shell (plastron), the scutes of which are separated by ar-

eas of skin, and which has only one rather indistinct hinge across it. Musk turtles are omnivorous but eat mostly animal food, including insects, snails, and carrion. The *Sternotherus* species are the common musk turtle, or stinkpot, *S. odoratus*; the razor-backed musk turtle, *S. carinatus*; and the loggerhead musk turtle, *S. minor*. Some classifications include a fourth species, the flattened musk turtle, *S. depressus*.

Muskegon [muhs-kee'-guhn] Muskegon is a city in western Michigan on Lake Michigan at the mouth of the Muskegon River. It is the seat of Muskegon County and has a population of 40,283 (1990). Muskegon is a port of entry and is highly industrialized, with petroleum refineries and diversified manufactures, including automobile parts, furniture, metal products, and heavy machinery. Muskegon's 130 km (80 mi) of waterfront, including about 13 km (9 mi) of public beaches, and excellent fishing areas attract a large tourist trade.

Muskegon began as a fur-trading post about 1812 but grew into a major logging center, nicknamed Sawdust City. Its location on the river and lake made it the outlet for an extensive dense forest region, and it became a major lumber shipping point. With the depletion of the forests by 1890, diversified industries developed.

muskellunge [muhs'-kuh-luhnj] The muskellunge, *Esox masquinongy*, is the largest member of the pike family, Esocidae. It is found in North America, now mostly in the Great Lakes region, but formerly it occurred commonly from eastern and central Canada to the upper Ohio Valley. An elongate, predatory fish with a mouth shaped into a duckbill-like snout containing large, conical teeth, the muskellunge can be distinguished from the pikes and pickerels by its large size—up to 1.5 m (5 ft) long and more than 32 kg (70 lb) in weight—and by its cheek and gill cover that have scales only on the upper halves. In the northern pike, the entire cheek but only the upper half of the gill cover is scaled; in the pickerel, both are fully scaled. Muskellunge like clear, cool, weedy, medium-sized waters. In early spring they enter tributaries to spawn, scattering their eggs into weedy shallows. Muskellunge are popular with anglers and were formerly fished commercially.

musket The musket was a large-caliber, smooth-bore firearm that was aimed and fired from the shoulder. The weapon, which first appeared in Spain in the mid-1500s, fired a lead ball weighing about 1.5 oz (42 g). Although it was lighter and more accurate than the older arquebus, it was still so heavy and long that each musketeer needed an aide who helped carry the weapon and its ammunition and prop it up on its stand. The first simple muskets were fitted with matchlocks as the refiring mechanism. The later wheel lock, a serrated wheel that struck sparks from iron pyrites, was too complicated and costly for rough use. The simpler flintlock, known in England as a snap-

The Brown Bess musket, made in four different patterns during the 18th and 19th centuries, was a smooth-bore .75-caliber British flintlock shoulder firearm to which a bayonet could be fixed. It was the British army's principal firearm from about 1690 to 1830.

hance, was produced in the late 1500s. Between 1645 and 1650 the snaphance flintlock action was improved, producing the Brown Bess, the musket used by the armies of Europe and America for nearly 200 years.

The Brown Bess was simple, cheap, and easy to manufacture, but like all muskets it had serious disadvantages. Apart from the complex loading procedure, the flintlock's efficiency was uncertain. Moreover, the musket's range was limited.

By 1836 the percussion lock and the copper cap had been introduced. The percussion system brought about perhaps the greatest single advance in the firearms. The system proved completely adaptable to the major change from muzzle to breech loading and to the transition from black powder to smokeless powders. The percussion system and pitched rifling marked the end for the musket.

Muskie, Edmund S. Edmund Sixtus Muskie, b. Rumford, Maine, Mar. 28, 1914, was U.S. secretary of state under President Jimmy Carter from May 1980 until January 1981, succeeding Cyrus Vance. He began his political career in the Maine House of Representatives (1947–51) and served as governor (1955–59) of that state. A liberal Democrat, Muskie was U.S. senator from Maine from 1959 until 1980; he was also the unsuccessful Democratic candidate for vice-president in 1968. He campaigned briefly for his party's presidential nomination in 1972.

Muskogee [muhs-koh'-gee] Muskogee, a city of 37,708 (1990) in eastern Oklahoma near the confluence of the Arkansas, Verdigris, and Grand rivers, is the seat of Muskogee County and an agricultural trade center. Established in 1872, Muskogee became (1971) a Gulf of Mexico port with the completion of the Arkansas River navigation system.

muskrat The muskrat, *Ondatra zibethicus*, in the family Cricetidae, is a semiaquatic rodent found in freshwater and saltwater marshes from Alaska through most of Canada and the United States. It was introduced into Europe for its fur but quickly became a pest. A dark-colored population in Newfoundland is often classified as a separate species, *O. obscurus*. Muskrats are stoutly built, reaching about 33 cm (13 in) long, plus a laterally flattened 29-cm (11-in) tail, and they weigh up to 1.8 kg (4 lb). The hind feet are partly webbed. The dense, glossy coat ranges in color from grayish brown to dark brown or

almost black. Muskrats live in a network of burrows in the banks of waterways or build houses of mounded vegetation in open water. They eat mainly plant material. Breeding is confined to the warmer months in the north, where a female may have three litters a year, but occurs year-round in the south. Gestation takes about 30 days, with usually three to seven young to a litter. The muskrat's fur is of prime commercial importance.

The muskrat dives and swims in its freshwater habitat by paddling with partially webbed hind feet. It builds a shelter in the water or burrows into the sides of earthen banks.

Muslim   see ISLAM

Muslim League The Muslim League, founded in 1906 as the All-India Muslim League, sought to defend the rights of the Muslim minority in predominantly Hindu British India and was instrumental in establishing the separate Muslim state of Pakistan on the Indian subcontinent. In 1916 the League and the overwhelmingly Hindu Indian National Congress formulated the Lucknow Pact, calling for greater Indian self-government with separate Muslim and Hindu electorates. After 1920, however, the organizations moved apart: the Congress became more militant while the League, led by Muhammad IQBAL and Muhammad Ali JINNAH, grew increasingly fearful that self-rule would mean oppression of Muslims by Hindus. This fear was strengthened when the Hindu-controlled governments chosen in the 1936–37 provincial elections declined to work with the League.

Although backed by Britain and sympathetic to continued British rule, the League had to alter its strategy as independence became an imminent possibility. In 1940 it voted to endorse the establishment of a separate Muslim state. Over vehement Hindu protests, Britain incorporated this proposal in its 1947 partition plan creating the independent nations of India and Pakistan. Initially, the League dominated Pakistani politics, but it subsequently split into factions and had ceased to be politically effective by 1970.

muslin Muslin is a firm, plain-weave cotton fabric first made in the city of Mosul (now in Iraq). One of the oldest cotton cloths, it is made today in a variety of weights and finishes, including such lightweight, loosely woven fabrics as gauze and cheesecloth, such sheer fabrics as voile and lawn, and such heavier-weight cottons as GINGHAM and percale. The term is also used for a white sheeting material that is heavier than percale but has fewer threads to the inch. The French mousseline is a silk or rayon fabric made in muslin's plain weave.

mussel Mussels are a group of aquatic, clamlike MOLLUSKS (class Pelecypoda or Bivalvia) found throughout the world. The name is most popularly used for the edible marine species in the genera *Mytilus* and *Modiolus*, family Mytilidae. Marine mussels live either partially buried in the sea bottom or attached to rocky surfaces by means of byssus threads. They have filibranch gills, in which the individual branches, or filaments, are united, and also held apart, by interlocking tufts of hairlike cilia. The familiar marine mussels are asymmetrical, with the posterior or end of the shells (valves) broad and rounded, and the anterior end smaller and pointed. The posterior halves of the valves contain a large adductor muscle that holds the valves closed.

The best-known freshwater mussels are species of *Anodonta* and *Unio*, family Unionidae, which burrow in the sand or mud of streams and lakes, with just the posterior tips of the shells exposed. They are characterized by a nacrous, or pearly, lining inside their shells and by their eulamellibranch gills, in which the individual branches are united by tissues into a sheet. Freshwater mussels typically pass through a larval parasitic stage, during which they infest fish.

Musset, Alfred de [mue-say'] One of the most paradoxical figures of French romanticism, Louis Charles Alfred de Musset, b. Paris, Dec. 11, 1810, d. May 2, 1857, parodied romantic poses and conventions in his first works, yet his trenchant sense of humor always remained secondary to an anguished search for ways to express feeling sincerely. The autobiographical nature of Musset's art has at its core his love affair (1833–35) with the writer George SAND, which was examined in novels by Sand herself and by Musset's brother Paul and was the pretext for Musset's *Confessions of a Child of the Century* (1836; Eng. trans., 1905). Musset's legacy is richest, however, in the ironies of narrative poems like *Contes d'Espagne et d'Italie* (Tales of Spain and Italy, 1830) and lyrics like *Les Nuits* (Nights, 1835–37) and *Souvenir* (1841), and most particularly in his plays. From the charm of such curtain raisers as *A Caprice* (1847; Eng.

trans., 1905) to the Shakespearean scope of *Lorenzaccio* (1834), first acted in 1896 by Sarah Bernhardt, Musset most fully exposed the finesse and resonance of his creative voice.

Mussolini, Benito [moos-soh-lee'-nee, bay-nee'-toh] Benito Mussolini, b. July 29, 1883, d. Apr. 28, 1945, was the founder of Italian FASCISM and premier (1922–43) of Italy, ruling as a dictator from about 1925. The son of an anticlerical, socialist blacksmith, he was influenced by such writers as Louis Auguste BLANQUI, Friedrich Wilhelm NIETZSCHE, and Georges SOREL. Mussolini became an itinerant schoolteacher and journalist and took as his wife a peasant, Rachele Guidi, who bore him five children.

When World War I began in 1914, Mussolini at first opposed Italy's involvement but soon reversed his position and called for Italy's entry on the side of the Allies. Expelled from the Socialist party for this stance, he founded his own newspaper in Milan, *Il popolo d'Italia,* which later became the organ of his Fascist movement. He served in the army until he was wounded in 1917.

On Mar. 23, 1919, Mussolini and other war veterans founded in Milan a nationalistic group called the Fasci di Combattimento, named for the ancient Roman symbol of power, the FASCES. The movement developed into a powerful "radicalism of the right," gaining the support of many landowners in the lower Po valley, industrialists, and army officers.

On Oct. 28, 1922, after the Fascists had marched on Rome, Mussolini secured a mandate from King VICTOR EMMANUEL III to form a coalition government. In 1925–26, the Fascist leader imposed a single-party, totalitarian dictatorship. His Corporative State came to terms with Italian capitalism but abolished free-trade unions. He ended conflict with the church by the Lateran Treaty of 1929, his most enduring legacy to Italy.

Benito Mussolini, who ruled Italy from 1922 until 1945, established the Fascist regime that provided a model for Adolf Hitler's German Third Reich. In 1936, Mussolini concluded an agreement with Germany that eventually resulted in Italy's disastrous participation in World War II. In April 1945 he was captured and executed by his fellow Italians.

In the mid-1930s, Mussolini turned to an aggressive foreign policy, conquering (1935–36) Ethiopia and helping Gen. Francisco FRANCO against the republicans in the SPANISH CIVIL WAR. Rapprochement (1936) with Germany was expanded into a military alliance (1939). In April 1939, Mussolini rashly ordered his armies to occupy Albania, but he kept Italy out of World War II until June 1940.

After a series of Italian military disasters in Greece and North Africa, the leaders of his party abandoned Mussolini. The king dismissed him on July 25, 1943, and had him arrested, but on September 12 the Germans rescued him, making him puppet head of a government in northern Italy. In April 1945, Mussolini and his mistress, Clara Petacci, tried to flee advancing Allied forces. Captured by Italian partisans at Lake Como, they were shot, and their bodies were hung in a public square in Milan. Although popular with most Italians until the late 1930s, *Il Duce* ("the leader") lost their support when he dragged his country into a war it was unprepared to fight.

Mussorgsky, Modest [mus-sohrg'-skee, moh-dest']
Modest Petrovich Mussorgsky, b. Karevo in Russia's Pskov Province, Mar. 21 (N.S.), 1839, d. Mar. 28 (N.S.), 1881, is best known as the composer of the opera *Boris Godunov*. He studied piano with Anton Herke, developing considerable skill as a performer and improviser. During the winter of 1856–57 he attended Aleksandr Dargomyzhsky's *musicales*, where he met César Cui, Mily Balakirev, and Vladimir Stasov. An ardent idealist at the age of 19, he resigned his commission in the Imperial Guard for a life of "meaningful endeavor"—music. (Later, from 1863 to 1867 and 1868 to 1880, he worked in the civil service.) By the early 1860s, "The Five"—Balakirev, Cui, Mussorgsky, Aleksandr Borodin, and Nikolai Rimsky-Korsakov—had coalesced and committed themselves to a nationalist Russian music.

Mussorgsky's commitment emerged primarily in opera. Concern for musical realism and sensitivity to broad social and moral issues appeared vividly in his songs of the 1860s—"The Seminarian," "The Outcast," and "The Orphan Girl"—but these elements gained cumulative

Modest Mussorgsky, a 19th-century Russian composer, sought to develop an unadorned national style in such works as the opera Boris Godunov *(1872) and the piano suite* Pictures from an Exhibition *(1874).*

power in his operas. In 1863–66 he set about adapting Gustave Flaubert's *Salammbô*, then turned to Nikolai Gogol's *The Marriage*, but completed neither. He started *Boris Godunov* in 1868. A first version was completed in 1869, but it was rejected by the Imperial Theaters because of its radical break with operatic convention. Mussorgsky remodeled the score in 1871–72. This definitive version was published in vocal score just before the opera's premiere in 1874. Mussorgsky was already writing *Khovanshchina*, another historical opera, and soon started the lighthearted *Fair at Sorochinsk*. (Rimsky-Korsakov completed *Khovanshchina*, along with editing and revising other works, including *Boris*; Cui completed *Fair*.) The 1870s also produced the song cycles *Sunless* and *Songs and Dances of Death* and the piano cycle *Pictures from an Exhibition*. Alcoholism wrecked Mussorgsky's health, and he died in Saint Petersburg.

Mussorgsky's music is distinctly Russian, yet it rarely quotes folk songs literally. Instead, characteristic elements from folk music are abstracted to synthesize an original style of melody based on formulaic figures, harmony derived from folk heterophony, and rhythm founded on the irregular patterns of certain folk genres. His concern for precise communication of personality and emotion led to a new type of vocal parlando that succeeds in reproducing the essence of Russian speech in the mouths of his operatic characters.

Mustang   The Mustang, an aircraft designed by Raymond Rice and Edgar Schmued for use in World War II, became one of the war's most successful fighter planes. The North American P-51 Mustang was evolved for ultimate large-scale service to an early-1940 specification of the British Air Purchasing Commission. The P-51, a single-seat, single-engine, low-wing monoplane with a 11.3-m (37-ft) wingspan and a laminar-flow airfoil section, incorporated many lessons learned from European air combat. The original Mustang was redesigned in 1942 as the P-51B, with a high-altitude, 1,380-hp Packard-Merlin engine; further modification produced the P-51D, which was equipped with a bubble canopy and was built in greater numbers (nearly 8,000 total) than all other Mustang models. The Mustang proved to be an extremely important interceptor and long-range escort. Various machine-gun combinations were fitted to the Mustang, and a rocket-firing version was developed. The plane was also engaged in ground attack and unarmed reconnaissance and was used as a fighter-bomber.

mustang   see HORSE

---

mustard   Mustard is the common name of annual plants of the genus *Brassica*, family Cruciferae, grown for their pungent seed and for their leaves, which are eaten as greens. Three species are commonly cultivated: black mustard, *B. nigra*; white or yellow mustard, *B. hirta*; and Indian mustard, or mustard greens, *B. juncea*. Mustard is native to southern Europe and southwestern Asia.

White mustard is cultivated for its seeds, which are a pungent food flavoring and a preservative. Mustard is used more than any other spice with the exception of pepper.

Whole mustard seeds are used as a pickling flavoring and to add pungency to many cooked foods. Powdered dry mustard develops a sharp, hot flavor when moistened. Prepared mustard is a mixture of powdered mustard with salt, spices, and lemon juice, with wine or vinegar to preserve the mustard's pungency. Mustard oil is used medicinally as an ingredient of liniments, stomach stimulants, and emetics.

mustard gas   see CHEMICAL AND BIOLOGICAL WARFARE

Mutanabbi, al- [moo-tah-nahb'-bee, ahl]   Al-Mutanabbi, b. Kufa, Iraq, 915, d. 965, is considered the greatest classical Arab poet. After studying in Damascus and living for a time among Bedouin, where he acquired the nickname "he who pretends to be a prophet," al-Mutanabbi reached Aleppo. There he joined the brilliant circle around the Hamdanid sultan Sayf al-Dawlah and for nine years dedicated panegyrics to his patron, who bestowed fame and fortune on him. After falling from favor, al-Mutanabbi was slain by brigands while traveling in Iraq.

---

mutation   Mutation describes an alteration of genetic information in an organism, involving changes in the genes or chromosomes. Mutation usually produces harmful effects, varying from decreased fitness to death of the organism. Many cancers and birth abnormalities, for example, are believed to be associated with mutations of somatic cells. Occasionally new genes or chromosomal rearrangements better adapt an organism to its environment; mutation in this sense actually supplies raw materials for natural selection, the fundamental process of biological EVOLUTION.

How Mutations Occur

Genes. Gene mutations are classified into the following types, according to changes in the nucleotide bases of deoxyribonucleic acid (DNA): substitution, deletion, addition, and transposition. Four different nucleotide bases constitute the DNA molecule: cytosine (C), thymine (T), adenine (A), and guanine (G). Genetic information is coded on bases; three consecutive bases form the triplet code, which is read, or translated, into an amino acid (see GENETIC CODE). In substitution mutation, any one of the bases may be replaced by any one of the others. Similarly, deletion and addition mutations involve removal and insertion, respectively, of one or more bases. Deletions or additions, which may cause frameshift mutations, usually produce greater effects than do other types of gene mutation, because a deletion or addition of one or two bases will cause misreading of the code from the point at which the change occurred onward throughout the rest of the gene's base sequence. Transposition is equivalent to chromosomal inversion, in which the arrangement of two or more nucleotide bases is reversed.

Chromosomes. Chromosomal mutation includes translocation, inversion, deletion, and duplication. Translocation occurs when a segment of one chromosome breaks off and becomes attached to a different chromosome set. Inversion results from a 180° change in direction of a chromosome segment. Duplication and deletion can involve either portions of chromosomes or whole chromosomes. Because of the large number of genes involved, chromosomal changes usually have drastic effects on the morphology, physiology, or behavior of an organism.

Spontaneous Mutations. Mutations occur in nature spontaneously. Origins or causes of spontaneous mutation are not yet completely clear. Some mutations may occur through errors in DNA replication; others may result from cosmic and terrestrial radiation or from the exposure of individuals to physical or chemical agents in their environment. For example, certain chemicals used commercially in food preservatives, cosmetics, and fertilizers are known to cause mutations.

In humans, many GENETIC DISEASES are brought about by the spontaneous appearance of a single dominant or recessive gene produced by mutation. The frequency of a genetic disease in a population is related to the mutation and selective value (measured by the number of offspring produced by mutant-gene carriers relative to the average number of offspring produced by normal persons) of the gene and its mode of inheritance. In general, diseases related to recessive genes are more frequent than those of dominant genes, because recessive genes are not exposed as much to the process of NATURAL SELECTION.

Protection from Mutation

Organisms have evolved the property of maintaining correct genetic information through physical and chemical means. The cytoplasmic and nuclear membranes of cells serve as physical barriers to prevent certain chemical compounds from entering the cells and damaging the DNA. If such compounds do enter, however, they can be inactivated by enzymes present in the cells. Further, certain enzymes of normal cells are able to repair some kinds of damage done to DNA molecules. The spontaneous occurrence of various mutations, however, indicates that the repair capacities of organisms are limited.

Evolution and Mutation

One of the most significant findings in modern genetic research is the discovery of the evolutionary impact of mutation through gene duplication, which is the addition of a base sequence identical to one already included in a gene, followed by nucleotide base substitution. Such mutations provide for species adaptation as well as for differences among evolving species. The controversial molecular-clock hypothesis, which suggests that there is some regularity in protein evolution, has been developed by some scientists in their studies of mutation rates and phylogenetic relationships.

Muti, Riccardo [moo'-tee]   The Italian conductor Riccardo Muti, b. July 28, 1941, succeeded Eugene Ormandy as music director of the Philadelphia Orchestra in 1980. Trained primarily in Milan, Muti won the Guido Cantelli conducting competition in 1967, beginning a rapid rise that included appointment as principal conductor of the Florence festival, Maggio Musicale, in 1969. He made his U.S. debut with the Philadelphia in 1972. Engagements with leading orchestras and opera companies have firmly established Muti as a major conductor of his time.

In 1990, Muti announced that he would leave the Philadelphia Orchestra in 1992, although he planned to continue as director at La Scala, the famed opera house in Milan, Italy.

mutiny   One of the most serious crimes categorized under MILITARY JUSTICE, mutiny is a revolt—usually concerted—against military authority in any branch of the armed services. Mutiny can also be committed on commercial or private ships. Mutiny, which in the United States may be punished by death, may involve various activities, such as an illegal attempt to seize authority on a ship, a refusal to obey orders, or desertion in the face of the enemy.

The 1797 British naval mutinies at Spithead and the Nore in England were major, fleet-wide revolts that had the ultimate effect of correcting serious abuses against the crews. Wide-scale revolutionary naval mutinies included those of the Russian navy at Kronshtadt in 1905 and 1917 and the German navy at Kiel in 1918. Army mutinies have also occurred. The largest were the INDIAN MUTINY (1857–58), in which the sepoys (Indian troops) of the British Indian Army rebelled, and the 1917 mutiny of French troops in the trenches during World War I. Smaller actions included the mutinies (1781) of nine Pennsylvania and New Jersey regiments during the American Revolution.

Mutiny on the Bounty   An unusually successful collaboration by two writers, Charles Nordhoff and James Norman Hall, *Mutiny on the Bounty* (1932) is a novel based on a famous mutiny that occurred on the H.M.S. BOUNTY, an English war vessel, in 1789. The master's mate, Fletcher Christian, led the revolt against the tyrannical captain, William BLIGH. The mutineers set Captain Bligh and his loyal crew members afloat in an open boat while they escaped first to Tahiti, then to Pitcairn Island. The novel has served as the basis for three films (1935, 1962, 1984), the earliest starring Charles Laughton and Clark Gable. Two sequels to the novel appeared in 1934.

mutual fund   A mutual fund is a company that invests most of its money in publicly traded securities— stocks and bonds of business corporations. A mutual fund—also called an investment, or unit, trust—obtains its capital by issuing and selling its shares (common stock) to investors, typically small individual investors, who are the company's shareholders.

Mutual funds are sometimes called open-end investment companies because they offer new shares for sale each day. Investors in a no-load mutual fund pay no sales charge (load or commission) when they purchase fund shares; investors buy the shares directly from the mutual fund. The purchase price of each share is equal to the net asset value (NAV) of the fund per share on the day of purchase. Investors in a load mutual fund pay a purchase price that is equal to the NAV plus a loading charge, or sales commission, usually amounting to about 8½% of the purchase price. Mutual-fund shareholders who wish to sell their shares are able to redeem them (usually at no cost) on any business day at the NAV.

Muybridge, Eadweard [my'-brij, ed'-wurd]   The Englishman Eadweard Muybridge, b. Edward James Muggeridge, Apr. 9, 1830, d. May 8, 1904, one of the great photographers of the American West, became even better known for his pioneering photographic studies of motion. Photographing throughout California in the 1860s and '70s, he made large, impressive landscapes of the Yosemite wilderness that won him initial fame. In 1872, Leland Stanford, the former governor of the state, bet a friend that once in every stride all four legs of a running horse were simultaneously off the ground. He hired Muybridge to settle the bet, and in 1877 Muybridge's pictures, which recorded the horse's motion in sequential frames, proved Stanford right. (The work took five years because it was interrupted while Muybridge was tried and acquitted for the murder of his wife's lover.) In 1879, Muybridge invented the zoopraxiscope, a machine that reconstructed motion from his photographs and a forerunner of cinematography. He published several volumes of photographic motion studies, including *Animal Locomotion* (1887), which contained 781 groups of sequential frames, and *The Human Figure in Motion* (1901).

Muzorewa, Abel T. [muz-oh-ray'-wuh]   The Zimbabwe (Rhodesia) black political leader Abel Tendekayi Muzorewa, b. Apr. 14, 1925, was elected Zimbabwe's first prime minister in June 1979. He had become Rhodesia's first black bishop in 1968. In 1971 he became president of the African National Council (ANC), opposed to the white minority government of Ian SMITH. Muzorewa joined Smith in the Rhodesian Transitional Executive Council in 1978 to prepare for a peaceful transfer of power to the black majority and in 1979 attended constitutional talks in London with Smith and rival black leaders Joshua NKOMO and Robert MUGABE. He remained head of the ANC after his defeat in the March 1980 elections and was later imprisoned (1983–84) by the Mugabe government.

MX missile The United States MX (MX—missile experimental) program has had a long and singularly controversial history. Since the 1960s, U.S. military experts have anticipated growing improvement in the accuracy and number of Soviet missile systems, to the point where they would be able to attack and destroy the concrete underground silos within which the land-based U.S. ICBM force is housed. It therefore seemed necessary to design a MIRV MISSILE with a mobility that would make it invulnerable to Soviet attack. In 1979, President Jimmy Carter decided to proceed with full-scale development of the MX, which weighs 86,200 kg (190,000 lb), carries 10 high-yield high-accuracy warheads, and has a range of 9,650 km (6,000 mi). The problem that has plagued the administrations of both Carter and his successor, Ronald Reagan—who called the MX the "Peacekeeper"—has been the mode whereby MX invulnerability will be achieved.

Such options as basing the MX on jumbo jets or giant dirigibles, or aboard small ships or submarines, were examined and rejected. President Carter chose a plan that would have based 200 MX missiles in the Nevada and Utah desert, mounted on movable launchers that would shuttle among about 4,600 underground shelters. Because 4,400 of the shelters would be empty at any one time, presumably missiles could not be targeted against the MX with any precision.

Cost and environmental considerations persuaded President Reagan to consider the "Dense Pack," in which a cluster of missiles would be placed in fortified silos within a small area; "deep basing," where the MX would be buried so deeply underground that it would be invulnerable; deploying the MX in silos defended by ANTIBALLISTIC MISSILES; or using lightweight patrol planes as mobile MX bases.

In 1983 a bipartisan commission recommended the deployment of 100 missiles in existing but newly hardened Minuteman silos. Congress approved in principle, although it held back from appropriating full funding for the program. By fiscal 1984, however, the MX program had already cost almost $10 billion. Congress in 1985 agreed to fund 50 missiles for deployment in fixed silos.

My Lai incident [mee ly] One of the grimmest episodes of the U.S. involvement in the VIETNAM WAR was the massacre of more than 300 unarmed Vietnamese civil-

ians by an American infantry company at the hamlet known as My Lai 4 on Mar. 16, 1968. The U.S. troops were brought by helicopter into a bitterly contested area of Quang Ngai province on South Vietnam's northeastern coast. Anticipating an engagement with an enemy military force, the Americans, under the command of Capt. Ernest L. Medina and Lt. William L. Calley, Jr., entered the village of Son My, and in the hamlet that they called My Lai 4 they lashed out at whomever they found—shooting mostly women, children, and old men.

It was not an isolated incident; while Calley's Charley Company was bringing destruction to My Lai 4, another army outfit, Bravo Company, was carrying out a similar mission at the nearby hamlet of My Khe 4. The U.S. Army was forced to initiate an official inquiry that resulted in murder charges against several members of Charley Company. Of the soldiers who were charged with the My Lai killings, only Lieutenant Calley was convicted by court martial. On Mar. 29, 1971, he was found guilty of the slaying of at least 22 Vietnamese civilians. No action was taken against the perpetrators of the smaller-scale massacre at My Khe.

Myanmar see BURMA

myasthenia gravis [my-uhs-thee'-nee-uh grah'-vis] Myasthenia gravis is a disease characterized by sporadic weakness of the muscles of the face and neck and, in later stages, weakness in the trunk and limbs. The age of onset is usually between 20 and 30 but can range from 10 to 70, with women being affected three times as often as men. Drooping eyelids, difficulty in swallowing, double vision, exhaustion on chewing, and general fatigue are common complaints. Respiratory weakness may occur and can be life-threatening. A tumor of the thymus gland in the chest is present in 15 to 20 percent of patients, particularly older males.

Myasthenia gravis is an AUTOIMMUNE DISEASE and is sometimes coexistent with other such diseases, including rheumatoid arthritis, systemic lupus erythematosus, and hyperthyroidism. In a myasthenia patient, the lymphocytes (see BLOOD) of the immune system produce a range of ANTIBODIES that attack and destroy sites on muscle cells that would otherwise receive acetylcholine molecules. Acetylcholine is the NEUROTRANSMITTER that links nerve to muscle, so that destruction of the muscle-cell sites prevents acetylcholine from inducing muscle contractions.

About 10 percent of myasthenia gravis patients die from the disease, but there is a good chance for stabilization and even some degree of recovery among those who survive the first three years after onset. Thus far little is known of the cause of the disease other than that it is not inherited or infectious. Research is under way to develop monoclonal antibodies to block the action of the receptor antibodies, but the range and varying potency of the antibodies concerned have presented difficulties. Myasthenia may be relieved by removal of the thymus and by drugs that inhibit cholinesterase, an enzyme that naturally breaks down acetylcholine.

(Above) *Excavations at Mycenae (1876–78) by Heinrich Schliemann revealed, among other royal objects, this beaten gold death mask.* (Right) *The grave circle at Mycenae, located just inside the palace walls, includes five royal shaft graves (1600 BC), where numerous Mycenaean artifacts were discovered.*

Mycenae [my-see'-nee]   Mycenae, capital of AGAMEM-NON in the epics of Homer, with defense walls built by the legendary Cyclops, was the most important center of AEGEAN CIVILIZATION on the Greek mainland in the Late Bronze Age (c.1600–1100 BC). Its situation on a hill dominating the Argive plain and the pass to Corinth in the eastern Peloponnesus may have contributed to Mycenae's rise to wealth and prominence. The great walls of the city and the famous Lion Gate, with its relief sculpture of confronting lions, have always remained visible.

In 1876, Heinrich SCHLIEMANN excavated a circular enclosure just inside the walls by the Lion Gate and found unplundered royal shaft graves of the 16th century BC containing gold treasures. In the 15th and 14th centuries BC, Mycenaean princes were evidently buried in circular tholos tombs, stone-built chambers with high corbeled vaults. The largest and most spectacular was known as the Treasury of Atreus (after the father of Agamemnon).

In the 13th century BC, Mycenae may have been the capital of an empire controlling the whole Aegean. About 1200 the palace and houses within the walls were destroyed by fire. The palace was never rebuilt, and Mycenae fell (c.1100 BC) to invasion. It afterward became an independent Dorian city-state. About 468 BC it was conquered by neighboring Argos.

mycology [my-kahl'-uh-jee]   Mycology is the science concerning fungi and their morphology, physiology, distribution, cultivation, classification, economic importance, and control. Medical mycology is the study of fungi that cause disease in humans or animals; this field includes diagnostic techniques, pathological effects, epidemiology, and treatment of fungi-caused disease.

mynah [my'-nuh]   Mynah, or myna, is the common name for 6 genera (12 species) of birds in the starling family, Sturnidae, order Passeriformes. The best known is the hill mynah, *Gracula religiosa*, native to India, Southeast Asia, Indonesia, and Malaysia. Its plumage is glossy black, its bill is orange, and it has yellow wattles beneath the eye and on the back of the head. It measures 24–37 cm (9–11 in) in length. The mynah can be trained to mimic human speech remarkably well and is popular as a pet. Other species include the golden-crested mynah,

The hill mynah has metallic black plumage with purple and green highlights and white wing patches. A fruit-eating forest dweller, the mynah has a large repertoire of sounds, including chuckles, shrieks, and whistles. In captivity, a trained mynah can imitate human speech, singing, and whistling.

Mino coronatus; the Papuan mynah, *Mino dumontii*; and the crested mynah, *Acridotheres cristatellus*.

myocardial infarction   see HEART DISEASES

myofacial pain dysfunction   see TMJ SYNDROME

myoglobin [my-uh-gloh'-bin]   Myoglobin is an animal protein that, in vertebrate animals, occurs only in red muscle tissues and gives the tissues their color. The myoglobin molecule resembles that of HEMOGLOBIN but is only one-fourth as heavy; it consists of a single iron-containing heme molecule attached to a single globin chain. Myoglobin has an even stronger affinity for oxygen than does hemoglobin, facilitating oxygen transfer from blood to muscle tissue for energy storage; it also releases oxygen more readily. Red muscle requires sufficient energy for sustained action; other muscle tissues are capable of rapid but not of sustained performance.

myopia [my-oh'-pee-uh]   Myopia, or nearsightedness, is an error of refraction in the eye that causes objects more than a short distance away to appear blurred. It usually results from the cornea of the eye being too far from the retina, so that images are focused in front of the retina. The error can be corrected for by concave EYEGLASSES or by CONTACT LENSES; severe cases of myopia are sometimes treated by a controversial surgical distortion of the cornea known as radial keratotomy (see EYE DISEASES).

Myrdal, Gunnar and Alva [mair'-dahl]   The Swedish sociologist and economist **Karl Gunnar Myrdal**, b. Dec. 6, 1898, d. May 17, 1987, shared the 1974 Nobel Prize for economics—the first one given in economics— with Friedrich von Hayek of Austria. The prize was awarded for their work on the theory of money and their analysis of social and economic relations. Myrdal, a professor at the University of Stockholm for many years, also served as executive secretary of the United Nations Economic Commission for Europe from 1947 to 1957. Among his published works are *An American Dilemma: The Negro Problem and Modern Democracy* (1944; rev. ed., 1962), *Asian Drama* (3 vols., 1968), and *Challenge of World Poverty* (1970). Myrdal at times collaborated with his wife, **Alva Reimer Myrdal**, b. Jan. 31, 1902, d. Feb. 1, 1986, a sociologist, former diplomat, and former Swedish cabinet member. She wrote and lectured on disarmament and was awarded the 1982 Nobel Peace Prize, with Alfonso García Robles of Mexico. Her books include *The Game of Disarmament* (1977).

Myron [my'-ruhn]   Myron, a Greek sculptor active in the second quarter of the 5th century BC, was famous for his *discobolus* (Museo Nazionale delle Terme, Rome), a bronze statue of an athlete hurling a discus. Myron's works are known only through Roman marble copies. The

discobolus can be securely identified because its distinctive pose was described by Pliny the Elder in the 1st century AD. Other works attributed to Myron include figures of Athena and Marsyas (Lateran Palace, Rome), the originals of which stood on the Acropolis, and a head of Perseus (British Museum, London).

myrrh [mur]   An aromatic, bitter-tasting gum RESIN obtained principally from a small thorny tree, *Commiphora myrrha* (family Burseraceae), native to Anatolia and northeast Africa, myrrh was highly prized in the ancient and medieval world as an ingredient of perfume, incense, cosmetics, and medicines. The Egyptians used it in embalming. The resin now finds limited medicinal use in tonics, dentifrices, and stomach remedies, and as an emollient for sore gums and mouth. An essential oil obtained from myrrh is an ingredient of perfume.

myrtle [murt'-ul]   Myrtles comprise about 16 species of evergreen shrubs or small trees of the genus *Myrtus* in the myrtle family, Myrtaceae. All but two species, one in southern Europe and one in Africa, are native to Florida and the West Indies. Leaves of myrtles are typically a shiny blue green and are strongly scented when crushed; the flowers, bark, and berries are also fragrant, and myrtle has been used in perfumery. The ancient Greeks considered myrtle sacred to the goddess Aphrodite and used it in festivals. The myrtle they used is *M. communis*. It grows to 4.5 m (15 ft) high, with dense, bushy foliage and solitary or sparsely blossomed clusters of white or pinkish flowers with many stamens. Each flower develops into a blue-black berry with the sepals (calyx) of the flower persisting at its top.

The term *myrtle* is also applied to a number of other unrelated plants, including the crape myrtle, *Lagerstroemia indica* (see LOOSESTRIFE); the PERIWINKLE, or running myrtle, *Vinca minor*; the sand myrtle, *Leiophyllum buxifolium*, an evergreen shrub with leathery leaves and pinkish flowers; and the southern BAYBERRY, or wax myrtle, *Myrica cerifera*.

Mysore (city) [my-sohr']   Mysore, a city in the state of Karnataka (formerly Mysore) in southern India, is situated approximately 137 km (85 mi) southwest of Bangalore. The city's population is 438,385 (1981). Mysore is an important manufacturing and commercial center, noted for silk and cotton textiles. It is located in a fertile valley near the sacred hill of the goddess Kali and is known for its many spacious parks.

Mysore was founded in the 16th century on the site of an ancient settlement. Nearby is Srirangapatna island, which was the capital of the state of Mysore in the 17th and 18th centuries. It has a Hindu temple dating from the 12th century, as well as a fort, mosque, and summer palace built by TIPPU SULTAN, who was killed (1799) in battle there by the British. The capital was then transferred to Mysore until 1831.

Mysore (state)   see KARNATAKA

Mysteries, Villa of the   see POMPEII

---

mystery, suspense, and detective fiction

Mystery, suspense, and detective fiction are modern expressions of venerable literary traditions. In mystery stories a vulnerable character is drawn into a mysterious situation that is revealed to be dangerous as well. Through tenacity, ingenuity, and luck the protagonist manages to expose sinister events. Unlike GOTHIC ROMANCES, mysteries reveal temporal rather than supernatural horrors. Suspense fiction emphasizes the vulnerability of the central character, the power of an adversary, and the immediate danger of the situation rather than the character's growing comprehension of it. Thrillers are structured in a similar way but emphasize action, so that the narrative evolves as a series of chases, entrapments, and escapes. Detective fiction substitutes a skeptical, aloof, intellectually aggressive investigator for the mystery's relatively naive protagonist. The detective story emphasizes the investigation and often focuses on the technical details related to the examination of clues, the character of the people involved, the psychology of the criminal, the ambience in which the crime took place, or the unique perspective of the detective. Most fictional detectives are outsiders who operate in a twilight zone between established authority and the underworld yet display skills and traits drawn from both.

Although the fascination with mysteries and detection can be traced to ancient times, distinct literary genres focusing on these matters did not emerge until the early 19th century. Before then, popular fiction dealing with unexplained murders and strange happenings were mixtures of dark fantasy, religious beliefs, and a growing knowledge of the urban, technological world. Mysteries took two forms in the early 19th century: one began to graft hereditary and psychological explanations onto gothic themes; the other used the trappings of the gothic to expose the furtive inner workings of cities, as in the works of the French writer Eugène Sue.

Edgar Allan POE, in such stories as "The Murders in the Rue Morgue" (1841), "The Mystery of Marie Rogêt" (1842), and "The Purloined Letter" (1844), perfected the "classic" detective form: the "locked-room story" in which a seemingly impossible crime has been committed and the detective relies on his or her superior perception, intellect, and often arcane knowledge to solve the mystery. After Poe the detective genre gained popularity with the work of Anna Katherine Green (1846–1935) and Mary Roberts Rinehart in America, Émile Gaboriau in France, and Wilkie COLLINS, Arthur Conan DOYLE, and G. K. CHESTERTON in England. Doyle's Sherlock Holmes epitomizes the classical detective, a brilliant professional drawn to cases through his interest in the problem, whereas the plots of John Dickson CARR'S novels demonstrate the intricacies to which the form lends itself. The classic story reached its greatest popularity in the 1930s and '40s with the work of such British masters as Dorothy L. SAYERS, Agatha CHRISTIE, Josephine TEY, and Margery ALLINGHAM, and such Americans as S. S. VAN DINE, Ellery QUEEN (pseudonym of Frederic Dannay and Manfred Lee), and Rex STOUT.

Where the detective is a part of established authority, the narrative is likely to be an occupational biography, a courtroom drama, or a police procedural that describes a way of doing rather than of knowing. The Inspector Maigret novels of the Belgian writer Georges SIMENON, the Martin Beck stories of the Swedish team Maj Sjöwall and Per Wahlöö, and the Inspector Wexford books of Ruth Rendell fall into this category, as do the Perry Mason stories of Erle Stanley Gardner. When the detective is assimilated into the intelligence world, the narrative shades over into spy fiction, as in the novels of Eric AMBLER or the James Bond stories of Ian FLEMING.

The hard-boiled detective story began to emerge in the stories of Gaboriau and in the Nick Carter stories written by various hands. Not until the pulp stories of the 1920s, however, did the hard-boiled form take on its most salient features. The hard-boiled world is fraught with implicit and explicit violence, and the hired private eye is tough and uncompromising. The hard-boiled detective story is largely associated with such Americans as Dashiell HAMMETT, Raymond CHANDLER, Mickey SPILLANE, and, more recently, John D. MACDONALD and Ross MACDONALD.

Anti-heroes abound in Patricia Highsmith's work, beginning with her *Strangers on a Train* (1950), but perhaps most notably personified by the elegant and amoral Ripley. In the stories of Emma Lathen (the pseudonym of Mary J. Latis and Martha Hennissart) the detective is an exceedingly well-mannered Wall Street banker. Dick Francis's heroes are usually jockeys. Lawrence Block's books feature a burglar or an alcoholic as protagonist, and Joseph Hansen's, a homosexual insurance investigator. Tony Hillerman's detective is a Navajo police officer.

---

mystery cults

The term *mysteries* is generally used to refer to those cults of the ancient world whose members believed that by means of the performance of particular secret rituals they would gain knowledge not available to the uninitiated and thus effect a mystical union with the divine. In contrast to traditional religion, which emphasized the gulf between God and humankind, the mystery cults promised a share in the life of the gods, most importantly in their immortality.

Because these cults focused on the search for eternal life, the central figures were usually gods who had died and were then reborn. The initiates thus guaranteed immortality for themselves by reenacting the death and rebirth of the divinity. The most important mysteries in Greece were the rites surrounding the goddess of agriculture, DEMETER, and her daughter PERSEPHONE. At Eleusis, a town outside Athens, the people established the ELEUSINIAN MYSTERIES, in which they reenacted Demeter's search for, and reunion with, Persephone after the latter's return from the underworld. By performing this ritual, as well as several others about which little is known, the initiates believed that they secured for themselves both the abundance of Demeter and a blessed life after death. Similar Greek cults revolved around Dionysus, the Greek god of fertility, and Orpheus.

In the Roman period many people belonged to mysteries that had been derived from Egypt, Syria, and Persia, such as the cults of Isis, Serapis, and Mithra (see Mithraism) and various gnostic sects (see Gnosticism).

mystery play   see Medieval Drama

mysticism   Mysticism in general refers to a direct and immediate experience of the sacred, or the knowledge derived from such an experience. In Christianity this experience usually takes the form of a vision of, or sense of union with, God; however, there are also nontheistic forms of mysticism, as in Buddhism. Mysticism is usually accompanied by meditation, prayer, and ascetic discipline. It may also be accompanied by unusual experiences of ecstasy, levitation, visions, and power to read human hearts, to heal, and to perform other unusual acts. Mysticism occurs in most, if not all, the religions of the world, although its importance within each varies greatly. The criteria and conditions for mystical experience vary depending on the tradition, but three attributes are found almost universally. First, the experience is immediate and overwhelming, divorced from the common experience of reality. Second, the experience or the knowledge imparted by it is felt to be self-authenticating, without need of further evidence or justification. Finally, it is held to be ineffable, its essence incapable of being expressed or understood outside the experience itself.

Modern philosophers and psychologists have studied the occurrence of mysticism. William James suggested that it may be an extension of the ordinary fields of human consciousness. The philosopher Henri Bergson considered intuition to be the highest state of human knowing and mysticism the perfection of intuition. Today scientists are interested in the ways in which certain drugs seem to induce quasi-mystical states. Recent studies have added to the understanding of mysticism without fully explaining it in psychological terms.

mythology   Myths are stories that narrate in an imaginative and symbolic manner the total and basic structures upon which a culture rests. This article will be limited in its treatment to the mythologies of the ancient Near East and India, Greek and Roman myths, and pre-Christian myths of pagan Western Europe. (See also Primitive Religion.)

Types of Myths

Myths may be classified according to the dominant theme expressed in the narrative. Some of the most important themes treated in myths are creation, the origin of gods and divine beings, and the renewal and rebirth of the world.

Creation Myths. The creation, or cosmogonic, myth is usually the most important myth of the culture because it relates how the entire world came into being. Not only the

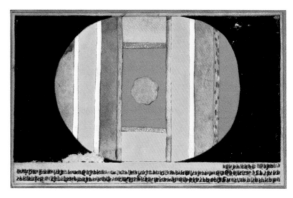

An 18th-century Indian miniature depicts the cosmic egg, a symbol of fertility found in many creation myths. In Hindu tradition this egg, created out of the waters, engenders the supreme being, Brahma. (Private collection.)

beings revealed in the myth but also the qualitative mode of creation becomes a model for all other forms of creation in the culture. Sometimes a deity will create *ex nihilo*, from out of nothing; in other cases, from a primordial chaos. In some myths creation emerges from a metamorphosis of embryonic forms within the earth or from water. Creation may also be seen as the result of violent acts and warfare among the gods. The activity of divine beings such as earth-divers who dive into primordial waters to secure a small piece of earth is found in other creation narratives. A widespread myth speaks of creation coming out of a cosmic egg that a deity has made for the perfection of the cosmos. In all these kinds of myths the mode of creation is part of the structure of a myth that symbolically sets the tone and style for many of the other meanings of the life of the society.

Almost all creation myths contain a structure of rupture—a place in the narrative that describes a happening that separates the primordial condition from the human condition. This mythic event may be due to the ignorance of the prehuman beings, or to a matter of forgetfulness, or to a conscious disobedience. In any case, this flaw is sufficient to establish a discontinuity between the creation at the beginning and the human condition as it is now lived. The nature of this flaw or rupture and the healing rituals of the society are correlative. (See Creation Accounts.)

Myths of the Origin of Deities. Specific deities may appear at the time of creation and are thus part of the narrative of creation myths. The oldest forms of these deities in myths of creation are often symbolized through the expressions of sky and earth. The sky may be a symbol of a father; the earth, a mother. The sky-father may appear as a *deus otiosus* (a distant or retiring deity), who upon creating the world retires from active participation or relationship to it, leaving this world open for other sacred manifestations. In some cases—for example, in Mesopotamian myths—new deities emerge as offspring of the union of earth and sky, and finally warfare ensues between the parents and offspring.

Other forms of deities give expression to the sacredness of particular spatial dimensions, the atmospheric deities of the sky—lightning, thunder, astral phenomena, rain—or deities of the underworld. Other deities express the sacredness of the topography; they reside in mountains, water, and vegetation. Another class of deities manifests techniques and crafts of the human community. In some cases they appear as cultural heroes bringing to the human community fire, the techniques of agriculture, or weaving. Notions of order are expressed in other deities. These notions may be symbolized in the rhythms of night and day; others are related to more general rules of social order and express the interrelationship of the social order and the more fundamental order undergirding the world itself.

Myths of Renewal and Rebirth. Whereas modern societies conceive of time as a linear process moving always into a new and infinite future, in primitive and traditional societies time was understood and experienced as a cyclical rhythm that at various intervals came to the end of a cycle and began again.

The basic order underlying this understanding of time was the creation of the world. The creation myth is a narrative that relates how the gods through the irruption of great creative power brought forth the world. At certain moments this creative power is thought to run down or to become overweighted with the actions of human and divine beings; it needs to be renewed. The renewal takes place at the end of a cycle when the society as a whole reexperiences the original creative act. During the ritual enactment of the creation all rules and conventions of the society are abolished; the original creation is that chaos of power out of which the proper conventions and institutions of the society later emerge.

Rituals of Kenosis, or emptying, portray the evacuating of the meaning of time as it approaches the end of a cycle. The wearing down of time at this moment produces noxious and defiling effects, and thus the appropriate response is an ascetic form of behavior accompanied by austerities. In the rituals of Plerosis, or the filling of time or the beginning again of the new time, dramas of excess and overabundance of power are portrayed in the rituals. Specific dramatic roles in these rituals imitate the power of deities in bringing about the renewal of the time of the cosmos. The interpenetration of the human imitation and cooperation with the deeds of the myth creates the dramatic character of the rituals. Rituals of this kind are common among the Mesopotamians, the Egyptians, and the early Greeks and in almost all traditional agricultural societies.

Ancient Near Eastern Mythologies

Mesopotamian Myths. The religion and culture of Mesopotamia are continuous over a 4,000-year period. Archaeological and literary materials exist from almost every period of this long past. The deities of the southeastern marshes (Sumer) were adopted by the Semitic peoples who came to dominate the area, the Akkadians (see Akkad), the Amorites, and the Assyrians (see Assyria).

In the earliest Mesopotamian mythology Dumuzi-abzu is a Sumerian deity of the marshes. His name means

"quickener of the young in the mother womb of the deep," and he is generally seen as a fertility deity. His sister, Geshtinanna, is the power in the grape, and his female consort is Inanna, who in this period symbolizes the "storehouse of dates."

Dumuzi (whose Semitic name is Tammuz) is the focus of a myth and cult that manifests fertility as the power in the date palm that appears in the spring. The sexual metaphors of Dumuzi's courtship of and marriage to Inanna, the tragedy and lamentation of his death, and the veneration and search for Dumuzi in the underworld by his sister and mother are part of this myth. In the myth and cult of Dumuzi, Mesopotamian religion portrays the characteristic vulnerability of humankind in confrontation with the manifestation of holiness in the forms of nature.

In the middle period (c.2500–c.1900 BC) the cycle of myths continues fertility motifs but in a muted form. The emphasis in these myths is on the origin, meaning, and authority of the ruler; historically they correspond to the use of collective organization among the city-states of Mesopotamia. The symbolism of fertility changes from one of simple sexual embrace to one of cosmic meaning—the power and violence of the thunderstorm that makes the rivers run. The source of the storm is Enlil, whose name means "lord wind." As power in the wind, he is an executive who presides over and directs actions that are beneficent to the human community. The highest authority in the pantheon is Anu (or An), the power in the sky. Anu's wife is Ki, the earth, and from their union are engendered trees, reeds, and other forms of vegetation. He is the father of Enki (later called Ea), who personifies the sacredness in the waters of rivers, rain, and marshes. Enki is identified with the Tigris and Euphrates rivers. His name means "lord of the soil," and in this name the power and necessity of sweet water to fructify the soil is intended. As such, a homology is made between Enki and human semen. Because of the connotations that are derived from his activity with water and soil in the form of clay, Enki is equally a deity who forms and gives shape; he is a molder, or sometimes he is understood as the archetype or the original form.

The form of Inanna (whose Semitic name is Ishtar) changes during this middle period. While retaining her symbolism as the storehouse of dates and consort of Dumuzi, she adds to this symbolism that of a goddess of war, the power in the rain, the evening and morning star, and the harlot. The variety of symbolisms attached to her becomes one of the symbols itself of her being (see MOTHER GODDESS). During this period the deities come to the fore as distinct forms whose power is one of dynamic energies acting and interacting with humans and other deities. The concern of the myths is with cosmic order, and the deities reveal themselves as part and parcel of this context.

In the late Assyrian-Babylonian period (7th century BC) a significant shift of emphasis occurs in which the relation of humankind to the created order emerges as a serious concern. During this period the myth-epics Enuma Elish and Gilgamesh appear. In Enuma Elish, the myth-epic tells the story of the birth of the gods and how human order proceeds from this prior origin of the gods. The hero of the story is MARDUK.

The birth of the gods begins from the commingling of Apsu, the fresh waters underground, and Tiamat, the salt water in the sea. From these waters Lahmu and Lahamu come forth. They engender Anshar and Kishar, who give birth to Anu, god of heaven. Anu makes Nudimmud, or Ea, god of earth, in his own image. Tiamat and Apsu remain in repose; the offspring move about and their activity creates a noise in heaven that disturbs Apsu. Tiamat takes the side of her offspring and attempts to allay the anger of Apsu. Apsu is inclined to forbear until his servant, Mummu, persuades him to insist on quieting the noisy offspring. Expecting an attack, Ea casts a magical spell over Apsu and, while he is sleeping, slays him. Ea then builds a dwelling over the place of Apsu's grave and lives with his wife, Damkina; their first son is Marduk.

Later in the story a group of the younger deities plot to avenge Apsu's death. They choose Kingu, the second husband of Tiamat, to lead them. The other younger deities meet and choose Marduk as their leader in battle against the forces of Tiamat and Kingu. Kingu becomes cowed at the sight of Marduk, but Tiamat is unafraid and the battle ensues with Marduk and Tiamat as combatants. Marduk slays Tiamat, cuts up her body into two pieces, making heaven out of one part and earth out of the other. He then fashions the other parts of the cosmos and assigns the other deities to rule over the cosmos.

The Gilgamesh epic is concerned more with the vicissitudes of the life of the city-state as played out in the story of the ruler of Uruk, Gilgamesh. Gilgamesh is a young, strong, and exceptionally intelligent ruler of Uruk. He is so exceptional, in fact, that he has no human equal and thus disturbs the city of Uruk because no one is capable of sharing his companionship. The people of Uruk entreat the gods to create an equal of Gilgamesh so that they can gain some peace. The gods respond by creating a counterpart to Gilgamesh in the form of Enkidu. Enkidu is equal to Gilgamesh in strength, youth, and intelligence, except that instead of being a city dweller, he is a savage

This tablet portrays a scene from the Epic of Gilgamesh, the legendary ruler of Uruk who undertakes an unsuccessful quest for the secret of immortality.

born in the wilds whose companions are wild animals.

Gilgamesh hears of the existence of Enkidu and seeks ways to entice him into the city. A trapper and a harlot are sent to the wilderness to seduce Enkidu into captivity. They succeed. The harlot seduces Enkidu, and after lying with her for six days and seven nights, he finds that the animals who were formerly his companions avoid him and that he has lost his capacity to communicate with them. The harlot then offers him her companionship, giving him clothes to wear. They move slowly toward the city, where they arrive during the wedding of Gilgamesh. Enkidu and Gilgamesh engage in physical combat. Enkidu wins, but in this victory he discovers someone equal to himself and thus a strong friendship is born.

Enkidu and Gilgamesh later go into the wilderness to destroy the giant or monster Huwawa. Upon return to the city Gilgamesh is tempted by Ishtar, daughter of the god of heaven, Anu. She offers Gilgamesh her hand in marriage. In refusing the marriage, Gilgamesh insults Ishtar for her infidelities and her inability to take care of a husband. Angered, Ishtar seeks vengeance upon Gilgamesh. She sends the bull of heaven to ravage Uruk, but Gilgamesh makes short work of him.

Later Enkidu becomes ill and dies. Gilgamesh, the conqueror of all things on earth, finds that he is helpless before death. He learns that one of his ancestors, Utnapishtim, knows the powers of eternal life and sets out to find him. After several adventures Gilgamesh arrives at his abode in a distant land. Utnapishtim, who is the sole survivor of the great DELUGE, tells Gilgamesh of a thorny plant growing in Apsu, the sweet waters underneath the earth, that gives eternal life. Gilgamesh dives to the bottom of the waters and secures the plant, but as he journeys home a serpent eats the plant; thus serpents, but not human beings, have eternal life. The two myths, Enuma Elish and Gilgamesh, both give a prominence to death in the life of the human community. In Enuma Elish death is the creative power that allows for a new cosmos; in Gilgamesh it is the pervasive inevitability of human life. In both cases death is seen as the ultimate limit to human existence.

Egyptian Mythology. In ancient Egypt the tendency was toward unity and stasis, not confrontation and tension. A text that exemplifies this attitude, while taking into account older historical and local traditions, is the theology of Memphis, recorded on the Shabaka Stone. The Memphite theology presents the teachings of MENES, who established (c.3000 BC) a new capital at MEMPHIS. In this theology all local and former mythological traditions are brought to their theological goal in the god PTAH. The text is a cosmology that describes the creation of the world and the unity of the land of Egypt as a process in the eternal ordering of the world. Ptah creates everything from notions that were in his heart and are then pronounced by his tongue. All things—the universe, living beings, justice, beauty, and so on—are created in this manner. The gods are also created in this way; coming forth first as concepts of Ptah's mind, they enter into the material forms of the world—stone, metal, wood—that have equally been created out of Ptah.

(Left) *A painted wooden stele dating from Egypt's late dynastic period shows the sun god Ra-Harakhte with a worshiper. One of the most prominent deities in the Egyptian pantheon, Ra-Harakhte is represented as a falcon crowned with a solar disk. By the 5th dynasty each pharaoh was revered as the son and incarnation of Ra-Harakhte.*

(Right) *The Canaanite god Baal, in his aspect as god of storms, is depicted on this relief stele (1300–1200 BC) from Ugarit, an ancient Phoenician city. A fertility and creator god, Baal headed the Canaanite pantheon and was revered in other Near Eastern cultures. (Louvre, Paris.)*

The Memphite theology takes over older local notions of creation, such as that of Hermopolis, which describes creation proceeding from eight primordial beings of chaos who inhabited the primeval slime. The four males are toads, and the four females snakes, forming the pairs of Nun and Naunet (primordial matter and primordial space); Kuk and Kauket (the illimitable and the boundless); Huh and Hauhet (darkness and obscurity); and Amon and Amaunet (hidden and concealed ones). These eight bring forth the sun, and in the Memphite theology they are said to come forth from Ptah himself.

Another part of the Memphite mythology takes up myths from the Old Kingdom about the gods HORUS and SET. These two deities contend for authority over Egypt; another deity, Geb, the earth-god, acts as mediator. Geb first partitions the country between the two, then, changing his mind, gives the entire country to Horus. In the Memphite theology the pharaoh Menes is identified with Horus. That theology also makes Geb homologous to Ptah, but in another mythological context Geb, the power in the earth, is supreme. He is the primeval hillock that is the symbol of the first creation. For the Egyptians the earth deity is male rather than female.

In the Old Kingdom mythology the sun Atum (or Aten) often appears as the first creator. He makes Shu and Tefnut (air and moisture) out of himself, and they in turn produce Geb and Nut (earth and sky). The children of the latter couple are OSIRIS, ISIS, Set, and Nepthys. Thus the first four deities establish the cosmos, and the later four are mediators between humans and the cosmos. Osiris is the symbol of the dead king, who is succeeded in the form of Horus, the living ruler. Isis is the consort of Osiris, and after his murder by Set she reconstitutes his body

and thus achieves for him eternal life; her ally in this role is Nepthys, the consort of Set. Horus, the son of Osiris and Isis, ultimately vanquishes Set, a symbol of antistructure or antiorder. Set is related to the desert of Upper Egypt. As a deity of clouds, he opposed Atum, the sun.

Although kingship appears as the pivot around which Egyptian mythology revolves, the key mythological themes are creation, procreation, revival, and the unity of the two lands of Upper Egypt and Lower Egypt.

Canaanite Mythology. The Canaanites are part of the group referred to in ancient times as the Western Semites; this group includes the Phoenicians, Ugarites, and Hebrews. One of the most prominent deities of the Canaanites, and indeed of all Western Semitic peoples, is the god El. Although *El* is often a generic name for deity, in certain mythological cycles El is a specific god. In some respects he resembles the deities Enlil of the Mesopotamians and Zeus of the Greeks. He is a father and creator and sometimes a divine warrior, but the dominant image of El is that of an old, wise patriarch and judge. He manifests great strength, but he is not an absolute ruler. Unlike the Mesopotamian deities, El does not manifest the power behind the phenomena of nature; he is seen rather as a deity whose homologies are found in the social life.

El's consorts are Asherah, ASTARTE, and Anat, all of whom are counterparts of the Mesopotamian Ishtar. Asherah and Astarte are El's wives or, in some contexts, his sisters; Anat is his daughter. Asherah is often referred to as a creator who gives birth to 70 deities. El, who is a sky deity, and Asherah, who represents earth, first produced the morning and the evening stars; two other sons are Yamm (the sea) and Mot (the underworld).

The most important deity after El is BAAL Haddad.

Baal Haddad is the son of Dagan, a god of rain, who probably originated in the region of the Middle Euphrates and was transmitted to the Western Semites through the Akkadians. The name *Baal Haddad* carries the connotation of rulership. He is a young, warlike god of wind and thunderstorms. Unlike El, he is not at all judicious, frequently creating situations from which he must be saved by female deities, in most cases Anat, who appears as his consort. In this respect he bears some resemblance to Dumuzi (Tammuz) among the Mesopotamians, who is also surrounded by female protectors and whose actions carry little ethical value.

In the mythological cycles Baal is pitted in warfare with El; this warfare may indicate that he is a later arrival in the area, the warfare being congruent to a change in the culture. Initially Baal and Anat seem to be members of the court of El; Anat is El's concubine, and Baal has become his cupbearer. In a sudden and surprise move Baal attacks El. Baal and his helpers defeat El in the abode of his mountain, Sapan, tying him down and castrating him. In this act the fertility of El is destroyed. In despair El calls out to his sons, and Yamm comes to his aid. El proclaims Yamm the lord and tells him that he must recover the gold and silver stolen by Baal in order to build himself a palace fit for a lord and possess the treasure. He must also fight Baal in order to avenge the defeat of his father, El, through blood vengeance.

Yamm is killed by Baal in the combat, and the obligation of blood vengeance then falls upon the next son, Mot. Mot succeeds in killing Baal in Baal's own palace. The death of Baal infuriates Anat, who implores Mot to restore Baal to life. When he refuses, she kills and dismembers him, scattering his remains over the land. Baal, now revived, undertakes a full-scale war against all the other gods, who are now referred to as the "sons of Asherah," and is victorious.

Mot too is revived and once again challenges Baal to single combat. In the midst of the fighting, however, the sun-goddess, Spsi (Shapash), intervenes, advising Mot that no further combat is needed because El is now on the side of Baal. El, always patriarchal and judicious, has discerned that Baal in his defeat and resurrection has manifested a new form of order; as a patriarchal deity El must uphold this new order. The decree is made that Baal will rule during the seasons of fertility and Mot during the seasons of sterility and drought.

Canaanite mythology in general and the mythical cycle of the combat of El and Baal in particular have several broad implications. In the first place, the geographical location and the historical period indicate that these myths are part of a wider mythological synthesis. Elements of Mesopotamian, Egyptian, Hittite, Hurrian, and Ugaritic myths are present in this cycle, which is thus a watershed for the understanding of myth and history during this period. Second, light is shed on the Hebrew Old Testament. Although the Old Testament contains a polemic against Baal, Asherah, and Astarte, some of the elements and practices of the Hebrews are best understood within the context of Canaanite mythology.

Indo-European Mythology

About the 2d millennium BC a group of peoples usually referred to as the Indo-Europeans, or ARYANS, began a series of massive migrations from their original homelands in the area north of the Black Sea. They eventually came to dominate most of Europe, the northern Near East, and the Indian subcontinent.

The development of Indo-European myth and the myths of the various subgroups display the rejection of an early sky-god in favor of a tripartite division of divine power reflecting the social structure of the peoples. This division consists of a magical-legal function, a warrior function, and the various functions of fertility and production, thus leading to the expectation of three supreme gods beneath whom the pantheon is organized. Various complications appear, however, the most important of which is the tendency to distribute the first function between two gods, one threatening and indifferent to the fate of humanity, and one specifically concerned with the proper ordering of human life and society. Another important feature is the ambiguity of the warrior god. As a warrior he must be great in battle, in order to protect the safety of cosmos and society, but in his victory his rage may become so great as to threaten the well-being of creation; thus the necessity of taming the powers of the warrior god through ritual and sacrifice. Variations on these themes will recur throughout the analysis of the myths of the Indo-European peoples.

Indian Mythology. The earliest development of Indo-European mythology for which evidence is plentiful comes from the Indian *Rig-Veda*, compiled probably at the end of the 2d millennium BC by the Aryans, who had

This South Indian woodcarving portrays one of the chief deities of Vedic mythology, Agni, the god of fire. The two faces of Agni symbolize his dual nature—beneficent and malevolent. He is holding a torch and a sacrificial spoon, emblems associated with the rituals of his fire cult. Agni personifies the creative fire of the universe and acts as a messenger between mortals and the gods. (Musée Guimet, Paris.)

overrun northern India (see VEDAS). At this time the high god was Varuna, the overpowering master of knowledge and magic, presiding over the changing spectacle of the universe. Often associated with him is Mitra, the sun-god, who takes the part of humankind, establishing laws and contracts and ensuring the well-being of society. The most important god of the *Rig-Veda*, however, is Indra, the warrior. These three, together with a large number of lesser gods, are Adityas, the children of the boundless goddess Aditi, perhaps an ancient mother of earth. Against the Adityas stand the Danavas, the children of Danu (the restrainer), the most important of whom is the great dragon Vritra. After many combats, trials, and treaties, Indra, the chosen champion of the Adityas, destroys Vritra with his thunderbolt, thus freeing the cosmic waters and making possible the creation, over which Varuna and Mitra will preside.

The mythology of India is in constant flux, however, and gods who have but a minor part in the *Rig-Veda* become important in later Vedic and other literature. One such is Prajapati, who comes to replace Varuna as arbiter of the cosmic order. By "heating" himself, Prajapati brings into being the hierarchy of the universe through either his sweat or his semen, thus establishing through his self-sacrifice the order of things that is perpetuated through the rituals and sacrifices of the priestly caste. Two other important deities connected with ritual are Agni and Soma. Agni is the god of fire, the illuminator and agent of sacrifice. The cult of fire, an ancient aspect of Indo-European religion, remained important in the religion and mythology of Iran. Soma, the god, is often indistinguishable from soma, the drink of the gods, which gives Indra the power to overcome the dragon. As both drink and god, Soma confers strength, insight, and immortality, as well as providing a form of union between the priest and divinity.

In later HINDUISM another triad appears: BRAHMA, the creator; VISHNU, the preserver; and SHIVA, the destroyer. Because his role is exclusively that of creator, Brahma's work is done, and he is a peripheral figure in the myths. Vishnu and Shiva are far more important. Vishnu, a minor god in the earlier period, is worshiped primarily in his avatars, or incarnations, as Rama and KRISHNA, the principal characters of the epics RAMAYANA and Mahabharata. In both of these the god takes on human form in order to heal a breach in the order of society, and thus the world in general, and by so doing reestablish the proper relation of humankind to divinity. He is consequently seen and worshiped as the loving savior of humanity.

Shiva, on the other hand, is an ambivalent figure, a loner who seeks knowledge through ascetic practice. He is in many ways a dangerous god, a destroyer, but at the same time represents the rejection of normal society and its ways by the ascetic, who seeks release from the world through mystical discipline.

Ancient Iranian religion shared the same Aryan heritage as Indian mythology. Mitannian sources from the late 14th century BC list Varuna, Mitra, and Indra as well as two Nasatyas, twin gods who represent the productive functions of society. By Achaemenid times (549–330 BC)

the triad was Ahura Mazda, Mithra, and a goddess called Anahita. Ahura Mazda became the central deity of ZOROASTRIANISM; Mithra, a lesser figure in Zoroastrianism, became the object of the separate cult of MITHRAISM.

Greek Mythology. The 12 major deities in the Olympian pantheon are ZEUS, HERA, ATHENA, HERMES, APHRODITE, HEPHAESTUS, ARES, APOLLO, ARTEMIS, POSEIDON, DEMETER, and DIONYSUS. Zeus is the most prominent deity of Greek mythology. He is clearly of Indo-European origin and is a celestial deity related to and symbolized by the sky and sky phenomena. He is the thunderbolt, a god of lightning, a god of rain. He is a ruler-father, sovereign, and controller.

In HOMER's *Iliad*, Zeus is referred to as the son of CRONUS, but Cronus is given no other prominence, and Zeus is frequently called father of the gods. Zeus is often related to various female consorts—at Eleusis his consort is Demeter; at Thebes, SEMELE; and at Argos, Hera. Each one of these female deities is a symbol of earth and fertility. In Homer, Zeus is a reigning god who sits on a throne at the top of Mount OLYMPUS. He is attended by his council of deities: Hera, Apollo, Poseidon, Artemis, and Athena. Each of these has his or her own dwelling on Olympus. The palace and walls were built by Hephaestus.

HESIOD's *Theogony* gives another story of Zeus. It provides a genealogy of the birth of the deities. The first god was URANUS, who mates with GAEA, the earth; from this union, the TITANS and CYCLOPS are born. The most important of these offspring is the Titan Cronus, who marries his sister Rhea. Cronus receives a prophecy that foretells his overthrow by one of his children; therefore when his children are born he immediately swallows them. The distressed Rhea is advised by her parents to go to Crete when she becomes pregnant again. She does so and on Crete gives birth to Zeus. Gaea becomes nursemaid to Zeus and devises a stratagem to save him from his father. She wraps a stone in clothing and presents it to Cronus as

This bronze statue (c.450 BC) is believed to represent the Greek god Zeus as he hurls his weapon, the thunderbolt. The supreme deity of Olympus, Zeus was a personification of highest power and rule. (National Museum, Athens.)

his new son. Upon ingesting the stone, Cronus disgorges it and all of the other children he had previously swallowed, including Hera, Poseidon, and Hades. Another element in the myth relates that the safety of Zeus is ensured by a group of divine beings called *kuretes* who dance around the young child, creating such a noise that the cries of the child cannot be heard by Cronus. This story of the birth of Zeus may be part of a chthonic religion that is related to the Mediterranean orgiastic traditions of Greece.

Zeus thus appears in the two mythological traditions, one Indo-European, the other Mediterranean (Minoan), as a sky-god belonging to invading Indo-Europeans. As the head of the pantheon he is symbolized by forms other than the sky, and through his marriages and amorous adventures he assimilates the indigenous deities to the Indo-European pantheon. The Titans may have been the ancient gods of the earth, and Hesiod's myth blends the two traditions into a single narrative.

Hera (*lady* in Greek) is the great goddess of the indigenous inhabitants of Greece before the Indo-European invasions. She symbolizes a matriarchal and polyandrous culture. As the great goddess, she annually takes a mate in a *hieros gamos* ("sacred marriage"), a ritual enactment of fertility and the coming of spring. Zeus, the sky-god of the Indo-Europeans, marries Hera at Argos, and this marriage becomes the archetype for monogamous patrilineal marriage and kinship. Hera becomes the goddess of marital virtue. Hesiod's version is that Hera was the sister of Zeus; when she is disgorged by Cronus, Zeus marries her.

Poseidon was originally an Indo-European deity and an elder brother to Zeus. He is often referred to as the producer of thunder but more often as the wild horse. In the time of Homer he was called earth-shaker, and this name may be related to the sound of horses' hooves.

Several stories tell of Poseidon's mating with goddesses in the forms of mares. In Arcadia, Demeter changes herself into a mare and is chased by Poseidon; from their mating is born PERSEPHONE and the horse Arion. Poseidon then becomes the god of the sea when he mates with the sea goddess Amphitrite.

Dionysus is not an Indo-European deity. Probably Phrygian in origin, the god and his cult traveled to Macedonia, then to Thessaly and Boeotia. The myth of his birth relates that his mother is Semele and that he was fathered by Zeus. When Hera, Zeus's wife, learns of Zeus's infidelity and the approaching birth, she disguises herself as Semele's nurse and convinces her to demand that Zeus reveal himself in the totality of his godliness to her. Zeus appears to Semele in the fullness of his thunder and lightning. The appearance strikes Semele dead, but just before her death Zeus snatches Dionysus from her womb, cuts open his thigh, and places the child therein; after nine months Dionysus is born from the thigh of Zeus. Dionysus is called the twice-born—from the womb of Semele and the thigh of Zeus.

Dionysus's appearance always seems to be accompanied by some violent activity that presents a threat to conventional order. As the center of an orgiastic mystical

A Greco-Roman relief depicts the visit of Dionysus, god of fertility and creator of wine, to the mortal Icarius. Icarius's hospitality earned him knowledge of the vine. (British Museum, London.)

cult, he tends to break the bonds of social life. EURIPIDES, in his drama *The Bacchae*, describes the Dionysian cult. (Dionysus is also called Bromios, the Boisterous, or BACCHUS.) The aim of the cult was to produce ecstasy—the experience of standing outside of oneself—or enthusiasm—the experience of being filled with the god. The heart of the Dionysian mystery was that the devotee and the god become identical. The majority of the cult followers were women, the MAENADS, those who had gone mad in their ecstasy. When the priest of Dionysus played on his flute, the devotees went into a frenzy, in which they were said to dismember animals.

Apollo stands in contrast to Dionysus. Whereas Dionysus orients his devotees to wild orgiastic rites, Apollo is the god of moderation and represents the legal or statutory meaning of religion. Apollo is foremost a god of law; he is described by Plato as the source of law. In his role as lawgiver, Apollo refers to the precedents of the gods and laws of the city.

Apollo has another side, however. Like Dionysus, he was related to the oracle of DELPHI, and his devotees there were enthusiastic and ecstatically possessed. W. K. C. Guthrie, in *The Greeks and Their Gods*, suggests that Apollo originated in Siberia and that the ecstatic powers attached to his cult were derived from the tribal shamanism of that area rather than from the Dionysian cult at Delphi. Because of the common ecstatic elements, Apollo's cult exerted a moderating influence on the distinctly non-Olympian religious experience of Dionysus.

Roman Mythology. The historical background out of which the myths of Rome emerge is similar in some aspects to that of the Greeks. There, too, the Indo-European elements were superimposed on the cultures of the indigenous peoples. In later periods cultural religious meanings from Greece, Syria, Iran, and Egypt played a role in Roman mythology. Nonetheless, Roman mythology has a special character and nature that can be delineated. Unlike Greek mythology, which is varied, complex, and rich in poetical and speculative allusions, Roman religion and Roman myths are prosaic, prudent, and precise in a legal and moral sense.

Roman mythology does not have a pantheon on the order of the Greek Olympians. It presents specific deities that are relatively well defined. Hardly anything is said about their mythic lives—births, infidelities, adventures, and relations among or between themselves. Rather, they tend to be venerated at certain times of the year or at certain places in the city or landscape.

At certain moments and places some manifestation of sacred power is expressed. Specific gods manifest themselves in ways particular to a town or region, or local heroes are elevated to the status of gods. Such local deities were catalogued in lists called *Indigitamenta*, which also prescribed the rituals appropriate to the worship of each.

A straightforward correspondence can be set up between the gods of the Greek pantheon and their Roman counterparts: Zeus-JUPITER; Hera-JUNO; Poseidon-NEPTUNE; Demeter-CERES; Apollo-Apollo; Artemis-DIANA; Athena-MINERVA; Hephaestus-VULCAN; Aphrodite-VENUS; Ares-MARS; Dionysus-Bacchus. This correspondence, however, barely scratches the surface of Roman mythology.

Beneath the great gods are the minor deities and demigods to whom a wide variety of festivals and sacrifices were dedicated throughout the Roman year. These are gods of specific functions, such as guarding or fostering the orchards, and they rarely figure in extended myths; they appear, however, in such works as Ovid's *Fasti* and *Metamorphoses*. Still more particular were the lares and PENATES, familiar deities who were thought to watch over the household hearth and cupboard. At this level it becomes apparent how the gods of the indigenous Latins and other pre-Indo-European peoples have been assimilated into a scheme that informs not only the Roman perception of the cosmos but also the day-to-day activity of the citizen.

In this context may be mentioned the myth-epics concerning the history of Rome. These include the AENEID of VERGIL, the ROMULUS AND REMUS cycle of stories, and the epics related to the Roman kings. By incorporating the traditions of Roman history into a grand scheme linking the Roman present with the mythic past and the hope of a glorious future, these stories form the clearest expression of the Roman love for order, stability, and strength evident throughout its mythology.

Norse (Germanic and Scandinavian) Mythology. Germanic and Scandinavian mythology have a common origin and structure; they will, therefore, be discussed in their unity. The main body of traditions is contained in the *Prose Edda* of SNORRI STURLUSON (*c.*1179–1241), an Icelandic historian who is considered the most accurate editor, redactor, and interpreter of the religious and mythological sources of the old Norse religion.

In the beginning was a great void (Ginnungagup). Before the Earth was formed, the world of death existed; in this world (Niflheim) was a great well, from which flowed 11 rivers. South of Niflheim existed an extremely hot world (Muspell) guarded by a giant called Sutr ("the Black"). The rivers of Niflheim froze, and these frozen rivers occupied Ginnungagup. Sparks from Muspell, however, fell on the rivers and melted them. Droppings from this melting took shape as YMIR, the giant, and from Ymir's sweat other giants, male and female, were formed.

Another version relates that the melting drops took the form of the primordial cow, Audumbla, who fed Ymir with her milk. The cow also licked the salty blocks of ice, shaping them into the form of the first man, who is called Buri. Buri has a son, Bor, who marries Bestla, daughter of a giant, Bolthorr; the children from this union are the gods ODIN, Vili, and Ve. Odin and his brothers kill Ymir and from his body fashion the Earth.

The gods endow two tree trunks with the qualities of wit, breath, hearing, vision, and so on. These tree trunks are the archetypes of the human race; the man is Askr (an ash tree) and the woman, Embla (a creeper). They next build ASGARD, the abode of the gods. Snorri describes in other versions how a great tree, Yggdrasil, the tree of fate, arises in the center of the world. Beneath the tree is the well of fate, which is described as feminine in form; the course of human life is decided here. In some versions, the council of the gods is convened around the tree. The tree is supported by three roots; one of these roots stretches to the underworld (HEL), another to the world of the frost-giants, and the last one to the world of human beings. The welfare of the entire world is dependent on the primordial tree, Yggdrasil.

The Norse deities are divided into two major groups, the Aesir and the Vanir. The most important of the Aesir are Odin, THOR, and sometimes Tyr. Their counterparts among the Vanir are Njord, FREY, and FREYA. The Vanir symbolize riches, fertility, and fecundity. They are associated with the earth and the sea as these symbolize sources of fecundity. The Aesir symbolize other values: Odin is a magician, chief among the gods, and a patron of heroes; Thor, who is god of the hammer, is an atmospheric deity of thunder who presides over work. In many of the Norse mythological cycles these two kinds of deities live in peace and engage in cooperative enterprises. Several important versions, however, report that in the distant past a fierce war was fought between the Aesir and the Vanir.

In the Norse cycles the conflict between the gods begins when Odin and Thor, the greatest of the gods, refuse

The Norse god Thor, whose name means "thunder," clutches the magical hammer that symbolizes his power in this bronze statuette (c.1000 AD). Thor was revered as a mighty warrior and as defender of the peasant. (National Museum of Iceland, Reykjavik.)

the full status of godhood to the Vanir. The latter entreat the Aesir by sending to them a woman, Gullveig (gold-drink, gold drunkenness), who corrupts them. War then breaks out. After both sides are exhausted, each side exchanges members of its group with the other; the Vanir send Njord and his son Frey, the Aesir, MIMIR and Hoenir. The truce is celebrated by a meeting at which all the gods spit into a bowl, creating a giant called Kvasir, who is the sign of peace and harmony among the deities. Kvasir is later sacrificed and from his blood a more potent drink for the gods is made. Kvasir thus becomes the drink that inebriates deities and gives inspiration to the poets.

An important mythological episode involves the deities BALDER and LOKI. Balder, one of the sons of Odin, appears as the essence of intelligence, piety, and wisdom. He holds court in a hall in heaven called Glitnir. Both gods and men come to him to settle legal disputes, and his judgments are reconciling and fair. Loki is a giant who is an Aesir by adoption. He and Odin have made a vow of friendship.

Balder has a very disturbing dream in which his life is threatened. Upon reporting this dream to the Aesir, his mother, FRIGG, exacts an oath from fire and water, all metals, bird and beast, and earth and stones that they will not harm Balder. After this the Aesir begin to amuse themselves by placing Balder in the midst of them and throwing darts and stones at him. Because of the oath Balder remains unharmed. When Loki sees this spectacle, he disguises himself as a woman and inquires of Frigg why Balder suffers no harm. Frigg tells him of the oath and also tells him of the one form of nature from which she did not exact the oath, the mistletoe. Loki immediately brings the mistletoe to the assembly of the Aesir and offers it to the blind god Hoder, brother of Balder, volunteering to direct his aim so that he can participate in the game. When the mistletoe strikes Balder, he falls dead. The Aesir want to take vengeance on the perpetrator of the deed, but because of the sanctity of the court they cannot.

Because Balder is not a warrior and does not die in battle, he does not go to VALHALLA, the hall of slain heroes, but into the domain of Hel, keeper of the dead. When Odin requests his release, Hel responds that if everything in the world both dead and alive weeps for Balder, then he can return to the Aesir; otherwise he will remain with Hel. The Aesir send messengers throughout the world requiring all nature, humanity, gods, and beasts to weep for Balder. All respond except a giantess, Thokk (Loki in disguise), whose refusal to weep forces Balder to remain in Hel's domain.

The Aesir finally succeed in capturing Loki and chaining him to prevent him from carrying out his evil tricks. The prediction is, however, that he will one day break these chains. This will be the sign for the loosing of all evil, monsters and giants, to attack the gods in the great battle of RAGNAROK, the twilight of the gods. Odin will be devoured by the wolf Fenrir, who will then be killed by Vidar, a son of Odin. Terrible fights will rage among the gods and the forces of evil until finally the primeval god Heimdall and Loki come face to face and kill each other.

The Earth will then be destroyed by fire, and the entire universe will sink back into the sea. This final destruction will be followed by a rebirth, the Earth reemerging from the sea, verdant and teeming with vegetation. The sons of the dead Aesir will return to Asgard and reign, as did their fathers.

Celtic Mythology. The CELTS originally inhabited an area in southern Germany and Bohemia. By the end of the 5th century BC they had expanded into the Iberian peninsula; in 390 BC they sacked Rome. In the east they went as far as Anatolia. In the west they migrated to Britain in the 5th century BC and Ireland in the 3d century BC. A great deal may be learned about the Celts from the archaeological materials left behind in the various countries where their culture dominated for several centuries. Most of the written documents of Celtic culture and religion are from Ireland and date from the 12th century AD, when they were written under Christian aegis.

As in the other Indo-European cultures, a clear tripartite structure appears in Celtic societal organization. The principal divisions are the king, the warriors, and the cattleherders. The religious hierarchy is also tripartite, consisting of the priestly DRUIDS, who also served as administrators; the vatis or filidh, experts in magic and divination; and the bards, who are concerned with oral literature and prose poetry. As a culture the Celts display counteracting tendencies: they seem to be autonomous, anarchic, and concerned for local traditions, but a basic unitary character is manifested in their social organization and mythological histories.

The Celtic pantheon is difficult to discern. The names of several hundred gods are known, but the majority appear to be local deities. During the Roman period, many Celtic deities were identified with Roman gods. One of the most important, called LUG in Ireland, was identified with Mercury.

The Irish mythological cycle can be divided into four major divisions. The first is the historical-mythological cycle. Two important texts are part of this cycle: the *Leabhar Gahbála* (Book of Invasions), a mythological history of Ireland; and the *Dinnshenchas* (History of Places), a mythological geography of Ireland. The main theme in the historical-mythological cycle concerns the peopling of Ireland and the fortunes of the Tuatha Dé Danann (People of the Goddess Danann), who were the mythological ancestors of the Irish.

The second division is the Ulster cycle. These myths are stories of the warriors of King Conchobar. The themes of those of honor and prestige revolve around heroic deeds and the hero CUCHULAIN (or Cúchulainn). The third division is that of Fenian. The Fenian cycle recounts the exploits of FINN MAC CUMHAIL and his companions and deals with the cult and institution of warriors. The last division deals with the institution and founding of the great and lesser kings of Ireland. The latter two divisions fall most readily into the category of folk tales and will not be discussed here.

In the historical-mythological cycle the story of the predecessors of the Irish settlement is told. The first

A Celtic stag god is surrounded by forms of animal life in this plaque from the Gundestrup Cauldron (AD c.100–300). Many varied nature deities were worshiped by the Celts. (National Museum of Denmark, Copenhagen.)

group to come to Ireland is led by a woman, Cesair; the majority of her group is composed of women. This group arrives before the great flood, and all are destroyed in the flood except one, Fintan, who in the form of a salmon, eagle, or hawk witnesses all of the later settlements. Fintan is the patron of the traditional lore and storytelling. The next group is led by Partholán, but he and all of his people die in a plague. A third group is led by Nemed; after suffering many vicissitudes, this group divides into three parts and abandons Ireland. Two of these groups, the Fir Bolg (Bolg Men) and the Tuatha Dé Danann, occupy the subsequent history. The Fir Bolg return to Ireland, which they divide into the five provinces of Ulster, Leinster, Munster, Connacht, and Meath; they also introduce kingship. When the Tuatha Dé Danann arrive, warfare ensues over possession of the land. One tradition states that after the First Battle of Mag Tuired, the Fir Bolg and Tuatha Dé Danann make peace and agree to live together in harmony. This outcome may reflect the classic Indo-European pattern.

The Tuatha are described as demigods; they are beautiful people, possessed with skill in music and the arts. They are always spoken about within a context of fabulous magical powers and wonders, which define the essence of their manifestation. A central theme in the myth of the Tuatha is that of the Second Battle of Mag Tuired. During the First Battle of Mag Tuired the king of the Tuatha, Nuada, is wounded. Because he is now physically blemished, he can no longer serve as king. The kingship is then given to his adopted son, Bres. Bres's father is a king of the Fomoire, a group of people with whom Nemed and his people had fought in previous times. Bres's mother, Eriu, is, however, a Tuatha. The choice of Bres is apparently an attempt to accomplish an alliance between the Tuatha and the Fomoire.

Bres, however, demands severe tribute from the Tuatha and persecutes them in many ways. A champion, Lug, arises from among the Tuatha; Lug is a master of all the arts of magic and warfare. Meanwhile Nuada, the blemished king, is restored to his kingship after he has been equipped with a silver arm. Nuada takes counsel with Lug, Dagda, the great god with the magic cauldron, and others concerning the preparations for warfare with the Fomoire. When the battle finally takes place, the Tuatha who are slain in the fighting are magically restored to life. Lug also uses magic to vanquish Balar "of the baleful eye." The Fomoire are routed. The life of the captured Bres is spared when he promises to advise on the proper times for sowing and reaping. Unlike similar battles in other Indo-European mythologies, the Second Battle of Mag Tuired does not end in a reconciliation and fusion of the two parties. The skills imparted by Bres, however, serve the same function of completing the functions needed in settled society.

The Tuatha are themselves later defeated by the Sons of Mil, the immediate ancestors of the Irish people. The Tuatha are said now to live in the underground of Ireland, in the fairy regions, where the fairies are subject to them. An analogous mythological history is related in the Welsh cycle of *The Four Branches of the Mabinogi*.

In the Ulster cycle the heroic accomplishments of Cuchulain are related. Cuchulain in some versions is said to be a foster child of Ulster, and in some respects his character is modeled on that of Lug of the historical-mythological cycle. He is described as a small black-browed man, beardless and full of gaiety. When he is in battle a remarkable change comes over him; he increases in size, and his body trembles and whirls about inside of his skin so that his frontal features are turned to the rear. He can draw one of his eyes back into his head, and his hair bristles on end, with a drop of blood on the end of each hair. When he is in a warrior frenzy he attacks anyone in the vicinity, friend and foe alike.

The central story of the Ulster cycle is the Cattle-raid of Cuailnge (*Táin Bó Cuailnge*). Queen Medb of Connacht and her vanguard attempt to steal the great bull, Donn Cuailnge, owned by the men of Ulster. She desires this bull so that her possessions will equal those of her husband, King Ailill, who owns a great white-horned bull, Finnbennach. Through the structure of this story the exploits of Cuchulain and his companions, Conall Cernach and Loegaire Buadach, are related. In the warfare against Queen Medb, Cuchulain realizes that he is fighting against supernatural forces that have been organized against him.

Before the last battle, the Great Carnage of Murthemne, Cuchulain realizes the contradictory workings of his *geasa*. The *geasa* is a kind of personal obligation or taboo that cannot be violated by the individual without suffering dire consequences. For example, the sorcerers of Queen Medb are cooking a dog when Cuchulain passes. One of his *geasa* obligates him to eat the food from any hearth that he passes; another of his *geasa* makes the meat of dog a forbidden food. When he eats the dog he feels some of his power leave him. In this manner he is depleted of his great powers and eventually is mortally wounded in battle. He is tied upright to a pillar so that he can die while standing.

Mytilene   see LESBOS

Nn

GERMAN-GOTHIC	RUSSIAN-CYRILLIC	CLASSICAL LATIN	EARLY LATIN	ETRUSCAN	CLASSICAL GREEK	EARLY GREEK	EARLY ARAMAIC	EARLY HEBREW	PHOENICIAN

N N/n is the 14th letter of the English alphabet. Both the letter and its position in the alphabet were derived from the Latin, which in turn had derived it from the Greek by way of the Etruscan. The Greeks call the letter *nu* and took its name, form, and position from a Semitic writing system. N/n is a voiced dental nasal continuant made with the point of the tongue against either the back of the upper teeth or the gum ridge behind the teeth, as in *no, honey,* and *knot.* Final *n* preceded by *m* is silent, as in *hymn* and *condemn,* but when a vowel sound is added, the *n* is sometimes pronounced (*hymnist*), sometimes not (*condemning*). When *n* is followed by *g,* the combination usually represents a different consonant—a voiced nasal continuant made similarly to *n,* but instead of the tip of the tongue being against the upper teeth, the back of the tongue is against the soft palate (velum), as in *ring* and *song.* In some words in which *g* or *k* follows *n,* the *g* or *k* is pronounced separately—as in *anger* and *ink.* In some words borrowed from Spanish, *n* is combined with a mark called a tilde. An *n* with a tilde (*ñ*) is pronounced like the *ni* in *onion* (*señor; cañon,* but also *canyon*).

NAACP see NATIONAL ASSOCIATION FOR THE ADVANCEMENT OF COLORED PEOPLE

Nabis [nah-bee'] The Nabis, a group of late-19th-century symbolist painters and poets in France, took their name from the Hebrew word *nabi* ("prophet" or "seer"), reflecting their interest in theosophy and the occult. Led by Paul Sérusier, the group followed doctrines discovered in the work of Paul Gauguin, such as synthetic form, flat, linear patterns, and arbitrary use of colors. The group's aesthetic and philosophical outlook was strongly influenced by the symbolists; like them, the Nabis felt that art should not reproduce the appearance of nature but ought to express the artist's inner world. The Nabis exhibited regularly as a group from 1891 to 1900, after which they drifted apart.

Nabokov, Vladimir [nah-baw'-kawv, vluhd-ee'-mir] One of the 20th century's master writers of fiction, Vladimir Vladimirovich Nabokov, b. Apr. 23 (N.S.), 1899, d. July 2, 1977, came from a family of Russian aristocrats. He learned English and French at a very early age and settled on a literary career while still in his teens. He was

The Russian-American novelist Vladimir Nabokov was one of the most brilliantly imaginative novelists of the 20th century. Nabokov first received international recognition with Lolita (1955) and was noted for his superb control of language and plot and for his satire of American mores.

Photo Jill Krementz © 1973

educated at the Tenishev Academy in his native Saint Petersburg (Leningrad); after the Russian Revolution, when he and his family went into exile, he continued his studies at Cambridge University, where he earned a B.A. in Slavic and Romance languages in 1922.

The years Nabokov spent among Russian émigré circles in Berlin (1922–37) and Paris (1937–40) constituted the first mature phase of his writing career. There he published nine complete Russian novels under the pseudonym V. Sirin. Brilliantly playful and inventive in style, tone, and point of view, these works—notably *Laughter in the Dark* (1932; Eng. trans., 1938), *Despair* (1936; Eng. trans., 1937), and *Invitation to a Beheading* (1938; Eng. trans., 1959)—revealed Nabokov's affinities with those writers, from Laurence Sterne to James Joyce, who had treated fiction as in part a game.

Before moving with his wife and son to the United States in 1940, Nabokov tested his skill as an English-language novelist by writing *The Real Life of Sebastian Knight* (1941). It, along with a stronger second English novel, *Bend Sinister* (1947), brought him both recognition (Guggenheim grants for writing in 1943 and 1952) and academic employment, first at Stanford, then at Wellesley, and finally at Cornell (1948–59), which provided the background for his satirical portrait of a bumbling Russian émigré professor, *Pnin* (1957).

Nabokov became famous in 1958 on publication of the American edition of his wildly amusing, highly idiosyncratic masterpiece *Lolita* (first published in Paris, 1955; film, 1962). This success gave him financial independence—he abandoned his teaching career for full-time writing and moved to Switzerland in 1959—and provided him with an opportunity to prepare English-language versions of his Russian novels. His reputation reached a peak with the appearance of *Pale Fire* (1962). Consisting of a 999-line poem supposedly written by a recently deceased American poet and an extensive commentary supposedly written by one of the poet's university colleagues, the novel becomes at another level the confession of a mad king exiled from a country much like Russia.

The idea of obsession with forbidden erotic pleasures found in *Lolita* was explored even more fully in *Ada* (1969), a fictional narrator's memoir, written when he is in his nineties, memorializing his long love affair with his sister. *The Enchanter*, an early novel using the Lolita theme, was brilliantly translated by Nabokov's son Dmitry and published in 1986.

Nabuco, Joaquim [nuh-boo-ku, zhwah-keem'] Joaquim Aurelio Barreto Nabuco de Araujo, b. Aug. 19, 1849, d. Jan. 17, 1910, a Brazilian writer and diplomat, was a leader in the fight to abolish slavery in Brazil. He helped secure a partial and gradual emancipation bill in 1871, founded the Brazilian Antislavery Society in 1880, and wrote extensively about slavery, which was finally abolished in Brazil in 1888. Although a monarchist, Nabuco served the Brazilian republic as ambassador to the United States (1905–10).

Nadar [nah-dahr'] Nadar, the pseudonym of Frenchman Gaspard Félix Tournachon, b. Apr. 6, 1820, d. Mar. 15, 1910, won fame as a journalist, caricaturist, and portrait photographer and was one of the liveliest personalities of Second Empire Paris. His caricatures first appeared in the 1840s in leading periodicals, and culminated in *Le Panthéon Nadar* (1854), a collection of 270 biting lampoons of contemporary figures. In 1853, as an aid to this continuing project, he began to make portrait photographs. Nadar's reputation as a spirited iconoclast was enhanced by his exploits in his enormous balloon, *Le Géant*—he had already made the world's first aerial photographs (1858) from a balloon—and by the loan of his studio to the impressionist painters for their first, notorious exhibition (1874).

Nadelman, Elie [nah'-dul-muhn] Elie Nadelman, b. Warsaw, Feb. 20, 1882, d. Dec. 28, 1946, was a Polish-American sculptor whose sophisticated neoclassical interpretations of ancient Greek art gained considerable attention in the early 20th century. On a trip to Munich in 1904, Nadelman first encountered classical sculpture and 18th- and 19th-century folk-art dolls. In Paris (1904–14), he became familiar with the work of Michelangelo and Auguste Rodin as well as with modern trends in art. His Parisian sculptures, often inspired by Hellenistic art, were primarily abstractions of the human form. Nadelman immigrated (1914) to the United States at the outbreak of World War I. His initial works, such as *Wounded Bull* (1915; Museum of Modern Art, New York City), were favorably received, partly because of the sponsorship of cosmetics queen Helena Rubinstein. The bronze *Man in The Open Air* (c.1915; Museum of Modern Art) and the elegant bronze and marble *Sur la Plage* (1917; Whitney Museum of American Art, New York City) are typical of Nadelman's mature sculpture.

Nader, Ralph Ralph Nader, b. Winsted, Conn., Feb. 27, 1934, is a lawyer who has, since the mid-1960s, been a leading figure in the U.S. CONSUMER PROTECTION movement. A graduate of Princeton and Harvard Law School, Nader began to gain national attention in 1966 after testifying before Congress on auto safety. He maintained that defective design was a major cause of accidents and injuries, a thesis presented in his book *Unsafe at Any Speed* (1965). His testimony was influential in the passage of the National Traffic and Motor Vehicle Safety Act (1966), which brought car design under federal control.

Nader's efforts were also instrumental in the passage of the Wholesome Meat Act (1967) and of legislation on issues such as natural-gas-pipeline safety and radiation-hazards control. By 1968 he had mobilized college students, nicknamed "Nader's Raiders," in study groups that investigated the activities of government regulatory agencies. These studies were organized in 1969 as part of Nader's Center for Study of Responsive Law. In 1971, Nader founded a consumer lobbying group, Public Citizen, Inc., which in turn sponsored other organizations.

Consumer advocate Ralph Nader testifies (May 1979) before a congressional subcommittee on environment, energy, and natural resources following an accident at Three Mile Island (Penn.) nuclear power plant. Since the 1960s, Nader has discovered and published information on many consumer hazards.

Nadir Shah [nah-dir' shah] One of the great Asian conquerors, Nadir Shah, b. Oct. 22, 1688, d. June 19, 1747, shah of Iran from 1736 to 1747, founded Iran's short-lived Afshar dynasty. A magnificent cavalry leader, he rose rapidly amid the chaos accompanying the disintegration of the Safavid dynasty, expelling Iran's Afghan rulers and placing (1732) Abbas III, the infant son of the last Safavid, on the throne, with himself as regent.

In 1736, Nadir assumed the imperial title. He warred with virtually all neighboring states. In the west he defeated the Ottoman Turks and took Baghdad in 1733; in the north he repulsed Russia in the Caucasus; in the east he smashed India's Mogul armies in 1739, occupied Delhi, and returned to Iran with booty that included the Koh-i-noor diamond and the Peacock Throne. A harsh, unskilled administrator who tolerated no opposition, Nadir Shah blinded his own son and heir. He was assassinated by disgruntled religious leaders and army officers.

Nag Hammadi Papyri [nahk hah-mah'-dee]

The Nag Hammadi Papyri are a group of gnostic documents that constitute the only significant body of gnostic works known to modern scholars. Discovered in a jar in a field near Chenoboskion, Egypt, in 1945, they include 49 treatises, of which 5 are duplicates. The treatises, which are Coptic translations from Greek originals, are bound in 13 leather volumes and have been variously dated between the 3d and 5th centuries AD. All but one are in the Coptic Museum in Cairo; the other is in the Jung Institute, Zurich.

Since their discovery the documents have been of primary importance in the study of GNOSTICISM, which was previously based largely on hostile reports by the early Fathers of the Church. Among the works are the *Gospel of Truth*, a treatise on Christian life and salvation, possibly by VALENTINUS; the *Apocryphon of John*, which reinterprets the first chapter of Genesis in cryptic mythological terms; and the *Gospel of Thomas*, a collection of sayings and discourses of Jesus.

Naga [nah'-guh]

In Hindu and Buddhist mythology a Naga is a deified serpent usually having a human head. Nagas are the guardians of raindrops, pearls, or the elixir of immortality, and their images are worshiped during droughts. Their women are believed to seduce mortal men. In Buddhist legend a Naga protected the Buddha from a storm after his enlightenment, and his alms bowl was a gift from the Nagas.

Nagaland

Nagaland is a mountainous state in northeastern India, bordering Burma to the east. It has an area of 16,488 km² (6,366 mi²) and a population of 774,930 (1981). Kohima is the capital. The economy is based on agriculture. A number of tribes occupying the Naga hills, known as the Naga, speak related Tibeto-Burman languages. Relations between various Naga lineages were traditionally ordered in terms of complex rules concerning marriage; feuds between lineages often involved the practice of head-hunting.

After Burmese domination, the Naga hills were taken over by the British between 1865 and 1880, and practices such as head-hunting were banned. Since then, the traditional culture of the Naga has been in decline, and

most of the Naga have converted to Christianity. When India became independent in 1947, Naga nationalists were unsuccessful in establishing a sovereign state. In response to various attempts to gain independence from Indian rule, including a series of military uprisings, Nagaland was made a separate Indian state in 1963. Despite a 1975 cease-fire accord and substantial economic aid, sporadic guerrilla activities continue.

Nagasaki [nahg-uh-sah'-kee]

Nagasaki, an industrial port city of Japan, is located on the western shore of Kyushu on the East China Sea, about 950 km (590 mi) southeast of Tokyo. The population is 449,149 (1987 est.). Nagasaki was the second of the two cities (the first being Hiroshima) on which an atomic bomb was dropped in World War II. Iron and steel production, machine building, metalworking, and shipbuilding are major manufacturing activities.

Nagasaki is Japan's oldest port. After Portuguese traders and missionaries arrived in the 16th century, it became a center of Christianity. The Dutch were permitted to establish a trading post in Nagasaki in 1609. From 1638 to the mid-19th century, when Japan was isolated from foreign contacts by the Tokugawa shogunate, Dutch traders were allowed to remain on an island in Nagasaki harbor; thus Nagasaki continued its commercial relations with the outside world. By the Kanagawa Treaty of 1859, Nagasaki became a treaty port.

On Aug. 9, 1945, a U.S. bomber dropped an atomic bomb on Nagasaki. The bomb missed its target, the Mitsubishi shipyards, but destroyed about half the city and killed approximately 75,000 people. A Peace Park commemorates the victims.

Nagorno-Karabakh [nah-gawr'-noh-kah-rah-bahk']

Nagorno-Karabakh is an autonomous oblast of Azerbaijan, in the USSR. Its capital is Stepanakert. Of its total population of 186,000 (1989 est.), 80 percent are ethnic Armenians. In 1988 and 1989, when the Soviet system began to loosen up under the Gorbachev regime, a movement for union with Armenia developed in Nagorno-Karabakh. Fighting erupted between Armenians and Azerbaijanis, and troops were sent to the area. The Soviet government vetoed any change in the status of Nagorno-Karabakh, which remained in a state of revolt.

Nagoya [nah-goh'-yah]

Nagoya is the fourth largest city in Japan, with a population of 2,149,517 (1989 est.). It is located on the Nobi plain at the head of Ise Bay in south central Honshu. An industrial city, Nagoya produces electrical machinery, precision instruments, automobiles, textiles, ceramics, chemicals, and plywood. Its port receives mostly raw materials and exports semimanufactured and manufactured goods. Train service connects Nagoya with Tokyo in the east and Osaka in the west. Nagoya is the home of Nagoya University (1939). Points of interest include the Nagoya Castle, built in

1610, an art museum, botanical gardens, and the Atsuta Shrine. During the Tokugawa period (1603–1868) Nagoya was a feudal castle town.

Nagpur [nahg'-poor]   Nagpur, a city in the state of Maharashtra, India, lies in the heart of the Deccan Plateau about 700 km (435 mi) east-northeast of Bombay. A transportation, trade, and industrial center, Nagpur has a population of 1,219,461 (1984 est.). Formerly the capital of Maratha Bhonslas (1743), of the British Central Province (1861–1947), and of the Madhya Pradesh state of India (1947–56), it is now the headquarters of Nagpur district. The University of Nagpur (1923) is there. Sitabaldi Hill Fort and the ruins of the Bhonsla Palace are historic landmarks.

Nagurski, Bronko [nah-gurs'-kee]   Bronislaw "Bronko" Nagurski, b. Rainy River, Ontario, Nov. 3, 1908, d. Jan. 7, 1990, was an American college and professional football player renowned as a hard-running fullback. Nagurski, who grew up in International Falls, Minn., was an All-American tackle and occasional fullback at the University of Minnesota during the years 1927–29. He joined the Chicago Bears in 1930 and played both positions until 1937. As a fullback the 6-ft 2-in (1-m 88-cm), 225-lb (102-kg) Nagurski earned a reputation as one of football's most unstoppable runners. He gained 4,031 yd (3,667 m) rushing during his career, and he was a capable passer as well. Nagurski became a charter member of the Pro Football Hall of Fame in 1963.

Nagy, Imre [nahj, im'-re]   A Hungarian Communist statesman, Imre Nagy, b. June 7, 1896, d. June 30, 1958, became the symbol of nationalism and independence in the HUNGARIAN REVOLUTION of 1956. A Communist since World War I, Nagy was in exile in the USSR from 1929 to 1944, when he returned to Hungary. He served in various ministerial positions, and in 1953 he became premier. He was ousted in 1955 for being too independent of Moscow. During the Hungarian Revolution he again became premier and proclaimed Hungary's neutrality. After the revolution was crushed, Nagy was arrested (November 1956) by the Soviets and later executed. In June 1989, Nagy was reburied in a state funeral attended by 300,000 people, and the following month the Hungarian Supreme Court repealed the treason verdict against him.

Nahum, Book of [nay'-uhm]   The Book of Nahum, seventh of the 12 minor prophetic books in the Old Testament of the Bible, probably dates from shortly after the destruction of Assyria in 612 BC, although the book is cast in the form of a prophecy of events yet to unfold.

The prophet Nahum described the conquest of the oppressive Assyrians by the Medes and Babylonians, presenting their fall as the righteous judgment of Yahweh.

Unlike other prophets, Nahum did not apply his condemnation of wickedness to Israel itself.

naiad [nay'-ad]   *Naiad* is the name given to the aquatic, gill-breathing NYMPH, or immature stage, of certain insects, including dragonflies, damselflies, mayflies, and stoneflies. These insects undergo a type of simple metamorphosis, called hemimetabolous metamorphosis, in which aquatic young become aerial adults without passing through a pupal stage.

nail (anatomy)   SEE HOOF, NAIL, AND CLAW

nail (carpentry)   Nails are fasteners used to attach wood to wood and to hold together other materials. Usually made of steel, they may also be made of brass, iron, and many other metals.

A nail has three parts: the head, which receives the driving blows; the shank, or body; and the point. Most nails have a broad, circular head; finishing nails have narrow heads, allowing them to be countersunk, or hidden in the wood; and upholstery nails have decorative heads. A brad is a nail with almost no head. The most common shank is round and smooth.

Early nails were hand-forged from copper, and later from bronze and iron; forging was common until the 19th

Different nails are made for special uses. Box nails are thinner than common nails of the same length and are used for hardwoods. Threaded or ringed nails provide increased grip strength. Plasterboard and roofing nails have wide heads to secure wallboards and shingles.

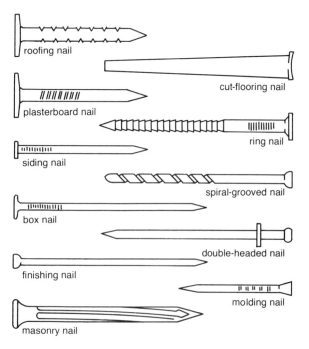

century. As early as the late 16th century, however, machines had been devised that could slice and flatten iron bars into strips called nail rods, out of which pointed, headed nails were forged. The wire-nail machine was invented (1835) by the French. Today almost all nails are cut out of metal wire and headed, pointed, threaded, and polished or galvanized by machine.

Naipaul, V. S. [ny-pawl]   The novelist and essayist Vidiadhar Surajprasad Naipaul, b. of Indian parents in Trinidad, Aug. 17, 1932, is among the greatest living writers of English. His early novels—notably *A House for Mr. Biswas* (1961)—focused on West Indian life. The theme of expatriate alienation is developed in *The Mimic Men* (1967) and *In a Free State* (1971). *Guerrillas* (1975) is the grim tale of a failed black-power movement on a West Indian island. *A Bend in the River* (1979) is a bleak description of life in postcolonial Africa. In *The Enigma of Arrival* (1987) he transforms the memories of his first years in England into fiction. Naipaul's essays are collected in such volumes as *India: A Wounded Civilization* (1977), *The Return of Eva Perón* (1980), and *Among the Believers: An Islamic Journey* (1981). *A Turn in the South* (1989) is Naipaul's leisurely rendition of a trip through the U.S. South.

Nairn [nairn]   Nairn is a former county in northeastern Scotland, along the southern shore of Moray Firth. The terrain is rugged, so agriculture is limited to livestock raising and dairying, except along the coast. Near Nairn, the former county town, is Cawdor Castle, the traditional site of King Duncan's murder by Macbeth. In 1975, during the administrative reorganization of Scotland, Nairn became a part of the HIGHLAND region.

Nairobi [ny-roh'-bee]   Nairobi, the capital city of Kenya, is located in the south central part of the country. Its population is 1,429,000 (1989 est.). The city is primarily an administrative and service center. Tourism centers on adjacent Nairobi National Park (1948), a noted game reserve. Due to its service facilities and excellent communications and transportation connections, Nairobi is the East African headquarters for many multinational operations. Industrial activity includes food processing, metal fabrication, and textile manufacturing. The National Museum of Kenya, the National Theater, and the University of Nairobi (1954) are in the city.

The city was founded as a railroad construction camp in the late 1890s. In 1905 it was made the capital of the British East Africa Protectorate, and in 1963 it became the capital of the independent nation of Kenya.

Naismith, James [nay'-smith]   Dr. James A. Naismith, b. Almonte, Ontario, Nov. 6, 1861, d. Nov. 28, 1939, invented the sport of basketball as an alternative to gymnastics while he was a physical-education instruc-

tor at the Young Men's Christian Association in Springfield, Mass. In December 1891, using peach baskets nailed to balconies at opposite ends of the gym, and a soccer ball, Naismith coached the first games. In 1892 he published a booklet containing the basic rules still in use today. Springfield's Basketball Hall of Fame (1959) is named for him.

Nakasone Yasuhiro   Nakasone Yasuhiro, b. May 27, 1918, was elected prime minister of Japan in November 1982, succeeding Suzuki Zenko. A member of the right wing of the ruling Liberal-Democratic party, he served in the House of Representatives and held a number of high government and party posts during the 1960s and 1970s. Nakasone, who became head of government with the political backing of former prime minister Tanaka Kakuei, insisted that Japan play an active role in international affairs befitting its stature as a world economic power. After he led his party to a landslide victory in the July 1986 parliamentary elections, a party rule requiring his retirement in 1986 was changed to extend his term to October 1987.

Namath, Joe [nay'-muhth]   Hall of Fame member Joe Willie "Broadway Joe" Namath, b. Beaver Falls, Pa., May 31, 1943, played U.S. professional football and was one of the most spectacular quarterbacks in the game's history. He played for the University of Alabama (1962–64) and professionally with the New York Jets. In 1969 he aroused strong feelings when he "guaranteed" that his team would defeat the heavily favored Baltimore Colts in Super Bowl III. He then directed the Jets to a 16–7 upset. Namath, who was hampered by knee injuries, set (1967) what was then a one-season record by passing for 4,007 yd. After 12 seasons with the Jets he was traded to the Los Angeles Rams, where he played for one year and then retired. During his 13-year career he completed 1,886 passes for 27,663 yd (25,295 m) and 218 touchdowns. Namath is a charismatic, colorful figure who has cultivated a second career in show business.

Namib Desert [nah'-mib]   The Namib Desert stretches along the southwest coast of Africa, from Angola in the north, through Namibia, into South Africa. The name means "place of nothing." About 1,700 km (1,060 mi) long and 100 km (60 mi) wide, covering an area of about 170,000 km^2 (85,640 mi^2), the desert is bordered by the Atlantic Ocean on the west and the Great Escarpment on the east. It rises from sea level to 914 m (3,000 ft). In the north deep canyons have been cut by ephemeral streams. Sands, varying from yellow to red in color, form dunes reaching 240 m (800 ft) in height. Annual rainfall averages only 25 mm (1 in), but high humidity results in fog and dew. Temperatures average 16° C (60° F). The desert is sparsely populated by SAN hunters and by KHOIKHOI, who herd sheep and goats. Diamonds, tungsten, and salt are mined.

REPUBLIC OF NAMIBIA

Land: Area: 824,290 km² (318,260 mi²), including Walvis Bay. Capital and largest city: Windhoek (1988 est. pop., 114,000).

People: Population (1990 est.): 1,452,951. Density: 1.8 persons per km² (4.6 per mi²). Distribution (1988): 30% urban, 70% rural. Official language: English. Major religions: Christianity, traditional religions.

Government: Type: republic. Legislature: National Assembly. Political subdivisions: regional councils.

Economy: GNP (1988): $1.19 billion; $950 per capita. Labor distribution (1987): commercial agriculture—16%; industry and commerce—17%; services—8%; government—11%; mining—4%. Foreign trade (1988): imports—$692 million; exports—$756 million. Currency: 1 South African rand = 100 cents.

Education and Health: Literacy (1984 est.): whites—100% ; blacks—38%. Universities (1990): 1. Hospital beds (1988): 7,542. Physicians (1988): 250. Life expectancy (1990): women—63; men—57. Infant mortality (1990): 71 per 1,000 live births.

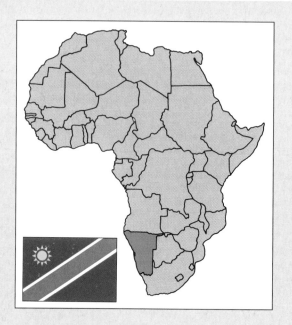

Namibia [nah-mib'-ee-uh] Namibia (formerly South West Africa) is a vast, sparsely populated country on the southwestern coast of Africa. It is bordered by Botswana and Zimbabwe on the east, Angola and Zambia on the north, and South Africa on the south. Namibia gained its independence on Mar. 21, 1990, after more than a century of foreign domination and international intervention. WINDHOEK is the capital.

Land, People, and Economy

Namibia is mainly arid or semiarid. The Namib Desert extends along the entire coastline. A semiarid mountainous plateau ranging in altitude from 1,000 to 2,000 m (3,280 to 6,500 ft) covers the central part of the interior. To the east are low-lying extensions of the KALAHARI DESERT and the Karoo desert. Along the border with Angola are bush-covered plains, including the fairly high rainfall areas of Kavango and the eastern CAPRIVI STRIP. The perennial rivers are on the borders: the ORANGE RIVER in the south and the Kunene, Kavango, ZAMBEZI, and Kwando-Linyanti rivers in the north. The country's high point, Brandberg, rises to 2,573 m (8,400 ft).

Although Namibia is one of the most sparsely populated countries in Africa, it has a diverse population. Its 11 ethnic groups are, in order of size: the Ovambo (who live primarily in the north and constitute nearly 50% of the total population), Kavango, whites (mainly persons of South African and German origin), HERERO, Damara, Nama (see KHOIKHOI), Coloureds, Capriviane, SAN, Bast-

ers, and Tswana. Most of the people live in the north, where they are engaged in subsistence agriculture. Many Ovambo men are employed as migrant laborers in white-owned mines and farms to the south, and unemployment is high. Because of the inequitable distribution of land and resources, the majority of the people are poor. (Before independence, Namibia had been run as an extension of South Africa. Whites owned 65% of all private property, and social services for blacks in rural areas had been seriously neglected.) In addition, the violence accompanying the independence struggle disrupted many aspects of normal life.

Namibia's economy is based on mineral exports—gem-quality diamonds and base metals—and agriculture and fisheries products. Much of the profit from exports has gone to South African or international interests. Almost all manufactured goods are imported. WALVIS BAY, Namibia's chief port, is still occupied by South Africa despite Namibian claims, and economic ties with South Africa remain strong. During the period of South African occupation, nearly 100,000 troops were stationed in Namibia; the government is heavily indebted because of high military expenditures during the 1980s. At independence, Namibia's new leaders declared their support for a mixed economy and sought foreign investment.

History and Government

The earliest known inhabitants of Namibia are the San, whose presence dates back about 11,000 years. In the mid-1400s, Bantu-speaking peoples from East Africa began migrating southwestward to Angola and northern Namibia. By the early 1700s, they had pushed into the central Namibian plateau.

The first European to visit the area, the Portuguese explorer Diogo Cão, arrived at Cape Cross in 1485. Soon after, the Dutch East India Company (see EAST INDIA COMPANY, DUTCH) began exploring the Namibian coast from its station at Table Bay. In 1773 the Cape government proclaimed Dutch sovereignty over Angra Pequina (Ludderitz), Halifax Island, and Walvis Bay. The Cape Colony and all its possessions were formally ceded to Britain in 1814.

By the early 1800s, British and German missionaries arrived in the interior. Namibia became a German colony (German South West Africa) in 1884, although the British had annexed Walvis Bay in 1878. The German settlers expropriated African lands and assigned Africans to reserves. Between 1904 and 1907, Herero and Nama rebellions against German land policies were brutally suppressed. The Herero were reduced from 80,000 to 15,000, and the Nama from 20,000 to 9,000.

During World War I, South African troops invaded Namibia and forced the Germans to surrender. Namibia (then South West Africa) was administered by South Africa under a League of Nations mandate. After World War II, in defiance of the international community, the South African government refused to hand over administration of Namibia to the United Nations. It ruled the territory di-

rectly for much of the period prior to independence and established a society based on separation of the races (APARTHEID). Nationalist resistance groups formed in the 1950s and '60s, and in 1966 the South West African Peoples Organization (SWAPO) took up arms. The UN General Assembly formally terminated the South African mandate in 1966 and changed the name of the territory to Namibia in 1968; UN Resolution 435 of 1978 set forth a formula for Namibian independence following UN-supervised elections. Pressure from the international community and escalation of the fighting along the Angolan border by Cuban forces persuaded South Africa in

(Above) *These women display banners celebrating Namibian independence, which finally became a reality on Mar. 21, 1990, with SWAPO leader Sam Nujoma as the first president.* (Below) *This giant variety of* Euphorbia *is one of the few large plants able to withstand the severe climate of the Namib desert.*

1988 to accept Resolution 435 as a framework for independence. A UN-supervised cease-fire took effect on Apr. 1, 1989, and elections were held in November for an assembly to prepare a constitution for an independent Namibia. The constitution established a multiparty democracy headed by an executive president limited to two 5-year terms and made the practice of apartheid a criminal offense. On Mar. 21, 1990, Namibia became an independent nation, with SWAPO leader Sam NUJOMA as executive president. The constituent assembly converted itself into the National Assembly (lower house of parliament). An upper house (the National Council) was to be created in 1992.

Namur [nah-moor'] Namur, a city in south central Belgium at the junction of the Sambre and Meuse rivers, is the capital of Namur province. It has a population of 103,104 (1988 est.). A rail and industrial center, Namur manufactures glass, leather, paper goods, steel, and cement. The city's historic churches include the 17th-century Church of Saint Loup and the Convent of the Sisters of Our Lady. First mentioned in the 7th century as a Merovingian fortress, Namur was the seat of the counts of Namur from 908 until 1420, when it passed to Burgundy. Much fought over in the wars of the 18th century, it passed back and forth between France and the Netherlands. In 1830 it became part of independent Belgium.

Nancy [nahn-see'] Nancy, the major commercial center of France's Lorraine region (see ALSACE-LORRAINE), is located on the Meurthe River and the Marne-Rhine Canal about 280 km (175 mi) east of Paris. The population of the city is 96,317 (1982); that of the metropolitan area is 306,982. Located in France's foremost iron-mining and industrial region, Nancy produces glassware, electrical equipment, metal products, tobacco, shoes, iron, beer, and textiles.

Nancy has long been a strategic site on the Paris-Strasbourg route. The focus of the city is an attractive public square developed by the architect Emmanuel Héré in the 18th century under a commission from Stanisław I Leszczynski, the former king of Poland who became duke of Lorraine (1737–66). The University of Nancy (1572) is in the city.

Nancy was the capital of the dukes of Lorraine from the 12th to the 18th century except for a short period of French control (1633–97). After the death of Stanisław in 1766, Nancy was reunited with France. It was occupied by the Germans during both world wars.

Nanjing (Nanking) [nan-jing] Nanjing, the capital of Jiangsu province, east central China, has a population of 2,390,000 (1988 est.). The city straddles the Chang Jiang at the western apex of an inverted triangle formed by itself, Shanghai (east), and Hangzhou (south). The triangle is the core of the fertile Chang Jiang delta. Nan-

jing's geographical position has made it the capital of many regional kingdoms and, at times, of the entire country. It received its present name in 1441.

Nanjing is the political, economic, cultural, and transportation center of Jiangsu province. Manufactures include chemicals, iron and steel, refined petroleum by-products, automobiles, machinery, textiles, electronics, cement, and processed food. The city is the site of Nanjing University (1902).

Nanjing is very rich in historical sites, relics, and scenic features, including the gates of the old city wall, the Xuanwu Lake, the Yuhua Terrace, the Mausoleum of Sun Yat-sen (founder of the Republic of China), the tombs of the Ming emperors, the Ziqin (Purple Gold) Hills, the Ling Ge Temple, and the Maizhou Lake.

Nanjing was the capital of the Six Dynasties (during the Period of Disunion, 220–589) and the early MING dynasty. In 1842 the Treaty of Nanjing, opening China to limited trade with the West, was signed there. Nanjing was the rebel capital (1853–64) during the TAIPING REBELLION and capital of the Republic of China from 1928 to 1937 and again from 1945 to 1949. When the city fell to the Japanese in 1937, at least 40,000 civilians were massacred in what became known as the "rape of Nanjing." Japan officially surrendered to China in Nanjing on Sept. 9, 1945. Communist forces captured the city in 1949 and transferred the capital to Beijing.

Nanni di Banco [nahn'-ee dee bahn'-koh] The Florentine sculptor Nanni di Banco (Giovanni di Antonio di Banco), b. c.1384, d. Feb. 12, 1421, was one of the most important artists of the early Renaissance and with Donatello and Lorenzo Ghiberti one of the founding fathers of Italian Renaissance sculpture. He was among the first masters to reject the formulas of the Late Gothic style and to look instead to ancient classical art for inspiration. The powerful, life-size statues of Nanni's major work, the heroic marble group entitled *Quattro Santi Coronati*, or *Four Crowned Saints* (c.1411–14), at Orsanmichele in Florence, show a new Roman-inspired grandeur and monumentality.

Nansen, Fridtjof [nahn'-suhn, frit'-yawf] Fridtjof Nansen, b. Oct. 10, 1861, d. May 13, 1930, was a Norwegian explorer of the Arctic, an oceanographer, and a humanitarian. Nansen made his first voyage through Arctic waters in 1882. In order to prove that the interior of Greenland was ice-covered, Nansen skiied (1888) across the island from east to west, becoming the first person to do so. To prove his theory that an ocean current flowed across the Arctic Ocean from Siberia, he proposed to drift with the pack ice across the North Pole in a specially constructed ice-resistant boat, the *Fram*. The expedition sailed north from Norway on June 24, 1893. The *Fram* froze in the waters off Siberia on Sept. 22 and began to drift; it reached Norway on Sept. 9, 1896. Nansen left the ship, hoping to reach the North Pole by skis, kayak, and dogsled, but when this proved impossible, he and his party returned to Norway. The expedition had, however, confirmed Nansen's original theory.

Following World War I, Nansen was appointed Norway's representative to the League of Nations, a post he held until his death. In 1921 he became the league's commissioner for refugees, and in recognition of his work he received the Nobel Peace Prize in 1922.

Nantes [nahnt] Nantes is a city in west central France, on the Loire River, about 360 km (225 mi) southwest of Paris and 55 km (35 mi) from the Bay of Biscay. The city has a population of 237,789 (1982). Nantes and its seaport, Saint-Nazaire, form a major industrial region of western France, concentrating on port activities and shipbuilding. A ship canal to Saint-Nazaire was built in 1891, and the port facilities in Nantes were improved following World War I. Other major industrial activities in Nantes include sugar and fish processing and textile, glass, iron, and ship-supply manufacturing.

Nantes was the main city of the Namnètes, an early Gallic tribe, prior to the conquest of Gaul by the Romans. Vikings (Normans) raided the area during the 9th century, causing extensive destruction. The city became part of the duchy of Brittany, which was formally incorporated in France in 1532. The Edict of Nantes, signed there in 1598, granted certain civil and religious liberties to Protestants. The Nantes area was of strategic importance during World War II, partly because of the Nazi submarine pens at Saint-Nazaire.

Nantes, Edict of The Edict of Nantes, establishing the legal toleration of Calvinism in Roman Catholic France, was authorized by King HENRY IV on Apr. 13, 1598. It resulted from hard bargaining with the HUGUENOTS (Calvinists) and marked the end of the Wars of Religion (see RELIGION, WARS OF).

The edict declared liberty of conscience and equality of legal and educational rights. It allowed French Protestants to hold government office and provided special courts to adjudicate disputes between the faiths. The Protestants were also given control of certain fortress towns, such as La Rochelle, whose garrisons were paid by the crown. Protestant public worship was allowed in these and other specified towns.

In the Peace of Alès (1629), which followed three revolts by the Huguenots, Cardinal RICHELIEU modified the edict; the Huguenots lost their capacity for armed self-defense. On Oct. 18, 1685, LOUIS XIV withdrew the edict and declared France entirely Catholic.

Nantucket Island Nantucket Island, which lies in the Atlantic Ocean about 40 km (25 mi) south of Cape Cod, is the southeasternmost point of Massachusetts. The island has an area of about 120 km^2 (45 mi^2) and a population of 6,012 (1990). With neighboring Muskeget and Tuckernuck islands, it forms Nantucket County. The principal village and port is Nantucket, notable for its

well-preserved colonial houses and whaling museum; other villages include Siasconset and Polpis. The historical buildings, sandy beaches, and resort facilities attract many summer vacationers.

Discovered in 1602, Nantucket was settled in 1659 by British Quakers. From 1664 to 1692 it was part of New York. During the 1700s and early 1800s, Nantucket was one of the world's great whaling ports.

---

napalm [nay'-pahm] A military incendiary substance, napalm is a mixture of gasoline and other fuels with a gelling agent. A napalm-armed bomb or a flamethrower broadcasts the burning substance over a wide area, where it adheres to whatever it touches and burns with an intense heat. Napalm was used during World War II and the Korean War, but its employment as the prime incendiary during the Vietnam War was widely protested, and a major napalm manufacturer, the Dow Chemical Company, was picketed and boycotted by members of the anti–Vietnam War movement. The word *napalm* is an acronym derived from the naphthenic and palmitic acids from which the gelling agent is made.

---

naphtha [naf'-thuh] Naphtha is any of various liquid hydrocarbon mixtures obtained from coal tar, petroleum, or oil shale. The use of controlled-temperature equipment yields naphthas of various boiling ranges. These distillation fractions, although mixtures themselves, are useful for dissolving or diluting other organic compounds. In addition to their use as solvents and diluents, naphthas are also used as raw material for the production of gasoline.

naphthalene see COAL TAR

Napier, John [nay'-peer] John Napier, b. 1550, d. Apr. 4, 1617, a Scottish mathematician, was the inventor of LOGARITHMS. In 1614, Napier published his *Mirifici logarithmorum canonis descriptio* (A Description of the Marvelous Canon of Logarithms), which contained a description of logarithms, a set of tables, and rules for their use. Napier hoped that, by means of his logarithms, he would save astronomers much time and free them from the "slippery errors" of calculations. His tables of logarithms of trigonometric functions were used for almost a century. Napier also made contributions to spherical trigonometry, found exponential expressions for trigonometric functions, and was influential in the introduction of the decimal notation for fractions.

Naples [nay'-pulz] Naples (Italian: Napoli), the capital of Naples province and of Campania region in southern Italy, is located about 190 km (120 mi) southwest of Rome. It has a population of 1,202,582 (1989 est.), making it the third largest city in Italy.

Contemporary City. Naples is the commercial and cultural heart of the *Mezzogiorno*, Italy's south, and an important highway and railroad junction. Its busy port handles more passenger traffic than any other port in the country. Industries manufacture iron and steel products, ships, electronics equipment, processed foods, textiles, leather goods, railroad machinery, and chemicals. Petroleum is also refined.

A major source of income is tourism. Visitors are attracted by Naples's warm climate, its natural beauty, and many nearby points of interest, which include Vesuvius, Pompeii, Herculaneum, and Capri. Within the city are five medieval castles and more than 200 churches, foremost of which is the Cathedral of San Gennaro (begun 8th century).

The University of Naples, founded in 1224, was one of the great centers of scholarship in the Middle Ages. Naples also has an academy of fine arts, the prestigious National Library, and the National Museum. The city has been traditionally associated with Italian music, especially with *bel canto* and with *opera buffa*, a comic opera that originated there in the mid-18th century. Among the contemporary musical institutions are a music school and a major opera company, housed in the Teatro San Carlo (built 1737).

Despite its great natural beauty, Naples has had some of the worst slum areas of Europe. After a catastrophic cholera epidemic in 1884, many parts of the city were demolished, but the slums were not eradicated. Since World War II considerable slum clearance and urban rebuilding have taken place, but the city's continuing population growth has resulted in a chronic housing shortage.

History. Founded by Greek colonists in about 600 BC, the original colony of Naples was soon replaced by a "new city"—hence the ancient name Neapolis. In the following centuries, Neapolis became a center of Greek culture in southern Italy. In 326 BC the city fell to the Romans, under whom it continued to prosper. The poet Vergil lived there in the 1st century BC, and many Roman emperors, including Nero in the 1st century AD and Hadrian and Marcus Aurelius in the 2d century, made Naples their favorite resort. After the collapse (476) of the Roman Empire, the city was conquered first by Ostrogoths, then by Lombards, and in the 6th century by Byzantines. From 763 until 1139, Naples was an independent duchy, but in 1139 the Norman rulers of Sicily annexed it to their domain. In 1282 the city became the capital of the Kingdom of Naples, which survived (despite periods of foreign domination) until 1860. It was then incorporated into the newly unified Italy.

Naples, Kingdom of   The Kingdom of Naples had its origins in the Norman-Swabian Kingdom of Sicily, founded by Roger II, king of Sicily, in the 12th century. With the accession of the Hohenstaufen Holy Roman emperor Henry VI to the throne of Sicily in 1194, the stage was set for a long series of conflicts between his son, Frederick II, and the papacy—especially popes Gregory IX and Innocent IV. Determined to eliminate the Hohenstaufen presence in Italy, the papacy offered the crown to Charles of Anjou in 1263; he ruled Naples and Sicily as Charles I from 1268.

In 1282 a revolt on the island of Sicily, the Sicilian Vespers, resulted in the separation of the island from the mainland kingdom; the Kingdom of Naples remained under the rule of the Angevins, while the Spanish house of Aragon was established in Sicily. In 1302, Charles II of Naples was forced to recognize Aragonese control of Sicily.

Following the death (1435) of Joan II, the last Angevin ruler of Naples, Alfonso V of Aragon defeated (1442) her adopted son, René of Anjou, and ushered in a period of Aragonese rule that lasted until the 18th century. This period was one of considerable cultural and economic development in the kingdom, although opposition to heavy taxes led to the establishment of the short-lived first Parthenopean republic in 1647. In the aftermath of the War of the Spanish Succession (1701–14), the Kingdom of Naples came under the rule of the Spanish Bourbons in the person of King Charles III. A Napoleonic army invaded the kingdom in 1799 and established the second brief Parthenopean republic; Napoleon I later (1806) gave the Neapolitan crown to his brother Joseph (see Bonaparte family), who was succeeded in 1808 by Joachim Murat, Napoleon's brother-in-law. The Spanish Bourbons were reestablished in the Kingdom of Naples in 1815, retaining their power until Italy was unified by the House of Savoy in 1860.

Napoleon I, Emperor of the French   (Napoléon Bonaparte) [nuh-poh'-lee-uhn]   Napoleon I, b. Aug. 15, 1769, d. May 5, 1821, known as Napoléon Bonaparte before he became emperor, was probably the most brilliant military figure in history. Rising to command of the French Revolutionary armies, he seized political power as first consul in 1799 and proclaimed himself emperor in 1804. He extended French rule over much of Europe, but he was finally defeated in 1814–15.

Early Life. Napoléon was born to Carlo and Letizia Buonaparte (see Bonaparte family) at Ajaccio, Corsica. He attended (1779–84) French military school at Brienne and in 1785 was commissioned a second lieutenant in artillery. Because of a conflict with the Corsican nationalist Pasquale Paoli, his family fled to Marseille in 1793. Bonaparte had welcomed the French Revolution in 1789, and in September 1793 he assumed command of an artillery brigade at the siege of Toulon. Promoted to general of brigade, Bonaparte was then assigned to the French army in Italy.

After the overthrow of the revolutionary leader Maximilien Robespierre in July 1794, Bonaparte was briefly imprisoned because he was identified with Robespierre's faction. Next year, on Oct. 5, 1795 (13 Vendémiaire under the Revolutionary calendar), a revolt against the National Convention broke out in Paris. Bonaparte, ordered by Paul Barras to defend the convention, and aided by Joachim Murat's cannons, routed the insurrectionists. In March 1796 he was appointed by the Directory commander of the Army of the Interior. Before taking up that post he married (March 9) Josephine de Beauharnais.

Italian and Egyptian Campaigns. Late in March 1796, Bonaparte began a series of operations against the Aus-

Napoleon I, emperor of the French, is portrayed by J. A. D. Ingres. A hero of the French Revolution, Napoléon Bonaparte staged the coup d'état of 18 Brumaire (1799) and rose to supreme power as first consul. On Dec. 2, 1804, he crowned himself emperor.

however, British admiral Horatio NELSON annihilated the French fleet at Abukir Bay. Thus cut off, Bonaparte continued his administrative reorganization and helped create the Institute of Egypt, which embarked on a methodical study of ancient Egypt. In the meantime, however, French forces in Europe were being defeated by the armies of the Second Coalition, and Bonaparte resolved to return to France.

First Consul. On Bonaparte's arrival in Paris on October 14, he joined Emmanuel SIEYÈS in a conspiracy to overthrow the Directory. On November 9 (18 Brumaire), Bonaparte was appointed commander of the Paris garrison and the following day accepted appointment as one of three consuls, with Sieyès and Pierre Roger Ducos. Bonaparte soon gained the position of first consul and began to concentrate power in his own hands.

During the rule of the CONSULATE more formidable legislation was completed than in any other comparable period in French history. Bonaparte centralized local government, pacified the rebellious regions of France, and participated in drawing the NAPOLEONIC CODE, a codification of the civil law. He initiated (1801) the CONCORDAT with Pope PIUS VII, which reestablished Roman Catholicism in France, and he created (1802) the order of the Legion of Honor to reward civil and military merit. Bonaparte also consolidated the national debt, balanced the budget, established the Bank of France, centralized tax collection, and created the Society for the Encouragement of National Industry. By creating the Université de France, he brought all higher education under centralized state control. His cultural concerns were reflected in the enlargement of the LOUVRE and the foundation of the Archives Nationales. These achievements were balanced by the restoration of French supremacy abroad. In June 1800, Bonaparte defeated the Austrians at Marengo, Italy, and concluded peace with them in the Treaty of Lunéville (Feb. 9, 1801). A year later the Treaty of Amiens (Mar. 27, 1802) ended war with Britain. On Aug. 2, 1802, Bonaparte was recognized by plebiscite as consul for life.

France then extended its influence into Holland (the Batavian Republic), Switzerland (the Helvetic Republic), and Savoy-Piedmont, and Bonaparte played the major role in the Imperial Recess (1803), by which the free cities and minor states of the HOLY ROMAN EMPIRE were consolidated. He also recovered Haiti (see LOUISIANA PURCHASE). As a result of these policies and his refusal to grant trade concessions to Britain, war with Britain was renewed in 1803.

Emperor. In February 1804 a British-financed plot to assassinate Bonaparte was uncovered by the former police minister Joseph FOUCHÉ. Of the leading conspirators, Jean Charles PICHEGRU died in prison and Jean Victor MOREAU fled the country. The Senate subsequently petitioned Bonaparte to establish a hereditary dynasty, and on Dec. 2, 1804, Napoleon crowned himself emperor. Believing in family ties, Napoleon placed his relatives on the thrones of several satellite states and also married them to some of the most distinguished families in Europe. In 1809, Bonaparte divorced Josephine because

trian and Sardinian armies in Italy. He won Lombardy from the Austrians, and as he was advancing on Vienna, the Austrians sued for an armistice, which was concluded at Leoben on Apr. 18, 1797. Bonaparte then negotiated the Treaty of Campo Formio (Oct. 17, 1797), ending the war of the First Coalition, the first phase of the FRENCH REVOLUTIONARY WARS. Apart from his military operations, Bonaparte also engaged in political affairs: he reorganized northern Italy to create (1797) the Cisalpine Republic and negotiated treaties with various Italian rulers.

The Directory then proposed that Bonaparte invade England, but he urged the occupation of Egypt in order to threaten British India. On May 19, 1798, he sailed out with an army of more than 35,000 troops on 350 vessels. Seizing Malta en route, he reached Egypt on July 1. He occupied Alexandria and Cairo, guaranteed Islamic law, and began to reorganize the government. On August 1,

NAPOLEONIC EMPIRE, 1812

- Napoleonic French Empire
- Dependent states
- French allies

0 — km — 1000
0 — mi — 600

Cartographic Production by Lothar Roth & Associates

she had borne him no male heir, and on Apr. 2, 1810, he married Marie Louise, daughter of the Austrian emperor Francis I. Within a year a son, François Charles Joseph Bonaparte, was born.

Meanwhile, Britain organized the Third Coalition against France (see NAPOLEONIC WARS), and Nelson destroyed most of the French-Spanish fleet in the Battle of TRAFALGAR (Oct. 21, 1805). After Napolean defeated the Austrians and Russians at the Battle of AUSTERLITZ (Dec. 26, 1805), Prussia put together the Fourth Coalition late in 1806; again Napoleon emerged victorious, and the allies had to sign the Treaties of TILSIT (July 7–9, 1807).

Obsessed with Britain's defiance, Napoleon imposed the Continental System (1806), a European-wide blockade of British trade. When Portugal refused to obey it, the French became embroiled in the Peninsular War; at the same time, Austria began the War of the Fifth Coalition, which culminated in the French victory at Wagram (July 5–6, 1809). Russia also refused to accept the Continental System, and Napoleon invaded it on June 23–24, 1812. The Russians were defeated at Borodino (September 7), but when the French reached Moscow a week later, the city was on fire. In Ocotober Napoleon ordered a retreat, and he barely managed to escape Russian encirclement. After the Russian debacle, the Sixth Coalition was formed in 1813, and Napoleon's fortunes began to turn; on October 16–19, he suffered a defeat in the so-called Battle of Nations at Leipzig, and on Mar. 31, 1814, the allies took Paris.

The Hundred Days. On April 6, Napoleon abdicated and was then exiled to the island of ELBA, where he introduced administrative, economic, and political reforms. Aware of France's dissatisfaction over the BOURBON restoration, however, Napoleon decided to return. Landing at Cannes on Mar. 1, 1815, he was greeted as the returning hero. King LOUIS XVIII fled abroad, and Napoleon occupied Paris on March 20, beginning the period called the Hundred Days. Although he proclaimed peaceful intentions, the allies immediately began to prepare for war. Napoleon then resolved to separate and attack the Prussian and Anglo-French armies in what is now Belgium but was defeated by the duke of WELLINGTON and Gebhard von BLÜCHER at WATERLOO on June 18, 1815. Abdicating for the second time on June 23, Napoleon was exiled to the island of SAINT HELENA, where he dictated his memoirs.

The Napoleonic legend was embellished by his followers, but even allowing for its exaggerations there remains no question that Napoleon I was a military genius. Although his ambition to dominate Europe cost France hundreds of thousands of lives, he created many of the institutions that form the country's modern basis. His tomb in the Invalides in Paris is a national shrine.

Napoleon III, Emperor of the French (Louis Napoléon Bonaparte) Napoleon III, b. Apr. 20, 1808, d. Jan. 9, 1873, was emperor of the French from 1852 to 1870, when he lost his throne in the FRANCO-PRUSSIAN WAR. The period of his reign is called the Second Empire.

Charles Louis Napoléon Bonaparte was the son of NAPOLEON I's brother Louis and Hortense de Beauharnais (see BONAPARTE family). On the death of Napoleon I's only son in 1832, Louis Napoléon asserted his claim to the imperial heritage. After the overthrow of King LOUIS PHILIPPE in the February Revolution of 1848, Louis Napoléon won election to the National Constituent Assembly. He soon announced his candidacy for the presidency of the Second Republic and in December was elected by an overwhelming majority.

On Dec. 2, 1851, Louis Napoléon, posing as the savior of French society from radical revolution, seized personal power. A year later he established the Second Empire and took the title Napoleon III. In 1853 he married the Spanish countess EUGÉNIE de Montijo de Guzmán; she bore him one son, Eugène Louis Napoléon, the Prince Imperial (1856–79).

In the 1850s Napoleon III governed as an authoritarian ruler. Beginning in 1860, however, he gradually transferred power to the legislature, and by 1870 France was essentially a parliamentary monarchy, the so-called Liberal Empire.

Rejecting the laissez-faire policies of his predecessors, Napoleon III undertook vast programs of public works, saw to the completion of the national railway network, encouraged formation of modern credit institutions, and negotiated a series of commercial treaties.

Foreign policy proved to be his undoing. In the 1850s, allied with Britain, he won victory over Russia in the CRIMEAN WAR and intervened in Italy (1859) in support of the nationalist war against Austria (see RISORGIMENTO). The 1860s brought a succession of reverses, however. The French endeavor (1861–67) to establish a Mexican empire under the Austrian archduke MAXIMILIAN was a di-

Napoleon III, born Louis Napoléon Bonaparte in 1808, was emperor of France from 1852 to 1870. His vast public works programs transformed Paris into a modern city and created a national rail network. Defeat in the Franco-Prussian War ended his reign.

Napoleonic Wars

The Napoleonic Wars were those waged between France under NAPOLEON I and various combinations of European nations from 1803 to 1815. They were a direct continuation of the FRENCH REVOLUTIONARY WARS (1792–1802). The object of the Allies was to halt French expansion, but only with overwhelming numbers did they finally defeat Napoleon in 1814–15.

The Treaty of Amiens (1802; see AMIENS, TREATY OF), which is usually taken to mark the end of the French Revolutionary Wars, brought only a lull in the conflict between France and the other European powers. New French encroachments led Britain to declare war in 1803. In 1805, Britain formed the Third Coalition with Austria, Russia, and Sweden. Napoleon, however, marched his army into Germany and forced the surrender (Oct. 20, 1805) of the Austrian forces at Ulm. He then advanced into Austria, occupied Vienna, and defeated the joint Austro-Russian army commanded by Marshal Mikhail KUTUZOV at the Battle of AUSTERLITZ (December 2), forcing Austrian withdrawal from the war. Shortly before, however, British admiral Horatio NELSON had annihilated a Franco-Spanish fleet in the Battle of TRAFALGAR (October 21); he had thus destroyed the French challenge to British seapower and removed the threat of a French invasion of Britain.

In 1806, in the war of the Fourth Coalition, the Prussian army was annihilated by Napoleon in the Battle of Jena-Auerstädt (Oct. 14, 1806). Napoleon then confronted the Russians at Eylau (Feb. 8, 1807) and again at Friedland (June 14). Both Prussia and Russia made peace in the humiliating Treaties of TILSIT (July 7–9).

In November and December, Napoleon's armies seized Portugal. Additional French troops occupied northern Spain, and Napoleon made his brother Joseph (see BONAPARTE family) king in May 1808. An insurrection soon encompassed the entire Iberian Peninsula, and in August the British sent a small force under Arthur Wellesley (later the duke of WELLINGTON) to support it. In 1810, Wellington's Anglo-Portuguese army finally turned back André MASSÉNA's French army on the outskirts of Lisbon in October. Wellington then took the offensive, winning the battles of Salamanca (July 22, 1812) and Vitoria (June 21, 1813). The Peninsular War ended when Wellington invaded France in late 1813.

In the meantime Austria had begun the War of the Fifth Coalition with France in April 1809, but its forces were crushed at Wagram on July 5–6.

In June 1812, Napoleon invaded Russia with forces numbering more than 450,000. The Russians under General Barclay de Tolly and later under Kutuzov retreated to Borodino. Both sides suffered staggering losses in battle there on September 7, and the Russians withdrew. Napoleon occupied Moscow on September 14, but Russian arsonists burned 80 percent of the city. The French evacuated the city on October 19, pursued by the Russian army. Napoleon withdrew from Russian territory with what was left of his starving army; only about 40,000 soldiers survived.

Following Napoleon's defeat in Russia, another coalition, the Sixth, was organized against him, and the wars

saster. In the meantime, Prussia became very powerful and defeated Austria in the SEVEN WEEKS' WAR of 1866. In 1870, Napoleon played into the hands of the Prussian chancellor Otto von BISMARCK, who provoked a French declaration of war. Defeated by the Prussians in the Battle of Sedan, Napoleon surrendered on Sept. 2, 1870. Two days later republicans in Paris proclaimed the Third Republic. After his release from Prussian captivity in 1871, Napoleon lived in retirement in England until his death.

Napoleonic Code

[nuh-poh-lee-ahn'-ik] The Napoleonic Code, or *Code Napoléon*, was the first successful attempt in modern times to produce a uniform national code of law arranged in logical order and expressed in clear, precise terminology. It was drawn up by a commission appointed by Napoleon Bonaparte in 1800, when he was First Consul of France, and was headed by Jean Jacques Régis de CAMBACÉRÈS. It was promulgated as the *Code Civil* in 1804. The code replaced the French law that had been a collection of ROMAN LAW, local customs, and ecclesiastical law.

As a codification of CIVIL LAW, it was divided—as was the Justinian Code—into three main parts dealing with persons, property, and rights and obligations. The first section covered civil and marital rights, protection of personal property, and education. The second section dealt with such topics as ownership of real property and eminent domain. Feudalism and class privileges were abolished. The third part of the code concerned inheritance, gifts, and contractual rights.

The *Code Civil* was followed by four other codes dealing with civil procedure (1807), commercial law (1808), criminal procedure (1811), and punishment (1811). It served as a model for codes in other countries, and a revised (1870) adaptation of the code is still in force in Louisiana.

of Liberation began under Russian leadership in 1813. After initial victories, Napoleon was defeated by the Allies at Leipzig (October 16–19). The Allies then entered France, and Paris capitulated on Mar. 31, 1814.

Napoleon abdicated and was exiled to the island of Elba, and the Congress of Vienna (see VIENNA, CONGRESS OF) convened to arrange a peace settlement. On Mar. 1, 1815, however, Napoleon returned to France. He organized an army to confront the English, Dutch, and Prussian forces in what is now Belgium. In the Battle of Waterloo (see WATERLOO, BATTLE OF) on June 18, Napoleon confronted the armies of the duke of Wellington and the Prussian marshal Gebhard BLÜCHER. Defeated, Napoleon retired to Paris, abdicated again, and was exiled permanently to Saint Helena.

Nara [nah'-rah] Nara, a noted historical city and the capital of Nara prefecture, Japan, lies about 40 km (25 mi) east of Osaka. The population is 338,842 (1988 est.). Nara is a major tourist and commercial center; there is also some light manufacturing. Founded in 706, ancient Nara was modeled after the Chinese Tang dynasty's capital of Xian. The city is the oldest capital of Japan; it was the seat of the imperial government from 710 to 784. Among the monuments to Chinese cultural influences in Japan is the Todai-ji (Todai Temple, completed 752), the site of the bronze Great Buddha. The Horyu-ji, built in 607, is the oldest Buddhist temple in Japan and is also believed to be the oldest wooden structure in the world.

Narbonne [nahr-buhn'] Narbonne is a city in southeastern France, 13 km (8 mi) from the Mediterranean Sea; its population is 38,222 (1982). The city is linked to the Mediterranean by canal. It serves as the trade center for the surrounding wine country and is known for Aude wines and honey. Landmarks include the unfinished Cathedral of Saint-Just (begun 1272); the 15th-century Gothic Cathedral of Saint-Sébastien; and the Palace of Archbishops (13th–14th century).

The first Roman colony in Gaul (founded 118 BC as Narbo Martius), the city was the capital of Gallia Narbonensis. Narbonne was subsequently occupied by the Visigoths, Saracens, and Franks. During the Middle Ages the southern part of the city was held by the counts of Toulouse while the north was under episcopal administration. In 1507, Narbonne was united with the French crown. During the Middle Ages Narbonne was a wealthy industrial city and Mediterranean port and an important center for Jews. Its decline resulted from the expulsion of the Jews (late 13th century), the plague (1310), and the silting up of the harbor.

Narcissus [nahr-sis'-uhs] In Greek mythology Narcissus was a beautiful youth who rejected all admirers, including the nymph ECHO, and fell in love with his reflection in a pool. He was finally transformed into the flower that bears his name. From this legend comes the term *narcissism*, meaning exclusive love of self. Psychoanalytic theory considers narcissism, which may or may not include sexual love, a normal phase of childhood; remnants of this phase in adulthood may be a factor in some neuroses.

narcissus The genus *Narcissus* of the amaryllis family, Amaryllidaceae, comprises about 26 species of spring- or fall-flowering herbs popularly called daffodils, narcissus, or jonquils. Native to Europe and North Africa, they all grow from a bulb that produces several long, narrow leaves and a single flower stalk. The flowers are usually white or yellow, with a narrow, tubular base (hypanthium), three petals and three petallike sepals (perianth), and a central cuplike appendage (corona, cup, or crown) that may be of contrasting color. Typically, a DAFFODIL has four to six flattened, grasslike leaves, and its flower stalk bears a single flower with a long, trumpetlike corona. A narcissus is similar, but its flattened flower stalk bears four to eight flowers with short coronas. A jonquil has two to four narrow, cylindrical, rushlike leaves, and its flower stalk bears two to six relatively small flowers with short coronas.

The narcissus is a plant popular for its cheerful-looking, fragrant flowers. Soleil d'Or (top) and Geranium (bottom) are two varieties.

narcotic see DRUG ABUSE

Nariño, Antonio [nah-reen'-yoh] Antonio Nariño, b. Apr. 9, 1765, d. Dec. 13, 1823, was a Colombian independence leader. Inspired by the French Revolution, he published (1793) his translation of the French Declaration of the Rights of Man—an action for which he was exiled. Nariño returned to Colombia in 1797 and was in jail or under house arrest until 1810, when the struggle for independence from Spain erupted. In 1811 he became president of the short-lived republic of Cundinamarca, one of the small states formed after the breakup of the viceroyalty of New Granada. After serving as vice-president of independent Colombia in 1821, he became a leader of the opposition to Simón Bolívar.

narodniki [nah-rawd'-ni-kee] The narodniki were 19th-century Russian populist intellectuals who believed that a peasant revolution could build socialism on the traditional agricultural commune, the *mir*. In a campaign known as "going to the people" (1873–74), they unsuccessfully tried to arouse the peasants (the *narod*, or people). In 1876 the narodniki formed a secret organization, Zemlya i Volya ("Land and Freedom"), which dispatched revolutionaries to live in rural areas. The terrorist Narodnaya Volya ("People's Will"), which emerged in 1879, assassinated Emperor ALEXANDER II in 1881. A more moderate faction, Chyorny Peredel ("Black Partition"), shifted its emphasis from the peasantry to urban workers in the 1880s, after its members became Marxists.

Narragansett [nair-uh-gan'-set] The Narragansett, a tribe of North American Indians who traditionally occupied Rhode Island, formed one of the most important Algonquian-speaking societies of the eastern seaboard. A horticultural people, they were organized as a chiefdom, with the leaders of their eight major villages subject to the chief of their largest village. The village, also called Narragansett, is now Kingston, R.I.

Because they escaped the epidemic that swept New England's other tribes in 1617, the Narragansett were able to expand their territory and incorporate remnants of other tribes. In 1674 they numbered more than 5,000. The following year, deeply engaged in KING PHILIP'S WAR, they lost 20 percent of their population and were forced by the English colonists to abandon their territory. Most joined the Abnaki and the Mahican. When they made peace with the colonists in 1682 they were resettled on land near Charleston, R.I., that later was made a reservation. There the population steadily declined. The Narragansett numbered about 2,050 in 1987.

Narragansett Bay Narragansett Bay, an inlet of the Atlantic Ocean on the Rhode Island coast, extends 45 km (28 mi) inland. Providence is at its northern extremity, and Newport is at the bay's southern end. Rhode, Prudence, and Conanicut islands are located in the bay, which is a resort and tuna-fishing center.

narrative and dramatic devices A narrative is an account in prose or verse of actual or fictional events. The term is generally restricted, however, to imaginative literature in which the link between reader and text is affected by the narrator—the teller of the story. In some works more than one narrator is used; in others the author functions as an all-seeing storyteller. The narrator may be a strongly defined and memorable character whose point of view affects the meaning of the work or may remain unobtrusive.

A drama requires no narrator because it is an imitation of action given by actors who impersonate characters on a stage. Although a dramatist may create a charac-

ter to represent his or her own point of view, the play bears no self-evident relation to the views of its author. In this respect drama makes a more immediate appeal to the senses, but the success of a theatrical presentation requires that the audience accept conventions by which, for example, the stage is a geographical setting, and the intervals between acts are long periods of time. Whereas drama is limited in setting, scope, and length by the constraints of the theater, narrative is bound only by the reader's and author's imaginations. Drama must unfold through dialogue, but novels may consist entirely of reported speech and description, analyze character at great length, or depict the background of events.

GLOSSARY OF TERMS

Act A division of the action of a play. Ancient Greek drama was not divided into acts, but the Roman poet Horace suggested a five-act structure, which was adopted by such 17th-century French neoclassical dramatists as Jean Racine. A three-act structure is common in 20th-century drama.

Allusion An implicit reference to people, events, or literary works that the author assumes the audience will recognize. Allusions are frequently used to enrich a work by enlarging its frame of reference.

Antagonist A figure who in drama or fiction opposes the hero or heroine—the protagonist (from the Greek *agon*, "a contest").

Archetype A symbol whose significance is universal. The term is derived from the psychological theories of Carl Jung, who posited the existence of a "collective unconscious" containing images that are recognized by all people.

Aside A remark made by a dramatic character directly to the audience that is inaudible to the other characters. The aside, like the soliloquy, is a convention allowing direct disclosure of inner thoughts.

Catastrophe The moment in a drama, particulary a tragedy, that ends the major conflict in the plot (from a Greek word meaning "overturning"). The death of the hero or heroine—or protagonist—usually occurs.

Catharsis In his *Poetics*, Aristotle refers to the purgation (*catharsis*) of pity and fear experienced by the audience of a tragedy. The term is thought to imply that tragedy produces an emotionally therapeutic effect.

Character A figure in a literary work having his or her own motives and capacity for distinctive speech and action. The figures in a chorus or mob are not regarded as characters.

Climax The point of crucial interest viewed with the greatest emotional intensity in a play or narrative. In tragedy it is the apex of the rising action, the high point of the hero or heroine's powers. It is sometimes synonymous with crisis.

Comic relief Comic dialogue or scenes that provide distraction or offer respite from the serious events of a tragedy but which often contribute to the action. Many of Shakespeare's tragedies employ it.

Crisis   In a play or narrative, the turning point in the fortunes of the protagonist, signaling the onset of the falling action in the plot. In tragedy sometimes synonymous with climax, the crisis leads to the catastrophe.

Decorum   The criterion of appropriate relationship between style and subject matter. In Renaissance and neoclassical criticism decorum regulated distinctions between the styles of literary genres: a grand style for epic poetry and tragedy, which dealt with noble character; a low, colloquial style for comedy, which depicted mundane events. Rules of decorum are constantly challenged and amended by writers who depart from accepted convention.

Denouement   The resolution, or clearing up, of the plot of a play or narrative (French for "unknotting"). In tragedy it is synonymous with catastrophe.

Deus ex machina   A Latin phrase meaning "god out of the machine," referring to the practice in ancient classical drama of lowering a deity onto the stage to resolve a crisis in the plot. The phrase is now applied to any improbable event used to extricate characters from difficulty.

Dialogue   An exchange of words between characters in drama or fiction. The term also refers to a literary form, such as the Socratic *Dialogues* of Plato, consisting entirely of spoken parts but not meant for stage presentation.

Diction   The words of which a literary work is composed and from which its individual tone and meaning are derived. Neoclassical critics considered only certain words ("poetic diction") appropriate for poetry.

Dramatic irony   In a narrative, a narrator introduces irony, but in drama most irony is situational. Dramatic irony occurs when the audience is apprised of facts hidden from a character or when a character's words or acts have an implication of which he or she is ignorant and the audience is aware.

Dramatic monologue   A poem in which a person speaks to an implied auditor or in soliloquy, creating a brief drama.

Exposition   The introductory material that in a play or narrative introduces the setting, characters, and other facts essential to the understanding of the work.

Hero and anti-hero   The protagonist of the work around whom the action revolves—usually, but not invariably, an admirable person. An anti-hero is a main character who disappoints the audience's expectations of an admirable hero or who deliberately reverses them.

In medias res   A Latin phrase meaning "in the middle of things," used by Horace in his *Art of Poetry* to indicate the most effective place in the action to begin a narrative, especially an epic.

Mimesis   A term derived from the Greek *mimos*, the actor in a play, meaning "imitation." According to Aristotle all forms of art imitate reality, not merely copying it but offering an ideal manifestation of the natural order. *Imitation* has often been used to signify adherence to classical literary models.

Persona   A Latin word originally signifying the masks worn by actors in ancient classical theater, the term now indicates the personality of the author as it appears in the work.

Plot   The pattern of events in a narrative or drama having a particular causal structure and unity of purpose or theme.

Point of view   A term used in criticism of prose fiction to designate the position from which the story is told. The two fundamental points of view are third-person narration, in which the narrator knows everything about the characters, and first-person narration, in which the narrator is a character within the story and has a limited perception of the action.

Prologue   A short speech at the beginning of a play introducing the characters or the theme, sometimes delivered by one of the actors speaking for the playwright.

Scene   The smallest subdivision of a play, or its setting.

Soliloquy   A device by which a dramatic character alone on the stage delivers a speech expressing thoughts, emotions, and intentions to the audience.

Style   A general term referring to an author's distinctive manner of expression. A definition of a particular style must take into account all the devices of language.

Subplot   Subsidiary action in a narrative or play that accompanies the main plot in a contrasting or complementary way.

Unities   In the *Poetics*, Aristotle said that a tragedy should have a single action, take place within a short time, and be confined to one location. Some Renaissance critics interpreted this strictly to mean that tragedy should observe unities of action, time, and place.

Narva [nar'-vuh]   Narva is a Soviet industrial city in Estonia, situated on the left bank of the Narva River. The population is 79,000 (1985 est.). Narva is a cotton-textile milling center. Nearby are a hydroelectric station and two large thermal-power stations based on local oil-shale deposits. The town was first settled by Danes in 1223. It was seized by the Swedes in the 16th century and passed to Russia in 1704. Its suburb of Ivangorod is part of Leningrad oblast.

Narváez, Pánfilo de [nar-vah'-ayth, pahn'-fee-loh day]   Pánfilo de Narváez, c.1470–1528, was a Spanish conquistador active in Cuba, Mexico, and Florida. He was an aide to Diego de VELÁZQUEZ DE CUÉLLAR in the conquest (1511–14) of Cuba and became a wealthy landowner there. Velázquez sent him to Mexico in 1520 to replace the insubordinate Hernán CORTÉS, but Cortés defeated Narváez and imprisoned him for two years. Narváez returned to Spain, where he was commissioned (1526) by the crown to settle Florida. His expedition reached Tampa Bay in April 1528 but, weakened by hunger and Indian attacks, was forced to depart. Narváez died at sea.

Narvik [nahr'-vik]   Narvik (1985 est. pop., 18,864) is a city and ice-free port in northern Norway, on the Ofotfjorden, opposite the Lofoten Islands. The city is a transshipment point for iron ore mined in northern Sweden. Fishing and tourism are also economically important. Founded (1887) as an ore port, the city was named Victoriahavn until 1898. During World War II, Narvik fell to the Germans on Apr. 9, 1940. After a prolonged assault a small Allied force recovered the port on May 28, but the force withdrew on June 9, and the Germans reoccupied Narvik.

narwhal [nar'-wuhl]   The narwhal, *Monodon monoceros,* and the beluga are the only species in the Monodontidae, one of the whale families. Narwhals have only two teeth, both embedded in the tip of the upper jaw. In the male, usually the left tooth develops into a narrow, spirally twisted tusk up to 2.8 m (9 ft) long. The function of this tusk is not known. Occasionally, the second tooth in males also develops into a small tusk, and the left tooth of females may become elongated. Narwhals vary in color from brownish to grayish or white, often with spots or mottling. A large narwhal may be 5 m (16 ft) long, exclusive of the tusk. Narwhals are found in Arctic seas and rivers, where they feed on cuttlefish, crustaceans, and fish.

NASA   see NATIONAL AERONAUTICS AND SPACE ADMINISTRATION

Nasby, Petroleum V. [naz'-bee]   Petroleum Vesuvius Nasby was the pseudonym of the journalist David Ross Locke, b. Vestal, N.Y., Sept. 20, 1833, d. Feb. 15, 1888. The satirical letters he published in the *Findlay* (Ohio) *Jeffersonian* during the Civil War attacked the Confederates by putting ludicrous proslavery arguments into the mouth of Nasby, a dissolute preacher. President Abraham Lincoln was among the many admirers of the character. Locke continued the fictional correspondence in the *Toledo Blade* until 1887.

Nash, Charles William   Charles William Nash, b. DeKalb County, Ill., Jan. 28, 1864, d. June 6, 1948, organized the automobile manufacturing firm that bore his name and that he directed until his death. In 1891 he started work as a trimmer for the Flint (Mich.) Road Cart Company and rose to a top executive position. In 1910 he became president of the Buick Motor Car Company, and in 1912, president of General Motors. He organized the Nash Motors Company in 1916. The company became the Nash-Kelvinator Corporation in 1937. In 1954, Nash-Kelvinator merged with the Hudson Motor Car Company to become American Motors Corporation.

Nash, John   John Nash, b. 1752, d. May 13, 1835, one of the leading British architects in the early 19th century, is best known for his grandiose urban designs for London's West End. He embodied in his architecture the ideals of the Picturesque—a favorite theory of the ro-

mantic movement that held that a structure and its surroundings must create a pleasing picture—and adapted its principles successfully to the practicalities of urban planning on a massive scale.

Nash entered into a highly successful partnership (1795–1802) with the gifted landscape designer Humphry Repton. Repton introduced Nash to the prince regent, later King George IV (r. 1820–30). Through his efforts, Nash was appointed (1806) architect to the Commission of Woods and Forests, a sinecure that led directly to the commission for the design of Regent's Park (begun 1810), and a processional way from the park to Buckingham Palace.

Nash dotted the idyllic parkland with villas and small mock-villages; he bordered the park with vast terraces and crescents of contiguous houses, incorporating them within gigantic, colonnaded palaces faced in white stucco. For the processional route Nash designed Park Crescent (1812), Oxford Circus (begun 1812), Regent Street (begun 1812), Piccadilly Circus (1819–20), Trafalgar Square (begun 1825), and Carlton House Terrace (begun 1827), and began (1825) the enlargement of Buckingham Palace as the route's terminus. Nash also refashioned (1815–23) the prince regent's seaside retreat, the Royal Pavilion at Brighton, into an Oriental pleasure palace.

Nash, Ogden   The American poet Frederic Ogden Nash, b. Rye, N.Y., Aug. 19, 1902, d. May 19, 1971, published an enormous amount of humorous verse, much of it in extravagantly rhymed couplets. Although his poems seem little more than casual wordplay, mixing the sophisticated and the commonplace, he actually revised them constantly. Two of his many popular collections are *Versus* (1949) and *You Can't Get There from Here* (1957). Besides writing 19 books of poetry, Nash collaborated with S. J. Perelman and composer Kurt Weill on the successful musical comedy *One Touch of Venus* (1943).

Nashe, Thomas   Among the first professional writers in England, Thomas Nashe, or Nash, 1567–1601, is notable for his early picaresque novel *The Unfortunate Traveller* (1594). His many satirical pamphlets and miscellaneous works, including *Lenten Stuff* (1599), are remarkable for their inventive language, vitality, and wit. His comedy *Summer's Last Will and Testament* (1600) has elements of a medieval morality.

Nashua [nash'-oo-uh]   Nashua (1990 pop., 79,662), an industrial city in southern New Hampshire located on the Merrimack and Nashua rivers, is the seat of Hillsboro County. Nashua's diversified industries produce asbestos, electronics, shoes, machinery, paper products, and chemicals. River College (1933) is located there.

Settled in 1656 on the site of an Indian trading post, it was part of Massachusetts until 1741. Textile mills, first opened in 1823, ensured the city's growth.

Nashville Nashville, the capital of Tennessee and seat of Davidson County, is located on the Cumberland River in the north central part of the state. In 1963 the Nashville and Davidson county governments were consolidated under a single charter providing for a mayor as administrative head and a 40-member legislative council. Nashville-Davidson has a population of 510,784 (1990) within an area of 1,380 km² (533 mi²). Its metropolitan area has a population of 985,026. Nashville is frequented by tourists, many of whom visit the popular entertainment complex Opryland U.S.A., home of the GRAND OLE OPRY.

Contemporary City. An important manufacturing center, Nashville produces chemicals, food products, shoes, machinery, automobile glass, metal products, apparel, textiles, airplane parts, and tires. The city has the nation's second largest recording industry and produces the largest volume of country-music records. Nashville is also a major publishing center, particularly for religious literature.

Because of its many educational institutions and numerous buildings constructed in Greek Revival style, Nashville has been called the "Athens of the South." A replica of the Athenian Parthenon, built in 1897, commemorates Tennessee's statehood. Among the city's institutions of higher learning are VANDERBILT UNIVERSITY and FISK UNIVERSITY. The tomb of President James K. Polk is on the grounds of the state capitol, which was completed in 1855. About 19 km (12 mi) east of the city is the Hermitage, President Andrew Jackson's home.

History. Nashville was founded in 1779 as Fort Nashborough in honor of the Revolutionary War general Francis Nash; it was renamed Nashville in 1784. It grew rapidly during the 19th century to become a thriving trade center. In 1843 it was made the permanent capital of Tennessee.

Nasr al-Din Shah [nah'-sur ahl-deen'] During the reign of Nasr al-Din, b. July 17, 1831, d. May 1, 1896, Iran's shah (emperor) between 1848 and 1896, well-intentioned but fumbling attempts were made to modernize Iran. Nasr al-Din succeeded his father, Muhammad Shah (1810–48; r. 1834–48). His chief minister, Mirza Taki Khan (d. 1852), crushed internal rebellions and introduced Western-style schools, military methods, communications, and economic development projects. These changes infuriated conservatives, however. Later the new mercantile class became disaffected when the shah sold to foreign developers the management rights to key economic activities and pocketed the proceeds. Nasr al-Din Shah was assassinated; he was succeeded by his son Muzaffar al-Din (1853–1907; r. 1896–1904).

Nassau (Bahamas) [na'-saw] Nassau, capital of the Bahamas, is located on the northern coast of New Providence island (1990 pop., 168,798). The city's warm, sunny climate; resort facilities, including gambling casinos; large harbor; and historic landmarks, such as the two 18th-century forts, have made it a popular tourist center. The city, settled in the mid-1600s, became an administrative center in 1671 and was heavily fortified in the 18th century to provide protection from the numerous attacks by the Spanish and by pirates.

Nassau (historical region) [nah'-sow] Nassau was an independent duchy situated in what is now Germany, between the Rhine River and the historic region known as Hesse. Early in the 12th century a count of Laurenburg built a castle at the town of Nassau; his descendant Walram (d. 1198) assumed the title count of Nassau. WIESBADEN was Nassau's principal city. One branch of the ruling family (the Ottonian line) acquired territories in the Netherlands; members included such famous Dutch leaders as William the Silent (see WILLIAM I, PRINCE OF ORANGE) and the William of Orange who became England's WILLIAM III.

The family's senior branch (the Walramian line) continued to rule in Nassau, which joined the Napoleonic Confederation of the Rhine and became a duchy in 1806. As a result of the Austro-Prussian War (1866), the duchy was annexed by Prussia. It then formed most of the district of Wiesbaden in the Prussian province of Hesse-Nassau. In 1950 most of the former duchy was incorporated in the new West German state of Hesse (now the German state of Hesse).

Nasser, Gamal Abdel [nah'-sur, guh-mahl' ab'-duhl] An Egyptian statesman and army officer, Gamal Abdel Nasser, b. Jan. 15, 1918, d. Sept. 28, 1970, was president of Egypt from 1954 to 1970. As a youth he became a revolutionary opposed to British rule in Egypt. By 1949 he had organized the revolutionary military group that forced King FAROUK from the throne in 1952. Gen. Muhammad Naguib became president and premier of the republic proclaimed in 1953, but in 1954, Nasser ousted Naguib and assumed those offices himself. A new constitution in 1956 greatly strengthened the presidency, and Nasser was elected president.

Nasser proposed an economic system known as Arab socialism. As part of this program he confiscated land from wealthy landowners. In 1956, after the United

Gamal Abdel Nasser was president of Egypt from 1954 until his death in 1970. A charismatic leader, he rallied not only Egyptian but pan-Arab nationalist sentiment, especially after his nationalization (1956) of the Suez Canal and the ensuing Franco-British-Israeli invasion of Egypt.

States and Britain withdrew their support for building ASWAN HIGH DAM, Nasser nationalized the Suez Canal Company. His action provoked an Israeli invasion of the Sinai Peninsula and an Anglo-French invasion of the Canal Zone (see ARAB-ISRAELI WARS; SUEZ CRISIS), but UN pressure forced the invaders to withdraw.

In 1958, Egypt and Syria merged, forming the United Arab Republic with Nasser as its head. The merger broke up in 1961, but Egypt retained the name as a symbol for Nasser's hopes for Arab unity, until 1971.

Egypt's relations with Israel continued to deteriorate after the 1956 invasion, and in 1967, Nasser precipitated a crisis by expelling UN peacekeeping forces from the Gaza Strip and by blockading Elat, Israel's only Red Sea port. On June 5, Israel launched an offensive that became known as the Six-Day War. Egypt's humiliating defeat led Nasser to attempt to resign, but massive demonstrations in his favor caused him to resume office. Thereafter, he became increasingly dependent on the USSR militarily and economically.

Nasser was the acknowledged leader of the Arab world and was much admired in the emerging Third World nations. He remains a great national hero to the Egyptian people, who credit him with achieving Egyptian independence after more than 2,000 years of foreign domination.

Nasser, Lake   Lake Nasser (now High Dam Lake; Lake Nubia in Sudan), a reservoir on the Nile River and the second largest artificial lake in the world, occupies 4,015 km^2 (1,550 mi^2) in southeast Egypt and northern Sudan. About 560 km (350 mi) long and 10 km (6 mi) wide, the lake was created during the 1960s when the ASWAN HIGH DAM was built across the Nile River.

Nast, Thomas [nast]   One of the first major American political cartoonists, Thomas Nast, b. Sept. 27, 1840, d. Dec. 7, 1902, is best known for his attacks in *Harper's Weekly* on William "Boss" Tweed and the corrupt Democratic machine in New York City in the early 1870s. Nast invented the idea of the elephant to represent the Republican party and popularized the use of the donkey to represent the Democratic party. He also invented the colorful costume that artists now give to Santa Claus. New techniques of art reproduction made Nast's wood-plate style obsolete, and his popularity had faded somewhat by the time he quit *Harper's Weekly* in 1886.

nasturtium [nuh-stur'-shuhm]   Nasturtiums are more than 50 species of somewhat succulent, usually climbing herbs of the genus *Tropaeolum* in the nasturtium family, Tropaeolaceae. Native to highland regions from Mexico to southern South America, they have rounded leaves that are attached at their centers to long stalks. The large, showy flowers are commonly red, orange, or yellow; each has five petals and an outer whorl of five sepals, the uppermost of which is a long, funnellike, nectar-bearing spur.

The leaves of the garden nasturtium, *T. majus*, are eat-

The nasturtium T. majus, a plant native to Peru, is grown in a flower garden or as a pot herb. Its stems and leaves are eaten raw in salads, and its seeds can be pickled and used like capers.

en, and its flower buds and fruits are used as seasoning or eaten pickled. *Nasturtium* is the genus name of watercress.

Natal (Brazilian city) [nuh-tahl']   Natal is a port city on the Atlantic coast of northeastern Brazil and is situated near the mouth of the Potengi River. The capital of the state of Rio Grande do Norte, the city has a population of 510,106 (1985). Its principal industries are salt refining and cotton-textile weaving; tourism is also important. The state university is located there.

Natal was established as a fortified Portuguese settlement in 1599. During World War II it was the site of a major air base along the United States–North Africa supply route.

Natal (South African province)   Natal, the smallest of the four provinces of South Africa, is bounded by the Indian Ocean in the east, Swaziland and Mozambique in the north, and Lesotho in the west. In 1985 there were 5,892,033 residents, the majority of whom were Bantu. KwaZulu, one of the Bantu homelands, covers about one-third of its 86,967-km^2 (33,578-mi^2) area. PIETERMARITZBURG is the capital, and DURBAN is the largest city. The terrain rises from a fertile coastal plain to the Drakensberg Range in the west. The economy is based on the cultivation and processing of sugarcane. Other industries include tanneries, petroleum refineries, and coal mining.

First settled by the British in 1824, Natal was contested by Bantu-speaking Zulu natives, British settlers, and Afrikaners. British annexation in 1843 prompted an Afrikaner exodus. Natal joined the Union of South Africa in 1910.

Natchez (Mississippi) [nach'-iz]   Natchez (1990 pop., 19,460) is a city in southwestern Mississippi, situated on bluffs above the Mississippi River. The seat of Adams County, Natchez is the shipping and industrial center for the surrounding agricultural and timber-producing region. Its industries produce textiles, wood and pulp products, and tires. The city's annual Spring Pilgrimage, offering a tour of about 30 antebellum homes and gardens, is a well-known tourist attraction.

Originally the site of a Natchez Indian village, Natchez was visited by the sieur de La Salle in 1682, and a settlement was founded in 1716. During the 19th century Natchez was an important river port and terminus of the Natchez trade. From 1798 to 1802 it served as Mississippi's territorial capital and from 1817 to 1821 as the state capital.

Natchez (people)   The Natchez, a tribe of North American Indians who lived on the east side of the lower Mississippi River, stressed rigid class distinctions in their social organization. Grand Village, for example, was the home of their ruler, the Great Sun, and of the head war chief, but the nobles and commoners lived beyond the nearby creek. Speakers of a Muskogean language, the Natchez in the 18th century lived in five towns and numbered 4,000. In 1713 the French set up a trading post near Grand Village, and in 1716 they built Fort Rosalie. When the French demanded land near White Apple Village, the tribe refused. They destroyed the French post and beat the commander to death with a wooden war club. The French retaliated the following year, but the Natchez escaped across the river. They dug in at Sicily Island, La., where they were ravaged by illness and death. Some then joined the CHICKASAW; others fled to the Coosa River. In 1832 the rest moved to Indian Territory. Today they have all but disappeared.

Natchitoches [nak'-i-tahsh]   Natchitoches (1990 pop., 16,609), a city on Cane River Lake in northwestern Louisiana, is the seat of Natchitoches Parish. Founded in 1714, the city is the oldest permanent settlement in Louisiana. It served first as a French fort and later as a cotton market. Its commercial role declined after 1832, when the Red River's course veered away from the city.

nation   A nation is a group of people bound together by language, culture, or some other common heritage and usually recognized as a political entity. Often the term *nation* is used synonymously with country or state, as in *United Nations*; however, *nation* implies more than the existence of boundaries or political institutions. In the 18th century, for example, when Poland was partitioned and ceased to exist as a state, the Poles continued to think of themselves as a nation.

Modern European nation-states came into being with the decline of the feudal era, as people began to give their loyalty to kings rather than to local lords and to cease identifying themselves in terms of the universalism of the church and Holy Roman Empire. The American and French revolutions identified nationhood with the people themselves rather than the sovereign. In the 19th and 20th centuries NATIONALISM became a strong political force as peoples everywhere sought independence and self-determination.

Nation, Carry Amelia   An American temperance advocate, Carry Amelia Moore Nation, b. Garrard County, Ky., Nov. 25, 1846, d. June 9, 1911, became famous for her destruction of saloons with a hatchet. Her crusade against liquor began in Medicine Lodge, Kans., in 1892. She became a "jail evangelist" for the Woman's Christian Temperance Union (WCTU) and concluded that alcoholism and crime were connected. Armed with a hatchet, she entered the "joints" (saloons) of Kansas and smashed bottles and furnishings. After initial success, her campaign of "hatchetation" provoked personal assaults and arrests. Rejected by the WCTU and without means of support, she eventually took to the vaudeville circuit in order to publicize her cause. She toured Britain in 1908–09 but returned to the United States ill and unable to continue her work.

National Academy of Sciences   The National Academy of Sciences (NAS)—a select, private body of distinguished scholars in the fields of science and engineering—is dedicated to the furtherance of science and its use for the general welfare. The NAS charter, passed by Congress and signed by President Lincoln on Mar. 3, 1863, stipulates that the academy should also act on request as official advisor to the U.S. federal government on questions of science and technology.

The NAS has grown from 50 to 1,500 members organized in 23 specialty sections and more than 350 active committees. Election to the academy is considered the capstone to a scientific career. A parallel body for distinguished engineers, the National Academy of Engineering (NAE), was established in 1964 under the NAS charter. It has about 1,200 members.

National Academy of Television Arts and Sciences   see EMMY AWARDS

National Aeronautics and Space Administration   The National Aeronautics and Space Administration (NASA) is the U.S. government agency responsible for the development of advanced aviation and space technology and for SPACE EXPLORATION. It is an independent civilian agency responsible directly to the president.

NASA's roots go back to 1914, when Smithsonian Institution secretary Charles D. Wolcott argued that a federal agency was needed to stimulate the growth of American aeronautics, which was then lagging behind European developments. The recognition of this deficiency led to the creation in 1915 of the National Advisory Committee for Aeronautics (NACA). In 1917, NACA opened its first research center, the Langley Memorial Aeronautical Laboratory, located in Hampton, Va. It was followed in 1941 by the Ames Aeronautical Laboratory near Palo Alto,

Calif., and in 1942 by the Aircraft Engine Research Laboratory at Cleveland, Ohio. These are now named the Langley, Ames, and Lewis Research Centers.

During the 1920s and '30s, NACA research turned the art of aeronautics into a disciplined engineering profession. It made possible many racing aircraft that influenced designs during World War II. The war brought a new urgency to NACA's mission, and its research helped make possible aircraft that gave the Allied nations a decided edge in aerial combat. Following the war NACA focused on jet propulsion and the attainment of higher altitudes and speeds. In 1947 the NACA X-1 broke the sound barrier, opening a new regime of flight.

The International Geophysical Year (July 1957–December 1958) brought intense competition between the army and the navy over which service would be chosen to attempt to orbit the first American artificial satellite. The navy was selected but failed at first when the Project VANGUARD schedule was accelerated with disastrous results because of the political pressures produced by the Soviet Union's successful orbiting of SPUTNIK *1*. The army later succeeded with EXPLORER *1*.

These diverse efforts—the air force also had a growing space program—made clear the need for a single agency to conduct nonmilitary space research. NACA was thus transformed into NASA by the National Aeronautics and Space Act of 1958. Either immediately or eventually transferred to NASA were the Project Vanguard personnel at the Naval Research Laboratory outside Washington, D.C., who formed the core of the Goddard Space Flight Center at Beltsville, Md., and the large booster development group at the Army Ballistic Missile Agency, which became the Marshall Space Flight Center at Huntsville, Ala. The JET PROPULSION LABORATORY at Pasadena, Calif., remained an independent contractor but was transferred from army to NASA authority. Other field centers include: the Dryden Flight Research Center, Edwards, Calif. (flight testing); the JOHNSON SPACE CENTER, Houston, Tex. (manned mission control); the KENNEDY SPACE CENTER, Cape Canaveral, Fla. (launch operations); the National Space Technology Laboratories, Bay Saint Louis, Miss. (rocket-

engine testing and Earth-resources studies); and the Wallops Flight Center, Wallops Island, Va. (sounding rockets).

During the 1960s, NASA grew rapidly with the APOLLO PROGRAM, the national effort to put an American on the Moon. The $25 billion project (see also GEMINI PROGRAM and MERCURY PROGRAM) employed more than 400,000 Americans at one point, either through NASA or its contractors (see AEROSPACE INDUSTRY). The agency budget shrank considerably after Apollo, but NASA was able to develop the SKYLAB space station and the VIKING Mars landers and to conduct other space and Earth-science programs. In the late 1970s and early 1980s, NASA developed the reusable SPACE SHUTTLE to make access to space cheaper and easier. The agency's management and quality-control procedures came under severe criticism, however, when the destruction of the Shuttle *Challenger* during launch in January 1986 caused NASA's first mission fatalities. The resulting delay in its programs lasted until September 1988, when Shuttle flights resumed.

National Association for the Advancement of Colored People

The National Association for the Advancement of Colored People (NAACP) is the oldest and largest civil-rights organization in the United States. Its aim is the "elimination of all barriers to political, educational, social and economic equality" for blacks and other racial minorities.

In 1905 a group of black intellectuals, led by W. E. B. DU BOIS, formed the Niagara Movement to demand full civil rights for blacks. Following bitter race riots in Springfield, Ill., the Niagara Movement joined with concerned white socialists and liberals to create the NAACP in 1909. The lawyer Moorfield Storey became its first president in 1910, and Du Bois edited its official organ, *Crisis*, from 1910 to 1934. Roy WILKINS succeeded Du Bois as editor. In 1955, upon the death of Walter WHITE (executive secretary, 1931–55), Wilkins became the organization's executive secretary (later director). In 1977 he was succeeded by Benjamin L. Hooks.

Since its inception the NAACP has emphasized legal action in areas such as employment, housing, voting, and education. Its lawyers have brought numerous test cases before the courts, of which the best known is the BROWN V. BOARD OF EDUCATION OF TOPEKA, KANSAS school desegregation case of 1954. Its headquarters is in Baltimore, Md.

National Association of Manufacturers

The National Association of Manufacturers (NAM) is a voluntary organization of U.S. industrial and business firms joined together to foster their trade, business, and financial interests, to promote greater communication among manufacturers, and to publicize the advantages of a free-enterprise economic system. The NAM was formed in 1895 to promote foreign trade, to facilitate the exhibition of American-manufactured products in other countries, to rehabilitate the merchant marine, to establish reciprocity and higher tariffs, and to promote the building of a canal in Central America.

All U.S. manned space missions are directed from the mission control room at NASA's Johnson Space Center near Houston, Tex.

national bank In the United States, national banks are federally chartered, privately operated institutions of the BANKING SYSTEM and are regulated by the FEDERAL RESERVE SYSTEM. They were originally authorized (1863–64) by Congress to help finance the Civil War through the sale of bond issues and to produce a stabler national currency by issuing paper notes redeemable by adequate reserves of specie. The financial panics of 1893 and 1907 led to the integration of national banks into the Federal Reserve System in 1913 and the replacement of their bank notes with Federal Reserve notes by 1935. CENTRAL BANKS, which are the national banks of many other countries, function in much the same way as the U.S. Federal Reserve.

National Book Awards The National Book Awards are granted annually for fiction and nonfiction. Between 1950 and 1979 the awards were sponsored by the National Institute of Arts and Letters and were given to distinguished books in seven categories. After a period (1980–86) as the American Book Awards, sponsored by the Association of American Publishers, the awards regained their original name and are now independently administered.

National Broadcasting Company see RADIO AND TELEVISION BROADCASTING

National Bureau of Standards The National Bureau of Standards, located in Gaithersburg, Md., was established by an act of Congress in 1901. Renamed the National Institute of Standards and Technology (NIST) in 1988, it provides the basis for U.S. MEASUREMENT standards and works to ensure accurate physical measurements and reliable data throughout the United States. NIST is involved in multiple projects in energy conservation and research, fire protection and prevention, and consumer safety.

National Collection of Fine Arts see SMITHSONIAN INSTITUTION

National Collegiate Athletic Association The National Collegiate Athletic Association (NCAA) is the organization that regulates the conduct of intercollegiate athletic competition in the United States. With over 1,000 colleges and universities as members, it sets guidelines for the recruiting and eligibility of athletes, maintains committees on 36 different sports, and arbitrates disputes between or among members in all athletic affairs. It also takes disciplinary action against institutions that violate its rules. Recent court decisions, however, have challenged this last power. The NCAA was founded in 1906 in response to public outrage at the violence that took place on the playing fields during the 1905 college football season. Its headquarters is in Overland Park, Kans.

National Conference of Christians and Jews The National Conference of Christians and Jews, with headquarters in New York City, is a nationwide ecumenical organization founded in 1928 to advance friendship and cooperation among Protestants, Catholics, and Jews. In its efforts to promote a fair society in which differences are respected and prejudices overcome, the conference helps diverse groups to discover their common ground and tries to develop the processes and strategies for solutions to areas of conflict.

National Congress of American Indians The National Congress of American Indians (NCAI) is a national, intertribal organization dedicated to the protection, conservation, and development of Indian land, mineral, timber, and human resources. It serves the legislative interests of Indian tribes, cooperates with the Bureau of Indian Affairs, and seeks to improve health, economic, and educational conditions for Indians. Founded (1944) in Denver, Colo., as a corporate body representing more than 50 tribes, it allows individual membership for those with tribal heritage and nonvoting membership for non-Indian associates. At the end of the 1980s, 155 tribes (representing 600,000 Indians) and 2,000 individuals were members. At present the largest native-American organization in the United States, the NCAI has been challenged by the formation of more-militant Indian organizations, such as the AMERICAN INDIAN MOVEMENT, the National Indian Youth Council, and regional associations of tribal groups that speak for Indian interests.

National Council of Churches The National Council of the Churches of Christ in the United States of America is a cooperative organization of which 32 Protestant and Orthodox churches are members. It was formally organized in 1950 by the union of several preexisting bodies, including the Federal Council of Churches (founded in 1908), the Foreign Missions Conference (1900), and the International Council of Religious Education (1907).

The purpose of the council is to foster cooperation among the churches and to provide a medium through which they can act together in matters of common concern. In public affairs these concerns include such issues as famine relief, civil rights, world peace, and racial conflict. The council is also concerned with a wide variety of church-related activities, such as home and foreign missions, Christian education, family life, and broadcasting and films.

The council is governed by a general assembly, which meets biennially, and a general board, which meets bimonthly. Its detailed work is conducted by a series of divisions and departments, each with its own specialized staff, functioning under a general secretariat. The council's headquarters is in New York City.

national debt National debt, or public debt, is money owed by a government to investors (individuals, businesses, nonprofit organizations, and other governments). The debt is incurred in order to finance budget deficits that occur whenever government spending exceeds tax revenues. In the past, such borrowing was generally greatest during major wars. In recent decades, government actions to promote high levels of employment, especially during severe recessions, have been the dominant factor in the growth of public debt. In the 1980s, however, very large income-tax cuts together with a sharp rise in defense spending generated the largest annual budget deficits in U.S. history, bringing the debt to an estimated $2.372 trillion in fiscal 1987. Although the term *public debt* is often used as a synonym for national debt, it also means the debt of state and local governments.

In order to attract funds from lenders with different investment objectives, the U.S. Treasury offers interest-bearing securities over a wide range of maturities, generally from 3 months to 30 years. Marketable securities—those which can be resold by the original buyer to someone else before the final maturity date—make up about three-quarters of the total federal debt. The Federal Reserve banks, as fiscal agents for the Treasury, sell the marketable securities and redeem them at maturity. To tap the funds of the smaller saver, the government offers SAVINGS BONDS, which are not marketable but can be cashed in before maturity with a penalty in the form of reduction of the interest rate paid. Because the available new funds for investment in any one year are limited, government borrowings reduce the amount of available funds that otherwise can be borrowed by the private sector. This heightened competition for investment funds, in the absence of offsetting factors, is likely to raise interest rates above the level that would have prevailed and also contributes to inflationary pressures.

Payments on the U.S. debt are made primarily to investors within the country. Some countries, particularly developing nations, have large external debts that require very substantial payments to be made abroad. Such externally held debts may cause BALANCE OF PAYMENTS difficulties and a decline in the standard of living if the payments are heavy. Servicing an internally held debt requires only the collection of taxes to cover the necessary interest. This may become a problem if the persons receiving the interest payments are a distinctly different group from those paying the taxes, because it then involves a redistribution of income that would not have occurred if there had been no debt.

National Education Association The National Education Association (NEA) is a professional organization of teachers, administrators, and others interested in education in the United States from elementary school through college. Its six program areas seek support for public education, human and civil rights, leadership in solving social problems, an independent united teaching organization, professional excellence, and economic and professional security for all educators. In 1966 it absorbed the predominantly black American Teachers Association, more completely integrating its Southern groups.

Originally called the National Teachers' Association, the NEA was organized in 1857 to improve the working conditions of teachers and "to promote the cause of popular education." It endorsed the growth of public education, helped obtain the establishment of the U.S. Office of Education, and lobbied for federal support of education and for separation of church and state. Its concern for the welfare of teachers was sharpened in the early 1960s by increased competition for membership from the AMERICAN FEDERATION OF TEACHERS. It has since participated in collective-bargaining elections in both schools and colleges and has conducted teachers' strikes.

National Farmers Organization The National Farmers Organization (NFO) was founded in 1955 by Jay Loghry, a feed salesman, to represent farmers in collective bargaining for farm commodity sales. It has actively supported a program of 100-percent PARITY for the farmer and has campaigned for substantial increases in the prices paid for hogs and cattle. The NFO has been extremely critical of government programs that, in its view, have failed to give the farmer enough help.

National Farmers Union The National Farmers Union (NFU), formally called the Farmers' Educational and Cooperative Union of America, was founded (1902) at Point, Tex., by Newt Gresham and nine other Texas farmers who desired a greater role in determining the prices they received. In its initial phase the NFU focused its activities on the poor farmers in the area. By 1956, however, the bulk of the union's membership was in the wheat-growing states of the Great Plains. The union favors a fairly active government role in agriculture and advocates high price supports rather than "flexible" ones. Among its other activities, the NFU has sponsored the establishing of farm cooperatives and has encouraged marketing through the union itself. It conducts educational programs and also lobbies for diverse legislative measures.

National Forest System The National Forest System is the aggregation of woodlands and grasslands and other designated areas in the United States and its possessions administered by the U.S. Forest Service. It includes 156 national forests, 19 national grasslands, and 15 land-utilization projects, covering more than 77 million ha (191 million acres). The system seeks to protect forage, recreational facilities, timber, water, and wildlife. Most land in the system is located in the western United States.

In 1891, Congress authorized the president to set aside forest reserves. Yellowstone Park Timber Reserve—now Shoshone National Forest—was the first to be established. From 1891 to 1905 the national forests were administered by the General Land Office of the Department of the Interior. The U.S. Forest Service was formed in 1905 as part of the Department of Agriculture to administer the lands.

National Foundation on the Arts and the Humanities

The National Foundation on the Arts and the Humanities, created by Congress in 1965, is an independent agency of the U.S. government. It includes the National Endowment for the Arts, the National Endowment for the Humanities, the Institute of Museum Services, and the Federal Council on the Arts and the Humanities. The last is intended to coordinate the activities of the two endowments, which make grants to individuals, groups, and organizations engaged in the arts and humanities.

The Federal Council has 20 members, including the two chairpersons of the endowments. Each endowment has its own council, composed of the chairperson and 26 other members. All council members are appointed by the president.

National Gallery, London see MUSEUMS, ART

National Gallery of Art

The National Gallery of Art in Washington, D.C., was conceived, founded, and endowed in 1937 by the collector Andrew W. MELLON. The original neoclassical marble building was designed by the architect John Russell Pope and opened to the public in 1941; the East Wing, designed by I. M. Pei, was completed in 1978. The collection focuses on the major schools of European and American painting, sculpture, graphic arts, and decorative arts from the 12th through the 20th century. The nucleus of the original collection was 21 masterpieces, once owned by Catherine II of Russia and purchased in the early 1930s by Mellon from the Hermitage Museum, Leningrad. *Ginevra dei Benci* (*c.*1475), the only painting by Leonardo da Vinci in the Western Hemisphere, is a highlight of the gallery's hold-

A monumental mobile by Alexander Calder is located in the central lobby of the East Wing of the National Gallery of Art. The new wing, designed by the architect I. M. Pei, was completed in 1978.

ings. The museum possesses a large library of books and periodicals in the fine arts and related fields, photographic archives, and conservation laboratories. It was also one of the first museums to produce (1984) a videodisc, with pictures of over 1,600 of its holdings.

National Geographic Society

The National Geographic Society is a U.S. scientific organization with headquarters in Washington, D.C. Organized by 33 explorers and scientists in 1888, it has since sponsored more than 500 major expeditions and research projects. It also publishes *National Geographic* magazine.

National Guard

The U.S. National Guard consists of volunteer army and air MILITIA units located in the separate states and subject to mobilization either by the governors of the states or by the U.S. president. Although state militias had existed since colonial times, the National Guard was established in its modern form by the Dick Act (1903), which provided that it be independent of the regular army and subject to call-up only by state governors. In 1916, however, the guard was made subject to federal mobilization. Under the National Defense Act of 1916, the U.S. Army was organized into three components: the regular army, the reserves, and the National Guard. Later amendments made the guard a reserve component of the army and required that it provide its members with at least 6 months of training. In 1947 an Air National Guard was also created.

The guard may be mobilized in individual states to deal with civil disturbances, such as the urban riots of the late 1960s, and with natural disasters, such as the eruption of Mount St. Helens in 1980. The guard may also fill in for striking police or fire personnel. It has been called up by the president in times of emergency, such as the Berlin crisis of 1961 and the GULF WAR in 1991. The Army National Guard has about 455,000 troops, and the Air National Guard about 115,000.

National Health Service

Great Britain's National Health Service (NHS) provides medical care on demand to all residents. The NHS was established in 1946 by legislation that created a three-part health-care structure: family physicians and dentists; specialist physicians and hospitals; and such local services as visiting-nurse and home-nursing care and maternity and child-welfare clinics. With the exception of small fees for such items as drug prescriptions, all services are funded out of general taxes. The vast majority of doctors and dentists have chosen to join the NHS and are paid a fixed fee per patient and supplemental allowances. Hospitals may also opt in or out of the system or reserve a portion of their beds for private-paying patients.

National Honor Society

The National Honor Society is an honorary society for students in grades 10 through 12, founded in 1921 by the National Association of Secondary School Principals, which directs it. In the late 1980s it had about 22,000 local chapters. Members are selected on the basis of scholarship, leadership, service, and character. Its offices are in Reston, Va.

national income   see INCOME, NATIONAL

National Institute of Mental Health   The most important U.S. government agency in the field of mental health, the National Institute of Mental Health was established by Congress in 1946. The NIMH seeks to promote mental health and to prevent and cure mental illness. It conducts and finances research on the biological, psychological, sociological, and epidemiological aspects of mental health and on the organization of mental-health services; it supports the training of mental-health personnel and the building and development of treatment facilities; and it works with state, regional, private, and other mental-health agencies, providing leadership, technical assistance, and often financial aid. The NIMH operates a research center in Bethesda, Md.

National Institutes of Health   The National Institutes of Health (NIH), most of which are located in Bethesda, Md., are a component of the Public Health Service, a division of the Department of Health and Human Services (see PUBLIC HEALTH). The NIH trace their origin to the Laboratory of Bacteriology, established in 1887. They conduct and support biomedical research into the causes, prevention, and cure of diseases and support research training and the development of research resources. NIH's components include national institutes for these medical specialities: aging; allergy and infectious diseases; arthritis and musculoskeletal and skin diseases; cancer; child health and human development; dental research; diabetes and digestive and kidney diseases; environmental health sciences; eye; general medical sciences; heart, lung, and blood; and neurological and communicative disorders and stroke.

National Labor Relations Act   The National Labor Relations Act, passed by the U.S. Congress in 1935, was intended to encourage and regulate collective bargaining between employers and employees. It was known as the Wagner Act for its principal author, Sen. Robert F. WAGNER, Sr., of New York. The act enumerated several "unfair labor practices" by employers, including interference with union organization attempts and discrimination against employees because of union activity.

Under the act an employer could informally recognize a particular union if the employer believed that it was the choice of a majority of the employees. Otherwise, a majority of the employees voting determined whether a union was wanted and, if so, what particular union they preferred. An employer was obligated to bargain exclusively with the appropriate union representatives. Administra-

tion of the act was entrusted to the National Labor Relations Board.

The National Labor Relations Act was declared constitutional by the Supreme Court in *National Labor Relations Board* v. *Jones & Laughlin Steel Corporation* (1937). The act was amended by the LABOR-MANAGEMENT RELATIONS ACT of 1947 (the Taft-Hartley Act) and by the LABOR-MANAGEMENT REPORTING AND DISCLOSURE ACT of 1959 (the Landrum-Griffin Act).

National Labor Relations Board   The National Labor Relations Board (NLRB) was established by the U.S. Congress in 1935 to administer the National Labor Relations Act (Wagner Act). Originally, the board consisted of three members, but membership was increased to five as a result of greater responsibilities given to the NLRB by the LABOR-MANAGEMENT RELATIONS ACT (Taft-Hartley Act) of 1947. The board has 33 regional offices and a general counsel with final authority over investigation, issuance, and prosecution of unfair-labor-practice complaints.

National Merit Scholarships   The National Merit Scholarship Foundation of Evanston, Ill., established in 1955, awards scholarships for college undergraduate study through its National Merit Scholarship Program. High school students who score well on a qualifying test are invited to apply for financial awards. About 6,000 scholarships, totaling $23 million, are given annually. Some of these are $2,000 nonrenewable awards, and the remainder are $250–8,000 awards, renewable for four years of college study. The corporation's National Achievement Scholarship Program for Outstanding Negro Students awards about 700 scholarships to black students each year, for a total of about $3 million. Scholarships are financed by funds from corporations, foundations, and colleges and universities.

National Museum of American History   see SMITHSONIAN INSTITUTION

National Oceanic and Atmospheric Administration   The National Oceanic and Atmospheric Administration (NOAA), with headquarters in Rockville, Md., reports and forecasts the weather in the United States and its possessions, issues warnings against such potentially destructive natural events as hurricanes and floods, conducts geodetic surveys, and provides a host of other services (see HYDROGRAPHY; OCEANOGRAPHY). A part of the Department of Commerce, NOAA was founded in 1970 during a government reorganization. It operates the National Ocean Survey, the NATIONAL WEATHER SERVICE, and the National Marine Fisheries Service.

National Organization for Women   The National Organization for Women (NOW), founded in 1966 with author Betty FRIEDAN as its first president, works to achieve "full equality for women in truly equal partnership with men." It has strongly supported the Equal Rights Amendment to the U.S. Constitution, and its major thrust has been toward eliminating prejudice and discrimination against women, using, among other techniques, litigation and political pressure. With headquarters in Washington, D.C., and some 800 local chapters, NOW has the largest membership of any women's civil rights organization in the world. The organization publishes a bimonthly newspaper, *National NOW Times*.

---

national parks A national park, according to international criteria, is a relatively large area—at least 1,000 ha (2,471 acres) or more—whose natural features and ecology are of great beauty, scientific interest, and recreational and educational value. National parks are protected by laws and are entered by visitors only under special conditions that preserve the features for which the parks were established.

Because much of the world's unique heritage is endangered, many countries are setting aside national parks as rapidly as possible. In the 1880s fewer than ten national parks existed in Australia, Canada, and the United States. By the late 1980s far more than 2,000 national parks and equivalent reserves had been established by more than 100 countries, with the number of new parks increasing each year.

U.S. National Park System

The national-park movement began in the United States in 1870 when a group of explorers recommended that a portion of the upper Yellowstone River region be set aside to protect its geothermal features, wildlife, forests, and unique scenery for future generations. The idea of preserving land for public use was not new, for there had long been public parks, but YELLOWSTONE, established in 1872, set the pattern for preserving large undisturbed ecosystems as national parks.

The idea caught on, and Congress established many new parks. Some were a gift from a state to the federal government, as in the case of YOSEMITE. Some were first established by presidential proclamation as national monuments. Some lands were given by individuals, notably John D. Rockefeller. Often commercial interests, especially the western railroads, actively promoted the creation of national parks.

Overseeing such a growing, complex domain proved so difficult at first that, from 1886 to 1916, the U.S. Army administered and protected the parks. In 1916, Congress created the National Park Service to oversee the park system. The national park system gradually grew in diversity by the addition of historic and prehistoric sites, together with battlefields, parkways, hiking trails, seashores, lakeshores, rivers, recreation areas, memorials, scientific reserves, and other areas. By the 1980s more than 300 of these diverse units, including the national parks themselves, made up the national park system and encompassed more than 32 million ha (79 million acres). More than half of these units are dedicated to historic preservation, but 95% of the area of the park system protects natural features.

Millions of people visit the U.S. national park service areas each year—364.6 million people in 1986. A number of parks, such as the EVERGLADES in Florida, basically protect biological features. A famous park preserving a geological phenomenon is GRAND CANYON in Arizona. Some national monuments, such as DEATH VALLEY in California and Glacier Bay in Alaska, have a larger land area than most national parks. Although the difference be-

(Left) *The Grand Canyon, an immense gorge carved by the Colorado River in northern Arizona, plunges to a depth of 1,700 m (5,577 ft).* (Center) *Frozen Lake, in Washington's Mount Rainier National Park, lies in a valley bordered by the Cascade Mountains.* (Right) *The Lower Falls, plunging 94 m (308 ft), is a major scenic attraction of Yellowstone National Park.*

tween national park and national monument status is frequently hazy, in general a national park is more outstanding in relation to the national heritage and usually more complex scientifically and historically.

A host of parks are important in U.S. history. Some of the better-known parts of the system include the STATUE OF LIBERTY, in New York City; the WHITE HOUSE in Washington, D.C.; INDEPENDENCE HALL and the LIBERTY BELL in Philadelphia; and Appomattox Court House in Virginia, where Lee surrendered to Grant.

Each park is under the direction of a superintendent directly responsible for all aspects of operating the park. He or she is usually assisted by a staff of rangers, naturalists, historians, administrative and maintenance personnel, and others. In Washington, D.C., the National Park Service is headed by a director who reports to the secretary of the interior. Funds to manage the park system and establish new areas are appropriated annually by Congress. Park facilities, such as hotels, restaurants, gasoline stations, stores, shops, and public transportation systems, are operated as private concessions granted by the federal government.

Canadian National Park System

The national park system of Canada began with the establishment of Banff National Park, Alberta, in 1885. Since then the total area of Canada's national parks has expanded to about 180,000 km^2 (69,498 mi^2). The system includes 32 national parks and 80 national historic parks and sites. As in the United States, most national parks are in the West. In general, management policies differ little from those in the United States. Bilingual programs (French and English) are evident nearly everywhere. About 25 million people visit Canada's national parks each year.

National Parks Elsewhere

Australia established its first park in 1879; New Zealand, in 1894. What was to become South Africa's famed 19,485-km^2 (7,523-mi^2) Kruger National Park first came under protection in 1898 (national park status: 1926). Sweden (1909), Russia (1911), France (1913), Switzerland (1914), and many other countries soon established parks. Great strides were made in the 1930s in Argentina, Chile, and Ecuador. Japanese officials, after visiting the United States, began (1934) to build a system that now occupies slightly more than 5% of the country's total land area. After World War II a number of outstanding African parks were set aside; some of the largest included Serengeti (Tanzania), Ruwenzori (Uganda), Tsavo (Kenya), Wankie (Zimbabwe), and Kafue (Zambia). Many of the world's highest and most scenic waterfalls, and many of the highest and most scenic mountains, are in national parks. Many parks constitute immense wild-animal reserves, as on the African plains. Some wildlife concentrations have great historic significance, such as those island species studied (1835) by Charles Darwin in what is now Galápagos National Park, Ecuador. Certain parks are important as the last refuges of animal species once nearly extinct.

The tendency of many governments has been to establish as many parks as possible before advancing civilization alters the character of natural environments. Developing countries place special emphasis on the economic benefits of national parks, especially through tourism. It can be difficult to find local experts who can plan and manage parks in developing countries, which sometimes do not possess the economic means to establish and maintain areas at national-park standards.

Problems and Prospects

Some of the problems associated with national parks result when the delicate balance of the natural environment is disrupted. One problem is the presence of exotic or introduced species that encroach on the habitats of native animals. Even native animals given protection may multiply so rapidly that their large numbers threaten to destroy the park environment. Other animal species may suffer, and plant and water resources are endangered.

The most challenging problems facing national parks result from human impact. Sometimes these problems originate outside the park. Acid rain, plus pollutants in rivers, the sea, and the air, bring into pristine park environments chemicals against which native life forms have evolved no protection. Overuse has placed strains on park environments in many countries, including the United States and Japan. Such problems as poaching of protected species have proved exceedingly difficult to control, especially in the big-game parks of East Africa. Special problems result when national parks occupy the home of traditional indigenous peoples. When indigenous peoples live within the parks, their economic and social systems are often threatened both by restrictive measures designed to protect the environment and by their contact with visitors. Some governments, therefore, allow the groups to retain varying degrees of control over the parks. In Australia, Kakadu National Park is the home of Aborigines whose tribal council gave the land in trust to the federal government for 99 years. The tribe members are allowed to hunt and decide where visitors may go.

As more wild areas are established, and even more are sought, a cry arises from miners, farmers, and developers: how much wilderness is enough? These conflicts are increasing as the world's resources become scarcer. Many national parks were created to preserve areas of outstanding scenic beauty, such as mountains. At the time of establishment it was often believed that the land was not economically usable. Many parks, however, do possess exploitable resources, and their control is a source of conflict between conservationists and developers. Conflicts over water are common and frequently result from proposed dams threatening parklands. In recent years many parks throughout the world have lost timber to the logging industry. Because public lands, often uninhabited, have been largely acquired for park purposes already, it is no longer as easy to establish parks.

Some countries, mostly developing nations, are now attempting to eliminate the adversary relationship between conservationists and developers before parks are established by integrating both preservation and long-

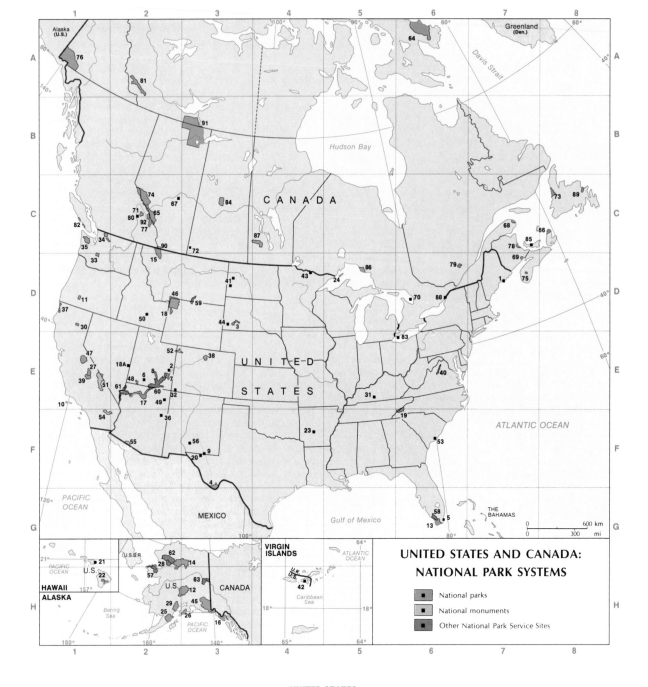

UNITED STATES AND CANADA: NATIONAL PARK SYSTEMS

- ■ National parks
- ■ National monuments
- ■ Other National Park Service Sites

UNITED STATES

No.	Location	Description
National Parks		
1	D-7	Acadia; Maine; 155 km² (60 mi²); Mount Desert Island and Atlantic coast; established 1919
2	E-2	Arches; Utah; 297 km² (115 mi²); natural arches formed by wind erosion; established 1971
3	D-3	Badlands; South Dakota; 985 km² (380 mi²); wind-eroded formations, fossils, and prairie grassland; established 1978
4	F-3	Big Bend; Texas; 2,866 km² (1,106 mi²); mountain and desert scenery along the Rio Grande; established 1944
5	G-6	Biscayne; Florida; 730 km² (282 mi²); 33 keys in a north-south chain, mostly reef and water; established 1980
6	E-2	Bryce Canyon; Utah; 145 km² (56 mi²); colorful eroded pinnacles; established 1928
7	E-2	Canyonlands; Utah; 1,366 km² (527 mi²); rock spires and mesas; established 1964

UNITED STATES (cont.)

No.	Location	Description
8	E-2	Capitol Reef; Utah; 979 km² (378 mi²); gorges, fossils, and cliff dwellings; established 1971
9	F-3	Carlsbad Caverns; New Mexico; 189 km² (73 mi²); largest natural caves yet discovered; established 1930
10	E-1	Channel Islands; California; 1,010 km² (390 mi²); five Pacific islands, sea birds, sea lion rookeries, plants; established 1980
11	D-1	Crater Lake; Oregon; 649 km² (250 mi²); lake in crater of extinct volcano; established 1902
12	H-3	Denali; Alaska; 19,016 km² (7,342 mi²); highest mountain in North America (Mt. McKinley), glaciers; established 1980
13	G-6	Everglades; Florida; 5,661 km² (2,186 mi²); subtropical wilderness with abundant wildlife; authorized 1934
14	G-2,3	Gates of the Arctic; Alaska; 30,351 km² (11,719 mi²); tundra wilderness, wild rivers, lakes; established 1980
15	D-2	Glacier; Montana; 4,102 km² (1,584 mi²); glaciers, lakes, and wildlife in Rocky Mountains; established 1910
16	H-3	Glacier Bay; Alaska; 13,052 km² (5,039 mi²); tidewater glaciers, rain forest, large variety of wildlife; established 1980
17	E-2	Grand Canyon; Arizona; 4,931 km² (1,904 mi²); canyon of the Colorado River; established 1919
18	D-2	Grand Teton; Wyoming; 1,257 km² (485 mi²); Teton Range of the Rocky Mountains; established 1929
18A	E-2	Great Basin; Nevada; 312 km² (120 mi²); scrubland, meadows, mountains, glacial lakes, bristlecone pine habitat; established 1987
19	E, F-6	Great Smoky Mountains; Tennessee and North Carolina; 2,105 km² (813 mi²); Appalachian uplands; established 1930
20	F-3	Guadalupe Mountains; Texas; 309 km² (119 mi²); mountains and limestone fossil reef; established 1972
21	G-1	Haleakala; Hawaii; 116 km² (45 mi²); extinct volcanic crater on Maui Island; established 1960
22	H-1	Hawaii Volcanoes; Hawaii; 927 km² (358 mi²); active volcanoes on Hawaii Island; established 1916
23	F-4	Hot Springs; Arkansas; 24 km² (9 mi²); 47 hot springs in the Ouachita Mountains; established 1921
24	D-5	Isle Royale; Michigan; 2,314 km² (893 mi²); island in Lake Superior; authorized 1931
25	H-2	Katmai; Alaska; 15,038 km² (5,806 mi²); lakes, forest, volcanoes, marshlands, wildlife; established 1980
26	H-2	Kenai Fjords; Alaska; 2,711 km² (1,047 mi²); major U.S. ice cap, glaciers, fjords, islands, rain forest; established 1980
27	E-1	Kings Canyon; California; 1,868 km² (721 mi²); canyons of the Kings River, Sierra Nevada peaks; established 1890
28	G-2	Kobuk Valley; Alaska; 7,082 km² (2,734 mi²); archaeological remains, sand dunes, Arctic wildlife; established 1980
29	H-2	Lake Clark; Alaska; 11,622 km² (4,487 mi²); Coast Ranges, wildlife, fishing area, volcanoes; established 1980
30	D-1	Lassen Volcanic; California; 430 km² (166 mi²); active volcano, hot springs, and geysers; established 1916
31	E-5	Mammoth Cave; Kentucky; 212 km² (82 mi²); cave system; established 1941
32	E-2	Mesa Verde; Colorado; 211 km² (81 mi²); prehistoric cliff dwellings; established 1906
33	D-1	Mount Rainier; Washington; 953 km² (368 mi²); glacier system on volcanic peak; established 1899
34	C-1	North Cascades; Washington; 2,043 km² (789 mi²); glaciers, waterfalls, and lakes; established 1968
35	C-1	Olympic; Washington; 3,701 km² (1,429 mi²); mountain wilderness, glaciers, and Pacific Ocean coast; established 1938
36	F-2	Petrified Forest; Arizona; 378 km² (146 mi²); petrified trees, parts of the Painted Desert, Indian ruins, and petroglyphs; established 1962
37	D-1	Redwood; California; 446 km² (172 mi²); redwood forests and Pacific Ocean coast; established 1968
38	E-3	Rocky Mountain; Colorado; 1,073 km² (414 mi²); Front Range of Rocky Mountains; established 1915
39	E-1	Sequoia; California; 1,629 km² (629 mi²); giant sequoia groves and Mount Whitney; established 1890
40	E-6	Shenandoah; Virginia; 789 km² (305 mi²); Blue Ridge Mountains and Skyline Drive; established 1935
41	D-3	Theodore Roosevelt; North Dakota; 285 km² (110 mi²); badlands along the Little Missouri River; established 1947
42	H-4	Virgin Islands; Virgin Islands; 59 km² (23 mi²); beaches and nearby hills on St. John; authorized 1956
43	D-4	Voyageurs; Minnesota; 882 km² (340 mi²); connecting lakes and forests; established 1975
44	D-3	Wind Cave; South Dakota; 114 km² (44 mi²); limestone caverns in Black Hills; established 1903
45	H-3	Wrangell-Saint Elias; Alaska; 36,199 km² (13,977 mi²); glaciers, mountains, rare wildlife; established 1980
46	D-2	Yellowstone; Wyoming, Montana, and Idaho; 8,983 km² (3,468 mi²); geysers, hot springs, lakes and waterfalls, and canyon of the Yellowstone River; established 1872
47	E-1	Yosemite; California; 3,080 km² (1,189 mi²); peaks, domes, and sequoia groves of the Sierra Nevada; established 1890
48	E-2	Zion; Utah; 593 km² (229 mi²); colorful canyon and mesas; established 1919

Major National Monuments

No.	Location	Description
49	E-2	Canyon de Chelly; Arizona; 339 km² (131 mi²); Indian remains in cliffs and caves; authorized 1931
50	D-2	Craters of the Moon; Idaho; 217 km² (84 mi²); volcanic formations; proclaimed 1924
51	E-1	Death Valley; California and Nevada; 8,367 km² (3,231 mi²); pictographs, geological formations, and lowest point in Western Hemisphere; proclaimed 1933
52	E-2,3	Dinosaur; Utah and Colorado; 854 km² (330 mi²); canyons and fossil remains; proclaimed 1915
53	F-6	Fort Sumter; South Carolina; 0.77 km² (0.3 mi²); Civil War fortress; authorized 1948
54	F-1,2	Joshua Tree; California; 2,266 km² (875 mi²); Joshua trees and desert wildlife, including desert bighorn; proclaimed 1936
55	F-2	Organ Pipe Cactus; Arizona; 1,338 km² (517 mi²); plants and animals of the Sonoran Desert; proclaimed 1937
56	F-2	White Sands; New Mexico; 585 km² (226 mi²); gypsum sand dunes; proclaimed 1933

Major National Recreation Areas and Preserves

No.	Location	Description
57	G, H-2	Bering Land Bridge; Alaska; 11,210 km² (4,328 mi²); remains of land bridge connecting Asia and North America; established 1980
58	G-6	Big Cypress; Florida; 2,307 km² (891 mi²); subtropical wildlife, adjacent to Everglades National Park; authorized 1974
59	D-3	Bighorn Canyon; Montana and Wyoming; 487 km² (188 mi²); canyon along the Bighorn River; established 1966
60	E-2	Glen Canyon; Utah and Arizona; 5,005 km² (1,933 mi²); includes Lake Powell; established 1972

UNITED STATES (cont.)

No.	Location	Description
61	E-2	Lake Mead; Arizona and Nevada; 6,057 km² (2,338 mi²); includes Lake Mead behind Hoover Dam and Lake Mohave behind Davis Dam; established 1964
62	G-2	Noatak; Alaska; 26,547 km² (10,250 mi²); mountain-ringed basin with diverse plant and animal life; established 1980
63	H-3	Yukon-Charley Rivers; Alaska; 10,198 km² (3,938 mi²); stretches of Yukon and Charley rivers; established 1980

CANADA

No.	Location	Description
64	A-6	Auyuittuq; Northwest Territories; 21,470 km² (8,290 mi²); fjords, mountains, glaciers, and the Penny Ice Cap; established 1972
65	C-2	Banff; Alberta; 6,641 km² (2,564 mi²); Canadian Rockies and hot springs; established 1885
66	C-8	Cape Breton Highlands; Nova Scotia; 950 km² (367 mi²); mountains along northern coast of Cape Breton Island; established 1936
67	C-2	Elk Island; Alberta; 195 km² (75 mi²); buffalo preserve; established 1913
68	C-7	Forillon; Quebec; 241 km² (93 mi²); tip of Gaspé Peninsula on Gulf of St. Lawrence; created 1970
69	D-7	Fundy; New Brunswick; 206 km² (80 mi²); hilly plateau overlooking Bay of Fundy; established 1948
70	D-6	Georgian Bay Islands; Ontario; 24 km² (9 mi²); 42 islands in Georgian Bay of Lake Huron; established 1929
71	C-2	Glacier; British Columbia; 1,353 km²)522 mi²); glaciers, lakes, and caverns in the Canadian Rockies; established 1886
72	C-3	Grasslands; Saskatchewan; 259 km² (100 mi²); short-grass prairieland; established 1981
73	C-8	Gros Morne; Newfoundland; 1,942 km² (750 mi²); coast of western Newfoundland with mountains, lakes, and dunes; decl. 1970
74	C-2	Jasper; Alberta; 10,878 km² (4,200 mi²); glaciers and lakes in the Canadian Rockies; established 1907
75	D-7	Kejimkujik; Nova Scotia; 381 km² (147 mi²); rolling landscape of inland Nova Scotia; established 1964-69
76	A-1	Kluane; Yukon Territory; 22,014 km² (8,500 mi²); St. Elias and Kluane Mountain ranges, glaciers, tundra, boreal forests, and lakes; established 1972
77	C-2	Kootenay; British Columbia; 1,406 km² (543 mi²); Canadian Rockies; established 1920
78	C-7	Kouchibouguac; New Brunswick; 225 km² (87 mi²); sand bars and lagoons on Kouchibouguac Bay; created 1969
79	D-6	La Mauricie; Quebec; 544 km² (210 mi²); Laurentian Mountains; created 1970
80	C-2	Mount Revelstoke; British Columbia; 263 km² (102 mi²); alpine ridges and plateau, glaciers, and lakes; established 1914
81	A-2	Nahanni; Northwest Territories; 4,765 km² (1,840 mi²); section of the Nahanni River; established 1972
82	C-1	Pacific Rim; British Columbia; 388 km² (150 mi²); beaches and islands on the west coast of Vancouver Island; created 1970
83	E-6	Point Pelee; Ontario; 15 km² (6 mi²); peninsula in Lake Erie with lagoons and marshes; established 1918
84	C-3	Prince Albert; Saskatchewan; 3,875 km² (1,496 mi²); forested region with lakes and rivers; established 1927
85	C-7	Prince Edward Island; Prince Edward Island; 32 km² (12 mi²); north coast of island; established 1937
86	D-5	Pukaskwa; Ontario; 1,878 km² (725 mi²); Precambrian topography on the Lake Superior shoreline; declared 1971
87	C-4	Riding Mountain; Manitoba; 2,978 km² (1,150 mi²); wooded plateau with glacial tarns; established 1929
88	D-6	St. Lawrence Islands, Ontario; 4.1 km² (1.6 mi²); mainland area and 17 of the Thousand Islands in the St. Lawrence River; est. 1914
89	C-8	Terra Nova; Newfoundland; 393 km² (152 mi²); rocky forested hills on the coast of Newfoundland; established 1957
90	C-2	Waterton Lakes; Alberta; 526 km² (203 mi²); Canadian Rockies with glacial features; established 1895
91	B-3	Wood Buffalo; Alberta and Northwest Territories; 44,900 km² (17,336 mi²); plains with buffalo herds; established 1922
92	C-2	Yoho; British Columbia; 1,313 km² (507 mi²); waterfalls and lakes in Canadian Rockies; established 1920

term resource needs in the planning stages. The actual location of the park becomes a key factor. In Brazil some national parks are surrounded by protected areas where multiple land use is permitted, thus "cushioning" the fragile inner environment while allowing controlled resource exploitation in the surrounding area.

Thus some long-range trends have become clear. Scores of governments have demonstrated a fundamental desire to conserve natural and historic places. Visitors are better informed about the world around them, and there is a more acute awareness of the economic benefits of national parks.

National party   The National party of South Africa was founded in 1914 by James Barry Munnik HERTZOG to protect and promote the interests of AFRIKANERS against what were considered the pro-British policies of the South African party, led by Louis BOTHA and Jan SMUTS. During the 1920s and 1930s a Nationalist-Labour coalition protected Afrikaner interests against rising black competition. The Nationalists returned to power in 1948, determined to promote rapid economic development, take South Africa out of the Commonwealth of Nations (withdrawal occurred in 1961), and ensure white supremacy.

Led successively by Daniel F. MALAN (1948–54), Johannes G. Strijdom (1954–58), Hendrik F. VERWOERD (1956–66), B. Johannes VORSTER (1966–78), Pieter Willem BOTHA (1978–89), and Frederik Willem DE KLERK (1989–), the National party formulated and implemented an APARTHEID policy of separate racial development to ensure white political and economic domination. This staunchly anti-Communist party, strongly supported by the Dutch Reformed church, has its strongholds in the former Boer republics, the Orange Free State and the Transvaal.

The National party banned many opposition groups, including (1960–90) the AFRICAN NATIONAL CONGRESS (ANC). Ultraconservative (*verkrampte*) party members defected to form the Herstigte Nasionale party (1969) and the Conservative party (1982), both of which oppose any relaxation of apartheid or the granting of national political rights to nonwhites. In 1990, as landmark talks between de Klerk and ANC leader Nelson MANDELA began, de Klerk urged the National party to open membership to all races and proposed dismantling apartheid as part of a broader settlement.

National Portrait Gallery   see SMITHSONIAN INSTITUTION

National Radio Astronomy Observatory   The National Radio Astronomy Observatory (NRAO), funded by the National Science Foundation and operated by Associated Universities, Inc., is the largest RADIO ASTRONOMY observatory in the United States. The NRAO has its headquarters and computing center in Charlottesville, Va., and maintains instruments in Green Bank, W.Va.; at Kitt Peak National Observatory, near Tucson, Ariz.; and in Socorro, N.Mex. One of the main instruments at Green Bank, a 91.5-m (300-ft) transit telescope that was the largest movable radio telescope in the world, began operating in 1962. It collapsed suddenly in 1988. Other instruments include a 43-m (140-ft) telescope (1965), the world's largest equatorially mounted radio telescope; a calibration horn antenna; an interferometer array of three 26-m (85-ft) dishes; and an 11-m (36-ft) millimeter-wave radio telescope. At a site 83 km (52 mi) west of Socorro, NRAO built (1981) a huge, movable, Y-shaped array of twenty-seven 25-m (82-ft) radio telescopes called the Very Large Array (VLA). The VLA has a resolution equivalent to that of a single dish about 30 km (20 mi) in diameter.

National Recovery Administration   The National Recovery Administration (NRA) was the keystone of the early NEW DEAL program launched by U.S. president Franklin D. Roosevelt to overcome the effects of the Depression of the 1930s. It was created in June 1933 under the terms of the National Industrial Recovery Act, a measure that Roosevelt considered "the most important and far-reaching ever enacted by the American Congress." The NRA permitted businesses to draft "codes of fair competition," subject to presidential approval, that regulated prices, wages, working conditions, plant construction, and credit terms. Businesses that complied were exempted from the antitrust laws, and workers were supposed to have the right to organize unions.

Using the slogan "We Do Our Part" and adopting the symbol of the Blue Eagle, the agency, under its first administrator, Gen. Hugh S. Johnson, obtained the voluntary cooperation of all major industries. In May 1935, however, the U.S. Supreme Court, in *Schechter Poultry Corporation* v. *United States*, unanimously declared the NRA unconstitutional on the grounds that the code-drafting process constituted an unwarranted delegation of legislative powers.

National Rifle Association of America   The National Rifle Association of America (NRA) was established in 1871 for people interested in the sport of SHOOTING with rifles and pistols. By 1988 the organization—which sponsors competitions and selects teams for international events, as well as conducting safety and education programs—had about 3 million members, including hunters, gunsmiths, gun collectors, police personnel, and target shooters. With headquarters and a strong lobby in Washington, D.C., the NRA wages a persistent and effective campaign against gun-control legislation, despite polls showing that the general public is in favor of such laws. The NRA succeeded in persuading Congress to reject major gun-control bills several times after the passage of the 1968 Gun Control Act; in 1986 Congress relaxed federal controls on firearms.

National Road   The National Road, also known as the Cumberland Road, was the first federal highway in the United States. Authorized by an act of Congress in 1806 and built from Cumberland, Md., to Vandalia, Ill., between 1811 and 1852, it was the chief road to the West for many years. Its most important segment—between Cumberland and Wheeling, on the Ohio River in present-day West Virginia—was completed in 1818. Portions of the road were turned over to the states after President James Monroe vetoed a bill authorizing repairs and tolls in 1822. After 1850 canals and railroads reduced the road's importance. It is now part of U.S. Route 40.

National Science Foundation   The National Science Foundation, an independent federal agency established in 1950, initiates and supports basic and applied research in the United States in all the scientific disciplines through grants and contracts to universities and research organizations. The foundation is headed by a 25-member National Science Board appointed by the president with the consent of the Senate. It funds such projects as the OCEAN DRILLING PROGRAM as well as the work of such national centers as the CERRO TOLOLO INTER-AMERICAN OBSERVATORY and the NATIONAL RADIO ASTRONOMY OBSERVATORY. The foundation also promotes programs in science education, fosters dissemination of scientific information, and takes part in international programs.

National Security Agency   The largest and most secret of the intelligence agencies of the U.S. government, the National Security Agency (NSA), with headquarters at Fort Meade, Md., has two main functions: to protect U.S. government communications and to intercept foreign communications. It protects government communications by enciphering messages and taking other measures to ensure their secrecy. In its foreign intelligence function the NSA marshals a vast corps of intelligence analysts who use sensitive electronic equipment to monitor, decipher, and translate the communications of foreign governments. It is able to follow space rocket launchings in the USSR and to overhear conversations between aircraft pilots and ground-control personnel in remote areas of the globe. The NSA was established in 1952 as a separately organized agency within the Department of Defense. It replaced the Armed Forces Security Agency.

National Security Council   The National Security Council (NSC) was established by the National Security Act of 1947 as part of the Executive Office of the president of the United States. Its purpose is to advise the president on national security matters taking into consideration the country's domestic, foreign, and military policies. Statutory members of the NSC are the president, the vice-president, and the secretaries of state and defense. Military advisor to the NSC is the chairman of the joint chiefs of staff; the intelligence advisor is the director of central intelligence. The NSC's staff of analysts is directed by the assistant to the president for national security affairs (or national security advisor). Holders of this position have included McGeorge BUNDY (1961–66), Henry KISSINGER (1969–77), and Zbigniew BRZEZINSKI (1977–81). Under President Ronald Reagan, the NSC staff engaged in operational activities that embroiled Reagan in the controversial IRAN-CONTRA AFFAIR. The then national security advisor John Poindexter had to resign. President George Bush chose Brent Scowcroft as his NSC advisor.

National Theatre   The National Theatre, in London, is three things: a concept, a company, and a theater complex. First proposed in the 1700s, the idea of a theater and an ensemble that would combine the best British talents to create definitive productions of dramas was finally approved by Parliament in 1949. Laurence OLIVIER became (1962) the first director of the company, which performed at the OLD VIC THEATRE for 12 years before moving to the new National Theatre on the south bank of the Thames River. Peter HALL, Olivier's successor, opened the complex, designed by Denys Lasdun, in 1976. The institution was renamed the Royal National Theatre in 1988.

National Weather Service   The National Weather Service, formerly the General Weather Service (1870–91) and the U.S. Weather Bureau (1891–1970), is a part of the National Oceanic and Atmospheric Administration. The service maintains several hundred meteorological, hydrological, and oceanographic facilities that issue a few million forecasts and warnings each year to the general public. The service operates the National Meteorological

Center in Camp Springs, Md.; the National Hurricane Center in Coral Gables, Fla.; and the National Severe Storms Forecast Center in Kansas City, Mo.

nationalism   Nationalism is a popular sentiment that places the existence and well-being of the nation highest in the scale of political loyalties. In political terms, it signifies a person's willingness to work for the nation against foreign domination, whether political, economic, or cultural. Nationalism also implies a group's consciousness of shared history, language, race, and values. Its significance lies in its role in supplying the ties that make the nation-state a cohesive viable entity.

Nationalism belongs to the modern world. Before the 18th century, people gave their loyalty to their communities, tribes, feudal lords, princes, or religious groups. Among the first modern manifestations of nationalism was the French Revolution (1789). Starting as a crusade for "liberty, equality, and fraternity," the French Revolution turned into a war of the French people against foreign aggressors. When Napoleon took power and began to create a French empire, people in other nations, from Spain to Russia, rose in defense of their nations against French imperialism.

After Napoleon's fall, nationalism continued to develop. At the Congress of Vienna (1814–15), Belgium was given to the Netherlands, but 15 years later the Belgians revolted and gained their national independence. In Italy the drive toward nationhood, led by Giuseppe MAZZINI, Camillo CAVOUR, and Giuseppe GARIBALDI, occupied much of the century. Germany, a grouping of states in 1815, was unified under Prussian chancellor Otto von BISMARCK in 1871. The many national groups in the Austrian empire became increasingly restive during the 19th century and finally achieved independence at the end of World War I. In the interwar years exaggerated German nationalism culminated in the excesses of NAZISM. Italian FASCISM was also based on strongly nationalistic principles.

The power of nationalism can be seen in the history of modern SOCIALISM, which began as an international workers' movement. When World War I broke out in 1914, the European socialist parties abandoned internationalism and supported their national governments. The Soviet Communists who took power in Russia in 1917 proclaimed the beginning of an international movement in behalf of working classes everywhere, only to become nationalistic as time went on. Communists in other countries, such as China and Vietnam, have developed their own types of nationalism.

Nationalism spread in Asia and Africa during the struggle against colonialism after World Wars I and II. Nationalist movements succeeded in such important countries as Egypt and India. Within the first 25 years after World War II, 66 new nations were created. Today nationalism remains a strong ideology, as evidenced by increasing demands for autonomy or independence by numerous national groups in the Soviet Union and some countries of Eastern Europe beginning in the late 1980s. Increasing international interdependence, global communication networks, and international organizations, however, tend to erode nationalist ties.

Native American Church The Native American Church is a religious body composed of Indians from several tribes mainly in the southwest United States. The church combines some teachings of traditional Christianity with the sacramental use of the drug PEYOTE. Peyote induces abnormal mental states or hallucinations when chewed, giving the user a sense of direct contact with God. The church's peyote ceremony is an all-night ritual. Since the turn of the century efforts have been made to curtail the use of peyote in this ritual, and in 1990 the U.S. Supreme Court ruled that it is not unconstitutional to prosecute church members for possession of peyote. The movement began about 1890 among the Kiowa Indians but soon spread. Since 1918 the Native American Church has been formally incorporated in several western states.

native Americans see INDIANS, AMERICAN

natural gas Natural gas, a flammable gas found within the Earth's crust, is a form of petroleum and is second only to crude oil in importance as a fuel. Natural gas consists mostly (88% to 95%) of the hydrocarbon METHANE (CH_4), but hydrocarbons higher in the methane series are usually present in the following proportions: ETHANE (C_2H_6), 3% to 8%; PROPANE (C_3H_8), 0.7% to 2%; BUTANE (C_4H_{10}), 0.2% to 0.7%; and PENTANE (C_5H_{12}), 0.03% to 0.5%. Other gases present include carbon dioxide (CO_2), 0.6% to 2.0%; nitrogen (N_2), 0.3% to 3.0%; and helium (He), 0.01% to 0.5%.

The hydrocarbons that make up natural gas are a component of in-ground PETROLEUM. Coal beds also contain appreciable quantities of methane, the principal component of natural gas (see COAL AND COAL MINING). Natural gas is produced on all continents except Antarctica. The world's largest producer is the USSR. The United States, Canada, and the Netherlands are also important producers.

The most efficient, least costly means of transporting natural gas is via pipeline. The United States has nearly 3.2 million km (2 million mi) of natural-gas pipeline, much of it built during World War II. The Siberian–Western Europe gas pipeline, completed in 1983, was built to exploit the natural gas reserves of the USSR, which are the largest in the world.

The gas may also be liquefied and transported in pressurized tanks. Liquefied natural gas (LNG) must be kept under very high pressures and at very low temperatures during transport but takes up far less space than the gas itself.

Uses. Aside from being a source of helium and carbon dioxide, natural gas is used primarily as a fuel and as a raw material in manufacturing. Domestically, it fuels furnaces and water heaters, clothes driers, and cooking stoves. It is used to fuel kilns for brick, cement, and ceramic tile; in glass making; for generating steam in water boilers; and as a clean heat source for sterilizing instruments and processing foods.

As a raw material in PETROCHEMICAL manufacturing, its uses are widespread. They include the production of sulfur, carbon black, and ammonia. Ammonia is used as a source of nitrogen in a range of FERTILIZERS, and as a secondary feedstock for manufacturing other chemicals including nitric acid and urea. ETHYLENE, perhaps the most important basic petrochemical produced from natural gas, is used in manufacturing plastics and many other products.

Future Prospects. Concern about the environmental damage caused by burning coal and oil, coupled with the fact of huge reserves of natural gas, has spurred new technologies that may increase the use of the gas, especially for generating elecricity. Natural gas may offer its greatest potential, however, as an alternative, cleaner fuel for vehicles, especially for the heavy vehicles now powered by diesel engines.

natural law Natural law is the concept of a body of moral principles—a system of justice—that is common to all humankind and, as generally posited, is recognizable by human reason alone. Natural law is therefore distinguished from—and provides a standard for—positive law, the formal legal enactments of a particular society.

The concept of natural law originated in the ancient Greeks' conception of a universe governed in every particular by an eternal, immutable law and in their distinction between what is just by nature and just by convention. STOICISM provided the most complete classical formulation of natural law. The Stoics argued that the universe is governed by LOGOS, or rational principle; they further argued that all humans have logos (reason) within them and can therefore know and obey its law. Because humans have the faculty of choice, they will not necessarily obey the law; if they act in accordance with reason, however, they will be "following nature."

Christian philosophers readily adapted Stoic natural-law theory, identifying natural law with the law of God. For Thomas AQUINAS, natural law is that part of the eternal law of God ("the reason of divine wisdom") which is knowable by humans by means of their powers of reason. Human, or positive, law is the application of natural law to particular social circumstances. Like the Stoics, Aquinas believed that human law that violates natural law is not true law.

With the secularization of society resulting from the Renaissance and Reformation, natural-law theory found a new basis in human reason. The 17th-century Dutch jurist Hugo GROTIUS believed that humans by nature are not only reasonable but social. Thus the rules that are natural to them—those dictated by reason alone (whether God exists or not)—are those which enable them to live in harmony with each other. From this argument Grotius developed the first comprehensive theory of international law.

John LOCKE argued that humans in the state of nature are free and equal, yet insecure in their freedom. When they enter society, by a SOCIAL CONTRACT, they surrender only such rights as are necessary for their security and for the common good. Each individual retains fundamental prerogatives drawn from natural law relating to the integrity of person and property. This natural-rights theory provided a philosophical basis for both the American and French revolutions.

During the 19th century natural-law theory lost influence as utilitarianism and Benthamism, positivism, materialism, and the historical school of jurisprudence gained ascendancy (see LAW). In the 20th century, however, it received new attention, partly in reaction to totalitarianism (see HUMAN RIGHTS).

natural selection   Charles DARWIN used the term *natural selection* in his 1859 essay *On the Origin of Species* to describe the process involving differential changes in gene frequencies within a population as a result of the differential ability of organisms to survive and reproduce in an environment. In evolutionary theory, this process constitutes the genetic basis of EVOLUTION.

Because some groups of individuals are better able to meet the challenges of a specific environment than are others, natural selection results in an unequal rate of survival and reproduction among the various genetic types (genotypes) in a species population. The preferential survival and reproduction of some groups go hand in hand with the elimination of others; as a result, the frequencies of specific genes among successive generations change. Natural selection, acting on the genetic variations pro-

The peppered moth (A), of Britain and western Europe lives on lichen-covered trees where its light color is effective camouflage. In industrial areas where trees became blackened by soot, however, darkened (B) or black (C) forms largely replaced the light forms through natural selection. Subsequent lowering of pollution reduced the number of the dark forms.

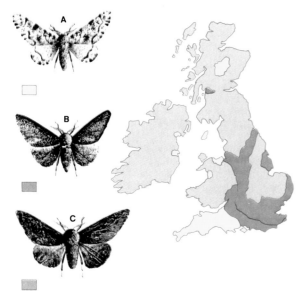

duced by MUTATION, is the most important of the forces that induce evolutionary change.

Natural selection may act as a stabilizing agent, a directional agent, or a disruptive agent. In stabilizing selection, environmental factors favor the existing traits of a population. Individuals that exhibit extreme variations of any critical characteristics are eliminated, and the population tends to become narrow in the expression of adapted traits. No evolutionary changes result; rather, the existing state of adaptation is maintained.

Directional selection occurs when environmental factors favor new traits or modifications of old traits. Directional selection results in evolutionary changes. It is, however, a relatively short-lived process; once a new adaptive state is reached the population enters the realm of stabilizing selection as long as the environmental factors remain unchanged.

Disruptive selection involves various environmental factors and a diversity of genotypes within the same area. When a population occupies a habitat that contains distinctly different types of soil conditions, food sources, or other factors, subpopulations may adapt to particular features of the area. Disruptive selection results in evolutionary changes; thereafter, the subpopulations settle into stabilizing selection.

See also: GENETICS; HEREDITY; POPULATION GENETICS; SEXUAL SELECTION.

naturalism (literature)   Naturalism was a late-19th- and early-20th-century literary movement. The term was adopted from philosophical naturalism, a form of materialism, by Émile ZOLA in the preface to the second edition of his novel *Thérèse Raquin* (1868; Eng. trans., 1886). Naturalism grew out of REALISM. To the realists' careful observation and mimetic depiction of external reality the naturalists added a particular view of humanity and a distinctive method of writing. They were strongly influenced by the natural sciences, especially Darwin's theory of evolution. The naturalists regarded heredity, environment, and the pressure of immediate circumstances as the mainsprings of action. Conditioned by forces beyond their control, people were seen as largely devoid of free will or moral choice. The naturalists also imitated scientific experimenters in clinically objective observation and dispassionate recording. Under the impact of Auguste Comte's POSITIVISM they sought out the constant laws of life. They were also affected by the consequences of the Industrial Revolution, notably the misery of the working classes in urban slums.

Naturalism was equally important in drama and narrative fiction. "Free" theaters were established to explore new techniques of acting and presentation: the Théâtre libre in Paris (1887), the Freie Bühne in Berlin (1889), the Independent Theatre Club in London (1891), and the Moscow Art Theater (1898). All these performed Henrik IBSEN's *Ghosts* (1881) with its exposure of unpalatable truths behind the lies of social conventions. Instead of the decorous "well-made play," naturalists favored the raw "slice of life," often using colloquial speech or dialect. Major naturalist plays include Leo TOLSTOI's *The Power of Darkness* (1886), August STRINDBERG's *The Father* (1887) and *Miss Julie* (1888), Gerhart HAUPTMANN's *Before Dawn* (1889) and *The Weavers* (1892), Maksim GORKY's *The Lower Depths* (1902), and George Bernard SHAW's *Plays Unpleasant* (1898).

In the naturalist novel the outstanding achievement is Zola's 20-volume series, *Les Rougon-Macquart* (1871–93). Under the subtitle "The Natural and Social History of a Family under the Second Empire," Zola traces the lives of two branches of a large and diverse family through five generations, showing how heredity, environment, and circumstances shape their actions. In his finest works, *L' Assommoir* (The Dram Shop, 1877) and *Germinal* (1885), meticulous documentation is combined with poetic imagination to transcend the limits of naturalism. Other European naturalist novelists were minor writers for the most part—George MOORE and Arthur Morrison in England, Michael Georg Conrad and Arno Holz in Germany, and Emilià Pardo Bazán in Spain. Of first-rank writers only Guy de MAUPASSANT, Flaubert's protégé, might be said to have learned naturalism from Zola.

American naturalism was influenced by Zola first through Frank NORRIS after his stay in Paris (1887–89) and later through James T. FARRELL, who aspired to give an integrated panorama of American life and is best known for his *Studs Lonigan* trilogy (1932–35). The native tradition of local-color regionalist writing (Hamlin Garland and Sherwood Anderson, for example), however, was an even stronger formative factor. Naturalism emerged later in the United States than in Europe, and it was more pragmatic and less doctrinaire. Much greater emphasis was placed on environment and less on heredity in determining behavior, and the pressure of circumstances was frequently financial. This is seen in works as diverse as Norris's *McTeague* (1899), Stephen CRANE's *Maggie, Girl of the Streets* (1893), Theodore DREISER's *An American Tragedy* (1925), and John STEINBECK's *Grapes of Wrath* (1939). All these novels are closely linked to native social and economic conditions in their analysis of the individual's struggle against the adverse situation into which forces outside his or her control have put the person. Like their European predecessors, the American naturalists sympathize with the "have-nots," often showing how they are exploited by the "haves."

Dreiser's *An American Tragedy*, with a defense lawyer pleading "You didn't make yourself" and shifting his client's guilt onto society, opened the writings of the American naturalists to political interpretation as an indictment of capitalism, but many American naturalists have also tempered their work with other important elements, notably romance and mythology. These are most evident in Norris, Steinbeck, and Jack LONDON among the novelists and in some of the early plays of Eugene O'NEILL.

naturalism (philosophy) Naturalism is a philosophical position that holds that all that exists is part of the spatio-temporal processes of nature, or, if any sort of nonnatural object may exist, it is known only through its effects within nature. As a system of natural processes, nature possesses a degree of orderliness that makes it intelligible, but it cannot be explained as a whole. Nor can it as a whole express moral value. Moral values, however, may emerge in the relation between human beings as one part of nature and the rest of nature. As part of nature, humans are subject to lawful natural processes; intelligence emerges from the active life of organisms within nature.

Differing views are held within naturalism regarding the general character of nature. Reductionistic naturalism, which predominated during the 17th, 18th, and 19th centuries, holds that all natural objects are reducible to objects as characterized by physical science. Contemporary naturalism, however, holds that all experienced objects and qualities are equally real within nature. As part of nature, human beings manifest spontaneity and freedom. Scientific method, as the method of natural inquiry, is a way of dealing with any content that reveals itself within nature.

naturalization Naturalization is the conferring of CITIZENSHIP by a country upon those who did not acquire that citizenship at birth. The 14th Amendment of the Constitution of the United States provides that "all persons born or naturalized in the United States . . . are citizens of the United States." The U.S. Constitution (Article I, Section 8) also empowers Congress to pass uniform laws for naturalization. Congress did so for the first time in 1790.

For all except veterans of the U.S. armed services, naturalization in the United States requires: (1) lawful entry for permanent residence; (2) five years residence or, for spouses of U.S. citizens, three years; (3) good moral character, as displayed during the period of residence; (4) attachment to the Constitution; (5) understanding of English, including an ability to read, write, and speak it except where physical disability prevents; (6) knowledge and understanding of the fundamentals of U.S. history and government; and (7) residence for six months in the district of the naturalization court.

An ALIEN seeking to become a U.S. citizen must make an application, be interviewed and investigated, and then file a formal petition for naturalization. Petitioners take an oath of allegiance and renounce their former nationality (see EXPATRIATION). They are also required to pledge to bear arms on behalf of the United States, or to perform noncombatant service in the armed forces, or do work of national importance under civilian direction when required by law. Veterans of the U.S. armed services may be naturalized without regard to residence if they meet certain requirements.

Naturalization in the United States confers all the rights of citizenship except the right to become president or, for a limited time, to run for congressional office. A naturalized citizen may run for the House of Representatives after seven years, and for the Senate after nine years. Aliens under the age of 16 may acquire citizenship upon the naturalization of their parents. Those between 16 and 18 who have citizen parents may be naturalized on the petition of their parents.

REPUBLIC OF NAURU

Land: Area: 21 km² (8 mi²). Capital: Yaren district.

People: Population (1990 est.): 9,202. Density: 438 persons per km² (1,150 per mi²). Distribution (1986): 100% urban, 0% rural. Official language: Nauruan. Major religions: Protestantism, Roman Catholicism.

Government: Type: republic. Legislature: Parliament. Political subdivisions: 14 districts.

Economy: GNP (1989): over $90 million; $10,000 per capita. Labor force (1980): phosphate industry—54%; government—46%. Foreign trade: imports (1984)—$73 million; exports—$93 million. Currency: 1 Australian dollar = 100 cents.

Education and Health: Literacy (1990): 99% of adult population. Universities (1988): none. Hospital beds (1983 est.): 200. Physicians (1980): 11. Life expectancy (1990): women—69; men—64. Infant mortality (1990): 41 per 1,000 live births.

Nauru [nah-oo'-roo]   Nauru, an island republic in the southwestern Pacific Ocean, is located just south of the equator and midway between Hawaii and Australia. An oval-shaped coral formation, the island covers about 21 km² (8 mi²). The average temperature is 29° C (84° F); annual precipitation is 2,000 mm (80 in).

Citizenship is limited to native Nauruans, who number about 5,000 and are chiefly of Polynesian, Micronesian, and Melanesian descent. They speak Nauruan, a language unrelated to the Polynesian or Micronesian linguistic families. Nauruans pay no taxes and enjoy free education, health care, and other social services. Many jobs, especially in the phosphate industry, are held by foreign contract laborers.

Nauru's prosperous economy is based on the export of phosphate rock, which is expected to cease in the mid-1990s. To provide for a secure economic future, the government has invested much of the phosphate revenue overseas in projects ranging from a skyscraper in Melbourne to phosphate plants in the Philippines and India. The country imports most foodstuffs and virtually all manufactured goods. Phosphate mining has rendered most of the island barren and unsuitable for agriculture without massive imports of topsoil. Nauru's attempts to purchase another Pacific island have foundered on the question of sovereignty, and in 1989 it filed suit to force Australia to pay to rehabilitate the area damaged by mining.

First visited by British navigators in 1798, Nauru was annexed by Germany in 1888. Following World War I the island was mandated to Britain, New Zealand, and Australia by the League of Nations. Occupied by the Japanese during World War II, the island later became a UN trusteeship administered by Australia. Phosphate mining made Nauru increasingly uninhabitable, so it was long thought that the people would have to be resettled elsewhere. They insisted on independence, granted in 1968. The government then took control of the phosphate industry and increased its profits.

Nauru is administered by a president chosen by the popularly elected legislative council. Hammer DeRoburt was president for most of the postindependence period.

NAURU

Railroad

+   Spot Elevation

National capital is underlined

City type size indicates relative importance

Scale 1:160,000

0   1   2   3 km

0   1   mi

© 1980 Rand M°Nally & Co.
A-591200-772   -1-1

nausea   Nausea is a disturbed body state marked by loss of appetite and, frequently, by vomiting. It is also often accompanied by a drop in blood pressure, increased salivation and perspiration, and feelings of faintness. Conditions that may induce nausea include intense pain, early stages of pregnancy, MOTION SICKNESS, FOOD POISONING AND INFECTION, and a wide range of diseases and other body disturbances.

Nautical Almanac   see NAVIGATION

nautiloid [naw'-tuh-loyd]   Nautiloids are a subclass, Nautiloidea, of cephalopod mollusks characterized by a complete outer shell that is internally divided into compartments by walls called septa. The line along which a septum attaches to the insides of the shell is called a suture. Nautiloid shells may be straight and slender, short and egg-shaped, or curled, and they may be weighted in various parts by additional deposits of shell material. All but 6 of the approximately 3,000 known species of nautiloids are extinct; the living nautiloids are often called pearly nautiluses (see NAUTILUS). Nautiloids appeared more than 500 million years ago and reached their greatest diversity from about 500 million to 425 million years ago.

Nautilus [naw'-tuh-luhs]   The name Nautilus was used for two important SUBMARINES, one the early-19th-century invention of Robert FULTON, which embodied features still used in modern submarines; the other, the first nuclear submarine, launched in 1954.

The world's first nuclear submarine was developed primarily through the determination of Admiral Hyman RICKOVER, who had recognized the applicability of nuclear energy to submarines as early as 1947, and who eventually—despite powerful opposition—secured the U.S. Navy's backing for the Nautilus program.

In a nuclear submarine, a nuclear reactor produces an intense heat that generates the steam necessary to drive the turbines, but does not consume oxygen or produce noxious gases. A single fuel charge can propel a vessel up to 640,000 km (400,000 mi). With the addition of equipment that transforms seawater into oxygen and fresh water, a nuclear submarine can remain submerged for many months.

The U.S.S. Nautilus was launched in January 1954. It was 98.4 m (323 ft) long, carried a crew of 105, and cruised at more than 20 knots (37 km/h; 23 mph) when submerged. Its cruise beneath the polar ice cap to the North Pole in August 1958 dramatically demonstrated the potential of nuclear submarines. In the years after the Nautilus launch, better-designed and better-armed submarines joined the U.S. nuclear fleet, while the Nautilus became increasingly costly to maintain. It was decommissioned in 1980 and is on public display at the Groton, Conn., shipyards, where it was originally built.

nautilus   The nautilus, also called the pearly nautilus or chambered nautilus, is a member of the mollusk class Cephalopoda. It is the only living cephalopod with a true external shell. (Cephalopods called paper nautiluses, or argonauts, are octopuses, genus Argonauta, that use a modified egg case as a shell.) The nautiluses, genus Nautilus, consist of six similar species found in tropical Indo-Pacific waters. They are nocturnal and commonly feed on crabs and carrion. Nautiluses have up to approximately 90 arms surrounding the head in two rings; males may have many fewer arms. Unlike octopuses, nautiluses lack ink sacs and also lack suckers on the arms. The shell, which is coiled upon itself and covers the inner whorls, is lined with mother-of-pearl and often colored white and reddish brown. It ranges from 10 to 27 cm (4 to 10.5 in) in diameter and is built in a series of compartments, with the animal occupying the latest and largest. A core of body tissues, called the siphuncle, passes through the other compartments and regulates the contained amounts of gas and fluid, thereby controlling the buoyancy of the shell.

Navajo [nah'-vuh-hoh]   The Navajo, or Navaho, constitute the largest American Indian tribe in the United States; their estimated population was 185,661 in 1989. Their principal reservation covers more than 62,000 km^2 (24,000 mi^2) in northeastern Arizona, northwestern New Mexico, and southeastern Utah. The Navajo speak a language belonging to the Athabascan linguistic family. Their name is derived from a Keresan Indian word; they originally called themselves Dinneh ("the people").

Early History.   Both the Navajo and their linguistic relatives, the APACHE, are comparative newcomers to the Southwest. They are thought to have arrived in the region

The first Nautilus submarine—shown in a cutaway view (A), and as it would appear (B) next to its modern namesake—was launched in 1800. It was driven by a hand-cranked propeller. The U.S. Navy's Nautilus (C), launched in 1954, was the world's first nuclear-powered submarine.

When completed, this Navajo artist's sand painting will be used in healing rituals, where its symbolic powers will be employed to cure an ailing person. Finely ground sand and mineral pigments are trickled through the artist's fingers in the creation of the elaborate sand paintings, which are destroyed at the end of the healing ritual.

not more than 500 years ago, moving south from the homeland of other Athabascan-speakers in northwest Canada and interior Alaska. Once in the Southwest the Navajo underwent a series of culture changes in adapting to a natural environment vastly different from that of the north and as a result of new contacts with long-established southwestern peoples, particularly the PUEBLO Indians.

The Navajo persistently raided the villages of the Pueblo Indians as well as those of the Spanish and, later, the Mexican colonists from the 1600s on. After the Anglo-Americans took possession of the Southwest the raids continued until 1863, when most of the Navajo were rounded up by militiamen under Col. Kit CARSON and sent to detention for four years at Fort Sumner, N.Mex. In 1868 a treaty was concluded with the Navajo, in which they agreed to settle on a reservation in their former homeland. They then numbered about 9,000.

The Navajo Tribal Council was founded (1923) in order for tribe members to deal collectively with the whites. Traditionally, the Navajo had had no centralized tribal government. Originally nomadic, they subsisted through hunting and gathering of wild-plant foods before learning techniques of dry farming (without irrigation) from the Pueblo peoples. Livestock, particularly sheep, acquired (early 17th century) from the Spanish, also became important in their economy.

Traditional Culture. The Navajo are considered to possess one of the best-preserved native-American cultures in North America. Their social structure is based on bonds of kinship, with descent traced through the mother. The preferred pattern is the extended family, consisting of at least two adult generations: an older woman and her husband and unmarried children, plus her married daughters and their husbands and children.

In the traditional Navajo worldview the universe is believed to contain hostile as well as friendly forces. If the universal harmony is disturbed, illness, death, or other disasters may result. The Navajo believe that all illness,

physical or mental, has supernatural causes, which can only be ascertained by a rite of divination. To effect a cure the doctor-priest or singer (*hatali*) prescribes one of many Navajo chants; in addition, the patient is often placed during the curing ceremony on an elaborate and beautifully colored sand painting, which depicts events in the life of the supernaturals. Certain Navajo ceremonies involve the ritual consumption of peyote (see NATIVE AMERICAN CHURCH).

The traditional Navajo dwelling is the hogan, usually six- or eight-sided, constructed of logs, and covered with earth. The most important Navajo craft is weaving of fine rugs, learned from the Pueblo by 1700 and traditionally performed on upright looms by women. Also important is silversmithing, learned in the 19th century from Mexican smiths; typical craft objects include beautifully worked silver and turquoise jewelry often decorated with squash blossom symbols.

At present the Navajo face persistent economic problems in their arid homeland. Their population continues to increase rapidly, despite high rates of infant and child mortality. Their subsistence economy continues to be based on agriculture, with almost every reservation family raising at least part of its food. In recent years sheep raising has been reduced because of the serious deterioration of the Navajo grasslands through overgrazing and erosion. The discovery of natural gas, uranium, and other minerals on the reservation has helped to provide new sources of tribal income, but the Navajo are still among the poorest native-American groups in the United States.

---

naval vessels   The word *naval*, from the Latin *nave*, "ship," originally had no intrinsic military connotation; a naval architect, for example, is still simply a designer of ships without reference to their types or uses. Nevertheless, in modern English, a naval vessel denotes a warship or, at the least, a noncombatant naval support vessel operated by uniformed personnel. This distinction, which excludes privately owned warships while encompassing unarmed vessels operating under governmentally sanctioned military authority, is a relatively recent one. In the period before the rise of the modern NAVY, the term *naval vessel* was roughly synonymous with warship.

Galleys

The earliest recorded specialized warships (as opposed to vessels used for both commerce and raiding) were Phoenician and Greek vessels of the 7th century BC. Like all warships for nearly 2,000 years, they used oars for maneuvering in combat and sails for cruising. These vessels were biremes, GALLEYS that had two banks of oarsmen and a ram at the bow to sink enemy ships by penetrating their hulls at the waterline. A galley in general is a long, slender vessel propelled by oars. By the 5th century BC the bireme had evolved into the trireme, literally a "three-er," a more specialized warship.

By 1250, Mediterranean naval warfare was dominated by galleys on which the oarsmen sat two to a bench on the same level. By the 1400s, these vessels had evolved

Phoenician bireme

Roman trireme

Viking longship

Sovereign of the Seas

U.S.S. *Constitution*

Among the earliest warships was the Phoenician bireme (c.700 BC), a galley with two banks of oarsmen and a square sail. Later Greek and Roman warships, such as the three-banked Roman trireme (c.100 BC), were built along similar lines. The Viking longship (AD c.900) carried 16 to 30 oarsmen on each side and had a large, square sail. Full-rigged men-of-war, such as the English Sovereign of the Seas (1637), were a refinement of the galleons built during the 16th century. The 44-gun frigate Constitution (1797) was one of the first six ships built for the U.S. Navy.

into triremes. By the late 1500s, the trireme was superseded by larger galleys, on which four or more oarsmen per bench pulled a single large oar. The first cannon appeared about 1200; by 1450 many war galleys mounted a large, fixed cannon that fired over the bow. Such centerline bow guns were soon adopted universally, often flanked by several smaller guns.

Sailing Warships

The first true warship in the full sense of the word—a deepwater vessel capable of carrying and effectively using a battery of heavy artillery—was the GALLEON. The galleon's hull form was derived in part from northern descendants of the Viking longship and in part from the war galley.

The full-rigged fighting ships of the Golden Age of Sail—from about 1650 through the Napoleonic Wars (1793–1815)—were straightforward developments of the galleon, with streamlined rigging and lower, stronger hulls to carry a greater weight of artillery. Broadside armament dictated line-ahead, follow-the-leader tactics, and ships that were capable of facing the enemy line of battle were termed ships of the line. By the 1760s the standard ship of the line was a '74, made to carry 74 guns, though it might carry more or fewer.

In addition to employment in the line of battle, ships of the line were used for convoy duties and to blockade enemy ports. Faster, smaller vessels—particularly FRIGATES, ship-rigged vessels of from 24 to 50 guns with a single covered gundeck—were designed for greater range.

Modern Era

The reign of the wooden sailing ship of the line was ended by technical and scientific advances, such as the STEAM ENGINE, shell-firing CANNON, and armor plate. By the 1840s, auxiliary steam power was common on warships. Shell guns—cannons firing an explosive projectile—enormously increased the destructive power of naval guns beginning in the 1820s, and rifled ARTILLERY improved range.

The initial response to these developments was armor, first used on an oceangoing warship in the French steam

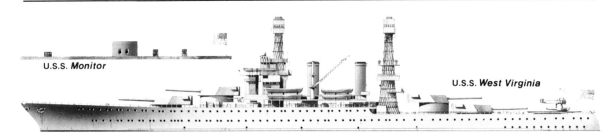

The ironclad U.S.S. Monitor *introduced the rotating gun turret into naval combat. The U.S.S.* West Virginia *(1923), a dreadnought-type battleship, carried a main battery consisting of eight 406-mm (16-in) guns mounted in four turrets.*

frigate *Gloire* in 1858. The first engagement between armored ships came in the U.S. Civil War between the Confederate ship *Virginia* (formerly the U.S.S. *Merrimack*) and the Union's turreted ironclad the *Monitor* (see MONITOR AND MERRIMACK). The rotating gun turret, an ingenious means of enabling a limited number of large cannons to direct their fire in a whole range of directions, was conceived independently and simultaneously in England and the United States and greatly affected warship design.

In the 1870s, iron construction gained acceptance and masts and sails were gradually abandoned as steam power became more dependable and efficient. Electricity was used for lighting; for communications and control; and, in the first practical SUBMARINES, for propulsion. Secure breech-loading mechanisms and the development of nitrocellulose propellants suddenly and dramatically increased the range, power, and rate of fire of naval guns. Broadside cannons gave way to a few powerful cannons mounted on rotating turrets. Improved steam engines led to the design of swift CRUISERS, both armored and unarmored.

With the invention of the self-propelled TORPEDO in the 1880s, large warships became vulnerable to small, swift torpedo boats (see PT BOAT). Quick-firing cannon and the torpedo-boat DESTROYER were developed in response. The perfection of the internal-combustion engine led to the airplane and to improved submarines.

Beginning of Twentieth Century

The symbol of naval warfare from the turn of the century until World War II was the dreadnought BATTLESHIP, named for H.M.S. *Dreadnought*, the first of its kind, launched in 1906. This type of battleship, with a turret-mounted main battery consisting of a limited number of the largest guns that could be mounted and dispensing with secondary armament, dominated naval warfare until the submarine and the AIRCRAFT CARRIER reached maturity. Battleships grew steadily in size and power, and sophisticated fire-control systems with optical ranging and electrical control were adopted; battleships continued to look much like *Dreadnought*, however, until they were retired in the 1950s.

Aircraft carriers, used tentatively in World War I, became major capital ships in World War II, deploying powerful squadrons of dive-bombers, torpedo bombers, and fighters (see AIRCRAFT, MILITARY). Carriers dominated fleet actions in the Pacific and were also important elsewhere. Today, carrier-centered task forces are a major component of the U.S. Navy. American nuclear-powered carriers

are the largest and most powerful surface warships currently in use. The Soviet navy relies on smaller carriers of the *Kiev* class equipped for protection of their surface fleet.

Submarines played a pivotal role in the Atlantic in World War I and in all oceans in World War II; antisubmarine warfare absorbed an increasingly large proportion of military resources. This trend is very much evident today and has been accelerated by the appearance of nuclear-powered submarines. Radar, sonar, and sophisticated electronic sensors became part of naval warfare, and smaller antisubmarine vessels such as frigates and corvettes were designed.

Since World War II, naval forces have been profoundly affected by the appearance of nuclear weapons, nuclear propulsion, and guided missiles. The nuclear-powered ballistic-missile submarine is now considered a capital ship in the navies of the United States, the Soviet Union, Great Britain, and France. All of these navies also have nuclear-powered attack submarines.

Ships of all types are now armed with guided antiship missiles whose range and power have rendered guns essentially obsolete as a means of engaging major naval units. Active, electronic defenses have replaced passive armor protection. Antiaircraft missiles have assumed the main burden of protecting individual ships from air attack, supplementing carrier-based interceptor aircraft—themselves armed with missiles—in the defense of carrier task forces. While enormously increasing the offensive potential of naval forces, nuclear weapons have also complicated the problem of fleet defense, calling into question the concept of massed task forces.

The importance of electronics and guided missiles has combined with nuclear propulsion to break down the traditional categories of combatant vessels. Today's capital ships, heirs of the sailing ship of the line and the armored battleship, are the attack carrier—large aircraft carriers with offensively oriented aircraft—and the ballistic missile submarine, some of which carry as many as several dozen intercontinental nuclear missiles. In a class by themselves are nuclear-powered attack submarines armed with sophisticated guided torpedoes, antiship missiles, and antisubmarine missiles.

Today the classification of surface warships is increasingly arbitrary, with emphasis on the ship's armament and electronic equipment rather than on the ship itself as in the past. Warship types overlap in size and function. Cruisers, destroyers, frigates, and corvettes (in order of size) all share many of the same antisubmarine and anti-aircraft duties. The picture has been further complicated by the appearance of helicopters, vertical takeoff and landing fighters, and, especially in the Soviet service, cruiser-carrier hybrids, which carry a powerful missile armament in addition to their aircraft. Fast missile boats, which evolved from PT boats, are in general service worldwide, often in the form of HYDROFOIL and air-cushion (surface effect) vessels (see AIR-CUSHION VEHICLE). Vessels engaged in mine warfare retain their importance.

The increasingly sophisticated logistic demands of naval operations have also brought about a proliferation of support vessels, both in types and in numbers. Oil TANKERS are still vital to fleets, as are munitions ships and replenishment vessels of all kinds. Fleet tugs, oceanographic survey ships, floating docks, and submarine tenders are only a few examples of essentially noncombatant but nevertheless vital naval vessels.

Navarre [nah-vahr']   Navarre, situated at the western end of the Pyrenees, was an independent Christian kingdom in Spain during the Middle Ages. The area now comprises the Spanish province of Navarre, with its capital at PAMPLONA, and the western section of the French department of Basses-Pyrénées.

Populated by the BASQUES, the kingdom began to emerge from obscurity in the late 8th century. For a time, Navarre's most famous king, SANCHO III (the Great; r. 1000–35), controlled Aragon, Castile, and León; he also developed the pilgrimage route leading westward to Santiago de Compostela. After his death the kingdom declined. In the 12th century the kings of Castile and Aragon even proposed to partition Navarre, but this plan was never carried out.

In 1234, Navarre came under the rule of the French family of the counts of Champagne, and for a time (1285–1328) the kings of France occupied the throne. In 1512, FERDINAND II of Aragon occupied most of Navarre, formally annexing it to Castile in 1515. The section north of the Pyrenees (Lower Navarre) remained independent under the French family of Albret until 1589, when Henry III of Navarre ascended the French throne as HENRY IV. Lower Navarre was then united with the French province of Béarn. Both the French kings (until 1789) and the Spanish monarchs (until 1833) used the additional title king of Navarre.

nave   see ARCHITECTURE; CATHEDRALS AND CHURCHES

navigation   Navigation is the art and science of conducting a ship, airplane, or spacecraft safely and expeditiously to a specific destination. In the broadest sense anyone faced with the problem of "finding the way" is a navigator, whether he or she travels on land, at sea, in the air, or in space.

Early Sea Navigation

It was not until the 12th century that the magnetic com-

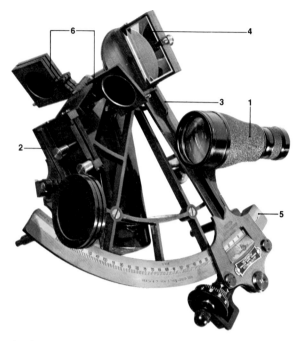

In using a sextant, a navigator first aims a telescope (1) and a half-silvered horizon glass (2) at the horizon. A pivoted index arm (3) and its attached index mirror (4) are moved until the horizon and the Sun or a star coincide in the telescope. The altitude of the Sun or star is read from a scale (5). Filters (6) are used to dim the Sun's light.

pass (see COMPASS, NAVIGATIONAL) was introduced, first to Mediterranean seamen. From that time it has been considered the most important aid to navigation. Before the advent of the compass, seamen estimated directions largely with reference to the wind, although strong evidence indicates that some Mediterranean voyagers used elementary astronomical principles for this purpose. Soon after the invention of the magnetic compass, marine charts appeared. The earliest form was the portolan chart drawn on a prepared animal skin. The portolan chart is characterized by a maze of sets of intersecting lines, each set formed by radial lines drawn from a common point. The lines, commonly called rhumblines, were used for ascertaining the direction in which to steer in order to reach a destination.

Knowledge of the rate at which a ship is traveling through the water is important if the navigator needs to estimate the time of arrival at a destination. In modern times any device used for this purpose is called a log, of which there are many varieties. The earliest printed reference to a log, dated as late as 1574, appears in the first native English manual of navigation, written by William Bourne of Gravesend. In earlier times the navigator judged the speed of the ship, without instrumental assistance, merely by observing the relative motion of the ship and the sea.

A record of courses steered and distances sailed on each course forms the ship's "reckoning"; a position obtained from such a record is a "dead reckoning" position. Because of the difficulty of determining actual courses and distances traveled, and because of the effects of wind and current, dead reckoning positions are usually inexact. Although this was not a serious handicap in the days when navigation was confined to the enclosed Mediterranean or coastal waters, when Portuguese seamen began their methodical exploration of the open Atlantic in the early 15th century, the primitive dead reckoning techniques were recognized as inadequate for long-distance ocean navigation.

The cosmographers whom the Portuguese prince HENRY THE NAVIGATOR gathered around him during the early days of the Age of Discovery are credited with providing seamen with a technique for finding latitude when out of sight of land. This technique represented the beginnings of modern nautical astronomy, the science by which terrestrial positions may be found from observations of heavenly bodies. The advantage of being able to use the latitude of the ship in these calculations, together with the record of courses and distances kept in the reckoning, enabled the seaman to increase the reliability of the ship's positions.

Determination of Latitude at Sea. The earliest astronomical method used by mariners for finding latitude involved measuring the altitude of the Pole Star or the Sun. The earliest instrument used for measuring these altitudes was the seaman's QUADRANT, a device with the shape of a quarter circle made of wood or brass and having two sights on one radial edge. The instrument, however, was not accurate when used on board a ship at sea. Another primitive instrument for measuring altitude that was designed for sea use was the mariner's ASTROLABE, but it, too, was of little use except in calm conditions.

The first instrument of practical use for measuring altitudes from the deck of a ship in rough seas was the cross-staff, also known as the JACOB'S STAFF, consisting of a graduated rod with a crossbar for sighting. The cross-staff was superseded for measuring Sun altitudes in the late 16th century by a novel device in the form of a shadow-staff, invented by the Elizabethan navigator Capt. John Davis and first described in his book *The Seamans Secrets* (1595). The Davis quadrant, known on the Continent as the English quadrant, evolved from the Davis backstaff. It was in general use at the time of the invention of the Hadley reflecting quadrant, developed in the early 18th century. (See *longitude* section below.)

Determination of Longitude at Sea. Finding latitude at sea is far simpler than finding longitude. Indeed, the problem of determining longitude at sea was not solved until the mid-18th century, when two methods came into use, both of which reached a state of practicability after a long period during which the methods were gradually improved. The first of these, known as the lunar-distance method, became available with the publication of the first official British Nautical Almanac for the year 1765. This almanac gave for the year, at intervals of 3 hours of Greenwich time, predicted angles (known as lunar distances) between the Moon and each of a small number of selected stars located on or near the Moon's monthly

circuit of the heavens. The mariner measured a lunar distance and compared it with the lunar distances in the almanac. The comparison enabled the mariner to determine the Greenwich time of the observation. The Greenwich time compared with local time (obtained from a simultaneous altitude observation of a heavenly body) gave the ship's longitude, the longitude of a place being proportional to the difference between Greenwich and local times. It was to facilitate the lunar method for finding longitude at sea that the mariner's SEXTANT was invented.

In the second method for finding longitude at sea a delicate mechanical timekeeper, now known as a CHRONOMETER, is used. The first satisfactory marine timepiece designed for determining longitude at sea was constructed by John Harrison in about 1750. When improved manufacturing methods made it possible to produce chronometers at relatively low prices, the lunar method became secondary for finding longitude at sea. Predicted lunar distances ceased to be given in the Nautical Almanac in the early part of the 20th century, and since that time the chronometer method for finding longitude has been standard in astronomical navigation.

Modern Air, Sea, and Space Navigation

In the early days of piloted flying machines, navigational techniques in the air were analogous to those of early seamen navigating by following the coastline: it was the recognition of ground marks that enabled the flying navigator to find the way. When long flights over the sea were first made, aviators, like seamen, used astronomical navigation for position finding. The need for speed in position finding on fast-flying aircraft led to a number of astronomical navigational improvements, especially in the field of navigation tables. These improvements were eagerly adopted, in turn, by mariners. In more recent times, when the relatively slow procedures used in astronomical navigation ceased to be suitable for air navigation (especially in wartime), the application of electronics and radio techniques to position finding brought about a new revolution in marine, as well as in air, navigation.

Radio Techniques. In addition to their increased use of sonic depth sounders and gyrocompasses, mariners soon took advantage of other technological advances. The first radio aid to navigation, initially used in the opening decade of the 20th century, was the radio time signal; this, in effect, made the chronometer redundant. In the 1920s medium-frequency-radio direction finding gave a new dimension to navigation by making it possible to find a ship's position from radio bearings of land-based transmitters. The world wars, especially World War II, gave great impetus to the advancement of navigation, as it did to other areas of science and technology. The problem of enemy detection, for example, in the air and at sea, led to the invention of RADAR techniques, using high-frequency radio energy. Radar in peacetime has been of great importance for safety in air and sea navigation when visibility is low. The problem of position finding in the air when visibility was poor led to the invention and development of several systems of navigation, some of which, at the present time, have all but superseded astronomical navigation.

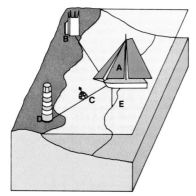

The position of a ship in sight of land can be found from the compass bearings of coastal objects. A map plot of azimuth lines from a vessel (A) to a tower (B) and a buoy (C) or light-house (D) indicates the ship's position at the point where the lines intersect. If depth charts are available, a depth sounding (E) will also indicate positions.

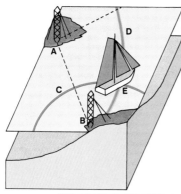

In hyperbolic navigation systems the difference in the arrival time of radio signals simultaneously transmitted to a ship from sources A and B in-dicates that the ship is situated at some point along hyperbolic line C. A third transmitter (not shown), also synchro-nized with A, is used to determine a second po-sition curve, D. The two curves intersect at the location of the ship, E.

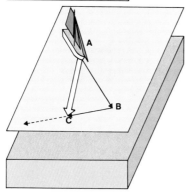

The dead-reckoning method estimates a ship's approximate position by calculating how far it has traveled from the last known position A along a course AB after a given time at a known speed. Addi-tional correction may be applied for a known or predicted ocean current in a direction BC, to fix the final position of the ship at point C.

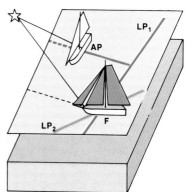

A ship's position can be calculated from altitude and azimuth readings of a star at two different times. Assuming the ship's position to be at point AP initially and at a different point some time later, lines of posi-tion LP$_1$ and LP$_2$ are calculated and drawn perpendicular to the respective bearing to the star. The two lines of position intersect at the ship's actual position F.

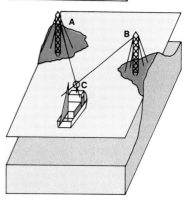

The dead-reckoning method estimates a ship's approximate position by calculating how far it has traveled from the last known position A along a course AB after a given time at a known speed. Additional correction may be applied for a known or predicted ocean current in a direc-tion BC, to fix the final position of the ship at point C.

In particular the invention in the 1940s and '50s of the method known as hyperbolic navigation has had the greatest influence on sea as well as air navigation. Hyper-bolic navigation, so called because the method involves lines of position in the form of hyperbolas, is based on the accurate measurement of the difference in times taken by radio signals transmitted from each of two fixed stations to reach an observer. The velocity of radio energy is con-sidered constant, so that distances traveled by radio en-ergy are proportional to the amounts of time taken. In-cluded in hyperbolic systems are the Decca Navigation System, Loran (Long-Range Navigation), Omega, and the satellite-based Global Positioning Systems.

The primary international AIRCRAFT navigational system is VOR (Very High Frequency Omni-Directional Range). Omnidirectional radio ranges are high-frequency signals that give bearings in all directions and—unlike earlier Low Frequency radio beacons—tell the pilot whether the plane is moving toward or away from the signal, as well as how distant the signal is. VOR has been combined with the military system known as TACAN (Tactical Air Navi-gation System), which provides distance, azimuth, and identification information.

Soon after the first artificial satellite had been launched in 1957, scientists, noting the change in the frequency of the radio signals transmitted from the satellites—the well-known DOPPLER EFFECT—invented the navigational system now known as TRANSIT. This system employs six satellites, each of which circles the Earth in polar orbit at a distance of about 965 km (600 mi) with a period of about 108 minutes. Each satellite is equipped with a magnetic memory that stores details of its orbit and posi-tion (its ephemeral data) for 12-hour periods. Details of the satellite's position—which a navigator receives di-rectly from the satellite—together with an observed Dop-pler shift as the satellite passes the observer's position, enables the navigator to find the ship's position to an ac-curacy of about 0.16 km (0.1 mi).

The NAVSTAR satellite system, part of the Global Po-sitioning System (GPS) developed by the U.S. military, is available for civilian use as well. Scientists have discovered how to use the satellites' signals to measure distances with a precision of 1 part per million, and further refinements may reduce the error to 0.1 part per million.

Inertial Navigation. The system known as inertial navigation is a sophisticated form of dead reckoning in which the motion of the ship, airplane, or spacecraft is sensed, so that the craft's position relative to its starting position is known at all times. Inertial navigation, which plays a vital role in space exploration, employs accelerometers to measure accelerations of the craft in each of three mutually perpendicular planes. The accelerometers are fitted to a device known as a stable platform, which has three planes of freedom, thereby maintaining a fixed orientation in space irrespective of the motion of the craft. The platform is stabilized by GYROSCOPES that sense the rotation of the platform relative to space.

The inertial system employed in submarines and surface craft is a self-contained system that functions independently of weather conditions that may hamper astronomical navigation and independently of radio energy, which may suffer natural interference or that caused by people. For these reasons such a system is of great strategic importance for military vessels. Its high cost, however, precludes its use in most commercial vessels and aircraft, although it has become standard equipment in large commercial airplanes.

Effects of Space Research. Recent research into GUIDANCE AND CONTROL SYSTEMS for space exploration has resulted in a large array of sophisticated navigational techniques being made available for terrestrial navigation. The navigation of space vehicles is conducted almost entirely by ground control. The navigation of aircraft also is becoming increasingly a matter of ground control, with the process of takeoff and landing largely in the hands of air traffic controllers. It is only in the case of ships that the navigators on board still control the movements of their respective vessels, but this, too, may change before long.

See also: AIRPORT; AVIATION; SHIP.

Navigation Acts The Navigation Acts, a series of statutes passed in the 17th century by the English Parliament, formed the basis of the trading system in the early, or first, BRITISH EMPIRE.

The act of 1651 required that all products from America, Asia, and Africa be imported into England and its possessions in ships manned predominantly by English subjects; European produce could be imported into England only in English ships or those of the country of origin. The Navigation Act of 1660 prohibited all foreign ships from trade between England and its colonies and restricted that trade to English-built and English-owned vessels with an English captain and a crew that was 75 percent English. It also enumerated certain commodities, such as sugar, tobacco, and dyes, that the colonies could export only to England or to another British colony. The Staple Act of 1663 forbade the shipping of European goods to the colonies except through England or Wales.

Originally aimed at excluding the Dutch from the profits of English trade, the Navigation Acts incorporated basic mercantilist assumptions that the volume of world trade was fixed and that colonies existed for the benefit of the parent country. The acts eventually aroused much hostility in the American colonies, where they were a target of the agitation before the AMERICAN REVOLUTION. They were finally repealed in 1849 after Britain had espoused the policy of FREE TRADE.

See also: MERCANTILISM.

Navratilova, Martina [nav-ruh-ti-loh'-vuh] Martina Navratilova, b. Prague, Czechoslovakia, Oct. 18, 1956, is a left-handed tennis star with a powerful forehand and an excellent serve and volley. In 1979 and 1982–86, Navratilova was the top-ranked woman player in the world. In 1975 she defected to the United States, eventually becoming a U.S. citizen. From that year on Navratilova has been a dominant doubles player, winning dozens of major titles, mostly with partner Pam Shriver; from 1983 to 1985 they won 109 consecutive matches, a victory streak unapproached in tennis history. Her ascent in singles competition began in 1978 and has produced 18 Grand Slam titles: 9 at Wimbledon (1978–79, 1982–87, 1990), 3 Australian (1981, 1983, 1985), 2 French (1982, 1984), and 4 U.S. Opens (1983–84, 1986–87). In 1984 she won 74 straight matches, another all-time record.

NAVSTAR [nav'-star] NAVSTAR, or NAVigation System using Time And Ranging, is the satellite portion of the U.S. Department of Defense Global Positioning System (GPS), expected to be fully operational in the 1990s. It will consist of 21 navigational satellites, with 3 in each of 6 circular orbital planes at an average altitude of 20,200 km (12,550 mi), plus three in-orbit and four on-ground spares. The system will be able to track objects with an accuracy of about 15 m (50 ft) anywhere in the world.

The GPS will provide worldwide, 24-hour service to an unlimited number of users on land, at sea, and in the air, if they have the required receivers. The system is initially for use by the armed forces, but civilian use is foreseen. Block 1 models are launched by Atlas rockets; Block 2 models are compatible with Space Shuttle launchings, but following the 1986 *Challenger* disaster other launch systems are also being used, such as the Delta rocket.

---

navy A navy consists of the ships, crews, and related personnel and equipment maintained by a country for purposes of war.

History

Early Development. In the Western world navies originated with Athens, whose fleet blocked an invasion by the Persian king XERXES I at the Battle of SALAMIS in 480 BC. Rome employed its navy to help destroy Carthage during the PUNIC WARS (264–146 BC). More than a century later, at the Battle of ACTIUM (31 BC), a Roman fleet defeated that of Mark ANTONY. For a thousand years after the fall of Rome, European nations displayed little interest in main-

The Bonhomme Richard, *commanded by the American John Paul Jones, battered the British frigate* Serapis *into surrender (Sept. 23, 1779) during the American Revolution.*

taining navies. The threat of Turkish expansion into the western Mediterranean finally forced Spain and the Italian states to forge a fleet that checked the Turks at the Battle of LEPANTO in 1571.

In the following century, Portugal, Spain, Holland, and Britain acquired or consolidated overseas empires, the protection of which required navies. The SPANISH ARMADA challenged England for dominance of the Atlantic in 1588, and Spain's defeat contributed to the emerging importance of Britain's Royal Navy. The British victory over the Dutch in the ANGLO-DUTCH WARS (1652–74) established Britain as the leading sea power of the world. The only serious contender to Britain was France, a rival repeatedly beaten in the SEVEN YEARS' WAR (1756–63), the FRENCH REVOLUTIONARY WARS (1792–1802), and NAPOLEONIC WARS (1803–15).

On Oct. 21, 1805, at Cape Trafalgar off the Spanish coast, Admiral Horatio NELSON's decisive defeat of the French fleet (see TRAFALGAR, BATTLE OF) eliminated France as a major naval power. For almost 100 years Great Britain remained the world's foremost sea power. Not until the rise of the German navy under Emperor William II (r. 1888–1918) did a serious rival to British maritime preeminence appear.

Nineteenth-Century Technological Transformation. During the Pax Britannica of 1815–1914, the navies of the Western powers and Japan underwent a fundamental technological transformation. In the mid-19th century, European navies began to experiment with steam propulsion, rifled breech-loading cannons, turrets, and protective armor plating. By 1890, when the German emperor initiated Germany's serious bid for naval greatness, the sail-driven, wooden, broadside-firing man-of-war that had been the mainstay of major European navies since the 1600s had been replaced by the steam-driven, heavily armored, heavily gunned, turreted BATTLESHIP. A decade later, in 1902, the German threat to Britain's maritime predominance was so great that Britain was forced to concentrate many of its capital ships in home waters.

U.S. Development. The 19th-century U.S. naval experience differed markedly from that of Europe. The AMERICAN REVOLUTION had bequeathed a strategic heritage of commerce raiding and coastal defense, as distinguished from the fleet engagements between large capital ships characteristic of British and, to a lesser extent, French strategy. When the United States was pitted against a stronger power, as in the Quasi-War with France (1798–1800) and the WAR OF 1812, commerce raiding proved the most effective strategy. The U.S. Navy also scored impressive successes in single-ship actions between FRIGATES, fast ships mounting about 50 guns. Only when facing a decidedly inferior power did the United States employ the British policy of attacking the enemy's fleet and blockading, bombarding, and invading hostile coasts. The United States was able to fight in this British fashion during the MEXICAN WAR (1846–48), the CIVIL WAR (1861–65), and the SPANISH-AMERICAN WAR (1898).

By the time of the Spanish-American War the United States had developed a "new navy" composed of steam-driven, steel-hulled cruisers and battleships. U.S. naval captain Alfred Thayer MAHAN published his first books on sea power in 1890 and 1892. These books were widely read throughout the world, and they helped insure international adoption of a strategy of capital-ship engagements, followed, if necessary, by amphibious landings.

World War I. By WORLD WAR I the United States had adopted the strategy and technology of the leading European naval powers. Whereas in the 19th century the United States had spread its frigates around the world in small squadrons designed to protect overseas Americans and their commerce in periods of peace, the navy in the early 20th century concentrated its battleships and their supporting CRUISERS and DESTROYERS in an Atlantic "battle fleet." The Panama Canal was begun in 1904 largely to insure unfettered movement of the fleet to the Pacific to protect the West Coast, Hawaii, or the Philippines from an enemy—envisioned always to be Japan. This "battle fleet," however, saw little significant action in World War I; the most important tasks proved to be the convoying of

The Japanese cruiser Mogame *was devastated by U.S. aircraft during the Battle of Midway (June 1942), one of the decisive naval engagements of World War II.*

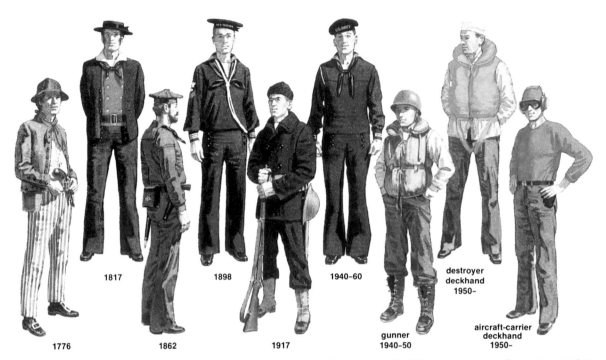

The various uniforms worn by sailors in the U.S. Navy over the past two centuries are illustrated above. The 1776 seaman wears an outfit common on merchant ships and war frigates at the time. In 1817 the navy adopted its first standard uniform (the winter version is shown), which remained virtually unchanged until the Civil War. The 1898 sailor wears his rank on his right sleeve and his ship's name on his cap. This uniform remained until World War I, when the watch cap and pea jacket were introduced. They are still worn today. The basic uniform from 1940 to 1960 differed little from that of 1898; it was modified, however, for certain tasks, as seen by the gunner's helmet and the goggles and earphones worn by the aircraft carrier deckhand. The destroyer deckhand still wears the traditional white hat introduced in 1910.

merchant ships threatened by German U-boats. Destroyers, the most effective escorts of convoys, determined the outcome of the naval struggle in the Atlantic. The great duel between the British and German battle fleets at Jutland in 1916 had little impact on the course of the war.

After World War I the leading naval powers reverted to the prewar pattern and launched a costly shipbuilding race. When the U.S. Congress proved reluctant to appropriate funds for a naval arms race, Secretary of State Charles Evans Hughes convened the WASHINGTON CONFERENCE (1921–22) to curtail the contest. Hughes managed to secure an agreement limiting the tonnage and construction of capital ships—generally defined as battleships—by the major navies of the world. The U.S. Navy was given parity with the Royal Navy of Great Britain. Japan ranked next as a world naval power, and France and Italy fell far behind. In 1935, Germany began full-scale rearmament, and the next year Japan renounced the Washington treaty. A new naval race began, focused once again on the battleship.

World War II. U.S. naval strategy in WORLD WAR II was determined by the Japanese naval air attack on PEARL HARBOR on Dec. 7, 1941; most of the battleships of the U.S. Pacific Fleet were destroyed or severely damaged. AIRCRAFT CARRIERS, previously considered valuable mainly

as scouts for battleships, now emerged as warships in their own right. The Pacific Fleet's carriers, which had been at sea during the Japanese attack, survived as the backbone of American naval power in the Pacific. The Pacific war became a combination of engagements between aircraft carriers, as at Midway (June 1942), and amphibious assaults, the latter beginning at Guadalcanal (August 1942–February 1943) and culminating with Iwo Jima (February–March 1945) and Okinawa (April–June 1945).

In the Atlantic, Allied naval strategy involved the convoying of merchant ships threatened by German SUBMARINES and amphibious landings in North Africa, Sicily, Italy, and France. No significant engagements took place between capital ships.

The Nuclear Age. At the close of World War II the U.S. Navy was incomparably the world's strongest. U.S. Air Force lobbyists argued, however, that future wars would be won with nuclear bombs, a strategy in which the navy had no role because nuclear bombs were at that time too large and heavy to be carried by carrier-based aircraft. The navy between 1947 and 1950 countered with plans for "supercarriers" but was unsuccessful. The KOREAN WAR (1950–53) changed this situation. The administration of Harry S. Truman considered Korea a Soviet-inspired feint intended to draw American attention from

Europe. It responded on both fronts; while strengthening the defense of Europe, the Truman administration also permitted the navy to build supercarriers and pressed the development of smaller and lighter atomic bombs. With the congressional authorization of the supercarrier *Forrestal* in 1952, the navy was included in a national nuclear strategy. In the event of a major war the supercarriers would share in attacking the enemy with nuclear weapons. In smaller, "limited" wars the navy would strike an enemy's warships with carrier-based aircraft, drop bombs on targets ashore, and launch amphibious landings under the protection of naval airplanes. Essentially, the limited-war strategy was followed in the Korean and Vietnam wars.

Concurrently with the development of supercarriers, the U.S. Navy, urged on by Hyman RICKOVER, also developed nuclear power plants for its ships. Nuclear reactors permit ships to travel at high speed for great lengths of time, thereby vastly increasing their range and making them relatively independent of vulnerable oil tankers or overseas fueling bases. The first nuclear power plant was placed aboard the submarine NAUTILUS in January 1954.

In the late 1950s, development of nuclear-powered submarines capable of launching the nuclear-tipped POLARIS ballistic missile was begun. In the 1960s and early 1970s the United States constructed 45 ballistic-missile submarines capable of firing Polaris or its longer-range successor, the POSEIDON. In the 1980s new submarines were commissioned to carry an even longer-range and larger ballistic missile, the TRIDENT. The U.S. Navy has also constructed several aircraft carriers and cruisers powered by nuclear reactors. The great cost of these ships, however, has limited their numbers.

Carriers, cruisers, destroyers, and submarines all proved their worth during the CUBAN MISSILE CRISIS of 1962, when U.S. naval superiority forced the Soviets to withdraw their nuclear missiles from Cuba. This motivated the Soviet Navy to build ballistic-missile submarines, expand its surface fleet, construct troop-carrying and antisubmarine aircraft carriers, and reach out for overseas bases and anchorages in the Mediterranean, the Indian Ocean, and Cuba. By 1987 the USSR had some 350 nuclear attack submarines, compared with 100 for the United States. Many observers, however, maintained that the fewer U.S. submarines were superior in quality. Expected in the mid-1990s is a new class of U.S. attack submarine, the SSN-21 Seawolf, featuring difficult-to-detect quiet operation.

President Ronald Reagan took office in 1981 vowing to build a 600-ship navy (up from 479 ships). Navy strategy focused on developing carrier battle groups—several cruisers and destroyers attached to an aircraft carrier in each group, with submarines operating on their own. Devastating missile attacks on ships during the FALKLAND

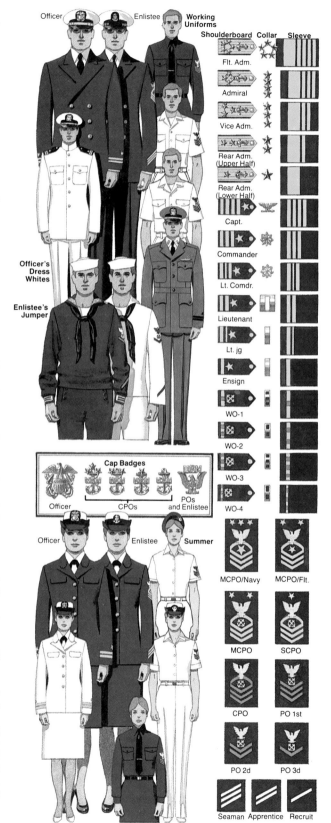

IMPORTANT SEA BATTLES OF HISTORY

Salamis (480 BC)	The Greek fleet, led by THEMISTOCLES, defeated the Persians.
Actium (31 BC)	The forces of Octavian (later Roman Emperor AUGUSTUS) defeated the sea and land forces of Mark ANTONY and CLEOPATRA.
Lepanto (1571)	Spanish and Italian ships defeated the Turks.
Spanish Armada (1588)	A Spanish fleet of 130 ships, the Armada, was defeated by the English in the English Channel.
Serapis vs. *Bonhomme Richard* (1779)	U.S. sea captain John Paul JONES and his *Bonhomme Richard* defeated the British frigate *Serapis* off the Yorkshire coast.
Chesapeake Bay (1781)	A French fleet bottled up English forces at Yorktown, Va. (see YORKTOWN CAMPAIGN), under Gen. Charles CORNWALLIS, who surrendered to the Americans, ending the American Revolution.
Trafalgar (1805)	A British fleet under Horatio NELSON defeated the French and Spanish fleets off Cape Trafalgar, Spain.
Lake Erie (1813)	An American fleet under Captain Oliver PERRY defeated a British force on Lake Erie, enabling Gen. William Henry HARRISON to defeat British land forces at the Thames River.
Navarino (1827)	British, French, and Russian fleets destroyed the combined Turkish and Egyptian fleets at Navarino (now Pylos), Greece.
Monitor vs. *Merrimack* (1862)	In the first engagement between ironclad ships, the MONITOR AND MERRIMACK, Union and Confederate vessels fought to a draw at Hampton Roads, Va.
Tsushima Straits (1905)	A Japanese fleet destroyed the Russian Baltic fleet.
Jutland (1916)	British and German fleets fought the largest naval battle of World War I, which left the British in command of the seas.
Pearl Harbor (1941)	Japanese carrier-based planes caught the U.S. Pacific Fleet by surprise and sank or severely damaged 19 naval vessels, including 8 battleships.
Midway (1942)	U.S. carrier-based aircraft destroyed 4 Japanese aircraft carriers.
Guadalcanal (1942)	U.S. seaborne forces made their first amphibious invasion of a Japanese-held island.
Leyte Gulf (1944)	U.S. fleets destroyed what remained of Japan's naval power. The Japanese lost 3 battleships, 4 carriers, 9 destroyers, and 10 cruisers.
Iwo Jima (1945)	U.S. forces captured an important Japanese air base in an amphibious assault.
Okinawa (1945)	U.S. naval vessels suffered heavy damages from Japanese kamikaze (suicide) planes during the final amphibious invasion of World War II.

ISLANDS war in 1982 and the IRAN-IRAQ WAR in 1987 demonstrated the vulnerability of surface ships to antiship missiles and rekindled a debate over the navy's role in high-tech warfare. During the GULF WAR in 1991, however, the navy clearly demonstrated its high-tech abilities with the launching of cruise missiles and the use of smart bombs by carrier-based planes.

U.S. Naval Organization

The U.S. Navy is under the operational command of the Joint Chiefs of Staff. Major commands of the U.S. Navy include the Pacific Fleet, which operates in the Pacific and Indian Oceans; the Atlantic Fleet, operating in the Atlantic and Mediterranean; Naval Forces, Europe; and the Military Sealift Command, which transports personnel and cargo for the Department of Defense and other agencies of government and also provides logistic support to the fleets. The sea commands are divided into fleets, including the Third Fleet in the eastern and middle Pacific, the Seventh Fleet in the western Pacific, the Sixth Fleet in the Mediterranean, and the Second Fleet in the western Atlantic.

American naval officers earn their commissions in one of three ways: by obtaining a college degree and subsequently attending Officers' Candidate School; by participating in a Naval RESERVE OFFICERS TRAINING CORPS program while enrolled in college; or by attending the U.S. Naval Academy.

Naxos [nahk'-sohs]   Naxos, a Greek island in the Aegean Sea, is the largest (about 44 km^2/170 mi^2) of the CYCLADES; it has a population of 14,037 (1981). The island produces a noted white wine, olives, and citrus fruit. Colonized by the Ionians, Naxos was captured by Persians in 490 BC; it joined the Delian League from which it revolted in 471 only to be captured by Athens, remaining under its control until 404. It passed to Venice in AD 1207, to the Turks in 1566, and to the Russians in 1770. Naxos joined independent Greece in 1830.

Nayarit [nah-yah-reet']   Nayarit is a mountainous state in west central Mexico, bordering the Pacific Ocean and including the Marías Islands. It has a population of 816,212 (1990) and an area of 26,979 km^2 (10,417 mi^2). The capital is Tepic, and the main port is San Blas. Crops include corn, beans, coffee, tobacco, sugarcane, and cotton. Livestock raising and some mining also take place. Nayarit has dense forests that attract many hunters.

Nayarit was conquered by the Spanish as late as the early 18th century. It was part of Guadalajara and Jalisco before becoming Tepic federal territory in 1884. Nayarit was made a state in 1917.

Nazarenes [naz'-uh-reenz]   The Nazarenes were a group of German artists who worked in Rome between 1810 and 1829 and attempted to revive the spirit of medieval Christianity in their painting. The guiding spirits of the group were Johann Friedrich Overbeck and Franz Pforr, who founded (1809) the semireligious Brotherhood of Saint Luke. Dubbed the Nazarenes because they wore their hair long, they led a communal existence in the spirit of medieval monastic life. Rejecting all art from the 16th century onward, they set as their ideal the painting of the Early Renaissance, and especially that of Albrecht Dürer, Perugino, and Raphael. The Nazarenes played a major role in the reevaluation of Early Renaissance art and also influenced the ideals of the Pre-Raphaelites.

Nazareth

Nazareth [naz'-uh-reth]   Nazareth is a town in Lower Galilee, Israel, near the Sea of Galilee. The population is 44,800 (1983 est.). Most of the inhabitants are Arabs. A regional market for the surrounding agricultural region, it produces textiles, pottery, and cigarettes. Tourism is of major importance. Historic landmarks include the Church of the Annunciation (first mentioned in 570, restored in 1730, and remodeled in 1966) with its Grotto of the Annunciation, and the Synagogue-Church on the traditional site where Jesus preached.

Nazareth has been inhabited since prehistoric times. It is sacred in Christian tradition because Jesus spent his childhood there. The town well, called Saint Mary's Well, dates from New Testament times. During the Crusades Nazareth was much fought over, changing hands several times. The Christians were expelled from the city in the 16th century when the Ottoman Turks took control. Allowed to return in the early 17th century, they formed the majority of the population until the 1970s.

Nazca

Nazca [nahs'-kah]   Nazca is the name given the culture that flourished from about 200 BC until about AD 600 on the southern coast of present-day Peru. Centered in the Nazca Valley, an almost rainless desert region broken by rivers from the Andean highlands to the east, Nazca culture continued many of the same traditions of the PARACAS culture that preceded it there. Textile arts, including the production of fine embroidered mantles, remained at a high level, and the Paracas-style clay panpipes were further refined. The ceramic technique of slip casting was mastered and used to form tubes for the panpipes and delicate spouts for jars. Nazca ceramics were extraordinarily fine, decorated with colorful stylized animals, plants, and human figures. Goldworking emphasized repoussé decoration of sheet gold, frequently to form masks attached to cloth-wrapped mummies. Many of the animal motifs that adorn ceramics, textiles, and gold were also executed as gigantic ground drawings, called Nazca Lines. The outlines of the animals as well as elaborate networks of straight lines were produced by removing the brownish stone from the Nazca plain, exposing the light earth underneath.

Nazi-Soviet Pact

Nazi-Soviet Pact   In the Nazi-Soviet Pact of Aug. 23, 1939, a vehemently anti-Communist Germany shocked the world by coming to terms with the USSR, a neces-sary preliminary to Hitler's imminent attack on Poland. The Soviets, having failed to achieve a working relationship with Britain and France, chose to make a deal with Nazi Germany instead. The pact, signed in Moscow by Joachim von RIBBENTROP for Germany and Vyacheslav MOLOTOV for the USSR, included a nonaggression and trade agreement, and a secret protocol that provided for a German-Soviet partition of Poland and cleared the way for the Soviet occupation of the Baltic states. World War II started within two weeks, and the pact remained in force until Hitler's invasion of the USSR in 1941.

Nazism

Nazism   Nazism refers to the ideology and policies espoused and practiced by Adolf HITLER and his National-sozialistische Deutsche Arbeiterpartei (National Socialist German Workers party) from 1921 to 1945. After a checkered beginning, the party gathered strength rapidly in the 1930s, and Hitler became chancellor and dictator in 1933 (see GERMANY, HISTORY OF). Although some tenets of Nazism, such as NATIONALISM and ANTI-SEMITISM, had existed earlier in German history, the Nazi ideology as a whole was a product of the beliefs of Hitler, articulated in his book MEIN KAMPF. Nazism had several elements: (1) A belief—with a pseudoscientific basis in the works of the comte de GOBINEAU, Houston Stewart CHAMBERLAIN, and Alfred ROSENBERG—in an Aryan German race superior to all others and destined to rule, together with a violent hatred of Jews that led to the establishment of CONCEN-

The Nazca Valley, along the southern coast of Peru, is covered with shallow troughs laid out to form animal shapes and geometric patterns. Anthropologists believe that the artworks, best viewed from the air, were created by Indians who inhabited the area more than a thousand years ago. The purpose of the drawings remains unclear, although scientists have speculated that the lines may form a giant calendar used for predicting astronomical phenomena.

TRATION CAMPS and to the HOLOCAUST. (2) An extreme nationalism that called for the unification of all German-
speaking peoples. This led to the occupation of Austria, a
German-speaking country, and of Czechoslovakia, which
had a large German minority. (3) A belief in some form of
corporative state socialism. (4) A private army, called the
SS (Schutzstaffel, or security echelon: see GESTAPO; SS).
(5) A youth cult that emphasized sports and paramilitary
outdoor activities. (6) The massive use of propaganda,
masterminded by Joseph GOEBBELS. (7) The submission
of all decisions to the supreme leader Adolf Hitler, and
the glorification of strength and discipline.

NBC   see RADIO AND TELEVISION BROADCASTING

NCAA   see NATIONAL COLLEGIATE ATHLETIC ASSOCIATION

N'djamena [uhn-jah'-may-nah]   N'djamena (or N'Djamena), formerly Fort-Lamy, is the capital and largest city
of Chad. The population of this agricultural trading center
is 500,000 (1988 est.). N'djamena lies at Chad's western border with Cameroon, 137 km (85 mi) south of Lake
Chad. The University of Chad (1971) is located there, as
well as the National Museum. The city was founded in
1900 as a French military post; its colonial origins are
reflected in the separate French and African quarters.

Ne Win, U [nay win, oo]   The Burmese soldier and political figure U Ne Win (formerly Maung Shu Maung), b.
May 14, 1911, was a military leader during World War II,
fighting first for the Japanese, then for the Allies. After
serving (1958–60) as prime minister, Ne Win deposed
the government of U Nu in 1962 and established a military dictatorship with himself first as prime minister and
then as civilian president under a new constitution
(1974). He resigned as president in 1981 but remained
head of the ruling Socialist Program party until 1988,
when he stepped down in the face of widespread discontent with the economic decline caused by his isolationist
and socialist policies. Later that year, as unrest continued, the army seized control.

Neagh, Lough [nay', lahk]   Lough Neagh, in central
Northern Ireland, is the largest lake in the British Isles.
Covering an area of 389 km^2 (150 mi^2), it averages 31
km (19 mi) long and 24 km (15 mi) wide. Fed primarily
by the Upper Bann, the Blackwater, and the Main rivers,
it is drained to the north by the Lower Bann. Fisheries
there are economically important. Mesolithic remains
from c.6000 BC have been found near the lake. A flood-
control project, completed in 1959, lowered the level of
the lake to 15 m (50 ft) above sea level.

Neanderthalers [nee-an'-der-tawl-urz]   The Neanderthalers (*Homo sapiens neanderthalensis*) were a widespread subspecies of PREHISTORIC HUMANS that inhabited

Europe and parts of Asia and North Africa from about
125,000 to about 40,000 years ago, immediately prior to
the appearance of anatomically modern humans (*Homo
sapiens sapiens*) throughout the world.

The first Neanderthal skeletal material was acciden-
tally discovered (1856) by quarrymen in a cave in the
Neander Valley, near Düsseldorf, Germany; it became the
first early-human fossil type to be recognized by science.
The British biologist Thomas Henry HUXLEY emphasized
the more primitive aspects of the fossil, suggesting it
formed a link between modern humans and the apes. By
stressing these features in his forceful defense of EVOLU-
TION, Huxley laid the foundations for a view of Neanderthalers as bent-kneed, half-witted, subhuman creatures.

In a detailed study of another Neanderthal fossil, the
French anatomist Marcellin Boule suggested that some of
the features of the Neanderthalers, such as the low fore-
head with strong brow ridges, were too extreme to have
evolved into the anatomically modern human species—
that the Neanderthalers represented a side branch of human evolution that became extinct about the time that
CRO-MAGNON MAN came into existence.

Many scientists continue to believe that the Neanderthalers became extinct. Others hold that in comparison
with older fossil forms, such as HOMO ERECTUS, the Neanderthalers share a great many physical traits with *Homo*

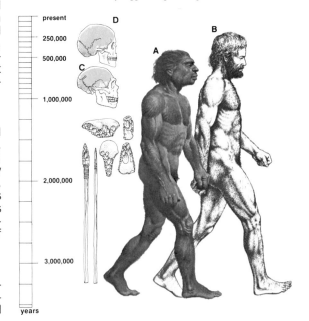

The Neanderthalers, Homo sapiens neanderthalensis, *lived about 125,000 to
40,000 years ago from western Europe and northern Africa to central Asia.
They take their name from the Neander Valley in Germany, where fossil bones
were discovered in 1856. Neanderthalers* (A) *were shorter and more thickly
built than modern humans,* Homo sapiens sapiens (B); *their long skulls* (C)
*had lower foreheads and heavier brow ridges (compare modern human skull,
D). Both subspecies share comparable posture and brain size. A sophisticated Neanderthal tool industry suggests high intelligence.*

sapiens sapiens. These shared traits—brain size, locomotor ability, manual dexterity, and the capacity for symbolic behavior—suggest that the Neanderthalers may have been the immediate ancestors of modern humans. Recent research indicating that the Neanderthalers had a capacity for speech supports this theory. Another view has emerged that the Neanderthalers and the Cro-Magnons actually coexisted in some areas for up to a few millennia before the Neanderthalers died out.

Throughout Europe, the Middle East, and North Africa, stone tools of the Middle Paleolithic MOUSTERIAN tradition have been discovered in association with Neanderthal remains. These tool assemblages exhibit superior workmanship over the preceding Acheulean industry. Evidence of ritualized behavior is reflected in the discovery of more than a dozen Neanderthal grave sites ranging from simple pit burials to stonelined tomb chambers.

—

Near East   *Near East,* an imprecisely defined term mostly used before World War II, usually refers to the African and Southwest Asian (and sometimes European) countries located around the Mediterranean's eastern shore. Today the term MIDDLE EAST is more common.

nearsightedness   see MYOPIA

—

Nebraska [nuh-bras'-kuh]   Nebraska lies immediately to the north of the geographic center of the conterminous United States, bounded on the north by South Dakota, on the west by Colorado and Wyoming, on the south by Kansas, and on the east by Iowa and Missouri. In area, Nebraska is the 16th largest of the 50 states.

The name of Nebraska comes from the Oto Indian word *nebrathka,* which means "flat water," referring to the Platte River. The nickname of "Tree Planters' State" was selected by the legislature in 1895 in official recognition of the pioneers' efforts in planting trees on the prairie. In 1945 the state's official nickname was changed to "Cornhusker State" in honor of the University of Nebraska's football team.

Land and Resources

Nebraska lies within two major physiographic regions of North America, the central lowlands and the GREAT PLAINS. In the central lowlands and along the Missouri River elevations average about 256 m (840 ft), rising to about 365 m (1,200 ft) in the northeast. Elevations also increase westward to about 915 m (3,000 ft) in the southwest and to about 1,525 m (5,000 ft) in the northwest. The highest elevation in the state is 1,654 m (5,426 ft), in Kimball County.

The topography changes from level to gently rolling prairie in the central lowlands. The eastern section of this area is a part of a glacial till plain that has been subjected to extensive weathering and erosion to form a well-developed drainage system. Farther west is the Sand Hill region, which is characterized by sand dunes covered with short grasses and is interspersed with numerous val-

leys and shallow lakes. The High Plains section of the Great Plains lies to the west and south of the Sand Hills region.

Soils. Deep, rich silt loams and sandy loams cover about 109,000 km^2 (42,000 mi^2) in the eastern third and southwestern quarter of Nebraska. These soils are especially noted for their fertility. The Sand Hill section has sandy or sandy loam soils used almost exclusively for grass cover and grazing. The use of irrigation has increased rapidly on these sandy soils. The High Plains, with its broad tablelands and extensive areas of bottom land, occupies about 39,000 km^2 (15,000 mi^2), mostly in the western panhandle. This westernmost section has a wide variety of loamy and sandy soils. The chief factor limiting the use of these fertile soils is the shortage of moisture, particularly in the west.

Drainage. The MISSOURI RIVER, following the state's northeastern and eastern border, is the eventual destination of all streams in Nebraska. The PLATTE RIVER is the state's longest river. The North Platte, flowing from Wyoming, and the South Platte, entering from Colorado, join near the town of North Platte and flow generally eastward to enter the Missouri about 20 km (12 mi) south of Omaha. Other major rivers include the Loup, Niobrara, and Republican rivers. Most major lakes within Nebraska are artificial.

Climate. Nebraska has light precipitation, relatively low humidity, hot summers, cold winters, and great variations in temperature and precipitation from year to year. Mean January temperatures are −5° C (23° F), while the July mean temperature is 24° C (76° F). The annual precipitation in the southeast averages 787 mm (31 in), in the central portion 584 mm (23 in), and in the panhandle 432 mm (17 in). About 77% of the precipitation falls during the months of April to September.

Vegetation and Animal Life. Natural vegetation ranges from tall prairie grass in the east to the short, drought-resistant grasses of the west. Trees are usually confined to major water courses and consist of broad-leaved deciduous species, especially elms and cottonwoods.

Animal life prior to European settlement included American bison, beaver, deer, pronghorn antelope, coyote, pheasant, quail, grouse, and a variety of migratory waterfowl. Although the numbers of many of these animals were seriously depleted, diligent conservation efforts have replenished some species so as to allow an open hunting season each year.

Resources. One of the great resources of Nebraska is the comparative abundance of easily accessible, high-quality groundwater. Although it currently is being withdrawn at a rate greater than that of annual recharge, the problem of a potential shortage is not yet acute.

People

The population growth rate of the state in recent decades has lagged behind the national average. Since the early 1930s the out-migration rate has tended to exceed the in-migration rate; the slight population gain is a result of natural increase. The rate of growth from 1970 to 1980 was a modest 5.7%, and from 1980 to 1990, 0.9%, far

AT A GLANCE

NEBRASKA

Land: Area: 200,356 km² (77,358 mi²); rank: 16th. Capital: Lincoln (1990 pop., 191,972). Largest city: Omaha (1990 pop., 335,795). Counties: 93. Elevations: highest—1,654 m (5,426 ft), in Kimball County; lowest—256 m (840 ft), Missouri River.

People: Population (1990): 1,584,617; rank: 36th; density: 7.9 persons per km² (20.5 per mi²). Distribution (1990): 66.1% urban, 33.9% rural. Average annual change (1980–90): +0.09%.

Government (1993): Governor: Ben Nelson, Democrat. U.S. Congress: Senate—2 Democrats; House—1 Democrat, 2 Republicans. Electoral college votes: 5. State legislature (unicameral): 49 legislators.

Economy: State personal income (1989): $24.9 billion; rank: 34th. Median family income (1989): $31,634; rank: 34th. Agriculture: income (1989)—$8.5 billion. Lumber production (1991, with Kansas): 11 million board feet. Mining (nonfuel): value (1988)—$91 million. Manufacturing: value added (1987)—$5.8 billion. Services: value (1987)—$5.6 billion.

Miscellany: Statehood: Mar. 1, 1867; the 37th state. Nickname: Cornhusker State; tree: western cottonwood; motto: Equality before the Law; song: "Beautiful Nebraska."

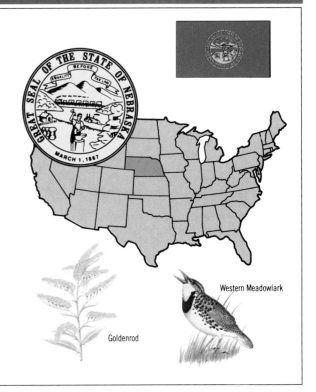

Western Meadowlark

Goldenrod

---

below the national growth rate of 10.2% of the same period. Nebraska is more rural in character than the nation as a whole. In 1990 only four cities in the state—GRAND ISLAND, LINCOLN, OMAHA, and Bellevue—had populations exceeding 25,000.

In addition to its rural nature Nebraska is comparatively homogeneous, with the vast majority of the population claiming European—particularly German—ancestry. The nonwhite population in 1990 was 97,827, only 6% of the total. Blacks account for about 60% of the minority population, and American Indians account for almost 13%. Persons of Spanish origin make up 2% of the state's population. More than two-thirds of the nonwhite population are concentrated in the Omaha urban area, with most of the remaining living in Lancaster and Thurston counties—the site of the Omaha and WINNEBAGO Indian reservations—or in Scotts Bluff County.

Nebraska's largest religious groups are the Roman Catholics, Methodists, and Lutherans.

Education. Nebraska has had a compulsory education law since 1891. Higher education is available at the University of Nebraska (1869), with its main campus at Lincoln, four state colleges, and several private colleges.

Culture. Major museums include the Museum of Natural History at the University of Nebraska in Lincoln, the Nebraska State Historical Society Museum in Lincoln, the Hastings Museum, the Pioneer Village in Minden, and the Strategic Aerospace Museum at Offutt Air Force Base, Omaha. Leading art galleries include the Joslyn Art Musuem in Omaha and the University of Nebraska gallery and sculpture garden in Lincoln. Omaha and Lincoln both support symphony orchestras. Omaha has several theaters, including the Orpheum Theatre, built in 1927 as a vaudeville house. It has been restored to its original opulence and now serves as the city's Performing Arts Center. The state's most important libraries are those of the University of Nebraska at Lincoln and the Omaha Public Library.

Historical Sites. The Homestead National Monument, located about 65 km (40 mi) south of Lincoln, commemorates the first farm plot to be claimed under the HOMESTEAD ACT of 1862. Chimney Rock National Historical Site and Scotts Bluff National Monument are important landmarks along the Overland Trail. Fort Robinson State Historical Park commemorates what was once an important military post during the Indian wars; CRAZY HORSE, chief of the Sioux, was killed there.

Recreation. State parks are located at Chadron, Niobrara, and Ponca. The state maintains more than 50 other lakes and recreation areas. Sports teams are supported with great intensity and pride, especially the "Cornhuskers" of the University of Nebraska at Lincoln.

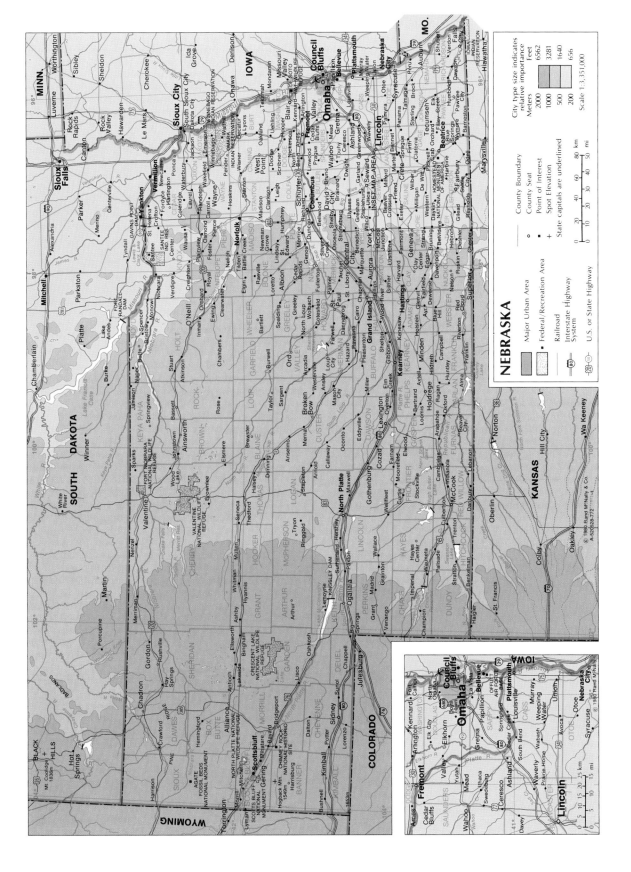

NEBRASKA

City type size indicates relative importance

Meters	Feet
2000	6562
1000	3281
500	1640
200	656

Scale 1:3,351,000

County Boundary
○ County Seat
■ Point of Interest
+ Spot Elevation
State capitals are underlined

Major Urban Area

Federal/Recreation Area

Railroad

Interstate Highway System

U.S. or State Highway

© 1980 Rand McNally & Co
A-520628-772

Cattle are penned in stockyards awaiting shipment to market in Omaha, one of the world's major meat-packing and processing centers. Beef is Nebraska's major farm product.

Communications. Nebraska's leading newspapers are the *Omaha World-Herald* and the *Lincoln Journal-Star*. The state also has numerous radio and television broadcasting facilities.

Economic Activities

The economic future of Nebraska is encouraging, especially in the areas of agriculture, manufacturing, and services. Agriculture and related activities, however, still dominate.

Agriculture. Nebraska ranks among the leading U.S. states in the value of total farm marketings, and nearly half of Nebraska's labor force is employed, directly or indirectly, in agriculture. Corn is a leading farm commodity of the state, along with cattle, hogs, and soybeans. Other important farm products are sorghum, hay, wheat, oats, barley, and rye.

Manufacturing. Nebraska's major industries are agriculturally based, engaged in the processing of meat, grain, and dairy products. Manufacturing has become increasingly diversified, with an emphasis on electric and electronic equipment, nonelectrical machinery, and chemicals. The major manufacturing areas of the state are the Omaha, Lincoln, and the Sioux City (Iowa) regions.

Mining. Petroleum, discovered in Nebraska in 1939, is the leading mineral produced in the state. The production of crude oil centers in the state's southwest and southwest panhandle. Other minerals exploited are sand and gravel, stone, and natural gas.

Energy. The low average cost of electricity in the state is a result of a user-owned, nonprofit system of power generation and transmission. Leading energy sources in the state are petroleum, natural gas, coal, and nuclear power.

Transportation and Tourism. The central location of Ne-

braska and the national road network that crosses it have facilitated tourism in the state. Omaha is an important rail center with several railroads and is a regional hub of air transportation. Omaha's Eppley Airfield is the state's busiest airport.

Nebraska has numerous state parks and recreation areas. Most tourists visit Nebraska while on their way to either eastern or western parts of the country.

Government

A state constitution was adopted on Oct. 12, 1875, and revised by a 1919–20 constitutional convention and through numerous amendments since that time. Nebraska is unique in that, since 1934, it has had a unicameral legislature. It consists of 49 nonpartisan members serving 4-year terms. Members of the executive branch are elected to 4-year terms on partisan ballots.

Justice is administered by a supreme court and by district, trial, county, and municipal courts, as well as certain special courts. The 93 counties are administered by either boards of supervisors or by boards of commissioners.

History

Archaeological excavations indicate the presence of prehistoric humans in Nebraska as early as 9000 BC. The PAWNEE Indian tribe was one of the first groups to be recorded in the area. Other Indian groups found by European explorers were the ARAPAHO, CHEYENNE, OMAHA, OTO, and SIOUX.

Pedro de Villasur and a party of Spanish soldiers were the first Europeans known to have reached Nebraska (1720), though some French fur traders and trappers had ventured upstream on the Missouri River by about 1700. The first Europeans to cross the state were probably Paul and Pierre Mallet, who traversed nearly the entire length of the modern state in their journey from the Missouri to Santa Fe, N.Mex., in 1739.

Spain, France, and Great Britain struggled for possession of the Nebraska region. France ceded all claims west of the Mississippi River to Spain in 1763, at the close of the Seven Years' War. Nebraska remained part of Spain until 1801, when Napoleon purchased the area for France. In 1803, Thomas Jefferson acquired the Louisiana Territory, which included present-day Nebraska, for the United States.

After the LOUISIANA PURCHASE the LEWIS AND CLARK EXPEDITION crossed the eastern edge of what was to become Nebraska. Later expeditions were led by Zebulon Montgomery PIKE (1806) and Stephen H. LONG (1820).

Numerous traders, trappers, missionaries, and travelers moved across Nebraska between 1800 and 1840. The famous OREGON TRAIL followed the Little Blue and Platte rivers through the state and was used by thousands of wagon trains from 1830 to 1870. The Mormon Trail to Utah and the Denver Trail to Colorado also crossed the area. From 1850 to 1860 steamboat navigation on the Missouri River was at its peak, only to fall off with the advent of rail travel in the 1860s.

Nebraska was part of the Territory of Indiana from Oct.

1, 1804, to July 4, 1805. From that time until Dec. 7, 1812, it was part of the Louisiana Territory. It then became part of the Territory of Missouri until 1821, when Missouri became a state and Nebraska part of an unorganized region usually called "Indian country." On June 30, 1834, the U.S. Congress defined the boundaries of this Indian country and passed the Indian Intercourse Act, which excluded white settlers and formalized relations between the United States and the Indians. The first congressional bill organizing the territory, the KANSAS-NEBRASKA ACT, was passed in 1854, and the first session of the territorial legislature met Jan. 16, 1855. Statehood was finally achieved in 1867.

The POPULIST PARTY controlled Nebraska's state government from 1890 to 1900. From that period until the 1930s, Nebraska's agricultural economy flourished. The Depression of the 1930s, coupled with a series of drought years, was especially severe in Nebraska. During the resultant DUST BOWL exodus, Nebraska lost nearly 4.5% of its population.

Since World War II the economy has revived, largely as a result of the spectacular growth in irrigation. During the mid-1980s Nebraska's economy suffered because of a widespread U.S. agricultural crisis. Low farm prices, heavy indebtedness, and low farmland values all contributed to the depression, which in Nebraska spread to farm-support businesses and banks. By the late 1980s, however, the state's agricultural economy was improving; there was a significant drop in farm debt, and land values were up. A drought interfered with the recovery, but its effects were ameliorated by the extensive irrigation. The service sector of the state's economy also has gained strength, a sign of diversification.

Chimney Rock rises 152 m (500 ft) above the North Platte River valley in western Nebraska. Visible from a distance of about 48 km (30 mi), it was a landmark for pioneers traveling on the Oregon Trail.

Nebuchadnezzar II, King of Babylonia [nebuh-kuhd-nez'-ur] Nebuchadnezzar II, son of Nabopolassar, founder of the Chaldean dynasty in BABYLONIA, reigned from 605 to 562 BC. Nebuchadnezzar helped his father destroy the power of ASSYRIA but is best remembered for his relations with the Jews and as the builder of the Hanging Gardens of Babylon. The Jewish Kingdom of JUDAH was positioned between two great powers—Egypt and Babylonia. It was unable to remain either independent or neutral; if it joined one side, it would be attacked by the other. In 597 and again in 586 when the kingdom was under Egyptian domination, Nebuchadnezzar besieged and captured Jerusalem. The second time, he destroyed the city and carried off the Jews into their long BABYLONIAN CAPTIVITY.

In Babylonia, but most conspicuously in Babylon itself, Nebuchadnezzar engaged in numerous building projects, fortifying the city and constructing many temples. A great step-pyramid, or ZIGGURAT, known as the Hanging Gardens, was later numbered among the SEVEN WONDERS OF THE WORLD.

The last years of Nebuchadnezzar's reign are obscure. Old, even senile, he was perhaps dethroned by his own son. The biblical Book of Daniel describes him as eating grass and undergoing a physical transformation in his final days. The Dead Sea Scrolls, however, suggest that it was not Nebuchadnezzar, but the last Chaldean king, Nabonidus (r. 556–539 BC), who was so afflicted.

nebula [neb'-yoo-luh] A nebula is a cloud of interstellar matter that may be observed by the light it emits, reflects, or absorbs. Nebulas are distinct from galaxies. The physical nature of nebulas was unknown until William Huggins observed (1864) the ORION NEBULA and found it to have a bright-line SPECTRUM indicating that it consists of a hot cloud of interstellar gas emitting light much as a neon or mercury-vapor lamp does. In the mid-1920s, Edwin P. Hubble demonstrated that other "nebulas" with continuous spectra are actually distant galaxies.

Most true nebulas have emission-line spectra similar to the Orion nebula. Their main energy source, which ionizes and heats interstellar gas and causes it to glow, is ultraviolet radiation emitted by very hot stars. The hottest main-sequence stars in our galaxy have temperatures of about 40,000 K and emit large amounts of high-energy ultraviolet radiation. Because the most abundant element in interstellar gas is hydrogen (H), much of the ultraviolet energy is absorbed in photoionizing the hydrogen, converting it to hydrogen ions (H^+) and electrons. The electrons created in this way may have high kinetic energies, so that the interstellar gas is heated by this photoionization process. Other elements in the gas such as helium, oxygen, carbon, neon, and nitrogen are also photoionized in the same way. Although nebulas with emission-line spectra are often called H II regions (meaning H^+ regions) because of the great abundance of the hydrogen ion, other ions are also present in lesser amounts.

Stars with temperatures below about 25,000 K do not

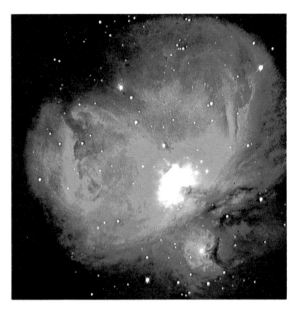

The Orion nebula is a huge cloud of gas and dust visible in the Orion constellation. Four hot stars, the Trapezium, near the brightest part of the nebula ionize the gas, causing it to glow.

emit enough high-energy ultraviolet radiation to appreciably ionize and heat interstellar gas. If such a star is located in an interstellar cloud rich in dust, however, light scattered by the dust makes the cloud visible. This is known as a reflection nebula. The gas in a reflection nebula does not glow, because it is not photoionized and heated. Highly evolved stars may themselves throw off shells of gas. These glowing shells are called planetary nebulas, although they do not contain interstellar materials.

Some dense interstellar clouds containing large amounts of dust completely cut off the light of stars beyond them. They appear as dark nebulas and are known as absorption nebulas. An example of this type is the Horsehead nebula in Orion.

Necho II, King of Egypt [nee'-koh]   Necho II, d. 593 BC, a pharaoh (r. 609–593 BC) of the 26th dynasty, sponsored the first known circumnavigation of Africa and an early, though unsuccessful, attempt to link the Mediterranean and Red seas by canal. He attempted to stem the expansion of resurgent BABYLONIA. He failed, however, in his efforts to aid collapsing Assyria and was himself defeated by the Babylonians at Carchemish (605). Thus, Egypt lost to Babylon its political and commercial advantages in Syria, Phoenicia, and Palestine. Abandoning Asia after 601, Necho strengthened the Egyptian navy for strategic and trading purposes and settled Greek mercenaries on Egyptian land in return for their services.

Necker, Jacques [ne-kair']   A wealthy Swiss Protestant banker in Paris, Jacques Necker, b. Sept. 30, 1732, d. Apr. 9, 1804, headed France's financial administration in 1776–81 and 1788–90, gaining great if fleeting popularity during the fiscal crisis that ushered in the FRENCH REVOLUTION. His wife's popular salon and his own writings in favor of mercantilism helped him win appointment by LOUIS XVI as director of the treasury (1776) and director general of finance (1777). He replaced the free-trade advocate A. R. J. TURGOT.

Necker's stringent economizing and his knack of borrowing outside court circles financed France's participation in the American Revolution. He was dismissed in 1781, however, partly because of the publication of a misleading budget (*Compte rendu*, 1781), which divulged courtier's pensions and disguised a soaring deficit as a slight surplus.

Recalled as finance minister in 1788, Necker gave the bourgeois third estate in STATES-GENERAL double representation without voting parity with the tax-exempt clergy and nobles—his famous "new year's gift." This "gift" helped polarize the assembly, however, and Necker was dismissed on July 11, 1789. He died in retirement near Geneva, survived by his famous literary daughter, Madame de STAËL.

nectarine   A subspecies of peach, the nectarine, *Prunus persica nectarina*, resembles the peach in tree, bud, and fruit characteristics, except that it has a smooth skin. Like the peach, it seems to have originated in China and to have reached Greece and Rome via the Middle East. It is believed to have been introduced into America by the Spaniards. California grows most of the nectarines raised in the United States. Nectarines are susceptible to attack by insects, and the fruit's tender skin is subject to scarring.

needlework   The term *needlework* refers to all types of crafts done with a needle, whether by hand or machine. It includes everything from plain sewing, which is the foundation of all forms of needlework, to elaborate ornamental stitchery.

EMBROIDERY is the art of decorating a background material, usually fabric, with designs using various ornamental stitches; cross-stitch is probably the oldest and most common form of decorative embroidery. Candlewicking, which originated in colonial North America, uses thread similar to the cotton used in the wicks of candles. Two popular types of embroidery produce very durable fabrics. In crewelwork, wool yarn of various colors is stitched onto a linen background. Needlepoint, or embroidery on an open-mesh base called a canvas, is used in making pictures, pillows, rugs, purses, and upholstery. BEADS AND BEADWORK are also used in ornamental needlework.

TAPESTRY, usually created by weaving a design directly into the material, can be extremely elaborate; an example is the magnificent medieval tapestry series *The Hunt of the Unicorn* (The Cloisters, New York City). The late-11th-century BAYEUX TAPESTRY, depicting the Norman invasion of England, is not a true woven tapestry but rather an embroidery. France, in particular, is noted for its fine tapestries, especially those of the GOBELINS factory (founded 1662).

Appliqué, the addition of pieces of fabric to the surface of a background material to form a design, is often used in conjunction with QUILTING. Two types of needlework related to weaving are CROCHET and KNITTING.

The art of making LACE, an ornamental openwork fabric, involves several different techniques. The two most important types of true lace are bobbin, or pillow, lace and needlepoint, or needle, lace. Lace can also be made using such techniques as MACRAMÉ, crochet, knitting, and tatting.

See also: FOLK ART.

Neel, Alice [neel]   The American portrait painter Alice Neel, b. Merion Square, Pa., Jan. 28, 1900, d. Oct. 13, 1984, is known for the psychological candor and sharpness of observation that characterize her work. Her highly individual style tends more toward expressionism than literal realism but at the same time portrays the distinctive traits of the subject. Of particular note are her paintings of the people of Spanish Harlem in New York City, for example, *T. B. Harlem* (1940; Graham Gallery, New York City).

Nefertiti [nef-ur-tee'-tee]   Nefertiti was the queen-consort of the controversial Egyptian king AKHENATEN (r. 1380–1362 BC) of the 18th dynasty. She appears to have lost favor with her husband after the 14th year of his reign. A famous bust of Nefertiti, dating from *c.*1363–1343 BC and made of painted limestone, is now in the Staatliche Museen, Berlin. It is a masterpiece of the new, naturalistic style in Egyptian art of the Amarna period. The Cairo Museum contains an unfinished quartzite head

This painted limestone portrait bust of Nefertiti, Egyptian queen and wife of the Pharaoh Akhenaten, dates from the Amarna period of the New Kingdom (18th dynasty). Nefertiti was actively involved in the religious reforms of Akhenaten, who sought to establish the monotheistic worship of the sun god, Aton, throughout Egypt. (Staatliche Museen, Berlin-Dahlem.)

of the same period that is also believed to represent Nefertiti.

Negev [neg'-ev]   The Negev is a desert occupying slightly more than half of Israel in the southern part of the country. A narrow wedge between Egypt and Jordan, it is 8 to 130 km (5 to 80 mi) wide and about 240 km (150 mi) long, covering an area of about 12,170 km^2 (4,700 mi^2). It stretches from BEERSHEBA in the north to the Gulf of Aqaba in the south, where ELAT has become an important port.

Consisting of sandy loam over limestone, the Negev is a plateau with an average elevation of 457 m (1,500 ft). Hot in summer and cold in winter, it receives less than 254 mm (10 in) of rain a year. Irrigation makes the northern part highly productive; wheat, barley, citrus fruits, and vegetables are grown there. The Negev also yields copper, phosphates, sulfur, kaolin, natural gas, and oil. The Desert Research Institute, a branch of Ben-Gurion University in Beersheba, works on projects concerned with development of the Negev.

---

negligence   Negligence, in law, is the inadvertent failure to act with the legally appropriate standard of care in a particular situation, in which injury or loss is sustained by another person to whom a duty of care is owed either contractually or by the standard of the actions of a "reasonable, prudent man." The concept became important in the early 19th century in its application to such problems as horse-and-buggy collisions, railroad accidents, and industrial injuries. Since then the range of activities and occurrences covered by negligence law has broadened to include motor-vehicle collisions (less important in recent years with the development of NO-FAULT INSURANCE), medical and legal MALPRACTICE, unsuccessful rescue attempts, and landowners' liability for injuries occurring on their property.

Negrito [nuh-gree'-toh]   Negrito (Spanish for "Little Negro") is used to identify the approximately 35,000 pygmies of Southeast Asia and Oceania, including the Andamanese, the Aeta of the Philippines, and the Semang of Malaysia. Other Negritos live in New Guinea. Their physical traits include a male height under five feet, dark brown to black hair that is curly to frizzy, skin color ranging from yellowish brown to black, and scant body hair. The traditional way of life of most Negritos is based on hunting and food gathering.

Negro, Rio [nay'-groh, ree'-oh]   Rio Negro, the largest tributary of the AMAZON RIVER, is a 2,253-km-long (1,400-mi) black-water river that begins as the Guainía River in eastern Colombia, flowing east, then south along the borders of Venezuela and Colombia. It flows into Brazil as the Rio Negro and joins the Amazon south of Manaus. Although its basin consists mostly of uninhabited swamps and forests, the river carries rubber, nuts, and skins. Its main tributaries are the Branco, Içana, and Uaupés.

Nehemiah   see EZRA AND NEHEMIAH, BOOKS OF

—

Nehru, Jawaharlal [nay'-roo, juh-wah-hahr-lahl'] Jawaharlal Nehru, b. Nov. 14, 1889, d. May 27, 1964, was the first prime minister of independent India and, with his mentor, Mahatma GANDHI, one of the two most influential political figures in that country in the 20th century. He was born at Allahabad, the son of Motilal Nehru (1861–1931), a lawyer who was also to be prominent in the nationalist movement. Nehru's childhood was one of privilege: he was tutored at home and then studied in England at Harrow School and Trinity College, Cambridge. He was admitted to the English bar and returned to India very westernized. There he married (1916) Kamala Kaul; their only child, Indira, was to become prime minister of India in 1966 (see GANDHI, INDIRA).

Nehru met Mohandas Gandhi in 1916 at an INDIAN NATIONAL CONGRESS party meeting. From then on, their lives were intertwined, although they differed on several points, largely because Nehru's international outlook clashed with Gandhi's more narrowly Indian views. Like Gandhi, Nehru became active in nationalist politics after the Amritsar massacre of 1919, becoming a leader of the more radical wing of the Congress party. In 1929 he was elected party president. Repeatedly arrested by the British for civil-disobedience strikes and other political actions, he spent half of the next 18 years in jail. After World War II he participated in the negotiations that eventually created the separate states of India and Pakistan. When India gained its independence on Aug. 15, 1947, Nehru became prime minister of India.

Nehru had to cope with the influx of Hindu refugees from Pakistan, the problem of integrating the princely states into the new federal structure, and war with Pakistan (1948) over Kashmir and with China (1962). In international affairs he pursued a policy of strict nonalignment. In January 1964, after 17 years in office, he suffered a stroke. He died four months later.

—

Nelson, Byron   John Byron Nelson, Jr., b. Fort Worth, Tex., Feb. 12, 1912, had perhaps an individual golfer's greatest year in 1945, when he won 19 tournaments—11 of them consecutively—averaged 68.33 strokes per round, and was the Associated Press Athlete of the Year. Nelson won the Masters twice (1937, 1942), the PGA twice (1940, 1945), and the U.S. Open once (1939).

—

Nelson, Horatio Nelson, Viscount   Horatio, Lord Nelson, b. Sept. 29, 1758, d. Oct. 21, 1805, was the most celebrated admiral in British history. He entered the Royal Navy at the age of 12 and was a captain by 1778. Britain's entry into the FRENCH REVOLUTIONARY WARS in 1793 gave him an opportunity to excel.

Horatio, Lord Nelson, British admiral, was renowned during his lifetime for brilliant tactical innovations in naval battles against the French and Spanish. Nelson was killed while winning a spectacular victory over the Franco-Spanish fleet at Trafalgar in 1805.

Nelson played a distinguished part in the defeat of the Spanish fleet off Cape Saint Vincent in 1797. The following year he achieved one of his most brilliant and crushing victories over the French fleet in the Battle of the Nile. Stationed next at Naples he began a celebrated liaison with Emma, Lady Hamilton, wife of the British ambassador there; she bore him a daughter in 1801. At the Battle of Copenhagen in 1801, Nelson put a telescope to his blind eye—he had been blinded in battle in 1794—to avoid seeing a signal from his commander, Sir Hyde Parker, that would have prevented him from crippling the Danish fleet.

On the renewal of war with France in 1803, Nelson was charged with blockading the French fleet at Toulon. Although he failed to prevent the French from breaking out and uniting with the Spanish fleet in 1805, he eventually brought the combined navies to battle. He was

Jawaharlal Nehru was prime minister of India from its independence in 1947 until his death in 1964. An extremely popular leader, Nehru strove for moderate socialist reforms within India and neutrality in international affairs.

killed in the resulting Battle of TRAFALGAR, but he lived long enough to know that his victory had saved Britain from the danger of a Napoleonic invasion. Lord Nelson's reckless courage and flamboyant manners masked a shrewd, strategic mind and a brilliant mastery of naval tactics. The *Victory*, his flagship at Trafalgar, is preserved at Portsmouth, England.

Nelson, Robert   Robert Nelson, b. Montreal, January 1794, d. Mar. 1, 1873, was a Canadian insurgent. A surgeon by profession, he sat (1827–30, 1834–38) in the legislature of Lower Canada and supported Louis Joseph PAPINEAU. Although he took no part in the REBELLIONS OF 1837, of which his brother Wolfred (1792–1863) was a leader, Nelson was nevertheless arrested. Released, he fled to the United States and formed a provisional government, which declared Canada a republic. In 1838 he led a small invasion of Canada that was easily repulsed. Nelson then practiced medicine in the United States.

Nelson River   The Nelson River is a 644-km-long (400-mi) river in north central Manitoba, Canada. It drains a basin of 1,150,000 km² (444,000 mi²). From its source, Lake Winnipeg, it flows northeastward and empties into Hudson Bay at Port Nelson. With the Bow and Saskatchewan rivers, it forms a river system extending to the Canadian Rockies. Long an important route for fur traders, the Nelson River was discovered in 1612 by the Welsh explorer Sir Thomas Button and was named for his sailing master.

nematode   Nematodes, or roundworms, are slender, cylindrical, unsegmented, and usually white animals. The nematode's body consists of little more than an outer tube and an inner tube joined together at the mouth and anus. The outer tube is the thin body wall, or epidermis, which is thickened at the top, bottom, and two sides into four internal ridges, or cords, running the length of the body. The body wall is covered by a multilayered cuticle and is lined internally by lengthwise muscles that are divided into four strips by the body-wall cords. The inner tube is the digestive tract, which may be muscularized at the front, or pharynx, and at the rear, or rectum. The space between the two tubes is called the pseudocoel and is filled with a fluid that moves freely as the worm wriggles.

In most nematodes the sexes are separate, and the reproductive organs loop back and forth in the fluid-filled pseudocoel. Some nematodes are hermaphroditic and self-fertilizing; others are parthenogenetic.

Some nematodes have ornamented body surfaces and can use these surface structures to crawl like earthworms. Others have long bristles (setae) that assist in gripping the surface to aid in caterpillarlike locomotion. Most nematodes, however, move by simple flexings of the body.

Nematodes live almost everywhere. Many kinds are free-living; most of these are less than 1 mm (0.04 in) long, and many are microscopic. A few marine forms may reach 5 cm (2 in) in length. The free-living forms feed on minute animals, including other nematodes, or on bacteria, algae, or fungi. They exist in enormous numbers in soil, fresh water, and the sea. Other nematodes are parasitic and may reach 2 m (7.5 ft) in length. Plant parasites may live within the tissue of the plant or attack it from the soil. Animal parasites, all internal, include the common "worms" of pet dogs and cats (see DISEASES, ANIMAL). About 50 species attack humans; roughly 12 of these are considered dangerous, including HOOKWORMS, trichina worms (see TRICHINOSIS), guinea worms, filariids (see FILARIASIS), EYE WORMS, and so-called roundworms.

About 12,000 species of nematodes have been described, but some authorities believe that there may be as many as 80,000 to possibly 500,000 different kinds in existence. Nematodes are sometimes considered a class, which, along with the rotifers and other classes, belongs to the phylum Aschelminthes, but most authorities consider them a distinct phylum, called either Nematoda or Nemathelminthes.

Nemerov, Howard   [nem'-uh-rawf]   The writer Howard Nemerov, b. New York City, Mar. 1, 1920, d. July 5, 1991, was best known for his ironic and witty verse found in such collections as *Mirrors and Windows* (1958), *The Blue Swallows* (1967), and *The Western Approaches* (1975). He was also a successful novelist—his *The Homecoming Game* (1957) was adapted into a play, *Tall Story* (1958), by Howard Lindsay and Russel Crouse—short-story writer, and essayist. His *Collected Poems* (1977) won the 1978 National Book Award and a 1978 Pulitzer Prize. Another poetry collection is *War Stories* (1987). Nemerov was appointed U.S. poet laureate in 1988 and reappointed to a second term in 1989.

Nemesis   [nem'-uh-sis]   In Greek and Roman mythology Nemesis was a goddess who brought retribution for evil deeds or undeserved good fortune. She was called the daughter of Nyx (Night) but was essentially the personification of an idea, rather than a mythological character.

Nemirovich-Danchenko, Vladimir Ivanovich   [nay-mee-roh'-vich-dahn'-cheng-koh]   Vladimir Ivanovich Nemirovich-Danchenko, b. Dec. 11 (N.S.), 1858, d. Apr. 25, 1943, a Russian director and drama teacher, was cofounder (1898) with Konstantin STANISLAVSKY of the MOSCOW ART THEATER. He brought to the new company his best pupils and directed many outstanding productions of plays by major Russian writers such as Anton Chekhov and Maksim Gorky as well as by European playwrights such as Henrik Ibsen and Gerhart Hauptmann.

neo-Nazi movements   Neo-Nazi movements promote the ideology of NAZISM, espousing white supremacy and anti-Semitism. Since World War II, small parties in several European countries, including Germany, have advocated Nazi tenets. The tiny American Nazi party, founded in 1959, gained notoriety for its racism (and Nazi regalia). Some later U.S. right-wing extremist groups, like the Aryan Nations and the Order, have been involved in violence; a member of the Order was convicted of the 1984 murder in Denver, Colo., of a Jewish radio-talk-show host.

---

neoclassicism (art) The neoclassical style dominated the arts from about 1750 until the mid-19th century. It originated in Britain, France, Italy, and Germany and was disseminated throughout the rest of Europe as far as Russia and to the United States. The style embraced architecture, painting, sculpture, the decorative arts, and even, toward 1800, clothing and jewelry.

The term *neoclassicism*, which was not used by the artists themselves, describes works heavily influenced by the art of classical antiquity. It was a reaction against the frivolity of the previous generation of rococo artists (see ROCOCO STYLE). The neoclassicists also hated the extravagant excesses of 17th-century BAROQUE ART AND ARCHITECTURE.

Classical antiquity had been an important model for European artists since the Renaissance, but in the mid-18th century its influence became particularly strong. Excavations at HERCULANEUM, POMPEII, and elsewhere in Italy produced a wealth of fresh material for the study of antiquity, particularly accurate engravings of sculptures, gems, cameos, paintings, buildings, and domestic objects. The linear style in which painted Greek vases were decorated and the absence of spatial depth in their compositions exercised a considerable influence on artists.

Theoretical treatises also contributed to the rise of neoclassicism, especially those of the German antiquarian and scholar Johann WINCKELMANN, who believed that modern artists should not produce mere copies of classical works, but should rather emulate the ancients by observing nature through their eyes.

Major painters such as Jacques Louis DAVID and Jean Auguste Dominique INGRES in France, produced outstanding portraits and history subjects. Major sculptors included the Italian Antonio CANOVA, the Dane Bertel THORVALDSEN, and the Englishman John FLAXMAN, who was also important for his outline drawings of scenes from the works of Homer, Aeschylus, and Dante. The portrait bust was handled with great skill by the Frenchman Jean Antoine HOUDON. Giovanni Battista PIRANESI's engravings of classical Roman ruins were among the finest of their kind. Leading architects who were also key figures in the development of the decorative arts included the Scot Robert ADAM, the German Karl Friedrich Schinkel, the Englishman John SOANE, and the Frenchman Claude Nicolas LEDOUX. Most neoclassical painters and sculptors believed that art should not only please the eye but also instruct the mind. This belief reinforced the academic hierarchy of artistic subject matter, which stressed the moral value of subjects drawn from the history and myths of classical Greece and Rome, and from the Old and New Testaments. Subjects drawn from postclassical literature

and history, and momentous contemporary events, were also acceptable. Portraits, landscapes, and still lifes were low in the hierarchy because they were deemed to be less edifying, but neoclassical artists continued to produce them.

The neoclassical style can be divided roughly into three phases. The first, lasting until about 1770, was influenced as much by the classicism of the 16th and 17th centuries as by a firsthand knowledge of classical art. Paintings combined elements borrowed from Nicolas Poussin and from antique Roman bas-reliefs; architectural styles owed as much to the designs of Andrea PALLADIO as to surviving Roman temples.

The second phase (*c.*1770–*c.*1825) made more direct use of classical sources. Before then, the austere simplicity of Greek vase painting and of Doric architecture had been too uncompromising for European and American taste. From the 1790s onward, however, the fundamental principles of GREEK ARCHITECTURE and GREEK ART were practiced in their purest form by such artists as Flaxman and Schinkel. During this second phase of neoclassicism a small number of artists, including Flaxman, Canova, and David, pioneered an appreciation of Italian late-medieval and Early Renaissance art, which had hitherto been neglected in the quest for the primitive, naive, and simple.

During the last phase of neoclassicism (*c.*1825–

Jean Auguste Dominque Ingres's Jupiter and Thetis *(1811), initially severely criticized, is now recognized as an early masterpiece. (Musée Granet, Aix-en-Provence.)*

*c.*1850) artists and designers sought inspiration, often indiscriminately, from a great diversity of sources, including other ancient cultures—Egypt, Persia, and India—as well as that of medieval Europe. This last phase saw the degeneration and decline of neoclassicism, although as an architectural style it continued to be used throughout the rest of the century for such public buildings as banks, museums, and railroad stations.

See also: CLASSICISM; GREEK REVIVAL; REGENCY STYLE.

neoclassicism (literature)   The classic status of ancient Greek and Roman literature has long been acknowledged, and any work that deliberately adopts their formal characteristics may therefore be called neoclassical (see also CLASSICISM). The term *neoclassicism*, however, is loosely used to describe the dominant characteristics of English literature written between about 1660 and 1780. The works of John DRYDEN, Alexander POPE, Jonathan SWIFT, John GAY, Oliver GOLDSMITH, Samuel JOHNSON, Joseph ADDISON, Edward Hyde, 1st Earl of CLARENDON, and many of their contemporaries exhibit the principles of order, clarity, and stylistic decorum that were formulated in the three major critical documents of the age: Dryden's *An Essay of Dramatic Poesy* (1668), Pope's *Essay on Criticism* (1711), and Johnson's *Lives of the Poets* (1779–81).

All these works insist that "nature" is the only true model and standard of writing—not the wild, spiritual nature of the romantic poets or the nature investigated by the modern scientist, but an ordered, harmonious universe that exhibits God's providential design. Although too vast for any individual's comprehension, nature had already been described by the ancient poets, among whom Homer was preeminent. Therefore the writer who imitates Homer is also describing nature. Many of the major poems of this period are adaptations of classical forms: MOCK EPIC, translation, and imitation. A large part of Pope's work belongs to this last category, which exemplifies the complexity of neoclassicism more thoroughly than does any other literary form of the period. In his satires and verse epistles Pope becomes an English Horace, adopting the Roman poet's informal candor and conversational civility and applying the standards of the AUGUSTAN AGE to his own time.

neodymium   Neodymium, a chemical element, is a silver white metal of the LANTHANIDE SERIES. Its symbol is Nd, its atomic number is 60, and its atomic weight is 144.24. One of its natural isotopes, ^{144}Nd, is radioactive. Discovered by Carl Auer von Welsbach in 1885, neodymium is used in electronics, in colored glass for astronomical lenses, in lasers, and in magnetic alloys.

neoimpressionism   see SEURAT, GEORGES

Neolithic Period [nee-oh-lith'-ik]   The Neolithic Period, or New Stone Age, refers to the stage of prehistoric cultural development that followed the PALEOLITHIC and transitional MESOLITHIC periods and preceded the BRONZE AGE. The term *Neolithic*, from the Greek *neos* ("new") and *lithos* ("stone"), was adopted (1865) by the English archaeologist Sir John Lubbock as a further refinement of the three-age system (Stone, Bronze, and Iron ages), the chronological framework in archaeology proposed (1836) by the Danish archaeologist Christian Thomsen. Lubbock recognized that the Stone Age should be divided into an earlier period (the Paleolithic), characterized by the use of chipped stone tools, and a later period (the Neolithic) marked by the introduction of ground and polished stone tools.

In the 1920s the English archaeologist Miles Burkitt ascribed to the Neolithic four characteristic traits; these included, in addition to the grinding and polishing of stone tools, the practice of agriculture, the domestication of animals, and the manufacture of pottery. Today agriculture and animal domestication are generally recognized as the hallmarks of Neolithic culture. The British prehistorian V. Gordon CHILDE termed the associated change from a hunting and gathering economy to one based on food production the *Neolithic Revolution*; he considered it the greatest advance in human history after the mastery of fire. The domestication of plants and animals provided prehistoric populations with a stable food supply, which in turn encouraged the establishment of permanent settlements resulting eventually in the rise of urban civilization.

In southwest Asia the cultivation of wheat and barley—the basic food cereals in the Western world—coupled with the domestication of food animals such as sheep, goats, pigs, and later cattle, first occurred in the period between 9000 and 5000 BC. The earliest known sites containing evidence of Neolithic culture traits associated with sedentism, or early settled life, are found in the FERTILE CRESCENT area of the Near East.

In the development of the Neolithic in Europe, the impulses toward early farming came mainly via the waterway routes from the Near East. The earliest known evidence of food production in Europe dates from about 6500 BC at the Greek site of Argissa-Maghula. By about 4000 BC cereal crops and cattle were introduced to western France and Switzerland, probably via the Mediterranean. Agriculture and domestic animal stock were in use in southern Scandinavia and in the northern European plains by about 3500 BC, pushing the remaining hunter-gatherer peoples farther north into the wilderness or influencing them to adopt the new, settled mode of life. At the extreme northwest corner of Europe from about 3500 BC on, the British Isles were at the receiving end of the Neolithic culture traits of many peoples arriving by sea and overland from the continent. (See EUROPEAN PREHISTORY.)

In eastern Asia archaeologists have traced an independent invention of ceramics and polished-stone use, with the development of a distinct form of agriculture based on rice and other native plants. Most of the domesticated animals appear to have been brought ultimately from the West, although chickens, pigs, and dogs could have been local domesticates in China. Farming appears to have been first developed along the Yellow River with

The Cucuteni-Tripolye, an important Neolithic culture, flourished in northern Romania and southwestern Russia about 3500–3000 BC. This drawing reconstructs the Cucuteni-Tripolye settlement at Hăbășești in Romania. The site, surrounded by defensive ditches, contains 44 rectangular houses arranged in a circular pattern. The houses were built of tree trunks covered with clay, and roofed with reed and thatch. Pottery was fired in closed top-draft kilns. The people of Hăbășești cultivated wheat and barley, and kept domesticated cattle, pigs, goats, and sheep. Hunting and gathering were also important sources of food. The Hăbășești settlers used such stone tools as axes, hoes, and flint-edged sickles; copper implements found at the site may reflect the influence of Anatolian Bronze Age culture.

the Yang-Shao culture, dating from about 4000 BC. Farther south in Thailand archaeologists have found evidence of ground-stone tools, pottery, and slate knives possibly used for rice harvesting dating from perhaps as early as 6800 BC, several thousand years before agriculture appeared in China. At Non Nok Tha, a mound site in northern Thailand on the Mekong River, evidence of sedentary farming was found dating from the 4th millennium BC.

In the New World animal domestication and agriculture based on maize, beans, and squash cultivation appeared by 2500 BC; the term *Neolithic* is generally not used, however, in the context of New World archaeology.

neon   Neon, a monatomic gas, is the second element of the noble gas series, Group 0 of the periodic table. The word *neon* is from the Greek *neos* meaning "new." Neon, symbol Ne, has an atomic weight of 20.179 and an atomic number of 10. The gas was discovered by Sir William Ramsay and Morris William Travers in 1898 in the residue from the distillation of liquid air. It is present in the Earth's atmosphere at concentrations of about 1 part in 65,000.

Natural neon consists of three isotopes. Its physical properties include a melting point of $-248.6°$ C, a boiling point of $-246.0°$ C (1 atmosphere pressure), and a gas density of 0.89990 g/l at 0° C. The electronic structure of neon includes a completed outer electron shell containing eight electrons, and the element shows little tendency to form compounds, although such ions as Ne_2^+, $(NeAr)^+$, $(NeH)^+$, and $(HeNe)^+$ have been observed in optical and mass spectrometric studies.

Like argon, krypton, and xenon, neon is obtained commercially as a by-product of the fractional distillation of liquid air. Liquid neon, with more than 40 times the refrigerant capacity, per unit volume, of liquid helium, is finding increasing application as an economical CRYOGENIC refrigerant. Neon gas emits a characteristic intense reddish orange glow in a vacuum discharge tube (see DISCHARGE, ELECTRICAL) and is therefore used effectively in display lighting. Neon is also used to make high-voltage indicators, lightning arrestors, wave meter tubes, television tubes, and more recently, gas lasers.

Neoplatonism Neoplatonism was a philosophical school that flourished in the Roman Empire in the 3d and 4th centuries AD. It also had a strong influence on religious thought during the Middle Ages and played a part in the development of modern Western philosophy. Neoplatonism originated in Alexandria, Egypt, where PLOTINUS, a Hellenized Egyptian, and his teacher, Ammonius Saccas (185–250), sought to revive Platonism (the thought of PLATO) as a viable contemporary philosophy. Its major development as a school, however, occurred in Rome, where Plotinus headed an influential philosophical academy from 244 to 270.

Plotinus was six centuries removed from Plato, and his writings show the influence of Pythagorean, Peripatetic, and Stoic ideas current in his own day. He was especially concerned to defend Plato and Platonism against the criticisms of Aristotle, but in doing so he accepted a number of Aristotle's own concepts. His main tactic was to show how Aristotle's categories and logic are inadequate to account for the whole of reality—both the things known by the intellect and those known by the senses.

The chief source for Neoplatonism is the *Enneads* (the Nines), 54 essays written by Plotinus during the period 254–67. They emphasize three points: the ultimate nonmaterial nature of reality; the possibility of gaining real knowledge about the world and its basic laws; and the unity, goodness, and sacredness of the universe. Affirming that all things in nature (souls) are alive, dynamic, and in a process of change (becoming), Plotinus argues that these processes themselves can have no higher significance unless it be established that there are higher fixed principles that do not themselves change. Order among such principles, however, cries out for belief in their inherence in some higher unifying element that possesses in itself a unity higher than any one of them. His resulting cosmology consists of several levels of reality, the lower of which are given meaning and significance by those above. At the lowest level is the material world; at the highest is the dynamic union, or fusion, of all higher principles (the One).

PORPHYRY, who was Plotinus's chief disciple, critic, promoter, and biographer, disagreed with Plotinus's rejection of Aristotle's categories (fundamental classes of being). Porphyry based his own form of Neoplatonism on a modified version of these categories, thus adding an even more Aristotelian character to later Neoplatonic thought.

Various other schools of Neoplatonism (for example, the Syrian, Athenian, Alexandrine, and Pergamene) emerged in addition to the Roman school. Some of them, like the Pergamene, engaged in theurgy, or magical practices. The next major intellectual development occurred in the 5th century with PROCLUS, a scholar of the Platonic Academy in Athens, which had adopted Neoplatonism at the end of the 4th century. His main innovation was to suggest that there must be also an internal, or "horizontal," dependency in each level of reality, so that the primal form of each level generates forms similar to itself.

In late antiquity and early medieval times philosophers of various religious traditions were attracted to and influenced by Neoplatonic thought. Among these were the Muslims al-KINDI, al-FARABI, and AVICENNA; the Christians ORIGEN, DIONYSIUS THE PSEUDO-AREOPAGITE, Saint AUGUSTINE, BOETHIUS, and John Scotus ERIGENA; and, in the Jewish tradition, Isaac ben Solomon Israeli, Dunash ben Tamim, and Solomon ben Judah IBN GABIROL (Avencebron). Augustine introduced a great number of Neoplatonic notions into Western Christian thought.

Plotinian Neoplatonism was revived in 15th-century Italy by the Florentine Academy, especially with the translation of the *Enneads* into Latin by Marsilio FICINO in 1492. The *Oration* (1486), on the dignity of man, by Ficino's pupil PICO DELLA MIRANDOLA is a classic of Renaissance humanism. In the same period, Neoplatonism was introduced into England by John Colet (1466–1519), who paved the way for the Cambridge Platonists of the 17th century.

Neoptolemus [nee-ahp-tahl'-i-muhs] In Greek mythology Neoptolemus, the son of ACHILLES, entered the TROJAN WAR after his father was killed. One of the greatest and cruelest of the Greek warriors during the sack of Troy, Neoptolemus killed Priam at the altar of Zeus and sacrificed Polyxena on the grave of Achilles. Andromache, Hector's widow, was taken by Neoptolemus as his concubine. Although in Homer's *Odyssey* he is described as returning safely from the war and afterward marrying Hermione, according to later accounts Neoptolemus was killed in Delphi at the shrine of Apollo; thus "the punishment of Neoptolemus" became a metaphor for poetic justice.

neorealism Neorealism as an Italian literary movement can be said to have begun in 1929 with Alberto MORAVIA's *Time of Indifference* (Eng. trans., 1932), a novel that unflinchingly addressed highly sensitive moral, social, and political issues during the early repressive years of Mussolini's dictatorship. The movement developed slowly until the overthrow of the fascist regime in 1943. Neorealist novels of the next 12 years focused on the plight of working-class people and thus represented a break with the elitist tradition that had characterized Italian literature for centuries. Neorealism, both as a style and as a political outlook, became even better known internationally through the 1940s and postwar films of Italian directors Luchino VISCONTI (*Ossessione*, 1942; *La Terra Trema*, 1948), Roberto ROSSELLINI (*Open City*, 1945; *Paisan*, 1946), and Vittorio DE SICA (*Shoeshine*, 1946; *The Bicycle Thief*, 1948; *Umberto D.*, 1952).

neoteny [nee-aht'-uh-nee] Neoteny is the permanent retention of larval characteristics in a sexually mature animal. The classic example is the tiger salamander, or AXOLOTL, *Ambystoma tigrinum*, found in the southwestern United States and in Mexico.

The term is also used to refer to retention of immature characteristics in a particular body structure of an adult animal.

KINGDOM OF NEPAL

Land: Area: 140,797 km² (54,362 mi²). Capital and largest city: Katmandu, or Kathmandu (1981 pop., 235,160).

People: Population (1990 est.): 19,145,800. Density: 136 persons per km² (352 per mi²). Distribution (1989): 7% urban, 93% rural. Official language: Nepali. Major religions: Hinduism, Buddhism.

Government: Type: constitutional monarchy. Legislature: House of Representatives; National Council. Political subdivisions: 14 zones.

Economy: GDP (1989): $2.9 billion; $158 per capita. Labor distribution (1988): agriculture and fishing—91.1%; manufacturing—0.5%; commerce and services—6.2%; construction—2.1%; government and public authorities—0.1%. Foreign trade (1989): imports—$724 million; exports—$374 million. Currency: 1 Nepalese rupee = 100 paisa (pice).

Education and Health: Literacy (1991): 30% of adult population. Universities (1991): 1. Hospital beds (1988): 4,021. Physicians (1988): 879. Life expectancy (1990): 50. Infant mortality (1990): 99 per 1,000 live births.

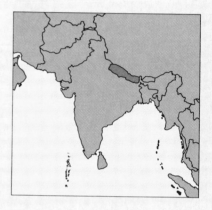

Nepal [nuh-pawl']   Nepal is an independent state occupying a salient, or projection, into India, by which it is surrounded on the east, south, and west. The northern border follows the approximate crest of the HIMALAYAS, which form the frontier with Tibet (China). KATMANDU is the capital.

Land and Resources

Nepal contains three distinct geographical zones. The southern lowland area known as the Terai is a mixture of forested and cultivated land that yields most of the country's grain. Midaltitude hills, mountains, and valleys are in the central sector. The Great Himalaya Range runs across the northern third of Nepal and is easily visible on a clear day from Katmandu at the head of the Nepal Valley, the largest lowland area in the central region. Many Himalayan peaks exceed 7,620 m (25,000 ft) in elevation; Mount EVEREST, at 8,848 m (29,029 ft), is the world's highest point. Temperatures correspond to the physiographic divisions, ranging from subtropical to alpine-arctic, and most of Nepal is adequately watered by monsoonal rains. At Katmandu, summer temperatures rarely exceed 32° C (90° F), and winters are mild. The average annual temperature is 18° C (65° F).

The variation in vegetation and fauna reflects altitudinal and climatic regions. Subtropical species dominate the Terai, including water buffaloes, hyenas, leopards, deer, and tigers found among bamboo and palm growth. Plant and animal species of the Himalayas are diverse.

Mounting population pressures and extensive deforestation have contributed to a serious erosion problem, reducing agricultural productivity and causing the silting and flooding of downstream rivers. Hydroelectric power potential has been scantily exploited.

People

The people of Nepal are dominantly Indo-Nepalese, and about one-fifth of the population is Tibeto-Nepalese. The Nepali and the Newars, the largest ethnic groups in the country, are the principal inhabitants of the greater Katmandu area. In the Himalayas, SHERPA and Bhutias—ethnologically related to the Tibetans—are in the majority. GURKHA inhabitants introduced Hinduism into the area. About 88% of Nepal's population are Hindu; the rest are Buddhists and Muslims.

In order to reduce a high illiteracy rate, the Nepalese government has instituted a system of free 5-year primary schools. Tribhuvan University (1960) is in Katmandu. Medical services are inadequate.

Economic Activity

Nepal's economy is mainly agricultural, with almost all of the work force engaged in farming. Mica is mined, and some timber is cut for sale. On the Himalayan slopes medicinal herbs are grown for a worldwide market. Katmandu has food processing factories, sawmills, and a jute mill. Other mechanized industries are underdeveloped.

Only about 18% of Nepal's land is cultivated, about a third is forested, and almost 40% is wasteland. The lead-

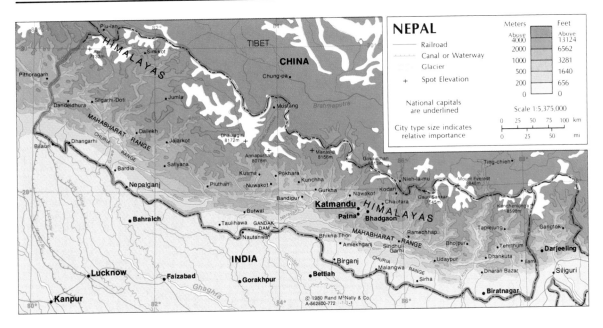

ing crops are sugarcane, rice, and maize, with some wheat, potatoes, and vegetables. Buckwheat is grown at higher altitudes. Land in the Nepal Valley and on hillside terraces is intensively cultivated and widely irrigated.

Tobacco is grown in the Terai, and the surplus is exported. Cardamom, grown in the eastern hills, rice, and oilseed are important exports. A few cows and buffaloes are kept, but animal husbandry is mostly limited to poultry raising. Most animals and animal products are imported. Trade is dominated by India, but some commerce has been developed with China and Bangladesh. Because of its need to import machinery, finished goods, and food, Nepal suffers a trade deficit.

Tourism has grown in importance since the 1960s. Katmandu, with its road and air links with India, attracts visitors with its examples of LAMAIST ART AND ARCHITECTURE. A growing number of hikers and mountain climbers are using Katmandu as a major base for expeditions to Mount Everest as well as for hiking tours in the Middle and High Himalayas.

Because of its rugged terrain, Nepal faces major transportation obstacles. Narrow-gauge railroads are confined to the Terai. An international airport is in Katmandu.

Government and History

Newars are thought to have lived in the Nepal Valley since the 4th century AD, developing a Hindu-Buddhist culture. The Gurkha principality was later established by RAJPUT warriors from India, and in 1769 they conquered lands beyond the present-day borders of Nepal. After incursions into northern India in which the Gurkhas were defeated, Nepal became a protectorate of the British government of India in 1816. In return for its loan of troops and other services to the British raj, Nepal was granted full independence in 1923. It has maintained its close

association with India since the latter gained independence in 1947.

Nepal has the world's only Hindu monarchy. Until 1951, however, the government was controlled by a hereditary prime ministership in the hands of the Rana family. The nation's first election was held in 1959, but in 1960, King Mahendra dismissed the cabinet, dissolved parliament, and banned political parties. The 1962 constitution calls for a nonparty *panchayat* (council) system of government; the highest legislative body is the National Panchayat. After a 1980 referendum approved a modified version of the *panchayat* system, direct parliamentary elections were held in 1981. A dispute with India led to India's closing of most border crossings from March 1989 to July 1990, and the resultant economic crisis fueled demands for political reform. After more than two months of violence, King Birendra Bir Bikram Shah Dev dissolved parliament. The opposition formed a multiparty interim government that took office on Apr. 19, 1990; a new constitution approved later that year created a constitutional monarchy. It vested executive power in the king and a council of ministers. A bicameral parliament with an elected lower house and a partially elected upper house held legislative power.

Nepalese art   see LAMAIST ART AND ARCHITECTURE

nephrite   see JADE

nephritis   see KIDNEY DISEASE

Neptune (mythology)   In Roman mythology Neptune was the chief god of the sea. He was originally a minor water deity, but as the Romans became seafarers he assumed greater importance and was identified with the Greek god POSEIDON.

Neptune (planet)

Neptune is the eighth planet from the Sun and the most remote of the gas giants of the outer SOLAR SYSTEM. During 1845 and 1846 the Englishman John Couch ADAMS and the Frenchman Urbain Jean Joseph Leverrier, unknown to each other, independently calculated where an eighth planet would have to be in order to explain slight perturbations in the orbit of URANUS. In Berlin on the night of Sept. 23, 1846, Johann Gottfried Galle and Heinrich Louis d'Arrest found a new planet within one degree of the position sent them by Leverrier. The equally good prediction of Adams, made a year earlier, met with unfounded skepticism in England and was not published until after the planet had been discovered.

During the months following the announcement of the discovery, an international controversy developed between English and French astronomers as to whom credit belonged and what the planet should be named. (Leverrier wanted to name it after himself.) Eventually the new planet was named Neptune, for the Roman sea god, and credit was given to both Adams and Leverrier for their calculations. Galileo actually may have spotted Neptune more than two centuries earlier, but he did not recognize it as a planet.

Appearance. Neptune reaches a maximum brightness in the Earth's night sky of magnitude 7.8, about five times too faint to be seen by the naked eye. In a large telescope the planet appears as a small blue disk, 2.3 seconds of arc in diameter. The best pictures of Neptune from Earth show discrete bright clouds and a bright haze over the south pole of the planet. The U.S. VOYAGER 2 spacecraft confirmed these sightings when it reached Neptune in 1989, flying less than 5,000 km (3,100 mi) above the planet's cloud tops on August 25. The spacecraft's cameras revealed many atmospheric features, including a large, dark storm system named the Great Dark Spot for its resemblance to the Great Red Spot of Jupiter.

Astronomical Data. The orbit of Neptune around the Sun is even more nearly circular than the Earth's orbit. The planet's average distance from the Sun is 4,497,000,000 km (2,794,000,000 mi), with an eccentricity of only 0.0086. The orbit is inclined 1° 46' to the ecliptic, or plane of the solar system, and the planet takes 164.793 years to make one trip around the Sun. Neptune's axis of rotation is tipped only 28° 48', which is not greatly different from Earth's 23° 30'.

The rotation period of Neptune's magnetic field, which is presumed to trace the rotation of the planet's core, was found by *Voyager 2* to be 16.11 hours. Most of the clouds on Neptune have longer periods of rotation, however, ranging from about 16 hours near the planet's south pole to more than 18 hours near the equator. This means that the jet-stream wind speeds on Neptune reach 2,400 km (1,500 mi) per hour, moving in a retrograde direction—that is, opposite to the direction of rotation. These are the strongest retrograde winds seen on any planet in the solar system.

Physical Characteristics. Neptune has a diameter of 49,500 km (30,750 mi) and a mass 17.22 times that of the Earth. This means that the planet is slightly smaller and heavier than Uranus. It has an average density of 1.67 g/cm^3, compared to Uranus's density of 1.21 g/cm^3.

The atmosphere of Neptune consists mainly of hydrogen and helium, but about 2.5–3% of the atmosphere is methane (CH_4). The cirrus clouds seen in the atmosphere probably consist of crystals of methane rather than of water ice, as seen in cirrus clouds on Earth. Methane's strong absorption features dominate the spectrum of the planet, giving Neptune its deep blue color. Because the effective temperature of Neptune is at least −218° C (−360° F), it, like Jupiter and Saturn but unlike Uranus, appears to have an internal energy source.

Satellites. The English astronomer William Lassell de-

The planet Neptune, seen as it would appear to the human eye, exhibits a number of atmospheric features. At the center of the disk is the Great Dark Spot, as wide as planet Earth, with a bright cloud along its southern boundary. A smaller bright cloud, some distance below, is called the "Scooter" because of its rapid motion relative to the other features.

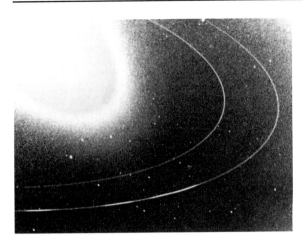

Circling Neptune's glare, the two brighter rings of the planet are clearly visible in this overexposed view.

tected Neptune's largest satellite, TRITON, less than a month after the discovery of the planet in 1846. In 1949, Dutch-American astronomer Gerard KUIPER discovered Nereid, a second Neptunian satellite. Both satellites had unusual orbits. Triton, unlike any other of the solar system's large satellites—it has a diameter of 2,705 km (1,680 mi), slightly smaller than Earth's Moon—moves in a retrograde direction around its primary, Neptune. Nereid, in turn, has the most eccentric orbit of any moon in the solar system. Its distance from Neptune varies from 1,400,000 to 9,700,000 km (900,000 to 6,000,000 mi). *Voyager 2* found that Nereid is about 340 km (213 mi) in diameter and reflects about 12% of the sunlight that falls on it. The unusual nature of Triton is discussed in the article of that title.

Voyager 2 also discovered six new satellites during its passage, giving Neptune a total of eight moons. One, 1989N1, is the largest of the newly discovered satellites. It has an irregular shape with an average diameter of about 400 km (250 mi). This makes it slightly larger than Nereid, but it is a much darker body, reflecting only about 6% of the sunlight that strikes it. It is also closer to Neptune, which is why it remained undiscovered while Nereid could be observed from Earth. The moon is gray in color, and hints of craterlike forms and groovelike lineations are seen on its surface.

Another satellite, 1989N2, is an irregularly shaped, dark object about 210 by 190 km (130 by 118 mi) in size. It reflects only 5% of the sunlight that falls on it, and it appears to have several craters 30–50 km (19–31 mi) across. The irregular outlines of 1989N1 and 1989N2 suggest that they remained cold and icy throughout much of their history. The two satellites orbit at distances of about 117,600 km (73,500 mi) and 74,000 km (46,300 mi) from Neptune, respectively. Little is known about the remaining small satellites: 1989N3 and 1989N4 orbit at distances of about 62,000 km (38,000 mi) and 52,000 km (32,000 mi), respectively; 1989N5 circles Neptune every 7.5 hours at a distance of 50,000 km (31,000 mi);

1989N6, with its 7.1-hour orbit, is the only new satellite with a noticeable inclination, being tilted 4.5° to the equatorial plane of Neptune.

Rings. The presence of rings around Neptune had been a subject of debate prior to the *Voyager* encounter. Several ground-based observations had suggested that irregular arcs, or strands of partial rings, orbited the planet. Studies of the probe's photographs, however, eventually revealed that five rings surround Neptune: two bright, narrow rings and three fainter, fuzzier sheets of orbiting materials. Some sections of the bright rings have significantly higher densities than others, and it was these "arcs" of higher density that had first been detected by Earth telescopes. The bright rings are located roughly at distances of 53,000 km (33,000 mi) and 63,000 km (39,000 mi). One broad ring is located at 42,000 km (25,000 mi), and another in a zone between the bright rings, while a third extended sheet perhaps fills the system between the planet and the inner broad ring.

neptunium   Neptunium, a silvery metal, is a chemical element of the ACTINIDE SERIES. Its symbol is Np, its atomic number is 93, and its atomic weight is 237.0482. The stablest and most important isotope is neptunium-237, which has a half-life of 2.2 million years. Neptunium occurs in nature in uranium ores, but only in very minute amounts. The element was first synthesized in 1940 when E. M. McMillan and P. Abelson bombarded uranium with neutrons and produced neptunium-239. Twelve other isotopes, all radioactive, have since been synthesized. Neptunium-237 is used in neutron-detection instruments.

See also: TRANSURANIUM ELEMENTS.

Nereus [nee'-ree-uhs]   In Greek mythology Nereus was a sea god who, in Homer's *Iliad* and *Odyssey* and Hesiod's *Theogony*, was called the Old Man of the Sea. He and the Oceanid Doris were the parents of the 50 sea nymphs known as the Nereids. In art the wise Nereus is often represented as wrestling with Hercules.

Neri, Saint Philip [nay'-ree]   Perhaps the most humanly attractive of the saints of the COUNTER-REFORMATION, Philip Neri, b. Florence, Italy, July 21, 1515, d. May 26, 1595, was the founder (1575) of the Congregation of the Oratory. Because of his charismatic effect on individuals he became known as the Apostle of Rome. His Congregation of the Oratory, where priestly members led a devotional life without vows, was approved by Pope Gregory XIII in 1575. The popular afternoon services that Philip designed at the Church of San Girolamo were the setting from which the musical form known as the oratorio developed. He was canonized on May 12, 1622. Feast day: May 26.

Nernst, Walther [nairnst]   The German physical chemist and inventor Hermann Walther Nernst, b. June

25, 1864, d. Nov. 18, 1941, was awarded the Nobel Prize for chemistry in 1920 for his discovery (1906) of the third law of thermodynamics, which states that entropy approaches zero as temperature approaches absolute zero. He introduced the Nernst equation (1889), which relates electric potential to various properties of the electric cell; the Nernst-Thomson rule (1893) that ions "fall apart" in water; and the Nernst lamp (1904), whose patent he sold for a million marks, but that was soon replaced by an improved version of Edison's light bulb. He also investigated the specific heat of solids at low temperature in connection with quantum theory and proposed the atom chain-reaction theory in photochemistry.

Nero, Roman Emperor [nee'-roh]

Nero Claudius Caesar, b. Dec. 15, AD 37, d. June 9, 68, ruled Rome from 54 to 68 and was one of its most infamous emperors. The son of Domitius Ahenobarbus and Caligula's sister AGRIPPINA II, Nero was adopted by the emperor CLAUDIUS I after the latter's marriage to Agrippina and succeeded him on the throne.

From the beginning, Agrippina vied for influence and power with the prefect of the Praetorian Guard, Burrus, and with Nero's former tutor, the philosopher SENECA. The first victim of the ensuing plots and counterplots was Claudius's son, Britannicus, who was poisoned in 55. Nero resented Agrippina's interference and had her murdered in 59. Burrus died in 62, and Seneca retired the same year.

From 62, Nero ruled unrestrained. Having divorced and murdered his first wife, Claudius's daughter, Octavia, Nero married (62) Poppaea Sabina, an ambitious intriguer. In 62 he revived the wide-ranging law of treason, and people were executed on suspicion of offense. In 64 a great fire ruined Rome. Nero lavishly rebuilt the city, but rumor held that he had started the fire himself to make room for his new palace and that he had recited poetry while watching the blaze. To avert this suspicion Nero

Nero, the last Roman emperor of the line of Julius Caesar, so mismanaged his empire and violated standards of justice that he faced widespread revolt. His excesses of personal vanity and violence included the murders of both family members and political opponents and persecution of the Christians. Nero committed suicide in AD 68.

blamed the Christians, thus initiating the first major Roman persecution of that sect. Executions increased in 65, when an assassination plot was uncovered. The poet Lucan, Seneca, the general Corbulo, and numerous senators lost their lives.

Nero scandalized Roman society by displaying in public his talents as a chariot driver, singer, and musician. As he devoted himself to artistic pursuits, the reins of power slipped from his hands. In 68 the governors of three provinces rose in an open revolt, and when the Praetorians also deserted him, Nero committed suicide. The historian Tacitus and the biographer Suetonius present a lurid picture of his reign.

Neruda, Pablo [nay-roo'-dah]

Pablo Neruda, b. Parral, Chile, July 12, 1904, d. Sept. 23, 1973, is one of the greatest Spanish-American poets of this century. His works have been translated into most modern languages, and he has received many honors and awards, including the Lenin Prize for Peace (1953) and the Nobel Prize for literature (1971). Born Ricardo Eliezer Neftalí Reyes y Basoalto, he grew up in Temuco, a southern region whose wilderness he would evoke constantly in his poetry. While in high school he became interested in anarchism and began using the pen name Pablo Neruda, for the 19th-century Czech poet Jan Neruda.

In 1921, Neruda went to Santiago to study French at the Pedagogical Institute of the University of Chile. There he led a bohemian life and dedicated himself to poetry at the expense of his studies, which he never finished. He won first prize in a literary contest in 1921 and three years later published *Twenty Love Poems and a Song of Despair* (1924; Eng. trans., 1969), a romantically tormented book that was to remain his most popular work. Following a long-standing Latin American tradition, the promising young poet was rewarded with consular positions, first in southern Asia (1927–32) and later in Latin America and Europe. While in Asia he wrote his powerful if enigmatic *Residence on Earth* (1933; Eng. trans., 1946), in which, under the influence of surrealism, he sang of anguish and solitude in an intensely personal style.

During the Spanish Civil War, Neruda sided with the Republican cause. Thenceforth he was no longer the hermetic poet of solitude but the accessible "poet of enslaved humanity." His socialist beliefs are reflected in *Tercera residencia* (Third Residence, 1947) and *Canto general* (General Song, 1950), a great epic poem of the Americas. Neruda told the rich story of his life in five volumes of verse (*Memorial de Isla Negra*, 1964) and in a volume of prose, published posthumously, *Confieso que he vivido* (I Confess that I Have Lived, 1974).

Nerval, Gérard de [nair-vahl', zhay-rahr' duh]

Gérard de Nerval was the pen name of the French romantic poet, novelist, and playwright Gérard Labrunie, b. Paris, May 22, 1808, d. Jan. 26, 1855. Possibly because his mother died in his infancy, the Great Mother Goddess constantly recurs under various guises in his writing, along with tarot cards, numerology, alchemy, astrology, and religious syncretism. At age 20, Nerval published a translation (1828) of the first part of *Faust* that won praise from Goethe himself. In 1841 he suffered the first attack of a mental illness that led to frequent confinement. His recognized masterpieces are the story of Adoniram in *Voyage en Orient* (Voyage to the East, 1843–51); the story of Sylvie in *Les Filles du feu* (Daughters of the Fire, 1854); the haunting *Aurelia* (1855; Eng. trans., 1932), about Nerval's dreams and madness; and the strange, densely written sonnets of *Les Chimères* (The Chimeras, 1854), of which "El Desdichado" is the best known. Nerval hanged himself in Paris on the site occupied today by the Sarah Bernhardt Theater.

nerve cell   see NERVOUS SYSTEM

nerve impulse   see REFLEX

Nervi, Pier Luigi [nair'-vee, pee-air' loo-ee'-jee]   The Italian architect-engineer Pier Luigi Nervi, b. June 21, 1891, d. Jan. 9, 1979, one of the most innovative and influential architects of the 20th century, demonstrated the aesthetic potential of lightweight, steel-reinforced concrete. Early in his career he established a reputation for designing boldly curving concrete structures such as his Giovanni Berta stadium in Florence (1929–32) and the weblike concrete airplane hangars he devised (1935–43) for the Italian air force.

In the mid-1940s he formulated the concept of lightweight steel grids held together by thin layers of concrete—a structural system whose lightness and malleability would allow a far greater freedom in handling than hitherto had been available with concrete. *Ferro-cemento*, as Nervi called his new material, was shown to its best advantage in his designs for three stadiums (1956–59) erected in Rome for the 1960 Olympics. In his later works Nervi frequently collaborated with other well-known modern designers: most notably with Marcel Breuer on the UNESCO headquarters building in Paris (1953–57), with Gio Ponti on the Pirelli Building in Milan (1955–59), and with Pietro Belluschi on the Cathedral of Saint Mary in San Francisco (completed 1970).

nervous system   A highly organized collection of cells known as nerve cells, or neurons, constitutes the nervous system, which is found in all higher forms of animal life. These nerve cells collect information from the environment by means of receptors. They coordinate the information with the internal activities of the organism in a process known as integration. They also store information in terms of MEMORY and generate adaptive patterns of behavior. Nervous systems vary greatly in form and complexity, ranging from simple nerve nets to elaborate, segmentally organized, and bilaterally symmetrical structures.

Unicellular animals, such as those of the phylum Protozoa, do not have nervous systems. Although these animals can produce coordinated responses to their environ-

ments, the fine gradations and various combinations of responses that characterize the nervous systems of higher animals are absent. Simple multicelled animals, such as sponges (phylum Porifera), can give localized responses to various types of stimulation, but because they lack nervous systems they do not have the ability to integrate signals and responses in such a way as to achieve flexibility and unity of action.

In animals with nervous systems the membrane properties of individual nerve cells are extremely specialized. As a result, electrochemical signals are able to carry information from one neuron to the next, often in complex patterns and combinations. Further, in more highly evolved forms of animal life many types of signals arise that involve both excitation and inhibition. These animal forms also have developed specialized regions within the nervous system for particular functions such as seeing, hearing, feeding, and mating.

The nervous system of higher organisms such as human beings is divided into a central system that comprises the BRAIN and SPINAL CORD, and a peripheral system that comprises the remaining nervous tissue. The central nervous system, coordinates the activity of the system as a whole (see diagram in HUMAN BODY). The motor nervous system innervates skeletal muscle, skin, and joints and controls voluntary actions, whereas the autonomic nervous system coordinates mainly involuntary actions such as heartbeat.

The study of the structure and function of nerve cells and networks of nerve cells used by organisms to receive, process, and act on information about their environment is called neurophysiology. Neurophysiological studies are largely concerned with the features of nerve cells, the origin and conduction of nerve impulses, the transmission of nerve impulses from one nerve cell to another, and the encoding and decoding of information as neural signals.

The Neuron

The basic building block of a nervous system is the neuron, or nerve cell, a cell that is specialized for the transmission of information into, within, and out of the animal. The human brain alone has about one trillion individual nerve cells, any one of which may have several thousand direct connections to other nerve cells in the system.

Structure and Function. A neuron of the human brain has three main regions: the cell body (soma; pl. somata), the dendrites, and the axon. The cell body ranges in size from 2 to 500 micra (or microns; symbol μ) in diameter. It contains the basic constituents of most animal CELLS: a nucleus, which has a nucleolus and chromosomes, and such cytoplasmic bodies as RIBOSOMES, MITOCHONDRIA, and endoplasmic reticulum. The dendrites are branched structures that have cytoplasmic continuity with the cell body. They function to receive signals from other nerve cells. The axon is a long fiber—up to 9 m (30 ft) in some whales—that is relatively uniform in diameter and often is covered with a myelin sheath. It normally serves to transmit information from one neuron to adjacent neurons.

Neurons of many animals also contain specialized structures that serve diverse functions. Nissl bodies con-

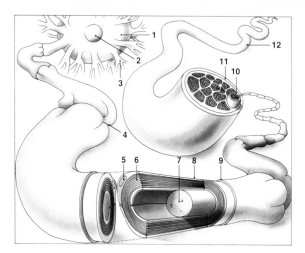

A typical peripheral nerve cell contains a cell body (1), or soma, with a nucleus (2) and dendrites (3), projections that bring impulses to the cell body. The axon (7), which conducts impulses from the cell body, is enclosed in a Schwann cell (nucleus shown, 5) which may secrete an insulating sheath of myelin (6). Constrictions in the myelin sheath are called nodes of Ranvier (4). A nerve fiber (8) is defined as the complex of axon and sheath. The endoneurium (9) is a delicate tissue between nerve fibers; the perineurium (10) surrounds each bundle of fibers; the epineurium (11) forms a sheath around the nerve (12).

tain ribonucleoproteins and are involved in protein synthesis. Fibrillar structures have neurofilaments and microtubules and appear to aid the transport of various substances throughout the neuron. Synaptic bulbs, often located at the ends of axons, seem to be involved with impulse transmission.

Receptors. Receptors are neurons that bring information into the nervous system. Classically, sensory reception has been divided into the five senses of hearing, vision, touch, taste, and smell. Today receptors are more commonly classified in terms of the physical forms of stimulation that excite them: chemoreception, electroreception, mechanoreception, photoreception, and thermoreception. Nociceptors are stimulated by damage to tissues.

How Neurons Operate

In spite of their physical diversity, most nerve cells operate in a similar way: they generate and carry two basic types of electrochemical signals known as graded potentials and spike discharges. Because of the unequal distribution of some ions across the nerve-cell membrane, an inactive nerve cell has what is known as a resting potential, with the inside of the cell having a negative charge with respect to the outside of the cell. When the neuron is depolarized, this potential difference is reduced, and the nerve cell propagates an impulse to the end of the fiber. The graded-potential change, caused by depolarization of the dendrites, moves along the branches toward the soma.

If the depolarization is great enough, one or more spike discharges are generated at the base of the axon and car-

ried toward the synaptic terminal. When the spikes reach synaptic bulbs, they induce the release of special chemical transmitters. These in turn give rise to graded, postsynaptic potentials in the dendrites or soma of the next neuron.

When a neuron's resting potential increases, the neuron becomes hyperpolarized and is less likely to carry messages. The neuron becomes inhibited rather than excited. Certain transmitters are excitatory, stimulating nerve-impulse propagation; others are inhibitory, causing hyperpolarization.

Myelin. The axons of many vertebrate neurons are covered with a myelin sheath, which acts like insulation on a wire and greatly promotes speed and reliability of nerve-impulse conduction. Humans with myelin deficiency, such as those afflicted with multiple sclerosis, may experience serious problems in nervous system functioning because of decreased speed and reliability of conduction.

Synaptic Cleft. The points of closest affinity and functional connection between neurons are known as synapses. Most neurons do not signal each other by direct anatomical contact. They are normally separated by a small synaptic cleft. NEUROTRANSMITTERS—chemical substances that effect impulses—are released into the synaptic cleft from the presynaptic terminals. They are received by the postsynaptic membrane of the receiving neuron. Occasionally, tight junctions exist, in which the transmission of information from one neuron to the next is primarily electrical, not chemical. Most common synapses occur between the axon of the sender cell and the dendrites or soma of the receiver cell. Synapses between two axons, dendrites, or somata also occur.

Types of Nervous Systems

Lower Organisms. Primitive nervous systems, such as those found in the nerve nets of coelenterates, do not have nerve-cell bodies that are grouped into ganglia or true brains. Individual neurons are poorly differentiated and not insulated by myelin sheaths, and the signals can travel in any direction across a synapse.

The flatworms (phylum Platyhelminthes) have a more highly ordered nervous system that is bilaterally symmetrical. The somata are collected into ganglia, and axons are grouped together, forming nerves. Flatworms receive environmental information by means of well-differentiated sense organs. The segmented roundworms (Annelida) show an even greater sophistication of nerves, controlled by a true brain. Highly complex and sophisticated patterns of nervous-system organization are apparent in insects and crustaceans (Arthropoda) and mollusks (Mollusca).

Vertebrates. In the various vertebrate species, sensory and motor nerve fibers are separated within the various spinal-cord segments. Clearly demarcated synaptic regions contain cell bodies (gray matter), and equally well-defined tracts of myelinated axons (white matter) exist. A large, well-organized brain coordinates all nervous-system functions.

Spinal Cord. A vertebrate spinal cord in cross-section resembles a gray butterfly—the gray matter with cell bodies and associated synapses is arranged within a white

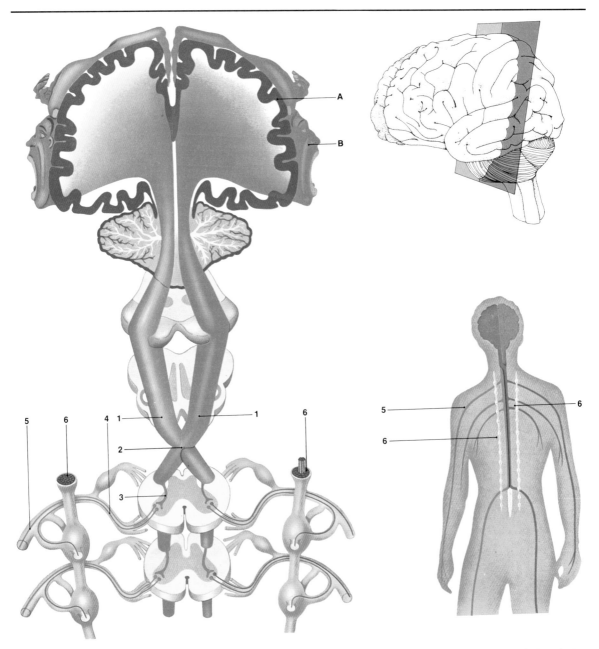

The motor nervous system controls the voluntary activity of the skeletal muscles. Integrated messages from motor centers in the spinal cord, brain stem, cerebellum, and cerebral cortex coordinate posture and movement. Many nerve cells that transmit impulses to muscles are located in motor areas near the surface of the cerebral cortex (A; from cross section of brain, above right), especially in the area known as the motor cortex. The body parts shown on the motor "homunculus" (B) are controlled by neurons at those locations on the cortex. The size of each body part is proportional to the amount of cortical area serving it. Nerve fibers from the cortex collect and descend through the spinal cord in corticospinal, or pyramidal, tracts. Because the two lateral corticospinal tracts (1), which contain 75% to 90% of the fibers, cross (2) in the medulla, each cerebral hemisphere mainly controls muscles on the other side of the body. The corticospinal tracts, each of which may contain more than a million fibers, give off fibers (3) at each level of the spinal cord. These fibers relay impulses to roots (4) of spinal nerves (5), which carry the messages directly to skeletal muscle fibers. The two sympathetic trunks shown (6) belong to the autonomic nervous system, which controls the involuntary actions of smooth and cardiac muscle and regulates the activity of glands.

oval, which contains the incoming (afferent) and outgoing (efferent) axons. In each segment sensory afferent fibers are concentrated into dorsal roots that are connected to associated ganglia outside of the spinal cord. Efferent fibers are concentrated in the ventral roots. The spinal cord's cervical, thoracic, lumbar, and sacral regions control incoming, integrative, and outgoing nervous functions for successive body parts.

Autonomic System. The spinal cord also houses and protects the two main branches of the autonomic nervous system, which controls involuntary, unconscious actions of smooth muscle and glands. These two branches are the sympathetic and parasympathetic systems. The thoracic and lumbar segments of the spinal cord contain nerves of the sympathetic system. The sympathetic system serves an adrenergic function, mobilizing the organism in a "fight or flight" reaction in emergencies. The parasympathetic system, located in cranial and sacral segments, is primarily cholinergic in function, serving to relax the organism.

Reflex

One of the more interesting and important features of the spinal cord is that even when it is separated from the brain, it can control fundamental integrative functions known as reflexes. A REFLEX can be considered schematically in terms of a sensory (receptor or afferent) cell that excites an interneuron, which in turn excites a motor (efferent) neuron. A variable lapse between the stimulus and the response reflects the time necessary to process the signal carried by the reflex afferent nerves. The strength of the response corresponds to a summation through time as well as over the different pathways. The response to a standard signal may take some time to develop fully. After the signal is removed the response may continue for a certain period of time. Different reflexes within the system interact with each other in complex patterns of mutual excitation and inhibition.

Feedback. Perhaps the most interesting feature derived from studies of nervous-system reflexes is the highly intimate and intricate connection between sensory inputs and motor outputs. The general principle of FEEDBACK control appears to be important for complex nervous-system functions. Mammalian muscle fibers, for example, contain specialized sensory cells (spindle organs) that convey to the spinal cord information concerning their current state of contraction. The output to these muscles from both the spinal cord and the brain depends, in part, on the signals from spindle fibers. Further, the brain can send special signals by way of the efferent system, which selectively changes the bias of these muscle spindles and affects the responsiveness of the muscle to signals of the motor neurons. Thus, sensory signals affect motor responses, which in turn affect sensory signals.

Operation of Neurons. At least four distinguishable classes of operation exist for the vertebrate nervous system. First, sensory inputs can generate the specific details of motor response, a direct transfer process. More commonly, the details of sensory input depend on the integration of afferent nerve stimulation as well as the cur-

rent state of responsiveness of interneurons and motor neurons. Afferent signals can also serve to trigger responses, the characteristics of which are basically inherent to the structure stimulated. Finally, integrative and motor cells can fire spontaneously, even in the absence of sensory input. In each case, the vertebrate spinal cord normally acts in cooperation with the brain.

The Brain

Myelencephalon. The brain connects with the spinal cord at the medulla, or myelencephalon, the site of the more primitive regulatory functions. Great fiber tracts between the brain and spinal cord cross in the medulla. The entrance and exit points of 12 cranial nerves, which serve a variety of somatic and visceral functions, are located in the medulla as well as in the next higher level of the brain, the pons.

Metencephalon, Cerebellum, and Mesencephalon. The pons (the metencephalon) and the cerebellum are responsible for many basic tasks of sensory and motor coordination. The next level of the brain, the mesencephalon (midbrain), is involved with still more complex functions of sensory-motor processing. The brain stem (medulla, pons, and midbrain) houses the reticular formation, a complex structure that combines many otherwise separate sensory and motor functions. The reticular formation also influences generalized levels of consciousness, including cycles of waking and sleeping.

Diencephalon. The diencephalon contains complex integrative structures, including the thalamus, which coordinates multiple sensory signals, and the hypothalamus, which plays a critical role in motivated behaviors, such as feeding, drinking, mating, and fighting. The hypothalamus is a major site of neurosecretion, connecting the nervous system to the endocrine (hormone) system by means of the pituitary.

Telencephalon. The telencephalon, largely the cerebrum, is the apex of sophisticated brain structure and undoubtedly plays a major role in the subtler emotional, coordinative, and intellectual functions.

Integration

The precision and intricacy of nervous-system architecture is well illustrated in the mammalian cerebellum, which plays an important role in various forms of sensory-motor coordination. Five types of neuron are located there and are distributed in precise relationship to one another, permitting excitation and inhibition for the control of a variety of skilled tasks. A similar ordered complexity is evident among the five cell types of the vertebrate retina. The highly ordered interactions among these cells process the rich details of the visual environment. Similarly impressive specializations are found in other receptors and central-nervous-system structures throughout all higher forms of animal life.

---

nervous system, diseases of the   Diseases of the nervous system comprise an assortment of afflictions that vary in terms of cause, areas of the nervous system involved, and disturbances of function. All levels of the BRAIN, SPINAL CORD, and peripheral nervous system can be affected. Manifestations of such diseases include diminished muscular strength with or without wasting, altered sensation, incoordination, and impaired bowel, bladder, or sexual functions. Disturbances in the regulation of heart rate, blood pressure, and respiration may occur. Movements may be diminished, abnormally increased, or involuntary.

Cerebral Disorders. Disorders of the cerebral hemispheres are characterized by seizures, decrease in intellectual functioning, confusion, disorientation, and profound derangements either in comprehension or in speaking or writing (APHASIA). Anomalies include gross underdevelopment, abnormal cortical convolutions (gyri), and other assorted malfunctions resulting in intellectual impairment or decreased life expectancy. HYDROCEPHALY, caused by a disturbance of cerebrospinal-fluid circulation or absorption in the cranial cavity, results in enlargement of the brain ventricles, thinning of the cerebral mantle, and MENTAL RETARDATION.

Congenital and Developmental Diseases. Congenital or developmental disorders (see BIRTH DEFECTS) include almost every imaginable anomaly of structure and function. For example, SPINA BIFIDA involves the incomplete closure of the embryonic neural tube, resulting in an incomplete vertebral-column roof. The spinal cord and its meningeal investments and roots may extrude through bony clefts, causing paralysis of the lower extremities, bowel, and bladder. An infection, such as MENINGITIS, can occur early in life, resulting in severe neurological impairment and, possibly, death. SYRINGOMYELIA, a progressive formation of a cavity in the spinal cord, is characterized by loss of perception of pain and temperature and later by weakness and wasting of the muscles. Maldevelopment of blood-vessel walls in the brain may underlie later development of aneurysms or vascular tumors, both of which may be responsible for cerebral hemorrhage.

CEREBRAL PALSY results from a defect in the developing fetal brain. It may be caused by such factors as infection, blood disorders, metabolic deficiencies, anoxia, or trauma. An increasingly recognized number of hereditary errors of metabolism—for example, PHENYLKETONURIA—cause enzyme deficiencies that result in abnormal accumulations of harmful chemicals. These excess chemical deposits often underlie mental retardation. One of the many significant mental-deficiency syndromes is DOWN'S SYNDROME, caused by a chromosomal abnormality that occurs at the time of fertilization.

Degenerative Diseases. Degenerative diseases commonly have dissimilar or unrelated pathologies. Frequently, the causes of these types of disorders are unknown. ALZHEIMER'S and Pick's diseases (so-called presenile dementias) are characterized by unremitting loss of cortical neurons with resultant cerebral atrophy. Loss of intellectual function (DEMENTIA), behavioral and personality changes, language and perceptual deficits, seizures, and disturbances of movement are common.

PARKINSON'S DISEASE is a degenerative disorder that involves the central gray matter of the brain (basal ganglia), resulting in deficiency of the neurotransmitter dopamine.

Many people infected by ENCEPHALITIS during the 1919–26 pandemic contracted a form of Parkinson's disease afterward. Many centrally acting psychotropic drugs, manganese, other toxins, and anoxic cerebral damage may produce parkinsonian syndromes. Symptoms include decreased spontaneous movement, increased muscle tone (rigidity), and rhythmic tremor at rest.

MULTIPLE SCLEROSIS is characterized by circumscribed areas of degeneration of myelinated nerve fibers. Eventually the nerve fiber (axon) loses the ability to function properly. The plaques become increasingly numerous, resulting in widespread neural disconnections. Symptoms include incoordination, weakness, disturbances of vision, and numbness. Progress of the disorder may be punctuated by long symptom-free periods.

Motor-neuron disease, such as AMYOTROPHIC LATERAL SCLEROSIS, is characterized by a rapid loss of cells within the areas of the brain and spinal cord responsible for the initiation of movement. Muscular weakness and degeneration with eventual paralysis ensue. Progressive muscular atrophy is a form of this disorder in which primarily the motor cells of the spinal cord are affected. MUSCULAR DYSTROPHY differs from motor-neuron disease in that the degeneration is restricted to the muscle itself and is usually transmitted genetically.

Genetic Diseases. HUNTINGTON'S CHOREA is an inherited disorder that affects primarily the adult. Dementia, behavioral changes, and abnormal, jerky movements (chorea) are its major symptoms, reflecting changes in the cerebral cortex and the basal nuclei. Hereditary spinal ataxias are disorders primarily affecting children and young adults. They are characterized by clumsy gait, incoordination, and muscular weakness. Wilson's disease affects copper metabolism. Excess copper deposits result in cerebral changes, impaired coordination (ataxia), tremors, and liver failure.

Infections. Practically all conceivable infectious organisms (bacteria, fungi, viruses, yeasts, and protozoans) have been known to infect the nervous system. Certain organisms—for example, pneumococci—are common invaders, whereas others are rare. Invasion may be by direct entry through penetrating wounds or by spreading throughout the circulatory system. The infection may be severe or relatively mild, depending on the particular pathogen and the immune response of the host. Acute, or infectious, chorea, also called Saint Vitus's dance, is similar to Huntington's chorea in its symptoms. Meningitis denotes invasion of the meningeal covering of the brain, spinal cord, and accessory blood vessels; encephalitis implies infection of the brain only; meningoencephalitis, which combines aspects of both disorders, commonly occurs. An abscess of the brain or spinal cord is a localized cavity that contains pus surrounded by a wall of inflammatory cells and scar tissue. The infective agents of kuru and Creutzfeldt-Jakob disease differ significantly from known viruses—they are capable of replication, are resistant to conventional sterilization, and have distinctive chemical characteristics. Infective agents of this type may possibly be implicated in other neurological diseases of as yet unknown cause (see VIRUS, SLOW).

Circulatory Disorders. The nervous system has high energy requirements and is imbued with an elaborate vascular bed and a rich blood supply. It is sensitive to impaired circulation or deficits in oxygen or glucose supply. STROKE is a result of localized circulatory impairment. It may result from occlusion of a major artery—or, less commonly, of a vein—that supplies a certain area of the brain, brain stem, or spinal cord. Stroke victims suffer from irreversible loss of brain function due to tissue damage. The obstruction to normal blood flow may occur because of hardening of the vessel wall (arteriosclerosis) or blood-clot formation (thrombus). A clot can become dislodged in one part of the circulatory system and travel to the brain, causing an obstruction known as an embolism. Hemorrhagic stroke principally occurs in patients afflicted with long-standing high blood pressure. In this case blood escapes under pressure from a damaged artery and intrudes massively upon the brain, destroying tissue. In addition, hemorrhage may result from a rupture of an aneurysm, a vascular anomaly, or a disturbance in clotting mechanisms.

Tumors. TUMORS can arise within the brain or spinal cord or occur in other body tissues and spread (by a process known as metastasis) to the nervous system. Gliomas constitute an important group of malignant tumors that appear to arise from the microscopic supportive tissue of the nervous system known as glia. Meningiomas and neuromas stem from the supportive investments of the brain and spinal cord and are generally nonmalignant. A variety of other primary tumors are recognized; they are named according to the tissue of origin, for example, pituitary tumors and vascular tumors. Metastatic tumors ordinarily are malignant but differ in tissue type depending on the site of origin. Representatives are pulmonary, breast, and melanomatous skin CANCERS.

Epilepsy. EPILEPSY is a periodic, paroxysmal disorder involving cerebral excitability. Symptoms are an alteration of consciousness often associated with excessive motor activity or disturbed sensory perception. Seizures are regarded as a symptom and not a disease. They result from a great variety of factors that alter cortical excitability.

Metabolic Disorders. Systemic metabolic disturbances produce wide-ranging effects on the nervous system, as exemplified by stupor or coma seen in liver disease, renal failure, and diabetes. Altered levels of calcium in the blood may produce convulsions. A type of periodic muscular paralysis relates to altered blood-potassium levels.

Poisoning. Toxic disorders include botulism, a type of food poisoning that causes muscular paralysis. Cerebral or peripheral nerve disease can be a result of lead, mercury, or arsenic poisoning. Ethyl alcohol, when abused, is a toxin of enormous importance. Alcoholics are subject to seizures and peripheral nerve, brain stem, cerebellar, cerebral, and optic-nerve degeneration (see ALCOHOL CONSUMPTION; ALCOHOLISM). Methyl-alcohol poisoning produces blindness by its direct effect on the optic nerve.

Injuries. Injuries can affect the nervous system at any level. In lumbar intervertebral disk disease the spinal nerve roots compress, producing pain, numbness, and weakness of the lower extremities. Spinal-cord damage from vertebral-column fracture can cause paraplegia, paralysis of the lower extremities, or quadriplegia, paralysis from the neck down. Injuries to the brain may result in seizures and intellectual, motor, sensory, visual, and language impairment. Accumulations over the brain of blood from torn intracranial vessels may cause death if not surgically relieved.

A less serious, but still debilitating, injury common to musicians and computer operators is CARPAL TUNNEL SYNDROME. Tendons in the carpal tunnel, a bone structure in the wrist, swell and prevent circulation to the thumb and first three fingers, causing numbness and sometimes pain. The problem is often caused by repetitive hand and wrist movements.

Nesbit, E. [nez'-bit] The English novelist Edith Nesbit, b. London, Aug. 15, 1858, d. May 4, 1924, is best known for her children's stories. Many of them—such as *Five Children and It* (1902), *The Phoenix and the Carpet* (1904), *The Railway Children* (1906; film, 1971), and *The Enchanted Castle* (1907)—have become classics. With her husband, Hubert Bland, and others, she helped found the Fabian Society.

Ness, Loch [nes, lahk] Loch Ness is a long, narrow, freshwater lake in the Highland region of northwestern Scotland. The lake extends approximately 37 km (23 mi) northeast along the Great Glen. Fed by the small Foyers, Enrick, and Oich rivers, it is drained at its northeastern end by the River Ness, which flows to Moray Firth 11 km (7 mi) away. The lake has a fairly uniform width of 1.6 km (1 mi) and reaches a maximum depth of 230 m (754 ft). It is part of the Caledonian Canal waterway system. Reports have persisted since the 7th century of a 12–15-m (40–50-ft) aquatic creature, the LOCH NESS MONSTER, in the loch.

Nesselrode, Karl Robert, Count [nyes-elrawd'-ye] Count Nesselrode, b. Dec. 14, 1780, d. Mar. 23, 1862, was foreign minister of Russia for 40 years under emperors ALEXANDER I and NICHOLAS I. He helped arrange the Treaties of TILSIT (1807) and, at the Congress of Vienna (1814–15; see VIENNA, CONGRESS OF), influenced Alexander I to favor the Bourbon restoration in France. In 1816 he became Russian foreign minister, sharing first the office with Count CAPO D'ISTRIA.

Under Nicholas I, who became emperor in 1825, Nesselrode advised the severe suppression of the Polish insurrection of 1830 and sent Russian troops to help Austria put down the Hungarian Revolution of 1848. His policy of maintaining the Ottoman Empire as a weak power contributed to the outbreak of the CRIMEAN WAR (1853–56).

Nestor [nes'-tur] In Greek mythology Nestor was a king of Pylos. A famous athlete in his youth, he distinguished himself in a battle that he entered on foot after his father had taken away his horses. In his old age Nestor led a fleet of 90 ships to the TROJAN WAR, where his wise counsel was esteemed by the younger Greek leaders. A Mycenaean palace located a short distance from modern Pylos is identified with the palace in which Nestor entertained Telemachus in Homer's *Odyssey.*

Nestorian church [nes-tohr'-ee-uhn] An ancient Christian body, the Nestorian church follows the teachings of Nestorius (see NESTORIANISM) and is today found in Iraq; Iran; Malabar, India; Syria; and Turkey. The church is also known as the Assyrian or East Syrian church, and its rite as the Chaldean or Assyrian, which is similar to other Eastern rites. After the condemnation of Nestorius's doctrine in 431 by the Council of Ephesus (see EPHESUS, COUNCIL OF), his followers settled in Persia. Nestorians reject all but the first two ecumenical councils held by the Christian church, honor Nestorius as a saint, and deny the title "Mother of God" to Mary. In their worship Nestorians use a sacramental bread that is believed to have come down from the dough used for the bread eaten at the Last Supper.

During the Middle Ages the Nestorians developed remarkably active missions in Arabia, India, Turkistan, China, and even Japan. Respected by the Mongolian khans, the Nestorian clergy can be credited with the toleration shown Christianity by Genghis Khan during the 13th century. The spread of Islam together with persecution of the church by Hindus and Chinese, however, led to the virtual disappearance of Nestorian Christianity in most of Asia. During the 19th and 20th centuries Nestorians suffered further attrition through massacres at the hands of Kurds and Turks; in Iraq and Turkey only a few communities now survive.

Nestorianism A 5th-century Christological heresy, Nestorianism takes its name from Nestorius, bishop of Constantinople (428–31), who argued against the Alexandrian use of the title *Theotokos,* meaning "God-bearer," or "Mother of God," for the Virgin Mary; for Nestorius, Mary was the mother of Christ only in his humanity. Theologians of the Antiochene school emphasized the humanity of Jesus Christ, the Alexandrian his deity. THEODORE OF MOPSUESTIA held that Christ's human nature was complete but was conjoined with the Word by an external union. Nestorius, Theodore's pupil, took up his teacher's position after his death.

Nestorius was condemned by the Council of Ephesus (431; see EPHESUS, COUNCIL OF), which was convened specifically to settle the dispute. There the *Theotokos* was officially affirmed and orthodox doctrine on the nature of Jesus Christ clarified: Christ was pronounced true God and true man, as having two distinct natures in one person—a position that was reaffirmed by the Council of Chalcedon (451; see CHALCEDON, COUNCIL OF).

Netherlandish art see FLEMISH ART AND ARCHITECTURE

Netherlands The Netherlands is a small independent European country located on the North Sea. It is often called Holland after a historic region now a part of the modern nation. Germany lies to the east; Belgium is to the south. The West FRISIAN ISLANDS lie offshore in the north. Trade, industry, intensive agricultural land use, and land reclamations provide for a high standard of living. The name is derived from the Dutch word *neder,* meaning "low," and the term *Low Countries* is used collectively for Belgium, Luxembourg, and the Netherlands. The capital is Amsterdam; the seat of government, The Hague, or 's Gravenhage. The Netherlands Antilles in the Caribbean is an integral part of the kingdom.

Land and Resources

The "Low Netherlands" in the north and west lies less than 1 m (3.2 ft) above sea level, while the "High Netherlands" in the south and east reaches an altitude of 321 m (1,053 ft) in the extreme southeast. Approximately a third of the entire country lies below sea level at high tide. Another 25% is so low-lying that it would be subject to inundation if it were not for the surrounding dunes and dikes and the regular pumping of excess water. An area surrounded by dikes where the water table can be controlled is called a polder. The lowest point is 6.7 m (22 ft) below mean sea level, immediately to the northeast of Rotterdam.

Soils. The soils of the High Netherlands, predominantly sandy with admixtures of gravel, require heavy additions of humus and fertilizers to be productive. The soils of the polders consist mainly of sea clay and bog peat; the clays are exceptionally fertile when desalinated and drained.

Climate. The Netherlands has a northern maritime climate. Because of its small size and low elevations, the country's regional climatic differences are negligible. Temperatures average 17° C (63° F) in July and 2° C (35° F) in January. Precipitation averages 762 mm (30 in) a year and varies little from year to year.

Drainage. Three of Europe's most important waterways—the MEUSE, RHINE, and Scheldt—enter the sea through a common delta in the southwest. A number of small lakes dot the polderlands, filling hollows from which peat was once removed for fuel. A network of canals and dikes provides an artificial drainage system that keeps the land dry. In ancient times floodwaters regularly invaded the lowlands, forcing people to build their homes on artificial mounds called *terpen.* During the Middle Ages dikes were built, enclosing lower-lying polders; in the 16th and 17th centuries windmills were used to pump excess water from the polders. Steam, and later diesel and electric, pumps made possible the reclamation of larger areas. In 1853 the Haarlemmeer was drained to create 162 km^2 (63 mi^2) of new land. The Zuiderzee Plan, begun in 1920, has provided 2,050 km^2 (792 mi^2) of new land in five polders—Wieringermeer (completed in 1930), the Northeast (1945), East Flevoland (1957), South Flevoland (1968), and Markerwaard (begun 1963). The freshwater IJSSELMEER was also formed.

KINGDOM OF THE NETHERLANDS

Land: Area: 41,863 km² (16,163 mi²), including 7,926 km² (3,060 mi²) of inland water. Capital and largest city: Amsterdam (1989 est. pop., 694,680).

People: Population (1990 est.): 14,936,032. Density: 440 persons per km² (1,140 per mi²). Distribution (1989): 89% urban, 11% rural. Official language: Dutch. Major religions: Roman Catholicism, Protestantism.

Government: Type: constitutional monarchy. Legislature: States-General. Political subdivisions: 11 provinces.

Economy: GNP (1989): $237 billion; $16,010 per capita. Labor distribution (1987): agriculture—5%; manufacturing and construction—23%; services and public administration—31%; transportation and communications—5%; trade—16%; others—20%. Foreign trade (1989): imports—$101 billion; exports—$110 billion. Currency: 1 gulden (guilder) or florin = 100 cents.

Education and Health: Literacy (1990): 100% of adult population. Universities (1987): 13. Hospital beds (1988): 94,000. Physicians (1989): 35,852. Life expectancy (1990): women—81; men—74. Infant mortality (1990): 7 per 1,000 live births.

The DELTA PLAN, a massive flood-control project begun in 1958, was completed in 1986. A series of dams and barriers were built, closing off from the sea the estuaries of the Rhine, Meuse, and Eastern Scheldt rivers, and creating the freshwater lakes Haringvliet and Grevelingen. Only the Western Scheldt and the New Waterway remain open for access to Antwerp (Belgium) and Rotterdam.

Vegetation and Animal Life. No areas of the virgin deciduous tree cover remain in the Netherlands, and only 8% of the total land area is wooded. The wildlife has also been greatly reduced. The Waddenzee is a world-renowned bird sanctuary.

Resources. Natural gas, discovered at Slochteren in the north in 1959, is the leading natural resource. Petroleum also occurs in the north and west, but production satisfies less than 5% of the nation's needs. Coal underlies Limburg Province, but production is unprofitable. Other mineral resources are salt, marl, peat, gravel, sand, and clay. The newly created freshwater IJssel, Haringvliet, and Grevelingen lakes add significantly to the water supply.

People

The Dutch are a homogeneous people of ancient Germanic origin, with some Celtic admixture. The most distinctive indigenous subgroup are the Frisians in the north. Principal immigrant subgroups include South Moluccans, Surinamese, and foreign workers from Mediterranean countries. Dutch, a Germanic language, is the official language; Frisian, a separate Germanic language, is taught along with Dutch in the schools of Friesland.

Religion. About 36% of the population in the Netherlands are Roman Catholic; 26% are Protestant, of which many (including the Dutch royal family) are of the Dutch Reformed church; and 35% have no professed religion. Jews constitute less than 1% of the population.

Until recently, Dutch society was strictly divided along religious lines, a phenomenon known as *verzuiling* (columnization). Catholics and Protestants not only sent their children to different schools, but also read different newspapers, shopped at different stores, and voted for different political parties. Today this separateness is less rigid.

Demography. More than 40% of the Dutch live in cities with 50,000 inhabitants or more, and nearly half the population are concentrated in an area known as Randstad Holland, stretching from Utrecht through Amsterdam, The Hague, and Rotterdam. The largest cities are AMSTERDAM, ROTTERDAM, The HAGUE, UTRECHT, EINDHOVEN, GRONINGEN, HAARLEM, and NIJMEGEN. The population density is one of the highest in the world. The population of the country as a whole has tripled since 1900, but today the growth rate is very low.

Education and Health. Children between ages 6 and 16 must attend school full time, and those leaving at 16 must continue their education for an additional two years on a part-time basis. About 70% attend private—mostly denominational— schools, and 30% public schools; both are financed in full by the state. Secondary education offers a choice of preparation for a university in a gymnasium, atheneum, or lyceum; a general course (chosen by the majority); or vocational training. The largest universities are those of LEIDEN (the oldest), Groningen, Amsterdam, and Utrecht.

Public and private health-insurance funds guarantee adequate health care for all; government expenditures for health-care facilities are traditionally high.

The Arts. The most famous Dutch literary figure is the 17th-century poet Joost van den VONDEL. Leading contemporary writers include the poets A. Roland Holst and J. C. Bloem and the novelist Simon Vestdijk. Major paint-

ers include Karel APPEL, Frans HALS, Piet MONDRIAN, REMBRANDT, Vincent VAN GOGH, and Jan VERMEER. The nation's historical heritage is apparent in more than 40,000 monuments, ranging from medieval castles, Gothic churches, and windmills to municipal fortifications from the 16th and 17th centuries.

The Amsterdam Concertgebouw Orchestra, long under the direction of Bernard HAITINK, is considered one of the world's finest. Major museums are Amsterdam's Vincent

Shops in historic Delft line one of the many canals that crisscross the city. Delft, located along the Schie River in the province of South Holland, is internationally known for delftware, a variety of fine tin-glazed earthenware.

van Gogh National Museum, Rijksmuseum, and Stedelijk and The Hague's Mauritshuis. (See DUTCH ART AND ARCHITECTURE; DUTCH AND FLEMISH LITERATURE.)

Economic Activity

From an early economy based on fishing and commerce, the western areas of the Netherlands later developed shipbuilding, diamond cutting, and industries manufacturing cocoa, chocolate, gin, and liqueurs from raw materials provided by overseas areas. The Industrial Revolution did not begin on a large scale until the Limburg coalfields were developed in the late 19th century. The Depression of the 1930s and the devastation of World War II left the nation impoverished, but recovery and expansion of trade and industry proceeded rapidly after 1950 through closer economic ties within the Benelux Economic Union, composed of Belgium, Luxembourg, and the Netherlands, and the EUROPEAN COMMUNITY (EC).

Manufacturing and Mining. Except for natural gas, the Netherlands must import all needed industrial raw materials. As a result, the major industrial regions have developed around the major port complexes of Rotterdam/Europoort and Amsterdam–North Sea Canal–IJmuiden. The leading manufactures are processed foods, metal and engineering products, electrical and electronic machinery and equipment, chemicals, petroleum products, and natural gas. Velsen, on the North Sea Canal, is the iron-and-steel center; Rotterdam, a leading petroleum refining center; and Eindhoven, a center for electronics. Food-processing plants are widely distributed, but the chemical manufacturers are highly localized—in Rotterdam, the center of the petrochemical industry, and in Limburg. The government seeks to direct new growth to the relatively undeveloped northeastern provinces and to such economically depressed areas as the former coal-mining region of south Limburg and the older, declining textile towns.

Energy. Coal, once a major energy source, is now relatively insignificant. The importance of petroleum has also declined with the increasing use of natural gas. The Netherlands has two nuclear power plants.

Agriculture. Dutch agriculture became increasingly more intensive and specialized after the shift to imported grains during the 1870s. The leading export products are butter and cheese—including varieties named for Dutch communities such as Edam and Gouda; tulips and other flower bulbs from the Haarlem area; hothouse crops such as tomatoes, cucumbers, and lettuce; and flowers.

Fishing. The main fishing ports are IJmuiden, Scheveningen, and Urk. The most valuable fish landed include sole and plaice; shrimps, mussels, and oysters are also caught.

Transportation. Most freight is transported by road along the Netherlands' extensive modern roadway network. About 25% moves by water, along about 4,850 km (3,014 mi) of the Rhine, Meuse, and other canalized waterways. The state-owned rail system is government subsidized for passenger travel to lure commuters from their increasing use of private automobiles. Royal Dutch Airlines (KLM) is the national airline, and Amsterdam's Schiphol airport is one of Europe's busiest.

Rotterdam/Europoort, connected to the North Sea by the enlarged New Waterway, is the largest and busiest port in the world. Amsterdam is linked to the North Sea at IJmuiden by the North Sea Canal and has access to the Rhine River by way of the Amsterdam-Rhine Canal opened in 1938. A 9,000-km-long (5,625-mi) pipeline network transports petroleum and natural gas from Rotterdam to other areas of the Netherlands and to Belgium, France, and Germany.

Trade. In most years exports slightly exceed imports in value. Exports include mineral fuels (petroleum products, natural gas), chemical products, machinery and transport equipment, and foodstuffs. Imports are crude petroleum, machinery, chemical products, and food-stuffs. The majority of the Netherlands' trade is with other EC members (especially Germany) and the United States. The Netherlands joined with Belgium and Luxembourg in 1948 to form the Benelux Customs Union, with other European nations in 1957 to form the EC, and with the other Benelux members in the Benelux Economic Union in 1958.

Government

The Kingdom of the Netherlands is a parliamentary democracy with a constitutional and hereditary monarchy. The head of state since 1980 is Queen Beatrix of the House of ORANGE. Executive power is vested in the crown (the monarch reigns but does not rule) and in a council of ministers (cabinet) responsible for formulating and carrying out government policy. Legislative authority rests with the crown and the States-General, a bicameral parliament consisting of a 150-member Second Chamber, chosen every 4 years by direct ballot, and a 75-member First Chamber, elected for 6-year terms by the 11 provincial councils. All Dutch citizens over the age of 18 may vote. Seats in the parliament are allocated among the parties on the basis of proportional representation, a system that usually results in the formation of multiparty coalition governments. Each of the 11 provinces is governed by a popularly elected provincial legislature headed by an appointed queen's commissioner.

History

Germanic tribes, including the Batavi and Frisians, occupied the area in pre-Roman times; in 12 BC the Romans extended their empire north as far as the Rhine River, remaining until about AD 300. The Franks and Saxons settled during the great Germanic migration beginning in the 5th century. The Franks absorbed the Batavi and subjugated the Frisians and Saxons during the 8th century to integrate the Netherlands into a wider European empire under the Frankish emperor CHARLEMAGNE. When the Frankish Empire disintegrated, most of the Netherlands portion passed eventually to the East Frankish Kingdom. Frankish rule progressively weakened, and at the same time Vikings invaded and pillaged the region.

Further fragmentation resulted from the emergence in the 10th century of a number of feudal, semiautonomous vassal states owing allegiance to the HOLY ROMAN EMPIRE. Among the more important of such states were the bishopric of Utrecht, the duchies of BRABANT and Gelre, and the lands held by the counts of Zeeland and the increasingly powerful counts of Holland. Consolidation began again after the dukes of Burgundy gained control in 1348, and under PHILIP THE BOLD many of the separate regions were reunited through marriages and purchases. In 1477, following the marriage of Philip's granddaughter and heir, MARY OF BURGUNDY, to MAXIMILIAN I, Holy Roman Emperor, the Burgundian possessions passed into Austrian Habsburg and—eventually—Spanish control.

Republic of the United Netherlands. In 1555–56, PHILIP II of Spain, an ardent Roman Catholic, inherited the Netherlands and the rest of the Spanish Empire from Holy Roman Emperor CHARLES V. From the beginning, Philip encountered strong anti-Spanish and anti-Catholic opposition, especially from the Dutch nobility and from Calvinists in the Protestant northern provinces.

In 1568 the disagreements erupted into a rebellion, the DUTCH REVOLT, led by WILLIAM I, Prince of Orange, resulting in the Eighty Years' War (1568–1648). In the course of the dispute, the seven northern provinces (Holland, Zeeland, Utrecht, Gelderland, Groningen, Friesland, and Overijssel) formed the United Provinces and proclaimed their independence from Spain in 1581—a claim unrecognized by Spain until the Peace of Westphalia (see WESTPHALIA, PEACE OF) in 1648. The predominantly Catholic southern provinces remained loyal to Spain and were subsequently distinguished as the Spanish Netherlands and then, after the War of the SPANISH SUCCESSION, as the Austrian Netherlands.

In the 17th century trade and shipping expanded greatly to create the golden age of the Netherlands. Through the Dutch East India Company (see EAST INDIA COMPANY, DUTCH), colonial territories were acquired in Ceylon (Sri Lanka), South Africa, Java, and Sumatra; meanwhile, the DUTCH WEST INDIA COMPANY, formed in 1621, assisted in the establishment of NEW NETHERLAND and the acquisition of territories in Brazil, Curaçao, and Saint Martin. As a result of the ANGLO-DUTCH WARS (1652–74) control of the seas was lost to England, along with New Netherland, in exchange for Suriname. A long period of decline set in during the 18th century. The end of the republic came in 1795, when the French set up the Batavian Republic (1795–1806), followed by the Kingdom of Holland (1806–10) under Napoleon's brother Louis Bonaparte (see BONAPARTE family) and in 1810 incorporated the lands into the French Empire.

The Netherlands, an important exporter of tulips since the 16th century, today devotes more than 5,900 ha (14,580 acres) to their cultivation. In addition to tulips, the nation exports a wide variety of ornamental bulbs.

Kingdom of the Netherlands. Reunification of the seven United Provinces with the southern (or Austrian) provinces as the Kingdom of the Netherlands under King WILLIAM I followed Napoleon's defeat in 1814 and was confirmed by the Congress of Vienna (see VIENNA, CONGRESS OF) in 1815. The unity of north and south was short-lived, and in 1830 the southern provinces withdrew and proclaimed their own independence, recognized in 1839, as the Kingdom of Belgium. The benevolent despotism of William I caused liberal reactions in the Netherlands, resulting in major democratic revision to the 1814 constitution in 1848 under WILLIAM II. Under WILLIAM III (r. 1849–90), additional reforms and limits on the monarchy were accomplished through the leadership of the distinguished Liberal statesman Johan Rudolf Thorbecke (1798–1872). When William died, his 10-year-old daughter WILHELMINA inherited the throne, her mother Emma acting as regent until the queen came of age in 1898.

Although neutral during World War I, the Netherlands encountered severe economic difficulties and was further weakened by the Depression of the 1930s. Liberalism declined during the interwar years of the 1920s and '30s, and coalitions of Catholic and Protestant political parties ruled. In World War II neutrality was again proclaimed, but German forces overran the nation in May 1940, their occupation claiming about 240,000 victims, many of them Jews. Much of the country was in ruins at the end of the war. In 1948, Queen Wilhelmina abdicated in favor of her daughter, Juliana, beginning a period of transformation for the Netherlands from a colonial power to a leading member of the European community of nations. Indonesia and Suriname gained their independence in 1949 and 1975, respectively.

On Queen Juliana's abdication in 1980, her daughter Beatrix became the sovereign. Since 1977 the country has been governed by a series of coalitions, first under Andreas van Agt, and from November 1982, under Christian Democrat Ruud LUBBERS, who was reelected in 1986 and 1989. Prime Minister Lubbers has pursued an austerity program, reducing government spending and selling off government-owned industries to compensate for revenue losses resulting from a period of declining economic activity.

Netherlands Antilles [an-til-eez]   The Netherlands Antilles, an autonomous part of the Netherlands, is a self-governing federation of five Caribbean islands. ARUBA had been the sixth member of the federation until Jan. 1, 1986, when it gained autonomy. The total land area 800 km^2 (308 mi^2), and the population is 183,503 (1990 est.). The two largest and most populated islands—CURAÇAO and Bonaire—lie off the Venezuelan coast. The other three—SAINT MARTIN (whose northern half belongs to France), Saba, and Saint Eustatius—are about 800 km (500 mi) to the northeast. The annual mean temperature in the Netherlands Antilles is 27° C (80° F), and rainfall varies from 560 mm (22 in) in the southern islands to 1,015 mm (40 in) per year in the northern group. The capital, WILLEMSTAD, is on Curaçao. The federation is governed by a prime minister and a legislative council.

The prosperous economy of the federation is based on tourism. Oil refining, once the principal industry, declined considerably in the 1980s. Natural resources are phosphates (Curaçao) and salt (Bonaire). Corn and pulses are grown.

The inhabitants are descendants of Indians, Dutch, Portuguese, Jews, and former African slaves. The inhabitants of the southern islands speak Papiamento (mixture of Dutch, Portuguese, Spanish, and African), and those of the northern group speak English. Illiteracy is almost nonexistent, and the standard of living is the highest in the Caribbean.

Originally inhabited by ARAWAK (in the south) and CARIB Indians (in the north), the islands were conquered by the Spanish in the 16th century and by the Dutch in the 17th century. They have been self-governing since 1954.

Neto, Agostinho António [ne'-too]   The Marxist poet and physician Agostinho António Neto, b. Sept. 17, 1922, d. Sept. 10, 1979, was president of the People's Republic of Angola from 1975 until his death. As a student he joined the Communist-dominated, anticolonial Democratic Unity Movement. Leading the Soviet-backed Popular Movement for the Liberation of Angola (MPLA) and with the active help of Cuban forces, he was victorious in a civil war against two other nationalist groups, the National Union for the Total Independence of Angola (UNITA) and the National Front for the Liberation of Angola (FNLA).

---

netsuke [net'-suh-kay]   A netsuke is a small carved toggle used in traditional Japanese male garb to fasten the cords of pouches or inro (medicine boxes) to the sash. They were fashionable items of middle-class dress during the Tokugawa period (1603–1867). Originally designed in the form of simple bamboo rings, netsuke eventually became finely detailed, diminutive works of sculpture, generally carved from ivory, horn, or wood, typically depicting human figures or subjects inspired by nature.

---

nettle   Nettle is the common name for a number of plants with bristly, usually stinging, hairs. A stinging hair is hollow and is tipped with a tiny, hard, brittle, bulbous cell that is able to penetrate the skin, where it breaks off to release the irritating liquid from secretory cells at the base of the hair.

The stinging nettle, *Urtica dioica*, of the nettle family, Urticaceae, has been cultivated for its linenlike fibers, and the newly arising young shoots and the pale green top leaves of older plants are simmered and eaten. The plant grows to about 1.8 m (6 ft) and has sharply toothed leaves and clusters of tiny greenish flowers.

Other plants called nettles include the bull nettle, *Cnidoscolus stimulosus*, of the spurge family, Euphorbiaceae; the hedge nettles, *Stachys*, and dead nettles, *Lamium*, both of the mint family, Labiatae; and the hackberries, *Celtis*, of the elm family, Ulmaceae, which are often called nettle trees.

Neuchâtel [nuh-shah-tel'] Neuchâtel is the capital of Neuchâtel canton, western Switzerland, on the northwestern shore of Lake Neuchâtel. Its population is 32,650 (1987). The city is the center of an important wine-producing region, and its industries manufacture watches, chocolate, tobacco products, and paper. Originally a Burgundian town, it was chartered in 1214. Its historical landmarks include a medieval castle and the Collegiate Church of Notre Dame (built 12th–13th centuries).

Neumann, Johann Balthasar [noy'-mahn, yoh'-hahn bahl-tah-zahr'] The brilliant and innovative German baroque architect Johann Balthasar Neumann, baptized Jan. 30, 1687, d. Aug. 18, 1753, created his two greatest works for the wealthy Schönborn family: the immense palace called the Würzburg Residenz and the astonishing Pilgrimage Church of Vierzehnheiligen (Fourteen Saints) near Bamberg. In addition, elsewhere in Germany and Austria, he designed 12 churches and 6 palaces. Neumann's originality is unmistakable in his masterly handling of light, space, and unusual forms. The core of the Würzburg Residenz is the awesome ceremonial staircase rising from a shadowy vestibule to a light-filled hall above. The Pilgrimage Church of Vierzehnheiligen (begun 1743, consecrated 1772) is a paradigm of German baroque church architecture. The massive cruciform edifice is seemingly conventional, but the interior is a vast, fantastical space drenched in light.

Neumann, Saint John Nepomucene After devoting his relatively short life to the spread of Catholicism in the United States, John Neumann, b. Prachatitz, Bohemia, Mar. 28, 1811, d. Jan. 5, 1860, became the first American bishop to be canonized. Although Neumann completed (1835) his seminary training in his homeland, he was ordained (1836) in the United States and served for four years in churches near Buffalo, N.Y. In 1840 he entered the Congregation of the Most Holy Redeemer, or Redemptorist monastic order, and gradually assumed greater supervisory burdens. In 1852 he was appointed bishop of Philadelphia.

Neumann's great organizational ability was reflected in such accomplishments as the building of 80 new churches and 100 schools, as well as in the growth of the number of students attending them. He was canonized in 1977. Feast day: Jan. 5.

neural network A neural network is a COMPUTER with an internal structure imitative of the human brain's interconnected system of neurons. In a neural network, TRANSISTOR circuits are the electronic analogue of neurons, and variable RESISTORS represent the synapses between the neurons (see NERVOUS SYSTEM).

Neural networks do not follow rigidly programmed rules, as more conventional digital computers do. Rather, they build an information base through a trial-and-error method. Pathways between individual circuits are "strengthened" (resistance turned down) when a task is performed correctly and "weakened" (resistance turned up) if performed incorrectly. In this way a neural network "learns" from its mistakes and gives more accurate output with each repetition of a task.

Simple neural networks were built in the late 1950s, but little progress was made in the field until more powerful PARALLEL PROCESSING techniques were developed a few decades later. Many researchers believe that sophisticated neural networks will one day be used for such ARTIFICIAL INTELLIGENCE tasks as PATTERN RECOGNITION and voice recognition.

neuralgia [nuh-ral-gee-uh] Neuralgia, a nervous-system disorder, involves sudden pain without inflammation and occurs along one or more peripheral nerve fibers. Neuralgia of the trigeminal nerve, characterized by intense facial pain, is known as TIC douloureux. Glossopharyngeal neuralgia and SCIATICA are two other common forms. Neuralgia can be a symptom of such disorders as diabetes, syphilis, malaria, and anemia. It can originate from viral infection, such as herpes zoster; compression of a nerve as a result of swollen arthritic joints; or poor blood supply. An amputated nerve axon attempting to regenerate can also cause neuralgia as the nerve becomes surrounded by scar tissue. This ball of tissue, known as a nerve tumor or neuroma, is endowed with pain receptors.

neurofibromatosis [noo'-roh-fy'-bruh-muh-toh'-sis] Neurofibromatosis is a genetic disorder that affects the growth of nerve cells. It can cause nonmalignant and sometimes massive tumors, called neurofibromas, to develop in the nervous system. The disorder affects about 1 out of every 4,000 persons, but most persons show only mild symptoms. (A rarer form affects about 1 out of every 50,000 persons.) About half of the offspring of a parent with the disorder develop it, but for many persons with the disorder no family history is known.

One early symptom of neurofibromatosis is the appearance of pigmented "café-au-lait" spots on the skin of the new-born infant. The disorder may thereafter affect a child's skeleton, leading to fractures and abnormal bone development, with SCOLIOSIS, or curvature of the spine, appearing in adolescence. Other more severe symptoms include growth disorders, learning disabilities, brain tumors, seizures, and malfunctions of the gastrointestinal system. Tumors of the optic and auditory nerves can cause impairments of vision and hearing, and impairments of other vital organs can become life-threatening. Treatment is thus far limited to relieving symptoms.

Neurofibromatosis has been called "Elephant Man's disease" because of the Englishman Joseph Carey Merrick (1862–90), who was exhibited for a while as the Elephant Man. His disfigurement was long attributed to neurofibromatosis, but he has recently been rediagnosed as having suffered from Proteus syndrome, a much rarer disease with worse physical effects.

neurology Neurology is the study of the anatomy, physiology, and pathology of the nervous system. A neurologist usually is a physician who specializes in diseases of the nervous system. The specialty overlaps to a degree the discipline of psychiatry because neurological disorders often produce symptoms of mental disorder.

neuron see NERVOUS SYSTEM

neurophysiology see NERVOUS SYSTEM

Neuroptera [nuh-rahp'-tuh-ruh] Neuroptera (Greek: *neuro*, "nerve"; *ptera*, "wings") is an order of about 4,300 insect species, including the LACEWINGS, alderflies, antlions, and dobsonflies. These soft-bodied insects have four similar membranous wings with many-branched veins. Many are predaceous in immature and adult forms and use sucking mouthparts.

neurosis A neurosis, in classic psychoanalytic theory (see PSYCHOANALYSIS), is a class of disorders characterized by maladaptive patterns of thinking, feeling, or acting. Neurotic behavior is rigid, repetitive, and self-defeating. Unlike individuals with psychoses, neurotics may function adequately in daily life even though they distort some aspect of reality, resulting in behavior that may be strange or offensive to others and unsatisfying to themselves. Sigmund Freud believed that isolated neurotic patterns occur in most "normal" individuals.

ANXIETY—a state of dread or discomfort lacking a distinct cause—is seen as both the main subjective feature of and the motivating force for neurosis. Freud believed that anxiety arises as a signal that some threat is being perceived, even below the threshold of awareness, and that this signal causes a redirection of behavior to avoid the threat. Reduction of anxiety is so rewarding that these avoidance maneuvers are resistant to change.

Freud divided neurosis into four subtypes: anxiety neurosis, anxiety hysteria (or PHOBIA), obsessive-compulsive neurosis (see OBSESSIVE-COMPULSIVE DISORDER), and HYSTERIA. Those suffering from anxiety neurosis have anxiety "attacks" for no readily apparent reason. Sufferers of anxiety hysteria have an unnatural fear of certain objects or situations that others perceive as being harmless. Those with obsessive-compulsive neurosis compulsively repeat certain acts or become obsessed by unwanted thoughts. Those with hysteria, an extreme form of neurosis, may suffer from amnesia, hallucinations, sleepwalking, or paralysis.

Freud's followers built upon his work by further subdividing and augmenting these basic categories, and neurosis was long an important diagnostic concept in the practice of PSYCHIATRY. As other causes for mental disorders were explored, however, the term *neurosis* gradually fell into disuse among many mental-health workers, although it remains an important concept in the practice of psychoanalysis.

Neurospora *Neurospora*, a genus of fungi in the phylum Ascomycetes, occurs commonly as a red mold on bread. It has a short life cycle, about 30 days, and multiplies profusely by asexual spores. The genus has been studied extensively and was used by biochemists George W. BEADLE and Edward L. TATUM to prove that genes act by controlling the synthesis of enzymes.

neurotransmitter A neurotransmitter is a chemical compound, secreted by a nerve cell (neuron), that either stimulates or inhibits the flow of an impulse between neurons (see NERVOUS SYSTEM). Shortly after a neurotransmitter completes its action, it is broken down by an enzyme. Acetylcholine and noradrenalin are examples of stimulatory neurotransmitters; gamma aminobutyric acid is an example of an inhibitor. Two other neurotransmitters, serotonin and dopamine, are stimulatory in some parts of the brain but inhibitory in others. Acetylcholine also stimulates muscle contraction wherever a neuron connects with a muscle. The effects of disruption of normal neurotransmitter function are observed in a number of diseases (see NERVOUS SYSTEM, DISEASES OF THE).

Neuss [noys] Neuss (1983 est. pop., 147,609) is a city in northwestern Germany, 8 km (5 mi) west of Düsseldorf in the state of North Rhine–Westphalia. Connected by the Erft Canal to the Rhine River, Neuss is accessible to small freighters. An important transportation and industrial center, it has a major grain market. Metal goods, machinery, chemicals, concrete, and fertilizer are manufactured there. The 13th-century Saint Quirinus Church and the Rathaus (1634–38) have been restored since World War II. Founded as Novaesium by the Romans in the 1st century BC, it was captured and renamed Niusa by the Franks. After being controlled by Napoleonic France, it became part of Prussia in 1816.

Neutra, Richard [noy'-truh] The architect Richard Josef Neutra, b. Vienna, Apr. 8, 1892, d. Apr. 16, 1970, brought the ideals and forms of the INTERNATIONAL STYLE in architecture to Southern California. His finest buildings, all in the Los Angeles area, were built shortly after he moved to California in 1926. They are notable for their evocative siting and creative use of building technology. The Lovell Health House (1929; Los Angeles) comprises large glass-and-concrete planes that step up a steep canyon wall. Its prefabricated steel frame was erected in less than 40 hours; its many balconies are suspended from the roof above each plane. By contrast, the von Sternberg House (1936; Northridge, Calif.) has a plan related to Frank Lloyd Wright's Prairie Houses, well suited to the flat site; its exterior is sheathed in aluminum-coated steel.

neutrality In international law a state of neutrality exists when a nation chooses not to take part in a war fought by other nations and pursues a nondiscriminatory and impartial policy toward those nations. Belligerent nations are expected to refrain from any interference in the land or territorial waters of the neutral state. Perpetual neutrality differs from temporary neutrality in that the former—as in the case of Switzerland—is set by multilateral treaty, whereas the latter is declared unilaterally. The concept of neutrality gained in importance with the extension of naval warfare and growing demands by nonbelligerent states to continue to trade freely. The right of neutral commerce, however, was limited by the development of international laws of BLOCKADE and CONTRABAND. George Washington proclaimed U.S. neutrality in 1793 during the French Revolutionary Wars; in 1935, Congress enacted the Neutrality Act, designed to prevent U.S. involvement in foreign wars. Because of growing international interdependence and charter obligations under the United Nations, neutrality is increasingly difficult to practice in the 20th century.

neutralization   see ACIDS AND BASES

neutrino   The neutrino, a neutral subatomic particle (see FUNDAMENTAL PARTICLES), was first postulated by Wolfgang Pauli as the elusive, invisible culprit in radioactive BETA DECAY responsible for the apparent violation of the law of conservation of energy. In the primary beta decay (emission of an electron from the nucleus of a naturally radioactive atom), the electrons are not all emitted with one and the same energy as would be expected if, in accord with basic quantum-mechanical ideas, the initial and final nuclei in the process had precise and definite energies. To resolve this dilemma Pauli proposed that the electron was accompanied by, and shared its energy with, a partner of small mass and zero electric charge: the *neutrino* (a name coined by Enrico Fermi to describe "the small, neutral one"). These and other properties preserved the conservation laws (of energy, momentum, and so on) and also explained the neutrino's elusiveness.

For approximately two decades conclusions regarding the existence and properties of the neutrino rested entirely on inferences. With the advent of powerful nuclear reactors, copious sources of (hypothetical) neutrinos became available. The reaction: neutrino + proton → neutron + positron (essentially the inverse of the familiar decay: neutron → proton + electron + antineutrino) was first observed by Clyde L. Cowan and Frederick Reines in 1957.

The chance of interaction between neutrinos and matter is extremely small because both the strong and electromagnetic interactions are absent here (see FUNDAMENTAL INTERACTIONS). For example, a neutrino of energy typical in beta decay can traverse the Earth with a likelihood of only about 1 in 200 million of interacting with matter.

Today neutrinos and antineutrinos are associated with a wide range of weak interaction processes in which fundamental particles of the LEPTON class are known to take part. Three different neutrinos are known, each associated with one of three charged leptons. A profound debate in modern physics centers on whether neutrinos have mass. If neutrinos have mass, they might constitute the so-called missing mass of the universe (see COSMOLOGY). The field of neutrino astronomy was expanded dramatically in 1987 by the appearance of a relatively nearby SUPERNOVA and the detection of neutrinos from the explosion.

neutron   The neutron may be regarded as one of the basic constituents of the ATOM, even though it (like all HADRONS) is a complex entity. When examined by high-energy probes, it exhibits a definite internal "structure" (see FUNDAMENTAL PARTICLES). The peculiar properties of a penetrating radiation emitted when some light elements, notably beryllium, were bombarded with alpha particles (from naturally radioactive substances) led James Chadwick in 1932 to interpret it as a stream of electrically neutral particles with mass similar to the proton's.

There had been earlier conjectures (1920) by Ernest Rutherford about, and searches for, a neutral composite entity comprising an electron and proton in closer association than in the usual neutral hydrogen atom. The newly discovered particle was at first regarded as potentially such an entity, until precise measurement showed that the neutron mass exceeded the mass of a proton and an electron combined. The close similarity, however, of the neutron to the proton (rather than to the neutral hydrogen atom) and, in particular, of their strong nuclear interactions (after allowance for the different electrical properties) led Werner Heisenberg (1934) to the notion of the neutron and the proton as twin particles. Furthermore, their properties were exactly those required to explain, in principle, the existence and properties of complex atomic nuclei. The close similarity with respect to mass, spin, and nuclear interactions are now regarded as one expression of isospin symmetry (see SYMMETRY, physics), which is characteristic of nuclear structures and interactions, and of strong (hadronic) interactions generally. Because the neutron is uncharged electrically, it can readily penetrate atoms and reach and interact with nuclei even when moving slowly. By elastic collisions with light nuclei, neutrons are moderated (slowed) in their passage through materials (especially hydrogenous compounds and carbon). The resulting slow neutrons provide a unique tool for probing the structure of bulk matter—a tool that is largely complementary to the X-ray probe, which responds particularly to heavy elements, whereas the neutron responds to light elements. Beams of neutrons now have a wide range of applications in science and technology.

neutron bomb   A neutron bomb is a special type of small HYDROGEN BOMB considered useful for battlefield or tactical conditions. It is also called an enhanced radiation (ER) weapon because the number of neutrons emitted is greater in proportion to the explosive force than in a conventional atomic or hydrogen bomb. A nuclear explosion releases energy in the form of nuclear radiation, thermal radiation, and blast. The nuclear radiation component, which includes alpha, beta, and gamma radiation as well as neutrons, can be increased relative to the other components by modification of the bomb design.

Because neutrons are uncharged particles, they travel great distances through matter until stopped or slowed, most likely by collision with light atoms. Humans are susceptible to injury from neutron irradiation because the body's water molecules contain the lightest atom, hydrogen. Structures, aside from having a higher proportion of heavier atoms, do not suffer biological changes and therefore are less prone to alteration from encounters with neutrons. A bomb that produces neutrons having a lethal or incapacitating range greater than the range of its thermal and pressure effects will, therefore, be more damaging to living things than to structures.

The ER concept came into prominence in the mid-1970s. Faced with the prospect of overwhelming Soviet superiority on the ground in the event of an invasion of Western Europe, the NATO countries, led by the United States, sought a means of effective defense. A desire to minimize the loss of lives and property of the invaded countries, while repelling the enemy from their soil, made a neutron warhead on a short-range missile or in an artillery shell seem an appropriate battlefield weapon, especially for use against tanks.

U.S. president Jimmy Carter approved (1978) the production of ER components. His successor, Ronald Reagan, ordered (1981) full assembly and stockpiling of the weapons. Completed neutron warheads were placed in 8-in (20.3-cm) artillery shells, with a range of about 24 km (15 mi), and in the Lance missile, which has a 120-km (75-mi) range. The European public actively opposed the deployment of ER weapons in their countries, and European leaders advised against the siting of neutron bombs on European soil.

neutron star   A neutron star is an extremely small, high-density star composed of tightly packed neutrons. The existence of neutron stars was first postulated in 1932, when Lev LANDAU suggested that a state of matter stable only at high densities might exist. Walter Baade and Fritz Zwicky suggested in 1934 that a SUPERNOVA explosion might leave a remnant in the form of a star consisting largely of neutrons, the stable state envisaged by Landau (see STELLAR EVOLUTION). In 1968, PULSARS, first discovered in 1967, were theorized to be rotating neutron stars, a view now widely accepted. The short period and the regularity of the pulses suggested a small, massive star of the kind predicted by theory. Neutron stars have masses of about one solar mass and radii of about 10 km (6.2 mi). Their mean densities are thought to be about 10^{14} times that of water.

Neutron stars are believed to have a solid crust, perhaps consisting of crystalline iron. Inside this crust there is probably a neutron-rich solid shell, and still deeper inside there is probably a superfluid material. The sudden slight changes that neutron stars show in their rotation period are thought to be caused by small, sudden changes in the star's structure.

Because of their identification with pulsars, rotating neutron stars are thought to have extremely strong mag-

netic fields. These fields must be involved in the radiation of the radio waves from pulsars, but exactly how this occurs is not yet understood.

Neva River [nee'-vuh]   The Neva River issues from Lake Ladoga in the northwestern USSR and flows 74 km (46 mi) west to the Gulf of Finland, forming a delta at Leningrad.

Nevada [nuh-vad'-uh]   Nevada, the westernmost intermountain state, is best known for its desert climate and legalized gambling. Bounded by California on the south and west, Oregon and Idaho on the north, and Arizona and Utah on the east, it is the seventh largest state; about 85% of its area is federally controlled, and only Alaska has more public land than does Nevada. Nevada is a sparsely populated state, but its population growth rate is one of the highest in the United States. The state capital is CARSON CITY. *Nevada* is a Spanish word meaning "snow covered." The nickname, Silver State, recalls Nevada's mining origins. Tourism is now the dominant sector of the economy, and the resort cities of Las Vegas and Reno have grown rapidly.

Land and Resources

Other than the SIERRA NEVADA in the extreme west and the Columbia Plateau in the far north, Nevada lies wholly within the GREAT BASIN, a plateau of isolated mountain ranges separated by arid basins. About 160 north-south-trending mountain ranges cross the state. The average elevation is 1,500 m (5,000 ft). The lowest and highest elevations are located, respectively, along the Colorado River and on Boundary Peak. Valleys between the mountains lie at high altitudes, usually at elevations of 1,200–1,800 m (3,800–6,000 ft), but somewhat lower in southern Nevada.

Nevada's topography reflects a complex geologic history that remains unstable; Nevada experiences earthquakes on occasion. Geothermal areas include the Beowawe Geysers in the north and Steamboat Geyser near Reno.

Soils. Mountain soils are thin and poorly developed, and arid valley soils are of low fertility, except for those near rivers, where alluvium provides fertile farmland. Salinization is severe, and many valleys contain dry lake beds too salty to support plant life.

Rivers and Lakes. Except for the COLORADO RIVER flowing southwest from Colorado and Utah and the COLUMBIA RIVER watershed in the north, Nevada lies in the Great Basin area of interior drainage with only a few small permanent rivers. The Humboldt River, 467 km (290 mi), is the state's longest. The Carson, Truckee, and Walker rivers drain the east slopes of the Sierra Nevada.

Nevada has more than 200 lakes, most of which are small reservoirs. Lake MEAD reservoir and Lake TAHOE are the largest bodies of water.

Climate. Nevada's location in the Sierra Nevada rain shadow makes it the driest state in the country. Annual precipitation averages 229 mm (9 in), varying from 76

NEVADA

Land: Area: 286,368 km^2 (110,567 mi^2); rank: 7th. Capital: Carson City (1990 pop., 40,443). Largest city: Las Vegas (1990 pop., 258,295). Counties: 17 and one independent city. Elevations: highest—4,005 m (13,140 ft), at Boundary Peak; lowest—146 m (479 ft), at the Colorado River.

People: Population (1990): 1,206,152; rank: 39th; density: 4.2 persons per km^2 (10.9 per mi^2). Distribution (1990): 88.3% urban, 11.7% rural. Average annual change (1980–90): +5.1%.

Government (1993): Governor: Bob Miller, Democrat. U.S. Congress: Senate—2 Democrats; House—1 Democrat, 1 Republican. Electoral college votes: 4. State legislature: 21 senators, 42 representatives.

Economy: State personal income (1989): $21.4 billion; rank: 38th. Median family income (1989): $35,837; rank: 18th. Agriculture: income (1989)—$235 million. Lumber production (1991): not available. Mining (nonfuel): value (1988)—$1.9 billion. Manufacturing : value added (1987)—$1.3 billion. Services: value (1987)—$11.3 billion.

Miscellany: Statehood: Oct. 31, 1864; the 36th state. Nicknames: Silver State and Sagebrush State; tree: bristlecone pine and single-leaf piñon; motto: All for Our Country; song: "Home Means Nevada."

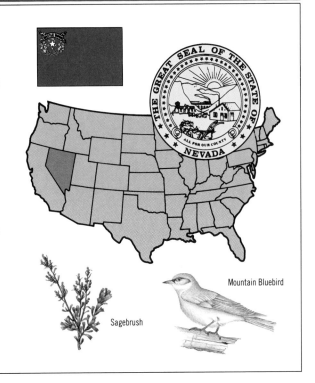

Mountain Bluebird

Sagebrush

---

mm (3 in) in the south to 737 mm (29 in) in the Sierra Nevada. Most water is derived from mountain snowmelt.

Nevada has extremely cold winters and very hot summers. Southern Nevada is a subtropical desert, with a July mean temperature of 30° C (86° F) and a January average of 6° C (43° F). Northwestern Nevada is cooler throughout the year, with a January mean of –1° C (30° F) and a July average of 22° C (71° F). Almost no rain falls in summer, but snow can occur between October and May. The northeast is the highest, coolest, and wettest region; its semiarid steppe climate supports sufficient vegetation for grazing.

Vegetation and Animal Life. Nevada's most common plant is sagebrush. Salt-tolerant soapweed and iodine bush grow in the mid-latitude desert and creosote bush in the southern desert. The most common mountain vegetation is a pine nut–juniper woodland. Aspen, mountain mahogany, sugar pine, and lodgepole pine grow at higher elevations. Bristlecone pines as old as 4,900 years have been found in the Toiyabe Range and on Wheeler Peak.

Indigenous mammals include mule deer, coyote, jackrabbit, various rodents, and wild horses. Meadowlarks, doves, chukars, pheasants, mountain bluebirds, and migratory waterfowl are common. More than 50 reptile species can be found in the desert, and rare desert pupfish inhabit several springs.

Resources. Nevada's most abundant resource is open space; only about 20% of its land is privately owned, and most public land is undeveloped. The state's limited water supply—two-thirds streamflow and one-third groundwater—is unevenly distributed and already committed, especially to irrigated agriculture. Nevada's major resources are minerals, including gold, copper, silver, lithium, mercury, tungsten, barite, magnesite, and gypsum.

People

Nevada's overall population density is low, but most of the state's residents live in just two metropolitan areas—LAS VEGAS and RENO. The population grew by nearly 64% during the 1970–80 decade and by nearly 51% during 1980–90, made up mostly of migration to these areas. Clark County alone has more than 60% of the state's residents. The racial composition of the population is mainly white, with blacks and Indians accounting for less than 10% of the population. Native tribes, including the Northern and Southern PAIUTE, Western SHOSHONI, and WASHO, live on several reservations and colonies statewide. The largest single religious group is the Roman Catholics, followed by the Mormons.

Education. More than three-quarters of the adult population in Nevada have completed high school. Institutions of higher learning include the University of Nevada

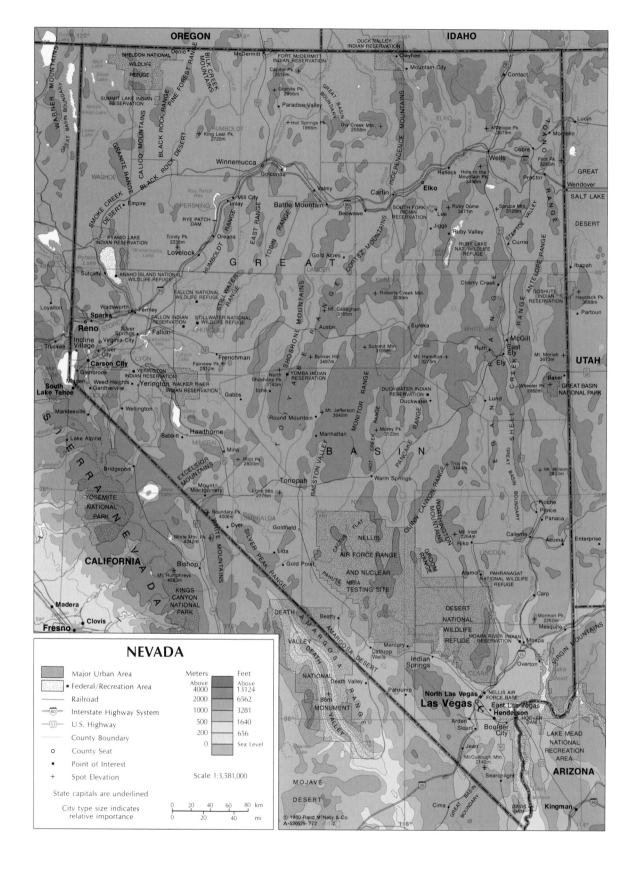

Nevada, the driest state in the United States, lies mostly in the Great Basin, an arid region east of the Sierra Nevada. Nearly half of the state has a desert climate.

(1864) at Las Vegas and at Reno, four community colleges, and two private colleges. Major scientific institutions include the Desert Research Institute, the Basque Studies Program in Reno, and the Nevada Atomic Test Site.

Culture. The state's major museums include the State Museum in Carson City, and the Fleischmann Atmospherium-Planetarium and Harrah's Automobile Collection, both in Reno. Las Vegas and Reno support symphony orchestras. Nevada's best-known historic sites are its 100 mining villages, most of which are now GHOST TOWNS; Virginia City is famous as the major focus of the state's early development. Parklands include DEATH VALLEY National Monument; Lake Mead National Recreation Area; and Great Basin National Park. The Jarbidge Wilderness and the Ruby Mountain scenic area are outstanding. Wildlife refuges include Anaho Island Refuge for pelicans in Pyramid Lake, the Ruby Lakes National Wildlife Refuge, and the Desert National Wildlife Refuge in Clark County. Ski slopes are near Crystal Bay, Ely, and Las Vegas.

Communications. Nevada's largest newspaper is the *Las Vegas Review-Journal*, and the most influential paper in northern Nevada is the *Reno Gazette-Journal*. The state also has numerous radio and television broadcasting facilities, including several cable television systems.

Economic Activities

Nevada's economy, built on mining, railroading, and ranching, has changed dramatically since World War II. The need for an industry requiring little water brought legalization of gambling in 1931, facilitating tourism's dominance of the economy.

Two-thirds of the state is administered by the U.S. Bureau of Land Management, mostly for grazing, mining, or dispersed recreation, and another 7% is national forestland. Only 1% of Nevada land is state-owned.

Agriculture. Livestock, mostly beef cattle with some sheep and dairy stock, make up about two-thirds of agricultural sales. Principal crops include barley, hay, potatoes, wheat, alfalfa seed, cotton, and oats. Much of the produce is used for fodder.

Mining. Nevada is an important mineral-producing state, leading the nation in the production of gold (the state's most valuable mineral), barite, magnesite, and mercury. Other major minerals produced include silver, copper, diatomite, fluorspar, iron ore, lithium, molybdenum, and perlite. Sand, gravel, and gypsum are also economically important.

Manufacturing. Nevada has a limited manufacturing sector. The chief products are chemicals, processed food, stone, clay, and glass products, electrical equipment, primary metals, nonelectrical machinery, and printing and publishing. Most manufacturing firms are located in the large urban areas. Henderson is the center of heavy industry.

Tourism. Tourism is Nevada's greatest source of income, drawing about 30 million visitors annually to the state's gambling facilities and scenic beauty. Principal gambling areas are Las Vegas, Reno, and Lake Tahoe, but casinos can be found in most counties. Nevada's liberal regulations for marriage and divorce bring in nonresidents, and the marriage and divorce rates are both high. Nevada's best-known attractions are the nightclubs associated with the hotel-casinos. Events for tourists include rodeos, the annual Basque Festival in Elko, and the National Championship Air Races in Reno. Hunting, fishing, camping, boating, and winter sports are also popular.

Transportation. The state's principal highways are Interstate 80 in the north and Interstate 15 in the south. Amtrak provides rail passenger service. Nevada's leading commercial air terminals are McCarran International Airport in Las Vegas and Reno-Cannon Airport.

Energy. Nevada exports electricity, principally from Clark County's several coal-fired plants and hydroelectric generators at HOOVER DAM on the Colorado River. Other Colorado River dams that provide electric power are the Davis and Glen Canyon dams.

Government

The Nevada constitution, adopted in 1864, has been amended many times. State revenues are derived primarily from gaming and sales taxes. The absence of an income or inheritance tax has attracted many wealthy residents.

In the bicameral legislature, state senators serve 4-year terms, and members of the assembly, 2-year terms. The governor and lieutenant governor serve 4-year terms, and each may belong to a different political party. The state judicial system has a supreme court, district courts, city courts, and justice courts, apportioned on a township basis. The state is divided into 17 counties and one independent city, Carson City. County commissions are responsible for all areas outside the incorporated towns.

The Republican party dominated Nevada politics from statehood until 1892, when the Silver party absorbed both the Democratic and Republican parties. These tradi-

The glittering nightlife of Las Vegas has become legendary because of its casinos, hotels, and nightclubs. The city's principal source of income is tourism.

tional parties reemerged by 1900, and neither has enjoyed sole dominance since that time.

History

The first residents of Nevada were Indians who entered the Great Basin about 12,000 years ago. Their descendants, a widely scattered hunting and gathering population, dominated the harsh region until relatively recent times. The first European to see Nevada was probably Francisco Garcés (1738–81), a Spanish Franciscan priest who reached the Colorado River while journeying through Spanish Mexico. In 1826, Jedediah Strong SMITH reached the Walker River and central Nevada, and the trapper Peter Skene Ogden (1794–1854) crossed the Humboldt and Carson basins in 1825. The first systematic observations of the region were made by John C. FRÉMONT from 1843 to 1845. In 1841 settlers journeying to the west coast began crossing the Humboldt Valley and the Forty Mile Desert, a route later followed by the Overland Stage Lines.

The Treaty of GUADALUPE HIDALGO (Feb. 2, 1848), which concluded the Mexican War, granted to the United States territory that included present-day Nevada. The Mormons founded the first permanent settlement at Genoa in the Carson Valley in 1849 and established a mission in the Las Vegas Valley in 1855. The pony express route crossed central Nevada in 1860–61.

Nevada's major period of growth followed the discovery of the COMSTOCK LODE at Virginia City in 1858, a strike that yielded $386 million in silver and gold by the time production stopped in 1921. Nevada Territory separated from Utah Territory in 1861, and statehood was granted on Oct. 31, 1864.

The first transcontinental railroad was completed across northern Nevada in 1869, with the Central Pacific Railroad gaining the valuable freighting from the Comstock mines. Mining camps flourished and died until, in

the early 1900s, the major Tonopah and Goldfield strikes established Nevada as a major source of industrial metals. Cattle ranching began in the 1860s, and sheep raising became important in the 1870s, both activities pursued by Basques.

Water supplies have been a concern. The Prior Appropriation Doctrine prevails over distributing the limited supply; water is granted to the earliest established users. In 1905 the first federal reclamation scheme was completed near Fallon to irrigate croplands with waters from the Truckee River. Urban growth has also increased water demands. Use of Colorado River water can meet the region's immediate needs, but river rights are limited. Nevada's future prosperity will depend on tourism and other industries that consume little water.

Rangeland suitable for the support of livestock has deteriorated, partly due to the expansion of the wild horse population following passage (1971) of the protective Wild Horse and Burro Act. Such problems moved the Nevada legislature to pass the "Sagebrush Rebellion" act in 1979 authorizing the state to sue for possession of federal lands.

Minerals continue to be important, but metal extraction remains a boom-and-bust operation. Although the 1978 shutdown of copper mines had little effect on the overall state economy, it had a severe impact on White Pine County.

Tourism remains Nevada's most important industry, although in the 1980s efforts toward diversification of the state's economy have met with some success. There is a continuing need for planning to control congestion, pollution, and housing costs so that Nevada can maintain a pleasant living environment.

Nevelson, Louise [nev'-ul-suhn] The American sculptor Louise Nevelson, b. Louise Berliawsky, in Kiev, Russia, Sept. 23 (N.S.), 1900, d. Apr. 17, 1988, was internationally known for her sculptural environments. Collecting old parts of furniture and other wooden odds and ends, she combined such objects into a famous series of black-box sculptures. Arranged like shelves along a wall, these assemblages achieve an almost musical effect of repetition and variation. These walls reached the height of their development in the 1950s, and in later years Nevelson turned to brighter materials—aluminum, steel, and plexiglass, as in *Transparent Sculpture VI* (1967–68; Whitney Museum, New York City)—and finishes—white and, later, gold. Both her wall-mounted and freestanding works retained her unique, detailed style. In 1977–78, Nevelson executed the Chapel of the Good Shepherd for Saint Peter's Lutheran Church, New York City.

Nevers, Ernie One of the great football players, Ernest Alonzo Nevers, b. Willow River, Minn., June 11, 1903, d. May 3, 1976, was elected to both the professional and the college Hall of Fame. For his career (1923–25) as an All-American at Stanford University, Nevers was voted the 1st-team fullback on the All-Time

All-American team for modern collegiate football (1919–69). His professional career was with the Duluth Eskimos (1926–27) and Chicago Cardinals (1929–31). On Nov. 28, 1929, he scored 40 points in a single game, a record that still stands.

Nevins, Allan [nev'-inz] Allan Nevins, b. Camp Point, Ill., May 20, 1890, d. Mar. 5, 1971, a leading American historian, taught at Columbia University (1928–58). A prolific writer, Nevins wrote, among other works, *Grover Cleveland* (1932) and *Hamilton Fish* (1936), both Pulitzer Prize winners; *John D. Rockefeller*, 2 vols. (1940); and a series on the U.S. Civil War, *The Ordeal of the Union*, 8 vols. (1947–71), for which he won (1972) a posthumous National Book Award. In 1948, Nevins established Columbia's oral history program. He was a founder (1954) of *American Heritage* magazine.

new age *New age* is a term popularized in the mid-1980s to describe a nebulous, quasi-religious set of beliefs that are an outgrowth of the 1960s COUNTERCULTURE and the 1970s "human potential movement" in the United States. The name alludes to the expectation of adherents, found particularly on the West Coast, that a new "spiritual" age is dawning in which humans will realize higher, more spiritual selves. New age encompasses a wide array of notions—SPIRITUALISM, ASTROLOGY, out-of-body experiences, reincarnation, and other occult disciplines, as well as unorthodox psychotherapeutic techniques and pseudoscientific applications of the "healing powers" of crystals and pyramids.

In music, *new age* refers to a meditative, almost invariably instrumental style with roots in Oriental, jazz, and classical music. Often derivative, new-age compositions can sound like minimalist music or like lush evocations of the natural environment. New-age music is meant to relax the listener.

New Bedford New Bedford is a city in southeastern Massachusetts and one of the seats of Bristol County (the others are Fall River and Taunton). Located where the Acushnet River enters Buzzards Bay, it has a population of 99,922 (1990), which includes a large Portuguese segment. Once an important whaling center and seaport, New Bedford is now a fishing port and an industrial city supporting textile, machine, rubber, and electrical-equipment industries. Landmarks are the Seamen's Bethel (1832), described in *Moby-Dick*, and the New Bedford Whaling Museum. Settled (1640) by Quakers, the town was incorporated as Bedford in 1787 and later renamed New Bedford. During the American Revolution it harbored American privateers; a water and land battle was fought there in 1778. The whaling industry reached its height in 1845, when 10,000 seafarers sailed on New Bedford whalers. A textile industry boom took place there from 1881 to the 1920s.

New Bern Located in eastern North Carolina at the confluence of the Neuse and Trent rivers, the city of New Bern is the seat of Craven County; it has a population of 17,363 (1990). New Bern is an important river port and trading center. Tryon Palace and Garden (1767–70), now restored, was the colonial capitol of North Carolina. Settled in 1710 by Swiss and German colonists, New Bern was the colonial capital from 1770 to 1774. Meeting there in 1774, the First Provincial Congress committed North Carolina to joining the revolutionary movement. During the Civil War, Union forces under Gen. A. E. Burnside occupied (March 1862) the city.

New Britain New Britain, the largest island in the Bismarck Archipelago in the southwestern Pacific, forms part of Papua New Guinea. The crescent-shaped island covers more than 37,810 km^2 (14,600 mi^2). Its population is 263,500 (1989 est.). Rabaul is the major city. Densely forested, New Britain has active volcanoes and mountains that rise to 2,300 m (7,546 ft). Economic activities include copra and cacao cultivation; logging; and coal, copper, gold, and iron mining. First visited by Europeans in 1700, New Britain became part of a German protectorate, New Pomerania, in 1884. In 1914, Australia gained control. Japan seized the island in 1942 for its chief base of operations in the southwestern Pacific. From 1945 to 1975 it was again administered by Australia.

New Brunswick (city in New Jersey) Located in eastern New Jersey at the head of navigation on the Raritan River, New Brunswick is the seat of Middlesex County and has a population of 41,711 (1990). The city is an industrial and shipping center noted for the production of pharmaceuticals—the firm of Johnson and Johnson was founded there in the late 19th century. It is also the home of Rutgers–The State University of New Jersey (1766). Settled in 1681 by the English, New Brunswick was named in 1730 in honor of King George II, who had been duke of Brunswick. During the American Revolution, Washington and his army stopped there in November 1776, when retreating from New York, and again during the summer of 1778.

New Brunswick (province in Canada) This Canadian Maritime Province is located on the eastern seaboard of North America, adjacent to the Gulf of St. Lawrence and the Bay of Fundy. With an area of 73,440 km^2 (28,355 mi^2), New Brunswick ranks eighth among the ten provinces both in size and in population. The province is named for the German duchy of Brunswick-Lüneburg (the electorate of Hanover), ruled by King George III of England when New Brunswick became a colony in 1784.

Land and Resources

The topography of New Brunswick is characterized by up-

NEW BRUNSWICK

Land: Area: 73,440 km² (28,355 mi²); rank: 8th. Capital: Fredericton (1991 pop., 46,466). Largest city: Saint John (1991 pop., 74,969). Municipalities: 114. Elevations: highest— 820 m (2,690 ft), at Mount Carleton; lowest—sea level, along the coasts of Bay of Fundy.

People: Population (1991): 723,900; rank: 8th; density: 10.1 persons per km² (26 per mi²). Distribution (1991): 47.7% urban, 52.3% rural. Average annual change (1986–91): +0.4%.

Government (1992): Lieutenant Governor: Gilbert Finn. Premier: Frank McKenna, Liberal. Parliament: Senate— 10 members; House of Commons—5 Liberals, 5 Progressive Conservatives. Provincial legislature: 58 members. Admitted to Confederation: July 1, 1867, one of the four original provinces.

Economy: (monetary figures in Canadian dollars): Total personal income (1990): $12.3 billion; rank: 8th. Median family income (1990): $378,118. Agriculture: farm cash receipts (1987)—$247.7 million. Fishing: landed value (1989)—$87.7 million. Forestry: lumber production (1988)—748.8 million board feet. Mining: value (1989)—$91 million. Manufacturing: value added (1988)—$2.1 billion.

lands—over the northern, western, and southern three-fifths of the province—and coastal lowlands, both part of the physiographic Appalachian Mountain region. From sea level along the Bay of FUNDY and the Gulf of ST. LAWRENCE, the land rises to more than 400 m (1,300 ft) in most of the uplands. The highest point in the province, Mount Carleton (820 m/2,690 ft), is located in the Miramichi Highlands, part of the New Brunswick Highlands.

Soils and Drainage. Soils range from loose sandy tills in the north to poorly drained clay loam tills in the south. In the New Brunswick Highlands soils are usually rocky loam tills, although in the northwest fertile loam tills are found.

The 673-km-long (418-mi) Saint John River flows the length of western New Brunswick. Other major rivers are the Restigouche, the Miramichi, and the Petitcodiac. Most lakes are in the New Brunswick Highlands, except Grand Lake in the lower Saint John River valley.

Climate. Annual precipitation ranges from 660 to 1,120 mm (26 to 44 in), about 15% to 30% falling as snow. Temperatures average 18° C (65° F) in July and –8° C (17° F) in January. The maritime influence produces cooler summers, warmer winters, and higher precipitation along the Bay of Fundy than in the rest of New Brunswick.

Vegetation and Animal Life. Nearly 90% of New Brunswick's total area is forested, mainly with spruce and fir. Common deciduous species are red and sugar maples, birches, and beeches. White-tailed deer, moose, beavers,

black bears, otters, and muskrat are common. The Miramichi River is considered one of the most important Atlantic salmon–fishing rivers in North America. Offshore sea life includes crab, cod, flounder, haddock, herring, lobster, pollock, and redfish. Coastal areas are visited by migratory waterfowl, seals, and even whales.

Resources. New Brunswick is rich in wood, hydroelectric power, and minerals in its uplands (coal, zinc, copper, lead, and silver).

People

The population is concentrated in the coastal areas and the Saint John River valley, with over 50% of the people classified as rural. More than half of the urban population are in the four largest cities—SAINT JOHN (1991 pop., 74,969), MONCTON (57,010), FREDERICTON (46,466; the capital), and BATHURST (14,409). New Brunswick has been losing population to central Canada, particularly Ontario.

Because about one-third of the population are of French-Canadian descent, in French-speaking districts French is the language of instruction in public schools. The University of New Brunswick and Saint Thomas University are located in Fredericton, a 2-year college of the University of New Brunswick is in Saint John, and Mount Allison University is situated in Sackville. The Université de Moncton and its affiliates are the provincial French-language institutions.

The provincial museum and the Regional Library are in Saint John. The Theatre New Brunswick, Fiddlehead Poetry Society, Beaverbrook Art Gallery, and the Provincial Archives are in Fredericton.

Among the province's historic buildings are the birthplace of Richard Bedford Bennett, the only New Brunswicker to become prime minister of Canada, and the summer home of U.S. president Franklin D. Roosevelt on CAMPOBELLO ISLAND. Popular attractions include the Roosevelt Campobello International Park and Fundy National Park.

Radio and television stations in New Brunswick broadcast in both English and French. The province has several daily newspapers—published in both languages—as well as a score of weekly newspapers.

Economic Activity

Historically, the economy of New Brunswick has been based on the timber industry. Toward the end of the 19th century, as shipbuilding declined and the timber markets generally stagnated, the province suffered economically. By the 1930s the pulp and paper industries had superseded timber in economic importance; pulp and paper production encouraged the development of hydroelectricity.

Long-range government-sponsored economic-development programs, begun in the 1960s, emphasized exploitation of the large copper, lead, zinc, and silver deposits in northeastern New Brunswick. The forestry industries have also been expanded; agriculture and fisheries have been modernized. Manufacturing, such as food processing, has increased. Nuclear power was more important in the 1980s than hydroelectricity or steam plants. Tourism is also of increasing economic importance in the province.

Transportation links are through the major ports of Saint John, Dalhousie, Newcastle, and Chatham, by road via the TRANS-CANADA HIGHWAY (612 km/380 mi), and by the Canadian National and Canadian Pacific railways (2,680 km/1,665 mi). Major airports are located at Moncton, Saint John, and Fredericton. New Brunswick's leading port is at Saint John.

Government

The nominal head of government is the lieutenant governor. The actual chief executive is the premier, who presides over an executive council (cabinet) made up of members of the majority party in the Legislative Assembly. The 58 members of this house of assembly are elected for a maximum term of 5 years. The judiciary consists primarily of a supreme court divided between Appeals and Queen's Bench courts.

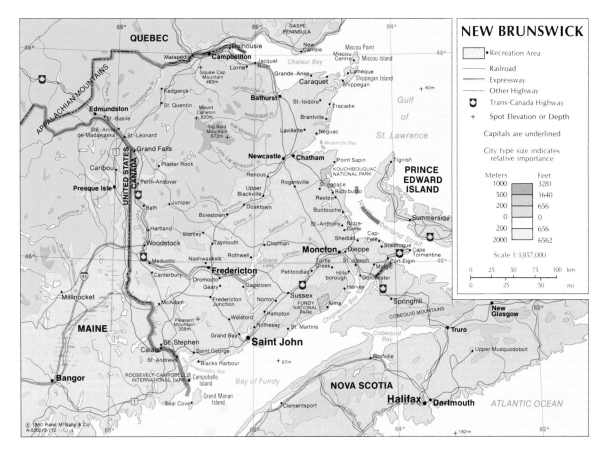

Rolling agricultural land of the Saint John River valley, the most fertile region of New Brunswick, is dotted with small farms that yield a variety of dairy products, livestock, and fruit. Most field crops are raised for livestock feed.

History

New Brunswick was occupied by archaic hunters and gatherers over 5,000 years ago. Portions of the coast were charted by Samuel de Champlain as early as 1604, and French settlers spread into the province during the late 17th and early 18th centuries (see ACADIA).

Following the Treaty of Paris in 1763 the area was annexed to the British province of Nova Scotia, and soon the Saint John region was settled by New Englanders. After the American Revolution their ranks were substantially augmented with more than 12,000 LOYALISTS.

In 1784, New Brunswick was established as a separate colony, and Fredericton was chosen as the capital. The port of Saint John prospered from timber and shipbuilding during the Napoleonic Wars (1803–15), and by 1824 the population of the colony reached 75,000. By the latter half of the 1800s, however, New Brunswick was thrust into a decline.

Despite considerable opposition within the colony, New Brunswick was one of the four original provinces to enter the national Confederation on July 1, 1867. The province soon became a captive market for Montreal and Toronto manufacturers. Saint John stagnated, and the province lagged behind much of Canada in economic growth.

Although the 20th century has been a period of revitalization of Saint John's port facilities, the redevelopment of the forest industry, and considerable modernization in all sectors, New Brunswick is still, in the words of its prominent historian W. S. MacNutt, the "Quiet Province" and remains close to nature and tradition.

Real advances, however, are certainly in evidence. Strong environmental concern, self-sufficiency in electric power, and a peaceful bicultural and bilingual duality all hold promise for a secure future.

New Caledonia The French Overseas Territory of New Caledonia lies 1,200 km (750 mi) east of Australia

and 1,300 km (870 mi) north of New Zealand. The territory, with a total land area of 19,103 km² (7,376 mi²), comprises the island of New Caledonia (16,750 km²/ 6,467 mi²), the Isle of Pines, Loyalty Islands, Huon Islands, Bélep Archipelago, Chesterfield Islands, and Walpole Island; only the first three are inhabited. The population is 164,173 (1989). About 45% of the people are indigenous Melanesians (Kanaks); the remainder are Europeans (34%), other Pacific islanders, and Asians. The capital and largest city is Nouméa (1989 pop., 65,110), where most Europeans live.

A mountain chain extending the length of New Caledonia island rises to 1,650 m (5,413 ft) at Mount Panié. The eastern slopes receive about 2,000 mm (80 in) of rainfall annually, approximately twice that of the western side. Average monthly temperatures range from 17° to 32° C (63° to 90° F). An offshore reef, the world's second largest, almost completely encircles the mostly volcanic island, which has about 30% of the world's known nickel reserves.

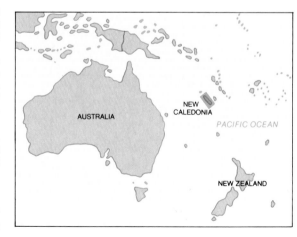

The first European to visit New Caledonia was James Cook, in 1774. France annexed New Caledonia in 1853 and sent prisoners there from 1864 to 1897. There were several Kanak uprisings protesting European land annexation prior to World War II, when New Caledonia was a major Allied base. The islands became a French overseas territory (and their people French citizens) in 1946. A boycott of the 1984 legislative elections by proindependence Kanaks and outbreaks of violence over the independence issue led to new elections in 1985. In 1988, French voters approved an increase in economic aid, the division of the territory into three autonomous provinces, and the holding of a local referendum on independence in 1998.

New Criticism The term *New Criticism* was not widely used until it became associated with the program announced in John Crowe Ransom's *The New Criticism* (1941). Ransom's critical methodology, which was derived from T. S. Eliot's essays of the 1920s and I. A. Richards's search for a more clinical language to describe the effects of poetry on the emotions, was taken up by Cleanth Brooks, Allen Tate, Robert Penn Warren, and R. P. Blackmur. The New Critics were united in an effort to free literary criticism from what they regarded as fallacious interpretations, including assessments of value and meaning based on impressionistic, emotional, and historical criteria. They insisted on the autonomy and uniqueness of the text, whose language could be clinically described only by reference to itself—not to the author's biography or to abstract concepts such as genre. In its effort to promote close analysis of literature and its concentration on the figurative uses of language, the New Criticism did much to encourage the study of literature as a specialized discipline.

New Deal The term *New Deal* refers to U.S. president Franklin D. Roosevelt's program (1933–39) of relief, recovery, and reform that aimed at solving the economic problems created by the Depression of the 1930s. The New Deal included federal action of unprecedented scope to stimulate industrial recovery, assist victims of the Depression, guarantee minimum living standards, and prevent future economic crises. At first the New Deal was concerned mainly with relief; the second New Deal, beginning in 1935, emphasized reform.

In each of its goals the New Deal was partially successful. The production controls and price supports managed by the National Recovery Administration and the Agricultural Adjustment Administration (both set up in 1933) helped put business proprietors and farmers back on their feet, but the nation's economy did not regain its 1929 level until the United States entered World War II. The Public Works Administration (formed in 1933) and the Works Progress Administration (formed in 1935) helped tide many of the jobless over hard times, but nearly 9.5 million remained unemployed in 1939. The Social Security Act (1935; see Social Security) created a system of old-age pensions and unemployment insurance, and the Fair Labor Standards Act (1938) established a federal Minimum Wage and maximum-hours policy; both laws, however, excluded millions of working people. By regulating banks and the stock market the New Deal eliminated the dubious financial practices that had helped precipitate the Great Depression, but Roosevelt's chief fiscal tool—deficit spending—proved not entirely effective in averting downturns.

After 1936 the New Deal was thrown increasingly on the defensive. The U.S. Supreme Court ruled that much of the New Deal legislation was unconstitutional, and the president's proposal (1937) to enlarge the court to make it more liberal and therefore more amenable to the legislation caused many members of Congress to desert the president. In addition a severe recession (1937–38) led many people to turn against New Deal policies. When World War II erupted in September 1939, Roosevelt grew increasingly reluctant to support reforms that, by antagonizing conservatives in Congress or alienating any bloc of voters, might jeopardize support for his foreign policy. No major New Deal legislation was enacted after 1938. The New Deal, however, had laid the foundation for a greater federal commitment to manage the economy and provide a system of programs to aid the poor.

New Delhi [del'-ee] New Delhi, the capital of the Republic of India, is located on the western bank of the Yamuna River in north central India. With an area of 41 km² (16 mi²) and a population of 271,990 (1981), the municipality is part of greater Delhi, which covers an area of 326 km² (126 mi²) and has a population of 8,380,000 (1991 prelim.). The Union Territory of Delhi encompasses greater Delhi and 258 surrounding villages.

Contemporary City. New Delhi is essentially an administrative sector with business and retail activities, and Old Delhi is largely a commercial and industrial center. New Delhi was designed (1912–14) by Sir Edwin Landseer Lutyens on a geometrical plan. The Rashtrapati Bhavan, or Presidential Palace (formerly the viceroy's residence and one of the largest palaces in the world), and India Gate are joined by the Raj Path (Kingsway), a wide highway lined with government buildings. The imposing Parliament House contains both houses of the Indian legislature.

Old Delhi, to New Delhi's north, is dominated by exquisite Indo-Islamic and Mogul architecture. Historic monuments include the 5th-century Iron Pillar and the early-13th-century Qutb Minar, a fine example of Indo-Islamic architecture. Examples of Mogul architecture include Humayun's Tomb (1565); the Red Fort (1638–48), containing the emperor's court and palaces; and the Jama Masjid (1650–56), the largest mosque in India (see Mogul art and architecture).

Delhi's diversified economy is dominated by the civil service. The leading industries in the city produce textiles, machinery, books and periodicals, transportation equipment, metal products, steel castings, and chemicals. The University of Delhi (1922), Jawaharlal Nehru University (1969), the National Museum of India, and

The Jantar Mantar Observatory, located in the center of New Delhi, was built during the 18th century. These brick and sandstone instruments were used in an attempt to combine European and classical Indian astronomy.

the Gandhi National Museum and Library are in the city.

History. Strategically located between the Punjab and Ganges plains, the Delhi site lies on the main invasion path from the west. At least nine sites in the vicinity, known as the Delhi Triangle, have been identified as former locations of capitals: mythological Indraprastha (pre-6th century BC) near the Purana Qula site; Dilli (1st century BC); Dhillika (736) at Lal Kot; Kilookai (1287–90) by the side of the Yamuna; Tughlukabad (1320–51); Firozabad (1354–88); Din Panah, later Purana Qula (1530–56); and magnificent Shah Jahanabad (1638–1857), today's Old Delhi. New Delhi is the most recent site. Delhi was pillaged by a succession of invaders: Timur in 1398; Nadir Shah in 1739; Abdali in 1756–57; Marathas in 1757, 1760, and 1772; and Rohilas in 1788. The British erected a cantonment nearby in 1803. In 1857, during the Indian Mutiny, Delhi was the scene of a major battle won by the British over native troops.

When Delhi replaced Calcutta as capital of British India in 1912, the city resumed its earlier significance after two centuries of decline. The Indian independence movement brought on violent demonstrations between 1919 and 1946. Mahatma Gandhi was killed there in 1948; the Rajghat memorial commemorates the site of his cremation.

New Democratic party   The New Democratic party (NDP) is a moderate left-wing Canadian political party that was founded in 1961 to replace the Cooperative Commonwealth Federation (CCF). Formed in Ottawa, the NDP elected Thomas C. DOUGLAS head of the party. In 1962 the NDP, which draws the bulk of its support from

the western provinces, won 19 seats in the federal House of Commons. Under the leadership (1975–89) of Ed Broadbent, the NDP won 32 seats in 1980, 30 in 1984, and 43 in 1988. In 1989 the NDP elected as leader Audrey McLaughlin, the first woman to head a Canadian national party.

New Economic Policy   A program allowing limited capitalism, the New Economic Policy (NEP) was introduced in the USSR by V.I. LENIN in 1921 to alleviate the economic failings and political discontent caused by the oppressive centralization of the civil war policies known as War Communism. In agriculture, the NEP replaced requisitions by force with taxes in kind and allowed peasants to sell their produce in a free market. Banks and large-scale industry remained state controlled, but small private enterprises were permitted. Economic productivity rose substantially, but in 1928 Joseph STALIN abandoned the NEP for forced collectivization of agriculture and rapid industrialization.

New England   New England, which consists of Maine, New Hampshire, Vermont, Massachusetts, Connecticut, and Rhode Island, is the northeasternmost region of the United States. The area is bounded by Long Island Sound on the south, the Atlantic Ocean on the east, the St. Lawrence River and Canada on the north, and New York State on the west. The Connecticut River is the area's longest river, and the Green and White mountain ranges form the major uplands. Boston is the regional metropolis.

New England Conservatory of Music   Founded in 1867 by Eben Tourjée, the New England Conservatory of Music in Boston is the oldest independent conservatory of music in the United States. The school, with both undergraduate and graduate divisions, is in effect an unofficial educational affiliate of the Boston Symphony Orchestra; of the more than 150 full- and part-time faculty members, several are members of the orchestra, and more than a third of the BSO musicians are former students of the conservatory. The principal concert facility is Jordan Hall (seating 1,019). Student ensembles include two orchestras, a ragtime ensemble (formed by Gunther Schuller), an electronic music group, and the conservatory chorus.

New France   That part of North America claimed by France from the 17th century until 1763 was called New France. It comprised, at its greatest extent, the Canadian Maritimes, the St. Lawrence–Great Lakes area, and the Mississippi and Ohio river valleys.

New Granada [gruh-nah'-duh]   New Granada, located in northwestern South America, was a Spanish colonial administrative area. It consisted of the present states of Colombia, Ecuador, Panama, and Venezuela, and its capital was BOGOTÁ. In 1538 the Spanish conqueror Gonzalo JIMÉNEZ DE QUESADA, who was from Granada, Spain, called the region surrounding present-day Bogotá the new kingdom of Granada. The original inhabitants of the area were CHIBCHA. The region became part of the viceroyalty of Peru as the captaincy general of New Granada in 1564.

The viceroyalty of New Granada was constituted in 1718, then abolished in 1724, but reestablished in 1740; it lasted until 1819. By the end of the 18th century the region was one of the cultural centers of the Spanish empire. It was also one of the first regions to rise against Spain in the early 19th century. Independence was declared in 1819, and Simón BOLÍVAR established the whole territory as Gran Colombia.

Venezuela and Ecuador seceded in 1830. The remaining territory became the Republic of New Granada in 1831. Its name changed several times, and in 1886 the name Republic of Colombia was adopted. Panama seceded in 1903.

New Guinea [gin'-ee]   New Guinea is an island in the southwestern Pacific Ocean just north of Australia. It is part of the eastern Malay Archipelago. The second largest island in the world (after Greenland), it is 2,414 km (1,500 mi) long east to west, and its maximum width is 644 km (400 mi) north to south. It has an area of about 790,000 km² (305,000 mi²). Politically, the island is divided in half: IRIAN JAYA—a province of Indonesia—is in the west and PAPUA NEW GUINEA—an independent country that includes several smaller islands—is in the east. The total population (1984 est.) is 4,150,000.

A complex system of rugged mountain ranges trends northwest-southeast, and much of the island remains unexplored. Jaya Peak, formerly called Mount Carstensz, in Irian Jaya is the highest peak, rising to 5,029 m (16,500 ft). The Sepik, Ramu, Mamberamo, Purari, Fly, and Digul are the principal rivers.

Rainfall—more than 2,540 mm (100 in) annually—is seasonal. Along the coast temperatures average 27° C (80° F) all year. Most of the terrain below the timberline is covered by tropical rain forest, where most of the indigenous people— Melanesians, Negritos, and Papuans— live in small villages.

Human beings probably entered New Guinea 50,000 years ago over a land bridge that linked the island with Asia. New Guinea was sighted by Portuguese navigators in 1512. The Dutch took possession of the western sector in 1828. The British established a protectorate in the southeast, and the Germans took control of the northeast in 1884. Australia assumed the administration of the British portion in 1905 and occupied the former German territory in 1914. Between 1942 and 1945, Japanese troops controlled the island. In 1946, Australia regained control of the eastern territory and administered it as a UN trusteeship until the independent nation of Papua New Guinea was formed in 1975. Irian Jaya (West New Guinea), once part of the Dutch East Indies, came under the control of Indonesia in 1962.

New Hampshire   New Hampshire lies between Maine on the east and Vermont on the west in northern New England. Its southern boundary, except for the southeast corner that provides New Hampshire's 29 km (18 mi) of Atlantic coastline, borders Massachusetts. New Hampshire's northern tip touches the Canadian province of Quebec. About 85% of New Hampshire is covered with woods. The state derives its name from the county of Hampshire, England, where Capt. John Mason, the founder and first proprietor of the colony, was governor of the English city of Portsmouth, for which New Hampshire's only port city is named.

Land and Resources

Topographically, the state's most conspicuous feature is the WHITE MOUNTAINS, whose 86 peaks in the north central part of the state are the highest mountain range in the northeastern United States. Eleven peaks in Coos County, five more than 1.6 km (1 mi) above sea level, form the Presidential Range, which culminates in Mount Washington at 1,917 m (6,288 ft; see WASHINGTON, MOUNT).

Immediately north of the White Mountain National Forest lies the high land of New Hampshire's North Country. Along the Vermont border, the Connecticut River valley provides New Hampshire's best farming country. In

NEW HAMPSHIRE

Land: Area: 24,219 km^2 (9,351 mi^2); rank: 46th.
Capital: Concord (1990 pop., 36,006). Largest city:
Manchester (1990 pop., 99,567). Counties: 10.
Elevations: highest—1,917 m (6,288 ft), at Mount
Washington; lowest—sea level, at the Atlantic coast.

People: Population (1990): 1,113,915; rank: 41st;
density: 47.8 persons per km^2 (123.7 per mi^2). Distribution (1990): 51% urban, 49% rural. Average annual
change (1980–90): +2.1%.

Government (1993): Governor: Steve Merrill, Republican. U.S. Congress: Senate—2 Republicans; House—1
Democrat, 1 Republican. Electoral college votes: 4. State
legislature: 24 senators, 400 representatives.

Economy: State personal income (1989): $22.4 billion;
rank: 36th. Median family income (1989): $41,628;
rank: 7th. Agriculture: income (1989)—$142 million.
Fishing: value (1989)—$10 million. Lumber production
(1991): 203 million board feet. Mining (nonfuel): value
(1988, partial data only)—$53 million. Manufacturing:
value added (1987)—$8.2 billion. Services: value
(1987)—$4.5 billion.

Miscellany: Statehood: June 21, 1788; the 9th state.
Nickname: Granite State; tree: white birch; motto: Live
Free or Die; song: "Old New Hampshire."

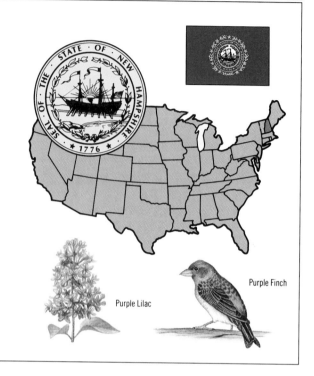

Purple Finch

Purple Lilac

the southeastern corner of the state, New Hampshire's
Eastern Slope descends gradually to the sea. The brief
New Hampshire coastline consists of sandy beaches in
addition to Portsmouth Harbor at the mouth of the Piscataqua River.

Soils. The most fertile soils in New Hampshire are
found in the lowlands of the Connecticut and Merrimack
river valleys. The Eastern Slope is covered with a moderately fertile soil, and the mountain areas are covered largely
with a sandy loam. The soil in the rest of the state consists primarily of relatively unproductive hardpan and till.

Rivers and Lakes. The CONNECTICUT RIVER rises from the
three Connecticut Lakes in Coos County and drains the
entire state west of the north-south divide. East of the divide, two northern systems—the Androscoggin and the
Saco—flow into Maine. Umbagog Lake straddles the
Maine border, furnishing the headwaters of the Androscoggin River. The Piscataqua drains the Eastern
Slope. Just to the south of the White Mountain area the
Lakes district forms a wide belt across the middle section
of the state. The largest of these lakes is Lake WINNIPE-
SAUKEE, source of the Merrimack River, which drains the
south central portion of the state into the Atlantic.

Climate. Temperatures generally run several degrees
cooler in the northern highlands than in the southern half
of the state. Mean monthly temperatures for January
range from −12° C (10° F) in the extreme north to −6° C

(21° F) in the south. Mean monthly temperatures for July
range from 16° C (61° F) in the north to about 21° C (70°
F) in the south. Average yearly precipitation, aside from
the 1,930 mm (76 in) atop Mount Washington, ranges
from Hanover's 914 mm (36 in) to Durham's 1,067 mm
(42 in). Much falls as snow.

Vegetation and Animal Life. New Hampshire is covered
generally with mixed hardwoods and evergreens. The
most common deciduous trees are maples and birches.
White pine predominates south of the White Mountains,
and spruce and fir to the north. Common wild animals include deer, black bear, bobcat, beaver, muskrat, mink,
red fox, skunk, otter, raccoon, porcupine, woodchuck, red
and gray squirrel, and chipmunk. The lakes and ponds,
more than 200 of which are stocked annually with trout
and salmon from state-operated hatcheries, contain
perch, pike, pickerel, trout, horned pout, and bass. More
than 300 species of birds have been recorded.

Resources. New Hampshire's chief resource today is
its scenery and the recreational potential of its hills,
mountains, forests, lakes, and ocean. Its timber resources
provide building materials, pulpwood, and firewood.
There is considerable water-power potential in the state.
New Hampshire's limited mineral resources include granite, feldspar, and mica. The resources of the seacoast
area include saltwater finned fish and shellfish, especially lobsters.

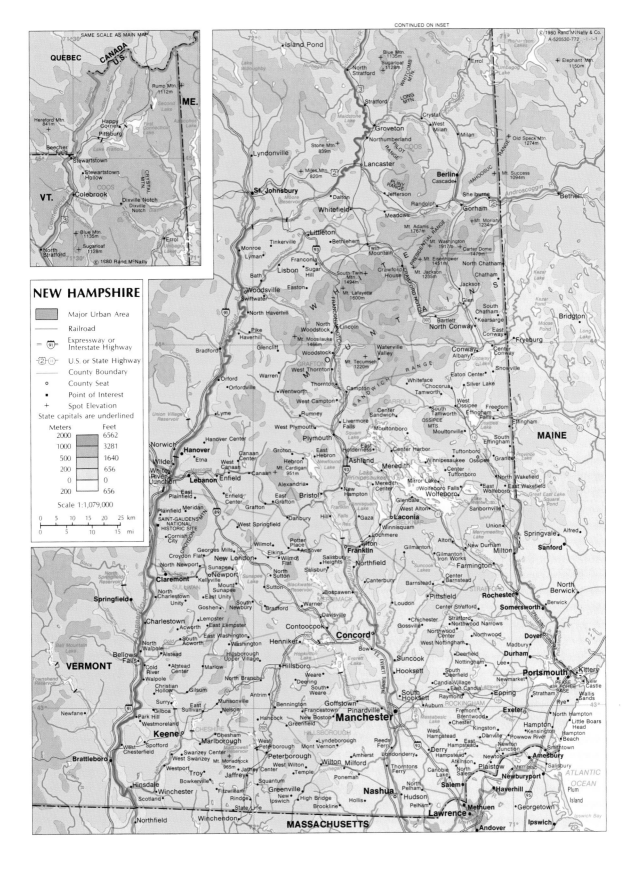

© 1980 Rand McNally & Co.
A-520530-772 - 1-1-1

QUEBEC
CANADA
U.S.
ME.

Rump Mtn.
1112m

Hereford Mtn.
841m

Happy
Corner
Pittsburg

Beecher
Falls

Stewartstown

Stewartstown
Hollow

COOS

VT.   Colebrook

Dixville Notch
Dixville
Notch

CRYSTAL
MTN.

Blue Mtn.
1135m

North
Stratford

Sugarloaf
1128m

Errol
Umbagog
Lake

SAME SCALE AS MAIN MAP

© 1980 Rand McNally

NEW HAMPSHIRE

- ▢ Major Urban Area
- ── Railroad
- ═⟨91⟩═ Expressway or Interstate Highway
- ⟨2⟩⟨1⟩ U.S. or State Highway
- ──── County Boundary
- ○ County Seat
- ■ Point of Interest
- + Spot Elevation

State capitals are underlined

Meters	Feet
2000	6562
1000	3281
500	1640
200	656
0	0
200	656

Scale 1:1,079,000

0 5 10 15 20 25 km
0   5   10   15 mi

Island Pond

North
Stratford

Blue Mtn.
Sugarloaf
1128m

Errol

Elephant Mtn.
1150m

Richardson
Lakes

Lake
Willoughby

Stratford

LONG
MTN.

WHITCOMB
MTN.

Crystal

West
Milan   Milan

Old Speck Mtn.
1274m

Bethel

Lyndonville

Groveton
Northumberland

Stone Mtn.
839m

Lancaster

COOS

PILOT
RANGE

Berlin
Cascade

Shelburne

Mt. Success
1094m

MAHOOSUC
RANGE

Androscoggin

St. Johnsbury

Whitefield

Dalton

Meadows

Miles Mtn.
820m

PLINY
RANGE

Jefferson

Randolph

Gorham

Mt. Moriah
1234m

Mt. Adams
1767m

Mt. Washington
1917m

Carter Dome
1479m

North Chatham

Chatham

Kezar
Lake

Littleton

Bethlehem

Twin
Mountain

Mt. Eisenhower
1451m

Mt. Jackson
1235m

Jackson

Glen

South
Chatham

Kearsarge

Bridgton

Monroe   Tinkerville

Franconia

Lyman

Bath   Lisbon

Sugar
Hill

South Twin
Mtn.
1494m

Crawford
House

PRESIDENTIAL RANGE

CRAWFORD NOTCH

Bartlett

East
Conway

Fryeburg

Woodsville
Swiftwater
Easton

Mt. Lafayette
1600m

North Conway

Center
Conway

Conway

Long
Lake

Pike
Haverhill

North Haverhill

Glencliff

North
Woodstock
Lincoln

Mt. Moosilauke
1466m

Woodstock

Waterville
Valley

Albany

Snowville

Bradford

Orford

Warren

West Thornton

Mt. Tecumseh
1220m

Whiteface
Chocorua

SANDWICH   RANGE

Eaton Center

Silver Lake

Orfordville

Thornton

Campton

Center
Sandwich

Tamworth

East
Ossipee

Freedom

West Campton

Rumney

Livermore
Falls

Moultonboro

OSSIPEE
MTS.

South
Tamworth

Effingham
Falls

Ossipee
Lake

South
Effingham

MAINE

Lyme

West Plymouth

Plymouth

East
Holderness

East
Hebron

Ashland

Squam
Lake

Center Harbor

Moultonville

Center
Ossipee

Tuftonboro

Granite

North Wakefield

East
Wakefield

Hanover Center

Hanover

Etna

Groton

Hebron

Mt. Cardigan
951m

Newfound
Lake

Meredith

Mirror Lake

Winnipesaukee

Tuftonboro

Great East
Lake

Wildex

White
River
Junction

Lebanon

Enfield

West
Canaan

Canaan
Center

Canaan

Alexandria

East
Grafton

Bristol

New
Hampton

Lake
Winnipesaukee

Meredith
Neck

Wolfeboro Falls

Wolfeboro

East
Wolfeboro

Sanbornville

East
Plainfield

Enfield
Center

Grafton

Danbury

Hill

Franklin
Falls
Res.

Gaza

Glendale

West Alton

Laconia

Union

Springvale

Alfred

Plainfield
Meriden
Kellyville

SAINT-GAUDENS
NATIONAL
HISTORIC SITE

Cornish
City

West Springfield

Potter
Place

Andover

Winnisquam

Lochmere

BELKNAP

Alton

Merrymeeting
Lake

New Durham

Milton

Sanford

Cornish
City

Georges Mills

Wilmot

Salisbury
Heights

Tilton

Franklin

Gilmanton

Gilmanton
Iron Works

Farmington

Springfield

North Newport
Croydon Flat

New London

Elkins

Wilmot
Flat

North
Sutton

Salisbury

Northfield

Canterbury

STRAFFORD

North
Berwick

Claremont

SULLIVAN

Sunapee

oNewport
Kellyville

Mount
Sunapee

East Unity

Goshen

South
Newbury

Sutton

Boscawen

Barnstead

Center
Barnstead

Pittsfield

Rochester

Somersworth

Berwick

North
Charlestown
Unity

Lempster
East Lempster

East Washington

Bradford

Warner

MERRIMACK

Loudon

Chichester

Center Strafford

Stratford

Northwood Narrows

Dover

Durham

Charlestown

Acworth

Washington

Davisville

Gossville

Northwood
Center

Northwood

Madbury

Bellows
Falls

North
Walpole

South
Acworth

Alstead

Hillsborough
Upper Village

Henniker

Concord

Bow

Suncook

West Nottingham

Deerfield

Lee

Newmarket

Portsmouth

Kittery

PEASE
AIR FORCE
BASE

New
Castle

Cold
River

Walpole

Christian
Hollow

Alstead
Center

Marlow

Gilsum

North Branch

Hillsboro

Weare

Deering

South
Weare

Hooksett

South
Hooksett

Raymond

South
Deerfield

Candia Village

East Candia

Nottingham

Epping

Stratham

Rye

Exeter

VERMONT

Munsonville

Nelson

Antrim

Bennington

Francestown

New Boston

Goffstown

Pinardville

Auburn

ROCKINGHAM

Fremont
Brentwood

Chester

Candia

North
Hampton

Little Boars
Head

Newfane

Silboa

East
Sullivan

Hancock
Greenfield

Manchester

West
Hampstead

Danville

Kingston

Hampton

Hampton
Beach

Park Hill
Westmoreland

Spofford

Chesham

West
Peterborough

Mont Vernon

Reeds
Ferry

Londonderry

Derry

East
Hampstead

Atkinson

Powwow River

Seabrook

West
Chesterfield

Keene

Marlborough

Mt. Monadnock
965m

Swanzey Center
West Swanzey

Peterborough

West Wilton

Amherst

Milford

Thorntons
Ferry

Canobie
Lake

North
Salem

Plaistow

Newton

Smithtown

Amesbury

Salisbury

Brattleboro

Westport
Troy

Bowkerville

Jaffrey Center

Temple
Wilton

Ponemah

Nashua

Hudson

North
Pelham

Salem

Newburyport

Plum
Island

Hinsdale

Winchester

Fitzwilliam

Rindge

Squantum

Greenville

New
Ipswich

High Bridge

Hollis

Brookline

Pelham

Haverhill

Scotland

Northfield

Winchendon

State
Line

Lawrence

Methuen

Georgetown

MASSACHUSETTS

Andover

Ipswich

ATLANTIC
OCEAN

Ipswich Bay

Mount Washington, the highest peak in New England (1,917 m/6,288 ft), is one of eight peaks in the Presidential Range of New Hampshire's White Mountains. Part of the Appalachian system, the White Mountains are the highest range in the northeastern United States.

People

The population density of New Hampshire is considerably greater than in the nation as a whole, with the majority of the inhabitants concentrated in the southern third of the state. The population increased by nearly 25% in the decade between 1970 and 1980 and 21% between 1980 and 1990. The Merrimack Valley is New Hampshire's most heavily populated geographical area and contains three of the state's principal cities: CONCORD, the state capital; MANCHESTER, the state's largest city; and NASHUA, which borders the Massachusetts line and, along with several nearby border towns, is absorbing much of the heavy population movement into southern New Hampshire.

The majority of the population is Protestant. In the 19th century a large migration of French-Canadian workers from Quebec occurred; it still continues to a lesser degree. Today a number of New Hampshire citizens speak French as a mother tongue, and nearly a third of the population is Roman Catholic, forming the largest single religious denomination. Beginning in the mid-19th century, waves of Irish, Greek, Italian, Finnish, Polish, and German immigration hit the state. The state's black population is small.

Education. DARTMOUTH COLLEGE, the ninth college founded in the American colonies, was established in 1769 and was moved to HANOVER in 1770 by the Reverend Eleazar WHEELOCK. The University of New Hampshire, which began as a land-grant college in 1866, moved to Durham in 1893. Phillips Exeter Academy (1781) is one of about 20 private preparatory schools in the state.

The Juvenile Library founded in Dublin in 1822 was the first free library in the United States, and in 1833 the first free public library in the United States supported by public funds was established at Peterborough. Since 1908, Peterborough has also been famous as the home of the MacDowell Colony, founded by the widow of Edward MACDOWELL, a composer, as a retreat for writers, composers, and artists.

Cultural Institutions. The Currier Gallery of Art and the Manchester Historic Association are located in Manchester. Dartmouth College is the site of the Hopkins Center for fine arts and theater, and Nashua also possesses an arts and sciences center.

Historic Sites and Recreation Areas. The home of the sculptor Augustus SAINT-GAUDENS at Cornish has been made a National Historic Site. There are many restored colonial homes, and Fort Constitution at New Castle has been preserved. Many state parks and forest preserves supplement the White Mountain National Forest. There are a number of major commercial ski areas throughout the state.

Communications. New Hampshire's best-known newspaper is the daily *Manchester Union Leader*. There are commercial radio and television broadcasting facilities, as well as public television and cable television systems.

Economic Activity

During the 1960s, the shoe, woodworking, textile, and apparel industries declined in productivity and employment while such industries as electronics, communications, and utilities and other services increased.

Manufacturing. The leading industries in the state are nonelectrical machinery, electrical and electronic products, shoes, pulp and paper, and plastics.

Energy. New Hampshire's electricity is supplied by coal-fired and oil-fired steam-generating plants and by hydroelectric facilities. Unit I of the nuclear generating plant at Seabrook was completed in 1986, but operations did not begin until 1990.

Tourism. Tourism is now the second most important sector in New Hampshire's economy. Among the state's major tourist attractions are the White Mountains, Lake Winnipesaukee, and Strawbery Banke, a restored village in Portsmouth. Skiing and water sports draw many visitors to the state.

Agriculture. Although agriculture is of limited importance to New Hampshire's economy, dairy and poultry products are the state's agricultural mainstays. Cattle, sheep, and horses are also raised. Apples and hay are the major crops, but corn, peaches, and maple syrup are also important.

Mining, Forestry, and Fishing. Mining is a minor economic activity in New Hampshire. Major minerals found in the state are granite, sand and gravel, and quartz.

Forests cover about 80% of the state. Lumber and wood products and the pulp and paper industry are the most important industries based on native resources. Trees of commercial importance are the balsam fir, hemlock, white pine, spruce, ash, basswood, beech, birch, elm, maple, and oak. On the coast there are marketable catches of shellfish, especially lobsters, and deep-sea fish. Saltwater fishing centers are in Hampton, Portsmouth, and Rye.

Transportation. New Hampshire has rail freight-carrier service, and a tourist attraction is the cog railway up Mount Washington. The state's highway system includes Interstate 93, the main north-south highway, part of which is the Everett Turnpike; the New Hampshire Turnpike, part of Interstate 95; and the Spaulding Turnpike. There is commercial air service to five cities.

Government and Politics

The present constitution, adopted in 1784 and amended many times since then, provides for an elective executive council, which must concur with the governor in all nominations and appointments.

Because representation in the state House of Representatives is based on towns, New Hampshire's General Court is the largest legislative body of any state; the 400 representatives and 24 senators serve two-year terms.

New Hampshire is unique in its lack of both a sales tax and a state income tax. The state relies for revenue on such state-sponsored enterprises as liquor sales, horse and dog racing, and the first state lottery in modern times (1964), and on taxes on beer and cigarettes, business profits, and taxes paid primarily by tourists and visitors.

Except in the state's 13 cities, local government is carried on at the town meeting. Between town meetings, the towns are governed by elected boards of selectmen.

The state's judicial system includes a supreme court, the highest court, and the main trial court known as the superior court. All judges are appointed.

From statehood (1788) until 1816, the Federalist party was in control of New Hampshire politics; then the Democrats dominated until the 1850s. From the Civil War onward the state's majority shifted to the Republican party. New Hampshire's presidential primary is the earliest in each presidential election year.

History

Recent archaeological discoveries suggest the presence of human life in the area about 10,000 years ago. At the time of the first English settlements in 1623, there probably were about 4,000 Indians within the present area of the state, more than half in the various tribes of the PENNACOOK Confederacy in the Connecticut and Merrimack valleys and the seacoast area. The rest, in the eastern White Mountains and the Saco Valley, were on the western edge of the Sokoki Confederacy and merged with the ABNAKIS of Maine. Friendly relations with the Pennacooks ceased at the time of KING PHILIP'S WAR (1675–76), and in 1676 most of the Pennacooks moved to Canada.

Colonial Period. English fishing and trading settlements began (1623) at Odiorne's Point—near the mouth of the Piscataqua—and at Dover Point, 13 km (8 mi) up the river. In 1629 the original proprietors of the whole area between the Merrimack and Kennebec rivers, Sir Ferdinando Gorges and Capt. John MASON, divided the area between them, Mason taking the area south of the Piscataqua, which he called New Hampshire. From 1641 to 1679, and again from 1690 to 1692, the New Hampshire settlements came under the jurisdiction of Massachusetts.

The decisive change in the importance and prospective fortunes of the province came in 1741 with the settlement of the long-disputed boundary with Massachusetts in New Hampshire's favor. A dispute with New York over the area west of the Connecticut River, the so-called New Hampshire Grants (present-day Vermont), was temporarily resolved in 1764.

In the first overtly hostile act of the American Revolution, an armed mob stormed the fort in Portsmouth Harbor in December 1774. In 1776, New Hampshire adopted its own constitution and was, therefore, the first colony to become wholly independent of Great Britain. In 1788, New Hampshire became the ninth state to ratify the U.S. Constitution.

Economic Development. During the early 17th century the economic life of New Hampshire was based on fishing and the exploitation of the rich native timber resources. Shipbuilding soon emerged as the leading industry and flourished throughout the 18th and 19th centuries. During the 18th century, as settlers pushed into the interior, agriculture on family farms began to rival Portsmouth-based commerce and shipbuilding as the chief economic activity of the province. The relocation of the state capital from Portsmouth to Concord in 1808 signified not only the end of the dominance of New Hampshire politics by the commercial interests of Portsmouth and Exeter but also that the center of population had moved inland.

The primacy of farming was short-lived, however, for as early as 1810 water-powered textile manufacturing arrived in New Hampshire. The textile industry reached its peak between 1910 and 1920 and then began a long decline, primarily because of competition from the South. Large-scale shoe manufacturing, which appeared after the Civil War, has also declined but not to the same extent. Since World War II, industries attracted by an underutilized labor force, low land costs (until recently), low taxes and few regulations, and New Hampshire's proximity to the large northeastern market have moved in to take the place of the departed woolen and cotton mills—often occupying the same buildings. An industrial group increasingly important to the state is the high-technology sector.

New Hampshire is trying to plan for a future that must balance a grave concern for continuing the quality of life to which most New Hampshire people are attached, with strong pressures for further economic development.

New Harmony   New Harmony (1990 pop., 846) is a community along the Wabash River in southwestern Indiana. A distribution center for a rich agricultural area, the town is an important historical site. The first settlement there was founded (1814) by the Harmony Society under the leadership of George Rapp, a German pietist preacher. Within 10 years they turned 12,140 ha (30,000 acres) of dense forests and swampland into choice farms. In 1825, however, the land was sold to Robert OWEN, who established the cooperative Community of New Harmony. Although the community disbanded in 1828, some members remained to create a notable intellectual center.

New Haven   New Haven is a port city located in south central Connecticut, on Long Island Sound at the mouth of the Quinnipiac River. The city, with a population of 130,474 (1990), is the center of a rapidly growing metropolitan area. The seat of New Haven County, the city is best known as the home of Yale University. Noted since the 19th century for the manufacture of firearms, transportation equipment, and hardware, New Haven also produces prestressed concrete, clothing, machinery, chemicals, and rubber products. Among its cultural attractions are the Yale Repertory Theatre, the Long Wharf Theatre, and Yale's museums—the Peabody Museum of Natural History, the Center for British Art, and the Art Gallery.

New Haven was founded in 1638 by the English Puritans John Davenport and Theophilus Eaton. In 1643 it became the chief town of a colony that encompassed the southwestern portion of present-day Connecticut. This colony joined with the Connecticut Colony in 1664. From 1701 to 1875, New Haven was the joint state capital with Hartford. Since 1957, New Haven has gained national attention for urban-renewal efforts.

New Hebrides   see VANUATU

New Ireland   New Ireland, the second largest island in the Bismarck Archipelago in the southwest Pacific, is part of Papua New Guinea. It covers 8,651 km^2 (3,340 mi^2). New Ireland and its adjacent islands have 79,800 inhabitants (1990 est.), mostly Melanesians. Kavieng is the administrative center and principal port. The densely forested Rossel Mountains form the spine of the island, reaching elevations of 2,108 m (6,916 ft). Major products include copra and cocoa.

New Ireland was thought to be part of New Britain from its first sighting by Europeans until 1767, when Philip Carteret discovered Saint George's Channel between the two islands. Renamed Neu Mecklenburg while a German protectorate (1884–1914), it was mandated to Australia in 1920. The island was occupied by the Japanese during World War II and then administered by Australia again until 1975.

New Jersey   New Jersey, a Middle Atlantic state located between New York on the north and east and Pennsylvania and Delaware on the west, occupies a peninsula bounded by the Delaware and Hudson rivers. The state's northern border is its only artificial limit. The Atlantic Ocean to the southeast provides an attractive and popular resort area. The "waistline" of the state is the corridor between New York City and Philadelphia, which has proved to be both a blessing and a curse. New Jersey's location has provided both impetus and market for agriculture, commerce, industry, and services, as well as cultural stimulation. Because of its location, however, New Jersey has suffered from a lack of identity, although that is changing now with growing awareness of the state's key position in the Northeast Corridor, or megalopolis. Among the smallest of states in size, New Jersey nevertheless ranks high in total population, and it is the most densely populated state.

Named for the island of Jersey, one of the Channel Islands, New Jersey was the 3d of the 13 colonies to enter the Union. Its capital, Trenton, was the site of Washington's first decisive victory of the American Revolution in 1776.

Land and Resources

New Jersey contains parts of the Atlantic Coastal Plain and the Appalachian Highlands, two major North American landforms. These can be further divided into five distinct sections, lying in parallel northeast-southwest bands.

The Outer Coastal Plain along the Atlantic, occupying about 46% of the state's area, is fringed with barrier islands, lagoons, and tidal marshes interrupted by estuarine rivers. The flat Pine Barrens cover about a third of the state inland from the coast.

The Inner Coastal Plain (about 13% of the state's area) is a strip of land that averages 20 km (12 mi) in width and slopes toward the Delaware River and Delaware Bay. Toward the northeastern end of this section are the Navesink Highlands, the highest mainland point on the Atlantic Coast.

The three sections of the Appalachian Highlands exhibit a pattern of ridges and lowlands. The northern portion contains lakes, ancient lake beds, and rock-abraded surfaces.

The Piedmont section, containing 20% of the land area and 70% of the population, shows the effects of human habitation with spreading suburbs, filled wetlands, and dense road networks found alongside primitive swamplands and rugged geologic Watchung Mountains and the PALISADES.

The Highlands (13% of the land) are characterized by narrow flat-topped ridges separated by small valleys containing lakes, such as Hopatcong, Mohawk, and Greenwood, that are used extensively for recreation.

The Ridge and Valley section, occupying less than 10% of the land, is dominated by flat-topped Kittatinny Mountain. At its northern end is High Point and at the southwestern end is the spectacular DELAWARE WATER GAP.

AT A GLANCE

NEW JERSEY

Land: Area: 22,590 km² (8,722 mi²); rank: 47th. Capital: Trenton (1990 pop., 88,675). Largest city: Newark (1990 pop., 275,221). Counties: 21. Elevations: highest—550 m (1,803 ft), at High Point; lowest—sea level, at Atlantic coast.

People: Population (1990): 7,748,634; rank: 9th; density: 402.3 persons per km² (1,042 per mi²). Distribution (1990): 89.4% urban, 10.6% rural. Average annual change (1980–90): +0.5%.

Government (1993): Governor: James J. Florio, Democrat. U.S. Congress: Senate—2 Democrats; House—7 Democrats, 6 Republicans. Electoral college votes: 15. State legislature: 40 senators, 80 representatives.

Economy: State personal income (1989): $183.9 billion; rank: 7th. Median family income (1989): $47,589; rank: 2d. Agriculture: income (1989)—$660 million. Fishing: value (1989)—$79 million. Lumber production (1991): less than 500,000 board feet. Mining (nonfuel): value (1988)—$242 million. Manufacturing: value added (1987)—$42.5 billion. Services: value (1987)—$43.6 billion.

Miscellany: Statehood: Dec. 18, 1787; the 3d state. Nickname: Garden State; tree: red oak; motto: Liberty and Prosperity; song: none.

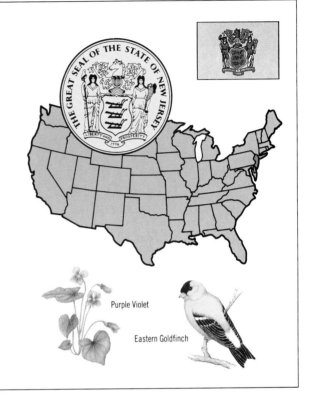

Purple Violet

Eastern Goldfinch

A fertile valley lies immediately to the east, part of a lowland that extends from Georgia to the St. Lawrence River.

Soils. Unconsolidated sand, silt, and clay are dominant in the coastal plain. Sandy loams have developed inland, and the highland areas are dominated by soils formed from the breakdown of shale, sandstone, and limestone.

Drainage. Northern New Jersey, once subjected to continental glaciation, exhibits drainage characteristics common in depositional areas. Disturbed drainage patterns have resulted in many lakes and erratic stream channels. The major rivers within the state—the Hackensack, Passaic, and Raritan—are located in the northern half of New Jersey. The Great Swamp National Wildlife Refuge area is a remnant of ancient Lake Passaic.

Drainage in southern New Jersey is less efficient than in the north, and extensive areas of porous sands in the Pine Barrens overlie a vast groundwater reservoir. Much of this southern region drains toward Delaware Bay or the DELAWARE RIVER. Swamps and bogs are common.

Climate. The interaction of cold, dry air masses from the northwest with warm, moist air masses from the south produces varied weather patterns in New Jersey. The July average temperature range is 21° to 24° C (70° to 76° F), and the January range is −2° to 3° C (26° to 37° F). Pre-

cipitation is evenly distributed through the year, with a slight maximum in late summer; amounts range from more than 1,270 mm (50 in) in the higher elevations to less than 1,020 mm (40 in) near the coast. Severe northeasterly storms in late winter and occasional hurricanes in the warm months cause considerable coastal damage.

Vegetation. The Highlands as well as the Kittatinny and Watchung ridges are forested, but the tree cover decreases yearly with urban encroachment. Oak-hickory forests dominate this area. The Pine Barrens are covered by an often-dwarfed pine-oak forest, dependent for its renewal on an ecological cycle in which forest fires are frequent. The Kittatinny Valley, the lowland of the Piedmont, and the Inner Coastal Plain are virtually devoid of tree cover.

Wildlife. Wildlife in New Jersey has been subjected to extensive human encroachment, yet many species survive. White-tailed deer remain, monitored and controlled by the state. Coyotes have returned, and beavers, muskrats, and river otters are still present. Squirrels, raccoons, skunks, and opossums are common in suburban areas. Coastal New Jersey is on the Atlantic Flyway, and many migrating bird species can be seen near the ocean, particularly in the Brigantine National Wildlife Refuge.

Resources. The Pine Barrens in the south contain de-

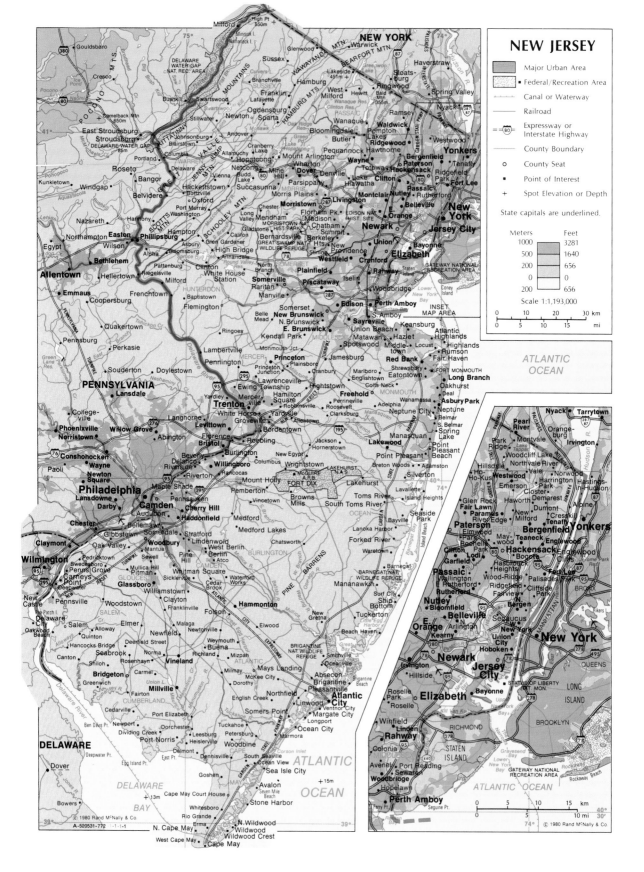

NEW JERSEY

Major Urban Area
Federal/Recreation Area
Canal or Waterway
Railroad
Expressway or Interstate Highway
County Boundary
○ County Seat
■ Point of Interest
+ Spot Elevation or Depth

State capitals are underlined.

Meters	Feet
1000	3281
500	1640
200	656
0	0
200	656

Scale 1:1,193,000

0   10   20   30 km
0   5   10   15 mi

INSET MAP AREA

ATLANTIC OCEAN

PENNSYLVANIA

DELAWARE

DELAWARE BAY

ATLANTIC OCEAN

© 1980 Rand McNally & Co.

A-520531-772   -1-1-1

posits of limonite (bog iron), sand, clay, and ilmenite (an ore of titanium). Greensand, used for water filters and fertilizers, is found in the southern interior. The north has deposits of sand, gravel, red sandstone, basalt, copper, magnetite iron, zinc, limestone, and slate.

People

New Jersey's population density is the highest of all the U.S. states. County densities, however, range from more than 10 times the state figure of 384 persons per km^2 (995 per mi^2) in Hudson to less than one-fourth in Sussex, Warren, Hunterdon, and Salem counties. In 1880 the state had more urban residents than rural, with a third of the population living in JERSEY CITY, NEWARK, AND Paterson. Since that time, although urbanization has increased greatly, the population has dispersed as New Jersey "suburbanized." At the center of the Northeast megalopolis, the state has only four cities with populations of more than 100,000: Newark, Jersey City, Paterson, and Elizabeth. Population growth during the 1980–90 decade was 5.2%, far below the national growth rate of 10.2% for the same period.

New Jersey has always had a diverse ethnic mixture. The population remained predominantly of northern European origin until the late 1800s, when southern and eastern Europeans made up most of the overseas arrivals. After the Civil War a migration of blacks from the South to unskilled industrial employment in the cities began; after 1890 the rate of increase of the black population was higher than that of the white population. Later, Hispanics, too, arrived in considerable numbers. In 1990, New Jersey's population was about 13% black and almost 10% of Spanish origin. Both groups were concentrated in the urban areas.

Nassau Hall (1756), a historic site of the Princeton University campus, was occupied by British troops during the American Revolution and was the site of several engagements during the Battle of Princeton (1777).

Roman Catholics form the largest religious group in the state. Urban areas show greater percentages of Roman Catholics and Jews than the more rural areas, where Protestants are dominant.

Education. Public education in New Jersey was established statewide in 1871. An 1875 constitutional amendment required the state to provide free public school education for all children between the ages of 5 and 18. A state supreme court revision in 1973 ruled that local property taxes could not serve as the primary source for school funding, so in 1976 a state income tax was instituted to pay for public education. State-supported institutions of higher education in New Jersey include Rutgers—The State University (1766), with its main campus at New Brunswick; the New Jersey Institute of Technology (1881) at Newark; the University of Medicine and Dentistry of New Jersey (1970), with facilities at Newark, Camden, and Piscataway; nine colleges; and a system of two-year community colleges. The state's private institutions include Drew University, Fairleigh Dickinson University, PRINCETON UNIVERSITY, Stevens Institute of Technology, and Seton Hall University.

Culture. The Garden State Ballet, the New Jersey Symphony Orchestra, and the New Jersey State Opera—all headquartered in Newark—are examples of the many performing arts units in New Jersey. The Papermill Playhouse—The State Theatre of New Jersey—is located in Millburn. The McCarter Theatre of Princeton University serves as a major regional repertory theater. Museums in New Jersey include the New Jersey State Museum in Trenton, the Newark Museum, the Paterson Museum, the Princeton University Art and Natural History museums, and Waterloo Village on the Morris Canal.

Historical Sites. New Jersey has preserved many historical sites, particularly those of the Revolutionary War periods. Morristown National Historical Park encompasses the Ford Mansion, the Wick House, and Jockey Hollow. Battlefield monuments have been erected at Monmouth, Princeton, Trenton, and Red Bank. Other historic sites include the Edison National Historic Site in West Orange and Walt Whitman's house in Camden.

Communications. New Jersey has its share of daily and Sunday newspapers; the *Newark Star Ledger* has the largest circulation of any state daily. Philadelphia and New York City newspapers are also widely read. Similarly, although New Jersey has locally based radio and television stations, there are large audiences in the state for broadcasts from neighboring New York and Pennsylvania.

Economy

Diversity has long been a characteristic of New Jersey's economy. No single source of income dominates. Since colonial times agriculture, commerce, and manufacturing have been present, but in changing proportions. The population, along with the large metropolitan markets nearby, has always been the state's own best customer for services. New Jersey, considered by many an industrial state, is also especially strong in the service industries.

Agriculture. Agriculture is decreasing in New Jersey, the traditional supplier of truck, dairy, and poultry products for the urban markets of New York and Philadelphia. Competition for land and labor have raised production costs while prices have remained comparatively low. The once-giant poultry industry has diminished drastically, but horse breeding has expanded. Truck crops remain important, although there is a trend toward grain production—particularly winter wheat—in an effort to minimize costs and lessen the need for migrant labor.

Forestry and Fishing. Forests in New Jersey support the limited production of wood for charcoal, industrial pallets, and locally used agricultural produce baskets. Commercial ocean fishing provides a variety of fish and shellfish, but coastal pollution has resulted in fish kills and the closing of many of the state's best shellfish beds.

Mining. Despite prolonged use and relative scarcity, New Jersey still has some exploitable minerals. Zinc is produced in the northwest, titanium is recovered from coastal sands, and magnesium is recovered from seawater off Cape May. Most important in both volume and income are construction materials, such as gravel, sand, clay, crushed stone, and limestone.

Manufacturing. Manufacturing provides about 25% of the gross state product. Chemicals and allied products comprise by far the most important industrial sector. Food processing and the manufacturing of electrical machinery and equipment also produce very significant revenues. An important adjunct to the manufacturing aspect of New Jersey's economy is industrial research, particularly in telecommunication and pharmaceutical fields.

Tourism. Tourism is a leading source of income in New Jersey. Within the state are portions of Gateway National Recreation Area, Delaware Water Gap National Recreation Area, Palisades Interstate Park, and four national wildlife refuges. The state-parks system maintains numerous parks, state forests, wildlife protection areas, and state marinas. The STATUE OF LIBERTY and ELLIS ISLAND are

within the New Jersey waters of New York Bay. New Jersey's shore resorts are famous. Casino gambling in Atlantic City has generated revenue for the state, but the casinos' effect on the resort town is questionable. Old inland summer resorts, particularly around Lake Hopatcong and Budd Lake, have become year-round residences for many inhabitants. Winter sports, particularly skiing, are commercially important. The Meadowlands Sports Complex is the home of professional football, ice hockey, and basketball teams. It also contains a track for Thoroughbred and harness racing.

Transportation. New Jersey's transportation links reinforce its image as a corridor. Much of the responsibility for port facilities is shared by neighboring states—involved through the Port Authority of New York and New Jersey and the Delaware River Port Authority of Pennsylvania and New Jersey. The ports of Newark and Elizabeth provide container and bulk cargo facilities. Nearby is Newark International Airport. The New York-Philadelphia corridor is served by passenger and freight rail facilities. Ferry service connects New Jersey with Delaware, and tunnels and bridges link New York and New Jersey. Internal transportation is almost entirely by an extensive network of highways. Commuter railroads cover about 800 km (497 mi).

Energy. New Jersey's electrical energy is derived principally from petroleum and coal; nuclear power is also significant. Most petroleum is imported. Exploration in the Baltimore Canyon off the coast of New Jersey was undertaken in hopes of locating recoverable petroleum or natural gas.

Government and Politics

New Jersey's third constitution, adopted in 1947, gives strong powers to the governor, who is elected for a 4-year term. Senators in the bicameral legislature serve 4-year

Small farms similar to this one near Boonton are common throughout the Piedmont Plain, a fertile belt traversing north central New Jersey. Although its economy is mainly industrial, the state is an important producer of such specialty crops as asparagus, cranberries, and broccoli.

terms and members of the General Assembly 2-year terms. For representation in both houses the state is divided into 40 electoral districts. Each district elects 1 senator and 2 members of the Assembly. Deadlocks between representatives of the rural south versus the suburban north often result when dealing with urban problems and tax issues. The chief justice administers the judicial system, which consists of a supreme court; a superior court comprising 3 divisions—chancery, law, and appellate; municipal courts; and other lower courts subject to legislative alteration.

New Jersey's 21 counties, governed by elected boards of freeholders, have no constitutional powers but are granted certain powers by the legislature.

Municipalities in New Jersey tend to be powerful, although they have no constitutional power. Five types of municipal organization exist: cities, boroughs, towns, townships, and villages.

The diversity that marks New Jersey in so many other ways is evident in the voting habits of its citizens. Historically, a near-equal number of Democrats and Republicans have been voted into the governor's office. Voters tend to choose a candidate rather than a party at all levels of government.

History

The earliest inhabitants of the New Jersey area are believed to have lived in the region as early as the 11th century BC. The inhabitants at the time of European arrival were Lenni Lenape, or DELAWARE, Indians—farmers, fishers, and hunters of the Algonquian language group.

The area was claimed by the English, French, and Dutch on the basis of explorations (1524–1623) by John Cabot, Henry Hudson, Giovanni da Verrazano, and Cornelius Mey. The Dutch established NEW NETHERLAND in what is now New York and New Jersey. The then-powerful Swedes established small settlements on the Delaware River; it is there that Swedish and Finnish settlers built what are thought to be the first log cabins in North America (see NEW SWEDEN). The earliest Dutch settlements in New Jersey were destroyed during Indian attacks. In 1660, under the direction of Gov. Peter Stuyvesant, the fortified village of Bergen—present-day Jersey City—became the first permanent New Jersey settlement.

In 1664, England began to press colonial claims, and the name New Jersey was first used in a deed that gave the area to John, Lord Berkeley, and Sir George Carteret. Except for a brief return to Dutch rule in 1673, New Jersey remained British until the American Revolution. In 1676 the colony was divided from northwest to southeast into West New Jersey (Berkeley's portion) and East New Jersey (Carteret's portion). West New Jersey, purchased by a group led by William Penn, served as a haven for persecuted English Quakers. East New Jersey attracted many New Englanders. These people, along with Dutch, Swedes, Scots, Irish, Germans, and French Huguenots, gave New Jersey greater cultural diversity than any other area. In 1702 the two proprietorships joined to form the royal colony of New Jersey.

During the colonial period industry began to grow in the Pine Barrens with the manufacture of iron and glass from local bog iron ores and sands. Iron was also produced in the northwest from local ores. Commerce was important, and New Jersey's highways were the best in the colonies because of its location between New York and Philadelphia and between the northern and southern colonies. Most of the population practiced subsistence agriculture, but specialization in truck crops began early in the areas closest to New York and Philadelphia.

New Jersey's strategic location and cultural diversity created many hardships during the American Revolution. Individual loyalties based on economy, religion, and cultural heritages resulted in a bitter local civil war within the larger conflict. Both British and colonial armies occupied, plundered, and marched repeatedly across the region. The major battles of TRENTON and MONMOUTH, along with many skirmishes, were fought in New Jersey. Washington's army spent two harsh winters at MORRISTOWN. For four months in 1783, because of a mutinous disturbance in Philadelphia, PRINCETON was the capital of the new country.

During the War of 1812 the need for rapid overland transport through the state resulted in road improvements that later provided routeways for railroads. Following the war large numbers of European immigrants arrived, swelling the populations of the state's cities. Although commerce remained the dominant economic sector until 1840, the state's industries expanded with increased demand and a growing labor force.

The sentiment of New Jersey's population was divided during the Civil War, with many people sympathetic to the Southern cause. The state did not support Abraham Lincoln in his reelection bid for the presidency in 1864, but cast its votes for George B. McClellan, a New Jersey Democrat.

During the 19th century, New Jersey gained attention as the location for significant inventions. John Stevens built the nation's first steam locomotive and the world's first steam ferry line in HOBOKEN during the early 1800s. Later in the century, Thomas Alva Edison set up his laboratory in New Jersey at Menlo Park and later at West Orange for work on the light bulb, phonograph, and motion pictures. The state's research tradition has continued into the present day, with such developments as the transistor in 1948 and the telecommunications satellite in 1962.

Because of its intensive industrialization and high population density, New Jersey has enacted legislation to protect the environment—one of the first states to do so. Special emphasis is placed on maintaining air quality and protecting coastal and wetlands areas. Predictions for New Jersey's future indicate continued growth, but at a somewhat slower pace. Its favorable location and skilled work force remain its finest assets for the years to come.

New Jerusalem, Church of the The 18th-century Swedish mystic Emanuel SWEDENBORG did not intend to establish a new form of Christianity, but his references to a "new Jerusalem" led to reading groups in Europe and the New World and, in 1787, to the founding in London of the New Jerusalem Church. The earliest leader of the movement in the United States was James Glen, and the church held its first American convention in Philadelphia in 1817. The General Convention of the New Jerusalem operates on democratic principles, with self-regulating societies deciding on a wide variety of worship services. Members of the convention are guided by Swedenborg's commentaries on the Bible, and they are vigorous in pursuing missionary activities.

In 1890 a dissident faction formed the General Church of the New Jerusalem. This group accepts Swedenborg's writings as having full divine authority, believing that their contents stem ultimately from God. Although the General Church, headquartered in Bryn Athyn, Pa., includes bishops.in its ruling structures, most decisions are reached after full and open discussion. A third group, also in Bryn Athyn, is called Nova Hierosolyma.

New London   New London (1990 pop., 28,540) is a city on Long Island Sound at the mouth of the Thames River in eastern Connecticut. It is a port, the location of a U.S. naval base, a manufacturing center where nuclear submarines are built, a popular summer resort, and an educational center. Connecticut College (1911), the United States Coast Guard Academy (1876), and the United States Submarine Officers' School are there.

New London was founded in 1646. During the Revolutionary War, in 1781, British troops under the command of Benedict Arnold burned the town; during the War of 1812 the harbor was blockaded by the British. As a 19th-century whaling port it rivaled New Bedford, Mass., in importance. Eugene O'Neill lived in New London and wrote his first plays there.

new mathematics   see MATHEMATICS, EDUCATION IN

New Mexico   New Mexico, located in the southwestern United States at the southern end of the Rocky Mountains, borders Mexico on the south, Arizona on the west, Colorado on the north, Oklahoma on the east, and Texas on the east and southeast. With regard to total area, it ranks fifth among the states in size. New Mexico's population, however, is considerably less than 1% of the total for the United States, ranking in the bottom third in number of inhabitants. Hispanics form more than 38% of the state's population, and Indians constitute nearly 9%. Like other southwestern states, New Mexico has been experiencing a large in-migration of Anglos from the midwestern and eastern states. Population growth of 28.1% between 1970 and 1980 and 16.8% from 1980 to 1990 shows a sharp increase when compared to the 6.9% between 1960 and 1970.

Initially explored and settled by Spaniards, the area remained a Spanish—and then Mexican—territory until U.S. annexation in 1846. Statehood was achieved in 1912.

The name *New Mexico* was given to the state to distinguish it from the independent nation to its south. Its scenic beauty and unique cultural characteristics are re-

flected in New Mexico's nickname, Land of Enchantment. Santa Fe, founded in 1609, is the state capital.

New Mexico has been a major contact point between three cultures—Indian, Spanish-Mexican, and Anglo-American. Historically a land of cattle and sheep ranching with some irrigated agriculture, the state is experiencing new growth based on tourism, retirement communities, aerospace and defense research, and the development of petroleum, natural-gas, coal, uranium, solar, and geothermal energy resources.

Land and Resources

New Mexico encompasses a variety of landforms, which may be divided into four major regions, all of which extend beyond its borders: the ROCKY MOUNTAINS, the GREAT PLAINS, the BASIN AND RANGE PROVINCE, and the COLORADO PLATEAU. In north central New Mexico are the southern Rocky Mountains, dominated by the San Juan and Sangre de Cristo ranges. The highest elevations in the state are found there. The RIO GRANDE flows between these two mountain systems and continues south to follow a small part of the boundary between New Mexico and Texas. Eastern New Mexico is made up of a section of the Great Plains, traversed by the CANADIAN RIVER and PECOS RIVER. A flat strip of land along the Texas border is known as the Llano Estacado (Staked Plains) or High Plains. Much of southern New Mexico is part of the basin and range province.

Several rugged north-south mountain ranges, particularly the Black, San Andres, Sacramento, and Guadalupe, are separated by basins, including the Jornada del Muerto and the Tularosa. The state's fourth region, a section of the Colorado Plateau, is in northwest New Mexico. It is a high-lying area with extensive valleys, deep canyons, mesas, buttes, and colorful sandstone formations.

Soils. Thin, granular, brownish gray desert soils cover most of New Mexico. Alluvial soils are found along narrow river valleys, and some podzols can be found at higher elevations.

Drainage. The Rio Grande is New Mexico's largest and longest river, flowing south through the state for a distance of 756 km (470 mi). Two-thirds of the eastern plains is drained by the Pecos River, which joins the Rio Grande in west Texas. Other rivers include the San Juan in the northwest and the Cimarron and the Canadian in the northern third of the eastern plains.

The Continental Divide passes through western New Mexico, but only the GILA RIVER and the San Juan flow toward the Pacific. A large area of closed drainage, characterized by salt pans and playa lakes, is found in the southwestern desert. Groundwater sources provide water for urban areas along the Rio Grande and are used in the eastern plains for irrigation. No sizable natural lakes exist in New Mexico, but marshlands have formed along the Rio Grande and Pecos River.

Climate. Three distinct climatic regions are discernible in New Mexico: the semiarid eastern plains, the western deserts, and the mountain areas, where conditions result in sharply increased moisture.

Aridity, warm-to-hot summers, and mild-to-cold winters are the dominant climatic characteristics of New

NEW MEXICO

Land: Area: 314,938 km^2 (121,598 mi^2); rank: 5th. Capital: Sante Fe (1990 pop., 55,859). Largest city: Albuquerque (1990 pop., 384,736). Counties: 33. Elevations: highest—4,011 m (13,161 ft), at Wheeler Peak; lowest—866 m (2,842 ft), at Red Bluff Reservoir.

People: Population (1990): 1,521,779; rank: 37th; density: 4.8 persons per km^2 (12.5 per mi^2). Distribution (1990): 73% urban, 27% rural. Average annual change (1980–90): +1.7%.

Government (1993): Governor: Bruce King, Democrat. U.S. Congress: Senate—1 Democrat, 1 Republican; House—1 Democrat, 2 Republicans. Electoral college votes: 5. State legislature: 42 senators, 70 representatives.

Economy: State personal income (1989): $20.1 billion; rank: 40th. Median family income (1989): $27,623; rank: 44th. Agriculture: income (1989)—$1.4 billion. Lumber production (1991): 139 million board feet. Mining (nonfuel): value (1988)—$1 billion. Manufacturing: value added (1987)— $1.7 billion. Services: value (1987)—$5.8 billion.

Miscellany: Statehood: Jan. 6, 1912; the 47th state. Nickname: Land of Enchantment; tree: piñon; motto: *Crescit Eundo* ("It Grows as It Goes"); song: "O Fair New Mexico."

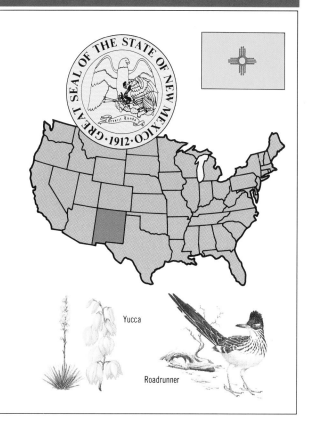

Yucca

Roadrunner

Mexico. Precipitation averages less than 400 mm (16 in), and summer temperatures often climb to 38° C (about 100° F). Snow covers the northern third of the state and the higher elevations in the winter months. The southwestern desert receives about 200 mm (8 in) of rain, yet precipitation exceeds 1,000 mm (39 in) in the Sangre de Cristo range in the north.

Vegetation and Animal Life. Mesquite and black grama grass are abundant in the lower Rio Grande and Pecos valleys and the southwestern part of the state below 1,400 m (4,500 ft). Blue grama grass, buffalo grass, piñon pine, and juniper grow in about 80% of the state. Ponderosa pine, blue spruce, Douglas fir, and alpine cover are found in the mountains at about 2,100 m (7,000 ft).

Native fauna includes the antelope, mule deer, white-tailed deer, elk, bear, and javelina, or peccary. Quail, ducks, and turkeys are also present. About 300 species of birds can be found, and numerous migratory waterfowl pass through the state or spend the winter there.

Resources. Surface water resources are limited because of overall low rainfall. Extensive aquifers are present, however, particularly below the eastern plains. New Mexico is rich in a number of minerals, including copper, gold and silver. New Mexico ranks first among the states in uranium, potash, and perlite production. Fuel resources include petroleum, natural gas, and extensive bituminous and subbituminous coal deposits. Also present are semiprecious turquoise, agate, jasper, and opal.

People

New Mexico is a sparsely settled state. Nearly one-third of the population lives in Bernalillo County—metropolitan ALBUQUERQUE. Only 6 cities other than Albuquerque— SANTA FE, LAS CRUCES, Roswell, Farmington, Clovis, and Rio Rancho—have populations in excess of 30,000.

The recent rapid growth of New Mexico is the result of in-migration from other states. This, coupled with an above-average reproduction rate, has placed New Mexico among the nation's fastest-growing states. The most rapidly growing areas are Albuquerque, Santa Fe, Las Cruces, Roswell, and the energy-producing region of the northwest.

The Hispanic population, 38% in the state as a whole, rises to more than 80% in 5 northern counties. Indians, most of whom are Pueblo, Navajo, or Apache, reside primarily on 4 reservations and in 19 pueblos; they are es-

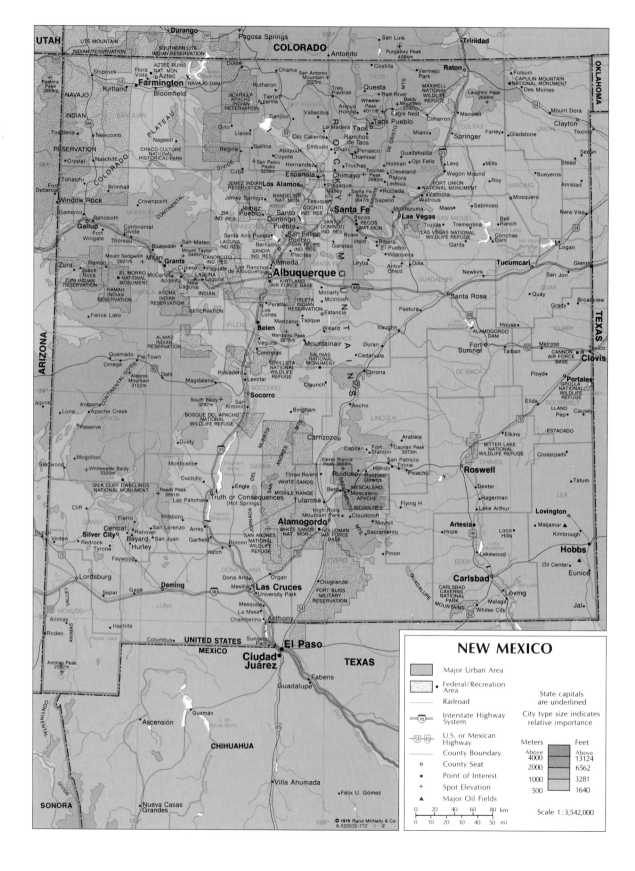

NEW MEXICO

Major Urban Area

Federal/Recreation Area

Railroad

Interstate Highway System

U.S. or Mexican Highway

County Boundary

○ County Seat

■ Point of Interest

+ Spot Elevation

▲ Major Oil Fields

State capitals are underlined

City type size indicates relative importance

Meters	Feet
Above 4000	Above 13124
2000	6562
1000	3281
500	1640

Scale 1:3,542,000

0 20 40 60 80 km
0 10 20 30 40 50 mi

© 1979 Rand McNally & Co.
A-520532-772

pecially numerous in the northwest counties McKinley and San Juan. About one-half of the population is Roman Catholic. Recent migrations of Anglo-Americans into New Mexico, however, have altered both the ethnic and religious character of the state.

Education. Education from the elementary grades through the university level is dominated by public institutions. Local school districts maintain primary and secondary education responsibility under the guidance of the State Board of Education. The state's six universities and colleges include the University of New Mexico (1889) at Albuquerque and New Mexico State University (1888) at Las Cruces. The College of Santa Fe (1947), St. John's College (1964), and the University of Albuquerque (1889) are important private institutions. The city of Albuquerque maintains the largest public library in New Mexico.

Culture. The SANTA FE OPERA, the Albuquerque Opera Theatre, and the Albuquerque Symphony Orchestra are nationally recognized music groups. Major museums of anthropology and Southwestern culture are maintained in Santa Fe and Albuquerque. The artist Georgia O'Keeffe used the area surrounding her home near TAOS as the subject for many of her works. Of special interest are the International Space Hall of Fame at ALAMOGORDO, the Robert Goddard Rocket Museum in Roswell, and the Living Desert State Park in Carlsbad.

Santa Fe, the second oldest city in the United States, maintains its colonial appearance. Other places of historical significance are the Indian pueblo villages, Mesilla, once the capital of Arizona Territory, and the Pecos Mission ruins.

Communications. The *Albuquerque Journal*, the *Albuquerque Tribune*, and the *New Mexican* of Santa Fe are the largest of the numerous daily newspapers in the state. New Mexico is well supplied with both AM and FM radio stations; television channels include educational operations as well as private, network-affiliated broadcasters.

Economic Activity

The economy of New Mexico has grown dramatically in recent years, mostly as a result of federal government operations within the state. Government employs about 25% of the work force. The federal government maintains many research centers in New Mexico, principally concerned with developing weapons or nuclear energy.

Agriculture. Agriculture contributes a small but still significant proportion to state revenues. Most of this income is derived from livestock products. Irrigated agriculture, made possible by dams and reservoirs on the Rio Grande, Pecos, San Juan, Canadian, and Cimarron rivers as well as from wells near Clovis and Portales, produces cotton, sorghum, pecans, corn, peanuts, pinto beans, lettuce, onions and chilies.

Forestry. Forests cover about 25% of New Mexico, but forestry is limited to small operations in the more humid mountains. Ponderosa pine, Douglas fir, and spruce are cut for timber.

Mining. New Mexico ranks among the leading U.S. states in mineral production. Petroleum, natural gas, and coal are the leading minerals in terms of their total value.

Copper, molybdenum, potash, and uranium also contribute to the state's economy.

Manufacturing. Mineral and agricultural processing, electronics and defense production, and weapons research and testing dominate New Mexico's industrial sector. Mineral processing is located close to areas of production near GALLUP, Artesia, Carlsbad, Grants, Raton, and Silver City. Defense-related research and industry are found in LOS ALAMOS and Albuquerque and at the WHITE SANDS MISSILE RANGE.

Tourism. Tourism is an increasingly important aspect of the state's economy. Desert landscapes, mountains, forests, and clear skies with spectacular sunsets provide a backdrop for the great cultural diversity of Indian pueblos, Spanish colonial settlements, abandoned mining camps, and modern cities. Carlsbad Caverns National Park and 9 national monuments are in the state. CHACO CANYON, with its many Indian ruins, is one of the most important pre-Columbian Pueblo sites in the Southwest. White Sands National Monument also attracts many tourists. Resort areas include the mountain fringe near Santa Fe and Taos, thermal mineral baths at Truth or Consequences, and winter sports centers in the Sangre de Cristo, Sandia, and Sacramento mountains.

Transportation. Two major east-west interstate highways as well as historic transcontinental railroad lines cross New Mexico. A north-south interstate highway connects El Paso, Tex., and Denver, Colo., passing through Las Cruces, Albuquerque, and Santa Fe. Major airlines serve Albuquerque, and commuter airlines connect that

The Rio Grande, the principal river of New Mexico, has its source in Colorado and flows south through New Mexico before emptying into the Gulf of Mexico.

city with outlying urban centers. Major railroad branches link the east-west trunk lines.

Energy. New Mexico is a major exporter of petroleum and natural gas. Coal and natural gas are the principal fuels used for the generation of electricity. Geothermal energy potential has been investigated, and solar energy has been applied to home and industrial heating and cooling.

Government

The New Mexico constitution, adopted in 1911, provides for executive, legislative, and judicial branches of government. The executive branch includes the governor and 9 other elected officials who serve for 4-year terms. The legislature is divided into a senate with 42 members elected to 4-year terms and a house of representatives whose 70 members serve 2-year terms. The judicial system includes probate courts, district courts, an appeals court, and a supreme court presided over by a chief justice and four associate justices. Each of the 33 counties is governed by a 3- or 5-member elected commission. Incorporated cities are governed by elected commissioners.

The Democratic party has dominated statewide politics in New Mexico since statehood in 1912. The governor's office was occupied by Republicans during most of the 1950s and part of the 1960s, however. In the 1970s and most of the 1980s the governorship was controlled by Democrats. During the same period the Democratic party predominated in the state legislature. In national presidential elections, New Mexico has always cast its electoral votes for the winning candidate except in 1976, when the Republicans carried the state and Democrat Jimmy Carter was elected president.

The Taos Pueblo, the oldest and northernmost of 19 pueblos in the Rio Grande Valley, is believed to have been founded about 1,000 years ago. This 5-story structure, known as San Geronimo de Taos, houses an agrarian community of Pueblo Indians.

History

Indians first lived in New Mexico about 20,000 years ago, developing the FOLSOM and Sandia cultures. Around AD 1000 the ANASAZI developed an advanced culture in northwestern New Mexico; the Mogollon Indians lived in the southwest. By about 1500 these groups had migrated, and the APACHE, COMANCHE, and NAVAJO moved in. The PUEBLO Indians—descendants of the Anasazi—cultivated maize, beans, and squash in irrigated plots along the Rio Grande.

The first white persons to visit present-day New Mexico were probably Álvar Núñez CABEZA DE VACA and some Spanish companions in 1536. The Franciscan priest Marcos de Niza and his black slave Esteban entered the area in 1539, searching for the Seven Golden Cities of CIBOLA (actually ZUNI villages that contained no particular wealth). Several other Spanish expeditions followed, including those of Francisco Vázquez de CORONADO and Antonio de Espejo. Juan de OÑATE entered in 1598 from New Spain, now Mexico, and the first European settlements were established at San Juan Pueblo in 1598 and Santa Fe in 1610.

Under Spanish colonial rule, and then under Mexico, the area remained a region of cattle and sheep grazing lands, with small farm villages along the Rio Grande and occasional mission settlements. The Spanish often treated the Indians harshly. In 1680 the Pueblos staged a great rebellion, but the Spanish regained control by the early 1690s. Relations with the UTE, Apache, Comanche, and Navajo tribes remained poor for most of the 18th century, and little economic development took place in the region.

In the early 1820s, New Mexico became a province of newly independent Mexico, and contact with the United States increased. Anglo-American traders from Kansas and Missouri opened the SANTA FE TRAIL in 1821. In 1822, William Becknell, an American trader, inaugurated travel along the route connecting New Mexico with Independence, Mo. In 1846, during the Mexican War, Gen. Stephen KEARNY took control of New Mexico for the United States. The Territory of New Mexico was organized in 1850, and the GADSDEN PURCHASE of 1853 added a strip of land to its south, fixing the present boundary between the United States and Mexico. In 1863, New Mexico was given its present boundaries upon the formation of the Arizona Territory.

Early in the Civil War, Confederate forces captured much of the area, but they were soundly defeated at Glorieta Pass near Santa Fe in March 1862 and withdrew soon after. Following the war, cattle and sheep ranching grew in importance.

New Mexico became effectively linked to the rest of the United States upon completion (1881) of the southern transcontinental railroad. Cattle ranching expanded, irrigated commercial agriculture developed, and mining operations brought new dimensions to the economy. On Jan. 6, 1912, New Mexico entered the Union as the 47th state. During the 1920s, mining—especially of petroleum and potash—increased, and tourism began to be economically important.

In recent decades new industries have moved to New Mexico. Military weapons development and testing became important during World War II; the first atomic bomb was exploded at Trinity Site in a remote area of New Mexico on July 16, 1945. Rocket and missile testing continues over a large area of southern New Mexico. Los Alamos was established as a scientific research community. In the postwar period several other major defense facilities were built in New Mexico.

Uranium was discovered in northwestern New Mexico in 1950. Mining of copper, coal, potash, and uranium—along with the extraction of petroleum and natural gas—has further diversified the economy. Additional irrigated croplands have also contributed to economic growth following the construction (begun in 1911) of dams and reservoirs on the state's rivers. The state's natural beauty has attracted both tourists and those seeking a retirement residence. In spite of the changes taking place in the rapidly growing state, New Mexico's people remain proud of their rich cultural heritage.

Jackson Square, the central plaza of New Orleans's celebrated French Quarter, faces Saint Louis Cathedral and structures dating from the period of Spanish rule.

New Netherland   New Netherland was the name given to the area of Dutch settlement in North America during the 17th century. In 1621 the DUTCH WEST INDIA COMPANY was granted a charter that included the right to establish colonies in the New World. The first permanent settlement was made in 1624. New Netherland was centered along the Hudson River Valley and included parts of what is now New York, New Jersey, Connecticut, and Delaware. From 1626 its capital was at New Amsterdam (now New York City). An English expedition forced Gov. Peter STUYVESANT to surrender New Netherland in 1664. The Dutch retook it in 1673, but it was permanently restored to England the following year by the Treaty of Westminster.

New Orleans   New Orleans is a city in southern Louisiana, located on the Mississippi River. Most of the city is situated on the east bank, between the river and Lake Pontchartrain to the north. Because it was built on a great turn of the river, it is known as the Crescent City. New Orleans, with a population of 496,938 (1990 est.), is the largest city in Louisiana and one of the principal cities of the South. The metropolitan area has a population of 1,238,816 (1990). It was established on the high ground nearest the mouth of the Mississippi, which is 177 km (110 mi) downstream. Elevations range from 3.65 m (12 ft) above sea level to 2 m (6.5 ft) below; as a result, an ingenious system of water pumps, drainage canals, and levees has been built to protect the city from flooding. The city covers a land area of 518 km^2 (200 mi^2). New Orleans experiences mild winters and hot, humid summers.

Contemporary City. The population of New Orleans, including Anglos, French, blacks, Italians, Irish, Spanish, and Cubans, reflects its cosmopolitan past. The CAJUNS, or Acadians, are descendants of French émigrés expelled from Nova Scotia (or Acadia) during the 18th century.

They speak their own French dialect. The port is one of the world's largest and ranks first in the United States in tonnage handled. Major exports are petroleum products, grain, cotton, paper, machinery, and iron and steel. The city's economy is dominated by the petrochemical, aluminum, and food-processing industries and by tourism.

The most important tourist event is MARDI GRAS, which is celebrated for a week before the start of Lent. The Superdome, an enclosed sports stadium, attracts major sporting events and is an element in achieving the city's position as a leading convention center. New Orleans is noted for its fine restaurants, for its Dixieland jazz, and for its numerous cultural and educational facilities. TULANE (1834), Dillard (1869), and Loyola (1849) universities are major institutions of higher learning. The French Quarter, or Vieux Carré (French for "old square"), is the site of the original city and contains many of the historic and architecturally significant buildings for which New Orleans is famous.

History. New Orleans was founded in 1718 by Jean Baptiste Le Moyne, sieur de Bienville, and named for the regent of France, Philipe II, duc d'Orléans. It remained a French colony until 1763, when it was transferred to the Spanish. In 1800, Spain ceded it back to France; in 1803, New Orleans, along with the entire Louisiana Purchase, was sold by Napoleon I to the United States. It was the site of the Battle of New Orleans (1815) in the War of 1812. Besieged during the Civil War by Union ships, the city fell on Apr. 25, 1862.

New Rochelle [roh-shel']   New Rochelle (1990 pop., 67,265) is a city in southeastern New York State; it is situated on Long Island Sound about 26 km (16 mi) northeast of New York City in Westchester County. Its proximity to New York City has made it a popular residence for commuters. Settled by French Huguenots in 1688, it assumed its present suburban role in the 1890s. Several monuments are dedicated to the patriot Thomas Paine, who lived in the town briefly.

New School for Social Research   Established in 1919, the New School for Social Research is a private coeducational institution in New York City offering graduate and undergraduate degrees. The school includes the Eugene Lang College, and its affiliate schools are the Parsons School of Design and the Otis Art Institute of Parsons. It has graduate studies in political and social science and management and urban professions. A service of the school is adult education.

New South Wales   New South Wales is a state on the east coast of Australia, between Queensland and Victoria, covering an area of 801,428 km² (309,433 mi²). The country's most populous state, it has a population of 5,543,500 (1986). More than 60% of the people live in greater SYDNEY, the capital.

New South Wales has three main north-south trending physical regions. The narrow strip of coastal lowlands is composed primarily of alluvium; sediments and igneous rocks characterize the eastern highlands and the interior western plains. The eastern highlands, part of the GREAT DIVIDING RANGE, is a series of plateaus with an average elevation of 760 m (2,500 ft), reaching a maximum elevation at Mount KOSCIUSKO, the highest point in Australia. The DARLING and MURRAY are the state's longest rivers. Mean annual temperatures range between 12° C and 21° C (53°–69° F). Rainfall averages 1,138 mm (45 in) annually, decreasing markedly in the northwest. Grass is the dominant vegetation in the vast semiarid interior. Forests of eucalyptus, pine, and tropical softwood are found on the coastal plain and in the highlands.

The people of New South Wales are almost entirely of European, especially British, ancestry. About 23,100 residents are Aborigines. The state's population is 80% urban, concentrated in the three major cities of NEWCASTLE, Sydney, and WOLLONGONG.

Agricultural products—especially wool, lamb, beef, and wheat—form the major economic sector. Mining is of traditional importance, and the state is a large producer of coal, silver, lead, and zinc. Industries produce machinery, food products, iron and steel, chemicals, and paper products. New South Wales's foreign trade is the largest of all Australia's states.

New South Wales was claimed for Great Britain in 1770 by the British explorer James COOK. Australia's first settlement was established in 1788 as the prison camp of Fort Jackson, on the site of present-day Sydney. During the 1820s immigration of free settlers surpassed the arrival of convicts. The search for additional sheep-grazing land was the major stimulus for exploration. The colony of New South Wales at first encompassed more than half the continent, but its dimensions shrank as other colonies were established. The colony became a state in 1901

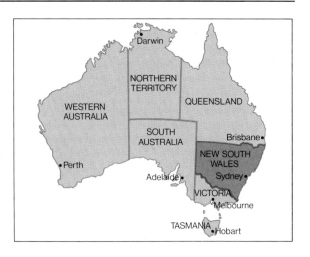

upon achievement of federation. The Australian Capital Territory, an enclave within New South Wales, was ceded in 1911.

New Spain   New Spain, from 1535 to 1821 a Spanish viceroyalty with headquarters at Mexico City, included for much of its history the present southwestern United States, Mexico, Florida, Central America, the Antilles, part of northern South America, and the Philippines.

New Stone Age   see NEOLITHIC PERIOD

New Sweden   New Sweden was a 17th-century American colony on the Delaware River, in what is now Delaware, New Jersey, and Pennsylvania. The New Sweden Company was founded in 1633 with joint Swedish and Dutch backing. In 1638 its first expedition, led by Peter MINUIT, established a settlement on the site of present-day Wilmington, Del., naming it Fort Christina in honor of the queen of Sweden. The colony later became an exclusively Swedish enterprise, and under governors Johan Björnsson Printz (1643–53) and Johan Claesson Rising (1654–55), it came into conflict with neighboring Dutch settlements. The Dutch under Peter STUYVESANT conquered the area in 1655 and made it part of NEW NETHERLAND.

New Testament   see BIBLE

New Thought   A religious movement that began in the United States in the late 19th century, New Thought stresses the power of the mind to heal disease and to improve life. Its individualistic orientation has hindered the development of centralized institutions. New Thought, however, has influenced many who claim no allegiance to its organizations. Phineas Parkhurst QUIMBY is considered the founder of New Thought, even though the movement incorporates ideas of other thinkers, including those of the American transcendentalists. Warren F. Evans (1817–89) and Julius A. Dresser (1838–93) spread Quimby's teachings. The magazine *New Thought*, which is still published, was begun in 1894. The National New Thought Alliance was formed in 1908, and the International New Thought Alliance (INTA) in 1914. The Unity School of Christianity, although not part of INTA, is a prominent New Thought movement.

new towns   The "new towns" approach to urban planning was first undertaken on a large scale in England after World War II to relieve overcrowding in London and other cities. It involved the establishment, by the government, of urban communities in outlying areas and was based on the idea of the GARDEN CITY, developed by Ebenezer Howard and others. The New Towns Act of 1946 provided that these developments should be viable, self-contained, largely autonomous units open to all people. All of the basic occupations were to be represented so that the needs of the residents might be met. The act also provided that housing, roads, schools, police and fire departments, and other urban necessities should be carefully planned to prevent problems caused by the haphazard growth of older cities. Thirty-two new towns now exist in England, Scotland, Wales, and Northern Ireland.

Highly successful in Great Britain, the new-towns idea has not caught on as well elsewhere. In the United States, for example, of 15 government-supported communities established during the 1960s and '70s, all but 5 failed because of poor planning, poor management, and rising costs.

New Wave   The term *New Wave* (in French, *Nouvelle Vague*) refers to the films of a group of French directors, including Jean Luc GODARD, Alain RESNAIS, François TRUFFAUT, and Claude Chabrol, who made their first feature films between 1958 and 1961. Most of them wrote for the film journal *Cahiers du Cinéma* and helped develop the *auteur* (director-oriented) theory of film criticism,

which advocated the personal and autobiographical approach used in such films as Truffaut's *The 400 Blows* (1959). These directors also emulated American genre films, such as the detective movie, and favored low-budget location shooting over studio filming.

The phrase *New Wave* was used to label a pop-music variant of the late 1970s that incorporated elements of punk rock (very fast tempos, very angry lyrics). The term may also occur in describing almost any minor development in such fields as fashion, art, or the dance.

New York (city)   New York, the largest city in the United States, lies at the mouth of the Hudson River on the southernmost extension of New York State. The city's population of 7,322,564 (1990) is divided among five boroughs, each of which is a county of New York State: MANHATTAN (New York County), BROOKLYN (Kings County), the BRONX (Bronx County), QUEENS (Queens County), and STATEN ISLAND (Richmond County). The five boroughs cover an area of 831 km^2 (321 mi^2). New York's metropolitan area (1990 pop., 18,087,251) includes Long Island and parts of southern New York State, northeastern New Jersey, and southwestern Connecticut.

The city's physical setting is a complex assortment of islands and parts of islands. Only the Bronx is on the mainland, and it is separated from Manhattan Island by the Harlem River. The borough of Queens is located on western Long Island and is separated from Manhattan and the Bronx by the East River. Brooklyn, also on Long Island, lies to the west and south of Queens. Staten Island, officially Richmond Borough until 1975, includes several small islands. Many other smaller islands dot the bays, rivers, and estuaries. Among the more important are ELLIS ISLAND, Governors Island, and Liberty Island (with the STATUE OF LIBERTY), and City, Randall's, Riker's, Roosevelt, and Ward's islands.

The core of the city is Manhattan, which is totally urban except for Central Park and other smaller parks. The most densely populated borough and the city's economic and cultural center, Manhattan is often considered to be synonymous with New York City.

The Brooklyn Bridge (left foreground) and the Manhattan Bridge are two of the three bridges across the East River linking Brooklyn with Manhattan. The most prominent structure of the Manhattan skyline is the 102-story Empire State Building.

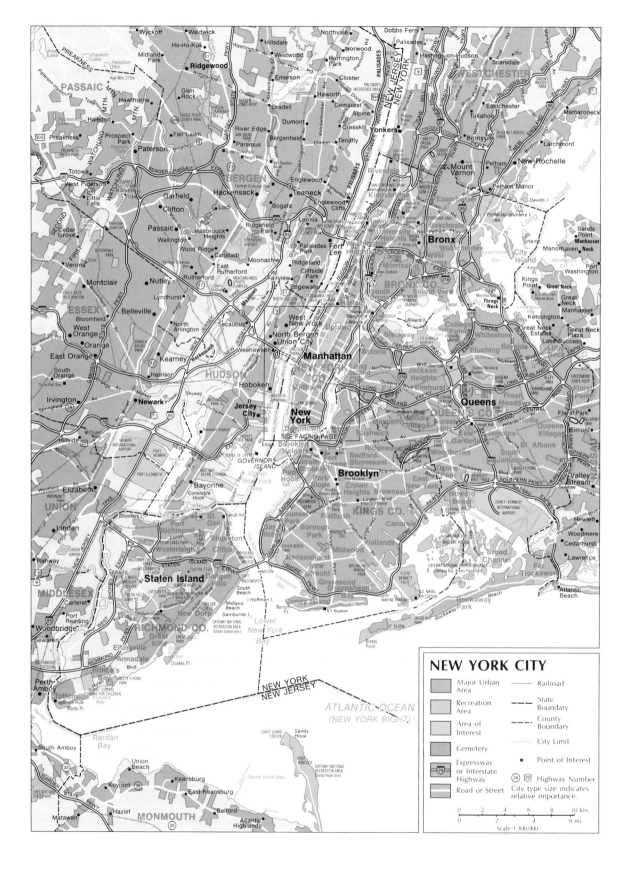

NEW YORK CITY

	Major Urban Area	——	Railroad
	Recreation Area	– – –	State Boundary
	Area of Interest	- - -	County Boundary
	Cemetery		City Limit
	Expressway or Interstate Highway	■	Point of Interest
	Road or Street	24 22	Highway Number

City type size indicates relative importance.

0   2   4   6   8   10 km
0   2   4   6 mi
Scale 1:300,000

Contemporary City

New York's ethnic composition is unusually diverse. The black community, 2,102,512 persons (1990), is the largest in the United States. Many blacks live in HARLEM, a section of Manhattan north of Central Park. The world's largest Jewish population lives in the metropolitan New York area. Both Little Italy and Chinatown are located in Lower Manhattan. Other major foreign-born groups include Russians, English, Irish, and Poles. Hispanics and Asians constitute the latest large-scale immigrant groups to settle in New York.

Economy. New York is the location of the headquarters for many leading U.S. business firms, as well as the U.S. television and radio broadcasting industry. Most banks and brokerage firms and the exchanges—the New York and American stock exchanges, the commodity exchanges, and the maritime exchange—are found in the WALL STREET area, a world financial center. The city is also the largest wholesale trade center in the United States. Retail trade in New York is centered in midtown Manhattan. The Bronx and Brooklyn also have important wholesaling and retailing districts. The city has more than 1,000 advertising agencies, many located on Madison Avenue. More than a third of the city's work force is engaged in tertiary or service occupations.

The garment and publishing industries are the two largest and best-known industries in New York, and petrochemicals, processed foods, metal goods, electrical machinery, and leather goods are also produced. New York attracts about 17 million tourists annually, who make a major contribution to the city's income.

Transportation. A hub of U.S. and world transportation, New York has one of the world's finest natural harbors. The port handled more than 155 million U.S. tons of cargo in 1990. The Port Authority of New York and New Jersey was established in 1921 by the two states in order to administer jointly the shared waterfront.

The city's major air-transportation facilities are the John F. Kennedy International Airport and La Guardia Airport, both of which are located in the borough of Queens. They are supplemented by Newark (N.J.) International Airport.

Pennsylvania Station and Grand Central Terminal in Manhattan are the chief rail terminals. The subway network serves all boroughs except Staten Island, which has a separate above-ground transit system. The boroughs are joined to each other and to New Jersey by tunnels and bridges. A ferry service links Manhattan and Staten Island.

Government and Education. New York's charter provides for a mayor, elected at large; five borough presidents; and a city council. The city operates the nation's largest public education system, with nearly 1,000 schools. The City University of New York (see NEW YORK, CITY UNIVERSITY OF) comprises 18 senior and junior colleges. Among the private universities are COLUMBIA, FORDHAM, NEW YORK, YESHIVA, and BARNARD COLLEGE. More than 100 hospitals and several major medical-research centers, including Rockefeller University and the Memorial Sloan-Kettering Cancer Center, are located in New York City.

Points of Interest. One of New York's most famous streets, Broadway begins in lower Manhattan at Battery Park and traverses the island for its entire length. Downtown, Broadway passes through the Wall Street and City Hall areas. At Broadway and 34th Street, Macy's, one of the world's largest department stores, marks the heart of the garment district. Seventh Avenue intersects Broadway immediately north of 42d Street at Times Square, the city's center for the legitimate theater.

Farther north on Broadway, between 62d and 66th Streets, is LINCOLN CENTER FOR THE PERFORMING ARTS. In the Columbia University area, north of 110th Street, is the Cathedral of SAINT JOHN THE DIVINE, the largest Gothic-style cathedral in the world. At the heart of Manhattan is CENTRAL PARK.

Fifth Avenue is known for its department stores and elegant residences. It is also the site of several world-famous art museums: the Frick Collection, the GUGGENHEIM MUSEUM, and the METROPOLITAN MUSEUM OF ART. Other New York museums include the American Museum of Natural History, the MUSEUM OF MODERN ART, and the Whitney Museum of American Art. SAINT PATRICK'S CATHEDRAL is across Fifth Avenue from ROCKEFELLER CENTER. The NEW YORK PUBLIC LIBRARY, with its major branch at 42d Street and Fifth Avenue, is one of the great research libraries of the world. The EMPIRE STATE BUILDING, at 34th Street and Fifth Avenue, was the world's tallest building from 1931 to 1971. Lower Fifth Avenue ends in Washington Square Park, a focal point of the area known as GREENWICH VILLAGE, long associated with the city's artistic community. South of Greenwich Village lies SoHo, also an artists' and writers' neighborhood. Lower Manhattan is the location of the WOOLWORTH BUILDING, the WORLD TRADE CENTER (its twin towers are the tallest buildings in the city), and Fraunces Tavern (1719). The United Nations Headquarters is on the East River at 42d Street.

The city's park system includes the BRONX ZOO; Central, Prospect, and Van Cortlandt parks; and botanical gardens in Brooklyn and the Bronx. Professional teams in basketball, hockey, baseball, and football, playing at Madison Square Garden, Shea Stadium, and Yankee Stadium, help make sports one of the major businesses in the city.

History

The New York area was probably visited in 1524 by Giovanni da Verrazano. In 1609, Henry Hudson explored the area before sailing up the river that now bears his name. The first Dutch settlers arrived on Manhattan in 1624. A more permanent settlement was made in 1625 and named New Amsterdam. The following year the island was bought from the local Indians by Peter MINUIT for the equivalent of $24. New Amsterdam became the principal community of the Dutch colony of NEW NETHERLAND. When the English seized New Amsterdam in 1664, they renamed both the city and the colony in honor of the duke of York (later King James II) and replaced the governor, Peter STUYVESANT.

The city continued to flourish under the British as a major mercantile center. New York became a bastion of resistance to royal authority, and in 1776, George Washington established his headquarters there. He was soon driven out by the British, however, and they retained control until the end of the American Revolution.

Following the American Revolution, from 1785 to 1790, New York served as the capital of the United States. There Washington was inaugurated president in 1789. New York was also the capital of New York State until 1796, when the seat of government was moved to Albany.

During the 18th century commerce and wealth drew people to the city. New roads, schools, newspapers, hospitals, and industries were founded, and the people began to move farther north from the Battery. In 1825 the ERIE CANAL opened, further boosting the city's commercial importance. By 1830 the population had grown to 200,000.

During the 19th century thousands of European immigrants arrived annually, and many stayed in the New York area. The New York Democratic political machine—TAMMANY HALL—exploited these new arrivals, offering jobs, housing, and gifts in return for votes. Not until the mayoral administration of Fiorello LA GUARDIA in the 1930s was the power of the political machine seriously challenged.

Despite the devastating DRAFT RIOTS of 1863, New York contributed greatly to the Northern cause during the Civil War and also prospered from the war effort. In 1898, New York became Greater New York, encompassing the present five boroughs. Expansion of the city's role and responsibilities continued until the 1970s, when New York faced increasingly serious problems. The tax base was eroded as many companies moved out of the city, and the middle class continued to move to the suburbs. With rising costs the city had to curtail services. By 1981, New York had regained its financial health, but in the ensuing years it had serious problems relating to a decayed infrastructure (water pipes, bridges); official corruption; environmental and social problems, including homelessness; and crime, often associated with illegal drug abuse.

New York (state)   New York, the largest of the Middle Atlantic states, is bordered on the east by Vermont, Massachusetts, and Connecticut, on the southeast by the Atlantic Ocean, on the south by New Jersey and Pennsylvania, on the west by Lakes Erie and Ontario and the Canadian province of Ontario, and on the north by the province of Quebec. Although New York does not rank even in the top half of all the U.S. states with regard to area, its 1990 census population was second overall to that of California.

In 1664 the colony passed from Dutch to British hands and was named New York for the duke of York (later King James II). Almost from its beginnings New York has been known as the Empire State. Until recently it led all other states in population, and it still leads in wholesale trade, transportation, and finance. Since the late 1980s, the state has experienced periods of slower economic growth than other parts of the country and of rising costs for social services and education.

Land and Resources

The ADIRONDACK MOUNTAINS, part of the Laurentian Mountain system, in northeastern New York, constitute about a quarter of the state and rise to elevations above 1,500 m (5,000 ft). Mount Marcy, the highest point in the state, has an elevation of 1,629 m (5,344 ft). West of the Adirondacks the Tug Hill Plateau is a tableland of low relief. Northeast of the Adirondacks the St. Lawrence–Champlain lowland forms a corridor between the Great Lakes and the Atlantic Ocean.

The Hudson River originates in the Adirondacks and flows south through its 16-to-32-km-wide (10-to-20-mi) valley. The Taconic Mountains, which lie along the eastern border of the state to the east of the Hudson, reach elevations above 610 m (2,000 ft). South of the Taconics the Manhattan Hills include most of Westchester County and Manhattan Island.

West of the Hudson River the Hudson highlands, about 305 m (1,000 ft) in elevation, extend southwest. The Triassic lowland is a wedge of low, rolling terrain just south of the Hudson highlands. Their best-known feature is the PALISADES, sheer cliffs of igneous rock forming the west bank of the Hudson River. The major features west of the Hudson, however, are part of the Appalachian Mountain system, which occupies nearly half the state in the south. The eastern part of this region is known as the CATSKILL MOUNTAINS. West of the Catskills the land is hilly, the central and lowest portion of the upland consisting of the Finger Lakes Hills, characterized by deep valleys. Near the extreme southwest corner of the state are the ALLEGHENY MOUNTAINS.

Soils. A broad belt of lime-rich soils extends eastward along the Erie–Ontario Lake plain, into the Mohawk and Hudson valleys, and along parts of the St. Lawrence valley. Most of the Adirondacks, Tug Hill Plateau, and Catskills are covered by shallow acid soils. On a large part of the Appalachian Plateau soils are deep and acid. Major stream valleys are generally composed of relatively fertile alluvial soils.

Climate. Mean annual precipitation for most of the state is about 889 to 1,143 mm (35 to 45 in). Along Lakes Erie and Ontario are belts of especially heavy snowfall. The Tug Hill Plateau, for example, receives more than 4,445 mm (175 in) of snow each winter—the heaviest snowfall east of the Rocky Mountains. Generally, January mean temperatures in the state are below 0° C (32° F), except in the New York City area, and July mean temperatures are about 21° C (70° F).

Rivers and Lakes. East of the Adirondacks is Lake CHAMPLAIN, on the border between New York and Vermont, and just south of it is Lake GEORGE. The FINGER LAKES are in central New York, and northeast of Syracuse is Lake Oneida.

New York's largest drainage basin consists of the Great Lakes–St. Lawrence systems, which carry the waters of much of western, central, and northeastern New York. The NIAGARA RIVER as well as the Genesee and the Black rivers are in this system. The HUDSON RIVER system drains

AT A GLANCE

NEW YORK

Land: Area: 141,089 km^2 (54,475 mi^2); rank: 27th. Capital: Albany (1990 pop., 101,082). Largest city: New York (1990 pop., 7,322,564). Counties: 62. Elevations: highest—1,629 m (5,344 ft), at Mount Marcy; lowest—sea level, at the Atlantic coast.

People: Population (1990): 18,044,505; rank: 2d; density: 147.1 persons per km^2 (381 per mi^2). Distribution (1990): 84.3% urban, 15.7% rural. Average annual change (1980–90): +0.28%.

Government (1993): Governor: Mario M. Cuomo, Democrat. U.S. Congress: Senate—1 Democrat, 1 Republican; House—18 Democrats, 13 Republicans. Electoral college votes: 33. State legislature: 61 senators, 150 representatives.

Economy: State personal income (1989): $378.3 billion; rank: 2d. Median family income (1989): $39,741; rank: 10th. Agriculture: income (1989)—$2.86 billion. Fishing: value (1989)—$51 million. Lumber production (1991): 380 million board feet. Mining (nonfuel): value (1988)—$696 million. Manufacturing: value added (1987)—$80 billion. Services: value (1987)—$114.1 billion.

Miscellany: Statehood: July 26, 1788; the 11th state. Nickname: Empire State; tree: sugar maple; motto: *Excelsior* ("Ever Upward"); song: "I Love New York."

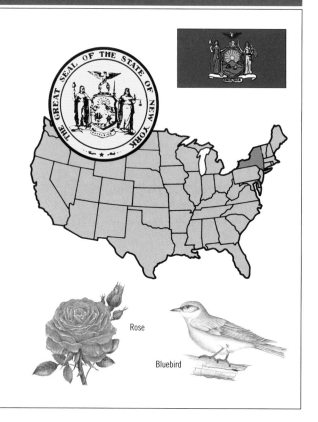

Rose

Bluebird

---

parts of eastern New York, reaching the Atlantic Ocean at New York Bay. Its largest tributary is the MOHAWK RIVER. Southwestern New York is drained by the ALLEGHENY RIVER system, which reaches the Gulf of Mexico by way of the Ohio and Mississippi rivers. Central New York is drained by the SUSQUEHANNA RIVER and its tributaries and by the DELAWARE RIVER basin, both flowing into Chesapeake Bay.

Vegetation and Animal Life. Trees cover 60% of the state. In the southeast oaks predominate, and in the higher Adirondacks spruce and fir predominate. Birch, sugar maple, basswood, ash, and yellow birch comprise the majority of trees in the rest of the state. Oaks are intermingled with the northern hardwoods in the Finger Lakes region and the Hudson Valley; the Ontario and St. Lawrence plains have an abundance of elm and red maple.

Animals commonly found in the state are the fox, raccoon, opossum, woodchuck, muskrat, deer, rabbit, and squirrel. The many species of birds that inhabit the region include the predatory hawks, eagles, and owls.

Resources. New York is endowed with adequate supplies of both surface and groundwater. The Adirondack region has some of the state's richest mineral deposits, such as iron, lead, and zinc. Petroleum and natural gas

are found near Lake Erie. New York's fertile valleys and plains produce varied agricultural products, especially fruit and dairy products. Commercial fishing is an important industry off Long Island.

People

The average population density is 142 per km^2 (367 per mi^2), but density ranges from less than 1 per km^2 (3 per mi^2) to more than 25,915 per km^2 (67,006 per mi^2) on Manhattan. More than 60% of the state's population are concentrated in the New York City urban area, and over 90% of the total population are urban. Other major urban areas include BUFFALO, ROCHESTER, SYRACUSE, ALBANY (the state capital), NIAGARA FALLS, UTICA, SCHENECTADY, BINGHAMTON, and TROY.

In 1990 the nonwhite population in the state was 25.6%, ranging from 48% in New York City to 5% in Binghamton. Blacks numbered 2,859,055 (15.9% of the population), Hispanics 2,214,026 (12.3%), and Asians and Pacific Islanders 693,760 (3.9%). The state's American Indian population was 62,651. Between 1980 and 1989, 854,000 immigrants, most of them from Latin America, the Caribbean, and Asia, settled in New York City alone. Roman Catholics make up by far the most nu-

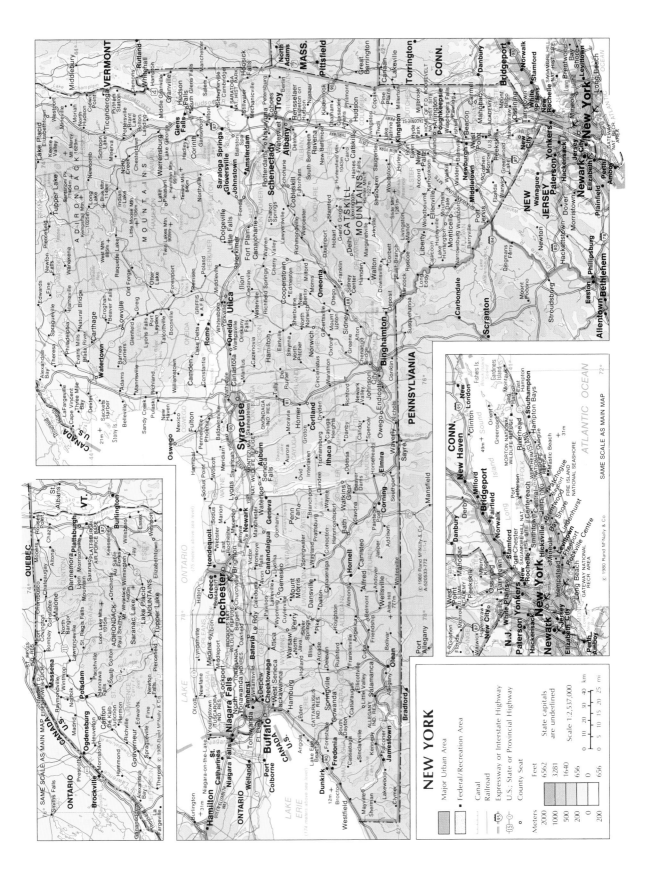

NEW YORK

Major Urban Area

Federal/Recreation Area

Canal

Railroad

Expressway or Interstate Highway

U.S., State or Provincial Highway

County Seat

State capitals are underlined

Scale 1:2,537,000

Meters	Feet	
2000	6562	
1000	3281	
500	1640	
200	656	
0	0	
200	656	

0 10 20 30 40 km
0 5 10 15 20 25 mi

© 1980 Rand McNally & Co.
A-500533-772-1-1-1

SAME SCALE AS MAIN MAP

© 1980 Rand McNally & Co.

The Bear Mountain Bridge spans the Hudson River at Bear Mountain State Park, a popular recreation area near New York City. The Hudson is one of the most commercially trafficked rivers in the northeast.

merous religious group in the state. The Jewish population is over 10% of the total.

Education. Education in New York is the responsibility of the 16 regents of the University of the State of New York, a body formed in 1784. Libraries, museums, and historical sites are regulated by the regents, and all professions, except law, are under their direction. The State University of New York (SUNY) was created in 1948 (see NEW YORK, STATE UNIVERSITY OF). The City University of New York (see NEW YORK, CITY UNIVERSITY OF) is also a public system. Private institutions of higher education in the state include COLUMBIA UNIVERSITY, FORDHAM UNIVERSITY, and NEW YORK UNIVERSITY, in New York City; CORNELL UNIVERSITY at ITHACA; SARAH LAWRENCE COLLEGE in Bronxville; SKIDMORE COLLEGE in SARATOGA SPRINGS; and VASSAR COLLEGE in Poughkeepsie; as well as the UNITED STATES MILITARY ACADEMY at West Point and the UNITED STATES MERCHANT MARINE ACADEMY at Kings Point.

Cultural Institutions. New York City is the focus of much of the nation's cultural and artistic life. In addition, Albany has the New York State Museum and the Albany Institute of History and Art. Binghamton has the Roberson Center for the Arts and Sciences; Buffalo has the Albright-Knox Art Gallery and the Buffalo Museum of Science. Corning has the famous Corning Glass Center, and the Rockwell-Corning Museum. In Rochester is the International Museum of Photography at George Eastman House, the Rochester Museum and Science Center, and the Memorial Art Gallery.

Historic Sites. New York has many restored colonial homes and historic sites, among them Sunnyside, the home of Washington Irving, in Tarrytown. The Franklin Delano Roosevelt National Historic Site in HYDE PARK is open to the public. The National Baseball Hall of Fame and Museum is in COOPERSTOWN. Fort TICONDEROGA, on the shores of Lake Champlain, has been restored.

The major vacation areas are NIAGARA FALLS, the Adirondack and Catskill mountains, the Finger Lakes and Great Lakes, Long Island, and New York City. The Catskill Park includes some of the wildest country in the Northeast. Fire Island is a National Seashore.

New York has several major sports teams, including the New York Jets and the Buffalo Bills (football); the New York Yankees and Mets (baseball); the New York Knickerbockers (basketball); and the New York Rangers, New York Islanders, and Buffalo Sabres (hockey).

Economic Activity

New York leads the nation in the banking, securities, and communications industries. Financial activities—including insurance—and real estate are the most important segments of the service industries. Manufacturing maintains great importance, but agriculture, mining, and forestry and fishing contribute only small amounts to the gross state product.

Manufacturing. New York is a leading manufacturing state. Buffalo specializes in heavy industry, and Rochester is the national leader in the manufacture of photographic and optical equipment. Syracuse produces primary metals, machinery, and paper; Utica-Rome, machinery and transportation equipment; Albany-Troy-Schenectady, paper; and Binghamton, computers and business machines. New York City is noted for its garment and publishing industries as well as for food processing. Leading industries statewide include making women's outerwear, publishing and printing periodicals, producing electronic components and computers and office machines, book publishing and printing, and manufacturing communications equipment.

Agriculture. New York ranks in the mid-range of U.S. states in the value of its agricultural production. Dairy products account for the bulk of all farm income. Important crops include apples, hay and corn for silage, and vegetables from truck farms.

Mining. Much of the value of New York's mineral production comes from nonmetallic minerals, including cement, stone, clays, sand and gravel, gypsum, garnets, salt, talc, and petroleum. New York is virtually the only U.S. producer of wollastonite (a paper and paint filler) and of emery. Metals include lead, zinc, iron, and silver.

Energy. Hydroelectric sources account for about one-quarter of the power generated in New York. Of the thermal power sources, about one-third comes from oil-fired plants and the remainder is more-or-less evenly divided among coal-fired plants, gas-fired units, and nuclear power plants.

Forestry and Fishing. New York's lumber production is centered in the Adirondacks and consists chiefly of softwoods. Elsewhere in the state hardwood is cut for specialized uses. New York also produces limited quantities of wood pulp.

Commercial fishing yields a small revenue, with marine fisheries around Long Island producing a variety of fish and shellfish.

Tourism. Tourism and recreation contribute much to the state's economy. Multitudes visit New York City, but many millions of tourists are attracted annually by the numerous state parks, campgrounds, and historical sites elsewhere in the state.

Transportation. New York has an extensive network of highways and roads, including the world's longest toll superhighway, the Gov. Thomas E. Dewey Thruway, with a length of 899 km (558 mi). A pioneering railroad state, New York has several thousand miles of railroad track traversing it.

The NEW YORK STATE BARGE CANAL system is a state-operated waterway totaling 840 km (522 mi). Other major navigable waterways are the Hudson River, the St. Lawrence River (via the Seaway), and Lakes Erie and Ontario. The port of New York is one of the world's biggest and busiest. Buffalo is a leading Great Lakes port.

With nearly 500 airports, New York can handle seaplanes and helicopters as well as long-distance aircraft. Besides the 3 New York City airports—Kennedy, La Guardia, and Newark (N.J.)—other large airports are Greater Buffalo International, Rochester-Monroe County, Syracuse Hancock International, and Albany County.

Government

The state government is organized under the constitution adopted in 1894, with subsequent amendments. The executive branch of government consists of the governor, elected to a 4-year term, assisted by 3 other elected officials—the lieutenant governor, the comptroller, and the attorney general.

The legislature consists of two houses, the senate and assembly. The 61 senators and 150 assemblymen are elected to two-year terms in even-numbered years.

New York is organized into 12 judicial districts; voters in each district elect varying numbers of justices to 14-year terms. These justices—more than 300 in all—form the supreme court; they sit individually. The appellate division of the supreme court is organized into 4 judicial departments with justices chosen by the governor. The court of appeals is the highest state court. It consists of a chief judge and 6 associates elected for 14-year terms.

Albany's capitol is seen at the far end of the new Empire State Plaza, a magnificent mall constructed to rejuvenate the city's downtown area.

A lighthouse dominates the coast of Montauk Point, New York's most easterly extremity. A state park surrounding the point offers such recreation as swimming, surf casting, deep-sea fishing, and hiking.

Local government exists in counties, cities, towns, villages, and special districts, the largest of which is the Port of New York Authority. Most cities and villages are governed by a mayor and a council.

History

Two Indian groups occupied what is now New York State when Europeans began exploration and settlement. ALGONQUINS, composed of several tribes, occupied much of the Hudson Valley, Manhattan, and Long Island, while the Iroquois controlled most of the rest of the state area. About 1570 the Iroquois formed the IROQUOIS LEAGUE, consisting of the CAYUGA, MOHAWK, ONEIDA, ONONDAGA, and SENECA tribes. The league dominated or conquered many other tribes in the region. In 1722 the TUSCARORA were added to the confederation.

The Colonial Period. This era began with the exploration of the Hudson River; Giovanni da VERRAZANO is believed to have sailed into New York Bay in 1524. In 1609, Henry HUDSON sailed as far as present-day Albany in the service of the Dutch. The first settlement was Fort Nassau (1614–18) at present-day Albany. In 1621 the DUTCH WEST INDIA COMPANY was chartered and empowered to establish the colony of NEW NETHERLAND. Between 1624 and 1626 a series of Dutch forts were established along the Hudson, from Fort Amsterdam on Manhattan to Fort Orange (replacing Fort Nassau) at Albany.

In 1664 the British sent a fleet to New York Harbor, and Peter STUYVESANT, the Dutch governor, surrendered the colony to the British, who renamed it New York after the duke of York. In 1664, New Jersey was separated from the rest of the colony. The boundary between New York and Connecticut was established basically as it exists today in 1665.

In 1688, New York and New Jersey were combined with the New England colonies in the Dominion of New England under Sir Edmund ANDROS. News of the Glorious Revolution in England and the overthrow of Andros in Boston encouraged a rebellion in New York led by Jacob LEISLER. He won control and ruled the colony for 2 years (1689–91) before royal authority was restored.

New York was a pivotal colony during the FRENCH AND INDIAN WARS. Its location near Canada exposed the colony to French attack, and British armies launched attacks on Montreal and Quebec from Albany. The final defeat of the French in 1761 established British control over what is now New York State.

New York also occupied a strategic position during the American Revolution. About a third of the major battles were fought in the state. To thwart the British drive for control of New York City, Gen. George WASHINGTON tried unsuccessfully in August 1776 to defend it against superior British forces led by Sir William HOWE. A series of battles lasted 3 months, and then the conflict shifted to New Jersey and Pennsylvania. The British drive along the Mohawk was thwarted by their defeat at the Battle of Oriskany, near Fort Stanwix (present-day Rome), in August 1777. In July 1777 the British general John BURGOYNE captured Crown Point, Ticonderoga, and Fort Edward. In October the Americans and British met in a decisive battle at Bemis Heights near Saratoga, where Burgoyne was forced to surrender (see SARATOGA, BATTLES OF).

Statehood and Economic Growth. During the Revolution a constitution was adopted in April 1777, creating New York State with its temporary capital at Kingston. In 1797, Albany became the capital. Alexander HAMILTON and John JAY, leaders of the New York delegation to the Constitutional Convention, were supporters of adoption of the federal Constitution. New York became the 11th of the 13 original states to ratify the new constitution on July 26, 1788.

By the end of the first quarter of the 19th century New York was exporting agricultural goods; manufacturing flourished; and New York City had become a leading trade and industrial center. Part of this growth resulted from the expansion of transportation facilities. In addition to the natural waterways, a system of turnpikes spread across the state. The ERIE CANAL, linking the Hudson River with Lake Erie, was completed in 1825. The first railway opened (1831) between Albany and Schenectady, and within another 25 years most parts of the state were linked by rail. Robert FULTON's first successful steamboat appeared on the Hudson River in 1807. By 1820, New York led all other states in population, and by 1850 it was the leading manufacturing state.

A democratization of New York society took place during the 1830s and '40s; suffrage was extended, and after the bitter ANTIRENT WAR, tenant farmers were given the opportunity to own the land they farmed. Slavery was abolished and women's rights, temperance, and educational and prison reform were pursued. Many of the nation's leaders arose in New York at this time, among them De Witt Clinton (see CLINTON family), Martin VAN BUREN, and William H. SEWARD. Horace GREELEY, another notable New Yorker, was among the leaders of the antislavery movement as the country moved toward the Civil War. During the war 500,000 New Yorkers fought, and 50,000 of them were killed.

After the war, economic development in New York proceeded at a rapid pace. Urbanization was also rapid, with huge numbers of immigrants from Europe pouring into the state. Along with these developments came such social ills as corporate malpractice, political corruption, unjust labor conditions, and inadequate social services.

Into this situation stepped the political institution known as TAMMANY HALL. In the 1780s a largely middle-class group was formed to combat the aristocratic Revolutionary leaders. By the mid-19th century the group was firmly in the hands of Irish politicians who dominated New York City politics, culminating in the control of the Democratic machine after 1868 by William Marcy TWEED. Republican control of upstate politics intensified the conflict, and such nationally prominent New Yorkers as Samuel J. TILDEN, Grover CLEVELAND, Theodore ROOSEVELT, Franklin D. ROOSEVELT, and Charles Evans HUGHES fought for reform of this machine. Investigations, such as the Seabury Commission (1931–32), and the mayoral administration of Fiorello H. LA GUARDIA (1934–45) in New York City saw the eventual curtailment of Tammany Hall power.

The Modern Era. Since World War II the gap between New York City and the upstate region has not closed. The city remains the focus of much of the economic, financial, and cultural life of the nation. The deepening financial woes of the nation's cities, with eroding tax bases and increasing needs for social services, make it likely that the state and New York City will become more closely linked.

Concern for the environment intensified during the 1960s as two Pure Waters Bond Acts were approved. Later, other programs made possible the acquisition of more forest wetlands, urban parks, and other ecologically or recreationally valuable areas and provided funding for the cleaning up of hazardous waste sites.

New York, City University of In 1961 the public liberal arts senior colleges of New York City came under the jurisdiction of the City University of New York Board of Higher Education. Several other colleges have been formed since that date. Until 1976, when tuition was imposed, the schools provided quality education free of charge to city residents who could not normally afford it. All the four-year colleges are coeducational. The colleges of CUNY are: **Bernard M. Baruch** (founded 1968), **City** (1847), **CUNY Graduate School and University Center** (1961), **Hunter** (1870), and **John Jay College of Criminal Justice** (1964)—all in Manhattan; **Lehman** (1931) in the Bronx; **College of Staten Island** (1955); **Brooklyn** (1930), **Medgar Evers** (1969), and **New York City Technical College**, all three in Brooklyn; **Queens** (1937), in Flushing; and **York** (1966), in Jamaica. The **Mount Sinai School of Medicine** (1963), in Manhattan, is also part of CUNY. There are also six community colleges in the system.

New York, State University of The State University of New York (SUNY) was established in 1948 to encompass all state-supported but unaffiliated colleges and universities outside New York City, whose public colleges and universities form part of the City University of New York (CUNY) system.

SUNY includes 4 university centers, 13 state colleges, and agricultural, technical, community, and specialized colleges. A board of trustees appointed by the governor controls the university system, and each constituent school has its own president. All the state schools are co-educational, and all four-year schools grant the bachelor's degree. Most award the master's degree, but the doctorate is given only by the university centers.

The university centers, which grant all undergraduate and graduate degrees, are at **Albany** (established 1844), which has schools or colleges of liberal arts, nursing, business, public affairs, library science, and education; **Binghamton** (1946), which has schools of liberal arts, nursing, education, and management; **Buffalo** (1846), with programs in liberal arts and schools of architecture, management, education, library studies, social work, and a Health Science Center; and **Stony Brook** (1957), with colleges of liberal arts and engineering and a Health Science Center.

Among the specialized schools within the state system are the **College of Environmental Science and Forestry** in Syracuse; the **New York Maritime College** in the Bronx; and the **Fashion Institute of Technology** in New York City. Colleges of Agriculture and Life Sciences, Human Ecology, and Veterinary Medicine, and the School of Industrial and Labor Relations at CORNELL UNIVERSITY are also divisions of SUNY.

New York City Ballet   The New York City Ballet (NYCB) has been the most consistently creative of American classical ballet companies since its inception in 1946—as the Ballet Society, until renamed in 1948. For many years the chief outlet for the choreographic genius of George BALANCHINE, NYCB, which began as a subscription venture without a permanent home, was brought

Peter Martins, a principal dancer, choreographer, and ballet master in chief of the New York City Ballet, is seen with other members of the company in a performance of George Balanchine's Stars and Stripes.

about through the efforts of Lincoln KIRSTEIN, the company's general director until 1989. In 1948 it accepted the city's invitation to become the resident company of New York City's Center Theater and in 1964 moved triumphantly into the New York State Theater in Lincoln Center for the Performing Arts.

A number of diverse choreographers have created works for the company, including Sir Frederick ASHTON, Antony TUDOR, Martha GRAHAM, Merce CUNNINGHAM, John Cranko, and John Taras. From 1949 to 1956, Jerome ROBBINS created several ballets for NYCB, among them the popular *Afternoon of a Faun* (1953), *The Cage* (1951), and *The Concert* (1956). In 1969, Robbins returned to the company, this time as ballet master, a position he shared with Balanchine and Taras. In the subsequent two decades he devoted most of his creative energies to NYCB, and served as co–ballet master in chief along with dancer-choreographer Peter MARTINS from 1983 until 1990, when Martins assumed sole control.

The company's principal claim to worldwide fame, however, is its repertoire of Balanchine ballets, a corpus of enormous richness and variety that ranges from the coolly classical *Concerto Barocco* (1941), to such daring extensions of classicism as *Agon* (1958), the experimental *Ivesiana* (1954), or the romantic *Vienna Waltzes*.

Through the School of American Ballet, founded in 1933, Balanchine was able to train a succession of brilliant dancers as the instruments of his creative will.

New York City Opera   A part of the New York City Center of Music and Drama, the New York City Opera made its debut in February 1944, in the center's building on West 55th Street, where it remained until February 1966. The company's objective is to offer adventurous repertory at modest prices; it has successfully explored the history of opera from Claudio Monteverdi to Hans Werner Henze. Laszlo Halász was the company's first artistic director (1943–51), followed by Joseph Rosenstock (1952–55), Erich LEINSDORF (1956), Julius Rudel (1957–79), and Beverly SILLS (1979–89), one of the outstanding singers whose careers were launched or furthered by the City Opera. During Rudel's long tenure the company moved to its present quarters, the New York State Theater at Lincoln Center, and gained considerably in stature. Eschewing the lavish sets and imported "star" singers favored by the Metropolitan Opera, the company emphasizes acting and a disciplined ensemble. From its beginnings the company has championed the cause of American composers and performers.

New York Philharmonic   The oldest of the orchestras still in existence in the United States was founded by the violinist Ureli Corelli Hill in April 1842 as the Philharmonic Society of New York. Its first concert took place on December 7 of the same year in the Apollo Rooms on Broadway. In 1866, Carl Bergmann emerged as the orchestra's first permanent conductor; his 19th-century successors included Leopold Damrosch, Theodore Thomas,

Anton Seidl, and Emil Paur. In the 20th century the Philharmonic's regular conductors and musical advisors have included Walter Damrosch (1902–03), Wassily Safonoff (1906–09), Gustav Mahler (1909–11), Joseph Stransky (1911–23), Willem Mengelberg (1921–30), Arturo Toscanini (1927–36), John Barbirolli (1937–42), Artur Rodzinski (1943–47), Bruno Walter (1947–49), Dimitri Mitropoulos (1949–57), Leonard Bernstein (1957–69, subsequently named laureate conductor for life), Pierre Boulez (1971–78), and Zubin Mehta (from 1978). Kurt Masur has been named to succeed Mehta in 1992.

Performing in nine different halls before 1892, the orchestra began in that year a long residence in Carnegie Hall; in 1962 it first occupied its current home, Philharmonic Hall (now Avery Fisher Hall) in Lincoln Center.

New York Public Library   The New York Public Library was created in 1895 by combining the Astor and Lenox libraries and the Tilden Trust. The first of these was founded in 1848 under the will of John Jacob ASTOR and opened to the public in 1854. The second was composed of the books and paintings collected by James Lenox (1800–80) and opened in 1887, and the third was established (1895) from the bequest of Samuel J. TILDEN.

The city of New York erected a building for the new library, which opened on May 23, 1911, with a stock of 1.2 million volumes. The library now contains about 44 million catalogued items, and its circulation facilities include about 80 branches. The Lincoln Center Library has the Dance, Music, and Theater Collections as well as the Rodgers and Hammerstein Archives of Recorded Sound. The central Harlem branch houses the Schomburg Center for Research in Black Culture.

New York State Barge Canal   The New York State Barge Canal is an 845-km (525-mi) inland waterway system within New York State. The system, completed in 1918, is dominated by the ERIE CANAL. The Champlain Canal connects the Erie with Lake Champlain, the Oswego Canal joins it with Lake Ontario, and the Cayuga-Seneca Canal connects it with Cayuga and Seneca lakes. A total of 57 locks enable ships to move goods to about 50 cities that serve as transshipment points to rail and truck routes.

New York Times, The   The New York Times is conceded to be the most authoritative daily newspaper in the United States. Its staff has won more Pulitzer Prizes than any other. Founded by Henry J. Raymond in 1851, the newspaper was taken over by Adolph Simon OCHS in 1896, and his descendants still run it. Arthur Ochs Sulzberger is the present publisher. A morning newspaper with a circulation (1987) of about 911,000 daily and 1,523,000 on Sundays, the New York Times is international in its outlook and progressive in its politics. Many people famous in the history of journalism have been associated with the Times, such as editor Carr Van Anda

(1864–1945), sportswriter Red SMITH, and reporter-columnists Arthur Krock (1887–1974), James RESTON, Harrison SALISBURY, and Russell BAKER. The Times played a leading role in publication of the PENTAGON PAPERS and in other tests of freedom of the press.

New York University   Established in 1831, New York University is a private coeducational institution in New York City. In addition to Washington Square College of Arts and Sciences and the Graduate School of Arts and Sciences, there are schools of law, education, business and public administration, and social work. The schools of medicine and nursing are at the medical center in Manhattan; the college of dentistry is nearby. One of America's most prestigious graduate schools of art history and archaeology is the university's Institute of Fine Arts, which also has an art conservation center.

New Zealand   [zee'-luhnd]   New Zealand, an island nation in the middle latitudes of the Southern Hemisphere, is the most physically isolated of the industrialized countries. Its nearest neighbor, Australia, is about 1,900 km (1,200 mi) to the northwest. New Zealand is bordered by the TASMAN SEA on the west and the South Pacific Ocean on the east. The country comprises two main islands, the North Island (114,469 km^2/44,197 mi^2) and the South Island (150,660 km^2/58,170 mi^2); Stewart Island (1,751 km^2/676 mi^2); and numerous tiny islands and islets, including the ANTIPODES ISLANDS and the Auckland Islands. In addition, New Zealand administers the ROSS DEPENDENCY in Antarctica and TOKELAU. NIUE and the COOK ISLANDS are self-governing, but New Zealand manages their external affairs, and their residents are citizens of New Zealand.

Land and Resources

The two major islands of New Zealand, which are separated by the narrow Cook Strait, could be considered parts of two separate continents. The North Island and the northwest corner of the South Island are carried on the same continental plate as India and Australia, while the South Island is on the Pacific plate. The two plates slide past each other in opposite directions along the Alpine Fault. This movement creates many earthquakes in New Zealand.

New Zealand is generally mountainous, with only about 30% of the land classified as flat or rolling. The North Island was shaped by internal volcanic activity and includes regions of boiling mud and steam, which are often harnessed for power and heat. The highest point on the island is Ruapehu volcano (2,797 m/9,176 ft). The South Island has about 20 peaks exceeding 3,000 m (9,840 ft). The highest, Mount Cook (3,764 m/12,349 ft), is part of the impressive Southern Alps range.

Climate.   The islands extend approximately 1,610 km (1,000 mi) from north to south, but the climate throughout the country is mild, and there is surprisingly little difference in temperature ranges between the North and the

NEW ZEALAND

Land: Area: 269,057 km^2 (103,883 mi^2). Capital: Wellington (1989 est. pop., 135,400). Largest city: Auckland (1989 est. pop.: city proper, 150,000; metropolitan area, 930,800).

People: Population (1990 est.): 3,295,866. Density: 12.2 persons per km^2 (31.7 per mi^2). Distribution (1990): 84% urban, 16% rural. Official language: English. Major religion: Christianity.

Government: Type: parliamentary democracy. Legislature: House of Representatives (Parliament). Political subdivisions: 241 boroughs, counties, and town and district councils.

Economy: GNP (1989): $40.1 billion; $10,588 per capita. Labor distribution (1990): commerce and services—37%; manufacturing—17%; agriculture and fishing—11%; construction—6%; government and public authorities—29%. Foreign trade (1990 est.): imports—$7.0 billion; exports—$9.1 billion. Currency: 1 New Zealand dollar = 100 cents.

Education and Health: Literacy (1987): virtually 100% of adult population. Universities (1987): 7. Hospital beds (1989): 29,352. Physicians (1987): 6,390. Life expectancy (1990): women—78; men—72. Infant mortality (1990): 10 per 1,000 live births.

South islands. January and February are the warmest months, and July is the coldest. Westerly winds from the Tasman Sea bring frequent rain. The North Island generally receives about 150 days of rain a year; the South Island averages 100 days. The South Island has both the wettest (the Southern Alps) and the driest (Central Otago) regions in the country.

Drainage. There are numerous lakes and rivers in New Zealand. The country's largest lake is Lake Taupo (606 km^2/243 mi^2), a crater lake on the North Island. Also on the North Island is the country's longest river, the Waikato. Most lakes and rivers on the South Island are fed by snow and glacier melts from the Southern Alps.

Plant and Animal Life. Scientists believe that New Zealand was once part of a supercontinent known as Gondwanaland and that its flora and fauna evolved in isolation for more than 100 million years after this land mass broke apart. About 84% of the country's native plants are found nowhere else. They include two of the world's oldest known plant forms, the puka and the kauri tree. Today's forests are dominated by evergreen beech and conifers.

New Zealand's isolation also had a profound impact on its animal life. Before the Maori arrived in about AD 900, there were only birds, lizards, frogs, and two species of bats on the islands. The tuatara is the only reptile that has survived since the age of the dinosaurs. With no predators, numerous species of flightless birds also flour-

ished. The kiwi, kakapo, and takatre can still be found in the forests; other species, such as the huge moas, were hunted to extinction by human beings and by predators introduced by humans.

Resources. New Zealand's most fertile soils are found in the Canterbury Plains near Christchurch and the Southland-Otego alluvial plains at the southern end of the South Island. New Zealand has more than 3 billion tons of coal reserves and abundant offshore natural-gas reserves. The country is also rich in hydroelectric potential. It was thought to lack petroleum until 1988, when a field estimated to contain 40 million barrels of petroleum was discovered in the western part of the North Island. Other resources include geothermal energy, iron sands, and limestone.

People

New Zealand is one nation and two peoples and is only now coming to grips with its biculturalism. The initial MAORI settlers are far outnumbered by people of European descent, primarily of English and Scottish heritage. The *pakeha* (the Maori word for European settlers) make up 86% of the total population. Maori constitute approximately 9%, and other Pacific islanders 3%. Immigration to New Zealand is not significant. A recent census revealed that 85% of the residents were New Zealanders by birth, and the country suffered a net out-migration of

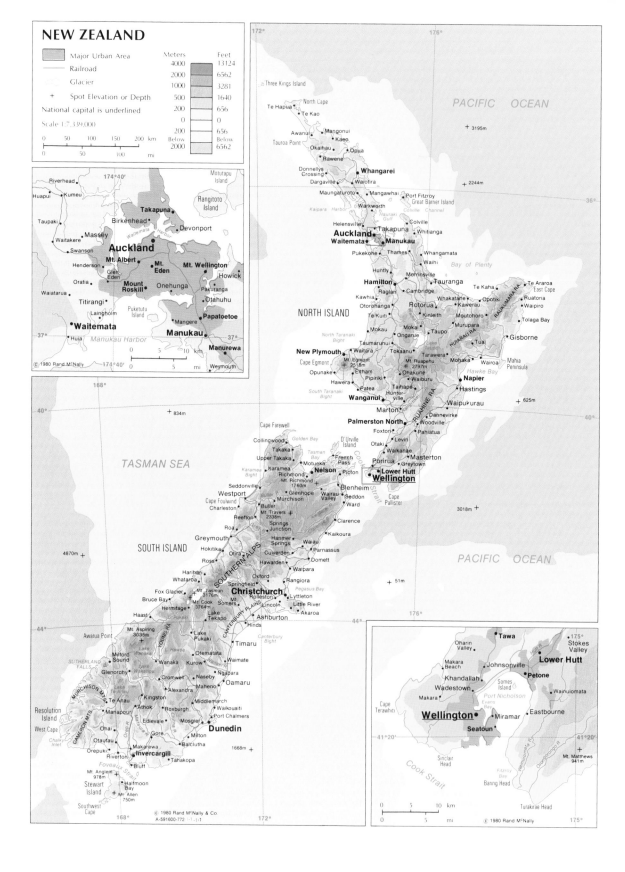

NEW ZEALAND

Major Urban Area
Railroad
Glacier
+ Spot Elevation or Depth
National capital is underlined

Scale 1:7,339,000

Meters	Feet
4000	13124
2000	6562
1000	3281
500	1640
200	656
0	0
200	656
Below 2000	Below 6562

0   50   100   150   200 km
0   50   100 mi

Auckland inset

Riverhead
Huapui
Kumeu
Taupaki
Waitakere
Massey
Swanson
Henderson
Glen Eden
Oratia
Waiatarua
Titirangi
Laingholm
Hua
Motutapu Island
Rangitoto Island
Takapuna
Birkenhead
Devonport
Waitemata Harbor
Auckland
Mt. Albert
Mt. Eden
Mount Roskill
Onehunga
Howick
Pakuranga
Otahuhu
Mangere
Puketutu Island
Waitemata
Manukau
Manukau Harbor
Papatoetoe
Manurewa
Weymouth

© 1980 Rand McNally
0   5   10 km
0   5 mi

North Island

Three Kings Island
North Cape
Te Hapua
Te Kao
Te Puia
Awanui
Mangonui
Kaeo
Okaihau
Opua
Tauroa Point
Rawene
Donnellys Crossing
Dargaville
Maungaturoto
Mangawhai
Helensville
Warkworth
Whangarei
Waiotira
Port Fitzroy
Great Barrier Island
Colville
Whitianga
Takapuna
Auckland
Waitemata
Manukau
Thames
Whangamata
Pukekohe
Waihi
Huntly
Morrinsville
Hamilton
Raglan
Cambridge
Tauranga
Te Kaha
Te Araroa
East Cape
Kawhia
Otorohanga
Rotorua
Whakatane
Kawerau
Opotiki
Ruatoria
Waipiro
Te Kuiti
Kinleith
Moutohora
Murupara
Tolaga Bay
Mokau
Mokai
Taupo
Ongarue
Lake Taupo
Gisborne
Taumarunui
Tokaanu
Tarawera
Mahia Peninsula
New Plymouth
Waitara
Mt. Egmont 2518m
Cape Egmont
Eltham
Ohakune
Waiburu
Mohaka
Wairoa
Opunake
Pipiriki
Taihape
Napier
Hawera
Patea
Hunterville
Hastings
Wanganui
Waipukurau
625m
Marton
Dannevirke
Woodville
Palmerston North
Foxton
Pahiatua
Levin
Otaki
Waikanae
Masterton
Porirua
Greytown
Lower Hutt
Wellington
Cape Palliser

South Island

834m
Cape Farewell
Collingwood
Takaka
Upper Takaka
Golden Bay
Tasman Bay
D'Urville Island
French Pass
Karamea
Richmond
Motueka
Nelson
Picton
Mt. Richmond 1760m
Blenheim
Seddonville
Glenhope
Murchison
Wairau Valley
Seddon
Westport
Buller
Ward
Cape Foulwind
Charleston
Mt. Travers 2338m
Clarence
Reefton
Springs Junction
Greymouth
Roa
Hanmer Springs
Waiau
Kaikoura
Hokitika
Otira
Culverden
Ross
Hawarden
Waipara
Harihari
Oxford
Whataroa
Springfield
Rangiora
Pegasus Bay
Fox Glacier
Mt. Tasman 3176m
Rolleston
Christchurch
Bruce Bay
Mt. Cook 3764m
Mt. Somers
Lyttelton
Hermitage
Lincoln
Little River
Haast
Lake Tekapo
Akaroa
Ashburton
Canterbury Plains
Hinds
Mt. Aspiring 3035m
Lake Pukaki
Canterbury Bight
Awarua Point
Lake Wanaka
Otematata
Waimate
Milford Sound
Wanaka
Kurow
Timaru
Glenorchy
Lake Wakatipu
Cromwell
Naseby
Ngapara
Maheno
Oamaru
Lake Te Anau
Kingston
Alexandra
Athok
Roxburgh
Middlemarch
Waikouaiti
Te Anau
Manapouri
Edievale
Mosgiel
Port Chalmers
Resolution Island
Onai
Gore
Dunedin
West Cape
Otautau
Edievale
Milton
1668m
Chalky Inlet
Orepuki
Makarewa
Balclutha
Riverton
Invercargill
Tahakopa
Bluff
Foveaux Strait
Mt. Anglem 978m
Halfmoon Bay
Stewart Island
Mt. Allen 750m
Southwest Cape

PACIFIC OCEAN
TASMAN SEA
3195m
2244m
4870m
3018m
51m
625m

© 1980 Rand McNally & Co.
A-591600-772

Wellington inset

Oharin Valley
Makara Beach
Tawa
Stokes Valley
Johnsonville
Lower Hutt
Makara
Khandallah
Petone
Wadestown
Somes Island
Wainuiomata
Cape Terawhiti
Port Nicholson
Evans Bay
Wellington
Miramar
Eastbourne
Seatoun
Sinclair Head
Mt. Matthews 941m
Cook Strait
Baring Head
Turakirae Head

0   5   10 km
0   5 mi
© 1980 Rand McNally

Shepherds pen a herd of sheep on one of the prosperous sheep ranches of the South Island's fertile eastern plain. New Zealand ranks among the world's foremost producers of dairy products, wool, and mutton.

more than 30,000 between 1982 and 1986 due to adverse economic conditions.

The official language is English. The Maori language, which has similarities to other Pacific island languages, is widely used by the Maori and is an important factor in the Maori cultural renaissance that has occurred since the late 1960s. Christianity is the dominant religion.

Demography. About 74% of the population live on the North Island, which is often described as a town, while only 25% live on the South Island, which is considered the country. The Maori population is increasing at a more rapid rate than that of non-Maoris. New Zealand is highly urbanized, with one in four New Zealanders living in the city and suburbs of AUCKLAND, but cities are not overcrowded and the overall population density remains low. Other cities include WELLINGTON (the capital), CHRISTCHURCH, and DUNEDIN.

Education and Health. The 1877 Education Act declared free, compulsory, and secular education for all. Preschool and kindergarten are provided before five years of compulsory elementary school begin at age six. Recently, the government established Maori-language kindergartens (*kohanga reo*) for Maori children. Most children attend two years of intermediate school. During the first two years of secondary school, students follow a general curriculum; the later years are more specialized. The largest of New Zealand's six universities are Massey University (1926), in Palmerston North, and the University of Auckland (1882). University admission is open to holders of a university entrance certificate (usually a four-year secondary-school qualification), and students who qualify for university study receive government scholarships. New Zealand also has many technical institutes, community colleges, and teacher-training colleges. The government sponsors extensive continuing- and adult-education programs.

New Zealand is a social-welfare state. Citizens are eli-

gible for unemployment benefits, retirement at age 60 with a pension equaling as much as 80% of average pay, and essentially free medical care.

The Arts. New Zealanders are very aware and proud of their two cultures. A major exhibit of Maori art, *Te Maori*, was assembled for showing in the United States in 1985. New Zealanders have made and continue to make contributions of international significance to literature, the visual arts, ballet, opera, and contemporary music. Authors such as Janet Frame, Katherine MANSFIELD, Sylvia Ashton-Warner, Ian Cross, Ngaio Marsh, M. K. Joseph, and Teri Hulme and the soprano Kiri TE KANAWA have won international acclaim.

Economic Activity

New Zealand is an advanced industrial state with an economy dependent on trade. Commodities were traditionally exported to Great Britain, but today New Zealand is attempting to build new markets, particularly in the Pacific region, to increase economic self-reliance and to restructure the economy to make it more responsive to world-market forces.

Agriculture. Although fewer than 1% of New Zealand's people are farmers, agricultural production has generated most of the nation's wealth. New Zealand is the world's third largest producer and second largest exporter of wool and produces approximately 50% of the world's lamb and mutton exports. Sheep in New Zealand outnumber people by nearly 20 to 1. There are also more than 8 million cattle, and the country is the world's largest and most efficient exporter of dairy products. New Zealand is also a

The government complex in Wellington, the capital of New Zealand, includes the Parliament House (foreground) and a building known as the Beehive, which contains many of the ministerial offices.

major exporter of fresh fruit, beef, and fish. The emphasis is on marketing food for specialized markets rather than on bulk exporting.

Mining, Manufacturing, and Services. In addition to the processing of agricultural products, goods manufactured in New Zealand include light engineering products, electronic equipment, textiles, leather goods, carpets, rubber and plastic products, glassware, and pottery. About 30% of New Zealand's exports are manufactured goods, and that percentage is increasing. The mining industry is relatively small. Construction materials (sand, gravel, and rock), limestone, and coal are mined; coal is exported to Japan and Korea. New technologies are being used to convert volcanic black sands to iron and other minerals. A significant portion of the labor force is employed in public and private service industries, including tourism.

Fishing and Forestry. New Zealand's rivers and lakes support more than 50 species of freshwater fish, and sport fishing is a popular tourist attraction. The country also has an important coastal fishing industry. Forestry products are another important source of income.

Energy. To reduce its dependency on imported petroleum, New Zealand has dramatically increased its exploration for new energy sources and has begun to exploit existing energy sources more efficiently. Hydroelectric power meets nearly 75% of national electricity needs, and coal reserves are abundant. New Zealand is also exploiting its natural-gas reserves; a pipeline carries natural gas from offshore throughout the North Island. The country also has the world's first synthetic-fuels plant, which converts natural gas to methanol and then to gasoline. This satisfies about 20% of the nation's primary oil requirements. Exploration for petroleum continues, and geothermal energy fields have been harnessed to produce heat and power.

Transportation and Trade. New Zealand's cities and towns are linked by a sophisticated road system. In addition, most areas are linked by air and rail. Air New Zealand and New Zealand Railways are both government owned. There are international airports at Auckland, Wellington, and Christchurch. The chief ports are Auckland, Wellington, Tauranga, Lyttelton, and Port Chalmers.

The primary exports are agricultural commodities. Automobiles and other manufactured goods and petroleum are the leading imports. Japan, Australia, and the United States purchase about 40% of New Zealand's exports and provide a substantial percentage of its imports.

Government

New Zealand is a parliamentary democracy. Like Great Britain, it has no written constitution. The legislature, which has been unicameral since 1950, comprises 95 members who serve 3-year terms. Ninety-one are elected by universal suffrage and four are elected from Maori electoral rolls. The British monarch, represented by a governor-general, is recognized as queen of New Zealand. Executive authority rests with a cabinet headed by a prime minister. The two major political parties are the La-

bour party (founded 1916), which originated most of the nation's social welfare and labor legislation, and the National party (founded 1931), which traditionally favors personal initiative, private enterprise, and the dismantling of extensive government controls. New Zealand was the first country to enfranchise women (in 1893), and all citizens aged 18 and over are eligible to vote. Counties, boroughs, district councils, and town districts are units of local government.

History

The first inhabitants of New Zealand, the Maori, are thought to have arrived in a series of migrations beginning in the 9th century AD. When discovered in 1642 by the Dutch navigator Abel Janszoon TASMAN, the Maori were cannibals in an advanced state of Neolithic civilization. They remained virtually unknown to Europe until rediscovered in 1769 by James COOK when he circumnavigated New Zealand.

In Cook's wake came escaped convicts and settlers from the penal settlement of New South Wales in Australia, European sealers and whalers, and traders from Port Jackson (now Sydney, Australia). The early European contacts with the Maori often resulted in massacres and licentious conduct. Continuing missionary reports of the harmful effects Europeans were having on the natives persuaded the British government to appoint a resident administrator for New Zealand. The first administrator, who arrived in 1833, proved ineffective, and Britain finally decided to take possession of the islands.

This decision was strengthened by suspicious activities of the French on the South Island and more particularly by precipitous private action of the New Zealand Company, founded by Edward Gibbon WAKEFIELD, in dispatching a survey party to purchase land from the Maori. In 1839 a naval captain, William Hobson (d. 1842), was

Under the Treaty of Waitangi, signed in 1840 by representatives of Great Britain and the Maori tribes of North Island, Britain recognized Maori territorial possessions in exchange for sole purchasing rights and Maori acceptance of British sovereignty.

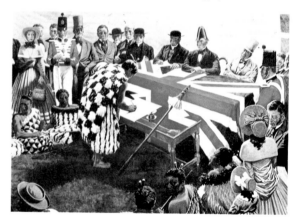

appointed lieutenant governor of New Zealand, which was then a part of New South Wales. He quickly concluded the Treaty of Waitangi (1840), by which the Maori chiefs signed over their tribal lands to Queen Victoria in return for her protection. In 1841, New Zealand became a separate colony with Hobson as governor.

European Settlement. The New Zealand Company founded the first permanent settlement at Port Nicholson (Wellington) in 1840 and later established settlements at Nelson (1841), New Plymouth (1841), Dunedin (1848), Otago (1850), and Canterbury (1850). The process of colonization led, especially on the North Island, to clashes with the Maori, who with good cause disputed the alleged purchase of land by the New Zealand Company. By the early 1870s, however, the efforts of Gov. George GREY, with the help of British troops, brought an end to the Maori Wars.

Meanwhile, the South Island, almost untroubled by land disputes, was being rapidly developed. The discovery of gold in Otago (1861) and in Westland (1865) brought not only wealth but also thousands of gold seekers to settle the land.

Self-Government. In 1846 the British Parliament passed an act (implemented 1852) providing for a General Assembly at Auckland, the capital until 1865, and six provincial councils. In 1856 cabinets became responsible to the elected legislature rather than to the governor.

By the 1870s the prosperity of the South Island and the pacification of the North Island encouraged Prime Minister Julius Vogel (1835–99) to borrow extensively from overseas for road and rail construction and the opening up of land for pasturing sheep and cattle. Obstructed in his plans by provincial councils, he abolished them in 1876 and moved the General Assembly to the new capital, Wellington.

In the 1880s falling export prices ended the spending spree begun by Vogel. Recovery was helped by the introduction of refrigerated cargo ships that stimulated production by the small farmers who were gradually transforming the now-peaceful North Island. Their greater political radicalism, moreover, enabled Liberal Prime Minister Richard J. SEDDON to make New Zealand a world leader in the introduction of progressive social reforms. These social advances contributed to New Zealand's firm refusal to join the less progressive Australian colonies in their Commonwealth Federation in 1901.

The World Wars. With years of prosperity through high export prices, New Zealand took little interest in international affairs and looked to the Royal Navy for its protection. As a token of loyalty in 1899 it sent volunteers to aid Britain in the South African War, and at the outbreak of World War I it gave immediate support in men and materials to the Allied cause. After the war New Zealand received a League of Nations mandate over ex-German Western Samoa and shared another, with Australia and Britain, over the island of Nauru.

Government-assisted migration from Britain began again in 1919 and continued until the late 1920s. The Depression of the 1930s caused severe unemployment and social distress, and rioting broke out in the cities. In 1934, small farmers and industrial workers elected the first Labour party government. Led by Michael SAVAGE, it introduced radical reforms, the most important of which was the Social Security Act of 1938.

The onset (1939) of World War II intensified demand for New Zealand's primary products. The Labour government, led by Peter Fraser (1884–1950) from 1940, dispatched an expeditionary force to join British troops, introduced conscription, and rationed essential goods. U.S. naval supremacy in the Pacific saved New Zealand from invasion after Japan entered the war in December 1941.

Postwar Governments. Since the war the National and Labour parties have vied with each other for office. The National party that came to power in 1949 under Sidney Holland (1893–1961) abolished the obsolete Legislative Council (upper house). Labour returned to office under Walter Nasy (1882–1968) in 1957. It averted an economic crisis through external loans but lost power in 1960 when it threatened sterner economies.

The new National prime minister Keith Holyoake created (1962) the unique post of OMBUDSMAN, a parliamentary commissioner whose task was to investigate complaints against government departments. Soon after Holyoake's resignation in 1972, Labour won another term under the leadership of Norman Kirk (1923–74). The National party returned to power in 1975 under Robert MULDOON, but as a national recession deepened, Labour party leader David LANGE became prime minister in 1984. Party infighting led to the resignation of Lange (August 1989) and his successor, Geoffrey Palmer (September 1990). Jim Bolger of the National party replaced Labour's Mike Moore as prime minister after his party won the October 1990 elections.

Foreign Affairs. A cultural revival among native Maori and an influx of Polynesian and Indochinese migrants have reinforced New Zealand's independent national identity as a Pacific nation, and the diversification of its overseas trade has necessitated greater interest and participation in international affairs. With its constitutional ties to Britain almost completely severed, except for the crown-appointed office of governor-general and limited appeal to the Privy Council, New Zealand has drawn closer to Australia. It was also a founding member of the now-defunct SOUTHEAST ASIA TREATY ORGANIZATION (1954) and sent combat troops to the Korean War and the Vietnam War. New Zealand advocates a nuclear-free Pacific, and its ban on visits to New Zealand ports by nuclear ships led the United States in 1985 to suspend its defense obligations to New Zealand under the ANZUS TREATY (1952).

——

Newark (Delaware) [noo'-urk]   Newark (1990 pop., 25,098), the second largest city in Delaware, is located 24 km (15 mi) southwest of Wilmington, the state's largest city. It is the site of the University of Delaware (1843). The economy is centered on a major automobile-assembly plant and light industries. Newark was founded in the late 1680s.

Newark (New Jersey)   Newark, the largest city in New Jersey and seat of Essex County, is located at the confluence of the Passaic River and Newark Bay. It is the center of northeastern New Jersey's industrial-urban complex and is part of the New York City urban area. The city has a population of 275,221 (1990); 1,824,321 (1990) persons reside in the metropolitan area.

Newark's industries produce paperboard, chemicals, leather goods, hand tools, jewelry, paint, plastics, processed foods, toys, and electrical equipment. Newark is the third largest insurance center in the United States, a banking center, a transportation hub, and the site of many state government offices. Concentrated along Newark Bay are Newark International Airport (1928), the port of Newark-Elizabeth (1914), major railroads, and a section of the interstate highway system. The port of Newark, administered by the Port Authority of New York and New Jersey, is the largest general cargo port in the nation and the largest container port in the world.

Newark is the home of the New Jersey Institute of Technology (1881), Essex County College (1966), the University of Medicine and Dentistry of New Jersey (1970), and campuses of Rutgers and Seton Hall universities. Cultural sites include Symphony Hall, the New Jersey Historical Society (1845), and the Newark Museum (1909), famous for its collection of Tibetan art. Among noteworthy historic sites are Trinity Cathedral (1743) and Plume House (1710).

Newark was founded in 1666 by colonists from Connecticut. In the 19th century it grew rapidly as a railroad and industrial center. Newark has been losing industries and jobs since the 1930s and population since 1950. Blacks became the majority race in the 1960s, a period when the city also experienced racial riots.

Newbery Medal   Named for John Newbery (1713–67), the English bookseller who was the first to publish books written for children, the Newbery Medal was established in 1921 and honors the American author of the most distinguished children's book of the year. The medal is presented annually by the American Library Association.

Newburgh   Newburgh (1990 pop., 26,454) is a city in southeastern New York on the west bank of the Hudson River, 93 km (58 mi) north of New York City. The Hudson River is deep enough at Newburgh to accommodate oceangoing vessels—the city was once a whaling town and a center for shipping. The city remains a distribution center for agricultural and dairy products; clothing, aluminum products, and paints are manufactured there. Settled in 1709, Newburgh was the headquarters (1782–83) of George Washington during the American Revolution. The building where he lived has been restored.

Newcastle   Newcastle, a city on the southeastern coast of Australia in New South Wales about 120 km (75 mi) northeast of Sydney, is located on a coastal plain at the mouth of the Hunter River. The city's population is 422,100 (1988 est.). As the major city in the extensive Hunter coalfield region, Newcastle is an important coal port, a center of the Australian iron and steel industry, and a commercial center for the region's wool, mutton, and milk. Other industries include shipbuilding and chemicals processing. The city is the seat of the University of Newcastle (1965). Newcastle was founded in 1804 as a British penal colony.

Newcastle, Thomas Pelham-Holles, 1st Duke of   Thomas Pelham-Holles, duke of Newcastle, b. July 21, 1693, d. Nov. 17, 1768, made adroit use of patronage and wielded considerable influence throughout his long political career during the period of Whig supremacy in 18th-century England. The older brother of the statesman Henry PELHAM, he inherited (1711) the vast estates of his uncle, John Holles, whose name he adopted. He was created duke in 1715. In 1724, Newcastle became a secretary of state, holding that position until 1754, when he briefly (until 1756) succeeded his brother as prime minister. He was prime minister again from 1757 to 1762, although William PITT the Elder was the de facto head of the government.

Newcastle upon Tyne [tyn]   Newcastle upon Tyne is a port city of northeastern England in the county of Tyne and Wear, on the River Tyne, about 13 km (8 mi) from the North Sea. It has a population of 279,600 (1988 est.). An important trade and shipping center, Newcastle has engineering, chemical, and petroleum-product industries and produces ships, iron and steel, soap, chemicals, and glass. It became famous in the 16th century as a shipping point for the region's coal mines. Landmarks include the 14th-century Cathedral Church of Saint Nicholas, the Guildhall (rebuilt 1655), and portions of the old town walls. The University of Newcastle upon Tyne (1963) and several museums are located there.

Newcastle dates to Roman times, when it was a military fort, Pons Aelius. A fortified castle was built in 1080 by Robert II, duke of Normandy and son of William the Conqueror, from which the settlement took its name. Since the 14th century, when a thriving textile industry developed, Newcastle has gradually emerged as one of England's most important commercial cities. Prior to 1974 it was a part of Northumberland county.

Newcomen, Thomas [noo'-kuhm-uhn]   The English ironmonger Thomas Newcomen, b. 1663, d. Aug. 5, 1729, initiated a revolution in the production of power when he developed (1712) an atmospheric STEAM ENGINE for pumping water from a Birmingham coal mine. Little is known about the inventor, but the circumstances behind his invention are clear. Coal had become an important fuel by 1700; however, traditional means of removing

AT A GLANCE

NEWFOUNDLAND

Land: Area: 405,720 km² (156,649 mi²); rank: 7th. Capital and largest city: St. John's (1991 pop., 75,770). Municipalities: 313. Elevations: highest—1,622 m (5,322 ft), at Mount Caubvick, Torngat Mountains; lowest—sea level, along the Atlantic coast.

People: Population (1991): 568,474; rank: 9th; density: 1.5 persons per km² (4.0 per mi²). Distribution (1991): 53.6% urban, 46.4% rural. Average annual change (1986–91): 0%.

Government (1992): Lieutenant Governor: Frederick W. Russell. Premier: Clyde K. Wells, Liberal. Parliament: Senate—6 members; House of Commons—5 Liberals, 2 Progressive Conservatives. Provincial legislature: 52 members. Admitted to Confederation: Mar. 31, 1949, the 10th province.

Economy: Total personal income (1990): $9.1 billion; rank: 9th. Median family income (1990): $35,334. Agriculture: farm cash receipts (1987)—$48.8 million. Fishing: value (1989)—$258.2 million. Forestry: lumber production (1988)—25.9 million board feet. Mining: value (1989)—$899 million. Manufacturing: value added (1988)—$844.8 million.

floodwater failed as coal mines grew deeper. Seeking to eliminate this problem, Newcomen and others finally produced a successful engine to pump out the water. Use of the engine spread rapidly throughout British mining districts. Newcomen's attempt to patent it, however, was blocked by a broad, earlier patent of Thomas Savery, under whose license Newcomen had to build his own engines.

Newfoundland The easternmost province of Canada, Newfoundland comprises the island of Newfoundland and the territory of LABRADOR on the mainland. Cape Spear is the island's easternmost point. The total area of the province is 405,720 km² (156,649 mi²), three times as large as the combined areas of the other MARITIME PROVINCES (Nova Scotia, New Brunswick, and Prince Edward Island). Newfoundland ranks seventh in size among the ten provinces and ninth in population, with 568,474 inhabitants (1991).

Land and Resources

Geologically, the island is an extension of the APPALACHIAN MOUNTAIN system, and Labrador comprises the eastern edge of the CANADIAN SHIELD. The interior of Labrador, a plateau, has been cut deeply by many large rivers. The coastal area is rugged and deeply indented with fjords. The highest elevations are on the north coast of Labrador, where the Torngat Mountains rise to about 1,620 m

(5,315 ft). In the west of the island the Long Range Mountains rise to 814 m (2,671 ft). The island's interior is rolling, with isolated ranges and peaks, and the eastern coasts are rugged. Located off the island's coast is the GRAND BANKS, one of the world's richest fishing beds.

Coarse and immature glacial till soils cover most of Newfoundland. Northern Labrador is mostly rocky. Boglands and heathlands are extensive in poorly drained and exposed areas.

Climate. January mean temperatures near St. John's, on Newfoundland Island, are –3.8° C (25° F). In western Labrador the January mean is –26° C (–15° F). Summers show less variation, with July mean temperatures ranging from 15° C (60° F) in the southeast to 10° C (50° F) in the northwest. During the summer, coastal areas are cooler due to the south-flowing Labrador Current. Arctic-drift ice blocks the northern areas during the winter and early spring. Precipitation totals 1,524 mm (60 in) in the southeast, grading to 432 mm (17 in) in the extreme north. Half the precipitation is snow in the north, but only about 20% falls as snow in the southeast.

Rivers and Lakes. Streams and thousands of lakes and ponds are clear and usually full. On the island, the Humber and Exploits rivers are used for floating logs to pulp and paper mills. The mighty CHURCHILL RIVER flows eastward across central Labrador and tumbles 76 m (250 ft) at Churchill Falls, where a huge hydroelectric plant is located.

Vegetation, Animal Life, and Resources. Forests cover

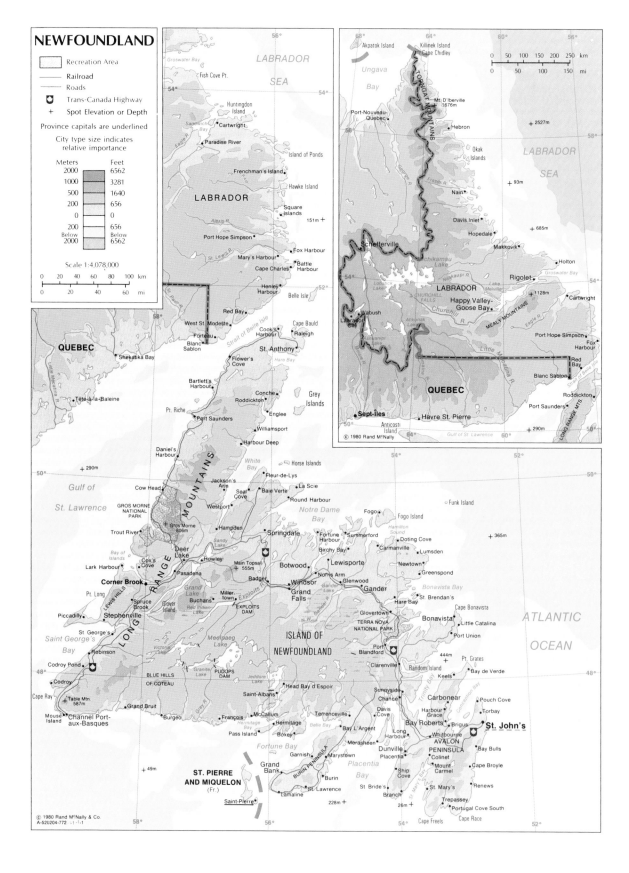

NEWFOUNDLAND

- ▭ Recreation Area
- ── Railroad
- ⸺ Roads
- ◖ Trans-Canada Highway
- + Spot Elevation or Depth

Province capitals are underlined

City type size indicates relative importance

Meters	Feet
2000	6562
1000	3281
500	1640
200	656
0	0
200	656
Below 2000	Below 6562

Scale 1:4,078,000

0 20 40 60 80 100 km

0 20 40 60 mi

© 1980 Rand McNally & Co.
A-520204-772 -1-1-1

Fish dry on a hill overlooking Hibbs Cove on the Porte de Grave Peninsula. Although Newfoundland's fishing industry has diminished during the 20th century, considerable quantities of lobster, salmon, and cod are exported.

more than 35% of the total area of the island and 30% of Labrador. Balsam fir and black spruce trees dominate. Extensive barren lands support blueberries and kalmia, and Newfoundland's numerous bogs are covered with sphagnum moss and sedges. The forests support fur-bearing animals, such as beaver, fox, lynx, and otter, as well as caribou, black bear, and moose. The rivers are rich in trout and salmon.

Newfoundland, which produces half of Canada's iron ore, has reserves exceeding 5 billion metric tons (5.5 billion U.S. tons). The province's topography and many rivers are particularly favorable for the development of hydroelectric power. Some zinc, lead, copper, gold, and silver is mined. Commercial fishing operations in cod, halibut, haddock, and flounder in the Grand Banks, as well as a commercial lobster industry, flourish.

The 1980s saw increased efforts to develop the province's offshore oil and gas resources. In 1985 test drilling near Grand Bruit raised hopes of a notably rich gold strike.

People

Newfoundland was colonized primarily by people of English and Irish stock. Population increase was slow through the early years, but a rise in opportunity during and since World War II has brought about significant expansion. The greatest population density is in the northern Avalon peninsula, where the capital, St. John's, is located. Corner Brook is located on the west coast of the island.

Education is free and compulsory for children from the ages of 7 to 16. Postsecondary education is provided by Memorial University of Newfoundland (1925) at St. John's, with a branch college in Corner Brook, and a trades college and a fisheries college, also at St. John's.

The vast areas of unspoiled and uninhabited land provide excellent opportunities for outdoor recreation. Tourism is important, and 2 national parks and numerous provincial parks provide excellent recreational facilities.

Economic Activity

The economy is primarily resource-based. About 415,000 metric tons (457,000 U.S. tons) of fish are caught annually. Large catches of deep-sea cod, redfish, and flounder are taken from the Banks; the fish are frozen for export. A shore fishery catches cod, salmon, lobster, herring, and squid.

Newfoundland accounts for 5% of Canadian mineral production. Iron ore is mined in western Labrador. On the island, copper, lead, zinc, and asbestos are mined, and limestone, gypsum, and pyrophyllite are quarried. Smaller resource-based industries include pulp, paper, plasterboard, cement, brick, and chipboard manufacturing. Shipbuilding is also important.

The huge hydroelectric complex at Churchill Falls in Labrador is one of the largest single generating plants in the world.

Agriculture is of minor importance. Potatoes, turnips, and cabbage are grown on the island, and dairy and beef cattle are significant in a few areas.

Roads reach almost all settlements on the island, but in Labrador they are few, and transportation is by sea, air, or by the modern rail system built to carry out iron ore. Six large airports, including the international airport at Gander, serve the areas of concentrated settlement.

St. John's, a port situated on the southeastern coast of the Avalon Peninsula, is the capital and largest city of Newfoundland. Settled during the early 1600s, St. John's is one of the oldest continuously inhabited cities in North America.

Government and History

The provincial Legislative Assembly sits at St. John's; it has 52 members. Newfoundland also elects seven members to the House of Commons in Ottawa.

Long before the advent of European settlement, a number of aboriginal tribes occupied different parts of the area. Recent archaeological finds near Port aux Choix on the west coast of Newfoundland Island show evidence of an ancient Indian culture (6500 BC). Several tribes of Indians and Eskimo later occupied the region.

As early as AD 986, Norse explorers are believed to have sailed in Newfoundland waters and may have established temporary settlements, including L'ANSE-AUX-MEADOWS. European explorers visited the area in the late 15th and early 16th centuries. John Cabot, a Venetian navigator sailing for King Henry VII of England, is believed to have sighted Newfoundland in 1497. In 1583, Sir Humphrey Gilbert claimed the territory in the name of Queen Elizabeth I, but the French contested England's claims until the Treaty of Paris of 1763 awarded the area to England.

Due to bankruptcy during the Great Depression, a commission government was appointed by Great Britain in 1934. It governed until 1949, when Newfoundland became the tenth province of Canada. Thereafter, the economy advanced rapidly with the development of iron mining in Labrador, but in the late 1970s and early 1980s there was a recession. With the development of the offshore Hibernia oil field, however, economic resurgence is anticipated.

Newfoundland (dog) The Newfoundland is a large, powerful breed of dog that resembles the Saint Bernard in general appearance. The average height for males is 70 cm (28 in); for females, 65 cm (26 in). Males weigh about 67.5 kg (150 lb), and females weigh 54 kg (120 lb). Newfoundlands have long coats, massive heads, small drop ears, bushy tails, and webbed toes. The coat is double. The undercoat is thick and soft, whereas the out-

The Newfoundland is an able water dog known to save drowning humans. It is also used as a draft and pack animal.

er coat is short and fine on the head, and long, flat, and dense on the body. The outer coat is coarse and oily. Newfoundlands are glossy black in color. Varieties with white and a black patch are known as Landseers.

The origins of the Newfoundland are uncertain, with the Great Pyrenees (brought to Newfoundland by Basque fishermen), French hounds, and the husky all being mentioned as ancestors. The breed emerged at the end of the 18th century in Newfoundland.

Newhouse, Samuel I. The American media mogul Samuel Irving Newhouse, b. New York City, May 24, 1895, d. Aug. 27, 1979, built a media empire that today includes numerous national magazines, radio and television stations, cable-TV systems, and one of the largest newspaper chains in the United States.

The son of Russian immigrants, Newhouse started as an office boy with the *Bayonne* (N.J.) *Times* and became a lawyer but soon turned permanently to journalism and began to build the Newhouse empire, which culminated in the acquisition of Booth Newspapers for $300 million cash in 1976.

In the 1950s, Newhouse began acquiring many already profitable enterprises, including Condé Nast, publisher of *Vogue*. In the 1980s his son S. I. Newhouse, Jr., bought The *New Yorker* and Random House. The Newhouse Foundation helps to support the Newhouse Communications Center at Syracuse University, one of the largest U.S. journalism schools.

Newman, Barnett The abstract expressionist Barnett Newman, b. New York City, Jan. 29, 1905, d. July 4, 1970, played a major role in the development of COLOR-FIELD PAINTING. Beginning in 1948 he painted huge canvases consisting of unified fields of pure color interrupted by one or two narrow vertical stripes of another color or tone, for example, *Stations of the Cross* (1958–66), a series of 14 black-and-white paintings. Newman eliminated form and the illusion of depth from his work, creating his effects solely with the use of pure color and the interaction between the field and the narrow stripe ("zip") or stripes. He also created several pieces of sculpture, including the steel *Broken Obelisk* (1963–67; The Rothko Chapel, Houston, Tex.).

Newman, Edwin The correspondent and writer Edwin Harold Newman, b. New York City, Jan. 25, 1919, began his journalistic career with the International News Service in 1941. After working for the United Press and the Columbia Broadcasting System (CBS), he joined the National Broadcasting Company (NBC) in 1956 and 10 years later won Peabody and Emmy awards as that network's critic-at-large. Newman's books *Strictly Speaking* (1974) and *A Civil Tongue* (1976) have established him as one of the country's most influential arbiters of good English usage and a stern critic of the abuse of language.

Newman, John Henry   A leader of the OXFORD MOVE-MENT and later a cardinal of the Roman Catholic church, John Henry Newman, b. Feb. 21, 1801, d. Aug. 11, 1890, was probably the most influential theologian of Victorian England.

Originally of an evangelical bent, Newman little by little turned toward high Anglicanism and then to Rome. With Hurrell Froude he visited Italy in 1832, and upon his return, inspired by John KEBLE's sermon "National Apostasy" (1833), he joined the effort to reform the Anglican church that resulted in the Oxford movement. The publication of his *Tract 90* (1841), arguing the essentially Catholic nature of the Thirty-nine Articles, raised such a furor among Anglicans that Newman withdrew for two years to Littlemore, a chapel attached to Saint Mary's. In 1843 he resigned his living and in 1845 was received into the Roman Catholic church. A year later he was ordained in Rome.

During his stay in Rome, Newman joined the Congregation of the Oratory, and after his return to England he established (1849) an Oratorian house in Birmingham. When the Catholic bishops of Ireland proposed to establish a national Catholic university, Newman served (1854–58) as its first rector, at this time developing the theories on education that appeared as *The Idea of a University* (1852). Frustrated by his experiences in Dublin, Newman returned to England and settled permanently at the Birmingham Oratory. Leo XIII made him cardinal in 1879.

A master of English prose style, Newman is best known for his influential *Essay on the Development of Christian Doctrine* (1845), his autobiographical masterpiece *Apologia Pro Vita Sua* (1864), and the *Grammar of Assent* (1870).

Newman, Paul   Paul Newman, b. Shaker Heights, Ohio, Jan. 26, 1925, is an actor whose charm and wit made him one of the most popular film personalities of the 1960s and '70s. He achieved success on the stage in *Picnic* (1953) and screen stardom in *The Long Hot Summer* (1958). His most notable screen roles have been in *The Hustler* (1961), *Sweet Bird of Youth* (1962), *Hud* (1963), *Cool Hand Luke* (1967), *Hombre* (1967), *Butch Cassidy and the Sundance Kid* (1969), *The Sting* (1973), *Absence of Malice* (1981), *The Verdict* (1982), *The Color of Money* (1986), and *Mr. and Mrs. Bridge* (1990). After his son Scott died (1978) from a drug overdose, he established (1980) the Scott Newman Foundation, which produces such educational films as *Doin' What the Crowd Does* (1982).

Newport   Newport is the seat of Newport County on the southern tip of the state of Rhode Island at the mouth of Narragansett Bay. The city has a population of 28,227 (1990).

The city was the site of a major U.S. naval base until 1974. The closing of the base severely hurt the local economy, which is now centered around the manufacture of electrical products and a summer influx of tourists.

Newport became a fashionable resort for the rich after the Civil War—many of the opulent "cottages" they built are now open to the public. Yacht races (including, through 1983, the AMERICA'S CUP) and tennis tournaments draw large crowds. The International Tennis Hall of Fame and Tennis Museum and the Touro Synagogue (1763), the oldest synagogue in the United States, are in Newport. From 1954 to 1971 the Newport Jazz Festival was held there.

Newport was founded in 1639 by groups fleeing religious intolerance in Massachusetts.

Newport Jazz Festival   The annual musical celebration known as the Newport Jazz Festival for more than 25 years attracted the foremost jazz artists, who played extended jam sessions for huge audiences. Organized by jazz promoter George Wein, the first festival was held on July 17 and 18, 1954, on the tennis court of the Newport Casino in Rhode Island, and included among its performers such stars as Ella Fitzgerald, Dizzy Gillespie, and Stan Kenton. By 1960 the festival had moved to a park, was held for 4 days and nights, and attracted thousands of jazz lovers. In 1969 and 1971, rock music groups and their followers brought disruption and riot to the town, which finally revoked permission to hold the festival in Newport. Subsequent festivals were held in New York City and other sites and were later called the Kool Jazz Festival.

Newport News   Newport News, an independent city in southeast Virginia, is located at the point where the James River enters HAMPTON ROADS harbor. Newport News has a population of 170,045 (1990). The city, along with nearby NORFOLK, is a major port of entry, and its shipyards have built or repaired some of the largest ships in the world. Each year the port facilities handle more than 27

The American actor Paul Newman appears in a scene from The Mackintosh Man *(1973). Newman is best known for his portrayals of ironic, independent characters. He also achieved critical success as the director of such films as* Rachel, Rachel *(1968), starring his wife, Joanne Woodward.*

million metric tons of grain, ores, oil, and coal. Manufactures include seafood products, construction materials, petroleum products, electronic equipment, textiles, and paper. Of interest are the Mariners Museum, Victory Arch, and the War Memorial Museum of Virginia. Christopher Newport College was founded in Newport News in 1960.

Settled by Irish colonists in 1621, Newport News remained small until 1880, when it became the coal-shipping terminus for the Chesapeake and Ohio Railroad; in 1886 the Newport News Shipbuilding and Dry Dock Company was established. During the Civil War, Union forces captured the city and built a fortified base.

newspaper   A newspaper, in a broad sense, is an unbound publication issued at regular intervals that seeks to inform, analyze, influence, and entertain. It can be published at various intervals but usually appears weekly or daily. The place of the newspaper in the overall journalistic enterprise is described in JOURNALISM.

There are several newspapers in the United States that have huge circulations (such as the *New York Daily News*, with more than 1 million, and the WALL STREET JOURNAL and *USA Today*, with about 2 million each), and there are small specialized newspapers (for example, country weeklies and college newspapers) with circulations of a few thousand at most. In addition to providing a varied assortment of news, opinion, and features, newspapers survive by publishing ADVERTISING. The newspaper is both a business, with a need to make a profit, and a public service. In the latter function U.S. newspapers are under the protection of the FREEDOM OF THE PRESS clause of the 1st Amendment of the U.S. Constitution.

Modern Newspapers

It is estimated that worldwide about 60,000 newspapers exist with a combined circulation of 500 million. Readership, however, is probably three times that because newspapers are shared, some are posted, and others are placed in libraries and other public sites. About 8,000 of these newspapers are dailies.

The newspaper requires well-qualified journalists. It usually has a managing executive, called the publisher or director, who may own the newspaper or at least is responsible for its overall success. The content managers, usually called editors, supervise the preparation of news and other editorial features. Probably the most familiar newspaper employee is the reporter, who gathers and presents the news and sometimes writes columns of opinion. There are also photographers, cartoonists and other artists, a variety of special writers and editors, and the advertising staff, who sell, write, and design advertisements for the newspaper.

Technological advances have greatly changed the procedures of newspaper production and PRINTING. "Hot metal" printing systems are now generally outmoded, replaced by offset printing produced by computerized phototypesetting. The newsroom once depicted in the movies is now more serene, with video-display terminals in place of the clattering manual typewriters. Layouts are pro-

duced with computers. Electronic technology also enables the *Wall Street Journal*, for example, to publish four regional editions daily.

Newspapers in the United States.   A wide variety of newspapers saturate the United States and compete with other communication media such as magazines and television. Of the nearly 1,800 U.S. dailies, with a circulation of about 75 million, those with the highest visibility and reputations are the serious general dailies such as the NEW YORK TIMES, WASHINGTON POST, and *Los Angeles Times*. There are also other internationally oriented dailies such as the *Christian Science Monitor*; thoughtful general-circulation dailies such as the *Boston Globe, Atlanta Constitution, Miami Herald*, and *Louisville Courier-Journal*; specialized dailies like the *Wall Street Journal*; popular mass-appeal dailies such as the *New York Daily News*; national general dailies like *USA Today* (founded in 1982); specialized trade dailies such as *Variety* (show business) and *Women's Wear Daily*.

Of the approximately 8,000 nondaily newspapers in the United States, there are popular-appeal weeklies such as New York's *Village Voice*, the family-oriented *Grit*, and the sensational *National Enquirer* and *Star*. There are newspapers for African Americans and other racial and cultural groups, for the military, for university students, for prison populations, and for hobbyists. In addition there are many suburban and rural weeklies, semiweeklies, and biweeklies, and a multiplicity of company, trade, and industrial newspapers.

Newspapers in Other Countries.   The idea of the free press fostered in the United States is shared in large degree by other English-speaking countries, Japan, and Western Europe. Press CENSORSHIP, however, was common enough in monarchical Europe in the 16th and 17th

Reporters at the Philadelphia Inquirer *type copy on electronic terminals that allow them to edit and correct as they write. Newspaper production has undergone great changes as a result of computer technologies.*

centuries. Today in many parts of the world—the Middle East, the USSR, Africa, and parts of Asia and Latin America—the press is controlled in one of two ways: either the government censors the press to protect itself, or, the government uses the press as a vehicle of PROPAGANDA.

Third World countries have complained about Western domination of the PRESS AGENCIES AND SYNDICATES that distribute most international news. Intense Third World feelings about Western "cultural imperialism" led UNESCO in 1980 to propose its New World Information Order, a program that would have included the licensing of journalists by UNESCO.

Newspaper quality, of course, is largely a matter of opinion, but informed international observers have consistently placed the following newspapers in the "elite," or quality class: the *Toronto Globe and Mail* of Canada; the TIMES, *Manchester Guardian*, and *Telegraph* of Britain; the *Neue Zuercher Zeitung* of Switzerland; the *Frankfurter Allgemeine* and the *Sueddeutsche Zeitung* of Germany; *Le Monde* and *Le Figaro* of France; *El País* and *ABC* of Spain; *Corriere della Sera* of Italy; *Svenska Dagbladet* of Sweden; PRAVDA and IZVESTIA of the USSR; *Renmin Ribao (People's Daily)* of China; *Asahi* and *Mainichi* of Japan; the *Indian Express, Statesman, Hindu*, and the *Times of India* of India; *Excélsior* of Mexico; *O Estado de S. Paulo* of Brazil; *El Mercurio* of Chile; *El Tiempo* of Colombia; *El Comercio* of Peru; and *La Nación* of Argentina.

History

The Germans were newspaper pioneers in Europe. Forerunners of newspapers as they are known today were published in the 15th century in Nuremberg, Cologne, and Augsburg. In the 16th and 17th centuries rudimentary newspapers spread throughout Germany and appeared elsewhere in Europe—Venice in 1562, the Low Countries in 1616, Britain in 1620, and France in 1631.

U.S. newspaper history can be divided into eight periods: (1) the colonial press, (2) the Revolutionary War press, (3) the political press, (4) the Penny Press, (5) New Journalism, or the press of personal editors, (6) the yellow press, (7) jazz journalism, and (8) the current period of consolidation.

The first newspaper in America was a Boston newssheet called *Publick Occurrences Both Forreign and Domestick* in 1690; it appeared only once. Early publishers of note in the American colonies were printers such as John CAMPBELL and James and Benjamin FRANKLIN. America's first regularly published newspaper was the *Boston News-Letter* (1704). A landmark event in U.S. journalism occurred in 1735 when John Peter ZENGER was tried for seditious libel but acquitted because he had printed the truth. The political tracts of John DICKINSON and others helped set the stage for the American Revolution.

The postrevolutionary political press reflected the partisan battles between the Federalists and the Republicans. Newspapers were fostering a national consciousness and developing political awareness. The Penny Press (1830s–1860s) provided human interest at a low price for the ordinary reader; leading examples were James

Gordon BENNETT's *New York Herald*, and Horace GREELEY's *Tribune*.

Following the Civil War came New Journalism, when the modern newspaper took form. Three men dominated this period of news-and-opinion journalism in which the editor's voice was prominent: Joseph PULITZER, William Randolph HEARST, and E. W. SCRIPPS. Intense competition—particularly between Pulitzer and Hearst—led in the 1890s to YELLOW JOURNALISM with its emphasis on sensationalism.

Jazz journalism refers to the proliferation of tabloid newspapers in the 1920s. Originally a term for a small newspaper format, "tabloid" came to designate a tabloid-size newspaper with a sensational approach to the news and with abundant illustrations. The first U.S. tabloid, the *New York Daily News*, is still the exemplar of the category.

Today, U.S. newspapers are caught up in a consolidation trend toward group ownership, which actually began after World War I. U.S. newspapers are increasingly falling into one of the 155 chains or groups (for example, Gannett, Knight-Ridder, Newhouse, Scripps-Howard, Hearst, and Thomson) and, according to many critics, are losing much of their distinctiveness and independence. At the turn of the century there were only 8 chains in the United States, controlling 27 daily newspapers and accounting for 10% of the country's circulation. By 1982, 155 chains controlled about two-thirds of the daily newspapers. By 1987 only about 50 U.S. cities had more than one separately owned and competing newspaper.

---

newsreel   Until the growth of television after World War II, newsreels—short films of various contemporary events—provided moviegoers with their "window on the world." These short films often were shown before the feature movie, although some theaters in the 1930s specialized in newsreels. Subject matter included sporting events and the activities of royalty and celebrities as well as headline news. At the height of their popularity they were seen by 40 million Americans each week. The newsreel was invented by the French photographer Charles Pathé, who began exhibiting them in New York in 1911. In early reels, the events were restaged, sometimes using actors, but as film technology improved, cameramen were sent to gather footage on location. The propaganda value of newsreels was recognized and exploited during both world wars. Televised news is the direct descendant of newsreels.

Newton, Sir Isaac   Sir Isaac Newton, the culminating figure in the scientific revolution of the 17th century, was born on Jan. 4, 1643 (N.S.; Dec. 25, 1642, O.S.), in the manor house of Woolsthorpe, near Grantham, Lincolnshire, England. Perhaps the greatest scientific genius of all time, Newton made fundamental contributions to every major area of scientific and mathematical concern to his generation.

Newton came from a family of modest yeoman farmers. His father died several months before he was born.

Isaac Newton, one of the most important figures in the history of science, made significant contributions in the fields of physics, astronomy, and mathematics. In his Principia *(1687) he explained the laws of motion and universal gravitation. Newton also developed the calculus and made important discoveries about the nature of light and color.*

Three years later his mother remarried and moved to a nearby village, leaving Isaac in the care of his maternal grandmother. Upon the death of his stepfather in 1656, Newton's mother removed him from grammar school in Grantham in hopes of training him to manage her now much-enlarged estate, but even then Newton's interests ran more toward books and mathematical diversions. His family decided that he should be prepared for the university, and he entered Trinity College, Cambridge, in June 1661.

Even though instruction at Cambridge was still dominated by the philosophy of Aristotle, some freedom of study was permitted in the student's third year. Newton immersed himself in the new mechanical philosophy of Descartes, Gassendi, and Boyle; in the new algebra and analytical geometry of Vieta, Descartes, and Wallis; and in the mechanics and Copernican astronomy of Galileo. At this stage Newton showed no great talent. His scientific genius emerged suddenly when the plague closed the university in the summer of 1665 and he had to return to Lincolnshire. There, within 18 months he began revolutionary advances in mathematics, optics, physics, and astronomy.

Calculus. During the plague years Newton laid the foundation for elementary differential and integral CALCULUS, several years before its independent discovery by the German philosopher and mathematician Gottfried LEIBNIZ. The "method of fluxions," as he called it, was based on his crucial insight that the integration of a function (or finding the area under its curve) is merely the inverse procedure to differentiating it (or finding the slope of the curve at any point). Taking differentiation as the basic operation, Newton produced simple analytical methods that unified a host of disparate techniques previously developed on a piecemeal basis to deal with such problems as finding areas, tangents, the lengths of curves, and their maxima and minima. Isaac Barrow, a Fellow of Trinity College and Lucasian Professor of Mathematics at the university, was so impressed by Newton's achievement that when he resigned his chair in 1669 to devote himself

to theology, he recommended that the 27-year-old Newton take his place.

Optics. Newton's initial lectures as Lucasian Professor dealt with OPTICS, including his remarkable discoveries made during the plague years. He had reached the revolutionary conclusion that white light is not a simple, homogeneous entity, as natural philosophers since Aristotle had believed. When he passed a thin beam of sunlight through a glass prism, he noted the oblong spectrum of colors—red, yellow, green, blue, violet—that formed on the wall opposite. Newton showed that the spectrum was too long to be explained by the accepted theory of the bending (or refraction) of light by dense media. The old theory said that all rays of white light striking the prism at the same angle would be equally refracted. Newton argued that white light is really a mixture of many different types of rays, that the different types of rays are refracted at slightly different angles, and that each different type of ray is responsible for producing a given spectral color. A so-called crucial experiment confirmed the theory. Newton selected out of the spectrum a narrow band of light of one color. He sent it through a second prism and observed that no further elongation occurred. All the selected rays of one color were refracted at the same angle.

These discoveries led Newton to the logical, but erroneous, conclusion that telescopes using refracting lenses could never overcome the distortions of chromatic dispersion. He therefore proposed and constructed a reflecting telescope, the first of its kind, and the prototype of the largest modern optical telescopes. In 1671 he donated an improved version to the Royal Society of London, the foremost scientific society of the day. As a consequence, he was elected a fellow of the society in 1672. Later that year Newton published his first scientific paper in the *Philosophical Transactions* of the society. It dealt with the new theory of light and color and is one of the earliest examples of the short research paper.

Because of a heated controversy over his optical work, Newton withdrew from public scientific discussion for about a decade after 1675, devoting himself to chemical and alchemical researches. He delayed the publication of a full account of his optical researches until 1703. Newton's *Opticks* appeared the following year. It dealt with the theory of light and color and with Newton's investigations of the colors of thin sheets, of "Newton's rings," and of the phenomenon of diffraction of light. To explain some of his observations he had to graft elements of a wave theory of light onto his basically corpuscular theory.

Gravitation. Newton's greatest achievement was his work in physics and celestial mechanics, which culminated in the theory of universal gravitation. Even though Newton also began this research in the plague years, the story that he discovered universal gravitation in 1666 while watching an apple fall from a tree in his garden is a myth. By 1666, Newton had formulated early versions of his three LAWS OF MOTION. His great insight of 1666 was to imagine that the Earth's gravity extended to the Moon, counterbalancing its centrifugal force. From his law of centrifugal force and Kepler's third law of planetary motion, Newton deduced that the centrifugal (and hence centripetal) force of the Moon or of any planet must decrease as the inverse square of its distance from the center of its motion. For example, if the distance is doubled, the force becomes one-fourth as much; if distance is trebled, the force becomes one-ninth as much. This theory agreed with Newton's data to within about 11%.

In 1679, Newton returned to his study of celestial mechanics when his critic and adversary the natural philosopher Robert HOOKE drew him into a discussion of the problem of orbital motion. Hooke is credited with suggesting to Newton that circular motion arises from the centripetal deflection of inertially moving bodies. Hooke further conjectured that since the planets move in ellipses with the Sun at one focus (Kepler's first law), the centripetal force drawing them to the Sun should vary as the inverse square of their distances from it. Hooke could not prove this theory mathematically, although he boasted that he could. Not to be shown up by his rival, Newton applied his mathematical talents to proving Hooke's conjecture. He showed that if a body obeys Kepler's second law (which states that the line joining a planet to the sun sweeps out equal areas in equal times), then the body is being acted upon by a centripetal force. This discovery revealed for the first time the physical significance of Kepler's second law. Given this discovery, Newton succeeded in showing that a body moving in an elliptical path and attracted to one focus must indeed be drawn by a force that varies as the inverse square of the distance. Later even these results were set aside by Newton.

In 1684 the young astronomer Edmond Halley, tired of Hooke's fruitless boasting, asked Newton whether he could prove Hooke's conjecture and to his surprise was told that Newton had solved the problem a full 5 years before but had now mislaid the paper. At Halley's constant urging Newton reproduced the proofs and expanded them into a paper on the laws of motion and problems of orbital mechanics. Finally Halley persuaded Newton to compose a full-length treatment of his new physics and its application to astronomy. After 18 months of sustained effort, Newton published (1687) the *Philosophiae naturalis principia mathematica* (The Mathematical Principles of Natural Philosophy), or *Principia*, as it is universally known.

By common consent the *Principia* is the greatest scientific book ever written. Within the framework of an infinite, homogeneous, three-dimensional, empty space and a uniformly and eternally flowing "absolute" time, Newton fully analyzed the motion of bodies in resisting and nonresisting media under the action of centripetal forces. The results were applied to orbiting bodies, projectiles, pendula, and free-fall near the Earth. He further demonstrated that the planets were attracted toward the Sun by a force varying as the inverse square of the distance and generalized that all heavenly bodies mutually attract one another. By further generalization, he reached his law of universal gravitation: every piece of matter attracts every other piece with a force proportional to the product of their masses and inversely proportional to the square of the distance between them.

Given the law of gravitation and the laws of motion,

Newton could explain a wide range of hitherto disparate phenomena such as the eccentric orbits of comets, the causes of the tides and their major variations, the precession of the Earth's axis, and the perturbation of the motion of the Moon by the gravity of the Sun. Newton's one general law of nature and one system of mechanics reduced to order most of the known problems of astronomy and terrestrial physics. The work of Galileo, Copernicus, and Kepler was united and transformed into one coherent scientific theory. The new Copernican world-picture finally had a firm physical basis.

With the publication of the *Principia*, Newton was recognized as the leading natural philosopher of the age, but his creative career was effectively over. After suffering a nervous breakdown in 1693, he retired from research to seek a government position in London. In 1696 he became Warden of the Royal Mint and in 1699 its Master, an extremely lucrative position. He oversaw the great English recoinage of the 1690s and pursued counterfeiters with ferocity. In 1703 he was elected president of the Royal Society and was reelected each year until his death. He was knighted (1708) by Queen Anne, the first scientist to be so honored for his work.

Newton died in London on Mar. 31 (N.S.; Mar. 20, O.S.), 1727, having singlehandedly completed the scientific revolution and molded much of the content and the image of modern science.

See also: GRAVITATION; PHYSICS, HISTORY OF.

Nexø, Martin Andersen- [nek'-su] Martin Andersen-Nexø, b. June 26, 1869, d. June 1, 1954, was a Danish novelist and short-story writer known for his proletarian themes. Born in the Copenhagen slums and reared as a shepherd boy and cobbler's apprentice on the remote Baltic island of Bornholm, he was intimately familiar with the hunger and poverty he so poignantly described in his novels. Three of his major works became classics: the novels *Pelle the Conqueror* (4 vols., 1906–10; Eng. trans., 1913–17) about a union organizer and *Ditte* (5 vols., 1917–21; Eng. trans., 1920–22) about a working-class girl and his memoirs, *Under the Open Sky: My Early Years* (1932–39; partial Eng. trans., 1938).

Ney, Michel [nay] The French marshal Michel Ney, b. Jan. 10, 1769, d. Dec. 7, 1815, rendered brilliant service to NAPOLEON I in many of the crucial campaigns of the NAPOLEONIC WARS. Ney enlisted in the cavalry in 1787 and was promoted rapidly. He was named marshal of France and given the 6th Corps in 1804. In 1805 he helped force the Austrian surrender at Ulm by his victory at Elchingen, and in 1808 he was sent to Spain, where he fought several brilliant rear-guard actions against the duke of WELLINGTON. In 1811 he was relieved of command after a quarrel with his commander, André MASSÉNA.

Appointed (1812) by Napoleon to command the 3d Corps in the Russian campaign, he fought admirably at Smolensk and Borodino and was made prince of the Moskova. He fought courageously to halt the allied invasion (1814) of France, but after the surrender of Paris urged Napoleon to abdicate. Later, Ney joined Napoleon during the Hundred Days. At the Battle of Quatre Bras he prevented Wellington's union with Gebhard BLÜCHER at Ligny, but at WATERLOO he was overwhelmed by the Prussian force. Following Napoleon's final abdication, Ney was excluded from the general amnesty. He was tried and condemned for treason by the house of peers and executed.

Nez Percé [nez purs or nay pair-say']   The Nez Percé (French for "pierced nose"), a Sahaptin-speaking tribe of North American Indians, occupied central Idaho and adjacent areas in Washington and Oregon. Their Plateau culture acquired Plains traits after the introduction (c.1700) of the horse stimulated trade and war contacts. Renowned as breeders of the Appaloosa, the Nez Percé were noted for their large horse herds. Scattered settlements of related families ranged from 10 to 75 persons. Local villages organized into a band were governed by a council of headmen and a war leader. Wealth in horses stimulated social ranking of families. War captives made up a slave class.

The fur trade began to change Nez Percé life by 1811. Prophets stressed the theme of strange people from the East who would bring vast changes. Presbyterian missionaries arrived in 1836, and pressures from white settlers forced land cessions in 1855 and 1863. Government failure to substantiate promises about a reservation precipitated open conflict in 1877. Chiefs JOSEPH and Looking Glass fought hard but eventually surrendered. In 1987 about 2,400 Nez Percé resided on or near a reservation in central Idaho.

Nezami, Nezamoddin Ilyas [nay-zah'-mee]   Nezamoddin Ilyas Nezami, b. Ganja, now Kirovabad, in the Caucasus, c.1140–c.1203, was the first great dramatic poet in the Persian language. Distinguished for originality of thought as well as clarity of style, he wrote both odes and romantic lyrics. His renown, however, rests on five longer poems: the philosophical *Treasury of Mysteries* (1174–75; Eng. trans., 1945); the romantic *Khusrau and Shirin* (1180), *Laila and Majnun* (1188; Eng. trans., 1836), and *Haft Paikar* (1197; Eng. trans., 1924); and *The Sikander Nama* (1200; Eng. trans., 1975), about Alexander the Great.

Ngo Dinh Diem [ngoh deen zee'-uhm]   Ngo Dinh Diem, b. Jan. 3, 1901, d. Nov. 2, 1963, was the first president of the Republic of (South) Vietnam. Diem served in the French colonial government of Emperor Bao Dai during the early 1930s but subsequently gave up his ministerial position. He remained aloof from political movements in Vietnam until after the Communist victory at Dien Bien Phu in 1954; a strong nationalist and anti-Communist, he was named that June as premier of Vietnam. In July the Geneva Agreements divided Vietnam in two, and with U.S. support, Diem continued to rule the

southern part. On Oct. 26, 1956, he proclaimed South Vietnam a republic and became its president. From the start Diem had to battle Communist forces. His hostility toward Buddhists and his family's prevailing influence in government led to popular discontent, and he was assassinated during a military coup.

Ngugi wa Thoing'o [uhn-goo'-gee]   James Ngugi wa Thoing'o, b. Kenya, Jan. 5, 1938, is considered the most important East African novelist. His first two novels, *Weep Not, Child* (1964) and *The River Between* (1965), concern the impact of colonialism, Christianity, and rebellion on the East African peoples. Both novels were influenced by the realism of West African writer Chinua ACHEBE. In *A Grain of Wheat* (1967), Ngugi's most successful novel, which deals with the Mau Mau rebellion, his style is more mature and is characteristic of his later works. His criticism of the Kenyan government in the novel *Petals of Blood* (1977) led to his imprisonment (1978–79) and to the prison diary *Detained* (1981). He has written two books in Kikuyu (the play *I Will Marry When I Want* and the novel *Devil on the Cross*, both 1980; Eng. trans., 1982) and the critical work *Decolonising the Mind* (1986).

Nguni [uhn-goo'-nee]   The term *Nguni* is generally used to refer to those Bantu-speaking peoples inhabiting the eastern part of South Africa. Nguni also designates the language subgroup spoken by the XHOSA, ZULU, Swazi, Pondo, Bhaca, Fingo, and Tembu, who together numbered about 13 million in the early 1990s. Although the Nguni peoples share a common language and culture, with regional variations, they are not a political entity. Typical cultural phenomena common to most Nguni include taboos against cousin marriages, an elaborate system of bride-price (lobola), widespread polygamy, and an aversion to eating fish. Residence was patrilocal, and inheritance of property and succession to office were also traced through the father's line. Similarly, the ancestral gods were part of the patrilineal system. Thus husbands and wives worshiped and propitiated different gods. The practice of magic, sorcery, and witchcraft, common to all Nguni, followed similar principles. Diviners played an important part in determining the causes of good and bad fortune as well as the nature of disease.

Prior to conquest by Europeans the Nguni practiced both agriculture and animal husbandry. With the decline of the traditional economy and political identity, every Nguni tribe, chiefdom, and kingdom has lost its autonomy. The majority have been transformed into an urban working class.

Nguyen Van Thieu [nuh-win' vahn tee-oo']   Nguyen Van Thieu, b. Apr. 5, 1923, was president of South Vietnam from 1967 until it was overrun by North Vietnamese forces in 1975. Thieu joined (1945) Ho Chi Minh's movement (Viet Minh) but left in opposition to its communist sympathies. He fought (1946–54) with the French against the Viet Minh and rose in the South Vietnamese Army. In 1963 he was one of the leaders of the coup against Ngo Dinh Diem. In 1965 he became military chief of state of South Vietnam, and he was elected president of a civilian government in 1967 and 1971. Until his resignation Thieu remained opposed to any political settlement with the North.

Ni Zan (Ni Tsan) [nee dzahn]   The Chinese painter, scholar, poet, and calligrapher Ni Zan, b. 1301, d. Dec. 4, 1374, was one of the Four Great Masters of the Yuan dynasty (1279–1368). Born into a wealthy family of Wuxi, in Jiangsu province, Ni enjoyed a life of leisure until 1352, when he dispersed all his property and took up residence on a houseboat, wandering around the Wuxi lakes. Ni's quiet, reclusive personality is reflected in the spare composition of his landscapes, from which human figures are absent. Executed in ink monochrome, his paintings exhibit a cool, tranquil quality, as in his masterpiece, *Rongxi Studio* (dated 1372; National Palace Museum, Taipei).

Niagara, Fort   see FORT NIAGARA

Niagara Falls [ny-ag'-ruh]   Niagara Falls are located north of Lake Erie on the Niagara River, between Ontario, Canada, and western New York. The falls provide an unparalleled natural spectacle for tourists as well as abundant energy for the region's highly diversified industries.

At Niagara Falls, one of the most spectacular natural features of North America, the Niagara River tumbles over the American Falls alone at a rate of 22.8 million liters (6 million gal) per minute.

Public parks and power stations have been built on both sides of the falls; two bridges span the water.

The falls were formed about 10,000 to 12,000 years ago, when the retreat of melting glaciers enabled water trapped in Lake Erie to flow northward to Lake Ontario, which is 99 m (326 ft) lower. Rapids precede the falls for 11 km (7 mi) before the river is divided by Goat Island into Horseshoe Falls (792 m/2,600 ft long at the crestline and 49 m/161 ft high) on the Canadian side and the American Falls (305 m/1,000 ft long and 51 m/167 ft high) on the U.S. side of the international boundary. Serious erosion of the American Falls crestline (hard dolomitic limestone underlain by softer shales and sandstone) has taken place. In 1969 the river water was temporarily diverted so that studies could be made on possible methods of slowing the erosional process. The first European to sight the falls was Father Louis Hennepin, in 1678.

Niagara Falls (city in New York)   Niagara Falls (1990 pop., 61,840) is a port city in western New York, on the bank of the Niagara River at Niagara Falls. Power supplied by the falls supports extensive heavy manufacturing in the area. Tourism is also an important economic factor. Settled by the French in the 1680s and captured by the British in 1759, Niagara Falls, N.Y., came into U.S. possession in 1805. It is the home of Niagara University (1856).

Niagara Falls (city in Ontario)   Niagara Falls (1986 pop., 72,107) is a Canadian port city located in Ontario on the Niagara River. The city is primarily a tourist center; its industries manufacture chemicals, cereals, fertilizers, and abrasives. Niagara Falls is also the headquarters for important hydroelectric power projects. Founded as Elgin in 1853, Niagara Falls was known as Clifton between 1856 and 1881 after the towns of Elgin and Clifton had merged. The 1963 merger with nearby Stamford Township greatly increased the city's area and population.

Niagara River   The Niagara River flows north from Lake Erie to Lake Ontario for about 56 km (35 mi), marking the boundary between the United States and Canada. About halfway along its course it drops 51 m (167 ft) at Niagara Falls. Below the falls the river enters Niagara Gorge to form the Whirlpool Rapids, providing an important source for hydroelectric power.

Niamey [nee-ah-may']   Niamey, the capital and largest city of Niger, is a busy river port strategically located where transportation routes cross the NIGER RIVER. Niamey has a population of 398,300 (1988). The city lies in a parched region on the edge of a desert in the southwest corner of the country, and the river is the focal point of the city's activity. Niamey is an agricultural and livestock market and a processing center.

Small hamlets occupied the site when it was chosen to replace Zinder as the French colonial capital in 1926.

Niamey has since grown into a major city that has drawn many immigrants from the hinterland.

Nibelungenlied

Nibelungenlied [nee-be-lung'-en-leet] The great medieval German epic the *Nibelungenlied* (*c*.1200) is based on the tales of the Norse Poetic EDDA and the *Völsunga Saga* but is less directly concerned with the gods than with heroic feats, royal revenge, and magical powers. SIEGFRIED, the hero who enters the territory of the Nibelung kings, takes all the symbols of power, including Queen Kriemhild, by prowess. Kriemhild and Brunhild of Iceland are played off against each other, and a series of complicated reprisals eventually leads to everyone's downfall. For his opera cycle *Der Ring des Nibelungen* (first produced in 1876), Richard Wagner drew on several versions of the story and overlaid them with elements of Greek tragedy.

See also: MYTHOLOGY.

Nicaea

Nicaea [ny-see'-uh] Nicaea (modern Iznik, Turkey), an important city of the Hellenistic-Roman kingdom of BITHYNIA, was founded in the 4th century BC by the Macedonian king ANTIGONUS I and was later expanded by King LYSIMACHUS. Lying astride busy trade routes to Galatia and Phrygia, Nicaea flourished as a commercial and cultural center.

The city achieved fame as the site of two Christian ecumenical councils. Surviving a brief occupation by Seljuks (1077–97), Nicaea later emerged as an imperial center, with Balkan holdings, after Constantinople fell to the Fourth Crusade in 1204. Founded by Theodore I Lascaris, the Nicaean empire preserved vital Byzantine traditions of scholarship and education until 1261, when Constantinople was able to resume its hegemony in the East.

Nicaea, councils of

Nicaea, councils of The two councils of Nicaea were ecumenical councils of the Christian church held in 325 and 787, respectively. The **First Council of Nicaea**, the first ecumenical council held by the church, is best known for its formulation of the Nicene Creed, the earliest dogmatic statement of Christian orthodoxy (see CREED). The council was convened in 325 by the Roman emperor Constantine I in an attempt to settle the controversy raised by ARIANISM over the nature of the Trinity. It was the decision of the council, formalized in the Nicene Creed, that God the Father and God the Son were consubstantial and coeternal and that the Arian belief in a Christ created by and thus inferior to the Father was heretical. Arius himself was excommunicated and banished.

The **Second Council of Nicaea**, the seventh ecumenical council of the Christian church, was convoked by the Byzantine empress Irene in 787 to rule on the use of saints' images and icons in religious devotion. At that time a strong movement known as ICONOCLASM, which opposed the pictorial representation of saints or of the Trinity, existed in the Greek church. At the prompting of Irene, the council declared that whereas the veneration of images was legitimate and the intercession of saints efficacious, their veneration must be distinguished from the worship due God alone.

Nicaragua

Nicaragua [nik-uh-rah'-gwah] Nicaragua, the largest nation in Central America, is bordered on the north by Honduras, on the south by Costa Rica, on the east by the Caribbean Sea, and on the west by the Pacific Ocean. Known as "the land of lakes and volcanoes," it contains Central America's two largest lakes and numerous active volcanoes. From 1979, when a revolution brought the SANDINISTA National Liberation Front (FSLN) to power, until the holding of democratic elections in 1990, Nicaragua was a focus of conflict in the region and tensions with the United States.

Land and Resources

Nicaragua's population is concentrated along the low, fertile Pacific coast; this area includes most of the major cities and produces cotton, cattle, sugarcane, and basic food crops. The cooler central highlands, where the bulk of the coffee crop is grown, reach 2,107 m (6,913 ft) at Pico Mogotón. The thinly settled Caribbean lowlands (see MOSQUITO COAST) add little to the economy. The Pacific-

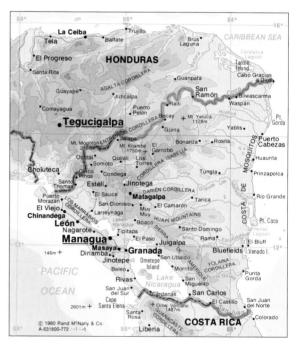

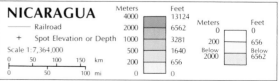

NICARAGUA	Meters	Feet		
—— Railroad	4000	13124	Meters	Feet
+ Spot Elevation or Depth	2000	6562	0	0
Scale 1:7,364,000	1000	3281	200	656
	500	1640	Below	Below
	200	656	2000	6562
	0	0		

AT A GLANCE

REPUBLIC OF NICARAGUA

Land: Area: 130,700 km^2 (50,464 mi^2), including 10,351 km^2 (3,997mi^2) of inland water. Capital and largest city: Managua (1985 est. pop., 682,111).

People: Population (1990 est.): 3,722,683. Density: 31 persons per km^2 (80 per mi^2). Distribution (1989): 60% urban, 40% rural. Official language: Spanish. Major religion: Roman Catholicism.

Government: Type: republic. Legislature: National Assembly. Political subdivisions: 17 departments, grouped into 9 administrative regions.

Economy: GNP (1988): $2.1 billion; $610 per capita. Labor distribution (1987): agriculture—32.4%; services—13.2%; trade—8.4%; manufacturing—8%; public administration—6.9%; other—31.1%. Foreign trade (1989 est.): imports—$550 million; exports—$250 million. Currency: 1 gold córdoba = 100 centavos.

Education and Health: Literacy (1986): 74% of adult population. Universities (1989): 4. Hospital beds (1988): 4,762. Physicians (1987): 2,086. Life expectancy (1990): women—62; men—61. Infant mortality (1990): 68 per 1,000 live births.

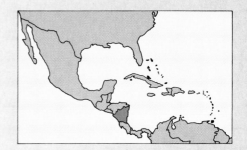

coast region is subject to severe earthquakes, which virtually destroyed the nation's capital, MANAGUA, in 1931 and 1972. All major rivers drain into the Caribbean.

The rainy season extends from May through November on the Pacific coast and in the highlands and longer in the east. Annual rainfall averages 1,207 mm (47.5 in) at Managua and 3,124 mm (123 in) at Puerto Cabezas and has reached 7,554 mm (297 in) at Bluefields. Temperatures average 27° C (80° F) along the coasts and are lower in the highlands.

Half of Nicaragua is covered by forests, including valuable hardwoods. Small amounts of gold and silver are produced.

People

About 77% of Nicaragua's population are mestizo (of mixed Spanish-Indian ancestry). Another 10% are of European descent, 9% are of African descent, and about 4% are Indians (see MISKITO). About 88% of Nicaraguans are Roman Catholic.

Nicaragua is the most urbanized nation in Central America; the largest cities are Managua, GRANADA, and LEÓN. The FSLN provided land and improved education and health care for the poor; a nationwide literacy campaign in 1980 raised official literacy to nearly 75%. Recent years have seen increases in dengue fever, malaria, and tuberculosis.

Economic Activity

Subsistence farming (rice, corn, and beans) and gold

mining formed the basis of the economy until the rise of coffee production late in the 19th century. After World War II cotton came to rival coffee as the principal export crop; cattle and sugar exports also increased. The creation of the Central American Common Market (CACM) in the 1950s spurred industrial development.

The decline of the Nicaraguan economy, which began in the 1970s with the rising costs of imported oil, was accelerated by the 1978–79 civil war. Under the FSLN, the state controlled prices, banks, imports, and access to foreign exchange. Conflicts between the state and private sectors, a massive foreign debt, spiraling inflation, a decline in regional trade, a U.S. economic embargo, and the costs of renewed civil conflict kept the economy severely depressed. U.S. economic aid was restored in 1990.

Government

The 1974 constitution was suspended after the 1978–79 civil war, and the FSLN soon came to monopolize effective political power, acting through a nine-member national directorate. A constituent assembly elected in 1984 drafted a new constitution that came into effect in 1987. A president is head of state and government. Both the president and members of the National Assembly are directly elected for six-year terms.

History

Before the first Spanish colonies were established in the early 1520s, Nicaragua was inhabited by numerous, competing Indian groups. Independence from Spain

Shantytowns grew up in the heart of downtown Managua, the capital of Nicaragua, after the city was almost totally destroyed by an earthquake in 1972. Much of the international aid sent to help rebuild the city was misappropriated by Somoza and his associates. The resentment among ordinary Nicaraguans was one of the factors contributing to Somoza's overthrow in 1979.

came in 1821, first as part of the Mexican empire, then as part of the CENTRAL AMERICAN FEDERATION. The federation collapsed by 1838, and rival Liberal and Conservative factions began violent struggles for power. U.S.-British rivalry over control of potential transoceanic canal routes aggravated the situation. In 1855 the Liberals invited William WALKER, a U.S. adventurer, to come to Nicaragua. Walker soon made himself president, but he was defeated in 1857 by a combined Central American army.

After several Conservative presidents, a Liberal revolution in 1893 brought to power Gen. José Santos Zelaya. In 1909 the United States supported a revolution that restored Conservative rule, and another U.S. military intervention took place in 1912. U.S. marines remained in Nicaragua until 1925 and returned in 1926 to halt another revolution, but their presence was opposed by Gen. Augusto César Sandino, who conducted a guerrilla war until the marines departed in 1933. Sandino was killed in 1934 by the U.S.-trained National Guard, and two years later, the Guard's commander, Gen. Anastasio Somoza García, seized power. When Somoza was assassinated in 1956, power was assumed by his sons, Luis and Anastasio (see SOMOZA family).

Nicaragua's economy grew under the Somozas, but massive corruption produced growing resentment. The murder of opposition leader Pedro Joaquín Chamorro in January 1978 sparked a nationwide uprising. When U.S.-sponsored mediation efforts failed to oust the Somozas, civil war spread, led by the Marxist guerrillas of the FSLN. The FSLN took power on July 9, 1979, and set up a broad-based coalition government. Tensions over Marxist elements in the FSLN's program, however, soon broke up the coalition. Moderate politicians, the private sector, and the leadership of the Roman Catholic church began to oppose the FSLN, which responded by tightening controls over the opposition. Conflicts with the United States also grew as the FSLN forged ties with Cuba and the Soviet bloc and

aided leftist guerrillas in El Salvador. Under President Ronald Reagan the U.S. government aided anti-Sandinista guerrillas, or "contras" (see IRAN-CONTRA AFFAIR).

FSLN leader Daniel ORTEGA SAAVEDRA was elected president in 1984, but much of the opposition boycotted the election. As civil conflict widened, the Nicaraguan government increased restrictions on the opposition and channeled scarce resources to the military, aggravating economic hardships. On Aug. 7, 1987, Ortega and the leaders of four other Central American nations signed a regional peace plan, and in 1989, Ortega committed Nicaragua to democratic changes. After an opposition coalition captured 55% of the vote in the Feb. 25, 1990, elections, amnesty was granted to both sides for crimes committed during the civil war, the U.S. economic embargo was lifted, and the contras were disbanded. Violeta Barrios de CHAMORRO, who succeeded Ortega as president on April 25, has since worked to reconcile the nation.

Nicaragua, Lake   Lake Nicaragua lies in southwestern Nicaragua. More than 160 km (100 mi) long, with a maximum depth of 61 m (200 ft), it is the largest freshwater lake in Central America. Once an arm of the Pacific Ocean, the lake still contains varieties of ocean creatures, including the only known freshwater sharks.

Nice [nees]   Nice is located on the Baie des Anges of the Mediterranean Sea about 160 km (100 mi) east of Marseille in southeastern France. The city's population is 377,085 (1982). For the past two centuries Nice has been a playground of France, Europe, and the world. The

Nice, a port and departmental capital in southeastern France, is one of the major resort centers on the French Riviera.

Alps just to the north protect the city from cold winter winds, and the mild climate is the major basis for the city's popularity as a resort.

Nice's harbor is filled with yachts, pleasure boats, fishing vessels, some merchant ships, and passenger ships that link Nice with the island of Corsica. Nice is located on a narrow coastal plain, but much of the city's growth has taken place on nearby slopes. The Château, a high hill on which a fortress stood until 1706, is now a park with tree-lined walks and vantage points from which to view the city, the harbor, and the Mediterranean. A 4-km (2.5-mi) flower-edged path called the Promenade des Anglais parallels the waterfront. The University of Nice was established in 1965. In addition to the resort business, olive oil, electrical equipment, viticulture supplies, furniture, textiles, brandy, tobacco, and straw hats are produced.

Nice was settled by the Greeks about 350 BC and became an important trading center. Control of the city has changed hands many times. It was wrested from Sardinia by the French in 1792, was reclaimed by Sardinia after the fall of Napoleon I in 1814, and was returned to France in 1860. The city was occupied by the Italians in 1940 and by the Germans from 1943 to 1945. Nice regained its reputation as a major tourist center in affluent postwar Europe.

Nicephorus, Saint [ny-sef'-uh-ruhs]

A patriarch of Constantinople, Nicephorus, c.758–829, became famous for his lifelong defense of the veneration of sacred images, or icons, in the struggle against ICONOCLASM. In 787 he represented Emperor Constantine VI at the Second Council of Nicaea (see NICAEA, COUNCILS OF). Appointed (806) to the patriarchate by Emperor Nicephorus I, he was subsequently deposed (815) by the iconoclastic emperor Leo V. Nicephorus was canonized in 847. Feast day: Mar. 13 (Western); June 2 (Eastern).

Nichiren [nee-chee'-rayn]

Nichiren, b. 1222, d. Nov. 4, 1282, a Japanese Buddhist monk of the Kamakura period, was the founder of the Japanese sect of Buddhism that still bears his name. As a young man he became convinced that the essence of the Buddha's teachings lay in the *Lotus Sutra* and in no other text; soon the chanting of "Namu Myoho Renge Kyo" ("Hail to the Marvelous Lotus Sutra") became the main devotional practice of his followers.

Nichiren combined his zeal for the *Lotus* with a prophetic quality, a fervent patriotism, and a fierce intolerance of other Buddhist sects. In the 20th century the Nichiren sect has gained renewed importance as the fountainhead of several of Japan's most dynamic "new religions," including the Risshokosei-kai and the Soka-gakkai.

Nicholas, Saint

Saint Nicholas, d. c.350, was a bishop of the Christian church of Myra, in Lycia, Anatolia, about whom little is known with certainty. He is some-times referred to as Saint Nicholas of Bari because his remains were supposedly translated there in 1087. His reputation for generosity and compassion is best exemplified in the legend that relates how Nicholas saved from a life of prostitution the three daughters of a poor man. On three separate occasions the bishop is said to have tossed a bag of gold through the family's window, thus providing a dowry to procure for each daughter an honorable marriage. The story provides the foundation for the custom, still followed in many countries, of giving gifts on the saint's feast day.

Saint Nicholas is the patron saint of Russia, of children, and of sailors. Feast day: Dec. 6.

Nicholas of Cusa [koo'-zah]

Exemplifying the Renaissance man, Nicholas of Cusa, b. Kues, Germany, 1401, d. Aug. 11, 1464, was a churchman, philosopher, theologian, and scientist. In 1437 he became a member of a papal legation to Constantinople; he was subsequently created a cardinal and made bishop (1450) of Brixen (Bressanone), Italy, and served as papal legate in Germany.

Nicholas's first and most important theological work, *De docta ignorantia* (On Learned Ignorance, 1440), argued that knowledge is learned ignorance, that wisdom lies in the recognition that the human mind is incapable of grasping the infinity of God, in whom all opposites are combined. Nicholas also wrote on astronomy, physics, and mathematics and is considered a precursor of the scientific revolution of Galileo and Sir Isaac Newton.

Nicholas I, Emperor of Russia

Emperor of Russia from 1825 to 1855, Nicholas I, b. July 6 (N.S.), 1796, d. Mar. 2 (N.S.), 1855, opposed the growth of liberalism and pursued a rigid reactionary policy. He succeeded his eldest brother, Emperor ALEXANDER I, whose unexpected death was followed in late 1825 by the mutiny known as the Decembrist Revolt (see DECEMBRISTS). Nicholas dispersed the rebels, and this inauspicious beginning turned his reign in the direction of repression.

Nicholas had a rigid sense of duty and order, believing himself to be responsible only to God—and his subjects to be similarly responsible to himself. This belief, expressed in his education minister's formula "Orthodoxy, autocracy, and nationality," embodied the spirit of his reign. The few concrete achievements of his reign, such as the creation of His Majesty's Own Chancery and the codification of the empire's laws by Mikhail SPERANSKY, reflected the concern of Nicholas for order and continuity. During much of his reign Nicholas also played the role of a "gendarme of Europe," suppressing a Polish rebellion in 1830–31 and helping Austria put down the Hungarian revolution of 1848–49. He died during the CRIMEAN WAR (1853–56).

Nicholas II, Emperor of Russia

Nicholas II, b. May 18 (N.S.), 1868, d. July 16–17, 1918, was the last

Nicholas II, last tsar of Russia, presided over a disintegrating government from 1894 until the Revolutions of 1917. His wife, Alexandra, under the influence of the monk Rasputin, encouraged Nicholas to appoint incompetent and reactionary ministers. The tsar and tsarina were executed, together with their children, in 1918.

emperor (1894–1917) of Russia. The eldest son of ALEXANDER III, Nicholas succeeded his father with the intention of continuing his autocratic rule but lacked Alexander's ability and strength of will. He wavered between severe repression and, in time of popular upheaval, grudging acceptance of limited reforms that he sought to withdraw after the turmoil subsided. A passive, retiring man who preferred family life to public affairs, Nicholas allowed his superstitious but strong-willed wife, ALEXANDRA FYODOROVNA, and her insidious advisor, Grigory RASPUTIN, great sway over government policy. Enlightened moderates such as Count Sergei WITTE were thus unable to promote the reforms needed to avert revolution.

Disastrous defeats in the RUSSO-JAPANESE WAR (1904–05) exposed the incompetence and corruption of the government and precipitated the RUSSIAN REVOLUTION OF 1905. In his October Manifesto (1905) Nicholas, advised by Prime Minister Witte, promised a constitutional government with a representative DUMA authorized to approve or reject all proposed laws. After revolutionary activity ebbed, however, Nicholas dismissed (1906) Witte, dissolved (1906, 1907) the first two Dumas when they showed an independent spirit, and subsequently reduced the Duma's role to that of an advisory body.

World War I proved Nicholas's undoing. In 1915 he took personal command of the army, giving Alexandra and Rasputin greater power at the court. Rumors of their unsavory activities, along with Russia's deteriorating military and economic situation, eroded public morale. Strikes and riots erupted in the capital, Petrograd (now Leningrad), in February (O.S.; March, N.S.) 1917, and on Mar. 2 (O.S.; Mar. 15, N.S.), Nicholas abdicated at the Duma's demand. Exiled to western Siberia and later the Urals region, he and his family were executed by the Bolsheviks.

See also: RUSSIAN REVOLUTIONS OF 1917.

Nicholas I, Pope Nicholas I, b. *c*.820, d. Nov. 13, 867, was pope from 858 to 867, succeeding on the death of Benedict III. An active proponent of papal leadership within the church, he intervened in Frankish affairs in 863–64 to force King LOTHAIR II to repudiate an adulterous relationship and reinstate his wife and also involved himself in the affairs of the archdiocese of Reims.

In 858 he refused to recognize PHOTIUS as patriarch of Constantinople because Photius's predecessor, Ignatius, had been illegally deposed and Nicholas wished to have him restored. This led to a bitter quarrel in which Photius declared (867) Nicholas deposed as pope. Feast day: Nov. 13.

Nicholas V, Pope Nicholas V, 1397–1455, was pope from 1447 to 1455, succeeding Eugenius IV. He was originally named Tommasso Parentucelli. As pope, Nicholas attempted to placate the various factions in Rome, Italy, and Europe and in 1448 reached a concordat with Holy Roman Emperor FREDERICK III. The acceptance of his policy by the rump Council of Basel led to the abdication of the antipope Felix V in 1449 and thus ended the schism within the church. Nicholas expressed his commitment to Renaissance ideals by undertaking an extensive building and renovation program in Rome, which was executed by many of the greatest artists of the day. His chief interest, however, was his library, for which his agents scoured Europe in pursuit of rare codices. The library formed the nucleus of the future Vatican Library.

Nichols, Mike Mike Nichols, pseudonym of Michael Igor Peschkowsky, b. Berlin, Nov. 6, 1931, made his initial appearance in the entertainment world as the partner of Elaine May in a highly successful, satirical cabaret act (1957–61). He then became a stage and film director. On Broadway he won Tony Awards for directing *Barefoot in the Park* (1963), *Luv* (1964), *The Odd Couple* (1965), *Plaza Suite* (1968), *The Prisoner of Second Avenue* (1971), and *The Real Thing* (1984). His first film was *Who's Afraid of Virginia Woolf?* (1966), followed by *The Graduate* (1967), for which he won an Academy Award. Nichols's films, known for flashy visual style and virtuoso performances, also include *Catch-22* (1970), *Carnal Knowledge* (1971), *Silkwood* (1983), and *Postcards from the Edge* (1990).

Nicholson, Ben The English artist Ben Nicholson, b. Apr. 10, 1894, d. Feb. 6, 1982, first painted realistic still lifes and seascapes, but he later developed his characteristic style of elegantly composed geometric studies in colored low relief, based largely on the shapes of circles and rectangles. The subtle surface textures of these works are notable, many of them relying for their effect on the grain of the underlying wood panels. Nicholson's abstraction often begins with a representational vision that he gradually coaxes and presses into abstract form until nothing is left but chaste ornament.

Nicholson, Jack Jack Nicholson, b. Neptune, N.J., Apr. 22, 1937, is an actor, director, and producer whose raffish, cynical wit made him a film hero. After gaining recognition as an alcoholic civil liberties lawyer in *Easy Rider* (1969), he starred in numerous films, including *Five Easy Pieces* (1970), *Carnal Knowledge* (1971), *Chinatown* (1974), *One Flew Over the Cuckoo's Nest* (1975; Academy Award for best actor), *The Shining* (1980), *The Postman Always Rings Twice* (1981), *Reds* (1981), *Ironweed* (1987), and *The Two Jakes* (1990). Nicholson's comedic talent was evident in *Terms of Endearment* (1983; Academy Award for best supporting actor), *Prizzi's Honor* (1985), *The Witches of Eastwick* (1987), and *Batman* (1989; as Batman's foe the Joker).

Nicias [nish'-ee-uhs] Nicias, c.470–413 BC, was an Athenian general and leader of the aristocratic party during the PELOPONNESIAN WAR. He fought loyally against Sparta although opposing the expansionist policies of the democratic party. After the death (422 BC) of CLEON he secured (421) the Peace of Nicias. Over Nicias's opposition, the Athenians resumed warfare with an expedition against Sicily in 415. Left in sole command by the recall of Alcibiades and the death of Lamachus, Nicias was crushed and then executed by the Syracusans.

nickel Nickel is a hard, silvery white metal, familiar from its use in coins but used mainly in alloys with other metals to improve their strength and corrosion resistance. A chemical element, nickel is a member of the transition series and belongs to Group VIIIB of the periodic table along with iron, cobalt, palladium, platinum, and five other elements. Its chemical symbol is Ni, its atomic number is 28, and its atomic weight is 58.71.

The Earth's crust contains 0.018% nickel, although the core is believed to be much richer. Meteorites can contain up to 20% nickel. Nickel was mined and used for centuries in impure form. The first fairly pure sample was prepared in 1751 by the Swedish chemist Baron Axel F. Cronstedt from an ore German miners called *Kupfernickel* ("Old Nick's copper").

Pure nickel is used in electron tubes and in the galvanic (plating) industry, where many objects must be coated with nickel before they can be chrome plated (see CHROMIUM). Most nickel is used in alloys where high resistance to corrosion is important, such as for chemical-reaction vessels and pump parts. Stainless steel, an alloy of iron and chromium, may contain up to 35% nickel. Special nickel alloys include alnico, Cunife, and cunico, used as permanent magnets, and nichrome, which is used as electrical heating elements in many household appliances. The U.S. coin known as the "nickel" actually has 75% copper and 25% nickel.

Nicklaus, Jack [nik'-luhs] Jack William Nicklaus, b. Columbus, Ohio, Jan. 21, 1940, is generally considered the greatest golfer in the history of the game. In 1986, at the age of 46, he became the oldest man ever to win the Masters.

Nicklaus won the Ohio Open at the age of 16. While still a student at Ohio State University, he won the National Amateur title in 1959 and 1961 and helped the U.S. team win the World Amateur title in 1960. In 1959 he helped the U.S. Walker Cup team defeat the British at Muirfield, Scotland.

After winning the NCAA title in 1961, Nicklaus turned professional. He won his first major victory a year later in the U.S. Open with a playoff victory over Arnold Palmer, becoming the youngest Open champion since Bobby Jones. In 1962 he also won the World Series of Golf. In 1963 he became the youngest golfer ever to win the Masters.

Nicklaus won more major championships (20) than any other golfer in history: the U.S. Amateur twice (1959, 1961); the Masters 6 times (1963, 1965, 1966, 1972, 1975, 1986); the Professional Golfers Association (PGA) championship 5 times (1963, 1971, 1973, 1975, 1980); the U.S. Open 4 times (1962, 1967, 1972, 1980); and the British Open 3 times (1966, 1970, 1978). He was named the PGA Player of the Year 5 times and was the leading money winner on the professional tour 8 times. His purses totaled more than $5 million. In 1979 a poll of U.S. sportswriters and broadcasters chose Nicklaus as the Athlete of the Decade.

The American golfer Jack Nicklaus lines up a putt during the 1980 Professional Golfers' Association (PGA) championship, in which he won his 19th Grand Slam victory. Nicklaus has won each of the four annual Grand Slam events—the Masters, the U.S. Open, the British Open, and the PGA—at least three times in his career, far surpassing his closest rivals.

Nicobar Islands [nik'-oh-bahr] The Nicobar Islands are a group of 19 small islands in the Bay of Bengal that form, with the ANDAMAN ISLANDS to their north, a union territory of India. The land area of the Nicobars is about 1,645 km² (635 mi²). The inhabitants, numbering a little more than 30,000 (1981), live on 12 of the islands: Great Nicobar, the largest and southernmost island, is virtually uninhabited. Port Blair, in the Andamans, is the territorial capital. The inhabitants, primarily tribal aborigines of Mongoloid stock, fish and grow coconuts and betel nuts. Tourism is also important.

The Nicobar Islands have been known to sailors since ancient times. They were occupied in the 17th, 18th, and 19th centuries by Danes, British, and French and were annexed by the United Kingdom in 1869. During World War II they were held by the Japanese from 1942 to 1945, and they became part of independent India in 1947.

Nicolet, Jean [nee-koh-lay']　Jean Nicolet, b. 1598, d. Nov. 1, 1642, was a French explorer who passed through the Straits of Mackinac and, in his search for fur pelts and the Northwest Passage, discovered (1634) Lake Michigan and Green Bay as well as the Fox River in the region that is now Wisconsin. He formed an alliance with the WINNEBAGO Indians, facilitating the establishment of a route for the northwestern fur trade. Nicolet drowned on his way to Trois Rivières (now in Quebec).

Nicosia [nik-uh-see'-uh]　Nicosia, the capital of Cyprus, lies in the north central part of that eastern Mediterranean island. Its population is 166,900 (1989 est.). Nicosia is a regional trading center where machine tools, textiles, tobacco products, pottery, and leather goods are manufactured. Tourism is important. Landmarks include the Church of Saint Sophia—now a mosque—which was begun in the 13th century, and the 15th-century Venetian walls. Nicosia is also the archepiscopal seat of the autonomous Church of Cyprus. Known as Ledra in ancient times, it was first mentioned in the 7th century BC. Nicosia was ruled by the Byzantines (330–1191), Lusignan kings (1192–1489), Venetians (1489–1571), Turks (1571–1878), and the British until 1960, when Cyprus became independent. Since 1974 the city has been divided into Greek and Turkish sectors.

nicotine [nik'-uh-teen]　Nicotine is an extremely poisonous, colorless, oily liquid alkaloid that turns brown on exposure to air. The most potent ingredient of the TOBACCO plant, *Nicotiana tabacum*, it is found mainly in the leaves. Nicotine can affect the human nervous system, causing respiratory failure and general paralysis. It may be absorbed through the skin. Only two or three drops (less than 50 mg) of the pure alkaloid placed on the tongue is rapidly fatal to an adult. A typical cigarette contains 15 to 20 mg of nicotine. The actual amount that reaches the bloodstream and hence the brain through normal SMOKING, however, is only about 1 mg. Nicotine is believed to be responsible for most of the short-term and many of the long-term effects of smoking and for the fact that tobacco smoking is such a powerful habit. Nicotine yields of cigarettes have declined by about 70 percent

since the 1950s, largely due to the popularity of filter-tipped varieties. Nicotine can be produced in quantity from tobacco scraps and is used as a pesticide. It is also converted to nicotinic acid, a member of the vitamin B group, for use as a food supplement.

Niebuhr, Reinhold [ryn'-hohld]　By common consent the leading native-born Protestant theologian in the United States in the 20th century, Reinhold Niebuhr, b. Wright City, Mo., June 21, 1892, d. June 1, 1971, not only influenced church and theological circles but also reshaped much of American thinking about society, politics, and the direction and meaning of history.

Following his graduation (1915) from Yale Divinity School he took a pastorate at Bethel Evangelical church in Detroit. There for 13 years he encountered the full force of modern social tensions and conflicts. Niebuhr saw in this encounter the unmasking of the optimistic idealism and self-confident rationalism of liberal culture—and of the liberal theology he had himself espoused.

In 1928 he began to teach at Union Theological Seminary in New York and in 1930 was appointed professor of Christian ethics. Initially influenced by Marxist insights, he became convinced of the sinfulness of humankind, the self-interestedness of society, and the irony of history. Niebuhr began, in the light of this new understanding, to reinterpret not only American democracy and civilization but also the classical theological symbols of creation, fall, incarnation, and final hope, providing a powerful modern interpretation, in Christian terms, of human nature and destiny.

Reinhold Niebuhr was a highly influential 20th-century American theologian. Known for his "neo-orthodox" theology, Niebuhr presented a theological interpretation of modern society that combined awareness of the tragic with hope based on divine goodness.

Nielsen, Carl [neel'-sen]　Denmark's greatest composer, Carl August Nielsen, b. June 9, 1865, d. Oct. 2, 1931, is important both as a nationalist and as a highly individual postromantic. The son of a house painter and village musician, Nielsen played in a military band as a boy and was able in 1884 to begin studies at the Copenhagen Conservatory. He earned his living as an orchestra violinist while gradually gaining attention and financial support through his compositions. As conductor (1908–14) of the Royal Opera and other groups, and as teacher and director (1915–27) at the Royal Conservatory, he came to dominate Danish musical life.

Long overshadowed by the work of Jean Sibelius, Nielsen's music has begun belatedly to receive international acclaim. He is most admired for his six symphonies, in which he developed—under the influence of Brahms and Johan Svendsen—a rich but unsentimental postromantic style and a highly personal use of the supposedly defunct key system that analysts have called "progressive tonality." Nielsen's other orchestral scores include a violin concerto and concertos for flute and clarinet. A master of chamber-music writing, he published four string quartets, two violin sonatas, and a famous wind quintet (1922). He composed with great imagination for piano, and in his last years he explored the organ, notably in his *Commotio* (1931). Nielsen was also an accomplished vocal composer; his songs have entered the Danish national heritage, and his masterful choral writing is shown in several major works. His two operas, the brooding character study *Saul and David* (1902) and the wise and witty comedy *Masquerade* (1906), have begun to receive attention outside Denmark. Nielsen also wrote essays and a memoir that is regarded as a classic of Danish literature.

Niemeyer, Oscar [nee'-my-ur]

Oscar Niemeyer, b. Dec. 15, 1907, is one of the founders of modern architecture in Brazil and with Lúcio Costa one of its acknowledged masters. Niemeyer was profoundly influenced by the INTERNATIONAL STYLE, especially by the work of Le Corbusier, who visited Brazil in 1936 to help design the Ministry of Education and Health building in Rio de Janeiro. Niemeyer worked with Le Corbusier and other architects on this design; he succeeded Costa as leader of the group.

Niemeyer's principal works in Brazil include his designs (1942–43) for the Casino, Yacht Club, and the Church of Saint Francis in Pampulha, all in a new section of Belo Horizonte. His larger projects included the Boavista Bank (1946) and the Sul America Hospital (1952–59), both in Rio de Janeiro, and the Palace of Industry (1951–54) in São Paulo. His career was crowned with the commission to design, from 1956 on, all the monumental buildings for BRASÍLIA,.

Niemöller, Martin [nee'-mur-lur]

A German Lutheran pastor, Friedrich Gustav Emil Martin Niemöller, b. Jan. 1, 1892, d. Mar. 6, 1984, became the symbolic figure of Protestant opposition to National Socialism in Germany. When Adolf Hitler came to power in 1933, Niemöller preached against the neopagan tendencies of the regime. In opposition to the government-sponsored German Christian church, he formed (1933) the Pastors' Emergency League. In 1934 this group constituted itself as the German Confessing church; at the Synod of Barmen (May 1934) it issued a declaration openly indicating its resistance to the Nazis. Arrested in 1937, Niemöller was confined at Sachsenhausen and then at Dachau. After the war he took part in the Stuttgart "Declaration of Guilt."

Niepce, Joseph Nicéphore [nee-eps']

The French inventor Joseph Nicéphore Niepce, b. Mar. 7, 1765, d. July 3, 1833, is credited with having made the first photograph. He first attempted to record a camera image in the early 1790s. The invention of lithography spurred Niepce to try reproducing pictures from other media; in 1816 he produced an impermanent camera image and six years later a permanent "heliograph." He was joined by Louis J. M. DAGUERRE in 1829, and they worked together until Niepce's death. Daguerre later sold their invention to the French government. Niepce also perfected the *pyréolophore*, an early combustion engine.

Nietzsche, Friedrich Wilhelm [nee'-che]

Friedrich Wilhelm Nietzsche, b. Oct. 15, 1844, d. Aug. 25, 1900, was a German philosopher who, together with Søren Kierkegaard, shares the distinction of being a precursor of EXISTENTIALISM.

In his first book, *The Birth of Tragedy* (1872; Eng. trans., 1968), Nietzsche presented a theory of Greek drama and of the foundations of art that has had profound effects on both literary theory and philosophy. In this book he introduced his famous distinction between the Apollonian, or rational, element in human nature and the Dionysian, or passionate, element, as exemplified in the Greek gods Apollo and Dionysus. When the two principles are blended, either in art or in life, man achieves a momentary harmony with the Primordial Mystery. This work, like his later ones, shows the strong influence of the German philosopher Arthur Schopenhauer, as well as Nietzsche's affinity for the music of his close friend Richard Wagner. What Nietzsche presented in this work was a pagan mythology for those who could accept neither the traditional values of Christianity nor those of Social Darwinism.

After resigning (1879) from his teaching position at the University of Basel, Switzerland, because of ill health, Nietzsche lived in Switzerland, Italy, and Germany for the

Friedrich Nietzsche was among the most influential figures of German philosophical thought. Nietzsche formulated the concept of the Übermensch, or "superman," whose creative impulses were propelled by the "will to power." He appears in a portrait by Edvard Munch. (Thielska Galleries, Stockholm.)

next two decades, writing extensively. In *Thus Spake Zarathustra* (1883–85; Eng. trans., 1954), his most celebrated book, he introduced in eloquent poetic prose the concepts of the death of God, the superman, and the will to power. Vigorously attacking Christianity and democracy as moralities for the "weak herd," he argued for the "natural aristocracy" of the superman who, driven by the "will to power," celebrates life on Earth rather than sanctifying it for some heavenly reward. Such a heroic man of merit has the courage to "live dangerously" and thus rise above the masses, developing his natural capacity for the creative use of passion.

Although these ideas were distorted by the Nazis in order to justify their conception of the master race, to regard Nietzsche's philosophy as a prototype of Nazism is erroneous. His criticism of the mediocrity and smugness of German culture led to a disintegration of his friendship with Richard Wagner as well as to a disassociation from his beloved Germany. To correct any misconceptions concerning the superman, Nietzsche published *Beyond Good and Evil* (1886; Eng. trans., 1967) and *On the Genealogy of Morals* (1887; Eng. trans., 1968).

Nietzsche became increasingly deranged in his later years. In 1889 he suffered a severe breakdown, from which he never recovered.

Niger [ny'-jur]   The Republic of Niger is a landlocked state on the southern edge of the Sahara in West Africa.

Niger is bounded by Algeria on the northwest, Libya on the northeast, Chad on the east, Nigeria and Benin on the south, and Burkina Faso (Upper Volta) and Mali on the west. NIAMEY is the capital.

Land and Resources

The topography of Niger consists of highlands and plains. The Aïr Massif (highest point: 1,073 m/3,520 ft), an extension of the Ahaggar (Hoggar) Mountains in Algeria, thrusts into central Niger. In the northeast the Djado, Mangueni, and Tchigaï plateaus join the Aïr with the Tibesti Massif of northwestern Chad. The sandy, rocky plains of the SAHARA extend to the east and west. A chain of arid plateaus in the SAHEL parallels the southern frontier. The major stream is the NIGER RIVER. Part of Lake Chad (see CHAD, LAKE) is in Niger's southeastern corner.

The climate is tropical. Most parts of the country experience highs of about 40° C (104° F) from February to May and lows of between 12° and 15° C (54° and 59° F) during December and January. The northern desert receives almost no rain, whereas enough rain falls in the area south of Gouré and Tahoua to support herding; in the south, rainfall is adequate (560 mm/22 in) for settled agriculture. In the northern Sahara region some vegetation is found only after the rare rainfall. Along the Niger and in the Sahel open savanna predominates. Fauna include antelope, panther, leopards, hyenas, crocodiles, and hippopotamuses.

Niger possesses important mineral resources. The

AT A GLANCE

REPUBLIC OF NIGER

Land: Area: 1,267,000 km² (489,191 mi²). Capital and largest city: Niamey (1988 pop., 398,300).

People: Population (1990 est.): 7,969,309. Density: 6.3 persons per km² (16.3 per mi²). Distribution (1988): 21% urban, 79% rural. Official language: French. Major religion: Islam.

Government: Type: republic. Legislature: National Assembly. Political subdivisions: 7 departments, 1 commune.

Economy: GNP (1988): $2.4 billion; $330 per capita. Labor distribution (1985): agriculture—90%; other—10%. Foreign trade (1988): imports—$441 million; exports—$371 million. Currency: 1 C.F.A. franc = 100 centimes.

Education and Health: Literacy (1991): 17% of adult population. Universities (1991): 2. Hospital beds (1986): 3,500. Physicians (1985): 160. Life expectancy (1990): women—53; men—48. Infant mortality (1990): 131 per 1,000 live births.

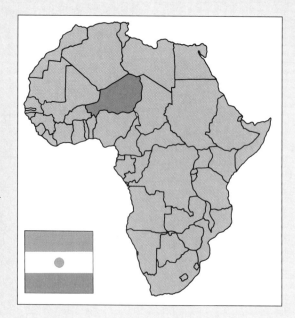

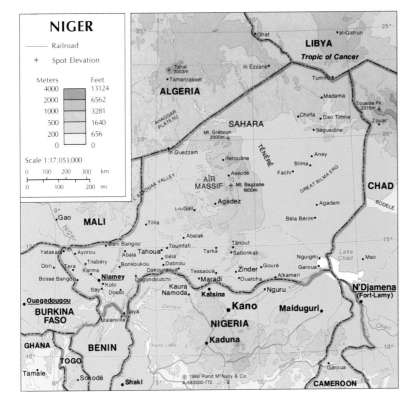

NIGER

— Railroad

+ Spot Elevation

Meters	Feet
4000	13124
2000	6562
1000	3281
500	1640
200	656
0	0

Scale 1:17,053,000

The remains of a medieval fortification stand near Agadez, a city in central Niger founded (11th century) as a station on the trans-Saharan trade routes. Remaining a trade center for the nomadic peoples of northern Niger, Agadez assumed new economic importance after the discovery of uranium in the nearby Arlit region.

most valuable is uranium, and reserves in the northwestern Arlit region are among the largest in the world. Some cassiterite, gypsum, phosphate, salt, iron, tin, tungsten, petroleum, and coal reserves also exist.

People

The peoples of Niger fall into five groups classified by language and livelihood. The arid north and center of the country are home to the TUAREG camel and goat herders, who speak Tamashek, a language related to Berber. Other pastoralists include the FULANI, a cattle-keeping group whose West Atlantic language indicates that their forebears came from Senegal. In the east and northeast live the Teda and Daza, herder-gatherers who speak Saharan languages. Related by language but not livelihood are the Kanuri, agriculturists of the southeast, many of whom are now urban dwellers. By far the most numerous ethnic group is the HAUSA (56%), settled agriculturists who live in the south. To the west are the Songhai-Djerma cultivators. The overwhelming majority of the people are Muslims; most others follow traditional religions. Hausa is the major lingua franca, especially for trade. French remains the official language, although it is spoken by only a small minority. Great variations in population density exist: the lowest densities are found in the desert regions, especially in the northeast, and the highest are found along the Niger River.

Educational and medical facilities are limited outside the larger cities. Although education is free and compulsory for all children from age 7 to age 15, only about 29% actually attend school. The University of Niamey was founded in 1971, and the Islamic University of West Africa at Say was inaugurated in 1987.

Economic Activity

The economy rests on subsistence agriculture, animal husbandry, and exploitation of Niger's mineral wealth. Although only about 3% of the land is cultivated, about 90% of the labor force is engaged in agriculture and herding. Millet, sorghum, and rice are the major subsistence crops. The production of peanuts, formerly the leading agricultural export, has declined. During the mid-1970s cotton cultivation was introduced in order to reduce dependence on a single agricultural export. The nomadic peoples in north and central Niger practice animal husbandry, but their livelihood was adversely affected by drought in 1968–74 and again in 1984–85 and by the closing of the border with Nigeria from 1984 to 1986.

Extraction of minerals for export is the leading industry. Manufacturing is limited to primary products—peanut oil and other processed foods, beer, cotton textiles, and cement. Uranium exports provide the major source of government revenue. In the 1980s, a drop in world demand for uranium forced the government to cut back on its ambitious development plans. The country has a large foreign debt and is heavily dependent on foreign aid.

History and Government

Fossils and artifacts in Niger testify to a long period of human habitation, and both Roman and later Arab historians described contact and trade with the region. During the Middle Ages the western part of present-day Niger formed part of the SONGHAI empire, established during the 7th century by Berbers, and had accepted Islam by the 11th century. Much of eastern Niger belonged to the state of KANEM-BORNU (14th–19th centuries). In the south city-states arose (c.14th century) among the Hausa and became southern termini for trans-Saharan commerce. During the early 19th century the Hausa states were conquered by Fulani under the Muslim reformer USMAN DAN FODIO.

In the 1890s the French signed treaties with the rulers of the Say, Gaya, and Dosso states, but Niger did not become a formal French colony within French West Africa until 1922.

In 1960 the colony gained its independence, and Hamani Diori, who had led the independence movement, became the first president. From 1968 to 1974 a severe drought took place throughout the Sahel, and Niger's residents, especially the nomadic peoples of the north, suffered severely. Diori governed until 1974, when a group of army officers accused him of mismanaging relief efforts during the Sahelian drought. A military and civilian council, headed first by Col. Seyni Kountoché (until his death in 1987) and later by Col. Ali Seybou, then ruled the country. In 1989 the first national elections since 1960 were held. Seybou was elected to a 7-year term as president under a new constitution establishing a second republic; in 1990, Seybou agreed in principle to amend the constitution to permit multipartyism.

Niger-Congo languages   see AFRICAN LANGUAGES

Niger River   Africa's third longest river, the Niger flows for 4,185 km (2,600 mi) through West Africa to empty into the Gulf of Guinea. Rising in the Fouta Djallon highlands of Guinea, it flows northeast into Mali, then east and southeast through Mali, Niger, and Nigeria. The Niger's watershed covers about 1,554,000 km^2 (600,000 mi^2).

The river's annual flooding has been harnessed by dams, at Sansanding and Ségou, Mali, and at Kainji, Nigeria. Between Ségou and Timbuktu, the river divides into many channels and lakes in a marshy region known as Maçina. The upper, middle, and lower courses of the Niger, all navigable, are separated by rapids. The Niger delta, the largest in Africa, forms at Aboh, Nigeria, about 240 km (150 mi) from the sea, and covers an area of about 36,260 km^2 (14,000 mi^2).

The Niger basin is sparsely populated except in areas of irrigated agriculture. Fishing is a major industry along the entire river, and there are rich petroleum deposits under the delta and offshore.

During the 12th to 15th centuries the Niger was the site of the Mali and Songhai empires. Mungo Park reached the river in 1796 and explored it in 1805. The Niger River

Commission was formed in 1963 to coordinate multinational projects.

Nigeria [ny-jir'-ee-uh]   The Federal Republic of Nigeria, located on the Atlantic coast in West Africa, is bordered by Benin on the west, Niger and Chad on the north, and Cameroon on the east. Nigeria is the most populous country in Africa. Lagos, the acting capital, is the largest city in sub-Saharan Africa. Nigeria is a country of immense physical and human diversity. Formerly a British colony, it derives its name from the Niger River. The country attained its independence on Oct. 1, 1960.

Land and Resources

The major physiographic feature of the country is the Niger River, which—with its principal tributary, the Benue River—forms a giant Y, dividing Nigeria into three regions. The highest point is Mount Dimlang (2,042 m/ 6,700 ft), near the border with Cameroon. The principal physical regions are the coastal plains and the Niger delta in the south, the Oyo-Yoruba upland in the southwest, the Udi plateau in the southeast, the Adamawa highlands along the eastern border, the Niger-Benue lowland, the high plains of Hausaland with the Jos plateau superimposed, and the Chad Basin in the extreme northeast.

Much of the surface consists of Precambrian rocks, which are more than 600 million years old. Many areas are overlain with younger sedimentary or volcanic rocks; recently deposited materials make up the coastline and the Niger Delta.

Along the coast, swamp soils are found. Inland are well-drained, excessively leached soils low in organic matter. Farther inland, rainfall and leaching diminish. In the north, sandy soils are formed from material blown in from the Sahara.

Climate. Climate is determined primarily by distance from the ocean. Rainfall varies from more than 3,300 mm (130 in) along the coast to less than 650 mm (26 in) along the northern border and falls mostly from May to September. Maximum temperatures range from 35° C (95° F) on the coast, where cloud cover is nearly continuous, to above 41° C (105° F) in the north. Minimum temperatures range from 22° C (72° F) in the south to 19° C (66° F) in the north.

Drainage, Vegetation, and Animal Life. The NIGER RIVER originates in the highlands of Guinea and flows northeast toward the Sahara before turning southward toward Nigeria, where it enters the Gulf of Guinea (see GUINEA, GULF OF) off Nigeria's southern coast about 4,200 km (2,600 mi) farther on. The Benue River is about 1,085 km (675 mi) in length. Other important rivers are the Cross, the Kaduna, and the Sokoto. Lake Chad (see CHAD, LAKE) occupies the extreme northeastern corner of the country.

Natural-vegetation distribution coincides with the climatic pattern. The three basic types are swamp forest in the delta and coastal zone, tropical rain forest in the humid south, and savanna in the subhumid middle belt and dry north. High population pressure precludes abundant animal life.

AT A GLANCE

FEDERAL REPUBLIC OF NIGERIA

Land: Area: 924,630 km² (357,000 mi²). Official capital: Abuja (1987 est. pop., 15,000); acting capital and largest city: Lagos (1989 est. pop., 1,274,000).

People: Population (1990 est.): 118,819,317. Density: 128 persons per km² (333 per mi²). Distribution (1986): 28% urban, 72% rural. Official language: English. Major religions: Islam, Christianity, traditional religions.

Government: Type: military rule. Legislature: National Assembly (suspended). Political subdivisions: 21 states, capital territory.

Economy: GNP (1989): $30.0 billion; $270 per capita. Labor distribution (1985): agriculture—58%; manufacturing—18%; trade—16%; public administration, services and finance—6%. Foreign trade (1989): imports—$5.7 billion; exports—$8.4 billion. Currency: 1 naira = 100 kobo.

Education and Health: Literacy (1985): 42%. Universities (1988): 24. Hospital beds (1986): 90,668. Physicians (1986): 16,003. Life expectancy (1990): women—49; men—48. Infant mortality (1990): 119 per 1,000 live births.

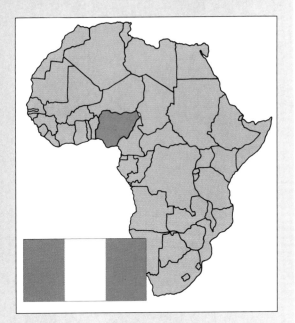

Resources. By far the most important resource is petroleum, although petroleum revenues dropped from a peak of $24 billion in 1980 to $7.1 billion in 1988. At present, production is confined to the offshore and delta areas, although exploration continues throughout the country. Other important minerals are coal, tin, columbite, and gold. About 15% of the total land area is forested, and 34% is under cultivation.

People

About 250 different ethnic groups live in Nigeria. Four ethnic groups together account for more than 70% of the total population: the FULANI and HAUSA live mainly in the north; the IBO (Igbo) predominate in the southeast and the YORUBA in the southwest. The EDO, Ibibio, Kanuri, Nupe, Tiv, Chamba, Ekoi, and Ijaw are smaller, but still important, groups.

Language and Religion. English is the official language, but outside the south and the cities it is little understood. Generally, each ethnic group has its own language, although neighboring peoples frequently speak mutually intelligible languages. Languages spoken by larger groups may have as many as 200 dialects.

Islam, introduced from the north during the 14th century, is the dominant religion in the north; Christianity is dominant in the south. The remainder of the people hold traditional religious beliefs.

Demography. Population statistics concerning Nigeria are widely disputed by demographers. The population is increasing rapidly despite recent government efforts to reduce the birthrate. The percentage of urban dwellers is also expanding rapidly. Major cities include LAGOS, IBADAN, KANO, Enugu, Kaduna, Ogbomosho, and Port Harcourt.

Education and Health. Six years of primary education are free and compulsory. Secondary school enrollments are limited, schools are generally overcrowded, and teacher shortages are common. More than 120,000 students were enrolled in Nigerian universities in 1986. Health-care facilities remain inadequate, especially in rural areas.

Culture. Nigeria has an artistic and cultural heritage unsurpassed in sub-Saharan Africa. Traditional dancing and singing are important to Nigerian culture, particularly in the south. Plastic arts include wood carving, the famous Benin bronzes, and weaving. The Federal Department of Antiquities directs a national system of museums containing art treasures that date to the Nok culture (*c.*500 BC–AD 200; see AFRICAN ART). Contemporary Nigerian authors have made significant contributions to AFRICAN LITERATURE; Wole SOYINKA was awarded the Nobel Prize for literature in 1986.

Economic Activity

The Nigerian economy is the largest in black Africa. Nigeria became a large-scale exporter of petroleum in the mid-1960s, fueling a period of rapid economic expansion. The agricultural sector, however, which had even earlier failed to keep pace with population growth, be-

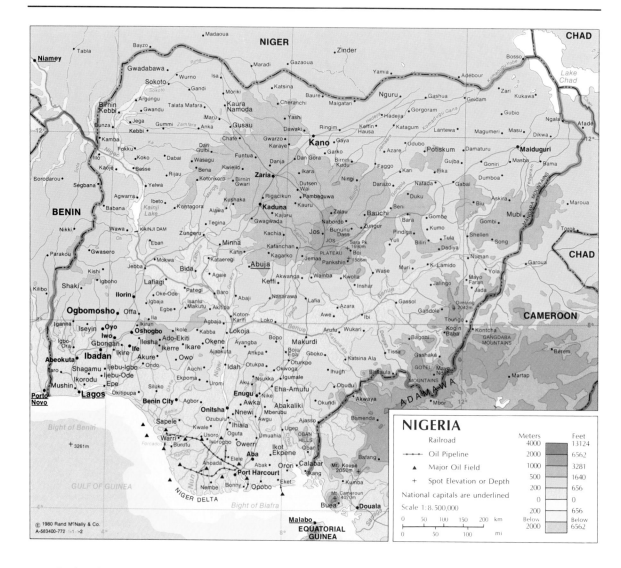

came further depressed. When world demand and prices for petroleum dropped in 1981, Nigeria's foreign-exchange earnings declined precipitously; per capita income declined 50% between 1985 and 1988. Foreign debt increased, factories slowed production or closed for want of imported raw materials and spare parts, and foodstuffs and various consumer goods became increasingly scarce and expensive. The government introduced a variety of austerity measures and attempted to encourage the growth of the agricultural sector and agro-based industries to reduce the dependence on petroleum.

Mining and Energy. Nigeria has about 1% of the world's proven petroleum reserves. By 1989 petroleum provided about 95% of all foreign-exchange earnings, compared with only 1.7% in 1959. Nigeria is also one of the world's largest tin producers, the leading producer of columbite, and a source of coal and limestone. Its iron ore deposits

supply the national steel industry. Electricity production is inadequate.

Agriculture, Forestry, and Fishing. The chief subsistence crops are yams, cassava, and cacao in the south and maize, guinea corn, rice, and millet in the north. The leading export crops are palm oil and kernels, cacao, rubber, and cotton. Obeche, abura, and mahogany are the main commercial trees. Lake Chad is the prime source of fish, followed by the Niger Delta and offshore waters.

Manufacturing. This sector of the economy contributed about 8% of the GDP in 1986. Important industries include oil refining, tin smelting, textile manufacturing, food processing, brewing, cement production, motor-vehicle assembly, sawmilling, and consumer-goods manufacturing.

Transportation. The general flow of transport is north-south, a reflection of both the export-oriented economy and the east-west agricultural belts. Railroads link Lagos and Port Harcourt with points in the north. Most shipping is handled at the port of Lagos.

History and Government

Northern and southern Nigeria (savanna and forest, respectively) have their own separate histories. Arab traders as early as the 8th century found African peoples who were highly organized, with cities and towns, a trading network, and a monarchical government. The earliest firsthand account is that of the Arab traveler IBN BATTUTA, who visited (1352–53) the western savanna zone. A series of kingdoms flourished in the savanna zone, beginning with the kingdom of Ghana (700–1350) in the west and moving eastward to the Hausa emirates (emerged c.1000), in present-day northern Nigeria.

In Yorubaland, in the southeast, archaeological evidence suggests a high degree of urbanization by the 11th century. Highly sophisticated bronze and brass sculptures by the Yoruba and Benin peoples indicate a high level of metallurgical skill (see BENIN, KINGDOM OF). In southeastern Nigeria the Ibo had by the 9th century developed a sophisticated society involved in trade and the arts.

European Era. The first Europeans to visit the Nigerian coast were the Portuguese. By the early 1500s the slave trade was well established. About 6.3 million slaves are estimated to have been transported from West Africa; of these, 23% came from the Slave Coast (western Nigeria, Benin, and Togo), and 42% came from the Niger Delta and the Cameroons.

Much of the British acquisition of Nigeria was accomplished by the Royal Niger Company under Sir George Goldie, and British claims to the Niger Basin were recognized by the other European powers at the Conference of Berlin in 1885. In 1914 the Colony and Protectorate of Nigeria was established, with Sir Frederick (later 1st Bar-

Kano, a state capital and the largest city of northern Nigeria, has been an important center of trans-Saharan commerce since its founding in the 10th century.

on) LUGARD as governor-general. There he established the policy of indirect rule, which became the keystone of administration throughout the British Empire. Colonial rule itself brought about changes that would ultimately lead to its demise; an educated African elite unwilling to remain colonial subjects soon emerged.

Independence and After. In 1960, Nigeria gained its independence. Initially, independent Nigeria was a federation composed of three regions—northern, western, and eastern—each represented in the federal government. The northern region, because of its large population, was able to dominate the entire country politically. Friction increased, especially between the Hausa in the north and the Ibo in the southeast, and resulted in a military coup led by easterners in January 1966. During the upheaval of 1966 many Ibo living in the north were killed, and many others fled to their traditional homeland in the southeast. The coup was viewed by many as an Ibo attempt to take over the country, and six months later another coup placed Gen. Yakubu GOWON (a non-Muslim northerner) in command. In 1967 the Ibos, under the leadership of Chukwuemeka Odumegwu OJUKWU, attempted to secede as the Republic of BIAFRA, which led to a bloody civil war that lasted until 1970, when the Ibo were defeated. In 1975 another military coup led to the elevation of Lt. Gen. Olusegun Obasanjo as head of state.

A new constitution came into force in 1979, when elections were held and the ruling military council transferred power to a civilian government headed by president Shehu Shagari. In December 1983, soon after his reelection, Shagari was overthrown in a coup led by Maj. Gen. Mohammed Buhari. Buhari was ousted in August 1985 in a bloodless coup led by army chief of staff Ibrahim Babangida, who continued his efforts to stem corruption and restructure the economy. Local elections were held in 1987 and 1988. A controversial constitution creating a two-party federal system was promulgated in 1989. In an effort to ease continuing religious and ethnic tensions, nine new states were created in 1991; the capital was formally transferred to Abuja, in the center of the country. State elections were held that year, and elections for a bicameral legislature, in July 1992. On October 7 the government suspended political activity pending an investigation of charges of fraud during the September presidential primaries. This raised questions about whether a return to civilian rule would take place as scheduled in 1993.

night blindness   Impairment of the vision normally possible in dim light is called night blindness, or nyctalopia. The condition may be an early sign of vitamin A deficiency, because that vitamin plays a major role in the cells of the EYE sensitive to dim light. Night blindness is also a manifestation of various eye disorders. It is often the earliest symptom of retinitis pigmentosa, a chronic and progressive inflammation of the retina. One form of the condition, called congenital stationary night blindness, is hereditary. Treatment of night blindness is aimed at treating the underlying disorder. In the case of vitamin deficiency, use of vitamin tablets or a diet rich in the pigments called CAROTENOIDS can help restore night vision, because the liver converts carotenoids into vitamin A.

night lizard   The night lizards, constituting the New World family Xantusiidae, are 11 or more species of small, soft-skinned lizards closely related to the geckos. They are generally gray or brown and about 13 cm (5 in) in length. They have small beadlike scales on the back and large rectangular scales on the belly. The eyes have vertical pupils and fused eyelids, and each eye is permanently covered by a windowlike transparent scale. Most species of night lizards are secretive and nocturnal, hiding in rocky outcroppings or under roots or logs and coming out at night to feed on insects and spiders. Night lizards bear their young alive and are truly viviparous. Usually two young are born, and in the desert night lizard, *Xantusia vigilis*, gestation is about three months.

night sight   The generic term for a variety of military devices that allow one to "see" at night, *night sights* operate on several principles: the optical magnification of the smallest amounts of light, infrared imaging, and thermal sensing systems that create images based on temperature differentials. The sniperscope, for example, was a device used by the Allied forces during World War II. It could sense infrared, or thermal, radiation from objects having a temperature differing only slightly from that of their surroundings.

The Starlight Scope, employing image-intensifying technology, was used extensively during the Vietnam War. The FLIR (Forward Looking Infrared), among the most technologically advanced sighting devices, senses the differences in the heat of objects on the ground and projects images of the objects on a screen. Useful in bad weather and at night, the FLIR can also detect camouflaged and concealed objects.

nighthawk   Nighthawk is the common name for several species of migratory New World birds related to the whippoorwill and the nightjars of the goatsucker family, Caprimulgidae. The common nighthawk, *Chordeiles minor*, is robin-sized, measuring about 25 cm (10 in) in length, and has dark plumage with white patches on its

The common nighthawk catches insects in midair. Laboratory tests show that 1 bird consumed 500 mosquitoes in a day and another bird consumed 2,175 flying ants.

long, pointed wings. It nests over much of North America and winters in South America. Like the other goatsuckers, it feeds on insects on the wing.

nightingale   Nightingales, comprising two species of the thrush family, Turdidae, are renowned for the beauty of their songs, often heard at night. The nightingale, *Luscinia megarhynchos*, measures 16 cm (6.5 in) in length and has a brown back, clear, pale underparts, and a reddish brown tail. It lives in dense thickets throughout western Europe and Anatolia. The thrush nightingale, *L. luscinia*, is similar to the nightingale but darker in color, with a less reddish tail and a lightly speckled breast. It lives in northeastern Europe and Siberia. Both species winter in Africa.

Nightingale, Florence   The English nurse Florence Nightingale, b. May 12, 1820, d. Aug. 13, 1910, is considered, because of her dedication to the care of war victims, the founder of modern nursing and a pioneer in sanitation and hygiene. Born in Florence, Italy, Nightingale obtained brief nursing training in the early 1850s. She was appointed supervisor of nursing at British army hospitals during the Crimean War. Her nursing care in Turkey and the Crimea revolutionized army medical care, greatly reduced mortality rates, and brought about strict sanitary and nursing standards. In 1860 she established a school for training nurses that became a model for nursing training. In 1907 she became the first woman awarded the British Order of Merit.

Florence Nightingale, a British nurse and reformer, established the modern nursing profession. Widely acclaimed for her services to the British troops during the Crimean War (1854–56), Nightingale founded (1860) one of the first nursing schools, the Nightingale School and Home for Nurses at Saint Thomas's Hospital, London.

nightmare   A nightmare is a vividly unpleasant, often violent dream that awakens the sleeping person. Like other dreams, nightmares occur during the stages of SLEEP known as REM (rapid eye movement) sleep (see DREAMS AND DREAMING).

About half of all children experience nightmares at some time, but the frequency of such dreams usually decreases with age. Some adults, however, have nightmares throughout their lives, and nightmares also tend to occur following periods of unusual STRESS. In general they are not taken as signs of sleep disorder or as indications of any particular physiological or psychological problems such as depression. More rarely, they may require treatment.

Night terrors, on the other hand, are considered disorders of arousal from sleep. These incidents of panicky arousal from non-REM (nondreaming) sleep also occur more frequently in children than in adults, especially in the very young.

nightshade Nightshade is the common name for a family of plants, Solanaceae, and particularly for the plants of one of its genera, *Solanum*. The genus *Solanum* comprises about 1,700 species of widely distributed annual and perennial herbs, many shrubs, and some trees. Poisonous alkaloids are present in many of these plants, including the common potato, *S. tuberosum*, which is perfectly safe to eat if cooked.

The common, or black, nightshade, *S. nigrum*, native to Europe but now widespread elsewhere, is an annual, weak-stemmed plant that may be prostrate or erect and grow to 75 cm (2.5 ft) in length. It has long-stalked, irregularly margined leaves and small white flowers with turned-back petals. Its fruit is a black berry. The bitter nightshade, *S. dulcamara*, is native to Eurasia but now grows wild in North America. In Europe it is often called the bittersweet, but it should not be confused with the American bittersweet, *Celastrus*. The leaves of the bitter nightshade are pointed and usually have two narrow lobes at the base. The flowers are small and violet in color, with turned-back petals and beaklike anthers. The oval berries are borne in drooping clusters and ripen into a brilliant red color. The related deadly nightshade, or BELLADONNA, *Atropa belladonna*, is cultivated for medicinal purposes in treating asthma and hyperacidity.

nihilism [ny'-ul-izm] Nihilism, a form of philosophical realism popular in Russia during the 1860s and '70s, reflected a scientific and materialist view of humankind and of its place in the physical world. Ivan TURGENEV, in his novel *Fathers and Sons*, was the first to apply the term to the young radicals of the era; he used it to describe the character Bazarov, who negated everything that could not be proved scientifically. As materialists and atheists, the nihilists saw contemporary society as existing apart from the harmony of nature, maintaining itself through hypocrisy and lies. Young Russians, therefore, sought to liberate humanity and transform society by behaving in accordance with their true natures.

Nijinsky, Vaslav [ni-zhin'-skee, vuh-slahf'] Vaslav Fomich Nijinsky, b. Kiev, Russia, Mar. 12 (N.S.), 1888, d. 1950, was one of the greatest male dancers in the

Vaslav Nijinsky, one of the 20th century's greatest dancers, is shown here in the role of the cavalier in Mikhail Fokine's ballet Les Sylphides. *Nijinsky achieved his greatest success as the premier dancer and choreographer of the Ballets Russes de Serge Diaghilev.*

history of BALLET. He joined (1907) the Imperial (Maryinsky) Ballet and was at once given solo roles. Nijinsky began to move in the aristocratic society of Saint Petersburg and in 1908 met Serge DIAGHILEV, who was to become his mentor.

Nijinsky performed in Europe with the BALLETS RUSSES DE SERGE DIAGHILEV during his summer vacations from the Imperial Ballet in 1909 and 1910. He had enormous success in such ballets as *Le Pavillon d'Armide* (1909), *Les Sylphides* (1909), and *Schéhérazade* (1910). During his 1911 season with the Imperial Ballet, Nijinsky was dismissed in a controversy over a costume. Nijinsky's new triumphs with Diaghilev's company in 1911 included the creation of the title roles in *Le Spectre de la Rose* (The Spirit of the Rose) and *Petrushka*.

Encouraged by Diaghilev, Nijinsky choreographed and danced in *L'Après-midi d'un Faune* (The Afternoon of a Faun, 1912), into which he introduced stylized movements that were derived from the poses and gestures observable in ancient Greek vase paintings and bas-relief sculptures. Nijinsky created two more ballets in 1913, *Jeux* (Games) and *Le Sacre du Printemps* (The Rite of Spring); both were highly innovative, and *Sacre* created a riot in the theater. Later in 1913 the company, without Diaghilev, sailed for a South American tour. Pursued by a young Hungarian named Romola de Pulszka, Nijinsky suddenly married her in Buenos Aires. When the tour was over, Diaghilev fired Nijinsky, supposedly for a breach of contract but in actuality out of jealousy over his favorite's defection.

Despite their falling-out, Diaghilev again secured Nijinsky for the Ballets Russes' North American tour of 1916–17, during which Nijinsky presented his last ballet, *Till Eulenspiegel* (1916), and danced the title role. He made his final appearance with the Ballets Russes during its 1917 South American tour. Nijinsky and his wife then settled in Switzerland; he was severely troubled by mental instability, which in 1919 was diagnosed as schizophrenia. Nijinsky spent the rest of his life in and out of mental institutions. His final three years were spent in London, where he died on Apr. 8, 1950.

Nijinsky's creative life was brief but exceedingly brilliant. A phenomenal master of technique, he had tremendous elevation, achieved without visible preparation. His combination of virtuosity and acting ability, allied with his innate sense of style, contributed to his legendary reputation.

Nijinsky's sister, the renowned choreographer Bronislava Nijinska (1891–1972), danced with him in the Maryinsky and Diaghilev companies. Some of her best-known works, such as *Les Noces* (The Wedding, 1923) and *Les Biches* (The Does, 1924), were created for the Ballets Russes. From 1938 she taught in California and choreographed for major ballet companies.

Nijmegen [nay'-may-guhn]

Nijmegen is a city in the eastern Netherlands on the Waal River; it has a population of 145,816 (1988 est.). Located near the German border, Nijmegen is an important transportation center. Industrial products include clothing and shoes, heavy machinery, electrical and heating equipment, and plastics. The city's university was founded in 1923.

Originally the Roman city of Noviomagus, Nijmegen is the oldest town in the Netherlands. Charlemagne built a palace there, remnants of which are still visible. After decades as a free imperial city, it became an active member of the Hanseatic League. Nijmegen is best known for the treaties concluded there in 1678–79, terminating the war of Louis XIV of France against the Dutch. The city suffered heavy bombardment during World War II, but several old buildings escaped damage. Since the war much new construction has taken place.

Nike [ny'-kee]

In Greek mythology Nike was the goddess of victory, who presided over all military and athletic contests. The counterpart of the Roman goddess Victoria, she was primarily an abstraction rather than a mythological figure but achieved great popularity following the Greek victories over the Persians in 480 BC. Represented in art as winged and standing on a globe, holding laurel and a palm branch, Nike was perhaps most perfectly realized in the Hellenistic sculpture known as the Nike of Samothrace (220–190 BC; Louvre, Paris), or the Winged Victory.

Nikolais, Alwin [ni'-koh-ly]

Choreographer, director, designer, and composer Alwin Nikolais, b. Southington, Conn., Nov. 25, 1912, is the creator of an innovative form of mixed-media theater. Since 1953 his Dance Theatre has presented programs that use movement as part of a grand design of electronic sound, elaborate props and costumes, and special lighting effects. Some works are abstract studies in dance design, such as *Tent* (1968); others, such as *Gallery* (1978), are marked by allegorical overtones. In 1989, Nikolais and director-choreographer Murray Louis merged their two companies, forming Nikolais and Louis Dance. They jointly choreographed *Segue*, which was premiered by the new company in 1990.

Nikon [nee'-kohn]

Patriarch of Moscow and all Russia from 1652 to 1660, Nikon, b. 1605, d. Aug. 27 (N.S.), 1681, was one of the most eminent figures in the history of the Russian Orthodox church. Nikon became involved in the internal drama of Russian Christianity in the 17th century. Faced with the necessity of revising the text of liturgical books, he decreed (1654) that such revisions be made in accordance with Greek liturgical books, which differed in some details from the Russian ones. This provoked the schism of the OLD BELIEVERS. Tiring of Nikon's authoritarian manner, Tsar ALEXIS had him deposed on political grounds (1660) and condemned by a council (1666). His liturgical reforms were, however, fully endorsed. After years of exile, Nikon was recalled to Moscow by Tsar Fyodor III; he died on the journey.

Nile River [nyl]

The Nile River of northeastern Africa, the longest river in the world, flows north for 6,650 km (4,132 mi) from the most distant headwaters of the White Nile in Burundi to the Mediterranean Sea, crossing Rwanda, Uganda, Sudan, and Egypt. Major tributaries, such as the Blue Nile, rise in the highlands of western Ethiopia, and smaller watercourses in Kenya and Tanzania also drain into the Nile. The drainage basin thus encompasses about 3,349,000 km^2 (1,293,000 mi^2). More than 3,200 km (2,000 mi) of the Nile are navigable.

The word *Nile* is probably derived from the Semitic root *nahal*, meaning "river valley." Although references to the Nile appear in the earliest records from the eastern Mediterranean region, the Nile's tributaries remained unknown in Europe and the Muslim world until the modern era. In 1613, Pedro Páez, a Spanish Jesuit, visited the headwaters of the Blue Nile; in 1860, the English explorer John SPEKE identified the southernmost source of the White Nile.

The River's Course. Relative to its great length, the Nile basin is narrow, reaching only 1,930 km (1,200 mi) at its widest point. The course of the Nile and its tributaries may be divided into eight major geographical regions from south to north. In the far south the lake region of East Africa gives rise to streams that ultimately form the headwaters of the White Nile. Some of these streams flow into Lake VICTORIA, Africa's largest lake; some flow into Lake ALBERT; they then unite at Kabalega Falls in Uganda. The second zone begins near the Sudan-Uganda border where the stream called the Bahr al-Jebel descends rapidly over rough terrain, eventually flowing into the third zone, a low, broad, marshy plain known as the Sudd about 160 km (100 mi) farther north. North of the Sudd the stream is called the White Nile; about 800 km (500 mi) long, the White Nile furnishes 29% of the Nile's total volume. The fourth and fifth zones are the Blue Nile and the Atbara rivers, the Nile's eastern tributaries, which drain the Ethiopian highlands and Lake TANA and provide the

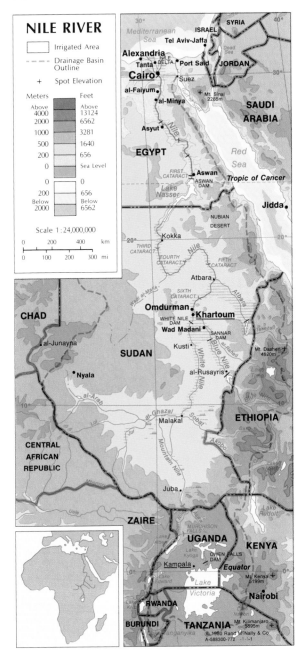

NILE RIVER

☐ Irrigated Area

- - - - Drainage Basin
Outline

+   Spot Elevation

Meters		Feet	
Above 4000		Above 13124	
2000		6562	
1000		3281	
500		1640	
200		656	
0		Sea Level	
0		0	
200		656	
Below 2000		Below 6562	

Scale 1 : 24,000,000

0   200   400   km

0   100   200   300   mi

Lake NASSER, one of the world's largest artificial lakes. In the seventh zone, between Aswan and the Nile Delta, the river flows for about 725 km (450 mi), irrigating lands that are cultivated to the shoreline. The eighth zone, north of Cairo, is the 160-km-long (100-mi) delta, formed by thousands of years of silt deposits. Here the Nile branches into many small streams and two major ones—the Rosetta and Damietta—which meander to the Mediterranean Sea.

History and Economy. The Nile basin did not always look as it does today. About 30 million years ago the Atbara may have been the main headstream. At that time streams in the southern portion of the drainage system flowed into the Sudd, which formed a large inland lake independent of the Nile. Much later, only 20,000 to 25,000 years ago, the East African lake system began draining north toward the Sudd, causing it to spill over and combine its watershed with that of the northern Nile. The region sheltered not only the ancient Egyptian civilization (see EGYPT, ANCIENT), which arose about 3100 BC, but also MEROË, the capital (656 BC–AD 320) of Cush and an early iron-working center; early Christian and Muslim states in southern Egypt and the northern Sudan; kingdoms such as Buganda, established during the 17th century in East Africa; and many smaller social and political units.

People living along the Nile and its tributaries include fishers and cultivators in the irrigated north and wetter south, nomads who raise cattle and camels in the northern Sudan, and cattle herders in the White Nile, Bahr al-Jebel, and East African lakes regions. Nearly 99% of Egypt's population live in the Nile valley and delta.

Irrigation began in the time of the ancient Egyptians, but the first dams were constructed only in 1861. The Aswan High Dam increased the amount of land under irrigation by about 20% and produces substantial electricity. Other dams in Sudan and Uganda provide hydroelectric power and surplus water during the dry season. Work on the Jonglei Canal, designed to divert the flow of the White Nile around the Sudd and provide additional water to Egypt and northern Sudan, was halted by civil war in 1984.

Nilsson, Birgit [nil'-suhn, bir'-git] The Swedish dramatic soprano Birgit Nilsson, b. May 17, 1918, is best known internationally for her Wagnerian roles, particularly as Brünnhilde in *The Ring of the Nibelung*. She studied singing in Stockholm, and from 1947 to 1951 she sang with the Stockholm Opera. She performed at the Glyndebourne Festival (England) in 1951 and sang Elsa in *Lohengrin* and Isolde in *Tristan and Isolde* at the Bayreuth Festival (Germany) in 1954 and 1957, respectively. Nilsson has appeared on most of the major opera stages of Europe. She made her American debut at the Hollywood Bowl in 1956, subsequently appearing with the San Francisco Opera and the Chicago Lyric Opera. Her Metropolitan Opera debut, as Isolde, took place in 1959. One of her biggest triumphs was her interpretation of the title role in Puccini's *Turandot*, which she first sang in Paris in 1968. After her retirement from the operatic stage in the early 1980s, Nilsson continued to give concert performances.

greatest amount of water to the main river. The sixth zone begins at Khartoum, Sudan, where the White Nile and the Blue Nile join, and continues to Aswan in southern Egypt. Along this stretch of the Nile, about 1,800 km (1,100 mi) long, the river makes a great S-shaped turn and is broken by the six cataracts, stretches of rapids and waterfalls. Aswan, located at the first cataract, is also the site of the ASWAN HIGH DAM (completed 1971), which created

Nimbus [nim'-buhs]   Nimbus, named for the meteorological term for rain clouds, was a second-generation series of weather satellites that followed TIROS. Seven satellites were launched between 1964 and 1978. *Nimbus 1*, launched Aug. 28, 1964, returned thousands of cloud-cover photographs, as did *Nimbus 2* in 1966. After a launch failure in 1968, *Nimbus 3* (Apr. 14, 1969) returned geodetic, infrared, television and cloud-cover data and was the first U.S. satellite to make repetitive day-and-night global atmospheric temperature measurements at various altitudes. *Nimbus 4* (Apr. 8, 1970), *Nimbus 5* (Dec. 11, 1972), and *Nimbus 6* (June 12, 1975) were similar to *Nimbus 3* but contained new and improved instrumentation. The last in the series, *Nimbus 7* (Oct. 24, 1978), was the first satellite to monitor the Earth's atmosphere for artificial and natural pollutants.

Nimbus, always using the most advanced instrumentation, could take pictures at night and during the day. During a typical day, 1,440 pictures were taken and stored on tape for subsequent readout to tracking stations on the ground. In addition, Nimbus carried an automatic picture-transmission system, including a TV camera that sent pictures shortly after they were taken.

As the technology of weather satellites advanced, instruments such as the high-resolution infrared radiometer were tested aboard Nimbus. Although not a camera, the radiometer can detect the difference between cloud and surface temperatures, thus permitting the construction of an image of cloud cover at night. Other experimental instruments included a variety of specialized spectrometers and radiometers, which significantly advanced the technology of weather satellites in determining temperature, ozone, and water-vapor profiles within the atmosphere, as well as variations of solar radiation and its effect on weather.

Nimeiry, Muhammad Gaafar al- [nim-air'-ee, gah-fahr' ahl]   Muhammad Gaafar al-Nimeiry, b. Jan. 1, 1930, leader of Sudan from 1969 to 1985, led the overthrow of the civilian government of Muhammad Mahgoub in May 1969. He became prime minister later that year and won presidential elections in 1971, 1977, and 1983. In 1972, Nimeiry ended a 17-year civil war between Sudan's Arab and Muslim north and its largely Christian and animist south. Following rising protests over economic issues and his imposition (1983) of Islamic law, Nimeiry was ousted in an April 1985 coup led by Sudanese defense minister Gen. Siwar al-Dahab.

Nîmes [neem]   Nîmes is the capital city of Gard department in Provence, southern France. Located about 105 km (65 mi) northwest of Marseille, today the city serves as a trade and industrial center where a wide variety of goods are produced. It has a population of 129,924 (1982).

Nîmes is best known, however, as one of the finest examples of the prosperous Gallo-Roman settlements located in southern France. The city, originally named Nemausus (for the local god of spring), served as a regional Celtic capital. In 121 BC the city came under Roman control. Soon after the residents received (c.28 BC) Roman citizenship, the city was replanned. A new city wall enclosed a forum with temples, an amphitheater, a watchtower, and a fountain sanctuary. The famous Pont du Gard was built in 19 BC. Under Hadrian (r. 117–38 AD) the city achieved great prosperity. The best-known monument of Nîmes is the Maison Carrée, a remarkably well-preserved Corinthian temple.

NIMH   see NATIONAL INSTITUTE OF MENTAL HEALTH

Nimitz, Chester W. [nim'-its]   The U.S. admiral Chester William Nimitz, b. Fredricksburg, Tex., Feb. 24, 1885, d. Feb. 20, 1966, planned the victorious war against the Japanese navy in World War II. A 1905 graduate of Annapolis, Nimitz served with the U.S. submarine force in World War I. He was put in command of the Pacific Fleet early in World War II and directed the U.S. victories at the battles of Midway (1942), the Philippine Sea (1944), and Leyte Gulf (1944). Nimitz was promoted (1944) to fleet (five-star) admiral and was a signer of the Japanese surrender document. From 1945 to 1947 he was chief of naval operations.

Nin, Anaïs [nin, uh-ny'-is]   An American novelist and diarist of Spanish and French descent whose work was neglected for many years, Anaïs Nin, b. Paris, Feb. 21, 1903, d. Jan. 14, 1977, collected a circle of discriminating admirers in Paris. The publication (1965) of her correspondence with Henry Miller sparked a more general interest, but her reputation was firmly established with the publication of the six-volume *Diary of Anaïs Nin* (1966–76), a remarkable record of a woman's journey toward psychic integration and artistic fulfillment. Nin's earlier novels, which the diaries illuminate, were influenced by surrealism; five of them, published between 1946 and 1958, are collected in *Cities of the Interior* (1959). Among her critical writings are *D. H. Lawrence: An Unprofessional Study* (1930), *The Novel of the Future* (1968), and *In Favor of the Sensitive Man* (1976), a collection of essays.

Nineteen Eighty-Four   George ORWELL's famous novel *Nineteen Eighty-Four*, written in 1949, is set in an imaginary state of the future where freedom of thought and action have utterly disappeared. Humans are under the constant scrutiny of the government, symbolized by Big Brother, whose posters everywhere warn that "Big Brother is Watching You." Children are taken from their parents, and love is strictly forbidden. The story centers on one couple's escape attempt and ultimate defeat at the hands of the secret police. Although *Nineteen Eighty-Four* is often thought of as science fiction, it is actually a notable work of utopian literature emphasizing what Orwell believed were the dangers inherent in modern bureaucratic society.

19th Amendment see Constitution of the United States; suffrage, women's

---

Nineveh [nin'-uh-vuh]   Nineveh, the capital of ancient Assyria, lies on the left bank of the Tigris River opposite present-day Mosul, Iraq. Prehistoric occupation of the site dates back to at least the 6th millennium BC. Holding an important position on the main river crossing in the fertile northern Mesopotamian plain, Nineveh was dominated in the 3d millennium BC by the Agade and Ur empires and in the 2d millennium by the Mitanni and Kassite empires. With the rise of Assyrian power in the late 2d millennium, the city became a royal residence and was finally established as the capital by King Sennacherib (r. 704–681 BC), who replanned the city and built for himself a magnificent palace. Sacked (612 BC) by the Medes, Nineveh declined, although occupation of the site continued through the Seleucid and Parthian periods until medieval times.

Sennacherib's city wall, more than 12 km (7.5 mi) long, enclosed an area of about 700 ha (1,730 acres); it was pierced by 15 great gates, 5 of which have been excavated. The northern Nergal Gate, with its original flanking bull colossi, has been restored. The palaces of Sennacherib and his grandson Ashurbanipal stand at Kuyunjik, the citadel of the site. Their walls and doorways were lined with sculptured reliefs, many of which are now in the Louvre, Paris, and the British Museum, London (including Ashurbanipal's famous Lion Hunt reliefs, now in the British Museum). Sennacherib's palace comprised at least 80 rooms. Archives of cuneiform tablets were found in both palaces, but the library of Ashurbanipal forms an unrivaled epigraphic source for current knowledge of Mesopotamian history. One of the greatest treasures of ancient Mesopotamia, it contains more than

During the reign (669–633 BC) of the Assyrian king Ashurbanipal, Nineveh flourished as the capital of his empire, which extended from Egypt to the Persian Gulf. Ashurbanipal is portrayed in a hunting scene in this relief from the royal palace. (British Museum, London.)

20,000 tablets and fragments, many of which are copies of ancient Mesopotamian texts such as the Sumerian Epic of Gilgamesh and the Babylonian Flood story.

Ningbo (Ning-po) [ning-boh]   Ningbo is a city in eastern Zhejiang province of China. It has a population of 1,050,000 (1988 est.). Located about 160 km (100 mi) south of Shanghai, Ningbo is the center of overland and river transportation in the eastern part of the province and the region's principal fishing port. A railroad links Ningbo with Hangzhou and with the national railroad network. Manufactures include steel, diesel engines, farm equipment, ships, textiles, and canned foods. The outer port handles coastal shipping.

Ningbo was settled in the 8th century and in 1842 became one of the first Chinese ports to be opened to international trade. It was occupied by the Japanese during World War II.

Ningxia (Ningsia) [ning-shyah]   Ningxia is an autonomous region in northern China. Its 66,400-km^2 (25,600-mi^2) area contains a population of 4,655,451 (1990). Approximately one-third of the population are Hui, or Chinese Muslims. Its capital and main city is Yinchuan (1982 pop., 576,000). The southern part of the region is a loess plateau, and the northern part is a flat plain that is well irrigated by the Huang He. Wheat, rice, sugar beets, fruits, and cotton are cultivated, and pigs and sheep are raised. Coal mining and wool and tool manufacturing round out the economy.

Inhabited before the 3d century BC, Ningxia was made part of the Tangut kingdom in the 11th century. Some of the area was captured by Genghis Khan during the 13th century. Once part of Gansu province, Ningxia province was formed in 1928 but reverted to Gansu in 1954. In 1958 the southern portion of the former province was made an autonomous region, and in 1970 the boundary was moved north to enlarge the autonomous region.

Ninian, Saint [nin'-ee-uhn]   Apostle to the Picts and Britons, Saint Ninian, c.360–c.432, a Briton, went to Rome as a youth and there was instructed in Christian doctrine and later ordained bishop. Sent to convert Scotland, Ninian established a church, *Candida Casa* ("White House"), dedicated to Saint Martin of Tours, in the Strathclyde region. It long served as a center of learning, and Ninian's tomb was a popular shrine in the Middle Ages. Feast day: Sept. 16.

9th Amendment see Bill of Rights; Constitution of the United States

---

Niobe [ny'-oh-bee]   In Greek mythology Niobe, the daughter of Tantalus, was the wife of King Amphion of Thebes and the mother of six sons and six daughters. Because she taunted Leto for having only two children—

ARTEMIS and APOLLO—Leto's twins avenged their mother by killing all of Niobe's offspring. The story of Niobe's never-ending tears and of Zeus turning her into stone is recounted in Ovid's *Metamorphoses*.

niobium [ny-oh'-bee-uhm] Niobium is a shiny-white, soft, metallic chemical element in Group VB of the periodic table; its symbol is Nb. The name of the element is derived from the Greek mythological Niobe, the daughter of Tantalus. Niobium has an atomic number of 41, an atomic weight of 92.9064, and 24 isotopes.

The element was discovered by Charles Hatchett in 1801 in a sample of ore sent to England more than a hundred years earlier by the first governor of Connecticut. The metallic element was first prepared in 1864 by Christian Blomstrand of Sweden by reduction of the heated chloride in a stream of hydrogen. Despite the adoption of the name *niobium* by the International Union of Pure and Applied Chemistry, the alternative name *columbium* is still used by metallurgists in the United States.

A ductile metal, niobium has a melting point of 2,468° C, a boiling point of 4,742° C, and a density of 8.51 g/cm^3 at 20° C. It exhibits valences of 2, 3, 5, and possibly 4 as well. It is used in superconductive magnets and as an alloying agent in carbon and alloy steels.

Nippur [nip-oor'] Nippur, at modern Nuffar, about 160 km (100 mi) southeast of Baghdad, Iraq, was the principal religious center of ancient SUMER. The city, bisected by a wadi and covering an area of about 79 ha (180 acres), was occupied almost continuously from c.4000 BC until the Islamic period (AD c.800). Although Nippur was never politically dominant, the Ekur precinct of Enlil (see MARDUK), chief god of the Sumerian pantheon and bestower of kingship, was maintained by Mesopotamian rulers until Neo-Babylonian times.

Much of the extant Enlil temple and adjacent ZIGGURAT was built (c.2100 BC) by Ur-Nammu of Ur. Of particular importance are the cuneiform archives from the west mound and scribal quarter, which give information on the economic and administrative life of Nippur. Excavation, begun in 1851 by Austen Layard, has progressed intermittently since 1889.

nirvana [nir-vah'-nuh] Although common to Hinduism, Jainism, and Buddhism, the notion of nirvana became a concept of central importance only in Buddhism, where it refers to the ultimate state attained by the Buddha and to the goal recognized by all Buddhists. Involving a release from samsara, or bondage to physical desire and pain, nirvana in Hinduism can be achieved only by a complete cessation of the cycle of death and rebirth. In Buddhism, by contrast, nirvana refers to the cooling, or blowing out, of the passions, especially the extinction of the selfish passions, a state of enlightenment that can be achieved either in this life or after death.

Nisei [nee-say] The Nisei ("second generation") are native-born American citizens who are the children of Japanese immigrants, the Issei. All of them faced harsh discrimination on the Pacific Coast, where they settled in large numbers. California passed (1913, 1920) alien land laws that barred the Issei from owning or leasing agricultural land and forbade them to purchase land in the names of their children, the Nisei.

Feared as potential saboteurs during World War II, 112,000 Japanese Americans, 70,000 of them Nisei, were evacuated from the West Coast by an executive order (Mar. 18, 1942) and placed in ten "relocation centers." In late 1944 the U.S. Supreme Court upheld the legality of the evacuation but also ruled that the prolonged detention of Japanese Americans whose loyalty had been ascertained was illegal.

Under a law passed in 1988, the U.S. government was to issue individual apologies for violations of civil liberties and constitutional rights and award $20,000 in tax-free payments to each eligible internee.

See also: ASIAN AMERICANS.

Nisqually [niz'-kwah-lee] The Nisqually tribe of North American Indians traditionally formed a division of the Puget Sound speakers of Coast SALISH languages. They occupied a number of villages on the Nisqually River and the middle and upper portions of the Puyallup River at the southern end of Puget Sound. Like all groups of the Puget Sound region, the Nisqually depended heavily on salmon runs for subsistence. Large multifamily shed-roof houses of cedar planks were built for shelter. Dugout canoes with low extended prow pieces were constructed for use on the Sound; shovel-nosed canoes, lacking the sharp vertical bow, were used on rivers. Concepts of hereditary rank separated chiefs and nobles from the lower class. All males and some women fasted in lonely places in the forest to acquire a guardian spirit who might bestow special powers for healing or prophecy, for skill at hunting, gambling, and warfare. An estimated 1,455 Nisqually were living on or near the Nisqually reservation in Washington State in 1987.

niter   see NITRATE MINERALS; SALTPETER

nitrate minerals The nitrates comprise a small class of rare minerals characterized by the presence of the nitrate ion (NO_3) as a major constituent. Their rarity in nature—only ten nitrate minerals are known—is explained by their ready solubility in water. The most common nitrates, soda niter ($NaNO_3$) and niter (KNO_3), are found in sheltered places and arid regions, such as desert environments and caves. Soda niter occurs abundantly in deposits in the coastal deserts of northern Chile, from whence the common name *Chile saltpeter* is derived. Niter, commonly called SALTPETER, was mined from caves in Tennessee, Kentucky, Alabama, and Ohio during the War of 1812 and the Civil War for use in the manufacture of gunpowder. Nitrates are now predominantly used in fertilizers.

nitric acid

Nitric acid, HNO_3, is a strong acid (see ACIDS AND BASES) and oxidant. It is sometimes called *aqua fortis*, Latin for "strong water." Pure nitric acid is a colorless liquid, although old solutions may acquire a yellow tinge as light decomposes some acid to nitrogen dioxide, a poisonous gas. Nitric acid attacks all base metals except aluminum, iron, and special chromium steels, all of which react initially to form a protective coating. A mixture of one part of nitric acid and about three parts of hydrochloric acid, HCl, by volume, is known as nitrohydrochloric acid, or *aqua regia*, which attacks all metals, even gold and platinum. Nitric acid is used to manufacture organic and inorganic nitrates and nitro compounds for use as fertilizers, dyes, explosives, and plastics.

nitrite

The term NITRITE refers to compounds containing the nitrogen-oxygen radical NO_2 and in particular to sodium nitrite, $NaNO_2$, which is used in the chemical industry, dyeing and bleaching processes, fertilizers, and photography. It has also served for centuries as a FOOD ADDITIVE in the curing of meat (see FOOD PRESERVATION). Its antimicrobial properties include inhibition of toxin production by the BOTULISM-causing bacillus *Clostridium botulinum*. It also contributes to and stabilizes the color of cured meats such as ham, bacon, and frankfurters. The discovery in the 1960s that nitrite can combine with amines in foods to form nitrosamines, which are proven carcinogens in laboratory animals, led to calls for banning its use, but by the mid-1980s the problem was determined as being mainly limited to bacon. In 1985 the U.S. Food and Drug Administration established lower limits of nitrite use in that product.

nitrogen

The chemical element nitrogen is a colorless, odorless gas. Its chemical symbol is N, its atomic number is 7, and its atomic weight is 14.0067. It is a member of Group VA in the periodic table. Nitrogen was discovered in 1772 by Daniel Rutherford in Scotland, and independently by Joseph Priestley and Henry Cavendish in England and Carl W. Scheele in Sweden. The French chemist Antoine L. Lavoisier proved that it was an element. The name *nitrogen* is derived from the Greek words *nitron* and *genes*, which mean "saltpeter-producing," because one of the most important nitrogen compounds then known was SALTPETER (potassium nitrate, KNO_3).

Occurrence. Nitrogen, the most abundant uncombined element, occurs as the diatomic molecule N_2. Air is 78.06% nitrogen gas by volume (75.5% by weight), and nitrogen is also found in gases from volcanoes, springs, and mines. The most important nitrogenous mineral is sodium nitrate, $NaNO_3$, also known as Chile saltpeter and Chile niter. The nitrogen used in industry is usually obtained by the fractional distillation of liquid air.

Uses. Nitrogen gas is relatively inert because of the stability of the nitrogen-nitrogen triple bond, $N\equiv N$. The primary use of nitrogen is in the synthesis of ammonia, which is then used to produce fertilizers, nitric acid, urea, hydrazine, and amines. Liquid nitrogen is used as a supercoolant in CRYOGENICS. Nitrogen gas is used to form an inert atmosphere in which reactive substances can be stored or processed. Nitrogen is also used to repress oxidation, for example, when coffee is roasted.

Nitrogen Chemistry. Because diatomic nitrogen is a very stable molecule, the gas usually forms compounds only at high temperatures or under high pressure. By passing a high-voltage electrical current through it, nitrogen gas can be split into highly unstable single nitrogen atoms that react readily with mercury, sulfur, phosphorus, and sodium, and with many organic compounds at room temperature. Nitrogen exhibits all oxidation states from −3 to +5 but is usually found in the −3, +3, or +5 oxidation state.

The production of a simple nitrogen compound from atmospheric nitrogen is known as *nitrogen fixation*. In industry, ammonia, nitrogen oxide, and cyanamide are produced by nitrogen fixation. In nature, nitrogen from the air is fixed by some bacteria and plants. It is then made available to all organisms through the NITROGEN CYCLE.

Compounds of Nitrogen. A number of elements react with nitrogen or ammonia to form nitrides. The valence of nitrogen in a nitride is −3. The nitrides can be divided into three groups: the ionic nitrides such as lithium nitride, Li_3N, which have high melting points and are readily hydrolyzed in water to the metal hydroxides and ammonia; the interstitial or metallic nitrides, such as titanium nitride, TiN, which are compounds of nitrogen and a transition metal and are good electrical conductors; and the covalent nitrides, such as boron nitride, BN, which are highly stable and in many cases have properties similar to those of diamonds.

With the exception of NF_3, the compounds formed by nitrogen with halogens are unstable and explosive. With oxygen, nitrogen forms oxides: nitric oxide, NO, nitrogen dioxide, NO_2, and its dimer, dinitrogen tetroxide, N_2O_4, are deadly gases. The damage they do to the breathing passages of the lungs often goes undetected until days after they are inhaled, when death may result because of edema, excessive fluid concentration in the lungs. A mixture of NO_2 and N_2O_4 is given off by automobiles and exists in smog. Nitrous oxide, N_2O, or laughing gas, is a colorless gas with a sweet taste and odor. When it is inhaled, nitrous oxide causes a feeling of intoxication, loss of pain sensation, and (eventually) unconsciousness. It is used as an anesthetic in minor surgery and in dentistry because its effects are short-lived. Nitrites, the salts derived from nitrous acid, HNO_2, and nitrates, the salts derived from NITRIC ACID, HNO_3, are valuable ingredients of fertilizers. The most extensively used nitrate is ammonium nitrate, NH_4NO_3, which is used in fertilizers, explosives, and matches and in producing nitrous oxide. Silver nitrate, $AgNO_3$, is used to produce the silver bromide needed in photography and to cauterize wounds.

Many nitrogen-hydrogen compounds are known. They include hydrogen azide, HN_3; hydrazine, $H_2N{-}NH_2$; ammonia, NH_3, and ammonium salts. Hydrogen azide is a poisonous, explosive liquid that is stable in aqueous solution. Hydrazine is a colorless liquid with a reducing action. It is used to synthesize organic compounds such as pharmaceuticals and rubber and, sometimes, as a rocket fuel. Lead azide, $Pb(N_3)_2$, a salt of hydrogen azide, is an important detonator in the explosives industry. It explodes when heated or upon percussion.

The many important and useful organic nitrogen compounds include proteins, urea, cyanamide, cyanides, and vitamins such as thiamine and riboflavin. Many explosives, such as TNT (trinitrotoluene), and aniline dyes are organic nitrogen compounds. Penicillin and some sulfa drugs contain nitrogen. Nylon, a polyamide, and Spandex, a polyurethane, contain nitrogen.

nitrogen cycle All living organisms participate in the nitrogen cycle, which encompasses the processes and chemical reactions involved in producing organic nitrogen from inorganic nitrogen and subsequently breaking down organic nitrogen back to the inorganic form.

Ammonification. The cycle begins when atmospheric nitrogen and hydrogen combine to form ammonia, NH_3; the electrical energy of lightning drives the reaction. Ammonia combines with rain and becomes available to green plants as dilute nitric acid, HNO_3. Ammonia is also derived from the breakdown of proteins that constitute plant and animal cells. This chemical, combined with the products of PHOTOSYNTHESIS, is used to form amino acids, which are the basic components of plant proteins. Animals eat the plant proteins, break them down into amino acids during the process of digestion, and recombine them to form their own particular forms of protein in order to build tissues and organs of their bodies.

Denitrification. Certain soil bacteria convert nitrogen-containing compounds into ammonia and atmospheric nitrogen, a process known as denitrification. These bacteria, known as denitrifying bacteria, obtain energy by breaking down not only the nitrogen compounds urea, $CO(NH_2)_3$, and uric acid, $C_5H_4N_4O_3$, that are excreted by living animals, but also the nitrogen compounds produced by decaying organic matter.

Nitrification. Several genera of bacteria, also living in the soil, are involved in the process of nitrification. Such bacterial genera as *Nitrosomonas* and *Nitrosococcus* convert ammonia into nitrites (NO_2). *Nitrobacter* species convert nitrites into nitrates (NO_3), which green plants then use in the production of amino acids. Two other common genera of soil bacteria, the anaerobic *Clostridium* and the aerobic *Azotobacter*, produce nitrites and nitrates from free nitrogen.

Nitrogen Fixation. Several species of bacteria, fungi, and blue-green algae are involved in the process of nitrogen fixation. These organisms convert organic nitrogen into ammonia, which is used by higher plants to manufacture complex nitrogen-containing compounds.

An important genus of nitrogen-fixing bacteria is *Rhizobium*, which forms nodules on the roots of legumes (members of the bean family). The bacteria obtain food from the legume, and the legume obtains abundant us-

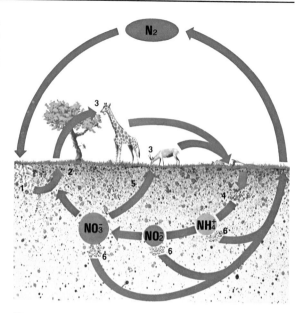

Nitrogen gas (N_2) in the air is converted into nitrates (NO_3^-) by nitrogen-fixing bacteria (1) in the soil. Plants absorb (2) nitrates, from which they obtain the nitrogen needed for growth. Herbivorous animals (3) feed on the plants. Bacteria and fungi (4) decompose the bodies of dead plants and animals, releasing ammonium (NH_4^+) compounds into the soil. Nitrifying bacteria convert these ammonium compounds into nitrites (NO_2^-), which are then converted into nitrates (NO_3^-) to be used (5) by plants. Denitrifying bacteria (6) convert the nitrogen compounds back into nitrogen gas.

able nitrogen compounds from the bacteria. For this reason legumes—such as clovers, alfalfa, beans, and peanuts—are excellent protein sources. Gardeners often inoculate the soil with appropriate species of *Rhizobium* when they are planting legumes in order to produce an abundant, high-quality crop.

Nitrogen Fertilizers. In 1902, Charles Bradley and Jesse Lovejoy succeeded in duplicating one of the natural processes for nitrogen-compound production by passing air through a powerful electric arc. Fritz HABER and Carl Bosch later developed a method for synthesizing ammonia from hydrogen and nitrogen; production of ammonia by the Haber-Bosch process began in 1911. These techniques have been used to manufacture nitrogen FERTILIZERS, which supplement the soil composition.

nitroglycerin [ny-truh-gli′-sur-uhn] Nitroglycerin (glyceryl trinitrate) is a pale yellow oil, highly unstable and toxic, first made in 1846 by the Italian chemist Ascario Sobrero. Alfred NOBEL's first attempts in 1863 to utilize its explosive power were unsuccessful because the extremely unstable nature of the substance precluded its safe transport, storage, and employment. In 1864, Nobel produced solid preparations by mixing nitroglycerin with porous substances such as kieselguhr, thus allowing the explosive to be employed as a safe, stable, blasting agent, namely dynamite.

In medicine, nitroglycerin is used as a vasodilator to reduce arterial tension, especially for the treatment of heart diseases such as angina pectoris. The basic pharmacological action of nitroglycerin is the nonspecific relaxation of all smooth muscle. A throbbing headache, experienced by dynamite factory workers, is the most characteristic symptom of nitroglycerin toxicity. After some time, immunity to the poison develops; immunity is rapidly lost, however, after exposure is discontinued.

Niue [nee-oo'-ay]   Niue, once called Savage Island, is a self-governing territory of New Zealand in the southwestern Pacific, about 2,300 km (1,400 mi) northwest of New Zealand. A coral island 23 km (14 mi) long and 16 km (10 mi) wide, Niue's area is 259 km^2 (100 mi^2). Alofi is its administrative center and only port. Niue's population of 2,400 (1987 est.), composed mostly of mixed Polynesians and Melanesians, has been declining because of emigration to New Zealand. Agriculture is hampered by a heavily wooded interior, rocky soil, and a lack of surface water, but the island exports coconut cream, copra, sweet potatoes, and bananas as well as woven goods. Niue is linked by air to New Zealand and Western Samoa.

Settled for at least 1,000 years, Niue was visited by James COOK in 1774. He was hostilely received by the natives—hence the name Savage Island. Annexed by New Zealand in 1901, Niue became a self-governing territory in 1974.

Nivelle, Robert Georges [nee-vel']   Robert Georges Nivelle, b. Oct. 15, 1856, d. Mar. 23, 1924, was commander in chief (December 1916–May 1917) of the French Army in World War I. From May to December 1916 he successfully defended Verdun, but his April 1917 offensive, in which he commanded the combined French and British armies, failed. Mutinies broke out in the French army, and on May 15, Nivelle was replaced by Gen. Henri Philippe PÉTAIN. In December he was transferred to North Africa.

Niven, David [niv'-en]   Hollywood's idea of the perfect, unflappable Englishman, David Niven, b. Kirriemuir, Scotland, Mar. 1, 1909, d. July 29, 1983, enjoyed more than 40 years of international stardom plus the benefits of three best-selling books—two autobiographies, *The Moon's a Balloon* (1971) and *Bring on the Empty Horses* (1975), and a novel, *Go Slowly, Come Back Quickly* (1981). His choicest performances were in *Bachelor Mother* (1939), *Raffles* (1940), *The Way Ahead* (1944), *A Matter of Life and Death* (1946), *Around the World in Eighty Days* (1956), and *Separate Tables* (1958), for which he won an Academy Award.

Nixon, Richard M.   Richard Milhous Nixon was the 37th president of the United States (1969–74). During his administration the United States withdrew its military forces from Vietnam and informally recognized the government of the People's Republic of China. The WATERGATE scandal that occurred at the beginning of his second term brought Nixon to the verge of IMPEACHMENT by the House of Representatives and led to his resignation, the first ever by a U.S. president.

Early Career. Born in Yorba Linda, Calif., on Jan. 9, 1913, Nixon was the second of Hannah and Francis Nixon's five children, all of whom were boys. Young Richard excelled in school, graduating second in his class from Whittier College (1934) and third in his class from Duke University law school (1937). From 1937 to 1942 he practiced law in Whittier, Calif. When the United States entered World War II, he served in the navy as a supply officer in the South Pacific.

Upon his return to Whittier after the war he entered politics, becoming the Republican candidate for Congress in California's 12th district. His first political campaign, in 1946, set the tone for many that would follow. Running against the liberal Democratic incumbent, Jerry Voorhis, Nixon suggested that Voorhis had dangerous left-wing tendencies. Nixon won easily and thereafter made anti-Communism one of his main political themes. As a new congressman he was assigned to the then relatively unimportant House Committee on UN-AMERICAN ACTIVITIES. He quickly attained national prominence by playing a central role in the committee's investigation of Alger HISS, a former high State Department official accused of carrying on espionage for the USSR during the 1930s. Nixon was reelected to the House in 1948. In 1950 he ran for the Senate, defeating the Democratic candidate, Congresswoman Helen Gahagan Douglas, against whom he leveled charges not unlike those he had used to unseat Voorhis 4 years earlier. When he entered the Senate, he was regarded as one of the brightest young stars of the Republican party. In 1952, at the age of 39, he was nominated by the party to be Dwight D. EISENHOWER's vice-presidential running mate.

Vice-Presidency. During the 1952 presidential campaign, Nixon once again employed the blistering anti-Communist language that had helped him gain national prominence. Midway in the campaign, however, he was nearly dropped from the ticket. Stories appeared in the press of an $18,000 fund that had been raised for Nixon by California businessmen. Nixon defended himself in a nationwide radio and television speech, denying that there was anything improper in his use of the money. The only gift that he had kept for himself was a cocker spaniel named Checkers. The "Checkers speech" brought an overwhelmingly favorable response from Republicans across the nation. Eisenhower kept him on the ticket, and the two were swept into office by a margin of more than 6 million votes over the Democratic ticket headed by Gov. Adlai E. Stevenson of Illinois.

In 1955, when Eisenhower suffered a heart attack,

AT A GLANCE

RICHARD MILHOUS NIXON
37th President of the United States (1969–74)

Born: Jan. 9, 1913, Yorba Linda, Calif.
Education: Whittier College (graduated 1934); Duke
    University Law School (LL.B. 1937)
Profession: Lawyer, Public Official
Religious Affiliation: Society of Friends (Quaker)
Marriage: June 21, 1940, to Thelma Catherine "Pat"
    Ryan (1912–   )
Children: Patricia (1946–   ); Julie (1948–   )
Political Affiliation: Republican
Writings: *Six Crises* (1962); *Memoirs* (1978); *The Real
    War* (1980); *Leaders* (1982); *Real Peace* (1984);
    1999: Victory without War (1988)
Vice-Presidents: Spiro T. Agnew (1969–73); Gerald R.
    Ford (1973–74)

Nixon filled in effectively for him until the president could resume his duties. The Eisenhower-Nixon ticket was reelected by another landslide in 1956. In 1959, Nixon opened the American National Exhibition in the USSR. There, in a model kitchen, he engaged in a debate with Nikita Khrushchev. This widely publicized "kitchen debate" enhanced Nixon's political stature.

In 1960, Nixon was the logical Republican choice to run for president. Campaigning against the Democratic nominee, John F. Kennedy, Nixon seemed to come off second best in a series of television debates. He lost the election by a little more than 100,000 votes. Two years later he was defeated for the governorship of California by the Democratic incumbent, Edmund G. ("Pat") Brown.

In the next few years Nixon worked as a partner in a New York law firm and traveled the country and the world. He tried again for the presidency in 1968, obtaining the nomination on the first ballot after winning a series of presidential primaries. This time, partly because the Democratic party was bitterly divided over the Vietnam War, Nixon won the election, narrowly defeating the Democratic nominee, Hubert H. Humphrey.

Presidency. In the White House, Nixon worked closely with his national security advisor (later, secretary of state), Henry Kissinger, forsaking his anti-Communist policies in favor of détente with the USSR and rapprochement with the Communist government of China. In 1969 he began the Strategic Arms Limitation Talks (SALT) with the Soviet Union. In February 1972 he made a historic trip to Beijing, thus reversing the U.S. policy of not recognizing the Communist government. In 1973, after 4 years of waging war in Vietnam—includ-

ing bombing raids on North Vietnam (1972) and the invasion (1970) of Cambodia—the administration managed to arrange a cease-fire that would last long enough to permit U.S. withdrawal from the Indochinese war zone. After the Arab-Israel War in 1973, the efforts of Henry Kissinger led to a cease-fire and troop disengagement in the Middle East. Domestically, Nixon cut back and opposed federal welfare services, proposed antibusing legislation, and used wage-and-price controls to fight inflation. A combination of domestic and international developments, notably the quintupling of oil prices by the Organization of Petroleum Exporting Countries (OPEC) in 1973, led to the economic recession of 1974–75.

In 1972, Nixon swept to an overwhelming victory in the presidential election against his Democratic challenger Sen. George S. McGovern—but, ironically, the seeds of political collapse had already been sown. During the campaign, a group of burglars working for the Committee to Re-elect the President broke into the headquarters of the Democratic National Committee at the Watergate office-apartment complex in Washington, D.C., apparently in search of political intelligence. Attempts by the White House to stop or frustrate the ensuing investigations ultimately failed when Nixon's own White House tape recordings revealed that the president and his assistants had engaged in an obstruction of justice. In the meantime he had been forced to drop Vice-President Spiro T. Agnew, who resigned in October 1973 after he was charged with corruption that began during his tenure as county executive of Baltimore, Md. As the revelations of wrongdoing piled up, Nixon became preoccupied with preserving his presidency. He jettisoned top assistants in the White House and fired Special Prosecutor Archibald Cox. After the Supreme Court required that he supply Cox's successor, Leon JA-WORSKI, with tape recordings of conversations with his advisors, the House Judiciary Committee voted to recommend approval by the full House of three articles of impeachment against the president. On Aug. 9, 1974, Nixon resigned his office and was succeeded by Vice-President Gerald R. FORD, whom he had selected to replace Agnew. A month after Nixon's resignation, Ford pardoned him for any crimes he might have committed as president. Nixon accepted the pardon but insisted that his mistakes had been personal and political, not criminal.

Nizer, Louis [ny'-zur]   Louis Nizer, b. London, Feb. 6, 1902, became one of the leading trial lawyers in the United States. He rose to prominence as general counsel for the Motion Picture Association of America. In his most famous case, Nizer represented (1954) author Quentin Reynolds in a libel suit against columnist Westbrook Pegler and the Hearst Corporation; he described the case in *My Life in Court* (1962).

Nkomo, Joshua [uhn-koh'-moh]   The Zimbabwe guerrilla leader and politician Joshua Nkomo, b. 1917, was a founder of the black nationalist opposition to the white minority government of Ian Smith. Nkomo became president of the Zimbabwe African People's Union (ZAPU) in 1961. In 1976 he joined with Robert MUGABE in the Patriotic Front, using Zambia as a base for guerrilla warfare against Smith and then against the government of Abel MUZOREWA. In 1979 a cease-fire and a new constitution providing for black majority rule were agreed upon. Nkomo's party, supported by the Ndebele minority, finished second to Mugabe's ZANU-PF in the 1980 elections. Mugabe appointed Nkomo to his cabinet but dismissed him in 1982. ZAPU and ZANU-PF merged in 1988, and Nkomo became a senior minister in Mugabe's unity cabinet.

Nkrumah, Kwame [uhn-kroo'-mah, kwah'-may] Francis Nwia Kofie Kwame Nkrumah, b. Sept. 21, 1909, d. Apr. 27, 1972, was the first president of Ghana and a leading proponent of anticolonialism and pan-Africanism. Born into the Akan tribe in what was then the Western Province of the Gold Coast, Nkrumah was educated at Achimota College, Accra, and later studied in the United States and at the London School of Economics. In 1947 he became secretary of the United Gold Coast Convention, a group newly formed to agitate for constitutional reform. Two years later he founded his own Convention People's party (CPP), a mass political party committed to direct action to secure self-government for the Gold Coast.

In 1950, after considerable violence, Nkrumah was detained by the British. His party won the colony's first general election in 1951, however, and Nkrumah was released to become leader of government business and, in 1952, prime minister. In the elections of 1956 the CPP defeated the National Liberation Movement, an Ashanti body advocating a federal form of government as against Nkrumah's design for a unitary state. The following year the Gold Coast became fully independent, changing its name to Ghana—the first of the new African states to attain independence after World War II.

Nkrumah served as prime minister of Ghana until 1960, when he assumed the presidency. In 1958 he convoked a conference of independent African states at Accra, and in 1961 he participated in the Casablanca Conference at which the heads of the radically minded African states adopted an African Charter condemning neocolonialism. During the Congo crisis of 1960–61, Nkrumah supported Patrice Lumumba. He also helped to bring about South Africa's withdrawal from the British Commonwealth in 1961. Within Ghana, however, Nkrumah's Second Development Plan (1959), entailing a good deal of state enterprise, turned out to be a failure. Widespread discontent ensued, and in 1966 the Ghanaian army seized power while Nkrumah was out of the country. The former leader went to live in Guinea and died in Romania.

NKVD   see KGB

No drama [noh]   No, also written Noh, is the oldest form of traditional Japanese drama. It consists of a highly refined, one-act dance performed by male actors. The word *no* in Japanese means "skill" or "accomplishment" and refers to those serious plays which grew out of the comic sketches and popular entertainments—Dengaku and Sarugaku—of the medieval period. No is profoundly religious in nature. The major character, or *shite*, is usually either a Shinto god, or a demon, or the spirit of a dead court noble or lady who is seeking salvation through the compassion of Buddha.

No is performed on a raised stage about 6 m (20 ft) square and covered with a roof supported by four pillars. Actors enter and exit on a connecting passageway, or *hashigakari*. The No stage is bare of scenery, and production is simple, in keeping with the austerity of Zen Buddhism, which No's samurai (warrior) patrons favored. Prose passages are chanted and verse sections are sung by the actors and a seated chorus, who are accompanied by the music of three drums and a flute. Vocal style is based on the chanting of Buddhist prayers. In contrast to the lively KABUKI dance, No movements are extremely slow in tempo. Gestures, especially those using the fan, may be symbolic of rain, wind, weeping, or drinking.

Some 240 No plays are still performed; these are divided into five groups according to the main character. A traditional program of five No plays—one from each group—alternating with four Kyogen comedies lasts all day.

no-fault insurance No-fault insurance, usually for automobile drivers, means that, regardless of who is to blame, claims payments are made by the insurance company to its own policyholder. This type of coverage eliminates the need to establish the blame for an accident as a prerequisite for a settlement. No-fault insurance also limits the amount of damages that an accident victim may be paid (although further lawsuits for serious-injury cases may be allowed); claims are paid quickly and are not large in amount. With no-fault insurance, automotive insurance becomes mandatory for all drivers. Motorists must carry liability insurance for themselves and the passengers in their car.

No-fault has been used in Saskatchewan, Canada, since 1946; Puerto Rico instituted it in 1970. In that same year Massachusetts was the first state to pass a no-fault insurance plan. Subsequently, many of the states adopted some form of no-fault insurance.

NOAA see NATIONAL OCEANIC AND ATMOSPHERIC ADMINISTRATION

Noah [noh'-uh] In the Bible, Noah, the tenth descendant of Adam, through Seth, is portrayed as the only righteous man in an age of iniquity (Gen. 6–9). Because God is determined to save him and his family from the impending DELUGE, Noah is commanded to build an ark and to take with him two of every creature. When the waters subside, Noah makes sacrifices to God and receives a fertility blessing and a divine COVENANT sealed by the rainbow. Noah had three sons: Shem, Ham, and Japheth. Ham saw his father naked, an offense for which he and his descendants, the Canaanites, were cursed by Noah.

Nobel, Alfred [noh-bel'] Alfred Bernhard Nobel, b. Oct. 21, 1833, d. Dec. 10, 1896, was a Swedish chemist, inventor, and industrialist whose most important invention, the explosive dynamite, earned a fortune for its inventor and provided the financial basis for the establishment of the Nobel Prize. With his father, Immanuel, himself an inventor and industrialist, Alfred Nobel began to manufacture NITROGLYCERIN in a factory near Stockholm in 1862. An explosion in 1864 killed five people, including Nobel's young brother, Emil. Searching for a safe way of handling nitroglycerin, Nobel discovered that an organic packing material—such as kieselguhr, the diatomaceous earth he eventually used—absorbed the liquid in nitroglycerin, reducing its volatility. In 1867 he patented this mixture under the name *dynamite*. In 1875, Nobel perfected blasting gelatin, which possessed more blasting force and greater stability than pure nitroglycerin. He introduced the smokeless powder ballistite in 1887. A skillful entrepreneur who received more than 355 patents, Nobel left most of his fortune to a foundation established for the awarding of the prizes that bear his name.

Alfred Nobel, founder of the Nobel Prizes, made his substantial fortune largely through the manufacture of the explosive dynamite, which he invented in 1866. A reclusive man and a pacifist, he established a fund of approximately $8.5 million to honor selected achievements benefiting humankind.

Nobel Prize Alfred Nobel left most of his fortune in trust, as a fund from which annual prizes would be awarded to those who, each year, conferred "the greatest benefit on mankind." The prizes, awarded since 1901, are administered by the Nobel Foundation in Stockholm. The prizes designated in Nobel's will were for physics, chemistry, physiology or medicine, literature, and peace. In 1969 a prize for economics endowed by the Central Bank of Sweden was added. Recipients in physics, chemistry, and economics are named by the Royal Swedish Academy of Sciences; those in physiology or medicine by the Caroline Institute; those in literature by the Swedish Academy; and those who contribute to peace by the Norwegian Nobel Committee appointed by Norway's Parliament.

The average value of each prize has grown from about $30,000 to about $1.2 million in 1992. Nobel laureates in literature have included historians, critics, and philosophers as well as novelists, poets, dramatists, and essayists. The peace prize has been awarded to individuals and to organizations.

NOBEL PRIZE WINNERS FOR ECONOMICS*

Year	Winner	Year	Winner
1969	Ragnar Frisch	1980	Lawrence R. Klein
	Jan Tinbergen	1981	James Tobin
1970	Paul A. Samuelson	1982	George J. Stigler
1971	Simon S. Kuznets	1983	Gerard Debreu
1972	Sir John R. Hicks	1984	Sir Richard Stone
	Kenneth J. Arrow	1985	Franco Modigliani
1973	Wassily Leontief	1986	James M. Buchanan
1974	Gunnar Myrdal	1987	Robert M. Solow
	Friedrich A. von Hayek	1988	Maurice Allais
1975	Tjalling C. Koopmans	1989	Trygve Haavelmo
	Leonid V. Kantorovich	1990	Harry M. Markowitz
1976	Milton Friedman		William F. Sharpe
1977	Bertil Ohlin		Merton H. Miller
	James E. Meade	1991	Ronald H. Coase
1978	Herbert A. Simon	1992	Gary S. Becker
1979	Sir Arthur Lewis		
	Theodore Schultz		

*See separate biographical articles on many of the Nobel Prize winners.

NOBEL PRIZE WINNERS*

Year	Literature	Physiology or Medicine	Chemistry	Physics	Peace
1901	René F. A. Sully-Prudhomme	Emil A. von Behring	Jacobus H. van't Hoff	Wilhelm K. Roentgen	Jean Henri Dunant Frédéric Passy
1902	Theodor Mommsen	Sir Ronald Ross	Emil Fischer	Hendrik A. Lorentz Pieter Zeeman	Élie Ducommun Charles Albert Gobat
1903	Bjørnstjerne Bjørnson	Niels R. Finsen	Svante A. Arrhenius	A. Henri Becquerel Pierre Curie Marie S. Curie	Sir William R. Cremer
1904	Frédéric Mistral José Echegaray	Ivan P. Pavlov	Sir William Ramsay	Lord Rayleigh	Institute of International Law
1905	Henryk Sienkiewicz	Robert Koch	Adolf von Baeyer	Philipp Lenard	Baroness Bertha von Suttner
1906	Giosuè Carducci	Camillo Golgi S. Ramón y Cajal	Henri Moissan	Sir Joseph Thomson	Theodore Roosevelt
1907	Rudyard Kipling	Charles L. A. Laveran	Eduard Buchner	Albert A. Michelson	Ernesto T. Moneta Louis Renault
1908	Rudolf C. Eucken	Paul Ehrlich Élie Metchnikoff	Sir Ernest Rutherford	Gabriel Lippman	Klas P. Arnoldson Fredrik Bajer
1909	Selma Lagerlöf	Emil T. Kocher	Wilhelm Ostwald	Guglielmo Marconi Karl F. Braun	Auguste Beernaert Paul H. B. B. d'Estournelles de Constant
1910	Paul von Heyse	Albrecht Kossel	Otto Wallach	Johannes D. van der Waals	International Peace Bureau
1911	Maurice Maeterlinck	Allvar Gullstrand	Marie S. Curie	Wilhelm Wien	Tobias M. C. Asser A. H. Fried
1912	Gerhardt Hauptmann	Alexis Carrel	Victor Grignard Paul Sabatier	N. G. Dalen	Elihu Root
1913	Sir Rabindranath Tagore	C. R. Richet	Alfred Werner	Heike Kamerlingh Onnes	Henri La Fontaine
1914		Robert Barany	T. W. Richards	Max von Laue	
1915	Romain Rolland		Richard Willstätter	Sir William H. Bragg Sir William L. Bragg	
1916	Verner von Heidenstam				
1917	K. A. Gjellerup Henrik Pontoppidan			C. G. Barkla	International Red Cross Committee
1918			Fritz Haber	Max Planck	
1919	C. F. G. Spitteler	Jules Bordet		Johannes Stark	Woodrow Wilson
1920	Knut Hamsun	S. A. S. Krogh	Walther Nernst	C. E. Guillaume	Léon Bourgeois
1921	Anatole France		Frederick Soddy	Albert Einstein	Karl Hjalmar Branting Christian L. Lange
1922	Jacinto Benavente y Martínez	A. V. Hill Otto Meyerhof	F. W. Aston	N. H. D. Bohr	Fridtjof Nansen
1923	W. B. Yeats	Sir Frederick G. Banting J. J. R. Macleod	Fritz Pregl	Robert A. Millikan	
1924	W. S. Reymont	Willem Einthoven		K. M. G. Siegbahn	
1925	G. B. Shaw		Richard Zsigmondy	James Franck Gustav Hertz	Sir Austen Chamberlain Charles G. Dawes
1926	Grazia Deledda	Johannes Fibiger	Theodor Svedberg	J. B. Perrin	Aristide Briand Gustav Stresemann
1927	Henri Bergson	Julius Wagner-Jauregg	Heinrich Wieland	A. H. Compton C. T. R. Wilson	F. É. Buisson Ludwig Quidde
1928	Sigrid Undset	C. J. H. Nicolle	Adolf Windaus	Sir Owen W. Richardson	
1929	Thomas Mann	Christian Eijkman Sir Frederick G. Hopkins	Sir Arthur Harden Hans von Euler-Chelpin	L. V. de Broglie	Frank B. Kellogg
1930	Sinclair Lewis	Karl Landsteiner	Hans Fischer	Sir Chandrasekhara V. Raman	Nathan Söderblom
1931	E. A. Karlfeldt	Otto H. Warburg	Carl Bosch Friedrich Bergius		Jane Addams Nicholas Murray Butler
1932	John Galsworthy	E. D. Adrian Sir Charles Sherrington	Irving Langmuir	Werner Heisenberg	
1933	I. A. Bunin	Thomas H. Morgan		P. A. M. Dirac Erwin Schrödinger	Sir Norman Angell

NOBEL PRIZE WINNERS* (cont.)

Year	Literature	Physiology or Medicine	Chemistry	Physics	Peace
1934	Luigi Pirandello	G. H. Whipple G. R. Minot W. P. Murphy	Harold C. Urey		Arthur Henderson
1935		Hans Spemann	Frédéric Joliot-Curie Irène Joliot-Curie	Sir James Chadwick	Carl von Ossietzky
1936	Eugene O'Neill	Sir Henry H. Dale Otto Loewi	P. J. W. Debye	C. D. Anderson V. F. Hess	Carlos Saavedra Lamas
1937	Roger Martin du Gard	Albert von Szent-Gyorgyi	Sir Walter N. Haworth Paul Karrer	C. J. Davisson Sir George P. Thomson	E. A. R. Cecil, Viscount Cecil
1938	Pearl S. Buck	Corneille Heymans		Enrico Fermi	Nansen International Office for Refugees
1939	F. E. Siilanpää	Gerhard Domagk	Adolf Butenandt Leopold Ružička	E. O. Lawrence	
1940-42†					
1943		E. A. Doisy Carl Henrik Dam	Georg von Hevesy	Otto Stern	
1944	J. V. Jensen	Joseph Erlanger H. S. Gasser	Otto Hahn	I. I. Rabi	International Red Cross Committee
1945	Gabriela Mistral	Sir Alexander Fleming E. B. Chain Sir Howard W. Florey	A. I. Virtanen	Wolfgang Pauli	Cordell Hull
1946	Hermann Hesse	H. J. Muller	J. B. Sumner J. H. Northrop W. M. Stanley	P. W. Bridgman	J. R. Mott Emily G. Balch
1947	André Gide	C. F. Cori Gerty T. Cori B. A. Houssay	Sir Robert Robinson	Sir Edward V. Appleton	American Friends Service Committee Friends Service Council
1948	T. S. Eliot	Paul H. Müller	Arne Tiselius	P. M. S. Blackett	
1949	William Faulkner	W. R. Hess Egas Moniz	William F. Giauque	Hideki Yukawa	John Boyd Orr, Baron Orr
1950	Bertrand Russell, Earl Russell	Philip S. Hench Edward C. Kendall Tadeus Reichstein	Otto Diels Kurt Alder	C. F. Powell	Ralph J. Bunche
1951	Pär F. Lagerkvist	Max Theiler	Edwin M. McMillan Glenn T. Seaborg	Sir John D. Cockcroft Ernest T. S. Walton	Léon Jouhaux
1952	François Mauriac	S. A. Waksman	A. J. P. Martin R. L. M. Synge	Felix Block E. M. Purcell	Albert Schweitzer
1953	Sir Winston L. S. Churchill	F. A. Lipmann Sir Hans A. Krebs	Hermann Staudinger	Frits Zernike	George C. Marshall
1954	Ernest Hemingway	J. F. Enders F. C. Robbins T. H. Weller	Linus C. Pauling	Max Born Walther Bothe	Office of the United Nations High Commissioner for Refugees
1955	Halldór K. Laxness	A. H. T. Theorell	Vincent du Vigneaud	Willis E. Lamb, Jr. Polykarp Kusch	
1956	Juan Ramón Jiménez	D. W. Richards, Jr. Ándre Cournand Werner Forssmann	Sir Cyril N. Hinshelwood Nikolai N. Semenov	W. B. Shockley W. H. Brattain John Bardeen	
1957	Albert Camus	Daniele Bovet	Alexander R. Todd, Baron Todd	Tsung Dao Lee Chen Ning Yang	Lester B. Pearson
1958	Boris L. Pasternak	Joshua Lederberg G. W. Beadle E. L. Tatum	Frederick Sanger	P. A. Cherenkov Igor Y. Tamm Ilya M. Frank	Georges Henri Pire
1959	Salvatore Quasimodo	Severo Ochoa Arthur Kornberg	Jaroslav Heyrovský	Emilio Segrè Owen Chamberlain	Philip J. Noel-Baker
1960	Saint-John Perse	Sir Frank M. Burnet P. B. Medawar	Willard F. Libby	D. A. Glaser	Albert J. Luthuli
1961	Ivo Andrić	Georg von Bekesy	Melvin Calvin	Robert Hofstadter R. L. Moessbauer	Dag Hammarskjöld
1962	John Steinbeck	J. D. Watson F. H. C. Crick M. H. F. Wilkins	M. F. Perutz J. C. Kendrew	L. D. Landau	Linus C. Pauling

NOBEL PRIZE WINNERS* (cont.)

Year	Literature	Physiology or Medicine	Chemistry	Physics	Peace
1963	George Seferis	Sir John Carew Eccles Alan Lloyd Hodgkin Andrew Fielding Huxley	Guilio Natta Karl Ziegler	Eugene Paul Wigner Maria Goeppert Mayer Hans Jensen	International Red Cross Committee League of Red Cross Societies
1964	Jean Paul Sartre	Konrad E. Bloch Feodor Lynen	Dorothy Mary Crowfoot Hodgkin	Charles Hard Townes Nikolai Gennadiyevich Basov Aleksandr Mikhailovich Prokhorov	Martin Luther King, Jr.
1965	M. A. Sholokhov	François Jacob André Lwoff Jacques Monod	Robert Burns Woodward	Richard Phillips Feynman Sin-itiro Tomonaga Julian Seymour Schwinger	United Nations Children's Fund
1966	S. Y. Agnon Nelly Sachs	Francis Peyton Rous Charles Brenton Huggins	Robert S. Mulliken	Alfred Kastler	
1967	Miguel Angel Asturias	Ragnar Granit Haldan Keffer Hartline George Wald	Manfred Eigen Ronald George Wreyford Norrish Sir George Porter	Hans Albrecht Bethe	
1968	Kawabata Yasunari	Robert W. Holley H. Gobind Khorana Marshall W. Nirenberg	Lars Onsager	Luis W. Alvarez	René Cassin
1969	Samuel Beckett	Max Delbrück Alfred D. Hershey Salvador E. Luria	Derek H. R. Barton Odd Hassel	Murray Gell-Mann	International Labor Organization
1970	Aleksandr I. Solzhenitsyn	Julius Axelrod Bernard Katz Ulf von Euler	Luis Federico Leloir	Louis Eugène Néel Hannes Alfvén	Norman E. Borlaug
1971	Pablo Neruda	Earl W. Sutherland, Jr.	Gerhard Herzberg	Dennis Gabor	Willy Brandt
1972	Heinrich Böll	Gerald M. Edelman Rodney R. Porter	Stanford Moore William Howard Stein Christian B. Anfinsen	John Bardeen Leon N. Cooper John Robert Schrieffer	
1973	Patrick White	Konrad Lorenz Nikolaas Tinbergen Karl von Frisch	Ernst Otto Fischer Geoffrey Wilkinson	Leo Esaki Ivar Giaever Brian D. Josephson	Henry A. Kissinger Le Duc Tho
1974	Eyvind Johnson Harry Martinson	Albert Claude George Emil Palade Christian de Duve	Paul J. Flory	Sir Martin Ryle Antony Hewish	Sean MacBride Sato Eisaku
1975	Eugenio Montale	Renato Dulbecco Howard M. Temin David Baltimore	John W. Cornforth Vladimir Prelog	Aage Bohr Ben R. Mottelson James Rainwater	Andrei D. Sakharov
1976	Saul Bellow	Baruch S. Blumberg D. Carleton Gajdusek	William N. Lipscomb	Burton Richter Samuel C. C. Ting	Mairead Corrigan Betty Williams
1977	Vincente Aleixandre	Rosalyn S. Yalow Roger Guillemin Andrew Schally	Ilya Prigogine	Philip W. Anderson Nevill Mott John H. Van Vleck	Amnesty International
1978	Issac Bashevis Singer	Daniel Nathans Hamilton Smith Werner Arber	Peter Mitchell	Peter Kapitza Arno A. Penzias Robert W. Wilson	Menachem Begin Anwar al-Sadat
1979	Odysseus Elytis	Allan M. Cormack Godfrey Hounsfield	Herbert C. Brown Georg Wittig	Sheldon Glashow Steven Weinberg Abdus Salam	Mother Teresa
1980	Czesław Miłosz	Baruj Benacerraf Jean Dausset George D. Snell	Paul Berg Walter Gilbert Frederick Sanger	James W. Cronin Val L. Fitch	Adolfo Pérez Esquivel
1981	Elias Canetti	Robert W. Sperry David H. Hubel Torsten N. Wiesel	Kenichi Fukui Roald Hoffmann	Nicolaas Bloembergen Arthur Schawlow Kai M. Siegbahn	Office of the UN High Commissioner for Refugees
1982	Gabriel García Márquez	Sune Bergstrom Bengt Samuelsson John R. Vane	Aaron Klug	Kenneth G. Wilson	Alfonso García Robles Alva Myrdal
1983	William Golding	Barbara McClintock	Henry Taube	Subrahmanyan Chandrasekhar William A. Fowler	Lech Wałesa
1984	Jaroslav Seifert	Georges J. F. Köhler Cesar Milstein Niels K. Jerne	R. Bruce Merrifield	Carlo Rubbia Simon van der Meer	Desmond Tutu

NOBEL PRIZE WINNERS* (cont.)

Year	Literature	Physiology or Medicine	Chemistry	Physics	Peace
1985	Claude Simon	Joseph L. Goldstein Michael S. Brown	Herbert A. Hauptman Jerome Karle	Klaus von Klitzing	International Physicians for the Prevention of Nuclear War
1986	Wole Soyinka	Rita Levi-Montalcini Stanley Cohen	Yuan T. Lee Dudley Herschbach John C. Polanyi	Ernst Ruska Gerd Binnig Heinrich Rorer	Elie Wiesel
1987	Joseph Brodsky	Susumu Tonegawa	Jean Marie Lehn Charles J. Pederson Donald J. Cram	K. Alex Müller J. Georg Bednorz	Oscar Arias Sánchez
1988	Naguib Mahfouz	Gertrude B. Elion George H. Hitchings Sir James Black	Johann Deisenhofer Robert Huber Hartmut Michel	Leon Max Lederman Melvin Schwartz Jack Steinberger	United Nations Peacekeeping Forces
1989	Camilo José Cela	J. Michael Bishop Harold E. Varmus	Sidney Altman Thomas R. Cech	Hans G. Dehmelt Wolfgang Paul Norman F. Ramsey	Dalai Lama
1990	Octavio Paz	Joseph E. Murray E. Donnall Thomas	Elias James Corey	Richard E. Taylor Jerome I. Friedman Henry W. Kendall	Mikhail S. Gorbachev
1991	Nadine Gordimer	Erwin Neher Bert Sakmann	Richard R. Ernst	Pierre-Gilles de Gennes	Daw Aung San Suu Kyi
1992	Derek Walcott	Edmond H. Fischer Edwin G. Krebs	Rudolph A. Marcus	George Charpak	Rigoberta Menchú

*See separate biographical articles on many of the Nobel Prize winners. †No prizes awarded 1940–42.

nobelium   Nobelium is a TRANSURANIUM ELEMENT, a radioactive metal of the ACTINIDE SERIES. Its symbol is No, its atomic number is 102, and the atomic weight of its stablest isotope (half-life, about 1 hour) is 259. Nobelium does not occur in nature. In 1957 a group of scientists from Great Britain, Sweden, and the United States claimed to have created element 102 and suggested that it be named nobelium for Alfred Nobel. Scientists at the Lawrence Radiation Laboratory in Berkeley, Calif., later created nobelium-254 by irradiating curium with high-energy carbon ions. Since then a total of 9 isotopes with masses ranging from 251 to 259 have been produced.

noble gases   see INERT GASES

Nobunaga [noh-boo-nah'-gah]   Nobunaga, also known as Oda Nobunaga, 1534–82, began the military unification of Japan, a process completed by HIDEYOSHI and IEYASU. The first of the "unifiers" was born into a *daimyo* (baronial) family of low rank in Owari province. By strategic marriages and by buying or conquering land, he came to control Owari by 1560. He then attacked the daimyo of neighboring provinces, adding to his domains.

In 1568, Nobunaga seized Kyoto and established Ashikaga Yoshiaki as the shogun. He then put down all opposition, particularly the powerful Buddhist establishment. In 1573 he deposed Yoshiaki, ending the Ashikaga shogunate and assuming personal control of the central provinces.

Between 1576 and 1579, Nobunaga built the great citadel of Azuchi. Aided by his general Hideyoshi, he also began to conquer the provinces of western Honshu. In 1582, however, Nobunaga was murdered by a disaffected aide in Kyoto.

nocturne   The nocturne is a 19th-century instrumental piece, usually for piano, characterized by an extended melody over a chordal accompaniment. Nocturnes are quiet, reflective pieces, written in a slow tempo, although sections may become loud and agitated. The genre may have originated with the 18th-century *notturno, nachtmusik*, or serenade, all of which were to be played at evening concerts. John Field wrote the first nocturnes for piano. Frédéric Chopin composed 19 of the best-known examples of the genre. Nocturnes have also been written for orchestra.

Nogales [noh-gah'-lays]   Nogales is a city and port of entry in southern Arizona, adjacent to Nogales, Mexico. The seat of Santa Cruz County, the city has a population of 19,489 (1990). The economy is based on mining and cattle raising. Tumacacori Mission (1696), the Coronado National Forest, and the ruins of the Guevavi Mission (1692) are nearby. Originally named Isaactown for Jacob Isaacson, who built an inn there in 1880, it was shortly renamed for the area's walnut trees (Spanish: *nogal*). Nogales was the scene of fighting against Pancho Villa in 1916 and 1918.

Noguchi, Isamu [noh-goo'-chee, ee-sah'-moo]   The American sculptor Isamu Noguchi, b. Los Angeles, Nov. 17, 1904, d. Dec. 30, 1988, is best known for his evocative abstract creations. On a grant from the Guggenheim

Isamu Noguchi, one of the most respected contemporary American sculptors, is seen with The Sun at Noon, a marble ring. Noguchi's work is characterized by the subtle blending of traditional Oriental principles and modern Western design.

Foundation, Noguchi went (1927) to Paris and worked with Constantin Brancusi. In the early 1930s in Peking he studied calligraphic drawing, an important element in much of his later sculpture.

Noguchi experimented with various materials, producing delicate works conducive to the play of light across and through their surfaces. These were admirably suited to the theater. Beginning in the 1930s and continuing almost until his death, he designed memorable sets and costumes for many of the dance productions of George Balanchine, Martha Graham, Merce Cunningham, and other choreographers.

During this period Noguchi created some of his most admired sculptures, particularly the marble *Kouros* (1944–45; Metropolitan Museum of Art, New York City), a complex, graceful work suggesting archaic Greek sculpture. His outdoor projects, which used principles of Japanese garden design to create versatile, elegant urban spaces, include two bridges for the Peace Park at Hiroshima (1952); the Garden of Peace (1952–58) of the UNESCO Building in Paris; and the Water Garden (1964–65) of New York City's Chase Manhattan Bank Plaza. Some 500 sculptures and other materials related to his career are gathered at the Isamu Noguchi Museum (opened 1986), in Long Island City, New York.

noise   The term *noise* is used widely in science and technology. Its general meaning in all such fields, as in everyday life, is of a useless or interfering signal of some form.

The most familiar use of the word is in acoustics, where it refers to sound waves that are unwanted or judged to be lacking in some desired quality (see SOUND AND ACOUSTICS). Such judgments are made relative to a given desired mixture of sound waves. The term *white noise* refers to a synthesized, uniform mixture of all audible wavelengths. This kind of mixture is used in electronic music, for example, as a source from which desired blends of sound waves are obtained. In SOUND RECORDING AND REPRODUCTION, *background noise* refers to all sound waves that are present in a given system in addition to the

desired sounds. Judgments of whether or not environmental sounds are noises are subjective, but the fact is that unwanted sounds can have severe psychological effects (see POLLUTION, ENVIRONMENTAL). Above certain levels of intensity, noises can also cause physical harm.

Such uses of the term *noise* have been extended to the fields of ELECTRICITY and ELECTRONICS and, in general, to all areas that involve some form of frequency range. Most broadly, the term *noise* is used in INFORMATION THEORY to refer to any form of disturbance of information-bearing signals, or to any meaningless addition to such signals. This does not, however, include redundant signals added as means of checking the accuracy of transmission.

Nolan, Sidney [noh'-luhn]   Sidney Nolan, b. Melbourne, Apr. 22, 1917, d. Nov. 27, 1992, was the major Australian artist of the 20th century and was best known for his paintings inspired by Australian history, folklore, and landscapes. Although he studied (1934–38) art at the school of the National Gallery of Victoria, Melbourne, Nolan was largely a self-taught painter. His first important works were a series of paintings (1946–47) based on the life of the Australian outlaw Ned Kelly; another Kelly series followed in 1955. A later series, *Leda and the Swan* (1960), was his first group of works with a non-Australian theme. Nolan left Australia for the first time in 1950 and traveled throughout Europe and the United States. In 1954 he exhibited his paintings at the Venice Biennale.

Noland, Kenneth [noh'-luhnd]   Kenneth Noland, b. Asheville, N.C., Apr. 10, 1924, was a prominent color-field painter in the 1950s who later turned (1960s) to hard-edge painting. Noland explored such techniques as applying liquefied paint to unprimed canvas to create stains or veils of color. In 1957 he began a series of target paintings that combined painterly brushwork with strictly structured compositions. By 1960 the targets were painted in a hard-edged manner, with bright, pure color rings, often separated by raw canvas. In the early 1960s, Noland experimented with the effects of unusual image placement and canvas shape in a series of brightly colored chevron and diamond paintings; these led to enormous horizontal striped paintings and plaid pictures.

Nolde, Emil [nohl'-de]   Emil Nolde, b. Emil Hansen, Aug. 7, 1867, d. Apr. 13, 1956, was one of the most consistently powerful of the German expressionist painters (see EXPRESSIONISM). His oil paintings, woodcuts, and watercolors are distinguished by their bold forms, bright colors, and emotional content.

In 1902 he married and changed his name to Nolde—the town in which he was born. He held his first one-person show in Dresden in 1905. In 1906–07 he was a member of Die BRÜCKE, but he had too individual a temperament to remain long with any group. After an illness in 1909, Nolde experienced a religious conversion. His brutal, ecstatic, but sometimes lyrical religious paintings,

In his Dancers with Candles *(1912), German expressionist Emil Nolde combined strident color, tortured form, and crusty surface texture to convey anxiety and struggle. (Nolde-Museum, Seebüll, Germany.)*

for example, *The Last Supper* (1909; Statens Museum for Kunst, Copenhagen), reflect the intensity of that experience.

In 1926, Nolde purchased a farm, where he spent his summers away from Berlin and where he retired in 1940 to escape Nazi persecution. His brooding, evocative paintings, such as *The Mill* (1932; Bayerische Staatsgemäldesammlungen, Munich), capture the desolate, haunting expanses of this rural landscape. In 1931 he was appointed to the Prussian Academy, and in 1934 he published his memoirs, *Years of Struggle*. After 1941, Nolde was forbidden to paint or exhibit his earlier work, but between 1938 and 1945 he executed a vast series of watercolors entitled *Unpainted Pictures*.

nolo contendere [noh'-loh kuhn-ten'-duh-ray]   Nolo contendere (Latin, "I do not wish to contend") is a plea in a criminal action. It has the same effect as a guilty plea in most respects, because it enters no defense against the charges. In a subsequent criminal trial, however, it is not counted as a previous conviction.

nomad   Nomads are people without permanent dwellings who migrate regularly according to their own detailed knowledge of exploitable resources. The term *nomad* (from the Greek, "to pasture") was originally used to refer

only to pastoralists—groups that migrate in an established pattern to find pasturelands for their domestic livestock—but it has since been generalized to include all nonsettled populations, of which there are three basic types. The first type comprises foraging populations who wander in search of their food. Typically, in these populations the women gather vegetable foods and the men hunt, except in the Arctic, where there is little or nothing to gather. These foraging populations constitute the simplest form of human society and are made up of small bands rarely exceeding 50 individuals. It is estimated that 99 percent of all humanity once lived in this way, even though food production was begun in some places as much as 10,000 years ago. HUNTER-GATHERER societies remain today only in a few marginal areas where they have taken refuge from more highly organized and technologically advanced peoples.

The second type, the most significant numerically and historically, comprises the pastoral nomads who move with their families, belongings, and herds of cattle, camels, sheep, or goats through an annual cycle of pastures whose availability is determined by the alternation of hot and cold or wet and dry seasons. For thousands of years, pastoral nomads have controlled vast areas from southern Africa to the Siberian Arctic. Because they can organize themselves in large or even very large numbers, as in the Mongol invasions, and because they are free of any fixed assets, they have played an important part in the history of Asia and Africa. With the development of nation-states, however, their traditional structure is breaking down.

The third type of population generally referred to as nomadic comprises GYPSIES, tinkers, and similar itinerants in urban and complex societies.

Nome [nohm]   Nome, a port city in western Alaska, lies on the south shore of the Seward Peninsula on Norton Sound. Its population of 3,500 (1990) is primarily Eskimo. Petroleum deposits have been discovered in the area. Commercial fishing, fur ranching, Eskimo handicrafts, and tourism are also economically important. Nome was founded in 1899 following a gold strike in a nearby creek.

nominalism   Nominalism is the designation usually applied to any philosophical system, ancient or modern, that denies all objectivity, whether actual or potential, to UNIVERSALS; in other words, nominalists grant no universality to mental concepts outside the mind. In this sense, the philosophical systems of Epicurus, William of Occam, George Berkeley, David Hume, and John Stuart Mill and of contemporary linguistic analysis may be called nominalistic in that they attribute universality only to words (*nomina*), mental habits, or concepts and maintain the objective existence only of the concrete, individual thing. Nominalism is simultaneously opposed to the philosophical idealism of Plato and to the moderate realism of Aristotle and Saint Thomas Aquinas. The principal objection of nominalists is to the attribution of objective existence to ideas formally as they exist in the mind and fundamentally (or potentially) as they exist in particulars having some similarity to each other in any given class or species.

nomination, political   see POLITICAL CONVENTION

▬

non-Euclidean geometry   Non-Euclidean geometry refers to two geometries—hyperbolic geometry and elliptic geometry. These geometries are based on the first four postulates of EUCLID but assume alternatives to his parallel postulate instead of assuming the postulate itself. The parallel postulate is equivalent to an assumption that there is exactly one line that is parallel to a given line m and contains a given point that is not a point of the line m. Hyperbolic geometry may be obtained by replacing Euclid's parallel postulate by an assumption that there are at least two lines that are parallel to a given line m and contain a given point that is not a point of the line m. Elliptic geometry may be obtained by replacing Euclid's parallel postulate by an assumption that no line exists that is parallel to a given line m and contains a point that is not a point of the line m. The three cases—(1) exactly one line (Euclidean geometry), (2) at least two lines (hyberbolic geometry), and (3) no lines (elliptic geometry)—represent all possibilities. The latter two are therefore known as non-Euclidean geometries.

Comparisons of the Geometries

The sum of the measures of the angles of a triangle is 180° in Euclidean GEOMETRY, less than 180° in hyperbolic geometry, and more than 180° in elliptic geometry (see Figure 1). The area of a triangle in hyperbolic geometry is proportional to the deficiency of its angle sum from 180°; the area of a triangle in elliptic geometry is proportional to the excess of its angle sum over 180°. In Euclidean geometry all triangles have an angle sum of 180° irrespective of their areas. Thus, similar triangles with different areas can exist in Euclidean geometry; this occurrence is not possible in either hyperbolic or elliptic geometry.

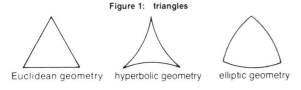

Figure 1:   triangles

Euclidean geometry   hyperbolic geometry   elliptic geometry

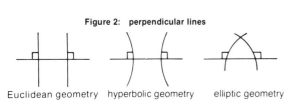

Figure 2:   perpendicular lines

Euclidean geometry   hyperbolic geometry   elliptic geometry

In two-dimensional geometries, lines that are perpendicular to the same given line are parallel in Euclidean

geometry, are neither parallel nor intersecting in hyperbolic geometry, and intersect at the pole of the given line in elliptic geometry. As indicated in Figure 2, the appearance of the lines as straight or curved depends on the postulates for the space.

Historical Development

Euclid postponed the use of his parallel postulate as long as possible and probably was a bit uneasy about it. For the next 2,000 years numerous attempts were made to prove the statement as a theorem. Many of the attempts involved statements that are now recognized as equivalent to the parallel postulate.

A proof of the parallel postulate by reductio ad absurdum was attempted by Girolamo Saccheri (1667–1733) in his work *Euclid Freed of Every Flaw*. Unfortunately, Saccheri's proof is not acceptable by present standards. However, Saccheri's work provided foundations for successful independent efforts by János BOLYAI and Nicolai LOBACHEVSKY in the development of hyperbolic geometry and of Georg RIEMANN in the development of elliptic geometry. Carl F. GAUSS appears to have recognized the existence of non-Euclidean geometries. Arthur Cayley and Felix Klein developed distance functions (metrics) for these geometries. In the 19th and 20th centuries the non-Euclidean geometries have been accepted as consistent geometries and have been extended to three and more dimensions and also to fractional dimensions (see GEOMETRY, FRACTAL).

The Geometry of the Universe

The recognition of the existence of the non-Euclidean geometries as mathematical systems was resisted by many people who—with an almost religious fervor—proclaimed that Euclidean geometry was the one and only geometry. Such attitudes reflect a failure to recognize that a geometry is a mathematical system that is determined by its assumptions. The truth of the geometry in the sense of representing our universe is a matter of observation. At the present time mathematicians are not even sure which of the three geometries provides the best representation of the entire universe. They do know that Euclidean geometry provides an excellent representation for the part of the universe that we inhabit. Unfortunately, all observed measurements are approximate. Thus, the sum of the angles of a triangle might someday be proved different from 180°, but this can never be proved by measurement.

The future of the universe is expected to be determined by whatever is the actual geometry of the universe. According to current theories in cosmology (see COSMOLOGY, astronomy), if the geometry is hyperbolic, the universe will expand indefinitely; if the geometry is Euclidean, the universe will expand indefinitely at escape velocity; and if the geometry is elliptic, the expansion of the universe will slow down and come to a halt; then the universe will start to shrink, possibly to explode again.

▬

Nonaligned Movement   The Nonaligned Movement consists of more than 100 nations, most of them in

Asia, Africa, and Latin America. Its members meet periodically to discuss matters of common interest and to adopt common policy resolutions. Although they are theoretically not aligned with either the United States or the USSR, many of them do in fact have close ties to one or the other, and this often causes dissension within the movement. Although the BANDUNG Conference, which brought 29 Asian and African nations together in Indonesia in 1955, was a precursor, the first Nonaligned conference met in 1961 in Belgrade, Yugoslavia, at the invitation of President Tito of Yugoslavia. In addition to Tito, other early leaders of the movement included Jawaharlal Nehru of India and Gamal Abdel Nasser of Egypt.

Nonconformists

In England and Wales, Nonconformists are Protestants (Presbyterians, Methodists, Baptists, Congregationalists, Quakers, and others) who do not belong (conform) to the established Church of England. The term originated in the 17th century, when it was used alternately with "Dissenters." Today Nonconformists are also called Free Churchmen.

Nonpartisan League

The Nonpartisan League was an American farmers' protest movement in the upper Midwest between 1915 and 1924. Founded by Arthur Charles Townley, a North Dakota farmer and socialist, the League advocated state ownership of grain elevators, flour mills, and packing plants. Its major successes were in North Dakota, where League candidate Lynn J. Frazier was elected governor in 1916, 1918, and 1920 and where the League's program was enacted in 1919. The league also spread to neighboring states, principally Minnesota, South Dakota, and Montana. Farm depression and antisocialist sentiment contributed to the League's rapid decline after World War I.

nonverbal communication

The transfer of information between persons without the use of words, nonverbal communication takes place by means of facial expressions, head movements, body positions and acts, tones of voice, clothing, and even odor. People need not be conscious of sending a message in order to communicate nonverbally, although some people, such as actors, politicians, and salespersons, make deliberate use of nonverbal communication to create particular effects. Often the receiver of a nonverbal message is unaware of it and knows only that he or she feels a certain way about the sender.

Nonverbal messages are usually statements about the immediate relationship. They often express emotions and reveal attitudes people hold toward their own bodies. Nonverbal messages qualify the words people use and, because they are less under conscious control, may even betray discrepancies between words and true feelings. Researchers have found that specific acts have specific meanings. Head and facial movements give the most information about the type of emotion being expressed;

body position and tension reveal the intensity of the feeling. Eye contact is especially important in signaling changes in ongoing interactions.

See also: ANIMAL COMMUNICATION; COMMUNICATION; SIGN LANGUAGE.

nonviolence   see PACIFISM AND NONVIOLENT MOVEMENTS

Nootka

[nut'-kuh]   The Nootka are North American Indians who lived along the seaward coast of Vancouver Island, Canada, and the Olympic Peninsula in Washington state. Nootka was first applied as a tribal name by the explorer Capt. James COOK. It now refers to all speakers of the language and to the language itself with its variants: standard Nootkan, Nitinat, and Makah (Cape Flattery). Nootka speakers are linguistically related to the KWAKIUTL; together they form the Wakashan language family (see INDIAN LANGUAGES, AMERICAN). Outstanding sea hunters as well as fishermen and woodworkers, the Nootka and a few imitators were the only Northwest Coast whalers.

Traditional Nootkan society consisted of economically self-sufficient local groups, each with a hereditary chief and nobility and commoners. The major Nootkan ceremonial enacted the seizing of those being initiated by Wolf Spirits, who returned them with hereditary decorations, songs, and dances. Warfare between tribes and even between confederacies was frequent, both for revenge and for control of natural resources.

Nootkan culture at the time of earliest European contacts is the best known of any Northwest Coast group. Captain Cook spent one month at Nootka Sound in 1778. A Spanish military post was built and maintained there (1789–96), and many explorers and traders wrote copious descriptions of the Indians. From an aboriginal population of over 10,000, Nootkan-speakers were reduced to 1,605 in 1939. In more recent years, their numbers increased to more than 4,500.

noradrenaline   see HORMONE, ANIMAL

Nordenskjöld, Adolf Erik, Baron

[noor'duhns-hurld]   Nils Adolf Erik Nordenskjöld, b. Nov. 18, 1832, d. Aug. 12, 1901, was a Swedish geologist, geographer, mineralogist, and explorer. Nordenskjöld made several voyages to the Arctic island of Spitsbergen (in SVALBARD). In 1870 he explored the inland ice of Greenland. From 1875 to 1876 he voyaged to the Kara Sea, an arm of the Arctic Ocean, and the Yenisei River, and from 1878 to 1880 he sailed around the Arctic coast of Europe and Asia, thus discovering the much-sought NORTHEAST PASSAGE. In 1883 he became the first person to penetrate the ice on the southeast coast of Greenland.

Nordenskjöld was professor of mineralogy at the Swedish State Museum from 1858 until his death. His son, Nils Erland Nordenskjöld (1877–1932), became well known as a cultural anthropologist of South and Central America, and his nephew Otto Nordenskjöld

(1869–1928) led scientific expeditions to southern South America (1895–97) and Antarctica (1901–04).

Norfolk (England) [nohr'-fuk] Norfolk is a county in eastern England bordering the North Sea on the east and the north. The rivers Wensum, Bure, Ouse, and Yare drain Norfolk's 5,368-km^2 (2,073-mi^2) area. The population is 744,400 (1988 est.). The principal towns are NORWICH, the county town, Great Yarmouth, King's Lynn, and Thetford. Grain, vegetable, and poultry (especially turkey) farming are the main occupations. Fishing, tourism, and the manufacture of agricultural machinery, footwear, and processed foods are also important to the economy. Sandringham, a home of the royal family, is located there. The region prospered during the Middle Ages because of its wool industry. Norfolk's area was expanded in 1974 to include a part of East Suffolk.

Norfolk (Virginia) Norfolk, Virginia's largest city, is located on the Elizabeth River, where it enters HAMPTON ROADS at Chesapeake Bay. The city's population is 261,229 (1990), and the Norfolk-VIRGINIA BEACH-NEWPORT NEWS metropolitan area has a population of 1,396,107. Norfolk, Newport News and PORTSMOUTH compose the Port of Hampton Roads. It is one of the world's largest coal ports and a leading Atlantic port in export tonnage. Norfolk alone is among the ten busiest ports in the country. The Norfolk Naval and Naval Air stations, together with the Norfolk Naval Shipyard in Portsmouth, constitute the world's largest operating naval base. The headquarters of the Atlantic Fleet, Second Fleet, NATO Supreme Allied Command Atlantic, and Fifth Naval District are located there. Norfolk is also a distribution, trade, financial, and, along with adjacent Virginia Beach, vacation center. Its major industries include shipbuilding and seafood processing. The city is also the home of Old Dominion University (1930) and Norfolk State College (1968).

Founded in 1682, Norfolk was burned by American colonists as a Tory stronghold in 1776. It was slowly rebuilt after the Revolutionary War. During the Civil War, following the famous battle between the *Monitor* and *Merrimack* in Hampton Roads in 1862, the city fell to Union forces.

Norfolk Island Norfolk Island is a territory of Australia located about 1,500 km (930 mi) northeast of Sydney in the southwest Pacific. The volcanic island covers 36 km^2 (14 mi^2) and has a population of 2,367 (1986). Kingston is the chief town and only port. The highest point is Mount Bates (318 m/1,043 ft). Tourism is the economic mainstay.

The island was discovered by Capt. James Cook in 1774. The British used it as a penal colony until 1855. In 1856 descendants of the *Bounty* mutineers were moved to Norfolk from Pitcairn Island at their request. Norfolk Island was made a federal territory of Australia in 1913.

Noriega, Manuel Antonio [nawr-yay'-gah] The Panamanian dictator Manuel Antonio Noriega Morena, b. 1934, became commander of Panama's Defense Forces in 1983 and subsequently installed and deposed presidents. In February 1988 he was indicted by two U.S. grand juries for drug trafficking and racketeering. As U.S.-Panamanian tensions mounted, he was finally ousted by U.S. troops on Dec. 20, 1989, and brought to the United States to stand trial.

norm, social A social norm is a standard of behavior expected by a particular group, such as wearing shoes to work. Norms are generally not written or legalized. No one norm is always obeyed; and no one person obeys all norms. However, norms suggest what behavior or role is appropriate to a given social situation, and many sociologists consider social institutions and society itself structures based on norms. Sociologists distinguish two kinds of norms: folkways (for example, not talking with one's mouth full), which can be violated without severe punishment, and mores (such as prohibitions against incest), which are so deeply rooted that few violate them.

See also: CONFORMITY; DEVIANCE.

normal distribution A normal distribution is a DISTRIBUTION of values described by a particular frequency curve called a normal curve (see figure). Because the shape resembles that of a bell, the curve is also known as a bell-shaped or bell curve. The normal distribution is often used in applications of PROBABILITY and STATISTICS.

The normal distribution is important for several reasons. First, many types of data tend to have approximately a normal distribution. The errors made in repeated careful measurements are normally distributed, so the normal distribution is used by scientists in the study of errors of observation. The normal distribution is often called a Gaussian distribution in honor of Carl F. GAUSS, who used it to analyze errors in astronomical observations. In psychology, many measurements have a normal distribution (see PSYCHOLOGICAL MEASUREMENT). Biological variables, such as measurements of the length or weight of individual members of a species, also often have an approximately normal distribution.

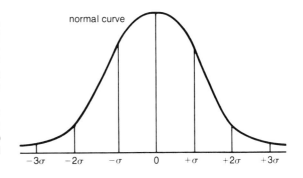
normal curve

−3σ   −2σ   −σ   0   +σ   +2σ   +3σ

Because test scores of many standardized psychological and educational tests (see EDUCATIONAL MEASUREMENT AND TESTING) follow or nearly follow a normal distribution, data relating to the normal curve have been tabulated, and systems for interpreting the scores have been developed. Units of the standard deviation, denoted by σ (see figure), are useful for measuring such tests, because each such unit corresponds to a particular fraction of all the scores in a group.

The second reason for the prominence of normal distributions is that many statistics that are not normal become approximately normal when a large number of observations are taken. The central limit theorem states that under very general conditions the mean of n number of observations will have a distribution of values that is closely approximated by a normal curve when n is large.

normal school   see TEACHING

normality   see CONCENTRATION

Norman, Jessye   Among the most highly acclaimed vocal artists, soprano Jessye Norman, b. Augusta, Ga., Sept. 15, 1945, is also one of the many talented U.S. singers whose careers were established in Europe. A first prize in a Munich competition led Norman to a lengthy contract with the Berlin Opera, beginning in 1969. Later, her association with Colin Davis, conductor of the BBC Symphony, resulted in several prize-winning recordings. In 1973, Norman made her New York debut. Her singing is notable for its taste, intelligence, and emotional depth. Norman is endowed with a magnificent stage presence.

Norman architecture   Norman architecture was a well-defined regional variant of Romanesque architecture (see ROMANESQUE ART AND ARCHITECTURE) that developed in Normandy about 1020 and in England following the Norman Conquest, lasting until about 1150. It inspired both the aesthetic and the technical advances of Gothic architecture (see GOTHIC ART AND ARCHITECTURE).

In Normandy the style developed from such early Romanesque churches as Saint Pierre (926–45) at Jumièges and the abbey church of Bernay (c.1017–40). Mont-Saint-Michel (1022–84) and Notre Dame (1028–67) at Jumièges are early examples of Norman style. Norman architecture is best exemplified, however, by the monastic churches of Caen—Saint-Étienne (c.1068–1115) and La Trinité (1062–c.1110), built as funerary monuments for William the Conqueror and his wife Matilda, respectively. La Trinité, typical of small churches in the style, is a basilican-plan structure (see BASILICA) with a series of parallel apses at the east end.

Saint-Étienne, a typical large Norman church, has a similar plan, sometimes called the Benedictine or the Norman plan. Above the nave arcades, here carried on alternating supports, the triforium arcades are equal in size to those below, and open on tribunes or galleries over the aisles. The arcaded clerestory above them is of approximately equal height with a passageway in front of the windows.

Norman architecture had influenced building in England before 1066—for example, at London's Westminster Abbey—but it became dominant after the conquest. Among the major monuments in this style are the cathedrals at Ely, Durham, Lincoln, Norwich, Peterborough, and Winchester. Most of the characteristic features of Saint-Étienne appear in these buildings, sometimes in slightly altered form. The passage in front of the clerestory windows and subsequent lightening of the walls appears in all the English examples. This feature may be the most important Norman contribution to English medieval architecture, directly anticipating Gothic construction. The major English contribution to Norman architecture is rib-vaulted masonry covering (see ARCH AND VAULT). The most significant early appearance in England of such vaults is at Durham Cathedral (begun 1093; see ARCHITECTURE).

Norman Conquest   see WILLIAM I, KING OF ENGLAND (William the Conqueror)

Normandy   [nohr'-muhn-dee]   The historic region of Normandy (French: Normandie) is located in northern France along the English Channel between Picardy on the east and Brittany on the west. It is predominantly agricultural, with camembert cheese a local specialty. The most famous spot in western Normandy is the offshore shrine of MONT-SAINT-MICHEL. Normandy's principal cities are CAEN, CHERBOURG, LE HAVRE, and ROUEN. The SEINE RIVER is the major waterway.

Normandy was part of ancient Gaul. Conquered by Julius Caesar in the 1st century BC, the area was incorporated into the Roman province of Lugdunensis in 27 BC. Franks overran the area during the 5th century. Beginning in the 9th century, NORMANS repeatedly raided the coast and began to settle there. In 911 the Normans were ceded the area by the French king CHARLES III. Their leader, Rollo, was recognized as the 1st duke of Normandy. The duchy became extremely powerful, and, in 1066, Duke William conquered England, being crowned there as WILLIAM I. On William's death, succession disputes among his sons divided Normandy and England, but the En-

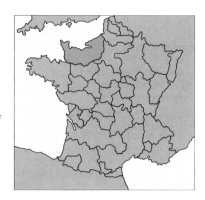

The shaded portion of the map indicates the location of Normandy, a former province of France that was divided among five administrative departments in 1791.

glish king HENRY I obtained Normandy in 1106.

Seized by Geoffrey Plantagenet, count of Anjou, in 1144, Normandy was reunited with England when Geoffrey's son, HENRY II, succeeded to the English throne in 1154. After 1204, when PHILIP II of France conquered the area, Normandy was a French possession, but the English twice invaded it during the HUNDRED YEARS' WAR (1338–1453). They were finally expelled in 1450. Normandy lost its status as a province in 1790 and was divided into the departments of Calvados, Eure, Manche, Orne, and Seine-Maritime. In World War II the Normandy Invasion was the first step in the Allied invasion of Europe.

Normandy Invasion   see WORLD WAR II

—

Normans   The Normans were VIKINGS, or Norse, who settled in western France in the 9th and early 10th centuries. In 911 the weak French monarchy under the Carolingian CHARLES III granted the lands at the estuary of the Seine River to Rollo, a Norwegian Viking, in return for an alliance against other Vikings, thus laying the foundation for the duchy of NORMANDY. Rollo's son and successor, William Longsword (d. 942), extended the duchy in the lower Seine region. The state created by these early Norman rulers was noted for its emphasis on strong ducal authority and the evolution of administrative and feudal institutions.

As early as the first half of the 11th century, some Normans sought adventure in Mediterranean lands. The numerous sons of Tancred of Hauteville entered the service of Lombard rebels against the Byzantine Empire in southern Italy. One of them, ROBERT GUISCARD, established himself as an independent ruler in Calabria and Apulia. Between 1060 and 1091 he and his brother, Roger I, undertook the conquest of Sicily from the Muslims. By 1139, ROGER II made good his effort to mold these Norman conquests into the kingdom of Sicily.

This Sicilian endeavor was matched by the Norman conquest of England. In 1066, Duke William II defeated the Anglo-Saxon king HAROLD II in the Battle of HASTINGS and assumed the English crown as WILLIAM I. Among his most notable accomplishments was the collection of data regarding the lands and households of England for the DOMESDAY BOOK. William enjoyed good relations with the church, especially with Archbishop LANFRANC of Canterbury, who brought the English church into line with continental developments. At his death in 1087, William bequeathed a strong government to his sons, WILLIAM II and HENRY I of England. The civil war between Henry's daughter, MATILDA, and his nephew, STEPHEN, disrupted the government, but order was restored by Matilda's son, HENRY II, who inaugurated (1154) the ANGEVIN dynasty in England. William the Conqueror had left Normandy to his eldest son, Duke Robert II (c.1054–1134), but it was seized by Henry I in 1106 and later became part of the Angevin domains.

In both England and Italy the Normans formed a warrior aristocracy and imposed their own social system (see FEUDALISM). However, they also adapted and developed local institutions, and their rule brought not only greater

Norman horsemen were a powerful military force in western Europe around AD 1100. Their armor included a long, chain-mail coat (hauberk), with a mail hood (coif); a conical, metal helmet with a face-guarding nasal bar extending over the nose; and a shield.

political stability but also a flowering of local culture. In England this development was most marked in the writing of history (see GEOFFREY OF MONMOUTH); in the kingdom of Sicily the Norman court was a center of interest in Greco-Arabic science. In both areas many examples of NORMAN ARCHITECTURE remain.

—

Norodom Sihanouk   [nohr-oh-duhm' sihuh-nuhk']
Norodom Sihanouk, b. Oct. 31, 1922, was king of Cambodia from 1941 to 1955, when he abdicated in favor of his father Norodom Suramarit. Sihanouk formed a mass movement that won every seat in the National Assembly in 1955. He served as prime minister in 1955–57 and, after his father's death in 1960, as head of state. He was deposed in 1970 by LON NOL and went into exile in Beijing. He served again as nominal head of state in the POL POT regime from April 1975 to April 1976, when he resigned and disappeared from public view. In 1978 he reappeared in China. He again allied himself with Pol Pot's KHMER ROUGE to oppose the 1979 Vietnamese invasion of Cambodia, helping in 1982 to form the anti-Vietnamese coalition government in exile that holds Cambodia's UN seat. With the withdrawal of the Vietnamese from Cambodia in 1989, Sihanouk participated in unsuccessful negotiations to end the war. He insisted on Khmer Rouge involvement in a future Cambodian government.

Norris, Frank   The American novelist Frank Norris, b. Benjamin Franklin Norris, Jr., Chicago, Mar. 5, 1870, d. Oct. 25, 1902, was a pioneer of NATURALISM in literature. His novels portray the demoralizing effects of modern technology on human fate. His best-known works, *The Octopus* (1901) and *The Pit* (1903), attack the railroad and wheat industries. These powerful but grim works, which contain much factual material on industrial practice and corruption at the turn of the century, are part of an intended trilogy that was to have included *The Wolf,* a novel about famine in Europe.

Norris was born to a wealthy Chicago family that moved to San Francisco during his childhood, and most of his novels are set in California. His first published work, *Moran of the Lady Letty* (1898), was followed by *McTeague* (1899), a shocking tale of how greed destroys human character.

Norris, George W.   George William Norris, b. Sandusky County, Ohio, July 11, 1861, d. Sept. 22, 1944, was a self-styled "fighting liberal" politician. Having settled in Nebraska in 1885, he was elected to the U.S. House of Representatives as a Republican in 1902.

Norris acted on behalf of the Nebraska farmers who sought federal regulation of big business and economic policies that favored farming interests. Speaker Joseph G. CANNON had blocked passage of reform legislation, and in 1910, Norris sponsored a resolution amending House rules that ended Cannon's dictatorial control of the House.

Norris served in the U.S. Senate from 1913 to 1943. Increasingly independent of Republican policies, he supported many of President Woodrow Wilson's measures. Although he opposed U.S. entry into World War I in 1917, he subsequently supported the war effort and tried to prevent wealthy corporations and citizens from making excess profits. In the 1920s he opposed Republican-administration policies that he felt hurt farmers and workers and attempted, although unsuccessfully, to create a federal farm price support system. The Norris–La Guardia Act (1932) curbed the use of injunctions in labor disputes and asserted the right of labor to organize and bargain collectively. Norris also sponsored the 20th Amendment to the Constitution (1933), which advanced the date of presidential inaugurations from March to January.

Norris is perhaps best known for his fight on behalf of public development of hydroelectric power. His bills providing for government operation of the Muscle Shoals facilities on the Tennessee River were vetoed by Presidents Calvin Coolidge (1928) and Herbert Hoover (1931). Franklin D. Roosevelt, however, did take up the project, and in 1933 the act creating the TENNESSEE VALLEY AUTHORITY was passed. Norris also wrote legislation encouraging rural electrification.

Norrköping [nohr'-chur-ping]   Norrköping (1989 est. pop., 119,370), a city and seaport in southeastern Sweden, is located where the Motala River flows into an inlet of the Baltic Sea about 130 km (80 mi) southwest of Stockholm. Sweden's main textile center, the city also produces ships, electrical equipment, paper, rubber products, and processed foods. Nearby Bronze Age rock carvings attract tourists as does the city's 16th-century castle. Norrköping was founded in the 14th century.

Norse language   see GERMANIC LANGUAGES

Norse mythology   see MYTHOLOGY

North, Lord   Frederick North, b. Apr. 13, 1732, d. Aug. 5, 1792, is remembered as the British prime minister who lost most of the American colonies. Commonly known as Lord North, a courtesy title given to him as the eldest son of an earl, he entered the House of Commons in 1754. In 1770, GEORGE III turned to him to form an administration of his own. His harmonious relations with the king and his ability to manage the House of Commons made his the longest-lived ministry since that of Sir Robert WALPOLE (served 1721–42).

North introduced the provocative INTOLERABLE ACTS (1774) in reprisal against the Boston Tea Party. However, once the American Revolution began, he lacked both the grasp of strategy and the control of his cabinet essential for the successful conduct of war. He tired of ministerial responsibility long before the British defeat at Yorktown compelled him to resign in 1782.

North's coalition in 1783 with his old opponent Charles James Fox earned him public odium and the bitter enmity of the king, who brought the ministry down by securing defeat of Fox's East India bill. North continued political activity, opposing William PITT the Younger, even after going blind in 1787. He succeeded his father as 2d earl of Guilford in 1790.

Frederick, Lord North, was prime minister of England during the rebellion of the American colonies. North, whose coercive policies following the Boston Tea Party helped precipitate the Revolution, sought to resign when the war began. Kept in office by George III, he resigned after the British defeat at Yorktown.

North Africa   North Africa, which includes Morocco, Tunisia, Algeria, and Libya, is also called the Maghreb ("west" in Arabic). It is a mountainous region bounded by

AT A GLANCE

NORTH AMERICA

Area: 24,249,000 km² (9,363,000 mi²); 16.4% of the world's land area.
Population: 416,000,000 (1988 est.); 8.2% of total world population. *Density*—17.5 per km² (44.4 per mi²).
Coastline: 155,236 km (96,459 mi).
Elevation: *Highest*—Mount McKinley (Denali), 6,194 m (20,320 ft); *lowest*—Death Valley, 86 m (282 ft) below sea level.
Northernmost Mainland Point: Tip of Boothia Peninsula, Northwest Territories, Canada, 70°30′ N.
Southernmost Point: Southeastern Panama, 7°15′ N.
Easternmost Mainland Point: Southeast coast of Labrador, Canada, about 55°42′ W.
Westernmost Mainland Point: Cape Prince of Wales, Alaska, 168°05′ W.
Principal Rivers: Missouri, Mississippi, Yukon, Rio Grande, Red, Arkansas, Colorado, Columbia, Peace, Saskatchewan, Mackenzie, Snake, Churchill, Ohio, St. Lawrence.
Principal Lakes: Superior, Huron, Michigan, Great Bear, Great Slave, Erie, Winnipeg, Ontario.
Principal Mountain Ranges: Rocky, Alaska ranges, Coastal ranges, Cascade, Sierra Nevada, Sierra Madre, Appalachian.
Principal Desert: Sonoran.
Political Divisions: 23 independent countries; 14 nonindependent political units.

the Mediterranean Sea on the north, the Sahara on the south, the Libyan Desert on the east, and the Atlantic Ocean on the west. The population, mostly Arabic-speaking Muslims, is of BERBER ancestry. Because of cultural, religious, and linguistic links, the area is sometimes considered part of the Middle East.

North America   North America is the larger of the two continents of the Western Hemisphere. The main body of this somewhat rectangular continent is extended in the northwest by the peninsula of Alaska and its Aleutian Island chain, in the northeast by the world's largest island (Greenland), in the southeast by Florida's peninsula, and in the southwest by Mexico and the land bridge to South America. The Caribbean islands are also often included in the physical definition of North America. Altogether, the continent's land area places it third in size among the seven continents, smaller only than Asia and Africa.

Alternative definitions of North America are also made on political or cultural grounds. Greenland, under Danish sovereignty and virtually without permanent human settlement, is often considered an extension of Europe. The small countries occupying the narrow isthmus between Mexico and South America may be treated separately as CENTRAL AMERICA. The Caribbean islands may be combined with Mexico and Central America and

described, collectively, as Middle America.

In the broadest definition, North America extends across 5,300 km (3,300 mi) from St. John's, Newfoundland, to the Pacific coast of Washington's Olympic Peninsula; and 5,600 km (3,500 mi) between the Arctic and the Gulf of Mexico, with an additional 2,300 km (1,400 mi) south across the land bridge to the Panama-Colombia border.

It is believed that humans first entered North America more than 20,000 years ago. They probably crossed a land bridge that appeared between Siberia and Alaska as sea levels dropped during the period of continental glaciation. Small groups of hunters and gatherers pushed human settlement south and eastward, eventually across the Central American land bridge and on into South America. Agriculture and permanent settlement in villages in the Western Hemisphere are thought to have begun in central Mexico about 7000 BC.

During the 10th century AD Norse and probably Irish explorers reached North America. The first uninterrupted European settlement, however, awaited Spanish occupation of the Caribbean and Middle American lands during the 16th century. French and English permanent settlements (begun in 1605 and 1607, respectively) proved to be the most durable of the other European contacts. Africans were carried to Caribbean plantations early in the Spanish occupation and introduced into English colonial

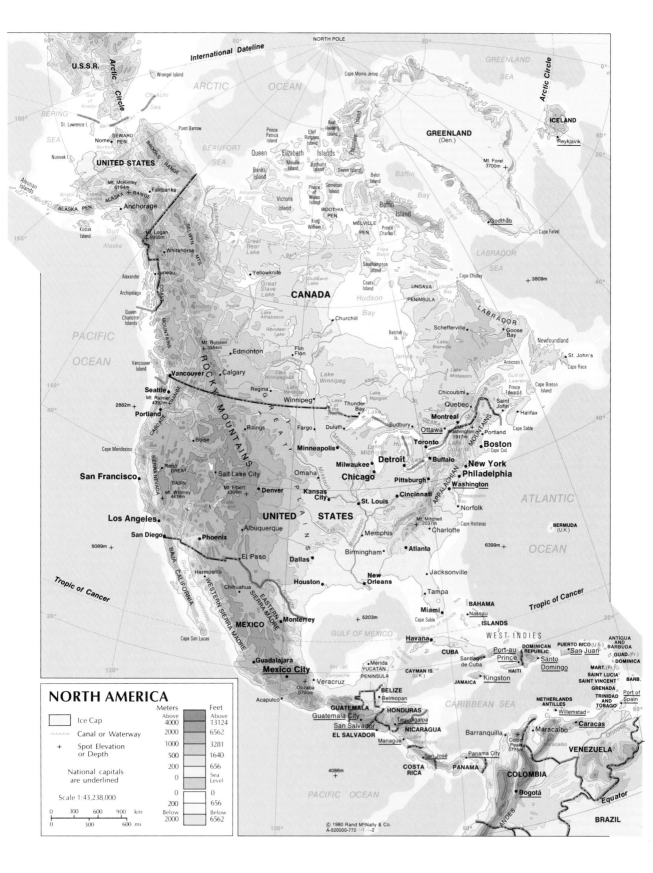

NORTH AMERICA

	Meters	Feet
Ice Cap	Above 4000	Above 13124
Canal or Waterway	2000	6562
+ Spot Elevation or Depth	1000	3281
	500	1640
National capitals are underlined	200	656
	0	Sea Level
Scale 1:43,238,000	0	0
	200	656
	Below 2000	Below 6562

0 300 600 900 km
0 300 600 mi

© 1980 Rand McNally & Co.
A-520000-772 -1-1-2

The Canadian Rockies rise above Honeymoon Lake in Jasper National Park. The park includes portions of the Columbia Icefield, the largest North American glacial ice field south of the Arctic Circle.

holdings in 1619. The tide of European migration continued for the next three centuries to fill much of the rest of North America.

Political independence in North America began with the United States (1776), and now most states are independent. Puerto Rico remains a U.S. territory, and a few Caribbean islands remain possessions of the United States, Britain, France, or the Netherlands. Canada became a nation in 1867.

Land

The natural regions of North America are typified by broad areas of apparently similar appearance and morphology. The entire western margin of the continent is paralleled by a series of mountain chains. The vast interior of the continent is dominated by gently rolling plains. The eastern side of the continent has both low mountain relief and, along the southeast coast, almost flat topography.

Western Uplands. The western margin of the continent is occupied by long ranges of mountains interspersed with high plateaus, narrow valleys, and broad interior basins. This region extends from the Arctic (in Alaska) through Mexico and the Central American isthmus to South America. There are two linear mountain regions: the more eastern is the ROCKY MOUNTAINS, and the more western section is a succession of rugged ranges (CASCADE RANGE, SIERRA NEVADA, and COAST RANGES) that parallel the Pacific coast. Between (and among) these mountainous margins are areas of lower relief punctuated in some places by smaller mountain ranges or cut deeply by rivers and streams to form spectacular canyonlands, such as the GRAND CANYON of the COLORADO RIVER. The southern extension of the continent is largely within this region, with the two major ranges in Mexico (Sierra Madre Occidental and Sierra Madre Oriental; see SIERRA MADRE) forming the margins of an interior plateau in the north and merging in the rugged south central portion of the country.

Except for a narrow high-rainfall zone along the northern Pacific margin, most of the region is dry but also subject to altitudinal climatic zonation.

The Rocky Mountains form the continental divide between Atlantic and Pacific Ocean drainage, but the arid GREAT BASIN of the western United States and a smaller portion of north central Mexico have interior drainage. Throughout the entire region, settlement is especially dependent on local water supplies or on the importation of water.

Canadian Shield. Located north of the GREAT LAKES and the estuary of the ST. LAWRENCE RIVER, and including Greenland, the CANADIAN SHIELD is a vast region of Precambrian metamorphic rock. Along the eastern side of the shield, as in the LAURENTIAN MOUNTAINS of Quebec and Labrador, shield topography remains rugged. Most of the remainder between the Arctic and the Great Lakes is a low-lying, moderately hilly landscape dotted with millions of small lakes and swampy bogs that freeze during the long winters. The general drainage is northward into HUDSON BAY or the Arctic Ocean, although the southern margins of the shield drain toward the Great Lakes and the St. Lawrence River. The southern portion of the shield is covered by a forest of needleleaf evergreens, whereas the northern portion (except where permanently ice-covered) is characterized by the low, brushy tundra.

Interior Plains. The immense Interior Plains of the continent reach from the Arctic almost to the Gulf of Mexico and have flat to moderately rolling topography. The region has a continental climate, characterized by a wide seasonal temperature range and periods of intermittent aridity. The western portion of the Interior Plains is often referred to as the GREAT PLAINS, with the remainder still called the Interior Plains.

The vegetation consists of grassland throughout the drier portion of the region, merging into what was originally a deciduous or a mixed coniferous-deciduous wood-

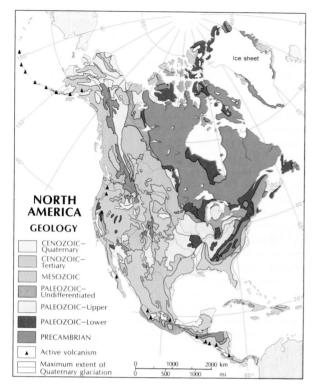

NORTH
AMERICA
GEOLOGY

CENOZOIC–
Quaternary
CENOZOIC–
Tertiary
MESOZOIC
PALEOZOIC–
Undifferentiated
PALEOZOIC–Upper
PALEOZOIC–Lower
PRECAMBRIAN
▲ Active volcanism
Maximum extent of
Quaternary glaciation

Ice sheet

NORTH
AMERICA
CLIMATIC ZONES

Tropical Wet
Tropical
Wet-Dry
Steppe
Desert
Mediterranean
Subtropical Humid
Marine West Coast
Continental Humid
Subarctic
Tundra
Ice sheet
Highlands-
undifferentiated

Arctic Bay
Anchorage
Seattle
Minneapolis
Los Angeles
El Paso
Houston
Monterrey
Havana
Belize City

land. The small portion of the plains in the far north shares the coniferous-to-tundra pattern found across the shield. The region's drainage pattern is largely into the MISSISSIPPI RIVER system, but some of the rivers flow across the shield into the Hudson Bay and eventually make their way into the Arctic-bound MACKENZIE RIVER.

Appalachian and Interior Highlands. The APPALACHIAN MOUNTAIN system occupies an area from Newfoundland and the Gulf of St. Lawrence almost to the Gulf of Mexico. Most of the Appalachian region is composed of a series of low, well-worn mountains or deeply dissected plateaus. The northern portion of the region offers a more jumbled and rounded relief pattern than the BLUE RIDGE MOUNTAINS and Ridge and Valley sections of the southern Appalachians. The natural vegetation is generally a mixed coniferous-deciduous forest. The region's climate ranges from the subarctic regime of Newfoundland to the humid subtropical conditions of the southern interior United States.

Atlantic and Gulf Lowlands. Bordering the continent on the south and east are a series of plains and low, rolling topography. From LONG ISLAND to Mexico's YUCATÁN PENINSULA and beyond, this region is primarily characterized by its low elevation and its proximity to the coast, although the Atlantic plain gives way inland to the gently hilly, fertile PIEDMONT PLATEAU. The region's summers are hot and humid, and winters, where seasonal variation is experienced, are relatively short and mild. The vegetation is extremely variable.

The Caribbean. Located almost entirely within the trop-

ics, the Caribbean islands experience a humid, tropical climate. It is this area, together with the Atlantic and Gulf Lowlands, that is most susceptible to hurricanes. Almost all the islands have a narrow coastal lowland that rises toward a mountainous interior. The dominant vegetation pattern is broadleaf evergreen with some broadleaf deciduous intermixture.

Resources

The agricultural resources of North America are immense, with much of this potential located in the United States and southern Canada. Almost all of the Interior Plains and the Atlantic and Gulf Lowlands regions are suitable for agriculture. Significant areas within the Western Uplands—wherever water is available—are valuable crop or pasture lands as are smaller sections of Middle America.

Mineral fuel resources—coal, petroleum, and natural gas—are found in abundance in North America. Extensive coalfields are located in the eastern half of the United States, and many other, smaller deposits are located throughout the eastern Rockies. Canada, too, has extensive reserves. The small deposits in northeastern Mexico are the only significant coalfields in Middle America.

About 13% of the world's reserves of petroleum and natural gas are found in North America. Deposits currently recognized in the United States represent roughly half of the total. The leading U.S. producing regions are in the south central plains and in a long arc along the Gulf Coast, although significant deposits also occur in California, Alaska, and elsewhere. Canada continues to discover sizable deposits, especially along the eastern margin of the Rockies. Mexico has almost twice the proven oil reserves of the United States.

North America's water resources are important for hydropower, irrigation, and transportation. Canada's hydropower potential is concentrated in the Laurentian Mountains of the shield and in the major rivers of the far West. Most of the remaining undeveloped hydro potential is in the West, concentrated principally on the COLUMBIA RIVER and its major tributaries. Much of Middle America's hydro potential remains to be developed. In the arid western region aqueducts carry water for irrigation and municipal needs across many hundreds of kilometers.

The navigable waterways of North America are exceptional. The Mississippi River and its tributaries provide access between the Gulf of Mexico and the heart of the Interior Plains. The Great Lakes are also navigable, and, with the development of the ST. LAWRENCE SEAWAY, the Great Lakes now connect the north central Interior Plains with the Atlantic Ocean.

North America also possesses an impressive array of high-quality metallic mineral deposits. Iron, nickel, copper, uranium, gold, and most other major metals are found in minable deposits, mostly in the shield and the Western Uplands. Bauxite, in short supply in North America, is found in the Ozarks and Jamaica. Of the economically important metallic minerals, only tungsten, tin, and chromi-

um are insufficiently concentrated on the continent.

As rich in resources as North America is, the high consumption, especially by the U.S. population, makes North America a net importer of virtually all major resources.

People

Of the 416 million people (1988 est.) in North America, almost 60% are located in the United States and another 20% live in Mexico. Almost all of Canada's 26 million people live within 200 km (125 mi) of the U.S. border. The remainder of the continent's population is divided between the Caribbean and Central American countries.

The Spanish were the first Europeans to arrive and by the early 16th century had established their control over the Aztec empire in the Valley of Mexico, the strategically important isthmus of Central America, and several of the larger islands in the Caribbean. Other European countries laid claim to sections of the Caribbean and subsequently established outposts along the Atlantic coast. The French early claimed the mouths of the two water routes to the interior, the St. Lawrence and Mississippi rivers, and the Dutch temporarily held the mouth of the Hudson River.

By 1750 the dominant European cultural patterns were established. Mexico and Central America were largely Spanish with a significant but diminished Amerindian influence (see INDIANS, AMERICAN). This Spanish region reached into what is now New Mexico and along much of the rest of the Gulf Coast. The Caribbean islands

(Left) *Death Valley, in southeastern California, is an arid, hot basin of mud and salt flats. Within the valley, at 86 m (282 ft) below sea level, is the lowest point in the Western Hemisphere.*

(Below) *This aerial photograph of the Mississippi River was taken a short distance from the river's headwaters at Lake Itasca in northern Minnesota. Although the Mississippi and its tributaries eventually form one of the largest river systems in the world, the river is only 3 m (10 ft) wide at this point.*

were very mixed culturally, and the composition was complicated further by the introduction of Africans and, later, Asian Indians in some colonial holdings. The French, soon to lose political control of all their North American claims, were well established along the middle St. Lawrence in what became Quebec and had a foothold in New Orleans at the mouth of the Mississippi. British settlement, scattered along the entire Atlantic coast between Spanish Florida and the St. Lawrence, included pockets of Dutch, French Huguenot, German, and Swedish settlers. The only other European presence of consequence was a thin strip of Russian control along the north Pacific coast.

During the 150 years following U.S. independence, many millions of immigrants arrived from Europe. During the first century of this period, most immigrants came from northwestern Europe. The British Isles continued to be a major source of settlers, with the Irish arriving in a strong wave between 1830 and 1860. Immigrants from Germany were the next most numerous. Late in the 19th century, following a small wave from Scandinavia in the 1880s, most new immigrants came from eastern and southern Europe. Many Chinese arrived in the mid- to late-19th century to help build the railroads. Since the 1920s most immigration to the United States has come from Latin America (see HISPANIC AMERICANS), Canada, and, more recently, Asia.

Canada, too, has received millions of immigrants, although the numbers have been much smaller than for the United States. Canadian immigrants have come primarily from Britain and the United States, with significant numbers from Eastern Europe, the USSR, Ireland, and Italy during some decades.

Most of the large Canadian cities have a mixture of European heritages among their populations, but the French-Anglo division is most pronounced. About 5.3 million French-speaking people live in Quebec province. In the rest of Canada—except for New Brunswick, in which about one-third of the population speak French, and in the far north, where Eskimo is important—English predominates.

Africans were imported as slaves to the Caribbean plantations and to the southern British colonies, probably by the millions. This population remained concentrated in the southern United States and the Caribbean regions until early in the 20th century, when blacks began to move to northern and western cities in large numbers. This migration wave, from the agrarian South to the urban North and West, apparently peaked about 1970 and began to taper off. Almost half of the black population of the United States continue to reside in the Southeast (see AFRICAN AMERICANS).

Demography and Urbanization. Differences in population growth rates are most marked between Middle America and the two larger northern countries. Annual rates of increase are 1.0% (1990) for the United States and 0.8% for Canada (1987 est.). Rates for mainland Middle America are 3 to 5 times the U.S. level, whereas rates for

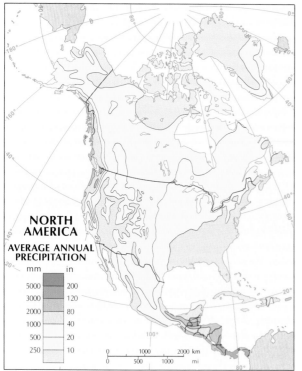

NORTH AMERICA

AVERAGE ANNUAL PRECIPITATION

mm	in
5000	200
3000	120
2000	80
1000	40
500	20
250	10

NORTH AMERICA

NATURAL VEGETATION

- Tropical rain forest
- Subtropical evergreen forest
- Temperate deciduous forest
- Taiga or Boreal forest
- Chapparal or Mediterranean scrub
- Tropical grassland and savanna
- Temperate grassland (prairie, steppe, pampa)
- Semidesert
- Desert
- Tundra
- Alpine tundra
- Ice sheet

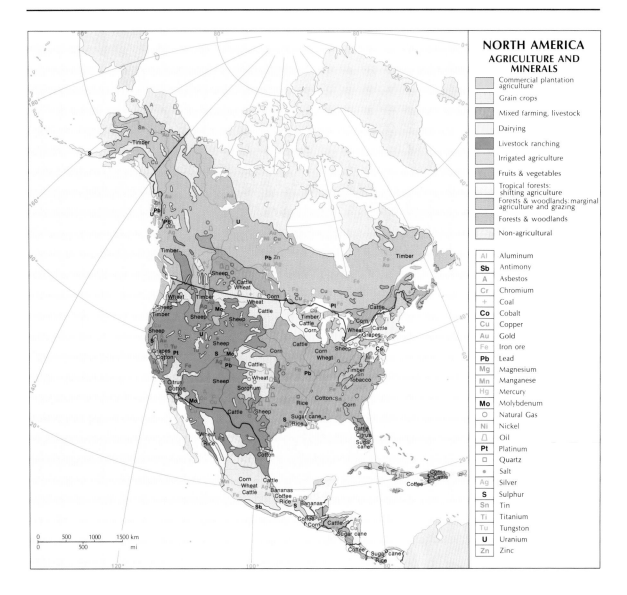

NORTH AMERICA
AGRICULTURE AND MINERALS

	Commercial plantation agriculture
	Grain crops
	Mixed farming, livestock
	Dairying
	Livestock ranching
	Irrigated agriculture
	Fruits & vegetables
	Tropical forests: shifting agriculture
	Forests & woodlands: marginal agriculture and grazing
	Forests & woodlands
	Non-agricultural

Al	Aluminum
Sb	Antimony
A	Asbestos
Cr	Chromium
+	Coal
Co	Cobalt
Cu	Copper
Au	Gold
Fe	Iron ore
Pb	Lead
Mg	Magnesium
Mn	Manganese
Hg	Mercury
Mo	Molybdenum
O	Natural Gas
Ni	Nickel
⌂	Oil
Pt	Platinum
▫	Quartz
•	Salt
Ag	Silver
S	Sulphur
Sn	Tin
Ti	Titanium
Tu	Tungsten
U	Uranium
Zn	Zinc

the Caribbean differ widely, with some relatively high and others roughly equal to the Canadian and U.S. rates.

Levels of urbanization vary sharply, with generally lower, although increasing, rates in Middle America than in the United States and Canada. Approximately three-quarters of the two northern countries' populations live in urban areas, whereas in much of the rest of North America the proportion ranges between 45% and 60%. Some countries have even lower rates, for example, Haiti at about 25%. The rate in Mexico, however, is about 70%. Mexico City alone contains more than 22% of the national population in its total urban area.

The U.S. and Canadian populations have been urban for decades, with major population shifts occurring among the large urban centers, and from central cities to the suburbs. In Canada the movement is from the cities in Ontario and Quebec to those in Alberta and British Columbia. In the United States the major shift has been from northeastern metropolitan areas to those located in the West and South.

Education. In the United States and Canada more than 50% of the persons older than 25 years have completed at least 12 years of schooling. In addition, more than 15% have completed at least 4 years of college. Virtually the entire populations of both countries are considered literate. In contrast, a large portion of the Middle American population does not finish primary school, and illiteracy rates remain high, probably over 50% in some countries, including Haiti and Guatemala.

Health. Using infant mortality as a general indicator of

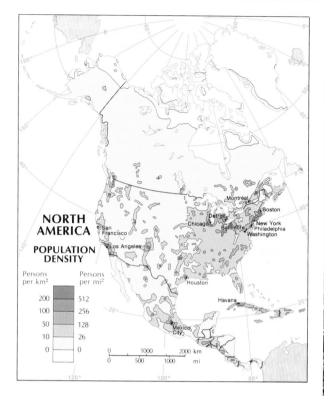

NORTH
AMERICA

POPULATION
DENSITY

Persons per km²		Persons per mi²
200		512
100		256
50		128
10		26
0		0

The Los Angeles metropolitan area is a complex of incorporated and unincorporated towns connected to each other by a vast highway system.

public health, only Northern and Western Europe, with several notable exceptions, have rates as low or lower than the two countries of temperate North America (about 8 deaths and 10.1 deaths per 1,000 live births in Canada and the United States, respectively). With life expectancy at birth approaching 75 years, mortality in the United States and Canada is more often caused by diseases of aging (heart disease, cancer, and stroke) than by infectious diseases. The rest of North America, on the other hand, must contend with many of the enervating and often fatal illnesses typical of the tropics. The infant mortality rate often exceeds 30 deaths per 1,000 live births.

Religion. Of those who regularly attend religious services in North America, the overwhelming majority are Christian. Together, the various Protestant religions dominate in the United States except in the Northeast and large eastern cities and the Southwest, where Roman Catholics are more numerous. In Canada, Quebec is largely Catholic while the other provinces are predominantly Protestant. Almost all of Middle America is predominantly Catholic. Sprinkled throughout North America, especially in Canada and the United States, are sizable Jewish communities and smaller groups of virtually every other religion.

Economy

Levels of economic development vary greatly over the continent. The economies of Canada and the United States employ well under one-tenth of their labor forces

in agriculture and one-third or less in industry, with the rest primarily employed in service industries. Fueled by oil revenues, Mexico's economy developed rapidly in the 1970s, but the fall of oil prices in the 1980s stalled this growth and plunged Mexico deeply into debt. About one-third of the workers remain engaged in agriculture. In most of the Middle American countries south of Mexico, more than half of the labor force is engaged in agriculture. In the Caribbean the pace of economic development is uneven, and unemployment rates are generally high. The agricultural sector employs about three-quarters of the labor force in some areas, although the tourism industry results in high service-sector employment.

Agriculture. North America's agriculture may be the most productive on Earth. The United States and Canada regularly export more wheat than the rest of the world combined. Wheat, corn, oats, soybeans, barley, and many other feed crops are grown regionally throughout the vast Interior Plains, with most used to feed the two countries' millions of cattle, hogs, and dairy cows. Specialty crops, such as tobacco, rice, and peanuts, are grown across the U.S. South. Fruit and vegetable production is concentrated in California, Texas, and Florida. Sugarcane is prominent in the Caribbean, as are coffee, cotton, and bananas in Central America.

In Central America ownership of large estates (haciendas), farmed by landless peasants, is concentrated in the hands of a small, wealthy, and politically powerful class. Scattered among the large holdings are very small subsistence plots farmed by low-income peasants. Following the Revolution of 1910 in Mexico, a land-reform program subdivided many of the largest haciendas into communally held farm villages known as *ejidos*.

Manufacturing. In North America the primary area of traditional industry, which produces such products as steel, automobiles, and machine tools, lies around the southern Great Lakes (Chicago, Gary, Detroit, Cleveland, Pittsburgh, Toronto, Hamilton). Other, smaller areas are numerous in the United States and Canada, but except for Mexico (Monterrey and Mexico City), there is little heavy industry in Middle America.

The continental distribution of lighter industry is similar, with most located in the two temperate countries. The traditional pattern of Great Lakes–Northeast United States concentration is changing rapidly. The new pattern is one of decentralization and dispersion with an emphasis on high-technology industries. Urban regions in the South and the West are growing. Industrialization is occurring in Mexico and, to a lesser degree, in Puerto Rico and Jamaica, but the rest of Middle America remains far behind.

Forestry and Fishing. More than one-third of Canada is forested, but most forests—with those in British Columbia the leading exception—are not easily accessible and are slow-growing woodlands of the northern boreal region. Almost 200 million ha (500 million acres) of commercial timberland are available in the United States; the most used are the pine forests of the Southeast and Pacific

The conical Popocatépetl volcano rises to a height of 5,452 m (17,887 ft) in Mexico's Cordillera de Anáhuac range. Popocatépetl, named for a pre-Columbian Indian term meaning "smoking mountain," has not erupted since the 19th century.

Corn, or maize, a grain believed to have originated in the Americas, ripens on a farm in Grant County, Wis. North America produces almost 50 percent of the world's corn.

Northwest. U.S. domestic consumption of wood as lumber and pulp exceeds supply, so much is imported from Canada. Central America has vast forests, but they are used selectively.

Shallow shelves, such as the Grand Banks and Georges Bank off the New England and Newfoundland coasts, are fished for cod, herring, flounder, and scallop. The southern Atlantic and Gulf coasts are fished for herring, sardines, shrimp, and oysters. Along the Pacific, in addition to cod and herring, salmon and flounder are prominent north of Point Reyes, Calif., while tuna is more important to the south. Fishing is locally important in the Caribbean and elsewhere.

Trade. The countries of North America, dominated economically by the United States, trade with each other more than with most other parts of the world. Canada's chief trading partner for both imports and exports is the United States. Similarly, the primary trading partner of the United States is Canada. All Middle American countries, except Cuba and Nicaragua, trade more intensively with the United States than with any other country. In general, raw materials and specialty crops flow into the United States from its neighbors, while manufactured products and basic foodstuffs are exported.

Recent Developments

The United States, which has long held a proprietary attitude toward the Western Hemisphere and especially toward North America, has rarely hesitated to involve itself directly in the political and economic affairs of other states on the continent. Central America, where extremes of wealth and poverty have resulted in much political instability, continues to attract U.S. intervention, although changing conditions have forced a modification in this approach to continental affairs.

Mexico's size and growth since 1960 have made it the dominant force within Middle America, and when Mexico's national policy toward other states in the region does not coincide with that of the United States, more U.S. accommodation is necessary than was formerly the case.

Revolutions in Cuba (1959) and Nicaragua (1979) and the signing of a treaty (1978) for gradual U.S. withdrawal from the PANAMA CANAL ZONE all showed that issues within the region were less likely to be settled solely from Washington. Nevertheless, strong, indirect U.S. involvement in Nicaragua and the U.S. intervention (1983) on the tiny island of Grenada demonstrated that the United States still considered the region part of its sphere of influence.

Two issues between the United States and Mexico illustrate their interdependence. As U.S. demands on the limited supply of irrigation water from the south-flowing Colorado River have increased, farmers south of the border have complained that an international river has been appropriated for only one country's needs. Bilateral discussions have so far failed to settle the issue. Second, the booming growth of southwestern U.S. cities has led many Mexicans, perhaps by the hundreds of thousands annually, to cross the border illegally in search of employment. The social, economic, and political issues involving these illegal migrants remained tangled and sensitive.

Within Canada, the boom economies of its western provinces threaten to draw the center of the national economy away from the traditional eastern Toronto-Montreal axis. The pull from the West has also exaggerated the country's regionalisms. Conflicts on provincial versus federal sovereignty emerged (1980–1987) over the issues of drafting the federal constitution and the pricing system for fossil fuels from Alberta. A plebiscite in Quebec reaffirmed (1980) its inclusion within the confederation of Canada but did not eliminate the need to address the underlying issue of bicultural equality.

Regional rivalries within the United States highlight major relocations in population and economic activity. Shifts in employment from heavy industry to high-technology industry have stimulated major growth spurts in the South and West, largely at the expense of the Northeast. Accompanying the clear benefits of regional economic growth, however, have been strains on local service structures and local cultures unaccustomed to such a rapid influx of people and economic demand. During the 1980s the large and skilled labor force in the Northeast attracted an increasing share of the new service and specialized technical jobs. In the arid West, debate has become more vigorous between proponents of full-scale development and those arguing for maintenance of balance with the environment's ability to absorb human demands. Ultimately, the supply of available water in the West will limit the number of people and economic activities within the region, but those who argue for slower regional growth are concerned that irreparable damage will have been caused by then.

See also: articles on individual physical features, cities, countries, states, and provinces; CANADA, HISTORY OF; MEXICO, HISTORY OF; UNITED STATES, HISTORY OF THE.

North American archaeology As Europeans began their conquest and settlement of North America from the 16th to the 18th century, a number of antiquarians suggested that multiple migrations must have taken place from the Old World within the then-accepted time restriction of biblical chronology (which dated the creation of the world at 4004 BC). Today the only view accepted by scholars is that humans first entered the New World from Asia by way of the BERING LAND BRIDGE, a landmass that existed during the Ice Age linking Siberia and Alaska in the area of what is now the Bering Strait. The only adequately documented evidence of a European presence in North America before the arrival of Columbus is that of the VIKINGS. They are known to have reached Newfoundland in about AD 1000 (see L'ANSE AUX MEADOWS), but they made no significant impact in the New World. In recent years a number of claims have been made regarding other European or Asiatic explorations of North America in pre-Columbian times, but none has been adequately substantiated through archaeological evidence.

Earliest Americans. All prehistoric human skeletal material found in North America belongs to the modern human species, *Homo sapiens sapiens*. Anatomically, the skeletal finds relate most closely to Mongoloid population groups of northeastern Asia. The earliest inhabitants of North America are thought to have occupied the continent about 12,000 years ago, although archaeologists disagree as to precisely when the original crossing from Asia may have occurred. Some have speculated that the migrations southward through North America may have begun 20,000 to 30,000 years ago.

Paleo-Indian Period. Although a small number of archaeological sites provide evidence of occupation dating from more than 12,000 years ago—notably MEADOWCROFT ROCKSHELTER in Pennsylvania, Fort Rock Cave in Oregon, and Wilson Butte Cave in Idaho—such sites have not yielded adequate evidence to identify a full cultural complex, and the actual age of the sites is still under debate. The earliest widespread complex is that of the hunting and gathering societies called Paleo-Indian. Remains of their stone and bone tool technology were first recognized during the 1920s and 1930s in the high plains of the Southwest, at sites near Folsom and Clovis in the east central part of New Mexico. Their distinctive grooved, or fluted, projectile points (see CLOVIS CULTURE; FOLSOM CULTURE) have since been found in the contiguous 48 states, southern Canada, north into Alaska, and northern Mexico. In western sites this cultural complex has been associated with extinct fauna, such as mammoths, mastodons, horses, and camelids, but at Eastern Woodlands sites such associations are not known.

Paleo-Indian groups lived in small bands of probably 30 to 40 individuals or as family units. Their lithic technology included projectile points on spears or dart shafts, knives, scrapers, drills, gravers, hammerstones, abraders, and some bone awls and beads. They occupied almost all of central North America beginning about 12,000 to 10,000 years ago, during a period when vegetation and animal life were adjusting to the climatic changes at the end of the Ice Age.

The following 7,000 years was a period of adaptation by native American populations to the diverse North American environments. It was marked by the develop-

(Above) *This carved shell gorget (AD 1200–1600) is an artifact of the pre-Columbian Southeast.*

(Right) *This caribou shinbone, discovered in Old Crow Basin in Canada's Yukon Territory, dates from c.25,000 BC, among the oldest for a North American artifact.* (Above) *This detail shows the serrated edge of the scraping tool.*

(Above left) *This hand, cut from sheet mica, was discovered in a burial mound constructed by members of the Eastern Woodlands Hopewell culture in Ohio. It dates from 1,500 years ago.* (Above right) *This intricately carved stone effigy pipe (AD 1200–1600) of a warrior beheading a victim was found at Spiro Mound in eastern Oklahoma.*

(Left) *These late Paleo-Indian projectile points, found in eastern North America, have a lanceolate shape typical of blades made after 7000 BC.*

ment of new tools, clothing, and shelter and intensive exploration for sources of raw materials and for plant and animal foods. During the long Archaic period major regional adaptations occurred in the Eastern Woodlands, the Plains, the Desert West, and also in California, the Northwest Plateau, and the Arctic.

Eastern Archaic. In the East, bands of hunter-gatherers moved north as far as Newfoundland and Labrador by 6000 BC, into Quebec, Ontario, and the prairie provinces, and on to the Canadian Shield as the vegetation and animal life moved north. Particularly favored were river valleys and lake areas, where aquatic foods could supplement those from the woods and prairies. The population gradually increased. Through time many changing varieties of projectile points, knives, drills, scrapers, milling stones, and other lithic tools were developed. Some of these, particularly projectile point styles, spread widely and are today used by archaeologists to indicate approximate contemporaneity of Archaic peoples.

The earliest known remains of houses are associated with the Archaic. Preserved clay impressions of mats and fabrics testify to a widespread production of these perishable items. Clothing was made from animal skins and from vegetable materials. In most Archaic burials the corpse is found in a flexed position, although cremation was also practiced.

Trade and exchange patterns existed across large stretches of the Eastern Woodlands, with items made from marine shells during the Late Archaic appearing as far north and west as Minnesota and Lower Canada. Evidence of tropical gourds and squash dating from the 3d millennium BC is found in Missouri, Kentucky, and Tennessee; these are the first indications of agricultural activities, introduced from northeastern MESOAMERICA.

The Plains Archaic was characterized by a primary emphasis on the hunting of bison, beaver, antelope, elk, deer, and smaller animals and by a continuation of the way of life established by the fluted-point hunters.

Desert Archaic. In the Desert or Western Archaic many groups maintained continuous occupation of caves and rock shelters over long periods. Preserved at DANGER CAVE in Utah and at other Desert Archaic sites were a number of organic artifacts: twined and coiled baskets, matting, sandals made from vegetable materials, wooden fire drills and hearths, animal-skin medicine pouches, cloth, hide moccasins, and feather robes. Characteristic lithic implements included a variety of notched and stemmed projectile points, drills, scrapers, and grinding and milling stones. Distinctive cultural complexes have been located at sites along the Pacific coast and along the streams flowing into the sea.

Arctic and Subarctic. In the Aleutians, mainland Alaska, and across the Canadian Arctic, small population groups developed their distinctive hunting and gathering cultures, which reflected their unique adaptations to the harsh local environments. In the Bering Strait area a coastal sea-mammal hunting complex evolved before 2000 BC, by which time early ESKIMO groups had spread eastward to northeastern Canada and Greenland. By this time Indian populations reliant on hunting and gathering were distributed in small groups through the interior forest and the tundra of the subarctic area.

Woodland Culture. About 1000 BC in Eastern North America, a number of pronounced cultural developments appeared that archaeologists identify as the prehistoric Woodland cultural complexes (see MOUND BUILDERS). These developments included burial in earthen mounds; the production of pottery, tubular pipes, new gorget forms, and a preponderance of ungrooved axes or celts; the increasing use of copper for ornaments; and a noticeable increase in the trade and exchange of raw materials and finished artifacts. In the Adena complexes (c.500 BC) of the central Ohio Valley, large mounds with elaborate log tombs and earthen circles were constructed, reflecting the growing importance of burial ceremonialism, particularly for important males of the society.

Throughout most of the East, sites of the Middle Woodland period, dating from the end of the 1st century BC to AD 300–400, reveal strong cultural links with the Hopewell sites of Ohio, which had gradually developed out of the Adena cultural complex. Other Middle Woodland groups whose material culture was less advanced also indicated a growth in population and an increasingly complex social organization.

Mississippian Culture. With the gradual decline and eventual disappearance of the Hopewellian during the mid-1st millennium AD, many local Late Woodland complexes appeared whose material culture was less spectacular but represented widespread changes in every facet of the way of life. Numerous indications have been found of a shift between AD 700 and 900 from an economy based primarily on hunting and gathering to one in which maize cultivation was increasingly important. Another important change was the introduction of the bow and arrow from the west. Settlements became more permanent, with house forms gradually becoming rectangular and with some villages having stockades or fortifications. In the Mississippi Valley and its major tributaries, stretching from St. Louis, Mo., to Vicksburg, Miss., several hundreds of the so-called Mississippian societies appeared. From 900 to 1400 many major sites existed, with populations ranging from a few hundred to several thousand. Impressive earthen platform mounds to support civic and ceremonial buildings were built, often around a central open plaza. Substantial rectangular dwellings were typically enclosed by a stockade. Although some mound burials were made, particularly for the elite of the societies, most of the dead were buried in cemeteries. Evidence of social stratification is indicated by the presence in burials of objects and clothing that are clearly symbolic of the deceased individual's leadership role in the society. In some areas warfare was apparently used to obtain dominance over neighboring groups in order to exact tribute and control over surplus production. Many historic Indian tribes are descended from these Mississippian societies, including the CHICKASAW, CREEK, and NATCHEZ.

Agricultural societies with populations of several hundred also developed in the river valleys of the Plains from

Kansas City, Mo., to Bismarck, N.Dak. They also had fortified villages, some with rectangular houses and some with circular earth lodges. Although they had an effective agricultural production, they continued to hunt bison and other Plains animals. Descendants of these Plains agriculturalists include the HIDASTA, MANDAN, OMAHA, PAWNEE, and WICHITA.

Southwest. In the Southwest, with the introduction first of maize from northwestern Mexico and then of pottery, settled village agriculturalists—the HOHOKAM in southeastern Arizona and the Mogollon in southwestern New Mexico—flourished during the first half of the 1st millennium AD. This village development spread north and became the initial phase of the ANASAZÍ societies beginning about AD 500. As these farming societies found ways to cultivate successfully in the dry environments of the Southwest, the population and cultural development grew remarkably with continuing stimuli from northwestern Mexico. From 700 to 1300 major centers developed throughout the Southwest, especially in CHACO CANYON in west central New Mexico; in the San Juan Valley of northwestern New Mexico and northern Arizona; around present-day Flagstaff in northwestern Arizona; and in the MESA VERDE area of southwestern Colorado. The construction of multiroom and multistory stone pueblo-type dwellings with subterranean ceremonial KIVA rooms, a rich and varied ceramic tradition, and the production of stone and bone tools and ornaments, baskets, mats, woven bags, and cotton cloth represent the climax of Anasazi culture. After 1300 a marked retraction of Anasazi societies into the

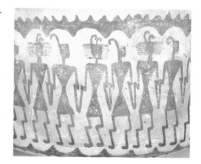

Two prominent prehistoric cultures of the American Southwest were the Hohokam and the Anasazi. (Right) The Hohokam created a red-on-buff pottery, exemplified by this decorated bowl. (Below) Cliff Palace, at Mesa Verde, Colorado, is the largest of the Anasazi cliff dwellings.

most favorable areas for agriculture occurred, probably the result of drier conditions. In these areas the Hopi, Zuñi, and Rio Grande Pueblo Indians have maintained many of their ancestors' ancient cultural patterns. By about 1500 the hunter-gatherer ancestors of the Apache and Navajo began to invade the Southwest from the north. Although they were often in conflict with the Pueblo groups, they gradually adopted elements of Pueblo culture, such as farming, weaving, and some religious ideology.

See also: Indians, American.

North American Indian art   see Indians of North America, art of the

North Atlantic Treaty Organization   The North Atlantic Treaty Organization (NATO) was established on Apr. 4, 1949, by representatives from 12 nations (Belgium, Canada, Denmark, France, Iceland, Italy, Luxembourg, the Netherlands, Norway, Portugal, the United Kingdom, and the United States; Greece and Turkey joined in 1952, the Federal Republic of Germany in 1955, and Spain in 1982) who gathered in Washington, D.C., to sign the North Atlantic Treaty, which had as its purpose the deterring of potential Soviet aggression in Europe. The signing of the treaty paved the way for the first peacetime alliance participated in by the United States.

The key article of the North Atlantic Treaty is Article 5: "The Parties agree that an armed attack against one or more of them ... shall be considered an attack against them all." NATO conformed to the provisions of Article 51 of the United Nations Charter—the right of collective defense—but NATO was also supposed to promote political, social, and economic ties among the members.

Although the impetus for the treaty was the increasing stridency of the COLD WAR, NATO at first had no military structure. The Korean War, however, which began in June 1950, was at first perceived by Western European countries as part of a worldwide Communist offensive, and this perception led to the establishment of a NATO military force. The major element of this force is the Allied Command Europe; Gen. Dwight D. Eisenhower was appointed (December 1950) its first commander—Supreme Allied Commander Europe (SACEUR). The command's headquarters, the Supreme Headquarters Allied Powers in Europe (SHAPE), is located in Brussels.

The chief policy-making body of NATO is the North Atlantic Council. Permanent representatives of participating countries meet at least once a week in Brussels. The North Atlantic Council also meets twice yearly in ministerial session. The secretary general chairs the council. When defense matters are discussed, the permanent representatives meet as the Defense Planning Committee (DPC). The council and the DPC have established a number of committees to deal with such matters as emergency planning and nuclear affairs. In addition to defense matters, the 16 nations cooperate in economic, scientific, cultural, and environmental problems.

The alliance, however, is primarily concerned with military defense. The Military Committee under the DPC, com-

In May 1989 the leaders of the North Atlantic Treaty Organization (NATO) countries gathered at NATO's headquarters in Brussels, to mark the 40th anniversary of the alliance.

posed of senior military representatives from each country—except Iceland, which has no military forces and is represented by a civilian, and France, which withdrew from the integrated military structure in 1966 while remaining a member of the Council—recommends to the DPC those defense measures it considers necessary and guides the three NATO military commands: the Atlantic, European, and Channel. The forces of member countries include those assigned in peacetime to the NATO commanders and those earmarked in event of war for those commands. The NATO commanders are responsible for the development of defense plans for their respective areas, for the determination of force requirements, and for the deployment and exercise of the forces under their command.

Major problems with which the alliance concerned itself over the years fall into four categories: problems associated with the military balance between Warsaw Pact forces and NATO forces; questions of strategic doctrine, such as the credibility of the nuclear deterrent and the use of tactical nuclear weapons; issues of standardizing military equipment, with an immediate effect on domestic arms production; and political disputes between members—such as those between Greece and Turkey—that tend to weaken the organization.

The fading of cold-war tensions in the late 1980s, followed by the dissolution of the Warsaw Pact military alliance in March 1991 and the staged withdrawal of Soviet troops from Eastern Europe, caused NATO leaders to reassess the Soviet threat to Europe and to implement plans to reorder the organization's military strategy.

North Cape   North Cape (Norwegian: Nordkapp) is a promontory on Mageroy Island in northern Norway. It is considered the northernmost point of Europe, although Knivskjellodden Island to the northwest is actually farther north. North Cape rises about 300 m (1,000 ft) above the Arctic Ocean. Tourists come to see the cliffs and the midnight sun in summer.

NORTH CAROLINA

Land: Area: 139,397 km² (53,821 mi²); rank: 28th. Capital: Raleigh (1990 pop., 207,951). Largest city: Charlotte (1990 pop., 395,934). Counties: 100. Elevations: highest—2,037 m (6,684 ft), at Mount Mitchell; lowest—sea level, at the Atlantic coast.

People: Population (1990): 6,657,630; rank: 10th; density: 52.5 persons per km² (136.1 per mi²). Distribution (1990): 50.4% urban, 49.6% rural. Average annual change (1980–90): +1.3%.

Government (1993): Governor: Jim Hunt, Jr., Democrat. U.S. Congress: Senate—2 Republicans; House—8 Democrats, 4 Republicans. Electoral college votes: 14. State legislature: 50 senators, 120 representatives.

Economy: State personal income (1989): $99.9 billion; rank: 13th. Median family income (1989): $31,548; rank: 36th. Agriculture: income (1989)—$4.6 billion. Fishing: value (1989)—$71 million. Lumber production (1991): 1.6 billion board feet. Mining (nonfuel): value (1988)—$529 million. Manufacturing: value added (1987)—$47 billion. Services: value (1987)—$19.4 billion.

Miscellany: Statehood: Nov. 21, 1789; the 12th state. Nicknames: Tar Heel State and Old North State; tree: pine; motto: *Esse Quam Videri* ("To Be Rather Than to Seem"); song: "The Old North State."

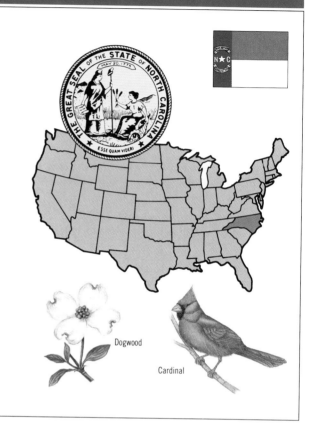

Dogwood

Cardinal

North Carolina   North Carolina occupies a median location along the Atlantic seaboard and is bounded on the south by South Carolina and Georgia, on the west by Tennessee, on the north by Virginia, and on the east by the Atlantic Ocean. In area, the state ranks 28th, and in population it ranks 10th. Raleigh is the state capital. North Carolinians are called Tar Heels, a nickname the origin of which is still debated. The state has a rich historical tradition on which, in part, a growing tourist industry is based. Traditionally agricultural with many tobacco plantations, the state was one of the first in the South to industrialize and now ranks high in industrial output.

Land and Resources

North Carolina is divided into three main physical provinces: the coastal plain, the Piedmont, and the mountains. The eastern boundary of the coastal plain is a chain of barrier islands, the Outer Banks, separated from the mainland by lagoons and salt marshes. The coastal plain is divided into the Tidewater area, which is quite flat, poorly drained and often marshy, and the inner coastal plain, which is higher, better drained, and better suited for agriculture.

The coastal plain merges with the gently rolling PIEDMONT at the FALL LINE. The Piedmont elevations range from 90 to 180 m (295 to 591 ft) in the east to 457 m (1,500 ft) at the Blue Ridge. The Piedmont encompasses about 45% of the area of the state, about the same percentage of the total area as the coastal plain.

The BLUE RIDGE MOUNTAINS, the beginning of the mountain province, rise above the Piedmont. In North Carolina the Appalachian chain reaches its zenith. More than 40 peaks are higher than 1,830 m (6,000 ft), and Mount Mitchell, at 2,037 m (6,684 ft), is the highest peak east of the Mississippi.

Soils. North Carolina soils are generally low in plant nutrients and minerals. Sandy soils dominate in the coastal plain, red clay in the Piedmont, and thin residual soils in the mountains. Heavy applications of lime and fertilizers are necessary for good yields, and continued care must be taken to prevent erosion.

Climate. The climate of North Carolina is generally mild, especially on the south coast. In the mountainous west the winters are more severe, but the summers are relatively cooler. January mean temperatures are 5° C

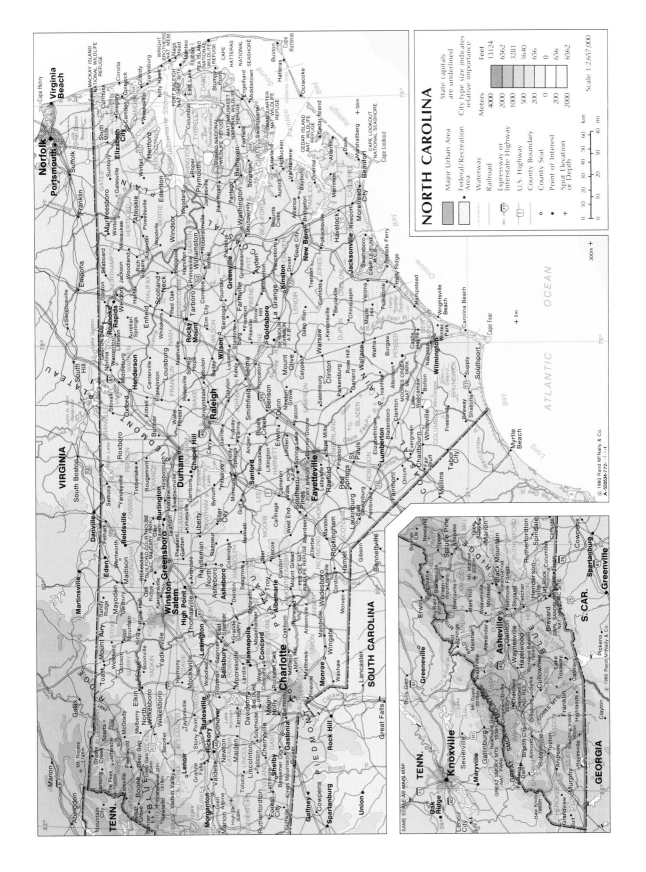

NORTH CAROLINA

State capitals are underlined

City type size indicates relative importance

	Meters	Feet
	4000	13124
	2000	6562
	1000	3281
	500	1640
	200	656
	0	0
	200	656
	2000	6562

Scale 1:2,657,000

Major Urban Area

Federal/Recreation Area

Waterway

Railroad

Expressway or Interstate Highway

U.S. Highway

County Boundary

County Seat

Point of Interest

Spot Elevation or Depth

0 10 20 30 40 50 60 km
0   10   20   30   40 mi

© 1980 Rand McNally & Co.
A-520534-772--1-1--1

SAME SCALE AS MAIN MAP

© 1980 Rand McNally & Co.

(42° F), and July temperatures average 24° C (75° F). The state is well watered, with from 1,016 to 2,032 mm (40 to 80 in) of rainfall yearly. The coastline is occasionally hit by hurricanes, especially on the Outer Banks.

Rivers and Lakes. Although the state has no major river, the area is drained by a dense network of streams in three distinct systems. The first of these rises west of the Blue Ridge, drains into the Gulf of Mexico through the Tennessee and Ohio rivers, and includes the French Broad and Little Tennessee rivers. The second system drains the Piedmont south and east through South Carolina and Georgia and includes the Catawba and Yadkin rivers. The third network, which includes the Cape Fear, Neuse, Roanoke, and Tar rivers, drains the Piedmont by way of the coastal plain into Albermarle and Pamlico sounds. Only the Cape Fear River flows directly into the Atlantic Ocean. The state has no large natural lakes and few sizable artificial reservoirs.

Vegetation and Animal Life. Most of the coastal plain and Piedmont is forested with pines, and hardwoods dominate in the mountains. The state has an abundance and diversity of wildlife, ranging from migratory waterfowl at the seashore to the deer, foxes, bears, and wildcats of the highest mountains.

Resources. Most of the state's mineral production consists of construction materials, except for a large phosphate deposit on the outer coastal plain. A favorable climate and moderately fertile soil give the state a valuable agricultural base, and climate and scenery encourage tourism. The numerous rivers, as well as the ocean and sounds, afford abundant sport and commercial fishing. The heavy rainfall, steep gradients, and topography all favor hydroelectric power, which has been important to North Carolina's industrialization.

People

The population of North Carolina is largely descended from the original Scottish, Irish, Welsh, French, and German settlers, as well as from the blacks brought to the region as slaves. In 1990 blacks formed 22% of the state's population. A smaller minority group is the Indians, who numbered 80,155 in 1990, mainly the CHEROKEE in the west and the Lumbee in the southeast. The population of the state is almost 50% Baptist.

The Piedmont has long been the most populous region, with somewhat more than half the state's population, followed by the coastal plain and the lightly populated mountains. Although highly industrialized, North Carolina has one of the lowest levels of urbanization in the country, 46%. The urban pattern of North Carolina is characterized by a small-town orientation. Most of the cities are clustered in the Urban Piedmont Crescent, extending in an arc from Raleigh to Charlotte, but none dominates. The largest urbanized center is CHARLOTTE, with only 5.9% of the state's population. The largest metropolitan area is GREENSBORO–WINSTON-SALEM–High Point, with a population of 942,091 (1990). Another urban complex is RALEIGH-DURHAM, with 735,480 (1990). Other important cities are ASHEVILLE, FAYETTEVILLE, and WILMINGTON.

Education. North Carolina ranks high among the states in the number of children enrolled in public schools (1,082,000 in 1988). Nearly two-thirds of educational funds come from state rather than local sources.

The University of North Carolina at CHAPEL HILL (UNC–CH), the nation's first operating state university, DAVIDSON COLLEGE, and DUKE UNIVERSITY are national leaders in higher education. The unusual proximity of Duke, UNC–CH, and North Carolina State led in 1958 to the establishment of Research Triangle Park. The combined libraries of the three universities has created one of the larger university book collections and was one reason for luring to the Park the National Center for the Humanities. Among North Carolina's numerous private colleges and universities is Wake Forest in Winston-Salem.

Cultural Attractions. Because North Carolina does not have very large cities, many of its cultural institutions are state supported—such as the North Carolina Symphony, headquartered in Raleigh. The North Carolina Museum of Art is also located in Raleigh. Charlotte has the small but distinctive Mint Museum of Art, and the Morehead Planetarium at Chapel Hill is one of the finest facilities of its kind in the United States.

Historic Sites. The long and rich history of the state has been preserved in a number of outstanding historic sites. The mystery of Sir Walter Raleigh's colony on Roanoke Island (see ROANOKE COLONY) has been memorialized in an outdoor drama entitled "The Lost Colony," and the fort has been rebuilt. Tryon Palace, the English governor's residence at New Bern, has been called the most beautiful building in the colonial Americas. The Moravian settlement of Old Salem has been restored. On the Outer Banks the Wright Brothers National Memorial commemorates America's first sustained flight.

Recreation. GREAT SMOKY MOUNTAINS National Park is visited by several million persons annually. Among the better-known mountain resort areas are Asheville and Boone, with nearby ski resorts where the introduction of snow-making machines has made skiing a Southern sport. The state has no major league sports teams, but college sports events, especially basketball, are extremely well attended.

Communications. North Carolina's first newspaper was the *North Carolina Gazette,* established in 1751. Major newspapers today are in Raleigh, Greensboro, Charlotte, and Winston-Salem. There are also numerous commercial and noncommercial radio and television broadcasting facilities and television cable systems in the state.

Economic Activity

In the course of a century North Carolina has been transformed from a largely agricultural economy to one that is highly industrialized. North Carolina is a leading producer of textiles, cigarettes, and furniture. Although the industrial mix is becoming more diversified, more than 35% of total industrial employment is still in the textile and apparel industries. In value added by manufacturing, the state is among the top ten in the nation.

Agriculture. North Carolina ranks high among U.S. states in farm income. Tobacco is the dominant component of the state's agriculture, along with other leading

Tobacco leaves are harvested at this farm near Lumberton, N.C. A major crop since colonial times, tobacco became the state's principal agricultural commodity during the early 20th century. Today a significant amount of the U.S. tobacco crop is grown there.

farm commodities—broilers, hogs, and turkeys. Principal crops grown in the state include sweet potatoes, peanuts, corn, grapes, pecans, apples, tomatoes, and soybeans. North Carolina's major agricultural counties are located on the coastal plain or among northern Piedmont counties. Cotton is grown in scattered areas along the South Carolina border.

Fishing and Forestry. A small fishing industry is based on the Atlantic coast. Flounder, striped bass, and menhaden are major finfish. The shellfish catch includes shrimp, oysters, and crab. A much larger forest-products industry provides raw materials for the furniture and pulp industries.

Mining and Energy. Sand, gravel, and crushed stone account for much of the state's mining industry, but the state is also a leader in the production of feldspar, lithium, mica, and phosphate rock. Most of North Carolina's energy comes from outside sources. Power requirements derive from petroleum, coal, natural gas, nuclear power, and hydropower.

Transportation. Wilmington and Morehead City, connected by the Atlantic Intercoastal Waterway, are the major ports. North Carolina is well served by highways, including five interstates. Today, trucks are more important than railroads in moving goods. The state is served by numerous railroads and commercial airports.

Tourism. The state's beaches and mountains have provided variety for North Carolina vacationers. Tourism has become one of the largest industries in the state. Outdoor recreation facilities attract most visitors.

Government

Government authority in North Carolina rests in the constitution adopted in 1971. A total of 100 counties and many municipalities are legally controlled by the state government, though these smaller units exercise a degree of local autonomy. The executive office in North Carolina is given less power than is the practice in most other states. The governor serves a 4-year term and may be reelected for a second term. The governor has no veto power. An ex-officio council of state advises the governor.

The legislature is made up of a 50-member senate and a 120-member house that are elected biennially. Supreme court and appellate, superior, and district court judges form the judiciary. The Democratic primary traditionally has been more important than the general election in the selection of state officials.

History

Although human settlement dates from 8000 BC, the first Europeans to visit the North Carolina coast were French explorers led by Giovanni da Verrazano in 1524. In 1526 a group of Spanish sailors established a temporary colony of more than 500 persons, probably at the mouth of the Cape Fear River. A 1540 expedition by Hernando de Soto crossed what is now western North Carolina before turning west to discover the Mississippi River.

It was the English, however, who made the first permanent European settlements in North Carolina, and the Roanoke Island settlement (1585–86) of Sir Walter RALEIGH was the first English colony in the New World. A second group set sail from England in 1587 but had vanished by 1590 when a supply ship arrived. The mystery of the colony's disappearance has never been solved. Among the settlers was the first child born of English parents in America, Virginia DARE.

The early European settlers came in contact with a number of Indian tribes as settlement spread westward, the most numerous groups encountered being the TUSCARORA. The natives fiercely resisted the whites before being defeated in 1713. The CATAWBA of the southern Piedmont were friendly. The Cherokee, living in the Appalachian Mountains, were the last major tribe to be confronted by the settlers.

Brightly colored synthetic materials are manufactured in large quantities at this North Carolina textile mill. With its readily available supply of raw cotton and its expanding chemical industry, North Carolina has continued to lead the nation in textile production.

Proprietary Period. The colonial period from 1663 to 1729 began when Charles II granted to eight lords proprietors that region lying between 31° and 36° north latitude and extending from the Atlantic Ocean to the South Seas. This region was later (1665) extended to 36°30' N to include the Albemarle settlers who had moved south from Virginia. As the Charleston settlement grew more rapidly, the territory began to be known as North and South Carolina. The northern territory was made a separate colony in 1712 and had its own governors until 1829. This boundary was not established until 1735. Bath, near the mouth of the Pamlico River, was the first town to be incorporated (1706). Settlement was generally confined to the coastal areas.

Royal Colony. In 1729, North Carolina became a crown colony. Until the outbreak of the Revolution in 1775, a more efficient government brought about increased settlement and greater prosperity. The population increased from 35,000 in 1729 to almost 350,000 in 1775, and settlement extended to the Blue Ridge Mountains and beyond. With this transmontane movement came the deep-seated differences between east and west that have continued to the present day. The colonial government was dominated by the eastern planters, and the more egalitarian and poorer west suffered from corrupt government and excessive taxes. The conflict resulted in the War of Regulation (see REGULATORS), in which the western insurgents were crushed by Gov. William Tryon (1729–88) at the Battle of Alamance Creek on May 16, 1771.

In 1747–48 the Spanish attacked the North Carolina coast. Troops from North Carolina assisted British troops in the capture of Fort Duquesne during the FRENCH AND INDIAN WAR (1754–63) and fought the Cherokee on the western frontier in 1760. Yet, North Carolina was among the leaders in resistance to British rule in the 1760s.

The American Revolution. British rule came to an end in North Carolina in May 1775. The Second Provincial Congress in 1775 established two regiments and a state government. The first battle of the Revolution in North Carolina was fought against Scottish Loyalists at Moore's Creek Bridge on Feb. 27, 1776. Later that year the Fifth Provincial Congress adopted a state constitution. North Carolina was the first colony to declare officially its readiness for independence and in April 1776 furnished ten regiments to the Continental army, as well as thousands of militiamen. At the same time it helped defeat the Cherokee and suppressed the Tory residents who made the revolution virtually a civil war in North Carolina. Despite its leadership in the Revolution, North Carolina was the next to last of the 13 original states to ratify the federal Constitution (November 1789). In 1789, North Carolina ceded its western territory, present-day Tennessee, to the federal government.

The 19th Century. The period from 1815 to 1835 was one of political and economic stagnation, with the oligarchic east in power at the expense of the more reform-minded west. The state's convention of 1835 resulted in a reapportionment that gave the west control of the state house of representatives, leaving the east in control of the senate. From 1835 until 1860 progress in transportation, education, tax reform, and women's rights, as well as agricultural expansion and greater prosperity, reversed the downward political and economic spiral and halted emigration.

The CIVIL WAR brought this improving trend to an end. North Carolina, though sympathetic to the South, was the last state to secede, on May 20, 1861. The battles of Fort Hatteras, Plymouth, Fort Fisher, and Bentonville, as well as Sherman's 1865 invasion and Johnston's surrender to Sherman near Durham on Apr. 26, 1865, were the most notable Civil War events in North Carolina. The political and social disruption caused by the war were exacerbated during RECONSTRUCTION.

In 1880 the state began to industrialize and to urbanize for the first time. The new industrialization brought additional jobs to the Piedmont but only modest prosperity because of low wages. Agricultural production increased, but farmers were burdened by low prices and heavy debt. By the turn of the century, major advances were made in the educational system. World War I boosted the economy and led to the establishment of important military bases, including FORT BRAGG.

Modern Period. During the early 1920s an exodus of textile mills from New England to the Carolinas took place, reforms in state government were instituted, and extensive construction projects began. Even during this period of prosperity, however, personal income still lagged, averaging only about half of the national mean. The Depression of the 1930s struck North Carolina early, and New Deal programs, particularly farm price supports, were important to economic recovery. World War II also gave the state's economy a boost.

North Carolina has profited in recent years from its location in the Sun Belt, though problems still remain. In-

comes are still low, agriculture remains dominated by tobacco, and the state's national primacy in textiles is vulnerable to foreign competition. Despite these problems, its
people have probably never been better prepared to face
the future.

North Dakota North Dakota, located at the center of
the North American continent, is bounded by Montana on
the west, South Dakota on the south, Minnesota on the
east, and the Canadian provinces of Manitoba and
Saskatchewan on the north. North Dakota encompasses
183,123 km² (70,704 mi²). The state ranks 19th in area
of the 50 states, and 47th in population (1990 pop.,
641,364). The name *Dakota* comes from a Sioux Indian
word meaning "allies." North Dakota is a significant agricultural producer and contributes lignite coal and petroleum reserves to regional and national demands for increased energy. The state is concerned with maintaining
the present quality of environment while developing its
resources.

Land and Resources

North Dakota is composed of three principal physiographic regions: the Red River Valley, the Drift Prairie,
and the Missouri Plateau. These regions rise from east to
west in a steplike fashion from 229 m (750 ft) in the Red
River Valley to the state's highest elevation of 1,069 m
(3,506 ft) at White Butte on the Missouri Plateau.

The Red River Valley is the former bed of glacial Lake
Agassiz. The North Dakota portion varies from 16 to 64
km (10 to 40 mi) in width from north to south along the
North Dakota and Minnesota border. The valley is relatively flat with an average elevation of 275 m (900 ft).
The Drift Prairie lies to the west of the Red River Valley in
the center of the state. It is separated from the Red River
Valley by the Pembina Escarpment in the north and the
Coteau des Prairies in the south. The land is generally
hilly, averaging 440 m (1,450 ft) in elevation, and broken
by numerous shallow coulees and lakes. The Missouri
Plateau lies to the southwest of the Drift Prairie, separated from it by the Missouri Escarpment and a hilly area
between the Missouri River and the escarpment known as
the Coteau du Missouri. Elevations average 655 m
(2,150 ft), and the land surface is irregular and rolling.
The rugged BADLANDS, with rock formations eroded by the
Little Missouri River, are found in this area, as are the
Killdeer Mountains, with buttes rising about 180 m (600
ft) above the prairie.

Soils vary across the state. In the Red River Valley,

AT A GLANCE

NORTH DAKOTA

Land: Area: 183,123 km² (70,704 mi²); rank: 19th.
Capital: Bismarck (1990 pop., 49,256). Largest city:
Fargo (1990 pop., 74,111). Counties: 53. Elevations:
highest—1,069 m (3,506 ft), at White Butte; lowest—
229 m (750 ft), at the Red River.

People: Population (1990): 641,364; rank: 47th; density: 3.6 persons per km² (9.3 per mi²). Distribution
(1990): 53.3% urban, 46.7% rural. Average annual
change (1980–90): -0.17%.

Government (1993): Governor: Ed Schafer, Republican. U.S. Congress: Senate—2 Democrats; House—1
Democrat. Electoral college votes: 3. State legislature:
53 senators, 106 representatives.

Economy: State personal income (1989): $9 billion;
rank: 49th. Median family income (1989): $28,707;
rank: 40th. Agriculture: income (1989)—$2.1 billion.
Mining (nonfuel): value (1988)—$19 million. Manufac-
turing: value added (1987)—$979 million. Services:
value (1987)—$2.1 billion.

Miscellany: Statehood: Nov. 2, 1889; the 39th state.
Nicknames: Flickertail State, Peace Garden State, and
Sioux State; tree: American elm; motto: Liberty and
Union, Now and Forever, One and Inseparable; song:
"North Dakota Hymn."

Wild Prairie Rose

Western Meadowlark

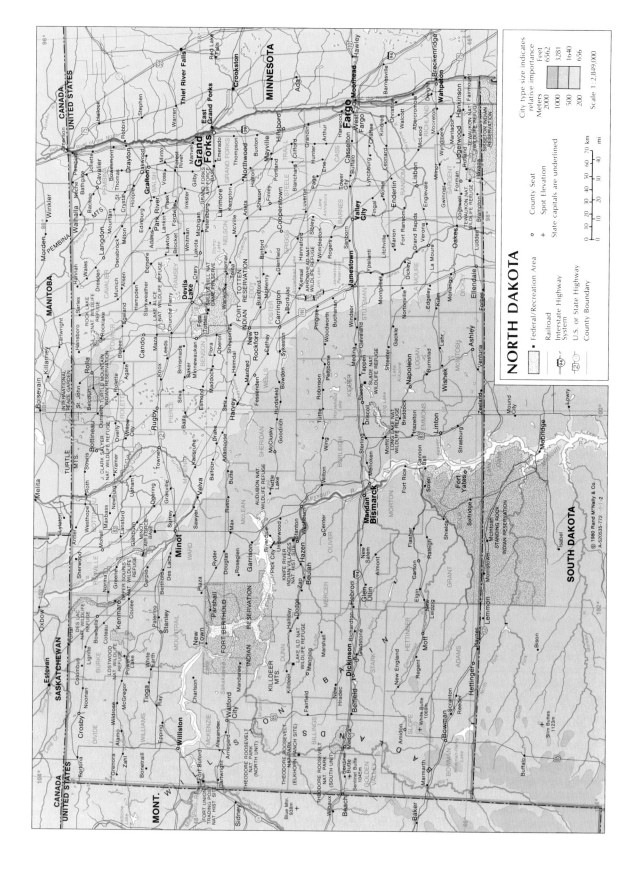

NORTH DAKOTA

Scale 1 : 2,849,000

City type size indicates relative importance

Meters	Feet
2000	6562
1000	3281
500	1640
200	656

● Federal/Recreation Area

○ County Seat

+ Spot Elevation

✶ State capitals are underlined

‑‑‑‑ Railroad

⊕94 Interrupted Highway System

⊙20 U.S. or State Highway

‑‑‑‑ County Boundary

© 1980 Rand McNally & Co.

A-520535-772 -11-2

rich chernozem (black) soils of excellent fertility are prominent. On the Drift Prairie, glacial soils are well suited for agricultural production. The chestnut or brown soils of the Missouri Plateau are less productive than the eastern soils formed under more humid conditions; these chestnut soils are productive when there is adequate moisture, but agricultural yields are lowered by moisture deficiency.

Climate. The climate of North Dakota ranges from humid-continental in the east to semiarid in the west and is characterized by hot summers and cold winters, low humidity and precipitation, and much wind and sunshine. Precipitation varies from an average of near 560 mm (22 in) in the east to less than 380 mm (15 in) in the southwest. Temperatures range from a July average of 21° C (70° F) to a January average of −14° C (6° F).

Rivers and Lakes. The Red River of the North and Souris River drain the northern and eastern parts of the state into Hudson Bay. The remaining 59% of the state is drained into the Gulf of Mexico by the MISSOURI RIVER, the James River, and their tributaries.

Lake Sakakawea, created by damming the waters of the Missouri River, is the largest water body in the state, covering 2,353 km² (909 mi²), and is 322 km (200 mi) long. The largest natural lake is Devils Lake.

Vegetation and Animal Life. Vegetation ranges from medium to tall varieties of prairie grass in the east to short varieties of prairie grass in the west. Trees are found mostly in river valleys, although the Turtle Mountains and Pembina Hills have a forest cover of oak and aspen. Antelope, deer, beaver, muskrat, and mink are found in the state, as are coyote and fox. Waterfowl, upland game birds, and songbirds are common. The federal government maintains two fish hatcheries, and several new species, including the coho salmon and lake trout, have been introduced into North Dakota waters.

Resources. North Dakota's mineral resources are vast and varied. Mineral fuels include lignite coal, natural gas, and petroleum. Other minerals include clay, sand and gravel, sulfur, potash, and salt. Conservation of North Dakota's resources, especially soil, has been a dominant consideration since the 1930s.

People

The average population density of North Dakota has always been one of the smallest in the United States. Slightly less than half of the population live in urban centers of 2,500 or more people; the leading cities are BISMARCK, FARGO, GRAND FORKS, and MINOT. More citizens are becoming categorized as urban as rural centers grow, farm numbers decrease, and farm size increases. The population grew dramatically from statehood (1889) until 1930, when depression and drought started a migration from the state. The 1930 population (680,845) has not been exceeded since.

The population is predominantly white, the only significant minority group being the native Americans, who constitute about 4% of the state's population. In terms of national origin, the largest groups are Scandinavian, Russian, German, and Canadian. Eight Christian denominations each have at least 3,000 members. The Lutheran and Roman Catholic faiths predominate.

Education and Cultural Activity. Free public education began in 1889. North Dakota has 9 institutions of higher education, as well as 2 public junior colleges and 5 private colleges. The University of North Dakota at Grand Forks, with a branch in Williston, and North Dakota State University at Fargo, with a branch at Bottineau, are the state's largest universities.

Institutions of higher education have tended to emerge as the focal points of cultural and artistic expression in the state. Fargo, Grand Forks, and Minot have symphony orchestras that make statewide appearances. The North Dakota Ballet is located in Grand Forks. The State Historical Museum is in Bismarck, and the North Dakota Heritage Center is on the State Capitol grounds. A summer school of fine arts is held annually at the International Peace Garden, which straddles the Manitoba-North Dakota border.

Historic Sites. North Dakota's historic sites reflect the frontier character of the state. Military forts include Fort Lincoln, the post from which Gen. George Custer departed for his fateful encounter at the Little Bighorn. The oldest settlement in North Dakota is at Pembina. The historic cattle town of Medora (est. 1883) in the Badlands of western North Dakota has been reconstructed.

Recreation. Theodore Roosevelt National Memorial Park, located in the Badlands, is one of the state's major tourist attractions, with hiking, trail riding, camping, and other facilities. The Turtle Mountains, located on the international boundary in the north central part of the state, are widely used for boating, fishing, swimming, and camping in the summer months and for cross-country skiing and snowmobiling during the winters. The International Peace Garden commemorates friendly relations between the United States and Canada.

Communications. North Dakota has daily and weekly newspapers, radio and television broadcasting facilities, and public and cable television systems. The state's leading newspapers originate in Fargo, Grand Forks, Minot, and Bismarck.

Economic Activity

The basic economic activities in North Dakota are agriculture, mining, manufacturing, and tourism. Manufacturing is concentrated on agricultural products and machinery.

Agriculture. North Dakota is a leading farm state. Crops account for much of the state's farm income, with wheat the major crop. North Dakota is typically the nation's leading producer of hard red spring wheat and durum wheat. Other important crops include oats, corn, soybeans, hay, sunflower seeds, flaxseed, barley, and rye. Cattle, hogs, sheep, turkeys, chickens, and dairy products are also valued commodities.

Mining and Energy. Petroleum is the most valuable mineral found in North Dakota. It first was discovered in 1951 and is produced primarily from wells located in a number of counties in the western part of the state. Natural-gas wells are also located in western North Dakota.

The Badlands of North Dakota are located in the extreme western portion of the state. These sedimentary mesas and valleys were eroded by wind and water to create the dramatic landscape.

The state ranks first in the nation in total coal reserves, although most of these are lignite (brown) coal. The coal deposits are found in western North Dakota. Major nonfuel minerals found in the state are sand and gravel. Southwestern North Dakota has large amounts of clay.

Most of North Dakota's electrical power is generated from steam plants that burn lignite coal. The hydroelectric power plant at Garrison Dam provides electricity as well. North Dakota also exports electricity to other midwestern states.

Manufacturing. Industry in North Dakota is based primarily on its agricultural products, and establishments such as flour mills, sugar-beet processing plants, and other food-processing establishments form the leading industrial group. Other industries include nonelectrical machinery; printing and publishing; stone, clay, and glass products; oil refining; and the processing of natural gas.

Transportation and Tourism. North Dakota is served by two major interstate highway systems. Interstate 94 travels east and west, passing near Fargo, Jamestown, and Bismarck; Interstate 29 extends north and south near North Dakota's eastern border. Major railroads servicing North Dakota are the Burlington Northern and the Soo Line. Several airlines provide transportation for the state. Tourists attracted to outdoor activities and exploration provide significant income and employment opportunities.

Government

The Omnibus Bill of Feb. 22, 1889, divided the Dakotas and allowed the formulation of a state constitution. A constitutional convention was held beginning on July 4, 1889, and on October 1 the constitution was voted upon and passed by the people. North Dakota was admitted to statehood on Nov. 2, 1889.

Governmental Institutions. The chief executive is the governor, who is elected to a 4-year term. The legislative as-

sembly consists of a 50-member senate and 100-member house of representatives. Senators are elected to 4-year terms and representatives to 2-year terms. The judicial system consists of a 5-member supreme court, 6 district courts, and 53 county magistrates. Additionally, there are numerous county justices and police magistrates.

The state is composed of 53 counties having organized townships. Each county elects county commissioners to 4-year terms and other officials to 2-year terms.

Politics. Though normally a Republican stronghold, North Dakota has had a tradition of independent politics, especially in times of agricultural distress. The POPULIST PARTY, led by William Jennings BRYAN, attracted much support there in the 1890s. In 1915 the NONPARTISAN LEAGUE

The Statue of Sacagawea, a memorial to the Indian woman who served as guide to the Lewis and Clark Expedition, appears in the foreground of this view of North Dakota's distinctive state capitol.

was organized, led by A. C. Townley, a socialist. The League controlled state government after 1916 and founded a state-owned bank, mill, and elevator. The state still controls these institutions. The League lost power in the 1920s. North Dakota has regularly voted for the Republican candidate in presidential elections since 1900, except for Woodrow Wilson in 1912 and 1916, Franklin D. Roosevelt in 1932 and 1936, and Lyndon B. Johnson in 1964.

History

As long as 15,000 years ago a hunting culture inhabited the region that is now North Dakota. In historic times Indian tribes of the region included the Dakota, usually called SIOUX, a name bestowed on them by others that means "enemies"; the HIDATSA, parent tribe of the CROW nation; the OJIBWA, who came west from the Great Lakes with French trappers; and the CHEYENNE, originally a pastoral people, who became nomadic as they were pushed west by the Sioux. The first European to visit the area was the sieur de LA VERÉNDRYE, a French fur trapper from Canada. In 1738 he met and lived with the MANDAN Indians near present-day Bismarck.

In 1742, La Veréndrye's sons returned to explore southwestern North Dakota in search of the great western sea. Lewis and Clark explored (1804–05, 1806) the Missouri River through North Dakota on their expedition to the Pacific and again on their return in 1806 (see LEWIS AND CLARK EXPEDITION). In 1812 colonists sponsored by the earl of SELKIRK arrived at Pembina as part of the larger RED RIVER SETTLEMENT. This first attempt to establish a permanent European settlement in the state failed, but Charles Cavaleer brought settlers to Pembina from Minnesota to form the first permanent agricultural colony in 1851.

The period from 1850 to 1870 was one of war with the Dakota Indians, who were being pushed west by European settlers in Minnesota and whose bison herds on the Dakota plains were being decimated. The Dakota Indians were eventually pushed into the Badlands, west of the Missouri River, and the Dakota Territory was opened to homesteading on Jan. 1, 1863. Joseph Rolette filed the first homestead in the northwestern Red River Valley in 1868. In 1871 railroads reached the Red River of the North from Duluth and Saint Paul, resulting in the emergence of Fargo, now the state's largest city. A flood of settlers homesteaded the area, and large-scale agriculture began. The period from 1878 to 1886 became known as the Dakota Boom, but settlement west and north of the Missouri River was stalled until the surrender of SITTING BULL, chief of the Sioux, at Fort Buford in 1881. North Dakota became the 39th state on Nov. 2, 1889.

Agriculture has grown dramatically since World War II and remains the mainstay of the state's economy. Resource development was highlighted in 1957 by the discovery of oil. The strategic importance of the state was enhanced during the 1960s by the establishment of air bases and intercontinental ballistic missile sites.

The energy crisis of the 1970s spurred increased exploration and development of the state's oil resources and the mining of its immense lignite reserves. The development of water projects in this area of variable precipita-tion remains a vital concern from the standpoints of environmental impact and economic benefit to the agricultural sector.

As a producer of agricultural and energy commodities, North Dakota will experience increasing demand for its products. The consequences of this demand, as reflected by agricultural commodity prices, economic stability, and quality of the natural and human environment, are the paramount concerns of the present.

North German Confederation   see GERMANY, HISTORY OF

North Pole   The North Pole is that location marking the northern end of the Earth's imaginary axis. It is found in the Arctic Ocean at 90° north latitude, where all meridians of longitude intersect. This is one of the two points on the Earth's surface that receive six months of continuous daylight followed by six months of continuous darkness. This geographical North Pole differs from the North magnetic pole (see EARTH, GEOMAGNETIC FIELD OF). Robert E. PEARY and Matthew A. Henson have generally been credited as the first to reach the North Pole, on Apr. 6, 1909.

North Sea   The North Sea is an arm of the Atlantic Ocean between Great Britain and the continent of Europe, covering an area of about 570,000 km^2 (220,000 mi^2). It is connected to the Atlantic by the ENGLISH CHANNEL to the south and between the Orkney Islands and Norway to the north; the Skagerrak provides access to the Baltic Sea.

Although depths of more than 730 m (2,400 ft) have been recorded, the North Sea's average depth is 94 m (308 ft). Shallow depths and currents make the sea unusually turbulent. In addition, it is subject to frequent winter gales.

The North Sea is of major economic importance to the European economy. Its fisheries yield more than 5% of the world's annual catch. More important are the vast petroleum and natural-gas deposits found beneath the sea floor since 1959 and exploited intensively since the 1970s.

The North Sea today covers a huge plain that as late as the Pliocene Epoch (2.5 million years ago) was an expanse of dry land. Melting ice sheets led to a rise in sea level, and at some time about 9000–8000 BC the land bridge broke, separating southeastern England from France. The present coastlines were established by about 1000 BC.

North Star   see POLARIS (astronomy)

North West Company   The North West Company was a fur-trading organization that flourished in Canada and the Great Lakes region of the United States in the late 18th and early 19th centuries. Following the acquisition of Canada by Great Britain at the end (1763) of the French and Indian War, British (mainly Scottish) and

American traders moved to Montreal to exploit the old French fur trade. These traders soon began to pool their interests in various partnerships; one such group eventually expanded to become the North West Company.

Throughout its 38 years of existence (1783–1821) the North West Company was never a chartered company like its older English rival, the HUDSON'S BAY COMPANY. It always remained a loose partnership of independent traders, including French Canadians, who accepted monopoly conditions as preferable to unrestricted competition. The partners, known as Nor'Westers, included those who spent the winter trading with the Indians in the West and the merchants who handled the trade from Montreal. They met annually at the western headquarters in Grand Portage (now in Minnesota) and later at Fort William (now Thunder Bay, Ontario).

In the relatively short period of its existence, the North West Company extended its activities to the Pacific and to the Arctic. Its trader-explorers, including Simon FRASER, Sir Alexander MACKENZIE, and David THOMPSON, opened up almost the whole of northwestern Canada. During the War of 1812 the company acquired Astoria, a post established by U.S. fur magnate John Jacob Astor on the Columbia River. The North West Company, however, overreached itself and soon became undercapitalized. Furthermore, as its trade routes became longer, its transport costs became higher than those of its English competitor, whose traders were able to send their furs through Hudson Bay.

Competition between the two organizations increased after the English company was taken over by the earl of SELKIRK in 1808. The rivalry sometimes reached the level of open warfare, especially over Selkirk's colony, the RED RIVER SETTLEMENT. In 1821 the British authorities virtually forced a merger of the two groups. Although the new company was known as the Hudson's Bay Company, the Nor'Westers were its dominant members.

Northampton (England) [north-amp'-tuhn] Northampton is a city in central England on the River Nene, 97 km (60 mi) northwest of London. This rapidly growing county town of Northamptonshire has a population of 169,800 (1985 est.). The city's long-famous shoe and leather industry has declined, and new industries have emerged, mainly engineering, brewing, and electronics. Northampton is famous for its churches, including Saint Sepulchre's (c.1110), one of four round churches in England. Originally an Anglo-Saxon village, Northampton became the site of a Norman castle, built during the 11th century, where parliaments were held from the 12th to the 14th century. In 1460, Henry VI was defeated by the Yorkists at Northampton.

Northampton (Massachusetts) Northampton (1990 pop., 29,289) is a city in west central Massachusetts on the west bank of the Connecticut River; it is the seat of Hampshire County. Its industries produce cutlery, hosiery, optics, and cable. Smith College (1871) and Clarke School for the Deaf (1867) are there. Settled in 1654,

Northampton grew after 1809, when a textile industry began there. Calvin Coolidge lived in Northampton.

Northamptonshire [north-amp'-tuhn-shir] Northamptonshire (Northants) is a county in central England with an area of 2,367 km^2 (914 mi^2) and a population of 570,300 (1988 est.). Its principal cities include Northampton (the county town), Corby, Kettering, and Wellingborough. Drained by the River Nene, the land is used primarily for the raising of livestock. Manufactures include iron and steel, processed foods, brewed products, and clothing. The county has many historic landmarks, including Sulgrave Manor, the home of U.S. president George Washington's ancestors.

The site of Roman settlements and later part of the kingdom of Mercia (by the 7th century), Northamptonshire became a center for religious dissenters during the 17th century. King Charles I was defeated (1645) at Naseby during the English Civil War and imprisoned (1647) at Holdenby.

Northcliffe, Alfred Harmsworth, Viscount Alfred Charles William Harmsworth, Lord Northcliffe, born near Dublin on July 15, 1865, d. Aug. 14, 1922, virtually revolutionized the newspaper and magazine publishing business in Great Britain between 1888 and his death. At the age of 23, Harmsworth published a magazine of his own called *Answers to Correspondents*. Featuring puzzles and games and offering prizes, it achieved almost instant success. His brother, Harold Harmsworth, three years younger, joined him in the enterprise, and from then on they worked together. The brothers started other magazines and in 1894 bought the ailing London *Evening News*. In 1896, Alfred Harmsworth established a morning halfpenny *Daily Mail*, introducing the modern "popular" daily in England with enormous success. It was followed by an illustrated tabloid-size *Daily Mirror* in 1903 and a *Continental Daily Mail* in Paris in 1905. In 1908 the brothers purchased controlling interest in the *Times*, the most respected daily in the world.

Harmsworth backed an Arctic expedition in 1894, offered prizes to encourage the development of motoring and aviation, and exercised great influence on public opinion and policy. He was knighted in 1904 and made a peer in 1905 as Baron Northcliffe, and in 1917 he was created Viscount Northcliffe of Saint Peter-in-Thanet.

Northeast Passage The search for a Northeast Passage connecting the Atlantic and Pacific oceans along the northern shores of Eurasia began when the English Muscovy Company, set up in 1553, sent out Sir Hugh Willoughby and Richard CHANCELLOR. Willoughby's ship was lost; Chancellor wintered in the White Sea and then reached Moscow. Between 1594 and 1597 the Dutch explorer Willem BARENTS made three voyages, rediscovering Spitsbergen and Bear Island and sailing east of Novaya Zemlya into the Kara Sea. Henry HUDSON's voyages between 1607 and 1609 reached polar ice that blocked further eastward passage.

Russian sailors finally found the passage in 1648 when Semen Ivanov Dezhnev sailed from the Kolyma River through what is now called the Bering Strait to the mouth of the Anadyr River on the Pacific Ocean. Vitus Bering, a Dane in the employ of Russia, sailed from the Pacific to the Arctic Ocean between 1725 and 1730.

The Swedish baron Nils A. E. Nordenskjöld made the first through-passage from west to east in the *Vega* in 1878–79. The USSR has mapped and explored the passage, now called the Northern Sea Route, and modern ice-breaking ships have extended its use through much of the year.

Northern Cross   see Cygnus

Northern Expedition

The Northern Expedition was the military campaign launched in 1926 by Kuomintang (Guomindang, or Nationalist) Chinese forces—which then included Communists—to eliminate the various warlords who dominated China and to unite the country. It was led by the Kuomintang army commander in chief Chiang Kai-shek. Halfway through the advance from Guangzhou to Beijing, Chiang initiated attacks on Communist activists and won absolute control of the Nationalist movement. The expedition ended in 1928 with the capture of Beijing and the establishment of the Kuomintang government over a unified China. Many of the major northern warlords were suppressed, but others retained considerable independence by nominally cooperating with the Nationalists.

Northern Ireland

Northern Ireland, part of the United Kingdom, occupies 14,120 km² (5,452 mi²), or about 17%, of the island of Ireland. Its six counties were part of the ancient northeastern Irish province of Ulster. The population of Northern Ireland is 1,575,000 (1987 est.). Belfast is the capital.

A dominant lowland centered on Lough Neagh (see Neagh, Lough) is almost surrounded by rugged mountains. The highest are the Antrim Mountains in the northeast, the Mourne Mountains in the southeast, and the Sperrin Mountains on the west. The Bann and the Shannon (see Shannon, River) are the two major rivers.

The region has cool winters, with January temperatures averaging 4° C (40° F). Summers are warm, with July average temperatures of 15° C (59° F). Annual precipitation exceeds 1,650 mm (65 in) in upland areas. The mild climate and abundant rain at all seasons enable grass to grow well, giving the landscape its rich, green color.

People and Economy

The otherwise homogeneous population of Northern Ireland is divided into two communities by religion: the Protestants, who constitute about 70% of the population, and the Roman Catholics, who form a minority of about

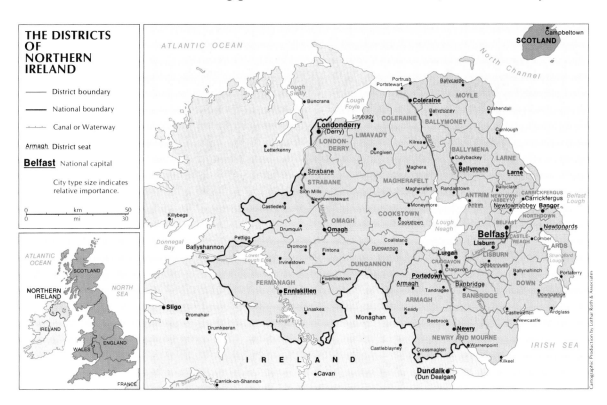

THE DISTRICTS OF NORTHERN IRELAND

—— District boundary

▬▬ National boundary

+−+−+ Canal or Waterway

Armagh District seat

Belfast National capital

City type size indicates relative importance.

30%. In general, the northeast is predominantly Protestant, and the areas bordering the Republic of Ireland are primarily Roman Catholic. The two groups are segregated in the larger cities.

Health-care, welfare, and educational facilities are similar to those in the rest of the United Kingdom. Queen's University (1845) in Belfast is Northern Ireland's oldest and largest institution of higher learning.

More than two-thirds of the land is used for agriculture, and most farms are small family holdings. Dairying is important, and most of the land is used for producing fodder for livestock. Barley and potatoes are also grown.

Two important industries developed during the 1800s: linen weaving and shipbuilding. Textile weaving, now dominated by synthetics, employs about one-fifth of the work force, especially in greater Belfast. Extensive shipyards lie along Belfast Lough, northeast of the city. Other industries include engineering, apparel manufacturing, and food processing.

History and Government

Northern Ireland owes its origin to the large-scale settlement of Scottish and English Protestants in Ulster during the early 1600s. They quickly became predominant over the native Catholic population. From the 19th into the 20th century, Catholics supported the Irish nationalist movement, but the Protestant majority in the north strongly opposed the formation of an Irish state in which they would become a small minority. In 1912, led by Sir Edward Carson, they organized armed volunteers in opposition to the Third Home Rule Bill. With Ireland on the brink of civil war, the British Liberal government excluded Ulster from the terms of the bill in 1914. Then World War I intervened.

Donegal Square is in the heart of Belfast, the capital of Northern Ireland. Since the late 1960s the city's life has been seriously disrupted by conflicts between Catholics and Protestants.

The Home Rule Bill of 1920 created separate parliaments for Ulster and the South. The Ulster Protestants accepted this settlement, but the Irish nationalists rejected it, eventually negotiating (1921) the treaty that created the Irish Free State in the south. Ireland was thus partitioned into a Protestant-dominated North, which remained part of the United Kingdom but with a separate legislature and considerable autonomy, and an independent South.

Northern Ireland was governed under the terms of the 1920 act until 1972. Protestant Unionists dominated the legislature and government (Stormont) and held economic power in the province to the virtual exclusion of the Roman Catholics. In 1968, Catholic civil rights demonstrations provoked Protestant attacks, and the simmering hostility between the two religious communities broke into open violence. British troops were sent in to maintain order in 1969, but hostilities increased as the IRISH REPUBLICAN ARMY became involved in the fray. In 1972 the British government suspended Stormont and imposed direct British rule.

Attempts in 1974 and 1982 to reestablish self-government on a more equitable basis were unsuccessful; an Anglo-Irish agreement (1985), which accorded the Irish government an advisory role in the affairs of Northern Ireland, was denounced as a sellout by the Unionists and as insufficient by the Nationalists. Meanwhile, violence and civil strife continued unabated, with the death toll rising to new heights in 1988.

northern lights   see AURORAS

Northern Rhodesia   see ZAMBIA

Northern Territory   The Northern Territory, an administrative region in north central Australia, has an area of about 1,340,000 km² (517,400 mi²), almost twice that of Texas, and a population of 155,800 (1988 est.). DARWIN is the capital and leading port. Two-thirds of the territory's residents are English-speaking Caucasians, most of whom live in Darwin and ALICE SPRINGS. The remaining third are Australian ABORIGINES who live on reservations that cover 20% of the territory. The population density of .07 per km² (0.2 per mi²) is one of the lowest in the world.

The landscape, from the relatively level coast bordering the Arafura and Timor seas, gradually rises to a plateau averaging 457 m (1,500 ft) in elevation. The highest point, Mount Zeil, reaches 1,510 m (4,955 ft). Temperatures are high: the average at Darwin is 29° C (84° F) in January and 24° C (76° F) in July. Most of the area is arid, with less than 255 mm (10 in) of rainfall annually, except for the northern monsoonal fringe, where the rainfall averages 1,525 mm (60 in) each year.

Cattle raising and the mining of metallic ores such as uranium, iron, manganese, copper, lead, and zinc are the mainstays of the economy. Agricultural products are raised for local consumption. Stuart Highway connects Darwin and Alice Springs.

The region around Port Darwin was permanently settled in the 1870s when gold was found in the Pine Creek

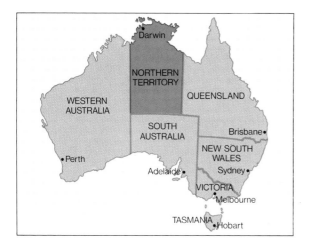

area, about 190 km (120 mi) southeast of Darwin. In 1911 the jurisdiction over the Northern Territory was transferred from South Australia to the commonwealth government. The Northern Territory was administered by the federal government until June 1978 when it came under partial self-rule. The region is expected to become a full-fledged state in the Australian Federation.

Northern War, Great The Great Northern War (1700–21) was a struggle for control of the Baltic region. Sweden, the dominant power in northern Europe when the war began, fought against an alliance of neighboring states intent on tearing apart its Baltic empire. Throughout most of the war the outstanding figure was CHARLES XII of Sweden, one of the greatest soldiers of all time. His opponents included PETER I of Russia, AUGUSTUS II of Poland (also the elector of Saxony), and FREDERICK IV of Denmark and Norway.

Sweden's rise to power in the 17th century had left that country surrounded by enemies. After Charles inherited (1697) the Swedish throne at the age of 14, Denmark, Saxony, and Russia formed an alliance and attacked (1700) Sweden. Charles, however, quickly drove the Danes from the war and then destroyed (November 1700) virtually the whole Russian army that was besieging Narva. Turning upon Augustus, Charles toppled him from the throne of Poland by 1704 and broke his power in Saxony by 1706.

In 1707, Charles marched against Russia. The Swedish army was decisively defeated at Poltava (July 1709). Charles fled to the Ottoman Empire, where he helped to inspire the Turkish attack on Russia (1710–11).

In the north, Denmark, Saxony, and Russia resumed their assault on Sweden and were soon joined by Hanover and Prussia. Russia seized Livonia, Estonia, and other lands around the Gulf of Finland while the other allies attacked Swedish possessions in Germany. When Charles returned to the north in 1714, he tried to pull his battered empire together but was killed (1718) during a campaign against Norway. Sweden was then forced to accept peace. The treaties of 1719–21 left Sweden with no overseas possessions except Finland, Wismar, and part of Pomerania and signaled the emergence of Russia as the strongest power in the Baltic region.

Northumberland, John Dudley, Duke of [north-um'-bur-luhnd] John Dudley, b. c.1502, d. Aug. 22, 1553, was the virtual ruler of England from 1549 to 1553. He was one of the councilors named by HENRY VIII to rule during the minority of EDWARD VI, who inherited the crown in 1547. Initially, Dudley acquiesced in the assumption of power by the protector, Edward Seymour, duke of SOMERSET, but in 1549 he overthrew Somerset and later ordered his execution. When Edward died in 1553, Northumberland attempted to divert the succession to his own daughter-in-law, Lady Jane GREY, but failed. Edward's half sister Mary Tudor (see MARY I) succeeded to the throne, and Northumberland was executed for treason.

Northumbria [north-um'-bree-uh] Northumbria, an Anglo-Saxon kingdom in northeastern England, was formed in the 7th century by the union of the kingdoms of Bernicia and Deira. Northumbria's rich cultural life (exemplified by the writings of Saint BEDE and the illuminated Lindisfarne Gospels) was destroyed by Danish raids in the 9th century.

Northwest Passage The search for the Northwest Passage—a route from Europe to Asia through the northern extremities of North America—was a long one. As early as 1534, Jacques CARTIER, the French navigator, explored the St. Lawrence River looking for a passage to China. Sir Martin FROBISHER discovered a body of water (Frobisher Bay) on what is now called Baffin Island in 1576 and thought it was the passage. Between 1585 and 1587, John DAVIS made three voyages, exploring the western shores of Greenland, Davis Strait, and Cumberland Sound. Henry HUDSON reached Hudson Bay in 1610 and was abandoned there by his mutinous crew. Between 1612 and 1615, Thomas Button, Robert Bylot, and William BAFFIN made three voyages to Hudson Bay—searching unsuccessfully for a passage to Asia.

Sir John Ross rediscovered Devon and Ellesmere islands in 1818. Sir William PARRY sailed through Lancaster Sound, the entrance to the passage, as far as Melville Island (1819–20) and through Hudson Strait to Fury and Hecla Strait (1821–23). Sir John FRANKLIN explored the Canadian Arctic coast between 1819 and 1821. Ross explored near Boothia Peninsula (1829–31). Franklin mounted an ambitious, ill-fated expedition that entered Lancaster Sound in July 1845; its last survivors died in 1848. Until 1854, when Eskimos told John Rae of Franklin's fate, more than 40 expeditions searched for Franklin's expedition. Robert McClure and his crew completed a passage from west to east in 1854, but partly by foot and sledge because of the thick ice. Not until the 20th century did a ship traverse the Northwest Passage. Roald AMUNDSEN sailed from Oslo on the *Gjøa* in 1903, spent almost two years on King William Island, and then followed the Canadian coast westward. He reached Cape Nome, Alaska, in August 1906.

A Royal Canadian Mounted Police schooner, *St. Roch,* traveled the passage from Vancouver, British Columbia, to Halifax, Nova Scotia, and back between 1940 and 1944. U.S. Coast Guard cutters, Canadian icebreakers, and the oil tanker *Manhattan* (1969) have also traversed the passage, but it is not now commercially useful.

Northwest Territories

Northwest Territories The Northwest Territories (NWT) includes all mainland Canada north of 60° north latitude between the Yukon Territory on the west and Hudson Bay on the east. It also encompasses all islands between the mainland and the North Pole. Eighteen of these islands are larger than Prince Edward Island, Canada's smallest province, and the largest, BAFFIN ISLAND, is more than twice as large as Great Britain. The NWT accounts for one-third of all Canada's land area.

Land and Resources

The CANADIAN SHIELD covers the eastern two-thirds of the NWT mainland and some of the southern Arctic islands. The western third of the mainland is part of the continental interior plains, marked on the west by the abrupt rise of the rugged Cordillera region with peaks exceeding 1,525 m (5,000 ft) in elevation. The eastern Arctic islands are mountainous, averaging approximately 2,000 m (6,500 ft) in elevation.

Most of the NWT lies north of the timberline, which extends southeast from the mouth of the MACKENZIE RIVER to HUDSON BAY at a point immediately south of 60° north latitude. The subarctic forest of spruce, pine, birch, and larch provides habitat for moose, caribou, bears, and beavers; musk-oxen, caribou (in summer), and Arctic foxes live on the tundra.

Long, cold winters occur everywhere. The January mean temperature is below –29° C (–20° F), with the lowest temperatures usually occurring in the Mackenzie Valley. The valley's summers are warm, however, with July temperatures averaging 16° C (60° F), in contrast to the Arctic islands, which average 4° C (40° F) in July. Precipitation everywhere is light, averaging 330 mm (13 in) annually on the mainland. On the islands precipitation ranges from 406 mm (16 in) in the southeast to as little as 50 mm (2 in) in the northwest.

The western mainland drains northward through the Mackenzie River system, which includes GREAT BEAR LAKE and GREAT SLAVE LAKE. The primary resources of the NWT are its wildlife, minerals, and petroleum and gas potential.

People

The NWT is the most sparsely settled area of Canada, most settlements consisting of only a few hundred people. In the Arctic sector Iqaluit, formerly Frobisher Bay

---

AT A GLANCE

NORTHWEST TERRITORIES

Land: Area: 3,426,320 km² (1,322,909 mi²). Capital and largest city: Yellowknife (1991 pop., 15,175). Municipalities: 44. Elevations: highest—2,773 m (9,098 ft), Mackenzie Mountains, unnamed peak; lowest—sea level, along the north coast and Hudson Bay.

People: Population (1991): 57,649; density: 0.017 persons per km² (0.045 per mi²). Distribution (1991): 36.7% urban, 63.3% rural. Average annual change (1986–91): +2.08%.

Government (1992): Commissioner: Dan Norris. Govt. leader: Nellie Cournoyea. Parliament: Senate—1 member; House of Commons—2 Liberals. Territorial legislature: 24 members. Admitted to Confederation: July 15, 1870.

Economic Resources (monetary figures in Canadian dollars): Furs: value (1990–91)—$1.8 million (including marten, mink, polar bear, lynx). Manufacturing: value added (1986)—$13.7 million. Fishing: value (1990–91)—$2 million (principally trout, arctic char, whitefish). Forestry: value (1989–90)—$2.2 million. Mining: value of metallic minerals (1990)—$881 million (lead, zinc, gold, cadmium, silver).

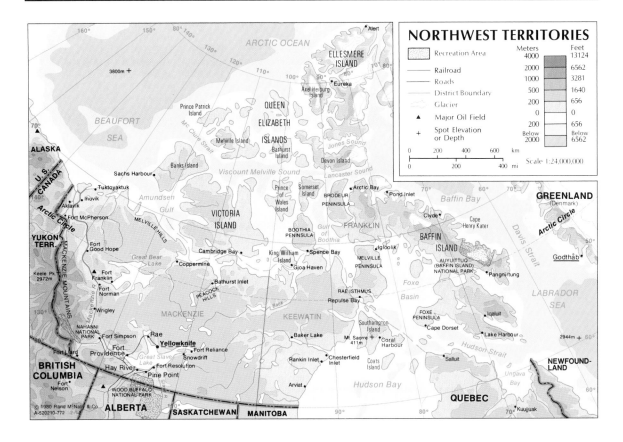

NORTHWEST TERRITORIES

	Recreation Area	Meters	Feet
		4000	13124
	Railroad	2000	6562
	Roads	1000	3281
	District Boundary	500	1640
	Glacier	200	656
▲	Major Oil Field	0	0
+	Spot Elevation or Depth	200	656
		Below 2000	Below 6562

Scale 1:24,000,000

(1991 pop., 3,552) is the only large center. In the Mackenzie Valley the largest settlements include YELLOWKNIFE, the capital and gold-mining city, Inuvik (3,206), Hay River (3,206), and Fort Smith (2,480).

About two-thirds of Canada's 27,290 (1986) Inuit (ESKIMO) live in the NWT's Arctic sector. Of the 30,530 NWT aboriginals, 57% are Inuit. About 11% are aboriginals of multiple origins. The Dene and métis populations (32%) and most Europeans live in the Mackenzie Valley. Since World War II almost all of the native peoples have abandoned their nomadic existence.

In the past, qualified students from the NWT, which had no universities, attended provincial universities without charge. In 1986, however, the Arctic Colleges Act established a college system in the NWT, with campuses in Fort Smith, Iqaluit, and Inuvik.

Economic Activity

Mining is the NWT's most important economic activity. Petroleum was discovered along the Mackenzie River in 1920, but recent interest has focused on the North Slope, offshore from the Mackenzie delta, and on the northwestern Arctic islands. Other areas of exploration include northwestern Baffin Island and the Davis Strait. Metallic minerals, including lead, zinc, and gold, are important revenue producers. Other economic activities include commercial

fishing on Great Slave Lake and trapping. Hydroelectric plants operate on the Snare and Taltson rivers.

Commercial water transport operates seasonally on the Mackenzie River system and in the southern Arctic waters. The only rail link with the south terminates at Hay River. A limited road system links the Mackenzie Valley to northwestern Alberta, and Inuvik was linked to Yukon roads in 1979. Fort Simpson was linked to the ALASKA HIGHWAY in 1984.

Government

The Northwest Territories consists of five regions—Baffin, Fort Smith, Inuvik, Keewatin, and Kitikmeot—governed by an elected legislature. In 1992, NWT voters approved the 1991 land-claims agreement negotiated by federal, territorial, and Inuit leaders, establishing Nunavut—a 2,000,144-km^2 (772,260-mi^2) territory in the eastern Arctic. The agreement, effective in 1999, gives the Inuit title to 350,000 km^2 (135,136 mi^2) of land, a cash settlement, limited mineral rights, and political domain of Nanavut. Western-Arctic Inuit had finalized an agreement in 1984. Negotiations between NWT's Dene-Métis and the federal government continue.

History

Native Indians belonged to a number of nomadic tribes,

Frobisher Bay, now called Iqaluit, is the largest town in the Arctic sector of the Northwest Territories. It was established (1943) as a U.S. air base. Most residents are Inuit (Eskimo).

most members of the Athabascan language group. The NWT was opened up by fur traders, explorers, and whalers in the 18th and 19th centuries, and prospectors in this century. It was held (1670–1870) by the HUDSON'S BAY COMPANY and was transferred to Canada in 1870. Since World War II the federal government has supported scientific research and social-economic development programs there. In 1989, Dan Norris became the first métis to become NWT commissioner.

Northwest Territory   The Northwest Territory, officially called the Territory Northwest of the River Ohio, was established by the Continental Congress on July 13, 1787, by the Northwest Ordinance. The region was later called the Old Northwest. Comprising the land west of Pennsylvania between the Ohio and the Mississippi rivers ceded to the U.S. government by individual states in the 1780s, the territory was later divided into the new states of Ohio, Indiana, Illinois, Michigan, Wisconsin, and part of Minnesota. The policies that were devised for the sale of land and for the government in this region established precedents for the settlement of the public domain across the whole of the United States.

The Land Ordinance of 1785 had provided for the survey and sale of mile-square sections of land. After the first sales, in the area that is now eastern Ohio, the federal government began to allow land companies to purchase huge areas farther down the Ohio River. Congress passed the Northwest Ordinance of 1787 to provide for the government of the entire region. The Ordinance was based in part on a plan drawn up by a committee headed by Thomas JEFFERSON in 1784. It stated that no fewer than three nor more than five states were eventually to be formed from the region and set down an orderly procedure for the creation of these new states. In the first stage the entire Northwest Territory would be ruled by a governor, a secretary, and three judges appointed by Congress; in the second stage, when the free adult males residing in one of the territories numbered 5,000, they could elect a territorial legislature and send a nonvoting delegate to Congress; and when the population of any territory reached 60,000, it would be eligible to enter the Union as a new state equal to the original states. Slavery was prohibited in the territory.

Ohio was the first state admitted (1803) to the Union from the Northwest Territory. U.S. control of the less populous frontier areas was challenged by the presence of British trading posts in the Northwest and was firmly established only in the aftermath of the War of 1812.

Northwestern University   Established in 1851, Northwestern University is a private coeducational institution with campuses in Evanston and Chicago, Ill. The university has a college of arts and sciences and schools of speech, journalism, music, education, and management (graduate). The law, medical, and dental schools are in Chicago.

Norton, Charles Eliot   An American scholar, translator, editor, critic, and influential Harvard professor (1875–98), Charles Eliot Norton, b. Cambridge, Mass., Nov. 16, 1827, d. Oct. 21, 1908, was a dominant figure in the Boston-Cambridge intellectual aristocracy of the late 19th century. He maintained close ties with many of the best-known European and American writers and scholars of the period. He edited the *North American Review* and in 1865 helped found the *Nation*.

Norwalk   Norwalk (1990 pop., 78,331) is an industrial city in southwestern Connecticut, situated on Long Island Sound at the mouth of the Norwalk River. Although it was long famous for its oysters and the production of felt hats, at present aircraft and space-vehicle components and electrical equipment are the principal manufactures.

Norwalk was settled in 1649. In 1779, during the Revolutionary War, the British burned the city. In 1913 eight adjoining towns were consolidated to create the present city of Norwalk.

Norway   Norway (Norwegian: Norge), known as the Land of the Midnight Sun, is located on the Scandinavian peninsula in northern Europe. Its long, craggy coast (3,420 km/2,125 mi) fronts the Atlantic Ocean for most of the country's length. To the southwest the North Sea separates Norway from the British Isles, and directly to

KINGDOM OF NORWAY

Land: Area: 323,878 km^2 (125,050 mi^2). Capital and largest city: Oslo (1990 est. pop., 457,818).

People: Population (1990 est.): 4,233,486. Density: 13.1 persons per km^2 (33.9 per mi^2). Distribution (1985): 73% urban, 27% rural. Official languages: two forms of Norwegian (Bokmål and Nynorsk). Major religion: Evangelical Lutheranism.

Government: Type: constitutional monarchy. Legislature: Storting. Political subdivisions: 19 counties.

Economy: GNP (1989): $92 billion; $21,850 per capita. Labor distribution (1989): agriculture, forestry, and fishing—6.1%; mining and manufacturing—15.9%; commerce—17.1%; banking and financial services—7.1%; transportation—7.8%; construction—6.8%; services and other—39.2%. Foreign trade (1989): imports—$18.7 billion; exports—$22.2 billion. Currency: 1 krone = 100 øre.

Education and Health: Literacy (1990): 100% of adult population. Universities (1989): 4. Hospital beds (1988): 24,493. Physicians (1988): 9,443. Life expectancy (1990): women—81; men—73. Infant mortality (1990): 7 per 1,000 live births.

the south the Skagerrak separates it from Denmark. On the landward side Norway shares a long border with Sweden and shorter borders in the north with Finland and the USSR. Lying directly northward is the Barents Sea, an arm of the Arctic Ocean.

The country's length from north to south is about 1,770 km (1,100 mi), but for much of the distance it is extremely narrow. Almost one-third of Norway lies within the Arctic Circle. In the northernmost city in Europe, HAMMERFEST, the sun shines almost continuously for 24 hours at the height of the summer. Most of Norway's terrain is marked by rugged mountains interrupted by narrow valleys.

Norway has one of the highest standards of living in the world. The discovery of petroleum and natural gas in the Norwegian section of the North Sea in the late 1960s increased prosperity further. Exports of petroleum and natural gas accounted for 39% of income from exports in 1989.

The Norwegian state was formed in the 9th century, but in 1397 it was united with Denmark and, for a brief period, with Sweden, in the Kalmar Union. The union with Denmark lasted until 1814, when Norway was ceded to Sweden. During the 19th century a strong nationalist movement within Norway led to the dissolution of the union with Sweden, and in 1905, Norway became an independent nation.

Land and Resources

The highest peak, Glittertinden, in the JOTUNHEIM range,

rises to 2,472 m (8,110 ft). The Dovrefjell and Langfjell ranges are in southern Norway. The only region that can be described as coastal lowland lies in the area surrounding OSLO, the capital city.

Along much of the coast sheer cliffs drop spectacularly to the sea, forming the FJORDS. The longest and deepest of these is the Sogne Fjord. About 150,000 offshore islands and rocks, including the Lofoten group, serve as a barrier that helps protect the coast from Atlantic storms.

Soils. Most soils were removed by glaciers during the Pleistocene Epoch, and new soil has not yet had time to form over the land. Peat is now found in surface hollows in the mountains. Glacial deposits that were spread over the valley floors have resulted in poor, stony soils.

Climate. The climate is temperate, and the severity of winter along the coast is moderated by southerly air currents brought in above the waters of the North Atlantic Drift, which is warmed by the Gulf Stream. The coastal region has a January average temperature that varies from about −1° C (30° F) in the north to more than 7° C (45° F) in the south. Winter temperatures drop sharply inland and readings below −18° C (0° F) are common. Summers are cool throughout the country, with averages at sea level no higher than 16° C (60° F) in July. Rainfall is high everywhere and drops below 1,017 mm (40 in) only in the southeast.

Drainage. The drainage system consists of many short rivers that drop steeply from the high regions and drain directly to the sea. Only in the southeast has a drainage

(Above) *Lapp chidren play on a hillside over-looking the harbor of Hammerfest, generally regarded as the most northerly city in Europe. Hammerfest, on the island of Kvaløya off the northern coast of Norway, lies almost 400 km (228 mi) inside the Arctic Circle.*

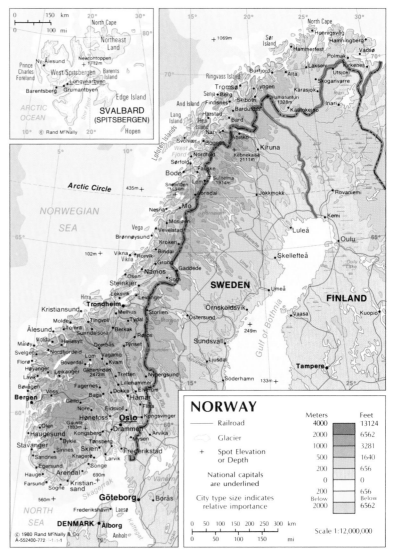

network evolved; here the Glåma, Lågen, and Rauma rivers join before entering the North Sea near Oslo.

Animal Life and Vegetation. The native fauna is rich and varied and includes reindeer, elk, wolf, and bear, as well as many varieties of smaller animals. The larger species, however, are found only in the remote north. Norway is a breeding ground for many varieties of birds that migrate to warmer climates during the winter. The rivers contain abundant salmon and trout, which are caught commercially.

Spruce and pine predominate, and hardy deciduous trees, such as birch and ash, are common at low elevations. In the mountains the growth is mainly heather, low bushes that yield abundant edible berries, and gnarled shrubbery.

Resources. Timber is the main natural resource. In addition, Norway has tremendous resources in its offshore petroleum and natural-gas fields as well as in the hydro-electricity-generating capacity of its numerous rapid rivers and waterfalls. Iron and copper and small reserves of the alloy metals are found.

People

Norway's population is primarily Nordic. The LAPPS, who constitute the indigenous population and are now a minority numbering about 20,000, are thought to be of Mongolian origin. LAPLAND, their home, extends across northern Scandinavia, but Kautokeino, Norway, is its center.

Language. Norwegian is a Germanic language closely related to both Danish and Swedish. Two mutually intelligible forms of the language exist in present-day Norway. Bokmål (formerly Riksmål) evolved from Danish, which was the only written language of Norway until about 1850. In an attempt to restore the connections with Old Norse, the philologist Ivan Andreas Aasen (1813–96) drew from the old rural dialects and created Landsmål. A struggle for supremacy between Landsmål (now Nynorsk) and Bokmål ensued, and although both languages are used, Bokmål is more widespread and is generally used in the press and in education. Currently an attempt is being made to fuse the two languages into one, called Samnorsk.

Demography. The population of Norway is increasing slowly. Both the birth and infant mortality rates are low, and life expectancy is among the highest in the world. Oslo, the largest city, is followed in size by BERGEN, TRONDHEIM, STAVANGER, Baerum, Kristiansand, and Drammen. About two-thirds of the population are concentrated in the valleys of the southeast and close to the coast in southern Norway. The overall density is the lowest in Europe, excluding Iceland.

Education and Health. Norway has a system of free education, compulsory to the age of 16. Beyond this age students have a choice between vocational training and continued high school education, which leads to university admission. Norway's universities, together with a number of professional and other institutions of higher education, are all free. More than 41,000 students, or 1% of the population, are enrolled in universities and professional schools.

The state operates a national health system, and much health care is free. Most of Norway's doctors are employed in hospitals. A system of social security helps to maintain an adequate standard of living for all and provides a basic retirement pension, irrespective of former income. Families with children under 16 years of age receive a yearly allotment for each child.

Literature and the Arts. The oldest Norwegian literature, the legends of the VIKINGS written in Old Norse, dates from the early Middle Ages and survives mainly in Icelandic writings (see ICELANDIC LITERATURE). The Norwegians who fled (c.850–75) from Norway during the reign of Harold I and colonized Iceland brought with them a large body of oral mythological poetry; these legends were eventually recorded and constitute the SAGAS and EDDAS of Old Norse literature. When a literary tradition again emerged it was in Danish. A distinctly Norwegian literary tradition began to take shape in the 19th century, receiving impetus from newly achieved independence (1814) from Denmark, and reached its peak in Henrik Arnold WERGELAND, Henrik IBSEN, and Bjørnstjerne BJØRNSON (Nobel Prize, 1903). The works of Knut HAMSUN (Nobel Prize, 1920) and Sigrid UNDSET (Nobel Prize, 1928) represent new and diverse strains in Norwegian literature. In the 20th century, literature began to reflect interest in Norwegian history and culture (see NORWEGIAN LITERATURE).

Norway has a strongly developed tradition of folk music. The most distinguished members of the 19th-century school of composers were Edvard GRIEG, Christian Sinding, and Johan Svendsen, all of whom made great use of traditional music. The painting of Edvard MUNCH has achieved worldwide recognition. Gustav VIGELAND produced a vast body of sculpture, which has been collected in Frogner Park in Oslo.

Economic Activity

Until late in the 19th century Norway remained a producer of primary goods: fish, timber, and farm products. Industrial development began about 1900, when the immense reserves of waterpower were put to use. Today Norway derives about 14% of its gross domestic product from manufacturing and less than 4% from agriculture.

Agriculture, Forestry, and Fishing. Agriculture is practiced in the fertile valleys on small farms averaging 17 ha (42 acres). Only about 3% of the land is arable and almost 75% is unproductive; mountain pastures (2%) permit livestock raising, particularly cattle raising, which is more important economically than the cultivation of crops. Dairying is also important. Forests account for 21% of the land, and many farmers engage in forestry to supplement income.

Norway has long been known for its fisheries. Fishing, including fish farming, forms the basis of the fish-processing industry, and fish and fish products are important exports.

Industry and Energy. Production of petroleum and gas has become the foremost industry with the discovery of offshore fields. Food, beverage, and tobacco processing rank second. The manufacture of transportation equipment, primarily ships and boats (the major export), ranks third, followed by the production of metal and metal products.

Norway has coal only on its Arctic islands of SVALBARD (Spitsbergen). Despite the petroleum being exploited from the North Sea, the chief energy source is still hydroelectric power.

Transportation. Norway's elongated shape and rugged terrain have made it difficult to maintain a transportation network, which is well developed only in the southeast. Coastal shipping is commonly used; the northern third of the country has no railroad, and traveling there is done by bus or automobile. The railroads are state owned. Aircraft are used to maintain contact with remote areas, and Norway is a part owner of Scandinavian Airlines System (SAS).

Trade. Petroleum and natural gas provide more than one-third of export earnings. Other important exports are metals and metal products, machinery and transportation equipment, and fish and fish products. Imports include machinery and transportation equipment, raw materials for industry, metals and metal products, and foodstuffs. Tourism also provides foreign exchange.

Government

Norway is a hereditary constitutional monarchy, with a constitution that was drafted in 1814. It gives broad powers to the king, but the council of ministers, headed by the prime minister, generally exercises this power as king in council. The 155 members of the Storting, or parliament, are elected for a fixed term of 4 years by all Norwegians 20 years of age or older. Election is by a form of proportional representation. The major political parties

Mountains rise steeply from the waters of the Geiranger Fjord, one of the many narrow bays that indent Norway's west coast. Formed when retreating glaciers deepened the existing river valleys, Norway's fjords are internationally famous for their dramatic beauty.

are the Labor party, the largest single party, and the Conservative party. The Labor party, which was responsible for creating the democratic-socialist welfare state, headed the government for 37 years during the period 1935–81. A debate about high taxes and rising inflation caused the Labor party to lose ground to center-right groups. The Conservatives under Kåre Willoch were in office from 1981 to 1986, when they were ousted by Labor, led by Gro Harlem BRUNDTLAND, Norway's first woman prime minister. Voted out of office in 1989, Brundtland was replaced by Jan Syse, but she returned to head a new government in November 1990.

Local administration is on the basis of 19 counties or provinces (*fylker*) and the cities of Bergen and Oslo. Norway is closely associated with the other Scandinavian countries in an informal alliance. In 1972 a referendum rejected membership in the European Community (EC), but Norway remained part of the EUROPEAN FREE TRADE ASSOCIATION (EFTA).

History

Norway was not settled until the climate ameliorated at the end of the Ice Age (*c.*7000 BC), allowing people to migrate both from Central Europe and from Asia. From the 8th century on, a number of small tribal kingdoms emerged, representing the beginnings of separate nation-states within Scandinavia. The bloody conflicts between the tribal groups, as well as a craving for adventure, prompted people to leave their lands in what is known as the Viking movement (9th to 11th century). Warriors from the *Viks,* or fjords, raided throughout western Europe and into the Mediterranean.

Unification. During the 10th century the country moved toward political unity. King HAROLD I conquered much of Norway, which his descendants ruled for two centuries. Among these kings were OLAF I, who sought to impose Christianity on the pagan country, and OLAF II (Saint Olaf), who succeeded in Christianizing Norway. This period was extremely troubled, and the country was often at war with the Swedes, Danes, and peoples in northern Britain. In the 12th century King SVERRE consolidated the power of the monarchy.

Prolonged peace did not come to Norway until the 13th century, under HAAKON IV. Iceland and Greenland were ruled by Norway at this time. King MAGNUS VI introduced a new code of legal practice, replacing the ancient system of *wergild* that had derived from pagan times. At the same time the country began to develop economically. Bergen and other coastal cities grew into important commercial centers, linked by trade with the HANSEATIC LEAGUE (which was eventually to dominate Norwegian trade completely).

Foreign Domination. Marriage ties linked Norway with both Sweden and Denmark. At the end of the 14th century the Norwegian royal house died out, and the nobles elected as their king, Eric of Pomerania, a grandnephew of MARGARET I of Denmark, the wife of Haakon VI. Eric ruled nominally for Margaret, who united Norway, Sweden, and Denmark by the Union of Kalmar.

This union did not last long; Sweden broke away in 1450, but Norway became linked even more closely to Denmark, of which it was little more than a province.

During the 18th century Danish control began to be relaxed; in 1814, Denmark ceded Norway to Sweden by the Treaty of Kiel at the end of the Napoleonic Wars. The Norwegians refused to recognize the change and demanded independence. The Swedish army invaded Norway, but a compromise was reached; under the Act of Union of 1814, Norway was allowed to retain the constitution that had been recently drawn up at Eidsvold, while remaining in personal union with Sweden under the Swedish king.

Independence. During the 19th century relations between Norway and Sweden were strained. Growing nationalism in Norway and increasing wealth made the country resentful of its dependent status. In 1905 the union with Sweden was peacefully dissolved, and a Danish prince, Carl, taking the name HAAKON VII, was elected king of Norway.

Norway remained neutral during World War I but in April 1940 was invaded without warning by the Germans. The Norwegians resisted German occupation forces and severe reprisals were inflicted by the Nazis in an attempt to halt the underground movement. During most of this period Norway was ruled by a puppet regime under the Norwegian Vidkun QUISLING, who had been nominated by Hitler. The Norwegian merchant fleet played a vital role in aiding the Allies. Although it lost half its fleet, the country recovered quickly after the war. In 1957, OLAF V ascended the throne on the death of his father, becoming the second monarch to rule over an independent Norway.

Norwegian art and architecture see SCANDINAVIAN ART AND ARCHITECTURE

Norwegian elkhound

The Norwegian elkhound is a typical member of the spitz group of dogs, with the characteristic erect ears, dense coat, wedge-shaped head, and bushy tail curled over the back. The national dog of Norway, it was developed to hunt moose (known as elk in Europe) and is also used to hunt bear and other large game and, on a long leash, to find and flush game birds. Ideally, males are 52 cm (20.5 in) high at the shoulder and weigh 25 kg (55 lb); females, 49.5 cm (19.5 in) and 22 kg (48 lb). The body is short and compact, with fairly long legs and small paws. The medium-length coat is thick and profuse, with a light gray, dense undercoat and a gray, black-tipped, close-lying outer coat. Only gray-colored elkhounds are accepted in American Kennel Club show competition.

Norwegian language see GERMANIC LANGUAGES

Norwegian literature

Norway did not achieve full political autonomy until 1905. This, coupled with the country's difficult terrain, may explain why Norwegian literature from its origins in the Viking age (800–1050) to the present has been imbued with a spirit of heroism, integrity, and self-identity.

The earliest Norwegian literature is a group of poems on mythological subjects, called the Elder, or Poetic, EDDA. It was written down in Old Norse during the Viking period by the Norwegian colonizers of Iceland. A more ornate and technically complicated poetry was composed by court poets, or skalds. SKALDIC LITERATURE was composed mainly in praise of the battle exploits of various chieftains.

The Learned Period. From the 16th through the 18th century, Norwegian literature was written in Danish, mainly by clerics and civil servants educated in Denmark. The two principal literary figures were Petter Dass in the 17th century and Ludvig, Baron HOLBERG in the 18th. Dass has given a vivid picture of life in the north of Norway in his poem *The Trumpet of Nordland* (1739; Eng. trans., 1954). Holberg was the first professional writer in Dano-Norwegian literature. Highly learned and an accomplished imitator, he wrote in a variety of genres.

National Romanticism (1814–70). After 1814, when their country was transferred from Danish to Swedish rule, Norwegian writers began to regard themselves as creators of a national literature. Henrik Arnold WERGE-

Norwegian literature has been dominated during the modern period by three writers. Henrik Ibsen (left) is considered the father of modern drama. His plays include A Doll's House *(1879) and* Hedda Gabler *(1890). Bjørnstjerne Bjørnson (center), a journalist and author, wrote "Yes, We Love This Native Land," a poem that became Norway's national anthem. Novelist Knut Hamsun (right) won the Nobel Prize in 1920.*

LAND, considered Norway's national poet, enthralled Norwegians with his monumental cosmological poem, *Skabelsen, mennesket, og messias* (Creation, Man, and Messiah, 1830). Johan Sebastian Cammermeyer Welhaven reproached Wergeland for his refusal to recognize the existence of a shared Dano-Norwegian cultural heritage, but the reproach had no noticeable effect, either on Wergeland or on such other writers as Peter Christen Asbjørnsen and Jørgen Engebretsen Moe, who were enthusiastically rediscovering Norway's past. Asbjørnsen and Moe published their celebrated *Norske folkeeventyr* (Norwegian Folk Tales) in 1842–44. Bjørnstjerne BJØRNSON also drew on folklore in his novellas of peasant life.

The Modern Period. Dramatist Henrik IBSEN is Norway's outstanding literary figure. In the 20th century two Norwegian novelists have won Nobel Prizes: Knut HAMSUN, most famous for *Growth of the Soil* (1917; Eng. trans., 1920), and Sigrid UNDSET, author of the epic novel *Kristin Lavransdatter* (1920–22; Eng. trans., 1923–27). Other eminent writers of this century include novelist John Bojer, poet Olaf Bull, novelist Olav Duun, playwright and novelist Nordahl Grieg, and novelist Tarjei Vesaas. More-recent authors of note are short-story writer Terje Stigen, novelist Jens Bjørnboe, poet Stein Mehren, and the feminist writer Bjørg Vik.

Norwich [nahr'-ich]   Norwich is a city in eastern England, on the River Wensum, about 55 km (95 mi) northeast of London. The county town of Norfolk and the regional capital of East Anglia, Norwich has a population of 122,300 (1985 est.). The city's once-famous textile industry has been largely replaced by the manufacture of boots and shoes. Other manufactures include farm machinery, chemicals, textiles, and food products. The city has 30 medieval churches, and a 12th-century castle has become a museum housing many paintings from the 19th-century Norwich school of landscape painting. Settled by the Saxons, Norwich was overrun by the Danes in 1004. The city became a thriving wool center in the 14th century.

Norwich terrier   The Norwich terrier is one of the smallest terrier breeds, ideally standing 25 cm (10 in) high at the shoulder and weighing 5 to 5.5 kg (11 to 12 lb). It is a compactly built, short-legged dog with a wide head, a short muzzle, and small, pointed ears; its tail is docked and carried high. Its double coat, which consists of a very short undercoat and a hard, wiry, close-lying outer coat, is commonly red but also may be wheaten, black and tan, or grizzle. The breed is thought to have originated about 1870 near Norwich in the county of Norfolk, England, where it was probably derived from small Irish terriers and possibly the border terrier and one or more other English or Scottish terrier breeds. Two types of Norwich terriers have been bred, one with erect ears, the other with hanging, or drop, ears. In 1965 the English Kennel Club recognized the drop-eared variety as a separate breed called the Norfolk terrier. The American Kennel Club followed suit in 1979.

nose   The nose, the site of the sense of smell (see TASTE AND SMELL), is the organ through which mammals take in air. It is supported by cartilage and bone, covered with skin, lined with a mucous membrane, and provided with muscle. A nasal septum divides it into two passages, each of which begins with a vestibule and contains a respiratory and olfactory region. The lining of the vestibule is continuous with the skin and contains hairs, sweat glands, and sebaceous (oil-producing) glands.

The respiratory region includes nearly all of the septum and the lateral walls of the nose. Goblet cells, which produce and secrete a watery mucus, are present in the lining, as is a type of erectile tissue, composed of large, thin-walled veins whose blood supply serves to warm incoming air. The olfactory region is located on the superior concha and adjacent septum. Olfactory cells are present in its lining and have delicate, slender processes (modified cilia) at their free surfaces. Odors from chemicals in the air are received by these processes. Nerve cells that impinge upon the olfactory cells convert the chemical information into nerve impulses and convey the sensory information to the brain.

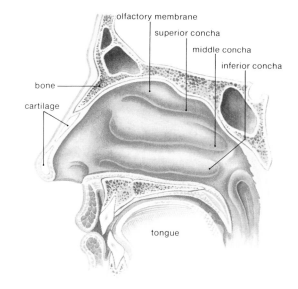

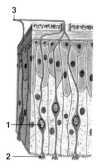

The nose is divided by the septum into two cavities, each containing three folds called conchae and lined with a mucous membrane. Air taken in through the nostrils is filtered by the cilia— small hairs in the mucous membrane—moistened by the mucus, and warmed by the blood vessels of the superior conchae. The olfactory membrane (detail), located in the mucous membrane of the superior conchae and adjacent part of the septum, contains olfactory cells (1), nerve cells sensitive to odors. Airborne chemicals interact with the ciliated endings (2) of these cells; nerve impulses then are carried by the olfactory nerve (3) to the brain.

nosocomial diseases [nohs-uh-koh'-mee-ul] Infections and disorders acquired in hospitals and in other health-care settings are called nosocomial diseases, after the Latin *nosocomium* for "hospital." Patients with weakened resistance are particularly prone to infections of the genital, urinary, and respiratory tracts and of surgical wounds. Common infections that can spread through hospitals include those caused by *Enterococcus, Escherichia, Klebsiella, Pseudomonas,* and *Staphylococcus* bacteria; the *Candida albicans* fungus; and hepatitis and herpes zoster viruses. Other nosocomial disorders include bedsores, which can develop in patients who remain in one bed position for long periods, and blood clots, which can occur in patients who remain inactive too long after surgery.

Nostradamus [nahs-truh-day'-muhs] Michael Nostradamus (Michel de Notredame), b. Dec. 14, 1503, d. July 2, 1566, was a French physician and astrologer whose predictions of the future have fascinated people for centuries. Nostradamus acquired a great reputation as a doctor by treating victims of the plague that ravaged that part of Europe, but he eventually turned more to astrology and metaphysics. In 1555 he completed the *Centuries,* a book of more than 900 predictions about the fate of France, the world, and celebrated persons of his time. The title of the book refers to the fact that the contents are arranged in sections of 100 verses each. An expanded version was published in 1558.

His prophecies are written as four-lined rhymed verses (quatrains) in vague, often cryptic language. His fondness for anagrams and his penchant for sprinkling his verses with Hebrew, Latin, and Portuguese words further complicates interpretation of his predictions. Some interpreters say the verses can be applied to anything, or nothing, whereas others claim that various verses foretold the Great Fire of London in 1666, the deaths of several monarchs, details of the French Revolution, the rise of Napoleon and Hitler, and World War II.

Because Nostradamus included very few dates in his prophecies and because, additionally, he did not organize them into a chronological order, the verses have been constantly reinterpreted since the time of their publication.

notary public A notary public is an official whose main duties, under British and American law, are to authenticate documents such as contracts and deeds. In most of the states of the United States notaries public are appointed by the governor. To qualify for the position a person must be of legal age, a resident of the state or county in which appointment is sought, and of good moral character.

Notre Dame de Paris (cathedral) [noh'-truh dahm duh pah-ree'] The cathedral of Paris, situated on the Île de la Cité and dedicated to the Virgin Mary, was begun in 1163. On completion of the choir in 1183, work was be-

Notre Dame de Paris (begun 1163), on the Île de la Cité, is one of the most celebrated Gothic cathedrals in France. Its exterior reveals a typical Gothic cross plan, with twin towers marking the entrance.

gun on the nave and completed about 1200. The appearance of the interior was radically transformed in the mid-13th century when the small clerestory windows typical of the Early Gothic style (see GOTHIC ART AND ARCHITECTURE) were enlarged downward and filled with High Gothic tracery. The enlargement caused the removal of the unusual triforium. Originally, the interior had the four-story elevation common to many Early Gothic churches. In his restoration (begun 1844), Eugène Emmanuel VIOLLET-LE-DUC reinstated the triforium and small clerestory windows in the eastern bay of the nave. The six-part rib vaults and the thin elements articulating the wall are also typically Early Gothic. From the exterior, however, the building appears to be High Gothic. Notable features include the profusion of colonnettes and tracery screens, the horizontal and vertical ordering of the facades, the imposing size of the rose windows, and the delicacy of the flying buttresses. All these elements were constructed in a series of building projects carried out between 1200 and 1260.

Notre Dame, University of [noh'-tur daym] Established in 1842 by the Congregation of the Holy Cross, but now governed by a predominately lay board of trustees, Notre Dame is a private coeducational university in Notre Dame, Ind. It has a law school and a graduate medieval institute and houses the Center for the Study of Man in Contemporary Society.

Nott, Eliphalet [naht, uh-lif'-uh-let] Eliphalet Nott, b. Ashford, Conn., June 25, 1773, d. Jan. 29, 1866, was an American college president and inventor. As president of Union College in Schenectady, N.Y., where he remained for 62 years (1804–66), Nott introduced the first elective courses and the first science course in an American liberal arts college; later he added courses in civil engineering. Among his inventions were the first anthracite-burning stove and the first steamboat to burn coal. Nott was also a leader in the temperance and abolitionist movements.

Nottingham

Nottingham [naht'-ing-uhm]   Nottingham is a city in north central England on the River Trent. The county town of Nottinghamshire, the city has a population of 273,500 (1988 est.). A transportation center, Nottingham manufactures pharmaceuticals, textiles and lace, cigarettes, and bicycles. The University of Nottingham (1948) is there. Nearby is Sherwood Forest, domain of the legendary Robin Hood. Settled in the 6th century by Anglo-Saxons, it was occupied by the Danes in the 9th century. Parliaments were held in the city in the mid-1300s. In 1642 the English Civil War began in Nottingham.

Nottinghamshire

Nottinghamshire   [naht'-ing-uhm-shir]   Nottinghamshire is a county in the east Midlands region of central England. Nottinghamshire covers 2,164 km² (836 mi²) and has a population of 1,007,700 (1988 est.). The TRENT is the principal river; the major towns include Nottingham (the county town), Newark, Mansfield, and Worksop. Most of the county is fertile lowland, and the main economic activity is farming. Coal, limestone, and gravel are mined, and there are small petroleum fields at Egmanton and Bothamsell. Textiles, bicycles, drugs, clothing, and tobacco products are manufactured. Occupied in prehistoric times, Nottinghamshire was the site of several Roman settlements and then became part of the kingdom of Mercia. Nottinghamshire came under the Danes by 878. The English Civil War began there in 1642. By the 18th century Nottinghamshire was a center of the textile industry.

Nouakchott

Nouakchott [nwahk-shuht']   Nouakchott, the capital, chief city, and transportation center of Mauritania, is located near the Atlantic coast of Africa. Its population (1987 est., 600,000) has grown rapidly in recent years due to drought in the surrounding countryside, and encroaching sand dunes threaten the city itself. Agricultural products, copper, and petroleum are exported from Nouakchott's deepwater port, completed in 1986. A new city whose construction began in the late 1950s, Nouakchott was selected as the capital in 1957, three years before Mauritania became independent.

noumenon   see KANT, IMMANUEL

noun   see PARTS OF SPEECH

nova

nova   A nova is a VARIABLE STAR whose luminosity suddenly increases by a factor of thousands or tens of thousands. Two or three novas are discovered each year and are named for the constellation and the year in which they appear. By the late 20th century, many hundreds of novas had been observed within our own galaxy, the Milky Way, as well as in extragalactic systems. Although the

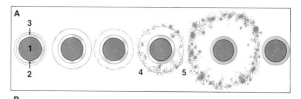

A nova is caused by instability in the outer layer of a star (A). Most stars contain an isothermal core of nitrogen or oxygen (1), surrounded by a layer containing hydrogen (2). Hydrogen atoms in this layer are constantly combining to form helium. If helium production occurs too rapidly, the surface layer (3) expands, creating a brief burst of energy (4, 5). The surplus helium is consumed, and the star returns to its normal size and luminosity. A nova may also be created in a binary system (B), when matter from the atmosphere of an expanding red star (6) passes to the atmosphere of a nearby white dwarf (7), producing a helium surplus in the smaller star.

term *nova* means "new star," novas are actually long-existing stars that suddenly flare into brilliance as seen in the Earth's sky. Novas are celestial phenomena distinct from SUPERNOVAS, which are in fact destructive explosions of massive stars; therefore supernovas, unlike novas, do not recur, because the stellar material has been dispersed by the explosion.

The sudden brightness of a nova occurs when a STAR's surface suddenly explodes, rapidly discharging an expanding shell of gas into space. Though the observed discharge appears spectacular, the star is not destroyed by its outburst. In fact, some novas are recurrent. Only a tiny fraction, perhaps 10^{-7}, of the star's entire mass is lost. Peak brightness tends to occur within 10 to 50 hours. Following a brief peak period, the nova begins to fade, reaching its original luminosity days, months, or perhaps years later. A transition stage early in the fading period is common. During this transition the luminosity may fluctuate between several different levels, drop sharply and then quickly recover, or simply decline gradually and evenly. Fading after the transition stage is characteristically gradual and slow.

Nova Scotia

Nova Scotia [noh'-vuh skoh'-shuh]   Nova Scotia (New Scotland), located on the eastern seaboard of Canada, comprises the Nova Scotia peninsula and CAPE BRETON ISLAND. It is bounded on the northwest by the Bay of FUNDY, on the north by the Gulf of ST. LAWRENCE, sharing only a short boundary with New Brunswick, and on the south, west, and east by the Atlantic Ocean. Nova Scotia has an area of 55,490 km² (21,425 mi²), making it 9th in size among the 10 Canadian provinces; in population it ranks 7th.

One of the first areas of the Western Hemisphere to be

NOVA SCOTIA

Land: Area: 55,490 km^2 (21,425 mi^2); rank: 9th. Capital and largest city: Halifax (1991 pop., 114,455). Municipalities: 66. Elevations: highest—532 m (1,745 ft), in Cape Breton Highlands; lowest—sea level, along the coast.

People: Population (1991): 899,942; rank: 7th; density: 17 persons per km^2 (44.1 per mi^2). Distribution (1991): 53.5% urban, 46.5% rural. Average annual change (1986–91): +0.62%.

Government (1992): Lieutenant Governor: Lloyd Crouse. Premier: Don W. Cameron, Progressive Conservative. Parliament: Senate—10 members; House of Commons—6 Liberals, 4 Progressive Conservatives, 1 Independent. Provincial legislature: 52 members. Admitted to Confederation: July 1, 1867, one of the original four provinces.

Economy (monetary figures in Canadian dollars): Total personal income (1990): $16.2 billion; rank: 7th. Median family income (1990): $39,863. Agriculture: farm cash receipts (1987)—$290.6 million. Fishing: landed value (1989)—$410.8 million. Forestry: lumber production (1988)—223.2 million board feet. Mining: value (1989)— $406.6 million. Manufacturing: value added (1988)— $1.8 billion.

visited by Europeans, Nova Scotia was long a battleground between British and French. Now it has shared in the decline of the traditional fishing and lumbering industries of the MARITIME PROVINCES, although its coal and tidal resources hold promise for the future.

Land and Resources

Geologically, Nova Scotia is part of the APPALACHIAN MOUNTAIN system. The Atlantic Upland—the largest physiographic region, stretching from Yarmouth to eastern Cape Breton—dips gently eastward to the Atlantic Ocean. It is poorly drained with thin, stony soils. The Cape Breton Highlands, Cobequid Mountains, and North Mountain have the highest relief. Lowland areas have been formed by the erosion of softer rocks or by reclamation of tidal marshland. The best agricultural lands are the glacial tills and alluvial soils, especially in the Annapolis Valley.

Short rivers dominate the drainage pattern. The largest watershed, drained by the Shubenacadie River, covers only about 2,600 km^2 (1,000 mi^2). Along the Fundy coast, where tides reach more than 15 m (50 ft), dikes have been constructed along the coast and lower river courses to prevent flooding and to reclaim farmland.

Climate. In winter the area is primarily influenced by Arctic air. The January mean temperature is about –3° C (27° F) in southwestern Nova Scotia, where the coast is influenced by warmer Gulf Stream water, but it decreases inland. The July mean temperature is about 18° C (64° F)

inland but is cooler on the coast. Mean annual precipitation ranges from 635 to more than 1,600 mm (25 to 63 in).

Resources. Forests, principally red spruce and balsam fir, cover nearly 80% of the land surface. Extensive coal deposits occur in Cape Breton and Cumberland counties. Gypsum, salt, and sand and gravel are also abundant. Unmined resources of lead, zinc, silver, celestite, and barite are also found in Nova Scotia. The extensive offshore continental shelf has a wealth of fish resources, proven natural-gas deposits, and potential petroleum reserves. The Bay of Fundy tides have enormous energy potential.

People

Nova Scotia's level of urbanization is lower than Canada's as a whole. Besides HALIFAX (the capital) and DARTMOUTH, the major towns are SYDNEY, Glace Bay, New Glasgow, Amherst, and Truro. English is spoken by 93% of the population and French by about 5%. Leading religious denominations include the Roman Catholic church, the United Church of Canada, as well as Anglicans, Baptists, Presbyterians, and Lutherans.

Halifax, the major center of learning and entertainment, is the site of Dalhousie University, Saint Mary's University, Mount Saint Vincent University, the University of King's College, and the Technical University of Nova Scotia; the Halifax City Regional Library; and a symphony orchestra, a theater, and an arts center.

The province has two national parks—Cape Breton

Highlands and Kejimkujik. The province's former military significance is reflected in restored defensive sites at Fort Anne (ANNAPOLIS ROYAL), Fortress Louisbourg (LOUIS-BOURG), and Citadel Hill (Halifax).

Leading daily newspapers in Nova Scotia include the *Halifax Chronicle-Herald* and its afternoon edition, the *Mail-Star*. Halifax is an important regional television production center.

Economic Activity

The traditional fishing, lumbering, and shipbuilding industries have declined since the 19th century, causing chronic unemployment in Nova Scotia. Leading industries now include coal mining; food and beverage processing; and the production of transportation equipment, paper and allied manufacturing, printed materials, fabricated metal, concrete and glass products, and textiles. Most heavy industry is located in Sydney, in Pictou County, in Halifax-Dartmouth, and on the Strait of Canso. Resource-processing industries produce the most important exports; they include lumber mills and other wood-using firms, pulp and paper plants, and fish-processing and agricultural-products plants.

Coal, the leading mineral, is found mainly in Cape Breton County. Other valuable minerals include salt, gypsum, sand, gravel, and stone. Offshore oil and gas exploration is in progress. In value of fish caught, Nova Scotia is a leading province. Lumbering traditionally has been important to the province's economy. The pulp and paper industry now far outweighs in importance and value the sawtimber industry.

Nova Scotia's leading agricultural activity is dairying.

The Canadian National Railway runs from Halifax to Amherst, and the TRANS-CANADA HIGHWAY has been completed to Sydney on Cape Breton Island. Ferries run from Yarmouth to Portland and Bar Harbor, Maine; across the Bay of Fundy from Digby to Saint John, New Brunswick; from Caribou to Prince Edward Island; and from Halifax and North Sydney to Newfoundland. Commercial airports provide both passenger and freight service. Halifax has maintained preeminence in the handling of cargo.

Government

The federal government appoints a lieutenant governor, but the provincial premier and his cabinet are the actual executive branch. Judges are federally appointed. The 52-member legislative assembly is elected to a maximum 5-year term. The province sends 10 members to the federal Senate and 11 members to the House of Commons.

History

Paleo-Indians inhabited the region about 8000 BC, and the VIKINGS were probably the first Europeans to visit the area. John CABOT is believed to have landed (1497) on Cape Breton Island. The first permanent European settlement was founded in 1605 at Port Royal (near present-day Annapolis Royal) by the French explorers Pierre du Gua, Sieur de MONTS, and Samuel de CHAMPLAIN. Throughout the 17th century, Nova Scotia—part of ACADIA—was a battleground for French and British colonial interests, and control of the region alternated between the

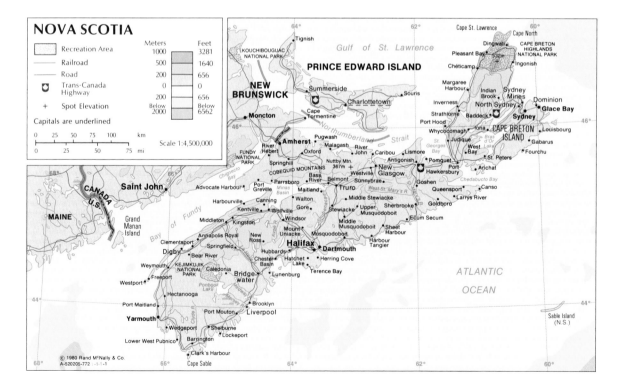

two powers. The French ceded the mainland portion to the British in 1713, and the British gained control over Cape Breton Island in 1763.

In 1755 the British expelled between 6,000 and 10,000 French-speaking Acadians for refusing to take an oath of allegiance to Britain, which included a promise to fight against France.

The establishment of a lucrative lumber and fish trade brought prosperity to the colony and stimulated population growth, so that by 1851 the colony had about 277,000 inhabitants. Following Confederation (1867), the population and economy grew less rapidly as fishing, shipbuilding, ship exporting, and agriculture entered a long period of decline. Today Nova Scotia's weakened economic base is reflected in low incomes and high unemployment.

Novalis [noh-vah'-lis]   Novalis is the pseudonym of Baron Friedrich von Hardenberg, b. May 2, 1772, d. Mar. 25, 1801, the outstanding creative poet of the first generation of German romanticism. The death in 1797 of his beloved, Sophie von Kühn, inspired his *Hymns to the Night* (1800; Eng. trans., 1948), which celebrates the mystical visions he had at her grave. His two narratives, *Henry of Ofterdingen* (Eng. trans., 1964) and *The Novices of Saïs* (Eng. trans., 1949), remained unfinished at his death and were published posthumously in 1802. Both tell of a youth's search, in nature and literature, for the world's inner meaning.

Novara [noh-vah'-rah]   Novara is the capital of Novara province in the Piedmont region of northwestern Italy, on the Agogna River about 45 km (28 mi) west of Milan. The city's population is 102,961 (1988 est.). Novara is an agricultural center, a rail hub, and a flourishing industrial city. Founded by Celts, it later became a Roman colony.

Novatian [noh-vay'-shuhn]   Novatian, *c*.200–*c*.258, a Roman theologian and the first writer of the Western church to use Latin, was an early antipope. He had himself consecrated bishop of Rome in 251 in opposition to Pope Cornelius. Novatian believed that Cornelius was too lenient toward those who had apostatized during the Decian persecution (249–50) and had then requested readmission to the church. Novatian was excommunicated, but his followers formed a schismatic sect that persisted for several centuries. Novatian himself was probably martyred in the persecution of Valerian.

Novaya Zemlya [noh'-vy-uh zim-lee-ah']   The island of Novaya Zemlya ("new land" in Russian), part of Archangel Oblast, USSR, lies in the Arctic Ocean between the Barents and Kara seas. Its total area of about 82,620 km^2 (31,900 mi^2) encompasses the two halves of the dominant island, which has been divided by a glaciated strait, Matochkin Shar. Fishing and fur trapping support small outposts along the deeply indented coastline.

Novaya Zemlya was probably known to Norse sailors and Novgorod hunters in the 11th century, but it was not mapped until the late 18th century. Soviet defense installations were established there after World War II.

novel   The term *novel* now refers to any extended narrative fiction in prose. The SHORT STORY, which usually deals with fewer incidents and characters, is distinguished from the novel primarily by its length. The word *novel* is derived from the Italian *novella,* a compact prose tale somewhat longer than a short story. In many European countries, however, a novel is known as a *roman,* suggesting its connection with the older form, ROMANCE—a narrative of a more legendary, poetic nature.

The Scope of the Novel. The novel evolved from a number of older forms of extended narrative. The most ancient of these, the EPIC, was succeeded in the Middle Ages by the romance. Renaissance verse drama, which represented a growing interest in the real world rather than an ideal, is also among the many antecedents, for the novel usually seeks to re-create everyday experience, to represent the world as it is rather than to evoke, like the romance, a legendary world. A novel may be set within the human mind, in a visionary future state, on a ship or a battlefield, in an aristocratic drawing room or a hovel, in a parliament or a church, in a court of law or a hospital. A novel may concentrate on the development of character while virtually ignoring plot (see NARRATIVE AND DRAMATIC DEVICES), as in some of the writings of James JOYCE and William FAULKNER. It may be carefully plotted in order to imitate the classical structure of TRAGEDY, as in the novels of Thomas HARDY, or to sustain suspense by the gradual disclosure of information, as in the detective stories (see MYSTERY, SUSPENSE, AND DETECTIVE FICTION) of Wilkie COLLINS. It may attempt a detailed portrayal of life and its shaping influences with the detached, objective perspective of science, as in the naturalistic novels of Émile ZOLA, or use the weapon of SATIRE in the hope of bringing about changes in society, as in the novels of Charles DICKENS.

The Origins of the Novel. The earliest narrative prose fiction was probably *Milesiaka,* written by the Greek ARISTIDES in the 2d century BC—a series of tales of his hometown. In Latin a number of works of prose fiction appeared, of which the most important were *The Golden Ass* of APULEIUS, and the *Satyricon* of PETRONIUS ARBITER. During the 3d century AD Longus wrote his *Daphnis and Chloë* (Eng. trans., 1587), a love story in Greek prose, and Heliodorus of Emesa composed a long, realistic love story in prose called *Aethiopica* (trans. as *Ethiopian Story,* 1961). With the appearance of the medieval romances and Italian novellas such as Giovanni BOCCACCIO's DECAMERON, formative influences on the modern novel had come into being.

The earliest prose narratives that can be called novels in the modern sense of the word were PICARESQUE NOVELS—sequences of episodic tales linked only by the presence of the protagonist, a charming rascal who lives by his wits. The great example of this form is Miguel de CERVANTES SAAVEDRA's satire DON QUIXOTE. Picaresque satire is also the mode of Henry FIELDING's earliest full-length

Honoré Daumier's etching of Don Quixote and Sancho Panza delineates the characters of each. Don Quixote de la Mancha (1605–15), Miguel de Cervantes Saavedra's finest work and one of the greatest novels in Western literature, epitomizes the picaresque novel. (Ny Carlsberg, Glyptotek, Copenhagen.)

novel, *Joseph Andrews* (1742). Other 17th- and early-18th-century influences—all of them French—on the English novel include the romances of Madeleine de SCUDÉRY, Paul Scarron's *Le Roman Comique* (The Comic Novel, 1651–57), the Comtesse de LA FAYETTE's *La Princesse de Clèves* (1678), Jean de LA FONTAINE's *Fables* (1668–94), Alain René LESAGE's *Gil Blas* (1715–35), Abbé PRÉVOST's *Manon Lescaut* (1731), and Pierre Carlet de Chamblain de MARIVAUX's *Marianne* (1731–41).

The English Novel. The English novel was quasi-dramatic in form and tragicomic in theme, reflecting Renaissance drama. John BUNYAN's *Life and Death of Mr. Badman* (1680) is printed as though the dialogue were the text of a play; Samuel RICHARDSON's *Pamela* (1740) is preceded by a list of characters. English writers of the 18th century, working in the tradition of classical literature, the romance, the picaresque tale, the novella, and such earlier English prose models as John LYLY's *Euphues* (1579), Sir Philip SIDNEY's *Arcadia* (1590), Aphra BEHN's *Oroonoko* (1688), and Bunyan's PILGRIM'S PROGRESS, discovered the form of the novel as it is known today.

Daniel DEFOE's ROBINSON CRUSOE and *Moll Flanders* (1722) are the first novels of incident in English; Samuel Richardson's *Pamela* (1740) and *Clarissa* (1747–48), the first novels of character. The latter are epistolary novels: the narrative consists entirely of an exchange of letters. The first great flowering of the English novel began with *Pamela* and ended three decades later with the publication of Tobias SMOLLETT's *Humphrey Clinker* and the death of Laurence STERNE, author of TRISTRAM SHANDY. Of the four leading novelists of these years, the most enduringly popular was Henry Fielding. His masterpiece, TOM JONES, appeared in 1749.

After the deaths of Fielding, Richardson, Sterne and Smollett, only the work of Oliver GOLDSMITH, Fanny BURNEY, and Ann RADCLIFFE stands out from the mass of GOTHIC ROMANCES, trivial novels of manners, and theological treatises dressed up as fiction. During the late 18th and early 19th centuries another kind of fiction came into vogue, the novel of sensibility. It stressed the importance of emotional consciousness and cultivated the capacity to be moved by the pathetic. Morbid sensibility—stimulated for its own sake as an end in itself—was the logical result of such a development, and when Jane AUSTEN wrote *Sense and Sensibility* (1811) it was in part to lampoon the cultivation of sentiment.

The 19th-Century English, French, and Russian Novel. Jane Austen and Sir Walter SCOTT were contemporaries, but while Scott was the most popular novelist in the world, Austen's novels remained obscure. He used the broad canvas of Scottish, English, and French history for his subject, while she focused on the restricted life of provincial towns and rural families. During the last hundred years, however, Scott's reputation has declined, whereas many regard Austen as the first modern novelist.

Austen died at a time when the writers who made the 19th century throughout Europe into the golden age of the novel were just coming into existence. Dickens, William Makepeace THACKERAY, Anthony TROLLOPE, Charlotte Brontë (see BRONTË family), and George ELIOT were all born within eight years of one another during the second decade of the century. Despite their individuality, they were primarily novelists of manners, chroniclers of their era, and instinctive proponents of artistic realism. The later Victorian novelists—Samuel BUTLER (1835–1902), George MEREDITH, Thomas Hardy, and George Robert GISSING, for example—felt less comfortable with their time and its values and questioned many of its basic assumptions. Hardy so outraged conventional opinion as to impel a bishop to burn *Jude the Obscure* (1895).

Identification with their time distinguishes the early Victorian novelists not only from their successors in England but also from many of their great European contemporaries. STENDHAL, Honoré de BALZAC, and Gustave FLAUBERT in France and Nikolai GOGOL, Ivan TURGENEV, Fyodor Mikhailovich DOSTOYEVSKY, and Count Leo TOLSTOI in Russia were far more radical and skeptical of the inevitability of poetic justice for all.

In terms of technique, the work of George Eliot, even more than that of Dickens or Hardy, was of seminal importance in the 19th century. An admirer of Jane Austen, Eliot extended the psychological possibilities of the novel further than her predecessor. Eliot's novels had a pro-

George Cruikshank's The Battle Royal in the Churchyard illustrates a mid-19th-century edition of Henry Fielding's comic novel Tom Jones (1749). Considered Fielding's masterpiece, this work exemplifies his theory of the novel as a "comic epic poem in prose."

Before the Murder, *one of Fritz Eichenberg's wood-cuts for a 1948 edition of Dostoyevsky's* Crime and Punishment (1866), *depicts Raskolnikov's mounting tension and desperation as he prepares to commit his crime. The psychological acuity and philosophical complexity of* Crime and Punishment *are characteristic of both Dostoyevsky and late-19th-century European novelists in general.*

found influence on Henry JAMES, who admired and imitated Eliot's psychological penetration while rejecting her assumption that fiction must teach morality by example or, as Trollope put it, take the place of the preacher in the pulpit. Eliot responded to European influences, but it was not until the 1880s, in the work of Meredith, Hardy, Gissing, and others, that continental fiction began to affect the English novel; by this time Zola had developed his influential theory of literary NATURALISM.

The American Novel. The American novel had come into being during the later 18th and early 19th centuries in the tales of Charles Brockden BROWN, the adventure stories of James Fenimore COOPER, and the mysteries of Edgar Allan POE. Cooper and Washington IRVING were the first American writers to achieve an international reputation, but the American novel came to maturity in the mid-19th century. Nathaniel HAWTHORNE, the greatest American romancer, published THE SCARLET LETTER in 1850, *The House of the Seven Gables* in 1851, and *The Blithedale Romance* in 1852; Herman MELVILLE, the greatest American allegorist, published his masterpiece, MOBY-DICK, in 1851. In the latter half of the 19th century the American novel, as written by James, Mark TWAIN, William Dean HOWELLS, and Stephen CRANE, equaled the achievements of English and European fiction.

Henry James. Taking Balzac, Flaubert, and George Eliot as his literary models and feeling that the United States offered too little cultural background and history for a writer to build on, James settled in England in the 1880s and lived there for the last 30 years of his life, producing several major novels. Ultimately following him into European exile, mostly for similar reasons, were such American writers as Edith WHARTON, Henry ADAMS, Gertrude STEIN, and T. S. ELIOT. No one could have been more attuned to the subtleties of the American character and American life than Twain, among whose many novels TOM SAWYER and HUCK-LEBERRY FINN have attained classic status. Few novels could be more different from one another than James's *Portrait of a Lady* and Twain's *Huck Finn,* written just a few years apart; yet each in its way exemplifies American realism,

and both testify to the independence of American fiction from the European tradition.

James's influence as novelist and critic is perhaps seen most clearly in the subtlety and care lavished on the novelist's craft by such 20th-century writers as James Joyce, Thomas MANN, Virginia WOOLF, and William Faulkner. James's greatest interest was in "point of view"—the perspective from which the novelist tells a story. Like Flaubert—the only other 19th-century novelist to write with depth and subtlety of the novel's theoretical concerns—James believed that the novelist should not obtrude into the narrative, that inconspicuousness would preserve the "air of reality." The novelist, James said, is not a romancer, as Hawthorne believed, but rather a historian, the biographer of his characters. To refer to other times, as in the historical novel, or to promulgate moral or social beliefs, preaching openly in the manner of Thackeray, Trollope, or George Eliot, is to remind the reader that the world of the novel is not the real world.

The earliest criticism of the novel concerned itself mainly with the moral implications of technique—with how to tell a story so that it would have the most salutary effect on its readers. Samuel JOHNSON felt that fiction ought to offer models of conduct. He was interested in art as a didactic medium and in the artist as instrument of moral instruction. Formal REALISM—the attempt to transcribe real life—was seen in the 18th century and well into the 19th as a means to alert the reader to the moral value of experience. Most Victorian novelists did not substantially differ from their Augustan predecessors in their preoccupation with the pedagogical value of art. Even Hardy, so often at odds with his time and its habits of mind, felt that the "true object" of reading fiction "is a lesson in life, mental enlargement from elements essential to the narratives themselves and from the reflections they engender."

With the critical writings of Flaubert and James the theory of the novel—and thus the novel itself—began to take a different tack. The novelist, they believed, should not be partisan, didactic, or obtrusive. Art should be imper-

Norman Rockwell's illustration for an edition of Mark Twain's The Adventures of Tom Sawyer (1876) *shows Tom embarking on a scheme to avoid whitewashing his aunt's fence.*

sonal. Flaubert's great interest, like James's, was in style and form; for Flaubert a novel could be aesthetically great regardless of its subject matter. At the beginning of the second half of the 19th century the notion of literature as a representation of existing reality was first questioned. Instead, literature began to assume autonomy as a creation of the artist's consciousness—self-referring and self-sustaining—no longer an imitation of life but a substitute for it.

The Modern Novel. Modern novelists have generally been less concerned with moral purpose than with abstract qualities of composition. Literary realism has attempted to represent mental states rather than to imitate the exterior world. James, insisting on psychological analysis of characters through dramatic form, on avoiding philosophical partisanship, and on the unobtrusiveness of the writer, set the standards. Aesthetic problems have certainly been a main concern of many of the 20th century's most important novelists. Marcel PROUST, Thomas Mann, James Joyce, Virginia Woolf, William Faulkner, and Albert CAMUS have indulged in technical experimentation, especially in the manipulation of time sequence, point of view, and symbols. The STREAM OF CONSCIOUSNESS novel, characteristic of the modern desire to probe the interior life of characters, is best exemplified by James Joyce's ULYSSES.

The work of such masters of the 20th-century English and American novel as Elizabeth BOWEN, F. Scott FITZGERALD, E. M. FORSTER, and Ernest HEMINGWAY has had surprisingly little effect on the mainstream of popular fiction.

The works of Cervantes, Richardson, and Dickens were best-sellers at the time of their publication, but this is rarely true of innovative modern novels. Among contemporary American novelists, Saul BELLOW, John DOS PASSOS, John HAWKES, Joseph HELLER, Norman MAILER, Bernard MALAMUD, Thomas PYNCHON, Philip ROTH, and J. D. SALINGER have reached wide audiences. Of these writers, however, only Mailer and Pynchon have made notable experiments with form, and one of the most popular modern novelists, Aleksandr SOLZHENITSYN, uses conventional narrative techniques.

This illustration by Henri Matisse was created for a 1935 edition of James Joyce's Ulysses *(1922). Considered a masterpiece of world literature, Ulysses revolutionized the subject and style of modern fiction. The book was banned in the United States until 1933.*

Since the publication of Proust's *À la Recherche du temps perdu* (1913–27) and Joyce's *Ulysses*, enormous changes have taken place in narrative technique, and writers of experimental fiction have shown comparatively little interest in the material world. In the writing of Hermann BROCH, Michel BUTOR, Albert Camus, Alain ROBBE-GRILLET, Franz KAFKA, Jean Paul SARTRE, and Virginia Woolf, reality is stylized or used merely as a setting for the novel's primary subject: the process of the individual consciousness. The passage of time has become, since the work of Proust, a major preoccupation of the novel. This ancient problem—the relation between fictional and real time—is at least as old as *Tristram Shandy,* but it is posed more urgently by Thomas Mann in *The Magic Mountain* and continues to engage many contemporary writers, who can no longer display Henry Fielding's confidence in the novelist's capacity to invent reality and whose search for new forms of expression reflects their desire to use the novel as an epistemological instrument.

———

novella and novelette [noh-vel'-uh]   The Italian word *novella*, meaning "tidings" or "news," referred during the Middle Ages to realistic, humorous, and frequently bawdy tales. In the hands of 14th- and 15th-century Italian writers such as Giovanni BOCCACCIO, Franco Sacchetti (*c.*1330–1400), and Matteo Bandello (*c.*1485–1561) the popular novella became an artful short tale of great literary distinction. The first writer of novellas in English was Geoffrey CHAUCER, who, like Boccaccio, wrote a collection of short narratives around a central theme in The CANTERBURY TALES. Italian novellas, like the closely related rhymed French FABLIAUX, were widely read in England, and several were used by William Shakespeare as sources for his plays.

By the late 19th century the novella, also known as novelette or by its French name *nouvelle*, had become a prose form. The novella has no strict formal characteristics and is best defined as a prose narrative longer than a SHORT STORY but shorter than a novel. Henry JAMES, who wrote of the "ideal, the beautiful and blest nouvelle," was attracted to the demanding constraints of the form and endowed it with the psychological complexity of his novels—*Daisy Miller* is among his finer works. Other notable novellas in English include Herman MELVILLE's *Billy Budd*, Joseph Conrad's HEART OF DARKNESS, and William FAULKNER's *The Bear*. Notable European examples of the form include Franz Kafka's *The Trial* and Thomas MANN's *Death in Venice*.

———

Noverre, Jean Georges [noh-vair']   The French choreographer and ballet reformer Jean Georges Noverre, b. Apr. 29, 1727, d. Oct. 19, 1810, was one of the first to realize the expressive and dramatic possibilities of ballet. His famous *Letters on Dance and Ballets* (1760; Eng. trans., 1930) urged more natural gestures, less exaggerated costumes, and the abolition of masks then worn by male dancers. Ignored in Paris, Noverre became ballet master at the Württemberg Ducal Theater in Stuttgart in 1760, creating his most important works, such as *Medée et Jason*

(1763), for that company. In Vienna from 1767 to 1774, he staged more than 50 ballets; he was finally named ballet master at the Paris Opéra in 1776. Noverre created 150 ballets and introduced the *ballet d'action* (narrative ballet).

Novgorod [nohv'-guh-ruht]   Novgorod is a city in Russia, a republic of the USSR. It is situated on the Volkhov River, just north of Lake Ilmen, in northwest European Russia. The population is 224,000 (1986 est.). One of the oldest Russian cities, Novgorod had an industrial rebirth in the 1960s, when it was selected as the site of one of the USSR's largest nitrogen fertilizer complexes. Because of Novgorod's long history, tourism is also important. A distinctive style of architecture flourished there from the 11th to the early 16th century. Among the structures that have been preserved are the kremlin, or walled fortress, and the Cathedral of Saint Sophia.

Novgorod was first mentioned in written chronicles dating from 859. It was then a settlement on a major north-south inland water trade route and a center of crafts industry and commerce. It was one of the most powerful Russian principalities, with a domain extending over most of northern Russia. Under Prince ALEXANDER NEVSKY, Novgorod defeated the Swedes on the Neva River in 1240 and the Teutonic Knights on icy Lake Peipus in 1242. After the rise of Moscow, Novgorod was merged in 1478 with the new Russian state. The city was badly damaged during World War II but has been rebuilt.

Novi Sad [noh'-vee sahd]   Novi Sad, a city in Serbia, Yugoslavia, is a major port on the Danube River located about 95 km (60 mi) south of Hungary and an equal distance west of Romania. The population is 170,800 (1981). A market center for a coal-mining and farming region, Novi Sad produces agricultural machinery, vegetable oil, pharmaceuticals, textiles, and ceramics. Novi Sad was settled c.1690 and served as an Austrian defense post against the Ottoman Turks during the 18th century. It was a leading political and cultural center of Serbs until World War I.

Novocain   see PROCAINE

Novosibirsk [noh-vuh-si-beersk']   Novosibirsk, the largest city in Siberia, is located in Russia, a republic of the USSR. It is situated at the junction of the Trans-Siberian Railroad and the Ob River in southwestern Siberia. The population is 1,436,000 (1989 est.).

Novosibirsk is a major manufacturing center, with a wide range of machinery plants, electronics factories, a tin smelter, and perfumeries. It is also an important educational and scientific research center. The USSR's largest opera house is located there.

The town was founded in 1896 in connection with construction of the Trans-Siberian Railroad and was originally called Novonikolayevsk (for Emperor Nicholas II). The present name dates from 1925 and means "new Si-

beria." Novosibirsk grew rapidly because of its favorable location near the KUZNETSK BASIN, the largest coal source in the USSR, and on major transportation lines.

NOW   see NATIONAL ORGANIZATION FOR WOMEN

Noyce, Robert   The scientist and entrepreneur Robert Norton Noyce, b. Burlington, Iowa, Dec. 12, 1927, d. June 3, 1990, was an inventor of the INTEGRATED CIRCUIT and played a large role in the development of the American electronics industry. Noyce earned a Ph.D. at the Massachusetts Institute of Technology and became a founder of Fairchild Semiconductor Company in 1957. There, in 1959, he worked out the design of an electronic network contained in a semiconducting chip; the same idea occurred independently that same year to Jack Kirby of Texas Instruments. Noyce and Kirby were both granted patents.

Noyes, John Humphrey [noyz]   An American religious radical and social reformer, John Humphrey Noyes, b. Brattleboro, Vt., Sept. 3, 1811, d. Apr. 13, 1886, founded experimental utopian communities that achieved a high degree of material success. While studying theology in the early 1830s, he became convinced of human perfectibility and of his own state of sinlessness. In Putney, Vt., Noyes established a community of Bible Communists who sought to spread the doctrine of perfectionism. After instituting the practice of free love within the community, he fled to central New York to escape prosecution for adultery. There, in 1848, he founded the ONEIDA COMMUNITY. Noyes established a eugenics program and promoted various lucrative enterprises at Oneida. In 1879, his authority waning, Noyes discarded Oneida's free-love system and moved to Canada to avoid prosecution.

Nu, U [noo, oo]   The Burmese statesman U Nu (formerly Thakin Nu), b. May 25, 1907, served as the first prime minister of independent Burma in 1948–58 and again in 1960–62. He was overthrown by the military leader U NE WIN in 1962 and kept in custody until 1966. In exile in Thailand, Nu organized (1969) a revolutionary movement against Ne Win. Forced to leave (1973) Thailand, Nu was allowed to return to Burma in 1980 after years in exile and joined the opposition during the 1988 uprising.

Nubia [noo'-bee-uh]   Nubia was a region of ancient northeastern Africa between the Nile's First Cataract, the confluence of the White Nile and Blue Nile (near present Khartoum), the Red Sea, and the Libyan desert. The ancient Egyptians occupied its northern area intermittently from about the 20th century to the 8th century BC and strongly influenced its culture. In the late 8th and early 7th centuries, Nubia, known to the Egyptians as CUSH, with its capital at Napata, ruled Egypt. In 671 the Assyrians invaded Egypt and soon after drove the Cushites back into Nubia. The Egyptians destroyed Napata in 590, but the Cushites established a new capital at MEROË and maintained an independent kingdom until about AD 350. In the 6th century AD, Nubia was Christianized, and it remained so until it was overrun by the Muslim Mamelukes of Egypt in the 14th century.

Nubian Desert [noo'-bee-uhn] The Nubian Desert, located in northeastern Sudan between the Red Sea and the Nile River, covers about 250,000 km² (97,000 mi²). A rocky plateau with a base of sandstone over granite and gneiss, it reaches its highest point (2,259 m/7,412 ft) at Jebel Oda in the east. Wadis form after the scanty rains, less than 125 mm (5 in) annually. The region has little vegetation and is sparsely populated.

---

nuclear energy Nuclear energy refers to the energy consumed or produced in modifying the composition of the atomic nucleus. This fundamental form of energy provides the ATOMIC BOMB and HYDROGEN BOMB with their enormous explosive force. It also produces power for electricity-generating plants throughout the world. Nuclear energy is seen by many as the source of inexpensive, clean power; but, because of the hazardous radiation emitted in producing that power and the RADIOACTIVITY of the materials used, others feel that it may not be a viable energy alternative to the use of fossil fuels or solar energy.

This article discusses the science involved in the release of nuclear energy, and the use of that science by the industries that produce electric power. The process by which nuclear-based electricity is produced is examined in NUCLEAR REACTOR, as are some of the safety issues. The by-products of nuclear energy production are described in NUCLEAR WASTE.

Basic Scientific Definitions

The processes that change the state or composition of matter are inevitably accompanied by the consumption or production of energy. Common processes such as combustion produce energy by the chemical rearrangement of atoms or molecules. For example, the combustion of methane (natural gas) releases 8 electron volts (eV). The electron volt is a unit of energy used by nuclear physicists and represents the gain in kinetic energy when an electron is accelerated through a potential drop of one volt.

The most well-known nuclear reaction is fission, in which a heavy nucleus combines with a neutron and separates into two other, lighter nuclei. A typical fission reaction using uranium-235 involves the combination of one neutron with uranium-235 to yield isotopes of strontium and xenon, 2 neutrons, and energy. The energy release in this case is about 200 million eV, a factor of 25 million greater than the combustion reaction of methane. (See FISSION, NUCLEAR.)

Another important nuclear reaction is fusion, in which two light elements combine to form a heavier atom, again with the release of enormous amounts of energy (see FUSION, NUCLEAR).

Nuclear power plants harness the enormous energy re-

leases from nuclear reactions for large-scale energy production. In a modern coal plant the combustion of one pound of coal produces about 1 kilowatt hour (kW h) of electric energy. The fissioning of one pound of uranium in a modern nuclear power plant produces about 3 million kW h of electric energy. It is the incredible energy density (energy per unit mass) that makes nuclear energy sources of such interest.

At present, only the fission process is used in the commercial production of energy, usually to make electricity, but also occasionally to produce steam for district heating or industrial applications. Fusion research has not yet produced a feasible power production technology.

Development of Fission Technology

The discovery of the fission process occurred in the late 1930s, the result of a long sequence of nuclear physics studies. The German scientists Otto HAHN and Fritz Strassman reported on an experiment involving neutron irradiation of uranium in early 1939. Subsequently, Otto Frisch and Lise MEITNER interpreted the experiment as the fissioning of uranium into lighter elements. The possibility of a self-sustaining chain reaction was apparent, and provided added impetus for accelerated research.

Secret government research into the military applications of nuclear fission began with World War II (see MANHATTAN PROJECT). The development of a weapon required that a self-sustaining fission reaction could be created and, further, that an adequate amount of fissionable material could be produced for use in a weapon. Both of these aspects were major undertakings, but they ended with a successful atomic bomb.

The concept of an energy source that promised extended naval voyages without refueling was also investigated. Under the direction of Hyman RICKOVER, a naval reactor program began in the late 1940s, and the first nuclear submarine, the NAUTILUS, was launched in 1954. An outstanding success, it proved the merits of nuclear propulsion for naval vessels. Its reactor was the prototype for the first commercial nuclear power plant, built in Shippingport, Pa., in 1957.

The decision to declassify much nuclear-related information in order to foster peaceful applications was made by President Dwight D. Eisenhower in 1953. Other nations joined in the search for peaceful uses for the atom, and the first international conference on nuclear energy was held in Geneva in 1955. In the United States the Atomic Energy Commission—founded in 1946 to oversee civilian uses of nuclear power—sponsored research on a host of reactor concepts that led to the birth of the civilian industry. Britain entered into the production of nuclear-fueled electricity in 1956. The first Soviet nuclear power plant came on line in 1954, and the French began construction of their first commercial plants in 1957. By the early 1960s nuclear power had been established as a viable commercial energy source.

Nuclear Energy Today

In the 50 years since the discovery of fission, nuclear power has become a major source of the world's electric energy. At the beginning of the 1990s there were 416 nuclear plants operating worldwide, generating about 17% of the world's electricity, with about another 130 in the design or construction stages. Nuclear plants operate in 27 nations, and 5 additional nations have them under construction.

The nuclear energy program in the United States is the world's largest: 108 operating plants (1989) have a capacity of about 100,000 MW and provide nearly 20% of U.S. power generation. Nuclear power is now the second largest source of U.S. electricity, exceeded only by coal, which provides about 55% of the country's electricity. Other contributors to electric generation include natural gas (9%), oil (6%), and hydropower (9%). The nuclear contribution is expected to reach about 25% during the 1990s. (See ENERGY SOURCES.)

Because few of the industrialized nations have adequate fossil-fuel resources, nuclear power has become an important source of supply for them as well. In addition, the dramatic increase in oil prices in the 1970s stimulated large investments in nuclear power.

In general, nuclear plants are more complex and costly to build than plants using fossil fuels; the cost of fuel, however, is significantly lower. On balance, the fuel-cost difference is such that nuclear electricity is cheaper than fossil electricity for most nations. For the industrialized countries of Europe and Asia the difference in cost may be as large as a factor of two.

The French Nuclear Program. The French nuclear program was begun in the 1940s, in order to create nuclear weapons capability. As in the U.S. program, the first French reactors were built for plutonium production. The first French commercial units, which used air as a coolant, were in operation by 1957. Their operation was a technical, but not an economic, success. As a result, in 1970, the French adopted the U.S. light-water technology. Subsequently, the French have built 54 domestic reactors, with 9 more under construction. The French standardized their designs to improve the efficiency of construction and operation. They have also built units for Belgium, South Africa, South Korea, and China.

The Japanese Nuclear Program. The Japanese also have a vigorous and successful nuclear program. Lacking any significant indigenous energy resources, in 1955 the Japanese government selected nuclear power as its major electric-supply technology. The program has carefully nurtured the internal capability to manufacture equipment and construct nuclear plants, to operate a high-quality power system, and to provide complete technology for the entire fuel cycle. The utilities in Japan have become leaders in plant operation; and by 2020 the nuclear-fueled portion of Japan's electric supply is expected to exceed 50%. In the future the Japanese plan to exploit the potential of BREEDER REACTORS, which convert nonfissionable U-238 into fissionable plutonium-239. A successful breeder reactor program could eliminate Japan's need to import any fuels for the production of electricity. To date, however, the cost of electricity from breeders exceeds the cost from conventional light-water reactors. The Japanese long-range policy assumes that uranium fuel will ultimately become scarce, making the breeder technology economical.

The Slowdown in Other National Programs. Nuclear power programs in most other countries have come to a virtual standstill. (In the United States there has not been an order for a new plant since the mid-1970s.) A major cause has been the move toward increased efficiency in the consumption of oil, and a drop in energy demand. Equally significant have been concerns about the safety of nuclear reactors, and an increasing awareness of the problems created by nuclear waste.

Public opinion remained largely favorable toward nuclear energy until the Three Mile Island (TMI) reactor accident in the spring of 1979, which caused a historic shift in attitudes toward nuclear power. The accident also had serious impacts on the licensing of new plants. Regulations were drastically modified to prevent a recurrence of the events of TMI. The modifications complicated the construction of new plants as well as the operation of existing plants. Construction times expanded from about 6 years to more than 12 years, and plant costs accelerated rapidly because of the new requirements.

Another factor contributing to the stagnation of new construction was the intervention by antinuclear groups in licensing proceedings for new plants. Such intervention has proven to be time consuming and costly to the industry, particularly for those plants in the late stages of construction, when interest costs mount on the billions that have been borrowed.

Although few other countries permit the extent of public intervention in licensing hearings that is allowed in the United States, all the major nuclear nations impose strict regulations on their nuclear energy programs. Nevertheless, studies indicate that, for the most part, the U.S. industry performs far less efficiently than do those in Switzerland, West Germany, France, and Japan. A key factor in their superior performance may be the cooperation that exists between the industries and their suppliers and regulators—a cooperation that, until recently, was not apparent in the United States.

In its early years, nuclear power was cost competitive with coal. Some of the cheapest sources of electricity in the United States today are nuclear plants built in the period before TMI. The current environment, however, has made nuclear power an uneconomical choice for U.S. utilities.

Chernobyl. The accident in April 1986 at the CHERNOBYL plant in the USSR was as devastating as a nuclear accident can be. A very large amount of radioactive material—between 30% and 50% of the total material in the reactor—was released. Radioactive fallout from the event spread, forcing the long-term evacuation of over 100,000 local people and causing the pollution of foods in large portions of Europe.

The Chernobyl reactor design uses water as a coolant and graphite as the moderator. This type of reactor is known to be hazardous and is used only in the USSR. (Such a design would not be licensed in the Western nations.) Nevertheless, like Three Mile Island, the accident has profoundly influenced worldwide public acceptance of nuclear power. It is too early to know whether or not the Chernobyl accident has permanently crippled the future of nuclear power in industrialized countries.

nuclear family The nuclear FAMILY, also known as the elementary, or conjugal, family, is a group linked by ties of marriage, the parent-child tie, and siblinghood. It consists of a man, a woman, and their socially recognized children, who may be their natural or their adopted offspring. The nuclear family includes only primary relatives (mother-wife, father-husband, son, daughter, brother, sister) and consists of only two generations. It is geographically mobile and is most characteristic of societies whose mode of subsistence puts a premium on mobility, notably hunter-gatherer societies and modern industrial societies. The nuclear family is not universal. Some societies favor the EXTENDED FAMILY, a form of the family or household group that is larger than the nuclear family. Within this larger structure the nuclear family then becomes an unacknowledged unit.

nuclear magnetic resonance Nuclear magnetic resonance is a phenomenon that is displayed by the nuclei of many kinds of atoms. When these atoms are placed in a static magnetic field and are subjected to electromagnetic radiation, the nuclei absorb the radiation's energy at certain frequencies characteristic of each atom. When materials are treated in this way, analyses of their absorption spectra can provide information for use in many fields of science. Chemists have employed NMR SPECTROSCOPY for several decades in studies of compounds and reactions. NMR imaging has become an important medical diagnostic technique.

nuclear medicine The use of isotopic or radioactive tracers to diagnose or treat disease is the branch of RADIOLOGY known as nuclear medicine. These radiographic techniques are valuable aids to and sometimes superior to X rays. Because of the very small amounts of radioactive substance utilized, patient exposure to radiation is usually minimal.

Both diagnostic studies and radiotherapeutic treatments may be performed using radioactive materials in a variety of pharmaceutical forms. Tiny amounts of compounds "tagged" with radioactive isotopes are introduced into the body either orally or by injection into a vein. These substances travel through the bloodstream to the specific organ or type of tissue being evaluated. The radiation that is released by the isotopes is detected by devices called scintillation cameras. Computers convert the data from these cameras to images that allow visualization of parts of organs that are not usually seen by normal X rays. By tracking how and where the radioactive compounds go, the nuclear-medicine physician is able to gain information about biological processes, such as in a heart scan, which determines if any areas of the heart are not receiving sufficient amounts of blood. Also, a therapeutic dose of radiation can be delivered to a specific organ for treatment.

Some examinations involve collecting specimens of blood, stool, or urine and measuring the radioactivity in them. In a RADIOIMMUNOASSAY a radioactive substance is placed in a blood sample to detect minute amounts of specific substances, such as antigens or hormones.

nuclear physics Nuclear physics is the study of the properties of the atomic nucleus (see ATOM). The nucleus, centrally located in the atom and surrounded by electrons, is composed of NEUTRONS and PROTONS, which current theory holds are themselves composed of QUARKS (see FUNDAMENTAL PARTICLES). Collectively called nucleons, they are bound tightly by the strong nuclear force (see FUNDAMENTAL INTERACTIONS). The experimental tools of nuclear physics are particle ACCELERATORS and DETECTORS. Applications include NUCLEAR ENERGY (see also FISSION, NUCLEAR; FUSION, NUCLEAR), nuclear weapons, and the use of radioisotopes in industry and medicine (see NUCLEAR MEDICINE; RADIOLOGY).

Nuclear Properties. A specific kind of nucleus is designated by writing $^A_Z X$. Here X is the chemical symbol of the element, Z is the ATOMIC NUMBER (the number of protons in the nucleus), and A is the MASS NUMBER (the combined number of protons and neutrons). Nuclei with the same number of protons but different numbers of neutrons are called ISOTOPES of one another. Nuclei containing certain numbers of protons or neutrons are particularly stable. The values of these numbers, called magic numbers, are 2, 8, 20, 28, 50, 82, and 126.

The properties of a nucleus include MASS, charge, size, shape, spin, and MAGNETIC MOMENT. The positive charge on the proton is of exactly the same magnitude as the negative charge on the electron. The mass of a nucleus is approximately the sum of the free masses of its particles. The attractive nuclear force, however, causes a small decrease in mass, called the MASS DEFECT (see BINDING ENERGY). The size of a nucleus is determined by bombarding it with some other particle and measuring its CROSS-SECTION by the probability of collision. The radius of a nucleus has been determined to be about $1.3 \times 10^{-13} A^{1/3}$ cm, where A is the mass number.

Neutrons and protons have spins, and their motions within the nucleus may contribute orbital angular momentum. The orbital angular momenta and spins of the nucleons combine according to the rules of QUANTUM MECHANICS to give the total spin of the nucleus. The rotation of the electrical charge of the nucleus creates a magnetic field. The field's strength is the magnetic moment of the nucleus. A nucleus is usually approximately spherical in shape, but some are ellipsoidal.

Nuclear Structure. The motions of the particles within a nucleus determine its properties. They cannot be calculated exactly, so physicists have invented simplified models from which properties can be predicted. One model assumes that the nucleus is similar to a charged liquid drop. The mass of a given isotope is primarily the sum of the free masses of its nucleons. Corrections are calculated for the nuclear binding, the surface tension of the drop, and the electrostatic repulsion of the protons in the nucleus, taking note also of the excess of neutrons over protons, and whether the nucleon number is odd or even. The resulting formula can be adjusted to fit closely all the measured masses of the known isotopes.

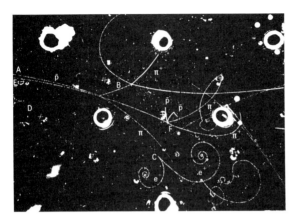

In a bubble chamber, an antiproton (A) and a proton (B) collide and are annihilated, leaving pions π^+ and π^-, a π^0 particle, and two photons. Electrons e^- and positrons e^+ collide at C to create a photon. Electron and positron orbits are seen at D. Particle (E) decays at F into two antiprotons and two pions π^+.

Some nucleus properties are explained by the shell model, which assumes that each nucleon moves in an average field created by all the other nucleons. Its permitted orbits, or energy levels, are then calculated by quantum mechanics.

Energy levels of some nuclei exhibit patterns of regularity. In the collective model of the nucleus, these properties are assumed to be determined by the motion of the nucleus as a whole. Finally, the unified model of the nucleus combines the effects of the collective and shell models to provide more comprehensive agreement with experimental observation.

Nuclear Reactions. When nuclei collide, the interaction may result in products different from the initial nuclei. The total momentum and angular momentum, however, must remain the same after the reaction. The total number of nucleons also remains unchanged, as does the total electric charge (see CONSERVATION, LAWS OF). A small but significant amount of mass (up to 1%) may be transformed into energy, or vice versa, during a reaction, but the total mass-energy is conserved as well. The conversion factor for mass into energy is the square of the velocity of light, as in $E = mc^2$, where c is the velocity—an extremely large number (see RELATIVITY).

In Niels BOHR's model of nuclear reactions, a bombarding particle penetrates a nucleus to form an intermediate compound nucleus that lasts only long enough for the energy and momentum of the incident particle to be shared among all the nucleons. In the direct interaction model, the incident particle is assumed to pass through the target nucleus relatively freely and to interact directly with only one or a small number of nucleons. The struck particle is ejected from the nucleus, and the incident particle may also reemerge.

Nuclear Forces. The strong nuclear force, carried only by the neutron and proton, is the strongest force known in nature. Its range is about one fermi, a distance of 10^{-13} cm. It weakens rapidly with distance and has little effect more than a few fermis from a nucleus. On the other hand, at distances smaller than about 0.4 fermi it becomes strongly repulsive. This region, called the hard core of the strong nuclear force, is responsible for the constant density of nuclear matter.

The weak nuclear force is involved in nuclear decay processes and in interactions involving the fundamental particles called NEUTRINOS. No complete theory combining the fundamental forces has yet been developed, but current theoretical work in particle physics is attempting to devise GRAND UNIFICATION THEORIES that will do so.

nuclear reactor   A nuclear reactor is a device in which a controlled nuclear fission chain reaction takes place. The fission reaction is initiated by the absorption of a neutron in a heavy nucleus, such as uranium-235 (U-235). The process produces additional neutrons that can be used to induce further fissions, thereby propagating the chain reaction. When the reactor materials are appropriately adjusted, it is possible for the chain reaction to be self-sustaining. Such a reaction, and the reactor itself, is called "critical." If there are insufficient neutrons being produced to sustain the process, then the reaction is "subcritical." Conversely, if too many neutrons are being produced, the reaction rate increases with time and the reaction is called "supercritical" (see NUCLEAR ENERGY).

Nuclear reactors are most commonly used to produce electric energy, although they are occasionally used as sources of thermal energy for heating. They are also designed as sources of neutrons used in research, or for the transmutation of elements. Reactors designed to produce materials for nuclear weapons by transmutation are called production reactors.

Energy from Fission

The energy released in the fission process takes several forms. Almost 85% of the energy produced is kinetic energy of the fission fragments. About 3% appears as the kinetic energy of the neutrons released, and another 3% as gamma-ray energy. All of the energy from these sources is released immediately and can be recovered from the reactor. A small amount of energy, about 5%, is carried away by neutrinos, which do not interact readily with matter. This fraction of the energy is lost from the reactor. Finally, about 6% of the total energy is obtained from the decay of radioactive fission fragments. This delayed source of energy plays a significant role in the safety of nuclear reactors. Long after the fission process has been shut off, the inventory of accumulated fission products will continue to produce energy, heating the reactor as it does so. Thus, it is essential to cool a reactor after shutdown.

Light-Water Reactors

The typical U.S. power reactor is termed a light-water reactor (LWR) because it uses water in the form of H_2O as a moderator and coolant. Another type of power reactor uses a type of water in which the hydrogen has been replaced by deuterium (D_2O) as a moderator; it is called a heavy-water reactor.

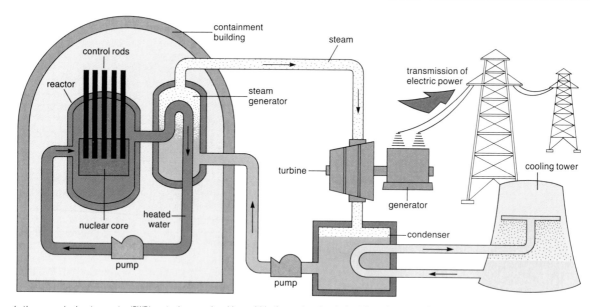

In the pressurized water reactor (PWR), water in an enclosed loop within the reactor absorbs heat from the energy of nuclear fission and becomes intensely hot. Because it is under pressure, however, it does not boil. In a heat exchange with loop one, water in a second loop, under lower pressure, is heated to boiling in a steam generator. The steam produced powers turbines that drive electricity-generators. Second-loop steam is condensed in a heat exchange with the third loop, which carries water from the cooling tower.

Reactor physicists are primarily concerned with finding means to promote the fission reaction so as to keep the reactor critical. This implies a careful balance between the neutron production rate (the fission rate) and the neutron loss rate. Neutrons are lost via two mechanisms: they may be captured by nuclei that do not fission, or they may simply migrate out of the region containing nuclear fuel.

The core of the reactor is the region that contains the nuclear fuel. Neutrons from the fission process are born with relatively high energy. However, the probability of a

neutron causing a fission in the fuel nuclei is much larger for low-energy, or slow, neutrons than for high-energy neutrons. In order to slow neutrons down, it is common to surround the fuel with a moderator. Moderators are made from light materials such as the hydrogen in water, deuterium in heavy water, or carbon in graphite. The physical arrangement of the fuel and moderator is a major element of reactor physics.

The LWR uses H_2O as the moderator and uranium dioxide, UO_2, as the fuel. The fissionable isotope of urani-

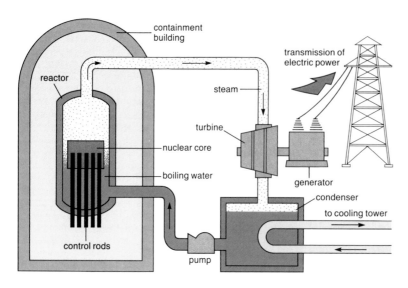

In the boiling-water reactor (BWR), the water within the reactor vessel is allowed to boil, and the steam produced is piped directly to the turbines. The steam rises to the top of the reactor vessel, and the control rods in the BWR are inserted into the reactor vessel from below—unlike the arrangement in a PWR. Both the boiling-water reactor and the pressurized-water reactor are called light-water reactors (LWRs). They form the largest class of reactors in the world.

um is U-235, which makes up only 0.7% of natural uranium. It is not possible to design a critical reactor using natural uranium. In order to increase neutron production, the U-235 concentration in the fuel is increased. Such fuel is called "enriched."

Fuel for an LWR has a relatively simple structure. Uranium is pressed into small cylindrical pellets that are stacked in zirconium alloy tubes—the "cladding"—about 3 m (10 ft) in length. The tubes are arranged in a "fuel assembly," a square array containing about 17 tubes on a side. A modern pressurized water reactor has about 200 fuel assemblies in its core.

Reactor control is achieved by carefully balancing the neutron production rate with the neutron loss rate, most commonly by adjusting the amount of neutron absorber, or control, in the core. Control materials—such as silver, indium, and cadmium, which are all highly absorbant to neutrons—are placed in rods with the same dimensions as the fuel rods; the set of control rods is inserted in the middle of the fuel assembly. The control rods are attached to a drive mechanism that moves them in and out of the core region. When reactor shutdown is desired, or when unexpected conditions are detected, the rods are inserted automatically into the core.

The core, including fuel assemblies, control rods, and moderator, is a very large system on the order of 4 m (13 ft) in diameter and 4 m high. The entire assemblage fits into a 12-m-high (40-ft), thick-walled steel pressure vessel, designed to withstand very high pressures, up to 2,500 psi. For LWRs, water is both the moderator and the coolant, that is, the agent used to remove fission energy from the core and transfer it to the electric generating segment of the system.

In the pressurized-water reactor (PWR)—a type of LWR—water is heated to a high temperature without boiling, by keeping the system under very high pressure. Water is piped into the pressure vessel and flows down the vessel sides to a region below the core. It then flows up through the core, gaining heat while keeping the core cooled. The heated water flows through pipes to a steam generator. The sets of pipes and associated pumps are called "loops." Typically, a large PWR has 3 or 4 loops.

Other Reactor Types

Over one-half of all nuclear-power reactors in the world are pressurized-water reactors. The second most common reactor, the boiling-water reactor (BWR), is also moderated and cooled with light water, which is permitted to boil within the reactor core. The steam emerging from the core is sent directly to a turbine rather than through a steam generator. The steam that enters into a BWR turbine is radioactive, however, and contaminates the turbine slightly. The major components such as the vessel, fuel, control rods, and coolant loops are quite similar to those in the PWR.

Reactors that use various gas coolants, rather than liquids, are collectively called gas-cooled reactors. The first plants of this type were built in Britain and France. The commercial versions used carbon dioxide (CO_2) as a coolant, and graphite for moderation. The designs are significantly different from those of LWRs. The fuel is usually uranium, but it is emplaced in steel tubes that are in turn embedded in graphite blocks. There are channels through the graphite for the very hot coolant gases to pass. Gas-cooled reactors have a higher thermodynamic efficiency than LWRs. They tend to be very large systems, however, and are costly to build. In addition, the hot gases cause corrosion on the surfaces within the reactor. In the early 1970s the French shifted their emphasis to LWR technology. Britain made a similar decision in the mid-1980s.

A different type of gas-cooled reactor has been under development in Germany and the United States and is called the high-temperature gas-cooled reactor, or HTGR. The significant change from earlier gas reactors is the adoption of helium as the coolant gas. Helium is chemically inert, and as a result causes little corrosion. The uranium fuel is embedded in graphite rather than steel, allowing the system to operate at very high temperatures, which promotes thermodynamic efficiency. A few HTGRs have been built to demonstrate the technology, although the economics of large plants has not been demonstrated.

The small HTGR, called a modular HTGR, or MHTGR, offers important safety advantages. Graphite has a very high heat capacity and melts at extremely high temperatures. If the decay heat stored in the core is sufficiently small, it may be possible for an MHTGR to withstand an accident in which coolant is prevented from reaching the core. Another argument made for the modular reactor is that total plant size can be increased in increments as the power demand increases. Thus, financial commitments can be kept small if the energy demand stops growing.

All the reactors described above are known as thermal reactors because the moderation slows the neutrons down to reach thermal equilibrium with the moderator. An entirely separate class of reactors are the "fast" reactors, in which there is no effort to moderate neutron energy.

The chance of a fast neutron causing a fission is much lower than that of a thermal neutron. However, if fast neutrons do cause a fission, more neutrons emerge, and in a carefully designed system the excess number of neutrons can be greater than one for each fission. The excess neutrons can be used to transmute nonfissionable species into fissionable species. The most common example is the transmutation of uranium-238 into plutonium-239. Under appropriate conditions it is possible to produce more fissionable material than is consumed in operating the reactor, and thus to breed fuel at a faster rate than it is being consumed. Such reactors are called "breeders," and they have been built and demonstrated in the United States, Great Britain, France, Germany, the Soviet Union, and Japan. (See BREEDER REACTOR.)

Nuclear Safety

As the reactor operates, a large inventory of radioactive isotopes accumulates. A fundamental objective of nuclear reactor design is to prevent accidents that could allow the escape of the RADIOACTIVITY. In order for fission products to reach the environment, several barriers must be overcome. For an LWR, the barriers are the fuel cladding, which is capable of withstanding pressures and tempera-

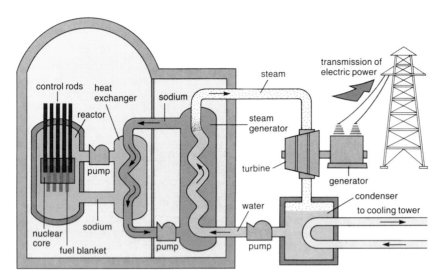

In the liquid-metal fast breeder reactor (LMFBR), the core holds not only the fuel and control-rod assemblies but also the fuel blanket, an array of rods containing uranium fuel that will be converted, or "bred," into plutonium by excess neutrons produced in the chain reaction. There is no moderator in the LFMBR, because its design requires "fast," or unmoderated, neutrons to breed plutonium. Liquid sodium is used as the reactor coolant and the heat-transfer medium. Sodium in a second loop absorbs heat from the sodium in the reactor, and transfers it to the third loop, containing the water used to generate steam. In a heat exchange, the fourth loop condenses the steam back to water, using cooler water from the cooling tower.

tures that are well beyond normal conditions; the pressure vessel, which is exceedingly strong, but does have numerous penetrations for the cooling water to enter and exit; and the containment building, designed to withstand substantial pressure.

In order for any barrier to be breached, the system must first become overheated. There are two possible ways for this to occur. The fission rate may grow too rapidly for the coolant to remove all of the energy being created, or the coolant system may fail. Excessive fission energy production is monitored by numerous sensors throughout the core region; if they detect a rapid rate of growth in the fission process, the control rods are automatically lowered into the core to absorb the fission products. The reactor shuts down.

The greatest threat to reactor safety is the loss-of-coolant accident, or LOCA. The fission process itself ceases if a reactor loses its cooling water because the reactor goes subcritical. However, the fuel continues to heat up due to stored thermal energy as well as from the decay heat of radioactive fission products. Without any coolant the cladding heats up and ultimately melts. Safety systems prevent the clad from overheating by providing emergency cooling water. Such systems are collectively known as emergency core cooling systems, or ECCSs. All such systems have multiple pathways for introducing water into the vessel under both high-pressure and low-pressure conditions.

Reactor Accidents

In spite of the installation of safety systems, there have been notable accidents at nuclear plants, both in the United States and in the USSR.

Three Mile Island. The most serious U.S. commercial reactor failure occurred on Mar. 28, 1979, at the Three Mile Island (TMI) reactor near Harrisburg, Pa. The accident began as a small-break LOCA in which a valve stuck open, allowing coolant to escape from the vessel. The ECCS operated as designed and provided makeup water

for the core. Unfortunately, the operators misinterpreted the information available to them and shut off the ECCS for several hours. The decay heat from the core boiled off the available water in the vessel, and without adequate cooling, the cladding and fuel started to melt. Before the operators resumed the flow of emergency coolant, a sizable portion of the core, about one-half to one-third, melted. The molten fuel and cladding dropped into the bottom of the vessel, which was full of water. This water was adequate to quench the molten material. The vessel itself held and kept all of the debris contained.

A sizable amount of gaseous fission products escaped from the vessel through the open valve into the containment building, which prevented its release. A small amount was also carried by coolant water that leaked out of the valve into the containment and then overflowed into an auxiliary building where the gases leaked into the environment. The releases were almost entirely noble gases, which are chemically inert and not retained within the human body. The health effects of the accident proved to be virtually undetectable against the normal incidence of background radiation.

Chernobyl. The accident at CHERNOBYL Unit 3 in the USSR in April 1986 has been the most serious of all nuclear accidents to date. Some uncertainty remains as to the sequence of events that led to the reactor catching on fire. The generally accepted scenario is that molten fuel came in contact with coolant water and reacted to generate huge volumes of steam that ruptured the piping. Subsequently, a second explosion occurred due to a chemical reaction of the incoming water and the hot metals and graphite in the core. This combination of events broke the barriers containing the fission products and allowed them to escape into the environment.

Nuclear Regulatory Commission The Nuclear Regulatory Commission (NRC) is an independent U.S.

government agency that is responsible for licensing and regulating civilian uses of nuclear materials. Its predecessor, the Atomic Energy Commission, was established in 1946 to succeed the Manhattan Engineer District of the Army Corps of Engineers, created during World War II to develop the atomic bomb (see MANHATTAN PROJECT). The NRC came into existence in 1975 under the provisions of the 1974 Energy Reorganization Act, along with the Energy Research and Development Administration (ERDA). ERDA was later abolished and its functions transferred to the Department of Energy.

The major concern of the NRC is the use of nuclear energy to generate electric power. It licenses the construction and operation of nuclear reactors and other nuclear facilities as well as the possession, use, processing, transport, handling, and disposal of nuclear materials. (The U.S. Department of Energy has authority over U.S. nuclear weapons plants.)

The NRC has been criticized for failing to take prompt action where nuclear plants were found to be violating the NRC's own standards; for failing to insure that workers were properly trained; and for lagging in its investigations of mismanagement and criminal activities at nuclear plants.

---

nuclear strategy Strategy is the art of acquiring, deploying, and using force for political purposes. Nuclear strategy involves the design, deployment, and doctrines governing nuclear weapons. Because they are so much more powerful than any armaments previously known, their introduction has required a rethinking of strategic principles.

Deterrence. The major political purpose of nuclear weapons, and the centerpiece of U.S. nuclear strategy, is deterrence, or prevention by threat. Nuclear weapons lend themselves particularly well to deterrence because they can inflict enormous damage on an enemy. Deterrence has become the principal—indeed, some would argue, the only—strategic purpose that nuclear weapons serve.

Nuclear deterrence is powerful because the punishment that the deterrer can inflict on the homeland of the aggressor is enormous. This property of nuclear arsenals is expressed by the term *assured destruction*, coined in the early 1960s to describe the standard that the U.S. nuclear arsenal had to meet. It had to have the capacity to destroy between one-fifth and one-third of the Soviet population and between one-half and three-fourths of Soviet industry in a retaliatory strike, even after absorbing an all-out Soviet attack. Both the United States and the USSR achieved this capacity in the 1960s. Theirs became a relationship whose stability was founded on the mutual capacity for assured destruction, the so-called balance of terror.

The easing of cold-war tensions during the later 1980s, the signing (1987) of the Intermediate-Range Nuclear Forces (INF) Treaty, and the continuing U.S.-Soviet negotiations on long-range nuclear missiles seemed, to many, to signal the waning of the era of nuclear threat through nuclear deterrence. Yet the strategy that has developed in conjunction with these weapons will probably continue to operate in some form as long as both sides maintain nuclear arsenals.

Nuclear Weapons. The vast majority of the world's nuclear explosives are in the possession of either the United States or the Soviet Union. These weapons may be classified in a number of different ways. They can be divided according to the physics of their explosive capacities: fission, or ATOMIC BOMBS, and fusion, or HYDROGEN BOMBS, which are far more powerful. Virtually all existing explosives are based on fusion.

Explosives can be distinguished according to their power, measured in tons of TNT equivalent. The power of fusion bombs is measured in millions of tons of TNT, or megatons; virtually all those in the inventories of the two great nuclear powers average one megaton or less.

Nuclear weapons may also be classified by their range, a classification that forms the basis for the ARMS CONTROL negotiations between the United States and the Soviet Union. Armaments of intercontinental range (intercontinental BALLISTIC MISSILES, or ICBMs, as well as long-range aircraft) have been the subject of the main negotiations, the SALT and START talks. ICBMs are based within each country or on submarines undersea (SLBMs). Prior to the INF Treaty, intermediate range weapons (IRBMs) were both based in and aimed at targets in Europe. Most battlefield, or tactical, nuclear weapons are also based in Europe. They have the shortest ranges of all.

The most important distinctions among nuclear weapons involve the delivery systems. Manned aircraft carry free-falling gravity bombs; land- or sea-based ballistic missiles are self-powered and self-guided; the hybrid CRUISE MISSILE, a small, pilotless drone, can be launched from land, ships, and even airplanes.

Delivery systems, in turn, may be categorized according to whether they reinforce or undercut deterrence. This depends on whether their characteristics make them better suited to swift, preemptive "first" strikes, which are considered incompatible with deterrence, or to retaliatory "second" strikes, which constitute the essence of deterrence. Convention has it that first-strike weapons are those suitable for attacking enemy weapons, while second-strike armaments are suitable for targeting enemy cities. Armaments aimed at cities are useful only in a retaliatory attack. Hence, these are deterrent armaments. Whether a weapon is better suited to a first or a second strike depends upon its vulnerability to preemptive attack, its speed, and its accuracy.

Weapons vulnerable to an enemy attack are first-strike weapons, since they would not be available for a retaliatory strike. Invulnerability, therefore, is the essence of deterrence. Submarine-launched missiles are the least vulnerable, because submarines cannot be tracked and destroyed. Missiles deployed on land have become increasingly vulnerable as targeting accuracy has improved.

Weapons that can move swiftly from launch to target are more useful for first strikes than slower ones. If a weapon is slow, warning of its approach is available to the other side. Ballistic missiles are swift and thus more suitable for first strikes—and less plainly weapons of deterrence—than are the slower cruise missiles.

Finally, weapons that are accurate lend themselves to

first-strike attacks. Greater accuracy is required to knock out hidden, protected missiles than to pulverize cities.

Evolution of Nuclear Strategy. The first atomic bombs, dropped on the cities of Hiroshima and Nagasaki in 1945, were used, like conventional bombs, to crush the morale of the Japanese. In the decade following the end of the war, nuclear weapons became more central to U.S. foreign policy, and their strategic purposes began to change. The United States undertook to defend Western Europe against Soviet attack, and the U.S. nuclear arsenal—the only one until the first Soviet nuclear test in 1949, and by far the larger one for a decade to come— was intended to offset the Soviet's large army and its advantage in nonnuclear weaponry.

After the Korean War, the U.S. government pledged to defend a number of Asian countries against Communism. It was decided to protect them by threatening a nuclear response to aggression of almost any kind—to deter a broad spectrum of challenges by the threat of "massive retaliation" in response to any of them. This strategy was altered as the USSR built its own arsenal of ICBMs. The U.S. government responded in two ways. First, it sought to protect the U.S. nuclear striking force against a Soviet preemptive attack. Second, it sought to develop forces that could resist Communist aggression of all types without resorting to nuclear war. This was the policy of "flexible response."

Flexible response remained the official U.S. doctrine from the 1960s on. The United States sought to deter a Soviet nuclear attack by the assured capacity for a devastating nuclear response, and to deter lesser forms of provocation with lesser armaments. Three important areas of uncertainty remained, however. First, if deterrence should fail, was it possible to fight and win a nuclear war? Second, did the simple capacity for assured destruction make for an adequate deterrent? Third, would new technologies change the basis for nuclear strategy?

Dilemmas of Nuclear Strategy. In a large-scale nuclear war, each side would suffer such catastrophic destruction that neither could regard the outcome as a victory. To provide a victory a nuclear war would therefore have to be severely limited. But the history of wars between great powers, especially in the 20th century, reveals a willingness to escalate.

Nuclear war would certainly create an environment more chaotic than any known before. Thus, even if both wished to do so, the great nuclear powers might quickly lose the means to limit the war's extent. In addition, the two governments are connected to their nuclear arsenals through complex electronic networks; these are vulnerable to attack and might not function properly in time of war. (See also ELECTROMAGNETIC PULSE.)

In the 1980s another prospective danger came to light. Scientists hypothesized that nuclear explosions might cause massive damage to the Earth's environment. They could create such intense fires and spew so much material into the air that the sunlight would be blocked out, producing a "nuclear winter" that could, in turn, have fatal consequences for all the planet's inhabitants. The possibility that this might occur has to be considered,

and is another element of uncertainty affecting the question of whether nuclear "victory" is possible.

The policies of the United States and the Soviet Union are ambiguous on the issue of victory. Both are well aware of the dangers and uncertainties surrounding nuclear war, and neither has shown any disposition to fight one.

Overabundance of Nuclear Weapons. Because they are so powerful, and can be invulnerable, relatively few nuclear weapons can give a country the capacity for assured destruction. Both the United States and the USSR have many more than the minimum necessary. The United States, especially, has strategic reasons for this surplus. It is committed to the nuclear protection of Western Europe and Japan. Assured destruction is generally reckoned adequate to deter a direct attack on the United States, but not sufficiently credible to deter one against a distant ally. The Soviets, it is feared, might not believe that the United States would risk the annihilation of Washington, D.C., to protect Bonn. The United States attempts to ensure the "credibility" of its commitment to Europe by "coupling" the U.S. nuclear arsenal to the defense of Europe, and by possessing nuclear firepower over and above the amount required for assured destruction.

Future of Deterrence. The viability of deterrence strategies could be threatened by one of several possible improvements in technology. The most conspicuous technical advances in nuclear weaponry in the 1970s, for example, involved the accuracy with which explosives could be aimed. Some weapons on both sides have become increasingly vulnerable to preemptive attack. Those carried by submarines are still protected. Neither side is close to possessing an antisubmarine capacity, but other kinds of technological advances, whose effects will be at the very least destabilizing, are at the beginnings of development.

The most important potential technological development is the means to defend against nuclear attack (see ANTIBALLISTIC MISSILE). Stability presently rests on the absolute supremacy of the offense, the essence of assured destruction. The development of an effective defense would make for a revolution in nuclear strategy.

The task of defense against nuclear attack is a difficult, perhaps an impossible, one. Each side has thousands of explosives, which can be launched from different directions, at different speeds, and with decoys to confuse a defense. To stop all of them is impossible, and if only one penetrated a defensive system, it could cause catastrophic damage.

Nevertheless, the idea of defense is logical and appealing. A world in which safety depended on mutual self-protection is much more attractive than the present world, where it is based on the mutual threat of annihilation. New technologies are constantly invented. Some of them, such as the space-based laser weapons that are being developed under the U.S. STRATEGIC DEFENSE INITIATIVE (the "Star Wars" program), are classed as defensive weapons; they are designed to destroy offensive nuclear missiles in space.

Lesser Nuclear Powers. Great Britain, France, and the People's Republic of China possess nuclear weapons.

Many smaller countries (Argentina, Brazil, India, Israel) have tested nuclear devices, or possess the technology to make them, and still others have been given nuclear weapons by one of the major powers. The belief that a particular nation might have a nuclear weapon has undoubtedly had some deterrent effect on its adversaries. This is perhaps the ultimate testimony to the strategic impact of nuclear weapons: deterrence is the product of the mere rumor that they exist.

nuclear waste   Nuclear waste refers to the entire array of radioactive materials created by all aspects of nuclear technology. The most widely known wastes are those produced by the civilian nuclear industry and the nuclear weapons program. Other sources include radioactive materials produced for medical, research, and industrial applications, and the contaminated sections of dismantled nuclear facilities.

Radioactive materials all decay by emission of various forms of radiation—gamma rays, alpha particles, electrons, positrons, and neutrons. A decay is characterized by the type of emission, the energy of the emitted radiation, and the rate at which decay occurs. The decay rate is usually measured in terms of the half-life, or the time required for one-half of the radioisotope present to decay. Half-lives for different isotopes may range from less than a millionth of a second to billions of years (see RADIOACTIVITY).

The concern with radioactive materials is that the emitted radiation may interact with the human body and cause damage to cells. The effects of exposure can be immediate or delayed, depending upon the amount of radiation received. Very small exposures may have no discernible effect; heavier exposures can cause a range of illnesses, from a mild, temporary sickness to death. Although thresholds had been established below which it was believed that there were no ill effects, the current consensus is that any irradiation will cause cell damage, and hence it should be assumed that there is no threshold (see RADIATION INJURY).

Types of Nuclear Wastes. Nuclear wastes are usually characterized by their physical and chemical properties and their sources of origin. In the United States all wastes from the nuclear defense program are termed *military wastes* and are usually treated separately. Civilian wastes with a low level of radioactivity are termed *low-level* wastes. These include slightly contaminated materials from nuclear-power facilities, research laboratories, hospitals, and industrial sites. A large source of low-level waste are mill tailings, the residues of uranium ores after the uranium has been extracted.

The major source of high-level waste, which contains large amounts of radioisotopes, is the spent fuel from nuclear power reactors. The reprocessing of fuel from civilian nuclear plants is the responsibility of the U.S. government, which has not yet established a reprocessing program. The spent fuel from military reactors is reprocessed, and the residues of this treatment are also high-level wastes.

The final waste category is called *transuranic waste*, which includes materials contaminated with human-made radioisotopes that have been created by the transmutation of uranium. The most common transuranic is plutonium. The amounts of radioactivity are usually small, but the transuranics emit alpha particles, which are particularly hazardous to human tissue. The greatest concern is that transuranic material might be inhaled and lodge in the lungs where it could do great damage.

Nuclear Waste Disposal. The disposal of low-level waste is technically simple since the activity of the material is quite low. A small amount of shielding, such as is provided by one meter of soil, is sufficient to protect human beings. The current storage methods are all some form of shallow land burial, and the concern is that water seepage may cause some materials to migrate out—a problem that might be solved by adequate design, management, and monitoring of the site.

In 1980, Congress gave states the primary responsibility for, and regulatory control over, their low-level wastes. The subsequent development of repositories has been a slow process, as states attempt to define appropriate controls.

High-level waste from spent nuclear fuel is a collection of many different radioisotopes with highly varying half-lives. It would require about 1,000 years for the total level of activity to decay down to the same level as the ore used to produce the fuel. Even after 1,000 years the composition of the fuel would be quite different from the ore, and would still require its isolation from human beings.

Nuclear wastes generated by weapons-production plants in the United States have been stored in shallow burials, in open pits and basins, or in large metal tanks that have begun to leak, contaminating soil and groundwater. Among possible solutions is the incineration at extremely high temperatures of contaminated soils and other solid wastes, producing a vitrified, or glassy, slag that, while still radioactive, can be more safely stored; and the treatment of liquid waste by mixing it with cement and burying it in concrete-lined pits.

Options for long-term storage all involve some form of burial. The concern with all forms of burial is that over long periods of time the enclosing materials will corrode and fail, allowing radioactive material to migrate into the water table or out into the atmosphere. Additionally, ground motion, such as would occur in an earthquake, might allow the escape of radioactivity. It has been suggested, however, that high-level wastes, vitrified at high temperatures or stored in corrosion-resistant canisters, might be placed underground in salt domes, tuff (ancient volcanic ash deposits), or granitic rock. Salt is of interest because the domes are theoretically free of water and should self-seal if disturbed by ground motion.

nuclear weapon   see ATOMIC BOMB; HYDROGEN BOMB; NEUTRON BOMB; NUCLEAR STRATEGY

nucleic acid   see GENE

nucleus   see CELL

nucleus, atomic   see ATOM; NUCLEAR PHYSICS

ILLUSTRATION CREDITS

The following list credits or acknowledges, by page, the source of illustrations used in this volume. When two or more illustrations appear on one page, they are credited individually left to right, top to bottom; their credits are separated by semicolons. When both the photographer or artist and an agency or other source are given for an illustration, they are usually separated by a slash. Those illustrations not cited below are credited on the page on which they appear, either in the caption or alongside the illustration itself.